Frommer's®

France 2012

by Alison Culliford, Joe Ray, Tristan Rutherford, Margie Rynn, Caroline Sieg, and Amelia Smith

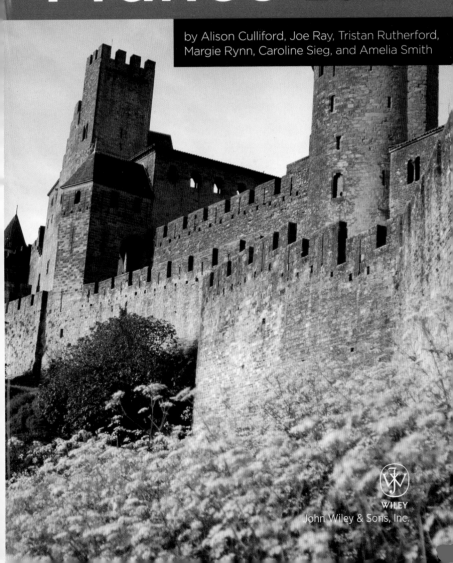

WILEY
John Wiley & Sons, Inc.

Published by:
Wiley Publishing, Inc.
111 River St.
Hoboken, NJ 07030-5774

ISBN 978-1-118-02742-4 (paper); 9781118075920 (paper); 9781118148426 (ebk); 9781118148433 (ebk); 9781118148440 (ebk)

Editor: Jamie Ehrlich
Production Editor: M. Faunette Johnston
Cartographer: Tim Lohnes
Photo Editor: Alden Gewirtz
Production by Wiley Indianapolis Composition Services

Front Cover Photo: Villandry Castle © Market Redondo
Back Cover Photos: LEFT: Horseback riding in the Camargue © Matthieu Colin. MIDDLE: Shopping in the city © Anne Ackermann / Aurora. RIGHT: The Pont du Gard in Languedoc-Roussillon © Kirsten Scully.

For information on our other products and services or to obtain technical support, please contact our Customer Care Department within the U.S. at 877/762-2974, outside the U.S. at 317/572-3993 or fax 317/572-4002.

Wiley also publishes its books in a variety of electronic formats. Some content that appears in print may not be available in electronic formats.

Manufactured in China

5 4 3 2 1

CONTENTS

List of Maps ix

1 THE BEST OF FRANCE 1

The Best Travel Experiences 2
The Best Romantic Escapes 4
The Best Driving Tours 5
The Best Châteaux & Palaces 7
The Best Museums 9
The Best Cathedrals 10
The Best Vineyards & Wineries 11
The Best Luxury Hotels 12
The Best Affordable Hotels 14
The Best Historic Places to Stay 15
The Best Upscale Restaurants 16
The Best Affordable Restuarants 18

2 FRANCE IN DEPTH 19

France Today 20
The Making of France 24
Art & Architecture 35
France in Popular Culture 41
Eating & Drinking in France 48
When to Go 54
FRANCE CALENDAR OF EVENTS 54
Tours 58

3 SUGGESTED ITINERARIES 61

THE REGIONS IN BRIEF 62
France in 1 Week 67
France in 2 Weeks 70
France for Families 73
A Wine Lover's Tour of Burgundy 76

4 PARIS 80

Orientation 81
NEIGHBORHOODS IN BRIEF 84
Exploring Paris 91
Where to Eat 136
The Top Cafes 162
Shopping in Paris 165
Entertainment & Nightlife 184
Where to Stay 193

5 SIDE TRIPS FROM PARIS 215

Versailles 216
Rambouillet 225
Chartres 227
Fontainebleau 232
Vaux-le-Vicomte 235
Disneyland Paris 237
Giverny 242
Chantilly 244
Senlis 247
Compiègne 249

6 THE LOIRE VALLEY 253

Orléans 255
Beaugency 260
Chambord 262
Blois 263
Cheverny 267
Valençay 268
Chaumont-sur-Loire 269
Amboise 271
Chenonceaux 275
Tours 277
Loches 283
Villandry 285
Langeais 287
Azay-le-Rideau 288
Chinon 290
Ussé 294
Fontevraud-l'Abbaye 294
Saumur 296
Angers 299

7 NORMANDY & MONT-ST-MICHEL 303

Rouen 304
Honfleur 312
Deauville 315
Trouville 320
Caen 322
Bayeux 326
The D-Day Beaches 329
Mont-St-Michel 333

8 BRITTANY 337

St-Malo 338
Dinard 343
Dinan 347
Quimper 349
Concarneau 353
Pont-Aven 355
Carnac 357
Nantes 359

9 THE CHAMPAGNE COUNTRY 366

La Ferté-sous-Jouarre 367
Château-Thierry 369
Condé-en-Brie 371
Reims 372
Epernay 380

10 ALSACE-LORRAINE 383

Strasbourg 384
La Route Du Vin (Wine Road) 396
Colmar 402
La Route des Cretes 407
Nancy 408
Domrêmy-la-Pucelle 414
Verdun 415

11 BURGUNDY 417

Auxerre 418
Vézelay 421
Avallon 423
Autun 425
Beaune 427
Dijon 431
Saulieu 437

12 **THE RHÔNE VALLEY** 439

Lyon 440
The Beaujolais Country 454
Roanne 456
Pérouges 458
Bourg-En-Bresse 459
Vienne 461
Valence 464
The Ardèche 465

13 **THE FRENCH ALPS** 469

Evians-les-Bains 470
Annecy 474
Aix-les-Bains 478
Grenoble 480
Courchevel 1850 484
Chamonix-Mont Blanc 487
Val d'Isére 492

14 **PROVENCE** 496

Orange 497
Avignon 501
Gordes 510
St-Rémy-de-Provence 514
Arles 517
Les Baux 523
Aix-en-Provence 526
Marseilles 533
Toulon 543
Iles d'Hyères 546

15 **THE FRENCH RIVIERA** 549

St-Tropez 550
Cannes 558
Mougins 569
Grasse 571
Biot 574
Juan-les-Pins 575
Antibes & Cap d'Antibes 578
Cagnes-sur-Mer 582
St-Paul-de-Vence 585
Vence 589

Nice 591
Villefranche-sur-Mer 606
St-Jean-Cap-Ferrat 607
Beaulieu-sur-Mer 610
Eze & La Turbie 613
Monaco 615
Roquebrune & Cap-Martin 626

16 LANGUEDOC-ROUSSILLON 628

Nîmes 629
Aigues-Mortes 636
Montpellier 638
Narbonne 643
Collioure 645
Perpignan 647
Carcassonne 651
Castres 655
Albi 657
Cordes-sur-Ciel 659
Toulouse 661

17 THE BASQUE COUNTRY 670

Pau 671
Bayonne 675
Biarritz 679
St-Jean-de-Luz 684

18 BORDEAUX & THE ATLANTIC COAST 688

Poitiers 689
La Rochelle 693
Cognac 700
Angoulême 703
Bordeaux 706
The Wine Country 715

19 THE DORDOGNE & THE LOT 720

Périgueux 721
Lascaux (Montignac) 726
Les Eyzies-De-Tayac 729
Sarlat-la-Canéda 732
Rocamadour 737
Cahors 740
Side Trip to Limoges 743

20 PLANNING YOUR TRIP TO FRANCE 747

Getting There 748
Getting Around 750
FAST FACTS: FRANCE 754

21 USEFUL TERMS & PHRASES 764

Glossary of French-Language Terms 764

Index 771

LIST OF MAPS

France 22

France in 1 Week 69

France in 2 Weeks 71

France for Families 75

A Wine Lover's Tour of Burgundy 77

Paris Neighborhoods 86

Paris's Top Attractions 93

Les Halles, the Louvre & Palais Royal (1er & 2e) 95

The Louvre 97

Marais, Ile St-Louis & Ile de la Cite (3e & 4e) 101

Notre Dame de Paris 103

The Champs-Elysees & Western Paris (8e, 16e, & 17e) 110

Restaurants near Opéra & Canal St-Martin (9e & 10e) 115

Pigalle & Montmartre (18e) 117

Belleville & Northeast Paris (19e & 20e) 119

The Latin Quarter & Southern Paris (5e & 13e) 123

St-Germain-des-Prés, Luxembourg & Montparnasse (6e & 14e) 127

Near the Eiffel Tower (7e & 15e) 129

Republique, the Bastille & Eastern Paris (11e & 12e) 153

Paris & the Ile de France 217

Versailles 219

Notre Dame de Chartres 229

The Loire Valley 255

Orléans 257

Tours 279

Normandy 305

Rouen 307

Mont-St-Michel 335

Brittany 339

Nantes 361

Champagne 369

Reims 373

Alsace-Lorraine 385

Strasbourg 387

Nancy 409

Burgundy 419

Dijon 433

The Rhône Valley 441

Lyon 443

The French Alps 471

Provence 499

Avignon 503

Palais des Papes 505

Arles 519

Aix-en-Provence 529

Marseille 535

The French Riviera 551

St-Tropez 553

Cannes 560

Nice 595

Monaco 617

Languedoc-Roussillon 631

Nîmes 633

Toulouse 663

The Basque Country 673

Bordeaux & the Atlantic Coast 691

Bordeaux 707

The Dordogne & the Lot 723

ABOUT THE AUTHORS

Alison Culliford was a journalist in London for 12 years before buying a one-way Eurostar ticket to Paris in 2001, and has never looked back. She worked in *Time Out*'s Paris bureau and now freelances as a travel journalist and guidebook author, taking every opportunity to discover the diverse regions of France by road, train, bicycle, and on foot.

Joe Ray has been writing and shooting food and travel stories for more than a decade. Based in Paris, he writes for major dailies and magazines around the world, along with restaurant critique with France's top critic, François Simon of Le Figaro. He is also a former winner of the Lowell Thomas Travel Journalist of the Year Award.

Tristan Rutherford moved to Nice and began a career in freelance travel journalism in 2002. He writes travel features for *Financial Times* and London's *Sunday Times Travel Magazine* among others, and lectures in travel journalism at Central Saint Martins in London. His hottest picks along the Cote d'Azur remain the 1€ no.100 bus from Nice to Monaco, the sandy beaches of Juan-les-Pins, and Nice's locals-only street market of Libération.

Margie Rynn has been living and writing in Paris for over 10 years. While she's not exactly assimilated, she did cross a major cultural threshold the day she realized she knew the lyrics to a Claude François tune. Margie is the author of *Pauline Frommer's Paris* and has written features for *Budget Travel*, *EasyJet*, and *Ryanair Magazine*, among other publications. She has also worked for the United Nations Environmental Program and acted in a Broadway show.

Caroline Sieg is half-Swiss, half-American, and her relationship with France began with childhood trips to Strasbourg to visit her Alsatian family. Later, she studied French, resided in Paris, and worked several seasons in a ski resort bordering France and Switzerland. These days, Caroline heads to France as often as possible—to ski, sniff out the best wine, cheese, and bread, or simply meander along quiet side streets.

Amelia Smith skipped the "tu" form of conjugation after her high school French teacher said the chances of her ever knowing an actual French person were close to none. Thirteen years after moving to France, she continues to address French family and friends like royalty. Her work has appeared in the *New York Times*, *Huffington Post*, and *The Daily Beast*, among others.

HOW TO CONTACT US

In researching this book, we discovered many wonderful places—hotels, restaurants, shops, and more. We're sure you'll find others. Please tell us about them, so we can share the information with your fellow travelers in upcoming editions. If you were disappointed with a recommendation, we'd love to know that, too. Please write to:

Frommer's France 2012
Wiley Publishing, Inc. • 111 River St. • Hoboken, NJ 07030-5774
frommersfeedback@wiley.com

AN ADDITIONAL NOTE

Travel information can change quickly and unexpectedly, and we strongly advise you to confirm important details locally before traveling, including information on visas, health and safety, traffic and transport, accommodations, shopping, and eating out. We also encourage you to stay alert while traveling and to remain aware of your surroundings. Avoid civil disturbances, and keep a close eye on cameras, purses, wallets, and other valuables. While we have endeavored to ensure that the information contained within this guide is accurate and up-to-date at the time of publication, we make no representations or warranties with respect to the accuracy or completeness of the contents of this work and specifically disclaim all warranties, including without limitation, warranties of fitness for a particular purpose. We accept no responsibility or liability for any inaccuracy or errors or omissions, or for any inconvenience, loss, damage, costs, or expenses of any nature whatsoever incurred or suffered by anyone as a result of any advice or information contained in this guide.

The inclusion of a company, organization or website in this guide as a service provider and/or potential source of further information does not mean that we endorse them or the information they provide. Be aware that information provided through some websites may be unreliable and can change without notice. Neither the publisher nor authors shall be liable for any damages arising herefrom.

FROMMER'S STAR RATINGS, ICONS & ABBREVIATIONS

Every hotel, restaurant, and attraction listing in this guide has been ranked for quality, value, service, amenities, and special features using a star-rating system. In country, state, and regional guides, we also rate towns and regions to help you narrow down your choices and budget your time accordingly. Hotels and restaurants are rated on a scale of zero (recommended) to three stars (exceptional). Attractions, shopping, nightlife, towns, and regions are rated according to the following scale: zero stars (recommended), one star (highly recommended), two stars (very highly recommended), and three stars (must-see).

In addition to the star-rating system, we also use seven feature icons that point you to the great deals, in-the-know advice, and unique experiences that separate travelers from tourists. Throughout the book, look for:

Special finds—those places only insiders know about

Fun facts—details that make travelers more informed and their trips more fun

Kids—best bets for kids and advice for the whole family

Special moments—those experiences that memories are made of

Overrated—places or experiences not worth your time or money

Insider tips—great ways to save time and money

Great values—where to get the best deals

The following abbreviations are used for credit cards:

AE American Express
DISC Discover
V Visa
DC Diners Club
MC MasterCard

TRAVEL RESOURCES AT FROMMERS.COM

Frommer's travel resources don't end with this guide. Frommer's website, **www.frommers.com**, has travel information on more than 4,000 destinations. We update features regularly, giving you access to the most current trip-planning information and the best airfare, lodging, and car-rental bargains. You can also listen to podcasts, connect with other Frommers.com members through our active-reader forums, share your travel photos, read blogs from guidebook editors and fellow travelers, and much more.

1

THE BEST OF FRANCE

France presents visitors with an embarrassment of riches—you may find yourself bewildered by all the choices. We've tried to make the task easier by compiling a list of our favorite experiences and discoveries. In the following pages, you'll find the kind of candid advice we'd give our closest friends.

THE best TRAVEL EXPERIENCES

- **Hunting for Antiques:** The 18th- and 19th-century French aesthetic was gloriously different from that of England and North America, and many objects bear designs with mythological references to the French experience. France has some 13,000-plus antiques shops throughout the country. Stop where you see the sign ANTIQUAIRE or BROCANTE.
- **Dining Out:** The art of dining is serious business in France. Food is as cerebral as it is sensual. Even casual bistros with affordable menus are likely to offer fresh seasonal ingredients in time-tested recipes that may add up to a memorable meal. For our favorite restaurants in France, see "The Best Upscale Restaurants" and "The Best Affordable Restaurants," later in this chapter.
- **Biking in the Countryside:** The country that invented La Tour de France offers thousands of options for bike trips. For a modest charge, trains in France will carry your bicycle to any point. **Euro-Bike & Walking Tours** (© **800/575-1540;** www.eurobike.com) offers some of the best excursions, including walking and cycling tours of areas such as Provence, Burgundy, and the Loire Valley. See chapter 20.

Biking in the French countryside. PREVIOUS PAGE: **A view of the Eiffel Tower.**

Window shopping at Chanel in Paris.

- **Shopping in Parisian Boutiques:** The French guard their image as Europe's most stylish people. The citadels of Right Bank chic lie on rue du Faubourg St-Honoré and its extension, rue St-Honoré. The most glamorous shops are along these streets, stretching between the Palais Royal to the east and the Palais de l'Elysée to the west. Follow in the footsteps of Coco Chanel, Yves Saint Laurent, and Karl Lagerfeld on the shopper's tour of a lifetime. See chapter 4.
- **Exploring the Loire Valley:** An excursion to the châteaux dotting the valley's rich fields and forests will familiarize you with the French Renaissance's architectural aesthetics and with the intrigues of the kings and their courts. Nothing conjures up the aristocratic *ancien régime* better than a tour of these landmarks. See chapter 6.
- **Paying Tribute to Fallen Heroes on Normandy's D-Day Beaches:** On June 6, 1944, the largest armada ever assembled departed on rough seas and in dense fog from England. For about a week, the future of the civilized world hung in a bloody and brutal balance between the Nazi and Allied armies. Today you'll find only the sticky sands and wind-torn, gray-green seas of a rather chilly beach. But even if you haven't seen *Saving Private Ryan* or *The Longest Day,* you can picture the struggles of determined soldiers who paid a terrible price to establish a bulkhead on the Continent. See "The D-Day Beaches" in chapter 7.
- **Climbing to the Heights of Mont-St-Michel:** Straddling the tidal flats between Normandy and Brittany, this Gothic marvel is the most spectacular fortress in northern Europe. Said to be protected by the archangel Michael, most of it stands as it did during the 1200s. See "Mont-St-Michel" in chapter 7.
- **Touring Burgundy During the Grape Gathering:** Medieval lore and legend permeate the harvests in Burgundy, where thousands of workers (armed with vintner's shears and baskets) head over the rolling hills to gather the grapes that have made the region's wines so famous. You can sample the local wines in the area restaurants, which always stock impressive collections. See chapter 11.
- **Schussing down the Alps:** France offers world-class skiing and luxurious resorts. Our favorites are Chamonix, Courchevel, and Megève. Here you'll find cliffs only experts should brave, as well as runs for intermediates and beginners. The après-ski scene roars into the wee hours. See chapter 13.
- **Marveling at the Riviera's Modern-Art Museums:** Since the 1890s, when Signac and Bonnard discovered St-Tropez, artists and their patrons have been

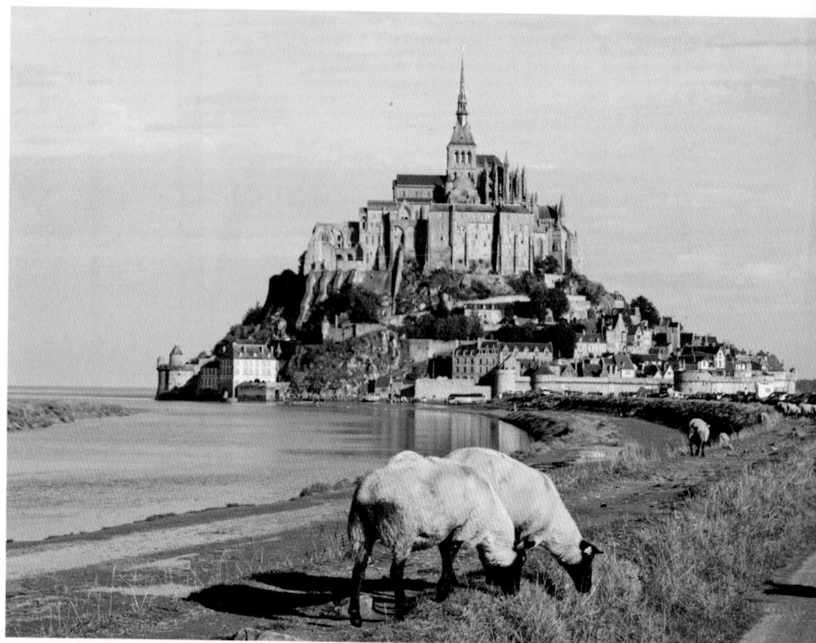

Mont-St-Michel.

drawn to the French Riviera. Experience an unforgettable drive across southern Provence, interspersing museum visits with wonderful meals, sunbathing, and stops at the area's architectural and artistic marvels. Highlights are Aix-en-Provence (Cézanne's studio), Biot (the Léger Museum), Cagnes-sur-Mer (the Renoir Museum), Cap-d'Antibes (the Grimaldi Château's Picasso Museum), La Napoule (the Henry Clews Museum), and Nice (the famed Matisse Museum and Chagall Museum). In addition, Monaco, St-Paul-de-Vence, and St-Tropez all have world-class modern art collections. See chapters 14 and 15.

THE best ROMANTIC ESCAPES

- **Deauville** (Normandy): Using the resort of Deauville to propel herself to stardom, Coco Chanel added greatly to its sense of glamour and romance. Try your hand at the casinos, ride horses, stroll along the elegant boardwalk, or simply revel in the resort's sense of style and nostalgia. See "Deauville" in chapter 7.
- **Belle-Ile-en-Mer** (Brittany): Consider an island escape with your significant other to Belle-Ile on the Brittany's Côte Sauvage (literally, "The Wild Side"). Stay in the Port de Goulphar and dine at the wonderful Table de La Desirade, sampling grilled lobster or cockles and zucchini between layers of potato rosettes. It's best enjoyed in the spring or fall, with a glass of wine on the water or with a collar flipped up in the off season as you stroll the cliffs above the sea. See p. 363.

Belle-Ile-en-Mer.

- **Talloires** (the French Alps): The bracing climate, the history that goes back to the Middle Ages, and the Gallic flair of the innkeepers make for a memorable stay. The accommodations include a converted medieval monastery, and the village's cuisine is superb. See "Talloires" in chapter 13.
- **Les Baux** (Provence): The isolated, cinematic setting of the ancient fortress of Les Baux had troubadours singing in its streets during the Middle Ages. Today it is no less romantic, with an abundance of hideaways within minutes of the village itself. See "Les Baux" in chapter 14.
- **St-Tropez** (Côte d'Azur): Any blonde feels like Brigitte Bardot in sunny St-Tropez, and the number of scantily clad satyrs and nymphs in town during summer could perk up the most sluggish libido. The real miracle here is that the charm of the place manages to survive its hype and the hordes of visitors. See "St-Tropez" in chapter 15.

THE best DRIVING TOURS

- **La Route des Crêtes** (Alsace-Lorraine): The Vosges, one of the oldest mountain ranges in France, once formed a boundary with Germany. Richly forested with hardwood trees and firs, they skirt the western edge of the Rhine and resemble the Black Forest. La Route des Crêtes (the Crest Road), originally chiseled out of the mountains as a supply line, begins west of Colmar, at the Col du Bonhomme. High points are Münster (home of the cheese), Col de la Schlucht (a resort with panoramas as far as the Jura and the Black Forest), and Markstein. At many points along the way, you can stop and strike out on a well-marked hiking trail. See "La Route des Crêtes" in chapter 10.
- **La Côte d'Or** (Burgundy): Stretching only 60km (37 miles) from Santenay to Dijon, this route is for wine lovers. Rows of terraced vines rise in tiers above the D122/N74/D1138 highways (La Route des Grands Crus),

passing through the towns of Puligny-Montrachet, Volnay, Beaune, Nuits-St-Georges, Vosne-Romanée, Gevrey-Chambertin, and Marsannay-la-Côte. Travel at your leisure, stopping to sample the noble vintages (look for the signs sprouting from the sides of the highway). See chapter 11.

- **The Gorges of the Ardèche** (the Rhône Valley): The river that carved these canyons (the Ardèche, a tributary of the Rhône) is the most temperamental French waterway: Its ebbs and flows have created the Grand Canyon of France. Riddled with alluvial deposits, grottoes, caves, and canyons more than 285m (935 ft.) deep, the valley is one of France's most unusual geological spectacles. A panoramic road (D290) runs along one rim of the canyons, providing views over a striking, arid landscape. Plan to park and walk a little on some of the well-marked paths. The drive, which you can do in a day even if you make frequent stops, stretches between Vallon-Pont-d'Arc and Pont St-Esprit. See "The Ardèche" in chapter 12.
- **La Route des Grandes Alpes** (the French Alps): One of the most panoramic drives in western Europe stretches south from the lakefront town of Evian to coastal Nice. You'll see Alpine uplands, larch forests, glaciers, and the foothills of Mont Blanc. Plan on driving 2 to 6 days, stopping in such towns as Morzine, Avoriaz, Chamonix, and Megève. The route covers 740km (459 miles) and crosses many of France's dramatic mountain passes. Some sections are passable only in midsummer. See chapter 13.

St-Tropez coastline.

La Côte d'Or.

THE best CHÂTEAUX & PALACES

- **Château de Chantilly/Musée Condé** (Ile de France): Anne de Montmorency, a constable of France who advised six monarchs, began this palace in 1560. To save money, he ordered the new building placed atop the foundations of a derelict castle. His descendants enlarged and embellished the premises, added the massive stables, and hired Le Nôtre to design gardens that later inspired Louis XIV to create similar, larger ones at Versailles. See p. 245.
- **Château de Versailles** (Ile de France): Versailles is the most spectacular palace in the world. Its construction was fraught with ironies and tragedies, and its costs were a factor in the bloodbath of the French Revolution. Ringed with world-class gardens and a network of canals whose excavation required an army of laborers, the site also contains the Grand and Petit Trianons, as well as miles of ornate corridors lined with the spoils of a vanished era. See p. 220.
- **Palais de Fontainebleau** (Ile de France): Since the days of the earliest Frankish kings, the forest has served as a royal hunting ground. Various dwellings had been erected for medieval kings, but in 1528, François I commissioned the core of the building that subsequent monarchs would

enlarge and embellish. Napoleon declared it his favorite château, delivering an emotional farewell to his troops from its exterior staircase after his 1814 abdication. See p. 232.

- **Château d'Azay-le-Rideau** (Loire Valley): Visitors are enthralled by this château's beauty. Poised above the waters of the Indre River, it boasts decorative remnants of medieval fortifications and an atmosphere that prefigures the Renaissance embellishments of later Loire Valley châteaux. See p. 288.
- **Château de Chambord** (Loire Valley): Despite the incorporation of feudal trappings in its layout, this château was built for pleasure—a manifestation of the successes of the 25-year-old François I. Begun in 1519 as the Loire Valley's most opulent status symbol, Chambord heralded the end of the feudal age and the dawn of the Renaissance. Construction dragged on for decades; during his lifetime, François stayed there for a total of only 7 weeks. See p. 262.
- **Château de Chenonceau** (Loire Valley): Its builders daringly placed this palace, built between 1513 and 1521, on arched stone vaults above the rushing Cher River. Two of France's most influential women, each of whom imposed her will on Renaissance politics and the château's design, fought over Chenonceau. Henri II gave the palace to his mistress, Diane de Poitiers. After the king's death, his widow, Catherine de Médicis, humiliated Diane by forcing her to move to a less prestigious château in nearby Chaumont. See p. 275.

Palais de Fontainebleau.

Château d'Azay-le-Rideau.

THE best MUSEUMS

- **Palais de Tokyo:** The Palais de Tokyo is a contemporary "art mall" that displays radical emerging art—even its hours (noon–midnight) are radical. After its 2011 renovation and expansion, the museum has become even more monumental, with double the exhibition space. You're bound to see thought-provoking exhibitions that you'd be unlikely to see elsewhere. See p. 113.
- **Musée du Louvre:** The Louvre's exterior is a triumph of French architecture, and its interior shelters an embarrassment of art, one of the greatest treasure-troves known to Western civilization. Of the Louvre's more than 300,000 paintings, only a small percentage can be displayed at one time. The museum maintains its staid dignity and timelessness even though thousands of visitors traipse daily through its corridors, looking for the *Mona Lisa* or the *Venus de Milo*. I. M. Pei's controversial Great Pyramid nearly offsets the grandeur of the Cour Carrée, but it has a real functional purpose. See p. 96.
- **Musée d'Orsay:** The spidery glass-and-iron canopies of a former railway station frame one of Europe's greatest museums of art. Devoted mainly to paintings of the 19th century, d'Orsay contains some of the most celebrated masterpieces of the French Impressionists, along with sculptures and decorative objects whose designs forever changed the way European artists interpreted line, movement, and color. This is also where *Whistler's Mother* sits in her rocker. See p. 131.
- **Centre Pompidou:** "The most avant-garde building in the world," or so it is known, is a citadel of modern art, with exhibitions drawn from more than 40,000 works. Everything seemingly is here—from Calder's 1928 *Josephine Baker* (one of his earliest versions of the mobile) to a re-creation of Brancusi's Jazz Age studio. See p. 103.

Musée Fabre.

- **Musée de la Tapisserie de Bayeux** (Bayeux, Normandy): This museum's star is a 900-year-old tapestry named in honor of medieval Queen Mathilda. Housed in a glass case, the Bayeux tapestry is a long band of linen embroidered with depictions of the war machine that sailed from Normandy to conquer England in 1066. See p.327.
- **Musée Historique Lorraine** (Nancy, Alsace-Lorraine): Few other French museums reflect a province as well as this one. Its collections include 16th-century engravings, 17th-century masterpieces by local painters, exhibits on Jewish history in eastern France, antique furniture, wrought iron, and domestic accessories. See p. 410.
- **Foundation Maeght** (St-Paul-de-Vence, Côte d'Azur): Established as a showcase for modern art by collectors Aimé and Marguerite Maeght, this avant-garde museum features works by Giacometti, Chagall, Braque, Miró, Matisse, and Barbara Hepworth. The multilevel design by the architect José Luís Sert boasts glass walls with views of the Provence landscape. See p. 586.
- **Musée Fabre** (Montpellier, Languedoc): This museum, which occupies a villa where Molière once presented some of his plays, acquired several new galleries, including an entire wing devoted to Pierre Soulages. It also displays one of the worthiest collections of French, Italian, and Spanish paintings in the south of France. See p. 640.
- **Musée Toulouse-Lautrec** (Albi, Languedoc): Henri Toulouse-Lautrec was born in Albi in 1864. Much to his family's horror, he moved to a scandalous area in Paris, where he created depictions of the Belle Epoque scene that are treasures today. Also on view in this expanding museum are works by Degas, Bonnard, and Matisse. See p. 658.

THE best CATHEDRALS

- **Notre-Dame** (Paris): This structure's stone walls symbolize the power of Paris in the Middle Ages. Begun in 1163, Notre-Dame is the cathedral of the nation and a triumph of medieval architecture. It's dazzling in the morning and at sunset, when its image reflects in the Seine. See p. 100.
- **Cathédrale Notre-Dame de Chartres** (Chartres, Ile de France): No less an artist than Rodin declared this cathedral a French Acropolis. Its site reputedly was holy for the Druids and the ancient Romans. Chartres is one of the world's largest cathedrals, one of the first High Gothic cathedrals, and one of the first to use flying buttresses. It also has possibly the finest stained-glass windows, more than 2,500 sq. m (26,910 sq. ft.) of glass whose vivid hues and patterns of light are truly mystical. See p. 228.
- **Cathédrale Notre-Dame de Rouen** (Rouen, Normandy): Consecrated in 1063 and rebuilt after a fire in 1200, parts of it are masterpieces of the Flamboyant Gothic style; others are plainer, though equally dignified. This cathedral was immortalized in the 19th century, when Monet painted a series of impressions of the facade. See p. 306.
- **Cathédrale Notre-Dame d'Amiens** (Amiens, the Ardennes): A lavishly decorated example of High Gothic architecture, this cathedral boasts a soaring nave whose roof is supported by 126 breathtakingly slender pillars. It was begun in 1220 to house the head of St. John the Baptist, brought back from the

Intricate French cathedral detail on the Cathédrale Notre-Dame d'Amiens.

Crusades. It is the largest church in France, surviving two world wars, despite fierce fighting nearby. Place Notre-Dame, Amiens. ✆ **03-22-71-60-50**.

- **Cathédrale Notre-Dame de Reims** (Reims, Champagne): One of France's first Christian bishops, St. Rémi, baptized Clovis, king of the Franks, on this site in 496. The church memorializing the event was conceived as a religious sanctuary where the French kings would be anointed; it was large, spectacular, and (in our eyes) rather cold. The coronation of every king between 815 and 1825 was celebrated here. Damaged by World War I bombings, the cathedral was restored by American donations during the 1920s and 1930s. See p. 372.

THE best VINEYARDS & WINERIES

- **Couly-Dutheil** (12 rue Diderot, Chinon; ✆ **02-47-97-20-20;** www.couly-dutheil-chinon.com): Many of its medieval cellars are carved into the rock undulating through the area's forests. Most production here involves Chinon wines (mostly reds), though its Bourgueil and St-Nicolas de Bourgueil wines are growing in popularity in North America. See "Chinon" in chapter 6.
- **Taittinger** (9 place St-Nicaise, Reims; ✆ **03-26-85-45-35;** www.taittinger.com): Taittinger is a grand *marque* of French champagne, one of the few still controlled by members of the family that founded it, in 1930. It's one of the most visitor-friendly houses. See p. 375.
- **Domaines Schlumberger** (100 rue Théodore-Deck, Guebwiller, near Colmar; ✆ **03-89-74-27-00;** www.domaines-schlumberger.com): Established

Tasting wine at Couly-Dutheil.

in 1810, these cellars blend early-19th-century brickwork and modern stainless steel; a visit will enhance your understanding of the subtle differences among wines produced by the seven varieties of grape cultivated in Alsace. See "Colmar" in chapter 10.

- **Domaine Maurice Protheau** (Château d'Etroyes, Mercurey; ✆ **03-85-45-10-84;** www.domaine-protheau-mercurey.fr): The 50 hectares (124 acres) of grapevines straddle at least two *appellations contrôlées* (a regulation system that ensures a wine has been produced where the bottle says), so you'll have a chance to contrast reds (both pinot noirs and burgundies), whites, and rosés produced under the auspices of both Rully and Mercurey. Headquarters is in a château built in the late 1700s and early 1800s. See "Autun" in chapter 11.
- **The Winegrowing Region around Bordeaux:** This area is among the most glamorous in France, with a strong British influence, thanks to centuries of trade with London- and Bristol-based dealers. One prestigious grower, **Société Dubosq,** Château Haut-Marbuzet, St-Estephe (✆ **05-56-59-30-54**), welcomes visitors who phone in advance of their arrival Monday to Saturday. Free visits to the cellars are followed by a complimentary *dégustation des vins* of whichever of the company's products a visitor requests. See p. 717.

THE best LUXURY HOTELS

- **Hôtel Ritz** (Paris; www.ritzparis.com; ✆ **800/223-6800** in the U.S. and Canada, or 01-43-16-30-30): This hotel occupies a palace overlooking the octagonal borders of one of the most perfect plazas in France: place Vendôme.

The decor is pure opulence. Marcel Proust wrote parts of *Remembrance of Things Past* here, and Georges-Auguste Escoffier perfected many of his recipes in its kitchens. See p. 194.

A room at the Hôtel Ritz.

- **Royal Monceau** (Paris; www.leroyalmonceau.com; ✆ **01-42-99-88-00**): This new Philippe Starck–designed gem has the whole city talking. It offers absolute luxury for contemporary jet-setters, including a Clarins spa, an indoor pool, a state-of-the-art cinema, edgy fashion, and a mobile sound studio that can be set up in any of the soundproofed rooms. See p. 198.
- **Château d'Artigny** (Montbazon, Loire Valley; www.artigny.com; ✆ **02-47-34-30-30**): The perfume king François Coty once lived and entertained lavishly at this mansion outside Tours—and you can do the same today in one of the poshest hotels in the Loire Valley. Experience the grandeur once enjoyed by Elizabeth Taylor and other celebs, taking in the weekend soirees and musical evenings. See p. 282.
- **Oustau de Baumanière** (Les Baux, Provence; www.oustaudebaumaniere.com; ✆ **04-90-54-33-07**): This Relais & Châteaux property is in the valley at the foot of Les Baux de Provence. Both the cuisine and the accommodations, some of which are in buildings dating from the 16th and 17th centuries, are superb. See p. 525.
- **Grand Hôtel du Cap-Ferrat** (St-Jean-Cap-Ferrat, Côte d'Azur; www.grand-hotel-cap-ferrat.com; ✆ **04-93-76-50-50**): The Grand Hôtel occupies 5.6 prime hectares (14 acres) on one of the world's most exclusive peninsulas. In a Belle Epoque palace, it has hosted royals, aristocrats, and wealthy wannabes since the turn of the 20th century. See p. 609.
- **Hôtel du Cap-Eden Roc** (Cap-d'Antibes, Côte d'Azur; www.hotel-du-cap-eden-roc.com; ✆ **04-93-61-39-01**): Built during the grand Second Empire and set on 8.9 hectares (22 acres) of splendidly landscaped gardens, this hotel is legendary, evoking the F. Scott Fitzgerald classic *Tender Is the Night.* Swimmers revel in a pool blasted from the dark rock of the glamorous coastline. See p. 580.
- **Hôtel Negresco** (Nice, Côte d'Azur; www.hotel-negresco-nice.com; ✆ **04-93-16-64-00**): Built in 1913 as a layered wedding cake in the château style,

Hôtel Negresco.

the Negresco was a lavish escape for the Edwardian era's most respected and most notorious figures, including Lillie Langtry, the longtime mistress of Britain's Edward VII. After her fall from grace, she sat in the lobby, swathed in veils, refusing to utter a word. Following renovations in early 2011, the hotel is better now than during its Jazz Age heyday. See p. 599.

- **Hôtel du Palais** (Biarritz, Basque Country; www.hotel-du-palais.com; ✆ **800/223-6800** in the U.S. and Canada, or 05-59-41-64-00): Delectably beautiful, this place was built in 1845 as a pink-walled summer palace for Napoleon III and his empress, Eugénie. The Belle Epoque fantasy has entertained such guests as Edward VII of England, Alfonso XIII of Spain, and the duke of Windsor. See p. 682.

THE best AFFORDABLE HOTELS

- **Hotel des Grandes Ecoles** (Paris; www.hotel-grandes-ecoles.com; ✆ **01-43-26-79-23**): In the heart of the Latin Quarter, and set within a luxuriant and peaceful little garden, this delightful hotel is a budget option boasting a unique, provincial charm. See p. 213.
- **Mama Shelter** (Paris; www.mamashelter.com; ✆ **01-43-48-48-48**): It might be off the beaten track, but this new Starck-designed hotel nonetheless attracts the in-crowd with its buzzing downstairs restaurant/bar space, high-tech set up, and low-cost rates. See p. 206.
- **Les Maisons de Léa** (Honfleur, Normandy; www.lesmaisonsdelea.com; ✆ **02-31-14-49-49**): It overlooks a Norman 18th-century port favored by the French novelist Flaubert. The amenities aren't grand, but the charming setting includes an appealing restaurant, and—more surprising—the price tag is reasonable. See p. 315.
- **Hôtel d'Avaugour** (Dinan, Brittany; www.avaugourhotel.com; ✆ **02-96-39-07-49**): Its exterior looks as antique as the fortifications ringing the medieval

Les Maisons de Léa.

La Maison Blanche.

harbor, but a major restoration transformed the interior into a cozy getaway on the Norman coast. Add aesthetic appeal, old-time flavor of Dinan's winding alleys, and views of the Channel, and you've got the ingredients for an affordable escape. See p. 348.

- **Ostellerie du Vieux-Pérouges** (Pérouges, Rhône Valley; www.hostelleriedeperouges.com; ✆**04-74-61-00-88**): This hotel, described as a museum of the 13th century, is one of the most significant in central France. Composed of a group of 13th-century buildings with low ceilings and thick walls, it evokes the France of another day and doesn't overcharge. See p. 459.
- **La Maison Blanche** (Montpellier; www.hotel-maison-blanche.com; ✆**04-99-58-20-70**): Evokes a French Creole ambience of New Orleans with its gingerbread trim. Bathrooms are spacious, for the most part, and the guest rooms are beautifully outfitted in oak. The price is right, too. See p. 641.

THE best HISTORIC PLACES TO STAY

- **Trianon Palace** (Versailles, Ile de France; www.trianonpalace.com; ✆**800/937-8461** in the U.S. and Canada, or 01-30-84-50-00): Louis XIV nearly bankrupted France during the construction of his nearby palace, but this hotel overlooking its gardens might have been even more influential. In 1919, the Treaty of Versailles was ratified by delegates who stayed in the same rooms that house guests today. You'll be pampered at this plush, elegant hotel, which boasts its own spa. See p. 223.
- **Château de Locguénolé** (Hennebont, Brittany; www.chateau-de-locguenole.com; ✆**02-97-76-76-76**): No professional decorator could accumulate the array of furnishings and artifacts that grace this Breton manor house, which has been occupied by the same family for 500 years. Some visitors think it's the most charming hotel in southern Brittany; you may agree. See p. 357.

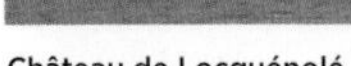

Château de Locguénolé.

Manoir du Stang.

- **Manoir du Stang** (La Forêt-Fouesnant, Brittany; www.manoirdustang.com; ✆**02-98-56-96-38**): Even the ivy that twines across the facade of this 16th-century Breton manor house looks as though it was planted by someone very important, very long ago. Formal gardens segue into forested parkland; modern amenities are juxtaposed with enviable antiques—the place is a gem that happens to be a glamorous hotel. See p. 352.
- **Château de Rochegude** (Rochegude, Provence; www.chateauderochegude.com; ✆**04-75-97-21-10**): During the thousand years of this château's existence, its owners have included popes, dauphins, and less prominent aristocrats who showered it with taste and money. Today each room is outfitted in a style inspired by a specific emperor or king. The setting is 10 hectares (25 acres) of parkland adjacent to the Rhône, outside Orange. See p. 500.
- **Château des Alpilles** (St-Rémy-de-Provence, Provence; www.chateaudesalpilles.com; ✆**04-90-92-03-33**): The Pichot family built this château in 1827, and it has housed many famous personages, including Chateaubriand. The luxurious hotel, modestly referred to as "a house for paying friends," is a showcase of luxury, refinement, and taste. See p. 515.

THE best UPSCALE RESTAURANTS

- **Passage 53** (Paris; ✆**01-42-33-04-35;** www.passage53.com.): Located inside the city's oldest covered passageway, this restaurant is bursting with postcard charm. It also has delicious, yet modern, cuisine, and just received its second Michelin star. See p. 138.
- **L'Arpège** (Paris; ✆**01-47-05-09-06;** www.alain-passard.com): Among the three-star Michelin splurges in Paris, we're most taken with this one. Chef Alain Passard's menu features pristine produce, raised on his farm and often picked in the morning and served the same day. See p. 159.
- **Lasserre** (Paris; ✆**01-43-59-02-13;** www.restaurant-lasserre.com): With its over-the-top opulence and retractable ceiling, this restaurant is an obvious setting for romance. See p. 144.

- **Les Crayères** (Reims, Champagne; ✆**03-26-82-80-80;** www.lescrayeres.com): This restaurant's setting is a lavish but dignified château with soaring ceilings and French Empire decor. Built in 1904 as the home of the Pommery family (of champagne fortune) and surrounded by a 5.6-hectare (14-acre) park, it's maintained by a staff that appreciates the nuances of service rituals. You can retire directly to your room after consuming a bottle or two of the region's bubbly. See p. ###.
- **A la Côte Saint Jacques** (Joigny, Burgundy; ✆**03-86-62-09-70;** www.cotesaintjacques.com): On the edge of Burgundy, beside the river Yonne, this is the quintessential *restaurant avec chambres.* Indulge your taste for well-prepared food and wine, and then totter off to one of the carefully furnished guest rooms in the historic compound. One of our favorite dishes is cassoulet of morels and frogs' legs, sublimely accompanied by a half-bottle of red burgundy. See p. 437.
- **L'Espérance** (Vézelay, Burgundy; ✆**03-86-33-39-10;** www.marc-meneau-esperance.com): In a farmhouse at the base of a hill (La Colline de Vézelay) that has been a holy site for thousands of years, L'Espérance is run by one of Europe's most famous chefs, Marc Meneau, and his wife, Françoise. The place combines country comforts with great sophistication. See p. 423.
- **Paul Bocuse** (Collonges-au-Mont-d'Or, near Lyon, Rhône Valley; ✆**04-72-42-90-90;** www.bocuse.fr.): Bocuse was the *enfant terrible* of French gastronomy through most of his youth. Today he's the world's most famous chef, catering to Europe's hardest-to-please customers. The cuisine is ostensibly Lyonnais, but Bocuse has never been limited by provincialism, and his mind wanders the world for inspiration. His signature dishes range from pigeon in puff pastry with foie gras to his notable black truffle soup. See p. 452.
- **La Maison Troisgros** (Roanne, Rhône Valley; ✆**04-77-71-66-97;** www.troisgros.com): The setting is the dining room of a once-nondescript hotel near a train station. The cuisine is a celebration of the agrarian bounty of France. Mingling regional specialties, the menu attracts diners from as far away as Paris. See p. 457.
- **Auberge du Père-Bise** (Talloires, French Alps; ✆**04-50-60-72-01;** www.perebise.com): A mysterious alchemy transformed a simple lakeside chalet into an illustrious restaurant. Beside Lac d'Annecy in eastern France, it's outfitted like a provincial home of local gentry, yet it serves elegant food favored by generations of patrons, including the Rothschilds. See p. 477.
- **Le Moulin de Mougins** (Mougins, Côte d'Azur; ✆**04-93-75-78-24;** www.moulin-demougins.com): Occupying a 16th-century olive mill in a Provence forest, this long-celebrated

Les Crayères.

destination is a showcase for Riviera foodies. The chef concocts what he calls the "cuisine of the sun," in celebration of sunny Provence. See p. 571.

THE best AFFORDABLE RESTAURANTS

- **La Crèmerie** (Paris; ✆**01-43-54-99-30;** www.lacremerie.fr): This old milk shop–turned–wine bar is an affordable choice for a romantic meal. It has beautiful tiles and an intimate atmosphere. See p. 157.
- **Breizh Café** (Paris; ✆**01-42-72-13-77;** www.breizhcafe.com): With incredible crepes and friendly service, this is the place to go when you want to fill up on authentic French comfort food for under 20€ a head. See p. 142.
- **Les Vapeurs** (Trouville, Normandy; ✆**02-31-88-15-24;** www.lesvapeurs.fr): An anomaly among the Norman coast's high-priced brasseries, this restaurant overlooking the port is no-frills, from its Art Deco decor to its fresh, well-priced seafood. Patrons enjoy the festive ambience. See p. 322.
- **L'Auberge du Pélican** (Dinan, Brittany; ✆**02-96-39-47-05**): Many visitors drive up from Paris for the day, followed by a dinner here in this old-fashioned Breton establishment, where even the bread is homemade. Dishes with an emphasis on fresh fish are based on time-honored recipes. See p. 355.

Brasserie de l'Ancienne Douane.

- **Brasserie de l'Ancienne Douane** (Strasbourg, Alsace-Lorraine; ✆**03-88-15-78-78;** www.anciennedouane.fr): In a city known for its Alsatian cuisine, this restaurant is a front-runner in the moderate category. In a medieval building, you can feast on the sauerkraut and foie gras of the region. See p. 399.
- **Au Chalet de Brou** (Bourg-en-Bresse, Rhône Valley; ✆**04-74-22-26-28**): In a town famous for its poultry, this restaurant sits across from the village church. It offers the local birds at amazingly low prices, and food critics travel here from all over France for the hearty roast chicken. See p. 460.
- **L'Isle Sonnante** (Aix-en-Provence, Provence; ✆**04-90-82-56-01**): In Paul Cézanne's hometown, this intimate bistro near the Palais de Papes is a favorite of locals and tourists alike. Look for innovative twists on Provençal classics such as rabbit with olives and calamari risotto with saffron. See p. 509.
- **Chez Servais** (Libourne, Bordeaux wine district; ✆**05-57-51-83-97**): As you're touring the wine district outside Bordeaux, one of your finest and best-value meals is likely to be in this little market town at the junction of the Dordogne and Isle rivers. The cuisine is a savory blend of classical and modern. See p. 716.

FRANCE IN DEPTH

The civilization and history of France and the French way of life—the savoir-faire of its people—lures travelers from all over the world to this country that covers an area smaller than Texas. You can get lost in France, lost in the sense that each region is so intriguing and varied that you may immerse yourself in one province for so long that you'll never have time to go on to see what's on the other side. France, often referred to as "the garden of Europe," is—perhaps more than any country in the world—a land to be savored. It's better to get to know intimately one, two, or three regions than try to explore them all. This is not a country to rush through on one of those quick bus tours ("If it's Tuesday, it must be Nice"). It is ideally explored by car, allowing you to stop whenever and wherever you wish.

No European country, not even England, can beat France in its pageantry of personalities, from Madame de Pompadour to Charles de Gaulle, from Jean-Luc Godard to Françoise Hardy, from Catherine de Médicis to Joan of Arc, from Napoleon to Victor Hugo. You'll be introduced to some of these figures in the pages ahead. Seeing where they lived, worked, loved, and became legends is part of the experience of going to France.

This guide is meant to help you decide where to go in France, but ultimately the most gratifying experience will be your own serendipitous discovery of France—sunflowers, a picnic in a poppy field, an hour spent chatting with a small winemaker—whatever it is that stays in your memory for years to come.

FRANCE TODAY

France remains one of the world's most hyped and written-about destinations. It can inspire a masterpiece—and has on countless occasions. Even the cantankerous James McNeill Whistler would allow his masterpiece, a portrait of his mother, to hang in no other city save Paris.

Although not large by North American standards (about the size of the state of Texas, or of Britain and Germany combined), France is densely packed with attractions, both cultural and recreational. Even better, it's permeated with style and known for its *joie de vivre.*

The French claim credit for developing the Gothic style of architecture and the cathedrals that stand as legacies of soaring stone for future generations. Creators of everything from palaces to subway stations have drawn at least some inspiration from designs inaugurated in France. However, despite the thrilling architectural monuments peppering the country's landscapes, it would be wrong

PREVIOUS PAGE: ***The Thinker* at Musèe Rodin.**

to assume that the culture's main contribution to the world is derived from stone, mortar, stained glass, and gilt. Its contributions to painting, literature, cuisine, fashion, and savoir-faire are staggering.

When other parts of Europe were slumbering through the Dark Ages, Provence was alive with creativity as Provençal poetry evolved into a truly lyrical, evocative, and (in some cases) erotic verse form. Despite the frequent absences of its monarchs, who sequestered themselves with their entourages in remote Loire Valley châteaux, Renaissance Paris developed into one of Europe's most cosmopolitan cities, embellishing itself with majestic buildings and sculpture.

> Impressions
>
> ***I tried to think it out. Why did Paris still draw us to its fascination, why did it draw those who felt themselves creative—talent or no talent? Why had it been, since Franklin, that all of us felt that we were freer there than elsewhere? Why did art, literature, and sex, and the feeding and drinking seem more genuine there? Generations of Americans had run a whole gamut of desires, hopes in Paris—all so opposite to those they had found at home, on the farm, in the city.***
>
> **—Stephen Longstreet,**
> ***We All Went to Paris* (1972)**

The passionate French tradition of scholarship helped build Europe's university system, synthesized the modern world's interpretation of human rights, helped topple one of the most powerful monarchies of all time, and justified the role of a post-revolutionary emperor (Napoleon) as conqueror of most of Europe.

As for style, it has always been foolhardy to try to compete with the French on their terms. The theatrical backdrops of the sometimes-silly Gallic monarchs have been interpreted by latter-day aesthetes as history's crowning achievement when it comes to conspicuous displays of wealth and prestige.

In politics and ideology, France has always been a leader and remains so today. Fueled by Enlightenment writings, whose most articulate voices were French, the 1789 Revolution toppled Europe's most deeply entrenched regime and cracked the foundations of dozens of other governments. After a period of murky maneuverings by diverse coalitions of strange bedfellows, post-revolutionary Paris became a magnet for the greatest talents of the 19th and early 20th centuries in many fields of endeavor.

Newcomers have commented (often adversely) on the cultural arrogance of the French. But despite its linguistic and cultural rigidity, France has received more immigrants and political exiles than any other European country. Part of this derives from France's status as one of Europe's least densely populated nations per square mile, and part of it from the tendency of the French to let others be until their actions become dangerous or obnoxious, not necessarily in that order.

This guidebook represents our effort to introduce first-time visitors to France's subtle pleasures and—if possible—to open new doors to those who might have already spent time here. We've set for ourselves the formidable task of seeking out France at its finest and condensing that information so you can access it easily. But the best need not always be the most expensive or the most chic or the most widely publicized.

If you're a first-timer, everything in Paris, of course, is new. But if you've been away for a long time, expect changes. Taxi drivers may no longer correct your fractured French, but address you in English—and that's tantamount to a

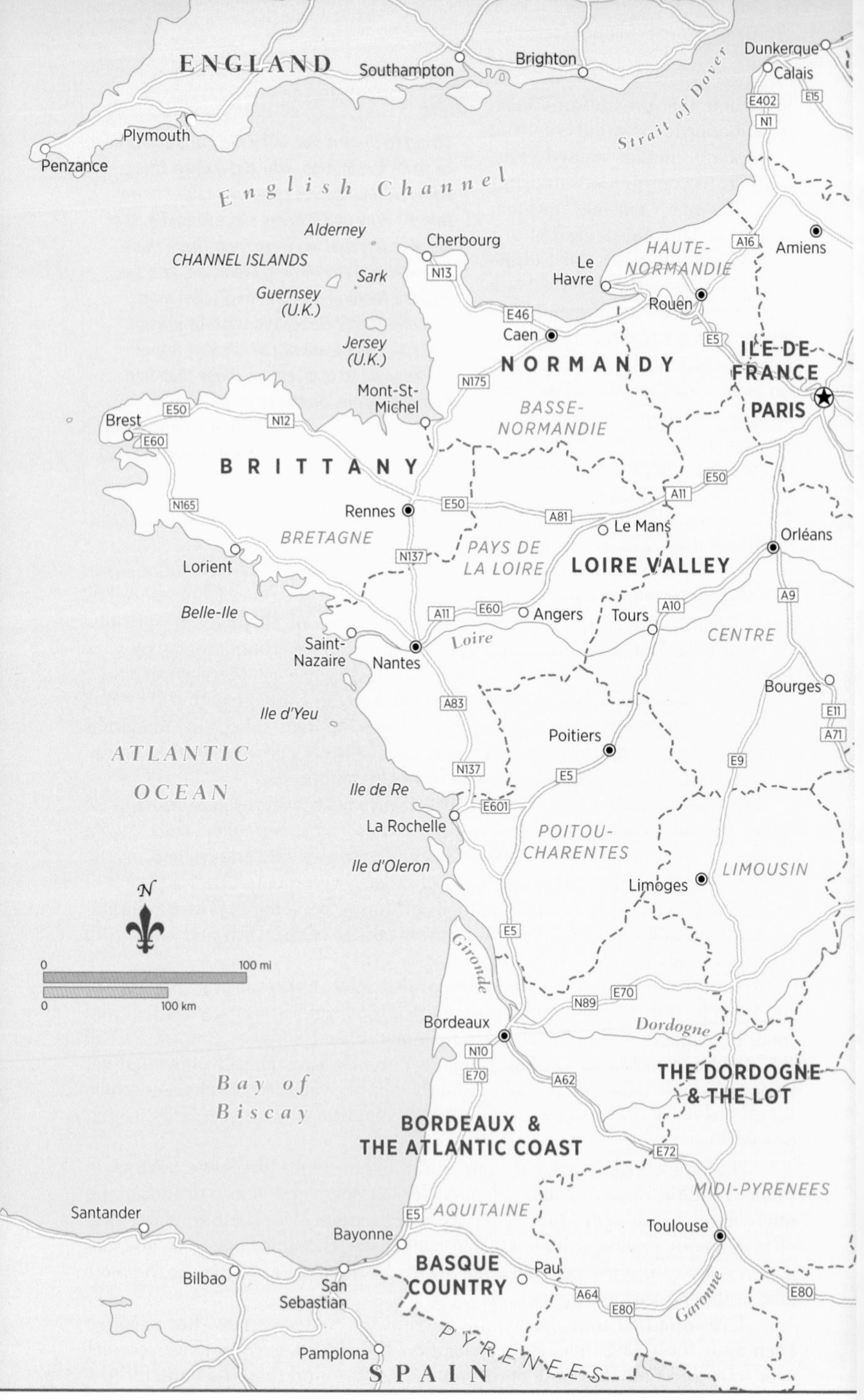
ENGLAND
Southampton
Brighton
Dunkerque
Calais
Plymouth
Penzance
Strait of Dover
English Channel
Alderney
CHANNEL ISLANDS
Sark
Guernsey (U.K.)
Jersey (U.K.)
Cherbourg
Le Havre
HAUTE-NORMANDIE
Amiens
Rouen
Caen
NORMANDY
ILE-DE-FRANCE
PARIS
Mont-St-Michel
BASSE-NORMANDIE
Brest
BRITTANY
Rennes
BRETAGNE
PAYS DE LA LOIRE
Le Mans
LOIRE VALLEY
Orléans
Lorient
Belle-Ile
Angers
Tours
CENTRE
Saint-Nazaire
Nantes
Loire
Bourges
Ile d'Yeu
Poitiers
ATLANTIC OCEAN
Ile de Re
La Rochelle
POITOU-CHARENTES
Ile d'Oleron
Limoges
LIMOUSIN
N
0
100 mi
100 km
Gironde
Bordeaux
Dordogne
THE DORDOGNE & THE LOT
Bay of Biscay
BORDEAUX & THE ATLANTIC COAST
MIDI-PYRENEES
AQUITAINE
Santander
Toulouse
Bayonne
BASQUE COUNTRY
Pau
Bilbao
San Sebastian
Garonne
Pamplona
PYRENEES
SPAIN
E402
E15
N1
A16
N13
E46
E5
N175
E50
N12
E60
A11
N165
E50
A81
N137
A11
E60
A10
A9
A83
E11
A71
N137
E5
E9
E601
E5
N89
E70
N10
E70
A62
E72
E5
A64
E80
E80

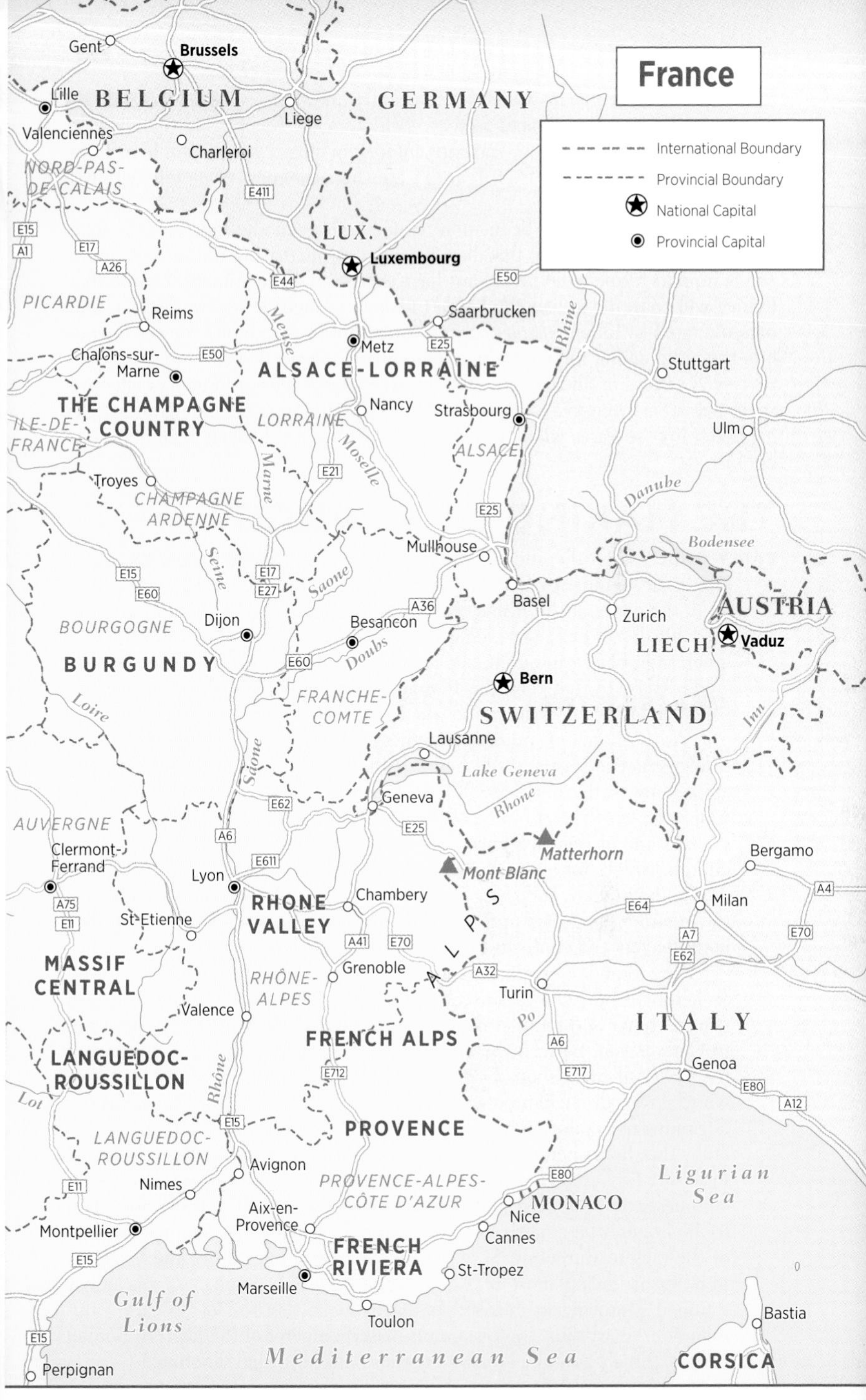

France
International Boundary
Provincial Boundary
National Capital
Provincial Capital
Gent
Brussels
BELGIUM
Lille
Liege
GERMANY
Valenciennes
Charleroi
NORD-PAS-DE-CALAIS
LUX.
Luxembourg
PICARDIE
Reims
Saarbrucken
Metz
Chalons-sur-Marne
ALSACE-LORRAINE
Stuttgart
THE CHAMPAGNE COUNTRY
Nancy
Strasbourg
ILE-DE-FRANCE
LORRAINE
Ulm
ALSACE
Troyes
CHAMPAGNE ARDENNE
Danube
Mullhouse
Bodensee
Basel
AUSTRIA
Zurich
BOURGOGNE
Dijon
Besancon
LIECH.
Vaduz
BURGUNDY
Bern
FRANCHE-COMTE
SWITZERLAND
Lausanne
Lake Geneva
Geneva
AUVERGNE
Matterhorn
Clermont-Ferrand
Mont Blanc
Bergamo
Lyon
RHONE VALLEY
Chambery
Milan
St-Etienne
ALPS
MASSIF CENTRAL
Grenoble
RHÔNE-ALPES
Turin
Valence
FRENCH ALPS
ITALY
LANGUEDOC-ROUSSILLON
Genoa
PROVENCE
Avignon
PROVENCE-ALPES-CÔTE D'AZUR
Ligurian Sea
Nimes
MONACO
Nice
Aix-en-Provence
Cannes
Montpellier
FRENCH RIVIERA
St-Tropez
Marseille
Gulf of Lions
Toulon
Bastia
Mediterranean Sea
CORSICA
Perpignan

revolution. More Parisians have a rudimentary knowledge of English, and the country, at least at first glance, seems less hysterically xenophobic than in past years. Part of this derives from Parisians' interest in music, videos, and films from foreign countries, and part from France's growing awareness of its role within a united Europe.

Yet France has never been more concerned about the loss of its unique identity within a landscape that has attracted an increasing number of immigrants from its former colonies. Many have expressed the legitimate concern that France will continue to lose the battle to keep its language strong, distinct, and unadulterated by foreign slang or catchwords. But as the country moves deeper into the millennium, foreign tourists spending much-needed cash are no longer perceived as foes or antagonists. *Au contraire:* The rancor of France's collective xenophobia has been increasingly redirected toward the many immigrants seeking better lives in Paris, where the infrastructure has nearly been stretched to its limits.

THE MAKING OF FRANCE

EARLY GAUL When the ancient Romans considered France part of their empire, their boundaries extended deep into the forests of the Paris basin and up to the edges of the Rhine. Part of Julius Caesar's early reputation came from his defeat of King Vercingetorix at Alésia in 52 B.C., a victory he was quick to publicize in one of the ancient world's literary masterpieces, *The Gallic Wars.* In that year, the Roman colony of Lutetia (Paris) was established on an island in the Seine (Ile de la Cité).

As the Roman Empire declined, its armies retreated to the flourishing colonies that had been established along a strip of the Mediterranean coast—among others, these included Orange, Montpellier, Nîmes, Narbonne, and Marseille, which retain some of the best Roman monuments in Europe.

As one of their legacies, the Roman armies left behind the Catholic church, which, for all its abuses, was the only real guardian of civilization during the anarchy following the Roman decline. A form of low Latin was the common language, and it slowly evolved into the archaic French that both delights and confuses today's medieval scholars.

The form of Christianity adopted by many of the chieftains was viewed as heretical by Rome. Consequently, when Clovis (king of northeastern Gaul's Franks and founder of the Merovingian dynasty) astutely converted to Catholicism, he won the approval of the pope, the political support of the powerful archbishop of Reims, and the loyalty of the many Gallic tribes who'd grown disenchanted with anarchy. (Clovis's baptism is viewed as the beginning of a collusion between the Catholic church and the French monarchy that flourished until the 1789 Revolution.) At the Battle of Soissons in 486, Clovis defeated the last vestiges of Roman power in Gaul. Other conquests that followed included expansions westward to the Seine, then to the Loire. After a battle in Dijon in 500, he became the nominal overlord of the king of Burgundy. Seven years later, his armies drove the Visigoths into Spain, giving most of Aquitaine, in western France, to his newly founded Merovingian dynasty. Trying to make the best of an earlier humiliation, Anastasius, the Byzantium-based emperor of the Eastern Roman Empire, finally gave the kingdom of the Franks his legal sanction.

After Clovis's death in 511, his kingdom was split among his squabbling heirs. The Merovingian dynasty, however, managed to survive in fragmented form for another 250 years. During this period, the power of the bishops and the great lords grew, firmly entrenching the complex hierarchies and preoccupations of what we today know as feudalism. Although apologists for the Merovingians are quick to point out their achievements, the feudalistic quasi-anarchy of their tenuous reign has been (not altogether unfairly) identified by many historians as the Dark Ages.

THE CAROLINGIANS From the wreckage of the intrigue-ridden Merovingian court emerged a new dynasty: the Carolingians. One of their leaders, Charles Martel, halted a Muslim invasion of northern Europe at Tours in 743 and left a much-expanded kingdom to his son, Pepin. The Carolingian empire eventually stretched from the Pyrénées to a point deep in the German forests, encompassing much of modern France, Germany, and northern Italy. The heir to this vast land was Charlemagne. Crowned emperor in Rome on Christmas Day in 800, he returned to his capital at Aix-la-Chapelle (Aachen) and created the Holy Roman Empire. Charlemagne's rule saw a revived interest in scholarship, art, and classical texts, defined by scholars as the Carolingian Renaissance.

Despite Charlemagne's magnetism, cultural rifts formed in his sprawling empire, most of which was eventually divided between two of his three squabbling heirs. Charles of Aquitaine annexed the western region; Louis of Bavaria took the east. Historians credit this division with the development of modern France and Germany as separate nations. Shortly after Charlemagne's death, his fragmented empire was invaded by Vikings from the north, Muslim Saracens from the south, and Hungarians from the east.

THE MIDDLE AGES When the Carolingian dynasty died out in 987, Hugh Capet, comte de Paris and duc de France, officially began the Middle Ages with the establishment of the Capetian dynasty. In 1154, the annulment of Eleanor of Aquitaine's marriage to Louis VII of France and subsequent marriage to Henry II of England placed the western half of France under English control, and vestiges of their power remained for centuries. Meanwhile, vast forests and swamps were cleared for harvesting (often by the Middle Ages' hardest-working ascetics, Cistercian monks), the population grew, great Gothic cathedrals were begun, and monastic life contributed to every level of a rapidly developing social order. Politically driven marriages among the ruling families more than doubled the size of the territory controlled from Paris, a city that was

Charlemagne.

increasingly recognized as the country's capital. Philippe II (reigned 1179–1223) infiltrated more prominent families with his genes than anyone else in France, successfully marrying members of his family into the Valois, Artois, and Vermandois. He also managed to win Normandy and Anjou back from the English.

Louis IX (St. Louis) emerged as the 13th century's most memorable king, though he ceded most of the hard-earned military conquests of his predecessors back to the English. Somewhat of a religious fanatic, he died of illness (along with most of his army) in 1270 in a boat anchored off Tunis. The vainglorious and not-very-wise pretext for his trip was the Eighth Crusade. At the time of his death, Notre-Dame and the Sainte-Chapelle in Paris had been completed, and the arts of tapestry making and stonecutting were flourishing.

During the 1300s, the struggle of French sovereignty against the claims of a rapacious Roman pope tempted Philip the Fair to encourage support for a pope based in Avignon. (The Roman pope, Boniface VIII, whom Philip publicly insulted and then assaulted in his home, is said to have died of the shock.) During one of medieval history's most bizarre episodes, two popes ruled simultaneously, one from Rome and one from Avignon. They competed fiercely for the spiritual and fiscal control of Christendom, until years of political intrigue turned the tables in favor of Rome and Avignon relinquished its claim in 1378.

The 14th century saw an increase in the wealth and power of the French kings, an increase in the general prosperity, and a decrease in the power of the feudal lords. The death of Louis X without an heir in 1316 prompted more than a decade of scheming and plotting before the eventual emergence of the Valois dynasty.

The Black Death began in the summer of 1348, killing an estimated 33% of Europe's population, decimating the population of Paris, and setting the stage for the exodus of the French monarchs to safer climes in such places as the Loire Valley. A financial crisis, coupled with a series of ruinous harvests, almost bankrupted the nation.

During the Hundred Years' War, the English made sweeping inroads into France in an attempt to grab the throne. At their most powerful, they controlled almost all the north (Picardy and Normandy), Champagne, parts of the Loire Valley, and the huge western region called Guyenne. The peasant-born charismatic visionary Joan of Arc rallied the dispirited French troops as well as the timid dauphin (crown prince), whom she managed to have crowned as Charles VII in the cathedral at Reims. As threatening to the Catholic Church as she was to the English, she was declared a heretic and burned at the stake in Rouen in 1431. Led by the newly crowned king, a barely cohesive France initiated reforms that strengthened its finances and vigor. After compromises among the quarreling factions, the French army drove the discontented English out, leaving them only the Norman port of Calais.

In the late 1400s, Charles VIII married Brittany's last duchess, Anne, for a unification of France with its Celtic-speaking western outpost. In the early 1500s, the endlessly fascinating François I, through war and diplomacy, strengthened the monarchy, rid it of its dependence on Italian bankers, coped with the intricate policies of the Renaissance, and husbanded the arts into a form of patronage that French monarchs continued to endorse for centuries.

Meanwhile, the growth of Protestantism and the unwillingness of the Catholic Church to tolerate it led to civil strife. In 1572, Catherine de Médicis reversed her policy of religious tolerance and ordered the St. Bartholomew's Day Massacre of hundreds of Protestants. Henri IV, tired of the bloodshed and fearful that a fanatically Catholic Spain would meddle in the religious conflicts, converted to Catholicism as a compromise in 1593. Just before being fatally stabbed by a half-crazed monk, he issued the Edict of Nantes in 1598, granting freedom of religion to Protestants in France.

THE PASSING OF FEUDALISM By now France was a modern state, rid of all but a few of the vestiges of feudalism. In 1624, Louis XIII appointed a Catholic cardinal, the duc de Richelieu, his chief minister. Amassing enormous power, Richelieu virtually ruled the country until his death in 1642. His sole objective was investing the monarchy with total power—he committed a series of truly horrible acts trying to attain this goal and paved the way for the eventual absolutism of Louis XIV.

Although he ascended the throne when he was only 9, with the help of his Sicilian-born chief minister, Cardinal Mazarin, Louis XIV was the most powerful monarch Europe had seen since the Roman emperors. Through first a brilliant military campaign against Spain and then a judicious marriage to one of its royal daughters, he expanded France to include the southern provinces of Artois and Roussillon. Later, a series of diplomatic and military victories along the Flemish border expanded the country toward the north and east. The estimated population of France at this time was 20 million, as opposed to 8 million in England and 6 million in Spain. French colonies in Canada, the West Indies, and America (Louisiana) were stronger than ever. The mercantilism that Louis's brilliant finance minister, Colbert, implemented was one of the era's most important fiscal policies, hugely increasing France's power and wealth. The arts flourished, as did a sense of aristocratic style that's remembered with a bittersweet nostalgia today. Louis's palace of Versailles is the perfect monument to the most flamboyantly consumptive era in French history.

Louis XIV.

Louis's territorial ambitions so deeply threatened the other nations of Europe that, led by William of Orange, they united to hold him in check. France entered a series of expensive and demoralizing wars that, coupled with high taxes and bad harvests, stirred up much civil discontent. England was viewed as a threat both within Europe and in the global rush for lucrative colonies. The great Atlantic ports, especially Bordeaux, grew and prospered because of France's success in the West Indian slave and sugar trades. Despite the country's power, the total number of French colonies diminished thanks to the naval power of the English. The rise of Prussia as a militaristic neighbor posed an additional problem.

THE REVOLUTION & THE RISE OF NAPOLEON Meanwhile, the Enlightenment was training a new generation of thinkers for the struggle against absolutism, religious fanaticism, and superstition. Europe was never the same after the Revolution of 1789, though the ideas that engendered it had been brewing for more than 50 years. On August 10, 1792, troops from Marseille, aided by a Parisian mob, threw the dimwitted Louis XVI and his tactless Austrian-born queen, Marie Antoinette, into prison. After months of bloodshed and bickering among violently competing factions, the two thoroughly humiliated monarchs were executed.

France's problems got worse before they got better. In the ensuing bloodbaths, both moderates and radicals were guillotined in full view of a bloodthirsty crowd that included voyeurs like Dickens's Mme. Defarge, who brought her knitting every day to place de la Révolution (later renamed place de la Concorde) to watch the beheadings. The drama surrounding the collapse of the *ancien régime* and the beheadings of Robespierre's Reign of Terror provides the most heroic and horrible anecdotes in the history of France. From all this emerged the Declaration of the Rights of Man, an enlightened document published in 1789; its influence has been cited as a model of democratic ideals ever since. The implications of the collapse of the French aristocracy shook the foundations of every monarchy in Europe.

Only the militaristic fervor of Napoleon Bonaparte could reunite France and bring an end to the revolutionary chaos. A political and military genius who appeared on the landscape at a time when the French were thoroughly sickened by the anarchy following their revolution, he restored a national pride that had been severely tarnished. He also established a bureaucracy and a code of law that has been emulated in other legal systems around the world. In 1799, at the age of 30, he entered Paris and was crowned first consul and master of France. Soon after, a decisive victory in his northern Italian campaign solidified his power at home. A brilliant politician, he made peace through a compromise with the Vatican, quelling the atheistic spirit of the earliest days of the Revolution.

Napoleon.

Napoleon's victories made him the envy of Europe. Beethoven dedicated his *Eroica* symphony to Napoleon—but later retracted the dedication when Napoleon committed what Beethoven considered atrocities. Just as he was poised on the verge of conquering all Europe, Napoleon's famous retreat from Moscow during the winter of 1812 reduced his formerly invincible army to tatters, as 400,000 Frenchmen died in the Russian snows. Napoleon was then defeated at Waterloo by the combined armies of the English, Dutch, and Prussians. Exiled to the British-held island of St-Helena in the South Atlantic, he died in 1821, probably the victim of an unknown poisoner.

THE BOURBONS & THE SECOND EMPIRE In 1814, following the destruction of Napoleon and his dream, the Congress of Vienna redefined the map of Europe. The new geography was an approximation of the boundaries that had existed in 1792. The Bourbon monarchy was reestablished, with reduced powers for Louis XVIII, an archconservative, and a changing array of leaders who included the prince de Polignac and, later, Charles X. New oppressions, however, didn't sit well in a France that had already spilled so much blood in favor of egalitarian causes.

In 1830, after censoring the press and dissolving Parliament, Louis XVIII was removed from power after yet more violent uprisings. Louis-Philippe, duc d'Orléans, was elected king under a liberalized constitution. His reign lasted for 18 years of calm prosperity during which England and France more or less collaborated on matters of foreign policy. The establishment of an independent Belgium and the French conquest of Algeria (1840–47) were to have resounding effects on French politics a century later. It was a time of wealth, grace, and expansion of the arts for most French people, though the industrialization of the north and east produced some of the 19th century's most horrific poverty.

A revolution in 1848, fueled by a financial crash and disgruntled workers in Paris, forced Louis-Philippe out of office. That year, Napoleon I's nephew, Napoleon III, was elected president. Appealing to the property-protecting instinct of a nation that hadn't forgotten the violent upheavals of less than a century before, he initiated a repressive right-wing government in which he was awarded the totalitarian status of emperor in 1851. Rebounding from the punishment they'd received during the revolution and the minor role they'd played during the First Empire, the Second Empire's clergy enjoyed great power. Steel production was begun, and a railway system and Indochinese colonies were established. New technologies fostered new kinds of industry, and the bourgeoisie flourished. And the baron Georges-Eugène Haussmann radically altered Paris by laying out the grand boulevards the world knows today.

By 1866, an industrialized France began to see the Second Empire as more of a hindrance than an encouragement to its expansion. The dismal failure of colonizing Mexico and the increasing power of Austria and Prussia were setbacks to the empire's prestige. In 1870, the Prussians defeated Napoleon III at Sedan and held him prisoner with 100,000 of his soldiers. Paris was besieged by an enemy who only just failed to march its vastly superior armies through the capital.

After the Prussians withdrew, a violent revolt ushered in the Third Republic and its elected president, Marshal MacMahon, in 1873. Peace and prosperity slowly returned, France regained its glamour, a mania of building occurred, the Impressionists made their visual statements, and writers like Flaubert redefined the French novel into what today is regarded as the most evocative in the world. As if as a symbol of this period, the Eiffel Tower was built as part of the 1889 Universal Exposition.

Émile Zola.

By 1890, a new corps of satirists (including Zola) had exposed the country's wretched living conditions, the cruelty of the country's vested interests, and the underlying hypocrisy of late-19th-century French society. The 1894 Dreyfus Affair exposed the corruption of French army officers who had destroyed the career and reputation of a Jewish colleague (Albert Dreyfus), falsely and deliberately punished—as a scapegoat—for treason. The ethnic tensions identified by Zola led to further divisiveness in the rest of the 20th century.

THE WORLD WARS International rivalries, thwarted colonial ambitions, and conflicting alliances led to World War I, which, after decisive German victories for 2 years, degenerated into the mud-slogged horror of trench warfare. Mourning between four and five million casualties, Europe was inflicted with psychological scars that never healed. In 1917, the United States broke the European deadlock by entering the war.

After the Allied victory, grave economic problems, plus the demoralization stemming from years of fighting, encouraged the growth of socialism and communism. The French government, led by a vindictive Georges Clemenceau, demanded every centime of reparations it could wring from a crushed Germany. The humiliation associated with this has often been cited as the origin of the German nation's almost obsessive determination to rise from the ashes of 1918 to a place in the sun.

The worldwide Great Depression had devastating repercussions in France. Poverty and widespread bankruptcies weakened the Third Republic to the point where successive coalition governments rose and fell with alarming regularity. The crises reached a crescendo on June 14, 1940, when Hitler's armies arrogantly marched down the Champs-Elysées, and newsreel cameras recorded French people openly weeping. Under the terms of the armistice, the north of France was occupied by the Nazis, and a puppet French government was established at Vichy under the authority of Marshal Pétain. The immediate collapse of the French army is viewed as one of the most significant

Impressions

Paris is a sphinx. I will drag her secret from her. —Mirabeau

humiliations in modern French history.

Charles de Gaulle.

Pétain and his regime cooperated with the Nazis in unbearably shameful ways. Not the least of their errors included the deportation of more than 75,000 French Jews to German work camps. Pockets of resistance fighters *(le maquis)* waged small-scale guerrilla attacks against the Nazis throughout the course of the war, and free-French forces continued to fight along with the Allies on battlegrounds like North Africa. Charles de Gaulle, the irascible giant whose personality is forever associated with the politics of his era, established himself as the head of the French government-in-exile, operating first from London and then from Algiers.

The scenario was radically altered on June 6, 1944, when the largest armada in history successfully established a bulkhead on the beaches of Normandy. Paris rose in rebellion even before the Allied armies arrived, and on August 26, 1944, Charles de Gaulle entered the capital as head of the government. The Fourth Republic was declared even as pockets of Nazi snipers continued to shoot from scattered rooftops throughout the city.

THE POSTWAR YEARS Plagued by the bitter residue of colonial policies that France had established during the 18th and 19th centuries, the Fourth Republic witnessed the rise and fall of 22 governments and 17 premiers. Many French soldiers died on foreign battlefields as once-profitable colonies in North Africa and Indochina rebelled. It took 80,000 French lives, for example, to put down a revolt in Madagascar. After suffering a bitter defeat in 1954, France ended the war in Indochina and freed its former colony. It also granted internal self-rule to Tunisia and (under slightly different circumstances) Morocco.

Algeria was to remain a greater problem. The advent of the 1958 Algerian revolution signaled the end of the much-maligned Fourth Republic. De Gaulle was called back from retirement to initiate a new constitution, the Fifth Republic, with a stronger set of executive controls. To nearly everyone's dissatisfaction, de Gaulle ended the Algerian war in 1962 by granting the country full independence. Screams of protest resounded long and loud, but the sun had set on most of France's far-flung empire. Internal disruption followed as vast numbers of *pieds-noirs* (French-born residents of Algeria recently stripped of their lands) flooded back into metropolitan France, often into makeshift refugee camps in Provence and Languedoc.

In 1968, major social unrest and a violent coalition hastily formed between the nation's students and blue-collar workers eventually led to the collapse of the government. De Gaulle resigned when his attempts to placate some of the marchers were defeated. The reins of power passed to his second-in-command, Georges Pompidou, and his successor, Valérie Giscard d'Estaing, both of whom continued de Gaulle's policies emphasizing economic development and protection of France as a cultural resource to the world.

THE 1980s & 1990s In 1981, François Mitterrand was elected the first Socialist president of France since World War II (with a close vote of 51%). In almost immediate response, many wealthy French decided to transfer their assets out of the country, much to the delight of banks in Geneva, Monaco, the Cayman Islands, and Vienna. Though reviled by the rich and ridiculed for personal mannerisms that often seemed inspired by Louis XIV, Mitterrand was reelected in 1988. During his two terms, he spent billions of francs on his *grands projets* (like the Louvre pyramid, Opéra Bastille, Cité de la Musique, and Grande Arche de la Défense), some of which are now beginning to fall apart or reveal serious weaknesses.

In 1992, France played a leading role in the development of the European Union (E.U.), 15 countries that will ultimately abolish all trade barriers among themselves and share a single currency, the euro. More recent developments include France's interest in developing a central European bank for the regulation of a shared intra-European currency, a ruling that some politicians have interpreted as another block in the foundation of a united Europe.

In April 1993, voters dumped the Socialists and installed a new conservative government. Polls cited corruption scandals, rising unemployment, and urban insecurity as reasons for this. The Conservative premier Edouard Balladur had to "cohabit" the government with Mitterrand, whom he blamed for the country's growing economic problems. Diagnosed with terminal prostate cancer near the end of his second term, Mitterrand continued to represent France with dignity, despite his deterioration. The battle over who would succeed him was waged against Balladur with epic rancor by Jacques Chirac, tenacious survivor of many terms as mayor of Paris. Their public discord was among the most venomous since the days of Pétain.

On his third try, on May 7, 1995, Chirac won the presidency with 52% of the vote and immediately declared war on unemployment. Mitterrand turned over the reins of government on May 17 and died shortly thereafter. But Chirac's popularity soon faded in the wake of unrest caused by an 11.5% unemployment rate, a barrage of terrorist attacks by Algerian Muslims, and a stressed economy struggling to meet European Union entry requirements.

A wave of terrorist attacks from July to September 1995 brought an unfamiliar wariness to Paris. Six bombs were planted, killing 7 people and injuring 115. In light of this, Parisians proved cautious, if not fearful. Algerian Islamic militants, the suspected culprits, may have brought military guards to the Eiffel Tower, but they failed to throw France into panic.

Throughout 1995 and early 1996, France infuriated everyone from the members of Greenpeace to the governments of Australia and New Zealand by resuming its long-dormant policy of exploding nuclear bombs on isolated Pacific atolls for testing purposes. This policy continued until public outcry, both in France and outside its borders, exerted massive pressure to end the tests.

In May 1996, thousands of Parisian workers took to the streets, disrupting passenger train service to demand a workweek shorter than the usual 39 hours. They felt that this move would help France's staggering unemployment figures. Employer organizations resisted this idea, claiming that even if the workweek were cut to 35 hours, businesses wouldn't be able to take on many new employees.

The drama of 1996 climaxed with the heat of the summer, when the police took axes to the doors of the Paris church of St-Bernard de la Chapelle. Nearly 300 African immigrants were removed by force from this place of refuge and deported. Strikes and protests continued to plague the country, and Chirac's political horizon became dimmer still—with a 12% unemployment rate and crime on an alarming increase. Terrorist scares continued to flood the borders of France throughout 1997, forcing a highly visible armed police force, as part of a nationwide program known as Vigipirate, to take to the streets of major cities. One of the unusual offshoots of the Vigipirate program involved the closing of the crypts of many of France's medieval churches to visitors, partly in fear of a terrorist bomb attack on national historic treasures.

In the latest power struggle between the Conservatives and the Socialists, in the spring of 1998, Conservatives were ousted in a majority of France's regional provinces, amounting to a powerful endorsement for Prime Minister Lionel Jospin's Socialist-led government.

In 1999, France joined with other European countries in adopting the euro as its standard of currency. The new currency accelerated the creation of a single economy comprising nearly 300 million Europeans, with a combined gross national product approaching 9€ trillion, larger than that of the United States.

France moved into the millennium by testing the practicality of new and progressive social legislation. On October 13, 1999, the French Parliament passed a new law giving legal status to unmarried couples, including homosexual unions. The law allows couples of same sex or not to enter into a union and be entitled to the same rights as married couples in such areas as housing, inheritance, income tax, and social welfare.

CONTEMPORARY POLITICS (2000–PRESENT) In February 2005, President George W. Bush flew to Europe to mend fences with some of his worst critics, notably French President Chirac. The two political foes found common ground on such issues as Syria and Lebanon, but Iraq remained a thorny problem. Chirac, a self-styled expert on cows after serving as a former agriculture minister, was not invited to Bush's Texas ranch. When asked why not, Bush enigmatically said, "I'm looking for a good cowboy."

Late in 2005, decades of pent-up resentment felt by the children of African immigrants exploded into an orgy of violence and vandalism. Riots began in the suburbs of Paris and spread around the country. Throughout France, gangs of youths battled the French police; torched schools, cars, and businesses; and even attacked commuter trains. Rioting followed in such cities as Dijon, Marseille, and Rouen. Most of the rioters were the sons of Arab and black African immigrants, Muslims living in a mostly Catholic country. The reason for the protests? Leaders of the riots claimed they live "like second-class citizens," even though they are French citizens. Unemployment is 30% higher in the ethnic ghettos of France.

In spring 2006, Jacques Chirac signed a law that made it easier for employers to fire workers, which set off massive demonstrations across France. Some one million protesters staged marches and strikes against the law, which was rescinded on April 10, 2006.

Against a backdrop of discontent regarding issues of unemployment, immigration, and healthcare, the charismatic Nicolas Sarkozy swept into the presidential office in May 2007. It remains to be seen whether his campaign promises to break from "politics as usual" translate into real change, especially for many of France's disenchanted youths.

Sarkozy, the combative son of a Hungarian immigrant, promised to reinvigorate ties with France's traditional ally, the United States. His election was followed by scattered violence throughout the country from anti-Sarkozy protesters. In 2005, he'd called rioters in Paris's immigrant-heavy suburbs "scum," which was blamed for the country's worst violence in 4 decades. Sarkozy has promised to be president of "all the French" during his administration.

Nicholas Sarkozy and Carla Bruni.

In all this muddle, Sarkozy found time to divorce a wife and take a beautiful new bride. A glamorous model-turned-singer, the sexy Carla Bruni, is the new first lady of France. "The Carla effect," as it's called in Paris, has decreased Sarkozy's popularity—along with his failure to revive France's ailing economy. The tabloids have had a field day with the first lady, whose former lovers include Mick Jagger, Eric Clapton, Donald Trump, even Laurent Fabius (a former French prime minister).

Beginning in 2008, a smoking ban in public places came into law throughout Paris and France in general. French authorities estimate that passive smoking kills about 13 people a day in France and ruled the situation unacceptable. Public places include transport stations, museums, government offices, and shops, but not streets or private places such as houses or hotel rooms. Those found in breach of the ban will be fined.

Many of the French became uncertain of their future as a European Union member in 2010. The financial instability in Greece and the continuing woes of debt-ridden Ireland, Italy, Spain, and Portugal contributed to the drop in the euro's value.

Politically, Sarkozy remains a divisive figure. His attempt to reform the pension system by raising the age of retirement from 60 to 62 caused a wave of strikes and protests across France in the autumn of 2010. Despite widespread opposition to the legislation, the French parliament approved the reforms in October 2010. Outside of politics, the French tend to look at Sarkozy's personal

Impressions

Paris (in each shape and gesture and avenue and cranny of her being) was continuously expressing the humanness of humanity. Everywhere I sensed a miraculous presence, not of mere children and women and men, but of living human beings.

—e e cummings

life with ridicule. His marriage to Italian–French pop singer Carla Bruni-Sarkozy and his holidays with the rich and famous have earned him the title of the "bling bling president," and stories of his aides putting boxes behind podiums to make him seem taller during his speeches have been met with derision. Given how badly Sarkozy is currently doing in the polls, it remains to be seen whether the French will give him a second chance and re-elect him in the upcoming 2012 French Presidential Election. One thing's for sure—he won't go without a fight.

ART & ARCHITECTURE

Art

France's art treasures range from medieval stained glass and Ingres portraits to Monet's Impressionist *Water Lilies;* its architecture encompasses Roman ruins and Gothic cathedrals, as well as Renaissance châteaux and postmodern buildings like the Centre Pompidou. This brief overview will help you make sense of it all.

PREHISTORIC, CELTIC & CLASSICAL (25,000 B.C.–A.D. 500)

After England's Stonehenge, Europe's most famous prehistoric remains are France's **Paleolithic cave paintings.** Created 15,000 to 20,000 years ago, they depict mostly hunting scenes and abstract shapes.

The **caves at Lascaux,** the Sistine Chapel of prehistoric art, have been closed since 1963, but experts have created a replica, Lascaux II. To see the real stuff, visit **Les Eyzies-de-Tayac,** which boasts four caves (Font de Gaume is the best). In the neighboring Lot Valley, outside Cahors, is the **Grotte du Pech-Merle,** with France's oldest cave art (about 20,000 years old). Little remains of the art of **Celtic** (ca. 1000 B.C.–A.D. 125) and **Roman** (A.D. 125–500) Gaul. Surviving items—small votive bronzes, statues, jewelry, and engraved weapons and tools—are spread across France's **archaeology museums.** Burgundy preserves the most of Celtic Gaul, including sites at **Dijon, Châtillon-sur-Seine, Alise-Ste-Reine,** and **Auxerre.** To see artifacts of Roman Gaul, visit the southern towns of **Nîmes, Arles, Orange, St-Rémy-de-Provence,** and **Vienne.**

ROMANESQUE (900–1100)

Artistic expression in medieval France was largely church related. Because Mass was in Latin, images were used to communicate the Bible's lessons to the mostly illiterate people. **Bas-reliefs** (sculptures that project slightly from a flat surface) were used to illustrate key tales that inspired faith in God and fear of sin (the *Last Judgment* was a favorite). These reliefs were wrapped around column capitals and fitted into the **tympanums,** or arched spaces above doorways (the complete door, tympanum, arch, and supporting pillars assemblage is the **portal**).

The best examples of Romanesque art include a *Last Judgment* tympanum by Gislebertus at **St-Lazare** in Autun; 76 Romanesque cloister capitals and one of France's best-carved 11th-century portals at **St-Pierre Abbey** in Moissac near Montauban; and the tympanum over the inner main portal of huge **Ste-Madeleine** in Vézelay. The **Bayeux Tapestry** (1066–77) is the most notable example of Romanesque artistry, 69m (226 ft.) of embroidered linen telling the story of William the Conqueror's defeat of the English.

GOTHIC (1100–1400)

Paris retains almost no art from the classical or Romanesque eras, but much remains from the medieval Gothic era, when artists created sculpture and stained glass for churches.

Outstanding examples include the **Cathédrale de Chartres** (1194–1220), a day trip from Paris, boasting magnificent sculpture and some of the best stained glass in Europe; the **Cathédrale de Notre-Dame** (1163–1250), with sculpture on the facade, an interior choir screen lined with deep-relief carvings, and three rose windows filled with stained glass; and **Sainte-Chapelle** (1240–50), a tiny chapel adorned with the finest stained glass in the world.

THE RENAISSANCE & BAROQUE (1450–1800)

Humanist thinkers rediscovered the wisdom of ancient Greece and Rome, while artists strove for naturalism, using newly developed techniques like linear perspective. The French had little to do with this movement, which started in Italy and was picked up only in Germany and the Low Countries. However, many Renaissance treasures are in French museums, thanks to collectors such as **François I.**

Not until the 17th-century **baroque** did a few French masters emerge. This period is hard to pin down. In some ways a result of the Catholic Counter-Reformation, it reaffirmed spirituality in a simplified, monumental, and religious version of Renaissance ideals. In other ways, it delved even deeper into classical modes and a kind of super-realism based on using peasants as models and the *chiaroscuro* (contrast of light and dark) of the Italian painter Caravaggio.

Paris's **Louvre** abounds with Renaissance works by Italian, Flemish, and German masters, including **Michelangelo** (1475–1564) and **Leonardo da Vinci** (1452–1519). Leonardo's ***Mona Lisa*** (1503–05), perhaps the world's most famous painting, hangs there. Great baroque and rococo artists include **Antoine Watteau** (1684–1721), a rococo painter of colorful, theatrical works; and **Jean-Honoré Fragonard** (1732–1806), a master of rococo pastel scenes, including the famous *The Bathers.*

NEOCLASSICAL & ROMANTIC (1770–1890)

As the baroque got excessive, the rococo got cute, and the somber Counter-Reformation got serious about the limits on religious art, several artists looked to the ancients for relief. This gave rise to a **neoclassical** artistic style that emphasized symmetry, austerity, clean lines, and classical themes.

The **romantics,** on the other hand, felt that both the ancients and the Renaissance had gotten it wrong and that the Middle Ages was the place to be. They idealized romantic tales of chivalry and the nobility of peasantry.

Some great artists and movements of the era, all with examples in the **Louvre,** include **Jean Ingres** (1780–1867), who became a defender of the neoclassicists and the Royal French Academy and opposed the romantics; **Theodore Géricault** (1791–1824), one of the great early romantics, who painted *The Raft of the Medusa* (1819), which served as a model for the movement; and **Eugène Delacroix** (1798–1863), whose *Liberty Leading the People* (1830) was painted in the romantic style.

IMPRESSIONISM (1870–1920)

Seeking to capture the *impression*, light made as it reflected off objects, the Impressionists adopted a free, open style; deceptively loose compositions; swift, visible brushwork; and often light colors. For subject matter, they turned to landscapes and scenes of modern life. You'll find some of the best examples of their works in the **Musée d'Orsay.**

Impressionist greats include **Edouard Manet** (1832–1883), whose groundbreaking *Picnic on the Grass* (1863) and *Olympia* (1863) helped inspire the movement with their harsh realism, visible brush strokes, and thick outlines; **Claude Monet** (1840–1926), who launched the movement officially in an 1874 exhibition in which he exhibited his Turner-inspired *Impression, Sunrise* (1874), now in the **Musée Marmottan; Pierre-Auguste Renoir** (1841–1919), known for his figures' ivory skin and chubby pink cheeks; **Edgar Degas** (1834–1917), an accomplished painter, sculptor, and draftsman—his pastels of dancers and bathers are particularly memorable; and **Auguste Rodin** (1840–1917), the greatest Impressionist-era sculptor, who crafted remarkably expressive bronzes. The **Musée Rodin,** his former Paris studio, contains, among other works, his *Burghers of Calais* (1886), *The Kiss* (1886–98), and *The Thinker* (1880).

POST-IMPRESSIONISM (1880–1930)

The smaller movements or styles of Impressionism are usually lumped together as "post-Impressionism." Again, you'll find the best examples of these works at the **Musée d'Orsay,** though you'll find pieces by Matisse, Chagall, and the cubists, including Picasso, in the **Centre Pompidou.** Important post-Impressionists include **Paul Cézanne** (1839–1906), who adopted the short brush strokes, love of landscape, and light color palette of his Impressionist friends; **Paul Gauguin** (1848–1903), who developed **synthetism** (black outlines around solid colors); **Henri de Toulouse-Lautrec** (1864–1901), who created paintings and posters of wispy, fluid lines anticipating Art Nouveau and often depicting the bohemian life of Paris's dance halls and cafes; **Vincent van Gogh** (1853–90), who combined divisionism, synthetism, and a touch of Japanese influence, and painted with thick, short strokes; **Henri Matisse** (1869–1954), who created **fauvism** (a critic described those who used the style as *fauves,* meaning "wild beasts"); and **Pablo Picasso** (1881–1973), a Málaga-born artist who painted objects from all points of view at once, rather than using such optical tricks as perspective to fool viewers into seeing three dimensions. The fractured result was **cubism.** You can see art from all of his periods at the **Musée Picasso** in the Marais.

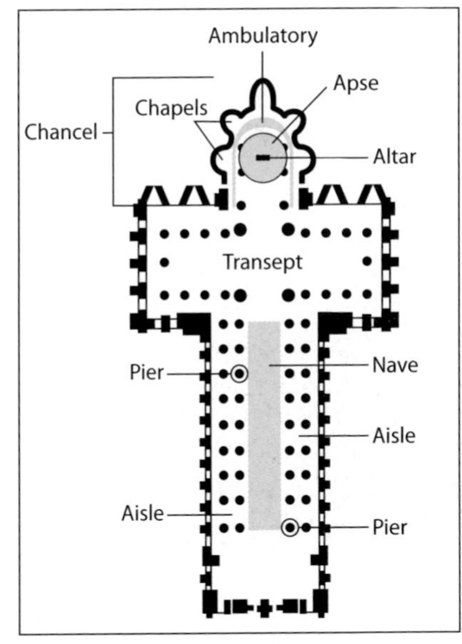

Church Floor Plan

Architecture

It's worth pointing out that very few buildings (especially churches) were built in one particular architectural style. These massive,

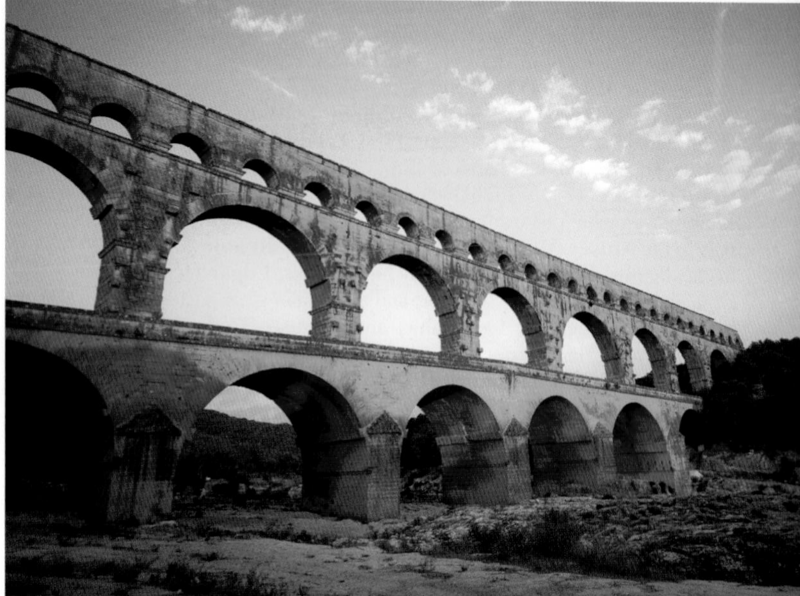

Pont du Gard, Nîmes.

expensive structures often took centuries to complete, during which time tastes would change and plans would be altered.

ANCIENT ROMAN (125 B.C.–A.D. 450)

Provence was Rome's first transalpine conquest, and the legions of Julius Caesar quickly subdued the Celtic tribes across France, converting it into Roman Gaul.

Nîmes preserves from the 1st century B.C. a 20,000-seat **amphitheater,** a **Corinthian temple** called the "Square House," a fine **archaeology museum,** and the astounding **pont du Gard,** a 47m-long (154-ft.), three-story aqueduct made of cut stones fitted together without mortar.

ROMANESQUE (800–1100)

The Romanesque style took its inspiration from ancient Rome (hence the name). Early Christians in Italy had adapted the basilica (ancient Roman law-court buildings) to become churches.

The **Cathédrale St-Bénigne** in Dijon was the first French Romanesque church, but of that era, only the crypt remains. The **Cathédrale St-Pierre** in Angoulême has a single large nave, a rounded apse with small radiating chapels, and a pair of transept mini-apses.

GOTHIC (1100–1500)

By the 12th century, engineering developments freed church architecture from the heavy, thick walls of Romanesque structures and allowed ceilings to soar, walls to thin, and windows to proliferate. Gothic interiors enticed churchgoers' gazes upward to high ceilings filled with light. Graceful buttresses and spires soared above town centers.

The best examples in and around Paris of the Gothic are **Basilique St-Denis** (1140–44), the world's first Gothic cathedral, in a Paris suburb; **Cathédrale de Chartres** (1194–1220), a Gothic masterpiece with some 150 glorious stained-glass windows; and, of course, **Cathédrale de Notre-Dame** (1163–1250), which possesses pinnacled flying buttresses, a trio of France's best rose windows, good portal carvings, a choir screen of deeply carved reliefs, and spiffy gargoyles.

Cathédrale Notre-Dame de Chartres.

RENAISSANCE (1500–1630)

In architecture, as in painting, the Renaissance came from Italy and was only slowly Frenchified. And as in painting, its rules stressed proportion, order, classical inspiration, and precision to create unified, balanced structures.

The Loire Valley and Burgundy are home to many Renaissance **châteaux.** Foremost is the Loire's **Château de Chambord,** started in 1519, probably according to plans by Leonardo da Vinci (who may have designed its double helix staircase). In contrast, the **Château de Chenonceau,** home to many a French king's wife or mistress, is a fanciful fairy tale built in the middle of a river. The best example in Burgundy is the **Château de Tanlay,** east of Chablis.

Château de Chambord.

CLASSICISM & ROCOCO (1630–1800)

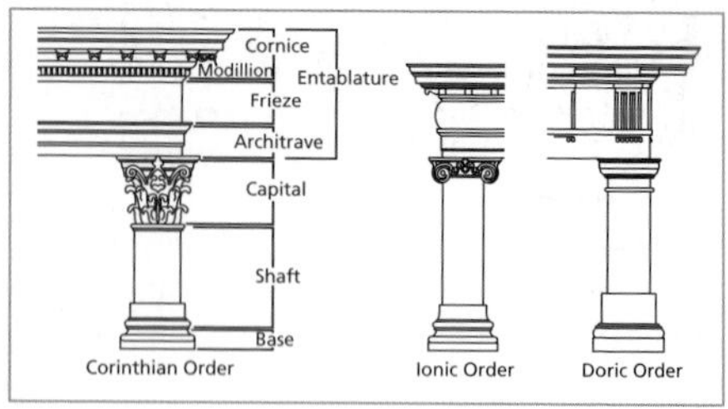

Classical Orders.

While Italy and Germany embraced the opulent baroque, France took the fundamentals of Renaissance **classicism** even further, becoming more imitative of ancient models. During the reign of Louis XIV, art and architecture were subservient to political ends. Buildings were grandiose and severely ordered on the Versailles model. Opulence was saved for interior decoration, which increasingly (especially in 1715–50, after the death of Louis XIV) became a detailed and self-indulgent **rococo** (*rocaille* in French). Externally, rococo is noticeable only in a greater elegance and delicacy.

Mansart built town houses, châteaux, and churches (**Val-de-Grâce** in Paris, the **Palais du Tau** in Reims) and laid out Dijon's **place de la Libération.** But the Parisian architect is chiefly remembered for his steeply sloping namesake, **"mansard" roofs.**

Louis Le Vau (1612–70) was the chief architect of the Louvre from 1650 to 1670 and of the **Château de Vaux-le-Vicomte** (1656–61) outside Paris, a gig that put him and his collaborators—including Mansart, interior decorator **Charles Le Brun** (1619–90), and the unparalleled landscape gardener **André Le Nôtre** (1613–1700)—on Louis XIV's radar and landed them the commission to rebuild **Versailles** (1669–85). Versailles is France's—indeed, Europe's—grandest palace.

THE 19TH CENTURY

Architectural styles in 19th-century Paris were eclectic, beginning in a severe classical mode and ending with an identity crisis torn between Industrial Age technology and Art Nouveau organic.

Identifiable styles include the neoclassical **First Empire,** with its strong lines often accented with a simple curve—the rage during Napoleon's reign; and **Second Empire,** which occurred during Napoleon III's reign, a reinterpretation of classicism in an ornate mood. During this period, Paris became a city of wide boulevards courtesy of **Baron Georges-Eugène Haussmann** (1809–91), commissioned by Napoleon III in 1852 to redesign the city. Haussmann lined the boulevards with simple six-story apartment blocks, such as elongated 18th-century town houses with continuous balconies wrapping around the third and sixth floors and mansard roofs with dormer windows.

The **Third Republic** expositions in 1878, 1889, and 1900 used the engineering prowess of the Industrial Revolution to produce such Parisian monuments as the Tour Eiffel and Sacré-Coeur.

Art Nouveau architects and decorators rebelled against the Third Republic era of mass production by creating asymmetrical, curvaceous designs based on organic inspiration (plants and flowers) in such media as wrought iron, stained glass, and tile.

The best examples are the **Arc de Triomphe** (1836), Napoleon's oversize imitation of a Roman triumphal arch, the ultimate paean to the classic era; **Tour**

Centre Pompidou.

Eiffel (1889), which **Gustave Eiffel** (1832–1923) slapped together to form the world's tallest structure, at 320m (1,050-ft.); and **Métro station entrances.**

THE 20TH CENTURY

France commissioned some ambitious architectural projects in the last century, most of them the *grand projets* of the late François Mitterrand. The majority were considered controversial or even offensive when completed.

At **Centre Pompidou** (1977), Britisher Richard Rogers (b. 1933) and Italian Renzo Piano (b. 1937) turned architecture inside out—literally—to craft Paris's eye-popping modern-art museum, with exposed pipes, steel supports, and plastic-tube escalators wrapping around the exterior; the **Louvre's glass pyramids** (1989) were created by Chinese-American architect I. M. Pei (b. 1917); and **Opéra Bastille** (1989) is a curvaceous, dark glass mound of space designed by Canadian Carlos Ott (b. 1947).

FRANCE IN POPULAR CULTURE

Books

There are numerous books on all aspects of French history and society—ranging from the very general, such as the section on France in the *Encyclopedia Americana,* International Edition (Grolier, 1989), which presents an excellent, illustrated overview of the French people and their way of life; to the very specific, such as Judi Culbertson and Tom Randall's *Permanent Parisians: An Illustrated Guide to the Cemeteries of Paris* (Chelsea Green, 1986), which depicts the lives of famous French and expatriates who are buried in Paris.

HISTORY In addition to the encyclopedia reference above, a broad overview of French history can be found in other encyclopedias and general history books. One very good one is *History of France,* by Guillaume de Bertier de Savigny and David H. Pinkney, a comprehensive history with illustrations and plenty of obscure but interesting facts.

Two books that present French life and society in the 17th century are Warren Lewis's *The Splendid Century* and Madame de Sévigné's *Selected Letters,* edited by Leonard W. Tancock, which contains imaginative and witty letters written to her daughter during the reign of Louis XIV. Simon Schama's *Citizens* is a long but enjoyable new history of the French Revolution.

Moving into the 20th century, *Pleasure of the Belle Epoque: Entertainment and Festivity in Turn-of-the-Century France,* by Charles Rearick, depicts public diversions in the changing and troubled times of the Third Republic. *Paris Was Yesterday, 1925–1939* is a fascinating collection of excerpts from Janet Flanner's "Letters from Paris" column of the *New Yorker.* Larry Collins and Dominique Lapierre have written a popular history of the liberation of Paris in 1944 called *Is Paris Burning?*

Finally, two unusual approaches to French history are Rudolph Chleminski's *The French at Table,* a funny and honest history of why the French know how to eat better than anyone and how they go about it, and *Paris: A Century of Change, 1878-1978,* by Normal Evenson, a notable study of the urban development of Paris.

TRAVEL Since 1323, some 10,000 books have been devoted to exploring Paris. One of the best is *Paris: Capital of the World,* by Patrice Higonnet. This book takes a fresh social, cultural, and political look at this City of Lights. Higonnet even explores Paris as "the capital of sex" and, in contrast, the "capital of art." The gang's all here, from Balzac to Zola.

Showing a greater fondness for gossip is Alistair Horne in his *Seven Ages of Paris.* From the Roman founding up to the student riots of 1968, this is one of the most amusing books on Paris we've ever read. Horne is not a timid writer. He calls the Palais de Chaillot fascistic and hideous, the Pompidou Center a horror. We even learn that a woman once jumped off the Eiffel Tower, bounced off the roof of a parked car, and survived.

In *The Flâneur: A Stroll Through the Paradoxes of Paris,* Edmund White wants the reader to experience Paris as Parisians do. Hard to translate exactly, *a flâneur* is someone who strolls, loafs, or idles. With White, you can circumnavigate Paris as whim dictates.

BIOGRAPHY You can get a more intimate look at history through biographies of historical figures. The best book yet on the architect who changed the face of Paris is *Haussmann: His Life and Times and the Making of Modern Paris,* by Patrick Camiller. Hugh Ross Williamson brings to life Catherine de Médicis in his *Catherine de Medici* by combining text and magnificent illustrations from the art of the 16th century. This queen of France was the dominant personality during her nation's religious wars and mother of three kings of France, a queen of Spain, and a queen of Navarre.

Representing a very different era are *A Moveable Feast,* Ernest Hemingway's recollections of Paris during the 1920s, and Morley Callaghan's *That Summer in Paris: Memories of Tangled Friendships with Hemingway, Fitzgerald and Some Others,* an anecdotal account of the same period. Another great read is *The Autobiography of Alice B. Toklas,* by Gertrude Stein. It's not only the account of 30 years in Paris, but also the autobiography of Gertrude Stein.

Simone de Beauvoir, by Deirdre Bair, was described by one critic as ". . . a biography *'à l'Americaine'*—that is to say, long, with all the warts of its subject unsparingly described." The story of the great feminist intellectual was based in part on tape-recorded conversations and unpublished letters.

Colette: A Life, by Herbert R. Lottman, is a painstakingly researched biography of the celebrated French writer and her fascinating life—which included not only writing novels and appearing in cabarets, but also dabbling in lesbianism and perhaps even collaborating with the enemy during the Nazi occupation.

THE ARTS Much of France's beauty can be found in its art. Three books that approach France from this perspective are *The History of Impressionism,* by John Rewald, which is a collection of writings about and quotations from the artists, illuminating this period in art; *The French Through Their Films,* by Robin Buss, an exploration of more than 100 widely circulated films; and *The Studios of Paris: The Capital of Art in the Late Nineteenth Century,* by John Milner. In the last, Milner presents the dynamic forces that made Paris one of the most complex centers of the art world in the early modern era.

Nightlife of Paris: The Art of Toulouse-Lautrec, by Patrick O'Connor, is an enchanting 80-page book with anecdotes about the hedonistic luminaries of Belle Epoque Paris, with paintings, sketches, and lithographs by the artist.

Olympia: Paris in the Age of Manet, by Otto Friedrich, takes its inspiration from the celebrated artwork in the Musée d'Orsay in Paris. From here the book takes off on an anecdote-rich gossipy chain of historical associations, tracing the rise of the Impressionist school of modern painting, but incorporating social commentary, too, such as the pattern of prostitution and venereal disease in 19th-century France.

FICTION The *Chanson de Roland,* edited by F. Whitehead, written between the 11th and 14th centuries, is the earliest and most celebrated of the "songs of heroic exploits." *The Misanthrope* and *Tartuffe* are two masterful satires on the frivolity of the 17th century by the great comic dramatist Molière. François-Marie Arouet Voltaire's *Candide* is a classic satire attacking the philosophy of optimism and the abuses of the ancient regime.

Gustave Flaubert.

A few of the masterpieces of the 19th century are *Madame Bovary,* by Gustave Flaubert, in which the carefully wrought characters, setting, and plot attest to Flaubert's genius in presenting the tragedy of Emma Bovary; Victor Hugo's *Les Misérables,* a classic tale of social oppression and human courage set in the era of Napoleon I; and *Selected Stories,* by the master of short stories, Guy de Maupassant.

Honoré de Balzac's *La comédie humaine* depicts life in France from the fall of Napoleon to 1848. Henry James's *The Ambassadors* and *The American* both take place in Paris. *The Vagabond,* by Colette, evokes the life of a French music-hall performer.

Tropic of Cancer is the semiautobiographical story of Henry Miller's years in Paris. One of France's leading thinkers, Jean-Paul Sartre, shows individuals struggling against their freedom in *No Exit and Three Other Plays.*

For more recent reads, you might pick up a tattered copy of *The Da Vinci Code* (if you haven't already read it) or David Sedaris's *Me Talk Pretty One Day,* revealing the viewpoint of an American tourist as he tries to absorb French culture.

Films

Although Americans understood—and very quickly, too—the commercial wealth to be made from films, the French are credited with the scientific and technical inventions that made them possible. French physicists had laid the groundwork for a movie camera as early as the mid-1880s, and the world's first movie was shown in Paris on December 28, 1895. Its makers were the Lumière brothers, who considered filmmaking a scientific oddity and stubbornly confined its use to the production of international newsreels. Later, a vaudevillian actor and illusionist, Georges Méliés, used film to convey plot and drama.

Charles Pathé and Léon Gaumont were the first to exploit filmmaking on a grand scale. Beginning in 1896, they produced and distributed their own films, building their company into a giant before World War I. When Gaumont made his first film, he enlisted his secretary, Alice Guy-Blanché, to create the plot, design the scenery, and direct it. She proved so successful that she was eventually promoted to the head of Paris's largest studio and became the world's first female director.

Before World War I the many talented actors arriving *en scène* included Max Linder, a popular French comic, whose style influenced Charlie Chaplin and helped him develop his keen sense of timing. After World War I, a flood of film imports from the United States and an economic depression slowed down the growth of French filmmaking.

By the 1920s, the French began to view filmmaking as an art form and infused it with surreal and dada themes. These were eventually named avant-garde and included experiments viewed (sometimes skeptically, sometimes encouragingly) in Hollywood and around the world. Examples include Man Ray's *Le retour à la raison* (1923), Fernand Léger's *Le ballet mécanique* (1924), and Jean Cocteau's *Le sang d'un poète* (1930).

The golden age of the French silent screen on both sides of the Atlantic was 1927 to 1929. Actors were directed with more sophistication, and technical abilities reached an all-time high. One of our favorite films—despite its mind-numbing length—is Abel Gance's sweepingly evocative masterpiece *Napoleon* (1927); its grisly battle scenes are easily as chilling as any war film made today. Other highlights from this era include René Clair's *Un chapeau de paille d'Italie* (*An Italian Straw Hat,* 1927), Carl Dreyer's *La passion de Jeanne d'Arc* (1928), and an adaptation of Emile Zola's *Thérèse Raguin* (1928) by Jacques Feyder.

Experiments with the early productions of "talkies" were less successful. One popular film director, Pagnol, declared outright that the role of films was to publicize to the masses the benefits of the theatrical stage. During this period, many of the counterculture's most gifted directors either left France altogether (as did René Clair, who emigrated to England in 1934) or died (Jean Vigo, *Zéro de Conduite*).

In 1936, the Cinémathèque Française was established to find and preserve old (usually silent) French films. By that time, French cinematographers had divorced themselves completely from the value system of the stage and had found a style of their own. An average of 130 films a year were made in France, by (among others) Jean Renoir, Charles Spaak, and Marcel Carne. This was also the era that brought such French luminaries as Claudette Colbert and Maurice Chevalier to Hollywood.

During World War II, the best-known (to Americans) of the French directors fled to Hollywood. Those who remained were heavily censored by the Vichy government. Despite that, more than 350 French films, many relating to long-past (and, therefore, uncontroversial) events were produced. Exceptions were Carne's *Les enfants du paradis* (*Children of Paradise,* 1945).

In 1946, France slapped a heavy quota system onto the importation of foreign (especially American) films. A semigovernmental film authority (le Centre national du Cinéma Français) financed independent French film companies and encouraged liaisons between the French and Italian film industries. Many directors who had supported the Vichy government's Nazi collaboration were soon accepted back into the cinematic community.

Two strong traditions—film noir and a return to literary traditions—began to flourish. Film noir included such existentially inspired nihilistic themes as André Cayatte's *Nous sommes tous des assassins* (*We Are All Assassins,* 1952) and Yves Allegret's *Dedée d'Anvers* (1948). Examples of the literary tradition include Bresson's *Journal d'un curé de campagne* (*Diary of a Country Priest,* 1951) and a film rendition of Stendhal's *Le rouge et le noir* (*The Red and the Black,* 1954), by Autant-Lara. By the 1950s, comedy adopted a new kind of genre with Jacques Tati's *Les vacances du Monsieur Hulot (Mr. Hulot's Holiday).* By the mid-1950s, French filmmaking ushered in the era of enormous budgets, a la Hollywood, and the creation of such frothy potboilers as *And God Created Woman,* which helped make Brigitte Bardot a celebrity around the world, contributing greatly to the image in America of France as a kingdom of sexual liberation.

By the late 1950s, François Truffaut, widely publicizing his auteur theories, rebelled with a series of short films (the most famous of which was *The 400 Blows,* 1959) that were partly financed by government funds, partly by wealthy benefactors. With Jean-Luc Godard (*A bout de soufflé,* or *Breathless,* 1960) and Claude Chabrol (*Le beau Serge,* 1959), they pioneered one of the most publicized movements in 20th-century French art, *la nouvelle vague.* In the early 1960s, dozens of new directors joined the movement, furiously making films, some of which are considered classics, others of which have been thrown into the dustbin of

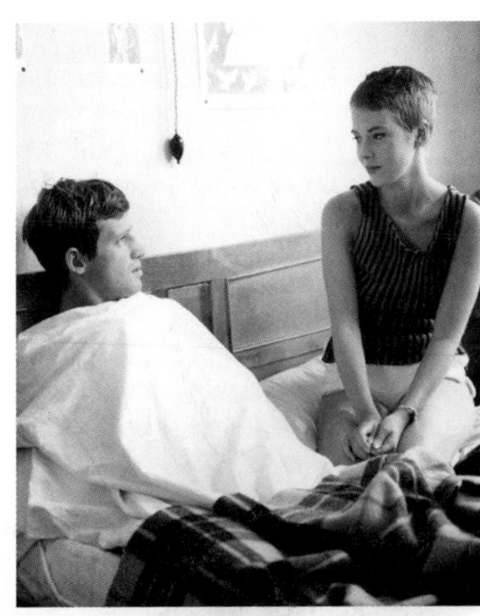
A scene from *A bout de soufflé.*

forgotten artistic endeavors. Enthusiastically endorsed by the counterculture on both sides of the Atlantic, these directors included Renais (*Muriel*), Roger Vadim, Agnès Varda (*Le Bonheur*), Jacques Demy (*Les parapluies de Cherbourg*), Louis Malle, Chris Marker, and Marguerite Duras (*Detruire, dit-elle*).

After a switch to political themes (Costa Gavras's Z) during the 1968 rebellions (and a politically motivated abandonment of the film festival at Cannes by at least a dozen prominent French directors), French cinema turned to comedy in the early 1970s. Examples include Buñuel's *Le charme discret de la bourgeoisie* (1972) and Yanne's *Tout le monde il est beau, tout le monde il est gentil* (1972).

Many American films—still shown rather frequently on TV—were filmed in Paris (or else used sets to simulate Paris). Notable ones have included the classic *An American in Paris,* starring Gene Kelly, and *Moulin Rouge,* starring José Ferrer as Toulouse-Lautrec. *Last Tango in Paris,* with Marlon Brando, was one of the most controversial films set in Paris. Woody Allen's acclaimed *Midnight in Paris* is the most recent film to celebrate the City of Lights. The film features beautiful shots of the city and includes cameos of iconic figures who lived in Paris in the 1920s.

Truffaut's *The Last Metro* and Clément's *Is Paris Burning?* gained worldwide audiences. *Betty Blue,* the stylish Jean-Jacques Beineix film about a torrid summertime love affair, was released in English in 1992. It was first shown in France in 1986 when it was that country's nominee for the Oscar as best foreign film.

One French film that continues to be popular is Jean-Pierre Jeunet's *Amélie,* which tugs at the heartstrings. You'll fall in love with those scenes shot in Montmartre. You can also rent *Le Placard,* by Francis Veber, starring Gérard Depardieu and dealing with gay life in French society.

The most recent French film to achieve world renown is *La Vie en Rose,* which won Marion Cotillard an Oscar in 2008 for her performance as "The Little Sparrow," Edith Piaf. This film documenting Piaf's tragic life is an astonishing immersion of one performer (Cotillard) into the body and soul of another (Piaf).

Music

You might not immediately think of music when you think of France, but music and France have gone together since the monks in the 12th century sang Gregorian chants in Notre-Dame. Troubadours with their ballads went all over France in the Middle Ages. In the Renaissance era, **Josquin des Prez** (c. 1440–1521) was the first master of the High Renaissance style of polyphonic vocal music. He became the greatest composer of his age, a magnificent virtuoso. **Jean-Baptise Lully** (1632–87) entertained the decadent court of Versailles with his operas. During the reign of Robespierre, **Claude-Joseph Rouget de Lisle** (1760–1836) immortalized himself in 1792 when he wrote *La Marseillaise,* the French national anthem. Regrettably, he died in poverty.

The rise of the middle class in the 1800s gave birth to both grand opera and *opéra comique.* Both styles merged into a kind of lyric opera, mixing soaring arias and tragedy in such widely popular hits as Bizet's *Carmen* in 1875 and St-Saën's *Samson et Dalila* in 1877.

During the romantic period of the 19th century, foreign composers moving to Paris often dominated the musical scene. **Frédéric Chopin** (1810–49) was half French, half Polish. He became the most influential composer for piano and even invented new musical forms such as the *ballade.* **Félix Mendelssohn**

(1809–47) had to fight against anti-Semitism to establish himself with his symphonies, concerti, and chamber music.

At the dawn of the 20th century, music became more impressionistic, as evoked by **Claude Débussy** (1862–1918). In many ways, he helped launch modernist music. His *Prélude à L'Après-midi d'un Faune* in 1894 and *La Mer* in 1905 were performed all over Europe. From Russia came **Igor Stravinsky** (1882–1971), who made *Time* magazine's list of the 100 most influential people of the 20th century. He achieved fame as a pianist, conductor, and composer. His *Le sacre du printemps (The Rite of Spring)* provoked a riot in Paris when it was first performed in 1913, with its pagan rituals.

A revolutionary artist, **Yves Klein** (1928–62) was called a "neo-Dada." His 1960 "The Monotone Symphony" with three naked models became a notorious performance. For 20 minutes, he conducted an orchestra on one note. Dying of a heart attack at the age of 34, Klein is considered today an enigmatic postmodernist. **Pierre Boulez** (b. 1925) developed a technique known as integral serialism using a 12-tone system pioneered in the 1920s. As director of the IRCAM institute at the Centre Pompidou, he has influenced young musicians around the world.

France took to American jazz like no other country. Louis Armstrong practically became a national hero to Parisians in the 1930s, and in 1949 Paris welcomed the arrival of Miles Davis. **Stéphane Grappelli** (1908–97), a French jazz violinist, founded the Quintette du Hot Club de France, the most famous of all-string jazz bands. **Django Reinhardt** (1910–53) became one of the most prominent jazz musicians of Europe, known for such works as "Belleville" and "My Sweet."

Some French singers went on to achieve world renown, notably **Edith Piaf** (1915–63), "The Little Sparrow" and France's greatest pop singer. Wherever you go in France, you will hear her "La Vie en Rose," which she first recorded in 1946. Born in 1924, **Charles Aznavour** remains an eternal favorite. He's known for his unique tenor voice with its gravelly and soulful low notes. **Jacques Brel** (1929–78), a singer-songwriter, has seen his songs interpreted by everybody from Frank Sinatra to David Bowie. A popular *chanson* singer, **Juliette Gréco** (b. 1927) became known as "the High Priestess of Existentialism" on Paris's Left Bank and was beloved by Jean-Paul Sartre. She dressed all in black and let her long, black hair hang free before coming to Hollywood and becoming the mistress of mogul Darryl Zanuck.

Frédéric Chopin.

Among rock stars, the French consider **Johnny Halladay** (b. 1943) their equivalent of Elvis Presley. He has scored 18 platinum albums, selling more than 100 million records. Another pop icon is **Serge**

Gainsbourg (1928–91). He was a master of everything from rock to jazz, to reggae. Upon his death, President François Mitterrand called him "our Baudelaire, our Apollinaire."

Artists with immigrant backgrounds often are the major names in the vibrant French music scene of today, with influences from French Africa, the French Caribbean, and the Middle East. Along with rap and hip-hop, these sounds rule the nights in the *boîtes* of France's biggest cities. **Khaled** (b. 1960), from Algeria, has become known as the "King of Raï." The most loved and influential French rapper today is **MC Solaar** (b. 1969); born in Senegal, he explores racism and ethnic identity in his wordplays.

EATING & DRINKING IN FRANCE

As any French person will tell you, French food is the best in the world. That's as true today as it was during the 19th-century heyday of the master chef Escoffier. A demanding patriarch who codified the rules of French cooking, he ruled the kitchens of the Ritz in Paris, standardizing the complicated preparation and presentation of haute cuisine. Thanks to Escoffier, with his legendary flare-ups and those of his French-born colleagues, whose kitchen tantrums have been the bane of many a socialite's life, the French chef for years has been considered a temperamental egomaniac, bearing single-handedly the burden of diffusing French civilization into the kitchens of the Anglo-Saxon world.

The demands of these chefs, however, aren't as far-fetched as they might seem, considering the intense scrutiny that has surrounded every aspect of France's culinary arts since the start of the Industrial Revolution.

Until the early 1800s, most French citizens didn't eat well. Many diets consisted of turnips, millet, fruits, berries, unpasteurized dairy products, and whatever fish or game could be had. Cooking techniques and equipment were unsanitary and crude, and starvation was a constant threat. Fear of famine was one of the rallying cries of the Revolution; everyone knows Marie Antoinette's "Let them eat cake" response to cries that the poor couldn't afford bread. (However, to be fair to Marie, this comment has been taken out of context. At the time, bread flour was much more expensive than cake flour, so her words weren't as callous as they might seem.)

At the foundation of virtually every culinary theory ever developed in France is a deep-seated respect for the *cuisine des provinces* (also known as *cuisine campagnarde*). Ingredients usually included only what was produced locally, and the rich and hearty result was gradually developed over several generations of *mères cuisinières.* Springing from an agrarian society with a vivid sense of nature's cycles, the cuisine provided appropriate nourishment for bodies that had toiled through a day in the open air. Specific dishes and cooking methods were as varied as the climates, terrains, and crops of France's many regions.

The revolution against Escoffier has been raging for so long that many of the early rebels are now returning to the old style of cookery, as exemplified by the boeuf bourguignon, the *blanquette de veau,* and the *pot-au-feu.*

Cuisine moderne is here to stay, and some restaurants feature both traditional and contemporary. The new cooking is often based on the classic principles of French cookery, but with a big difference. Rich sauces, for example, are eliminated. Cooking times that can destroy the best of fresh ingredients are considerably shortened. The aim is to release the natural flavor of food without covering it with heavy layers of butter and cream. New flavor combinations in this widely expanding repertoire are often inspired.

The most promising trend for those who don't want to sell the family homestead is to patronize one of the *neo-bistrots* springing up across France. Some of the top chefs of Paris, have opened these more simplified bistros where haute cuisine isn't served, just good-tasting and often regionally inspired dishes. Chefs have fun creating these more affordable menus, perhaps borrowing dishes that their *grande-mère* taught them.

Volumes have been written about French gastronomy—our comments are meant to be a brief introduction only. More than ever, young *chefs du cuisine* are making creative statements in the kitchen, and never in the history of the country has there been such an emphasis on superfresh ingredients. One chef we know in Paris has been known to shut down his restaurant for the day if he doesn't find exactly what he wants in the marketplace that morning.

There is a vast array of expensive restaurants in France that exist almost exclusively for the tourist trade. Luckily, there are others—hundreds of others. Paris, which is said to have more restaurants than any other city on Earth, has many good, reasonably priced ones. And they aren't hard to find. Once you arrive in the countryside, except for the French Riviera and certain citadels of haute cuisine, food prices become more reasonable.

CUISINE BOURGEOISE & HAUTE CUISINE Cuisine bourgeoise and its pretentious cousin, haute cuisine, were refinements of country cooking that developed from the increased prosperity brought on by 19th-century industrialization. As France grew more affluent, food and the rituals involved in its preparation and presentation became one of the hallmarks of culture. And as refrigerated trucks and railway cars carried meats, fish, and produce from one region to another, associations were formed and entire industries spawned, revolving around specific ingredients produced in specific districts. The country's wines (demarcated with "Appellation d'Origine Contrôlée"); lamb from the salt marshes of Pauillac; poultry from Bresse in Burgundy; and melons, strawberries, apples, and truffles from specific districts command premiums over roughly equivalent ingredients produced in less legendary areas.

France often names a method of preparation (or a particular dish) after its region of origin. Dishes described as *à la normande* are likely to be prepared with milk, cream, or cheese or with Calvados, in honor of the dairy products and apple brandy produced in abundance within Norman borders. **Cassoulet** (a stewed combination of white beans, duck, pork, onions, and carrots) will forever be associated with Toulouse, where the dish originated. And something cooked *à la bordelaise* has probably been flavored with ample doses of red bordeaux (along with bone marrow, shallots, tarragon, and meat juices).

Other than caviar (which the French consume in abundance but don't produce), the world's most elegant garnish is **truffles,** an underground fungus with a woodsy, oaky smell. Thousands of these are unearthed yearly from the Dordogne and Périgord forests, so if your menu proclaims a dish is *à la périgourdine,* you'll almost certainly pay a premium for the truffles and foie gras.

And what's all the fuss about **foie gras?** It comes from either a goose or a duck (the rose-hued gooseliver is the greater delicacy). The much-abused goose, however, has a rough life, being force-fed about a kilogram (2¼ lb.) of corn every day in a process the French call *gavage*. In about 22 days, the animal's liver is swollen to about 25 ounces (in many cases, far more than that). When prepared by a Périgourdine housewife (some of whom sell the livers directly from their farmhouses to passing motorists), it's truly delicious. Foie gras is most often served with truffles; otherwise, it's called au naturel.

Regional Cuisines

What exactly is "French food"? That's a hard question to answer. Even cities have their own specialties.

Gastronomy alone would be good enough reason for going to the Loire Valley. From Nantes to Orléans, the specialties are many, including, for example, shad cooked with sorrel, Loire salmon, chitterling sausage, lark pâté, goat's milk cheese, partridge, rillettes (shredded and potted pork), herb-flavored black pudding, plus good Loire wines, including rosés.

The Normans are known not only as good soldiers, but as hearty eaters. Their gastronomic table enjoys world renown. Many Parisians drive up for *le weekend* just to sample the cuisine. Harvested along the seacoast are sole, brill, mackerel, and turbot. Shellfish are also common, especially those fat black mussels, the prawns of Cherbourg, the demoiselles of Dieppe. Try also Madame Poulard's featherweight omelet, sole *normande* (stewed in rich cream), tripe *à la mode de Caen,* chicken from the Auge Valley, and duckling from Rouen. Normandy apples, especially those from the Auge Valley, produce a most potent cider. Matured in oaken casks, the apples also are turned into Calvados, a sort of applejack, a distillation of cider flavored with hazelnuts. A true Norman drinks this cider spirit at breakfast. Benedictine, the liqueur made at Fécamp, also enjoys acclaim. The rich Norman Camembert is imitated but never equaled. Pont l'Evêque cheese has been known here since the 13th century. The Livarot is just fine for those who can get past the smell.

The province of Brittany offers sublime seafood, the mainstay of its diet, including Aulne salmon, pike (best with *beurre blanc*), scallops, trout, winkles, cockles, spiny lobsters, and Lorient sardines. The pré-sale (salt-meadow lamb) is the best meat course, traditionally served with white beans. The finest artichokes come from Roscoff, the most succulent strawberries from Plouogastel. Nearly every village has its own crêperie, specializing in those paper-thin pancakes with an infinite variety of fillings. Savory crapes are most often made with buckwheat. Oysters are ubiquitous and fantastic, with the best coming from Cancale (p. 343)—splurge and try the flat, green-tinged *plates*. Breton food is washed down with cider (perhaps inferior to the Norman variety, but quite good nevertheless). Unlike much of France, the province lacks wine, except for Muscadet, a light white wine produced from the vineyards around the old Breton capital of Nantes in the lower Loire Valley.

The cuisine of Alsace-Lorraine has been influenced by Germany, as reflected by its sauerkraut garni, its most popular dish. It is also the home of foie gras, an expensively delicious treat. The Savoy, in the French Alps, also has many specialties, many using rich cream and milk, which makes the cuisine heavy but tasty. Game such as woodcock is common.

Some of the best food and best wines are found in Burgundy. You'll also see written *"à la Bourgogne"* after a dish, which means bourguignon—cooked in a red-wine sauce and often garnished with buttonhole mushrooms and pearl onions.

Cassoulet.

Lyon is regarded as the gastronomic capital of France. For example, tripe lyonnaise is known around the world. Lyonnais sausage is also well known, and the city's many famous dishes include *quenelles* (fish dumplings, often made with pike).

The Périgord and Dordogne regions are known for their foie gras and truffles. Many farmers' wives sell foie gras—from goose or duck—directly from their kitchen doors. Even if you don't like foie gras, you'll surely want to try the fish from the rivers of the Dordogne, along with morels, strawberries, and flap mushrooms—called *cèpes*—from the field.

Gourmets, not just beach lovers, go to the Riviera. The food, especially fish, can be exceptionally good. It also tends to be expensive. Bouillabaisse, said to have been invented by Venus, is the area's best-known dish. Each chef has his or her own ideas on the subject. *Rascasse* (rockfish), a fish found only in the Mediterranean, is very popular. One of the best seafood selections, *rouget* (red mullet) sometimes appears on fancy menus as *becasse de mer* (sea woodcock). Yet another is *loup de mer* (bass), cooked with fennel. Aioli, mayonnaise with a garlic-and-olive-oil base, is usually served with hors d'oeuvres or boiled fish. Other specialties include *soupe au pistou* (vegetable soup with basil), *salade Niçoise* (likely to include other items, but traditionally made with tomatoes, green beans, olives, tuna, anchovies, and radishes), *pain bagnat* (bread doused in olive oil and served with olives, anchovies, and tomatoes), and ravioli, which needs no explanation.

MEALS & DINING CUSTOMS In many of the less expensive places described in this guide, the menu will be handwritten, in French only. Don't let that intimidate you. Nor should you be timid about ordering dishes without knowing precisely what they are. You'll get some delightful surprises. We know a woman who wouldn't have dreamed of asking for escargots if she'd realized they were snails cooked in garlic sauce. As it was, she ate this appetizer in a spirit of thrift rather than adventure—and has been addicted to it ever since. As for vegetables, the French regard them as a separate course and eat them apart from the meat or poultry dishes. But we wouldn't advise you to order them especially unless you're an exceptionally hearty eater. Most main courses come with a small helping, or *garni,* of vegetables anyway.

As a rule, it's better to order an aperitif—often the house will have a specialty—rather than a heavy drink such as a martini before a classic French dinner. Vodka or scotch can assault your palate, destroying your taste buds for the festive repast to come. Allow plenty of time for a gourmet dinner. Orders are often prepared individually, and it takes time to absorb the wine and the flavors.

Most meals consist of several small courses. You can begin, for example, with hors d'oeuvres or a light *potage* (soup). The classic restaurant used to serve a small order of fish after the appetizer, then the meat or poultry course, but nowadays it's likely to be either fish or meat. A salad follows the main course, then a selection of cheese (there are now more than 1,000 registered French cheeses) and dessert (often a fruit concoction or a sorbet). In this book, prices are given for fixed-price or a la carte main courses.

If you find the food "too rich, with too many sauces," that may be because you've been overdoing it. Elaborately prepared gourmet banquets should not be consumed for both lunch and dinner, or even every day. Sometimes an omelet or a roast chicken can make a delightful light meal, and you can "save up" for your big dining experience.

WINE French cookery achieves palate perfection only when lubricated by wine, which is not considered a luxury or even an addition, but rather an integral part of every meal. Certain rules about wine drinking have been long established in France, but no one except traditionalists seems to follow them anymore. "Rules" would dictate that if you're having a roast, steak, or game, a good burgundy should be your choice. If it's chicken, lamb, or veal, you would choose a red from the Bordeaux country, certainly a full-bodied red with cheese such as Camembert, and a blanc-de-blanc with oysters. A light rosé can go with almost anything, especially if enjoyed on a summer terrace overlooking the Seine.

Let your own good taste—and, sometimes almost as important, your pocketbook—determine your choice of wine. Most wine stewards, called sommeliers, are there to help you in your choice, and only in the most dishonest of restaurants will they push you toward the most expensive selections. Of course, if you prefer only bottled water, or perhaps a beer, then be firm and order either without embarrassment. Some restaurants include a beverage in their menu rates *(boisson compris),* but that's only in the cheaper places. Nevertheless,

Bottles of Burgundy.

some of the most satisfying wines we've drunk in Paris came from unlabeled house bottles or carafes, called a *vin de la maison.* In general, unless you're a real connoisseur, don't worry about labels and vintages.

> ### Impressions
>
> ***Mummie & I about live in this here kafe. We feed on choucroute garnie, which is fried sauerkraut trimmed with boiled potatoes, a large slice of ham & a fat hot dog—yum, yum, werry excillint. And mummie & I come every day & eat the stinkin' stuff, & all our friends hold their noses & pass us by till we've finished.***
>
> **—Edna St. Vincent Millay**

When in doubt, you can rarely go wrong with a good burgundy or bordeaux, but you may want to be more adventurous than that. That's when the sommelier can help you, particularly if you tell him or her your taste in wine (semidry or very dry, for example). State frankly how much you're willing to pay and what you plan to order for your meal. If you're dining with others, you may want to order two or three bottles with an entire dinner, selecting a wine to suit each course. However, Parisians at informal meals—and especially if there are only two persons dining—select only one wine to go with all their platters, from hors d'oeuvres to cheese. As a rule of thumb, expect to spend about one-third of the restaurant tab for wine.

WINE LABELS Since the latter part of the 19th century, French wines sold in France (and sometimes elsewhere) have been labeled. The general label is known as *appellations contrôlées.* These controls, for the most part, are by regions such as Bordeaux and the Loire. These are the simple, honest wines of the district. They can be blended from grapes grown at any place in the region. Some are composed of the vintages of different years.

In most cases, the more specific the label, the better the wine. For example, instead of a Bordeaux, the wine might be labeled MEDOC (pronounced *may*-doc), which is the name of a triangle of land extending some 81km (50 miles) north from Bordeaux. Wine labels can be narrowed down to a particular vine-growing property, such as a Château Haut-Brion, one of the most famous and greatest of red wines of Bordeaux (this château produces only about 10,000 cases a year).

On some burgundies, you are likely to see the word *clos* (pronounced "cloe"). Originally, that meant a walled or otherwise enclosed vineyard, as in Clos-de-Bèze, which is a celebrated Burgundian vineyard producing a superb red wine. *Cru* (pronounced "croo," and meaning "growth") suggests a wine of superior quality when it appears on a label as a *vin-de-cru.* Wines and vineyards are often divided into crus. A grand cru or premier cru should, by implication, be an even more superior wine.

Labels are only part of the story. It's the vintage that counts. Essentially, vintage is the annual grape harvest and the wine made from those grapes. Therefore, any wine can be a vintage wine unless it is a blend. But there are good vintages and bad vintages. The variation between wine produced in a "good year" and wine produced in a "bad year" can be great, and even noted by the neophyte.

Finally, champagne is the only wine that can be correctly served through all courses of a meal—but only to those who can afford its astronomical cost.

WHEN TO GO

The best time to visit France is in the spring (Apr–June) or fall (Sept–Nov), when things are easier to come by—from Métro seats to good-tempered waiters. The weather is temperate year-round. July and August are the worst for crowds. Parisians desert their city, leaving it to the tourists.

Hotels used to charge off-season rates during the cold, rainy period from November to February; now they're often packed with business travelers, trade fairs, and winter tour groups, and hoteliers have less incentive to offer discounts. Airfares are still cheaper during these months, and more promotions are available. They rise in the spring and fall, peaking in the summer, when tickets cost the most.

In even-numbered years, don't come to Paris during the first 2 weeks of October without a confirmed hotel room. The weather's fine, but the city is jammed for the auto show.

Weather

France's weather varies from region to region and even from town to town. Despite its latitude, Paris never gets very cold. Snow used to be rare, though the last three winters have been very snowy. The hands-down winner for wetness is Brittany. Brest (known for the mold—probably caused by the constant damp—that adds flavor to its blue cheeses) receives a staggering amount of rain between October and December. May is the driest month.

The Mediterranean coast in the south has the driest climate. When it does rain, it's heaviest in spring and autumn. (Cannes sometimes receives more rainfall than Paris.) Summers are comfortably dry—beneficial to humans, but deadly to vegetation, which (unless it's irrigated) often dries and burns up in the parched months.

Provence dreads *le mistral* (an unrelenting wind), which most often blows in the winter for a few days but can last for up to 2 weeks.

Paris's Average Daytime Temperature & Rainfall

	JAN	FEB	MAR	APR	MAY	JUNE	JULY	AUG	SEPT	OCT	NOV	DEC
TEMP. (°F)	38	39	46	51	58	64	66	66	61	53	45	40
TEMP. (°C)	3	4	8	11	14	18	19	19	16	12	7	4
RAINFALL (IN.)	3.2	2.9	2.4	2.7	3.2	3.5	3.3	3.7	3.3	3.0	3.5	3.1

France Calendar of Events

For an exhaustive list of events beyond those listed here, check http://events.frommers.com, where you'll find a searchable, up-to-the-minute roster of what's happening in cities all over the world.

JANUARY

Monte Carlo Motor Rally (Le Rallye de Monte Carlo). The world's most venerable car race. For information, call the Monaco Tourist Office (© **377/93-15-26-00;** www.acm.mc). Usually mid-January.

FEBRUARY

Carnaval of Nice. Parades, boat races, music, balls, and fireworks are all part of this celebration. The climax is the 114-year tradition of burning King Carnaval in effigy, after *Les Batailles des Fleurs* (Battles of the Flowers), when teams pelt each other with blooms. For details, contact the Nice Convention and Visitors Bureau (✆ **08-92-70-74-07;** fax 04-92-14-46-49; www.nicecarnaval.com). Late February to early March.

MARCH

Foire du Trône, on the Reuilly Lawn of the Bois de Vincennes, 12e, Paris. This mammoth amusement park operates daily from 2pm to midnight. Call ✆ **01-46-27-52-29,** or visit www.foiredutrone.com. End of March to end of May.

International Ready-to-Wear Fashion Shows (Le Salon International de Prêt-à-Porter), Parc des Expositions, Porte de Versailles, 15e, Paris. See what you'll be wearing next season. Call ✆ **01-44-94-70-00,** or visit www.pretparis.com. Early March.

APRIL

International Marathon of Paris. Runners from around the world compete. Call ✆ **01-41-33-14-00,** or visit www.parismarathon.com. Early April.

Les 24 Heures du Mans Moto. This motorcycle race is on a grueling 4km (2½-mile) circuit 4.5km (2¾ miles) south of Le Mans. For information, call l'Automobile Club de l'Ouest (✆ **02-43-40-24-24**) or the Le Mans Ticket Office (✆ **04-73-91-85-75;** www.lemans.org). Mid-April.

MAY

Antiques Show. The annual *Cinq Jours de l'Objet Extraordinaire* show features more than 100 galleries and antiques stores displaying their collections in seven streets on the Left Bank, Carré Rive Gauche. For information, call ✆ **01-42-60-70-10,** or visit www.carrerivegauche.com. Mid-May to early June.

Cannes Film Festival (Festival International du Film). Movie madness transforms this city into a media circus. Admission to the films in competition is by invitation only. Other films play 24 hours a day. Contact the Festival International du Film, 3 rue Amélie, Paris 75007 (✆ **01-53-59-61-00;** www.festival-cannes.com). Two weeks before the festival, its administration moves to the Palais des Festivals, esplanade Georges-Pompidou, Cannes 06400. Mid-May.

Monaco Grand Prix de Formule. Hundreds of cars race through the narrow streets and winding roads in a blend of high-tech machinery and medieval architecture. Call ✆ **377/93-15-26-00** or 377/92-16-61-16, or visit www.acm.mc. Mid-May.

French Open Tennis Championship, Stade Roland-Garros, 16e, Paris (Métro: Porte d'Auteuil). The open features 10 days of men's, women's, and doubles tennis on the hot, red, dusty courts. For information, call ✆ **01-47-43-48-00,** or visit www.fft.fr. Late May to early June.

JUNE

Prix du Jockey Club and Prix Diane-Hermès, Hippodrome de Chantilly. Thoroughbreds from as far away as Kentucky and Brunei compete in this race. On race days, dozens of trains depart from Paris's Gare du Nord for Chantilly, where racegoers take free shuttle buses to the track. Call ✆ **01-49-10-20-30,** or visit www.france-galop.com for information on these and other Chantilly events. Early June.

Cinéscénie de Puy du Fou, *son-et-lumière,* Château du Puy du Fou, Les Epesses (La Vendée), Brittany. A cast of 2,500 actors, dozens of horses, and laser shows celebrate the achievements of the Middle Ages. Call ✆ **02-51-64-11-11,** or visit www.puydufou.com. Early June to early September.

Festival de St-Denis. A surge of music in the burial place of the French kings, a grim early Gothic monument in Paris's northern suburb of St-Denis. Call ✆ **01-48-13-06-07,** or visit www.festival-saint-denis.fr. Early June to July.

Les 24 Heures du Mans Voitures, for stock cars, is in the same circuit as the April motorcycle rally, but on a 13km (8-mile) radius. For information, call l'Automobile Club de l'Ouest (✆ **02-43-40-25-55**), or contact the Le Mans Ticket Office (✆ **08-92-69-72-24;** www.lemans.org). Mid-June.

Gay Pride Parade, place de la République to place de la Bastille, Paris. A week of expositions and parties climaxes in a parade patterned after those in New York and San Francisco, followed by a dance at the Palais de Bercy. For more information about gay pride and any other aspect of gay, lesbian, and transgendered life in and around Paris, contact Lesbian and Gay Pride Ile de France, 3 rue Perrée, Box 8, Paris 75003 (✆/fax **01-72-70-39-22;** www.inter-lgbt.org). Late June.

JULY

Colmar International Festival, Colmar. Classical concerts are held in public buildings of one of the most folkloric towns in Alsace. Call ✆ **03-89-20-68-97,** or visit www.festival-colmar.com. First 2 weeks of July.

Les Chorégies d'Orange, Orange. One of southern France's most important lyric festivals presents oratorios, operas, and choral works in France's best-preserved Roman amphitheater. Call ✆ **04-90-34-24-24,** or visit www.choregies.asso.fr. Early July to early August.

Fête Chopin, Paris. Everything you've ever wanted to hear by the Polish exile, who lived most of his life in Paris. Piano recitals take place in the Orangerie du Parc de Bagatelle, 16e. Call ✆ **01-45-00-22-19,** or visit www.frederic-chopin.com. Early July.

Les Nocturnes du Mont-St-Michel. This is a sound-and-light tour through the stairways and corridors of one of Europe's most impressive medieval monuments. Call ✆ **02-33-60-14-30,** or check out www.monuments-nationaux.fr for more information. Performances are Monday through Saturday evenings from early July to late August.

Tour de France. Europe's most hotly contested bicycle race sends crews of wind tunnel–tested athletes along an itinerary that detours deep into the Massif Central and ranges across the Alps. The finish line is on the Champs-Elysées. Call ✆ **01-41-33-14-00,** or visit www.letour.fr. First 3 weeks of July.

Festival d'Avignon. This world-class festival has a reputation for exposing new talent to critical scrutiny and acclaim. The focus is usually on avant-garde works in theater, dance, and music. Many of the dance and theater performances take place in either the 14th-century courtyard of the Palais des Pâpes or the medieval Cloître (cloister) des Carmes. For information, call ✆ **04-90-27-66-50,** or visit www.festival-avignon.com. Last 3 weeks of July.

Bastille Day. Celebrating the birth of modern-day France, the nation's festivities reach their peak in Paris with street fairs, pageants, fireworks, and feasts. In Paris, the day begins with a parade down the Champs-Elysées and ends with fireworks at Montmartre. July 14.

Paris Quartier d'Eté. For 4 weeks, music rules the Arènes de Lutèce and the Cour d'Honneur at the Sorbonne, both in the Quartier Latin. The dozen or so concerts are grander than the outdoorsy setting; they include performances by the Orchestre de Paris, the Orchestre National de France, and the Baroque Orchestra of the European Union. Call

Getting Tickets

Global Tickets can order tickets to many of the musical and theatrical events at the Avignon festival, as well as other cultural happenings throughout France. You'll pay a hefty fee (as much as 20%) for the convenience. Contact Global at 234 W. 44th St., Ste. 1000, New York, NY 10036 (✆ 800/669-8687; www.keithprowse.com).

✆ **01-44-94-98-00,** or visit www.quartierdete.com. Mid-July to mid-August.

Nice Jazz Festival. The most prestigious jazz festival in Europe. Concerts begin in the afternoon and go on until late at night (sometimes all night) on the Arènes de Cimiez, a hill above the city. Contact the Nice Tourist Office (✆ **08-92-70-75-07;** www.nicejazzfestival.fr). Mid-July.

Festival d'Aix-en-Provence. A musical event par excellence, with everything from Gregorian chant to melodies composed on synthesizers. Recitals are in the medieval cloister of the Cathédrale St-Sauveur. Expect heat, crowds, and traffic. Contact the Festival International d'Art Lyrique et Académie Européenne de Musique (✆ **04-42-17-34-34;** www.festival-aix.com). Throughout July.

AUGUST

Festival Interceltique de Lorient, Brittany. Celtic verse and lore are celebrated in the Celtic heart of France. The 150 concerts include classical and folkloric musicians, dancers, singers, and painters. Traditional Breton *pardons* (religious processions) take place in the once-independent maritime duchy. Call ✆ **02-97-21-24-29,** or check www.festival-winterceltique.com. Early August.

SEPTEMBER

La Villette Jazz Festival. Some 50 concerts are held in churches, auditoriums, and concert halls in the Paris suburb of La Villette. Past festivals have included Herbie Hancock, Shirley Horn, and other international artists. Call ✆ **01-40-03-75-75,** or visit www.lavillette.com. Early to mid-September.

Festival d'Automne, Paris. One of France's most famous festivals is one of its most eclectic, focusing mainly on modern music, ballet, theater, and art. Contact the Festival d'Automne (✆ **01-53-45-17-00;** www.festival-automne.com). Mid-September to late December.

OCTOBER

Paris Auto Show, Parc des Expositions, Porte de Versailles, 15e, Paris. This is the showcase for European car design, complete with glistening metal, glitzy attendees, lots of hype, and the latest models. Check *Pariscope* for details, or contact the French Government Tourist Office (see "Fast Facts," p. 754). You can also get information by calling ✆ **01-56-88-22-40** or visiting www.mondial-automobile.com. Two weeks in October (dates vary).

Perpignan Jazz Festival. Musicians from everywhere jam in what many consider Languedoc's most appealing season. Call ✆ **04-68-35-37-46,** or visit www.jazzebre.com. Month of October.

Prix de l'Arc de Triomphe, Hippodrome de Longchamp, 16e, Paris. France's answer to England's Ascot is the country's most prestigious horse race, culminating the equine season in Europe. Call ✆ **01-49-10-20-30,** or visit www.france-galop.com. Early October.

NOVEMBER

Armistice Day, nationwide. In Paris, the signing of the document that ended World War I is celebrated with a military parade from the Arc de Triomphe to the Hôtel des Invalides. November 11.

Les Trois Glorieuses, Clos-de-Vougeot, Beaune, and Meursault. Three Burgundian towns stage the country's most important wine festival. Though you may not gain access to many of the gatherings, tastings and other amusements will keep you occupied. Reserve early, or visit as day trips from nearby villages. Contact the Office de Tourisme de Beaune (✆ **03-80-26-21-30;** www.ot-beaune.fr). Third week in November.

DECEMBER

Christmas Fairs, Alsace (especially Strasbourg). More than 60 villages celebrate a traditional Christmas. The events in Strasbourg have continued for some 430 years. Other towns with celebrations are Münster, Sélestat, Riquewihr, Kaysersberg, Wissembourg, and Thann. Call ✆ **03-89-24-73-50,** or visit www.tourism-alsace.com. Late November to December 24.

The Boat Fair (Le Salon Nautique de Paris). Europe's major exposition of what's afloat, at Salon Nautique de Paris, 52–54 quai de Dion-Bouton, 15e, Paris (✆ **01-47-56-50-00;** www.salonnautiqueparis.com; Métro: Porte de Versailles). Ten days in early December.

Fête des Lumières, Lyon. In honor of the Virgin Mary, lights are placed in windows through the city. Call ✆ **04-72-10-30-30,** or visit www.lumieres.lyon.fr. Early December through early January.

Fête de St-Sylvestre (New Year's Eve), nationwide. In Paris, this holiday is most boisterously celebrated in the Quartier Latin. At midnight, the city explodes. Strangers kiss and boulevard St-Michel and the Champs-Elysées become virtual pedestrian malls. December 31.

TOURS

In a country as diverse and popular as France, there are numerous options.

Adventure & Wellness Trips

BALLOONING The world's largest hot-air-balloon operator is **Buddy Bombard's Private Europe,** 333 Pershing Way, West Palm Beach, FL 33401 (✆ **800/862-8537** or 561/837-6610; fax 561/837-6623; www.buddybombard.com). It maintains about three dozen hot-air balloons, some in the Loire Valley and Burgundy. The 5-day tours, costing $8,940 per person (double occupancy), incorporate food and wine tasting and all meals, lodging in Relais & Châteaux hotels, sightseeing, rail transfers to and from Paris, and a daily balloon ride over vineyards and fields.

Bonaventura Balloon Co., 133 Wall Rd., Napa Valley, CA 94573 (✆ **800/FLY-NAPA** [359-6272] or 707/944-2822; fax 707/944-2220; www.bonaventuraballoons.com), meets you in Paris and takes you on the high-speed train to Burgundy, where your balloon tour begins. It carries you over the scenic parts of the region. Guests stay in a 14th-century mill, now an inn owned by a three-star chef.

BARGE CRUISES Before the advent of the railways, many crops, building supplies, raw materials, and finished products were barged through France on a series of rivers, canals, and estuaries. Many of these waterways retain their old-fashioned locks and pumps, allowing shallow-draft barges easy access through the idyllic countryside.

French Country Waterways, Ltd., P.O. Box 2195, Duxbury, MA 02331 (✆ **800/222-1236** or 781/934-2454; www.fcwl.com), leads 1-week tours through Burgundy and Champagne. For double occupancy, the price ranges from $6,995 to $8,195.

Le Boat, 93 N. Park Place Blvd., Clearwater, FL 33759 (✆ **800/992-0291** or 800/734-5491; fax 727/530-9747; www.leboat.com), focuses on regions of France not covered by many other operators. The company's luxury crafts fit through the narrow canals and locks of Camargue, Languedoc, and Provence. Each 6-night tour has 10 passengers in five cabins outfitted with mahogany and brass, plus meals prepared by a Cordon Bleu chef. Prices vary widely.

Go Barging (© **800/394-8630;** www.gobarging.com) operates Great Island Voyages, featuring river cruise ships. Fares start at $4,590 per person (double occupancy) for a 6-night cruise, including room, breakfast, and dinner. Bicycles are carried on board for sightseeing trips. This company also offers cruises in the Loire Valley and the south of France.

BICYCLING TOURS Some of the best cycling tours of France are offered by **VBT (Deluxe Bicycle Vacations),** 614 Monkton Rd., Bristol, VT 05443 (© **800/245-3868;** www.vbt.com), which offers trips in five of the most scenic parts of France. These range from Burgundy (which combines a barge tour) to the Loire Valley, even Provence and the Normandy Coast. Packages are priced from $3,295 to $4,170 per person.

Classic Adventures, P.O. Box 143, Hamlin, NY 14464 (© **800/777-8090;** fax 585/964-7297; www.classicadventures.com), sponsors 6- to 10-day spring and fall tours of the Loire Valley and the Dordogne. Accommodations are upscale, and tours are van supported and escorted. The 6-day tour, including room, breakfast, and dinner, is $3,449 per person for the Loire Valley.

Euro-Bike & Walking Tours, P.O. Box 81025, Billings, MT 59108 (© **800/575-1540** or 406/655-4591; www.eurobike.com), offers 10-day tours in the Dordogne ($4,298 per person), 11-day tours in Provence ($4,498 per person), and 8-day tours of the Loire ($3,498 per person). All are escorted and include room, breakfast, and dinner.

Go-today.com (a division of Europe Express), 19021 120th Ave. NE, Ste. 102, Bothell, WA 98011 (© **800/227-3235;** www.go-today.com), has biking and walking tours of Bordeaux, Burgundy, the Dordogne, the Loire Valley, and Provence. An 8-day self-guided bike tour is $1,750 per person, double occupancy. All tours include overnight accommodations and most meals. Guided tours include van support and a guide; on nonguided tours, you'll always have the name of an English-speaking local contact.

Cooking Schools

The famous/infamous Georges-Auguste Escoffier (1846–1935) taught the Edwardians how to eat. Today the Hôtel Ritz maintains the **Ritz-Escoffier Ecole de Gastronomie Française,** 38 rue Cambon, Paris 75001 (© **01-43-16-30-30;** www.ritzparis.com), which offers demonstration classes of the master's techniques on Saturdays. These cost 135€ to 225€ each. Courses, taught in French and English, start at 1,000€ for 1 week, up to 11,400€ for 6 weeks.

Le Cordon Bleu, 8 rue Léon-Delhomme, Paris 75015 (© **800/457-2433** in the U.S., or 01-53-68-22-50; www.cordonbleu.edu), was established in 1895 and is the most famous French cooking school—where Julia Child learned to perfect her *pâté brisée* and *mousse au chocolat.* The best-known courses last 10 weeks, after which you are awarded a certificate. Many enthusiasts prefer a less intense immersion and opt for a 4-day workshop or a 2-hour demonstration class. Enrollment in either is first come, first served; costs start at 47€ for a demonstration and start at 920€ for the 4-day workshop. Classes are in English.

Language Classes

The **Alliance Française,** 101 bd. Raspail, Paris 75270 (© **01-42-84-90-00;** fax 01-42-84-91-01; www.alliancefr.org), a nonprofit organization with a network of 1,100 establishments in 138 countries, offers French-language courses to some 350,000 students. The school in Paris is open all year; month-long courses range from 400€ to 900€, depending on the number of hours per day. Request information and an application at least 1 month before your departure. In North America, the largest branch is the **Alliance Française,** 53 W. Jackson Blvd., Ste. 1225, Chicago, IL 60604 (✆ **312/431-1889;** www.afusa.org).

A clearinghouse for information on French-language schools is **Lingua Service Worldwide,** 42 Artillery Dr., Woodbury, CT 06798 (✆ **800/394-LEARN** [5327] or 203/263-6294; www.linguaserviceworldwide.com). Its programs are available in many cities throughout France. They cost $1,043 to $2,940 for 2 weeks, depending on the city, the school, and the accommodations.

Music Tours

One outfit that coordinates hotel stays in Paris with major musical events, usually in at least one (and often both) of the city's opera houses, is **Dailey-Thorp Travel,** P.O. Box 670, Big Horn, Wyoming 82833 (✆ **800/998-4677** or 307/673-1555; fax 307/674-7474; www.daileythorp.com). Sojourns tend to last 3 to 7 days and, in many cases, tie in with performances in other cities (usually London, Berlin, or Milan). Expect accommodations in deluxe hotels such as the Hôtel du Louvre or the Hôtel Scribe, and a staff that has made arrangements for all the nuts and bolts of your arrival in, and artistic exposure to, Paris.

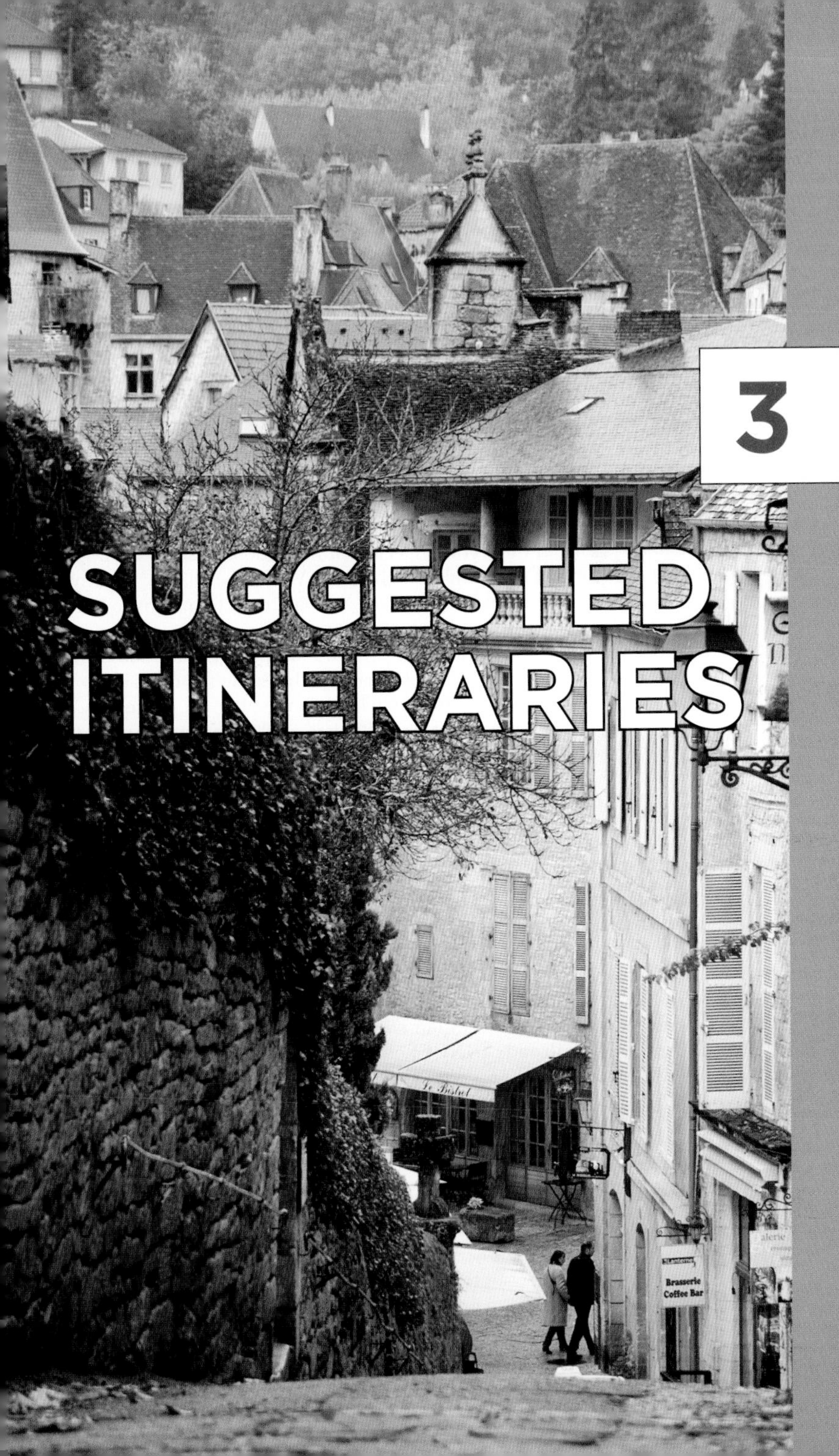

3 SUGGESTED ITINERARIES

I f you have unlimited time, one of the world's great pleasures is getting "lost" in France, wandering about at random, making new discoveries every day off the beaten path. But few of us have this luxury, and so below we present both 1- and 2-week itineraries to help you make the most of your time.

France is so vast and so treasure filled that you can't even skim the surface in 1 or 2 weeks, so relax and don't even try. Instead, we recommend that you enjoy the nuggets—Paris, Versailles, and Mont-St-Michel—among other allures, saving the rest for another day. You may also review chapter 1, "The Best of France," to find out what experiences or sights have special appeal to us and then adjust the itineraries to suit your particular travel plans.

France ranks with Germany in offering Europe's fastest and best-maintained superhighways, and it also has one of the fastest and most efficient public transportation systems in the world, especially in its national train system. For example, the highlights of Normandy and the Loire Valley (the château country) are just 1 or 2 hours away from Paris by train. You can travel from Paris to Nice on the Riviera in 5½ hours—or fly much more quickly, of course.

The itineraries that follow take you to some major attractions and some charming towns. The pace may be a bit breathless for some visitors, so skip a town or sight occasionally to have some chill-out time—after all, you're on vacation. Of course, you can use any of these itineraries as a jumping-off point to develop your own custom-made trip.

THE REGIONS IN BRIEF

Though France's 547,030 sq. km (211,209 sq. miles) make it slightly smaller than the American state of Texas, no other country has such a diversity of sights and scenery in such a compact area. A visitor can travel through the north's flat, fertile lands; the Loire Valley's green hills; the east's Alpine ranges; the Pyrénées; the Massif Central's plateaus and rock outcroppings; and the southeast's Mediterranean coast. Even more noteworthy are the cultural and historical differences that define each region.

Destinations in France are within easy reach from Paris and each other. **French National Railroads (SNCF)** offers fast service to and from Paris—though trains tend to crawl on routes that do not serve the capital. The train trip from Paris is 4 hours to Alsace, 5 to the Alps, 7 to the Pyrénées, and 8 to the Côte d'Azur—and the newer TGVs (high-speed trains) cut that travel time dramatically.

You'll find nearly 71,000km (about 44,020 miles) of roads, mostly in good condition. Try not to travel the Route Nationale network all the time. Nearly all of France's scenic splendors are along secondary roads.

A "grand tour" of France is nearly impossible for the visitor who doesn't have a lifetime to explore. If you want to get to know a province, try to devote at least a week to a specific region; you may have a more rewarding trip if you concentrate

PREVIOUS PAGE: **A street in the town of Sarlat-le-Canèda, Dordogne.**

Giverny.

on getting to know two or three areas at a leisurely pace rather than racing around trying to see everything. To help you decide where to spend your time, we've summarized the highlights of each region for you.

ILE DE FRANCE (EXCLUDING PARIS) The Ile de France is an island only in the sense that rivers—with odd-sounding names such as Essonne, Epte, Aisne, Eure, and Ourcq—and a handful of canals delineate its boundaries (about an 81km/50-mile radius from the center of Paris). France was born in this temperate basin, where the attractions include **Paris, Versailles, Fontainebleau, Notre-Dame de Chartres,** and **Giverny.** Despite industrialization (and Disneyland Paris), pockets of charm remain, including the forests of Rambouillet and Fontainebleau, and the artists' hamlet of Barbizon. For more information, see chapter 5.

THE LOIRE VALLEY This area includes two ancient provinces, Touraine (centered on Tours) and Anjou (centered on Angers). It was beloved by royalty and nobility until Henry IV moved his court to Paris. Head here to see the most magnificent castles in France. Irrigated by the Loire River and its many tributaries, the valley produces many superb wines. For more information, see chapter 6.

NORMANDY This region will forever be linked to the 1944 D-day invasion. Some readers consider a visit to the D-day beaches the most emotionally worthwhile part of their trip. Normandy boasts 599km (371 miles) of coastline and a maritime tradition. It's a popular weekend getaway from Paris, and many hotels and restaurants thrive here, especially around the casino town of **Deauville.** Normandy's great attractions include the **Rouen** cathedral, the abbey of **Jumièges,** and medieval **Bayeux.** For more information, see chapter 7.

BRITTANY Jutting into the Atlantic, the westernmost region (and one of the poorest regions) of France is known for its rocky coastlines, Celtic roots, frequent rain, and ancient dialect, akin to the Gaelic tongues of Wales and Ireland. Many French vacationers love the seacoast (rivaled only by the Côte d'Azur) for its sandy beaches, cliffs, and relatively modest—by French standards—prices. **Carnac** is home to ancient Celtic dolmens and burial mounds, and the region's most sophisticated resort, **La Baule,** is near some of Brittany's best beaches. For more information, see chapter 8.

CHAMPAGNE Every French monarch since A.D. 496 was crowned at **Reims,** and much of French history is linked with this holy site. In the path of any invader wishing to occupy Paris, Reims and the Champagne district have seen much bloodshed, including the World War I battles of the Somme and the Marne. Industrial sites sit among patches of forest, and vineyards sheathe the steep sides of valleys. The 126km (78-mile) road from Reims to Vertus, one of the **Routes du Champagne,** takes in a trio of winegrowing regions that produce 80% of the world's bubbly. For more information, see chapter 9.

THE ARDENNES & NORTHERN BEACHES In summer, French families arrive by the thousands to visit Channel beach resorts such as **Le Touquet-Paris-Plage.** This district is quite industrialized and has always suffered in wars. Its best-known port, Calais, was a bitterly contested English stronghold for centuries. Calais is now the port of disembarkation for ferries, hydrofoils, and Channel Tunnel arrivals from Britain. **Notre-Dame Cathedral** in **Amiens,** the medieval capital of Picardy, is a treasure, with a 42m-high (138-ft.) nave—the highest in France.

ALSACE-LORRAINE Between Germany and the forests of the Vosges is the most Teutonic of France's provinces: Alsace, with cosmopolitan Strasbourg as its capital. Celebrated for its cuisine, particularly its foie gras and choucroute, this area is home to villages with half-timbered designs that make you think of the Black Forest. If you travel the Route de Vin (Wine Road), you can visit towns such as **Colmar, Riquewihr,** and **Illhaeusern,** famous for great food and wine. Lorraine, birthplace of Joan of Arc, witnessed many battles during the world wars. Its capital, **Nancy,** is the guardian of a grand 18th-century plaza, place Stanislas. The much-eroded peaks of the Vosges forest, the closest thing to a wilderness in France, offer lovely hiking. For more information, see chapter 10.

BURGUNDY Few trips will prove as rewarding as several leisurely days spent exploring Burgundy, with its splendid old cities such as **Dijon.** Besides its famous cuisine (*boeuf* and *escargots à la bourguignonne*), the district contains, along its Côte d'Or, hamlets whose names (Mercurey, Beaune, Puligny-Montrachet, Vougeot, and Nuits-St-Georges) are synonymous with great wine. For more information, see chapter 11.

THE RHÔNE VALLEY A fertile area of Alpine foothills and sloping valleys in eastern and southeastern France, the upper Rhône Valley ranges from the French suburbs of the Swiss city of Geneva to the northern borders of Provence. The district is thoroughly French, unflinchingly bourgeois, and dedicated to preserving the gastronomic and cultural traditions that have produced some of the most celebrated chefs in French history.

Vineyards in Burgundy.

Only 2 hours by train from Paris, the region's cultural centerpiece, **Lyon,** is France's "second city." North of here, you can travel the Beaujolais trail or head for Bresse's ancient capital, **Bourg-en-Bresse,** which produces the world's finest poultry. You can explore the Rhône Valley en route to Provence. Try to visit the medieval villages of **Pérouges** and **Vienne,** 27km (17 miles) south of Lyon; the latter is known for its Roman ruins. For more information, see chapter 12.

THE FRENCH ALPS This area's resorts rival those of neighboring Switzerland and contain incredible scenery: snowcapped peaks, glaciers, and Alpine lakes. **Chamonix** is a famous ski resort facing **Mont Blanc,** western Europe's highest mountain. **Courchevel** and **Megève** are more chic. During the summer, you can enjoy such spa resorts as **Evian** and the restful 19th-century resorts ringing **Lake Geneva.** For more information, see chapter 13.

PROVENCE One of France's most popular destinations stretches from the southern Rhone River to the Italian border. Long frequented by starving artists, *la bourgeoisie,* and the downright rich and famous, its premier cities are **Aix-en-Provence,** associated with Cézanne; **Arles,** famous for bullfighting and van Gogh; **Avignon,** the 14th-century capital of Christendom; and **Marseille,** a port city established by the Phoenicians that today is the melting pot of France. Quietier and more romantic are villages such as **St-Rémy-de-Provence, Les Baux,** and **Gordes.** The strip of glittering beach towns along Provence's southern edge is known as the **Côte d'Azur,** or the French Riviera (see the following section). For more information, see chapter 14.

THE FRENCH RIVIERA (CÔTE D'AZUR) The resorts of the fabled Côte d'Azur (Azure Coast, or Blue Coast) still evoke glamour: **Cannes, St-Tropez, Cap-d'Antibes,** and **St-Jean-Cap-Ferrat.** July and August are the most buzzing months, while spring and fall are still sunny but way more laid-back. **Nice** is the biggest city and most convenient for exploring the area. The principality of **Monaco** occupies only about 2 sq. km (¾ sq. mile) but has enough sights, restaurants, and glamour to go around. Along the coast are some sandy beaches, but many are pebbly. Topless bathing is common,

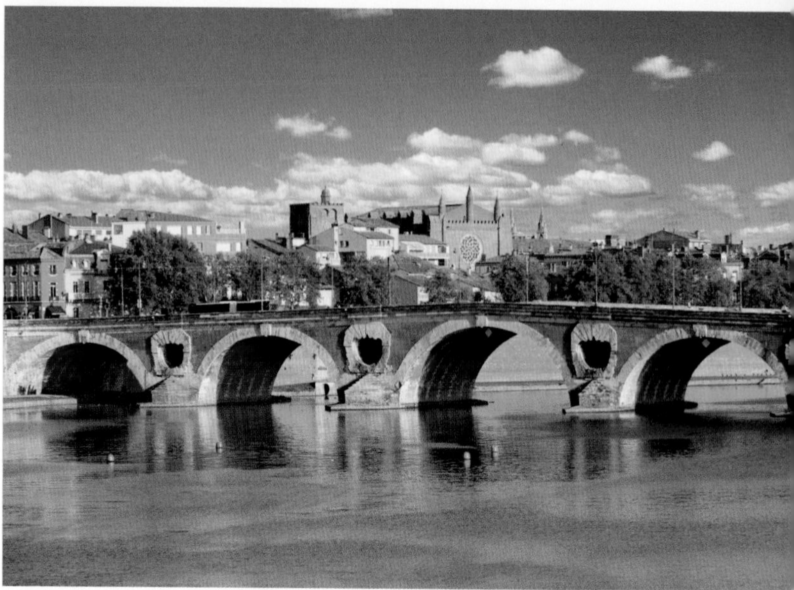
Pont Neuf, Toulouse.

especially in St-Tropez, and some of the restaurants are citadels of conspicuous consumption. Dozens of artists and their patrons have littered the landscape with world-class galleries and art museums. For more information, see chapter 15.

LANGUEDOC-ROUSSILLON Languedoc may not be as chic as Provence, but it's less frenetic and more affordable. **Roussillon** is the rock-strewn French answer to Catalonia, just across the Spanish border. The **Camargue** is the marshy delta formed by two arms of the Rhône River. Rich in bird life, it's famous for its grassy flats and such fortified medieval sites as **Aigues-Mortes.** Also appealing are **Auch,** the capital of Gascony; **Toulouse,** the bustling pink capital of Languedoc; and the "red city" of **Albi,** birthplace of Toulouse-Lautrec. **Carcassonne,** a marvelous walled city with fortifications begun around A.D. 500, is the region's highlight. For more information, see chapter 16.

THE BASQUE COUNTRY Since prehistoric times, the rugged Pyrénées have formed a natural boundary between France and Spain. The Basques, one of Europe's most unusual cultures, flourished in the valleys here. In the 19th century, resorts such as **Biarritz** and **St-Jean-de-Luz** attracted the French aristocracy; the empress Eugénie's palace at Biarritz is now a hotel. Four million Catholics make annual pilgrimages to the city of Lourdes. In the villages and towns of the Pyrénées, the old folkloric traditions, permeated with Spanish influences, continue to thrive. For more information, see chapter 17.

BORDEAUX & THE ATLANTIC COAST Flat, fertile, and frequently ignored by North Americans, this region includes towns pivotal in French history (**Poitiers, Angoulême,** and **La Rochelle**), as well as wine- and liquor-producing villages (**Cognac, St-Emilion,** and **Sauternes**) whose names are celebrated around the world. **Bordeaux,** the district's largest city, has an economy based on wine merchandising and showcases grand 18th-century architecture. For more information, see chapter 18.

THE DORDOGNE & THE LOT The splendid Dordogne River valley has been a favorite vacation spot since Cro-Magnon peoples were painting bison on cave walls in **Lascaux.** Today visitors flock to the valley to marvel at prehistoric sites near **Les Eyzies-de-Tayac** and to ramble through exquisite villages like **Sarlat-le-Canéda** and **Beynac-et-Cazenac.** The land of truffles and foie gras, Périgord has long been famed as a gastronomic mecca, while nearby **Cahors** is celebrated for its rich red wine. For more information, see chapter 19.

THE MASSIF CENTRAL The rugged heartland of south-central France, this underpopulated district contains ancient cities, unspoiled scenery, and an abundance of black lava, from which many buildings were created. The largest cities are **Clermont-Ferrand** and **Limoges**—the medieval capitals of the provinces of the Auvergne and the Limousin. **Bourges,** a gateway to the region and once capital of Aquitaine, has a beautiful Gothic cathedral. For information on a side trip to Limoges, see chapter 19.

FRANCE IN 1 WEEK

The title of this tour is a misnomer. There is no way you can see France in 1 week. But you can have a memorable vacation in Paris and see other highlights of France in a week if you budget your time carefully. One week provides enough time—barely—to visit the major attractions of Paris, such as the **Musée du Louvre** (world's greatest art gallery), the **Eiffel Tower,** and **Notre-Dame.** After 2 days in Paris, head for the former royal stamping grounds of **Versailles,** followed by Normandy (an easy commute from Paris), visiting such highlights as **D-day beaches,** the cathedral city of **Rouen** (where Joan of Arc was burned alive), the tapestry of **Bayeux,** and the incredible monastery of **Mont-St-Michel.**

DAYS 1 & 2: Arrive in Paris ★★★

Take a flight that arrives in Paris as early as possible on **Day 1.** Check into your hotel and hit the nearest cafe for a pick-me-up café au lait and a croissant before sightseeing. Take the Métro to the Palais Royal–Musée du Louvre for a visit to the **Musée du Louvre** (p. 96). Spend at least 2 hours here viewing world-class masterpieces such as Leonardo da Vinci's *Mona Lisa.* After leaving the Louvre, walk south toward the **Quays of the Seine,** spending an hour taking in the tree-shaded banks and panoramic vistas of Paris. Head for that island in the Seine, **Ile de la Cité,** to explore its attractions, including **Ste-Chapelle** (p. 106) and the monumental **Notre-Dame** (p. 100) and its gargoyles. As the evening fades, head for the **Eiffel Tower** for the greatest cityscape view in Europe.

On **Day 2,** arrive at the **place de la Concorde** and its Egyptian obelisk, and take a stroll up the 1.8km (1-mile) avenue of French grandeur, the **Champs-Elysées,** until you reach the **Arc de Triomphe** (p. 107), which you can scale for another panoramic view of Paris. Afterward, head for the **Ile St-Louis** (p. 85), which, after Cité, is the second

Basilique du Sacré-Coeur.

Eglise St-Maclou.

island in the Seine. Lacking monumental attractions, this little isle is a sight in itself, with quays to stroll and small side streets where you can discover hidden wonders such as antiques shops and little bistros.

After lunch in one of those bistros, visit **Musée d'Orsay** (p. 131) and the world's greatest collection of Impressionist paintings. As the afternoon fades, head for **Basilique du Sacré-Coeur** (p. 116) for a crowning view of Paris as the sun sets. Have a final dinner in a Montmartre cafe.

DAY 3: A Day Trip to Versailles ★★★

Having survived 2 days in the capital of France, bid an adieu and take the RER Line C to the **Versailles/Rive Gauche station.** You can spend a full day at Versailles—and then some—or else you can see the highlights in 3 hours, including the Grands and Petits appartements, the glittering Hall of Mirrors, Gabriel's Opera House, the Royal Chapel, and the Gardens of Versailles, which contain the Grand and Petit Trianons.

DAY 4: Normandy's Capital of Rouen ★★★

Take an early train to Rouen and check into a hotel. Spend at least 2 hours exploring the city's ancient core, especially its **Cathédrale Notre-Dame** (p. 306), immortalized in paintings by Monet. Stand at the **place du Vieux-Marché** (p. 309), where Joan of Arc was executed for heresy in 1431, and then visit the **Eglise St-Maclou** (p. 307), a 1432 church in the Flamboyant Gothic style. After lunch, rent a car for the rest of your trip and drive to **Giverny** (p. 242)—it's only 60km (37 miles) southeast of Rouen. At Giverny, visit the **Claude Monet Foundation** (p. 243), returning to your hotel in Rouen for the night.

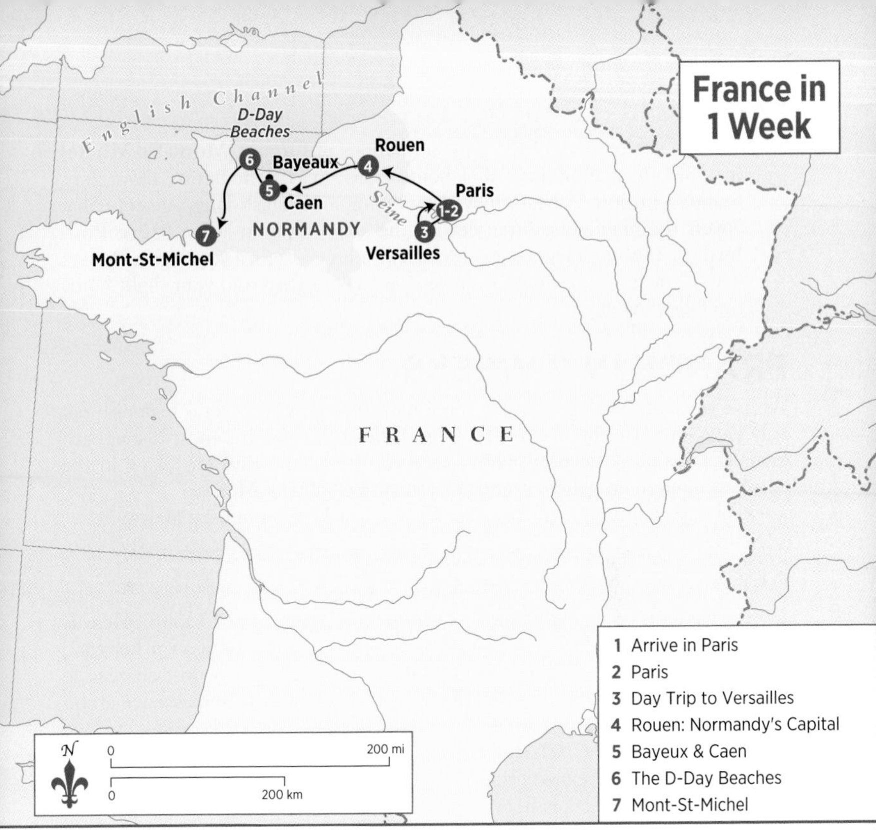

DAY 5: Bayeux ★★ & Caen ★★★

Strike out toward Bayeux, stopping en route to visit **Abbaye de Jumièges**, one of the most evocative ruins in France. Even with a stopover, you can easily be in the city of Caen in time for lunch before visiting **Abbaye aux Hommes** (p. 323), founded by William the Conqueror. After Caen, continue west to the city of **Bayeux,** where you can arrive in time to view the celebrated **Musée de la Tapisserie de Bayeux** (p. 327). Stay overnight in Bayeux.

DAY 6: The D-Day Beaches ★★

Reserve this day for exploring the D-day beaches, where Allied forces launched "the Longest Day," the mammoth invasion of Normandy in June 1944 that signaled the beginning of the end of Hitler's Third Reich.

From Bayeux, head east to explore the coastline. Your voyage of discovery can begin at the seaside resort of Arromanches-les-Bains, where you can visit the **Musée du Débarquement** (p. 331), **Omaha Beach** (p. 332), and the **Normandy American Cemetery** (p. 332). You can have lunch in the town of Grandcamp-Maisy (p. 332), later checking out **Utah Beach.**

That evening, drive to **Mont-St-Michel** (less than 2 hr. away) and overnight in the pedestrian village on "the Rock," giving you plenty of time for an early-morning visit to this popular attraction. If it's summer, you can also take an illuminated night tour.

DAY 7: Mont-St-Michel ★★★

You can explore one of the great attractions of Europe, **Mont-St-Michel** (p. 333), in a minimum of 3 hours. This great Benedictine monastery, founded in 966, is best enjoyed by taking an English-language tour that covers the highlights. After viewing the abbey, drop in at **La Mère Poulard** (p. 336) for a legendary omelet. After lunch, return your car to Rouen, where you'll find frequent train service back to Paris and your flight home the following day.

FRANCE IN 2 WEEKS

With 2 weeks to explore France, you'll have time to visit several regions—not only Paris, but also the best of the Loire Valley châteaux, the most history-rich town of Provence (Avignon), and several resorts on the Riviera, taking in the beaches, modern art galleries, and even the principality of Monaco.

For days 1 through 7, follow the "France in 1 Week" itinerary, above.

DAY 8: Orléans–Gateway to the Loire Valley ★

Leave Paris on an early train to **Orléans** (trip time: 1 hr., 15 min.). Heavily bombed in World War II, Orléans is a fairly dull town. Rent a car here and drive west to the **Château de Chambord** (p. 262), the largest château in the Loire Valley, representing the apogee of the French Renaissance architectural style. Allow 2 hours for a visit. Back on the road again, continue southwest to the **Château de Blois** (p. 264), called "the Versailles of the Renaissance" and a virtual illustrated storybook of French architecture. Stay overnight in Blois.

DAY 9: Amboise ★★ & Chenonceau ★★★

In the morning, continue southeast from Blois to **Amboise,** where you can check into a hotel for the night. Visit the 15th-century **Château d'Amboise** (p. 271), in the Italian Renaissance style, and also **Clos-Lucé** (p. 272), last residence of Leonardo da Vinci. In the afternoon, drive southeast to the **Château de Chenonceau** (p. 275), famous for the French dames who have occupied its precincts, including Diane de Poitiers (mistress of the king) and Catherine de Médicis (the jealous queen). You can spend 2 hours at the château before driving back to Amboise for the night.

Château d'Amboise.

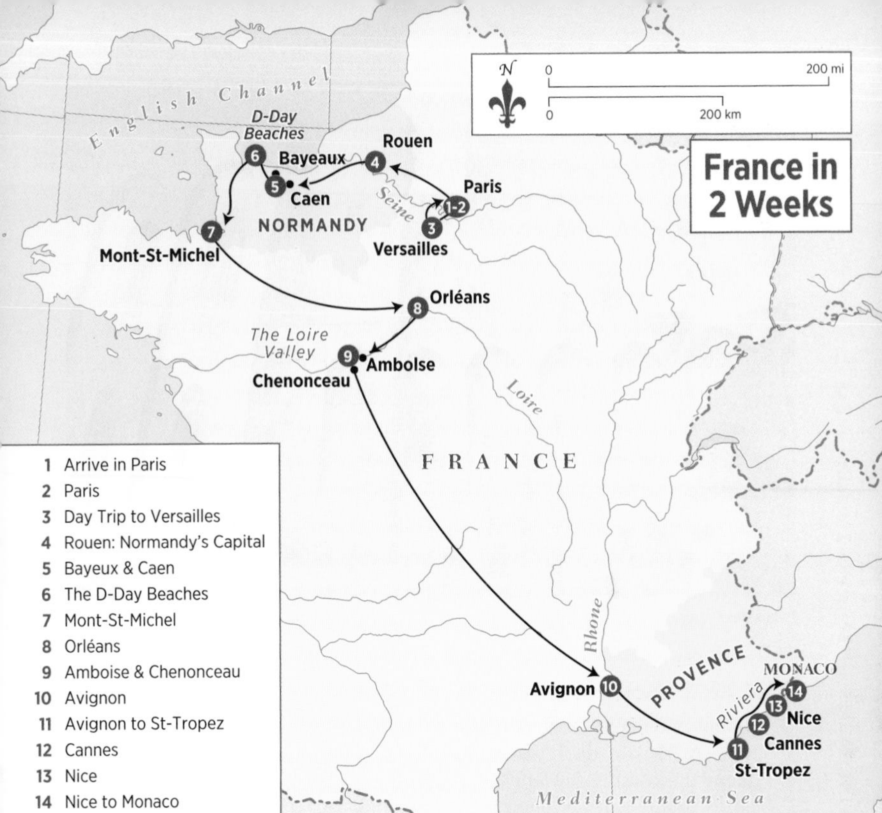

DAY 10: Avignon, Gateway to Provence ★★★

From Amboise, get an early start and drive east to Orléans to return your rental car. You now face a choice: take an early train from Orléans to Paris's Gare d'Austerlitz, then the Métro or a taxi to the Gare de Lyon, and hop on to a TGV bound for Avignon (2½ hours); or, perhaps more simply, take a train from Orléans to Lyon and then change trains for Avignon.

Check into a hotel in **Avignon,** one of Europe's most beautiful medieval cities. Before the day fades, you should have time to wander through the old city to get your bearings, shop for Provençal souvenirs, and see one of the smaller sights, such as the **Pont St-Bénézet** (also known as the Bridge of Avignon). See p. 502.

DAY 11: Avignon to St-Tropez ★★

In the morning, spend 2 hours touring the **Palais des Papes** (p. 504), the capital of Christendom during the 14th century. After lunch in one of Avignon's cozy bistros or cobblestoned outdoor cafes, rent a car and drive to **St-Tropez** (p. 550). If it's summer, get in some beach time and spend a good part of the early evening in one of the cafes along the harbor, indulging in that favorite French pastime of people-watching.

Palais des Papes.

DAY 12: Cannes, Capital of the Riviera Chic ★★★

Before leaving St-Tropez in the morning, check out the Impressionist paintings at **Musée de l'Annonciade** (p. 554). Drive 50km (31 miles) east along the coast until you reach Cannes.

Assuming it's summer, get in some time at the beach, notably at **Plage de la Croisette** (p. 559), and feel free to wear your most revealing swimwear. In the afternoon, take the ferry to **Ile Ste-Marguerite** (p. 563), where the "Man in the Iron Mask" was imprisoned. You can visit his cell. That evening, you may want to flirt with Lady Luck at one of the plush **casinos** (p. 568).

DAY 13: Nice, Capital of the Riviera ★★★

It's only a 32km (20-mile) drive east from Cannes to **Nice,** the Riviera's largest city. After checking into a hotel (the most affordable along the Riviera), stroll through **Vieille Ville** (p. 569), the Old Town, beginning at the foot of "the Rock." Enjoy a snack of *socca,* a round crepe made with chickpea flour that's sold steaming hot by street vendors. Then head for the **promenade des Anglais** (p. 593), the wide boulevard along the waterfront. Stop in at one of the grand cafes along the water for a light lunch. In the afternoon, head for the best of the hill towns above Nice, **St-Paul-de-Vence,** only 31km (19 miles) to the north. Here you can wander its ramparts in about 30 minutes before descending on the greatest modern art museum in the Riviera, the **Foundation Maeght** (p. 586).

Continue over to Vence (p. 589) for a visit to **Chapelle du Rosaire** (p. 589), where the great Henri Matisse created his artistic masterpiece for some Dominican nuns. From there, it's just 24km (15 miles) southeast to Nice.

Have dinner at a typical bistro, serving a traditional Niçoise cuisine with its inevitable Italian influences.

DAY 14: Nice to Monaco ★★★

While still overnighting in Nice, head east for the most hair-raising but thrilling drive in all of France, a trip along the **Grande Corniche** highway that stretches 31km (19 miles) east from Nice to the little resort of **Menton** near the Italian border. Allow 3 hours for this trip. Highlights along this road include **Roquebrune—Cap-Martin** and **La Turbie.** The greatest view along the Riviera is at the **Eze Belvedere,** at 1,200m (3,936 ft.).

FRANCE FOR FAMILIES

France offers many attractions for kids. Perhaps your main concern with having children along is pacing yourself with museum time. Our suggestion is to limit **Paris** to 2 days and then spend a day wandering the spectacular grounds and glittering interiors of **Versailles,** 2 days in **Disneyland Paris,** and 2 days on the **Riviera.**

DAYS 1 & 2: Paris ★★★

Take the kids for a morning visit to **Notre-Dame** (p. 100). The highlight is climbing the 387 narrow and winding steps to the top of one of the towers for a fabulously Quasimodo view of the gargoyles and Paris. After a visit, head for the **Eiffel Tower** (p. 133). In addition to scaling this fantastic monument, you can order lunch—allow at least 2 hours for your visit, one just to access the elevators on levels one and two. Food is available at the Altitude 95 restaurant on the first floor, but it's a bit pricey for most families. A first-floor snack bar and a second-floor cafeteria offer the best values for the family on a budget.

After touring the tower, take the kids for a donkey ride in the nearby **Champ de Mars,** which also stages the best puppet shows.

In the afternoon, take the children for a stroll through the **Jardin des Tuileries** (p. 92), where there are more donkey rides, ice-cream stands, and a marionette show. At the circular pond, you can rent a toy boat.

On **Day 2,** visit the **Musée du Louvre** (p. 96). Even if your child is not a museum buff and bores easily, he or she will surely be intrigued by the many displays. Over the years, we've observed that, even more than the paintings, kids are fascinated by the Egyptian art and antiquities displayed in the Sully and Denon wings, a total of 7,000 items, the largest exhibition of such artifacts outside of Cairo.

After the Louvre, take the Métro to Porte de la Villette, where you can spend 2 or 3 hours at **Cité des Sciences et de l'Industrie** (p. 119). The mammoth structure is home to a planetarium, a 3-D cinema, video workshops, and interactive exhibits.

Space is too tight in this book to document all activities in Paris of interest to children, but you'll want to spend a good 2 hours in the **Jardin d'Acclimatation,** in the northern part of the Bois de Boulogne. The visit starts with a ride on a narrow-gauge train through a stretch of wooded park, and attractions include a zoo, a house of mirrors, a puppet theater, a playground, and kiosks selling waffles.

As the afternoon fades, head for **Butte Montmartre,** with its fiesta atmosphere. Take the Métro to Anvers and walk to the funicular, the cable

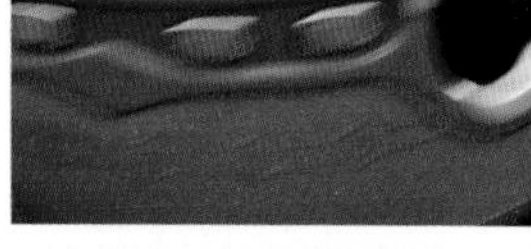

A ride at Jardin d'Acclimatation.

Place du Tertre, Montmartre.

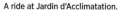

car that carries you to the **Basilique du Sacré-Coeur** (p. 116). Once you arrive at "the top of Paris," follow the crowds to the **place du Tertre,** where a Sergeant Pepper–style band often blasts off-key, and you can have a local artist create a sketch of your kids. Finally, reward your brood with ice cream sold on the square.

DAY 3: Versailles ★★★

Tear yourself away from the glories of Paris for a day spent at the **Château de Versailles** (p. 220). Take the RER line C to the Versailles/Rive Gauche station. Kids delight in the Hall of Mirrors and in the grand apartments. Take the children for a walk through the garden, where they can visit the hamlet where the ill-fated Marie Antoinette strolled with her lambs. You can buy the makings of a picnic lunch in Paris and enjoy it on the grounds, or else you can purchase fast food at one of the stalls placed in discreet corners of the garden.

Return to Paris in time to pay a quick visit to the **Musée National d'Histoire Naturelle** (p.121). Dinosaur-loving kids will enjoy the huge skeletons, and they'll also discover a menagerie of animals in their simulated natural habitats.

DAYS 4 & 5: Disneyland Paris ★★

Disneyland Paris is the top family vacation destination in France. Allow a full day to see the highlights of the park, plus another day to absorb its secondary adventures. Our recommendation is to visit **Main Street, U.S.A., Frontierland,** and **Adventureland** on the first day, saving **Fantasyland, Discoveryland,** the entertainment center at **Village Disney,** and **Sleeping Beauty Castle** for the second day. You can stay in the Disney hotels

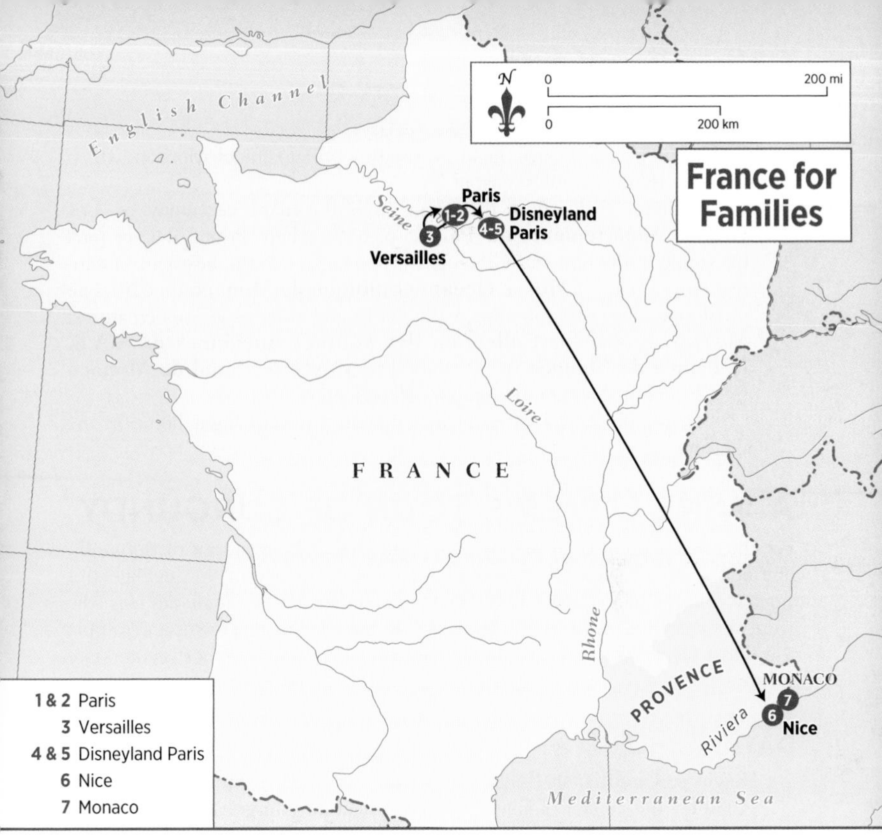

on-site, coming in various price ranges from very expensive to budget. The RER commuter express train A takes you from Etoile in Paris to Marne-la-Vallée/Chessy in 45 minutes.

DAY 6: Nice ★★★

Return to Paris and fly to Nice, capital of the French Riviera. If you flew Air France transatlantic, Nice can often be attached as a low-cost extension of your round-trip fare.

In Nice, you can check into your hotel for 2 nights, as the city has the most affordable hotels on the Riviera. Set out to explore this old city. The people-watching on the Riviera alone is likely to leave your kids wide-eyed. Beware that they'll see plenty of skin, as topless bathing is rampant. There's always a lot of free entertainment in summer along the boardwalk in Nice, called the **promenade des Anglais** (p. 593).

In the afternoon, journey to the hill town of **St-Paul-de-Vence** (p. 585). This is the most evocative of the hill towns of Nice, and children delight in touring the ramparts and strolling along the pedestrian-only rue Grande. You can have a late lunch in the cafeteria of the **Foundation Maeght** (p. 586), the Riviera's greatest modern-art museum.

Return to Nice for the evening and take your kids for a stroll through the Old Town, dining in a typical Niçoise bistro.

DAY 7: Monaco ★★★

While still based in Nice, head for the tiny principality of Monaco, which lies only 18km (11 miles) east of Nice.

Children will enjoy the changing-of-the-guard ceremony at **Les Grands Appartements du Palais** (p. 619), where Prince Rainier took his young bride, film star Grace Kelly, years ago. But the best part of Monaco for kids is the **Musée Océanographique de Monaco** (p. 620), one of Europe's biggest aquariums, with sharks and other exotic sea creatures. Monaco also has the **Collection des Voitures Anciennes de S.A.S. le Prince de Monaco** (p. 619) and the **Musée National de Monaco** (p. 620), with a mammoth antique doll collection.

Return to Nice that night and prepare for your flight home in the morning.

A WINE LOVER'S TOUR OF BURGUNDY

For the aficionado or even the lover of French landscapes, a tour of Burgundy, one of the world's greatest wine-producing regions, is one of the highlights of France. Burgundian vintages have been called *le vin des rois, le roi des vins* (the wine of kings, the king of wines). You can tour the winemaking towns and sample the finest of chardonnays and pinot noirs along the way. The best centers are **Dijon** (capital of Burgundy), **Beaune, Auxerre,** and **Autun.**

DAY 1: Chablis to Auxerre ★★

Begin at **Chablis,** in Burgundy's northwestern edge. Vineyards surround Chablis, the capital of Basse Bourgogne (Lower Burgundy). The town is now more famous for its wine than for its monuments, but it has two historic churches: Eglise St-Martin and Eglise St-Pierre. Chablis is not worth an overnight stop, though 15km (9¼ miles) to the west, along D965, in the hamlet of **Tonnerre,** is **Saint-Père,** one of the best restaurants in the province. After a meal, backtrack about 24km (15 miles) west on D965 (passing through Chablis) to **Auxerre** (p. 418).

Scene of many pivotal moments in French history, Auxerre is the site of one of France's most impressive churches, the Gothic **Cathédrale St-Etienne** (p. 419). Stay overnight in Auxerre.

DAY 2: Vézelay ★★

Drive south from Auxerre along N151 and then east on D951 to the hamlet of **Vézelay** (p. 421). If there's one must-see Romanesque church in France, it's here. Park at the bottom of the village and climb the cobblestone main street. At the base of the hill is **L'Espérance** (p. 423), one of the best restaurants in the world. It's closed Tuesday and at lunch Wednesday, so plan your itinerary accordingly.

You can spend the night in Vézelay, drive 9.5km (6 miles) east on D957 to **Avallon,** or continue south for 56km (35 miles) on well-signposted country roads to **Château-Chinon.** Wherever you spend the night, plan an early departure the following day.

DAY 3: Autun ★★

From Château-Chinon, drive east 32km (20 miles) on D978 to visit one of the oldest towns in France, **Autun** (p. 425).

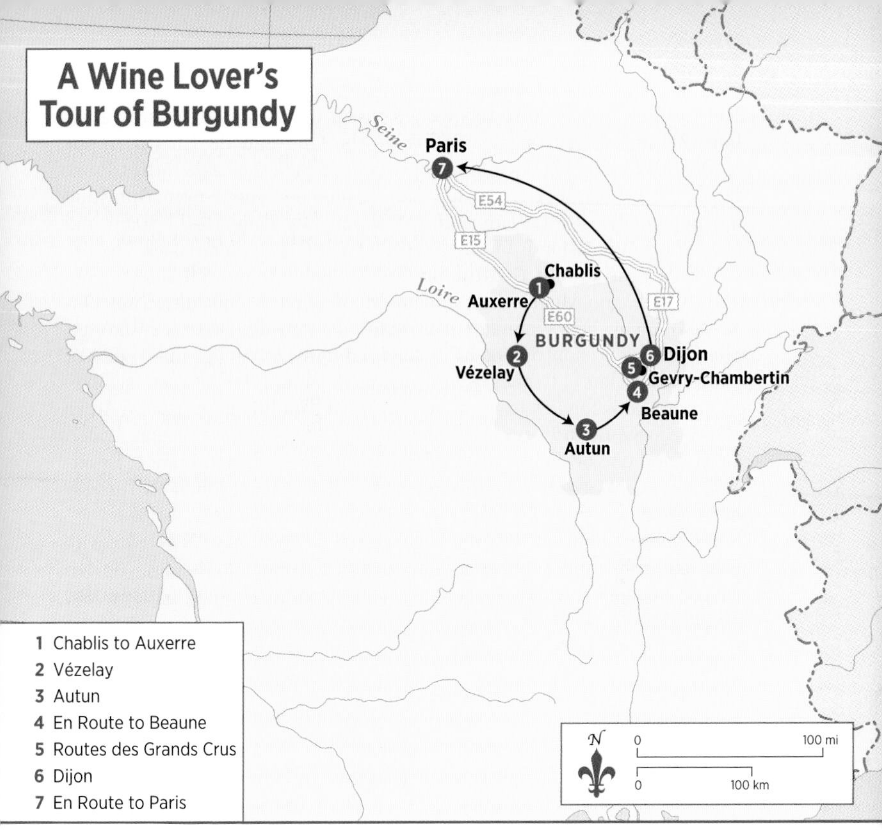

En route, you may wish to take this detour: Heading east on D978 toward Autun, turn right (south) at Arleuf, going right onto D500. At a fork, turn right toward Glux and follow arrows to Mont Beuvray on D18. Take D274 to reach the summit. After 3km (1¾ miles) of climbing, you'll be at **Oppidum of Bibracte,** home of Eduens, a Gallic tribe. Here Vercingetorix organized the Gauls to fight Caesar's legions in A.D. 52. At this altitude (840m/2,755 ft.), you'll have a splendid view of the wine country of Autun and Mont St-Vincent. Leave Mont Beuvray on D274 and continue northeast to Autun.

At Autun, you'll find a historic town with ruins left by the ancient Romans, as well as a cathedral built in 1120 to hold the remains of St. Lazarus. Spend the night here.

DAY 4: En Route to Beaune ★★

Start early in Autun, and be prepared for tours of châteaux, fortresses, vineyards, and other historic sites. Your route will be loaded with appealing detours, so be as flexible as possible as you negotiate a labyrinth of country roads toward Beaune.

Leave Autun on D973 east. After 9.5km (6 miles), turn left onto D326 toward Sully. Here you'll find the **Château de Sully,** once known as the Fontainebleau of Burgundy; it's closed to the public, but a view from the outside may satisfy you. The gardens are open Easter to September daily

8am to 6pm. Leave Sully, following signs to the village of **Nolay.** About 4km (2½ miles) past Nolay, you'll reach the **Château de La Rochepot** (✆ **03-80-21-71-37;** www.larochepot.com), a medieval-style fortress built during the Renaissance (July–Aug daily 10am–noon and 2–6pm; Apr–June and Sept daily 10–11:30am and 2–5:30pm; Oct daily 10–11:30am and 2–4:30pm). Admission is 6€ for adults and 3.50€ for children ages 6 to 14.

Now head toward **Beaune** on D973, passing some well-known vineyards: Chassagne-Montrachet, Puligny-Montrachet, Meursault, Auxey Durresses, Volnay, and Pommard. En route, you can detour to a restaurant whose setting is as intriguing as its food. **Chagny,** 43km (27 miles) east of Autun and 18km (11 miles) southwest of Beaune, rarely attracts sightseers; and serious foodies from all over stop at **Lameloise,** 36 place d'Arnes (✆ **03-85-87-65-65**), for lamb filet in a rice crepe, Bresse pigeon, lemon soufflé, and one of the broadest selections of burgundies in France. Reservations are required. It's closed Wednesday all day and at lunch on Tuesday and Thursday.

Continue north to Beaune on D973, which changes to N741. You can overnight in Beaune (p. 427). If you arrive early enough in the day, you can explore Beaune's historic attractions in 2½ hours, including **Musée des Beaux-Arts** (p. 428).

Even more intriguing for the wine connoisseur is a visit to one of the cellars for a tour and a tasting. Our favorite is **Marché aux Vins** (p. 428), housed in a former church. Its cellars are in ancient tombs under the 14th-century church.

DAY 5: Route des Grands Crus ★★★

The road visited on this trip is called the Route des Grands Crus (Road of the Great Wines).

Route N74 continues north 44km (27 miles) to Dijon, but you can make a full day of it because of the stopovers along the way.

This route takes you along the most celebrated vineyards of the **Côte d'Or,** which actually stretch from Dijon in the north to Santenay southwest of Beaune, a distance of 60km (37 miles). This is a region of France's greatest wines, and each village has some claim to fame.

As you head north from Beaune, the first village is **Aloxe-Corton,** where Charlemagne once owned vineyards. The emperor is honored with "a white wine of great character," Corton-Charlemagne, which is still produced here.The N74 continues north to the village of **Vougeot,** known for the quality of its red wines.

In Vougeot, you can visit **Château du Clos-de-Vougeot** (✆ **03-80-62-86-09**), surrounded by France's most celebrated vineyards. The 12th-century château maintains a cellar, open for visits year-round (Apr–Sept Mon–Fri 9am–6:30pm and Sat–Sun 9am–5pm; Oct–Mar Mon–Fri 9am–5pm, Sat–Sun 9–11:30am and 2–5pm). Admission is 3.50€ for adults and 2.60€ for students and children 8 and older.

The N74 continues north to Dijon, but you can branch off onto D122 to Chambolle-Musigny, where you'll see signs directing you to the town of **Gevrey-Chambertin,** which lies only 10km (6¼ miles) south of Dijon. Nine of the region's 33 Grands Crus are produced here.

Visit the village's main attraction, **Le Château de Gevrey-Chambertin,** constructed by the lords of Vergy in the 10th century. In the 13th

Aloxe-Corton.

A view over Dijon.

century, the decaying castle was expanded by the powerful monks of Cluny. The great hall is impressive, with exposed ceiling beams. Look for the guards' room in the watchtower and the collection of vintage wines in the vaulted cellars. English-language tours, ending with a tasting of the prize vintages, cost 14€. The château is open Monday, Thursday, and Friday 10am to noon and 2 to 5pm, Saturday and Sunday 11am to noon and 2 to 6pm. For more information, call ✆ **03-80-51-84-85.**

The D122 takes you north into **Dijon** (p. 431), where you can spend the night (or a second night, if your schedule allows). It takes 4 hours to explore Dijon. If you arrive early enough in the day, you can see half of the town's attractions, visiting the rest of the sights the next morning.

DAY 6: Dijon ★★★

Surrounded by some of the world's most splendid vineyards, Dijon was the former seat of the powerful dukes of Burgundy. A university town and regional center today, it has had a long and rich history. Its monumental attraction is the **Musée des Beaux-Arts** (p. 432), housed in an old palace and showcasing a stunning collection of European art from the 14th to the 19th centuries. Next, pick up a map at the **Office de Tourisme** (p. 431) and walk through the historic core of this ancient city. Or, better yet, in our view, spend the day touring the magnificent wine country around Dijon (see "Side Trips from Dijon," p. 435).

DAY 7: En Route to Paris

Dijon is one of the major transportation hubs in this part of France, and you can easily return to Paris from here. If you're driving, the distance is 312km (193 miles), which you can do in a morning, reaching Paris to the northwest in time for lunch.

4 PARIS

From the Louvre to the Eiffel Tower, Paris is home to some of the world's most famous museums and monuments. While all of these sights are well worth visiting, the city itself is much more than a mere collection of buildings. Visiting Paris is as much about soaking up the atmosphere as sightseeing. With all the layers of history, it's easy to forget that Paris is a 21st-century capital, but some of the more recent additions to the city, such as the Vélib biking scheme, have injected Paris with a new sense of dynamism.

Each of Paris's 20 arrondissements possesses a unique style and character. Our guide to the different neighborhoods of Paris will give you an insight into the city and help you decide where you want to stay and what you want to see. Once you arrive in Paris, try to explore as many neighborhoods as you can in order to appreciate the diversity of the city. If you have only a few days, you'll probably spend most of your time in the center of Paris, seeing the major sites. In a week, you'll be able to wander off the beaten track and explore some of Paris's neighborhoods in a bit more depth. And if you can stay for several weeks, you'll soon be an expert on *la vie parisienne*.

ORIENTATION

Arriving

BY PLANE

Paris has two international airports: **Aéroport d'Orly,** 13km (8 miles) south of the city, and **Aéroport Roissy–Charles de Gaulle,** 22km (14 miles) northeast. A shuttle (19€) makes the 50- to 75-minute journey between the two airports about every 30 minutes.

CHARLES DE GAULLE AIRPORT (ROISSY) At Charles de Gaulle (✆ **01-48-62-12-12,** or 39-50 in France), foreign carriers use Aérogare 1, while Air France uses Aérogare 2. From Aérogare 1, you take a moving walkway to the passport checkpoint and the Customs area. A *navette* (shuttle bus) links the two terminals.

Fast RER (Réseau Express Régional) trains depart the airport and **Roissy rail station** every 10 minutes between 5am and midnight for Métro stations, including Gare du Nord, Châtelet, Luxembourg, Port-Royal, and Denfert-Rochereau. A typical fare from Roissy to any point in central Paris is 8.20€ per person (5.60€ children 4–10). Travel time from the airport to central Paris is around 35 to 40 minutes.

You can also take an **Air France shuttle bus** (✆ **08-92-35-08-20** or 01-48-64-14-24; www.cars-airfrance.com) to central Paris for 15€ one-

FACING PAGE: **Walkers along the Seine.**

way. It stops at the Palais des Congrès (Port Maillot) and continues to place Charles-de-Gaulle–Etoile, where subway lines can carry you to any point in Paris. That ride, depending on traffic, takes 45 to 55 minutes. The shuttle departs about every 20 minutes between 5:40am and 11pm.

The **Roissybus** (✆ **01-58-76-16-16**), operated by the RATP, departs from the airport daily 6am to 11:45pm and costs 8.60€ for the 45- to 50-minute ride. Departures are about every 15 minutes, and the bus leaves you near the corner of rue Scribe and place de l'Opéra in the heart of Paris.

A **taxi** from Roissy into the city will cost about 47€ to 60€; from 8pm to 7am, the fare is 40% higher. Long orderly lines for taxis form outside each of the airport's terminals.

ORLY AIRPORT Orly (✆ **01-49-75-52-52,** or 39-50 in France) has two terminals—Orly Sud (south) for international flights and Orly Ouest (west) for domestic flights. A free shuttle bus connects them in 3 minutes.

Air France buses leave from exit E of Orly Sud and from exit F of Orly Ouest every 12 minutes between 6am and 11:30pm for Gare des Invalides; the fare is 9€ one-way, 14€ round-trip. Returning to the airport (about 30 min.), buses leave both the Montparnasse and the Invalides terminal for Orly Sud or Orly Ouest every 15 minutes.

Another way to get to central Paris is to take the RER from points throughout central Paris to the station at Pont-de-Rungis/Aéroport d'Orly for a per-person one-way fare of 6€, and from here, take the free shuttle bus that departs every 15 minutes from Pont-de-Rungis to both of Orly's terminals. Combined travel time is about 45 to 55 minutes.

A **taxi** from Orly to central Paris costs about 30€ to 50€, more at night. Don't take a meterless taxi from Orly; it's much safer (and usually cheaper) to hire one of the metered cabs, which are under the scrutiny of a police officer.

BY TRAIN

Paris has six major stations: **Gare d'Austerlitz,** 55 quai d'Austerlitz, 13e (serving the southwest, with trains to and from the Loire Valley, Bordeaux, the Pyrénées, and Spain); **Gare de l'Est,** place du 11-Novembre-1918, 10e (serving the east, with trains to and from Strasbourg, Reims, and beyond, to Zurich and Austria); **Gare de Lyon,** 20 bd. Diderot, 12e (serving the southeast, with trains to and from the Côte d'Azur [Nice, Cannes, St-Tropez], Provence, and beyond, to Geneva and Italy); **Gare Montparnasse,** 17 bd. Vaugirard, 15e (serving the west, with trains to and from Brittany); **Gare du Nord,** 18 rue de Dunkerque, 15e (serving the north, with trains to and from London, Holland, Denmark, and northern Germany); and **Gare St-Lazare,** 13 rue d'Amsterdam, 8e (serving the northwest, with trains to and from Normandy). Buses operate between the stations, and each station has a Métro stop. For

The Paris Airport Shuttle

The **Paris Airport Shuttle** (✆ **01-53-39-18-18;** fax 01-53-39-13-13; www.parisshuttle.com) is the best option. It charges 25€ for one person or 19€ per person for two or more going to and from Charles de Gaulle or Orly. Service is daily 6am to 11pm. Both shuttles accept American Express, Visa, and MasterCard, with 1-day advance reservations required.

train information and to make reservations, call ✆**08-92-35-35-35,** or **36-35** in France, between 8am and 8pm daily. From Paris, one-way rail passage to Tours costs 30€ to 51€; one-way to Strasbourg costs 55€ or 80€, depending on the routing.

Warning: The stations and surrounding areas are usually seedy and frequented by pickpockets, hustlers, hookers, and addicts. Be alert, especially at night.

BY BUS

Most buses arrive at the **Eurolines France** station, 28 av. du Général-de-Gaulle, Bagnolet (✆**08-92-89-90-91;** www.eurolines.fr; Métro: Gallieni).

BY CAR

Driving in Paris is *not* recommended. Parking is difficult and traffic dense. If you drive, remember that Paris is encircled by a ring road, the *périphérique.* Always obtain detailed directions to your destination, including the name of the exit on the *périphérique* (exits aren't numbered). Avoid rush hours.

The major highways into Paris are A1 from the north; A13 from Rouen, Normandy, and other points northwest; A10 from Spain and the southwest; A6 and A7 from the French Alps, the Riviera, and Italy; and A4 from eastern France.

Visitor Information

The **Paris Convention and Visitors Bureau** (✆**08-92-68-30-00;** .35€ per minute; www.paris-info.com) has offices throughout the city, with the main headquarters at 25–27 rue des Pyramides, 1er (Métro: Pyramides). It's open Monday through Saturday 10am to 7pm (June–Oct from 9am), Sunday and holidays from 11am to 7pm. Less comprehensive branch offices include Clémenceau Welcome Center, corner of avenue Champs-Elysées and avenue Marigny (8e; Métro: Champs-Elysées), open April 6 to October 20 daily 9am to 7pm. **Espace Tourisme Ile-de-France,** in the Carrousel du Louvre, 99 rue de Rivoli, 1er (Métro: Palais-Royal–Louvre), open daily 10am to 6pm; in the **Gare de Lyon,** 20 bd. Diderot, Paris 12e (Métro: Gare de Lyon), open Monday through Saturday 8am to 6pm; in the **Gare du Nord,** 18 rue de Dunkerque, 10e (Métro: Gare du Nord), open daily 8am to 6pm; and in **Montmartre,** 21 place du Tertre, 18e (Métro: Abbesses or Lamarck-Caulaincourt), open daily 10am to 7pm. You can walk in at any branch to make a hotel reservation; the service charge is free. The offices are extremely busy year-round, especially in midsummer, so be prepared to wait in line.

City Layout

Compared to many capitals, Paris is surprisingly compact. The river Seine divides the city into the *Rive Droite* (**Right Bank**) to the north and the *Rive Gauche* (**Left Bank**) to the south. The larger Right Bank is where you find the city's business sector, stately monuments, and high-fashion industry. The smaller Left Bank has the publishing houses, universities, and a reputation as bohemian because students, philosophers, and creative types have been congregating here for centuries.

Paris is divided into 20 numbered municipal districts called **arrondissements.** The layout of these districts follows a distinct pattern. The first (abbreviated 1er for *premier*) *arrondissement* is the dead center of Paris, comprising an area around Notre-Dame and the Louvre. From there, the rest of the districts spiral outward, clockwise, in ascending order, like a snail shell. The lower the *arrondissement* number, the more central the location. If you want to be within walking distance of all the major sites and monuments, be sure to stay in one of the first eight arrondissements. There are only six arrondissements—the 5e, 6e, 7e, 13e, 14e, and 15e—on the Left Bank. The Right Bank is much larger, and it is comprised of the remaining 14 arrondissements.

Most city maps are divided by arrondissement, and addresses include the arrondissement number (in Roman or Arabic numerals and followed by *éme* or *e,* as in *10éme*). Arrondissement numbers are key to locating an address in Paris, and this book lists addresses the way they appear in Paris, with the arrondissement number following the specific street address (for instance, 29 rue de Rivoli, 4e, is in the fourth arrondissement). Paris also has its own version of a zip code. The mailing address for a hotel is written as, for example, "Paris 75014." The last two digits, 14, indicate that the address is in the 14th arrondissement—in this case, Montparnasse. Arrondissements are indicated on the blue enamel street signs, above the street name.

Finding an address can be a complicated process in Paris, but once you know the arrondissement in which an address is located, finding that spot is much easier. Numbers on buildings running parallel to the Seine usually follow the course of the river east to west. On north–south streets, numbering begins at the river. To enter a building, you'll usually need a code for the outside door. Once inside, you'll need a letter indicating which staircase to take, the floor number, and the position of the apartment (right, left, last door, and so forth). *Bis* and *ter* after a building number are the equivalent of *b* or *c* and indicate a separate address.

A good way to orientate yourself is the Métro. As you're rarely more than 10 minutes' walk away from a Métro station, it's easy to work out which part of Paris you're in by finding your nearest station.

There is a pull-out map showing Paris's neighborhoods at the back of this book. For a more detailed map of Paris, we recommend *Paris Pratique par arrondissement,* available at newsstands and bookshops for around 7€. This guide provides you with a Métro map and maps of each arrondissement, with all streets listed and keyed. Free maps of the Paris Métro, bus, and RER networks are available at all Métro stations.

Neighborhoods in Brief

THE RIGHT BANK

LES HALLES, LOUVRE & PALAIS ROYAL (1ER & 2E) Home to some of Paris's most important sites, the area around the **Louvre** and **Palais-Royal** is one of the most visited (but least residential) parts of the city. Whether you're strolling through the **Jardin des Tuileries** or admiring the classic beauty of **place Vendôme,** this is one of the most elegant neighborhoods in the city. It's also one of the most luxurious, with designer boutiques filling the arcades of the Palais-Royal and *haute couture* lining the sidewalks of **rue St-Honoré. Rue de Rivoli,** the main street running through the 1st arrondissement, is one of the busiest streets in Paris, full of shops, cafes, and restaurants. For a little peace and quiet, head south for a walk along the banks of the Seine or take refuge in the gardens of the Palais-Royal.

North of the Palais-Royal is the **Bourse** (stock exchange). You'll find fewer tourists, but it still remains close to the center of the action. Like most financial districts, it's bustling and lively during the week but much quieter at weekends. To the east is **Sentier,** the traditional center of the wholesale clothing trade, and the picturesque, cobbled market street, **rue Montorgueil.** For a more classic shopping environment, explore the various passages (covered arcades) that the 2nd arrondissement is famous for.

Although the area around the **Forum des Halles** is currently being redeveloped by architect David Mangin, it remains one of central Paris's least attractive neighborhoods. The huge underground shopping center and Métro/RER station means that Les Halles is always hectic and heaving with people. It's not the safest area, and it's worth avoiding at night. The same is true of the seedy rue St-Denis, just east of Les Halles, as this is one of Paris's red light districts.

LE MARAIS, ILE ST-LOUIS & ILE DE LA CITÉ (3E & 4E) Located in the heart of the city, Paris's two islands could not be more different from each other. Although the **Ile de la Cité** does have some quieter spots, such as the Square du Vert-Galant, it is dominated by the majestic Gothic cathedral **Notre-Dame** and is visited by thousands of tourists every day. The **Ile St-Louis,** with its aristocratic town houses, is much calmer and more picturesque. Far removed from the hustle and bustle of Paris, the *quais* of the Ile St-Louis are perfect for a romantic stroll.

Having avoided Haussmann's 19th-century transformation of Paris, **Le Marais** has a more intimate atmosphere than other parts of Paris. The neighborhood became fashionable in the early 17th century when Henri IV commissioned the beautiful **place des Vosges,** and it is full of aristocratic mansions (known as *hôtels particuliers*) that were built by the French aristocracy. After the French Revolution, the area fell into disrepair, but in 1962, under Culture Minister André Malraux's law that permitted the preservation of historic quarters, Le Marais underwent a process of restoration; today it is one of Paris's trendiest neighborhoods.

Stretching across the 3rd and 4th arrondissements, the southern part of Le Marais is a lively area, full of elegant boutiques and small, contemporary art galleries. It's a great area for wining and dining, and very popular on Sundays as, unlike many other parts of Paris, most of the shops here are open. The area around **rue des Rosiers** has long been home to the city's Jewish community, while the **rues St-Croix-de-la-Bretonnerie, des Archives,** and **Vieille-du-Temple** are the center of Paris's gay and lesbian life. The northern part of the Le Marais, around rue de Bretagne, is more up and coming but considerably quieter than the 4th.

CHAMPS ELYSÉES & WESTERN PARIS (8E, 16E & 17E) One of the most famous avenues in the world, the tree-lined avenue **des Champs Elysées** is the embodiment of Parisian grandeur. While strolling along the Champs Elysées may be something of a disappointment thanks to the fast-food restaurants, overpriced cafes, and chain stores, leading off to the south are **avenue George V** and **avenue Montaigne,** home to *haute couture* boutiques and several of Paris's most luxurious hotels. Above the Champs Elysées, around **boulevard Haussmann,** you'll find a busy, commercial district and fewer tourists.

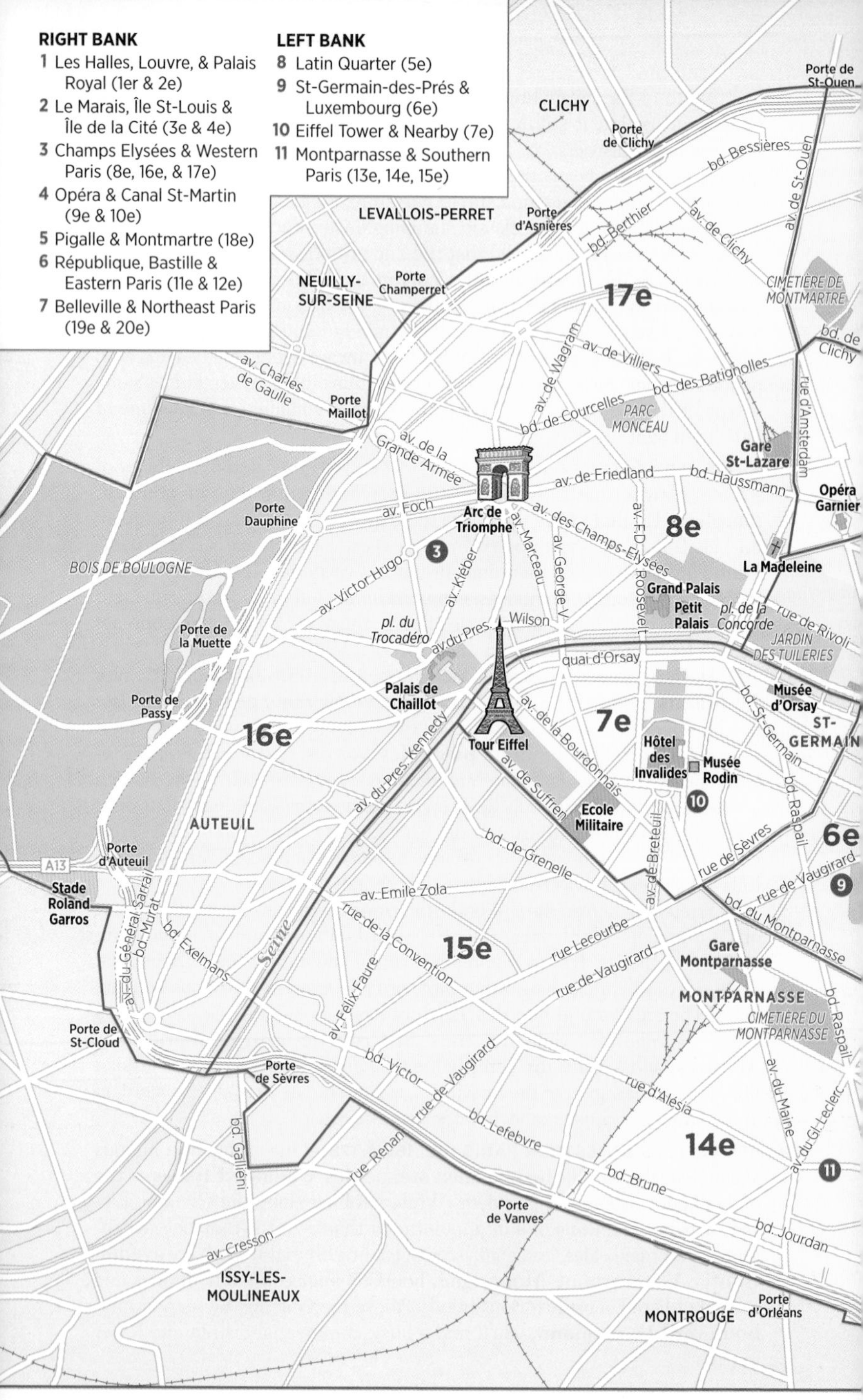
RIGHT BANK
1 Les Halles, Louvre, & Palais Royal (1er & 2e)
2 Le Marais, Île St-Louis & Île de la Cité (3e & 4e)
3 Champs Elysées & Western Paris (8e, 16e, & 17e)
4 Opéra & Canal St-Martin (9e & 10e)
5 Pigalle & Montmartre (18e)
6 République, Bastille & Eastern Paris (11e & 12e)
7 Belleville & Northeast Paris (19e & 20e)
LEFT BANK
8 Latin Quarter (5e)
9 St-Germain-des-Prés & Luxembourg (6e)
10 Eiffel Tower & Nearby (7e)
11 Montparnasse & Southern Paris (13e, 14e, 15e)
CLICHY
LEVALLOIS-PERRET
NEUILLY-SUR-SEINE
BOIS DE BOULOGNE
AUTEUIL
ISSY-LES-MOULINEAUX
MONTROUGE
MONTPARNASSE
ST-GERMAIN
17e
8e
16e
7e
6e
15e
14e
Arc de Triomphe
Tour Eiffel
Palais de Chaillot
Grand Palais
Petit Palais
pl. de la Concorde
JARDIN DES TUILERIES
Musée d'Orsay
Hôtel des Invalides
Musée Rodin
Ecole Militaire
La Madeleine
Opéra Garnier
Gare St-Lazare
Gare Montparnasse
CIMETIÈRE DE MONTMARTRE
CIMETIÈRE DU MONTPARNASSE
PARC MONCEAU
Stade Roland Garros
Porte de St-Ouen
Porte de Clichy
Porte d'Asnières
Porte Champerret
Porte Maillot
Porte Dauphine
Porte de la Muette
Porte de Passy
Porte d'Auteuil
Porte de St-Cloud
Porte de Sèvres
Porte de Vanves
Porte d'Orléans
pl. du Trocadéro
Seine
A13

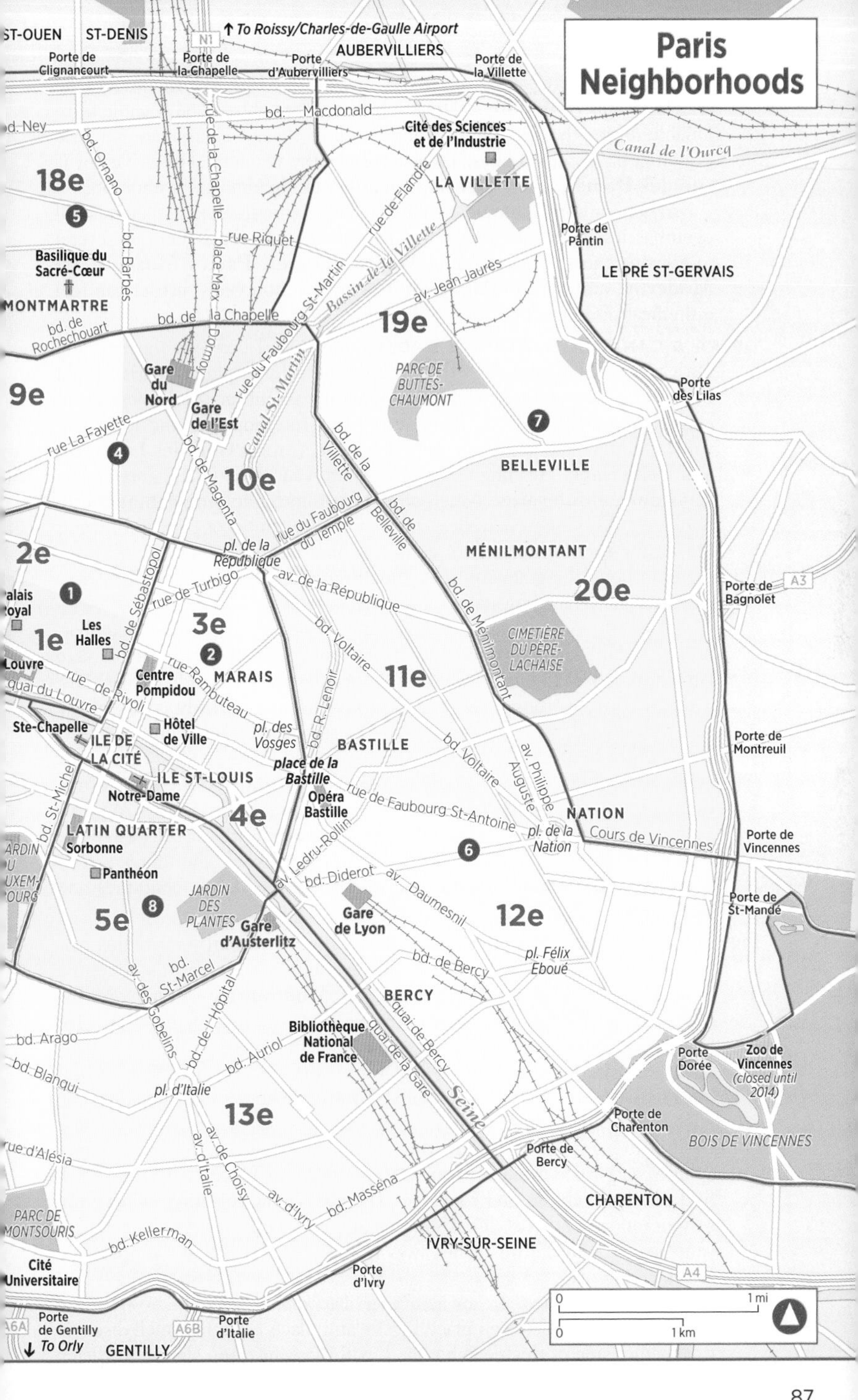

Paris Neighborhoods
ST-OUEN
ST-DENIS
To Roissy/Charles-de-Gaulle Airport
AUBERVILLIERS
Porte de Clignancourt
Porte de la-Chapelle
Porte d'Aubervilliers
Porte de la Villette
bd. Macdonald
Cité des Sciences et de l'Industrie
Canal de l'Ourcq
LA VILLETTE
18e
Basilique du Sacré-Cœur
MONTMARTRE
Porte de Pantin
LE PRÉ ST-GERVAIS
19e
PARC DE BUTTES-CHAUMONT
Porte des Lilas
BELLEVILLE
9e
Gare du Nord
Gare de l'Est
10e
MÉNILMONTANT
2e
20e
Porte de Bagnolet
1e
Les Halles
3e
MARAIS
Louvre
Centre Pompidou
CIMETIÈRE DU PÈRE-LACHAISE
11e
Ste-Chapelle
ILE DE LA CITÉ
Hôtel de Ville
BASTILLE
Porte de Montreuil
ILE ST-LOUIS
place de la Bastille
Opéra Bastille
Notre-Dame
4e
NATION
LATIN QUARTER
Sorbonne
Panthéon
Porte de Vincennes
5e
JARDIN DES PLANTES
Gare d'Austerlitz
Gare de Lyon
12e
Porte de St-Mandé
BERCY
Bibliothèque National de France
Seine
Porte Dorée
Zoo de Vincennes (closed until 2014)
13e
Porte de Charenton
BOIS DE VINCENNES
Porte de Bercy
CHARENTON
PARC DE MONTSOURIS
IVRY-SUR-SEINE
Cité Universitaire
Porte d'Ivry
Porte de Gentilly
Porte d'Italie
To Orly
GENTILLY
0 1 mi
0 1 km

Heading north, you'll come to the picturesque **Parc Monceau** and the area known as **Batignolles.** This sophisticated neighborhood became fashionable during the 19th century and is full of elegant Haussmannian-style buildings and wide avenues. Today it's a wealthy, residential area. Nearby is **rue des Dames,** where there are a number of hip bars and restaurants.

There's a similar atmosphere in the 16th arrondissement, which is full of embassies, diplomats, and exclusive residences. Although there are several interesting museums, including **Musée Guimet, Paris's Musée d'Art Moderne,** and the hip **Palais du Tokyo,** this bourgeois district can feel quite far from the action.

OPÉRA & CANAL ST-MARTIN (9E & 10E) Sandwiched between the 2nd and 18th arrondissements, the 9th is a good base for exploring Paris's Right Bank. The area around the **Opéra Garnier** is one of the busiest, most commercial areas of Paris. It's a great place for shopping, and it's where you'll find the famous 19th-century department stores **Galeries Lafayette** and **Printemps.** Heading east from Opéra, you come to the area known as **Grands Boulevards,** which stretches from boulevard Montmartre to boulevard de Bonne Nouvelle. This was the epicenter of cafe and theater life during the 18th and 19th centuries, and although there is still lively nightlife here, the grandeur of Grands Boulevards has faded and the area can seem rather shabby and unauthentic.

The 10th arrondissement is one of Paris's most multiethnic neighborhoods, and the streets around **rue du Faubourg Saint-Denis** are home to large numbers of Indians, Pakistanis, Bangladeshis, West Indians, Africans, and Turks. It's a vibrant, thriving area, and **Passage Brady** is one of the best places in Paris to eat Indian and Pakistani food. However, the streets around Strasbourg St-Denis, Gare du Nord, and Gare de l'Est are not the safest parts of the city and should be avoided late at night. The main attraction of the 10th is the increasingly popular Canal Saint Martin. With its picturesque footbridges and cobbled, tree-lined *quais,* this is the ideal place for a summer picnic or Sunday stroll. There's a very *bobo* (short for *bourgeois bohemian*) atmosphere around here, thanks to the stylish boutiques and trendy bars and cafes.

PIGALLE & MONTMARTRE (18E) Located on a hill, Montmartre's winding, narrow streets are a far cry from the wide avenues and boulevards of central Paris. Despite its distance from the center, **Montmartre**—or *la butte* (the hill), as it is affectionately referred to by locals—is one of the city's most popular neighborhoods for visitors and residents alike. At the end of the 19th century, Montmartre was full of avant-garde writers and artists, including Picasso, van Gogh, and Toulouse-Lautrec, who were attracted by the cheap rents and cheap booze. Despite the busloads of tourists who climb the hill to visit **Sacré Coeur,** this area has retained its bohemian atmosphere, and if you avoid the tourist traps—such as place du Tertre—you'll find plenty of charm and romance. There's a great selection of bars and restaurants around **rue des Abbesses** and **rue Lepic,** and one of the advantages of being a little farther away from the center is that the prices are lower.

Around **Pigalle** there are a number of good bars and well-known music venues. However, between place Pigalle and place Blanche, you'll discover the seedier side of this neighborhood, with flashing neon signs advertising sex shops and adult-only cinemas. To the east of the 18th, around rue de la Goutte d'Or and Barbès Rochechouart, there is a large North African community. There's a lively atmosphere here, but it's quite hectic, particularly on Saturdays, when there is a popular fruit and vegetable market. If you do get off the Métro here, be wary of pickpockets. Located on the northernmost edge of the 18th is the city's most famous flea market, the **Marché aux Puces de Clignancourt.**

RÉPUBLIQUE, BASTILLE & EASTERN PARIS (11E & 12E) Until a few decades ago, the 11th and 12th arrondissements were home to Paris's working-class population. Despite the fact that this neighborhood has become gentrified, both place de la Bastille and place de la République remain symbolic places for the French Left and are often the scenes of large public demonstrations.

Politics aside, **République** and **Bastille** are well connected in terms of public transport and are popular places to go out at night. Although many of the bars around place de la Bastille are overpriced and over-rated, the area between Goncourt, Menilmontant, Parmentier and Oberkampf is young and hip, and boasts some of the best nightlife in the city. As you head farther south, the 11th becomes increasingly quiet and residential.

Place de la Bastille is dominated by the modern **Opéra Bastille,** which was met with mixed reactions when it opened in 1989. To the east is **rue du Faubourg St-Antoine,** which has been the center of the furnituremakers district for centuries. It's now a pleasant shopping street, but if you go up some of the side streets, you can still find some artisans at work. In the southern part of the 12th is **Bercy Village.** Up until the 1980s, wine was unloaded from boats and stored in warehouses here, but the warehouses were recently renovated and are now home to shops and bars.

BELLEVILLE & NORTHEAST PARIS (19E & 20E) Traditionally a working-class district, **Belleville** is home to large numbers of immigrants. North African Muslims and Jews, many of Tunisian origin, live alongside Chinese and Vietnamese immigrants, and Belleville is Paris's second Chinatown. Sadly, Paris property prices mean that this area, like many others before it, is slowly being gentrified. There's a lively atmosphere in Belleville, and if you climb rue de Belleville, the park at the top of the hill offers spectacular views of Paris.

The 19th is not the most attractive of Paris's arrondissements, but there are some places that are worth visiting. At the top of Canal St-Martin is **Bassin de la Villette,** where two MK2 cinemas (MK2 is one of Paris's biggest movie theater chains) face each other across the canal. There's a pleasant atmosphere here during the summer, when people gather outside the local bars, picnicking or playing *pétanque.* If you continue along the Canal de l'Ourcq, you'll reach **Parc de la Villette,** which hosts an outdoor cinema festival in the summer and a jazz festival in September. A little farther south is one of Paris's loveliest green spaces, the **Parc des Buttes Chaumont.** If you continue south, the 19th becomes the 20th, a sprawling, predominantly residential district, some parts of which are not easily accessible on the Métro. There are a couple of good bars and music venues dotted around the 20th, but its main attraction is definitely **Père Lachaise Cemetery,** where the likes of Jim Morrison, Edith Piaf, and Chopin are buried.

THE LEFT BANK

LATIN QUARTER (5E) From a historical perspective, the Latin Quarter is not to be missed. From the Roman settlement of Lutetia to the heady days of May '68, layers of Parisian history are visible in the 5th arrondissement. Home to the **Sorbonne**—the administrative center of the University of Paris—the Latin Quarter has been associated with education and learning since the Middle Ages. Parts of it, particularly around rue Mouffetard and place de la Contrescarpe, are filled with students, and there are a lot of arthouse cinemas here that give the neighborhood an offbeat, indie vibe. As you head farther south, you can see the quieter, more residential side of the 5th.

Its popularity with the expat community in the 1920s—Ernest Hemingway, Henry Miller, and James Joyce, among others—gave the Latin Quarter a Romantic, literary edge. To relive this era, head to the charming English-language bookshop **Shakespeare & Company** (p. 172), on rue de la Bûcherie. Sadly, however, very little of this Latin Quarter remains, and many visitors are disappointed by how tacky and commercial parts of the 5th have become. The area around place St-Michel and rue de la Huchette, although very central, is one of most touristy parts of the city. If you're looking for an authentic Parisian experience, avoid eating or drinking in any of the bars and restaurants around here.

ST-GERMAIN-DES-PRÉS & LUXEMBOURG (6E) Now one of the city's most exclusive neighborhoods, St-Germain oozes *Rive Gauche* glamour. For most of the 20th century, the area around the Eglise-St-Germain-des-Prés was the intellectual heartland of Paris, and everywhere you turn, you'll encounter historic and literary associations. Here you'll find three of Paris's most famous cafes, all within a few meters of one another. Known as **The Golden Triangle,** the **Brasserie Lipp, Les Deux Magots,** and **Cafe de Flore** were frequented by the likes of Hemingway and Picasso in the 1920s, and Jean-Paul Sartre and Simone de Beauvoir in the 1950s. Nowadays, you'll find more *haute couture* (Christian Dior, Louis Vuitton, and more) than highbrow culture.

There's a lively atmosphere in the narrow streets around St-Germain and **Odéon,** which boasts some great bars and restaurants. It gets much quieter toward the charming **Jardin du Luxembourg,** a 24-hectare (59-acre) park, the design of which is based in the Boboli Gardens in Florence. Full of 19th-century park furniture and allegorical statues, it's one of Paris's loveliest parks.

EIFFEL TOWER & NEARBY (7E) Despite the fact that many people hated it when it was showcased at the 1889 Great Exhibition, the **Eiffel Tower** has become Paris's most famous symbol. The panoramic views from the top, and the sheer magnificence of the structure itself, attract thousands of visitors everyday. But where there are tourists, there are pickpockets, and you should be very vigilant when strolling around beneath the tower. Similarly, the Champ de Mars attracts some dodgy characters, and it's not the safest place to hang out after dark.

The 7th arrondissement is a calm, elegant neighborhood. In the center, you'll find **Hôtel des Invalides,** where Napoleon's body was interred; the **Assemblée Nationale** (National Assembly); and a number of key government ministries. Although there are a lot of civil servants running around—or being chauffeured around—during the week, there's very little life at the weekends. There's a bit more of a buzz on either side of Invalides. The area around **rue St-Dominique** and **rue de Grenelle** is quite lively, and **rue Cler** is a popular, well-heeled market street full of gourmet food shops and classy cafes. On the other side of the 7th, you'll find the elegant shopping street **rue du Bac** and, on the rue des Sèvres, the beautiful, 19th-century department store **Le Bon Marché.**

MONTPARNASSE & SOUTHERN PARIS (13E, 14E & 15E) Montparnasse is a busy, commercial neighborhood dominated by the rather ugly **Montparnasse Tower,** which was built in the 1970s. It's still reasonably close to central Paris and is very well connected in terms of public transport. Along boulevard Montparnasse, you'll find several famous Art Deco brasseries—La Coupole, Le Select, and Le Dôme—which were patronized by the all the movers and shakers of the interwar period, including Hemingway, Picasso, Lenin, and Trotsky.

As you head south, the 14th becomes increasingly residential and there's very little to see or do down here. The same is true for the 15th arrondissement, with the exception of the lively shopping district around **Métro La Motte Picquet Grenelle** and **rue du Commerce.** However, as you head east, you'll see quite a different side of Paris in the 13th arrondissement. As residential as the 14th and 15th, it's one of the few districts in the city where there are modern, high-rise tower blocks. Home to Paris's principal **Chinatown,** the area around place d'Italie, Tolbiac, and Olympiades is a great place to come for authentic Chinese and Vietnamese food.

EXPLORING PARIS

The city of Paris has a long history: There has been civilization here for more than 2 millennia, ever since Julius Caesar's troops invaded the city in 52 B.C., snatching power from the Gaulish tribe the *Parisii.* Two thousand years of art, architecture, war, religion, and politics—not to mention power, passion, and intrigue—have left its mark on the city. Paris counts hundreds of museums and

The New Les Halles

For 8 centuries, **Les Halles** was the city's primary wholesale fruit, meat, and vegetable market. In the 19th century, Zola famously called it "the belly of Paris." The smock-clad vendors, beef carcasses, and baskets of vegetables all belong to the past, for the original market was torn down in the early '70s and relocated to a massive steel-and-glass edifice at Rungis, a suburb near Orly. Today Les Halles includes the city's chief transportation hub and a major shopping complex, the **Forum des Halles** (1–7 rue Pierre-Lescot, 1er). This large mall, much of it underground, contains shops, restaurants, and movie theaters. In 2010, the City of Paris embarked on a massive 810-million-euro renovation program, which will overhaul the underground shopping and transportation zones, as well as the garden above. Renovations are slated to be completed in 2016, but the complex should remain open and operational during the renovations. For more information, visit www.parisleshalles.fr.

monuments. It's a city that can transport you back centuries, where you can lose yourself in the labyrinth of Royal power and opulence or get captivated by the violence of the French Revolution. Or, the city can bring you up-to-date, with the most avant-garde art, design, and architecture that the world has to offer today. But the special thing about Paris is that just walking the streets feels like visiting the world's most magical museum.

Area by area, the following pages will highlight the best that Paris can offer, from iconic sights known the world over to quirky museums and hidden gardens, from 1,000-year-old castles to galleries celebrating the most challenging contemporary art.

The Right Bank

LES HALLES, LOUVRE & PALAIS ROYAL (1E & 2E)

Crowned by the Louvre, this central area that flanks the Seine packs in a high density of important museums, centered on the magnificent former royal palace and its expansive Jardin des Tuileries. Though the Louvre is on top of most visitors' to-do lists, don't forget that there are also some wonderful smaller museums close by, and great shopping, too.

Jardin des Tuileries ★★ ☺ GARDEN The spectacular statue-studded Jardin des Tuileries, bordering place de la Concorde, is as much a part of Paris as the Seine. Le Nôtre, Louis XIV's gardener and planner of the Versailles grounds, designed the gardens. Some of the gardens' most distinctive statues are the 18 enormous bronzes by Maillol, installed within the Jardin du Carrousel, a subdivision of the Jardin des Tuileries, between 1964 and 1965, under the direction of Culture Minister André Malraux.

About 400 years before that, Catherine de Médici ordered a palace built here, the **Palais des Tuileries;** other occupants have included Louis XVI (after he left Versailles) and Napoleon. Twice attacked by Parisians, it was burned to the ground in 1871 and never rebuilt. The gardens, however, remain. In orderly

Jardin des Tuileries.

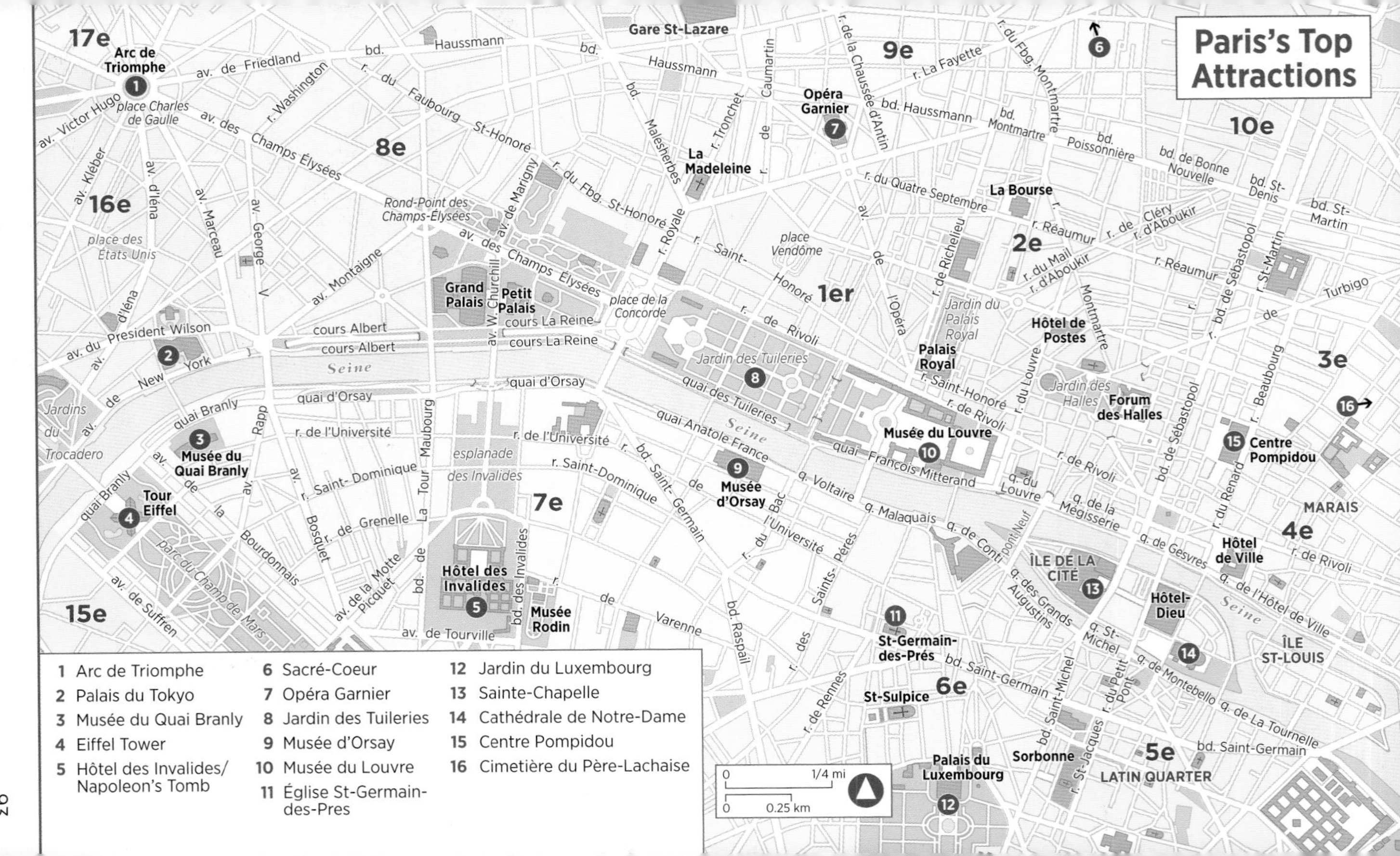
Paris's Top Attractions
1 Arc de Triomphe
2 Palais du Tokyo
3 Musée du Quai Branly
4 Eiffel Tower
5 Hôtel des Invalides/ Napoleon's Tomb
6 Sacré-Coeur
7 Opéra Garnier
8 Jardin des Tuileries
9 Musée d'Orsay
10 Musée du Louvre
11 Église St-Germain-des-Pres
12 Jardin du Luxembourg
13 Sainte-Chapelle
14 Cathédrale de Notre-Dame
15 Centre Pompidou
16 Cimetière du Père-Lachaise
0 1/4 mi
0 0.25 km

French manner, the trees are arranged according to designs, and even the paths are arrow straight. Bubbling fountains break the sense of order and formality.

Each summer, over the months of July and August, the parks hosts a traditional **funfair** (www.feteforaine-jardindestuileries.com) alongside rue de Rivoli—be sure to take a Ferris wheel ride for excellent views.

Near place de la Concorde, 1er. ✆ **01-40-20-90-43.** Free admission. Daily Apr–May 7am–9pm; June–Aug 7am–11pm; Sept 7am–9pm; Oct–Mar 7:30am–7:30pm. Métro: Tuileries or Concorde.

Jeu de Paume ★★ MUSEUM After knowing many roles, this museum, in the northeast corner of the Tuileries gardens, has become a national center for photography and video, exploring "the world of images, their uses, and the issues they raise" from the 19th to the 21st centuries. It is one of the finest museums of its type in the world and presents ever-changing exhibitions, many of them daringly avant garde.

Originally, in this part of the gardens, Napoleon III built a ball court on which *jeu de paume,* an antecedent of tennis, was played—hence the museum's name. The most infamous period in the gallery's history came during the Nazi occupation, when it served as an "evaluation center" for works of modern art. Paintings from all over France were shipped to the Jeu de Paume; art condemned by the Nazis as "degenerate" was burned.

1 place de la Concorde, 8e. ✆ **01-47-03-12-50.** www.jeudepaume.org. Admission 8.50€ adults, 5.50€ students and children. Tues noon–9pm; Wed–Fri noon–7pm; Sat–Sun 10am–7pm. Métro: Concorde.

Musée de l'Orangerie ★★ MUSEUM In the Tuileries stands another gem among museums. It has an outstanding collection of art and one celebrated work on display: Claude Monet's exquisite *Nymphéas* (1915–27). The two galleries were purpose built by the French State to house eight massive murals by Monet, in which water lilies float amorphously on the canvas. The paintings are displayed as the artist intended them to be—lit by sunlight in large oval galleries that evoke the shape of the garden ponds at his former Giverny estate.

Monet's *Nympheas* at Musèe de l'Orangerie.

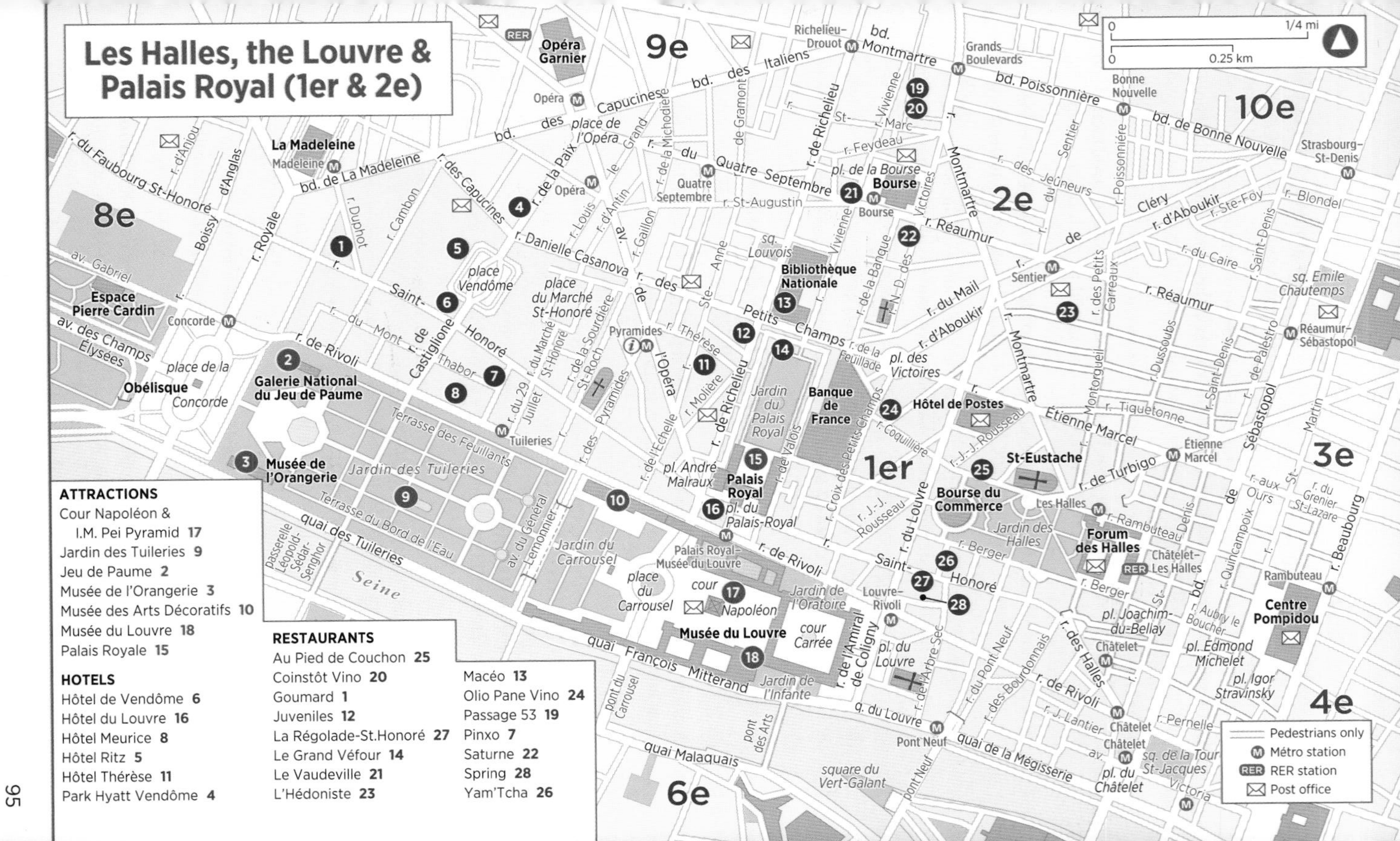
Les Halles, the Louvre & Palais Royal (1er & 2e)
0 1/4 mi
0 0.25 km
Pedestrians only
Métro station
RER station
Post office
ATTRACTIONS
Cour Napoléon & I.M. Pei Pyramid 17
Jardin des Tuileries 9
Jeu de Paume 2
Musée de l'Orangerie 3
Musée des Arts Décoratifs 10
Musée du Louvre 18
Palais Royale 15
HOTELS
Hôtel de Vendôme 6
Hôtel du Louvre 16
Hôtel Meurice 8
Hôtel Ritz 5
Hôtel Thérèse 11
Park Hyatt Vendôme 4
RESTAURANTS
Au Pied de Couchon 25
Coinstôt Vino 20
Goumard 1
Juveniles 12
La Régolade-St.Honoré 27
Le Grand Véfour 14
Le Vaudeville 21
L'Hédoniste 23
Macéo 13
Olio Pane Vino 24
Passage 53 19
Pinxo 7
Saturne 22
Spring 28
Yam'Tcha 26

Creating his effects with hundreds and hundreds of minute strokes of his brush (one irate 19th-c. critic called them "tongue lickings"), Monet achieved unity and harmony, as he did in his Rouen Cathedral series and his haystacks. Artists with lesser talent might have stirred up "soup." But Monet, of course, was a genius. See his lilies and evoke for yourself the mood and melancholy as he experienced them so many years ago. Monet continued to paint his water landscapes right up until his death in 1926, although he was greatly hampered by failing eyesight.

The renovated building also houses the art collections of two men, John Walter and Paul Guillaume, who are not connected to each other, except that they were both married at different times to the same woman. Their collection includes more than 24 Renoirs, including *Young Girl at a Piano*. Cézanne is represented by 14 works, notably *The Red Rock,* and Matisse by 11 paintings. The highlight of Rousseau's nine works displayed here is *The Wedding,* and the dozen paintings by Picasso reach the pinnacle of their brilliance in *The Female Bathers*. Other outstanding paintings are by Utrillo (10 works in all), Soutine (22), and Derain (28).

It is possible to buy a joint ticket to both Musée d'Orsay (p. 131) and Musée de l'Orangerie, which is valid for 4 days and costs 13€.

Jardin des Tuileries, 1er. ✆ **01-44-77-80-07.** www.musee-orangerie.fr. Admission 7.50€ adults, 5€ students 25 and younger. Free 1st Sun of every month. Wed–Mon 9am–6pm. Métro: Concorde.

Musée des Arts Décoratifs ★★ MUSEUM In the northwest wing of the Louvre's Pavillon de Marsan, this imposing museum is home to a treasury of furnishings, fabrics, wallpaper, objets d'art, and items displaying living styles from the Middle Ages to the present. Notable are the 1920s Art Deco boudoir, bath, and bedroom done for couturier Jeanne Lanvin by the designer Rateau, plus a collection of the works donated by Jean Dubuffet. Decorative art from the Middle Ages to the Renaissance is on the second floor; collections from the 17th, 18th, and 19th centuries occupy the third and fourth floors. The fifth floor has specialized centers, such as wallpaper and drawings, and exhibits detailing fashion, textiles, toys, crafts, and glass trends. The space also includes a lovely ground-floor shop, **107Rivoli** (p. 170), selling all sorts of craft pieces; and a restaurant, Le Saut du Loup, which boasts an outdoor eating area in the Tuileries Gardens.

Palais du Louvre, 107 rue de Rivoli, 1er. ✆ **01-44-55-57-50.** www.lesartsdecoratifs.fr. Admission 9€ adults, 7.50€ ages 18–25, free for children 17 and younger. Tues, Wed, and Fri 11am–6pm; Thurs 11am–6pm; Sat–Sun 10am–6pm. Métro: Palais-Royal or Tuileries.

Musée du Louvre ★★★ MUSEUM The Louvre is the world's largest palace and museum, and it houses one of the greatest art collections ever. To enter, pass through I. M. Pei's controversial 21m (69-ft.) **glass pyramid ★**—a startling though effective contrast of the ultramodern against the palace's classical lines. Commissioned by the late president François Mitterrand and completed in 1989, it allows sunlight to shine on an underground reception area with a complex of shops and restaurants.

People on one of those "Paris-in-a-day" tours try to break track records to get a glimpse of the Louvre's two most famous ladies: the beguiling ***Mona Lisa*** and the armless ***Venus de Milo*** **★★★**. The herd then dashes on a 5-minute stampede in pursuit of ***Winged Victory*** **★★★**, the headless statue discovered at Samothrace and dating from about 200 B.C. In defiance of the assembly-line

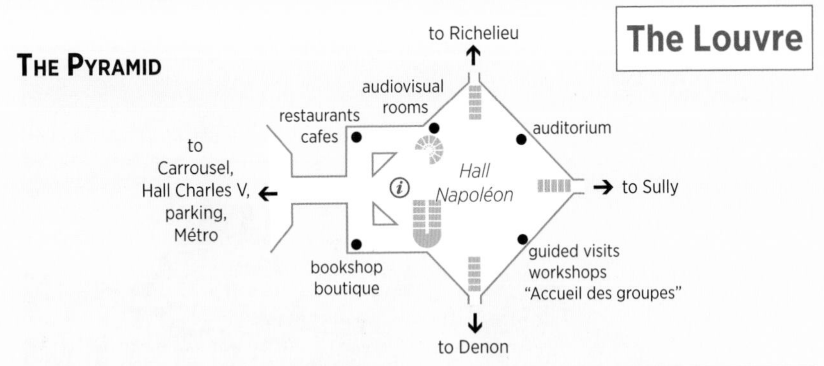

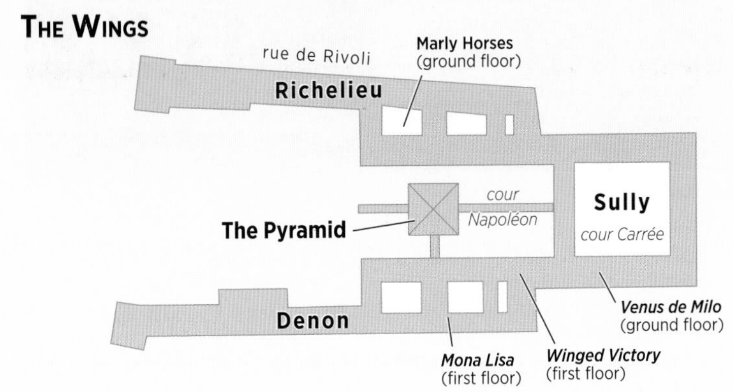

theory of art, we head instead for David's ***Coronation of Napoleon,*** showing Napoleon poised with the crown aloft as Joséphine kneels before him, just across from his ***Portrait of Madame Récamier*** ★, depicting Napoleon's opponent at age 23; she reclines on her sofa agelessly in the style of classical antiquity.

Then a big question looms: Which of the rest of the 30,000 works on display would you like to see? Between the Seine and rue de Rivoli, the Palais du Louvre suffers from an embarrassment of riches, stretching for almost a kilometer (half a mile). In the days of Charles V, it was a fortress, but François I, a patron of Leonardo da Vinci, had it torn down and rebuilt as a royal residence. Less than a month after Marie Antoinette's head and body parted company, the Revolutionary Committee decided the king's collection of paintings and sculpture should be opened to the public. At the lowest point in its history, in the 18th century, the Louvre was home for anybody who wanted to set up housekeeping. Laundry hung in the windows, corners were pigpens, and families built fires to cook their meals in winter. Napoleon ended all that, chasing out the squatters and restoring the palace. In fact, he chose the Louvre as the site of his wedding to Marie-Louise.

So where did all these paintings come from? The kings of France, notably François I and Louis XIV, acquired many of them, and others were willed to or purchased by the state. Many contributed by Napoleon were taken from reluctant donors: The church was one especially heavy and unwilling giver. Much of

Musée du Louvre.

Napoleon's plunder had to be returned, though France hasn't yet seen its way clear to giving back all the booty.

The collections are divided into seven departments: Egyptian Antiquities; Oriental Antiquities; Greek, Etruscan, and Roman Antiquities; Sculpture; Painting; Decorative Arts; and Graphic Arts. If you don't have to do Paris in a day, you might want to visit several times, concentrating on different collections or schools of painting. Those with little time should take a guided tour.

Acquired by François I to hang above his bathtub, Leonardo's ***La Gioconda (Mona Lisa)*** ★★★ has been the source of legend for centuries. Note the guard and bulletproof glass: The world's most famous painting was stolen in 1911 and then found in Florence in 1913. At first, both the poet Guillaume Apollinaire and Picasso were suspected, but it was discovered in the possession of a former Louvre employee, who'd apparently carried it out under his overcoat. Two centuries after its arrival at the Louvre, the *Mona Lisa* in 2003 was assigned a new gallery of her own. Less well known (but, to us, even more enchanting) are Leonardo's ***Virgin and Child with St. Anne*** ★ and the ***Virgin of the Rocks.***

After paying your respects to the "smiling one," allow time to see some French works stretching from the Richelieu wing through the entire **Sully wing** and even overflowing into the **Denon wing.** It's all here: Watteau's ***Gilles*** with the mysterious boy in a clown suit

Leaping over the Louvre Line

If you don't want to wait in line for tickets to the Louvre, you can order tickets in advance by calling ✆ **08-92-68-46-94** or visiting **http://louvre.fnacspectacles.com**; tickets can be mailed to you, or you can pick them up at any Paris branch of the FNAC electronics chain. You can also order advance tickets and take a virtual tour at **www.louvre.fr**. Note that the Louvre is open until 10pm on Wednesdays and Fridays—usually a quiet time to visit.

Contemporary Art & the Louvre

With all those centuries-old masterpieces grabbing the spotlight, the museum's contemporary works can get overlooked—but they're worth seeking out. In 2010, the museum unveiled a painted ceiling in the Salle des Bronzes by American artist Cy Twombly, the third contemporary artist who was commissioned to install a permanent work at the Louvre. (He was preceded by contemporary artists Anselm Kiefer and François Morellet.) Twombly's painting appears on the ceiling of one of the Louvre's largest galleries, and it covers more than 350 sq. m (3,767 sq. ft.). The ceiling depicts an immense blue sky that is dotted with spheres and white insets inscribed with the names of famous Greek sculptors.

staring at you; Fragonard's and Boucher's rococo renderings of the aristocracy; and the greatest masterpieces of David, including his stellar 1785 ***The Oath of the Horatii*** and the vast and vivid ***Coronation of Napoleon.*** Only Florence's Uffizi rivals the Denon wing for its Italian Renaissance collection—everything from Raphael's ***Portrait of Balthazar Castiglione*** to Titian's ***Man with a Glove.*** Veronese's gigantic ***Wedding Feast at Cana*** ★, a romp of Venetian high society in the 1500s, occupies an entire wall (that's Paolo himself playing the cello).

Of the Greek and Roman antiquities, the most notable collections, aside from the *Venus de Milo* and *Winged Victory,* are fragments of a **Parthenon frieze** (in the Denon wing). In Renaissance sculpture, you'll see Michelangelo's ***Esclaves (Slaves),*** originally intended for the tomb of Julius II but sold into other bondage. The Denon wing houses masterpieces such as Ingres's ***The Turkish Bath,*** the **Botticelli frescoes** from the Villa Lemmi, Raphael's ***La Belle Jardinière,*** and Titian's ***Open Air Concert.*** The Sully wing is also filled with old masters, such as Boucher's ***Diana Resting After Her Bath*** and Fragonard's ***Bathers.***

The **Richelieu wing** ★★★ houses northern European and French paintings, along with decorative arts, sculpture, Oriental antiquities (including a rich collection of both Islamic and Far Eastern Art), and the Napoleon III salons. One of its galleries displays 21 works that Rubens painted in a space of only 2 years for Marie de Médici's Palais de Luxembourg. The masterpieces here include Dürer's ***Self-Portrait,*** van Dyck's ***Portrait of Charles I of England,*** and Holbein the Younger's ***Portrait of Erasmus of Rotterdam.***

When you tire of strolling the galleries, you may like a pick-me-up at the Richelieu Wing's **Cafe Richelieu** (✆**01-47-03-99-68**) or, under the arcades and overlooking Pei's pyramid, at **Cafe Marly,** 93 rue de Rivoli, 1er (✆**01-49-26-06-60**). Boasting Napoleon III opulence, the Marly is a perfect oasis. Try a cafe crème, a club sandwich, a pastry, or something from the bistro menu.

34–36 quai du Louvre, 1er. Main entrance in the glass pyramid, Cour Napoléon. ✆ **01-40-20-53-17,** 01-40-20-50-50 for operator, or 08-92-68-46-94 for advance credit card sales. www.louvre.fr. Admission 10€, children 17 and younger free, free to all 1st Sun of every month. Sat–Mon and Thurs 9am–6pm; Wed and Fri 9am–10pm. 1½-hr. English-language tours (Mon and Wed–Sun) 9€, 6€ children 12 and younger with museum ticket. Métro: Palais-Royal–Musée du Louvre.

Palais Royal ★★ HISTORIC BUILDING The Palais Royal was originally known as the Palais Cardinal, for it was the residence of Cardinal Richelieu,

Louis XIII's prime minister. Richelieu had it built, and after his death it was inherited by the king, who died soon after. Louis XIV spent part of his childhood here with his mother, Anne of Austria, but later resided at the Louvre and Versailles. The palace was later owned by the duc de Chartres et Orléans (see Parc Monceau, p. 113), who encouraged the opening of cafes, gambling dens, and other public entertainment. Today the building is occupied by the French Culture Ministry.

The lovely **Jardin du Palais Royal** is at the center of the arcaded former palace and features a fountain and gardens. Don't miss the main courtyard, close to rue St-Honoré, with the controversial 1986 Buren sculpture—280 prison-striped columns, oddly placed. The arcades of the Palais Royal have become a high fashion destination over the last few years, with high-end boutiques like Marc Jacobs and Stella McCartney.

Rue St-Honoré, 1er. No phone. Free admission. Gardens daily 7:30am–dusk. Métro: Palais Royal–Musée du Louvre.

LE MARAIS, ILE ST-LOUIS & ILE DE LA CITÉ (3E & 4E)

This historic neighborhood, home to royalty and aristocracy in the 17th and 18th centuries, preserves exceptional architecture—some of it dating back to the Renaissance. Its narrow, winding streets are from another age. While it features some blockbuster attractions, including the **Hôtel de Ville** and the **Centre Pompidou,** the Marais is notable for its density of charming smaller museums, where you hopefully won't be fighting through crowds. The two islands in the Seine, Ile St-Louis and Ile de la Cité, set the stage for some impressive medieval monuments, the **Cathédrale de Notre-Dame,** the **Conciergerie,** and the glorious **Sainte-Chapelle.**

Cathédrale de Notre-Dame ★★ CHURCH Notre-Dame is the heart of Paris and even of the country itself: Distances from the city to all parts of France are calculated from a spot at the far end of place du Parvis, in front of the cathedral, where a circular bronze plaque marks **Kilomètre Zéro.**

The cathedral's setting on the banks of the Seine has always been memorable. Founded in the 12th century by Maurice de Sully, bishop of Paris, Notre-Dame has grown over the years, changing as Paris has changed and often falling victim to whims of taste. Its flying buttresses (the external side supports, giving the massive interior a sense of weightlessness) were rebuilt in 1330. Though many disagree, we feel Notre-Dame is more interesting outside than in, and you'll want to walk all around it to fully appreciate this "vast symphony of stone." Better yet, cross over the Pont au Double to the Left Bank and view it from the quai.

The histories of Paris and Notre-Dame are inseparable. Many prayed here before going off to fight in the Crusades. The revolutionaries who destroyed the Galerie des Rois and converted the building into a secular temple didn't spare "Our Lady of Paris." Later Napoleon crowned himself emperor here, yanking the crown out of Pius VII's hands and placing it on his own head before crowning his Josephine empress (see David's *Coronation of Napoléon* in the Louvre). But carelessness, vandalism, embellishments, and wars of religion had already demolished much of the previously existing structure.

The cathedral was once scheduled for demolition, but because of the popularity of Victor Hugo's *Hunchback of Notre-Dame* and the revival of interest in the Gothic period, a movement mushroomed to restore the cathedral to its original

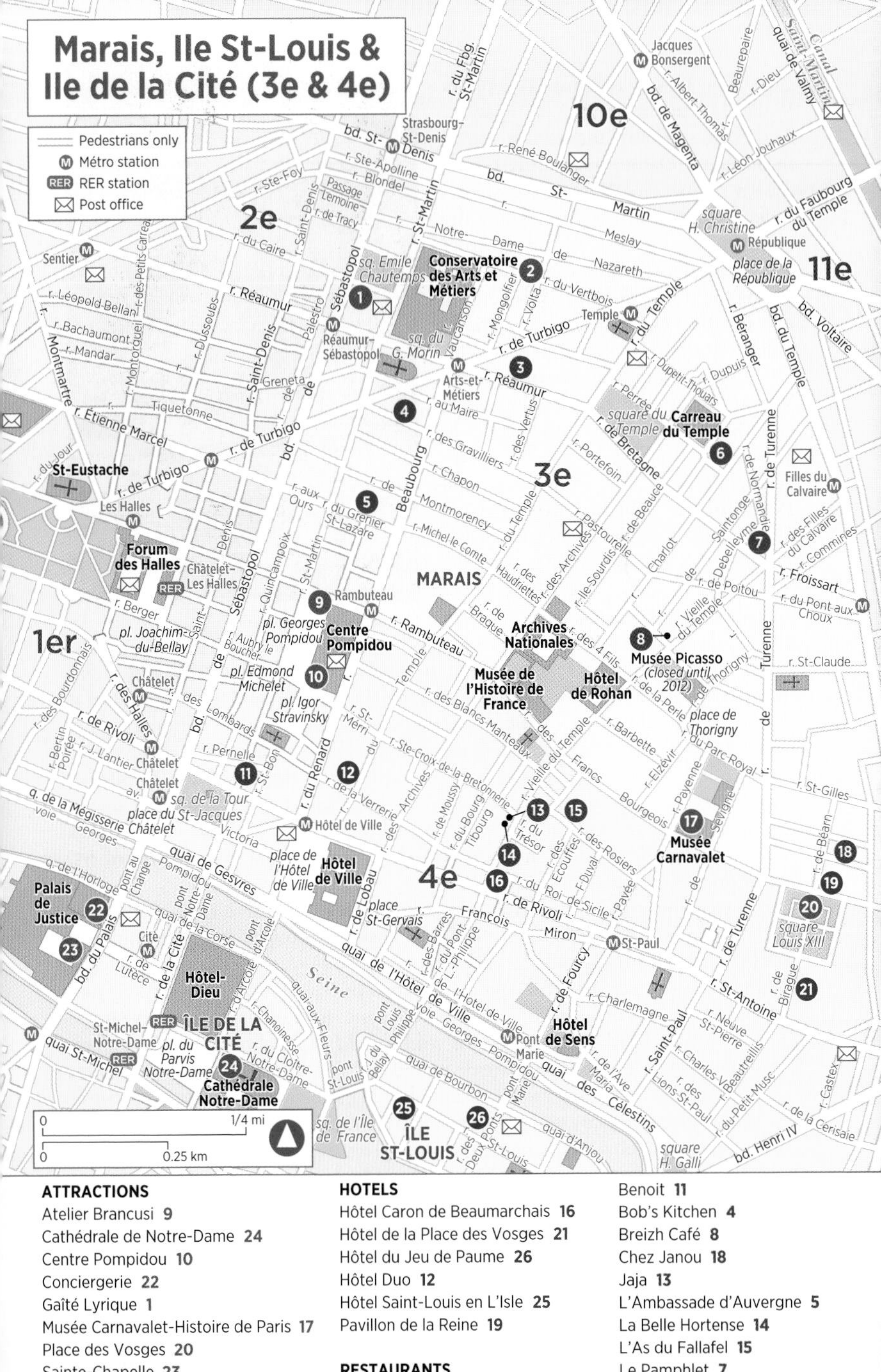

ATTRACTIONS
Atelier Brancusi **9**
Cathédrale de Notre-Dame **24**
Centre Pompidou **10**
Conciergerie **22**
Gaîté Lyrique **1**
Musée Carnavalet-Histoire de Paris **17**
Place des Vosges **20**
Sainte-Chapelle **23**

HOTELS
Hôtel Caron de Beaumarchais **16**
Hôtel de la Place des Vosges **21**
Hôtel du Jeu de Paume **26**
Hôtel Duo **12**
Hôtel Saint-Louis en L'Isle **25**
Pavillon de la Reine **19**

RESTAURANTS
Au Bascou **3**
Benoit **11**
Bob's Kitchen **4**
Breizh Café **8**
Chez Janou **18**
Jaja **13**
L'Ambassade d'Auvergne **5**
La Belle Hortense **14**
L'As du Fallafel **15**
Le Pamphlet **7**
Tartes Kluger **6**

glory. The task was completed under Viollet-le-Duc, an architectural genius. The houses of old Paris used to crowd in on Notre-Dame, but during his redesign of the city, Baron Haussmann ordered them torn down to show the cathedral to its best advantage from the parvis. This is the best vantage for seeing the three sculpted 13th-century portals (the Virgin, the Last Judgment, and St. Anne).

Cathédrale de Notre-Dame.

On the left, the **Portal of the Virgin** depicts the signs of the zodiac and the coronation of the Virgin, an association found in dozens of medieval churches. The restored central **Portal of the Last Judgment** depicts three levels: The first shows Vices and Virtues; the second, Christ and his Apostles; and, above that, Christ in triumph after the Resurrection. The portal is a close illustration of the Gospel according to Matthew. Over it is the remarkable **west rose window ★★**, 9.5m (31 ft.) wide, forming a showcase for a statue of the Virgin and Child. On the far right is the **Portal of St. Anne,** depicting scenes such as the Virgin enthroned with Child; it's Notre-Dame's best-preserved and most perfect piece of sculpture. Equally interesting (though often missed) is the **Portal of the Cloisters** (around on the left), with its dour-faced 13th-century Virgin, a survivor among the figures that originally adorned the facade. (Alas, the Child she's holding has been decapitated.) Finally, on the Seine side of Notre-Dame, the **Portal of St. Stephen** traces that saint's martyrdom.

If possible, see Notre-Dame at sunset. Inside of the three giant medallions warming the austere cathedral, the **north rose window ★★** in the transept, from the mid–13th century, is best. The main body of the church is typically Gothic, with slender, graceful columns. In the **choir,** a stone-carved screen from the early 14th century depicts such biblical scenes as the Last Supper. Near the altar stands the 14th-century ***Virgin and Child* ★**, highly venerated among Paris's faithful. In the **treasury** are displayed vestments and gold objects, including crowns. Exhibited is a cross presented to Haile Selassie, former emperor of Ethiopia, and a reliquary given by Napoleon. Notre-Dame is especially proud of its relics of the True Cross and the Crown of Thorns.

To visit the **gargoyles ★★** immortalized by Hugo, you have to scale steps leading to the twin **towers,** rising to a height of 68m (223 ft.). When there, you can inspect devils (some giving you the raspberry), hobgoblins, and birds of prey. Look carefully, and you may see hunchback Quasimodo with Esmeralda.

Approached through a garden behind Notre-Dame is the **Mémorial des Martyrs Français de la Déportation de 1945 (Deportation Memorial),** out on the tip of Ile de la Cité. Here birds chirp and the Seine flows gently by, but the memories are far from pleasant. The memorial commemorates the French citizens who were deported to concentration camps during World War

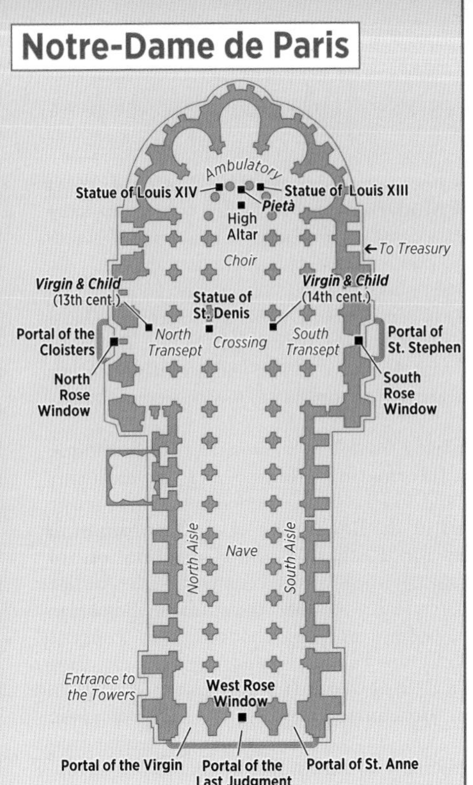

II. Carved into stone are these blood-red words (in French): "Forgive, but don't forget." The memorial is open Monday to Friday 8:30am to 9:45pm, and Saturday to Sunday 9am to 9:45pm. Admission is free.

6 place du Parvis Notre-Dame, 4e. ✆ **01-53-10-07-02.** www.notredamedeparis.fr. Admission free to cathedral. Towers 8€ adults, 5€ seniors and ages 13–25, free for children 12 and younger. Treasury 3€ adults, 2.20€ seniors, 1.60€ ages 13–25, free for children 12 and younger. Cathedral year-round daily 8am–6:45pm (Sat–Sun 7:15pm). Towers and crypt daily 10am–6pm (until 11pm Sat–Sun until June–Aug). Museum Wed and Sat–Sun 2–5pm. Treasury Mon–Fri 9:30am–6pm; Sat 9:30am–6:30pm; Sun 1:30–6:30pm. Métro: Cité or St-Michel. RER: St-Michel.

Centre Pompidou ★★★ MUSEUM When it first opened in the 1970s, Centre Pompidou was hailed as "the most avant-garde building in the world," and today it still continues to pack in the art-loving crowds—about six million people visit it each year.

Conceived by former French president Georges Pompidou and designed by architects Renzo Piano and Richard Rogers, this building originally opened in 1977, and it underwent a major renovation in 2000, which expanded and improved the space. The building's exterior is very bold: brightly painted pipes and

Pont Neuf

Don't miss the ironically named Pont Neuf (New Bridge) at the tip of the Ile de la Cité island, opposite Notre-Dame. The span isn't new—it's Paris's oldest bridge, begun in 1578 and finished in 1604. In its day, it had two unique features: It was paved, and it wasn't flanked with houses and shops. Actually, with 12 arches, it's not one bridge but two (they don't quite line up)—one from the Right Bank to the island and the other from the Left Bank to the island. At Musée Carnavalet (p. 106), a painting called *The Spectacle of Buffoons* shows what the bridge was like between 1665 and 1669. Duels were fought on it, the nobility's great coaches crossed it, peddlers sold their wares, and entertainers such as Tabarin went there to seek a few coins from the gawkers. As public facilities were lacking, the bridge also served as a de facto outhouse.

ducts crisscross its transparent facade (green for water, red for heat, blue for air, and yellow for electricity), and an outdoor escalator flanks the building, freeing up interior space for exhibitions.

Inside, the big attraction is the impressive **Musée National d'Art Moderne (National Museum of Modern Art) ★★**, which is home to some 40,000 works from the 20th and 21st centuries—though only about 850 works can be displayed at one time. If you want to view some real charmers, seek out Calder's 1926 ***Josephine Baker,*** one of his earlier versions of the mobile, an art form he invented. You'll also find two examples of Duchamps's series of Dada-style sculptures he invented in 1936: ***Boîte en Valise*** (1941) and ***Boîte en Valise*** (1968). And every time we visit, we have to see Dalí's ***Hallucination Partielle: Six Images de Lénine sur un Piano*** (1931), with Lenin dancing on a piano.

Other attractions inside the Centre Pompidou include the **Bibliothéque Publique d'Information (Public Information Library),** a vast public library with a huge collection of French and foreign books, periodicals, films, music records, slides, and more; the **Institut de Recherche et de Coordination Acoustique-Musique (Institute for Research and Coordination of Acoustics/Music),** which brings together musicians and composers; the **Atelier Brancusi ★**, a mini-museum that re-creates the Jazz Age studio of Romanian sculptor Brancusi; a movie theater; performance halls that often host concerts and events; shops; and restaurants. Centre Pompidou holds regularly changing public exhibitions and events, so check their website for information.

Outside there is a large, open **forecourt,** which is a free "entertainment center" often featuring mimes, fire-eaters, circus performers, and sometimes musicians. Don't miss the nearby **Stravinsky fountain,** containing mobile sculptures by Tinguely and Niki de Saint Phalle.

Place Georges-Pompidou, 4e. ✆ **01-44-78-12-33.** www.centrepompidou.fr. Admission 12€ adults, 9€ students, free for children 17 and younger. Wed–Mon 11am–10pm. Métro: Rambuteau, Hôtel de Ville, or Châtelet–Les Halles.

Conciergerie ★★ HISTORIC BUILDING London has its Bloody Tower, and Paris has its Conciergerie. Even though the Conciergerie had a long regal history before the Revolution, it was forever stained by the Reign of Terror and lives as an infamous symbol of the time when carts pulled up constantly to haul off fresh supplies of victims of Dr. Guillotin's wonderful little invention.

Much of the Conciergerie was built in the 14th century as an extension of the Capetian royal Palais de la Cité. You approach through its landmark twin towers, the **Tour d'Argent** (where the crown jewels were stored at one time) and **Tour de César,** but the **Salle des Gardes (Guard Room)** is the actual entrance. Even more interesting is the dark and foreboding Gothic **Salle des Gens d'Armes (Room of People at Arms),** utterly changed from the days when the king used it as a banquet hall. However, architecture plays a secondary role to the list of prisoners who spent their last days here. Few in its history endured tortures as severe as those imposed on Ravaillac, who assassinated Henri IV in 1610. In the Tour de César, he received pincers in the flesh and had hot lead and boiling oil poured on him like bath water before being executed. During the Revolution, the Conciergerie became a symbol of terror to the nobility and enemies of the State. A short walk away, the Revolutionary Tribunal dispensed a skewed, hurried justice—if it's any consolation, the jurists didn't believe in torturing their victims, only in decapitating them.

Conciergerie.

After being seized by a crowd of peasants who stormed Versailles, Louis XVI and Marie Antoinette were brought here to await their trials. In failing health and shocked beyond grief, *l'Autrichienne* ("the Austrian," as she was called with malice) had only a small screen (sometimes not even that) to protect her modesty from the gaze of guards stationed in her cell. By accounts of the day, she was shy and stupid, though the evidence is that, on her death, she displayed the nobility of a true queen. (What's more, the famous "Let them eat cake," which she supposedly uttered when told the peasants had no bread, is probably apocryphal—besides, at the time, cake flour was less expensive than bread flour, so even if she said this, it wasn't meant coldheartedly.) It was shortly before noon on the morning of October 16, 1793, when the executioners arrived, grabbing her and cutting her hair, as was the custom for victims marked for the guillotine.

Later the Conciergerie housed other prisoners, including Mme. Elisabeth; Mme. du Barry, mistress of Louis XV; Mme. Roland ("O Liberty! Liberty! What crimes are committed in thy name!"); and Charlotte Corday, who killed Marat while he was taking a sulfur bath. In time, the Revolution consumed its own leaders, such as Danton and Robespierre. Finally, one of Paris's most hated men, public prosecutor Fouquier-Tinville, faced the guillotine to which he'd sent so many others. Among the few interned here who lived to tell the tale was American Thomas Paine, who reminisced about his chats in English with Danton.

1 quai de l'Horloge, 4e. ✆ **01-53-40-60-80.** www.monum.fr. Admission 7€ adults, 4.50€ ages 18–25, free for children 17 and younger. Mar–Oct daily 9:30–6pm; Nov–Feb daily 9am–5pm. Métro: Cité, Châtelet, or St-Michel. RER: St-Michel.

Gaîté Lyrique ★ ☺ CULTURAL INSTITUTION This modern cultural institution, which is devoted to exploring mixed-media and digital art forms, opened in March 2011 to much fanfare. This museum hosts rotating exhibits that range from music and multimedia performances to design, fashion, and architecture, to new media—there's even an interactive room dedicated to video games. This forward-thinking institution is located within a beautifully restored and updated 19th-century Parisian theater in the heart of the city.

3 bis rue Papin, 3e. www.gaite-lyrique.net. Métro: Réaumur Sébastopol.

Musée Carnavalet-Histoire de Paris ★★ ☺ MUSEUM If you enjoy history, but history tomes bore you, spend some time here for insight into Paris's past, which comes alive in such details as the chessmen Louis XVI used to distract himself while waiting to go to the guillotine. The comprehensive and lifelike exhibits are great for kids. The building, a Renaissance palace, was built in 1544 and later acquired by Mme. de Carnavalet. François Mansart transformed it between 1655 and 1661.

The palace is best known for one of history's most famous letter writers, Mme. de Sévigné, who moved here in 1677. Fanatically devoted to her daughter (she moved in with her because she couldn't bear to be apart), she poured out nearly every detail of her life in her letters, virtually ignoring her son. A native of the Marais district, she died at her daughter's château in 1696. In 1866, the city of Paris acquired the mansion and turned it into a museum. Several salons cover the Revolution, with a bust of Marat, a portrait of Danton, and a model of the Bastille (one painting shows its demolition). Another salon tells the story of the captivity of the royal family at the Conciergerie, including the bed in which Mme. Elisabeth (the sister of Louis XVI) slept and the Dauphin's exercise book.

Exhibits continue at the **Hôtel le Peletier de St-Fargeau,** across the courtyard. On display is furniture from the Louis XIV period to the early 20th century, including a replica of Marcel Proust's cork-lined bedroom with his actual furniture, including his brass bed. This section also exhibits artifacts from the museum's archaeological collection, including some Neolithic pirogues, shallow oak boats used for fishing and transport from about 4400 to 2200 B.C.

23 rue de Sévigné, 3e. ✆ **01-44-59-58-58.** www.carnavalet.paris.fr. Free admission. Special exhibits from 5€ adults, 4.20€ students and children. Tues–Sun 10am–6pm. Métro: St-Paul or Chemin Vert.

Place des Vosges ★★ ☺ SQUARE The exquisite place des Vosges was built by Henri IV and inaugurated in 1612 to celebrate the wedding of Louis XIII to Anne of Austria. It is Paris's oldest planned square and is in the heart of the Marais, actually marking the division between the 3rd and 4th arrondissements. Lined with large buildings of red brick and blue-tiled roofs, the square was previously named place Royale under the reign of Henri IV, then place des Fédérés, place de la Fabrication-des-Armes, and place de l'Indivisibilité during the French Revolution. It was only in 1800 that it was given the name it has today, in honor of the French department, the Vosges. Adorned with Linden trees, water fountains, and an equestrian statue of Louis XIII, it makes a charming spot for a picnic *en famille*. There's free Wi-Fi here, too.

4e. Métro: St-Paul.

Sainte-Chapelle ★★★ CHURCH Countless writers have called this tiny chapel a jewel box, yet that hardly suffices. Go when the sun is shining, and you'll need no one else's words to describe the remarkable effects of natural light on Sainte-Chapelle. You approach the church through the Cour de la Sainte-Chapelle of the Palais de Justice.

Begun in 1246, the bi-level chapel was built to house relics of the True Cross, including the Crown of Thorns acquired by St. Louis (the Crusader King, Louis IX) from the emperor of Constantinople. (In those days, cathedrals throughout Europe were busy acquiring relics for their treasuries, regardless of their authenticity. It was a seller's, perhaps a sucker's, market.) Louis IX is said to

Place des Vosges.

have paid heavily for his relics, raising the money through unscrupulous means. He died of the plague on a crusade and was canonized in 1297.

You enter through the ***chapelle basse* (lower chapel),** used by the palace servants; it's supported by flying buttresses and ornamented with fleur-de-lis designs. The king and his courtiers used the ***chapelle haute* (upper chapel),** one of the greatest achievements of Gothic art; you reach it by ascending a narrow spiral staircase. On a bright day, the 15 stained-glass windows seem to glow with Chartres blue and wine-colored reds. The walls consist almost entirely of the glass, 612 sq. m (6,588 sq. ft.) of it, which had to be removed for safekeeping during the Revolution and again during both world wars. In the windows' Old and New Testament designs are embodied the hopes and dreams (and the pretensions) of the kings who ordered their construction. The 1,134 scenes depict the Christian story from the Garden of Eden through the Apocalypse; you read them from bottom to top and from left to right. The great rose window depicts the Apocalypse.

Sainte-Chapelle stages **concerts** from March to November daily at 7 and 8:30pm; tickets cost 19€ to 25€. Call ✆ **01-44-07-12-38** from 11am to 6pm daily for details.

Palais de Justice, 4 bd. du Palais, 4e. ✆ **01-53-40-60-80.** www.monum.fr. 8€ adults, 5€ ages 18–25, free 17 and younger. Mar–Oct daily 9:30am–6pm; Nov–Feb daily 9am–5pm. Métro: Cité, St-Michel, or Châtelet–Les Halles. RER: St-Michel.

CHAMPS-ELYSÉES & WESTERN PARIS (8E, 16E & 17E)

Money and power dominate this neighborhood and its emblematic avenue, the Champs-Elysées. There is also a wealth of exceptional museums here from **Musée d'art Moderne,** a testament to Paris's Modernist glory days, to the **Palais de Tokyo,** a pioneering contemporary art space.

Arc de Triomphe ★★ MONUMENT At the western end of the Champs-Elysées, the Arc de Triomphe suggests an ancient Roman arch, only it's larger.

Arc de Triomphe.

Actually, it's the biggest triumphal arch in the world, about 49m (161 ft.) high and 44m (144 ft.) wide. To reach it, *don't try to cross the square,* Paris's busiest traffic hub. With a dozen streets radiating from the "Star," the roundabout has been called by one writer "vehicular roulette with more balls than numbers," death is certain! Take the underground passage, and live a little longer.

Commissioned by Napoleon in 1806 to commemorate the victories of his Grand Armée, the arch wasn't ready for the entrance of his empress, Marie-Louise, in 1810 (he divorced Josephine because she couldn't provide him an heir). It wasn't completed until 1836, under the reign of Louis-Philippe. Four years later, Napoleon's remains, brought from St-Helena, passed under the arch on their journey to his tomb at the Hôtel des Invalides. Since then, it has become the focal point for state funerals. It's also the site of the tomb of the Unknown Soldier, in whose honor an eternal flame burns.

The greatest state funeral was Victor Hugo's in 1885; his coffin was placed under the arch, and much of Paris came to pay tribute. Another notable funeral was in 1929 for Ferdinand Foch, commander of the Allied forces in World War I. The arch has been the centerpiece of some of France's proudest moments and some of its most humiliating defeats, notably in 1871 and 1940. The memory of German troops marching under the arch is still painful to the French. Who can forget the 1940 newsreel of the Frenchman standing on the Champs-Elysées weeping as the Nazi storm troopers goose-stepped through Paris? The arch's happiest moment occurred in 1944, when the liberation-of-Paris parade passed beneath it. That same year, Eisenhower paid a visit to the tomb of the Unknown Soldier, a new tradition among leaders of state and important figures. After Charles de Gaulle's death, the French government (despite protests from anti-Gaullists) voted to change the name of this site from place de l'Etoile to place Charles de Gaulle. Today it's often known as place Charles de Gaulle–Etoile.

Of the sculptures on the monument, the best known is Rude's *Marseillaise,* or *The Departure of the Volunteers.* J. P. Cortot's *Triumph of Napoléon in 1810* and Etex's *Resistance of 1814* and *Peace of 1815* also adorn the facade. The monument is engraved with the names of hundreds of generals (those underlined died in battle) who commanded French troops in Napoleonic victories.

You can take an elevator or climb the stairway to the top, where there's an exhibition hall with lithographs and photos depicting the arch throughout its history, as well as an observation deck with an exceptional view.

Place Charles de Gaulle–Etoile, 8e. ✆ **01-55-37-73-77.** www.monum.fr. Admission 9€ adults, 5.50€ for those 18–24. Apr–Sept daily 10am–11pm; Oct–Mar daily 10am–10:30pm. Métro: Charles-de-Gaulle–Etoile. Bus: 22, 30, 31, 52, 73, or 92.

Bois de Boulogne ★★ ☺ PARK One of the most spectacular parks in Europe is the **Bois de Boulogne,** often called the "main lung" of Paris. Horse-drawn carriages traverse it, but you can also drive through. You can discover its hidden pathways, however, only by walking. You could spend days in the Bois de Boulogne and still not see everything.

Porte Dauphine is the main entrance, though you can take the Métro to Porte Maillot as well. West of Paris, the park was once a forest kept for royal hunts. It was in vogue in the late 19th century: Along avenue Foch, carriages with elegantly attired and coiffured Parisian damsels would rumble along with their foppish escorts. Nowadays, it's more likely to attract run-of-the-mill picnickers. (Be careful at night, when hookers and muggers proliferate.)

When Napoleon III gave the grounds to the city in 1852, they were developed by Baron Haussmann. Separating Lac Inférieur from Lac Supérieur is the **Carrefour des Cascades ★** (you can stroll under its waterfall). The Lower Lake contains two islands connected by a footbridge. From the east bank, you can take a boat to these idyllically situated grounds, perhaps stopping off at the cafe/restaurant on one of them.

Restaurants in the *bois* are numerous, elegant, and expensive. The **Pré Catelan ★** contains a deluxe restaurant of the same name (**✆01-44-14-41-00;** www.precatelanparis.com), occupying a gem of a Napoleon III–style château, and also a Shakespearean theater in a garden planted with trees mentioned in the bard's plays. Nearby is **La Grande Cascade** (**✆01-45-27-33-51**), once a hunting lodge for Napoleon III.

Jardin d'Acclimatation (**✆01-40-67-90-82;** www.jardindacclimatation.fr), at the northern edge of the park, is for children, with a zoo, an amusement park, and a narrow-gauge railway (see listing below for more information).

Two racetracks, the **Hippodrome de Longchamp ★★★** and the **Hippodrome d'Auteuil,** are in the park. The Grand Prix is run in June at Longchamp (the site of a medieval abbey). Fashionable Parisians always turn out for this, the women in their finest haute couture. To the north of Longchamp is the **Grand Cascade,** an artificial waterfall.

In the western section of the *bois,* the 24-hectare (59-acre) **Parc de Bagatelle ★** (**✆01-43-28-47-63**) owes its existence to a bet between the comte d'Artois (later Charles X) and Marie Antoinette, his sister-in-law. The comte wagered he could erect a small palace in less than 3 months, so he hired nearly 1,000 craftsmen (cabinetmakers, painters, Scottish landscape architect Thomas Blaikie, and others) and irritated the locals by requisitioning all shipments of stone and plaster arriving through Paris's west gates. He won his bet. If you're here in late April, it's worth visiting the Bagatelle just for the tulips. In late May, one of the finest rose collections in Europe is in full bloom.

16e. Métro: Porte d'Auteuil, Les Sablons, Porte Maillot, or Porte Dauphine.

Grand Palais ★★ HISTORIC BUILDING Built for the 1900 Universal Exhibition, this giant exhibition hall spans a total area of 72,000 sq. m (775,001 sq. ft.), with the biggest glass roof in Europe—an elegant lighting solution, since the building was constructed prior to electricity. After years of renovations, the Grand Palais reopened in 2007, and today it hosts a changing array of sporting and cultural events, including FIAC (Paris's annual contemporary art fair), the Hermès horse jumping competition, and fashion shows; check their website for events. The Grand Palais faces the Petit Palais.

1 av. Géneral Eisenhower, 8e. **✆ 01-44-13-17-17.** www.grandpalais.fr. Opening hours and admission prices vary according to the exhibitions and events. Métro: Champs-Elysées Clémenceau.

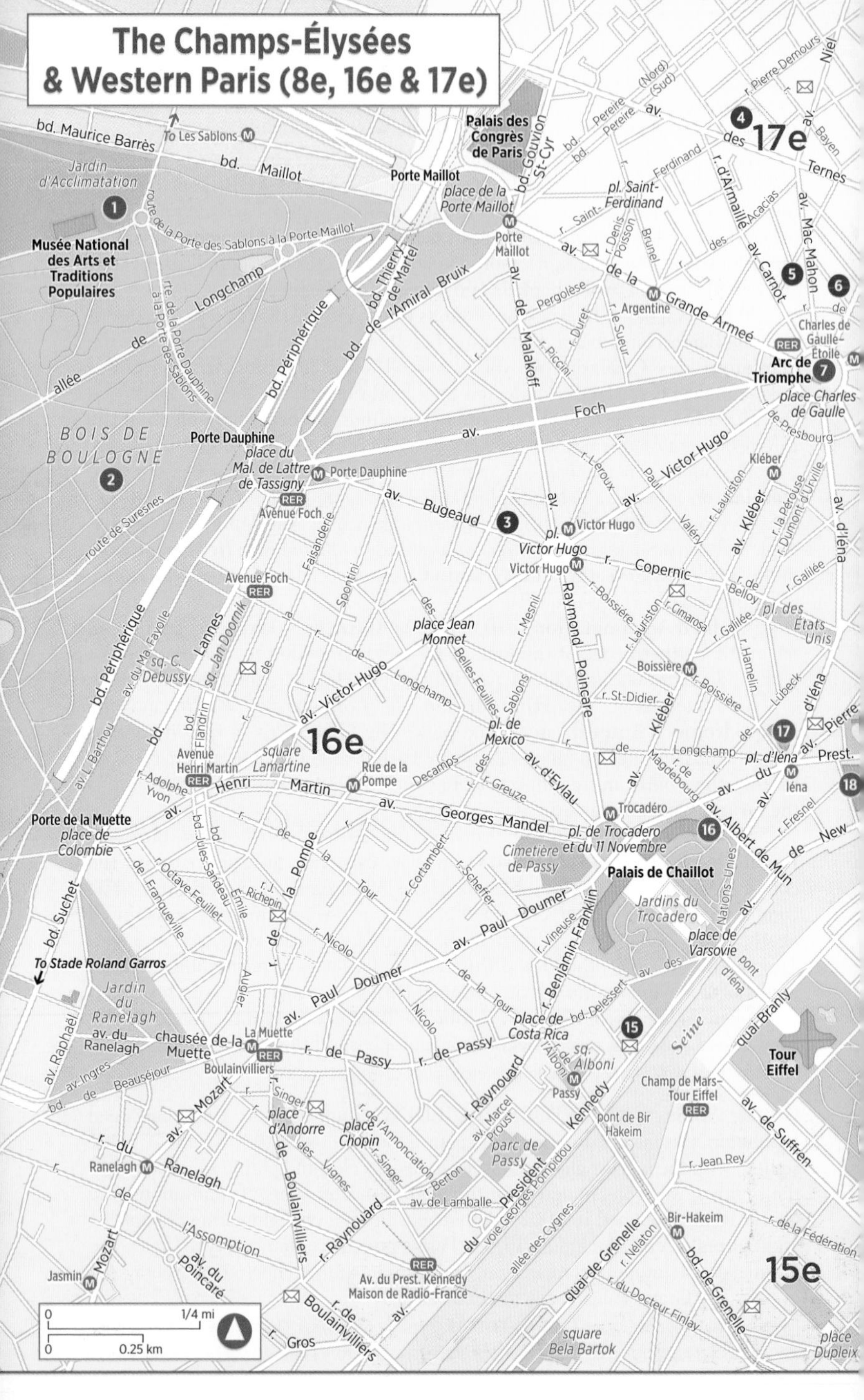
The Champs-Élysées & Western Paris (8e, 16e & 17e)
17e
16e
15e
Palais des Congrès de Paris
Porte Maillot
place de la Porte Maillot
Musée National des Arts et Traditions Populaires
Jardin d'Acclimatation
BOIS DE BOULOGNE
Porte Dauphine
place du Mal. de Lattre de Tassigny
Arc de Triomphe
place Charles de Gaulle
Charles de Gaulle-Étoile
pl. Victor Hugo
place Jean Monnet
pl. de Mexico
square Lamartine
Porte de la Muette
place de Colombie
pl. d'Iéna
pl. des États Unis
pl. de Trocadero et du 11 Novembre
Palais de Chaillot
Jardins du Trocadero
place de Varsovie
Cimetière de Passy
Tour Eiffel
Champ de Mars-Tour Eiffel
Seine
Jardin du Ranelagh
place de Costa Rica
sq. Alboni
parc de Passy
place d'Andorre
place Chopin
Av. du Prest. Kennedy Maison de Radio-France
square Bela Bartok
place Dupleix
To Les Sablons
To Stade Roland Garros
0 1/4 mi
0 0.25 km

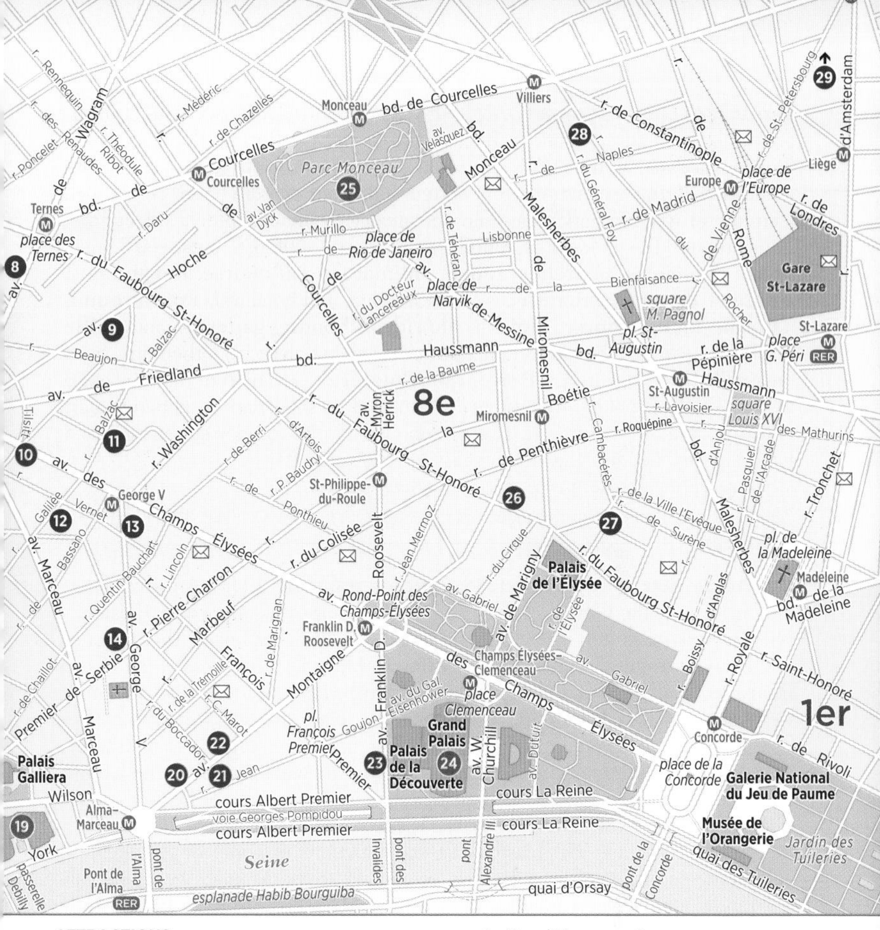

ATTRACTIONS

Arc de Triomphe **7**
Bois de Boulogne **2**
Grand Palais **24**
Jardin d'Acclimatation **1**
La Cité de l'Architecture et du Patrimoine **16**
Musée d'Art Moderne de la Ville de Paris **19**
Musée National des Arts Asiatiques Guimet **17**
Palais du Tokyo **18**
Parc Monceau **25**

HOTELS

Best Western Premier Regent's Garden **4**
Fouquet's Barrière **13**
Four Seasons Hotel George V **14**
Hôtel Balzac **11**
Hôtel Galileo **12**
Hôtel le Bristol **26**
Le Pavillon des Lettres **27**
Le Royal Monceau **9**
Plaza Athénée **22**
Relais Monceau **28**
Renaissance Paris Arc de Triomphe **8**

RESTAURANTS

Bar des Théâtres **21**
Guy Savoy **6**
La Maison Blanche **20**
L'Atelier Etoile de Joël Robuchon **10**
Lasserre **23**
L'Astrance **15**
Le Bristol **26**
Le Cinq **14**
Le Hide **5**
Les Tablettes **3**
Pierre Gagnaire **11**
Restaurant Plaza Athénée (Alain Ducasse) **22**

Jardin d'Acclimatation ★ ☺ AMUSEMENT PARK/GARDEN This 20-hectare (49-acre) children's park in the northern part of the Bois de Boulogne is the kind of place that amuses tykes and adults but not teenagers. The visit starts with a ride on a narrow-gauge train from Porte Maillot to the Jardin entrance, through a stretch of wooded park. The train operates at 10-minute intervals daily from 10:30am until the park closes; round-trip fare costs 2.70€. En route, you'll find a **house of mirrors,** an **archery range,** a **miniature golf course, zoo animals,** a **puppet theater** (performances Wed, Sat–Sun, and holidays), a **playground,** a **hurdle-racing course, junior-scale rides, shooting galleries,** and **waffle stalls.** You can trot the kids off on a **pony** (Sat–Sun only) or join them in a **boat** on a mill-stirred lagoon. **La Prévention Routière** is a miniature roadway operated by the Paris police: Youngsters drive through in small cars equipped to start and stop, and are required by two genuine gendarmes to obey street signs and light changes. Inside the gate is an easy-to-follow map.

In the Bois de Boulogne, 16e. ✆ **01-40-67-90-82.** www.jardindacclimatation.fr. Admission 2.90€, free for children 3 and younger. Apr–Sept daily 10am–7pm; Oct–Mar daily 10am–6pm. Métro: Sablons.

La Cité de l'Architecture et du Patrimoine ★ ☺ MUSEUM After a decade-long makeover, the City of Architecture and Heritage was opened by President Nicolas Sarkozy in 2007. With its trio of galleries and vast space, the museum is the largest architectural museum in the world. It lies in the east wing of the Palais de Chaillot on a hill overlooking a curve of the Seine, with panoramic views of Paris in all directions. The Eiffel Tower looms just across the river.

Exhibits are devoted to 12 centuries of French architecture, the most stunning of which is the reproduction of the stained-glass window ★★ in the Gothic cathedral at Chartres. Other exhibits include a walk-in replica of Le Corbusier's mid-20th-century Cité Radieuse in Marseille.

In all there are 350 plaster cast reproductions of some of the greatest achievements in French architecture, going back to the Middle Ages. One gallery reproduces France's remarkable paintings and frescoes from the 12th to 16th centuries. A third gallery is devoted to modern architecture right up to a turn-of-the-millennium cultural center in New Caledonia in the South Pacific. Children can build their own architectural masterpieces with LEGOs and other materials.

1 place du Trocadéro, 16e. ✆ **01-58-51-52-00.** www.citechaillot.fr. Admission 8€ adults, 5€ students, free ages 18 and younger. Wed and Fri–Mon 11am–7pm; Thurs 11am–9pm. Métro: Trocadéro.

Swing ride at the Jardin d'Acclimatation.

Musée d'Art Moderne de la Ville de Paris ★★ MUSEUM Paris's Modern Art Museum borders the Seine and is, in fact, housed in the Eastern Wing of the monumental Palais de Tokyo (p. 113), a building designed for the 1937 World Fair. The museum opened in 1961, and it is home to works of modern art, including Henri Matisse's *The Dance,* Pierre Bonnard's *Nude in the Bath* and *The Garden,* and Fernand Léger's *Discs.* There are also works by Chagall, Rothko, Braque, Dufy, Picasso, Utrillo, and Modigliani. Seek out Pierre Tal Coat's ***Portrait of Gertrude Stein,*** and keep Picasso's version of this difficult subject in mind. The museum also presents excellent ever-changing exhibits on individual artists from all over the world or on contemporary international trends.

11 av. du Président-Wilson, 16e. ✆ **01-53-67-40-00.** www.mam.paris.fr. Free admission to general collections, temporary exhibition admission 5€–7€. Tues–Sun 10am–6pm. Métro: Iéna or Alma-Marceau.

Musée National des Arts Asiatiques-Guimet ★★ MUSEUM This is one of the most beautiful Asian museums in the world, and it houses one of the world's finest collections of Asian art. Some 3,000 pieces of the museum's 45,000 works are on display. The Guimet, opened in Lyon but transferred to Paris in 1889, received Musée Indochinois du Trocadéro's collections in 1931 and the Louvre's Asian collections after World War II. The most interesting exhibits are Buddhas, serpentine monster heads, funereal figurines, and antiquities from the temple of Angkor Wat. Some galleries are devoted to Tibetan art, including fascinating scenes of the Grand Lamas entwined with serpents and demons.

6 place d'Iéna, 16e. ✆ **01-56-52-53-00.** www.guimet.fr. Admission 7.50€ adults, 5.50€ students, free for ages 17 and younger. Wed–Mon 10am–6pm. Métro: Iéna.

Palais de Tokyo ★★★ ☺ MUSEUM This art center, which opened in 2002, is one of the most original and avant garde in Europe. Dedicated to "emerging" art and artists, the Palais de Tokyo emphasizes edgy, contemporary art and ideas. Its monumental raw concrete architecture immediately sets it apart from a classic museum, and its opening hours (noon to midnight) are radical, too. The installations and vast open spaces invariably appeal to kids. The exhibits change frequently, so check to see what's showing—perhaps a video or sculpture exhibition, fashion events, or performance art. The space also includes a bookshop, a cafeteria, and a first-rate restaurant and bar. The museum is currently undergoing a renovation and expansion, which will double the the museum's exhibiton space.

13 av. du Président-Wilson, 16e. ✆ **01-47-23-54-01.** www.palaisdetokyo.com. Admission 6€ adults, 4.50€ students, free for ages 18 and younger. Tues–Sun noon–midnight. Métro: Iéna.

Palais de Tokyo.

Parc Monceau ★ PARK Much of Parc Monceau is ringed with 18th- and 19th-century mansions, some evoking Proust's *Remembrance of Things Past.* Carmontelle designed it in 1778 as a

The Canal St-Martin

The Canal St-Martin is a picturesque waterway that connects the river Seine, near the Bastille, to the Canal de l'Ourcq, near the Villette in the 19th arrondissement. When Parisians talk about *le canal,* they are usually referring to the popular stretch of the Quais Jemmapes and Valmy, which begins just above République and runs up by the Gare de l'Est. The canal was inaugurated in 1825 with the aim of bringing fresh drinking water to the heart of the city. During the 19th and early 20th centuries, this water highway attracted much commerce and industry to the surrounding areas. Painter Alfred Sisley was inspired by this canal—you can admire his painting *Vue du Canal Saint-Martin à Paris* (1870) at Musée d'Orsay (p. 131). After almost being destroyed in the 1970s to make way for more roads, the canal was classified as a historic monument in 1993, and today visitors can explore the canal at their leisure. If you'd like to take a scenic boat tour of the canal, contact **Paris Canal** (© **01-42-40-96-97**; www.pariscanal.com) or **Canauxrama** (© **01-42-39-15-00**; www.canauxrama.com).

private hideaway for the duc d'Orléans (who came to be known as Philippe-Egalité), at the time the richest man in France. The duke was noted for his debauchery and pursuit of pleasure, so no ordinary park would do. It was opened to the public in the days of Napoleon III's Second Empire.

Monceau was laid out with an Egyptian-style obelisk, a medieval dungeon, a thatched farmhouse, a Chinese pagoda, a Roman temple, an enchanted grotto, various chinoiseries, and a waterfall. These fairy-tale touches have largely disappeared except for a pyramid and an oval naumachia fringed by a colonnade. Now the park is filled with solid statuary and monuments, including one honoring Chopin. In spring, the red tulips and magnolias are breathtaking.

35 bd. de Courcelles, 8e. www.paris.fr. Free admission. 8am–sunset. Métro: Monceau or Villiers.

OPÉRA & CANAL ST-MARTIN (9E & 10E)

The impressive **Opéra Garner** dominates its dynamic neighborhood, which delivers perhaps more opportunities for outstanding retail experiences than for cultural ones. But perhaps the greatest attraction here is the picturesque **Canal St-Martin** itself.

Opéra Garnier ★★ OPERA HOUSE This Neo-Baroque masterpiece was built in 1875, under Napoleon III, by architect Charles Garnier and was known as the Palais Garnier. The stunning grand foyer, restored in 2004, is lined with mirrors and adorned with crystal chandeliers; it resembles the famous Galerie des Glaces at Versailles. It has a magnificent painted ceiling by Paul Baudry portraying themes from the history of music. The gilded auditorium has 1,900 seats and is lit by an immense crystal chandelier that hangs below a once-controversial ceiling painted by Marc Chagall in the 1960s. Today the venue is home to the fine Paris Opera Ballet.

8 rue Scribe, 9e. © **01-40-01-17-89.** www.operadeparis.fr. Admission 9€ adults, 5€ students, free for children 9 and under. Daily 10am–5pm. Métro: Opéra.

PIGALLE & MONTMARTRE (18E)

Perched on the city's highest point, the **Sacré-Coeur** basilica may be the area's only significant monument, but Montmartre's cobblestone streets and unique,

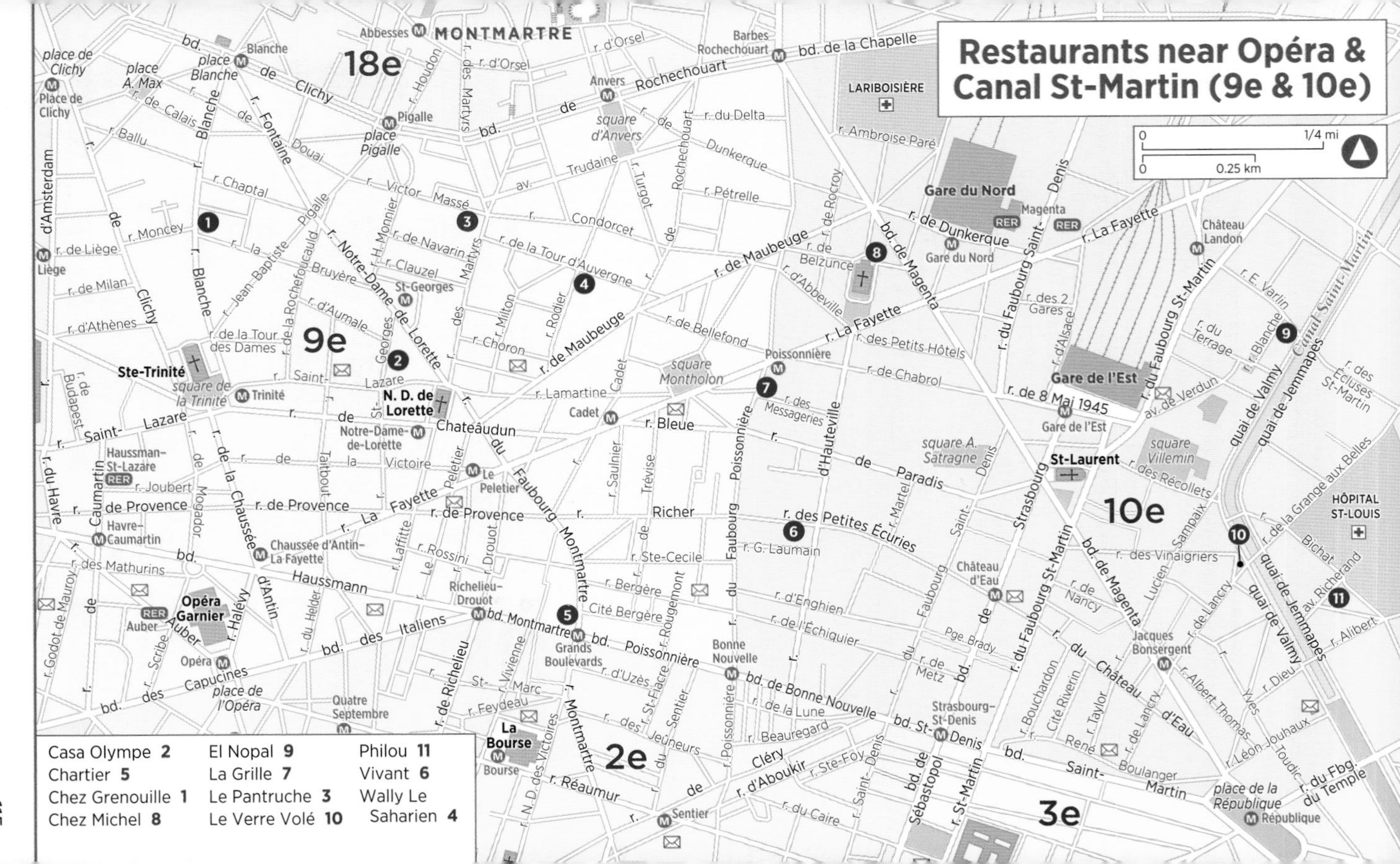
Restaurants near Opéra & Canal St-Martin (9e & 10e)
Casa Olympe 2
Chartier 5
Chez Grenouille 1
Chez Michel 8
El Nopal 9
La Grille 7
Le Pantruche 3
Le Verre Volé 10
Philou 11
Vivant 6
Wally Le Saharien 4

villagelike architecture are an attraction in themselves. The harmless red light district of neighbouring Pigalle can't be reduced to a single attraction either, but it is an exciting area to explore.

Basilique du Sacré-Coeur ★★ ☺ CHURCH Sacré-Coeur is one of Paris's most characteristic landmarks and has been the subject of much controversy. One Parisian called it "a lunatic's confectionery dream." An offended Zola declared it "the basilica of the ridiculous." Sacré-Coeur has had warm supporters as well, including poet Max Jacob and artist Maurice Utrillo. Utrillo never tired of drawing and painting it, and he and Jacob came here regularly to pray. Atop the *butte* (hill) in Montmartre, its multiple gleaming white domes and campanile (bell tower) loom over Paris like a 12th-century Byzantine church. But it's not that old. After France's 1870 defeat by the Prussians, the basilica was planned as a votive offering to cure France's misfortunes. Rich and poor alike contributed money to build it. Construction began in 1876, and though the church wasn't consecrated until 1919, perpetual prayers of adoration have been made here day and night since 1885. The interior is brilliantly decorated with mosaics: Look for the striking Christ on the ceiling and the mural of his Passion at the back of the altar. The stained-glass windows were shattered during the struggle for Paris in 1944 but have been well replaced. The crypt contains what some of the devout believe is Christ's sacred heart—hence, the name of the church. Kids will delight in taking a turn on the merry-go-round, then taking the funiculaire up the hill to the church.

Insider's tip: Although the view from the Arc de Triomphe is the greatest panorama of Paris, we also want to endorse the view from the gallery around the inner dome of Sacré-Coeur. On a clear day, your eyes take in a sweep of Paris extending for 48km (30 miles) into the Île de France. You can also walk around the inner dome, an attraction even better than the interior of Sacré-Coeur itself.

Place St-Pierre, 18e. ✆ **01-53-41-89-00.** www.sacre-coeur-montmartre.com. Free admission to basilica, joint ticket to dome and crypt 5€. Basilica daily 6am–11pm; dome and crypt daily 9am–6pm. Métro: Abbesses; take elevator to surface and follow signs to funicular.

Detail on a Montmartre building.

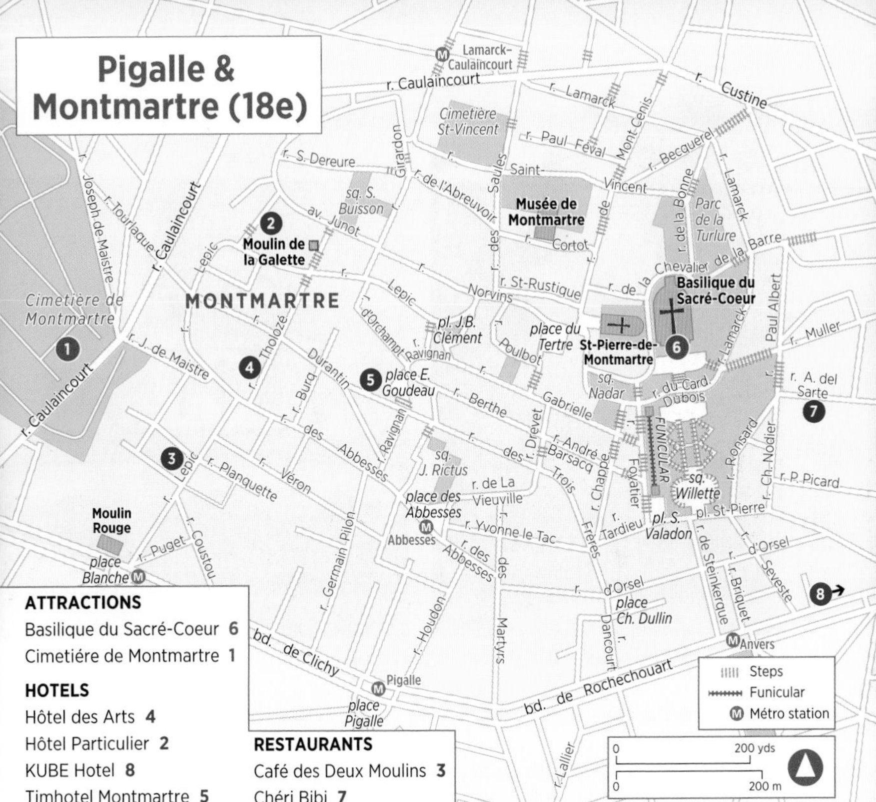

Cimetière de Montmartre ★ CEMETERY This cemetery, established in 1795, lies west of Montmartre and north of boulevard de Clichy. Russian dancer **Vaslav Nijinsky,** novelist **Alexandre Dumas *fils*,** Impressionist **Edgar Degas,** and composers **Hector Berlioz** and **Jacques Offenbach** are interred here, along with **Stendhal** and lesser literary lights such as **Edmond** and **Jules de Goncourt** and **Heinrich Heine.** A more recent tombstone honors **François Truffaut,** film director of the *nouvelle vague* (new wave). We like to pay our respects at the tomb of **Alphonsine Plessis,** heroine of *La Dame aux Camélias,* and **Mme. Récamier,** who taught the world how to lounge. **Emile Zola** was buried here, but his corpse was exhumed and promoted to the Panthéon in 1908. In 1871, the cemetery was used for mass burials of victims of the Siege and the Commune.

20 av. Rachel (west of the Butte Montmartre and north of bd. de Clichy), 18e. ✆ **01-53-42-36-30.** Mon–Fri 8am–6pm; Sat 8:30am–6pm; Sun 9am–6pm. Métro: La Fourche.

BELLEVILLE & NORTHEAST PARIS (19E & 20E)

Located on the edge of Paris, **La Villette** not only encompasses Paris's biggest park, Parc de la Villette, but it is also an exceptional 21st-century cultural compound including museums, concert halls, circus tents, and exhibition spaces which host a great year-round program. The lure of this former industrial zone is its outdoor attractions, including the renowned **Père-Lachaise cemetery.** Note that the area around the Belleville Métro station is also home to one of the city's bustling Chinatowns.

Chopin's grave at the Cimetèire du Père-Lachaise.

Basilique du Sacré-Coeur.

Cimetière du Père-Lachaise ★★★ ☺ CEMETERY When it comes to name-dropping, this cemetery knows no peer; it has been called the "grandest address in Paris." Everybody from Sarah Bernhardt to Oscar Wilde to Richard Wright is resting here, along with Honoré de Balzac, Jacques-Louis David, Eugène Delacroix, Maria Callas, Max Ernst, and Georges Bizet. Colette was taken here in 1954; her black granite slab always sports flowers, and legend has it that cats replenish the roses. In time, the "little sparrow," Edith Piaf, followed. The lover of George Sand, poet Alfred de Musset, was buried under a weeping willow. Napoleon's marshals, Ney and Masséna, lie here, as do Frédéric Chopin and Molière. Marcel Proust's black tombstone rarely lacks a tiny bunch of violets (he wanted to be buried beside his friend/lover, composer Maurice Ravel, but their families wouldn't allow it).

Some tombs are sentimental favorites: Love-torn graffiti radiates 1km (½ mile) from the grave of Doors singer **Jim Morrison** and could appeal to jaded teens. The great dancer **Isadora Duncan** came to rest in the Columbarium, where bodies have been cremated and "filed" away. If you search hard enough, you can find the tombs of that star-crossed pair **Abélard** and **Héloïse,** the ill-fated lovers of the 12th century—at Père-Lachaise, they've found peace at last. Other famous lovers also rest here: A stone is marked **Alice B. Toklas** on one side and **Gertrude Stein** on the other, and eventually, France's First Couple of Film were reunited when **Yves Montand** joined his wife, **Simone Signoret.**

Covering more than 44 hectares (109 acres), Père-Lachaise was acquired by the city in 1804. Nineteenth-century sculpture abounds, as each family tried to outdo the others in ostentation. Monuments also honor Frenchmen who died in the Resistance or in Nazi concentration camps. Some French Socialists still pay tribute at the **Mur des Fédérés,** the anonymous gravesite of the Communards who were executed in the cemetery on May 28, 1871. When these last-ditch fighters of the Commune, the world's first anarchist republic, made their final desperate stand against the troops of the French government, they were overwhelmed, lined up against the wall, and shot in groups. A few survived and lived hidden in the cemetery for years, venturing into Paris at night to forage for food.

A free map of Père-Lachaise is available at the newsstand across from the main entrance.

16 rue de Repos, 20e. ✆ **01-55-25-82-10.** www.pere-lachaise.com. Mon–Fri 8am–6pm; Sat–Sun 8:30am–6pm (closes at 5pm Nov to early Mar). Métro: Père-Lachaise or Philippe Auguste.

Cité des Sciences et de l'Industrie ★★ ☺ MUSEUM A city of science and industry has risen here from unlikely ashes. When a slaughterhouse was built on the site in the 1960s, it was touted as the most modern of its kind. It was abandoned in 1974, and the location on the city's northern edge presented the government with a problem. What could be built in such an unlikely place? In 1986, the converted premises opened as the world's most expensive ($642 million) science complex, designed to "modernize mentalities" in the service of modernizing society. It is located within the Parc de La Villette compound (see below).

The place is so vast, with so many exhibits, that a single visit gives only an idea of the scope of the Cité. Busts of Plato, Hippocrates, and a double-faced Janus gaze silently at a tube-filled riot of high-tech girders, glass, and lights. The sheer dimensions pose a challenge to the curators of its constantly changing exhibits. Some exhibits are couched in

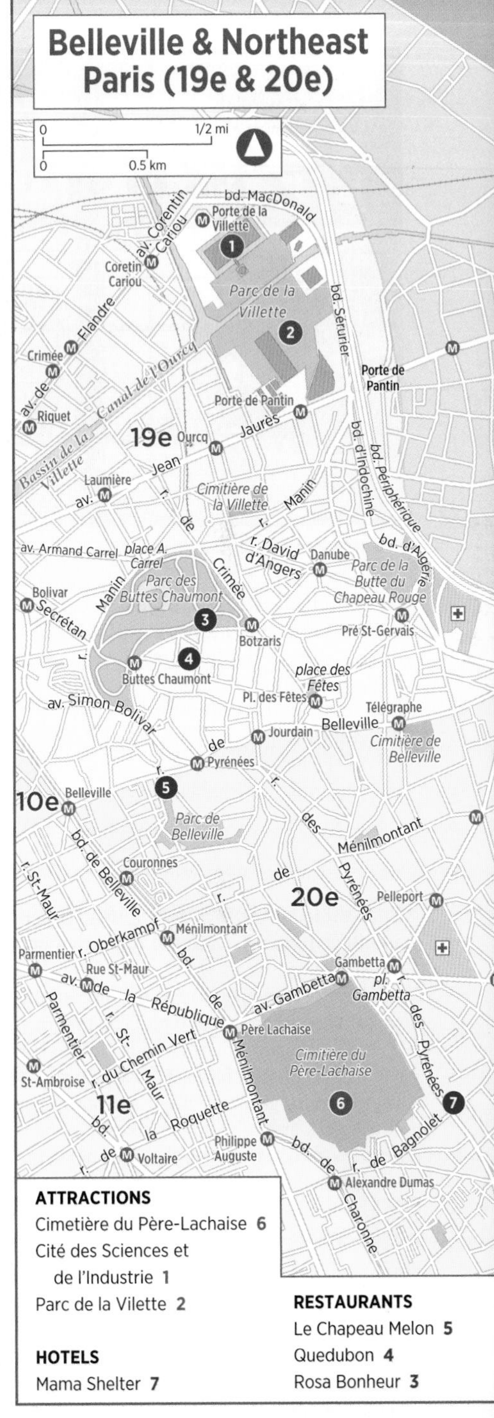

Cité des Sciences et de l'Industrie.

Gallic humor—imagine using the comic-strip adventures of a jungle explorer to explain seismographic activity. **Explora,** a permanent exhibit, occupies the three upper levels of the building and examines four themes: the universe, life, matter, and communication. The Cité also has a **multimedia library,** a **planetarium,** and an **"inventorium"** for kids. The silver-skinned geodesic dome, called **La Géode**—a 34m-high (112-ft.) sphere with a 370-seat theater—is the city's IMAX theater, regularly screening 3-D films on a giant 400-sq.-m (4,306-sq.-ft.) screen.

In the Parc de La Villette, 30 av. Corentine-Cariou, La Villette, 19e. ✆ **01-40-05-70-00.** www.cite-sciences.fr. Varied ticket options 11€–21€ adults, 8€–16€ ages 7–24, free 6 and younger. Tues–Sat 10am–6pm; Sun 10am–7pm. Métro: Porte de La Villette.

Parc de la Villette ★★★ PARK This modern 21st-century park, designed by architect Bernard Tschumi, cleverly combines nature and architecture. Twice the size of the Jardin des Tuileries, it is Paris's largest park. The Canal de l'Ourcq runs through the park, feeding into various waterfalls, fountains, and ponds. Two walkways crisscross the park: The first runs from the Porte de Pantin to the Porte de la Villette, and the second is elevated and runs along the southern bank of the canal. The park is famous for its 26 red "follies," a contemporary version of the 18th-century gazebo, which are both ornamental and functional. In the center of the park are large grassy areas known as the "circle" and the "triangle," where people can relax; during the summer, the "triangle" hosts a popular outdoor cinema program.

211 av. Jean Jaurès, 19e. ✆ **01-40-03-75-75.** www.villette.com. Daily 6am–1am. Métro: Porte de Pantin or Porte de la Villette.

The Left Bank

LATIN QUARTER (5E)

This leafy neighborhood is defined by the medieval university at its heart: the Sorbonne. In fact, it gets its name from the Latin the students spoke in their classes there up until 1793. The Roman occupation, from 52 B.C. until 486 A.D., remains visible, too; rue Saint-Jacques and boulevard Saint-Michel mark the former Roman cardo, and you can explore Roman ruins at the Cluny Museum.

Musée National d'Histoire Naturelle (Museum of Natural History) ★ ☺ MUSEUM This museum in the Jardin des Plantes, founded in 1635 as a research center by Guy de la Brosse, physician to Louis XIII, has a range of science and nature exhibits. At the entrance of the **Grande Gallery of Evolution,** two 26m (85-ft.) skeletons of whales greet you. Kids will love the display containing the skeletons of dinosaurs and mastodons, dedicated to endangered and vanished species. Galleries specialize in paleontology, anatomy, mineralogy, and botany. Within the museum's grounds are **tropical hothouses** containing thousands of species of unusual plant life and a **menagerie** with small animals in simulated natural habitats.

36 rue Geoffrey, 5e. ✆ **01-40-79-54-79.** www.mnhn.fr. Admission 9€ adults; 7€ students, seniors 60 and older, and children 4–13. Wed–Mon 10am–6pm. Métro: Jussieu or Gare d'Austerlitz.

Musée National du Moyen Age/Thermes de Cluny (Musée de Cluny) ★★ MUSEUM Along with the Hôtel de Sens in the Marais, the Hôtel de Cluny is all that remains of domestic medieval architecture in Paris. Enter through the cobblestoned **Cour d'Honneur (Court of Honor),** where you can admire the flamboyant Gothic building with its vines, turreted walls, gargoyles, and dormers with seashell motifs. First the Cluny was the mansion of a rich 15th-century abbot, built on top of and next to the ruins of a Roman bath. By 1515, it was the residence of Mary Tudor, widow of Louis XII and daughter of Henry VII and Elizabeth of York. Seized during the Revolution, the Cluny was rented in 1833 to Alexandre du Sommerard, who adorned it with medieval artworks. After his death in 1842, the government bought the building and the collection.

This collection of medieval arts and crafts is superb. Most people come to see ***The Lady and the Unicorn*** tapestries ★★★, the most acclaimed tapestries of their kind. All the romance of the age of chivalry—a beautiful princess and

The Lady and the Unicorn tapestries at the Musée National du Moyen Age.

her handmaiden, beasts of prey, and house pets—lives on in these remarkable yet mysterious tapestries discovered only a century ago in Limousin's Château de Boussac. Five seem to deal with the senses (one, for example, depicts a unicorn looking into a mirror held by a dour-faced maiden). The sixth shows a woman under an elaborate tent with jewels, her pet dog resting on an embroidered cushion beside her, with the lovable unicorn and his friendly companion, a lion, holding back the flaps. The background forms a rich carpet of spring flowers, fruit-laden trees, birds, rabbits, donkeys, dogs, goats, lambs, and monkeys.

The other exhibits range widely: Flemish retables; a 14th-century Sienese *John the Baptist* and other sculptures; statues from Sainte-Chapelle (1243–48); 12th- and 13th-century crosses, chalices, manuscripts, carvings, vestments, leatherwork, jewelry, and coins; a 13th-century *Adam*; and recently discovered heads and fragments of statues from Notre-Dame de Paris. In the fan-vaulted medieval chapel hang tapestries depicting scenes from the life of St. Stephen.

Downstairs are the ruins of the **Roman baths,** from around A.D. 200. The best-preserved section is seen in room X, the frigidarium (where one bathed in cold water). Once it measured 21 × 11m (69 × 36 ft.), rising to a height of 15m (49 ft.), with stone walls nearly 1.5m (5 ft.) thick. The ribbed vaulting here rests on consoles evoking ships' prows. Credit for this unusual motif goes to the builders of the baths, Paris's boatmen. During Tiberius's reign, a column to Jupiter was found beneath Notre-Dame's chancel and is now on view in the court; called the *Column of the Boatmen,* it's believed to be the oldest sculpture created in Paris.

6 place Paul Painlevé, 5e. ✆ **01-53-73-78-00.** www.musee-moyenage.fr. Admission 8.50€ adults, 6.50€ youths 18–25. Wed–Mon 9:15am–5:45pm. Métro: Miromesnil or St-Philippe-du-Roule.

Panthéon ★★ CHURCH Some of the most famous men in French history (Victor Hugo, for one) are buried here on the crest of the mount of St-Geneviève. In 1744, Louis XV vowed that if he recovered from a mysterious illness, he'd build a church to replace the Abbaye de St-Geneviève. He recovered but took his time fulfilling his promise. It wasn't until 1764 that Mme. de Pompadour's brother hired Soufflot to design a church in the form of a Greek cross with a dome reminiscent of St. Paul's in London. When Soufflot died, his pupil Rondelet carried out the work, completing the structure 9 years after his master's death.

After the Revolution, the church was converted to a "Temple of Fame" and became a pantheon for the great men of France. Mirabeau was buried here, though his remains were later removed. Likewise, Marat was only a temporary tenant. Voltaire's body was exhumed and placed here—and allowed to remain. In the 19th century, the building changed roles so many times—a church, a pantheon, a church again—that it was hard to keep its function straight. After Hugo was buried here, it became a pantheon once again. Other notable men entombed within are Rousseau, Soufflot, Zola, and Braille. Only one woman has so far been deemed worthy of placement here: Marie Curie, who joined her husband, Pierre. Most recently, in 1996, the ashes of André Malraux were transferred to the Panthéon because, according to former French president Jacques Chirac, he "lived [his] dreams and made them live in us." As Charles de Gaulle's culture minister, Malraux decreed that the arts should be part of the lives of all French people, not just Paris's elite.

Before entering the crypt, note the striking frescoes: On the right wall are scenes from Geneviève's life, and on the left is the saint with a white-draped head looking out over medieval Paris, the city whose patron she became, as well as Geneviève relieving victims of famine with supplies.

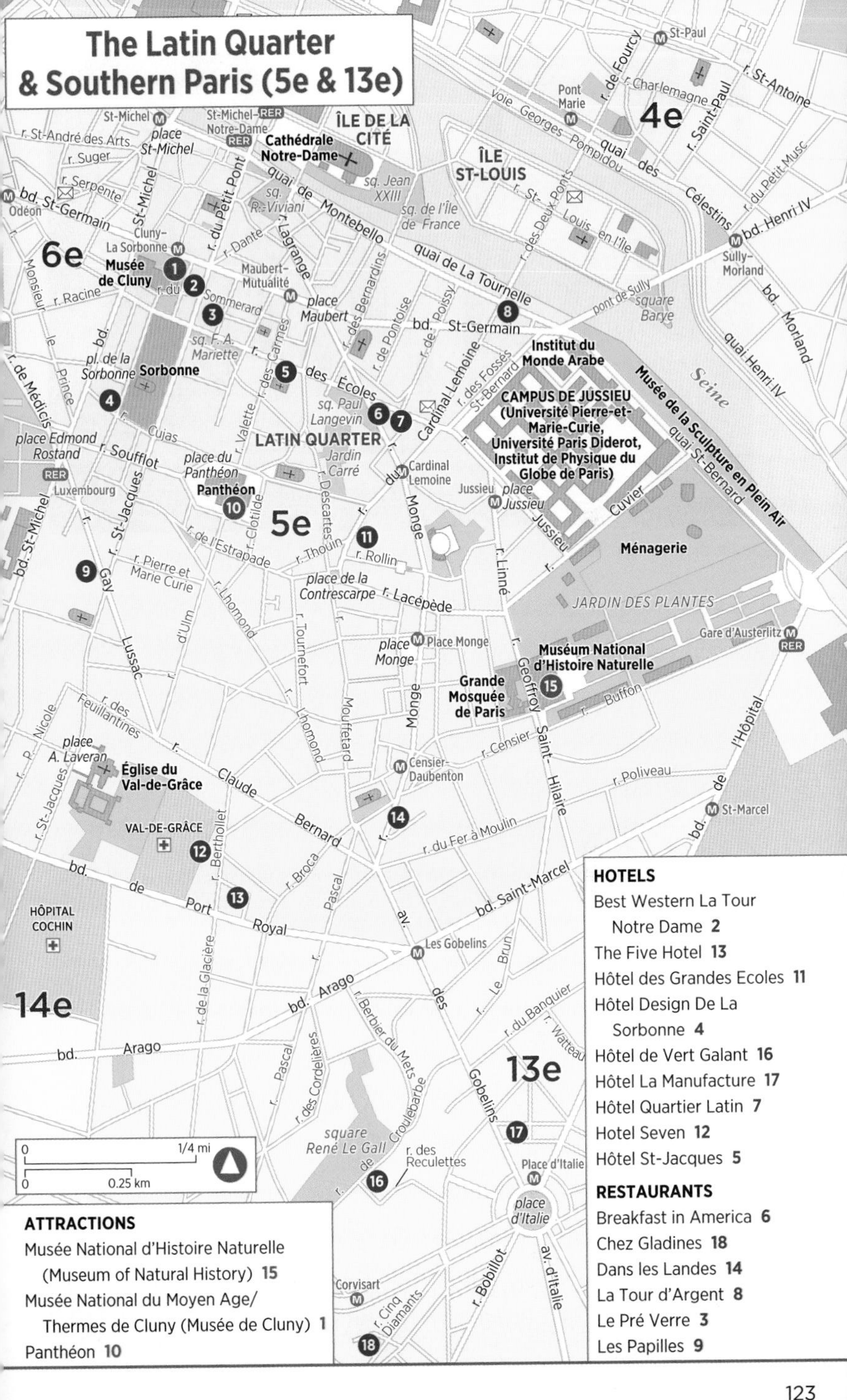
The Latin Quarter & Southern Paris (5e & 13e)
ÎLE DE LA CITÉ
Cathédrale Notre-Dame
ÎLE ST-LOUIS
4e
6e
5e
13e
14e
LATIN QUARTER
Musée de Cluny
Sorbonne
Panthéon
Institut du Monde Arabe
CAMPUS DE JUSSIEU (Université Pierre-et-Marie-Curie, Université Paris Diderot, Institut de Physique du Globe de Paris)
Musée de la Sculpture en Plein Air
Ménagerie
JARDIN DES PLANTES
Muséum National d'Histoire Naturelle
Grande Mosquée de Paris
Église du Val-de-Grâce
VAL-DE-GRÂCE
HÔPITAL COCHIN
Seine
0 1/4 mi
0 0.25 km
ATTRACTIONS
Musée National d'Histoire Naturelle (Museum of Natural History) 15
Musée National du Moyen Age/ Thermes de Cluny (Musée de Cluny) 1
Panthéon 10
HOTELS
Best Western La Tour Notre Dame 2
The Five Hotel 13
Hôtel des Grandes Ecoles 11
Hôtel Design De La Sorbonne 4
Hôtel de Vert Galant 16
Hôtel La Manufacture 17
Hôtel Quartier Latin 7
Hotel Seven 12
Hôtel St-Jacques 5
RESTAURANTS
Breakfast in America 6
Chez Gladines 18
Dans les Landes 14
La Tour d'Argent 8
Le Pré Verre 3
Les Papilles 9

Inside the Panthéon.

Place du Panthéon, 5e. ✆ **01-44-32-18-00.** www.monum.fr. Admission 8€ adults, 5€ ages 18–25, free for children 17 and younger. Apr–Sept daily 10am–6:30pm; Oct–Mar daily 10am–6pm (last entrance 45 min. before closing). Métro: Cardinal Lemoine or Maubert-Mutualité.

St-Germain-des-Prés & Luxembourg (6e)

This neighborhood in the 6th arrondissement was the postwar home of existentialism, associated with great writers and philosophers Jean-Paul Sartre, Simone de Beauvoir, Albert Camus, and an intellectual bohemian crowd that gathered at **Cafe de Flore** or **Les Deux Magots** (p. 90). St-Germain-des-Prés still retains an intellectually stimulating bohemian street life, full of many interesting bookshops, art galleries, *caveau* (basement) clubs, bistros, and coffeehouses. But the stars of the area are two churches, **St-Germain-des-Prés** and **St-Sulpice,** and **Musée National Eugène Delacroix.**

Jardin du Luxembourg ★★ ☺ GARDEN Hemingway once told a friend that the Jardin du Luxembourg "kept us from starvation." He related that in his poverty-stricken days in Paris, he wheeled a baby carriage (the vehicle was considered luxurious) through the garden because it was known "for the classiness of its pigeons." When the gendarme went across the street for a glass of wine, the writer would eye his victim, preferably a plump one; lure him with corn; "snatch him, wring his neck"; and hide him under the blanket. "We got a little tired of pigeons that year," he confessed, "but they filled many a void."

The Luxembourg has always been associated with artists, though children, students, and tourists predominate nowadays. Watteau came this way, as did Verlaine. In 1905, Gertrude Stein would cross them to catch the Batignolles/Clichy/Odéon omnibus, pulled by three gray mares, to meet Picasso in his studio at Montmartre, where he painted her portrait.

Marie de Médici, the wife of Henri IV, ordered the **Palais du Luxembourg** built on this site in 1612, shortly after she was widowed. A Florentine by birth, the regent wanted to create another Pitti Palace, where she could live with her "witch" friend Leonora Galigal. Architect Salomon de Brossee wasn't entirely successful, though the overall effect is Italianate. Alas, the queen didn't get to enjoy the palace, as her son, Louis XIII, forced her into exile when he discovered she was plotting to overthrow him. She died in poverty in Cologne. For her palace, she'd commissioned 21 paintings from Rubens, which glorified her life, but they're now in the Louvre. It is extremely difficult to visit the palace because it is the chamber of French senators. A few visits are organized throughout the year, but there is no schedule. But you can call ✆ **01-44-54-19-49** and take a chance. Even so, when tours are offered, only 30 tickets are available. The cost is 8€ per person.

You don't really come to the Luxembourg to visit the palace; the gardens are the attraction. For the most part, they're in the classic French tradition: well groomed and formally laid out, the trees planted in patterns. Urns and statuary on pedestals—one honoring Paris's patroness, St. Geneviève, with pigtails reaching to her thighs—encircle a central water basin. Kids can sail a toy boat, ride a pony, or attend an occasional Grand Guignol puppet show. And you can join a game of *boules* (lawn bowling) with a group of men who wear black berets and have Gauloises dangling from their mouths.

Place Edmond Rostand, place André Honnorat, rue Guynemer, rue de Vaugirard, 6e. 8am–dusk. Métro: Odéon. RER: Luxembourg

St-Germain-des-Prés ★★ CHURCH It's one of Paris's oldest churches, from the 6th century, when a Benedictine abbey was founded here by Childebert, son of Clovis. Alas, the marble columns in the triforium are all that remain from that period. The Normans nearly destroyed the abbey at least four times. The present building has a Romanesque nave and a Gothic choir with fine capitals. At one time, the abbey was a pantheon for Merovingian kings. Restoration of the site of their tombs, **Chapelle de St-Symphorien,** took place in 1981, when unknown Romanesque paintings were discovered on the triumphal arch. Among the others interred here are Descartes (his heart, at least) and Jean-Casimir, the king of Poland who abdicated his throne. The Romanesque tower, topped by a 19th-

Jardin du Luxembourg.

century spire, is the most enduring landmark in St-Germain-des-Prés. Its church bells, however, are hardly noticed by the patrons of Les Deux Magots across the way.

3 place St-Germain-des-Prés, 6e. ✆ **01-55-42-81-33.** www.eglise-sgp.org. Free admission. Mon–Sat 8am–7:45pm; Sun 9am–8pm. Métro: St-Germain-des-Prés.

Gregorians Unplugged

St-Germain-des-Prés stages wonderful concerts on the Left Bank; it boasts fantastic acoustics and a marvelous medieval atmosphere. The church was built to accommodate an age without microphones, and the sound effects will thrill you. For more information, call ✆ 01-55-42-81-33 or visit www.eglise-sgp.org. Arrive about 45 minutes before the performance if you'd like a front-row seat. Tickets are 15€ to 50€.

St-Sulpice ★★ CHURCH Pause first outside St-Sulpice. The 1844 fountain by Visconti displays the sculpted likenesses of four bishops of the Louis XIV era: Fenelon, Massillon, Bossuet, and Flechier. Work on the church, at one time Paris's largest, began in 1646. Though laborers built the body by 1745, work on the bell towers continued until 1780, when one was finished and the other left incomplete. One of the priceless treasures inside is Servandoni's rococo **Chapelle de la Madone (Chapel of the Madonna),** with a Pigalle statue of the Virgin. The church has one of the world's largest organs, comprising 6,700 pipes; it has been played by musicians such as Marcel Dupré and Charles-Marie Widor.

The real reason to come here is to see the Delacroix frescoes in the **Chapelle des Anges (Chapel of the Angels),** the first on your right as you enter. Look for his muscular Jacob wrestling (or dancing?) with an effete angel. On the ceiling, St. Michael is having some troubles with the Devil, and yet another mural depicts Heliodorus being driven from the temple. Painted in Delacroix's final years, the frescoes were a high point in his baffling career. If these impress you, pay the painter tribute by visiting Musée Delacroix (see above).

Rue St-Sulpice, 6e. ✆ **01-42-34-59-98.** Free admission. Daily 8:30am–8pm. Métro: St-Sulpice.

EIFFEL TOWER & NEARBY (7E)

The **Eiffel Tower** has become a symbol for Paris itself. After admiring and climbing the elegant structure, stroll west along the river to two other important attractions: **Musée du Quai Branly** and **Musée d'Orsay.**

Hôtel des Invalides/Napoléon's Tomb ★★ HISTORIC BUILDING In 1670, the Sun King decided to build this "hotel" to house soldiers with disabilities. It wasn't an entirely benevolent gesture, considering that the men had been injured, crippled, or blinded while fighting his battles. When the building was finally completed (Louis XIV had long been dead), a gilded dome by Jules Hardouin-Mansart crowned it, and its corridors stretched for miles. The best way to approach the Invalides is by crossing over the Right Bank via the early-1900s Pont Alexander-III and entering the cobblestone forecourt, where a display of massive cannons makes a formidable welcome.

Before rushing on to Napoleon's Tomb, you may want to visit the world's greatest military museum, **Musée de l'Armée.** In 1794, a French inspector started collecting weapons, uniforms, and equipment, and with the accumulation of war material over time, the museum has become a documentary of man's self-destruction. Viking swords, Burgundian battle axes, 14th-century blunderbusses, Balkan *khandjars,* American Browning machine guns, war pitchforks, salamander-engraved Renaissance serpentines, a 1528 Griffon, musketoons,

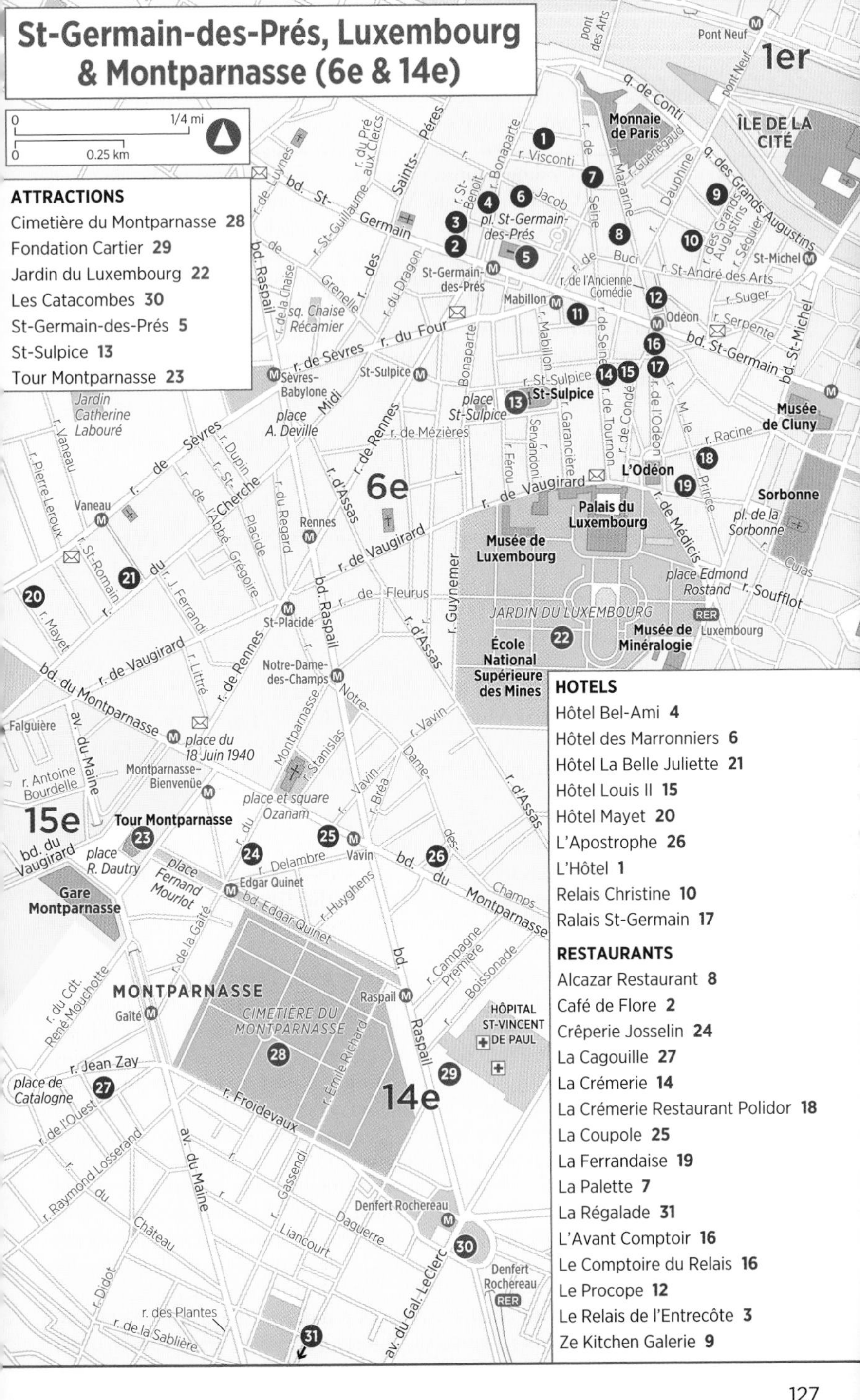

St-Germain-des-Prés, Luxembourg & Montparnasse (6e & 14e)
0
1/4 mi
0
0.25 km
ATTRACTIONS
Cimetière du Montparnasse 28
Fondation Cartier 29
Jardin du Luxembourg 22
Les Catacombes 30
St-Germain-des-Prés 5
St-Sulpice 13
Tour Montparnasse 23
HOTELS
Hôtel Bel-Ami 4
Hôtel des Marronniers 6
Hôtel La Belle Juliette 21
Hôtel Louis II 15
Hôtel Mayet 20
L'Apostrophe 26
L'Hôtel 1
Relais Christine 10
Ralais St-Germain 17
RESTAURANTS
Alcazar Restaurant 8
Café de Flore 2
Crêperie Josselin 24
La Cagouille 27
La Crémerie 14
La Crémerie Restaurant Polidor 18
La Coupole 25
La Ferrandaise 19
La Palette 7
La Régalade 31
L'Avant Comptoir 16
Le Comptoir du Relais 16
Le Procope 12
Le Relais de l'Entrecôte 3
Ze Kitchen Galerie 9
1er
6e
14e
15e
Pont Neuf
pont des Arts
q. de Conti
Monnaie de Paris
ÎLE DE LA CITÉ
q. des Grands Augustins
St-Michel
bd. St-Germain
pl. St-Germain-des-Prés
St-Germain-des-Prés
Mabillon
Odéon
r. de Buci
r. St-André des Arts
r. de l'Ancienne Comédie
r. Jacob
r. Visconti
r. Bonaparte
r. de Seine
r. Mazarine
r. Dauphine
r. des Saints-Pères
r. de Grenelle
r. du Dragon
r. du Four
r. de Sèvres
Sèvres-Babylone
St-Sulpice
place St-Sulpice
sq. Chaise Récamier
Jardin Catherine Labouré
place A. Deville
r. de Rennes
r. de Mézières
r. de Vaugirard
r. de Tournon
r. de Condé
r. de l'Odéon
r. Racine
Musée de Cluny
L'Odéon
Sorbonne
pl. de la Sorbonne
Palais du Luxembourg
Musée de Luxembourg
r. de Médicis
place Edmond Rostand
r. Soufflot
JARDIN DU LUXEMBOURG
Luxembourg
Musée de Minéralogie
École National Supérieure des Mines
r. Guynemer
r. d'Assas
r. de Fleurus
bd. Raspail
Rennes
Vaneau
St-Placide
Notre-Dame-des-Champs
r. Notre-Dame-des-Champs
r. Vavin
bd. du Montparnasse
place du 18 Juin 1940
Falguière
av. du Maine
r. Antoine Bourdelle
Montparnasse-Bienvenüe
Tour Montparnasse
place et square Ozanam
Vavin
r. Delambre
Edgar Quinet
bd. Edgar Quinet
place R. Dautry
place Fernand Mourlot
Gare Montparnasse
r. de la Gaîté
MONTPARNASSE
Gaîté
CIMETIÈRE DU MONTPARNASSE
Raspail
r. Campagne Première
r. Boissonade
HÔPITAL ST-VINCENT DE PAUL
r. Jean Zay
place de Catalogne
r. de l'Ouest
r. Froidevaux
r. Raymond Losserand
r. du Château
r. Gassendi
r. Liancourt
r. Daguerre
Denfert Rochereau
av. du Gal. LeClerc
r. Didot
r. des Plantes
r. de la Sablière

grenadiers . . . if it can kill, it's enshrined here. As a sardonic touch, there's even the wooden leg of General Daumesnil, the governor of Vincennes who lost his leg in the battle of Wagram. Oblivious to the irony of committing a crime against a place that documents man's evil nature, the Nazis looted the museum in 1940.

Among the outstanding acquisitions are suits of armor worn by the kings and dignitaries of France, including Louis XIV. The best are in the new Arsenal. The most famous one, the "armor suit of the lion," was made for François I. Henri II ordered his suit engraved with the monogram of his mistress, Diane de Poitiers, and (perhaps reluctantly) that of his wife, Catherine de Médici. Particularly fine are the showcases of swords and the World War I mementos, including those of American and Canadian soldiers—seek out the Armistice Bugle, which sounded the cease-fire on November 7, 1918, before the general cease-fire on November 11. The west wing's Salle Orientale has arms of the Eastern world, including Asia and the Mideast Muslim countries, from the 16th century to the 19th century. Turkish armor (look for Bajazet's helmet) and weaponry, and Chinese and Japanese armor and swords are on display.

Then there's that little Corsican who became France's greatest soldier. Here you can see the death mask Antommarchi made of him, as well as an oil by Delaroche painted at the time of Napoleon's first banishment (April 1814) and depicting him as he probably looked, paunch and all. The First Empire exhibit displays Napoleon's field bed with his tent; in the room devoted to the Restoration, the 100 Days, and Waterloo, you can see his bedroom as it was at the time of his death on St. Helena. The Turenne Salon contains other souvenirs, such as the hat Napoleon wore at Eylau, the sword from his Austerlitz victory, and his "Flag of Farewell," which he kissed before departing for Elba.

You can gain access to **Musée des Plans-Reliefs** through the west wing. This collection shows French towns and monuments done in scale models (the model of Strasbourg fills an entire room), as well as models of military fortifications since the days of the great Vauban.

A walk across the Cour d'Honneur (Court of Honor) delivers you to the **Eglise du Dôme,** designed by Hardouin-Mansart for Louis XIV. The architect began work on the church in 1677, though he died before its completion. The dome is the second-tallest monument in Paris (the Tour Eiffel is the tallest, of course). The hearse used at the emperor's funeral on May 9, 1821, is in the Napoleon Chapel.

To accommodate **Napoleon's Tomb ★★★**, the architect Visconti had to redesign the church's high altar in 1842. First buried on St-Helena, Napoleon's remains were exhumed and brought to Paris in 1840 on the orders of Louis-Philippe, who demanded that the English return the emperor to French soil. The remains were locked inside six coffins in this tomb made of red Finnish porphyry, with a green granite base. Surrounding it are a dozen Amazon-like figures representing Napoleon's victories. Almost lampooning the smallness of the man, everything is done on a gargantuan scale. In his coronation robes, the statue of Napoleon stands 2.5m (8¼ ft.) high. The grave of the "King of Rome," his son by second wife Marie-Louise, lies at his feet. Surrounding Napoleon's Tomb are those of his brother, Joseph Bonaparte; the great Vauban, who built many of France's fortifications; World War I Allied commander Foch; and the *vicomte* de Turenne, the republic's first grenadier (actually, only his heart is entombed here).

Place des Invalides, 7e. ✆ **01-44-42-37-72.** www.invalides.org. Admission to Musée de l'Armée, Napoleon's Tomb, and Musée des Plans-Reliefs 9€ adults, 7€ students, free for children 17 and

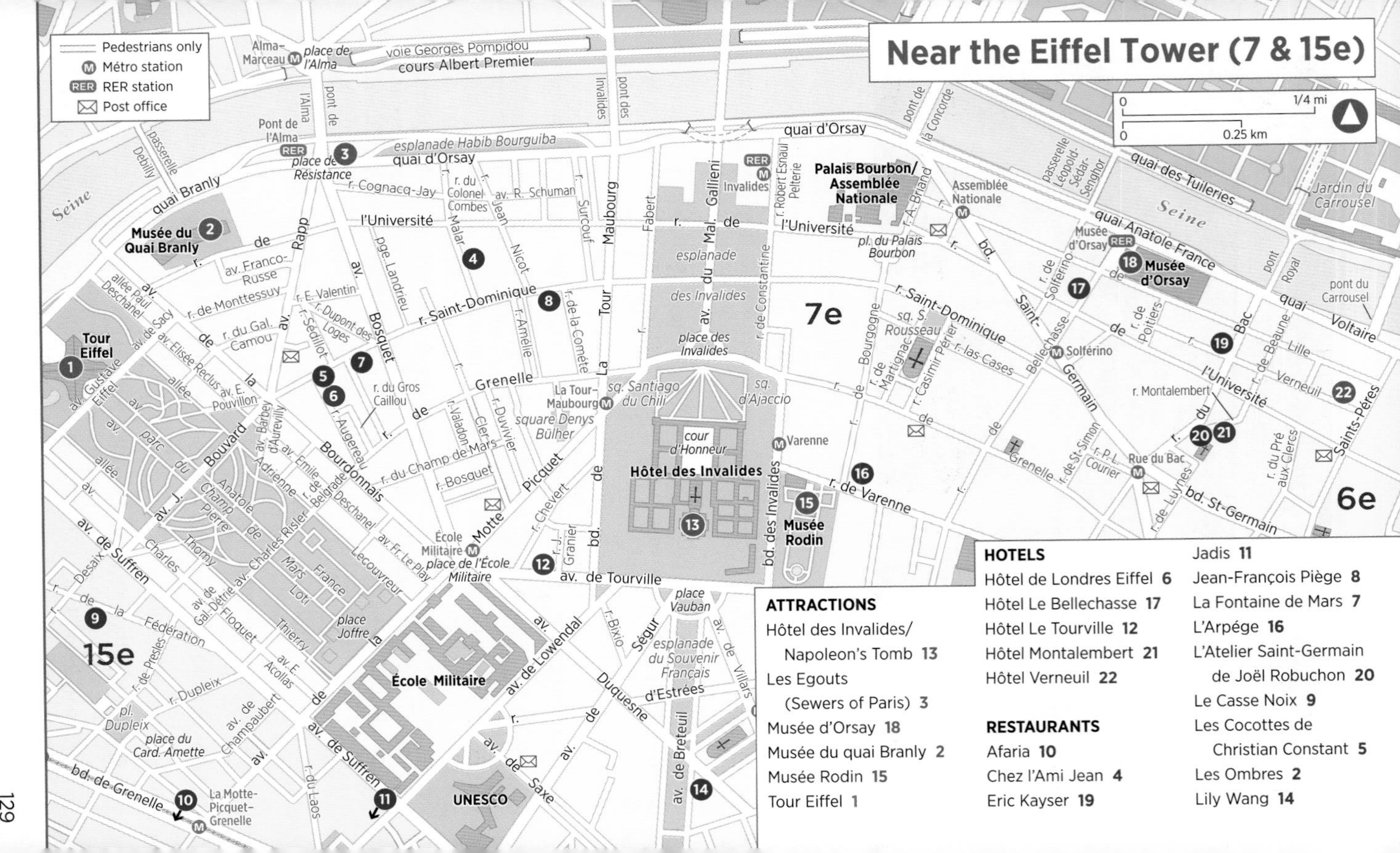

Near the Eiffel Tower (7 & 15e)
Pedestrians only
Métro station
RER station
Post office
ATTRACTIONS
Hôtel des Invalides/
Napoleon's Tomb 13
Les Egouts
(Sewers of Paris) 3
Musée d'Orsay 18
Musée du quai Branly 2
Musée Rodin 15
Tour Eiffel 1
HOTELS
Hôtel de Londres Eiffel 6
Hôtel Le Bellechasse 17
Hôtel Le Tourville 12
Hôtel Montalembert 21
Hôtel Verneuil 22
RESTAURANTS
Afaria 10
Chez l'Ami Jean 4
Eric Kayser 19
Jadis 11
Jean-François Piège 8
La Fontaine de Mars 7
L'Arpége 16
L'Atelier Saint-Germain
de Joël Robuchon 20
Le Casse Noix 9
Les Cocottes de
Christian Constant 5
Les Ombres 2
Lily Wang 14

Napoleon's Tomb.

younger. Oct 1–Mar 31 Mon–Sat 10am–5pm, Sun 10am–5:30pm; Apr 1–Sept 30 Mon and Wed–Sat 10am–6pm, Sun 10am–6:30pm, Tues 10am–9pm; June–Aug daily 10am–7pm. Closed New Year's Day, May 1, Nov 1, and Christmas. Métro: Latour-Maubourg, Varenne, Invalides, or St-Francois-Xavier.

Les Egouts ★ ☺ OFFBEAT SITE Some sociologists assert that the sophistication of a society can be judged by the way it disposes of waste. If so, Paris receives good marks for its mostly invisible sewer network. Victor Hugo is credited with making them famous in *Les Misérables:* Jean Valjean takes flight through them, "all dripping with slime, his soul filled with a strange light." Hugo also wrote, "Paris has beneath it another Paris, a Paris of sewers, which has its own streets, squares, lanes, arteries, and circulation."

In the early Middle Ages, drinking water was taken directly from the Seine, and wastewater poured onto fields or thrown onto the unpaved streets transformed the urban landscape into a sea of rather smelly mud. Around 1200, the streets were paved with cobblestones, and open sewers ran down the center of each. These open sewers helped spread the Black Death, which devastated the city. In 1370, a vaulted sewer was built on rue Montmartre, draining effluents into a Seine tributary. During Louis XIV's reign, improvements were made, but the state of waste disposal in Paris remained deplorable.

During Napoleon's reign, 31km (19 miles) of sewer were constructed beneath Paris. By 1850, as the Industrial Revolution made the manufacture of iron pipe and steam-digging equipment more practical, Baron Haussmann developed a system that used separate channels for drinking water and sewage. By 1878, it was 580km (360 miles) long. Beginning in 1894, the network was enlarged, and laws required that discharge of all waste and storm-water runoff be funneled into the sewers. Between 1914 and 1977, an additional 966km (599 miles) were added. Today the network of sewers is 2,093km (1,298 miles) long.

The city's sewers are constructed around four principal tunnels, one 5.5m (18 ft.) wide and 4.5m (15 ft.) high. It's like an underground city, with the street names clearly labeled. Sewer tours begin at Pont de l'Alma on the Left Bank, where a stairway leads into the city's bowels. Visiting times might change during bad weather, as a storm can make the sewers dangerous. The tour consists of a film, a small museum visit, and then a short trip through the maze. ***Warning:*** The smell is pretty bad, especially in summer, but kids should love the gross-out factor.

Pont de l'Alma, 7e. ✆ **01-53-68-27-81.** Admission 4.20€ adults; 3.40€ seniors, students, and children 5–16; free for children 4 and younger. May–Sept Sat–Wed 11am–5pm; Oct–Apr Sat–Wed 11am–4pm. Métro: Alma-Marceau. RER: Pont de l'Alma.

Musée d'Orsay ★★★ MUSEUM Architects created one of the world's great museums from an old rail station, the neoclassical Gare d'Orsay, across the Seine from the Louvre and the Tuileries. Don't skip the Louvre, of course, but come here even if you have to miss all the other art museums in town. The Orsay boasts an astounding collection devoted to the watershed years 1848 to 1914, with a treasure-trove by the big names plus all the lesser-known groups (the Symbolists, Pointillists, Nabis, Realists, and late Romantics). The 80 galleries also include Belle Epoque furniture, photographs, objets d'art, and architectural models.

A monument to the Industrial Revolution, the Orsay is covered by an arching glass roof allowing in floods of light. It displays works ranging from the creations of academic and historic painters such as Ingres to romanticists such as Delacroix, to neorealists, including Courbet and Daumier.

The museum's Impressionist and post-Impressionist galleries, as well as the four floors of the "Pavillon Amont," recently underwent a major renovation, which enlarged exhibition spaces and improved displays. The Impressionists still draw the crowds to this museum. Led by Manet, Renoir, and Monet, the Impressionists shunned ecclesiastical and mythological set pieces for a light-bathed Seine, faint figures strolling in the Tuileries, pale-faced women in hazy bars, and even vulgar rail stations such as the Gare St-Lazare. And the Impressionists were the first to paint that most characteristic feature of Parisian life: the sidewalk cafe, especially in the artists' quarter of Montmartre.

The most famous painting from this era is Manet's 1863 ***Déjeuner sur l'herbe (Picnic on the Grass),*** whose forest setting with a nude woman and two fully clothed men sent shock waves through respectable society when it was first exhibited. Two years later, Manet's ***Olympia*** created another scandal by depicting a woman lounging on her bed and wearing nothing but a flower in her hair and high-heeled shoes; she's attended by an African maid in the background. Zola called Manet "a man among eunuchs."

One of Renoir's most joyous paintings is here: the ***Moulin de la Galette*** (1876). Degas is represented by his paintings of racehorses and dancers; his 1876 cafe scene, ***Absinthe,*** remains one of his most reproduced works. Paris-born Monet was fascinated by the effect of changing light on Rouen Cathédrale and brought its stone bubbles to life in a series of five paintings; our favorite is ***Rouen Cathédrale: Full Sunlight.*** Another celebrated work is by an American, Whistler's ***Arrangement in Grey and Black: Portrait of the Painter's Mother,*** better known as ***Whistler's Mother.*** It's said that this painting heralded modern art, though many critics denounced it at the time because of its funereal overtones. Whistler was content to claim he'd made "Mummy just as nice as possible."

You'll also see works by Matisse, the Cubists, and the Expressionists in a setting once used by Orson Welles to film a nightmarish scene in *The Trial,* based on Kafka's unfinished novel. You'll find Millet's sunny wheat fields, Barbizon landscapes, Corot's mists, and Tahitian Gauguins.

1 rue de Bellechasse or 62 rue de Lille, 7e. ✆ **01-40-49-48-14.** www.musee-orsay.fr. Admission 8€ adults, 5.50€ ages 18–24, free ages 17 and younger. Joint ticket to this museum and Musée de l'Orangerie (p. 94) 13€. Tues–Wed and Fri–Sun 9:30am–6pm; Thurs 9:30am–9:45pm. Closed New Year's Day and Christmas. Métro: Solférino. RER: Musée d'Orsay.

Musée du quai Branly ★★★ ☺ MUSEUM The architect, Jean Nouvel, said he wanted to create something "unique, poetic, and disturbing." And so he did with the opening of this $265 million museum, which took a decade to launch. There was even scandal: The terra-cotta figures from Nigeria turned out to be smuggled. At long last, under one roof nearly 300,000 tribal artifacts from Africa, Asia, Oceania, and the Americas have been assembled. Galleries stand on sculpted pillars that evoke totem poles. Set in a lush, rambling garden on the Left Bank in the shadow of the Eiffel Tower, this is the greatest museum to open in Paris since Pompidou.

Housed in four spectacular buildings with a garden walled off from the quai Branly are the art, sculpture, and cultural materials of a vast range of non-Western civilizations, separated into different sections that represent the traditional cultures of Africa, East and Southeast Asia, Oceania, Australia, the Americas, and New Zealand. The pieces here come from the now-defunct Musée des Arts Africains et Oceaniens, from the Louvre, and from Musée de l'Homme. Temporary exhibits are shown off in boxes all along the 183m-long (600-ft.) exhibition hall.

Incredible masterpieces are on display made by some very advanced traditional civilizations; some of the most impressive exhibits present tribal masks of different cultures, some of which are so lifelike and emotional in their creation that you can feel the fear and elation involved in their use, which is well documented by descriptions in English. The exhibitions are very engaging for children. Allow 2 hours for a full visit; also take a stroll in the carefully manicured garden, or have a cafe au lait in the small cafeteria across from the main building. There are numerous entrances to the museum grounds from the area near the Eiffel Tower; the main entrance is on quai Branly.

27–37 quai Branly and 206–208 rue de Université, 7e. ✆ **01-56-61-70-00.** www.quaibranly.fr. Admission 8.50€ adults, 6€ seniors and students 18–26, free for children 17 and younger. Tues–Wed and Sun 11am–7pm; Thurs–Sat 11am–9pm. Métro: Alma-Marceau. RER: Pont d'Alma.

Musée Rodin ★★ ☺ MUSEUM Today Rodin is acclaimed as the father of modern sculpture, but in a different era, his work was labeled obscene. The world's artistic taste changed, and in due course, in 1911, the French government purchased Rodin's studio in this gray-stone, 18th-century mansion in the Faubourg St-Germain. The government restored the rose gardens to their 18th-century splendor, making them a perfect setting for Rodin's most memorable works.

In the courtyard are three world-famous creations. Rodin's first major public commission, ***The Burghers of Calais,*** commemorated the heroism of six citizens of Calais who in 1347 offered themselves as a ransom to Edward III in return for ending his siege of their port. Perhaps the single best-known work, ***The Thinker,*** in Rodin's own words, "thinks with every muscle of his arms, back, and legs, with his clenched fist and gripping toes." Not completed when

Rodin died, ***The Gate of Hell,*** as he put it, is "where I lived for a whole year in Dante's *Inferno.*"

Inside, the sculptures, plaster casts, reproductions, originals, and sketches reveal the freshness and vitality of a remarkable artist. You can almost see his works emerging from marble into life. Everybody is attracted to ***Le Baiser (The Kiss),*** of which one critic wrote, "The passion is timeless." Upstairs are two versions of the celebrated and condemned ***Nude of Balzac,*** his bulky torso rising from a tree trunk (Albert E. Elsen commented on the "glorious bulging" stomach). Included are many versions of his ***Monument to Balzac*** (a large one stands in the garden), Rodin's last major work. Other significant sculptures are the soaring ***Prodigal Son; The Crouching Woman*** (the "embodiment of despair"); and ***The Age of Bronze,*** an 1876 study of a nude man modeled after a Belgian soldier. (Rodin was falsely accused of making a cast from a living model.) Generally overlooked is a room devoted to Rodin's mistress, Camille Claudel, a towering artist in her own right. She was his pupil, model, and lover, and created such works as ***Maturity, Clotho,*** and the recently donated ***The Waltz*** and ***The Gossips.*** The little alley behind Musée Rodin winds its way down to a pond with fountains, flower beds, and even sand pits for children. It's one of the most idyllic hidden spots in Paris.

In the Hôtel Biron, 79 rue de Varenne, 7e. ✆ **01-44-18-61-10.** www.musee-rodin.fr. Admission 6€ adults, 5€ ages 18–25, free for children 17 and younger. Apr–Sept Tues–Sun 9:30am–5:45pm; Oct–Mar Tues–Sun 10am–5:45pm. Métro: Varenne, Invalides, or St-Francois-Xavier.

Tour Eiffel ★★★ ☺ MONUMENT This is without doubt one of the most recognizable structures in the world. Weighing 7,000 tons, but exerting about the same pressure on the ground as an average-size person sitting in a chair, the wrought-iron tower wasn't meant to be permanent. Gustave-Alexandre Eiffel, the French engineer whose fame rested mainly on his iron bridges, built it for the 1889 Universal Exhibition. (Eiffel also designed the framework for the Statue of Liberty.) Praised by some and denounced by others (some called it a "giraffe," the "world's greatest lamppost," or the "iron monster"), the tower created as much controversy in the 1880s as I. M. Pei's glass pyramid at the Louvre did in the 1980s. What saved it from demolition was the advent of radio—as the tallest structure in Europe, it made a perfect spot to place a radio antenna.

TIMEOUT AT THE tower

To see the Eiffel Tower best, don't sprint—approach it gradually. We suggest taking the Métro to the Trocadéro stop and walking from the Palais de Chaillot to the Seine to get the full effect of the tower and its surroundings; then cross the Pont d'Iéna and head for the base, where you'll find elevators in two of the pillars—expect long lines. (When the tower is open, you can see the 1889 lift machinery in the east and west pillars.) You visit the tower in three stages: The first landing provides a view over the rooftops, as well as a cinema museum showing films, restaurants, and a bar. The second landing offers a panoramic look at the city. The third landing gives the most spectacular view; Eiffel's office has been re-created on this level, with wax figures depicting the engineer receiving Thomas Edison.

The tower, including its antenna, is 317m (1,040 ft.) high. On a clear day, you can see it from 65km (40 miles) away. An open-framework construction, the tower unlocked the almost unlimited possibilities of steel construction, paving the way for skyscrapers. Skeptics said it couldn't be built, and Eiffel actually wanted to make it soar higher. For years it remained the tallest man-made structure on Earth, until skyscrapers like the Empire State Building surpassed it.

Tour Eiffel.

We could fill an entire page with tower statistics. (Its plans spanned 5,400 sq. m/58,125 sq. ft. of paper, and it contains 2.5 million rivets.) But forget the numbers. Just stand beneath the tower, and look straight up. It's like a rocket of steel lacework shooting into the sky.

From December to February, it is possible to ice-skate inside the Eiffel Tower. Skating takes place on an observation deck 57m (187 ft.) above ground. The rectangular rink is a bit larger than an average tennis court, holding 80 skaters at once. Rink admission and skate rental are free, after you pay the initial entry fee below.

To get to **Le Jules Verne** (✆ **01-45-55-61-44**), the second-platform restaurant, take the private south foundation elevator. You can enjoy an aperitif in the piano bar and then take a seat at one of the dining room's tables, all of which provide an inspiring view. The menu changes seasonally, offering fish and meat dishes that range from filet of turbot with seaweed and buttered sea urchins to veal chops with truffled vegetables. Reservations are recommended.

Champ de Mars, 7e. ✆ **01-44-11-23-23.** www.tour-eiffel.fr. Admission to 2nd landing 8€, 3rd landing 13€. Stairs to 2nd floor 4.50€. Sept–May daily 9:30am–11:45pm; June–Aug daily 9am–12:45am. Sept–June stairs open only to 6:30pm. Métro: Trocadéro, Ecole Militaire, or Bir Hakeim. RER: Champ de Mars–Tour Eiffel.

Tour Eiffel Bargain

The least expensive way to see the Tour Eiffel (www.tour-eiffel.fr) is to walk up the first two floors, at a cost of 4.50€ adults, or 3.50€ ages 25 and younger. That way, you also avoid the long lines waiting for the elevator—although the views are less spectacular from this platform. If you dine at the tower's own 58 Tour Eiffel (✆ 01-45-55-20-04), an Eiffel restaurant on the first floor, management allows patrons to cut to the head of the line.

MONTPARNASSE & SOUTHERN PARIS (13E, 14E & 15E)

For the "Lost Generation," life centered on the cafes of Montparnasse, at the border of the 6th and 14th arrondissements. Picasso, Amedeo Modigliani, Man Ray, and Hemingway frequented this neighborhood, as did Fitzgerald when he was poor (when he was rich, you'd find him at the Ritz). Today Montparnasse plays second fiddle to St-Germain-des-Prés, though the Jean Nouvel–designed **Fondation Cartier** remains a real standout.

Cimetière du Montparnasse ★ CEMETERY In the shadow of the Tour Montparnasse, this debris-littered cemetery is a burial ground of yesterday's celebrities. A map to the left of the main gateway will direct you to the gravesite of its most famous couple, **Simone de Beauvoir** and **Jean-Paul Sartre.** Others resting here include **Samuel Beckett; Guy de Maupassant; Pierre Larousse** (famous for his dictionary); **Capt. Alfred Dreyfus;** auto tycoon **André Citroën;** sculptors **Ossip Zadkine** and **Constantin Brancusi;** actress **Jean Seberg;** composer **Camille Saint-Saëns;** photographer **Man Ray;** poet **Charles Baudelaire,** who wrote about "plunging into the abyss, Heaven or Hell"; and American intellectual and activist **Susan Sontag,** who was interred here in 2005.

3 bd. Edgar-Quinet, 14e. ✆ **01-44-10-86-50.** Mon–Fri 8am–6pm; Sat 8:30am–6pm; Sun 9am–6pm (closes at 5:30pm Nov–Mar). Métro: Edgar-Quinet.

Les Catacombes ★ HISTORIC INTEREST Every year, about 50,000 visitors explore some 910m (2,985 ft.) of tunnel in these dank catacombs to look at six million ghoulishly arranged, skull-and-crossbones skeletons. First opened to the public in 1810, this "empire of the dead" is now illuminated with electric lights over its entire length. In the Middle Ages, the catacombs were quarries, but by the end of the 18th century, overcrowded cemeteries were becoming a menace to public health. City officials decided to use the catacombs as a burial ground, and the bones of several million persons were transferred here. In 1830, the prefect of Paris closed the catacombs, considering them obscene and indecent. During World War II, the catacombs were the headquarters of the French Resistance.

1 place du Colonel Henri Rol-Tanguy, 14e. ✆ **01-43-22-47-63.** www.catacombes-de-paris.fr. Admission 8€ adults, 6€ seniors, 4€ ages 14–25, free for children 13 and younger. Tues–Sun 10am–5pm. Métro: Denfert-Rochereau.

Les Catacombes.

Fondation Cartier ★★ MUSEUM This is a special place. The fine jeweler Cartier commissioned Pritzker Architecture Prize–winning architect Jean Nouvel to design a headquarters for its art foundation, and the result in an airy glass-and-steel structure. Once you enter the building—passing under a vertical plant wall—you will encounter a range of themed exhibitions from both French and international artists. The foundation is known for presenting art from stars better known for their success in other fields, like Patti Smith or David Lynch. There is also a wild-looking garden surrounding the building, which is a pleasure to walk through.

261 bd. Raspail, 14e. ✆ **01-42-18-56-50.** www.fondation.cartier.fr. Admission 8.50€ adults, 5.50€ students and seniors. Tues–Sun 11am–8pm (until 10pm Tues). Métro: Raspail.

Tour Montparnasse ☺ ARCHITECTURE Completed in 1973 and rising 206m (676 ft.) above the skyline, Tour Montparnasse was denounced by some as "bringing Manhattan to Paris." The city soon passed an ordinance outlawing any further structures of this size in the heart of Paris. Today the modern tower houses an underground shopping mall, as well as much of the infrastructure for the Gare de Montparnasse rail station. You can ride an elevator up to the 56th floor (where you'll find a bar and restaurant) and then climb three flights to the roof terrace. The terrific view encompasses virtually every important Paris monument, including Sacré-Coeur, Notre-Dame, and La Défense.

33 av. de Maine, 15e. ✆ **01-45-38-52-56.** www.tourmontparnasse56.com. Admission 11€ adults, 8€ students, 4.70€ children 7–15, free for children 6 and younger. Apr–Sept daily 9:30am–11:30pm; Oct–Mar daily 9:30am–10:30pm. Métro: Montparnasse-Bienvenüe.

WHERE TO EAT

Paris has always been a haven for high-rolling gastronomes who collect luxury restaurants like playing cards. That's still the case today. Whether you're looking for an opulent culinary experience or edgy, provocative cooking, Paris's range of quality restaurants—from three-star restaurants to casual bistros—remains unmatched by any other city in the world.

Although Paris has long been home to high-end gourmet restaurants, a growing number of affordable, high-end bistros serving gourmet food have entered Paris's culinary scene. For more than a decade now, chefs who have trained under three-star chefs have been leaving these "palace" restaurants to open more reasonably priced neo-bistrots, where you can get a three-course meal for about 30€ to 40€. Combining classic technique with an emphasis on fresh, seasonal ingredients, this new generation of chefs is revitalizing the culinary scene.

One important challenge remains, even at the informal bistro level: getting in. Paris restaurants tend to be small in size, and they rarely offer multiple seatings during a lunch or dinner service. The result is a smaller number of available seats, and these are often reserved in advance. Reservations are a very good idea at most of the restaurants we recommend, but you needn't worry about booking weeks in advance. The majority will have space if you call the same day or a few days in advance. Ask your hotel concierge to help if you can't manage the telephone, but don't shy away from this step if food is an important part of your Paris visit. The quality of what you can "stumble in" and find, versus what you can experience when you reserve, is radically different.

The Right Bank

LES HALLES, LOUVRE, & PALAIS ROYAL (1ER & 2E)

Les Halles takes its name from the soaring food pavilions that once stood on this spot as part of the city's largest outdoor market. That market, which writer Emile Zola famously nicknamed "the belly of Paris," has since moved to the suburbs, but Les Halles still has plenty of gourmet offerings today. Three of the city's most heralded newcomers—Yam'Tcha, Spring, and La Régalade–St-Honoré—have opened here in recent years. Just to the north, the 2nd arrondissement has also become a hotbed of restaurant activity, with Saturne, Frenchie, and Passage 53 drawing foodies from all across the city.

A dish at Le Grand Véfour.

Very Expensive

Le Grand Véfour TRADITIONAL FRENCH Tucked inside the Palais Royal and boasting one of the most beautiful restaurant interiors in Paris, Le Grand Véfour remains a history-infused citadel of classic French cuisine. This restaurant has been around since the reign of Louis XV. Napoleon, Danton, Hugo, Colette, and Cocteau dined here—as the brass plaques on the tables testify—and it's still a gastronomic experience. Guy Martin, chef for the past decade, continues to serve the restaurant's signature dishes like Prince Ranier III pigeon and truffled oxtail parmentier alongside new dishes that feature more contemporary flavors like yuzu and tonka bean. Other specialties are noisettes of lamb with star anise, Breton lobster with fennel, and cabbage sorbet in dark-chocolate sauce. The desserts are often grand, such as the *gourmandises au chocolat* (medley of chocolate), served with chocolate sorbet.

17 rue de Beaujolais, 1er. ✆ **01-42-96-56-27.** www.grand-vefour.com. Reservations required far in advance. Main courses 75€–125€; fixed-price lunch 88€, dinner 268€. AE, DC, MC, V. Mon–Fri 12:30–1:45pm and 8–9:30pm. Closed Aug 2–30. Métro: Louvre-Palais-Royal or Pyramides.

Expensive

Goumard SEAFOOD Opened in 1872, this landmark is one of Paris's leading seafood restaurants, with much of its seafood arriving daily from Brittany. Seafood platters—laden with mussels, crabs, shrimp, and many different oysters—are a specialty here. Fresh fish, like Dover sole with buttery potatoes, and roasted lobster with celery root purée and chestnut cream, are other delicious options. With polished wooden panels and a collection of Lalique crystal fish in artificial aquariums, the decor creates the impression of being on a transatlantic ocean liner. The unusual restrooms, with commodes designed by Art Nouveau master cabinetmaker Majorelle, have been classified as a historic monument.

9 rue Duphot, 1er. ✆ **01-42-60-36-07.** www.goumard.com. Reservations required far in advance. Main courses 29€–82€; fixed-price menus 39€ and 59€. AE, DC, MC, V. Daily 11:30am–12:30am. Métro: Madeleine or Concorde.

Passage 53 ★★ MODERN FRENCH After a stint at L'Astrance (p. 144), chef Shinichi Sato joined forces with famous butcher Hugo Desnoyer to open this petite restaurant inside the city's oldest covered passage. Start with a splash of Jacquesson Champagne before diving into a tasting menu that might begin with pink cubes of raw veal topped with a bracing and briny raw oyster. Up next, you might be served some pristine fish or a *civet* (a type of stew) of wild hare served with chocolate sauce. Flavors are bold and clear, and the technical skill on display is impressive. End the meal with a delicious tart with the thinnest possible pastry crust.

53 passage des Panoramas, 2e. ✆ **01-42-33-04-35.** www.passage53.com. Reservations recommended. Fixed-price lunch 45€, dinner 85€. Tues–Sat noon–10pm. Métro: Grands Boulevards.

Saturne ★★ MODERN FRENCH The young chef at the helm of this new restaurant is devoted to his ingredients, sourcing them carefully and cooking them with a sense of respectful restraint. Sven Chartier's cooking is bright and fresh, and at times his food looks more similar to Nordic cuisine than the French tradition in which he trained. The blonde-wood decor and glass roof create an airy environment where diners can enjoy the sparse compositions, like mackerel with charred leeks and squid with blinis and oyster mousse. The wine list assembled by sommelier Ewan Lemoigne leans toward natural, organic wines.

17 rue Notre-Dame-des-Victoires, 1er. ✆ **01-42-60-31-90.** Reservations recommended. Fixed-price dinner 37€, lunch 35€. MC, V. Mon–Fri noon–2pm and 8–10pm. Métro: Bourse.

Spring ★★ MODERN FRENCH The most media-hyped restaurant in Paris was created by young American chef Daniel Rose. Spring initially opened in a remote Pigalle location, but after garnering rave reviews from French critics, Rose moved the restaurant to this new space near the Louvre. Today Spring has a 16th-century wine cave, an underground wine bar with vaulted ceilings, an open kitchen, and a sleek modern dining room. The fixed-price tasting menu is improvisational—it changes nearly every day—but it might begin with a little beignet of fried sole, followed by roasted pigeon or sweetbreads with wild mushrooms. Desserts are deconstructed and usually come in threes—it might be a crustless lemon tart or berries floating in a tea made from the pit of a peach. The wine list is well chosen, but it offers only a few moderately priced bottles.

6 rue Bailleul, 1er. ✆ **01-45-96-05-72.** www.springparis.fr. Reservations required. Main courses lunch 40€–60€; fixed-price lunch 23€, dinner 64€. MC, V. Wed–Fri noon–3pm and 8–10:30pm; Tues and Sat 8–10:30pm. Métro: Louvre-Rivoli.

Yam'Tcha ★★★ MODERN FRENCH/CHINESE A seat at this modern restaurant, on an ancient side street in Les Halles, is one of the city's most difficult to reserve. That has something to do with the small number of tables, but it is mostly due to the fact that Chef Adeline Grattard has received almost universal acclaim for her Franco-Chinese cooking. After spending time at the Michelin three-starred restaurant L'Astrance, Grattard set out on her own in 2009 and has been solidly booked ever since. The dishes on her prix-fixe menus reflect the seasons and change regularly; a recent menu included a flash-seared lobster with corn coulis, and a bouillon of beef with foie gras that one French critic called "the best dish of the year." Both wine and tea pairings (*Yam'Tcha* means "Drink Tea") are available. Reserve a month in advance for lunch and more than 3 months in advance for dinner.

4 rue Sauval, 1er. ✆ **01-40-26-08-07.** Reservations required far in advance. Fixed-price lunch 50€, dinner 85€. AE, MC, V. Métro: Louvre-Rivoli.

Moderate

Au Pied de Cochon TRADITIONAL FRENCH Their famous onion soup and namesake specialty (grilled pigs' feet with béarnaise sauce) still lure visitors, and where else in Paris can you get such a good meal at 3am? Other specialties include a platter named after the medieval patron saint of sausage makers, *la temptation de St-Antoine,* which includes grilled pig's tail, pig's snout, and half a pig's foot, all served with béarnaise and *pommes frites;* and *andouillettes* (chitterling sausages) with béarnaise. Two flavorful but less unusual dishes: a *jarret* (shin) of pork, caramelized in honey and served on a bed of sauerkraut; and grilled pork ribs with sage sauce. On the street outside, you can buy fresh oysters.

6 rue Coquillière, 1er. ✆ **01-40-13-77-00.** www.pieddecochon.com. Main courses 18€–50€. AE, DC, MC, V. Daily 24 hr. Métro: Les Halles or Louvre.

Coinstôt Vino WINE BAR This cool wine bar occupies a corner spot in the historic Passage des Panoramas—Paris's oldest covered passage, if not its prettiest. Stop here for a glass or bottle of "natural" wine—unfiltered and unsulphured—from Guillaume Duprés's eclectic wine list. The menu is made up mainly of small plates; you'll find everything from oysters in season to cheese and charcuterie. There are usually also a few hot dishes. There are tables and counter seats in the main room, as well as some seating out in the passage.

26 passage des Panoramas, 2e. ✆ **01-44-82-08-54.** Reservations recommended. Main courses 15€–35€. MC, V. Mon noon–2pm; Tues–Fri noon–2pm and 6–11pm; Sat 6–11pm. Métro: Grands Boulevards.

Frenchie ★★ 🎁 MODERN FRENCH Greg Marchand acquired the nickname Frenchie when he left his native France to work for Jamie Oliver in England and later at New York's Gramercy Tavern. In 2009, Marchand returned to Paris and opened up this tiny bistro in an unfashionable part of the Sentier. Word spread quickly about the delicious and wonderfully priced cuisine, and Frenchie began to win various "Best Bistro" awards and features in magazines. As a result, this simple place requires booking (at least) several months in advance. Marchand's cooking remains astonishingly good. Starters like house-smoked fish with pickled vegetables are bright and clean, and main dishes like duck with blood orange and dandelion manage to be both comforting and provocative. Desserts, like a cheesecake composed of *Brillat Savarin* (a delicious triple cream cheese), are never too sweet.

5 rue du Nil, 2e. ✆ **01-40-39-96-19.** Reservations required far in advance. Fixed-price dinner 38€. MC, V. Mon–Fri 7–10:30pm. Métro: Sentier.

La Régalade-St-Honoré ★★ TRADITIONAL FRENCH/BISTRO It used to be that fans of the bistro La Régalade had to travel to the southern edge of the 14th arrondissement in order to enjoy the cooking of Bruno Doucet. Not anymore. In 2010, Doucet opened a second restaurant under the Régalade banner right on the rue Saint-Honoré. Now you can enjoy famously comforting dishes like sautéed morel mushrooms in cream with parsley and crispy croutons, or farm-raised pork belly with a creamy interior and crispy skin. Just like at the restaurant down south, the same "help-yourself" crock of homemade pork terrine arrives with *cornichons* (gherkin pickles) and butter as you sit down to the table. Desserts, as you can imagine, are sometimes hard to face after all that pork fat, but they're included in the three-course prix fixe for a remarkable 33€.

123 rue Saint-Honoré, 1er. ✆ **01-42-21-92-40.** Reservations required. Fixed-price dinner 33€. MC, V. Mon–Wed noon–2:30pm and 7–10:30pm; Thurs–Fri noon–2:30pm and 7–11:30pm. Métro: Louvre-Rivoli.

La Tour de Montlhéry (Chez Denise) ★★ TRADITIONAL FRENCH/BISTRO Diners looking for the classic Paris bistro experience come to this raucous old dining room near Les Halles. Chez Denise (as the locals call it) stays open late and serves sturdy platters of *côte de boeuf* (a giant rib steak), grilled marrow bones, and brochettes of grilled meat so long they look like swords. The long-aproned waiters are used to encountering English speakers, but Chez Denise hasn't yet lost its baudy, authentic local vibe. This might not be, however, the place to bring your vegetarian friend.

5 rue des Prouvaires, 1er. ✆ **01-42-36-21-82.** Reservations recommended. Main courses 22€–25€; fixed-price dinner 50€. MC, V. Mon–Fri noon–3pm and 7:30pm–5am. Closed July 15–Aug 15. Métro: Les Halles.

Le Vaudeville BRASSERIE Adjacent to La Bourse (stock exchange), this brasserie retains its marble walls and Art Deco carvings from 1918. In summer, diners can eat on a terrace adorned with geraniums. The place is boisterous and informal, often welcoming groups of six or eight diners at a time. The roster of platters includes a salad of crayfish and asparagus points, grilled Dover sole, smoked salmon, sauerkraut, and grilled meats—there's even stewed calf's head. Three dishes reign as enduring favorites: fresh grilled codfish with mashed potatoes and truffle juice, fresh *escalope* of warm foie gras with grapes or raspberries, and fresh pasta with morels. While the decor isn't quite as stunning as at Bofinger, Le Vaudeville is generally thought to have some of the best food among the surviving Paris brasseries.

29 rue Vivienne, 2e. www.vaudevilleparis.com. ✆ **01-40-20-04-62.** Reservations recommended in the evenings. Main courses 16€–30€; fixed-price menu 40€–50€. AE, DC, MC, V. Daily noon–3pm and 7pm–1am. Métro: Bourse.

L'Hédoniste MODERN FRENCH This contemporary restaurant was opened in late 2010 by a French food writer and his wife. The pair renovated a charming spot in the Sentier and brought in Sébastien Dubrulle to run the kitchen. Dubrulle's cooking can be both inventive (marinated sea scallops with radish and turnip) and comforting (duck confit on a bed of whipped potatoes with toasted hazelnuts). The wine list reflects the current demand among Parisians for natural (organic, unadulterated) wine and contains many reasonably priced bottles.

14 rue Léopold Bellan, 2e. ✆ **01-40-26-87-33.** www.lhedoniste.com. Reservations recommended. Main courses 23€–24€. MC, V. Tues–Sat 12:30–2pm and 8–10pm. Métro: Sentier.

Macéo MODERN FRENCH With a light and airy dining room overlooking the entrance to the Palais Royal, Macéo is a beautiful setting for lunch or dinner. Chef Thierry Bourbonnais produces food that's consistently delicious, like scallops with parsnip purée, leeks, and dates; and seared venison with winter vegetables. This place also provides a vegetarian tasting menu—something that's almost unheard of in meat-obsessed Paris. Mark Williamson (who owns the nearby Willi's Wine Bar) has put together an outstanding wine list here. Make time after your meal for a stroll in the gardens of the Palais Royal (p. 99).

15 rue des Petits-Champs, 1er. ✆ **01-42-97-53-85.** www.maceorestaurant.com. Reservations recommended. Main courses 26€–30€; fixed-price dinners 33€, 38€, and 48€. Mon–Fri noon–2pm and 7:30–11pm; Sat 7:30–11pm. Métro: Pyramides.

Pinxo SOUTHWESTERN FRENCH/BISTRO This is the informal bistro that's associated with Alain Dutournier's much more expensive Carré des Feuillants restaurant. At Pinxo, diners are encouraged to use their hands (*pinxo* means "to pinch" in the chef's southwestern dialect) and to share with their tablemates. This is relatively easy because anything that appears on a plate is replicated three times, often with variations. The cuisine is robust and celebrates the prized Aquitaine breed of cow—you can have it grilled, sliced thin as carpaccio, or served with black truffles. Other delicious options include milk-fed lamb from the Pyrénées and a baby squid stuffed with pigs' feet, porcini mushrooms, and coco beans. The decor at Pinxo is minimal, with a wooden floor, white walls, and views that extend directly into an all-black open kitchen.

Can You Dine Badly in Paris?

The answer is an emphatic yes. Our mailbox fills with complaints from readers who've encountered haughty service and paid outrageous prices for swill. Often these complaints are about restaurants catering to tourists. Avoid them by following our suggestions or looking in nontouristy areas for new discoveries. If you ask Parisians for recommendations, specify that you're looking for restaurants where *they* would dine, not where they think you, as a tourist, would dine.

In the Plaza-Paris-Vendôme Hôtel, 9 rue d'Alger, 1er. ✆ **01-40-20-72-00.** www.pinxo.fr. Reservations recommended. Main courses 19€–28€; fixed-price lunch 21€. AE, MC, V. Daily 12:15–2:30pm and 7:15–11:30pm. Métro: Tuileries.

Inexpensive

Juveniles SCOTTISH/INTERNATIONAL A short stroll from the Louvre and the Opéra, Juveniles is the domain of Tim Johnston, a friendly Scotsman who offers hearty food and one of the most international wine lists in the city. Diners come here for both haggis and traditional French charcuterie, along with cooked sausages and buttery mashed potatoes. The cheeses are pungent, and the food pairs well with the full-bodied Australian and Spanish red wines that are stacked in wooden crates all around. The staff is bilingual and friendly.

47 rue de Richelieu, 1er. ✆ **01-42-97-46-49.** Reservations recommended. Main dishes 8€–18€; tapas 6€–13€. MC, V. Mon–Sat 7–11pm and Tues–Sat noon–3pm. Métro: Pyramide or Palais Royal.

Olio Pane Vino ITALIAN Francesco, the ruggedly handsome guy who runs this place, is the embodiment of Italian hospitality. He's pretty good in the kitchen, too, turning out new fresh pasta creations each day to satisfy devoted customers who come back regularly. Order a glass of Prosecco and an antipasti platter to start—it might include bresaola with Parmesan, grilled vegetables, or *vitello tonnato* (veal covered in a creamy tuna-flavored cream sauce)—and then choose from one of the several pasta dishes on offer every day. Good tiramisu and a fun crowd make this a hard place to dislike. The central location near Les Halles doesn't hurt, either.

44 rue Coquillière, 1er. ✆ **01-42-33-21-15.** Reservations recommended. Main courses 13€–17€. MC, V. Mon–Wed and Sat noon–2:45pm; Thurs–Fri noon–2:45pm and 7:45–10:30pm. Métro: Les Halles.

LE MARAIS, ILE ST LOUIS & ILE DE LA CITÉ (3E & 4E)

The Marais is packed with contemporary galleries and cutting-edge fashion boutiques, but our favorite restaurants in this neighborhood are utterly traditional, serving classic dishes from areas such as the Basque region (Au Bascou) or Brittany (the Breizh Cafe). Any stroll through the historic Jewish quarter around the rue des Rosiers requires a stop at L'As du Fallafel for the beloved (and messy) falafel sandwich.

Expensive

Benoit TRADITIONAL FRENCH There's something weighty about this historical monument; every mayor of Paris has dined here since the restaurant was founded in 1912. Today Benoit is owned by the Alain Ducasse group, and therefore prices are a bit higher than you'd normally expect for bistro fare, but the food is still delicious. Traditional crowd-pleasers include turbot roasted in the Basque style, filet of sole, and *tête de veau* (head cheese) with a *ravigote* sauce.

20 rue St-Martin, 4e. ✆ **01-42-72-25-76.** Reservations required. Main courses 24€–43€; fixed-price lunch 38€. AE, DC, MC, V. Daily noon–2pm and 7:30–10pm. Métro: Hôtel-de-Ville.

Moderate

Au Bascou BASQUE The succulent cuisine of France's "deep southwest" is the specialty here, where art objects, paintings, and tones of ocher celebrate the beauty of the region, and hanging clusters of pimentos add spice to the air. Try *pipérade basquaise* (a spicy omelet loaded with peppers and onions), pimentos stuffed with purée of codfish, and *axoa* (a stew of veal shoulder, peppers, and onions). Also noteworthy are the *soupions* (baby squid) sautéed with chorizo.

38 rue Réaumur, 3e. ✆ **01-42-72-69-25.** Reservations recommended. Main courses 17€; fixed-price lunch menu 19€. AE, DC, MC, V. Mon–Fri noon–2pm and 7:30–10:30pm. Métro: Arts-et-Métiers.

Jaja MODERN FRENCH/BISTRO Tucked into a charming courtyard in the southern Marais, this new bistro has quickly become a favorite among the foodies and style hounds of the neighborhood. It's a place to be seen, sure, but also a place to eat well for not much money, especially at lunch. Jaja's take on the hot dog (an artisanal sausage topped with pungent cheese) and the croque-monsieur (ham and cheese grilled sandwich) are playful and delicious. Stick to the basics here, and wash them down with wine from Jaja's very well-curated wine list.

3 rue Sainte-Croix-de-la-Bretonnerie, 4e. ✆ **01-42-74-71-52.** www.jaja-resto.com. Reservations recommended. Main courses 15€–24€; fixed-price lunch 16€. Mon–Sun noon–2:30pm and 8–11pm. Métro: Hotel de Ville.

L'Ambassade d'Auvergne AUVERGNAT/TRADITIONAL FRENCH When you enter this rustic tavern through a bar that's heavy with oak beams, hanging hams, and ceramic plates, you feel immediately like you've been transported to the Auvergne. This homey restaurant showcases the culinary bounty of France's most isolated region, which produces some outstanding charcuterie and cheese. For mains, try the pork braised with cabbage, turnips, and white beans; or grilled tripe sausages with mashed potatoes and Cantal cheese with garlic. Nonpork specialties include pan-fried duck liver with gingerbread, perch steamed in verbena tea, and roasted rack of lamb with wild mushrooms.

22 rue de Grenier St-Lazare, 3e. ✆ **01-42-72-31-22.** www.ambassade-auvergne.com. Reservations recommended. Main courses 17€–23€; fixed-price menus 38€, 55€, and 65€. AE, MC, V. Daily noon–2pm and 7:30–10:30pm. Métro: Rambuteau.

Le Pamphlet SOUTHWESTERN FRENCH/TRADITIONAL FRENCH Alain Carrère has been called the most under-rated chef in town, and his restaurant remains one of the only places you find nice linens, polite service, and classic cooking for less than 45€ a head. The menu changes regularly, but it might begin with rillettes of rabbit with crayfish, a thick cream of crabmeat soup garnished with baby peas, or a thin potato tart with marinated wild salmon and fine herbs. Mains might include fresh fish or properly cooked risotto.

38 rue Debelleyme, 3e. ✆ **01-42-72-39-24.** Reservations required, usually 48 hr. in advance for dinner. Fixed-price menu 35€–45€. MC, V. Tues–Fri noon–2:30pm and 7:30–11pm; Sun–Mon 7:30–11pm. Métro: Filles du Calvaire.

Inexpensive

Bob's Kitchen VEGETARIAN Join the mix of bobos, fashion types, and Anglos at a communal table at this playful "bio" (organic) cantine for a refreshing, organic, and vegetarian lunch. Giant salads with greens and grains, a satisfyingly spicy veggie burger, curries, and soups are featured on the revolving menu. Wash it down with a shot of wheatgrass or a freshly made smoothie. Go early on the weekends, to avoid the brunch crunch.

74 rue des Gravilliers, 3e. ✆ **09-52-55-11-66.** www.bobsjuicebar.com. Reservations not required. Lunch 3.50€–8.50€. Mon–Fri 8am–3pm; Sat–Sun 10am–4pm. Métro: Arts et Metiers.

Breizh Cafe ★ CRÊPERIE/CAFE This popular spot in the Marais serves crêpes like you've never had them before. Run by a Breton-Japanese couple, this warm and modern wood-paneled space that is decorated with funky Japanese art has friendly service and quality food. Start with oysters or go straight to a savory buckwheat *galette,* which is crisp and nutty and filled with high-quality organic ingredients, such as farm-fresh eggs, Bordier butter, and seasonal produce. Sip on one of the artisanal ciders, and save room for a sweet crêpe, drizzled with chocolate or salted butter caramel. Reservations highly recommended.

109 rue Vieille du Temple, 3e. ✆ **01-42-72-13-77.** www.breizhcafe.com. Reservations recommended. Main courses 5.50€–11€. MC, V. Wed–Sat noon–11pm; Sun noon–10pm. Métro: Filles du Calvaire.

L'As du Fallafel ★ FALAFEL/LIGHT FARE You can distinguish the "king of falafel" from other pretenders on the street by the presence of a long line snaking away from the dark green shopfront. Join the line (it moves fast) for a sandwich to go, or push through into one of two dining rooms and ask for a table. There are many options on the menu, including chicken Shawarma and lamb kabobs, but you want the falafel sandwich. Stuffed with light and crispy balls of falafel (fried chickpeas) and topped with grilled eggplant and fresh salad, this really is one of the most delicious cheap bites in town. With a plate of fries to share and an Israeli beer, you can escape for less than 10€ per person. Note that L'As is closed Friday night and all day Saturday, to honor the Jewish Sabbath.

34 rue des Rosiers, 4e. ✆ **01-48-87-63-60.** Reservations not accepted. Main courses 5€–16€. Sun–Thurs 11am–11:30pm; Fri 11am–5pm. Métro: St-Paul.

Tartes Kluger TRADITIONAL FRENCH/BAKERY Occupying a loftlike space in the northern Marais, Tartes Kluger is a wonderful place to stop for lunch in between visits to the surrounding galleries and fashion boutiques. Two long communal tables are littered with glossy magazines and populated mostly by chic young women. They come to dine on Catherine Kluger's savory tarts (similar to a quiche), which are made from organic ingredients. Tarts include flavors such as feta, zucchini, and Parmesan or duck confit with turnips and potatoes, and are served with a fresh green salad. Finish up with a sweet tart, such as mango coconut, almond plum, or dark chocolate mousse.

6 rue de Forez, 3e. ✆ **01-53-01-53-53.** www.tarteskluger.com. Reservations not required. Tarts 5€–7€; fixed-price lunch 12€; brunch 25€. MC, V. Mon–Thurs 11am–7pm; Fri–Sat 11am–8pm; Sun 11am–4pm. Métro: Temple.

CHAMPS-ELYSÉES & WESTERN PARIS (8E, 16E & 17E)

The posh avenues that radiate from the Champs Elysées are home to some of the most expensive and elegant dining in the city. If you're looking to splurge on a lavish gastronomic experience, this is the right neighborhood. Dress sharp and be ready to drop at least 100€ per head, unless you book a table in the moderate category.

Very Expensive

Guy Savoy ★★ TRADITIONAL FRENCH Guy Savoy is undoubtedly one of the top chefs in France, and his namesake restaurant caters to diners who want a three-star experience they can understand. You won't find molecular hijinx or a ton of unfamiliar ingredients here—just beautiful dishes composed of luxury ingredients and accented by what many feel is the best service in town. The signature starter is a bowl of truffled artichoke soup topped with shavings of aged Parmesan and served with a truffle buttered–brioche for dipping. The menu changes seasonally but might include baby peas with poached quail's egg, or Breton lobster served inside a cloud of (dry ice) vapor. Don't be shy when the outstanding cheese cart comes around, because the kind servers are happy to box up any desserts that you don't manage to finish.

18 rue Troyon, 17e. ✆ **01-43-80-40-61.** Fax 01-46-22-43-09. www.guysavoy.com. Reservations for dinner required 1 month in advance, 2–3 days in advance for lunch. Main courses 75€–230€; fixed-price lunch 110€; *menu dégustation* (tasting menu) 298€, 360€, and 480€. AE, DC, MC, V. Tues–Fri noon–2pm; Tues–Sat 7–10:30pm. Métro: Charles-de-Gaulle–Etoile or Ternes.

Lasserre TRADITIONAL FRENCH This elegant restaurant was a bistro before World War II and has since become a legend. The main salon stretches two stories high, with a mezzanine on each side. Tall, silk-draped arched windows frame the tables set with fine porcelain, gold-edged crystal glasses, and silver candelabras. The ceiling is painted with white clouds and a cerulean sky, but in good weather, the staff slides back the roof to reveal the real sky. The faces of Audrey Hepburn and Marlene Dietrich have given way to young British royals and statuesque models from Brazil. Chef Christophe Moret, who previously worked under Ducasse at the Plaza Athenée, is a master of taste and texture, and he's brought renewed life to this swank citadel. Try the langoustines in a ginger-lime spiked seafood bouillon; young pigeon stuffed with truffles and served with turnips in lapsang-souchong tea; or the Brittany lobster with chestnut, salsify, and pumpkin.

17 av. Franklin D. Roosevelt, 8e. ✆ **01-43-59-02-13.** www.restaurant-lasserre.com. Fax 01-45-63-72-23. Reservations required far in advance. Main courses 56€–95€; fixed-price lunch 75€, dinner 185€. AE, MC, V. Thurs–Fri noon–2pm; Mon–Sat 7:30–10pm. Closed Aug. Métro: Franklin-D-Roosevelt.

L'Astrance ★★★ MODERN FRENCH This small and charming spot is owned by two former employees (some say "disciples") of megachef Alain Passard, scion of L'Arpège; Christophe Rohat supervises the dining room, while Pascal Barbot is a true culinary force in the kitchen. The menu changes seasonally but might include an unusual form of "ravioli," wherein thin slices of avocado encase a filling of seasoned crabmeat, all of it accompanied by salted almonds and a splash of almond oil. Other delights to the palate include turbot flavored with lemon and ginger, or sautéed pigeon with potatoes au gratin. The signature dish is a galette of thinly sliced raw mushrooms and verjus-marinated foie gras with hazelnut oil and lemon confit.

4 rue Beethoven, 16e. ✆ **01-40-50-84-40.** Reservations required months in advance. Main courses 24€–38€; fixed-price lunch 70€–120€, dinner 120€–290€. AE, DC, MC, V. Tues–Fri 12:15–1:30pm and 8:15–9pm. Closed Aug. Métro: Passy.

Le Bristol ★★ MODERN FRENCH Inside one of the most opulent three-star dining rooms in Paris, in the Bristol Hotel (p. 198), the cuisine of Chef Eric Frechon continues to delight even the most experienced gastronomes. Frechon is particularly gifted with seafood, as evidenced by dishes like sole stuffed with mushrooms and cooked in mussel jus, wild turbot served with a ravioli of pork lard and clams, and sea bass with oyster tartare. Another excellent dish is veal sweetbreads cooked in a tobacco leaf and served with a purée of anise-scented Jerusalem artichoke. Superb service and a strong wine list complete what is widely regarded as one of the best fine dining experiences in Paris.

112 rue Faubourg St-Honoré, 8e. ✆ **01-53-43-43-40.** www.lebristolparis.com. Reservations required. Main courses 68€–240€; fixed-price lunch 85€, dinner 230€. AE, MC, V. Daily 12:30–2:30pm and 7–10:30pm. Métro: Miromesnil.

Le Cinq ★★ MODERN FRENCH Since it was established in 1928 in honor of the king of England, there has always been a world-class dining venue associated with the Hotel George V. Today the grand decor of this high-ceilinged room evokes the Grand Trianon at Versailles. Critics have been lavishing Chef Eric Briffard with praise, saying that he's a shoe-in to regain the restaurant's third Michelin star. Briffard trained under both Joël Robuchon and Alain Ducasse, and cooks with precision and expertise. The menu changes frequently, but you may start with something like abalone and razor clams with algae butter and fried watercress, and move on to a main dish of venison with smoky bacon and a chocolaty peppercorn sauce.

In the Four Seasons Hotel George V, 31 av. George V, 8e. ✆ **01-49-52-71-54.** www.fourseasons.com. Reservations recommended 4 weeks in advance for dinner, 1 week in advance for lunch. Main courses 78€–135€; fixed-price lunch 78€–160€, dinner 160€–230€. AE, DC, MC, V. Daily 12:30–2:30pm and 7–10:30pm. Métro: George V.

Pierre Gagnaire ★★★ MODERN FRENCH Veteran food writer Patricia Wells once said "there is no chef more creative than Pierre Gagnaire," and that sentiment has been echoed by countless other writers and fans. Of all the three-star chefs working in Paris today, Gagnaire is by far the most playful and experimental. He spent years collaborating with molecular gastronomy pioneer Hervé This to create boundary-pushing dishes with unusual textures and forms. The menu changes regularly, but recent meals have featured lobster hidden under brightly colored blankets of vegetable gel, and raw clams on a bed of sweet-and-sour pumpkin. One tip if you plan to order a la carte: Each *plat* is actually made up of four to five dishes, so ordering both a starter and a main dish may yield more food than you could possibly eat. Perhaps it's not a bad thing that the desserts here are not as strong as you'll find at other three-star restaurants.

6 rue Balzac, 8e. ✆ **01-58-36-12-50.** Fax 01-58-36-12-51. www.pierre-gagnaire.com. Reservations required. Main courses 65€–165€; fixed-price lunch 105€, dinner 265€. AE, DC, MC, V. Mon–Fri noon–1:30pm; Sun–Fri 7:30–10pm. Métro: George V.

Restaurant Plaza Athénée (Alain Ducasse) ★★ TRADITIONAL FRENCH This three-star restaurant bears the name of internationally renowned chef Alain Ducasse and serves as the flagship of his restaurant empire. The globe-trotting chef is rarely here himself, but he has left his kitchen in the capable hands of Christophe Saintagne. A special emphasis is placed on "rare and precious ingredients"; the chef whips up flavorful and very expensive combinations of caviar, lobster, crayfish, and truffles (both black and white). Dishes may include sea scallops with salsify and black truffles, duck liver "pot au feu," or sole meunière with Belgian endives. The wine list is superb, with selections deriving from the best vintages of France, Germany, Switzerland, Spain, California, and Italy. The dining room, designed by Patrick Jouin and featuring a jaw-dropping "deconstructed" chandelier, is among the most beautiful in Paris.

In the Hôtel Plaza Athénée, 25 av. Montaigne, 8e. ✆ **01-53-67-65-00.** Fax 01-53-67-65-12. www.alain-ducasse.com. Reservations required 4–6 weeks in advance. Main courses 70€–175€; fixed-price menu 260€–360€. AE, DC, MC, V. Thurs–Fri 12:45–2:15pm; Mon–Fri 7:45–10:15pm. Closed mid-July to Aug 25 and 10 days in late Dec. Métro: Alma-Marceau.

Expensive

La Maison Blanche PROVENÇAL/TRADITIONAL FRENCH Jacques and his twin brother, Lauren Pourcel, were two of the most famous chefs in the southerly province of Languedoc before heading north to Paris. The setting of this place would be the envy of any restaurant in the world: Positioned on the uppermost (seventh) floor of the Art Deco–style Theatre des Champs-Elysées, it has contemporary white and purple decor, sweeping views across the Seine, and two dining rooms. Clientele tends to be rich, non-French, and a bit pretentious, but with brilliant food and a sublime setting, who cares? The menu changes with the inspiration of the chefs and the seasons, but stellar examples include filet of John Dory in candied lemon vinaigrette with stuffed olives, and a rack of Aveyron lamb with cracked wheat and mushroom compote.

15 av. Montaigne, 8e. ✆ **01-47-23-55-99.** www.maison-blanche.fr. Reservations required. Main courses 38€–73€; fixed-price lunch 55€. AE, DC, MC, V. Mon–Fri noon–2pm; daily 8–11pm. Métro: Alma-Marceau.

L'Atelier Etoile de Joël Robuchon ★★ MODERN FRENCH Chef Joël Robuchon recently expanded his empire with the addition of this second Atelier restaurant inside the Drugstore Publicis complex. Diners flock to this new location, just off the Champs-Elysées, for its high-flying gastronomy served by way of small sharable plates in a fun, unstuffy setting. Critics have raved about dishes of foie gras in port jelly with Parmesan cream, sea urchin with wasabi mousse, and black cod in a bouillon of daikon radish and yuzu zest. As the original Left Bank

Chinatown, Paris Style

Although it's not widely known, Paris does, in fact, have a Chinatown. Quartier Chinois, a 5-minute walk from place d'Italie, centers on avenue d'Ivry in the 13th arrondissement. (To get there, take the Métro to Porte d'Ivry or place d'Italie in the 13e.) About 250,000 Asian people live in the Quartier Chinois, and a slew of Asian food stores, restaurants, and markets cater to the growing population. Tang Frères (44 av. d'Ivry, 13e; ✆ 01-44-06-61-86) is the largest Asian-food market in Europe—here you'll find rows of teas and spices from China. Spend a morning exploring here and stick around for lunch at Le Mer de Chine (159 des Rentiers, 13e; ✆ 01-45-84-22-49), serving the best Cantonese cuisine in Paris.

location, reservations are accepted here only for lunch or for extremely early and late dinner seatings; for everyone else, it's first come, first served.

133 av. des Champs Elysées, inside the Publicis complex, 8e. ✆ **01-47-23-75-75.** www.joel-robuchon.net. Reservations accepted for lunch at 11:30am and 2pm, and dinner at 6:30pm. Small plates 14€–65€; nine-course tasting menu 150€. AE. Métro: Etoile.

Les Tablettes ★ MODERN FRENCH/PROVENÇAL In a spot formerly occupied by La Table de Joël Robuchon, Chef Jean-Louis Nomicos recently opened Les Tablettes, a modern restaurant where the menu is presented on an iPad (*tablette,* in French). Nomicos's cooking has a modern edge but is firmly based in the classic French tradition (he was most recently at Lasserre, p. 144). Loyalty to his Provençal roots is evident in dishes like sea scallops with bouillabaisse jus, and filet of beef with black olives. The signature dish that has critics raving, however, is a "royale" of sea urchin and fennel. The 58€ lunch menu, which includes water, wine, and coffee, is a great introduction to fine dining in Paris.

16 av. Bugeaud, 16e. ✆ **01-56-28-16-16.** www.lestablettesjeanlouisnomicos.com. Reservations recommended. Main courses 65€–165€; fixed-price lunch 58€, dinner 80€. Daily noon–2:30pm and 7:30–10:15pm. Métro: Victor Hugo.

Moderate

Bar des Théâtres TRADITIONAL FRENCH Its local patrons in the 8th arrondissement have long called this bar/restaurant "The Temple of the God Steak Tartare." For those daring souls who still eat this blood-rare red meat specialty, this long-established restaurant is said to make the best dish. Even though it's situated in the most lethally priced district of Paris, over the years it has kept its prices reasonable. Across the street is the Théâtre des Champs-Elysées, and many of its performers, especially actors and musicians, make the bar their "local" while appearing here. The chef also specializes in a delectable *magret de canard* (breast of duckling), and you can even order caviar and foie gras, but those items would put this into a very expensive category. Better settle for the sauerkraut.

6 av. Montaigne, 8e. ✆ **01-47-23-34-63.** Reservations recommended. Main courses 13€–22€. AE, DC, MC, V. Daily noon–1am. Closed Aug. Métro: Alma Marceau.

Le Hide 🎁 TRADITIONAL FRENCH This bistro near the Eiffel Tower was included in a recent top 10 list by *Le Figaro* (a local newspaper) of "overlooked tables" whose high quality merits more media attention. The still-hidden restaurant takes its name from Chef Hide Kobayashi, who describes his food as French bistro cooking. The cuisine is certainly French, but a few recipes hint at his Japanese origins. Kobayashi perfected his craft in the kitchens of some of the world's greatest chefs, including Joël Robuchon. The menu changes regularly, and main courses, like fricassee of rabbit with mustard or sweetbreads in cream with truffles, all carry the same price tag. In a neighborhood full of expensive and unmemorable restaurants, Le Hide provides well-executed French bistro cuisine at an affordable price.

10 rue du General Lanrezac, 17e. ✆ **01-45-74-15-81.** www.lehide.fr. Reservations required. Main courses 16€; fixed-price menu 22€–29€. MC, V. Mon–Fri noon–3pm and Mon–Sat 7–10:30pm. Métro: Charles-de-Gaulle–Etoile.

OPÉRA & CANAL ST-MARTIN (9E & 10E)

This area is filled with good-value bistros and wine bars, and is populated by a younger, cooler set. Le Verré Vole and Vivant serve meals centered on natural wine, and Philou is a notable new, affordable bistro.

Expensive

Wally Le Saharien ALGERIAN Head to this dining room—lined with desert photos and tribal artifacts crafted from ceramics, wood, and weavings—for an insight into the spicy, slow-cooked cuisine that fueled the colonial expansion of France into North Africa. The prix-fixe dinner menu begins with a trio of starters: spicy soup, stuffed and grilled sardines, and a savory pastilla of pigeon in puff pastry. Next comes any of several kinds of couscous or a *méchouia* (slow-cooked tart). Merguez, the cumin-laden spicy sausage of the North African world, factors importantly into any meal, as do homemade pastries.

36 rue Rodier, 9e. ✆ **01-42-85-51-90.** Reservations recommended. Main courses 35€–57€; fixed-price lunch 21€, dinner 44€. MC, V. Tues–Sat noon–2pm and 7–10:30pm. Métro: Anvers.

Moderate

Casa Olympe PROVENÇAL/GREEK Serious foodies make their way to the 9th to feast on the wares of an original cook. Olympe Versini earned a Michelin star at the age of 29 and dazzled some of the most discerning palates of *tout* Paris in Montparnasse before opening this unassuming 32-seat dining room. Critics cite the earthiness of her cooking as evoked by her duck ravioli bathed in a jus reduction or her heavenly foie gras terrine brazenly studded with split vanilla beans. From head to hoof, she serves most parts of the pig—and does so with gusto. Her langoustine ravioli is modish but not excessively so, and her beef tenderloin with peppercorn sauce is one of the best versions of this time-honored dish.

48 rue St-Georges, 9e. ✆ **01-42-85-26-01.** www.casaolympe.com. Reservations required. Fixed-price menu 33€ and 43€. MC, V. Mon–Fri noon–2pm and 8–11pm. Métro: St-Georges.

Chez Michel ★★ BRETON Chef Thierry Breton prepares outstanding dishes from his native Brittany for diners that come from all over Paris and through the nearby Eurostar train hub at Gare du Nord. Breton recently ripped out a few tables and installed a massive oven in the dining room itself. He's now offering a four-course prix-fixe menu with homey options like braised lamb, a chicken pot pie that's studded with foie gras, and other slow-baked specialties. For dessert, try the copious rice pudding or the awe-inspiring Paris-Brest.

10 rue de Belzunce, 10e. ✆ **01-44-53-06-20.** Reservations required. Fixed-price menu 32€. MC, V. Tues–Fri 11:45am–3pm and Mon–Fri 6:45pm–midnight. Métro: Gare du Nord.

La Grille SEAFOOD/TRADITIONAL FRENCH This nine-table restaurant, with its historically classified 200-year-old wrought-iron grills, seems to be a holdover from another age. For at least a century after the French Revolution, fishermen from Dieppe used this place as a springboard for carousing and cabaret-watching after delivering their fish to Les Halles market. Since the late 1960s, the charming, outspoken M. and Mme. Cullérre have run this restaurant. The holy grail at La Grille is an entire turbot prepared tableside with an emulsified white butter sauce. Other recommended dishes are seafood terrine, *boeuf bourguignon* (braised beef in red wine sauce), and a brochette of scallops in white butter.

80 rue du Faubourg-Poissonnière, 10e. ✆ **01-47-70-89-73.** Reservations required. Main courses 17€–66€. AE, MC, V. Mon–Sat noon–2:15pm and 7:30–9:30pm. Métro: Poissonnière.

Le Pantruche ★ 🎁 TRADITIONAL FRENCH/BISTRO This new bistro near Pigalle received rave reviews when it opened in early 2011, impressing critics with the friendly atmosphere, affordable prices, and better-than-average bistro fare. Dishes include a rich celery root soup, tender glazed beef cheeks, oyster tartare, and a classic Grand Marnier soufflé. Although it's dressed like a humble neighborhood joint, Franck Baranger's cooking puts Le Pantruche in another league altogether.

3 rue Victor Massé, 9e. ✆ **01-48-78-55-60.** Reservations recommended. Fixed-price dinner 32€; fixed-price lunch 17€. Mon–Fri noon–2:30pm and 7:15–10:30pm. Métro: Pigalle.

Le Verre Volé ★★ WINE BAR/MODERN FRENCH This wine bar, along the charming Canal Saint-Martin, has been open for more than 10 years, but it recently added a second dining room annex and brought in some real culinary talent in the form of Chef Delphine Zampetti. The sharable plates of charcuterie and cheese are still on the menu, but more inventive fare like octopus carpaccio, smoked swordfish, and pâté en croute with pigeon and foie gras are also on offer. Select a bottle of wine from the shelves that line the walls, and enjoy it (for a nominal corkage fee) in this informal and fun setting. It may be a casual place, but the popularity of the Verre Volé requires that you reserve in advance.

67 rue de Lancry, 10e. ✆ **01-48-03-17-34.** www.leverrevole.fr. Reservations recommended. Main courses 25€–30€; plate of the day 16€. MC, V. Daily 12:30–2pm and 7:30–10:30pm. Métro: Jacques Bonsergent.

Philou ★★ TRADITIONAL FRENCH/BISTRO Residents of the Canal Saint-Martin neighborhood rejoiced when Philippe Damas opened this charming bistro in 2010. This reasonably priced bistro serves superior bistro cooking, like sautéed porcini mushrooms, roasted grouse stuffed with foie gras, steak with root vegetables, and a delicious Mont Blanc (chestnut) dessert. The wine list wins major points for including many affordable but respected small producers. Service, which usually includes a visit from the amiable chef, is attentive and kind, and the updated bistro interior is very cool. All in all, one of our favorite openings in recent years.

12 av. Richerand, 10e. ✆ **01-42-38-00-13.** Reservations recommended. Fixed-price lunch 15€, dinner 25€. Tues–Sat noon–2:30pm and 8–10:30pm. Métro: Jacques Bonsergent.

Vivant ★ TRADITIONAL FRENCH/ITALIAN Reflecting the mixed heritage of owner Pierre Jancou, this new restaurant in an up-and-coming part of the 10th arrondissement serves homey French and Italian fare. Jancou has a gift for uncovering and restoring beautiful historic spaces (his previous projects include Racines (in the 2nd) and La Crèmerie (in the 6th; p. 157), and Vivant—dressed up in colorful tiles that date from 1903—is no exception. As soon as you enter the door, you hear the swish-swish of a Berkel slicing machine—cured Italian ham is a requisite beginning to any meal here. Jancou is a major figure in the natural wine movement, and the wine list offers some of the most interesting, hard-to-find bottles in the country. Complete your visit with an espresso pulled from the most beautiful 1950s coffee machine you've ever seen.

43 rue des Petites Ecuries, 10e. ✆ **01-42-46-43-55.** Main courses 15€–25€. MC, V. Mon–Fri noon–2:30pm and 8–10:30pm. Métro: Château d'Eau.

Inexpensive

Chartier TRADITIONAL FRENCH/BRASSERIE Opened in 1896, this unpretentious *fin-de-siècle* restaurant is now an official historic monument featuring a whimsical mural with trees, a flowering staircase, and an early depiction of an airplane (it was painted in 1929 by an artist who traded his work for food). The menu follows brasserie-style traditions, including items you might not dare to eat—beef tartare, chitterling sausages, tongue of beef with spicy sauce—as well as some classic temptations, like duck confit. The waiter will steer you through such dishes as *choucroute* (sauerkraut), *pavé* (a thick slice of rump steak), and at least five kinds of fish. High gastronomy this isn't, but you can't beat Chartier for a cheerful night on the cheap.

7 rue du Faubourg Montmartre, 9e. ✆ **01-47-70-86-29.** www.restaurant-chartier.com. Main courses 9€–12€. AE, DC, MC, V. Daily 11:30am–10pm. Métro: Grands-Boulevards.

El Nopal MEXICAN There are only two stools at this tiny taqueria, but in good weather you can take your burritos, tacos, quesadillas, and freshly mashed guacamole to go, and find a spot along the nearby Canal Saint-Martin for your picnic. The tortillas are handmade, the salsa is hot, and the *aqua fresca* hits the spot on a sunny day. The grilled steak or chicken tacos are fantastic, but almost everything can be made vegetarian. Just ask: Claudia and Alejandro speak at least three languages.

3 rue Eugène Varlin, 10e. ✆ **07-86-39-63-46.** Reservations not required. Main courses 6.50€. Mon–Thurs 11:30am–3pm and 6–10pm; Fri 11:30am–3pm and 6–11pm; Sat 5–11pm; Sun 11:30am–9pm. Métro: Chateau Landon.

PIGALLE & MONTMARTRE (18E)

Montmartre today is home to a good number of reputable restaurants. However, if you're looking for a good meal, avoid the place du Tertre, where hopeful portrait artists sit waiting for tourists with their easels.

Moderate

Chéri Bibi TRADITIONAL FRENCH Decorated with flea-market finds and featuring an affordable menu of classic French fare, Cheri Bibi has become the unofficial cantine for the young and artsy Montmartre crowd. The chalkboard menu includes rustic dishes like *boudin noir* (blood sausage), *andouillette*, head cheese, and steak-frites. This might not be the place to bring a vegetarian friend. A crowd often gathers around the restaurant's zinc bar just to sip wine, sometimes spilling out onto the sidewalk that lies just below the eastern slope of the Sacré Coeur.

15 rue André del Sarte, 18e. ✆ **01-42-54-88-96.** Reservations recommended. Main courses 15€–30€; fixed-price lunch 10€–20€, dinner 19€–24€. Mon–Sat 8pm–midnight. Métro: Barbes-Rochechouart.

Le Bal Cafe ★ ENGLISH Brunch-loving Parisians have flipped for the traditional English breakfast that's served on the weekends here. Tucked inside a cultural center and photography museum near place de Clichy, Le Bal Cafe is more than just eggs and bacon (and scones, kippers, kedgeree, and pancakes). The chef, who used to work at London's renowned Saint John restaurant, prepares an impressive array of modern British cuisine, with dishes like guinea hen with endives, lamb shoulder with carrots, and head cheese with prunes. The sturdy fare is complemented by a well-chosen and affordable wine list. Kill time waiting for your reservation by browsing the adjoining bookstore or taking in some of the wonderful photography exhibits at the center.

6 impasse de la Défense, 18e. ✆ **01-44-70-75-51.** www.le-bal.fr. Reservations not required. Main courses 5.50€–21€; brunch 3.50€–12€. MC, V. Wed–Sat noon–2:30pm and 8–10:30pm; Sun brunch 11–4pm. Métro: Clichy.

RÉPUBLIQUE, BASTILLE & EASTERN PARIS (11E & 12E)

With a mix of working-class families, hipsters, and *bobos,* the area between République and Nation is diverse, young, and fun. It's also one of the best food neighborhoods in the city. The atmosphere in these places is casual and buzzing, the waiters tend to be handsome and unshaven, and the wine is mostly natural. Don't let the informality trick you into believing that you don't need to book in advance.

Expensive

La Gazzetta ★ MODERN FRENCH Within one of the prettiest bistro settings in all of Paris, and just down the street from the bustling outdoor food market at Aligre, Chef Petter Nilsson is serving some of the city's most avant-garde cuisine. The beautiful dining room, with its soft lighting, leafy palm trees, and dark polished wood, suggests a place serving classic bistro fare. But Nilsson's dishes are anything but traditional. A recent meal featured a soft poached egg floating in a broth of anise-scented cardoon that was spiked with briny mullet roe. That was followed by rare beef with purslane, and veal knuckle with sea urchin and verbena. For fans of experimental cooking, the seven-course dinner dégustation, at 50€, is one of the city's best values.

29 rue de Cotte, 12e. ✆ **01-43-47-47-05.** www.lagazzetta.fr. Reservations recommended. Fixed-price lunch 16€, dinner 38€ and 50€. Tues–Sat noon–2pm and 8–11pm. Métro: Ledru-Rollin.

Le Chateaubriand ★★★ MODERN FRENCH Chef Inaki Aizpitarte is the unofficial leader (and handsome poster boy) of France's neo-bistro movement, and Le Chateaubriand was recently rated the 11th best restaurant in the world by *Restaurant Magazine,* the highest ranking for any French restaurant. Aizpitarte's regularly changing 45€ prix-fixe menu offers no choices, but open-minded diners are rewarded with some of the most innovative flavor pairings in Paris. Not every single plate is a winner, but usually at least three of four dishes tend to be brilliant. If you don't have a reservation, you can try to score a seat at the second seating, which begins around 10pm.

129 av. Parmentier, 11e. ✆ **01-43-57-45-95.** Reservations required. Fixed-price dinner 45€. AE, DC, MC, V. Tues–Sat 8–11:30pm. Métro: Goncourt.

Moderate

Astier TRADITIONAL FRENCH/BISTRO Open since 1956, old-fashioned Astier has managed to avoid becoming a relic, thanks to thoughtful preparations of classics like wild boar terrine, rabbit rillettes, filet of sole, duck confit, roast chicken, and tarte tatin, plus a legendary cheese tray. With red-checked tablecloths, original woodwork, and cafe curtains, it's a picture-postcard version of a Paris bistro, without the surly waiters.

44 rue Jean-Pierre Timbaud, 11e. ✆ **01-43-57-16-35.** www.restaurant-astier.com. Reservations recommended. Fixed-price lunch 26€, dinner 30€. Open every day 12:45–2:15pm and 7:30–10:30pm. Métro: Parmentier.

L'Ebauchoir TRADITIONAL FRENCH Tucked into a neighborhood rarely visited by foreigners, this bistro features a 1950s decor that is so out it's in; with buffed aluminum trim and plaster-and-stucco walls tinted dark orange-yellow and bordeaux, the place might remind you of a factory canteen. Specialties include a pigeon roasted in bacon fat and red wine, filet of perch in chorizo cream, lamb chops with black olive tapenade, and a grandmotherly rice pudding cake.

43 rue de Citeaux, 12e. ✆ **01-43-42-49-31.** www.lebauchoir.com. Reservations recommended for dinner. Main courses 14€–25€; fixed-price lunch 14€, dinner 23€. AE, MC, V. Tues–Sat noon–2:30pm; Mon–Sat 8–11pm. Métro: Faidherbe-Chaligny.

Le Bistrot Paul Bert ★★ BISTRO/TRADITIONAL FRENCH Ask any local food writer to name their favorite classic bistros, and there's a very good chance that they will direct you here. The chalkboard menu is long and changes with the seasons, but a typical meal might begin with a plate of sunny-side-up eggs with truffle cream and shaved black truffle, followed by one of the city's best steak-frites (it's crowned with a glistening morsel of marrow), and ending with a generous slice of *tarte tatin* (apple tart) and its accompanying pitcher of thick crème fraîche. The decor is a jumble of wooden tables, cracked tile floors, flea market finds, and a polished zinc bar—exactly how you imagine a neighborhood bistro should be. The crowd is predominantly local, although the staff is used to dealing with the occasional food-minded traveler. The wine list features many unusual and affordable bottles from small wine producers.

18 rue Paul Bert, 11e. ✆ **01-43-72-24-01.** Reservations required. Fixed-price lunch 17€, dinner 34€. Tues–Sat noon–2pm and 7:30–11pm. Métro: Faidherbe-Chaligny.

Le Repaire de Cartouche TRADITIONAL FRENCH Chef Rudolph Paquin is a towering red-cheeked man whose facility with game cookery is known far and wide. A stop here during an autumn visit is almost obligatory for fans of fowl and other wild forest animals. Paquin is also known for his impressive *carte des vins* (wine list), and wine enthusiasts come regularly to eat well while making their way through the chef's treasure-studded cave. Service can at times be a little gruff, which is a shame because it detracts from the often spectacular food and wine.

8 bd. des Filles du Calvaire, 11e. ✆ **01-47-00-25-86.** Reservations recommended. Main courses 18€–29€. MC, V. Tues–Fri noon–2pm and 7:30–11pm; Sat noon–2pm and 7:30–11:30pm. Métro: St-Sebastian Froissart.

Mansouria MOROCCAN One of Paris's most charming Moroccan restaurants occupies a restored building midway between place de la Bastille and place de la Nation. The minimalist decor combines futuristic architecture with bare sand-colored walls, accented only with sets of antique doors and portals from the sub-Sahara. Look for eight different varieties of couscous and six different *tagines,* including versions with chicken, beef, lamb, and vegetables.

11 rue Faidherbe, 11e. ✆ **01-43-71-00-16.** www.mansouria.fr. Reservations recommended. Main courses 17€–26€; fixed-price dinner 28€–36€. AE, MC, V. Wed–Sat noon–2pm; Mon–Sat 7–11pm. Métro: Faidherbe-Chaligny.

Inexpensive

Al Taglio PIZZA This Paris pizzeria does as the Romans do; the pizza here is sold by weight from rectangular pies, with a variety of fresh toppings, including zucchini and ham, a straightforward margherita, and a potato and truffle cream that is not to be missed. The room is bright and minimally decorated, with communal tables and a well-sized terrace where you'll see locals, students, and families diving into the slabs, which are served on wooden boards with not enough napkins. A short Italian wine list and gelato from Pozzetto round out the offerings.

2 bis rue Neuve Popincourt, 11e. ✆ **01-43-38-12-00.** Reservations not accepted. Pizza sold by the slice, 11€–30€ per kilo. MC, V. Sun–Thurs noon–11pm; Fri–Sat noon–midnight. Métro: Parmentier.

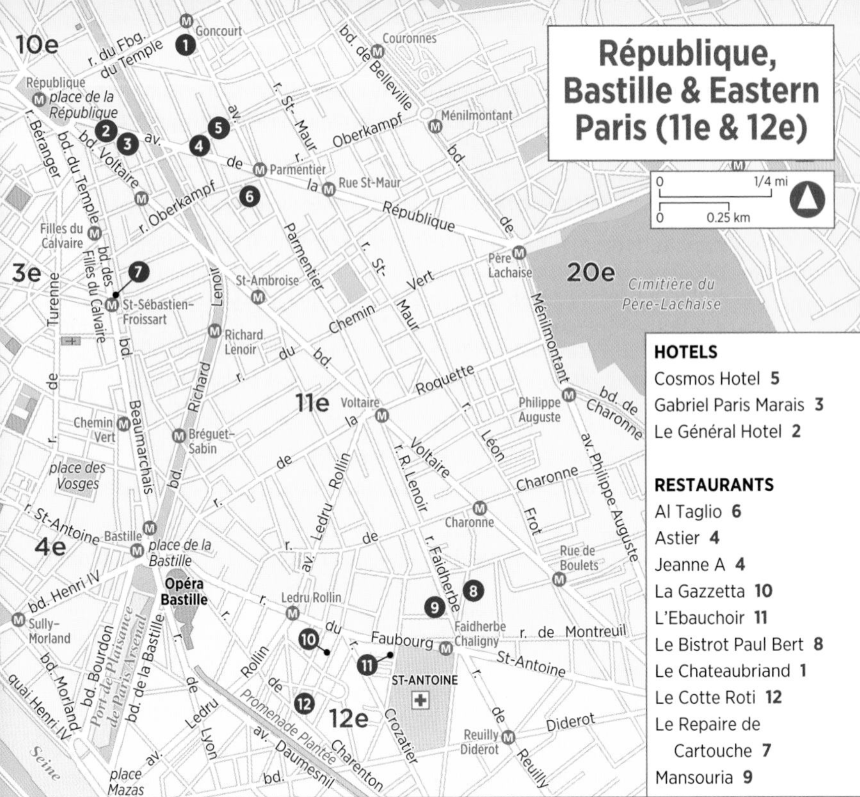

Jeanne A ★ TRADITIONAL FRENCH/WINE BAR This new restaurant/wine bar/takeaway shop represents a new trend in Paris, providing an informal place to eat and drink well for not a lot of money. Run by the renowned Astier restaurant next door (p. 151), Jeanne A turns out spit-roasted meats (Challans duck or crispy-skinned chicken) served with salad and a heaping portion of *potato gratin dauphinois*. These mains are book-ended by delicious charcuterie and an impressive selection of artisanal cheeses, and complemented by wines that are both easy drinking and easily priced. Order by the glass of the magnum (that's two bottles' worth), and take home what you're not able to drink.

42 rue Jean-Pierre Timbaud, 11e. ✆ **01-43-55-09-49.** Reservations recommended. Main courses 12€–17€; Thurs–Mon 10:30am–10:30pm. MC, V. Métro: Parmentier.

BELLEVILLE & NORTHEAST PARIS (19E AND 20E)

Between the two parks of Belleville and Buttes-Chaumont lie some of the city's most quirky, delightful, and wine-centered restaurants.

Moderate

Le Baratin ★ TRADITIONAL FRENCH/BISTRO Argentinian-born Chef Raquel Carena has created a neighborhood institution with Le Baratin, serving her imaginative bistro fare to both locals and foodies. Carena cooks from the heart, changing her menu regularly to reflect the seasons and her current inspiration. The value is most compelling at lunch, when one can enjoy a leisurely two-course affair for only 16€, to be followed by a stroll in the nearby Parc de Belleville. There is an impressive wine cave here, managed by Raquel's famously grumpy husband, Philippe Pinoteau.

3 rue Jouye-Rouve, 20e. ✆ **01-43-49-39-70.** Reservations recommended. Fixed-price lunch 16€, dinner 38€. MC, V. Tues–Fri noon–2:30pm and 8–11pm; Sat 8–11pm. Métro: Pyrénées.

Le Chapeau Melon ★ 🎁 MODERN FRENCH/WINE BAR Olivier Camus, the co-founder of Le Baratin (see above), has created one of our favorite wine bars in the city. Perched high up on the Belleville hill, not far from the beautiful Parc des Buttes-Chaumont, Le Chapeau Melon serves a no-choice four-course tasting menu for a remarkable 32€. Bright dishes like langoustine carpaccio or vitello tonnato are often followed by slow-braised beef or lamb, signaling your move from white to red wine. The shelves that line the walls are stocked with bottles from some of the most renowned producers of natural wine, and you can buy them to take away or drink them here for a modest corkage fee.

92 rue Rébeval, 19e. ✆ **01-42-02-68-60.** Reservations recommended. Prix-fixe dinner 32€. MC, V. Wed–Sun 8pm–1am. Métro: Pyrénées.

Rosa Bonheur 🎁 ☺ TAPAS This restaurant inside the Parc des Buttes Chaumont boasts a sprawling terrace and one of the best panoramic views in town. A huge crowd gathers to drink and nibble tapas outside, but the menu also features main dishes such as stuffed and grilled shrimp, lamb and carrot stew, and monkfish with sage sauce. The real reason to visit is for the relaxed and friendly ambiance, though—and the possibility of strolling through the city's largest and wildest park before or after your meal. That park, plus an indoor play area and kids' menu, makes Rosa Bonheur a great family option, too.

2 av. de la Cascade, 19e. ✆ **01-42-00-00-45.** www.rosabonheur.fr. Tapas from 5€–8€; fixed-price menus 29€ and 35€; children's menu 14€. MC, V. Reservations not accepted. Wed–Sun noon–midnight. Métro: Botzaris.

The Left Bank

LATIN QUARTER (5E)

This neighborhood, stretching south from the river near Notre-Dame to the market street of Mouffetard, is one of the oldest and best preserved in the city. The chefs who have set up shop here most recently are not content to merely perpetuate tradition. Some restaurants, like Le Pré Verre, are using foreign spices and techniques to update traditional French recipes, while others, like Dans Les Landes and Les Papilles, are trying to relax the rules and make restaurant dining a less formal experience.

Very Expensive

La Tour d'Argent ✋ TRADITIONAL FRENCH Although its reputation as the best in Paris has long been eclipsed, dining here remains an unsurpassed event—not because of the food, but because of its history and its view of the flying buttresses of Notre-Dame. A restaurant of some sort has stood on this site since 1582: Mme. de Sévigné referred to a cafe here in her letters, and Dumas used it in one of his novels. The fame of La Tour d'Argent spread during its ownership by Frédéric Delair, who in the 1890s started the practice of issuing certificates to diners who ordered *caneton* (pressed duckling). The birds are numbered: The first was served to Edward VII in 1890, and now the number has surpassed 1.2 million. For decades, the restaurant was owned by Claude Terrail, but after he died in 2006, his son, André, took over. A good part of the menu is devoted to duck, but the kitchen, of course, knows how to prepare other dishes. There are plenty of other places nearby where you can order food even better than that served here—and at only half the price.

15–17 quai de la Tournelle, 5e. ✆ **01-43-54-23-31.** Fax 01-44-07-12-04. www.latourdargent.com. Reservations required far in advance. Main courses 60€–75€; fixed-price lunch 65€. AE, DC, MC, V. Tues–Sat noon–1pm and 7:30–9pm. Métro: St-Michel or Pont Marie.

Moderate

Dans Les Landes ★ SOUTHWESTERN FRENCH This new spot from Julien Duboué (of Afaria, in the 15th arrondissement; p. 161) is named after the southwestern French region that inspired the chef's long list of tapas and small plates. Go for grilled quail breasts or the unmissable fried chipirions (small squid that are crisp, golden, and dusted with smoky pepper). Duboué's southwestern take on the spring roll—rice paper stuffed with foie gras, duck breast, and salad —is also compelling. Finish with an unusual dessert of warm anise-scented liquor with toasted crème anglaise.

119 bis rue Monge, 5e. ✆ **01-45-87-06-00.** Reservations recommended. Tapas 6€–15€; plat du jour 16€. MC, V. Mon–Sat noon–11pm. Métro: Censier-Daubenton.

Le Pré Verre ★ MODERN FRENCH/ASIAN FUSION Around the corner from the Sorbonne, in the heart of the Latin Quarter, sits a refreshing restaurant where you can get seriously good food at an affordable price. The Delacourcelle brothers are firmly based in the French tradition, but many of their chosen flavorings are inspired by Asia. In a welcoming, relaxed, and convivial atmosphere, tables are placed so close together that you're literally dining and rubbing elbows with your neighbors. For starters, dig into a well-flavored terrine—like the one made with layers of foie gras and mashed potatoes—or oysters marinated with ginger and poppy seeds or scallops with cinnamon. Main courses might include suckling pig with aromatic spices and crisp-cooked cabbage, or roasted codfish.

8 rue Thenard, 5e. ✆ **01-43-54-59-47.** www.lepreverre.com. Reservations required. Main courses 18€; fixed-price lunch 13€–29€, dinner 29€. MC, V. Tues–Sat noon–2pm and 7:30–10:30pm. Closed Aug. Métro: Maubert-Mutualité.

Les Papilles ★ TRADITIONAL FRENCH/BISTRO One of the most exciting additions to Paris's culinary scene is this bustling combination bistro/wine shop run by Bertrand Bluy. The fixed-price menu offers great value (four courses for 31€) but no choices. Dishes are comforting and often served family style from a cast-iron pot in the center of the table. Wine is available by the glass, but patrons are encouraged to choose a bottle from the nearby shelves and pay just a small corkage fee above retail price. This is a great place to try a good bottle because you're not paying for the usual restaurant markup on the wine.

30 rue Gay-Lussac, 5e. ✆ **01-43-25-20-79.** www.lespapillesparis.fr. Reservations not needed. Market menu 31€; fixed-price dinner 80€. AE, MC, V. Mon–Sat noon–3pm and 7–11pm. Métro: Luxembourg.

Inexpensive

Breakfast in America ☺ AMERICAN Connecticut-born Hollywood screenwriter Craig Carlson opened this replica of a down-home U.S.-based diner in 2003, building it with funds from members of the California film community who donated memorabilia from their films. Its self-proclaimed mission involves dispensing proper rib-sticking American breakfasts and diner food to Parisians. The setting replicates a 1950s-era railway car, replete with scarlet-and-black Naugahyde banquettes, faux windows with mirrored insets, and an unabashedly Americanized staff. Breakfast (heaping portions of the egg-and-waffle-and-bacon combinations, as well as omelets) is served throughout the day and evening. Also available are half a dozen variations of burgers, tacos, club sandwiches, and BLTs.

17 rue des Ecoles, 5e. ✆ **01-43-54-50-28.** Reservations not accepted. Breakfast platters 7€–11€; lunch and dinner platters and "blue-plate specials" 8€–12€; fixed-price Sun brunch 16€. MC, V. Daily 8:30am–10:30pm. Métro: Cardinal Lemoine or Jussieu.

ST-GERMAIN-DES-PRÉS & LUXEMBOURG (6E)

Our favorite restaurants in Saint-Germain are classic bistros, serving traditional French fare with a few modern accents. Le Comptoir du Relais and Ze Kitchen Galerie are run by notable chefs and require advance reservations, but the rest of our restaurant recommendations here are more casual and accept walk-ins or same-day bookings.

Expensive

Ze Kitchen Galerie ★ INTERNATIONAL/MODERN FRENCH Chef William Ledeuil trained in haute Parisian gastronomy under Chef Guy Savoy before brazenly opening up his own place right next door to Savoy's Les Bouquinistes. The setting is a colorful loft space in an antique building with an open showcase kitchen. Most of the paintings on display are for sale (the place doubles as an art gallery). Menu items, as with the paintings, change about every 5 weeks: Appetizers are subdivided into pastas, soups, and fish; and main courses are divided into meats and fish that are usually *à la plancha* (grilled). For starters, try the octopus with lemon grass and kalamenji. A pasta dish might feature homemade linguini with Bouchot mussels and dried fish eggs, and other mains of the moment include grilled mackerel with miso and Challans duck with mostarda and plums. Dessert could be the restaurant's "cappuccino of the month," a frothy dessert concoction with ingredients that change with the seasons.

4 rue des Grands-Augustins, 6e. ✆ **01-44-32-00-32.** www.zekitchengalerie.fr. Reservations recommended. Main courses 30€–35€; fixed-price lunch with wine 27€–39€, dinner 80€. AE, DC, MC, V. Mon–Fri noon–2:30pm; Mon–Sat 7–11pm. Métro: St-Michel or Pont-Neuf.

Moderate

Alcazar Restaurant TRADITIONAL FRENCH This high-tech place, funded by British restaurateur Sir Terence Conran, is Paris's sleekest brasserie. It features a red-and-white futuristic decor in a street-level dining room and a busy upstairs bar (La Mezzanine de l'Alcazar). The menu includes rack of veal sautéed with wild mushrooms, roasted rack of lamb with thyme, and shellfish and oysters from the waters of Brittany. The wines are as international and diverse as you'd expect.

62 rue Mazarine, 6e. ✆ **01-53-10-19-99.** www.alcazar.fr. Reservations recommended. Main courses 17€–33€; fixed-price lunch 20€–32€, dinner 43€; Sun brunch 32€. AE, DC, MC, V. Daily noon–2:30pm and 7pm–1am. Métro: Odéon.

La Ferrandaise TRADITIONAL FRENCH This restaurant near the Luxembourg Gardens is the place for anyone in search of meat-and-potatoes cooking done right. In celebration of a certain tasty cow from the Auvergne region, La Ferrandaise is decorated with photos of the namesake breed. Beef dishes are in the spotlight here, presented in various forms from steak to *pot au feu,* but heirloom pork and seasonal game offer some variety, too. Don't leave without trying the cheese plate—it includes many raw-milk varieties from central France that you won't find anywhere else.

8 rue de Vaugirard, 6e. ✆ **01-43-26-36-36.** www.laferrandaise.com. Reservations recommended. Fixed-price lunch 15€ and 32€, dinner 32€ and 44€. MC, V. Mon–Fri noon–3pm and 7–11:30pm; Sat 7–11:30pm. Métro: Odéon.

Le Comptoir du Relais ★★ TRADITIONAL FRENCH/BISTRO Le Comptoir is the domain of Yves Camdeborde, the pioneering chef who kicked off the "bistronomy" movement when he left a three-star kitchen to open his own bistro at the edge of the city. He sold La Régalade (which remains good) years ago to open this "counter," serving guests of the attached hotel and foodies who book dinner months and months in advance. Lunch is an easier table to score because reservations are not accepted—just line up before the doors open at noon and you're likely to get a table. All this fuss can be attributed to Camdeborde's well-executed bistro cuisine that reflects his southwestern roots and is made from high-quality ingredients. It's comfort food with a touch of luxury, and it will spoil you for all subsequent bistros.

9 carrefour de l'Odéon, 6e. ✆ **01-44-27-07-97.** Reservations required for dinner weeknights; reservations not accepted for lunch and weekends. Main courses 27€–35€ weekends; fixed-price dinner 50€ weeknights. MC, V. Daily noon–2am. Métro: Odéon.

Le Relais de l'Entrecôte ☺ TRADITIONAL FRENCH/STEAK For those who are tired of making decisions, Le Relais de l'Entrecote has only one question for you: "La cuisson?" Tell them how you like your steak done ("bien cuit" for medium well, "à point" for medium rare, or "saignant" for rare), and then sit back and let the show begin. You'll start with a fresh green salad and then proceed to the main event: a giant silver platter of steak, doused in an addictive "secret sauce" and served with crispy golden fries. That platter is refillable, by the way—you can expect to see your server return with a second helping once you've finished. Desserts, if you can find the strength, are classic and delicious, including profiteroles and crème brulée. The crowd that gathers inside the pretty-postcard dining room includes tourists, locals, and chefs; it also includes plenty of families with kids.

20 rue St-Benoît, 6e. ✆ **01-45-49-16-00.** www.relaisentrecote.fr. Reservations not required. Daily noon–3pm and 7–11pm. Fixed-price lunch and dinner 25€. MC, V. Métro: St-Germain-des- Prés.

Inexpensive

La Crèmerie 🎁 TRADITIONAL FRENCH New Yorker Serge Mathieu was an architect when he first entered Pierre Jancou's wine bar La Crèmerie. But after only one visit, he began pleading to take over this tiny 19th-century creamery. Jancou moved on to open two other restaurants, but La Crèmerie, with its ceiling of handpainted silk under glass, is still a destination for great wine and small plates. The charcuterie and cheeses are exceptional, but you can also dine on foie gras, oysters, delicately smoked tuna, and a spectacular chocolate fondant. Take note that La Crémerie doesn't serve any hot food except for grilled vegetables.

9 rue des Quatre Vents, 6e. ✆ **01-43-54-99-30.** www.lacremerie.fr. Reservations not needed. Meals from 20€. MC, V. Tues–Sat 10:30am–10pm; Sun 11am–2:30pm; Mon 2–8pm. Métro: Odéon.

La Crémerie Restaurant Polidor ☺ TRADITIONAL FRENCH/BISTRO Crémerie Polidor is the most traditional (and heavily touristed) bistro in the Odéon area, serving *cuisine familiale*. Its name dates from the early 1900s, when it specialized in frosted cream desserts, but the restaurant can trace its history to 1845. The Crémerie was André Gide's favorite, and Joyce, Hemingway, Valéry, Artaud, and Kerouac also dined here. Peer beyond the lace curtains and brass hat racks to see drawers where, in olden days, regular customers used to lock up their cloth napkins. Try the day's soup followed by kidneys in Madeira sauce, *boeuf bourguignon, confit de canard,* or *blanquette de veau.* For dessert, order a chocolate, raspberry, or lemon tart.

39 rue Monsieur-le-Prince, 6e. ✆ **01-43-26-95-34.** www.polidor.com. Main courses 11€–20€; fixed-price menu 22€–32€. No credit cards. Daily noon–2:30pm; Mon–Sat 7pm–12:30am; Sun 7–11pm. Métro: Odéon.

L'Avant Comptoir ★ WINE BAR/SOUTHWESTERN FRENCH This shoe-box-sized wine bar is just steps from the Odéon and run by bistro maestro Yves Camdeborde. Next door to his seminal restaurant Le Comptoir, this place sells crepes and sandwiches during the day and hors d'oeuvres to a raucous crowd at night. Basque and Béarnais-inspired nibbles include fried croquettes stuffed with from Eric Ospital's renowned Iberian ham, a filling cod brandade, oxtail canapés with horseradish cream, and chicken hearts grilled with garlic and parsley. Plates of charcuterie are meant to be eaten (and shared) with the crocks of Bordier butter and cornichons that line the counter. No more than a dozen people can crowd into this place at a time, and there are no chairs.

3 Carrefour de l'Odéon, 6e. No phone and no reservations accepted. Main courses 3€–7€. MC, V. Daily 9am–1am. Métro: Odéon.

EIFFEL TOWER & NEARBY (7E)

The chic 7th arrondissement is home to some of the city's most respected and innovative chefs, including Alain Passard (L'Arpège), Jean-François Piège, and Joël Robuchon. A table at one of their celebrated tables doesn't come cheap, but you'll never forget the experience. There are several *bistronomique* restaurants here, too, including Les Cocottes and Chez l'Ami Jean, where gastronomes can go for a memorable meal at more modest prices.

Very Expensive

Jean-François Piège ★ MODERN FRENCH This new restaurant, above the bustling brasserie Thoumieux, is the newest stage for chef Jean-François Piège. After leaving the palatial kitchens of Les Ambassadeurs, Piège partnered with Thierry Costes to open a hotel and restaurant complex near Invalides. His namesake restaurant is an intimate 20-seat showcase, which has been enthusiastically welcomed by the critics. Piège's cooking has been called witty and precise, and funky decor by India Mahdavi—featuring brightly colored sofas with black-and-white accents—has garnered almost as much attention as the food.

79 rue St-Dominique, 7e. ✆ **01-47-05-49-75.** www.jfpiege.com. Reservations recommended. Main courses 37€–69€. MC, V. Daily noon–midnight. Métro: La Tour Maubourg.

L'Arpège ★★★ MODERN FRENCH Chef Alain Passard made waves years ago when he decided to put vegetables, not meat, in the spotlight at his three-star restaurant, L'Arpège. Although meat is still featured on the menu, his dedication to carrots and turnips was something previously unseen. This pristine produce, which he raises on a farm near Le Mans, is often picked in the morning and served the same day in Paris. Uneaten food from his restaurant makes the return journey to become compost. Food politics aside, the flavors that Passard coaxes from these vegetables (often with the welcome addition of butter and cream) are truly remarkable. Service is discreet, as one expects at a restaurant frequented by diplomats and executives, and the dining room, with etched glass, burnished steel, and pearwood paneling, is beautiful, if a bit dated. Don't miss the cheese course, served on a giant polished plank of wood, or the *tarte aux pommes bouquet de roses* (a tart composed of apple ribbons rolled into tiny rosettes).

84 rue de Varenne, 7e. ✆ **01-47-05-09-06.** Fax 01-44-18-98-39. www.alain-passard.com. Reservations required 2 weeks in advance. Main courses 48€–180€; fixed-price lunch 125€, dinner 420€. AE, DC, MC, V. Mon–Fri 12:30–2:30pm and 8–10:30pm. Métro: Varenne.

Expensive

L'Atelier Saint-Germain de Joël Robuchon ★★ MODERN FRENCH World-renowned chef Joël Robuchon came out of a short-lived retirement in 2003 in order to open this ground-breaking culinary workshop on the left bank. He recently added the words "Saint-Germain" when he opened a second Atelier near the Arc de Triomphe (p. 146). This original location remains packed with gastronomes who want to eat well without the fuss implied by a three-star restaurant. Sitting informally upon high stools at a U-shaped bar, you can order the tasting menu or a series of sharable small plates like sea bream carpaccio, caviar with smoked eel and horseradish, grilled marrow bones, and the famous Robuchon mashed potatoes. Reservations are accepted for the extremely early and late seatings only (at 11:30am and 2pm for lunch, and 6:30pm for dinner); these spots are booked well in advance. Otherwise, it's first come, first served.

5 rue Montalembert, 7e. ✆ **01-42-22-56-56.** Reservations required. Main courses 27€–68€; dinner tasting menu 150€. AE, MC, V. Métro: Rue du Bac.

Les Ombres INTERNATIONAL/MODERN FRENCH Architect Jean Nouvel named this museum rooftop restaurant for the shadows cast by the Eiffel Tower looming nearby. You dine under a canopy of "metallic lace" inspired by the tower itself. A late dinner is practically a spectacle, as the tower twinkles for the first 10 minutes of every hour. Fortunately, the chefs don't just rely on the view. The head chef, Arno Busquet, trained under the great Joël Robuchon and creates eclectic dishes like foie gras with spiced mango chutney or guinea fowl stuffed with creole sausage and served with an apple cabbage purée. Other delights include a lamb shoulder with fennel, tarragon, and coco beans; and lard-roasted cod with clams and leeks.

Musée du Quai Branly, 27 quai Branly, 7e. ✆ **01-47-53-68-00.** www.lesombres-restaurant.com. Reservations required. Main courses 28€–43€; fixed-price lunch 38€, dinner 65€. MC, V. Daily noon–2:30pm and 7–10:30pm. Métro: Pont de l'Alma.

Moderate

Chez l'Ami Jean ★ BASQUE/SOUTHWESTERN FRENCH This restaurant was originally opened by a Basque nationalist in 1931, but it was Chef Stéphane Jego who really put the bistro on the map. Jego maintained the original decor (if one can call wood panels and sports memorabilia a decor) but turned L'Ami Jean into a destination for *cuisine bistronomique*—high-caliber cooking served in a homey neighborhood setting. Reserve in advance and arrive hungry because the Basque dishes served here are anything but light—even the fish dishes here are accented by foie gras and chorizo. However much you may have already eaten, say yes to the cheese plate with Basque brebis (sheep's milk cheese) and black cherry preserves, and finish with a heaping bowl of *riz au lait* (rice pudding).

27 rue Malar, 7e. ✆ **01-47-05-86-89.** www.amijean.eu. Reservations required. Main courses 20€–40€; fixed-price dinner 35€, 42€, and 60€. MC, V. Tues–Sat noon–2pm and 7pm–midnight. Closed Aug. Métro: Invalides.

La Fontaine de Mars BISTRO/SOUTHWESTERN FRENCH Visiting Americans began rushing to book tables shortly after President Obama and his first lady dined at this classic French bistro. One of the old-school bistros of Paris, it's been a venerable institution since it first opened in 1908, but it's never had this kind of business before. The cooking leans toward the southwest, with dishes like cassoulet, foie gras, and duck breast figuring prominently on the menu. Starters include *escargots* (snails) and *oeufs au Madiran* (eggs baked with red wine and bacon), and the dessert list is full of classics like *île flottante,* crème brûlée, and dark chocolate mousse.

129 rue Saint Dominique, 7e. ✆ **01-47-05-46-44.** www.fontainedemars.com. Reservations required. Main courses 17€–30€. AE, MC, V. Daily noon–3pm and 7:30–11pm. Mètro: Ecole Militaire.

Les Cocottes de Christian Constant ★ TRADITIONAL FRENCH Take a seat at the long counter or a high table for Christian Constant's updated comfort food—almost all of it served in cast-iron *cocottes* (casseroles). Begin with a plate of sliced Ospital ham; then move on to scallops with endive and orange butter sauce, potato-stuffed pigs' feet, or a seasonal vegetable cocotte. Desserts include an oversize waffle with chantilly cream and Constant's signature chocolate tarte. Reservations are not accepted, which can actually be an advantage in Paris.

135 rue St. Dominique, 7e. No phone. Reservations not accepted. Main courses 20€–35€. MC, V. Mon–Sat noon–4pm and 7–11pm. Métro: École Militaire.

Lily Wang CHINESE This audacious new Chinese restaurant is backed by the notorious Costes family and reflects the current obsession in Paris with anything Asian. The stylishly kitsch and dimly lit dining room features velvet curtains, glowing lanterns, and laquered furniture in shades of red and black. One French critic compared Lily's looks to that of a Chinese escort working in Saint-Tropez. Dishes like fried pork ravioli, pork tenderloin marinated in fish sauce, and smoky jian-jiao are undisputably delicious, but the steep prices put Lily's charms out of reach for budget-minded diners.

40 av. Duquesne, 7e. ✆ **01-53-86-09-09.** Reservations recommended. Main courses 23€–39€. MC, V. Daily noon–3pm and 7–11pm. Métro: Saint-François-Xavier.

Inexpensive

Eric Kayser ★★ BAKERY/LIGHT FARE If you're in the 7th arrondissement for breakfast or lunch, a good refueling stop is this bakery, bar, and cafe. Kayser's forte is bread making—he is known for the long fermentation of his dough. He's always coming up with new ideas for his breads, including one made with apricots and pistachios, and another with chorizo. This Alsatian baker offers many luxe breads and pastries, and breakfast is a delight here. At lunch you have a choice of 20 different combinations of *tartines* (open-faced sandwiches), and teatime features gourmet snacks such as a sweet tartine with meringue and chestnuts.

18 rue du Bac, 7e. ✆ **01-42-61-27-63.** MC, V. Tues–Sun 7am–8pm. Métro: Bac or Musée d'Orsay.

MONTPARNASSE & SOUTHERN PARIS (13E, 14E & 15E)

The largely residential 15th arrondissement has exploded with restaurants in recent years. Although this area may seem remote, those who venture here are rewarded with a large selection of fabulous and affordable bistros.

Moderate

Afaria ★ BASQUE/BISTRO Many visitors skip the 15th arrondissement, but Afaria is a good reason to go there. Chef Julien Duboué lures eaters from all over town to this dull corner of the 15th with his bright Basque cooking. The bistro, which he runs with his wife, Céline, includes a bar where locals nibble tapas at a communal table, and a dining room with wooden tables decked in cheerful red and white tablecloths. Traditional recipes are revisited with an imaginative twist, including spicy pumpkin soup with scallops and artichokes, terrine of venison with fig chutney, and rosy charred duck breast on the bone served over smoking grapevines.

15 rue Desnouettes, 15e. ✆ **01-48-56-15-36.** Reservations required. Main courses 17€–19€; fixed-price lunch 22€–26€. MC, V. Tues–Sat noon–2:30pm and Mon–Sat 7–11pm. Métro: Convention.

Jadis ★ TRADITIONAL FRENCH/BISTRO Shortly after it opened in 2009, the French daily newspaper *Le Figaro* hailed Jadis as "the best bistrot of the autumn." In the up-and-coming 15th arrondissement, Chef Guillaume Délage uses fresh seasonal ingredients to resuscitate "forgotten" bistro dishes from the past; start with an egg poached in red wine sauce, and move on to beef Stroganoff or stuffed breast of veal. Délage's nose-to-tail approach to cooking makes use of the whole animal, so don't be surprised to see cock's comb or kidney on the menu. Desserts, like the bittersweet chocolate soufflé and coffee-flavored *pot de crème,* are pure comfort.

208 rue de la Croix Nivert, 15e. ✆ **01-45-57-73-20.** www.bistrot-jadis.com. Reservations required. Main courses 21€; fixed-price lunch 25€, dinner 34€. AE, MC, V. Mon–Fri 12:15–2:30pm and 7:15–10:30pm. Métro: Convention.

La Cagouille SEAFOOD Don't expect to find meat at this temple of seafood—owner Gérard Allamandou refuses to feature it. Everything about La Cagouille is a testimonial to a modern version of the culinary arts of La Charente, the flat, sandy district on the Atlantic south of Bordeaux. In a trio of oak-sheathed dining rooms, you'll sample seafood prepared as naturally as possible, with no fancy sauces or elaborate techniques. Try such dishes as fried filet of sole, grilled John Dory, or warm cockles. Red mullet might be sautéed in oil or baked in rock salt. The name derives from the regional symbol of La Charente, the sea snail, whose preparation elevates its namesake to a fine culinary art. Look for a vast list of wines and cognacs.

10–12 place Constantin-Brancusi, 14e. ✆ **01-43-22-09-01.** www.la-cagouille.fr. Reservations recommended. Main courses 16€–60€; fixed-price lunch 23€–38€, dinner 38€. MC, V. Daily noon–2:30pm and 7:30–10:30pm. Métro: Gaité.

La Régalade ★★ TRADITIONAL FRENCH/BISTRO The *bistronomique* movement started here, under Chef Yves Camdeborde (who now works at Le Comptoir du Relais, p. 157), when people flocked to this sweet little bistro, with its cracked tile floors, polished wood, and burgundy banquettes, to taste excellent food in a low-key setting. Since then, the bistronomy movement has taken off, and Paris now boasts a large number of places that combine bistro ambience and prices with excellent culinary skills and ingredients. In 2006, Camdeborde sold La Regalade to Bruno Doucet, who has maintained the tradition and become a respected chef in his own right. Meals here begin with a help-yourself crock of homemade terrine, served with bread and cornichons, and continue with starters like foie gras in asparagus bouillon, or marinated sea scallops with basil and

Parmesan. Mains are comforting, like carmelized pork belly with mashed potatoes, or sea bream with carmelized fennel and black olives. Dessert could be a stinky Reblochon cheese or a molten Guanaja chocolate cake.

14 av. Jean-Moulin, 14e. ✆ **01-45-45-68-58.** Reservations recommended. Fixed-price menu 30€–50€. MC, V. Tues–Fri noon–2:30pm; Mon–Fri 7–11:30pm. Closed Aug. Métro: Alésia.

Le Casse Noix TRADITIONAL FRENCH/BISTRO After cooking for 6 years at La Régalade (p. 139), Chef Pierre-Olivier Lenormand opened his own *bistronomique*—a place that serves high-caliber food in a casual setting—in 2010. The decor is nostalgic, and the traditional French cooking is sincere and generous. Dishes like smoked chestnut soup, Iberian pork belly with choucroute of turnips, and the classic *petit salé aux lentilles* (lentils with smoky ham) are followed by crowd-pleasing desserts like *île flottante*. The wine list includes a good selection by the glass, as well as many moderately priced bottles. This is a good option if you're looking for an affordable, traditional bistro that's not yet overrun with tourists.

56 rue de la Fédération, 15e. ✆ **01-45-66-09-01.** www.le-cassenoix.fr. Reservations recommended. Fixed-price lunch 20€, dinner 32€. Mon–Fri noon–2:30pm and 7:30–10:30pm. Métro: Dupleix.

Inexpensive

Chez Gladines BASQUE Penny-pinchers climb the cobblestone hill of the Butte aux Cailles to dine on the large portions at this dive. The setting is laid back (actually, a bit grimy), but the food is hearty and authentic. This may not be the place to go to impress a date, but you can gorge on Gladines's giant "salads" (which consist of meat, cheese, garlic potatoes, and a few leaves of lettuce) and main dishes like *pipérade* (Basque-style scrambled eggs with vegetables), cassoulet, potatoes with ham and Cantal cheese, and our favorite, ham in a creamy sauce with layers of gratin-style potatoes that have been fried in duck fat. It's a bit leaden, but devotees love it.

30 rue des Cinq Diamants, 13e. ✆ **01-45-80-70-10.** Reservations not accepted. Main courses 8€–15€; fixed-price lunch 9€. No credit cards. Daily noon–3pm and 7pm–midnight; Sun noon–4pm. Closed 3 weeks in July. Métro: Corvisart or Place d'Italie.

Crêperie Josselin ★ ☺ CRÊPERIE Josselin is just one of maybe 20 crêperies that are concentrated around the "gateway to Brittany" Montparnasse train station, but it stands above all others as the city's best. The Breton manning the griddle knows exactly how to achieve the lacy, golden edges of a perfect galette, and he's not shy with the butter. Our idea of a perfect lunch (especially after too much wine the night before) is Josselin's *complete*—a buckwheat galette stuffed with egg, cheese, and ham—washed down with a ceramic bowl of hard cider and followed by a salted-butter caramel crêpe. Priced at just 10€, that set menu is one of the best deals in town. The easy prices, continuous service, and wide range of flavor combinations make this a great option for children as well.

67 rue du Montparnasse, 14e. ✆ **01-43-20-93-50.** Reservations not required. Crepes 5€–10€; fixed-price menu 10€. Tues–Sun noon–11pm. Métro: Montparnasse-Bienvenüe.

THE TOP CAFES

As surely everyone knows, the cafe is a Parisian institution. Parisians use cafes as combination club/tavern/snack bars, almost as extensions of their living rooms.

They're spots where you can sit alone and read your newspaper, do your homework or write your memoirs, and meet a friend or lover. Above all, cafes are for people-watching.

Now, just a few words on cafe etiquette: It's very likely that you won't receive a menu, because the options in most cafes are identical. The assumption, which is tricky for travelers, is that you already know what you want. Your bill will probably arrive with your order, but you're not expected to pay until you leave. *Service compris* means the tip is included in your bill, so it isn't necessary to tip extra. Still, tips are appreciated, but keep them small—a tip of small change (20 centimes–1€) is more than enough if you're having only a few drinks.

Cafe de Flore This is perhaps the most famous cafe in the world, still fighting to maintain a Left Bank aura despite hordes of visitors from around the world. Jean-Paul Sartre—the granddaddy of existentialism, a key figure in the Resistance, and a renowned cafe-sitter—often came here during World War II. Wearing a leather jacket and beret, he sat and wrote his trilogy, *Les Chemins de la Liberté* (The Roads to Freedom). Camus, Picasso, and Apollinaire also frequented the Flore. The cafe is still going strong, although the existentialists have been mostly replaced by tourists.

172 bd. St-Germain, 6e. ✆ **01-45-48-55-26.** www.cafe-de-flore.com. Cafe espresso 5€; glass of beer 9€; snacks from 16€; full meal 25€–45€. AE, DC, MC, V. Daily 7:30am–1:30am. Métro: St-Germain-des-Prés.

Cafe des Deux Moulins *Amélie* was a quirky low-budget film that was nominated for five Oscars and was seen by more than 25 million people around the world following its release in 2001. The film was set in Montmartre, and the cafe featured in the film has developed into a mandatory stopping-off place for the constantly arriving "cult of Amélie." In the film, Amélie worked as a waitress at the Cafe des Deux Moulins. The musty atmosphere, with its 1950s decor, mustard-colored ceiling, and lace curtains, has been preserved—even the wall lamps and unisex toilet. The menu has retained classic, hearty dishes like calf's liver, green frisée salad with bacon bits and warm goat cheese, and pigs' brains with lentils. They also serve hamburgers, with or without a fried egg on top.

15 rue Lepic, 18e. ✆ **01-42-54-90-50.** Main courses 11€–17€. MC, V. Daily 7am–2am. Métro: Blanche.

La Belle Hortense This is the most literary cafe in a neighborhood (the Marais) that's loaded with literary antecedents and references. It contains an erudite and accessible staff; an inventory of French literary classics, as well as modern tomes about art, psychoanalysis, history, and culture; and two high-ceilinged, 19th-century rooms with little changed since the days of Baudelaire and Balzac. Near the entrance is a zinc-covered bar that sells glasses of wine. If you're fluent in French, you might be interested in attending a reading, a book signing, or a lecture. Some kind of public gathering, conducted only in rapid, colloquial French, is scheduled every Tuesday, Wednesday, and Thursday, usually at 8pm.

31 rue Vieille du Temple, 4e. ✆ **01-48-04-71-60.** Glass of wine 4€–10€; coffee 1.50€; *plats du jour* 12€–24€. MC, V. Daily 5pm–2am. Métro: Hôtel-de-Ville or St-Paul.

La Coupole Born in 1927 and once a leading center of artistic life, La Coupole is now the epitome of the grand Paris brasserie in Montparnasse. Former patrons include Josephine Baker, Henry Miller, Dalí, Calder, Hemingway, Fitzgerald, and Picasso. At one of its sidewalk tables, you can sit and watch the passing scene and order a coffee or a cognac VSOP. The food is quite good, despite the fact that the dining room resembles an enormous rail-station waiting room. Try main dishes such as *sole meunière,* a very good rump steak, fresh oysters, shellfish, grilled lobster with flambéed whisky sauce, or curried lamb. The waiters are as rude and inattentive as ever, and the patrons would have it no other way.

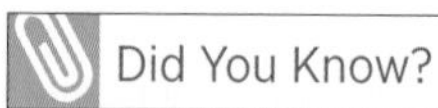

Did You Know?

You'll pay substantially less in a cafe if you stand at the counter rather than sit at a table, partly because there's no service charge, and partly because clients tend to linger at tables.

102 bd. du Montparnasse, 14e. ✆ **01-43-20-14-20.** www.flobrasseries.com. Breakfast buffet 14€–19€; main courses 20€–40€. AE, DC, MC, V. Daily 8am–1am (breakfast buffet Mon–Fri 8:30–10:30am). Métro: Vavin.

La Palette ★ The interior of this cafe, inhabited by amiably crotchety waiters, consists of tiled murals installed around 1935 advertising the virtues of a brand of liqueur that's no longer manufactured. If you happen to drop in during mealtime, you'll have a limited selection of salads and *croque monsieur* (toasted ham and cheese), plus one *plat du jour,* always priced at 15€, which may include roast beef, lamb stew, fish, or lamb. The real reason to come, though, is the terrace, a beautiful outdoor space not far from the river, where you can get a real sense of the village life in Saint-Germain.

43 rue de Seine, 6e. ✆ **01-43-26-68-15.** Sandwiches, omelets, and *plats du jour* 6€–15€. MC, V. Cafe and bar daily 8am–2am. Restaurant daily noon–3pm. Métro: Mabillon or St-Germain-des-Prés.

Le Procope To fans of French history, this is the holy grail of Parisian cafes. Opened in 1686, it occupies a three-story town house categorized as a historic monument. Inside, nine salons and dining rooms, each of whose 300-year-old walls have been carefully preserved and painted a deep red, are available for languorous afternoon coffee breaks or old-fashioned meals. Menu items include platters of shellfish, onion soup *au gratin, coq au vin* (chicken stewed in wine), duck breast in honey sauce, and grilled versions of various meats and fish. Every day between 3 and 6pm, the place makes itself available to sightseers who come to look but not necessarily eat and drink at the site that welcomed such movers and shakers as Diderot, Voltaire, George Sand, Victor Hugo, and Oscar Wilde. Especially charming is the ground-floor room outfitted like an antique library.

La Belle Hortense.

13 rue de l'Ancienne-Comédie, 6e. ✆ **01-40-46-79-00.** www.procope.com. Reservations

recommended. Coffee 3€; glass of beer 5€–7€; main courses 20€–29€. AE, DC, MC, V. Daily 10:30am–1am. Métro: Odéon.

SHOPPING IN PARIS

Paris is, of course, a world-famous shopping destination—and for good reason. The city marries art and commerce, elevating an afternoon of window shopping into a high-culture experience. Parisian department stores sell everything you could ever want under one elegant roof, while specialty shops hold countless small treasures, from jeweled safety pins to handcrafted candles. But true shoppers come to Paris for the fashion—Chanel, Dior, Hermès, and Louis Vuitton call Paris home. The city is also home to iconic cosmetic and perfume houses, as well as endless gourmet food shops. But you don't have to buy anything to appreciate shopping in Paris: Peer in the *vitrines* (window displays), keep an eye out for new trends, and return home with a whole new interepretation of style.

Business Hours

Usual shop hours are Monday to Saturday from 10am to 7pm, but hours vary, and Monday mornings don't run at full throttle. Small shops sometimes close for a 2-hour lunch break, and some do not open at all until after lunch on Monday. Thursday is the best day for late-night shopping, with stores open to 9 or 10pm.

Sunday shopping is limited to tourist areas and flea markets, though there's growing demand for full-scale Sunday hours. The department stores are now open on the 5 Sundays before Christmas. The **Carrousel du Louvre** (✆ **01-43-16-47-10**), a mall adjacent to the Louvre, is open daily 10am to 8pm. The tourist shops lining rue de Rivoli across from the Louvre are open on Sunday, as are the antiques villages, flea markets, and specialty events. Several food markets enliven the streets on Sunday. For our favorites, see the box "Food Markets" (p. 169). Most of the shops along the Champs-Elysées stay open on Sunday.

Note: Many independent stores close for about a month at the height of summer, from late July to late August.

Great Shopping Areas

LES HALLES, LOUVRE & PALAIS ROYAL (1E & 2E) Subterranean shopping mall **Les Halles** is a short stroll from major shopping strip **rue de Rivoli.** Both these destinations are a who's who of the major international fashion chains, including H&M, Zara, Sephora, Etam, and Gap. At another end of the 1st is the **Palais Royal,** just north of the Louvre and one of the city's best shopping secrets. The 18th-century arcade of boutiques flanks the garden of a former palace and includes some of the hottest names in fashion and accessories. It signals the beginning of the busy part of rue St-Honoré to the south, and to the north, behind the Palais Royal, is another sophisticated shopping destination, **place des Victoires,** which joins up with to the east with the **Etienne-Marcel** shopping neighborhood, known for its jeans and streetwear. In the 19th century, this area became known for its *passages,* glass-enclosed shopping streets—in fact, the world's first shopping malls. They were also the city's first buildings to be illuminated by gaslight. Many have been torn down, but a dozen or so have survived. The **Passage de Grand Cerf,** between 145 rue St-Denis and 10 rue Dussoubs (Métro:

Etienne-Marcel), is filled with everything from ethnic-chic to jewelry and accessory shops. **Place Vendôme** is the city's fine jewelery quartier, set like a crown around the mythical Ritz hotel.

LE MARAIS, ILE ST LOUIS & ILE DE LA CITÉ (3E & 4E) The Marais provides two dramatically different shopping experiences. The Lower Marais is concentrated around **rue des Francs-Bourgeois,** where you'll find a succession of charming fashion, accessories, and beauty stores. But don't be afraid to strike off into the neighborhood's medieval warren of twisting streets chockablock with up-to-the-minute fashions and trends. The Northern Marais, concentrated around **rue de Bretagne,** is a hotbed of independent French designers. Some in-the-know shoppers are skipping St-Germain and St-Honoré and heading here instead, for guaranteed cutting-edge fashion and design.

CHAMPS-ELYSÉES & WESTERN PARIS (8E, 16E & 17E) The heart of the international designer parade is here on the Right Bank. **Rue du Faubourg St-Honoré** was the traditional miracle mile until recent years, when many of the exclusive shops shunned it for the even more deluxe **avenue Montaigne** at the other end of the arrondissement. (It's a long but pleasant walk from one fashion strip to the other.) Paris's most glamorous shopping street is lined with almost unspeakably fancy shops, and in a few hours, you can see Dior, Chanel, and everything in between. The neighboring **Champs-Elysées** shouts "teen scene," with mass-market flagships. The zone around the **Madeleine** hosts many fine speciality food shops.

OPÉRA & CANAL ST-MARTIN (9E & 10E) These two neighborhoods offer wildly different shopping experiences. Opera has at its beating heart the "other" two department stores: Le Printemps and Les Galeries Lafayette, built in a row along **boulevard Haussmann.** Their commercial energy draws many other big names and chains. The sleepy Canal St-Martin offers boho local charm along little streets rue de Marseille, Beaurepaire, the Quais de Valmy, and Jemmapes.

PIGALLE & MONTMARTRE (18E) Villagey Montmartre's charming winding streets, fanning out around Abbesses, are filled with small speciality shops in design, fashion, jewelery, and food. Wander along rue des Abbesses, down rue Houdon, and up rue des Martyrs for a sweet afternoon of discovery.

RÉPUBLIQUE, BASTILLE & EASTERN PARIS (11E & 12E) Shopping in Bastille is concentrated on and around **rue du Faubourg St-Antoine,** which heads east from place de la Bastille and counts big names and chains; and winding streets nearby, like **rue de Charonne.** The **Viaduc des Arts,** running parallel to avenue Daumesnil, is a collection of about 30 specialist craft stores occupying a series of narrow vaulted niches under what used to be railroad tracks.

BELLEVILLE & NORTHEAST PARIS (19E & 20E) Not a shopping zone, tourists come here to soak up the cosmopolitan atmospheres and explore speciality shops from the city's various immigrant communities.

LATIN QUARTER (5E) More of a residential neighborhood, the Latin Quarter is better known for its major sights—the Luxembourg Gardens and the Sorbonne University—than for its shopping strips. However a host of specialist bookshops, which feed the local student population, remain a real draw.

Place Vendôme.

ST-GERMAIN-DES-PRÉS & LUXEMBOURG (6E) This area is the soul of the Left Bank and is one of the most famous shopping districts in Paris. In this traditionally more literary neighborhood, high-fashion addresses are gradually taking over the bookshops, and the Left Bank now rivals classic Right Bank shopping zones like St-Honoré and avenue Montaigne. Wander avenue St-Germain, rue St Sulpice, rue du Cherche Midi, rue du Vieux Colombier, rue Bonapart, and rue Jacob down to the Seine, or gourmet paradise rue de Buci, for some elevated shopping experiences.

EIFFEL TOWER & NEARBY (7E) The city's most glamorous department store, Le Bon Marché, sets the scene for another high-voltage shopping experience. If much of this neighborhood is more dedicated to culture and architecture than fashion, along its eastern edge, some of the glamour of adjacent St-Germain rubs off, and around **rue du Bac** and **rue du Grenelle,** you'll find all that wealth can buy.

MONTPARNASSE & SOUTHERN PARIS (13E, 14E & 15E) Located behind St-Germain, this neighborhood is dominated by both Paris's only skyscraper and France's tallest building, the Montparnasse tower, and a major railway station. Montparnasse might be worth a trip for the major shopping center located under the tower and the shopping along adjacent **rue de Rennes.**

Malls & Markets

Carrousel du Louvre ★★ If you want to combine an accessible location, a fun food court, boutiques, and plenty of museum gift shops with a touch of culture, don't miss the Carrousel. Always mobbed, this is one of the few venues allowed to open on Sunday. There's an Apple Store, Starbucks, Virgin Megastore, a branch of L'Occitane, and several other emporiums for conspicuous consumption. Check out Fragonard or Pylones for original souvenir ideas. Open daily 10am to 8pm. 99 rue de Rivoli, 1er. ✆ **01-43-16-47-10.** www.carrouseldulouvre.com. Métro: Palais-Royal or Musée du Louvre.

Le Forum des Halles This major transport and shopping hub draws suburban Parisians to its subterreanean labyrinth of chain stores, including H&M, Zara, and Muji, as well as a heated swimming pool and cinema multiplex. Open

Monday to Saturday 10am to 8pm. 101 Porte Berger, 1e. www.forumdeshalles.com. Métro: Châtelet-Les Halles.

Marché aux Fleurs ★ Artists and photographers love to capture the Flower Market on canvas or film. The stalls are ablaze with color, and each is a showcase of flowers, most of which escaped the perfume factories of Grasse on the French Riviera. The Flower Market is along the Seine, behind the Tribunal de Commerce. On Sunday, it becomes the poetic **Marché aux Oiseaux (Bird Market).** Open daily 8:30am to 4pm. Place Louis-Lépine, Ile de la Cité, 4e. No phone. Métro: Cité.

Marché aux Puces de la Porte de Vanves ★★ This weekend event sprawls along two streets and is the best flea market in Paris—dealers swear by it. There's little in terms of formal antiques and furniture. It's better for old linens, vintage Hermès scarves, toys, ephemera, costume jewelry, perfume bottles, and bad art. Asking prices tend to be high, as dealers prefer to sell to nontourists. On Sunday, there's a food market one street over. Open Tuesday to Sunday 7am to 5pm. Av. Georges-Lafenestre, 14e. No phone. Métro: Porte de Vanves.

Marché aux Puces St-Ouen de Clignancourt ★ Paris's most famous flea market is a grouping of more than a dozen flea markets—a complex of 2,500 to 3,000 open stalls and shops on the northern fringe of the city, selling everything from antiques to junk, from new to vintage clothing. The market begins with stalls of cheap clothing along avenue de la Porte de Clignancourt. As you proceed, various streets will tempt you. Hold on until you get to rue des Rosiers; then turn left. Vendors start bringing out their offerings around 9am Saturday to Monday and take them in around 6pm. Hours are a tad flexible, depending on weather and crowds. Monday is traditionally the best day for bargain seekers—attendance is smaller and merchants demonstrate a greater desire to sell.

First-timers always want to know two things: "Will I get any real bargains?" and "Will I get fleeced?" It's all relative. Obviously, dealers (who often have a prearrangement to have items held for them) have already skimmed the best buys. And it's true that the same merchandise displayed here will sell for less in the provinces. But for the visitor who has only a few days to spend in Paris—and only half a day for shopping—the flea market is worth the experience.

Dress casually and show your knowledge if you're a collector. Most dealers are serious and get into the spirit of things only if you speak French or make it clear you know what you're doing. The longer you stay, and the more you chat and show your respect for the goods, the more room you'll have for negotiating. Most of the markets have restroom facilities; some have central offices to arrange shipping. Cafes, pizza joints, and even a few restaurants

Marché aux Fleurs.

Food Markets

Outdoor markets are plentiful in Paris. Some of the better known are the **Marché Buci** (see below); the **rue Mouffetard market,** open Tuesday to Sunday from 9:30am to 1pm and Tuesday to Saturday from 4 to 7pm (6e; Métro: Monge or Censier-Daubenton); and the **rue Montorgueil market,** behind the St-Eustache church, open Monday to Saturday from 9am to 7pm (1er; Métro: Les Halles). The trendiest market is **Marché Biologique,** along boulevard Raspail, a tree-lined stretch lying between rue de Rennes and rue du Cherche-Midi, 6e. It's open Sunday from 8:30am to 6:30pm (Métro: Montparnasse).

are scattered around. ***Note:*** Beware of pickpockets and teenage troublemakers while shopping the market. Open Saturday to Monday 9am to 7pm. Av. de la Porte de Clignancourt, 18e. No phone. www.marchesauxpuces.fr. Métro: Porte de Clignancourt (turn left, cross bd. Ney, and then walk north on av. de la Porte Montmartre).

Marché Ave du Président Wilson ★ Even if you don't buy anything, this open-air market is worth a visit to browse. Parisians flock here to purchase some of the most exotic kinds of vegetables sold in the city, everything from purple cauliflower to sunflower-yellow zucchini. One stallmaster even sells a type of heirloom pea, Kelvedon Marvel, that was a particular favorite of Louis XIV, who preferred eating them to bedding one of his mistresses. A major attraction here is a vegetable stall operated by **Joel Thiebault** (✆ **01-44-24-05-77;** www.joelthiebault.fr), who supplies the city's best restaurants. Open Wednesday and Saturday from 7am to 2:30pm. On av. du Président Wilson btw. place d'Iena and rue Debrousse, 16e. No phone. Métro: Iena or Alma-Marceau.

Marché des Enfants Rouges ★ This charming covered fresh food market is the oldest in Paris and dates from 1777. In the heart of the rapidly gentrifying Northern Marais neighborhood, it's a lively place for stocking up on picnic supplies (organic, if you like), including wine and flowers, or for sitting down for a bite at any of the food stands. We recommend trad French dishes at L'Estaminet, in the western corner, or the excellent Japanese canteen Taeko, on the eastern edge. Open Monday to Saturday 8:30am to 7:30pm, Sunday 8:30am to 2pm. 39 rue de Bretagne, 3e. ✆ **01-42-72-28-12.** Métro: Filles du Calvaire.

Shopping A to Z

ANTIQUES, COLLECTIBLES & VINTAGE

Le Louvre des Antiquaires ★★ Across from the Louvre, this store offers three levels of fancy knickknacks and 250 vendors. It's just the place if you're looking for 30 matching Baccarat-crystal champagne flutes from the 1930s, a Sèvres tea service from 1773, or a signed Jean Fouquet gold-and-diamond pin. Too stuffy? No problem. There's always the 1940 Rolex with the aubergine crocodile strap. Prices can be high, but a few reasonable items are hidden here. What's more, the Sunday scene is fabulous, and there's a cafe with a variety of lunch menus. Pick up a free map and brochure of the premises from the information desk. Open Tuesday to Sunday 9am to 7pm. Closed Sunday. 2 place du Palais Royal, 1er. ✆ **01-42-97-27-27.** www.louvre-antiquaires.com. Métro: Palais-Royal.

Le Louvre des Antiquaires.

ART & CRAFTS

Artcurial ★ Set within minimalist showrooms in one of the most spectacular 19th-century mansions in Paris, this is one of the best outlets in Europe for contemporary art. Since it was established in 1975, it has represented megastars such as Man Ray and the "enfant terrible" of France's postwar intelligentsia, Jean Cocteau. Today the names of showcased artists read like a who's who of contemporary art: Arman, Sonia Delaunay, and Niki de Saint Phalle for painting and sculpture; Claude Lalanne for jewelry design; and Matta for contemporary carpets. Technically, it's an auction house, similar in some ways to Sotheby's and Christie's, albeit with a specialization in modern and contemporary art, vintage photographs by "important" photographers, antique books and posters, and sculpture. Despite an address that might be among the most expensive in the world (the intersection of av. Montaigne and Champs-Elysées), the place is more welcoming than its location implies. A great arts bookshop and a recently renovated daytime cafe provide respite from the shops. Open Monday to Friday 10am to 7pm, Saturday 11am to 7pm. 7 rond-point des Champs-Elysées, 8e. ✆ **01-42-99-20-20.** www.artcurial.com. Métro: Franklin-D-Roosevelt.

107Rivoli ★★ Inside the city's Decorative Arts Museum, itself located within a wing of the Louvre, this ground-floor store presents a wonderful selection of contemporary ceramic, textile, glass, and design pieces; a great collection of books dedicated to the arts, architecture, fashion, and design; and pieces inspired by the current exhibitions. Great for inspired souvenir shopping. Open Monday to Sunday 10am to 7pm. 107 rue de Rivoli, 1er. ✆ **01-42-60-64-94.** www.lesartsdecoratifs.fr. Métro: Palais-Royal.

Sennelier ★ This historic address has been keeping the city stocked in quality art supplies for over 120 years. Three generations of Senneliers have been

Village St-Paul

This isn't an antiques center, but a cluster of dealers in their own hole-in-the-wall hideout. It really hops on Sunday. Bring your camera, because inside the courtyards and alleys is a dream vision of hidden Paris: dealers in a courtyard selling furniture and other decorative items in French-country and formal styles. The rest of the street, stretching from the river to the Marais, is also lined with dealers. Open Thursday to Monday 11am to 7pm. 23–27 rue St-Paul, 4e. No phone. www.village-saint-paul.com. Métro: St-Paul.

providing students from the neighboring art school with the best pigments, from this rickety shop on the quais overlooking the river. Patron Gustave developed a range of oil pastels praised by artists such as Cézanne, Degas, and Chagall, and are still famous in the art world today. Open Monday 2 to 6:30pm, and Tuesday to Saturday 10am to 12:45pm and 2 to 6:30pm. Closed Sunday. 3 Quai Voltaire, 7e. ✆ **01-42-60-72-15.** www.magasinsennelier.com. Métro: St-Germain-des-Prés.

BOOKS

If you like rare and unusual books, there's not only the choice of the city's exceptional bookshops; you also have the choice to patronize one of the *bouquinistes,* the owners of those army-green stalls that line the Seine (on the Left Bank between the Quai de la Tournelle and Quai Malaquais, and on the Right Bank between Pont Marie and the Quai du Louvre). This is where tourists in the 1920s and 1930s went to buy "dirty" French postcards. You might get lucky and come across a treasured first edition that was banned for decades in the United States.

Galignani Sprawling over a large street level and supplemented by a mezzanine, this venerable wood-paneled bookstore has thrived since 1810. Enormous numbers of books are available in French and English, with a special emphasis on French classics, modern fiction, sociology, and fine arts. Looking for English-language translations of works by Balzac, Flaubert, Zola, or Colette? Most of them are here; if not, they can be ordered. Open Monday to Saturday 10am to 7pm. 224 rue de Rivoli, 1er. ✆ **01-42-60-76-07.** www.galignani.com. Métro: Tuileries.

Librairie le Bail-Weissert Paris is filled with rare book shops, but this one has the best collection of atlases, rare maps, and engravings from the 15th century to the 19th century. The shop sells original topographical maps of European and world cities, along with various regions of Europe. There's also a superb collection of architectural engravings. Open Monday to Friday 10am to 12:30pm and 2 to 7pm, Saturday 2 to 6pm. 13 rue Frederic Sauton, 5e. ✆ **01-43-29-72-59.** www.librairie-lebail.fr. Métro: Cluny–La Sorbonne.

7L ★ Monsieur Karl "Hyperactive" Lagerfeld is not only the creative director of Chanel, the city's emblematic fashion label, but also a prolific photographer and publisher. Here is where he sells his coffee-table tomes on art, architecture, photography, and design, in an elegant space designed by Japanese starchitect Tadao Ando. Open Tuesday to Saturday 10:30am to 6:45pm. Closed Sunday and Monday. 7 rue de Lille, 7e. ✆ **01-42-92-03-58.** www.galignani.com. Métro: St-Germain-des-Prés.

Shakespeare and Company.

Shakespeare and Company ★ The most famous bookstore on the Left Bank is Shakespeare and Company, on rue de l'Odéon, home to Sylvia Beach, "mother confessor to the Lost Generation." Hemingway, Fitzgerald, and Stein were frequent patrons, as was Anaïs Nin, the diarist noted for her description of struggling American artists in 1930s Paris. Nin helped her companion, Henry Miller, publish *Tropic of Cancer,* a book so notorious in its day that returning Americans who tried to slip copies through Customs often had them confiscated as pornography. (When times were hard, Nin herself wrote pornography for a dollar a page.) Long ago, the shop moved to rue de la Bûcherie, a musty old place where expatriates still swap books and literary gossip, and foreign students work in exchange for modest lodgings. Monday nights host free readings; check the program on their site. Open daily 10am to midnight. 37 rue de la Bûcherie, 5e. ✆ **01-43-25-40-93.** www.shakespeareandcompany.com. Métro: St-Michel.

Village Voice Bookshop This favorite of expatriate Yankees is on a side street in the heart of the best Left Bank shopping district, near some of the gathering places described in Gertrude Stein's *The Autobiography of Alice B. Toklas.* Opened in 1981, the shop is a hangout for literati. Its name has nothing to do with the New York weekly. Regular author events are publicized on their website. Open Monday 2 to 8pm, Tuesday to Saturday 10am to 8pm, Sunday 2 to 7pm. 6 rue Princesse, 6e. ✆ **01-46-33-36-47.** www.villagevoicebookshop.com. Métro: Mabillon.

CLOTHING & ACCESSORIES

Women's

Agnès b ★ Agnès b's take on relaxed but elegant urban fashion has been winning over Parisians, and the rest of the planet, since the 1970s. She produces collections for the whole family; note that you will find her menswear collections on sale around the corner at Agnès b. Homme (1 rue Dieu, 10e). There are numerous other addresses scattered around the city. Open Monday 1 to 7pm, Tuesday to Saturday 11am to 7pm. Closed Sunday. 13 rue de Marseille, 10e. ✆ **01-42-06-66-58.** www.agnesb.com. Métro: Jacques Bonsergent.

Balenciaga ★ Creative director Nicolas Ghesquière took control of this floundering but mythical *maison* in 1997 and immediately brought the label up-to-date. For the last 15 years, his visionary designs are splashed across the pages of fashion magazines from Milan to Tokyo. His taste for futuristic chic is visible right down to the boutique's decor, a kind of moonscape developed in collaboration with French artist Dominique Gonzalez-Foerster. Note that a dedicated menswear store is located on the Left Bank, at 5 rue de Varenne, 7e. Open Monday to Saturday 10am to 7pm. 10 av. George V, 8e. ✆ **01-47-20-21-11.** www.balenciaga.com. Métro: Alma-Marceau.

Bensimon ★ This popular French label designs wearable fashion and sportswear for the whole family. They also produce an important range of accessories, including a model of canvas sneaker that has become a cult summer classic. Just down the street, at no. 8 rue des Francs Bourgeois, you'll find Home Autour du Monde, stocking their ethnic-chic interiors range. Open Monday to Saturday 11am to 7pm, Sunday 1:30 to 7pm. 12 rue des Francs Bourgeois, 3e. ✆ **01-42-77-06-08.** www.bensimon.com. Métro: St-Paul.

Chanel ★ If you can't have the sun, the moon, and the stars, at least buy something with Coco Chanel's initials on it—either a serious fashion statement or something fun and playful. Karl Lagerfeld's designs come in all flavors and have added a subtle twist to Chanel's classicism. This mythical flagship store is located just behind the Ritz, where Mlle. Chanel once lived. Check out the beautiful staircase of the *maison* before you shop the two-floor boutique—where a series of rooms display Chanel fashion, accessories, beauty products, and perfumes, including store exclusives. It's well worth a peek. Open Monday to Saturday 10am to 7pm. 31 rue Cambon, 1er. ✆ **01-42-86-28-00.** www.chanel.fr. Métro: Tuileries or Madeleine.

French Trotters A temple to urban chic, this multibrand sells hot international fashion and accessories for men and women, from brands including local talents Jerome Dreyfuss, Le Mont Saint Michel, Les Prairies de Paris, Martin Margiela, Tila March, A.P.C., Comme des Garçons, and Maison Fabre. French Trotters also develops collaborations on limited-edition pieces available exclusively in store. Note that Little French Trotters, selling designer children's wear, is open next door, at no. 28. Open Monday 2:30 to 7:30pm and Tuesday to Saturday 11:30am to 7:30pm. 30 rue Charonne, 11e. ✆ **01-47-00-84-35.** http://frenchtrotters.fr. Métro: Bastille or Ledru-Rollin.

Givenchy ★ Hubert de Givenchy made fashion news around the world with his establishment, in 1962, of his couture company for elegant women. Today the Italian designer Riccardo Tisci continues the Givenchy traditions, but with a distinctly contemporary take on ready-to-wear. This flagship, overseen by Tisci himself in partnership with Brit architect Jamie Fobert, presents the brand's range of women's wear, menswear, and accessories, in an exquisite gallerylike space where five pods display the cutting-edge collections. Monday to Saturday 10am to 7pm. 28 rue Fbg-St-Honoré, 8e. ✆ **01-42-68-31-00.** Métro: Concorde. Other location: 3 av. George V, 8e. ✆ **01-44-31-50-00.** www.givenchy.fr. Métro: George V. Givenchy Hommes: 56 rue François Premier, 8e. ✆ **01-40-76-07-27.** Métro: Alma-Marceau.

Hermès ★★ France's single most important status item is a scarf or tie from Hermès. Patterns on these illustrious scarves, retailing from about 220€, have recently included the galaxies, Africa, the sea, the sun, and horse racing and breeding. But the choices don't stop there—this large flagship store sells beach towels and accessories, dinner plates, prêt-à-porter for men and women, the complete collection of Hermès fragrances (including their 24 Faubourg, named after this mythic address), and saddles; a package of postcards could be the least expensive item sold. Outside note the horseman on the roof with his scarf-flag flying. The illustrious brand opened a magnificent new flagship on the Left Bank in late 2010, which concentrates more on homewares than the fashion lines, and features a bookshop, florist, and pricey cafe (17 rue de Sèvres, 6e; ✆ **01-42-22-80-83;** Mon–Sat 10:30am–7pm). Open Monday to Saturday 10:30am to 7pm. 24 rue du Faubourg St-Honoré, 8e. ✆ **01-40-17-46-00.** www.hermes.com. Métro: Concorde.

Isabel Marant ★★ With her elegant but wearable urban fashion, Isabel Marant has defined this generation of Parisian chic, and now exports to all the fashion capitals. This is her original store, opened back in 1996 when the Bastille neighborhood was where it was at. Here you'll find her signature range of trendy looks, sporting ethnic and vintage details, for women and children. Open Monday to Saturday 10:30am to 7:30pm. Closed Sunday. Also at 47 rue Saintonge, 3e, and 1 rue Jacob, 6e. 16 rue Charonne, 11e. ✆ **01-49 29-71-55.** www.isabelmarant.tm.fr. Métro: Bastille or Ledru-Rollin.

JC de Castelbajac JC/DC's vivid, multicolored world borrows from different cultural universes, like pop music and pop art. He's been working on transforming the cultural zeitgist into fun and wearable fashion since the 1970s, and he's still on the map. Open Monday to Saturday 11am to 7pm. 10 rue Vauvilliers, 1er. ✆ **01-40-41-00-30.** http://jc-de-castelbajac.com. Métro: Châtelet-Les Halles. Other location: 61 rue des Saint Pères, 6e.

L'Eclaireur ★ You might feel like you're stepping into an art gallery when you enter this, the latest address in this prestige string of multibrand emporiums created by the pioneering Mme. and M. Hadida. Their beautifully curated selection of high-end fashion is available in five exceptional stores around Paris. This Marais address was designed by Belgian artist Arne Quinze and conceived of as a multimedia experience, or a sculpture, rather than a simple store. You'll discover women's wear from designers like Rick Owens, Maison Martin Margiela, Lanvin, Dries Van Noten, and Balenciaga. Open Monday to Saturday 11am to 7pm. 40 rue Sévigné, 3e. ✆ **01-48-87-10-22.** www.leclaireur.com. Métro: St-Paul.

Sonia Rykiel ★★ The emblematic Left Bank fashion designer has been dressing the independent and audacious women of St-Germain-des-Prés since 1968. Her modern wardrobe of elegant, comfortable clothes is instantly recognizable, with its bestselling signature range of stripey knits. So you'll find a piece of the city's fashion history in this glamourous two-floor flagship. Open Monday to Saturday 10:30am to 7pm. 175 bd. St-Germain, 6e. ✆ **01-45-49-13-10.** Métro: St-Germain-des-Prés. www.soniarykiel.fr/.

Uniqlo All of Paris, it seems, worships at this temple to the low-cost basic. The cult Japanese brand sells men's and women's fashions over three floors and is particularly revered for its range of well-cut jeans, plus its winter collection of cut-price cashmere and down jackets. The colorful, upbeat designs appeal to teenagers, but the premium range designed by Jil Sander targets their mothers. Open Monday to Saturday 10am to 8pm (Thurs to 9pm). 17 rue Scribe, 9e. ✆ **01-58-18-30-55.** www.uniqlo.com. Métro: Havre-Caumartin or Chausséé d'Antin-La Fayette.

Zadig & Voltaire This trendy young French brand is doing well at capturing a contemporary European rock 'n' roll spirit. This spacious first-floor store, overlooking place St-Sulpice in the heart of the Left Bank, displays its popular collections of up-to-date luxury: perfectly worn jeans, comfortable cashmeres, and biker boots for men, women, and children. Monday to Saturday 10:30am to 7:30pm. 1 rue du Vieux Colombier, 6e. ✆ **01-43-54-72-56.** www.zadig-et-voltaire.com. Métro: St-Sulpice.

Men's

Citadium A whole department store over four floors, dedicated to streetwear and "lifestyle" for men. You'll find all the usual international suspects, like North Face, Adidas, and Diesel, but also quality local brands, including Petit Bateau,

Veja, and The Kooples. The Beaubourg branch is smaller but more central. Monday to Saturday 10am to 8pm (Thurs to 9pm). 50/56 rue Caumartin, 9e. ✆ **01-55-31-74-00.** www.citadium.fr. Métro: Havre-Caumartin. Other location: 33 rue Quincampoix, 4e. ✆ 01-70-06-99-89. Métro: Rambuteau.

Sandro Homme If you want to resemble the nonchalently elegant gentlemen you see lounging around Parisian cafes, this newish Paris label is for you. You'll find flannel pants in tones of charcoal or chocolate, merino turtlenecks, leather biker jackets, woolen suits, and silk scarves. There's no compromising on style, but prices remain reasonable. The brand has a string of stores dedicated to their equally appealing women's wear. Open Monday to Saturday 10:30am to 7pm. 11 rue des Francs Bourgeois, 4e. ✆ **01-44-59-84-51.** www.sandro-paris.com. Métro: St-Paul.

Children's

Bonpoint ★★ 🎁 This stylish brand helps parents transform their darlings into models of well-tailored conspicuous consumption. Though you'll find some garments for real life, the primary allure of the place lies in its tailored, fairly traditional—and expensive—garments by the "Coco Chanel of the children's garment industry," Marie-France Cohen. This breathtaking flagship is located inside a mansion set around an interior courtyard and includes a secret cafe with chairs outside under the trees. Open Monday to Saturday 10am to 7pm. 6 rue de Tournon, 6e. ✆ **01-41-51-98-20.** www.bonpoint.com. Métro: Odéon.

Bonton ★ This fun three-floor emporium includes a candy counter, a hairdresser, a retro photo booth, toys, books, a basement knick-knack and interiors department, plus the French label's signature collections of trendy kidswear for boys and girls, from birth to age 16. It's hard to walk out empty handed. Open Monday to Saturday 10am to 7pm. 5 bd. des Filles du Calvaire, 3e. ✆ **01-42-72-34-69.** Métro: Filles du Calvaire.

Shoes & Accessories

Christian Louboutin A pair of iconic red-soled Louboutins are all any party girl needs on her pretty, pedicured feet. Sarah Jessica Parker from iconic '90s TV series *Sex & The City* helped launch the brand on the English-speaking market. The brand's deliciously romantic Paris flagship, inside a 19th-century covered market, is the perfect context to admire the iconic towering stillettos. Open Monday to Saturday 10:30am to 7pm. 19 rue Jean-Jacques Rousseau, 1er. ✆ **01-42-36-05-31.** www.christianlouboutin.com. Métro: Louvre-Rivoli.

Louis Vuitton ★★ Its luggage is among the most famous and prestigious in the world, a standard accessory aboard the first-class cabins of aircraft flying transatlantic and transpacific. Not content to cover the world's luggage with his initials, Vuitton also creates breathtaking ready-to-wear lines for men and women, as well as bags and other leather accessories, writing instruments, and travel products. The Champs-Elysées flagship rivals the Eiffel Tower as a destination for jetloads of flushed Japanese tourists, and note that the building includes a quality exhibition space (free entry) on its top floor (entry via rue Bassano). Open Monday to Saturday 10am to 8pm, Sunday 11am to 7pm. 101 av. Champs-Elysées, 8e. ✆ **01-53-57-52-00.** Métro: George V. Other location: 6 place St-Germain-des-Prés, 6e. ✆ 01-45-49-62-32. Métro: St-Germain-des-Prés.

Maison Fabre ★ Three generations of the Fabre family have taken this family-owned glove factory in rural France to the pages of the world's finest fashion magazines. The recently revamped brand sells an exquisite range of gloves, for day and night, summer or winter, that will wow your friends back home. Open Monday to Saturday 10am to 7pm. 128–129 Galerie de Valois, 1er. ✆ **01-42-60-75-88.** www.maisonfabre.com. Métro: Palais-Royal. Other location: 60 rue des Saints Pères, 7e.

Morabito This glamorous leather purveyor was originally established by an Italian entrepreneur on place Vendôme in 1905. In the 1990s, it was partially acquired by an organization in Tokyo. Today, from a site on the glamorous rue François-Premier, it sells chicer-than-thou handbags. Morabito also has suitcases—some of the best in Paris—for men and women. Open Monday to Saturday 10am to 7pm. 259 rue St-Honoré, 1er. ✆ **01-53-23-90-40.** www.morabitoparis.com. Métro: George V.

Vintage Clothing

Didier Ludot ★ Fashion historians salivate when they're confronted with an inventory of vintage haute couture. In this frenetically stylish shop, albeit at prices that rival what you'd expect to pay for a serious antique, you'll find a selection of gowns and dresses created between 1900 and 1980 for designing women who looked faaabulous at Maxim's, at chic cocktail parties on avenue Foch, in Deauville, or wherever. Open Monday to Saturday 11am to 7pm. 24 Galerie de Montpensier, in the arcades surrounding the courtyard of the Palais Royal, 1er. ✆ **01-42-96-06-56.** Métro: Palais-Royal.

Kiliwatch ★ The city's biggest central vintage emporium will not disappoint. Everything from secondhand jeans and military wear, to Hermès scarves and couture pieces. Plus, there's a great arts book corner. Open Tuesday to Sunday 11am to 7pm, Monday 2 to 7pm. 64 rue Tiquetonne, 1er. ✆ **01-42-21-17-37.** http://espacekiliwatch.fr. Métro: Etienne-Marcel.

Discount Stores

L'Habilleur ★ This northern Marais institution discounts last season's collections of quality brands, including the Italian knit brand Roberto Collina or French fashion for men and women by Paul and Joe and Antik Batik. The garments are impeccably maintained and most aesthetically organized by their color, creating a rainbow of fashion opportunities. Open Tuesday to Saturday 11am to 7pm. 44 rue du Poitou, 3e. ✆ **01-48-87-77-12.** Métro: St-Sébastien Froissart.

Réciproque ★ Forget about serious bargains: Celebrate what could be your only opportunity to own designer clothing of this caliber. Within a series of six storefronts side by side along the same avenue, you'll find used clothing from every major name in fashion, along with shoes, accessories, menswear, and wedding gifts. Everything has been worn, but some items were worn only on fashion runways or during photo shoots. Open Tuesday to Saturday 11am to 7pm. 89–101 rue de la Pompe, 16e. ✆ **01-47-04-30-28.** www.reciproque.fr. Métro: Pompe.

Lingerie

Chantal Thomass ★★ This lingerie brand sells luxury French underwear for the contemporary pin-up with a penchant for suspenders and corsets. The boutique is a delicious burlesque boudoir lined in pink satin. Open Monday to Saturday 10am to 7pm. 211 rue St-Honoré, 1er. ✆ **01-42-60-40-56.** www.chantalthomass.fr. Métro: Tuileries.

Erès ★★ Minimal collections of luxury French lingerie and swimwear flaunt a subtle palette and high prices. Open Monday to Saturday 10am to 7pm. 4 bis, rue du Cherche Midi, 6e. ✆ **01-45-44-95-54.** www.eresparis.com. Métro: St-Sulpice.

Princesse Tam-Tam ★ This quality lingerie chain sells quality seasonal collections of sexy French underthings for all ages and budgets. Open Monday to Saturday 10am to 7pm. 31 rue des Abbesses, 18e. ✆ **01-42-52-34-99.** www.princesse-tamtam.com. Métro: Abbesses.

Jewelry

Bijoux Blues ★ 🎁 This Marais boutique offers unique jewelry handmade in Paris with a variety of different materials, including Austrian and bohemian crystals, natural and semiprecious stones, pearls, coral, and mother-of-pearl. Custom requests are welcomed for individually designed pieces. The store offers jewelry at what the staff calls "atelier prices." Open Tuesday to Saturday noon to 7pm, Sunday 2 to 6pm. 30 rue St-Paul, 4e. ✆ **01-48-04-00-64.** www.bijouxblues.com. Métro: St-Paul.

Bijoux Burma If you can't afford any of the spectacular and expensive bijoux at the city's world-famous jewelers, come here to console yourself with some of the best fakes anywhere. This quality costume jewelry is the secret weapon of many a Parisian woman. Open Monday to Saturday 10:30am to 6:45pm. 50 rue François-Premier, 8e. ✆ **01-47-23-79-93.** www.bijouxburma.com. Métro: Franklin-D-Roosevelt.

Dior Joaillerie ★★ The talented Parisian aristocrat with the dreamy name Victoire de Castellane launched Dior's fine jewelery department in 1998. Colored stones, bright enamels, and flower and insect motifs are some of the signature elements. Discover her astounding, dreamy collections displayed within a jewel box of a store installed on the magnificent place Vendôme. Open Monday to Saturday 11am to 7pm. 8 place Vendôme, 1er. ✆ **01-42-96-30-84.** www.diorjoaillerie.com. Métro: Tuileries.

Van Cleef & Arpels ★ Years ago, Van Cleef's designers came up with an intricate technique that remains a vital part of its allure—the invisible setting, wherein a band of sparkling gemstones, each cut to interlock with its neighbor, creates an uninterrupted flash of brilliance. Come browse with the rich and famous. Open Monday to Friday 10:30am to 7pm, Saturday 11am to 7pm. 22 place Vendôme, 1er. ✆ **01-53-45-35-50.** www.vancleef-arpels.com. Métro: Opéra or Tuileries.

CONCEPT STORES

Antoine & Lili ★ This brighly colored string of stores sells the Paris brand's range of ethnic-inspired ready-to-wear for women, plus children's collections, toys, and homeware; there's even a bright canteen to refuel. The spirit of the cosmopolitan Canal St-Martin might reside here. Open daily 11am to 7pm. 95 quai de Valmy, 10e. ✆ **01-40-37-41-55.** www.antoineetlili.com. Métro: Jacques-Bonsergent.

Centre Commercial ★ An innovative new collaborative, fair-trade concept store set up by the ethical French trainer brand Véja. The elegant space includes fashion for men and women, from like-minded brands including Gloverall, Grenson, Saint-James, or Leaf, plus vintage furniture, second-hand bicycles, and a book and music corner. Open Monday 2 to 7:30pm, Tuesday to Saturday 11am to 7:30pm. 2 rue de Marseille, 10e. ✆ **01-42-02-26-08.** www.centrecommercial.cc. Métro: Jacques-Bonsergent.

Colette ★★ Named after the great French writer, Colette is a swank citadel for a la mode fashion. It buzzes with excitement, displaying fashions by some of the city's most promising young talent, including Marni and Lucien Pellat-Finet. This is for the sophisticated international shopper who'd never be caught dead shopping at Galeries Lafayette and the like. Not to be overlooked are home furnishings by such designers as Tom Dixon and even zany Japanese accessories. Even if you don't plan to buy anything, check out the basement "water bar," with its fresh quiches, salads, and cakes, plus three dozen brands of bottled water. Open Monday to Saturday 11am to 7pm. 213 rue St-Honoré, 1er. ✆ **01-55-35-33-90.** www.colette.fr. Métro: Tuileries or Pyramides.

Le 66 ★★ This appealing labyrinthine space in an arcade off the Champs-Elysées provides some welcome relief from the hysteria on the Avenue. Explore the considered selection of edgy fashion and accessories for men and women at your leisure. Discover the latest pieces from a giant list of local and international brands. There's also a satellite Kiiliwatch vintage bazaar on-site. Open Monday to Saturday 11am to 8pm, Sunday 2 to 8pm. 66 av. des Champs-Elysées, 8e. ✆ **01-53-53-33-80.** www.le66.fr. Métro: George V or Franklin D Roosevelt.

Merci ★★ This airy, three-floor style superstore brings together a tightly edited selection of furniture, homeware, fashion, and beauty. There's a delicious and healthy basement canteen overlooking a courtyard herb garden, and a literary cafe on ground level, too, for further refreshments. This imposing address in the Northern Marais exemplifies the neighborhood's panache and creativeness, and you don't know whom you might run into. Open Monday to Saturday 10am to 7pm. 11 bd. Beaumarchais, 3e. ✆ **01-42-77-00-33.** www.merci-merci.com. Métro: Saint Sébastien-Froissart.

Spree ★ 🎁 Possibly the best store in Montmartre, Spree has been doing its bohemian thing since 2000 and slowly drawing other quality retail to the vicinity. This relaxed concept store presents an inspiring fusion of fashion and accessories, art and design, with pieces from talents including Isabel Marant, Tsumori Chisato, Vanessa Bruno, Jerome Dreyfuss, Acne, and APC. The staff are warm and helpful. Open Monday to Saturday 11am to 7:30pm and Sunday 3 to 7pm. 16 rue Vieuville, 18e. ✆ **01-42-23-41-40.** www.spree.fr. Métro: Abbesses.

DEPARTMENT STORES

Le Bon Marché ★★ This Left Bank landmark has worked hard positioning itself as the most exclusive of the city's departments stores. Its modest size makes it manageable to wander the exclusive selection of fashion for men, women, and children; cosmetics and perfumes; furniture; upscale gifts; and housewares. It also boasts one of the largest food halls in Paris, which should not be missed. The magnificent displays of the finest fresh and preserved produce from France and around the world are a feast for the senses. Open Monday to Wednesday and Saturday 10am to 8pm, Thursday and Friday 10am to 9pm. 22–24 rue de Sèvres, 7e. ✆ **01-44-39-80-00.** www.lebonmarche.fr. Métro: Sèvres-Babylone.

Les Galeries Lafayette ★ Opened in 1896, with a lobby capped by an early-1900s stained-glass cupola classified as a historic monument, the family-owned Galeries Lafayette remains Paris's most popular department store. This store could provision a small city, with everything from perfume to fashion: thousands of racks of clothing for men, women, and children; and a staggering array of cosmetics, and perfumes. Also in the complex is **Lafayette Gourmet,** one of the fanciest grocery stores in Paris, selling culinary exotica at prices usually lower than those at Fauchon; **Lafayette Sports; Galeries Lafayette Mariage** (for wedding accessories); and two other general-merchandise stores, both known simply as **GL.** The floor above street level has a concentration of high-end, corners, including Cartier, Vuitton, and Prada. The **Galerie des Galeries,** is located within this luxury department and presents regular-quality contemporary art exhibitions (free entry). At the street-level **Welcome Desk,** a multilingual staff will tell you where to find various items in the store, where to get a taxi back to your hotel, and so on. Across the street, at 35 bd. Haussmann, you'll find the three-story **Lafayette Maison,** dedicated to the home. Open Monday to Wednesday and Friday to Saturday 9:30am to 8pm, Thursday 9:30am to 9pm. 40 bd. Haussmann, 9e. ✆ **01-42-82-34-56.** Métro: Chaussée d'Antin. RER: Auber.

Printemps ★ Take a look at the elaborate facade of this store for a reminder of the Gilded Age. Inside the merchandise is divided into housewares **(Printemps Maison),** women's fashion **(Printemps de la Mode),** and men's clothes **(Le Printemps de l'Homme).** Since a change in ownership in 2006, the Printemps has been chasing a serious luxury market and now displays a cavalcade of high-end brands across its selection. Inside is a magnificent stained-glass dome through which turquoise light cascades into the sixth-floor **La Brasserie Printemps,** where you can have a coffee or a full meal. Interpreters at the Welcome Service in Printemps de la Mode will help you find what you're looking for, claim your VAT refund, and so on. Printemps also has a tourist discount card, offering a flat 10% discount. Open Monday to Wednesday and Friday to Saturday 9:35am to 7pm, Thursday 9:35am to 9pm. 64 bd. Haussmann, 9e. ✆ **01-42-82-50-00.** www.printemps.com. Métro: Havre-Caumartin. RER: Auber or Haussmann–St-Lazare.

Printemps.

FOOD & DRINK

Bread & Cakes

Pierre Hermé ★★ The cult of the macaroon, a delicate sweet biscuit, has swept the city over the last few years, and M. Hermé is one of its pioneers. From this elegant Left Bank flagship, you will find Pierre Hermé's full range, with original flavor combinations like passionfruit and chocolate, or wasabi and strawberry. There is also an incomparable selection of cakes, to eat in, take away, or simply admire. Open daily 10am to 7pm. 72 rue Bonaparte, 6e. ✆ **01-43-54-47-77.** www.pierreherme.com. Métro: St-Sulpice.

Poilâne ★★ One of Paris's best-loved bakeries, Poilâne hasn't changed much since it opened in 1932. Come here to taste and admire the beautiful loaves of bread decorated with simple designs of leaves and flowers that'll make you yearn for an all-but-vanished Paris. Specialties include apple tarts, butter cookies, and a chewy sourdough loaf cooked in a wood-fired oven. Breads can be specially wrapped to stay fresh during your journey home. Cherche-Midi location open Monday to Saturday 7:15am to 8:15pm; Grenelle location open Tuesday to Sunday 7:15am to 8:15pm. 8 rue du Cherche-Midi, 6e. ✆ **01-45-48-42-59.** www.poilane.fr. Métro: St-Sulpice. Also 49 bd. de Grenelle, 15e. ✆ **01-45-79-11-49.** Métro: Dupleix.

Cheese

Barthélémy ★ This historic cheese monger has been supplying the country's presidents since 1973 with an incredible range of speciality produce from the four corners of France. Their speciality? The Mont d'Or, a creamy cow's milk cheese from the Alps available between September and May. Open Tuesday to Saturday 7:30am to 7:30pm. 51 rue de Grenelle, 7e. ✆ **01-42-22-82-24.** Métro: Rue du Bac.

Chocolate

Christian Constant ★★ Opened in 1970, Christian Constant sells some of Paris's most delectable chocolates by the kilo. Each is a blend of ingredients from Ecuador, Colombia, or Venezuela, usually mingled with scents of spices and flowers such as orange blossoms, jasmine, the Asian blossom ylang-ylang, and vetiver and *verveine* (herbs more usually used to brew tea). Open daily 9am to 8pm. 37 rue d'Assas, 6e. ✆ **01-53-63-15-15.** Métro: St-Placide.

Chocolates at Christian Constant.

Jean-Paul Hévin ★★ One of the great chocolatiers of Paris, its owner has mastered the fusion of *chocolat* with *fromage* (cheese, of course). Sweet, luscious chocolates with tart cheeses such as Camembert and Roquefort are infused to satisfy both the cheese fan and the chocolate lover's sweet tooth. Savory chocolates are also served without cheese. New offerings—unique in Paris—have caused this place to become one of the most acclaimed in Europe for chocolate devotees. Open Monday to Saturday 10am to 7:30pm. 231 rue St-Honoré, 1er. ✆ **01-55-35-35-96.** www.jphevin.com. Métro: Tuileries or Concorde.

Speciality

Fauchon ★★★ At place de la Madeleine stands one of the city's most popular sights—not the church, but Fauchon, a hyper-upscale mega-delicatessen that thrives within a city famous for its finicky eaters. In the original store (26 place de la Madeleine), you'll find a *pâtissier* and *boulangerie,* for breads and pastries; and a *traiteur,* for fresh produce, including cheeses, terrines, pâtés, caviar, and fruits. Prices are steep, but the inventories—at least, to serious foodies—are without equal. The selection of cakes is mouth-watering; try one of their famous *éclairs,* with new flavor combinations each season. Or try a *Paris-Brest,* a ring in the shape of a bicycle wheel that's loaded with pastry cream, almond praline, buttercream, and hazelnut paste capped with almonds. At the second, neighboring address (30 place de la Madeleine), you'll discover an *épicerie* (for jams, crackers, pastas, and exotic canned goods), a *confiserie* selling chocolates and confectionary, a wine cellar, plus two dining areas (a casual basement lunch space, La Cantine, and upstairs more formal dining at Le Cafe). At some of the counters, you'll indicate to attendants what you want from behind glass display cases and get an electronic ticket, which you'll carry to a *caisse* (cash register). Surrender your tickets, pay the tally, and then return to the counter to pick up your groceries. In other cases, you simply load up a shopping basket with whatever you want and pay for your purchases at a cash register, just as you would at any grocery store. Open Monday to Saturday 9:30am to 7pm. 26 and 30 place de la Madeleine, 8e. ✆ **01-70-39-38-00.** www.fauchon.com. Métro: Madeleine.

Hédiard ★★ Another fine Parisian delicatessan, this 1850 temple of *haute gastronomie* has a more traditional style than its neighbor, Fauchon. The old-fashioned decor is a series of red and black salons filled with towering displays of exotic and speciality foodstuffs, giving the store the look of an early-1900s spice emporium. Hédiard is rich in coffees, teas, jams, and spices. They have a quality wine cellar, and the fresh produce department displays exotic fruit and vegetables from the four corners of the planet, in all seasons. Open Monday to Friday 8am to 10pm, Saturday noon to 10:30pm. 21 place de la Madeleine, 8e. ✆ **01-43-12-88-99.** www.hediard.fr. Métro: Madeleine.

Maison de la Truffe ★ 🎁 Cramped and convivial, the layout of this shop was modeled after a Parisian's fantasy of an affable, cluttered, old-fashioned butcher shop in Lyon. It's *the* source for foie gras, caviar, black and white truffles, and other high-end foodstuffs. Artfully assembled gift baskets are a house specialty. One corner is devoted to a restaurant where many (but not all) of the dishes contain the costly items (especially truffles) sold in the shop. Examples include noodles or risottos with truffles, and caviar with all the fixings. The restaurant is open Monday to Saturday noon to 6pm and 7 to 11pm. The store is open Monday to Saturday 10am to 9pm. 19 place de la Madeleine, 8e. ✆ **01-42-65-53-22.** www.maison-de-la-truffe.com. Métro: Madeleine or Auber.

Wines

Lavinia ★ This is the largest wine-and-spirits store in Europe, opened in 2002 to great acclaim in Paris. Spread over three floors near place de la Madeleine, it stocks more than 3,000 brands of French wine and spirits, along with more than 2,000 brands from other parts of the world. A simple lunch-only restaurant is on-site, as is a tasting bar. Wine sales here are big business and reflective of France's marketing ideas that regard wine as a part of life. This is the only place in Paris where you can buy a good bottle of South Dakota wine. But who would want to? Open Monday to Saturday 10am to 8pm. 3–5 bd. de la Madeleine, 1er. ✆ **01-42-97-20-20.** www.lavinia.fr. Métro: Madeleine.

Nicolas 🎁 This is the flagship store of this chain of wine boutiques, and as such, its vintages are likely to be more esoteric and rare than what you'd find in any of the other 400 or so members of its chain. Scattered over three floors of a large space near La Madeleine are fairly priced bottles of mainstream wines such as Alsatian Gewürztraminers and Collioures from Languedoc-Roussillon. Nicolas also stocks some exceptionally rare vintages, such as a Romanée-Conti from Burgundy. Open Monday to Saturday 9:30am to 8pm. 31 place de la Madeleine, 8e. ✆ **01-42-68-00-16.** www.nicolas.com. Métro: Madeleine.

HOUSEWARES

Ceramics, China & Porcelain

Astier de Villatte ★★ This impossibly charming two-story shop sells a range of white, uncompromisingly hand-made earthenware in a range of designs inspired by 18th-century styles. There are regular special collections in collaboration with other Paris creatives, and a corner devoted to all sorts of other objects that appeal to the owners, from postcards to scented candles. Astier de Villatte also produces a cult range of annual diaries and notebooks. Everything they do radiates good taste. Open Monday to Saturday 11am to 7:30pm. 173 rue Saint-Honoré, 1e. ✆ **01-42-60-74-13.** www.astierdevillatte.com. Métro: Palais Royal.

Manufacture Nationale de Sèvres ★★ Once endorsed and promoted by the mistresses of Louis XV, Sèvres today manufactures only 4,000 to 5,000 pieces of porcelain every year. Of these, many are reserved as replacements for government and historical entities. Located a short walk beyond the western edge of Paris's 16th arrondissement, in the suburb of Sèvres, it maintains a sales outlet for the porcelain manufactured inside. Open Monday to Saturday 10am to 5pm. 2 place de la Manufacture, Sévres 92310. ✆ **01-46-29-22-10.** Métro: Pont-de-Sèvres. More centrally located is the organization's sales outlet near the Louvre, at 4 place André Malraux, 1er (✆ **01-47-03-40-20**). Métro: Palais-Royal. Tues–Fri 11am–7pm, Mon and Sat 2–7pm.

Crystal

Baccarat ★★ Opened in 1764, Baccarat is one of Europe's leading purveyors of full-lead crystal. They sell luxury jewelry pieces based on colored crystal and precious gems, tableware, glassware, and contemporary chandeliers and other crystal light fittings. The most prestigious outlet is on place de la Madeleine, but the exquisite Philippe Starck–designed **Maison Baccarat,** at 11 place des Etats-Unis, 16e, is larger and includes **Musée Baccarat**. Branches are open Tuesday to Friday 10am to 7pm, Monday and Saturday 10am to 7:30pm. 11 place de la Madeleine, 8e. ✆ **01-42-65-36-26.** www.baccarat.fr. Métro: Madeleine. Also 11 place des Etats-Unis, 16e. ✆ **01-40-22-11-22.** Métro: Boissière.

Lalique ★★ This historic crystal manufacturer is known for its smoky frosted-glass sculpture, Art Deco crystal, and unique perfume bottles. The shop sells a wide range of merchandise, including leather belts with Lalique buckles and silk scarves, designed to compete directly with those sold by Hermès. You'll also find a branch inside the Carrousel du Louvre. Open Monday to Saturday 10am to 7pm. 11 rue Royale, 8e. ✆ **01-53-05-12-81.** www.cristallalique.fr. Métro: Concorde.

Kitchenware

Dehillerin ★ Established in 1820, Dehillerin is Paris's most famous cookware shop, in the "kitchen corridor" around Les Halles, where all the city's chefs once came to stock up on provisions at the central fresh food market. The shop has a professional, though dusty, feel to it, but don't be intimidated. Equipped with the right tools from Dehillerin, you, too, can learn to cook like a master chef. Open Monday 9am to 12:30pm and 2 to 6pm, and Tuesday to Saturday 9am to 6pm. 18–20 rue Coquillière, 1er. ✆ **01-42-36-53-13.** www.e-dehillerin.fr. Métro: Les Halles.

MUSIC

FNAC ★ This is a large chain of music, books, and electronics stores known for their wide selection and discounted prices. Great for the traveler—you'll find everything you need for your computer, iPod, or digital camera. Most branches include digital photo development services. Stock up on French music in the CD department, or browse the book shelves. Seven branches are in Paris, with the largest being at 136 rue de Rennes, Montparnasse. Other locations include rue St-Lazare, avenue des Champs-Elysées, Forum des Halles, avenue des Ternes, and avenue d'Italie. All are open Monday to Saturday 10am to 7:30pm except Champs-Elysées, which is open daily noon to midnight. 136 rue de Rennes, 6e. ✆ **08-25-02-00-20.** www.fnac.com. Métro: St-Placide.

PERFUME & MAKEUP

Diptyque ★★ This contemporary Parisian perfumeur and candle maker has a truly unique range of aromatic plant-based scents, including best-sellers Philosykos, a woody blend of fig tree leaves and white cedar, and Tubéreuse, an intoxicating blend based on the heady Tuberose flower. They also do regular collaborations with Paris's creative icons on their cult-scented candles. Open Monday to Saturday 10am to 7pm. 34 bd. St-Germain, 5e. ✆ **01-43-26-77-44.** www.diptyqueparis.com. Métro: Maubert-Mutualité.

Francis Kurkdjian ★★ 🎁 One of the latest arrivals on the Paris perfume scene. Francis Kurdjian has created scents for many of the most famous French perfumers, including Guerlain, Dior, and Gaultier, over the past 15 years. In 2009, he set up his own *maison* and here sells an elegant range of scents for men and women, along with scents for the home and your laundry, and even perfumed bubble blowers for the kids. The store itself is a delightful homage to the city of Paris, inspired by its zinc roofs and gilded monuments. Open Monday to Saturday 11am to 7pm. 5 rue d'Alger, 1er. ✆ **01-42-60-07-07.** www.franciskurkdjian.com. Métro: Tuileries.

Salons du Palais Royal, Shiseido ★★ 🎁 Shiseido, the world's fourth-largest maker of cosmetics and skincare goods, has become more prominent, thanks to the efforts of its star parfumer, Serge Lutens. Here, in this special, secret place, it stocks more than 20 exclusive unisex fragrances created by Lutens, including one of its latest, Jeux de Peau, a nostalgic spicy scent inspired by the smell of hot bread and butter! Don't be afraid to wander in and ask for some scent strips. Open Monday to Saturday from 10am to 7pm. 142 Galerie de Valois, Palais Royal, 1er. ✆ **01-49-27-09-09.** www.salons-shiseido.com. Métro: Palais-Royal.

STATIONERY

Cassegrain ★ Nothing says elegance more than thick French stationery and notecards. Cassegrain, originally an engraver in 1919, offers beautifully engraved stationery, most often in traditional patterns, and business cards engraved to order. Several other items for the desk, many suitable for gifts, are for sale as well; there are even affordable pencils and pens, leather wallets, and small desk-top accessories. Open Monday to Saturday 10am to 7pm. 422 rue St-Honoré, 8e. ✆ **01-42-60-20-08.** www.cassegrain.fr. Métro: Concorde.

TOYS & GAMES

Au Nain Bleu ★ This is the largest, oldest, and most centrally located toy store in Paris. More important, it's probably the fanciest toy store in the world. But don't panic—in addition to the expensive stuff, you'll find rows of cheaper items on the first floor. Open Monday 2 to 7pm, Tuesday to Saturday 10am to 7pm. 5 bd. Malesherbes, 8e. ✆ **01-42-65-20-00.** www.aunainbleu.com. Métro: Concorde or Madeleine.

ENTERTAINMENT & NIGHTLIFE

It seems that every resident of this luminous city has a higher education in pleasure. Whatever your diversional whim, Paris can answer it. As its nickname indicates, Parisian streets and monuments remain illuminated all night. Restaurants won't expect you before 8pm, and by midnight, the party is just getting started at hundreds of bars or dance clubs throughout the city.

The Performing Arts

Home to a broad range of performing arts, Paris showcases everything from world-renowned opera and classical concerts to the edgy and contemporary theater. Recently, the Opéras Garnier and Bastille have been kicking out classics, such as Pucinni's *Madam Butterfly* and *Tosca,* as well as hosting performances from the Russian ballet powerhouse, the Bolshoi Theater. Look to companies like that of the Odéon Théâtre de L'Europe (www.theater-odean.fr) to push the theatrical envelope by showing a trilogy of Greek tragedies by Aeschylus during the same season as punk legend Patti Smith reading passages from her autobiography, *Just Kids.*

LISTINGS Announcements of shows, concerts, and operas are plastered on kiosks all over town. You'll find listings in the weekly ***Pariscope,*** an entertainment guide with an English-language section, or in ***L'Officiel des Spectacles,*** available at newstands. Also check out **en.parisinfo.com**, the city's official English-language tourism website. The "What's On" section has detailed listings for every concert and show in town. ***Note:*** Performances tend to start later in Paris than in London or New York—from 8 to 9pm—and Parisians tend to dine after the theater.

GETTING TICKETS Your best bet for cheap tickets is to try the theater's box office. Or head for discount agencies such as the **Kiosque-Théâtre,** 15 place de la Madeleine, 8e (✆ **01-42-65-35-64;** www.kiosquetheatre.com; Métro: Madeleine), offering leftover tickets for up to 50% off on the day of performance. Tickets for evening shows sell Tuesday to Saturday from 12:30 to 8pm; for matinees, Sunday 12:30 to 4pm. Other branches are in the basement of the Châtelet–Les Halles Métro station and in front of Gare Montparnasse.

Another option is **FNAC,** at 136 rue de Rennes, 6e (✆ **08-25-02-08-02;** Métro: St-Placide); or 1–7 rue Pierre-Lescot, in the Forum des Halles, 1er (✆ **08-25-02-00-20;** Métro: Châtelet–Les Halles). The Virgin Megastore type of chain sells music, movies, electronics, and books, as well as tickets for festivals, concerts, and the theater. You can pick up your stubs at the *billitterie* (ticket booth) of any of these locations or online at www.fnacspectacles.com. Another great website for reduced-price tickets is **www.ticketnet.fr**.

The easiest (and most expensive) way to get tickets is to ask your concierge to arrange for them. A service fee is added, but it's a lot easier if you don't want to waste precious hours in Paris trying to secure often hard-to-get tickets.

THEATER

Comédie-Française ★★ Those with even a modest understanding of French can delight in a sparkling production of Molière at this national theater, established to keep the classics alive and to promote important contemporary authors.

Nowhere else will you see the works of Molière and Racine so beautifully staged. The box office is open daily from 11am to 6pm, but the hall is dark from mid-July to early September. In 1993, a Left Bank annex was launched, the **Comédie Française-Théâtre du Vieux-Colombier,** 21 rue du Vieux-Colombier, 4e (✆**01-44-39-87-00**). Though its repertoire varies, it's known for presenting serious French dramas and the occasional foreign adaptation. Discounts are available if you reserve in advance. 2 rue de Richelieu, 1er. ✆ **08-25-10-16-80.** www.comedie-francaise.fr. Tickets 12€–38€. Métro: Palais-Royal or Musée du Louvre.

Cité de la Musique.

OPERA, DANCE & CLASSICAL CONCERTS

Cité de la Musique ★★★ This testimony to the power of music has been the most widely applauded, the least criticized, and the most innovative of the late François Mitterrand's *grands projets*. At the city's northeastern edge in what used to be a run-down neighborhood, this $120-million stone-and-glass structure incorporates a network of concert halls, a library and research center for the study of all kinds of music, and a museum. The complex hosts a rich variety of concerts, from Renaissance music through 19th- and 20th-century works, including jazz and traditional music from nations around the world. There's a beautiful cafe on-site if you'd like to sip some wine on the sunny terrace before your concert. 221 av. Jean-Jaurès, 19e. ✆ **01-44-84-45-00,** or 01-44-84-44-84 for tickets. www.cite-musique.fr. Tickets 20€–39€ for 4:30 and 8pm concerts. Métro: Porte de Pantin.

Opéra Bastille ★★ This controversial building—it has been called a "beached whale"—was designed by Canadian architect Carlos Ott, with curtains by Japanese designer Issey Miyake. Since the house's grand opening in July 1989, the Opéra National de Paris has presented works such as Mozart's *Marriage of Figaro* and Tchaikovsky's *Queen of Spades*. The main hall is the largest of any French opera house, with 2,700 seats, but the building also contains two smaller concert halls, including an intimate 250-seat room that usually hosts chamber music. Both traditional opera performances and symphony concerts are presented here, along with both classical and modern dance. 2 place de la Bastille, 4e. ✆ **08-92-89-90-90** or 01-40-01-17-89. www.operadeparis.fr. Tickets 5€–180€ opera, 8€–89€ dance. Métro: Bastille.

Opéra Garnier ★★★ Once the haunt of the Phantom, this is the premier venue for dance and once again for opera. Charles Garnier designed this 1875 rococo wonder during the heyday of the French Empire; the facade is adorned with marble and sculpture, including *The Dance*, by Carpeaux. Following a year-long renovation, during which the Chagall ceiling was cleaned and air-conditioning

Opéra Garnier.

was added, the facade gleams as it did for Napoleon III. You can see the original gilded busts and statues, the rainbow-hued marble pillars, and the mosaics. The Opéra Garnier combines ballet and opera, and provides one of the most elegant evenings you can spend in the City of Light. Because of the competition from the Opéra Bastille, the Garnier has made great efforts to present more up-to-date dance works such as choreography by Twyla Tharp, Agnes de Mille, and George Balanchine. The box office is open Monday to Saturday from 10:30am to 6:30pm. Place de l'Opéra, 9e. ✆ **08-92-89-90-90** or 01-40-01-18-50. www.operadeparis.fr. Tickets 5€–180€ opera, 8€–89€ dance. Métro: Opéra.

Salle Pleyel ★★★ New York has Carnegie Hall, but for years, Paris lacked a permanent home for its orchestra—that is, until several years ago, when the restored Salle Pleyel opened once again. Built in 1927 by the piano-making firm of the same name, Pleyel was the world's first concert hall designed exclusively for a symphony orchestra. Ravel, Debussy, and Stravinsky performed their masterpieces here, only to see the hall devastated by fire less than 9 months after its opening. The original sound quality was never recovered because of an economic downturn. In 1998, real estate developer Hubert Martigny purchased the concert hall and pumped $38 million into it, restoring the Art Deco spirit of the original and also refining the acoustics it once knew. Nearly 500 seats were removed to make those that remained more comfortable. The Orchestre Philarmonique de Radio France and the Orchestre de Paris now have a home worthy of their reputations, and the London Symphony Orchestra makes Pleyel its venue in Paris. The box office is open Monday to Friday 10am to 6pm. 252 rue du Faubourg-St-Honoré, 8e. ✆ **01-42-56-13-13.** www.sallepleyel.fr. Tickets 10€–160€. Métro: Miromesnil.

The Bar Scene

WINE BARS

The wine bar, or *bar à vin,* is a welcome departure from sitting down at a typical cafe or restaurant. They are often calm and warmly decorated, and many have regional themes. All offer diverse wines and serve simple small dishes—perfect for those in the mood for a snack with their drinks without the commitment to a full-blown meal.

5e Cru ★ 🎁 This shabby-chic spot, with only three pine tables as well as a few barrels converted to dining stations, is a favorite of the *le Fooding* crowd. Jean de Toalier serves more wines than just "fifth-growth" bottles, as the name suggests, and boasts that he's got "every *terroir* of France covered" in his kitchen, offering more than 150 different French wines. You can get a simple menu, or daily small plate special, for 14€; a glass of wine for 3€ to 8€; and a bottle for as low as 8€, rarely more than 60€. Open Tuesday to Friday 10:30am to midnight, Saturday 3pm to 1am. 7 rue du Cardinal Lemoine, 5e. ✆ **01-40-46-86-34.** www.5ecru.com. Métro: Jussieu.

Les Bacchantes This place prides itself on offering more wines by the glass—at least 90—than any other wine bar in Paris; prices range from 3€ to 6€. It also does a hefty restaurant trade in well-prepared *cuisine bourgeoise,* with main courses costing 14€ to 28€. Its cozy, rustic setting—with paneling, and chalkboards announcing vintages and platters—attracts theatergoers before and after performances at the Théâtre Olympia. Wines are mainly from France, but you'll also find examples from neighboring countries. Open Monday to Saturday noon to 3pm and 7pm to 2am. 21 rue Caumartin, 9e. ✆ **01-42-65-25-35.** Métro: Havre-Caumartin.

Willi's Wine Bar ★★ In an odd way, this is the granddaddy of the modern wine bar, opened in 1980 and still popular among local bankers and flashy tourists. There are more than 250 varieties of wine to choose from, ranging from the reasonably priced glasses, at around 8€, to the outrageous but delicious, costing upward of 20€ per glass. A fixed-price menu ranges from 22€ to 28€ at lunch, and 35€ at dinner. The restaurant is open Monday to Saturday noon to 2:30pm and 7 to 11pm, the bar Monday to Saturday noon to midnight. 13 rue des Petits-Champs, 1er. ✆ **01-42-61-05-09.** www.williswinebar.com. Métro: Bourse, Pyramides, or Palais-Royal.

BARS & PUBS

You will find Parisians enjoying their drink at any of the ubiquitous cafes throughout town (many of which double as bars and often an extension of personal living rooms). Nonetheless, there are plenty of nooks set up in the more traditional Anglo-centric style of drinking establishment—and some cafes function more like a bar than anything else. Our selections below are among the best places to enjoy a beer or cocktail, in part because of the interesting crowds they draw. Paris is also home to quite a few grand-luxe, world-class bars: Those at the **Plaza Athénée** and the **Ritz,** for example, are among the grandest in the world and provide a uniquely Parisian experience. Of course, you would never show up in sneakers at such an establishment (or without a titanium-level credit card). As a general rule, bars and pubs are open daily from 11am to 2am.

Bar Hemingway/Bar Vendôme In 1944, during the liberation of Paris, Ernest Hemingway made history by ordering a drink at the Ritz Bar while gunfire from retreating Nazi soldiers was still audible in the streets. Today the Ritz commemorates the event with bookish memorabilia, rows of newspapers, and stiff drinks. Look for the bar's entrance, and homages to other writers such as Proust, near the hotel's rue Cambon entrance. If you develop a thirst in the daytime, when Bar Hemingway isn't open, head for Bar Vendôme, near the hotel's place Vendôme entrance. The setting is just as cozy and woodsy, albeit a bit more grand. Open daily 6:30pm to 2am. In the Hôtel Ritz, 15 place Vendôme, 1er. ✆ **01-43-16-30-30.** Métro: Opéra or Concorde.

Cafe Charbon In many ways the social center of trendy Oberkampf, this former Belle Epoque dance hall has big wooden banquets, distressed mirrors, and pleasantly vaulted ceilings. Spacious but often crowded, it's a great place to start off your evening bar crawl along rue Oberkampf. Open Sunday to Thursday 9am to 2am, and Friday to Saturday 9am to 4am. 109 rue Oberkampf, 11e. ✆ **01-43-57-55-13.** Métro: Parmentier or Ménilmontant.

Experimental Cocktail Club This cosmopolitan lounge could have been lifted directly from the speakeasy craze that has struck New York for the past few years. Their cocktails are spot-on, and the crowd is fashionable—starchitect Philippe Starcke and actor Adrien Grenier have been spotted sipping drinks here late into the evening. Drinks start at 12€. Open daily from 6pm to 2am, until 5am Friday and Saturday. 37 rue St-Sauveur, 2e. ✆ **01-45-08-88-09.** www.experimentalcocktailclub.com. Métro: Sentier.

Le Bar This classy, historic joint is all glamour and fabulousness, with a shocking 21st-century decor. It will cost you a small fortune to drink a few centiliters of champagne, but for some, it's definitely worth it. Dress to the nines if you're going—but if you're planning on making the trip, you already knew that. Drinks start at 20€. Hotel Plaza-Athénée, 25 av. Montaigne, 8e. ✆ **01-53-67-66-65.** Métro: Alma-Marceau.

The Frog and the Princess It's loud, crowded, and sweaty in this English-style pub. You'll be surrounded by students and sports enthusiasts, and most will speak English. It's so un-Parisian that it has become an especially Parisian place to go, especially if you're an "anglophile" of sorts or enjoy a good pint. A definite place to try to catch a game, match, or whatever your countrymen consider the sporting event of the day. Open Monday to Thursday from 5:30pm to 2am, and from noon to 2am Friday and Saturday. 9 rue Princesse, 6e. ✆ **01-40-51-77-38.** www.frogpubs.com. Métro: S-Germain-des-Prés/Mabillon.

Music & Cabaret

Paris is still a late-night mecca, and both the quantity and variety of music exceed that of other cities. Nowhere else will you find such a huge, mixed array of jazz dives, cabaret, and music halls.

CABARETS

Decidedly expensive, these places give you your money's worth by providing lavishly spectacular floor shows. They generally attract an older crowd and are definitely not youth oriented.

The Crazy Horse Since 1951, this sophisticated strip joint has thrived, thanks to good choreography and a sly, coquettish celebration of the female form. The Crazy Horse has been getting more attention in recent years ever since the famous burlesque performer Dita Von Teese decided to make it her home away from home in Paris. Shows last less than 2 hours. You'll find a small number of women among the audience of mainly businessmen. Shows Sunday to Friday 8:15 and 10:45pm, Saturday at 7, 9:30, and 11:45pm. 12 av. George V, 8e. ✆ **01-47-23-32-32.** www.lecrazyhorseparis.com. Reservations recommended. Entry 100€ for the show alone; show/dinner packages 175€–209€. Métro: George V or Alma Marceau.

Folies-Bergère The Folies-Bergère has been an institution since 1869. Josephine Baker, the African-American singer who danced in a banana skirt and threw bananas into the audience, became "the toast of Paris" here. According to legend, the first GI to reach Paris at the 1944 Liberation asked for directions to the club. Don't expect the naughty and slyly permissive, skin-and-glitter revue that used to be the trademark of this place. In 1993, that all ended with a radical restoration of the theater and a reopening under new management. Today it's a conventional 1,600-seat theater devoted to a frequently changing roster of big-stage performances in French, many of which are adaptations of Broadway blockbusters. Josephine Baker may have once performed topless here with her bananas, but those looking for nudity today should head to the Lido or the Crazy Horse. 32 rue Richer, 9e. ✆ **01-44-79-98-60** or 08-92-68-16-50. www.foliesbergere.com. Tickets 25€–84€. Métro: Grands-Boulevards or Cadet.

Lido de Paris The Lido competes with the best that Las Vegas has to offer. In explaining the concept of *Bonheur,* the Lido's current production, artistic director Pierre Rambert invites us to imagine "a bird-woman arriving on her cloud of fathers from a shore where happiness does not exist." She then discovers joy through the "four worlds of women, Paris, India, and the cinema." Don't worry if that doesn't make any sense, because you're really there just to see the topless Bluebell Girls anyway. 16 av. des Champs-Elysées, 8e. ✆ **01-40-76-56-10,** or 800/227-4884 in the U.S. www.lido.fr. Tickets for the show alone 70€; dinner/show packages 140€–280€. Price includes half-bottle of champagne per person. Métro: George V.

Moulin Rouge This place is a camp classic. The establishment that Toulouse-Lautrec immortalized is still here, but the artist would probably have a hard time recognizing it today, surrounded as it is by so many tour buses. Colette once created a scandal here by offering an on-stage kiss to Mme. de Morny, but shows today have a harder time shocking audiences. Try to get a table—the view is much better on the main floor than from the bar. What's the theme? It's strip routines and the saucy sexiness of *la Belle Epoque,* and of permissive Paris between the wars. Handsome men and girls, girls, girls, virtually all topless, keep the place going. Dance finales usually include two dozen of the belles doing a topless cancan. Revues begin nightly at 9 and 11pm. 82 bd. Clichy, place Blanche, 18e. ✆ **01-53-09-82-82.** www.moulinrouge.fr. Tickets for the show alone 80€–90€; dinner/show packages 150€–180€. Métro: Blanche.

Moulin Rouge.

CHANSONNIERS

Chansonniers (literally, "Songwriters") provides a bombastic musical satire of the day's events. A combination of parody and burlesque, it's a time-honored

Parisian institution. Songs are often created on the spot, inspired by the "disaster of the day."

Au Lapin Agile Picasso and Utrillo patronized this little cottage near the top of Montmartre, then known as the Cabaret des Assassins, and it has been painted by many artists, including Utrillo. You'll sit at carved wooden tables in a dimly lit room with walls covered by bohemian memorabilia and listen to French folk tunes, love ballads, army songs, sea chanteys, and music-hall ditties. You're encouraged to sing along. Open Tuesday to Sunday 9pm to 2am. 22 rue des Saules, 18e. ✆ **01-46-06-85-87.** www.au-lapin-agile.com. Cover (includes 1 drink) 24€ adults, 17€ students under 26 years. Métro: Lamarck Caulaincourt.

LIVE MUSIC

La Maroquinerie ★ This divey little club atop the Ménilmontant hill is the place to catch local and international music artists before they blow up big and start playing La Cigale. The roster leans heavily toward the indie rock genre, but there are electro and folk acts in the mix, too. An attached restaurant and bar with a pretty outdoor courtyard is a good place to hang before and after the show. 23 rue Boyer, 20e. ✆ **01-40-33-64-85.** www.lamaroquinerie.fr. Tickets 10€–18€. Métro: Ménilmontant.

Le Gibus One of the original venues for the French punk-rock scene (yes, apparently they had their own in the 1970s), this place pulls in the under-40s and remains one of the best-known rock clubs in Paris. It opens every night as late as a concert hall and dance club, entertaining its diverse medley of counterculture Parisians and visitors. The themes are constantly rotating; there might be a live rock band or even a drag show presented as part of the evening's rhythms. The crowd is often mixed, and there are some gay-themed nights, but it's best to check on the website to see if there are any scheduled. Other nights of the week, this place tends to be the venue for private parties or for loosely scheduled rock or pop concerts. 18 rue du Faubourg du Temple, 11e. ✆ **01-47-00-78-88.** www.gibus.fr. Cover 15€–20€. Métro: République.

JAZZ CLUBS

The great jazz revival that long ago swept America is still going strong here, with Dixieland, Chicago, bop, and free-jazz rhythms being pounded out in dozens of cellars, mostly called *caveaux,* where music lovers of all ages gather to listen to jazz.

Caveau des Oubliettes ★ It's hard to say which is more intriguing—the entertainment and drinking or the setting. An *oubliette* is a dungeon with a trap door at the top as its only opening, and the name is accurate. Located in the Latin Quarter, just across the river from Notre-Dame, this night spot is housed in a genuine 12th-century prison, complete with dungeons, spine-tingling passages, and scattered skulls, where prisoners were tortured and sometimes pushed through portholes to drown in the Seine. The *caveau* is beneath the subterranean vaults that many centuries ago linked it with the fortress prison of Petit Châtelet. Today patrons laugh, drink, talk, and flirt in the narrow *caveau* or else retreat to the jazz lounge. There's a free jam session every night, perhaps Latin jazz or rock. At some point on Friday and Saturday nights, concerts are staged, sometimes with a cover charge. Open daily 5pm to 4am. 52 rue Galande, 5e. ✆ **01-46-34-23-09.** www.caveaudesoubliettes.fr. Métro: St-Michel.

La Chapelle des Lombards The club's proximity to the Opéra Bastille seems incongruous, considering the African/Caribbean jazz and Brazilian samba that's the norm. It's a magnet for South American and African expatriates, and the rhythms and fire of the music propel everyone onto the dance floor. Open daily 11:30pm to dawn. 19 rue de Lappe, 11e. ✆ **01-43-57-24-24.** www.la-chapelle-des-lombards.com. Free entry Sun–Thurs; 20€ Fri–Sat. Women free Fri before midnight. Métro: Bastille.

Le Petit Journal Montparnasse This is one of the best jazz supper clubs in Paris. Music lovers come here for dinner and a show, although you can also visit just for drinks and the music (a lot cheaper). Dinner guests are given preferred seating; other patrons usually sit at the bar. Open 8pm to 2am Monday to Saturday. 13 rue du Commandant Mouchotte, 14e. ✆ **01-43-21-56-70.** www.petitjournalmontparnasse.com. 3-course dinner and show 60€; cover (without dinner) 25€, including first drink. Métro: Gare Montparnasse.

Le Sunset/Le Sunside ★ This is a dual temple of jazz, one of the hottest addresses on the after-dark scene in Paris, lying between the Forum des Halles and the Centre George Pompidou. The Sunset Jazz Club, created in 1983, is dedicated to electric jazz and international music, whereas Sunside, launched in 2001, is devoted to acoustic jazz, for the most part. Some of the most innovative names in European jazz appear here regularly, along with jazz legends, many from abroad. Both clubs form a single complex, with two concerts every night. Open Monday to Saturday 9:30pm to 1am. 60 rue des Lombards, 1er. ✆ **01-40-26-46-60.** www.sunset-sunside.com. Tickets 20€–22€. Métro: Châtelet.

New Morning ★ Jazz maniacs come to drink, talk, and dance at this enduring club. It's sometimes a scene, attracting such guests as Spike Lee and Prince. Recent bookings have included Robin McKelle, The Klezmatics, Patricia Barber, and folk rock acts like Steve Earle. It opens nightly at 8pm, with concerts beginning at 9pm. 7 rue des Petites-Ecuries, 10e. ✆ **01-45-23-51-41.** www.newmorning.com. Cover 18€–26€. Métro: Château-d'Eau.

Dance Clubs

From the dance halls of the can-can to the raucous and energetic jazz clubs of the 1920s, Parisians have historically made it a point to get out at night and go dancing. Stepping into a Parisian club (known as *les boites de nuit,* or just *une boite*) today is one of the best ways to experience a night on the town in the City of Lights. The French love their fashion, so dressing to impress is obligatory. Check ***Time Out: Paris*** or ***Pariscope*** for current offerings. Most clubs don't really get going until at least 11pm, if not later.

Batofar ★ While most clubs never last more than a few years before the crowds move on, somehow Batofar remains fresh and consistently full. The fact that it sits on a converted barge floating on the Seine must have something to do with it. On good nights, you'll see hundreds of gyrating dancers moving to house, garage, techno, and live jazz by groups that fly in from Morocco, Senegal, and Germany. Beer costs about 8.50€ a bottle. Open Tuesday to Saturday from 6pm to 4am. Closed November to March. Facing 11 quai François Mauriac, 13e. ✆ **01-53-14-76-59.** www.batofar.org. Cover free–15€, depending on the band or DJ. Métro: Quai de la Gare.

Le Baron ★ Once the most expensive brothel in Paris, much of Le Baron's original decor remains, including the 1920s-era tile of frolicking nude ladies, sexy red

Le Baron.

walls, and tasseled lamps. It's long been regarded as the playground of the rich and bored, or sometimes just fabulous and occasionally androgynous. The dance floor is one of the most packed in Paris, with some of the world's most beautiful people. Drinks are costly, but so is being trendy. It's open daily 11pm to 6am, although hours can vary. 6 av. Marceau, 8e. ✆ **01-47-20-04-01.** www.clublebaron.com. Cover free–15€, depending on the event and the night of the week. Métro: Champs-Elysées.

Le Bataclan You'll never have trouble finding this place, considering its colorful exterior inspired by Chinese architecture. Inside is an equally awe-inspiring and massive space, perfect for big dance parties or concerts. Le Bataclan hosts an eclectic bevy of shows, from Swedish trip-hop star Jay Jay Johanson to indie-leaning rock groups like Morcheeba, MGMT, and Yeasayer; they also host the monthly gay-themed (but mixed) parties *Follievores* and *Crazyvores.* 50 bd. Voltaire, 11e. ✆ **01-49-23-96-33.** Cover varies depending on the show. Métro: Oberkampf.

Nouveau Casino Some Paris-watchers consider this the epitome of the hyper-hip countercultural scene that blossoms along rue Oberkampf every night. In a former movie theater adjacent to the Cafe Charbon, it's a large, drafty space centered on a dance floor and an enormous bar crafted to resemble an iceberg. Live concerts take place nightly between 8pm and 1am; on Friday and Saturday, the party continues from 1am till dawn, with a DJ who spins some of the most avant-garde dance music in Paris. 109 rue Oberkampf, 9e. ✆ **01-43-57-57-40.** www.nouveau-casino.net. Entry free–30€ for some concerts. Métro: St-Maur, Parmentier, or Ménilmontant.

Showcase Set almost unbelievably beneath the Pont Alexandre III, this may be the only club you'll ever enter that's literally under a bridge. Unique location aside, they have DJs and live bands, and gorgeous lighting along the endlessly long bar. Expect a crowd with champagne bottles, Gucci blazers, and impossibly high heels. While live bands are all over the map, the DJs play mostly electro, house, and disco beats. Open Friday and Saturday nights from 11pm until 7am. Port des Champs-Elysées, under the Pont Alexandre III. ✆ **01-45-61-25-43.** www.showcase.fr. Cover free–15€. Métro: Invalides.

Gay & Lesbian Bars & Clubs

Paris has a vibrant gay scene, centered on **Le Marais, Les Halles,** and, to some extent, **Bastille.** The area with the greatest concentration of gay and lesbian clubs, restaurants, bars, and shops lies between the Hôtel-de-Ville and Rambuteau Métro stops. Gay dance clubs come and go so fast that even the magazines devoted to them, such as ***2x*** and ***Illico***—distributed free in the gay bars and bookstores—have a hard time keeping up. For lesbians, there is ***Lesbia Magazine.*** Also check out ***Têtu*** and ***PREF*** (*Préférences*) magazines, sold at most newsstands.

Le Central Established in 1980 in a 300-year-old town house, Le Central is a staple of gay men's life in the Marais, and the only "official" gay hotel. Outfitted with decor of battered paneling and windows that wrap around on two sides, it attracts local residents who make the place their hangout, along with goodly numbers of attractive male tourists and the Parisians who appreciate them. You'll meet people from all over in this place, some inevitably from your home. Open Monday to Friday from 4pm to 2am, Saturday to Sunday from 2pm to 2am. 33 rue Vieille-du-Temple, 4e. ✆ **01-48-87-99-33.** www.hotelcentralmarais.com. Métro: Hôtel-de-Ville.

Le Cox This place gets so busy early in the evening that the muscled, tank-top-wearing crowd overflows out onto the sidewalk. This is where you'll find a dependably mixed gay crowd in Paris—from hunky American tourists to sexy Parisians. You may also want to check out **Open Cafe,** another gay club next door. 15 rue des Archives, 4e. ✆ **01-42-72-08-00.** www.cox.fr. Métro: Hôtel de Ville.

Le Duplex This welcoming bar is a good choice if loud club music isn't your cup of tea. Usually amid jazz and some hip rock, actual conversation can take place; the clientele is mostly local and quite friendly. 25 rue Michel Le Comte, 3e. ✆ **01-42-72-80-86.** www.duplex-bar.com. Métro: Rambuteau.

Le Raidd ★ The bartenders here may be hunks, and so are most of the patrons. Be prepared for attitude galore. A special feature is a Plexiglas shower box where nude shower boys flaunt their assets throughout the night. It's shoulder-to-shoulder action here, with pickup possibilities at every turn. Only the best dressed can expect to get invited in at the door. Open daily 5pm to 5am. 23 rue du Temple, 4e. ✆ **01-92-77-09-88.** www.raiddbar.com. Métro: Hôtel-de-Ville or Rambuteau.

Le 3w Kafe The 3w means "Woman with Woman." This is the best-known lesbian bar in the Marais, where an unattached woman usually has little trouble finding a drinking buddy. On weekends there's dancing downstairs, with a DJ in control of the sounds. Straight men are welcome, but only if accompanied by a woman. Gay men are admitted without problem. Open Wednesday to Sunday 5pm to 2am, Friday and Saturday 5pm to 4am. 8 rue des Ecouffes, 4e. ✆ **01-48-87-39-26.** Métro: St-Paul.

WHERE TO STAY

Naturally, the most-visited city in the world boasts an overwhelming number of hotels, which range from mythical palaces including the Ritz and the Crillon to dives so repellent that even George Orwell, author of *Down and Out in Paris and London,* wouldn't have considered checking in. (Of course, you won't find those in this guide!) We include deluxe places for those who can afford to live like the Sultan of Brunei, as well as a wide range of moderate and budget choices for the rest of us.

The Right Bank

LES HALLES, LOUVRE & PALAIS ROYAL (1ER & 2E)

Located on the right bank, this area is the *très chic* center of Paris. This part of Paris—by the Seine river and clustered around the Louvre—boasts exquisite monuments, boulevards, gardens, and shopping.

Very Expensive

Hôtel de Vendôme ★★ This luxury boutique hotel sits on one of Paris's most prestigious addresses, place Vendôme, surrounded by the city's finest jewelers. The soundproof rooms are opulent and designed in classic Second Empire style, with prestige beds and well-upholstered, hand-carved furnishings. Suites have generous space and such extras as blackout draperies and quadruple-glazed windows. The security is fantastic, with TV intercoms, and the service is warm and professional. This hotel is a short walk from the Louvre and Tuileries gardens.

1 place Vendôme, Paris 75001. www.hoteldevendome.com. ✆ **01-55-04-55-00.** Fax 01-49-27-97-89. 29 units. 535€–865€ double; 835€–1,525€ suite. AE, DC, MC, V. Parking 27€. Métro: Concorde or Opéra. **Amenities:** Restaurant; piano bar; babysitting; concierge; room service. *In room:* A/C, TV, hair dryer, minibar, MP3 docking station, free Wi-Fi.

Hôtel Meurice ★★★ This landmark lies between place de la Concorde and the Grand Louvre, facing the Tuileries Gardens. The hotel is more media-hip, style-conscious, and better located than the George V. Since the 1800s, it has welcomed the royal, the rich, and even the radical. The mad genius Salvador Dalí made the Meurice his headquarters. And in 2008, that other mad genius, Philippe Starck, overhauled the hotel's public areas, bringing an exquisite contemporary touch of the surreal to the lobby and downstairs bar and restaurant. Each room is individually decorated with period pieces, fine carpets, Italian and French fabrics, marble bathrooms, and modern features. Our favorites, and the least expensive, are the sixth-floor rooms. Some have painted ceilings of puffy clouds and blue skies, along with canopy beds. Suites are among the most lavish in France.

228 rue de Rivoli, Paris 75001. www.meuricehotel.com. ✆ **01-44-58-10-10.** Fax 01-44-58-10-15. 160 units. 665€–1,030€ double; from 1,150€ junior suite; from 1,800€ suite. AE, DC, MC, V. Parking 27€. Métro: Tuileries or Concorde. **Amenities:** 2 restaurants; bar; babysitting; concierge; health club and spa; room service. *In room:* A/C, TV/DVD, fax, hair dryer, minibar, Wi-Fi (20€ per day).

Hôtel Ritz ★★ The Ritz is Europe's greatest hotel, an enduring symbol of elegance on one of Paris's most beautiful and historic squares. César Ritz, the "little shepherd boy from Niederwald," converted the Hôtel de Lazun into a luxury hotel in 1898. With the help of the culinary master Escoffier, he made the Ritz a miracle of luxury. In 1979, the Ritz family sold the hotel to Mohammed al Fayed, who refurbished it and added a cooking school. The hotel annexed two town houses, joined by an arcade lined with display cases representing 125 of Paris's leading boutiques. The public salons are furnished with museum-caliber antiques. Each guest room is uniquely decorated, most with Louis XIV or XV reproductions; all have fine rugs, marble fireplaces, tapestries, brass beds, and more. Ever since Edward VII got stuck in a too-narrow bathtub with his lover, the tubs at the Ritz have been deep and big.

15 place Vendôme, Paris 75001. www.ritzparis.com. ✆ **01-43-16-30-30,** or 800/223-6800 in the U.S. and Canada. Fax 01-43-16-31-78. 159 units. 550€–870€ double; 800€–4,370€ suite. AE,

DC, MC, V. Parking 48€. Métro: Opéra, Concorde, or Madeleine. **Amenities:** Restaurant; 4 bars; babysitting; concierge; state-of-the-art health club; indoor pool; room service. *In room:* A/C, TV/DVD; hair dryer, minibar, Wi-Fi (25€ per day).

Park Hyatt Vendôme ★★★ American interior designer Ed Tuttle took five separate Haussmann-era buildings and wove them into a seamless entity to create this citadel of 21st-century luxury living. High ceilings, colonnades, and interior courtyards speak of the buildings' former lives, but other than the facades, all is completely modern inside—not just contemporary, but luxe modern. The third Hyatt in Paris, this palace enjoys the greatest and most prestigious location in "Ritz Hotel country." Graced with modern art, it is filled with elegant fabrics, huge mirrors, walk-in closets, and mahogany doors. Bedrooms and bathrooms are spacious and state-of-the-art, with elegant furnishings and glamorous bathrooms with "rain showers," plus separate tubs.

5 rue de la Paix, Paris 75002. www.paris.vendome.hyatt.com. ✆ **01-58-71-12-34,** or 800/492-8804 in the U.S. and Canada. Fax 01-58-71-12-35. 168 units. 800€–910€ double; from 1,010€ suite. AE, DC, DISC, MC, V. Métro: Tuileries or Opéra. Free parking. **Amenities:** 2 restaurants; bar; babysitting; concierge; health club and spa; room service. *In room:* A/C, TV/DVD, CD player, hair dryer, minibar, Wi-Fi (19€ per day).

Expensive

Hôtel du Louvre ★ When Napoleon III inaugurated this hotel in 1855, it was described as "a palace of the people, rising adjacent to the palace of kings." In 1897, Camille Pissarro moved into a room with a view that inspired many of his landscapes; its decor features marble, bronze, and gilt. The guest rooms are filled with souvenirs of the Belle Epoque, along with elegant fabrics, carpeting, double-glazed windows, comfortable beds, and wood furniture. Suites provide greater dimensions and better exposures, as well as such upgrades as antiques, trouser presses, and robes.

Place André-Malraux, Paris 75001. www.hoteldulouvre.com. ✆ **01-44-58-38-38,** or 800/888-4747 in the U.S. and Canada. Fax 01-44-58-38-01. 177 units. 200€–700€ double; 300€–750€ junior suite. AE, DC, MC, V. Parking 20€. Métro: Palais-Royal–Louvre or Louvre–Rivoli. **Amenities:** Restaurant; bar; babysitting; concierge; exercise room. *In room:* A/C, TV, minibar, free Wi-Fi.

Moderate

Hôtel Thérèse ★★ Close to the Louvre, place Vendôme, and the Tuileries Gardens, this hotel combines French charm with English classicism. The library and bar evoke a London club with wood-paneled walls and plush armchairs, but the lounge is adorned with Parisian art. It's government-rated three stars but seems more like four stars in ambience, style, and comfort. Owner Sylvia de Lattre, who likes shades of pistachio and royal blue, trolled the flea markets for paintings and prints to personalize each bedroom. The rooms are unpretentious but filled with quality furnishings, from the soft, efficient lighting by Philippe Starck to the natural wool quilts.

5–7 rue Thérèse, Paris 75001. www.hoteltherese.com. ✆ **01-42-96-10-01.** Fax 01-42-96-15-22. 43 units. 155€–320€ double. AE, MC, V. Métro: Musée du Louvre. **Amenities:** Library/bar; room service. *In room:* A/C, TV, hair dryer, free Wi-Fi.

LE MARAIS, ILE ST-LOUIS & ILE DE LA CITÉ (3E & 4E)

This busy neighborhood includes the city's gay and Jewish quarters. Most of the important contemporary galleries are here, too. You'll find a concentration of great stores from independent local labels in the northern Marais, around rue de Bretagne. But it's the architecture that really sets this area apart, as it conserves buildings dating back to the Renaissance.

Expensive

Hôtel du Jeu de Paume ★ This small-scale hotel encompasses a pair of 17th-century town houses accessible through a timbered passageway from the street outside. The hotel is located on the incredibly quaint and charming Ile St-Louis in the Seine and is just a 5-minute walk from Notre-Dame. Originally, the hotel was a clubhouse used by members of the court of Louis XIII, who amused themselves with *les jeux de paume* (an early form of tennis) nearby. Public areas are outfitted in a simple version of Art Deco. Renovated in 2010, guest rooms now have a sleek contemporary style, with elegant materials such as oak floors and fine craftsmanship. Some have wooden beamed ceilings. The rooms are a bit larger than those of some nearby competitors. All bathrooms are new. The most luxurious units are the five duplexes and two junior suites, each individually decorated and opening onto an indoor courtyard.

54 rue St-Louis-en-l'Ile, Paris 75004. www.jeudepaumehotel.com. ✆ **01-43-26-14-18.** Fax 01-40-46-02-76. 30 units. 285€–360€ double; 360€–560€ suite. AE, DC, MC, V. Métro: Pont Marie. **Amenities:** Bar; babysitting; concierge; exercise room; room service. *In room:* A/C, TV, hair dryer, minibar, free Wi-Fi.

Hôtel Duo ★ Fashionistas flock to this restored hotel in the Marais, which is one of the cutting-edge places to stay in Paris. The location is convenient to Centre Pompidou, Notre-Dame, and the Louvre. The building has been in the family of Veronique Turmel since 1918. In 2002, she decided to completely convert the interior while retaining the facade. Original architectural features, including exposed beams, old stones, and hardwood floors, remain intact; but a modern and stylish look includes Wengé-wood furnishings, white walls, and bronzed sconces—old-world charm in a tasteful and refined setting. The midsize bedrooms are completely up-to-date, with beautiful and comfortable furnishings. The so-called breakfast "cave" is a charming room with slipcovered chairs and sea-grass matting.

11 rue du Temple, Paris 75004. www.parishhotelleduo.com. ✆ **01-42-72-72-22.** Fax 01-42-72-03-53. 58 units. 200€–380€ double; 400€–550€ suite. AE, DC, MC, V. Métro: Hôtel-de-Ville. **Amenities:** Exercise room; room service. *In room:* A/C, TV, hair dryer, free Wi-Fi.

Pavillon de la Reine ★★ This is the kind of hidden gem that Frommer's readers love, opening onto the most romantic square in Paris. In days of yore, the 1612 mansion was a gathering place for the likes of Racine, La Fontaine, Molière, and Mme. de Sévigné. You enter through an arcade that opens onto a small garden. The Louis XIII decor evokes the heyday of the square itself, and iron-banded Spanish antiques create a rustic aura. Each guest room is individually furnished in a historic or modern style. Some units are duplexes with sleeping lofts above cozy salons.

28 place des Vosges, Paris 75003. www.pavillon-de-la-reine.com. ✆ **01-40-29-19-19.** Fax 01-40-29-19-20. 56 units. 330€–450€ double; 600€–800€ suite. AE, MC, V. Métro: Bastille. **Amenities:** Bar; concierge; room service. *In room:* A/C, TV, minibar, free Wi-Fi.

Moderate

Hôtel Caron de Beaumarchais ★ Built in the 18th century, this good-value choice features floors of artfully worn gray stone, antique reproductions, and elaborate fabrics based on antique patterns. Primrose-colored guest rooms evoke the taste of the French gentry in the 18th century, when the Marais was the scene of high-society dances and even duels. Most rooms retain their original ceiling beams. The smallest units overlook the courtyard, and the top-floor rooms are tiny but have panoramic balcony views across the Right Bank.

12 rue Vieille-du-Temple, Paris 75004. www.carondebeaumarchais.com. ✆ **01-42-72-34-12.** Fax 01-42-72-34-63. 19 units. 145€–185€ double. AE, MC, V. Métro: St-Paul or Hôtel-de-Ville. **Amenities:** Breakfast room; babysitting. *In room:* A/C, TV, hair dryer, minibar, free Wi-Fi.

Hôtel Saint-Louis en l'Isle ★ Proprietors Guy and Andrée Record maintain a charming family atmosphere at this antiques-filled hotel in a 17th-century town house. The hotel represents an incredible value, considering its prime location on Ile St-Louis. Expect cozy, slightly cramped rooms, each with a small bathroom. With mansard roofs and old-fashioned moldings, the top-floor units sport tiny balconies that afford sweeping views. The breakfast room is in the cellar, which has 17th-century stone vaulting.

75 rue St-Louis-en-l'Ile, Paris 75004. www.saintlouisenlisle.com. ✆ **01-46-34-04-80.** Fax 01-46-34-02-13. 19 units. 140€–220€ double. MC, V. Métro: Pont Marie or St-Michel-Notre-Dame. **Amenities:** Babysitting; concierge; smoke-free rooms. *In room:* A/C, TV, hair dryer, free Wi-Fi.

Inexpensive

Hôtel de la Place des Vosges ★ Built about 350 years ago, during the same era as the majestic square for which it's named (a 2-min. walk away), this is a well-managed, small-scale property with reasonable prices and lots of charm. The structure was once used as a stable for the mules of Henri IV. Entirely renovated in 2010, many of the small guest rooms have beamed ceilings, flatscreen TVs, and a sense of cozy, well-ordered efficiency. The most desirable and expensive room is top-floor no. 60, overlooking the rooftops of Paris, with a luxurious bathroom. Patches of chiseled stone in various parts of the hotel add a decorative touch.

12 rue de Birague, Paris 75004. www.hotelplacedesvosges.com. ✆ **01-42-72-60-46.** Fax 01-42-72-02-64. 16 units. 90€–160€ double. AE, DC, MC, V. Métro: Bastille. **Amenities:** Room service. *In room:* TV, hair dryer, free Wi-Fi.

CHAMPS-ELYSÉES & WESTERN PARIS (8E, 16E & 17E)

This is where most of the city's money and power is concentrated. The "Golden Triangle" (av. Montaigne, George V, and the Champs-Elysées) is bling-bling heaven, with all the major fashion labels jostling for position. It's also a business neighborhood, so get ready to navigate the suits.

Very Expensive

Fouquet's Barrière ★★★ This deluxe boutique hotel on the corner of the Champs-Elysées may lack the historic cachet of the neighboring George V or Plaza Athénée, but it's a more contemporary brand of glitz and glamour. Standing alongside its namesake, the legendary restaurant Fouquet's, it offers some of the most luxurious and spacious bedrooms in Paris, its decor dominated by ceiling-high padded headboards in shiny gold. The hotel contains such novel features as waterproof floating TV remotes in the bathtub and a bedside button that, when pressed, will summon your butler. There's one butler to every eight guests, and the service is the best in Paris. That butler even arrives to unpack your luggage and serve you champagne.

46 av. George V, Paris 75008. www.fouquets-barriere.com. ✆ **01-40-69-60-00.** Fax 01-40-69-60-05. 107 units. 750€–1,300€ double; 1,100€–1,700€ junior suite; 1,700€–3,600€ suite. AE, MC, V. Métro: George V. Parking 45€. **Amenities:** 2 restaurants; 2 bars; concierge; health club and spa; indoor pool; room service. *In room:* A/C, TV/DVD, hair dryer, minibar, free Wi-Fi.

Four Seasons Hotel George V ★★★ ☺ In its latest reincarnation, with all its glitz and glamour, this hotel is one of the best in the world. The George V opened in 1928 in honor of George V of England, grandfather of Queen Elizabeth. During the liberation of Paris, it housed Dwight D. Eisenhower. The guest rooms are about as close as you'll come to residency in a well-upholstered private home where teams of decorators have lavished vast amounts of attention and money. The beds rival those at the Ritz and Meurice in comfort. The largest units are magnificent; the smallest are, in the words of a spokesperson, *"très agréable."* Security is tight—a fact appreciated by sometimes notorious guests. The staff pampers children with bathrobes, bedtime milk and cookies, and even special menus.

31 av. George V, Paris 75008. www.fourseasons.com. ✆ **800/332-3442** in the U.S. and Canada, or 01-49-52-70-00. Fax 01-49-52-70-10. 245 units. 750€–1,095€ double; from 1,795€ suite. Parking 40€. AE, DC, MC, V. Métro: George V. **Amenities:** 2 restaurants; 2 bars; babysitting; concierge; health club and spa; room service. *In room:* A/C, TV/DVD, CD player, hair dryer, minibar, Wi-Fi (22€ per day).

Hôtel le Bristol ★★★ This palace is near the Palais d'Elysée (home of the French president), on the shopping street parallel to the Champs-Elysées. The 18th-century Parisian facade has a glass-and-wrought-iron entryway, where uniformed English-speaking attendants greet you. Hippolyte Jammet founded the Bristol in 1924, installing many antiques and Louis XV and XVI furnishings. The guest rooms are opulent, with antiques or well-made reproductions, inlaid wood, bronze, crystal, Oriental carpets, and original oil paintings. Personalized old-world service is rigidly maintained here—some guests find it forbidding; others absolutely adore it.

112 rue du Faubourg St-Honoré, Paris 75008. www.lebristolparis.com. ✆ **01-53-43-43-00.** Fax 01-53-43-43-01. 187 units. 670€–980€ double; 990€–1,600€ junior suite; from 1,900€ suite. AE, DC, MC, V. Free parking. Métro: Miromesnil or Champs-Elysées. **Amenities:** 2 restaurants; bar; babysitting; children's programs; concierge; health club and spa; indoor pool; room service. *In room:* A/C, TV/DVD, CD player, hair dryer, minibar, Wi-Fi (21€ per day).

Le Royal Monceau ★★★ This five-star Raffles hotel opened in late 2010 and immediately wowed Paris with its luxurious chic interiors designed by Philippe Starck. The decor is contemporary but is still in tune with the Art Deco heritage of the building. The spacious rooms offer all the comfort and amenities that you would expect from a hotel of this caliber, but still have a relaxed vibe. There's even an electric guitar in each room, if you feel like expressing your inner rock star. The hotel has a unique commitment to contemporary art: It regularly hosts art exhibitions, has a fully stocked art bookstore, and publishes a sophisticated website (www.artforbreakfast.com) that gives an insider's perspective on the Paris art scene. The hotel offers cutting-edge fashion in its satellite L'Éclaireur store. The icing on the cake? Star *pâtissier* Pierre Hermé is responsible for the desserts.

37 av. Hoche, Paris 75008. www.leroyalmonceau.com. ✆ **01-42-99-88-00.** Fax 01-42-99-89-00. 160 units. 780€–930€ double; 1,200€–10,000€ suite. AE, DC, MC, V. Métro: Ternes. **Amenities:** 2

restaurants; bar; cigar lounge; children's programs; concierge; electric guitar; health club; movie theater; indoor pool; room service; spa. *In room:* A/C, TV/DVD, hair dryer, MP3 docking station, minibar, free Wi-Fi.

Plaza Athénée ★★★ The Plaza Athénée, an 1889 Art Nouveau marvel, is a landmark of discretion and style. About half the celebrities visiting Paris have been pampered here; in the old days, Mata Hari used to frequent the place. **Salon Gobelins** (with tapestries against rich paneling) and **Salon Marie Antoinette,** a richly paneled and grand room, are two public rooms that add to the ambience of this lavish hotel. There's also a calm, quiet interior courtyard draped with vines and dotted with geraniums. The quietest guest rooms overlook a courtyard with awnings and parasol-shaded tables; they have ample closet space. Some rooms overlooking avenue Montaigne have views of the Eiffel Tower. The hotel is also home to **Alain Ducasse au Plaza Athénée,** where Alain Ducasse presents a gourmet French menu. During Paris Fashion Week, the bar becomes the event's unofficial HQ.

25 av. Montaigne, Paris 75008. www.plaza-athenee-paris.com. ✆ **866/732-1106** in the U.S. and Canada, or 01-53-67-66-65. Fax 01-53-67-66-66. 191 units. 830€–935€ double; 1,600€–1,700€ junior suite; 1,850€–22,000€ suite. AE, MC, V. Parking 28€. Métro: Franklin-D-Roosevelt or Alma-Marceau. **Amenities:** 5 restaurants; bar; babysitting; concierge; state-of-the-art health club; room service. *In room:* A/C, TV/DVD, CD player, hair dryer, minibar, Wi-Fi (24€ per day).

Expensive

Best Western Premier Regent's Garden ★★ Near the convention center (Palais des Congrès) and the Arc de Triomphe, the Regent's Garden boasts a proud heritage: Napoleon III built this château for his physician. Renovated in 2008, the hotel prides itself on its sustainability; it was awarded a prestigious European Eco-Label for its efforts in preserving the environment by reducing the consumption of water, gas, electricity, and waste. The smart guest rooms feature tall soundproof windows, traditional French furniture, and modern textiles—the environmental approach extends to the guest rooms, as the duvets in each room are made from fair trade cotton. Even breakfast is composed of organic ingredients. Guests have access to a neighboring fitness center and spa, Eclipse & Vous. A garden with ivy-covered walls and umbrella-shaded tables makes for a perfect place to meet other guests. The hotel is smoke-free throughout.

6 rue Pierre-Demours, Paris 75017. www.hotel-regents-paris.com. ✆ **800/528-1234** in the U.S., or 01-45-74-07-30. Fax 01-40-55-01-42. 40 units. 290€–440€ double; from 490€ suite. AE, DC, MC, V. Parking 20€. Métro: Ternes or Charles-de-Gaulle–Etoile. **Amenities:** Babysitting; spa. *In room:* A/C, TV, hair dryer, minibar, free Wi-Fi.

Hôtel Balzac ★★★ Built for the director of the Paris Opéra in 1853, and once home to Balzac himself, this is a luxurious, intimate town-house hotel overlooking the Champs-Elysées. Vibrant, warm colors such as plum and copper prevail throughout the elegant bedrooms, furnished with tasteful modern pieces of varying styles. The hotel manages to recapture the romantic era, but with a cutting modern edge. It underwent a multimillion-euro restoration in 2007 to attract guests who like five-star comfort but not commercial palace hotels. For atmosphere, the hotel has lithographs depicting Balzac and scenes from his works, including *La Comédie Humaine.*

6 rue Balzac, Paris 75008. www.hotelbalzac.com. ✆ **01-44-35-18-00.** Fax 01-44-35-18-05. 70 units. 350€–600€ double; 790€–870€ junior suite; from 870€ suite. AE, MC, V. Parking 23€.

Métro: Champs-Elysées. **Amenities:** Restaurant; bar; health club and spa; indoor pool; room service. *In room:* A/C, TV/DVD, hair dryer, minibar, Wi-Fi (22€ per day).

Le Pavillon des Lettres ★ If you're a literature fan, this hotel—Paris's first literary-themed hotel—might just be the place for you. Located in the 8th arrondissement, this charming boutique hotel opened in 2010 and is owned by the same owners of the Pavillon de la Reine. It features 26 rooms—one for each letter of the alphabet. Each room is dedicated to the life and work of great writers, from Anderson to Proust, to Zola, and you'll find excerpted texts from these writers printed on the bedroom walls. The comfortable rooms are designed to encourage relaxation and are decorated in metallic tones. Lounge in the hotel's library over a well-thumbed classic, and when you're tired of reading, just step outside to reach the many nearby shops and restaurants in the thick of the Right Bank.

12 rue des Saussaies, Paris 75008. www.pavillondeslettres.com. ✆ **01-49-24-26-26.** Fax 01-49-24-26-27. 26 units. 300€–340€ double; 460€ suite. AE, DC, MC, V. Métro: Madeleine. **Amenities:** Restaurant; bar; library; room service. *In room:* A/C, TV, MP3 docking station, minibar, free Wi-Fi.

Renaissance Paris Arc de Triomphe ★★ On the site of the once-famous Theatre de l'Empire, this cutting-edge hotel with its intriguing modern interiors lies only steps from the Arc de Triomphe and the Champs-Elysées. The top-floor rooms and suites open onto large terraces with panoramic views over the heart of Paris. The upscale hotel rooms and suites are spacious, tastefully decorated, and outfitted with the latest in-room technology. Its all-glass exterior has made this a distinctive landmark, even though it opened only in 2009. This is definitely a trendy and hip hotel, so it's probably not the best for kids. The on-site Makassar Lounge (a restaurant) blends French bistro flavors with authentic Indonesian dishes. The hotel is smoke-free.

39 av. de Wagram, 75017 Paris. www.marriott.com. ✆ **01-55-37-55-37.** Fax 01-55-37-55-38. 108 units. 289€–599€ double; from 429€ suite. Parking 35€. Métro: Charles-de-Gaulle–Etoile. **Amenities:** Restaurant; bar; concierge; exercise room; room service. *In room:* A/C, TV/DVD, hair dryer, minibar, Wi-Fi (7€ per hr.).

Moderate

Hôtel Galileo ★ This is one of the 8th's most charming hotels. Proprietors Roland and Elisabeth Buffat have won friends from all over with their Hôtel des Deux-Iles and Hôtel de Lutèce on St-Louis-en-l'Ile. A short walk from the Champs-Elysées, this town house is the epitome of French elegance and charm. The medium-size rooms are a study in understated taste. Within this hotel, rooms with numbers ending in 3 (specifically, 103, 203, 303, 403, and 503) are more spacious than the others. Rooms 501 and 502 have private glassed-in verandas that you can use even in winter.

54 rue Galilée, Paris 75008. www.galileo-paris-hotel.com. ✆ **01-47-20-66-06.** Fax 01-47-20-67-17. 27 units. 130€–185€ double. AE, DC, MC, V. Métro: Charles-de-Gaulle–Etoile or George V. *In room:* A/C, TV, hair dryer, minibar, free Wi-Fi.

Relais Monceau ★ Finding an elegant but affordable hotel in the overpriced 8th is always a challenge, but Relais Monceau is an inviting choice. A 19th-century town house with two private courtyards has been discreetly restored with a respect for the past, although all the modern amenities have been installed. A government-rated three-star hotel, it takes its name from the nearby

Parc Monceau. The midsize bedrooms are furnished with elegance and taste, and are spread over three floors. There are also several large public guest areas as well.

85 rue du Rocher, Paris 75008. www.relais-monceau.com. ✆ **01-45-22-75-11.** Fax 01-45-22-30-88. 51 units. 110€–198€ double; 195€–264€ suite. AE, MC, V. Métro: Champs-Elysées. **Amenities:** Bar. *In room:* A/C, TV, hair dryer, minibar, free Wi-Fi.

Inexpensive

Hôtel Eldorado If you're looking for something to criticize, you might well find it here. But if you're an intrepid bargain hunter and don't mind living in an offbeat neighborhood on the border of Montmartre, this is one of the best cheap hotels in an overpriced city. Of course, don't expect an elevator to take you to a room with a TV, phone, or air-conditioning. But the price is right. The manager, Anne Gratacos, continually decorates the hotel with flea market finds, including Buddha busts and Art Deco armoires. The most spacious and evocative units are in a separate pavilion separated from the main structure by a garden patio with a restaurant, Bistrot des Dames.

18 rue des Dames, Paris 75017. www.eldoradohotel.fr. ✆ **01-45-22-35-21.** Fax 01-43-87-25-97. 33 units, 23 with private bathroom. 70€–80€ double with bathroom; 80€–90€ triple with bathroom. AE, MC, V. Parking 25€. Métro: Place de Clichy. **Amenities:** Restaurant. *In room:* No phone, free Wi-Fi.

OPÉRA & CANAL ST-MARTIN (9E & 10E)

Two of Paris's major department stores are located just above Opéra, and they set the tone for this dynamic shopping district, which extends north via the gourmet Martyrs strip right up to the bright lights of Pigalle. The adjacent Canal St-Martin neighborhood, over to the east, has a different vibe altogether, with bohemian locals lingering over coffee by the leafy canal.

Very Expensive

Hotel Banke ★★ In the tradition of Derby Hotels Collection, this luxurious boutique hotel is art oriented. Works of art adorn both the public rooms and the accommodations. The building dates from the Belle Epoque era and contains a majestic hall from that time, which is embellished with a great mosaic. Bedrooms are midsize to spacious and decorated with antique art and an avant-garde design. The on-site spa focuses on a self-styled "purification and regeneration of your internal ecology." Bathrooms, for the most part, are very spacious. The staff is also extremely friendly, a rarity in Paris. The terrace opens onto a panoramic view of Sacré-Coeur and the Opéra.

Hotel Banke.

20 rue Lafayette, 75009 Paris. www.derby-hotels.com/Banke-Hotel-Paris. ✆ **01-55-33-**

22-22. Fax 01-55-33-22-28. 94 units. 630€ double; 1,265€ suite. AE, DC, MC, V. Métro: Opéra. **Amenities:** 2 restaurants; bar; exercise room; room service; smoke-free rooms; spa w/steam room and sauna. *In room:* A/C, TV, hair dryer, minibar, free Wi-Fi.

Moderate

Hotel Amour ★★ This hotel oozes streetwise chic and attitude. One critic claimed that, thanks to the hotel bar being frequented by young European fashionistas, each flaunting his and her respective allure and neurosis, "waiting in a queue for the toilets has never been so entertaining." Each bedroom is decorated by a celebrity friend of the owner (like Sophie Calle, Marc Newson), so the trendy decor varies widely, from a minimalist white-on-white decor with touches of faux baroque, to disco balls, to graffiti written directly on the walls. The relaxed downstairs bar and restaurant are a great destination at any time for seeing and being seen. The ivy-covered courtyard is perfect for sipping champagne on warm days or nights.

8 rue Navarin, Paris 75009. www.hotelamourparis.fr. ✆ **01-48-78-31-80.** 20 units. 150€–170€ double; 280€ duplex. AE, MC, V. Métro: St-Georges. **Amenities:** Restaurant; bar; room service. *In room:* A/C, minibar, no phone, free Wi-Fi.

Hôtel Arvor St Georges ★★ This fresh, contemporary hotel is located in the charming New Athens neighborhood, off the tourist beat and nestled below Montmartre. Back in the 19th century, this neighborhood was frequented by Romantic artists like Victor Hugo, George Sand, and Frédéric Chopin, but today the neighborhood is a gourmand's paradise, with the restaurant-lined rue des Martyrs nearby. The hotel is relaxed and comfortable, and you'll feel like a guest in a chic Parisian's private home as you flip through some of the art and photography titles over a cup of coffee in the airy downstairs lobby. The tasty breakfast (9€) is served here or outside in the flower-filled patio when the weather is nice. The rooms have a clean designer style, and the six suites boast views over Paris to the Eiffel Tower. Service is friendly and professional.

8 rue Laferrière, Paris 75009. www.arvor-hotel-paris.com. ✆ **01-48-78-60-92.** Fax 01-48-78-16-52. 30 units. 125€–190€ double. AE, DC, MC, V. Métro: St-Georges. **Amenities:** Bar; room service. *In room:* TV, hair dryer, free Wi-Fi.

Hôtel Langlois ★ This hotel used to be known as Hôtel des Croises, but when it was used as a setting for the Jonathan Demme film *The Truth About Charlie* (2002), the hotel owners changed the name to match the one used in the film. It's a well-proportioned, restored town house with a main stairwell and a spacious landing. An antique wrought-iron elevator running up the center of the building adds an old-fashioned Parisian touch. The rooms are well proportioned and spacious; those in the front get the most light. Units in the rear are darker but quieter. Rooms, with their aura of *Ecole de Nancy* (a florid Art Nouveau style), have well-chosen antiques, tasteful rugs and fabrics, and even an occasional fireplace.

63 rue St-Lazare, Paris 75009. www.hotel-langlois.com. ✆ **01-48-74-78-24.** Fax 01-49-95-04-43. 27 units. 140€–150€ double; 190€ suite. AE, DC, MC, V. Métro: Trinité. **Amenities:** Breakfast room; room service. *In room:* A/C, TV, hair dryer, minibar, free Wi-Fi.

Inexpensive

Hotel All Seasons Paris Gare de l'Est Magenta Opposite the Gare de l'Est railway station, this hotel lives up to its name. It is truly a hotel for all seasons and a great convenience for passengers disembarking at Gare de l'Est, which has good taxi, bus, and Métro links to all of Paris. All Seasons is the budget chain link of the famous French hotel group Accor, and, as such, it's aimed at both vacationers and business travelers who seek affordable rates. The bedroom furnishings are fairly standard, except for the bedding, which emphasizes "anti-stress" quilts and pillows made with carbon threads said to channel the body's electricity. Breakfast is called "as much as you wish," and there is unlimited tea, coffee, and mineral water. Magazines and games for children are available. The hotel is smoke-free.

87 bd. de Strasbourg, Paris 75010. www.accorhotels.com. ✆ **01-42-09-12-28.** Fax 01-42-09-48-12. 32 units. 95€–115€ double. Rates include breakfast. MC, V. Métro: Gare de l'Est. **Amenities:** Room service. *In room:* A/C, TV, hair dryer, free Wi-Fi.

Hôtel Chopin Enter this intimate, offbeat hotel through a passageway that includes a toy store, a bookstore, the exit from Musée Grevin, and the architectural trappings of its original construction in 1846. Just off the Grands Boulevards, this old-fashioned hotel evokes the charm of yesteryear. In honor of its namesake, the Chopin has a piano in its reception area. The inviting lobby welcomes you behind its 1850s facade of elegant woodwork and Victorian-era glass. In the style of the Paris of long ago, the comfortably furnished bedrooms open onto a glass-topped arcade instead of the hysterically busy street, so they are rather tranquil. We prefer the bedrooms on the top floor, as they are larger and quieter, with views over the rooftops of Paris. The least expensive bedrooms lie behind the elevator bank and get less light.

10 bd. Montmartre or 46 passage Jouffroy, Paris 75009. www.hotel-chopin.com. ✆ **01-47-70-58-10.** Fax 01-42-47-00-70. 36 units. 92€–106€ double; 125€ triple. AE, MC, V. Métro: Grands-Boulevards. **Amenities:** Free Wi-Fi. *In room:* TV, hair dryer.

Hôtel Particulier.

PIGALLE & MONTMARTRE (18E)

The wedding-cake Sacré-Coeur basilica crowns the city's highest point, on the summit of Montmartre. A neighborhood apart in Paris, with a rich artistic history and all the charm of a village, Montmartre runs into Pigalle below, a harmless red light district with a high concentration of concert and club venues.

Very Expensive

Hôtel Particulier ★★★ No hotel in Paris seems quite as special as this one, lying between avenue Junot and rue Lepic and nestled in a "secret" passageway called le passage du Rocher de la Sorcière (the Witch's Rock Passage). Modern Paris meets Old Montmartre in this Directoire mansion from the 18th century, and the marriage is harmonious. Louis Bénech, one of the landscape architects who renovated the Tuileries, created the intimate gardens of the hotel. Each of the five suites has a different personality, the work of various artists that range in decor from an erotic window by Philippe Mayaux to poems and hats by Olivier Saillard. The most unusual is the suite Curtain of Hair, a loft created in the attic with images of the long hair of photographer Natacha Lesueur. The downstairs bar has exceptional cocktails.

23 av. Junot, Paris 75018. www.hotel-particulier-montmartre.com. ✆ **01-53-41-81-40.** Fax 01-42-58-00-87. 5 units. 390€–590€ suite. MC, V. Métro: Blanche. **Amenities:** Bar; breakfast room; garden. *In room:* A/C, TV, hair dryer, free Wi-Fi.

Expensive

KUBE Hotel ★ Design-savvy clients appreciate the way the architect (Raymond Morel) made repeated use of the cube, a form that the owners refer to as "the most modern of shapes." The hotel occupies the six-story premises of what was built in the late 1800s as the administrative headquarters of a now-defunct brewery (*Les bières de la Meuse*), deep inside Paris's grungy industrial heartland. There's a restaurant and a dance lounge on street level, where a DJ regularly spins tunes. Bedrooms (and everything else about the place) seem to revel in the geometry of the cube. Rectangular beds are lit from below and appear to float. Expect shag-covered sofas, fuzzy faux-fur slippers in tones of high-voltage yellow, and a sense of compact efficiency. Also on the premises is the Ice Kube Bar, a deep-cooled conversational oddity whose bartop is fashioned from—you guessed it—ice.

1-5 Passage Ruelle, Paris 75018. www.kubehotel.com. ✆ **01-42-05-20-00.** Fax 01-42-05-21-01. 41 units. 250€–400€ double; 500€–900€ suite. Parking 15€. Métro: La Chapelle. **Amenities:** Restaurant; bar; exercise room. *In room:* A/C, TV, hair dryer, free Wi-Fi.

Moderate

Timhotel Montmartre ★ Another address in the reliable Timhotel chain, this two-star hotel is located in a charming square in Montmartre. The hotel is next door to the historical Bateau Lavoir building, where Picasso had a studio for many years and painted his masterpiece *Les Demoiselles d'Avignon.* The hotel rooms are decorated in a fairly basic and impersonal style, but they're clean. Rooms on the fourth and fifth floors offer excellent views over the rooftops of Paris and Sacré-Coeur. Note that the hilltop location means that it can be a steep climb up from the closest public transport stops.

11 place Emile Goudeau, Paris 75018. www.timhotel.com. ✆ **01-42-55-74-79.** Fax 01-42-55-71-01. 59 units. 130€–160€ double. AE, DC, MC, V. Métro: Abbesses. **Amenities:** Breakfast room; concierge. *In room:* A/C (in some), TV, hair dryer, free Wi-Fi.

Inexpensive

Hôtel des Arts ★ In the center of Montmartre between place du Tertre and the Moulin Rouge, this hotel lies in a delightful quarter of Paris once made famous by poets and painters. It has a warm, welcoming atmosphere, and in a former life, it was a dormitory for the dancers of the Moulin Rouge. As you might expect, the rooms are small yet comfortable, with country-style curtains and bedspreads. Opt for one of the four bedrooms on the sixth floor for a panoramic view of Paris. As night falls, the area around the hotel often has its share of sex workers, although the hotel itself is a safe destination.

5 rue Tholozé, Paris 75018. www.arts-hotel-paris.com. ✆ **01-46-06-30-52.** Fax 01-46-06-10-83. 50 units. 70€–140€ double. AE, MC, V. Métro: Blanche. **Amenities:** Breakfast room. *In room:* TV, free Wi-Fi.

RÉPUBLIQUE, BASTILLE & EASTERN PARIS (11E & 12E)

Paris's former industrial heart has been converted into a string of cosmopolitan neighborhoods with a bohemian vibe.

Moderate

Gabriel Paris Marais ★★ This chic boutique hotel calls itself Paris's first "detox hotel," a concept devoted to "well-being and regeneration." One example of this is that some accommodations are outfitted with Night Cove, a system that uses sound and light to encourage natural sleeping patterns; the rooms are also soundproofed to ensure a restful night. You can continue to detox with an organic breakfast and spa treatments in their Bioo Detox Room. Located close to place de la République and Canal St-Martin, this hotel offers small to midsize comfortably furnished rooms with modern amenities and stylish lighting. In the surrealist but harmoniously decorated "detox bar," guests can order a large choice of antioxidant drinks and teas.

25 rue du Grand-Prieure, Paris 75011. www.gabrielparismarais.com. ✆ **01-47-00-13-38.** 41 units. 155€–280€ double. AE, DC, MC, V. Métro: République. **Amenities:** Cafeteria; room service; small spa. *In room:* A/C, TV/DVD, hair dryer, minibar, MP3 docking station, free Wi-Fi.

Le Général Hotel ★ As the neighborhood around place de la République, Canal St-Martin, and rue Oberkampf becomes increasingly attuned to Paris's sense of counterculture chic, this is a good example of that neighborhood's improving fortunes. Opened within the premises of a rundown hotel that was radically renovated and decorated by noted designer Jean-Philippe Nuel, the hotel's upbeat interior revolves around prominent rectilinear lines, spartan-looking decors, and an intelligent distribution of spaces. The result is a seven-story hotel with floors linked by two separate elevator banks and pale, monochromatic beige-and-off-white color schemes, and with furniture that is either dark (rosewood toned) or pale (birch or maple toned).

5–7 rue Rampon, Paris 75011. www.legeneralhotel.com. ✆ **01-47-00-41-57.** Fax 01-47-00-21-56. 46 units. 157€–252€ double. AE, MC, V. Métro: République. **Amenities:** Bar; exercise room; room service; sauna. *In room:* A/C, TV, hair dryer, free Wi-Fi.

Inexpensive

Cosmos Hotel This no-frills option in the heart of the animated Oberkampf neighborhood has got to be one of the best deals in town. The simply furnished rooms are clean and have fresh towels provided on a daily basis. The staff is helpful, and the hotel is also home to a little furry feline mascot. The only downside is that the hotel can be noisy on the weekends as people spill out of the busy local bars and restaurants.

35 rue Jean-Pierre Timbaud, Paris 75011. www.cosmos-hotel-paris.com. ✆**/Fax 01-43-57-25-88.** 36 units. 67€ double; 75€ triple. AE, MC, V. Métro: Parmentier. *In room:* TV, hair dryer, free Wi-Fi.

BELLEVILLE & NORTHEAST PARIS (19E & 20E)

Not many tourists venture to these cosmopolitan areas, located deep in the city's old industrial heartland. But up-and-coming Belleville includes one of the city's Chinatowns, a new wave of contemporary art galleries, and the must-see Buttes Chaumont park.

Moderate

Libertel Canal St-Martin ★ This hotel consists of three small typical Parisian buildings, which are connected by a charming courtyard and a small garden. The largest building was entirely renovated in 2008, and the Villa Cosi was renovated in 2010. Though small, guest rooms are clean and contemporary, with flatscreen TVs and Wi-Fi access. Located in the Canal St-Martin neighborhood, the hotel is near some charming shops and restaurants, as well as the beautiful Buttes-Chaumont Park; it is also very close to the Jaurés Métro stop. The hotel is entirely smoke-free.

5 av. Secrétan, Paris 75019. www.hotel-canal-st-martin.com. ✆ **01-42-06-62-00.** Fax 01-42-40-64-51. 69 units. 105€–145€ double. Rates include breakfast. MC, V. Métro: Jaurès. **Amenities:** Breakfast room. *In room:* A/C (in most), free Wi-Fi.

Mama Shelter ★★ Even though it's located off the beaten track, this recently opened Philippe Starck–designed hotel attracts the in-crowd, with its buzzing downstairs restaurant-bar space, sleek design, and high-tech features. The stylish yet simple rooms are equipped with iMac computers, offering on-demand movies, Internet access, and television programs. Plus, the low rates make the rooms a great value. This is a place for the young and hip, and the bar is a local hot spot.

109 rue de Bagnolet, Paris 75020. www.mamashelter.com. ✆ **01-43-48-48-48.** Fax 01-43-48-48-49. 170 units. 89€–199€ double. Rates include breakfast. MC, V. Free parking. Métro: Gambetta. **Amenities:** Restaurant; bar; babysitting; bike rental; concierge. *In room:* A/C, iMac, microwave, minibar, free Wi-Fi.

Inexpensive

St-Christopher's Inn ★ Located on the picturesque Bassin de la Villette, which connects the Canal St-Martin to the Seine, this massive hostel—opened in 2008—is close to some great bars, cinemas, restaurants, and clubs. It is particularly lovely in summer, when the banks of the canal come to life. The hostel is home to an animated bar called Belushi's.

159 rue Crimée, Paris 75019. www.st-christophers.co.uk/paris-hostels. ✆ **01-40-34-34-40.** Fax 01-40-34-31-38. www.st-christophers.fr. 70 units. 75€–100€ double. Rates include breakfast. MC, V. Métro: Crimée or Laumière. **Amenities:** Restaurant; bar; bike rental. *In room:* Free Wi-Fi.

The Left Bank

LATIN QUARTER (5E)

This is where it was all happening in May 1968. The Sorbonne University is at the heart of this Left Bank neighborhood, which gets its name from the Latin the students and professors spoke there until the end of the 18th century. To feed those minds, the area also boasts some of the city's best specialty bookshops. This neighborhood dates back to the time when the Romans ruled—Paris was conquered by the Romans in 52 B.C.—and the area still conserves Roman ruins, which you can explore at the Cluny Museum.

Mama Shelter.

Expensive

Hôtel Design de la Sorbonne ★★ Located near the Sorbonne University and a short walk from the Luxembourg Gardens, this boutique hotel is stylish and comfortable. Though small, guest rooms are sleek and trendy, and are decorated in bold colors and patterns; rooms feature new bathrooms and modern amenities like Apple iMac computers. The owners, who manage several other quality hotels in Paris, demonstrate inventiveness through the hotel design—look down at the floor to read excerpts from French literary classics woven into the hotel's carpets. The hotel is smoke-free.

6 rue Victor Cousin, Paris 75005. www.hotelsorbonne.com. ✆ **01-43-54-58-08.** Fax 01-40-51-05-18. 38 units. 250€–340€ double. AE, DC, MC, V. Métro: Cluny–La Sorbonne. RER: Luxembourg. **Amenities:** Breakfast room. *In room:* A/C, TV, Apple iMac, hair dryer, minibar, free Wi-Fi.

Hotel Seven ★★ Run by the same team as the Five Hotel (see below), this luxury concept hotel is not for the faint hearted, taking the commitment to exceptional interiors a step beyond. Each room and suite is totally unique, with evocative names like Marie Antoinette, The Black Diamond, and On/Off; in the Levitation rooms, the bed is actually suspended off the floor. Each room is well appointed and might include a complimentary bottle of champagne, an MP3 docking base, an espresso machine, a large flatscreen TV, luxurious beds and linens, and designer bath products. Couples looking for a romantic setting will enjoy this hotel. The only downside is the slightly off-the-beaten path location.

20 rue Berthollet, Paris 75005. www.sevenhotelparis.com. ✆ **01-43-31-47-52.** Fax 01-43-36-41-40. 37 units. 327€–397€ double; 737€–1,107€ suite. AE, DC, MC, V. Métro: Les Gobelins. **Amenities:** Bar, breakfast room, room service. *In room:* A/C, TV, hair dryer, MP3 docking station, minibar, free Wi-Fi.

Moderate

Best Western La Tour Notre-Dame ★ In the heart of the Sorbonne district, this restored Latin Quarter hotel rises seven floors over a 17th-century vaulted cellar where breakfast is served. A hotel of Rive Gauche character, it is ideally situated for Left Bank living, lying between St-Germain-des-Prés and the cathedral of Notre-Dame, opposite the Sorbonne and the Cluny Museum. Bedrooms, many with exposed beams, have been given a decorator's touch, and they are adorned with certain Romantic accents. Liberty prints and Empire-era furniture decorate many of the bedrooms, which are beautifully maintained. A Vélib bike hire station is located just outside the front door.

20 rue du Sommerard, Paris 75005. www.la-tour-notre-dame.com. ✆ **01-43-54-47-60.** Fax 01-43-26-42-34. 48 units. 171€–245€ double. AE, DC, MC, V. Métro: Cluny–Sorbonne. RER: Saint-Michel or Notre-Dame. **Amenities:** Bar. *In room:* A/C, TV, hair dryer, minibar, free Wi-Fi.

The Five Hotel ★ 🎁 A charmer among Left Bank boutique hotels, the Five is named for the 5th arrondissement and lies in a restored 1800s town house on a U-shaped street off boulevard de Port-Royal. The funky interior design, including a red leather paneled hall or a red-painted gas fireplace, is not to everyone's taste. The rooms are individually designed in various colors (blood red or Halloween orange, for example), and tiny white lights evoke a planetarium. Of course, if you want a room the color of a prune, that, too, is available. A Chinese lacquer artist, Isabelle Emmerique, has certainly been busy here. Some rooms are small, but all the beds are exceedingly comfortable.

3 rue Flatters, Paris 75005. www.thefivehotel.com. ✆ **01-43-31-74-21.** Fax 01-43-31-61-96. 24 units. 202€–340€ double; 392€ suite. AE, MC, V. Métro: Bastilel or Gobelins. **Amenities:** Bar; room service. *In room:* A/C, TV, hair dryer, free Wi-Fi.

Hôtel Quartier Latin Between the Sorbonne and Musée de Cluny, this hotel captures the flavor of the Paris literati better than any other in Paris. Its original decor was conceived in 1997 by Didier Gomez, who referred to it as "contemporary with cultural references." That means walls stenciled with passages from Victor Hugo or photographs of Colette and André Gide. Even the breakfast room is stocked with bookshelves, and its ceiling inscribed with quotes from Baudelaire. Bibliomania continues in the lobby, which is filled with floor-to-ceiling bookcases. Bedrooms are decorated comfortably and tastefully in blue and white, with such delicacies as linen curtains, along with fine wood furnishings, plus white-tiled bathrooms. In all, this is a "novel" hotel and ideal for bookworms.

9 rue des Ecoles, Paris 75005. www.hotelquartierlatin.com. ✆ **01-44-27-06-45.** Fax 01-43-25-36-70. 29 units. 187€–248€ double; 242€–310€ junior suite. AE, MC, V. Métro: Cardinal Lemoine. Parking nearby 20€. **Amenities:** Babysitting; room service. *In room:* A/C, TV, hair dryer, minibar, free Wi-Fi.

Hôtel St-Jacques ★ Try for a room with a balcony view of Notre-Dame and the Panthéon. The Belle Epoque atmosphere of the hotel was made famous in the movie *Charade* (1963), which starred Cary Grant and Audrey Hepburn. Jean-Paul and Martine Rousseau, the owners, welcome you to this old-fashioned Latin Quarter gem, filled with Second Empire overtones, including frescoes in the breakfast room and lounge, 18th-century ceiling murals in some of the bedrooms, wedding cake plasterwork, and corridors painted with *trompe l'oeil* marble. Bedrooms are generally spacious and have been attractively and comfortably restored. Street-side rooms can be a bit noisy.

35 rue des Ecoles, Paris 75005. www.paris-hotel-stjacques.com. ✆ **01-44-07-45-45.** Fax 01-43-25-65-50. 26 units. 142€–247€ double; 176€ triple. AE, DC, MC, V. Métro: Maubert-Mutualité. **Amenities:** Babysitting. *In room:* A/C TV, hair dryer, free Wi-Fi.

Inexpensive

Hôtel des Grandes Ecoles ★ Few hotels in the neighborhood offer so much low-key charm at such reasonable prices. It's composed of a trio of high-ceilinged buildings, interconnected via a sheltered courtyard where in warm weather, singing birds provide a worthy substitute for the TVs deliberately missing from the rooms. Accommodations, as reflected by the price, range from snug, cozy doubles to more spacious chambers. Each room is comfortable, but with a lot of luggage, the very smallest would be cramped. The decor is old fashioned, with feminine touches such as flowered upholsteries and ruffles. Many have views of a garden where trellises and flower beds evoke the countryside.

75 rue de Cardinal-Lemoine, Paris 75005. www.hotel-grandes-ecoles.com. ✆ **01-43-26-79-23.** Fax 01-47-47-65-48. 51 units. 115€–140€ double. Extra bed 20€. MC, V. Parking 30€. Métro: Cardinal Lemoine, Jussieu, or Place Monge. RER: Port-Royal, Luxembourg. **Amenities:** Babysitting; room service. *In room:* Hair dryer, free Wi-Fi.

ST-GERMAIN-DES-PRÉS & LUXEMBOURG (6E)

This glamorous neighborhood is home to great shops and cafes. Intellectuals like Simone de Beauvoir and Jean-Paul Sartre put St-Germain on the map postwar, when they and their friends had high-minded conversations at cafes like Les

Deux Magots or Cafe de Flore. The area still draws many of the city's artists and thinkers, and most of the modern art galleries are here, too.

Very Expensive

Hotel Bel-Ami ★★ This four-star hotel was designed expressly to appeal to fashion-conscious patrons in the heart of the Left Bank cafe district. Its name translates as "Handsome (Male) Friend." You'll get the feeling that this is an arts-conscious hotel whose minimalist public areas were built only after months of careful design by a team of trend-following architects. Expect color schemes of lilac walls, acid-green sofas, copper-colored tiles, bleached ash, and industrial-style lighting fixtures. Bedrooms contain a palette of earth tones, such as pistachio ice cream or pumpkin pie, and an almost aggressively minimalist, even Cubist, design. Bathrooms are artfully spartan. The suites and first-floor rooms have all been recently renovated.

7–11 rue St-Benoît, Paris 75006. www.hotel-bel-ami.com. ✆ **01-42-61-53-53.** Fax 01-49-27-09-33. 112 units. 425€ double; 1,050€ suite. AE, DC, MC, V. Métro: St-Germain-des-Prés. **Amenities:** Bar; concierge; espresso bar; exercise room. *In room:* TV, minibar, free Wi-Fi.

Relais Christine ★★ This hotel welcomes you into a former 16th-century Augustinian cloister. From a cobblestone street, you enter a symmetrical courtyard and find an elegant reception area with sculpture and Renaissance antiques. Each room is uniquely decorated with wooden beams and Louis XIII–style furnishings; the rooms come in a range of styles and shapes. Some are among the Left Bank's largest, with extras such as mirrored closets, plush carpets, and some balconies facing the courtyard. The least attractive rooms are in the interior. Bed configurations vary, but all mattresses are on the soft side, offering comfort with quality linens.

3 rue Christine, 75006 Paris. www.relais-christine.com. ✆ **01-40-51-60-80.** Fax 01-40-51-60-81. 51 units. 390€–500€ double; 580€–900€ duplex or suite. AE, DC, MC, V. Free parking. Métro: Odéon or St-Michel. **Amenities:** Honor bar; babysitting; concierge; exercise room; room service; spa. *In room:* A/C, TV/DVD, hair dryer, minibar, free Wi-Fi.

Expensive

Hotel La Belle Juliette ★★ This luxury hotel, which opened in Saint-Germain-des-Prés in 2011, stands out for its chic interior design by local textile designer Anne Gelbard. The hotel is inspired by the life of Juliette Récamier, a 19th-century French socialite whose Parisian salon drew intellectuals and artists. Guest rooms feel very contemporary while still paying homage to the 19th century and Mme. Récamier, with sophisticated color combinations, luxurious fabrics, original engravings, and restored antiques. Yet the rooms are also completely modern, with Apple iMac computers for entertainment.

92 rue du Cherche Midi, Paris 75006. www.hotel-belle-juliette-paris.com. ✆ **01-42-22-97-40.** Fax 01-45-44-89-97. 34 units. 300€–450€ double; 620€–1,050€ suite. AE, DC, MC, V. Métro: St-Germain-des-Prés. **Amenities:** Restaurant; bar; room service; spa. *In room:* A/C, iMac, hair dryer, minibar, free Wi-Fi.

L'Apostrophe ★ This Rive Gauche boutique hotel lies near Cafe de Flore and Cafe des Deux-Magots, once the favorite literary haunts of some of France's most celebrated writers. This hotel pays homage to that tradition, becoming the first Parisian "poem hotel," an establishment devoted to the aesthetic, the beauty, and the mysteries of writing. On the ground floor is painted the story of *One*

Thousand and One Nights. The first floor is devoted to the markings that predate writing. On the second floor are signs indicating the alphabet, calligraphy, and music. The third floor is devoted to books and posters. A stay here is like no other in Paris. Bedrooms are beautifully decorated and comfortable, though a bit small. Be aware that the shower and water basin are actually in the room—there is no separate bathroom.

3 rue de Chevreuse, Paris 75006. www.apostrophe-hotel.com. ✆ **01-56-54-31-31.** 16 units. 149€–290€ standard double; 199€–350€ double with a Jacuzzi. Métro: Vavin. **Amenities:** Bar. *In room:* A/C, TV/DVD, CD player, hair dryer, free Wi-Fi.

L'Hôtel ★ Ranking just a notch below the Relais Christine (see above), this is one of the Left Bank's most charming boutique hotels. It was once a 19th-century fleabag whose major distinction was that Oscar Wilde died in one of its bedrooms, but today's guests aren't anywhere near destitution. Guest rooms vary in size, style, and price; all have decorative fireplaces and fabric-covered walls. All the sumptuous beds have tasteful fabrics and crisp linens. About half the bathrooms are small, tubless nooks. Room themes reflect China, Russia, Japan, India, or high-camp Victorian. The Cardinal room is all scarlet, the Viollet-le-Duc room is neo-Gothic, and the room where Wilde died is Victorian.

13 rue des Beaux-Arts, Paris 75006. www.l-hotel.com. ✆ **01-44-41-99-00.** Fax 01-43-25-64-81. 20 units. 280€–370€ double; 640€–740€ suite. AE, DC, MC, V. Métro: St-Germain-des-Prés. **Amenities:** Restaurant; bar; babysitting; room service. *In room:* A/C, TV/DVD, hair dryer, minibar, free Wi-Fi.

Relais St-Germain ★★ It's difficult to exaggerate the charm of this deeply personalized and intimate hotel created from side-by-side 17th-century town houses. You'll navigate your way through a labyrinth of narrow and winding hallways to soundproofed bedrooms that are spacious, and artfully and individually decorated in a style that evokes late-19th-century Paris at its most sensual. Two of the rooms have terraces. Come here for a discreet escape from the anonymity of larger, less personalized hotels and for an injection of boutique-style Parisian charm. Even *Vogue* magazine referred to this place as "an oasis of Left-Bank charm." We heartily agree. The owner of the hotel is one of the city's best chefs; hotel guests have priority booking at the attached restaurant, Le Comptoir, where Parisians often wait 6 months for a reservation.

9 Carrefour de l'Odéon, Paris 75006. www.hotelrsg.com. ✆ **01-43-29-12-05.** Fax 01-46-33-45-30. 22 units. 285€–370€ double; 395€ suite. Rates include breakfast. AE, DC, MC, V. **Amenities:** Restaurant. *In room:* A/C, TV/DVD, hair dryer, minibar, free Wi-Fi.

Moderate

Hôtel des Marronniers In the heart of St-Germain-des-Prés, this is one of those hidden gems that is nestled in the back of a courtyard on a street lined with antique stores. At the rear of this "secret" address is a small garden with a veranda, where you can linger over afternoon tea. Some of the rooms open onto views of the steeple of the church of St-Germain-des-Prés. The midsize bedrooms are furnished with period pieces placed under exposed beams and enveloped by fabric-covered walls in rich tones.

21 rue Jacob, Paris 75006. www.paris-hotel-marroniers.com. ✆ **01-43-25-30-60.** Fax 01-40-46-83-56. 37 units. 180€–195€ double. MC, V. Métro: St-Germain-des-Prés. *In room:* A/C, TV, hair dryer, free Wi-Fi.

Hôtel Louis II ★ In an 18th-century building on rue St-Sulpice, this elegant boutique hotel offers guest rooms decorated in modern French tones. Afternoon drinks and morning coffee are served in the reception salon, where gilt-framed mirrors, fresh flowers, and antiques radiate a provincial aura, as though something out of Proust. The generally small soundproofed rooms with exposed beams and lace bedding complete the impression. Many visitors ask for the romantic attic rooms.

2 rue St-Sulpice, Paris. 75006 www.hotel-louis2.com. ✆ **01-46-33-13-80.** Fax 01-46-33-17-29. 22 units. 195€–220€ double; 310€ junior suite. AE, DC, MC, V. Métro: Odéon. **Amenities:** Bar; room service. *In room:* A/C, TV, hair dryer, minibar, free Wi-Fi.

La Villa St-Germain ★ This hotel's facade resembles those of many of the other buildings in the neighborhood. Inside, however, the decor is a minimalist ultramodern creation rejecting traditional French aesthetics. The public areas and guest rooms contain Bauhaus-like furniture; the lobby's angular lines are softened with bouquets of leaves and flowers. Most unusual are the tubs, with decidedly postmodern stainless steel and pink, black, or beige marble.

29 rue Jacob, Paris 75006. www.villa-saintgermain.com. ✆ **01-43-26-60-00.** Fax 01-46-34-63-63. 31 units. 160€–370€ double; from 470€ suite. AE, DC, MC, V. Métro: St-Germain-des-Prés. **Amenities:** Bar; babysitting; room service. *In room:* A/C, TV, hair dryer, minibar, Wi-Fi (5€ per day).

Inexpensive

Hotel Mayet ★ This budget hotel has a great location close to shopping heaven, Le Bon Marché and St-Germain. The compact rooms are clean, comfortable, and contemporary, designed in a bordeaux-and-gray color scheme. The low-key lobby sets the scene: Deep, comfortable sofas are set against a brightly painted wall with some original graffiti by Parisian artist André. There's an iMac computer in the lobby with Internet access. Service goes the extra mile.

3 rue Mayet, Paris 75006. www.mayet.com. ✆ **01-47-83-21-35.** Fax 01-40-65-95-78. 23 units. 130€–150€ double. Rates include breakfast. AE, DC, MC, V. Métro: Duroc. **Amenities:** Bar, breakfast room. *In room:* A/C, minibar, TV, free Wi-Fi.

EIFFEL TOWER & NEARBY (7E)

Running along the Seine on the Left Bank, from Musée d'Orsay to the Eiffel Tower and opposite the Louvre, this elegant residential neighborhood counts M. Karl Lagerfeld as one of its well-heeled inhabitants.

Very Expensive

Hôtel Montalembert ★★ The elegant Montalembert dates from 1926, when it was built in the Beaux Arts style. Its beige, cream, and gold decor borrows elements of Bauhaus and postmodern design. The guest rooms are spacious except for some standard doubles that are small unless you're a very thin model. Frette linens decorate roomy beds topped with cabana-stripe duvets that crown deluxe French mattresses, and bathrooms boast L'Occitane products.

3 rue de Montalembert, Paris 75007. www.montalembert.com. ✆ **800/786-6397** in the U.S. and Canada, or 01-45-49-68-68. Fax 01-45-49-69-49. 56 units. 300€–520€ double; 650€–900€ suite. AE, DC, MC, V. Parking 33€. Métro: Rue du Bac. **Amenities:** Restaurant; bar; concierge; access to nearby health club; room service. *In room:* A/C, TV, hair dryer, minibar, Wi-Fi (29€).

Expensive

Hôtel Le Tourville ★★ This is a well-managed, personalized town house between the Eiffel Tower and Les Invalides. It originated in the 1930s as a hotel and was revitalized much later into the charmer of today. Bedrooms offer original art, antique furnishings or reproductions, and wooden furniture covered in modern, sometimes bold, upholsteries. Four of the rooms, including the suite, have private terraces. Beds are queens or twins, each of which was recently replaced. The staff is well trained, with the kinds of personalities that make you want to linger at the reception desk. Breakfast is the only meal served, but you can get a drink in the lobby.

16 av. de Tourville, Paris 75007. www.hoteltourville.com. ✆ **01-47-05-62-62.** Fax 01-47-05-43-90. 30 units. 210€–300€ double; 380€–470€ suite. AE, MC, V. Métro: Ecole Militaire. **Amenities:** Bar; concierge; room service. *In room:* A/C, TV, hair dryer, free Wi-Fi.

Moderate

Hôtel de Londres Eiffel ★★ Small and charming, this independently run hotel is just a 2-minute walk from the Eiffel Tower. Completely renovated, it is "dressed" in colors of yellow and raspberry, which is far more harmonious and elegant than the combination sounds. In a residential district (one of the best in Paris), the bedrooms are midsize and tastefully decorated, each with an individual decor. The top floors open onto views of the illuminated Eiffel Tower at night.

1 rue Augereau, 75007 Paris. www.londres-eiffel.com. ✆ **01-45-51-63-02.** Fax 01-47-05-28-96. 30 units. 185€–220€ double; 380€ suite. AE, DC, MC. Parking 34€. Métro: Ecole Militaire. **Amenities:** Concierge. *In room:* A/C, TV, hair dryer, minibar, free Wi-Fi.

Hôtel Le Bellechasse ★★ 🎁 This gem of a hotel, seconds on foot from Musée d'Orsay, is still one of the city's most fanciful designer hotels. It's the creation of couturier Christian Lacroix, who let his imagination go wild. A stay here is like wandering into a psychedelic garden. Each guest room is different, in a pastiche of colors with baroque overtones. One French critic called Lacroix's designs "magpie sensibility," perhaps a reference to one room where top-hatted, frock-coated Paris dandies with butterfly wings wrap around both walls and ceilings. The helpful staff is part of the fun—that and taking a bath in a fiberglass tub.

8 rue de Bellechasse, Paris 75007. www.lebellechasse.com. ✆ **01-45-50-22-31.** Fax 01-45-51-52-36. 34 units. 160€–245€ double. MC, V. Métro: Solferino. RER: Musée d'Orsay. **Amenities:** Dining room (breakfast). *In room:* A/C, TV/DVD, CD player, hair dryer, minibar, MP3 docking station, free Wi-Fi.

Hôtel Verneuil ★★ 🎁 Small-scale and personal, this hotel, in the words of a critic, "combines modernist sympathies with nostalgia for *la vieille France*" (old-fashioned France). Built in the 1600s as a town house, it is a creative and intimate jumble of charm and coziness inside. Expect a mixture of antique and contemporary furniture; lots of books; and, in the bedrooms, *trompe l'oeil* ceilings, antique beams, quilts, and walls covered in fabric that comes in a rainbow of colors.

8 rue de Verneuil, Paris 75007. www.hotelverneuil.com. ✆ **01-42-60-82-14.** Fax 01-42-61-40-38. 26 units. 178€–240€ double. AE, DC, MC, V. Métro: St-Germain-des-Prés. **Amenities:** Bar; babysitting; room service. *In room:* A/C (in some), TV, hair dryer, minibar, free Wi-Fi.

MONTPARNASSE & SOUTHERN PARIS (13E, 14E & 15E)

Back in the early days of the 20th century, Montparnasse was a hotbed of creativity. Between World War I and World War II, artists, expats, and extravagant figures like Kiki de Montparnasse and Gertrude Stein reinvented the world in the bars and cafes of the area.

Moderate

Hôtel La Manufacture ★ 🎁 With good rooms and decent prices, this place is a real find. Lying on a small street near place d'Italie in the 13th arrondissement, it is only 10 minutes by Métro from the stations at Montparnasse and Gare de Lyon. Small to midsize bedrooms are decorated in printed fabrics and soothing pastels. The most desirable room is no. 74 because of its distant views of the Eiffel Tower. This restored 19th-century building has a wrought-iron door and is graced with iron lamps, wicker chairs, oak floors, and bright paintings. It contains a number of old-fashioned armoires called *chapeau de gendarme* (police hat).

8 rue Philippe de Champagne (av. des Gobelins), Paris 75013. www.hotel-la-manufacture.com. ✆ **01-45-35-45-25.** Fax 01-45-35-45-40. 56 units. 145€–195€ double; 310€ triple. AE, DC, MC, V. Métro: Place d'Italie. **Amenities:** Bar; room service. *In room:* A/C, TV, hair dryer, Wi-Fi (10€ per 3 hr.).

Inexpensive

Hôtel du Vert Galant Verdant climbing plants and shrubs make this family-run hotel feel like an *auberge* (inn) deep in the French countryside. The smallish guest rooms have tiled or carpeted floors, unfussy furniture, and (in most cases) views of the private garden or the public park across the street. One of the hotel's best aspects is the Basque restaurant next door, the Auberge Etchegorry, sharing the same management; hotel guests receive a discount.

41 rue Croulebarbe, Paris 75013. www.vertgalant.com. ✆ **01-44-08-83-50.** Fax 01-44-08-83-69. 15 units. 90€–130€ double. AE, MC, V. Parking 15€. Métro: Corvisart or Gobelins. RER: Gare d'Austerlitz. **Amenities:** Restaurant; room service. *In room:* TV, hair dryer, minibar, free Wi-Fi.

Near the Airports

ORLY

Moderate

Hilton Paris Orly Airport ★ Boxy and bland, the Hilton at Orly is a well-maintained and convenient business hotel. Noise from incoming planes can't penetrate the guest rooms' sound barriers, giving you a decent shot at a night's sleep. (Unlike the 24-hr. Charles de Gaulle Airport, Orly is closed to arriving flights from midnight to 6am.) The midsize rooms are standard for a chain hotel; each has been renovated.

Aéroport Orly, 267 Orly Sud, Orly Aérogare Cedex 94544. www.hilton.com. ✆ **800/445-8667** in the U.S. and Canada, or 01-45-12-45-12. Fax 01-45-12-45-00. 351 units. 90€–250€ double; 300€ suite. AE, DC, MC, V. Parking 14€. Transit to and from airport by complimentary shuttle bus. **Amenities:** Restaurant; bar; airport transfers; babysitting; concierge; exercise room; room service. *In room:* A/C, TV/DVD, hair dryer, Wi-Fi (17€ per 12 hr.).

Inexpensive

Air Plus This 1990s hotel offers standard rooms that are comfortable, insulated against airport noise, and a bit larger than you might expect. The location is in an out-of-the-way, leafy residential zone. It is connected with Orly by 10-minute complimentary shuttle-bus rides, which can be irregular, so it's worth checking the timetable with the hotel directly.

58 voie Nouvelle (near the Parc Georges Mélliès), Orly 94310. www.hotelairplus.com. ✆ **01-41-80-75-75.** Fax 01-41-80-12-12. 72 units. 70€–110€ double. AE, DC, MC, V. Free parking. Transit to and from airport by complimentary shuttle bus. **Amenities:** Restaurant; airport transfers; room service. *In room:* A/C, TV, hair dryer, free Wi-Fi.

CHARLES DE GAULLE

Moderate

Novotel Convention & Wellness Roissy CDG ★★ ☺ This comfortable four-star hotel located on the airport grounds is ideal for business travelers or for people who need to be near the airport to make a flight. The hotel offers a Wellness Club, with a heated pool, hammam, sauna, gym, and beauty treatments to help exhausted travelers unwind. There are regular free shuttles that go between the hotel and the airport.

Allée des Vergers, Roissy 95700. www.novotel.com. ✆ **01-30-18-20-00.** Fax 01-34-29-95-60. 289 units. 129€–295€ double. AE, DC, MC, V. Free shuttles from 5:15am–12:30am btw. the RER/TGV train stations at Paris CDG airport and the hotel. Transit to and from airport terminals by free shuttle. Parking 21€ per day. **Amenities:** Restaurant; bar; babysitting; concierge; exercise room; indoor pool; room service. *In room:* A/C, TV, hair dryer, minibar, free Wi-Fi.

Inexpensive

ibis Paris CDG Terminal Roissy Conveniently located near CDG's Terminal 3, this two-star hotel is the cheapest option near the airport. Freshly renovated, the hotel rooms are clean and comfortable, though they are decorated in that bland aesthetic common to airports.

Roissy Aéroport, Roissy en France 95701. www.ibishotel.com. ✆ **01-49-19-19-19.** Fax 01-49-19-19-21. 556 units. 79€–139€ double. AE, DC, MC, V. Parking 16€ per day. Transit to and from airport by complimentary shuttle bus. **Amenities:** 2 restaurants; bar; room service. *In room:* A/C, TV, hair dryer, minibar, free Wi-Fi.

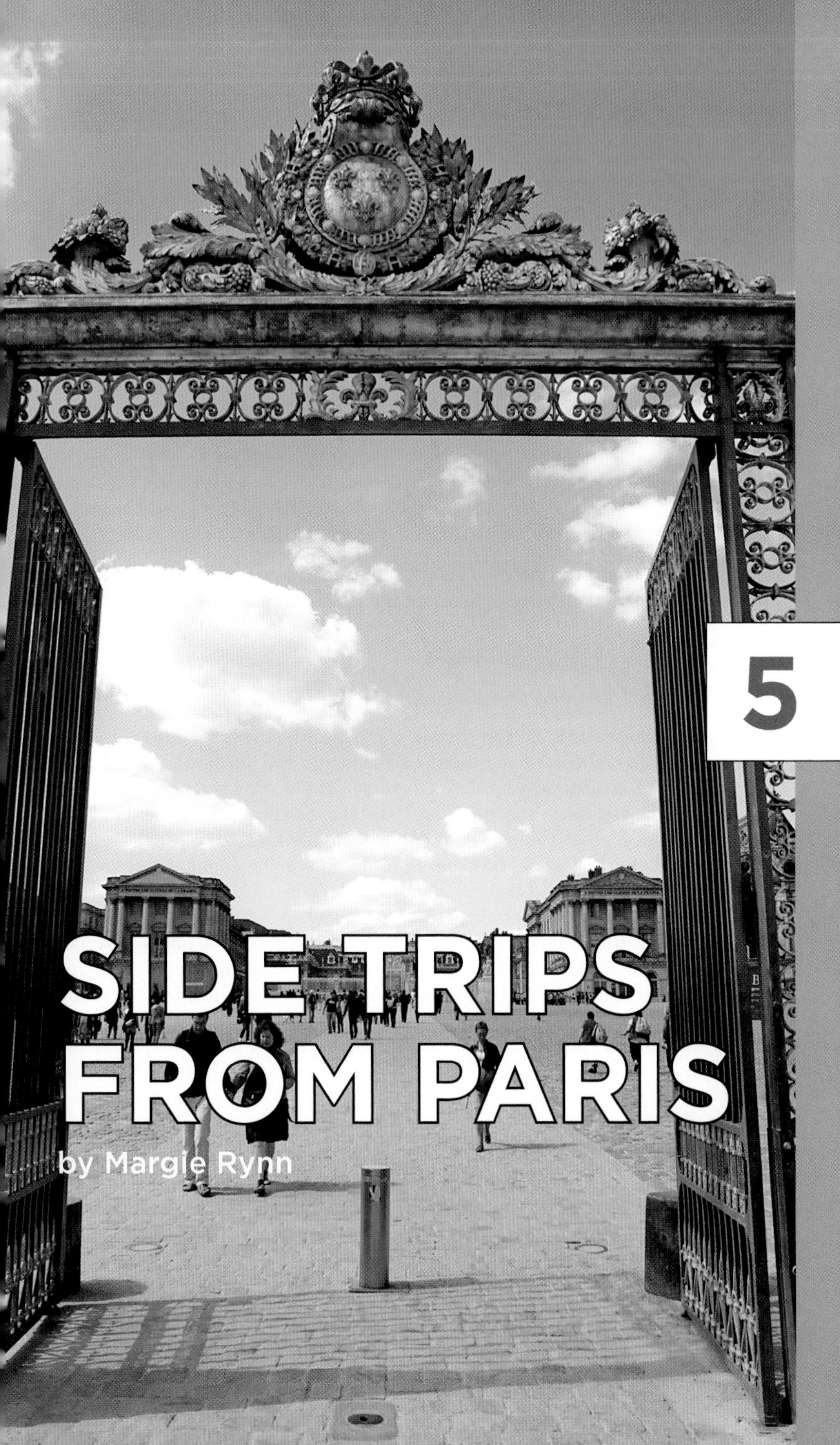

5

SIDE TRIPS FROM PARIS

by Margie Rynn

Château de Versailles, the Cathédrale Notre-Dame de Chartres, and the Palais de Fontainebleau draw countless tour buses to this region. They're the stars of the Ile de France. Some lesser-known but equally stunning spots also await you. You'll find everything from medieval towns, Gothic cathedrals, and an 18th-century château, to forests such as Fontainebleau and Chantilly, sleepy villages, and an African game reserve. For kids of all ages, there's Disneyland Paris. Finally, this region is a haven for artists, so you can visit the painted worlds of Corot, Renoir, Degas, Monet, and Cézanne.

You can experience everything we describe here on a day trip or an overnight from Paris. For even more day trips, check out the latest edition of *Frommer's Paris.*

VERSAILLES ★★★

21km (13 miles) SW of Paris; 71km (44 miles) NE of Chartres

Back in the *grand siècle,* all you needed was a sword, a hat, and a bribe for the guard at the gate. Provided you didn't look as if you had smallpox, you'd be admitted to the Château de Versailles, where you could stroll through salon after glittering salon and watch the Sun King, gossiping, dancing, plotting, and flirting. Louis XIV was accorded about as much privacy as an institution.

Today Louis XIV would be shocked to find 5.4 million commoners visiting the chateau each year and happy families regularly picnicking along the Grand Canal. What was once the terrain of the elite is now open to the masses, who are invited to enjoy the 7,000 paintings, 2,900 sculptures, and 2,500 objets d'art that decorate the castle and its vast grounds. With over 2,000 rooms and 787 hectares (1,944 acres) of grounds, Versailles' upkeep is a Herculean feat, and parts of the domain are still not open to the public. But thanks to a massive, multidecade restoration project (see box below), visitors will have even more to visit in years to come.

Essentials

GETTING THERE To get to Versailles, catch the **RER** line C to Versailles–Rive Gauche at the Gare d'Austerlitz, St-Michel, Musée d'Orsay, Invalides, Ponte de l'Alma, Champ de Mars, or Javel stop, and take it to the Versailles/Rive Gauche station. The trip takes 35 to 40 minutes. Make sure you take the train marked "Versailles/Rive Gauche" and not "Versailles Chantier," which takes a round-about route and will leave you on the other end of town, a long walk from the château. The round-trip fare is 6.10€; **SNCF trains**

PREVIOUS PAGE: **Château de Versailles.**

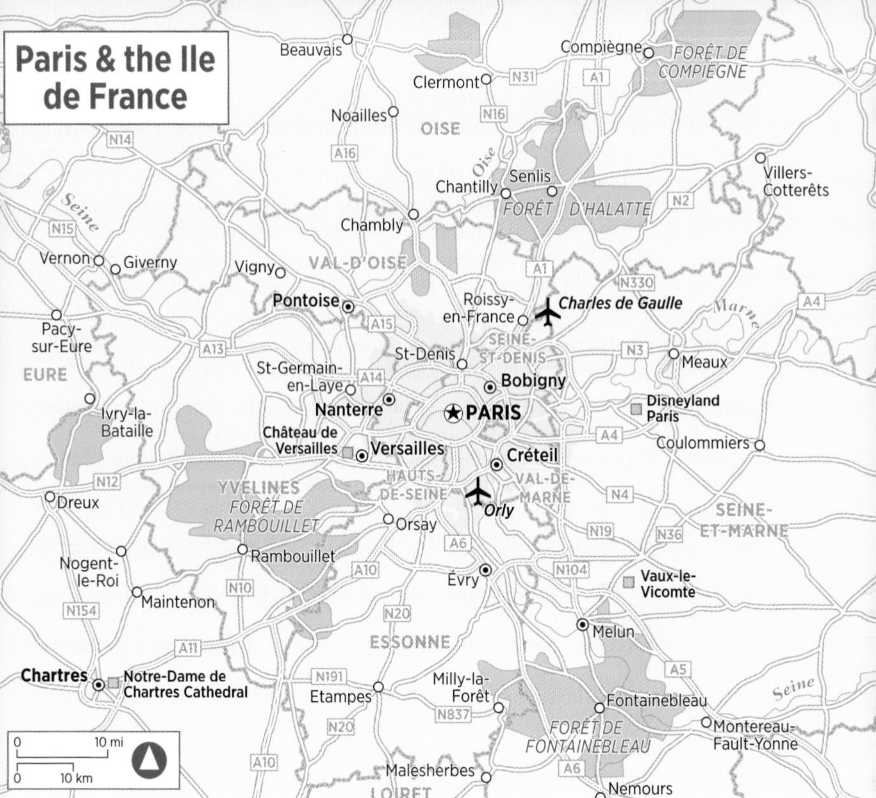

make frequent runs from Gare St-Lazare and Gare Montparnasse in Paris to Versailles. Trains departing from Gare St-Lazare arrive at the Versailles/Rive Droite railway station; trains departing from Gare Montparnasse arrive at Versailles/Chantiers station, a long walk, as mentioned.

Both Versailles/Rive Gauche and Versailles/Rive Droite stations are within a 10-minute walk of the château, and we recommend the walk as a means of orienting yourself to the town, its geography, its scale, and its architecture. Directions to the château are clearly signposted from each railway station.

If you're **driving,** take the *périphérique* (the ring road around Paris) to the autoroute A13 (direction Versailles/Rouen); take exit 5 to Versailles Centre and park on place d'Armes in front of the château.

TICKETS The **Château Passeport** offers access to the entire domaine (palace, Trianons, Domaine de Marie Antoinette, and temporary expositions) and costs 25€ from April to October and 16€ from November to March. If you are feeling less ambitious, the **Palace Ticket** (Billet Château) will let you in to just the palace and the temporary exhibits, and includes an audioguide in English. Both tickets include access to the gardens. Buying tickets in advance will save you headaches and extra lines at the entrance; tickets can be purchased online on the chateau's website (www.chateauversailles.fr) or through the Fnac bookstores (www.fnac.com; ✆ **08-92-68-36-22**). You can also buy tickets in person at any Fnac store (branches all over Paris—visit the website for locations). During the renovations, various parts of the domaine may be closed from time to time; check the chateau's website to see what's open the day you are visiting.

If you hold the **Paris Museum Pass**, admission is free to the château. The pass also lets you use the priority entrance so you don't have to wait in line to get in. Due to the ongoing renovations at the château, this privilege may occassionally be revoked, and you'll be obliged to stand in line with everyone else.

VISITOR INFORMATION The **Office de Tourisme** is at 2 bis av. de Paris (✆ **01-39-24-88-88;** fax 01-39-24-88-89; www.versailles-tourisme.com).

EVENING SPECTACLES Every summer, usually on Saturday nights between June and August, the palace grounds are the setting for "Les Grandes Eaux Nocturnes" a program of fireworks and illuminated fountains. Starting around 9pm, ticket holders get to stroll around and visit colorfully lit bosquets, fountains, and statues and gaze at fireworks set to music. Tickets are 17€ to 21€. Before the fountains start, for an extra 13€ to 18€ you can enjoy 50 minutes of "La Serenade," period dancing and music in the Hall of Mirrors. Tickets for these events can be purchased on the same day at the entrance to the gardens from 10am to 7:30pm.

Periodically, usually for a few highly publicized dates in late summer or early fall, there are open-air spectacles or concerts at the fountain of Neptune, near the boulevard de la Reine entrance to the grounds. Sometimes these take the form of a densely choreographed fireworks display featuring prerecorded classical music and hundreds of live players; sometimes they are exclusive concerts by big-name dance companies or performing artists. Ticket prices range from 35€ to 55€.

Since it reopened after an extensive restoration, big names in classical music, theater, and dance are filling the stage at the magnificent Opéra Royal. In 2011, Cecila Bartoli and John Malkovich were on the program; reserve well in advance and expect royal ticket prices (45€–100€). Tickets

A RETURN TO FADED glory

In 2003, the French government embarked on a massive 500€ restoration of Versailles and its splendid gardens that is scheduled to continue until 2020. The attraction—one of the most visited in Europe—remains open during the restoration, but don't be surprised to see scaffolding or notices of closings in certain parts of the domaine. The grand design of the architects is to make the palace, dating from the 17th century, look much as it did when it was home to Louis XIV, XV, and the ill-fated XVI. Some features will be removed, such as a wide staircase ordered built by King Louis-Philippe in the château's last major rebuilding in the 1830s. Other features will be added, including a replica of the *grille royale* (a gilded royal insignia that was part of the entrance gate) that was torn out after the 1789 Revolution. Facilities for visitors with disabilities will also improve.

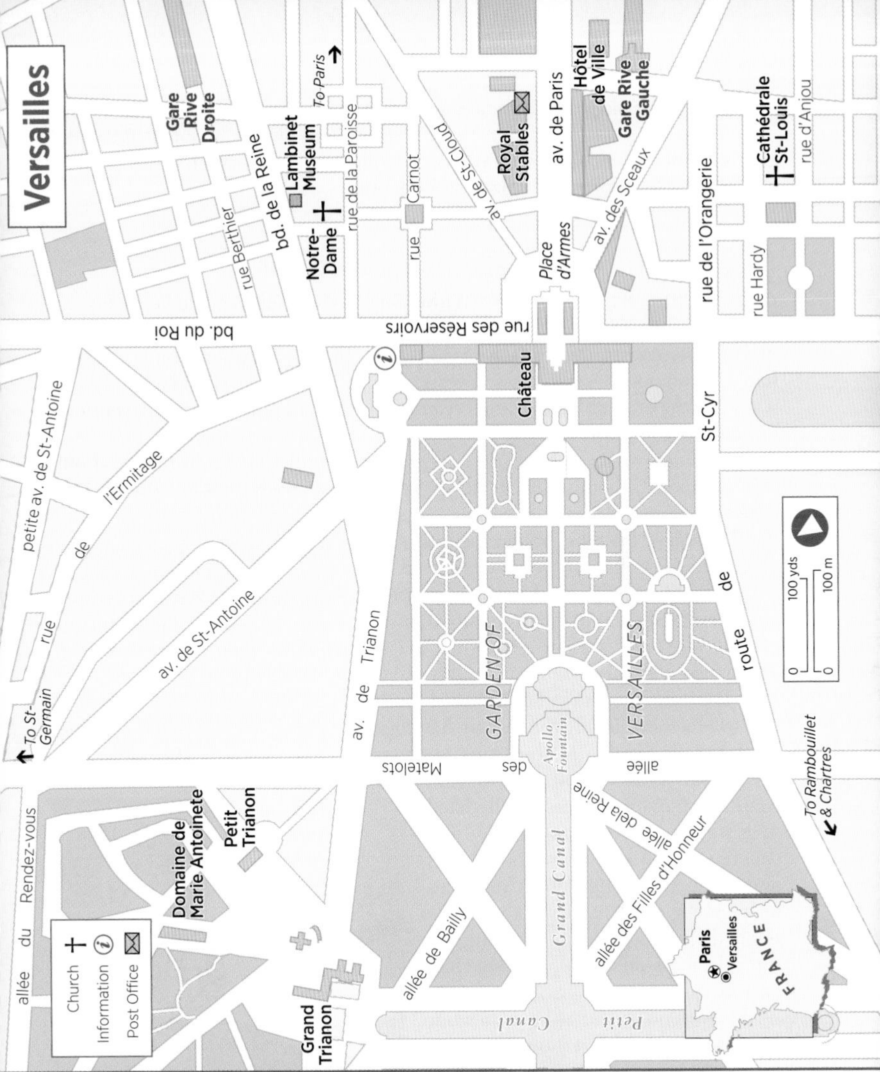

can be purchased online at www.chateauversailles-spectacles.fr, by phone at ✆ **01-30-83-78-89,** or through Fnac (see above).

DAYTIME SPECTACLES Saturdays and Sundays from April through October, between 11am and noon and 3:30 and 5pm, Versailles broadcasts classical music throughout the park and opens the valves on as many fountains as are currently in operation as part of a program known as "Les Grandes Eaux Musicales de Versailles." The spectacles showcase the landscaping vision of the palace's designers and encourage participants to walk, promenade, or meander the vast park, enjoying the juxtaposition of supremely grand architecture with lavish waterworks. Admission to the part of the park where the fountains are playing is 8€ for adults and 6€ for ages 6 to 18. Music and fountains are also on display during "Les Jardins Musicaux," a similar event that takes place on Tuesdays from July through September from 9am to 5:30pm (adults 7€, ages 6–18 6€). Tickets can be purchased at the garden entrance from 9am to 5pm. For information, visit www.chateauversailles-spectacles.fr or call ✆ **01-30-83-78-89.**

Exploring the Château & Gardens

Château de Versailles ★★★ Within 50 years, the Château de Versailles was transformed from Louis XIII's hunting lodge into an extravagant palace. Begun in 1661, its construction involved 32,000 to 45,000 workmen, some of whom had to drain marshes and move forests. Louis XIV set out to build a palace that would be the envy of Europe and created a symbol of opulence copied, yet never duplicated, the world over.

Wishing (with good reason) to keep an eye on the nobles of France, Louis XIV summoned them to live at his court. Here he amused them with constant entertainment and lavish banquets. To some he awarded such tasks as holding the hem of his robe. While the aristocrats played at often-silly intrigues and games, the peasants on the estates sowed the seeds of the Revolution.

When Louis XIV died in 1715, his great-grandson Louis XV succeeded him and continued the outrageous pomp, though he is said to have predicted the outcome: *"Après moi le déluge"* (After me, the deluge). His wife, Marie Leszczynska, was shocked by the blatant immorality at Versailles.

The next monarch, Louis XVI, found his grandfather's behavior scandalous—in fact, on gaining the throne, he ordered that the "stairway of indiscretion" (secret stairs leading to the king's bedchamber) be removed. The well-intentioned but weak king and his queen, Marie Antoinette, were well liked at first, but the queen's frivolity and spending led to her downfall. Louis and Marie Antoinette were at Versailles on October 6, 1789, when they were notified that mobs were marching on the palace. As predicted, *le déluge* had arrived.

Château de Versailles.

Napoleon stayed at Versailles but never seemed fond of it. Louis-Philippe (who reigned 1830–48) prevented the destruction of the palace by converting it into a museum dedicated to the glory of France. To do that, he had to surrender some of his own riches. Decades later, John D. Rockefeller contributed toward the restoration of Versailles, and work continues today.

The magnificent **Grands Appartements ★★★** are in the Louis XIV style; each bears the name of the allegorical painting on the ceiling. The best known and largest is the **Hercules Salon ★★**, with a ceiling painted by

The Gardens of Versailles.

François Lemoine, depicting the Apotheosis of Hercules. In the **Mercury Salon** (with a ceiling by Jean-Baptiste Champaigne), the body of Louis XIV was put on display in 1715; his 72-year reign was one of the longest in history.

The most famous room at Versailles is the 73m-long (239-ft.) **Hall of Mirrors ★★★**. Begun by Mansart in 1678 in the Louis XIV style, it was decorated by Le Brun with 17 arched windows faced by beveled mirrors in simulated arcades. On June 28, 1919, the treaty ending World War I was signed in this corridor. The German Empire was proclaimed here in 1871. In 2007, a $16-million makeover was completed, returning the Hall of Mirrors to much as it was during the reign of the Sun King. The restoration marked the first time in more than 3 centuries that the hall was restored from top to bottom. Even so, hawk-eyes will notice nips and tucks. But Frédéric Didier, the chief architect of France's monuments, claimed, "All the wrinkles in her face tell a story."

The royal apartments were for show, but Louis XV and Louis XVI retired to the **Petits Appartements ★★** to escape the demands of court etiquette. Louis XV died in his bedchamber in 1774, a victim of smallpox. In a second-floor apartment, which you can visit only with a guide, he stashed away first Mme. de Pompadour, and then Mme. du Barry.

Louis XVI had a sumptuous **Library,** designed by Jacques-Ange Gabriel. Its panels are delicately carved, and the room has been restored and refurnished. The **Clock Room** contains Passement's astronomical clock, encased in gilded bronze. Twenty years in the making, it was completed in 1753. The clock is supposed to keep time until the year 9999. At age 7, Mozart played for the court in this room.

Gabriel designed the **Opéra ★★** for Louis XV in 1748, though it wasn't completed until 1770. In its heyday, it took 3,000 candles to light the place. After two years of renovations, the Opéra reopened to the public and performances in 2009. Hardouin-Mansart built the harmoniously gold-and-white **Royal Chapel** in 1699, dying before its completion. Louis XVI married Marie Antoinette here in 1770, while he was the dauphin.

In 2005, a previously off-limits section of the vast palace was opened to the public for the first time by an act of Parliament. Among the rooms opened up is the mammoth **Battle Gallery,** which, at 119m (390 ft.), is the longest hall at Versailles. The gallery displays monumental paintings depicting all of France's great battles, ranging from the founding of the monarchy by Clovis, who reigned in the 5th and 6th centuries, through the Napoleonic wars in the early 19th century.

Spread across 100 hectares (247 acres), the **Gardens of Versailles ★★★** were laid out by landscape artist André Le Nôtre. At the peak of their glory, 1,400 fountains spewed forth. One of the most famous, located at the base of the Grand Canal, is the Apollo Fountain, by Jean-Baptiste Tuby, which features the god rising out of the water in his chariot pulled by four horses. Le Nôtre created a Garden of Eden using ornamental lakes and canals, geometrically designed flower beds, and avenues bordered with statuary. On the mile-long Grand Canal, Louis XV used to take gondola rides with his favorite of the moment.

A walk across the park takes you to the pink-and-white-marble **Grand Trianon ★★**, designed by Hardouin-Mansart for Louis XIV in 1687. Traditionally, it has been lodging for VIPs, though de Gaulle wanted to turn it into a weekend retreat. Nixon slept here in the room where Mme. de Pompadour died. The original furnishings are gone, replaced today by mostly Empire pieces.

In 2006, the 34-hectare (84-acre) **Domaine de Marie-Antoinette** opened, offering a glimpse into the private life of the ill-fated queen. Encompassing the Petit Trianon, its gardens, and the queen's private "hamlet," complete with cows and a dairy, the estate can be visited separately or as part of the "Chateau Passport" package. Gabriel, the designer of place de la Concorde in Paris, built the **Petit Trianon ★★** in 1768 for Louis XV. Louis used it for his trysts with Mme. du Barry. In time, Marie Antoinette adopted it as her favorite residence, a place to escape the rigid life at the main palace. Many of the current furnishings, including a few in her rather modest bedchamber, belonged to the ill-fated queen. After redecorating, she commissioned an English garden, complete with a pavilion where she often dined and a marble-columned structure known as the Temple of Love, as well as Belvédère Hall, where small recitals were held. Other sites include a delicate wooden and papier-mâché minitheater where the queen performed and an artificial grotto where she held private encounters.

Les Grandes Ecuries (the Stables) stand immediately opposite the château's main front facade, where horses and carriages of the kings were housed. Today the Académie de Spectacle Equestre is housed here, directed by Bartabas, whose equestrian theater company, Zingaro, has garnered world fame. Visitors can watch a team of up to a dozen students, with their mounts, strut their stuff during hour-long riding demonstrations within the covered 17th-century amphitheater of the historic stables. Hour-long demonstrations are conducted Saturdays and Sunday and certain Thursdays at 11:15am (12€). On some weekend afternoons, a more elaborate "equestrian ballet" is on offer; tickets to those shows are 25€. If you want to visit the stables without seeing a show, they are open for visits between 10am and noon daily; tickets are 6€. For more information and ticketing, visit the Académie's website: www.bartabas.fr/Academie-du-spectacle-equestre.

✆ **01-30-83-78-00.** www.chateauversailles.fr. Passport 18€–25€ adults, Palace Ticket 15€ adults, Domaine de Marie Antoinette (includes both Trianons) 10€ adults; free for ages 18 and under. Palace: Apr–Oct Tues–Sun 9am–6pm; Nov–Mar Tues–Sun 9am–5pm. Domaine de Marie Antoinette: Tues–Sun noon–6pm. Grounds daily dawn to dusk.

Musée Lambinet ★ Often overlooked by visitors to Versailles, the Musée Lambinet is filled with treasures seized from the French court during the Revolution. After a major overhaul, the museum reopened in 2010, displaying all the antiques, the carved wood paneling, even religious art and other objets d'art so beloved by Marie Antoinette and the mistresses of Louis XV. The sumptuous mansion from 1751 is also filled with paintings (no great masterpieces, however), weaponry, and rare porcelain (look for the Du Barry rose).

54 bd. de la Reine. ✆ **01-39-50-30-32.** www.musee-lambinet.com. Admission 4€ adults, free for ages 18 and under. Sat–Thurs 2–6pm.

Shopping

Founded by the Sun King himself, Louis XIV, **Marché Notre-Dame,** place du Marché Notre-Dame, is the major public market in Versailles, housed in a series of red-brick buildings. The present look dates from the 19th century. Indoor shops selling local cheeses, meats, and fresh fruits are open daily from 7am to 7pm, but the outdoor stalls in the center of the square flourish only on Tuesday, Friday, and Sunday, from about 9am to 2pm. It's best to go before noon; some of the stalls start shutting down in the early afternoon.

Close to the mammoth market, **Passage de la Geôle** (✆ **01-30-21-15-13;** www.antiques-versailles.com) is open Friday to Sunday 10am to 7pm, housing antiques shops selling furniture and objets d'art at "all prices."

Where to Stay

VERY EXPENSIVE

Trianon Palace ★★★ This luxe hotel is the grandest in the Ile de France, and after its 2008 renovation, it has a more modern feel, with redesigned public and private rooms. A Westin property, it was built in 1910 on land that had sheltered a Capucine monastery during the *ancien régime*. The setting is lovely—the 2-hectare (5-acre) garden borders the gardens of the Petit Trianon at Versailles. In 1919, it was the headquarters of the peace conference of Woodrow Wilson, Lloyd George, Georges Clemenceau, and other world leaders. Since then, guests have included John D. Rockefeller, Queen Elizabeth II, and Marlene Dietrich, who made headlines by wearing pants in the dining room. The hotel is in a classically designed palace and connected to a late-20th-century annex (Le Pavillon) by an underground tunnel. Accommodations in both buildings are decorated in traditional style with reference to château living, using rich fabrics and a mixture of antiques and reproductions. Amenities and electronic accessories are top of the line. The hotel has also joined with Guerlain to create an outstanding spa.

1 bd. de la Reine, Versailles 78000. www.trianonpalace.com. ✆ **800/937-8461** in the U.S. and Canada, or 01-30-84-50-00. Fax 01-30-84-50-01. 199 units. 229€–359€ double; from 639€ suite. AE, DC, MC, V. Parking 20€. **Amenities:** 2 restaurants; cafe; bar; babysitting; health club; indoor pool; room service; sauna; spa; tennis courts. *In room:* A/C, TV, hair dryer, Internet (7€ per hr.), minibar.

MODERATE

Novotel Château de Versailles A 15-minute walk north of one of the side wings of the château, this chain hotel, built in 1988, has a modern facade with columns and large windows. It's not too expensive and is a convenient choice for visitors to Versailles. All bedrooms have been recently renovated and sport a contemporary style.

4 bd. St-Antoine, Le Chesnay 78150. www.novotel.com. ✆ **01-39-54-96-96.** Fax 01-39-54-94-40. 105 units. 99€–159€ double; 165€–185€ suite. Children 16 and under stay free in parent's room. AE, DC, MC, V. Parking 11€. **Amenities:** Restaurant; bar; room service. *In room:* A/C, TV, hair dryer, minibar, free Wi-Fi.

Where to Eat

VERY EXPENSIVE

Gordon Ramsay au Trianon ★★★ FRENCH/INTERNATIONAL The *enfant terrible* of chefs, Gordon Ramsay, has invaded Versailles and is king of the roost at this stylish restaurant inside the swanky Trianon Palace Hotel. He is a master at traditional French cooking done in a modern style and changes his menu frequently to take advantage of the best and the freshest in any season. No one does filet of turbot like Ramsay. But the same could be said of his pan-fried John Dory with crab cannelloni in basil emulsion. He stuffs delectable ravioli with langoustines, and you can toss a pork belly his way, and he'll create a culinary masterpiece for you. The service, the setting, everything here is a delight. The food is of the highest order—and so are the prices. In summer, you can dine under the canopy on the front terrace.

In the Hotel Trianon Palace, 1 bd. de la Reine. ✆ **01-30-84-55-55.** www.trianonpalace.com. Reservations required. Main courses 55€–70€; fixed-price menu 170€. AE, DC, MC, V. Fri–Sat noon–2pm; Tues–Sat 7–10:30pm. Closed 1 week in Jan, 1 week in Mar.

MODERATE

Le Potager du Roy ★ MODERN FRENCH Philippe Letourneur spent years perfecting a distinctive cuisine that now adds novelty to the dining scene in Versailles. Letourneur rotates his skillfully prepared menu with the seasons. Examples are fresh foie gras, roasted duck with *navarin* of vegetables, and roasted codfish with roasted peppers in the style of Provence. Looking for something unusual and earthier? Try fondant of beef jowls in red wine.

1 rue du Maréchal-Joffre. ✆ **01-39-50-35-34.** Reservations required. Fixed-price menu 27€–34€. AE, MC, V. Tues–Sat noon–2pm and 7:30–10pm.

INEXPENSIVE

La Flottille One of the few restaurants inside the château's grounds (at the head of the Grand Canal), it has a sweeping view over some of Europe's most famous landscaping. Both restaurant and snack-bar service are available. In warm weather, the traditional French cuisine is also served at outside tables. Reservations are recommended.

Parc du Château, Versailles 78000. ✆ **01-39-51-41-58.** Fax 01-39-50-51-87. www.laflotille.fr. Main courses 18€–22€; fixed-price menu 28€. AE, MC, V. Daily noon to château closing.

Le Resto du Roi ★ MODERN FRENCH In an 18th-century building overlooking the western facade of Versailles, this bistro recently got a new owner and a chic makeover in tones of cream and chocolate. The new chef, Olivier Pariaud, has updated the menu as well, which features high-quality bistro classics made with fresh seasonal ingredients. Old-fashioned *blanquette de veau* (veal stew) shares the stage with roasted Provençal-style scallops and grilled sea bass. Warm-weather meals can be taken on the ample terrace overlooking the château.

1 av. de St-Cloud. ✆ **01-39-50-42-26.** Reservations required. Main courses 15€; fixed-price menus 20€–36€. AE, MC, V. Daily 11:45am–2:30pm and 7–10:30pm.

Versailles After Dark

O'Paris Pub, 15 rue Colbert, off place d'Armes (✆ **01-39-50-36-12;** www.puboparis.com), is an Irish pub where you can order the best brews in town. A bit more upmarket, **Bar à Vins-Restaurant Le Ducis,** 13 rue Ducis (✆ **01-30-21-93-76**), provides a mellow atmosphere on a summer evening, with tables spilling onto a side street. A bottle of wine and a good companion should get you through an evening, enhanced perhaps by a plate of food selected from the chalkboard menu.

RAMBOUILLET

55km (34 miles) SW of Paris; 42km (26 miles) NE of Chartres

Once known as La Forêt d'Yveline, the **Forest of Rambouillet ★** is one of the loveliest forests in France. More than 19,000 hectares (46,930 acres) of greenery stretch from the valley of the Eure to the high valley of Chevreuse, the latter rich in medieval and royal abbeys. Lakes, copses of deer, and even wild boar are some of the attractions of this "green lung." Most people, however, come here to see the château, which you can visit when it's not in use as a "Camp David" for French presidents.

Château de Rambouillet.

Essentials

GETTING THERE **Trains** depart from Paris's Gare Montparnasse every 30 minutes throughout the day for a 35-minute ride. Information and train schedules can be obtained by contacting the Transilien suburban train service (✆ **3658,** .23€ per minute; www.transilien.com). By **car,** take N10 southwest from Paris, passing Versailles along the way.

VISITOR INFORMATION The **tourist office** is at the Hôtel de Ville, place de la Libération (✆ **01-34-83-21-21;** www.rambouillet-tourism.com).

Seeing the Château

Château de Rambouillet ★ Stately and elegant, the château is surrounded by formal French gardens and a park, and is located in one of the most famous forests in France. While its origins lie deep in the Middle Ages, most of the facades were reconstructed in the 19th century, and the interiors date from the 16th. Superb woodwork is used throughout, and the walls are adorned with tapestries, many from the era of Louis XV. François I, the Chevalier king, died of a fever here in 1547 at age 52. When the château was later occupied by the comte de Toulouse, Rambouillet was often visited by Louis XV, who was amused (in more ways than one) by the comte's high-spirited wife. Louis XVI eventually acquired the château, but Marie Antoinette found it boring and called it "the toad." In his surprisingly modest boudoir are four panels representing the continents.

After the Revolution, the Bonaparte family moved in, leaving behind the emperor's ornate bathroom, decorated with Pompean frescos. Before his final exile to the remote island of St-Helena, Napoleon insisted on spending a final night at Rambouillet, where he secluded himself with his meditations and memories.

In 1830, the elderly Charles X, Louis XVI's brother, abdicated the throne at Rambouillet as a mob marched on the château and his troops began to desert him. From Rambouillet, he embarked for a safe but controversial haven in England. Afterward, Rambouillet fell into private hands. At one time, it was a fashionable restaurant attracting Parisians by offering gondola rides. Napoleon III returned it to the Crown. In 1896, it was designated a residence for the presidents of the republic. In 1944, Charles de Gaulle lived here briefly before giving the order for what was left of the French army to join the Americans in liberating Paris. In more recent years, major political figures like Boris Yeltsin, Nelson Mandela, and Hosni Mubarak have been château guests.

Two must-sees in the park include the **Queen's Dairy,** built for Marie Antoinette and sporting a romantic artificial grotto; and the **Shell Cottage,** a "humble" thatched cottage built for the Princess de Lamballe, whose interior is decorated with an astounding array of seashells, marble, and mother-of-pearl.

It takes about 2 hours to see the château at Rambouillet.

Parc du Château. ✆ **01-34-83-00-25.** www.monuments-nationaux.fr. Admission 7€ adults, 4.50€ students 18–25, free for children 17 and under. Apr–Sept Wed–Mon 10am–noon and 2–6pm; Oct–Mar Wed–Mon 10am–noon and 2–5pm.

Where to Eat

La Poste TRADITIONAL FRENCH On a street corner in the town's historic center, this restaurant dates from the mid–19th century, when it provided meals and shelter for the region's mail carriers. The two dining rooms have rustic beams and old-fashioned accents that complement the flavorful old-fashioned

 Through an Enchanted Forest

Rambouillet and its forests can provide a verdant interlude. If you've exhausted the idea of a ramble through the gardens that surround the château (or if they're closed because of a visit from the president of France), consider a visit to the Rochers d'Angennes, rocky hillocks that remain as leftovers from the Ice Age. To reach them, park your car on the D107, where you'll see a sign pointing to the Rochers et Etang d'Angennes, about 4km (2½ miles) north of the hamlet of Epernon. Walk along a clearly marked trail through a pine forest before you eventually reach a rocky plateau overlooking the hills and a pond *(l'Etang d'Angennes)* nestled into the surrounding countryside. Round-trip, from the site of your parked car to the plateau and back, your promenade should take between 30 and 45 minutes.

food. Tasty menu items include a fricassee of chicken and crayfish, and noisettes of lamb "prepared in the style of a roebuck," with a *grand Veneur* sauce (made with red wine, autumn berries, a touch of vinegar "to make it acidic," and crème fraîche). Also popular are civets of both *une biche* (female venison) and rabbit during hunting season.

101 rue du Général-de-Gaulle. ✆ **01-34-83-03-01.** Reservations recommended Sat–Sun. Main courses 18€–20€; fixed-price menus 24€–36€. AE, MC, V. Tues–Sun noon–2pm; Fri–Sat and Tues–Wed 7–9:30pm. Closed 1st week of Jan and Sept.

CHARTRES ★★★

98km (61 miles) SW of Paris; 76km (47 miles) NW of Orléans

Many observers feel that medieval architecture reached its pinnacle in the world-renowned cathedral at Chartres. Come to see its architecture, its sculpture, and—most of all—its stained glass, which gave the world a new color, Chartres blue.

The ancient town of Chartres also played a role in World War II. Jean Moulin, who was then the prefect of the Eure et Loir, was brought to Chartres and then tortured by the Nazis when he refused to sign a document stating that French troops committed atrocities. Moulin went on to become a hero of the Resistance and friend of de Gaulle; he was tortured to death by Klaus Barbie in 1943 and is buried in the Panthéon in Paris. To view the town's monument to Moulin, head down rue du Cheval-Blanc from the cathedral until it becomes rue Jean-Moulin (the monument is ahead on your right). Other street names, including boulevard de la Résistance, commemorate the World War II resistance movement. Allow 1 hour for the cathedral, 1½ hours for the town.

Essentials

GETTING THERE From Paris's Gare Montparnasse, **trains** run directly to Chartres, taking around an hour. Tickets cost 28€ round-trip and can be bought at the station. Call ✆ **3635** or visit www.voyages-sncf.com for more information. If **driving,** take A10/A11 southwest from the *périphérique* and follow signs to Le Mans and Chartres. (The Chartres exit is clearly marked.)

VISITOR INFORMATION The **Office de Tourisme** is on place de la Cathédrale (✆ **02-37-18-26-26;** fax 02-37-21-51-91; www.chartres-tourisme.com).

Seeing the Cathedral

Cathédrale Notre-Dame de Chartres ★★★ Rodin reputedly once sat for hours on the sidewalk, admiring the cathedral's Romanesque sculpture. His opinion: Chartres is the French Acropolis. When it began to rain, a kind soul offered him an umbrella—which he declined, so transfixed was he.

The cathedral's origins are uncertain; some suggest it grew up over a Druid site that later became a Roman temple. As early as the 4th century, a Christian basilica was here. A fire in 1194 destroyed most of what had then become a Romanesque cathedral, sparing the western facade and crypt. The cathedral today dates principally from the 13th century, when it was rebuilt with the efforts of kings, princes, churchmen, and pilgrims from all over Europe. One of the world's greatest High Gothic cathedrals, it was the first to use flying buttresses.

French sculpture in the 12th century broke into full bloom when the **Royal Portal ★★★** was added. The portal is a landmark in Romanesque art. The sculptured bodies are elongated, often formalized beyond reality, in long, flowing robes. But the faces are amazingly (for the time) lifelike, occasionally betraying Mona Lisa smiles. In the central tympanum, Christ is shown at the Second Coming, with his descent depicted on the right, his ascent on the left. Before you enter, admire the Royal Portal and walk around to both the North Portal and the South Portal; both date from the 13th century. They depict such scenes as the expulsion of Adam and Eve from the Garden of Eden.

Inside is a celebrated choir screen (parclose); work on it began in the 16th century and lasted until 1714. The niches, 40 in all, contain statues illustrating scenes from the life of the Madonna and Christ—everything from the Massacre of the Innocents to the Coronation of the Virgin.

But few rushed visitors ever notice the screen; they're too transfixed by the light from the **stained glass ★★★**. Covering an expanse of more than 2,600 sq. m (28,000 sq. ft.), the peerless glass is truly mystical. It was spared in both world

Inside the Cathédrale Notre-Dame de Chartres.

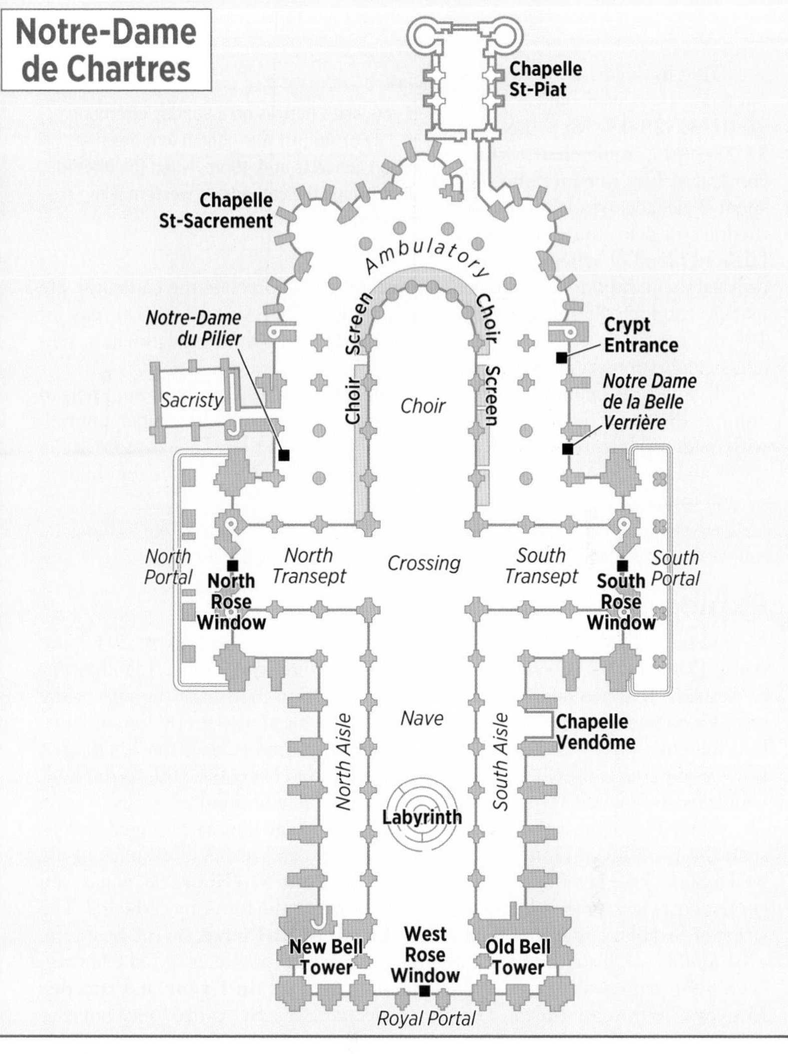

wars because of a decision to remove it piece by piece. Most of it dates from the 12th and 13th centuries. It's difficult to single out one panel or window—depending on the position of the sun, the images change constantly; however, an exceptional one is the 12th-century *Vierge de la Belle Verrière (Virgin of the Beautiful Window)*, on the south side. Of course, there are three fiery rose windows, but you couldn't miss those even if you tried.

The nave—the widest in France—still contains its ancient labyrinth. The wooden *Notre-Dame du Pilier (Our Lady of the Pillar)*, to the left of the choir, dates from the 14th century. The crypt was built over 2 centuries, beginning in the 9th. Enshrined within is *Notre-Dame de Sous Terre (Our Lady of the Crypt)*, a 1976 Madonna that replaced one destroyed during the Revolution.

Try to take a tour conducted by Malcolm Miller (✆ **02-37-28-15-58;** fax 02-37-28-33-03; millerchartres@aol.com), an Englishman who has spent 3 decades studying the cathedral and giving tours in English. His rare blend of scholarship, enthusiasm, and humor will help you understand and appreciate the cathedral. He usually conducts 75-minute tours at noon and 2:45pm Monday to Saturday for 10€ per person or 5€ per student. Tours are canceled during pilgrimages, religious celebrations, and large funerals.

A Free Concert

If you visit Chartres on a Sunday afternoon in July or August, the church features free organ concerts at 4:45pm, when the filtered light brings the cathedral's western windows to life.

If you're fit enough, don't miss the opportunity, especially in summer, to climb to the top of the tower. You can visit the crypt, gloomy and somber, but rich with medieval history, only as part of a French-language tour. The cost to visit the tower and the treasury is 7€ for adults, 4.50€ for ages 18 to 25, free for children 17 and under.

16 Cloître Notre-Dame. ✆ **02-37-21-22-07.** www.monuments-nationaux.fr. Free admission to cathedral. Daily 8:30am–7:30pm. There are 2 tours daily, at 11am and 4:15pm.

Exploring the Town

Next to the cathedral is the **Musée des Beaux-Arts de Chartres ★**, 29 Cloître Notre-Dame (✆ **02-37-90-45-80**), open May 2 through October 3 Wednesday to Monday 10am to noon and 2 to 6pm (closed Sun morning); the rest of the year, it's open only until 5pm. Admission is 3.10€ for adults, 1.60€ for students, free for children 18 and under. In a former Episcopal palace, the building at times competes with its exhibitions. The collection covers the 16th to the 20th centuries and includes works by Zurbarán, Chardin, and Soutine.

At the foot of the cathedral, the lanes contain gabled houses. Humped bridges span the Eure River. From the Bouju Bridge, you can see the lofty spires in the background. Our favorite stroll is along **rue du Pont-St-Hilaire ★**, where you get the best views of the old rooftops that lie beneath the towering cathedral. The street of St-Hilaire is east of the Gothic **church of St-Pierre,** on rue St-Pierre, a 10-minute stroll south of the cathedral. Two evocative streets of old Chartres, each a 3-minute walk south of the cathedral, are **rue du Cygne** and **rue des Ecuyers.** To the east, the most charming old *quartier* is **St-André,** once home to cobblers and tanners. Most of the buildings are restored but date from the 1700s and are known for their embossed doorways crowned by bull's-eye glass.

Shopping

Your best shopping bet in Chartres is place des Epars. This pedestrian area is home to most of the apparel shops and even some haute couture boutiques. Many shops selling regional items line the narrow streets that fan southeast from the cathedral. Along rue Noël-Balay is a small mall with about 15 interesting shops, which can also provide a dry respite if it's raining.

At **Galerie du Vitrail,** 17 Cloître Notre-Dame (✆ **02-37-36-10-03;** www.galerie-du-vitrail.com), you'll find a huge selection of stained glass. **Lassaussois Antiquités,** 17 rue des Changes (✆ **02-37-21-37-74**), specializes in antique objets d'art and contemporary furnishings.

Where to Stay

Grand Monarque Best Western The most appealing and desirable hotel in Chartres occupies an imposing civic monument whose 600-year-old foundations and infrastructures were "gentrified" sometime in the 19th century with white stucco, neoclassical detailing, and touches of the baroque. Functioning as an inn since its original construction in the 15th century, and expanded and improved many times since then, the hotel remains under the direction of a local family. It attracts guests who enjoy its old-world charm—such as Art Nouveau stained glass and Louis XV chairs in the dining room. The guest rooms are decorated with reproductions of antiques; most have sitting areas.

22 place des Epars, Chartres 28005. www.bw-grand-monarque.com. ✆ **800/528-1234** in the U.S., or 02-37-18-15-15. Fax 02-37-36-34-18. 60 units. 107€–185€ double; 215€–245€ suite. AE, DC, MC, V. Parking 8€. **Amenities:** 2 restaurants; bar; room service. *In room:* A/C (in some), TV, hair dryer, minibar, free Wi-Fi.

Hôtel Châtelet This modern hotel has many traditional touches. The rustic guest rooms are inviting, with reproductions of Louis XV and Louis XVI furniture. The larger, more expensive units face a garden and avoid street noise. But many windows along the front (street) side of the hotel open onto a view of the cathedral. Each room comes with a tidy, tiled bathroom with shower and tub. In chilly weather, there's usually a fire burning in one of the salons. Breakfast is the only meal served, but numerous restaurants are close by.

6–8 av. Jehan-de-Beauce, Chartres 28000. www.hotelchatelet.com. ✆ **02-37-21-78-00.** Fax 02-37-36-23-01. 48 units. 107€–134€ double. Extra person 25€. AE, MC, V. Parking 8€. **Amenities:** Bar; room service. *In room:* TV, hair dryer, minibar, free Wi-Fi.

Where to Eat

La Vieille Maison ★★ MODERN FRENCH Even if the food here wasn't superb, the 14th-century building could be visited for its historical value. The dining room, outfitted in the Louis XIII style, is centered on a narrow ceiling vault, less than 2m (6½ ft.) across, crafted of chiseled white stone blocks during the 800s. Bruno Letartre, who has been dubbed a *maître cuisinier de France,* supervises the cuisine. The menu changes four or five times a year, reflecting the seasonality of the Ile de France and its produce. Some good examples include a lasagna with lobster and scallops, and beef in a Bordeaux wine sauce. Dessert raves go to a hot Grand Marnier soufflé.

5 rue au Lait. ✆ **02-37-34-10-67.** www.lavieillemaison.fr. Reservations recommended. Main courses 32€–38€; fixed-price menu 29€–45€. MC, V. Tues–Sun noon–2:15pm; Tues–Sat 7–9:30pm.

Le Geôrges ★★ FRENCH The most upscale and delicious dining experience in Chartres is in the Grand Monarque, a hotel with roots that date from the 15th century, when the site served food and drink (not as elegant as what you'll find today) to weary travelers and postal workers. Today's diners feast in a formal, high-ceilinged dining room outfitted in soft reds and grays. Menu items change with the seasons but might include savory portions of crispy langoustines with fennel and vanilla, freshly grilled scallops, or a superb beef Rossini. Another specialty is John Dory served with ginger, lemongrass, and coconut bouillon. Desserts are sumptuous, and the chef is known locally for his Grand-Marnier soufflé.

In the Grand Monarque Best Western, 22 place des Epars. ✆ **02-37-18-15-15.** Reservations recommended. Main courses 18€–36€; fixed-price menus 48€–85€. AE, DC, MC, V. Tues–Sun noon–2pm; Tues–Sat 7–10pm.

Chartres After Dark

For an evening of theater or modern dance from September to June, try the **Théâtre de Chartres,** place de Ravennes (✆ **02-37-23-42-79;** www.theatredechartres.fr). For dancing, go to **Le Privilège,** 1 place St-Pierre (✆ **02-37-35-52-02**), where you'll find a range of dance music from zouk to disco.

FONTAINEBLEAU ★★★

60km (37 miles) S of Paris; 74km (46 miles) NE of Orléans

French kings originally came to Fontainebleau because of its proximity to great hunting. In the 16th century, François I invited a bevy of Italian artists and architects to convert it from a hunting lodge into a Renaissance palace. It was here that France was introduced to the Italian Mannerist style of painting and decoration that gave birth to the School of Fontainbleau.

Napoleon stood on the horseshoe-shaped exterior staircase and bade farewell to his army before his departure to exile on Elba. That scene has been the subject of countless paintings, including Vernet's *Les Adieux.*

Set in 20,000 hectares (49,400 acres) of verdant forest, Fontainebleau remains a country retreat for Parisians who come for horseback riding, picnicking, and hiking. It's not as crowded with tourists, so it's more peaceful than Versailles. Allow 2½ hours to see everything in Fontainebleau.

Essentials

GETTING THERE **Trains** to Fontainebleau depart from the Gare de Lyon in Paris. The trip takes 40 minutes each way and costs 8.05€ one-way. Fontainebleau's railway station lies 3km (1¾ miles) north of the château, in the suburb of Avon. A local bus (marked CHATEAU and part of line A) makes the trip to the château at 15-minute intervals Monday through Saturday and at 30-minute intervals on Sunday; the fare is 1.80€ each way. If you're **driving,** take A6 south from Paris, exit onto N191, and follow signs.

VISITOR INFORMATION The **Office de Tourisme** is at 4 rue Royale, Fontainebleau (✆ **01-60-74-99-99;** www.fontainebleau-tourisme.com), opposite the main entrance to the château.

Seeing the Château & Gardens

Musée National du Château de Fontainebleau ★★★ Starting in the 12th century, a parade of French rulers used the Palais de Fontainebleau as a resort, hunting in its magnificent forest. Under François I (who reigned in 1515–47), the hunting lodge was enlarged into a royal palace in the Italian Renaissance style. Many artists, including Cellini, came from Italy to work for the French monarch.

Under François I's patronage, the School of Fontainebleau (led by the painters Rosso, Fiorentino, and Primaticcio) increased in prestige. These artists adorned one of the most outstanding rooms at Fontainebleau: the 63m-long (207-ft.) **Gallery of François I ★★★**. Surrounded by pomp, François I walked the length of his gallery while artisans tempted him with their wares, job seekers asked favors, and courtesans attempted to lure him from the duchesse d'Etampes. The stucco-framed panels depict such scenes as Jupiter carrying off Europa, the Nymph of Fontainebleau (with a lecherous dog peering through the reeds), and the king holding a pomegranate, a symbol of unity. Everywhere is the salamander, symbol of the Chevalier King.

Musée National du Château de Fontainebleau.

If it's true that François I built Fontainebleau for his mistress, then Henri II, his successor, left a memorial to the woman he loved, Diane de Poitiers. Sometimes called the Gallery of Henri II, the **Ballroom (La Salle de Bal) ★★★** is the château's second splendid interior. The monograms H & D are interlaced in the decoration. At one end of the room is a monumental fireplace supported by two bronze satyrs, reproduced in 1966 (the originals were melted down during the Revolution). A series of 16th-century frescoes depict mythological subjects.

An architectural curiosity is the **Louis XV Staircase ★★**. Primaticcio originally decorated the ceiling for the bedroom of the duchesse d'Etampes. When an architect added the stairway, he simply ripped out her bedroom floor and used the ceiling to cover the stairway. Of the preserved Italian frescoes, one depicts the Queen of the Amazons climbing into Alexander the Great's bed.

Fontainebleau found renewed glory under Napoleon. You can wander much of the palace on your own, visiting sites that evoke his 19th-century heyday. They include the throne room, the room where he abdicated (the abdication document displayed is a copy), his offices, his bedroom (look for his symbol, a bee), and his bathroom. Some of the smaller rooms, especially those containing his personal mementos and artifacts, are accessible by guided tour only. The furnishings in the grand apartments of Napoleon and Josephine are marvelous.

The **Musée Chinois (Chinese Museum),** which is open only erratically, usually, but not always, on weekends, holds the Empress Eugénie's collection of Chinese treasures, including Far Eastern porcelain, jade, and crystal.

After your trek through the palace, visit the **gardens** and especially the carp pond; the gardens, however, are only a prelude to the forest of Fontainebleau and not nearly as spectacular as those surrounding Versailles.

Place du Général-de-Gaulle. ✆ **01-60-71-50-70.** www.musee-chateau-fontainebleau.fr. Combination ticket including *grandes appartements*, Pope's rooms, Renaissance rooms, chapel, Napoleon museum and *Gallerie de Diane*, and audioguide 10€ adults, 8€ students 18–25, free for children 17 and under. Ticket to *petits appartements* 6.50€ adults, 5€ students 18–25, free for children 17 and under. Apr–Sept Wed–Mon 9:30am–6pm; Oct–Mar Wed–Mon 9:30am–5pm.

 Hiking Along Trails Left by French Kings

The Forest of Fontainebleau is riddled with *sentiers* (hiking trails) made by French kings and their entourages who went hunting in the forest. A trail guidebook is available at the tourist information center (see above). Bike paths also cut through the forest. You can rent bikes at A La Petite Reine (32 rue des Sablons; ✆ 01-60-74-57-57), located in the center of town, near the bus stop. The cost of a regular bike is 5€ per hour or 15€ per full day. The kiosk is open Tuesday through Saturday 9am to 7:30pm, and Sunday from 9am to 6pm.

Where to Stay

Hôtel Aigle-Noir ★ This mansion, once the home of Cardinal de Retz, sits opposite the château. The formal courtyard entrance has a high iron/board grille and pillars crowned by black eagles. It became a hotel in the 1760s and is the finest lodging in Fontainebleau. The rooms are decorated with Louis XVI, Empire, or Régence-era antiques or reproductions, with plush beds and elegant bathroom amenities. Enjoy a drink in the Napoleon III–style bar.

27 place Napoleon-Bonaparte, Fontainebleau 77300. www.hotelaiglenoir.com. ✆ **01-60-74-60-00.** Fax 01-60-74-60-01. 53 units. 170€–240€ double; 320€–380€ suite. AE, DC, MC, V. Parking 10€. **Amenities:** Bar; exercise room; room service. *In room:* A/C, hair dryer, minibar, free Wi-Fi.

Hôtel de Londres With a historic 1850s-era facade, this hotel enjoys one of the best locations in town for anyone who's fascinated by the architecture of the château of Fontainebleau. It's directly in front of the cour des Adieux, site of Napoleon's farewell to his troops before his exile to Elba. It's been owned and managed by the same family for three generations. The well-maintained rooms are tastefully and cozily outfitted with a mix of modern and period furniture, and have extralong beds. Other than breakfast, no meals are served.

1 place du Général-de-Gaulle, Fontainebleau 77300. www.hoteldelondres.com. ✆ **01-64-22-20-21.** Fax 01-60-72-39-16. 16 units. 100€–170€ double; 180€–350€ suite. AE, MC, V. Closed 1 week in Aug and Christmas through 1st week in Jan. **Amenities:** Bar. *In room:* A/C (in about half of the rooms), TV, hair dryer, minibar, free Wi-Fi.

Hôtel Napoleon A short walk from the château, this hotel has far fewer amenities than the Aigle Noir (above) but is still a solid choice for classic lodgings. The airy lobby opens out onto the leafy courtyard garden. An inviting bar features an ornate oval ceiling, Louis-Philippe chairs, and a neoclassical fireplace. The renovated guest rooms are mostly modern, with some reproduction antique furniture. All are comfortable, but those facing the garden courtyard are larger and more tranquil.

9 rue Grande, Fontainebleau 77300. www.hotelnapoleon-fontainebleau.com. ✆ **01-60-39-50-50.** Fax 01-64-22-20-87. 57 units. 165€ double; 260€ suite. AE, DC, MC, V. Parking 9€. **Amenities:** Restaurant; bar; room service. *In room:* TV, hair dryer, minibar, Wi-Fi (5€ per 45 min.).

Where to Eat

In addition to the options below, **La Table des Maréchaux,** in the Hôtel Napoleon (see above), is a superb choice.

Auberge de la Croix d'Augas ★ 🎁 SAVOYARD Located in the forest of Fontainebleau, just 2km (1¼ miles) from the town center, this country inn features specialties from Savoy, an Alpine region known for its fondues, raclettes, and tartiflettes. Potatoes, cheese, and ham feature heavily in these stick-to-your-ribs dishes, but don't worry—there are salads and pasta plates for the faint of heart, as well as your classic steak-frites fare. The setting is truly rustic, including checked tablecloths and hanging copper pots; weather permitting, tables are set up outside on the terrace or under the veranda.

Exit Fontainebleau on bd. de Maréchal Foch (Rte. D606) to Rte. D116, about 1km (½ mile) into the forest. ✆ **01-64-23-49-25.** Main courses 9.70€–20€; fixed-price menu 19€; children's menu 9€. MC, V. Daily noon–2pm and 7–10pm.

Chez Bernard ★ TRADITIONAL FRENCH The premier dining choice in Fontainebleau has a covered terrace overlooking the château and the cour des Adieux. Chef Bernard Crogiez's cuisine is meticulous, with an undeniable flair. Seasonal specialties come and go on the menu, but you can be sure to find baked snails in garlic-flavored cream sauce, roasted *magret* of duck with cassis sauce, *rognon de veau* (veal kidneys) with mustard sauce, and sautéed scallops à la Provençal.

3 rue Royale. ✆ **01-64-22-24-68.** www.chez-bernard.fr. Reservations required. Main courses 14€–29€; fixed-price lunch Mon–Fri only 15€; fixed-price dinner 25€. AE, MC, V. Tues–Sun noon–2pm; Mon–Sat 7:30–9:30pm. Closed 2 weeks in Aug and 1 week in Dec.

VAUX-LE-VICOMTE ★★★

47km (29 miles) SE of Paris; 19km (12 miles) NE of Fontainebleau

Back in the 17th century, Louis XIV's finance minister, Nicolas Fouquet, built a castle that was so exquisite it turned the young king green with envy, prompting him to build an even more splendid palace—a certain Versailles. It's easy to see what got Louis so riled up—the architecture and grounds of this small château are utterly harmonious and elegant, reflecting the finest esthetics of the epoch.

Essentials

GETTING THERE Though it's close to Paris, Vaux-le-Vicomte is hard to reach by mass transit. By **car,** take the N6 to the A5 autoroute and get off at Saint Germain-Laxis, 1km (½ mile) from the château (around 50 min.). By **train,** take the 30-minute ride from Gare de Lyon to Melun (15€ round-trip), and then a taxi from the station 6.5km (4 miles) to Vaux-le-Vicomte (15€ each way). On weekends and holidays between April and October, there is a shuttle bus ("Châteaubus") from the Melun train station (3.5€ per person). Once there, allow 2 hours to see the château.

The nearest **tourist office** is in Melun, at 18 rue Paul Doumer (✆ **01-64-52-64-52;** www.ville-melun.fr); it's open Monday 1:30 to 6pm, Tuesday to Saturday 10am to 12:30pm and 1:30 to 6pm.

Seeing the Château

Château de Vaux-le-Vicomte ★★★ "On August 17, at 6 in the evening, Nicolas Fouquet was the King of France; at two in the morning, he was nobody." So Voltaire summed up the tragic events of the fateful day in 1661 when Fouquet gave a sumptuous party for King Louis XIV, his court, and the crème de la crème of French society. Thinking he was honoring his king, Fouquet went all out—after showing off the latest improvements to his splendid castle, he served a fabulous meal, presented a new comedy by Moliére, and set off fireworks to wow his guests. The king, who had enough of being upstaged by his flamboyant minister, had other ideas. Shortly thereafter, Fouquet was arrested on trumped-up charges of embezzlement and imprisoned for life. The king seized the castle, confiscated its contents, and hired its artists and architects to work on Versailles.

Château de Vaux-le-Vicomte.

Vaux-le-Vicomte was eventually released to Fouquet's widow, and the castle has remained in private hands ever since. The ancestors of the current owners, Patrice and Cristina de Vogüé, bought the palace in 1875, when they started a much-needed restoration program.

Today the view of the château from the main gate reveals the splendor of 17th-century France. On the south side, a majestic staircase sweeps toward the gardens, designed by Le Nôtre. The Grand Canal, flanked by waterfalls, divides the greenery. The château has been lovingly restored and furnished with 17th-century artwork and furniture. The entrance hall leads to 12 staterooms, including the oval rotunda, left in its unfinished state, as it was the night of Fouquet's arrest. Many rooms are hung with Gobelin tapestries and decorated with painted ceilings and wall panels by Le Brun, and sculptures by Girardon. The "simple visit" ticket includes the staterooms, the huge basement and wine cellar, the servants' dining room, the copper-filled kitchen, and the gardens; an extra 2€ gets you the "Vaux-le-Vicomte Pass," which also includes Fouquet's personal apartments and a view from the dome.

Included in either ticket is entrance to the château's carriage museum, **Musée des Equipages,** in the stables. Some 25 restored 18th- and 19th-century carriages are on display, each accessorized with mannequin horses and people.

Candlelight evenings, **Soirées aux Chandelles,** take place every Saturday from May to mid-October between 6pm and midnight. During the events, the electric lights go out and thousands of candles illuminate both the château and its gardens. The effect is mystical, a memorable re-creation of the way of life that prevailed during the building's heyday. Admission for the "simple visit" during candlelight evenings is 17€ for adults, 15€ for students and children 6 to 15, free for children 5 and under; add another 2€ for the Pass. Except for a couple of weeks during the Christmas season (check website for schedule), the château is closed from November through March.

77950 Maincy. ✆ **01-64-14-41-90.** www.vaux-le-vicomte.com. Admission "simple visit" 14€ adults, 11€ students and children 6–16, free for children 5 and under. Vaux-le-Vicomte Pass

16€ adults, 13€ students and children 6–16, free for children 5 and under. Apr–June Thurs–Tues 10am–6pm; July–Aug daily 10am–6pm. Closed Nov–Mar, except for certain days during the Christmas holidays, generally the last 2 weeks of Dec.

Where to Eat

Auberge de Crisenoy MODERN FRENCH You are more likely to find locals from Melun than fellow visitors at this *auberge,* and that's part of its charm. Behind the solid stone walls of a former private home, the two dining rooms (on separate floors), plus an additional 10 tables on a mezzanine, overlook a garden. The menu items are based on modern interpretations of French classics and change every 3 months. The best examples include foie gras with white grapes, toast, and compote of apples; *filet l'agneau* stuffed with onions, pears, and new onions; and well-seasoned cassoulet of snails and sweetbreads, served in a copper pot placed directly on the table.

23 Grande Rue, Crisenoy. ✆ **01-64-38-83-06.** Reservations recommended. Fixed-price lunch Tues–Fri 21€; fixed-price menu 32€ and 49€. MC, V. Tues–Sun noon–1:30pm; Tues and Thurs–Sat 7:30–9pm. Closed 1 week at Christmas, 1 week in Mar, and 3 weeks in Aug. From Vaux-le-Vicomte, follow N36 toward Meaux for 2.5km (1½ miles).

La Table de Saint Just TRADITIONAL FRENCH You're bound to be charmed while dining at this elegant 17th-century farmhouse, whose oak beams and exposed stone walls were once associated with the nearby **Château de Vaux-le-Pénil.** Menu items change with the seasons but may include foie gras with figs served with spice bread; lobster with green apples; scallops roasted with truffles; and roasted rack of lamb with moussaka of fresh vegetables.

11 rue de Libération, Ferme Saint Just, Vaux-le-Pénil. ✆ **01-64-52-09-09.** www.restaurantlatablesaintjust.com. Reservations recommended. Main courses 33€–48€; fixed-price menu 46€ and 90€. AE, MC, V. Tues–Sat noon–1:30pm and 7:30–9pm. Closed 3 weeks in Aug, 2 weeks at Christmas, and 1 week at Easter. From Vaux-le-Vicomte, drive 5.5km (3½ miles) west, following signs to Melun, then to Maincy, and then to Vaux-le-Pénil.

DISNEYLAND PARIS ★

32km (20 miles) E of Paris

After provoking some of the most enthusiastic and controversial reactions in recent French history, the multimillion-dollar Disneyland Paris opened in 1992. It's one of the world's most lavish theme parks, conceived on a scale rivaling that of Versailles. European journalists initially accused it of everything from cultural imperialism to the death knell of French culture.

But after godly amounts of public relations and financial juggling, Disneyland Paris has become one of France's top tourist attractions, with 15 million visitors annually. About 50% of the visitors are French, half of that from Paris. Disneyland Paris basically looks, tastes, and feels like the ones in California and Florida.

Situated on a 2,000-hectare (4,940-acre) site (about one-fifth the size of Paris) in the suburb of Marne-la-Vallée, the park incorporates the most successful elements of its Disney predecessors and European flair. The park in Florida is larger than the Paris property, with a greater number of attractions and rides, but Disneyland Paris does a decent job of re-creating the Magic Kingdom. In 2002, the Paris park added **Walt Disney Studios,** focusing on the role of movies in popular culture. Take 1 day for the highlights, 2 days for more depth.

Essentials

GETTING THERE The RER A commuter **train** stops within walking distance of the park. Board the RER A in Paris at Charles-de-Gaulle–Etoile, Auber, Châtelet–Les Halles, Gare de Lyon, or Nation. Make sure you are taking the branch that terminates at Marne-la-Vallée/Chessy (as opposed to Boissy-St-Leger) and get off at the last stop. The trip takes about 40 minutes from central Paris. The round-trip fare is 13€. Trains run daily every 10 to 20 minutes from 5:30am to midnight.

Shuttle buses connect Orly and Charles de Gaulle airports with each hotel in the resort. Buses depart the airports every 30 to 45 minutes. One-way transport to the park from either airport is 17€ for adults, 13€ for children 3 to 11.

If you're **driving,** take A4 (direction "Metz/Nancy") east from Paris and get off at exit 14, DISNEYLAND PARIS. Parking begins at 15€ per day but is free if you stay at one of the park hotels. A series of moving sidewalks speeds up pedestrian transit from parking areas to the park entrance.

VISITOR INFORMATION All the hotels we recommend offer general information on the theme park. For details and reservations at any of its hotels, contact the **Disneyland Paris Guest Relations Office,** located in City Hall on Main Street, U.S.A. (✆ **01-60-30-60-53** in English, or 08-25-30-60-30 in French; www.disneylandparis.com). For information on Disneyland Paris and specific details on the many other attractions and monuments in the Ile de France and the rest of the country, contact the **Maison du Tourisme,** just next to the TGV train station and Disney Village (✆ **01-60-43-33-33**).

ADMISSION Admission varies depending on the season. In peak season, a 1-day, one-park ticket costs 54€ for adults, 49€ for children 3 to 12, free for children 2 and under; a 2-day park-hopper ticket is 113€ for adults, 102€ for kids; and a 3-day park-hopper ticket is 159€ for adults, 117€ for kids. There are lots of package deals including park entry and hotel stay. Peak season is from mid-June to mid-September, as well as Christmas and Easter weeks. Entrance to Disney Village is free, though there's usually a cover charge at the dance clubs.

HOURS Hours vary throughout the year but most frequently are 10am to 7pm. Be warned that autumn and winter hours vary the most; it depends on the weather. It's good to phone ahead if you're contemplating a visit at this time.

Seeing Disneyland

Disneyland Paris is a total vacation destination. In one enormous unit, the park includes five "lands" of entertainment; a dozen hotels; a campground; an entertainment center (**Disney Village,** with 11 restaurants of its own); a 27-hole golf course; and dozens of restaurants, shows, and shops. The Disney Village entertainment center is illuminated by a spectacular gridwork of lights suspended 18m (59 ft.) above the ground. The complex contains dance clubs, shops, restaurants (one of which stages a dinner spectacle based on the original *Buffalo Bill's Wild West Show*), bars for adults trying to escape their children, a French Government Tourist Office, and a post office.

Visitors stroll amid flower beds, trees, reflecting ponds, fountains, and a large artificial lake flanked with hotels. An army of smiling employees and Disney characters—many of whom are multilingual, including Buffalo Bill, Mickey and

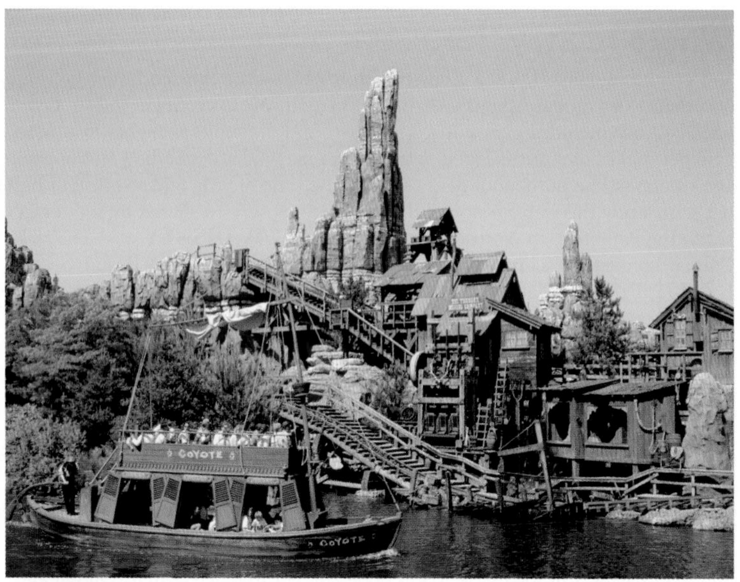

Disneyland Paris.

Minnie Mouse, and, of course, the French-born Caribbean pirate Jean Laffite—are on hand to greet the thousands of *enfants.* You'll see characters from *Aladdin, The Lion King, Pocahontas,* and *Toy Story.* As Disney continues to churn out animated blockbusters, look for the newest stars to appear in the theme park.

Main Street, U.S.A., abounds with horse-drawn carriages and barbershop quartets. Steam-powered railway cars embark from the Main Street Station for a trip through a Grand Canyon diorama to **Frontierland,** with its paddle-wheel steamers reminiscent of Mark Twain's Mississippi River. Other attractions are the **Big Thunder Mountain** roller coaster and the ghosts and ghouls of **Phantom Manor.**

The park's steam trains chug past **Adventureland**—with its swashbuckling **Pirates of the Caribbean,** stomach-churning **Indiana Jones and the Temple of Doom,** and the kinder, gentler **Aladdin's Magic Carpet**—to **Fantasyland.** Here you'll find the **Sleeping Beauty's Castle,** whose pinnacles and turrets are an idealized (and spectacular) interpretation of French châteaux. In its shadow are Europeanized versions of *Blanche Neige et les Sept Nains* (Snow White and the Seven Dwarfs), Peter Pan, Dumbo, Alice (from Wonderland), the Mad Hatter's Teacups, and Sir Lancelot's Magic Carousel.

Visions of the future are in **Discoveryland,** where tributes to invention and imagination draw from the works of Jules Verne, H. G. Wells, and the *Star Wars* series. Favorites here include hyperfast **Space Mountain** and **Buzz Lightyear's Lazer Blast.**

FASTPASS Those Long Lines

Disneyland Paris has instituted a program that's done well at the other parks. With the FASTPASS system, visitors to the various rides reserve a 1-hour time block. Within that block, the waiting is usually no more than 8 minutes.

Where to Stay

You can easily make Disney a day trip from Paris—the transportation links are excellent—or you can spend a night . . . or two. Most overnight guests take a package that includes park entry, breakfast, and a couple of nights in a hotel. The per-night hotel prices listed below can range wildly, depending on the package you book, the number of days you stay, the time of year, and so on. Your best bet is to study the website or call the reservations service shared by the resort's seven theme hotels. In North America, call ✆ **407/W-DISNEY** [934-7639]. In France, contact the **Central Reservations Office,** Euro Disney Resort, S.C.A., B.P. 105, F-77777 Marne-la-Vallée Cedex 4 (✆ **08-25-30-60-30;** www.disneylandparis.com).

VERY EXPENSIVE

Disneyland Hotel ★★ At the park entrance, this flagship four-story hotel has a Victorian facade, with red-tile turrets and jutting balconies. The spacious guest rooms are plushly furnished but evoke the image of Disney, with cartoon depictions and candy-stripe decor. The beds are king-size, double, or twin; in some rooms, armchairs convert to beds. Accommodations in the rear overlook Sleeping Beauty's Castle and Big Thunder Mountain. Some less desirable units open onto a parking lot. The luxurious bathrooms have marble vanities, showers and tubs, and twin basins. On the Castle Club floor, you get free newspapers, all-day beverages, and access to a well-equipped private lounge.

Disneyland Paris, B.P. 111, Marne-la-Vallée Cedex 4 F-77777. www.disneylandparis.com. ✆ **01-60-45-65-89.** Fax 01-60-45-65-33. 495 units. 530€–860€ double; from 775€ suite. AE, DC, MC, V. **Amenities:** 2 restaurants; bar; cafe; babysitting; health club w/indoor pool; room service; sauna; spa. *In room:* A/C, TV, hair dryer, Internet (5€ per 15 min.), minibar.

EXPENSIVE

Newport Bay Club ★★ You expect to see the reincarnation of Joe Kennedy walking along the veranda, with its slated roofs, awnings, and pergolas. It's very Hyannisport here. It's also the biggest hotel in France. With a central cupola, balconies, and a blue-and-cream color scheme, it recalls a harborfront New England hotel (ca. 1900). The layout features nautically decorated rooms in various shapes and sizes. The most spacious are the corner units.

Disneyland Paris, B.P. 105, Marne-la-Vallée Cedex 4 F-77777. www.disneylandparis.com. ✆ **01-60-45-55-00.** Fax 01-60-45-55-33. 1,093 units. 245€–460€ double; from 370€ suite. AE, DC, MC, V. **Amenities:** 2 restaurants; bar; health club; indoor and outdoor pools; room service; sauna. *In room:* A/C, TV, minibar, Wi-Fi (15€ per day).

MODERATE

Hotel Cheyenne/Hotel Santa Fe ☺ Next door to each other near a re-creation of Texas's Rio Grande, these Old West–style lodgings are the resort's least expensive hotels. The Cheyenne consists of 14 two-story buildings along Desperado Street; the desert-themed Santa Fe encompasses four "nature trails" winding among 42 adobe-style pueblos. The Cheyenne is a favorite among families, offering a double bed and bunk beds. Children have an array of activities, including a play area in a log cabin with a lookout tower and a section where you can explore the "ruins" of an ancient Anasazi village. The only disadvantage, according to some parents, is the absence of a pool.

FOR THOSE WITH another DAY: WALT DISNEY STUDIOS

Next to Disneyland Paris, **Walt Disney Studios** takes guests on a behind-the-scenes interactive discovery of film, animation, and television.

The main entrance to the studios, called the **Front Lot,** consists of Disney Studio 1, an elaborate sound stage complete with film props, shops, and restaurants. The **Art of Disney Animation** allows visitors to learn the trade secrets of Disney animators, and the **Production Courtyard** lets guests take a look behind the scenes of film and TV production. On the **Studio Tram Tour,** guests are plunged into the heart of a film shoot for "Catastrophe Canyon." Finally, the **Back Lot** is home to special effects and stunt workshops. A live stunt show features cars, motorbikes, and jet skis.

This ode to Hollywood and the films it produced since the end of its "golden age" has a roller coaster, the **Rock 'n' Roller Coaster,** featuring the music of Aerosmith, which combines rock memorabilia with high-speed scary twists and turns (completely in the dark); and a reconstruction of one of the explosion scenes in the Hollywood action film *Armageddon.*

More recently constructed, but charging the same prices, is the nearby **Kyriad Hotel,** a chain hotel designed for families that evokes the aesthetics and layout of a French country inn. Whenever the Cheyenne and the Santa Fe are full, Disney usually directs the overflow to the Kyriad.

Disneyland Paris, B.P. 115, Marne-la-Vallée Cedex 4 F-77777. www.disneylandparis.com. ✆ **01-60-45-63-12** (Cheyenne) or 01-60-45-79-22 (Santa Fe). Fax 01-60-45-62-33 (Cheyenne) or 01-60-45-78-33 (Santa Fe). 2,000 units. Hotel Cheyenne 135€–280€ double; Hotel Santa Fe 115€–250€ double. AE, DC, MC, V. **Amenities:** Restaurant; bar; Internet (15€ per 100 min.). *In room:* A/C, TV.

Where to Eat

Disneyland Paris offers a gamut of cuisine in more than 45 restaurants and snack bars. You can live on burgers and fries, or you can experiment at the following upscale restaurants.

Auberge de Cendrillon TRADITIONAL FRENCH A master of ceremonies wearing a plumed tricorn hat, embroidered tunic, and lace ruffles welcomes you to the dining room in Cinderella's castle. There are corny elements, but the chefs go out of their way to make French cuisine a big deal. For the most part, they succeed admirably. Appetizers like the warm goat-cheese salad with lardons or the smoked salmon platter will put you in the mood for main dishes like roast loin of lamb with a zesty mustard sauce or sautéed veal medallions. There is only a fixed-price menu, but it offers several choices. Dinner is served only on Saturday night and during certain holiday periods; for this reason, it is easier to reserve for lunch.

Fantasyland. ✆ **01-64-74-24-02.** Reservations recommended. Fixed-price menu 59€ adults, 25€ children. AE, DC, MC, V. Sun–Fri noon–4:30pm; Sat 6–8:30pm.

California Grill ★★ ☺ CALIFORNIAN/FRENCH The resort's showcase restaurant serves cuisine that's the equivalent of the fare at a one-Michelin-star restaurant. Even French food critics are impressed with oysters prepared with leeks and salmon. We also applaud the appetizer of foie gras with roasted red peppers and the roasted pigeon with braised Chinese cabbage and black-rice vinegar. Another winning selection is fresh salmon roasted over beechwood and served with a sprinkling of walnut oil, sage sauce, asparagus, and fricassee of forest mushrooms. Many items are specifically for children. If you want a quiet, mostly adult venue, go here as late as your hunger pangs will allow; the restaurant is open only for dinner.

In the Disneyland Hotel. ✆ **01-60-45-65-76.** Reservations required. Fixed-price menu 55€–71€; children's menu 17€–20€. AE, DC, MC, V. Daily 6:30–10:15pm.

Inventions INTERNATIONAL This may be the only buffet restaurant in Europe where animated characters from the Disney films (including Mickey and Minnie) go table-hopping. With views over a park, the restaurant contains four enormous buffet tables devoted to starters, shellfish, main courses, and desserts. Selections are wide, portions can be copious, and no one leaves hungry. Don't expect *grande cuisine*—that's the domain of the more upscale California Grill (see above), in the same hotel. What you'll get is a sense of American bounty and culinary generosity, with ample doses of cartoon fantasy. Brunch is on offer on Sundays.

In the Disneyland Hotel. ✆ **01-60-45-65-83.** Buffet 51€ adults, 26€ children 6–11, 20€ children 3–5. Fixed-price lunch menu 360€ adults, 18€ children 6–11, 16€ children 3–5. Brunch (Sun only) 58€ adults, 27€ children. AE, DC, MC, V. Daily 12:30–3pm and 6–10:30pm.

Disneyland After Dark

The premier theatrical venue is **Le Legende de Buffalo Bill,** in Disney Village (**✆ 01-60-45-71-00**). The twice-per-night stampede of entertainment recalls the show that once traveled the West with Buffalo Bill and Annie Oakley. You'll dine at tables arranged amphitheater style around a rink where sharpshooters, runaway stagecoaches, and dozens of horses and Indians ride fast and perform alarmingly realistic acrobatics. A Texas-style barbecue, served in an assembly line by waiters in 10-gallon hats, is part of the experience. Despite its corny elements, it's not without its charm. Wild Bill is dignified and the Indians are suitably brave. Shows start at 6:30 and 9:30pm; the cost (dinner included) is 59€ to 71€ for adults and 45€ to 57€ for children 3 to 11.

GIVERNY

81km (50 miles) NW of Paris

On the border between Normandy and the Ile de France, the Claude Monet Foundation preserves the estate where the great painter lived for 43 years. The restored house and its gardens are open to the public. Budget 2 hours to explore the museum and gardens at Giverny.

Essentials

GETTING THERE Take the **train** from Paris's Gare St-Lazare to the Vernon station (45-min. ride; 13€ each way). From Vernon, you can take either the **shuttle bus** (15-min. ride, timed to leave about 5 or 10 min. after the train arrives; 2€ each way), the **local bus** no. 240 (timed to leave about 15 min. after the train arrives; 2€ each way), or a **taxi** for the remaining 7km (4¼ miles) to Giverny. If you are feeling plucky, you can **walk** or **bicycle** to Giverny along a pretty bike path (bike rental at the Vernon train station). If you're **driving,** take the A14 autoroute, merging into the A13 toward Rouen. Take exit 14 at Vernon/Bonnières, and then follow the signs to Bonnières and cross the Seine to Bennecourt. From here, a direct road with signs leads to Giverny. Expect it to take about an hour; try to avoid weekends.

Show Me the Monet

Claude Monet Foundation ★★★ Born in 1840, the French Impressionist was a brilliant innovator, excelling in presenting the effects of light at different times of day. Some critics claim that he "invented light." His paintings of the Rouen cathedral and of water lilies, which one critic called "vertical interpretations of horizontal lines," are just a few of his masterpieces.

Monet came to Giverny in 1883. Many of his friends visited him at this house (known as Le Pressoir), including Clemenceau, Cézanne, Rodin, Renoir, Degas, and Sisley. When Monet died in 1926, his son, Michel, inherited the house but left it abandoned. The gardens became almost a jungle, inhabited by river rats. In 1966, Michel died and left house and gardens to the Académie des Beaux-Arts. It wasn't until 1977 that Gerald van der Kemp, who restored Versailles, decided to work on Giverny. A large part of it was restored with gifts from U.S. benefactors, notably the late Lila Acheson Wallace, former head of *Reader's Digest*.

The house is open to the public. It contains Monet's collection of 18th- and 19th-century Japanese prints, as well as antique (though not original) furnishings. From the painter's bedroom window, you'll have a stunning view of the gardens. You can stroll the garden and view the thousands of flowers, including the *nymphéas*. The Japanese bridge, hung with wisteria, leads to a setting of weeping willows and rhododendrons. Monet's studio barge was installed on the pond.

84 rue Claude-Monet, Giverny 27620. ✆ **02-32-51-28-21.** www.fondation-monet.com. Admission 8€ adults, 5€ students and children 7–12, free for children 6 and under. Daily 9:30am–6pm. Closed Nov–Mar.

Claude Monet Foundation.

Where to Stay

La Musardière A short walk from Monet's museum and gardens, this family-run hotel is in a former manor house. A scenic park filled with ancient trees surrounds the hotel and restaurant. The mansard-roofed building dates from 1880 and was around in

Monet's time. Many of the antique features and architectural adornments are still in place. *Musardière* is French for a place for "idling or dawdling along," and that is just what you do here. Each medium-size guest room, attractively and comfortably furnished, has a small bathroom with tub or shower. The hotel also operates its own restaurant and crêperie, where fixed-price menus cost 26€ and 36€.

123 rue Claude-Monet, Giverny 27620. www.lamusardiere.fr. ✆ **02-32-21-03-18.** Fax 02-32-21-60-00. 10 units. 81€–93€ double; 136€ suite. MC, V. Free parking. Closed Nov to mid-Mar. **Amenities:** Restaurant; bar. *In room:* TV, hair dryer, free Wi-Fi.

Where to Eat

Baudy FRENCH We hesitate to recommend this place because of the never-ending tour buses arriving from Paris, but it's a local legend and deserves a look. During the town's 19th-century heyday, the American painters used the pink villa as their lodging. In Monet's time, this place was an *epicerie-buvette* (casual hangout) run by the painter's friends Angelina and Gaston Baudy. Metcalf was the first artist to arrive on Mme. Baudy's doorstep, and in time, a string of other painters followed. Artists such as Cézanne could be found wandering around the rose garden here. The place no longer has its "legendary two tables," at which Mme. Baudy fed the artists, but it plays host to virtually all visitors to Giverny, feeding them simply prepared, traditional French cuisine, including big, freshly made salads and a changing array of hot food.

81 rue Claude-Monet. ✆ **02-32-21-10-03.** Reservations recommended. Main courses 14€–16€; fixed-price menu 23€. MC, V. Daily 10am–9:30pm. Closed Nov–Mar.

Restaurant Les Fleurs ★ FRENCH This pleasant, popular restaurant does a large percentage of its business with art lovers. The Claude Monet Foundation is just across the river in Giverny. On the main street of Vernon, 4.8km (3 miles) southwest of the museum, the restaurant focuses on flavorful, familiar *cuisine bourgeoise* that many diners remember fondly from their childhood. Menu items include fresh fish such as sea bass served with saffron sauce; a flavorful risotto of the day; and sweetbreads braised with Parmesan. Other dishes include fresh scallops with cocoa; a platter devoted to different preparations of duckling; and a variety of meats grilled, simply and flavorfully, *à la plancha.*

71 rue Carnot, Vernon. ✆ **02-32-51-16-80.** Reservations recommended. Main courses 18€–30€; fixed-price menu 27€–54€. AE, MC, V. Wed–Sun noon–2pm; Tues–Sat 7:30–10pm. From the Claude Monet Foundation in Giverny, drive 5km (3 miles) southwest, crossing the Seine, and follow signs to Vernon.

CHANTILLY ★★★

42km (26 miles) N of Paris; 50km (31 miles) SE of Beauvais

This is a resort town for Parisians who want a quick weekend getaway. Known for its frothy whipped cream and its black lace, it also draws visitors to its racetrack and château.

Two of the great French horse races, **Le Prix du Jockey Club** and the **Prix Diane,** take place at the Hippodrome on the first and second Sundays of June, respectively. Thoroughbreds from as far away as Kentucky and Brunei, as well as entrants sponsored by old and new European money, compete in a very civil format that's broadcast throughout France.

Essentials

GETTING THERE **Trains** depart frequently for Chantilly from Gare du Nord in Paris. The ride takes about 30 minutes; the round-trip cost is 15€. On race days, free shuttle buses take fans from the Chantilly station to the track. Alternatively, RER line D will get you from Métro stop Châtelet–Les Halles to Chantilly in about 45 minutes.

VISITOR INFORMATION The **Office de Tourisme** is at 60 av. du Maréchal-Joffre (✆ **03-44-67-37-37;** www.chantilly-tourisme.com).

Seeing the Château & Museums

Château de Chantilly/Musée Condé ★★★ Once the seat of the grand Condé, head of the Bourbon-Condé dynasty, this château and the museum within it are on an artificial lake. Approach on the same forested drive that Louis XIV rode for a banquet prepared by his chef, Vatel. (One day when the fish didn't arrive on time, Vatel committed suicide.) The château is French Renaissance, with gables and towers, but part was rebuilt in the 19th century. A forest once filled with stag and boar skirts it.

In 1886, the château's owner, the duc d'Aumale, bequeathed the park and palace to the Institut de France, along with his art collection and library. The château houses sumptuous furnishings as well as works by artists such as Memling, Van Dyck, Botticelli, Poussin, Watteau, Ingres, Delacroix, Corot, Rubens, and Vernet. See Raphael's *Madonna of Lorette, Virgin of the House d'Orléans,* and *Three Graces* (sometimes called the *Three Ages of Woman*). A series of about 40 miniatures represents the foremost French painter of the 15th century, Jean Fouquet. A copy of the rose diamond that received worldwide attention when it was stolen in 1926 is occasionally on display in the jewel collection. One of the most celebrated Condé acquisitions is the Limbourg brothers' *Les Très Riches Heures du Duc de Berry,* a 15th-century illuminated manuscript, which is not always on view.

The château was built about 1560 by Jean Bullant for a member of the Montmorency family. The stables (see below), a hallmark of French 18th-century

Château de Chantilly.

architecture, were constructed to house 240 horses, with adjacent kennels for 500 hounds. If you have time, take a walk in the garden laid out by Le Nôtre. A hamlet of rustic cottages and the Maison de Sylvie, a graceful building constructed in 1604 and rebuilt by Maria-Felice Orsini, are in the park.

If you don't want to see the château and its museum, you can visit the gardens (6€; free for 17 and under). Once you're in the garden, you can ride a motorized "train" (touristy and loaded with children) through the park (5€ for adults, 3€ for children), or take a boat ride on the château's ornamental lake (12€ per hr. for up to 4 people).

Chantilly. ✆ **03-44-62-62-62.** www.chateaudechantilly.com. Admission to the château, museum, and gardens 12€ adults, free for children 17 and under accompanied by an adult. Nov–Mar Wed–Mon 10:30am–5pm (park until 6pm); Apr–Oct Wed–Mon 10am–6pm (park until 8pm).

Les Grandes Ecuries/Musée Vivant du Cheval ★★ This museum occupies the restored Grandes Ecuries, the stables built between 1719 and 1735 for Louis-Henri, prince de Bourbon and prince de Condé, who occupied the château. Besides being fond of horses, he believed in reincarnation and expected to come back as a horse in his next life, so he built stables fit for a king.

The stables and an adjoining kennel fell into ruin, but they've been restored as a museum of the living horse, with thoroughbreds housed alongside old breeds of draft horses, Arabs and Hispano-Arabs, and farm horses. Exhibits trace the horse's association with humans and include a blacksmith shop and displays of saddles, equipment for the care of horses, and horse-race memorabilia.

At press time, the museum was undergoing more restorations and was scheduled to reopen in late 2012. Meanwhile, the stables continue to present themed equestrian shows; see the website for exact hours and prices.

Chantilly. ✆ **03-44-27-31-80.** www.museevivantducheval.fr. Equestrian shows Wed–Mon 11am and/or 2pm. Admission 11€–21€.

Where to Stay

Best Western Hôtel du Parc This hotel built in 1987 is in the center of town, close to a host of restaurants and sights. There are grander châteaux in Chantilly, but if you want a midtown location, this is your finest choice. The contemporary lobby, dominated by mirrors and chrome, gives way to an inviting bar, with plenty of dark wood and leather. The medium-size guest rooms have built-in furnishings and glass doors that open onto private balconies. About half of the small bathrooms have both tub and shower. Overall, expect a no-frills experience that's pleasant but nothing special.

36 av. du Maréchal-Joffre, Chantilly 60500. www.bestwestern.fr. ✆ **800/528-1234** in the U.S. and Canada, or 03-44-58-20-00. Fax 03-44-57-31-10. 57 units. 120€–180€ double; 160€–320€ suite. AE, DC, MC, V. Parking 10€. **Amenities:** Bar; room service. *In room:* TV, hair dryer, free Wi-Fi.

Château de la Tour ★★ A wealthy Parisian banking family built this elegant turn-of-the-20th-century château with a 4.8-hectare (12-acre) park as a weekend getaway. During World War II, it was the home of the German l'Etat Major, and in 1946, it became a luxury hotel. The likes of Edith Piaf, Tino Rossi, and Jean Gabin met and mingled in the restaurant. Today celebrities and sports personalities still frequent the château. In 1990, it gained a new wing; guests can choose rooms with a modern flavor or a more traditional ambience. All units are large and feature hardwood floors, high ceilings, and first-class furnishings, and three-quarters of the units are air-conditioned. Public areas feature two wood-burning fireplaces.

Chemin de la Chaussée, Gouvieux 60270. www.lechateaudelatour.fr. ✆ **03-44-62-38-38.** Fax 03-44-57-31-97. 41 units. 160€–190€ double; 190€–265€ suite. AE, DC, MC, V. Free parking. **Amenities:** Restaurant; bar; babysitting; free bikes; outdoor pool; room service; tennis court. *In room:* A/C (in 31 rooms), TV, hair dryer, minibar, free Wi-Fi.

Where to Eat

The restaurant at the **Château de la Tour** (see above) is open to the public for lunch and dinner.

La Ferme de Condé TRADITIONAL FRENCH The most appealing restaurant in Chantilly is in a 100-year-old stone-sided former Anglican church. It's on the periphery of town, about 1.6km (1 mile) north of the château. Antique farm implements, racks of wine bottles, and barrels give the space a cozy feel. The cuisine is old-fashioned, with variations based on seasonal ingredients and the chef's inspiration. Look for fresh oysters from Brittany or homemade foie gras, followed by duck *magret* with honey and spices, or succulent sweetbreads with morels. Two other delights include a fresh lobster salad and homemade smoked salmon.

42 av. du Maréchal-Joffre. ✆ **03-44-57-32-31.** www.lafermedeconde.fr. Reservations recommended. Main courses 15€–44€; fixed-price menus 25€–28€. AE, DC, MC, V. Daily noon–2pm and 7–10:30pm.

SENLIS ★★

52km (32 miles) S of Paris; 100km (62 miles) S of Amiens

Sleepy Senlis, which some Parisians treat as a suburb, is a quiet township surrounded by forests. Its memories are many and regal. Hugh Capet, founder of the Capetian dynasty that fathered all the Louis, was elected king here in 987. The town belonged to his royal descendants through the centuries until the monarchy finally ended in 1830. You can tie a visit to this town with a trek to Chantilly (see above). Today the core of Vieux Senlis is a medieval bonanza that attracts visitors from all over the world. Budget 2 hours to see Senlis.

Essentials

GETTING THERE From Paris's Gare du Nord, you can take a **train** to Chantilly (see above), and from the station take the SNCF **bus** (marked SENLIS), which has a schedule that coincides with the arrival of trains from Paris. You can also take the TER regional **train** from Gare du Nord to Creil and transfer to the SNCF bus to Senlis. The round-trip bus and train fare is 19€ to 24€, depending on the route. Total travel time from downtown Paris to Senlis should be around an hour but can be longer, depending on connections; visit the SNCF website (www.voyages-sncf.com) for schedules.

VISITOR INFORMATION The **Office de Tourisme** is on place parvis Notre-Dame (✆ **03-44-53-06-40;** www.senlis-tourisme.fr).

Seeing the Sights

Medieval streets loaded with antique masonry and evocative doorways run throughout the city. One of the most interesting is the **rue du Chat-Harét;**

from its center, it affords a view over the ruined château and the Gallo-Roman foundations. The **rue des Cordeliers** is the site of a (since demolished) medieval convent, and nos. 14 and 10 on that street are particularly beautiful and old, but neither is open to the public.

Rue du Chat-Harét, Senlis.

Cathédrale Notre-Dame de Senlis ★★ This cathedral has a 13th-century spire that rises 78m (256 ft.) and dominates the countryside. The severe western facade contrasts with the Flamboyant Gothic southern portal. A fire swept the structure in 1504, and much rebuilding followed. Damaged during the Revolution, the church, whose origins date from 1153, was restored in the 19th century. Before you enter, walk around to the western porch to see the sculptures. Depicted in stone is a calendar of the seasons, along with scenes showing the ascension of the Virgin. The builders of the main portal imitated the work at Chartres. In the forecourt are memorials to Joan of Arc and Marshal Foch.

3 place Notre-Dame. ✆ **03-44-53-01-59.** Free admission. Daily 8:30am–7pm.

Parc du Château Royal and Musées de la Vénerie (Hunting Museum) et des Spahis ★ A short walk from the cathedral stands this curious archaeological ruin. Its stones have more royal associations than virtually anywhere else in France. The most impressive aspect remaining today is a massive Gallo-Roman wall, in some places more than 6m (20 ft.) tall. It encircles an area of about 6 hectares (15 acres), some of them occupied by parts of medieval Senlis. Of the wall's 28 original watchtowers, 16 remain. Within the circumference, the best-preserved fortification of its kind in France, are the ruins of a château that was occupied, or at least visited, by virtually every monarch of France from Hughes Capet (in the 10th c.) to Henri IV (late Renaissance). Abandoned by the monarchs around 1600, the château was demolished after the French Revolution. Today you can wander freely among the ruins, imagining the grandeur of life as it used to be.

The complex's highlight, in the verdant park that surrounds the ruin, is the **Prieuré St-Mauritius,** a monastery that not only honors a saint, but also was founded by one, Louis IX. It houses the **Musée de la Vénerie (Hunting Museum),** where you'll see hunting-related works of art from the 15th century to the present. Exhibits include arms, horns, trophies, drawings, engravings, and old hunting suits and costumes, all of which evoke the passion and pageantry that used to surround royal hunting expeditions. You can visit the museum only as part of a 1-hour tour (in French); tours begin every hour on the hour.

In another building lies the **Musée des Spahis,** a small museum dedicated to the North African cavalry troops of the French army. The Spahi troops were first recruited from Algeria, Tunisia, and Morocco in 1831, when those countries were still French colonies, and served in both World Wars. A unit was posted in Senlis for 30 years in this former house, which now displays trumpets, banners, and the striking uniforms of this unique cavalry division.

Senlis. ✆ **03-44-32-00-81.** www.ville-senlis.fr. Free admission to the park. Admission to the Hunting and Spahi Museums, including guided tour, 2€ adults, 1€ adults over 60 and students 24 under, free 15 and under. Mon and Thurs–Fri 10am–noon and 2–6pm; Wed 2–6pm; Sat–Sun 11am–1pm and 2–6pm.

Musée d'Art et d'Archéologie At press time, this museum was getting a thorough overhaul and was scheduled to reopen in 2012. Housed in a former Episcopal palace, the museum contains a fine collection of Gallo-Roman artifacts from the region, as well as rare sculptures and church art from the Middle Ages. The collection also features paintings, some by local artists working in an untrained style that art historians refer to as "naive," executed between the 17th and 20th centuries.

Place du Parvis. ✆ **03-44-32-00-83.** Admission 2€ adults, 1€ students and children 16–18, free for children 15 and under. Mon and Thurs–Fri 10am–noon and 2–6pm; Wed 2–6pm; Sat–Sun 11am–1pm and 2–6pm.

Where to Stay & Eat

Hostellerie de la Porte Bellon In a town of lackluster inns, this is a good oasis for the night. The stately but relatively inexpensive hotel was built as a convent 300 years ago and later functioned as a coaching inn. A short walk east of Senlis's historic core, it has three floors of big-windowed guest rooms and a facade dotted with old-fashioned shutters and window boxes filled with pansies and geraniums. At the entrance is an unusual 19th-century glass vestibule inspired by an English greenhouse. The hotel interior is undergoing an overhaul after a recent change of ownership; the cheerful but ordinary rooms will be getting a fresh look.

51 rue Bellon, Senlis 60300. www.portebellon.fr. ✆ **03-44-53-03-05.** Fax 03-44-53-29-94. 17 units. 80€–93€ double; 245€ 3-bedroom suite. AE, MC, V. Closed 1st 2 weeks of Jan. **Amenities:** Restaurant; bar. *In room:* TV, free Wi-Fi.

La Vieille Auberge TRADITIONAL FRENCH This building has held a restaurant since 1558, when it served greasy food to wayfarers and pilgrims headed for the nearby cathedral. Today, considerably cleaned up, it has Louis-Philippe furniture and one large candlelit dining room that consists of three separate spaces. During warm months, guests can sit on a small terrace. The menu features classic French dishes with modern touches, like fricassée of sweetbreads in a sauce made with sesame and balsamic vinegar, or duck magret with Espelette pepper and fresh foie gras.

8 rue Long Filet. ✆ **03-44-60-95-50.** www.lavieilleauberge-senlis.com. Reservations recommended Fri–Sat. Main courses 17€–25€; fixed-price menu 23€–35€. MC, V. Wed–Mon noon–1:45pm; Wed–Sat and Mon 7–9:30pm. Closed 3 weeks in Jan and 3 weeks in July.

COMPIÈGNE ★★★

81km (50 miles) N of Paris

A visit to this Oise River valley town is usually combined with an excursion to Senlis, (see above), some 32km (20 miles) away. Like Senlis, this town north of Paris lives for its memories—not all pleasant. It was here that Hitler purportedly

Château de Compiègne.

danced his "jig of joy" on June 22, 1940, when the humiliated French government surrendered to Germany. After the war, it was revealed that the film clip that shocked the world was actually a hoax; the "dance" was manufactured by the director of the Canadian department of information and propaganda, who manipulated the film.

But most come to celebrate the town's royal heritage. Graced with two royal castles in its environs, there are several centuries' worth of history to visit, not to mention the 14,160-hectare (34,975-acre) forest of Compiègne. With its majestic vistas, venerable trees, and ponds, it merits exploration.

Essentials

GETTING THERE **Trains** run frequently from the Gare du Nord in Paris. The ride takes 40 to 60 minutes. The station is across the river from the town center. A round-trip ticket costs 27€. If you're **driving,** take the Paris–Lille motorway (A1 or the less convenient E15) for 81km (50 miles).

VISITOR INFORMATION The **Office de Tourisme** is located on the Place de l'Hôtel-de-Ville (✆ **03-44-40-01-00;** www.compiegne-tourisme.fr).

Seeing the Sights

An imposing statue of **Joan of Arc,** who was taken prisoner at Compiègne by the Burgundians on May 23, 1430, stands in the town square.

Château de Pierrefonds ★★ One of the Compiègne forest's most evocative medieval buildings lies 12km (7½ miles) north of the town. (To reach it from the center, follow signs to Soissons.) Originally built in the 1100s as a château-fortress, it was partially destroyed in the 17th century and was in ruins when it was bought by Napoleon for a pitance. In 1857, his nephew, Napoleon III, asked Viollet-Le-Duc, monument restorer par excellence, to not only fix it up, but rebuild it. The result is not entirely authentic, but impressive. Surrounded by a moat, it looks feudal, with rounded towers capped by funnel-shaped pointed roofs. Artifacts from the Middle Ages are displayed inside. Save time for a stroll through the tiny village of Pierrefonds at the base of the château. Here, half-timbered houses recall the château's medieval heyday.

Rue Viollet-Le-Duc in the Forêt de Compiègne. ✆ **03-44-42-72-72.** www.pierrefonds.monuments-nationaux.fr. Admission 7€ adults, 4.50€ students 18–25, free for ages 17 and under. May–Aug daily 9:30am–6pm; Sept–Apr Tues–Sun 10am–1pm and 2–5:30pm.

Musée de la Figurine Historique (Museum of Historical Figurines) ★ Housed in one of Compiègne's finest monuments, the Flamboyant Gothic Hôtel de Ville, built from 1499 to 1503, this museum showcases a collection of about 100,000 tin soldiers, from a Louis XIV trumpeter to a World War II soldier. The Battle of Waterloo, staged in miniature on a landscape with thousands of figurines, is depicted in all its gore.

28 place de l'Hôtel-de-Ville. ✆ **03-44-40-72-55.** www.musee-figurine.fr. Admission 3€ adults, 1.50€ students and children 7–18, free for ages 6 and under. Tues–Sat 9am–noon; Tues–Sun 2–6pm (until 5pm Nov–Feb).

Musée National du Château de Compiègne ★★★ In its heyday, Compiègne attracted royalty and two Bonaparte emperors. But this wasn't always a place of pageantry. Louis XIV once said: "In Versailles, I live in the style befitting a monarch. In Fontainebleau, more like a prince. At Compiègne, like a peasant." But the Sun King returned again and again. His successor, Louis XV, started rebuilding the château, based on plans by Gabriel. The king died before work was completed, and Louis XVI and Marie Antoinette expanded it.

Napoleon's second wife, Marie-Louise, arrived at Compiègne to marry him; in a dining room, which you can visit only on the guided tour, she had her first meal with the emperor. Accounts maintain that she was paralyzed with fear of the older man (Napoleon was in his 40s; she was 19). After dinner, he seduced her and is said to have only increased her anxiety.

During the Second Empire, Compiègne reached its pinnacle. Under Napoleon III and Eugénie, the hunting season was the occasion for balls and parties. Women in elegant hoop skirts danced to Strauss waltzes; Offenbach's operas echoed through the chambers and salons; and Eugénie, who fancied herself an actress, performed in the palace theater for her guests.

On the tour, you'll see the gold-and-scarlet Empire Room, where Napoleon spent many a troubled night, and his library, known for its secret door. In the Queen's Chamber, Marie-Louise used the "horn of plenty" bed.

In addition to the Imperial apartments, there are two museums stashed in the wings of the castle, both of which can be visited only on a guided tour (in French). The **Musée National de la Voiture (National Automobile Museum)** exhibits about 150 vehicles, from Ben-Hur chariots to a Citroën "chain-track" vehicle. The **Musée du Second Empire** is devoted to sculpture, paintings, and furniture from Napoleon III's glory days (1852–1870), including works by Meissonier, Giraud, and Carpeaux.

Place du Général de Gaulle. ✆ **03-44-38-47-02.** www.musee-chateau-compiegne.fr. Admission (including access to museums) 6.50€ adults, free for adults and children 25 and under. Wed–Mon 10am–6pm.

Wagon de l'Armistice (Wagon du Maréchal-Foch) ★★ In 1940, in one of the most perverse twists of fate in European history, Hitler forced the vanquished French to capitulate in the same rail coach where German officials signed the Armistice on November 11, 1918. The triumphant Nazis transported the coach to Berlin and then to Ordüff in the Thuringian Forest, where an Allied bomb destroyed it in April 1945. Seven kilometers (4¼ miles) into the forest of Compiègne lies the **Clarière de l'Armistice,** a clearing where the original coach came to a stop, and where today you can visit a replica that recounts the events of 1918 and 1940 in graphic detail, assisted by newspapers, photos, maps, and slide shows.

Rte. de Soissons, Compiègne. ✆ **03-44-85-14-18.** http://armistice.chez-alice.fr. Admission 4€ adults, 2€ children 7–13, free for children 6 and under. Apr to mid-Oct Wed–Mon 10am–noon and 2–6pm; mid-Oct to Mar Wed–Mon 10am–noon and 2–5pm.

Where to Stay

Hostellerie du Royal-Lieu ★ This half-timbered inn is the best choice for food and lodging close to the town, about 2km (1¼ miles) away. Guest rooms are medium in size, sleekly designed, and the bathrooms are tidily organized. The rooms and the restaurant's terrace overlook a garden. Meals in the elegantly rustic dining room may include pistachio-coated filet of sole, or pigeon stuffed with truffles and foie gras.

9 rue de Senlis, Compiègne 60200. www.host-royallieu.com. ✆ **03-44-20-10-24.** Fax 03-44-86-82-27. 15 units. 140€ double; 160€ suite. AE, MC, V. Follow signs southwest toward Senlis until you reach rue de Senlis, a 5-min. drive east of the town center. Free parking. **Amenities:** Restaurant; bar; room service. *In room:* TV, hair dryer, free Wi-Fi.

Where to Eat

The restaurant at the **Hostellerie du Royal-Lieu** (see above) is also open to the public.

La Part des Anges ★ FRENCH Our favorite restaurant in Compiègne occupies two warmly decorated dining rooms within a tile-roofed building from the early 1990s in the commercial center of town. Jean-Jacques Moissinac heads the kitchen, while his English-speaking wife, Marie-Hélène, tends to service in the dining room. The decor creates an old-fashioned warmth, with tapestry fabrics, indirect lighting, and a floor covered with antique beige-and-brown ceramic tiles. Items likely to appear on the menu include lobster-stuffed ravioli, sautéed sea scallops, mixed grill with tarragon butter, and homemade foie gras with figs. The place lies within a 10-minute walk of the château, the Hôtel-de-Ville, and most of the town's historic monuments.

18 rue de Bouvines. ✆ **03-44-86-00-00.** www.lapartdesanges60.com. Reservations recommended. Main courses 20€–27€; set-price menus 30€–60€. AE, MC, V. Tues–Fri and Sun noon–1:30pm; Tues–Sat 7:30–9pm. Closed 3 weeks in Aug, 1 week btw. Christmas and New Year's Day.

6

THE LOIRE VALLEY

by Margie Rynn

Cutting across the heart of France, the Loire River runs along a fertile valley filled with stunning castles, vineyards, and landscapes straight out of a fairy tale. François I, France's ultimate Renaissance king, made Amboise his capital, and he and his court left a spectacular legacy of castles and monuments all over the area. The epoch's most famous Italian artists, including Leonardo da Vinci, were invited to build and decorate these masterpieces, and today the entire valley has been declared a World Heritage Site. But the Loire quenches more than just château fever: Follow the rivers Loire, Cher, Vienne, and Indre to discover sleepy hamlets tucked into the pastoral terrain.

Sightseeing Start your tour of the châteaux of the Loire Valley at **Azay-le-Rideau,** a dreamy Renaissance castle that seems to float in a pond dotted with lily pads. Then move on to **Château d'Ussé,** said to be the model for the castle in Perault's *Sleeping Beauty.* Or trail Joan of Arc to **Chinon,** where the martyr begged the Dauphin to fight the English during the Hundred Years' War. The monumental **Château de Chambord** features a forest of chimneys and pepper-pot turrets, as well as a massive double staircase; while the gardens of **Villandry** dazzle with acres of intricate ornamental flowerbeds.

Eating & Drinking The Loire Valley is home to some of the world's most prestigious wine appellations, from Vouvray to Saumur-Champigny and dozens of others around **Saumur, Angers,** and **Tours.** The dining is world class as well, from smart Michelin-starred restaurants to rustic *auberges,* where you can sample scrumptious regional specialties like pikeperch in wine and butter sauce, or local products like Sainte-Maure goat cheese and *rillettes,* a buttery pork pâté.

History The Loire abounds in history. A parade of famous figures marched across the valley at one time or another, from Julius Caesar to Richard the Lionhearted. At the hauntingly beautiful Abbaye Royale de Fontevraud, the largest medieval abbey in France, you can see the tombs of four members of the royal house of Plantagenet. In Amboise, you can visit the house where Leonardo da Vinci spent his final days. Angers's striped slate and tufa château houses the Apocalypse tapestry, a 14th-century masterwork that is over 90m (300 ft.) long.

Active Pursuits The Loire Valley is relatively flat and crisscrossed with cycling paths, including the 800km-long (496-mile) Loire à Vélo trail, so you can easily bike from one château to another and stay at bike-friendly hotels associated with the trail. You'll pass through jewel-like villages, enjoy the natural riches of the Loire ecosystem, and be tempted by the offerings of wineries you'll pass along the way.

PREVIOUS PAGE: **Château de Chenonceau.**

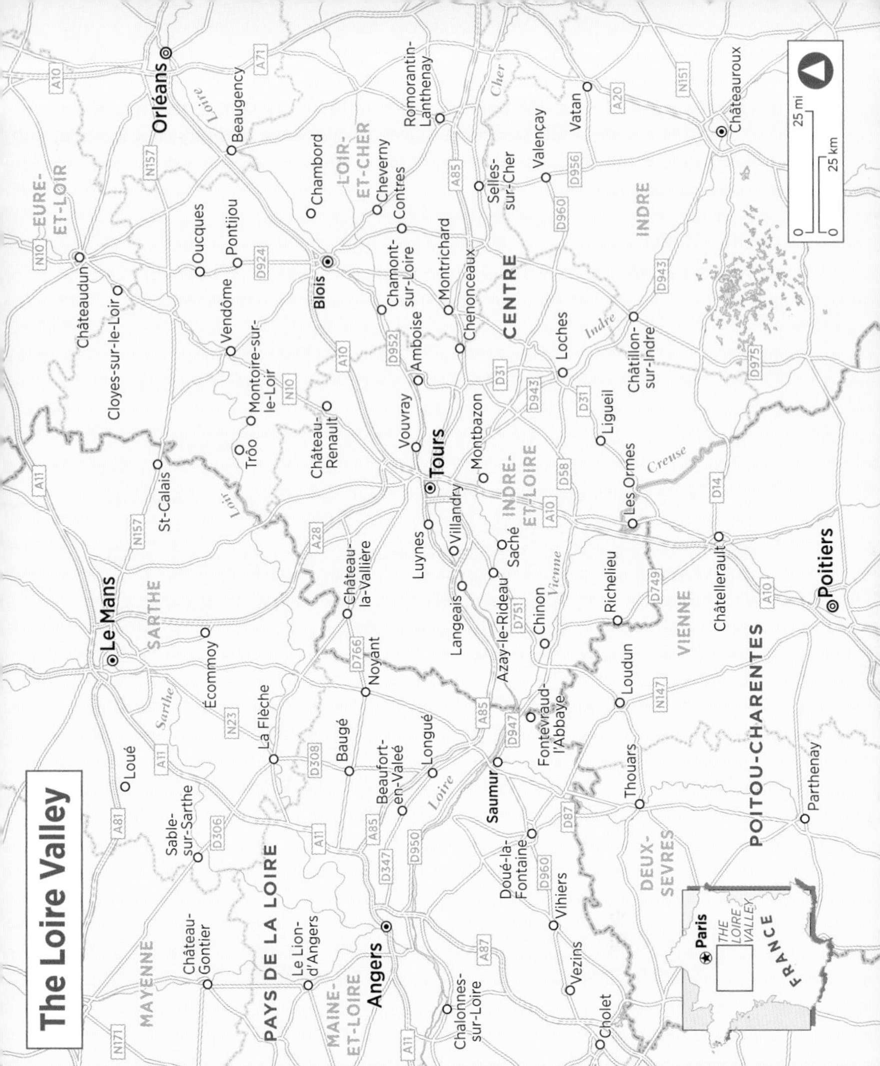

Trains serve some towns, but the best way to see this region is by car. There are **two regional tourist offices** that can help you plan your stay: **Comité Régional de Tourisme Val de Loire,** 37 av. de Paris, Orléans 45000 (✆ **02-38-79-95-28;** www.visaloire.com), and **SEM Régionale des Pays de la Loire,** 1 place de la Galarne, BP 80221, Nantes 44202 Cedex 2 (✆ **02-40-48-24-20;** www.westernloire.com).

ORLÉANS ★

119km (74 miles) SW of Paris; 72km (45 miles) SE of Chartres

After suffering damage in World War II, many Orléans neighborhoods were rebuilt in dull styles, so visitors who hope to see how it looked when the Maid of Orléans (Joan of Arc) was here are likely to be disappointed. In the last few decades, this city of 115,000 lost a lot of its prominence to Tours, but a recent urban makeover has brought a resurrection, with new streetcars, pedestrian areas, and public gardens.

Essentials

GETTING THERE About two **trains** per hour arrive from Paris's Gare d'Austerlitz (1 hr., 10 min; 18€ one-way); there are also a dozen connections from Tours

BIKING YOUR WAY through THE LOIRE

After 10 years and several million euros, 650km (404 miles) of bike paths are now available for your cycling pleasure along the banks of the Loire. Thanks to a vast program called **"La Loire à Vélo"** (The Loire on a Bike), you can now safely pedal from Sancerre to the sea on a dedicated bike path past châteaux, villages, and natural areas. Relatively flat, the path was designed primarily for low-key cycling with family and friends, and is linked to cycling-friendly hotels and bike rental outfits along the way (look for the ACCUEIL VÉLO signs). When finished, the project will include 800km (496 miles) of bike paths and hook up to an even more massive project called EuroVelo 6, a cycling path that leads all the way to the Black Sea.

La Loire à Vélo has partnered with various tourist offices and travel agencies to offer a range of bike-trip packages that include hotel, meals, bike rental, and baggage transport (very important if you don't want to haul extra weight). For more information, visit their site (in English), www.cycling-loire.com, or one of the two regional tourist offices (listed above). The website also has a detailed information on dozens of bike-rental outfits along the route, as well as brochures and links to guidebooks on various sections of the path.

One of the better-known outfitters is **Detours de Loire,** 35, rue Charles Gille, Tours (✆ **02-47-61-22-23;** www.locationdevelos.com), which has three other shops in Blois, Saumur, and Nantes, as well as 20 or so associated outlets up and down the Loire à Vélo circuit. This means that you can pick up your bike in one town and leave it in any partner outlet along the way, without having to worry about returning the bike to the place where you rented. If you are arriving in the Loire Valley by train, the four main shops are all located close to the town station. Prices for all-purpose bikes are from 14€ to 21€ per day, with discounts for multiple-day rentals. A 300€ deposit (usually a credit card imprint) is required. Detours de Loire can also organize hotel-bike packages, deliver your bike to your accommodations, and store your baggage while you are out pedaling. ***Note:*** Most outlets are open only from April to October.

BikeToursDirect, 1638 Berkley Circle, Chattanooga, TN (✆ **877/462-2423**), has six Loire Valley tours, including a three-stage program that, when linked together, takes cyclists from Orléans to the Atlantic. BikeToursDirect represents overseas bike tour operators whose low overhead and frequent departures allow them to offer prices as much as 70% below those of United States bike-tour companies. Self-guided tours start at 665€ per person, based on double occupancy, and include hotels, breakfasts, rental bikes, luggage transfers, and detailed route information.

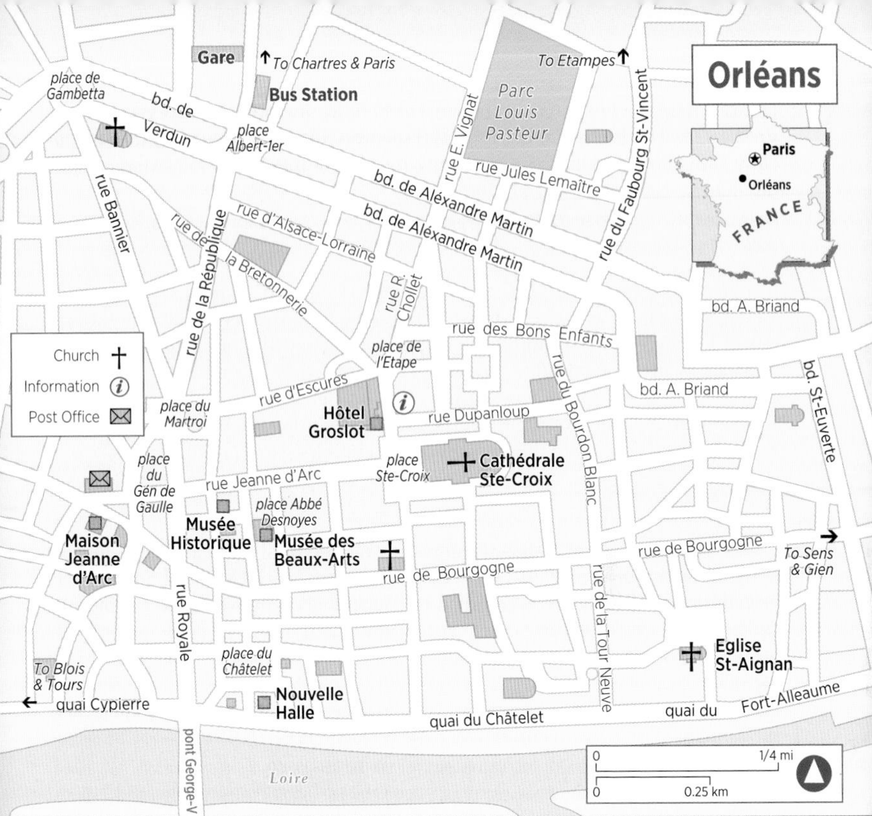

(50–70 min.). The one-way fare from Tours to Orléans is about 18€. Orléans lies on the road between Paris and Tours. If you're **driving** from Paris, take A10 south; from Tours, take A10 north.

VISITOR INFORMATION The **Office de Tourisme** is at 2 place de L'Etape (✆ **02-38-24-05-05;** www.tourisme-orleans.com).

Exploring the Town

Orléans is the chief town of Loiret, on the Loire, and beneficiary of many associations with the French aristocracy. It gave its name to ducs and duchesses of Orléans. In 1429, **Joan of Arc** relieved the city from a siege by the Burgundians and the English. That deliverance is celebrated every year on May 8, the anniversary of her victory. An equestrian statue of Jeanne d'Arc stands on place du Martroi. From the square, you can drive down rue Royal (rebuilt in 18th-c. style) across pont George-V (erected in 1760). A simple cross marks the site of the Fort des Tourelles, which Joan of Arc and her men captured.

Near rue Royale is **place du Châtelet,** with many boutiques, including a Galeries Lafayette. Look for fashionable clothing, jewelry, books, and leather goods. For antiques, walk along **rue de Bourgogne,** where a host of dealers sell everything from objets d'art to furniture.

Cathédrale Ste-Croix ★ Begun in 1287, after an earlier Romanesque church here collapsed from old age, the cathedral was burned by the Huguenots in 1568.

Henri IV laid the first stone of the present building in 1601, and work continued until 1829. The cathedral boasts a 17th-century organ and woodwork from the early 18th century in its chancel, the masterpiece of Jules Hardouin-Mansart and other artists associated with Louis XIV.

Place Ste-Croix. ✆ **02-38-77-87-50.** Free admission. May–Sept daily 9:15am–6pm; Oct–Apr daily 9:15am–noon and 2–6pm.

Eglise St-Aignan One of the most frequently altered churches in the Loire Valley, St-Aignan was consecrated in 1509 in the form you see today. It possesses one of France's earliest vaulted hall crypts, complete with polychromed capitals. Scholars of pre-Romanesque art view are interested in its rare 10th- and 11th-century aesthetics. Above ground, the church's Renaissance-era choir and transept remain, but the Protestants burned the nave during the Wars of Religion. In a wood-carved shrine are the remains of the church's patron saint.

Place St-Aignan. No phone. Crypt can be visited only on a guided tour; sign up at the tourist office.

Hôtel Groslot This Renaissance mansion was begun in 1550 and embellished in the 19th century. François II (the first husband of Mary, Queen of Scots) lived here during the fall of 1560 and died on December 5. Between the Revolution and the mid-1970s, it functioned as the town hall. Marriage ceremonies, performed by the town's magistrates, still are held here. It was here that Charles IX met his lovely Marie Touchet. The statue of Joan of Arc praying was the work of Louis Philippe's daughter, Princesse Marie d'Orléans. In the garden, you can see the remains of the 15th-century Chapelle St-Jacques.

Place de l'Etape (northwest of the cathedral). ✆ **02-38-79-22-30.** Free admission. July–Sept Mon–Fri and Sun 9am–6pm, Sat 5–8pm; Oct–June Mon–Fri and Sun 10am–noon and 2–6pm, Sat 5pm–7pm.

Musée des Beaux-Arts ★★ A museum of mostly French, but also Italian, Dutch, and Flemish works dating from the 15th to 20th centuries. The collection includes paintings by Tintoretto, Correggio, and Van Dyke, as well as a fine array of portraits, including one of Mme. de Pompadour by Drouais. A room dedicated to pastels includes works by Quentin de la Tour and Chardin.

1 rue Fernand Rabier. ✆ **02-38-79-21-55.** Admission 3€ adults, 1.50€ students, free for children 18 and under. Tues–Sun 10am–6pm.

Hôtel Groslot.

Shopping

Vinegar making was one of the city's main industries from the Middle Ages well into the 20th century. You can buy some of the famous Orléans vinegar north of town at **Martin Pouret,**

236 Faubourg Bannier, Fleury-les-Aubrais (✆ **02-38-88-78-49;** www.martin-pouret.com). The family-owned business dates from 1797. The current M. Pouret is the only person in the region carrying on the slow, traditional vinegar-making method. You can do a wine tasting at one of the region's most comprehensive wine merchants, **Cave de Marc & Sebastien,** 7 place du Châtelet (✆ **02-38-62-94-11;** www.cavedemarcetsebastien.fr), in the heart of the commercial center, just north of the Loire and west of rue Royale.

Where to Stay

Best Western Hôtel d'Arc This four-story hotel, built in the 1920s, has an Art Deco facade and old-fashioned elevator. It sits in the middle of the town and is close to the railway station and the pedestrian-only shopping streets. The guest rooms feature ceiling moldings and paneling. Most are of average size; the largest units have numbers that end in 2. Most rooms are peaceful, but avoid those that face rue de la République, which tend to be noisy. Although the hotel has no restaurant, it serves breakfast in an ornate room with a carved marble fireplace.

37 ter rue de la République, Orléans 45000. www.hoteldarc.fr. ✆ **02-38-53-10-94.** Fax 02-38-81-77-47. 35 units. 104€–171€ double. AE, DC, MC, V. **Amenities:** Room service. *In room:* TV, hair dryer, minibar, free Wi-Fi.

Hôtel de l'Abeille A touch of the 19th century lingers in these cozy lodgings—bedrooms are decorated with period prints and antique armoires, and even the façade of the building has a certain fin-de-siècle flourish. The hotel has been in the family for four generations; the feeling here is of a grand old house that is open to visitors. Not that this is a luxury palace, mind you: Lodgings are simple but clean and comfortable. There's a pretty roof garden with a view of the cathedral for lazing about on sunny days. You'll notice a Joan of Arc theme on the walls; the hotel owners collect artworks that celebrate Orléans' favorite liberator.

64 rue Alsace-Lorraine, Orléans 45000. www.hoteldelabeille.com. ✆ **02-38-53-54-87.** Fax 02-38-62-65-84. 27 units. 79€–98€ double; 98€–130€ family suite. AE, DC, MC, V. Parking 7€. **Amenities:** Bar; room service. *In room:* TV, hair dryer, free Wi-Fi.

Hôtel Mercure Orléans ★ If you seek modern comfort, this is the town's top choice. Along the river, adjacent to pont Joffre, the eight-story bandbox structure is within walking distance of place du Martroi and its Joan of Arc statue. Though rather impersonal—it's favored by businesspeople—it provides some of the best rooms in the city. Most units are in chain hotel style and of medium size. The on-site restaurant serves French and Loire Valley specialties.

44 quai Barentin, Orléans 45000. www.accorhotels.com. ✆ **02-38-62-17-39.** Fax 02-38-53-95-34. 111 units. 124€–163€ double; 195€ suite. AE, DC, MC, V. Parking 5€. **Amenities:** Restaurant; bar; babysitting; outdoor pool; room service. *In room:* A/C, TV, hair dryer, minibar, free Wi-Fi.

Where to Eat

Chez Jules ★ TRADITIONAL FRENCH This small bistro may not look like much, but it serves some of the best regional cuisine in the city. Tables are limited, so it's important to reserve in advance. Given the quality of the cuisine, prices are very reasonable. Try the eggplant caviar with ratatouille for an opener, or perhaps marinated mussels and beets or a goat cheese pastry. Look for a changing array of seafood dishes, depending on availability. One specialty is parmentier of pigeon with foie gras. The menu is seasonally adjusted.

136 rue de Bourgogne. ✆ **02-38-54-30-80.** Reservations required. Main courses 18€–22€; fixed-price lunch 19€, dinner 25€–33€. AE, MC, V. Tues–Sat noon–2pm and 7–9:30pm. Closed 2 weeks in July.

La Vieille Auberge ★ MODERN FRENCH You can dine inside in a stylish interior or, if the weather's right, order your food in a lovely garden. The restaurant is housed in a building from the 17th century, and all the food is prepared fresh daily by skilled chefs. The menu changes with the season to take advantage of the freshest available ingredients, which may include lobster, oysters, game (in autumn), shellfish, and lamb.

2 rue du Faubourg St-Vincent. ✆ **02-38-53-55-81.** www.la-vieille-auberge.net. Reservations recommended. Main courses 18€–35€; fixed-price lunch 25€, dinner 35€–49€. AE, MC, V. Mon–Thurs noon–2pm and 7–9:30pm; Fri–Sat noon–2pm and 7–10pm; Sun noon–2pm.

Orléans After Dark

You'll find most of the action in the bars along **rue de Bourgogne** and a handful of places on **rue Bannier.** A trendy young crowd drinks the night away at **Le Moog,** 245 rue de Bourgogne (✆ **02-38-54-93-23**), in a modern setting of stainless steel and bordello red lighting, with pop music playing in the background. There's also a terrace for fair weather. A few streets over is one of the better jazz clubs, **Paxton's Head,** 264 rue de Bourgogne (✆ **02-38-81-23-29**), with a down-home English pub feel. **Havana Café,** 28 place du Châtelet (✆ **02-38-52-16-00**), crawls with some of the city's most attractive and available 20- to 30-year-olds. This joint serves strong, party-colored drinks and loud music.

BEAUGENCY ★

150km (93 miles) SW of Paris; 85km (53 miles) NE of Tours

On the right bank of the Loire, the town of Beaugency boasts a long 12th-century bridge with 23 arches, said to have been built by the Devil himself. A major medieval event took place here: the 1152 annulment of the marriage of Eleanor of Aquitaine and her cousin, Louis VII. She then married Henry II of England, bringing southwestern France as her dowry, an act that set off the Hundred Years' War. This remarkable woman was the mother of Richard the Lion-Hearted. (The film *The Lion in Winter* dramatizes these events.) Allow 2 hours to see Beaugency.

The 15th-century **Château Dunois** is currently closed for renovations and may not reopen again until 2012 or beyond, so you'll have to see it from its exterior. The château is brooding and impressive, its historical links stretching back to almost-mystical medieval antecedents. It was built on the foundations of an earlier 10th-century fortress that belonged to the lords of Beaugency, whose feudal power extended throughout the region. Astride the street (la rue du Pont) that leads to one of the château's secondary entrances, the Voûte St-Georges (St. George's Vault) is an arched gateway from the earlier château.

More medieval moodiness is on hand at **La Tour César,** a 36m-tall (118-ft.) castle keep that is all that remains of an 11th-century citadel. A fine example of Romanesque military architecture, the interior of this five-story structure is in ruins.

Eglise Notre-Dame, place Saint-Fermin, a 12th-century abbey, was rebuilt after it was burned during the Wars of Religion (1562–1598). You can still

Beaugency.

see traces of its original Romanesque architecture in the chancel and transept. Nearby, the 16th-century **Tour St-Fermin,** a bell tower with a panoramic view of the valley, is famous for its bells, which ring out a traditional tune three times a day.

The 10th-century **Eglise St-Etienne,** place du Martroi, is one of the oldest churches in France. Now deconsecrated, it is owned by the municipality and is open only for temporary exhibitions of painting and sculpture.

Essentials

GETTING THERE If you're **driving** from Blois to Beaugency, take N152 northeast. About 20 **trains** per day run between Beaugency and either Blois or Orléans; each trip takes about 20 minutes, and the one-way fare ranges from 5.50€ to 6.10€. For railway information, visit www.voyages-sncf.com or dial ✆ **36-35.** From Orléans, there are about four to eight **buses** a day that go to Beaugency. For bus schedules and information, visit www.ulys-loiret.com or contact the tourist office (see below).

VISITOR INFORMATION The **Office de Tourisme** is at 3 place du Dr-Hyvernaud (✆ **02-38-44-54-42**).

Where to Stay & Eat

Abbaye de Beaugency ★ This three-star hotel offers the most historic accommodations in Beaugency. Built in 1640 as a monastery, it retains the stone window and door frames of its original construction and an elegant brick facade that may remind you of a château. A hotel since 1935, it sits beside the Loire, and all rooms have either partial or full views of the river. Guest rooms are large and bright; the decor includes lots of exposed beams and nice period touches.

2 quai de l'Abbaye, Beaugency 45190. www.hotel-abbaye-beaugency.com. ✆ **02-38-45-10-10.** Fax 02-38-44-98-14. 19 units. 99€–159€ double; 169€ suite. MC, V. **Amenities:** Bar; room service. *In room:* TV, minibar, free Wi-Fi.

La Tonnellerie ★ 🎁 About 1.5km (1 mile) south of the center of Beaugency, this well-managed hotel is intimate and charming. It was originally built as a manor house in the 19th century, and it retains its original L-shaped design, walled garden, and sense of the era of Balzac and Flaubert. Rooms are comfortable and traditional, furnished with reproduction antiques and period prints. The restaurant serves regional classics; main courses run 19€.

12 rue des Eaux-Bleues, Tavers, Beaugency 45190. ✆ **02-38-44-68-15.** Fax 02-38-44-10-01. www.tonelri.com. 20 units. 105€–180€ double; 174€–210€ suite. AE, MC, V. Closed Dec 13–Jan 31. Take A10, exit at Beaugency, and then take N152 to Beaugency/Tavers. **Amenities:** Restaurant; bar; outdoor pool. *In room:* TV, hair dryer, free Wi-Fi.

CHAMBORD

191km (118 miles) SW of Paris; 18km (11 miles) E of Blois

The **Château de Chambord** ★★★ (✆ **02-54-50-40-00;** www.chambord.org) is the culmination of François I's two biggest obsessions: hunting and architecture. Built as a "hunting lodge," this colossal edifice is a masterpiece of architectural derring-do. Some say Leonardo da Vinci had something to do with it, and when you climb the amazing double spiral staircase, that's not too hard to believe. The staircase is superimposed upon itself so that one person may descend and a second ascend without ever meeting. While da Vinci died a few months before construction started in 1519, what emerged after 20 years was the pinnacle of the French Renaissance, the largest château in the Loire Valley. The castle's proportions are of an exquisite geometric harmony, and its fantastic arrangement of turrets and chimneys makes it one of France's most recognizable chateâux.

Construction continued for decades; François I actually stayed at the château for only a few weeks during hunting season. After he died, his successors, none too sure what to do with the vast, unfurnished, and unfinished castle, basically abandoned it. Finally, Louis XIII gave it to his brother, who saved it from ruin; Louis XIV stayed there on several occasions and saw to restorations, but not a single monarch ever really moved in. The state acquired Chambord in 1932, and restoration work has been going on ever since.

Four monumental towers dominate Chambord's facade. The three-story keep has a spectacular terrace from which the ladies of the court used to watch the return of their men from the hunt. While many of the vast rooms are empty, several have been restored and filled with an impressive collection of period furniture and objects, giving an idea of what the castle looked like during the periods when parts of it were occupied. The château is in a park of more than 5,260 hectares (12,992 acres), featuring miles of hiking trails and bike paths, as well as picnic tables and bird-watching observation posts.

The château is open daily April to September 9am to 6:15pm, and October to March 9am to 5:15pm (until 7pm mid-July to mid-Aug). Admission is 9.50€ for adults and free for ages 17 and under accompanied by an adult. Allow 1½ hours to visit the château.

Essentials

GETTING THERE It's best to **drive** to Chambord. Take D951 northeast from Blois to Saint Dyé, turning onto the rural road to Chambord. You can also rent a **bicycle** in Blois and ride the 18km (11 miles) to Chambord, or take a **tour** to Chambord from Blois in summer. From May to September, **Transports**

Bedroom of Ludwig XIV at Château de Chambord.

du Loir et Cher (✆ **02-54-58-55-44;** www.tlcinfo.net) operates bus service to Chambord.

VISITOR INFORMATION The **Maison de Tourisme,** on place Saint Louis (✆ **02-54-33-39-16**), is open April to October.

Where to Stay & Eat

Hôtel du Grand-St-Michel Across from the château, and originally built as a kennel for the royal hounds, this inn is the only one of any substance in the tiny village. Try for a front room overlooking the château, which is dramatically floodlit at night. Accommodations are plain but comfortable, with provincial decor. Most visitors arrive for lunch, which in summer is served on a terrace. High points from the menu include pheasant with chestnuts (in late autumn and winter), grilled scallops with caramelized cauliflower and wild mushrooms, and several local pâtés and terrines, including coarsely textured, flavorful rillettes of regional pork.

103 place St-Louis, Chambord 41250, near Bracieux. www.saintmichel-chambord.com. ✆ **02-54-20-31-31.** Fax 02-54-20-36-40. 40 units. 61€–102€ double; 85€–114€ triple. MC, V. Free parking. Closed 2 weeks in Jan. **Amenities:** Restaurant; Internet; tennis court. *In room:* TV.

BLOIS

180km (112 miles) SW of Paris; 60km (37 miles) NE of Tours

The star attraction in this town of 52,000 is the **Château de Blois ★★★**, but if time remains after a visit to the château, you may want to walk around the town. It's a piece of living history, with cobblestone streets and restored white houses with slate roofs and red-brick chimneys. Blois (pronounce it "Blwah") hugs a hillside overlooking the Loire. Some of its "streets" are mere alleyways originally laid out in the Middle Ages, or lanes linked by a series of stairs. Allow 1½ hours to see Blois.

Essentials

GETTING THERE A dozen or so **trains** run from Paris's Gare de Austerlitz every day (1hr., 45 min.; 26€ one-way), and several others depart from the Gare Montparnasse, which involves a change in Tours (around 1hr., 50 min.; 31€–62€). From Tours, trains run almost every hour (trip time: 40 min.), at a cost of 9.80€ one-way. For information and schedules, visit www.voyages-sncf.com or dial ✆ **36-35.** From June to September, you can take a **bus** (✆ **02-54-58-55-44;** www.tlcinfo.net) from the Blois train station to tour châteaux in the area, including Chambord, Chaumont, Chenonceau, and Amboise. If you're **driving** from Tours, take RN152 east to Blois, which runs along the Loire; if you want to get there fast, take the A10 autoroute. If you'd like to explore the area by **bike,** check out **Traineurs de Loire,** 1 rue Chemonton (✆ **02-54-79-36-71;** www.traineursdeloire.com). Rentals start at 6€ per hour, 13€ per day.

VISITOR INFORMATION The **Office de Tourisme** is at 23 place du Château (✆ **02-54-90-41-41;** www.bloispaysdechambord.com).

Exploring the Town & the Château

If you have time for **shopping,** head for the area around **rue St-Martin** and **rue du Commerce** for high-end items such as clothing, perfume, shoes, and jewelry. Find a one-of-a-kind piece of jewelry, have something created by the master jeweler **Philippe Denies,** 3 rue St-Martin (✆ **02-54-74-78-24**). If you prefer antique jewelry, stop by **Antebellum,** 12 rue St-Lubin (✆ **02-54-78-38-78**), and browse its selection of precious and semiprecious stones set in gold and silver. If you want to acquire a copy of tapestries like the ones at the nearby châteaux, you'll find a wide range at **Tapisserie Langlois,** Voûte du Château (✆ **02-54-78-04-43**). Chocoholics flock to **Jeff de Bruges,** 77 rue du Commerce (✆ **02-54-74-26-44;** www.jeff-de-bruges.com), and **Max Vauché,** 50 rue du Commerce (✆ **02-54-78-23-55;** www.maxvauche-chocolatier.com). On Saturday all day, a **food market** is on place Louis XII and place de la République, lining several blocks in the center of town at the foot of the château.

Château de Blois ★★★ A wound in battle earned him the name Balafré (Scarface), but he was quite a ladies' man. In fact, on the misty morning of December 23, 1588, Henri I, the duc de Guise, had just left a warm bed and the arms of one of Catherine de Médicis's ladies-in-waiting. His archrival, King Henri III, had summoned him, but when the duke arrived, only the king's minions were about. The guards approached with daggers. Wounded, the duke made for the door, where more guards awaited him. Staggering, he fell to the floor in a pool of his own blood. Only then did Henri emerge from behind the curtains. "Mon Dieu," he reputedly exclaimed, "he's taller dead than alive!" The body couldn't be shown: The duke was too popular. Quartered, it was burned in a fireplace.

The murder of the duc de Guise is only one of the events

> **Let the Horse Lead the Way**
>
> **You can take a 25-minute horse-and-buggy ride through the old town of Blois for 6€ for adults and 4€ for children 2 to 12. The carriage departs from place du Château during April, May, June, and September from 2 to 6pm daily; in July and August, it leaves daily from 11am to 7pm. For more details, call the tourist office.**

Blois.

associated with the Château de Blois, begun in the 13th century by the comte de Blois. Blois reached the apex of its power in 1515, when François I moved to the château. For that reason, Blois is often called the "Versailles of the Renaissance," the second capital of France, and the "City of Kings." Blois soon became a palace of exile. Louis XIII banished his mother, Marie de Médicis, to the château, but she escaped by sliding into the moat down a mound of dirt left by the builders.

If you stand in the courtyard, you'll find that the château is like an illustrated storybook of French architecture. The Hall of the Estates-General is a beautiful 13th-century work; Louis XII built the Charles d'Orléans gallery and the Louis XII wing from 1498 to 1501. Mansart constructed the Gaston d'Orléans wing between 1635 and 1637. Most remarkable is the François I wing, a French Renaissance masterpiece, containing a spiral staircase with ornamented balustrades and the king's symbol, the salamander.

The château presents a *son-et-lumière* show in French from May to September, usually beginning at 10pm (except in June and July, when it starts at 10:30pm); on Wednesday nights, the show is in English. As a taped lecture plays, colored lights and readings evoke the age in which the château was built. The show costs 7€ for adults, 4€ for children 6 to 17, and is free for children 5 and under.

Blois 41000. ✆ **02-54-90-33-33.** www.chateaudeblois.fr. Admission 8€ adults, 6.50€ students, 4€ children 6–17, free for children 5 and under. July–Aug daily 9am–7pm; Apr–June and Sept daily 9am–6:30pm; Oct daily 9am–6pm; Nov–Mar daily 9am–12:30pm and 1:30–5:30pm.

Where to Stay

Some of the best rooms in town are at **Le Médicis** (see "Where to Eat," below).

Côté Loire–Auberge Ligérienne About a 5-minute walk from Blois Castle, these B&B-like lodgings include impeccably maintained rooms decorated with an interesting mix of antique headboards, country throw rugs, and 1930s shipping posters. There is a low-key maritime theme here, which makes sense for a hotel that sits on the edge of a river that served as a major transportation link up until the 19th century. Parts of this small inn were constructed in the 12th, 15th, and 16th centuries, which explains the narrow stairways and exposed beams.

One of the owners does double duty as chef: There is a tiny restaurant on the ground floor that features fresh, local ingredients.

2 place de la Grève, Blois 41000. www.coteloire.com. ✆ **02-54-78-07-86.** Fax 02-54-56-87-33. 8 units. 56€–79€ double. MC, V. **Amenities:** Bar, restaurant. *In room:* TV, hair dryer, free Wi-Fi. Closed Jan.

Mercure Centre ★ This is one of the best-located hotels in Blois—three stories of reinforced concrete and big windows beside the quays of the Loire, a 5-minute walk from the château. Though rooms never rise above the chain format, they attempt a modern look and are roomy and soundproof.

28 quai St-Jean, Blois 41000. www.mercure.com. ✆ **02-54-56-66-66.** Fax 02-54-56-67-00. 96 units. 90€–245€ double. AE, DC, MC, V. Parking 7€. Bus: Quayside marked PISCINE. **Amenities:** Restaurant; bar; babysitting; Jacuzzi; indoor pool; room service; sauna. *In room:* A/C, TV, hair dryer, minibar, free Wi-Fi.

Where to Eat

Au Rendez-vous des Pêcheurs ★★ TOURAINE/SEAFOOD This restaurant occupies a 16th-century house and former grocery a short walk from the château. Chef Christophe Cosme enjoys a reputation for quality, generous portions, and creativity. He prepares two or three meat dishes, including roasted Sologne pigeon on a caramelized cauliflower pancake, and seared Charolais steak with potatoes Maxime. These appear alongside a longer roster of seafood dishes, such as poached filet of local *sandre* (a freshwater fish; "zander" in English) served with celery root and chestnut gratin, and steamed freshwater pike in papillote with gnocchi.

27 rue du Foix. ✆ **02-54-74-67-48.** www.rendezvousdespecheurs.com. Reservations required. Main courses 29€–37€; fixed-price menu 30€–69€. AE, MC, V. Tues–Sat 12–2:30pm; Mon–Sat 7–10pm. Closed 1 week in Jan and the first 2 weeks of Aug.

Le Médicis ★ TRADITIONAL FRENCH Members of the Garanger family maintain one of the most sophisticated inns in Blois, just 1km (½ mile) from the château. It's ideal for a gourmet meal or an overnight stop. Fresh fish is the chef's specialty. Typical main courses are asparagus in mousseline sauce, scampi ravioli with saffron sauce, and *suprême* of perch with morels. Chocolate in many manifestations is the dessert specialty. The Garangers rent 10 elegant rooms with air-conditioning, TV, minibar, and hair dryer. Double rates are 87€ to 150€.

2 allée François 1er, Blois 41000. ✆ **02-54-43-94-04.** Fax 02-54-42-04-05. www.le-medicis.com. Reservations required. Main courses 18€–36€; fixed-price menu 23€–72€. AE, MC, V. Daily noon–1:15pm and 7–9pm. Closed Jan and Sun night and Mon Nov–Mar. Bus: 2.

L'Orangerie du Château ★★★ ☺ TOURAINE Next to the château, one of the castle's former outbuildings holds the grandest and best restaurant in the area, with a floral-themed dining room. Faithful customers and the most discerning foodies visiting Blois delight in the filet mignon with truffles. You can also sample a lovely waffle of potatoes with marinated salmon, or perfectly roasted monkfish flavored with fresh thyme. Everything tastes better with a Sauvignon de Touraine. For dessert, our favorite is melted chocolate and pistachio with crème fraîche.

1 av. Jean-Laigret. ✆ **02-54-78-05-36.** www.orangerie-du-chateau-fr. Reservations required. Main courses 23€–37€; fixed-price menu 34€–78€; children's menu 14€. AE, MC, V. Thurs–Tues noon–1:30pm; Thurs–Sat and Mon–Tues 7:15–9:15pm. Closed mid-Feb to mid-Mar.

Blois After Dark

There's not much in the way of nightlife in Blois, but you could saunter down to the fun and friendly **L'Hendrix Café,** 1 rue du Puits-Châtel (✆ **02-54-58-82-73**), for a drink. Another possibility is **Le Velvet Jazz Lounge,** 15 bis rue Haute (✆ **02-54-78-36-32;** www.velvet-jazz-lounge.com), off rue Denis Papin. This is part of a 13th-century abbey but is now a venue for weekly jazz concerts. Otherwise, this is a classy joint for a drink.

CHEVERNY

192km (119 miles) SW of Paris; 19km (12 miles) SE of Blois

The upper crust heads to the Sologne area for the hunt as if the 17th century had never ended. However, 21st-century realities—like formidable taxes—can't be entirely avoided, so the **Château de Cheverny ★★★** (✆ **02-54-79-96-29;** www.chateau-cheverny.fr) opens its rooms to visitors.

Unlike most of the Loire châteaux, Cheverny is the residence of the original owner's descendants. The family of the vicomte de Sigalas can trace its lineage from Henri Hurault, the son of the chancellor of Henri III and Henri IV, who built the château in 1634. Designed in classic Louis XIII style, it is resolutely symmetrical, with square pavilions flanking the central pile. Its elegant lines and sumptuous furnishings provoked the Grande Mademoiselle, otherwise known as the Duchess of Montpensier, to proclaim it an "enchanted castle."

You, too, will be impressed by the antique furnishings, tapestries, and objets d'art. A 17th-century French artist, Jean Mosnier, decorated the fireplace with motifs from the legend of Adonis. The Guards' Room contains a collection of medieval armor; also on display is a Gobelin tapestry depicting the abduction of Helen of Troy. In the king's bedchamber, another Gobelin traces the trials of Ulysses. Most impressive is the stone stairway of carved fruit and flowers.

Fireplace in the Guards' Room at the Château de Cheverny.

The château is open daily November to March 9:45am to 5pm, April to June and September 9:15am to 6:15pm, July and August 9:15am to 6:45pm, and October 9:45am to 5:30pm. Admission is 7.50€ for adults, 5.40€ for students under 25, 3.60€ for children 7 to 14, and free for children 6 and under. Allow 2 hours for your visit.

Essentials

GETTING THERE Cheverny is 19km (12 miles) south of Blois, along D765. It's best reached by **car** or on a **bus tour** (April–Aug only) from Blois with **TLC Transports du Loir et Cher** (✆ **02-54-58-55-44;** www.tlcinfo.net). Bus no.

4 leaves from the railway station at Blois once or twice per day; see the TLC website for the schedule. You can also take a **taxi** (✆ **02-54-78-07-65**) from the railway station at Blois.

VISITOR INFORMATION The **Maison de Tourisme** is at 12 rue Chêne des Dames (✆ **02-54-79-95-63;** www.bloispaysdechambord.com).

Where to Stay & Eat

Les Trois Marchands TRADITIONAL FRENCH This coaching inn, more comfortable than St-Hubert (see below), has been handed down for many generations. Jean-Jacques Bricault owns the three-story building, which has a mansard roof, a glassed-in courtyard, and sidewalk tables under umbrellas. In the tavern-style main dining room, the menu may include foie gras, lobster salad, frogs' legs, fresh asparagus in mousseline sauce, game dishes, or fish cooked in a salt crust. The inn rents 24 well-furnished, comfortable rooms with TVs for 42€ to 55€ for a double.

60 place de l'Eglise, Cour-Cheverny 41700. www.hoteldes3marchands.com. ✆ **02-54-79-96-44.** Fax 02-54-79-25-60. Dining room main courses 18€–47€; fixed-price menu 22€–45€. AE, DC, MC, V. Tues–Sun 7am–11pm. Closed Sun night Dec–Mar.

St-Hubert TRADITIONAL FRENCH About 500m (1,640 ft.) from the château, this inn was built in the 1950s in the provincial style. The least expensive menu (served only at lunchtime Mon–Fri) may include terrine of wild boar with pistachios, poached ray with mustard sauce, and walnut tart with vanilla ice cream. The most expensive menu may list scallop carpaccio with lavender, braised ris de veau with langoustines, cheeses, and fresh fruit sorbet with sparkling wine. The St-Hubert offers 20 conservatively decorated rooms with TVs for 55€ to 65€ for a double. Each room comes with free Wi-Fi.

122 rte. Nationale, Cour-Cheverny 41700. www.hotel-sthubert.com. ✆ **02-54-79-96-60.** Fax 02-54-79-21-17. Main courses 18€–22€; fixed-price menu 18€–37€; children's menu 12€. AE, MC, V. Daily noon–2pm and 7–9pm. Closed Sun night off season.

VALENÇAY

233km (144 miles) SW of Paris; 56km (35 miles) S of Blois

Château de Valençay ★★ (✆ **02-54-00-10-66;** www.chateau-valencay.fr) is one of the Loire's most handsome Renaissance châteaux. Talleyrand acquired it in 1803 on the orders of Napoleon, who wanted his minister of foreign affairs to receive dignitaries in style. The d'Estampes family built Valençay in 1520. The dungeon and west tower are of this period, as is the main body of the building, but other wings were added in the 17th and 18th centuries. The effect is grandiose, with domes and turrets.

The apartments are sumptuously furnished, mostly in the Empire style, but with Louis XV and Louis XVI trappings as well. A star-footed table in the main drawing room is said to have been the one on which the final agreement of the Congress of Vienna was signed in June 1815 (Talleyrand represented France).

A 45-minute audioguide visit gives detailed explanations of the castle's history and decor. After your visit to the château, you can walk through the garden and deer park. There are plenty of activities here for kids, including a giant labyrinth, a miniature farm, a playground, and, in high season, historic reenactments (at 3, 4, and 5pm).

Admission to the castle, car museum, and park is 11€ for adults, 8€ for students, 2.50€ for children 4 to 6, and free for ages 3 and under. The château is open daily mid-March to April 10:30am to 6pm, May 10am to 6pm, June 9:30am to 6:30pm, July and August 9:30am to 7pm, September 10am to 6pm, October to November 9 10:30am to 5:30pm. Allow 1½ hours to see the castle.

Within 200m (656 ft.) of the château, the **Musée de l'Automobile de Valençay,** route du Blois, 12 av. de la Résistance (✆ **02-54-00-07-74;** http://museedevalencay.voila.net), features a collection of more than 60 antique automobiles. Of special interest is a Bédélia (ca. 1914). The tandem-style automobile (the driver rode behind the passenger) with a pulley-operated two-speed gearshift is the rarest in the collection. The Bédélia, like 80% of the cars in the collection, was made in France. The museum is open from March to November.

Essentials

GETTING THERE If you're **driving** from Tours, take A85 east, turning south on D956 (exit 13 to Selles-sur-Cher) to Valençay. From Blois, follow D956 south.

VISITOR INFORMATION The **Office de Tourisme** is at 2 av. de Résistance (✆ **02-54-00-04-42**).

Where to Stay & Eat

Hôtel Le Relais du Moulin The town's best overnight choice is a 5-minute walk from the entrance to the château. It's also immediately adjacent to a stream and the now-disabled water wheel of an 18th-century textile mill that, during the age of Talleyrand and Napoleon, produced fabrics for curtains, clothing, and upholsteries. The hotel is in a modern building with a cream-colored façade; rooms are simple but functional, in tones of pale yellow and soft red, with views that overlook the château, the river, vineyards, and/or the verdant grounds. Fixed-price menus in the dining room cost from 14€ to 32€ and focus on traditional and well-prepared French food.

94 rue Nationale, Valençay 36600. www.hotel-lerelaisdumoulin.com. ✆ **02-54-00-38-00.** Fax 02-54-00-38-79. 54 units. 67€–70€ double. AE, MC, V. Closed Nov–Mar. **Amenities:** Restaurant; bar; exercise room; indoor pool; sauna. *In room:* TV, minibar (in some).

CHAUMONT-SUR-LOIRE

200km (124 miles) SW of Paris; 40km (25 miles) E of Tours

On the morning when Diane de Poitiers first crossed the drawbridge, the **Château de Chaumont ★★** (✆ **02-54-51-26-26;** www.chaumont-jardin.com) looked grim. Henri II, her lover, had recently died. The king had given her Chenonceau, but his angry widow, Catherine de Médicis, forced her to trade her favorite château for Chaumont, with its battlements and pepper-pot turrets. Inside, portraits reveal that Diane deserved her reputation as forever beautiful. Another portrait—of Catherine looking like a devout nun—invites unfavorable comparisons.

The chateau belonged to the Amboise family for 5 centuries. In 1465, when one of them, a certain Pierre, rebelled against the rule of Louis XI, the king had the castle burned to the ground as a punishment. Pierre and his descendents rebuilt for the next few decades. Overlooking the Loire, it's approached by a long walk up from the village through a tree-studded park. The castle's architecture spans the period between the Middle Ages and the Renaissance, and the vast rooms still evoke the 16th and 17th centuries. In the bedroom occupied by Catherine de Médicis, you can see a portrait of the Italian-born queen. The superstitious Catherine housed her astrologer, Cosimo Ruggieri, in one of the tower rooms (a portrait of him remains). He reportedly foretold the disasters awaiting her sons. In Ruggieri's room, a tapestry depicts Medusa with a flying horse escaping from her head.

In 1992, the chateau's grounds became the setting for the **International Garden Festival,** a world-renowned gathering of cutting-edge landscape designers that lasts from mid-April to mid-October that is open to the public. Each year, a dozen different gardens are created, using thousands of different plants and innovative garden designs. Since 2008, the château has also been a site for contemporary art and photography exhibits; check the website for this year's program. Entrance to the festival is 9.50€ for adults, 7.50€ for children 12 to 18, 4.50€ for children 6 to 11, and free for 5 and under.

The château is open daily November through March 10am to 5pm, April through June 10am to 6:30pm, July through August 10am to 7pm, September 10am to 6:30pm, and October 10am to 6pm. Admission is 9€ for adults, 6€ for children 12 to 18, 3.50€ for children 6 to 11, and free for ages 5 and under. Allow 2 hours to see Chaumont castle and its park, more if you are visiting the festival.

Essentials

GETTING THERE Several **trains** per day travel to Chaumont from Blois (trip time: 10–15 min.) and Tours (about 40 min.). The one-way fare is 3.30€ from Blois, 7.70€ from Tours. The railway station serving Chaumont is in Onzain, a nice 1½-mile walk north of the château. For train schedules and ticketing information, call ✆ **36-35** or visit www.voyages-sncf.com.

VISITOR INFORMATION The **Office de Tourisme** is on rue du 24 Maréchal-Leclerc (✆ **02-54-20-91-73;** www.chaumont-sur-loire.eu).

Where to Stay & Eat

Hostellerie du Château Visitors to the château who want to stay close to the castle can stay at this completely renovated half-timbered inn located directly in front of the gateway to the château. Accommodations open onto the riverbank of the Loire; ask for a room with a view. The rooms are modestly yet comfortably furnished. In the summer, you can enjoy regional specialties in the restaurant and swim in the terrace-flanked pool.

2 rue Maréchal de-Lattre-de-Tassigny, Chaumont-sur-Loire 41150. www.hostellerie-du-chateau.com. ✆ **02-54-20-98-04.** Fax 02-54-20-97-98. 15 units. 64€–80€ double. MC, V. **Amenities:** Restaurant; bar; outdoor pool; room service. *In room:* TV, hair dryer, free Wi-Fi. Closed mid-Nov to mid-Mar.

Le Domaine des Hauts de Loire ★★ Less than 3km (1¾ miles) from the Château de Chaumont, this property sits on the opposite side of the Loire. The manor house was built by the owner of a Paris-based newspaper in 1840 and called, rather coyly, a "hunting lodge." It's the most appealing stopover in the neighborhood, with rooms decorated in Louis Philippe or Empire style. More than half of the rooms are in the slightly less desirable half-timbered annex that was originally the stables.

The stately dining room's menu includes a salad of sautéed eel with shallot vinaigrette, local *sandre* (a freshwater fish) quenelles with crayfish, guinea hen with chestnut ravioli, bream with truffles, and lobster with rum. Main courses range from 48€ to 68€, with fixed-price menus ranging from 55€ to 150€.

Medallions at the Château de Chaumont.

Rte. d'Herbault, Onzain 41150. www.domainehautsloire.com. ✆ **02-54-20-72-57.** Fax 02-54-20-77-32. 36 units. 130€–290€ double; 320€–550€ suite. AE, DC, MC, V. Closed Dec–Feb. **Amenities:** Restaurant; bar; outdoor pool; room service. *In room:* TV, hair dryer, minibar, Wi-Fi (10€ per hr.).

AMBOISE ★★

219km (136 miles) SW of Paris; 35km (22 miles) E of Tours

Amboise is on the banks of the Loire in the center of vineyards known as Touraine-Amboise. The good news: This is a real Renaissance town. The bad news: Because it is so beautiful, tour buses overrun it, especially in summer. Many townspeople still talk about Mick Jagger's purchase of a nearby château. An earlier resident of the town was Leonardo da Vinci, who spent his last years here.

Essentials

GETTING THERE About a dozen **trains** per day leave from both Tours and Blois. The trip from Tours takes 20 minutes and costs 5€ one-way; from Blois, it takes 20 minutes and costs 6.30€ one-way. Several conventional trains a day leave from Paris's Gare d'Austerlitz (trip time: about 2 hr., 15 min.), and several TGVs depart from the Gare Montparnasse, with a change to a regular train at St-Pierre-des-Corps, next to Tours (trip time: 1 hr., 30 min.). Fares from Paris to Amboise start at 23€. For information, call ✆ **36-35** or visit www.voyages-sncf.com.

If you prefer to travel by bus, **Fil Vert Buses** (www.touraine-filvert.com), which operates out of Gare Routière in Tours, just across from the railway station, runs about six to eight **buses** every day between Tours and Amboise. The one-way trip takes about 45 minutes and costs 1.70€.

If you're **driving** from Tours, take the D751, following signs to Amboise.

VISITOR INFORMATION The **Office de Tourisme** is on quai du Général-de-Gaulle (✆ **02-47-57-09-28;** www.amboise-valdeloire.com).

Exploring the Town

Château d'Amboise ★★ This 15th-century château, which dominates the town, was the first in France to reflect the Italian Renaissance. Built on a rocky spur separating the valleys of the Loire and the Amasse, it is associated with Charles VIII, who in 1492 rebuilt the medieval castle in a combination of Gothic and Renaissance styles.

Amboise.

You enter on a ramp that opens onto a panoramic terrace fronting the river. At one time, buildings surrounded this terrace, and fetes took place in the enclosed courtyard. The castle fell into decline during the Revolution, and today only about a quarter of the once-sprawling edifice remains. You first come to the Flamboyant Gothic **Chapelle de St-Hubert,** distinguished by its lacelike tracery and where you can visit the **tomb of Leonardo da Vinci,** who died in Amboise. Tapestries cover the walls of what's left of the château's grandly furnished rooms, which include **Logis du Roi (King's Apartment).** It was built against the **Tour des Minimes** (also known as the Tour des Cavaliers), which was noteworthy for its ramp up which horsemen could ride. The other notable tower is the Heurtault, which is broader than the Minimes, with thicker walls.

✆ **02-47-57-00-98.** www.chateau-amboise.com. Admission 9.70€ adults, 8.30€ students, 6.30€ ages 7–14, free for children 7 and under. Daily as follows: Jan 9am–12:30pm and 2–4:45pm; Feb 9am–12:30pm and 1:30–5pm; Mar 9am–5:30pm; Apr–June 9am–6:30pm; July–Aug 9am–7pm; Sept–Oct 9am–6pm; Nov 2–15 9am–5:30pm; Nov 16–Dec 31 9am–12:30pm and 2–4:45pm.

Château du Clos-Lucé ★ Within 3km (1¾ miles) of the base of Amboise's château, this brick-and-stone building was constructed in the 1400s. It later served as a retreat for Anne de Bretagne, who, according to legend, spent a lot of time praying and meditating. Later, François I installed "the great master in all forms of art and science," Leonardo himself. Da Vinci lived here for 3 years, until his death in 1519. (The paintings of Leonardo dying in François's arms are probably symbolic; the king was supposedly out of town at the time.) Today the site functions as a small museum, offering insights into Leonardo's life and a sense of the decorative arts of the era. The manor contains furniture from his era; examples of his sketches; models for his flying machines, bridges, and cannon; and even a primitive example of a machine gun.

2 rue de Clos-Lucé. ✆ **02-47-57-00-73.** www.vinci-closluce.com. Mar–Nov 15 admission 13€ adults, 9.50€ students, 7.50€ children 6–18, 34€ family ticket (2 adults, 2 children), free for children 5 and under; Nov 16–Feb admission 10€ adults, 7.50€ students, 6.50€ children 6–18, 28€ family ticket (2 adults, 2 children), free for children 5 and under. Jan daily 10am–6pm; Feb–June daily 9am–7pm; July–Aug daily 9am–8pm; Sept–Oct daily 9am–7pm; Nov–Dec daily 9am–6pm.

Nearby Attractions

The region around Amboise has attractions that resemble a mix of Disney's Magic Kingdom and the court of the Renaissance kings. The most frequently visited attraction, the **Aquarium du Val de Loire,** Parc des Mini-Châteaux (✆ **02-47-23-44-44;** www.aquariumduvaldeloire.com), lies 9.5km (6 miles) west of Amboise. It has more than 10,000 freshwater and saltwater fish, including about a half-dozen sharks. Admission is 14€ for adults and 9.50€ for children 4 to 14; it's open daily 10:30am to 6pm January through March and September through December, 10:30am to 7pm April through May, 10am to 7pm June through July, and 10am to 8pm July through August. The aquarium is closed from November 15 to 26 and January 11 to 29.

At the same address (same phone) is the **Parc des Mini-Châteaux,** which holds replicas of France's most famous castles, built at 1⁄30 the size of the originals. Chambord, for example, is less than 3.5m (11 ft.) tall. It's all very patriotic —a sort of learning game that teaches French schoolchildren the glories of their *patrimoine* (heritage) and collects some of the most celebrated architecture in Europe. Admission is 14€ for adults, 9.50€ for students and children 4 to 14, and free for children 3 and under. The Parc des Mini-Châteaux is open daily 10:30am to 7pm April through May, 10am to 7pm June through August, 10:30am to 6pm September through November 14. The park is closed from mid-November through March.

To get here from Amboise, follow signs to Tours and take RD751 along the southern bank of the Loire. The aquarium is 1km (½ mile) beyond the village of Lussault-sur-Loire (it's clearly marked).

Where to Stay

Best Western Le Vinci Loire Valley This modern-design boutique hotel stands only a 3-minute ride from the historical center of Amboise. Everything is bright and airy here, from the lounges to the cozy, well-furnished bedrooms. A sleek contemporary look prevails, enlivened by some modern statuary. The hotel serves a substantial buffet breakfast in a brightly decorated modern room.

12 av. Emile Gounin, Amboise 37400. www.vinciloirevalley.com. ✆ **02-47-57-10-90.** Fax 02-47-57-17-52. 26 units. 78€–95€ double. AE, DC, MC, V. Free parking. **Amenities:** Breakfast room. *In room:* A/C, TV, minibar, free Wi-Fi.

Le Château-de-Pray ★ This château 1.6km (1 mile) west of the town is flanked by imposing towers that date from the 13th century. You'll find antlers, hunting trophies, and a paneled drawing room with a fireplace and a collection of antique oils. Rooms in the main building are conservative and comfortable; many of the beds sport canopies. The more spacious guest rooms are near the ground floor. Try to avoid the four rooms in the 1990s annex; they're impersonally furnished and lack character. The restaurant, open to nonguests, offers fixed-price menus (52€–65€) with excellent Loire cuisine; reservations are required.

Rue de Chargé 37400. www.chateaupray.com ✆ **02-47-57-23-67.** Fax 02-47-57-32-50. 19 units. 145€–195€ double; 225€–245€ suite. AE, DC, MC, V. Free parking. Closed 2nd half of Nov and 3 weeks in Jan. **Amenities:** Restaurant; babysitting. *In room:* TV, hair dryer, free Internet.

Le Choiseul ★★★ This 18th-century mansion, in the valley between a hillside and the Loire, harbors the best hotel in Amboise and serves its best cuisine. Guest rooms, 25 of which are air-conditioned, are luxurious; though modernized, they retain their old-world charm. The small bathrooms contain combination tub/showers. The formal dining room has a view of the Loire and welcomes nonguests who phone ahead. The restaurant is superb; the menu features classic and regional French, utilizing the freshest ingredients. Lunch ranges from 27€ to 41€, with dinner going for 45€ to 80€. The grounds showcase a garden with flowering terraces.

36 quai Charles-Guinot, Amboise 37400. www.le-choiseul.com. ✆ **02-47-30-45-45.** Fax 02-47-30-46-10. 32 units. 108€–305€ double; 365€ suite. AE, DC, MC, V. **Amenities:** Restaurant; bar; bicycles; outdoor pool; room service. *In room:* A/C, TV, hair dryer, minibar, free Wi-Fi.

Le Clos d'Amboise Up until recently, this 16th-century mansion was the home of a very fortunate doctor. While the inside has been restructured, the 3,000-sq.-m (32,292-sq.-ft.) garden has been carefully preserved, including its 100-year-old magnolia trees and a cedar of Lebanon that witnessed the French Revolution. A small pool is discreetly tucked into a corner of the park. A 5-minute walk to the center of town, this hotel offers calm and comfort, with airy rooms decorated with a pleasant mix of modern and antique furniture. There is a small sauna and exercise room for post-sightseeing rest and relaxation.

27 rue Rabelais, Amboise 37400. www.leclosamboise.com. ✆ **02-47-30-10-20.** Fax 02-47-57-33-43. 19 units. 95€–149€ double; 290€ suite with private garden. AE, MC, V. Free parking. **Amenities:** Bar; fitness room; sauna. *In room:* A/C, TV, minibar, free Wi-Fi.

Le Fleuray ★★ One of the most appealing hotels in the region is this well-maintained ivy-covered manor house, a few minutes' drive from Amboise. Managed by the Newingtons, a family of English expatriates, it was built in the mid-1800s as the centerpiece of a farm. It's a marvel of country-living grandeur, partly because of the masses of geraniums, marigolds, and flowering vines that adorn the masonry in warm weather. Guest rooms are dotted with antique accessories evoking an elegant but not terribly formal English country house. There's plenty to do on the extensive grounds: Aside from a swimming pool and Jacuzzi, there is a tennis court, 9-hole golf course, and children's play area.

Don't miss the restaurant—it's one of the best in the area and is manned by a hot young chef. Items on the fixed-price menus (29€–49€) include marinated leeks with Serrano ham, duck foie gras with champagne and figs, and calamari stuffed with chorizo and served with green olive confit.

Rte. D74, Cangey 37530, near Amboise. www.lefleurayhotel.com. ✆ **02-47-56-09-25.** Fax 02-47-56-93-97. 23 units. 78€–146€ double. MC, V. Free parking. From Amboise, take the D952 on the north side of the river, following signs to Blois; 12km (7½ miles) from Amboise, turn onto D74, in the direction of Cangey. **Amenities:** Restaurant; bar; free bikes; golf course; Jacuzzi; massage; outdoor pool; room service; tennis court. *In room:* TV, hair dryer.

Le Manoir Les Minimes ★★ This restored 18th-century mansion is a welcoming, cozy hotel built on the foundation of an ancient convent. On the river's edge, in the shadow of the château, it is surrounded by acres of gardens. Inside, furnishings are elegant in both the public and private rooms, with much use made of antiques. You can dine in the garden if weather permits. The most desirable rooms are in the main building; a comfortable, well-furnished trio of units is in an annex, although these lack character. No. 10 is a particularly beautiful corner suite with panoramic views. Many of the second-floor bedrooms open onto views of the Loire. The best-value rooms are smaller and on the third floor. Each room has unique decor and comes with an elegant bathroom with tub.

34 quai Charles Guinot, Amboise 37400. www.manoirlesminimes.com. ✆ **02-47-30-40-40.** Fax 02-47-30-40-77. 15 units. 129€–200€ double; 285€–485€ suite. MC, V. **Amenities:** Breakfast room. *In room:* A/C, TV, minibar, free Wi-Fi.

Le Manoir Saint Thomas ★ Antonella and Bertrand Pautout have installed a four-star hotel in a manor that dates originally from the 12th century. The living conditions have never been better around here; there's even a heated swimming pool in the garden. Rooms are spacious, with luxury bathrooms, and are completely modernized, although the antique character has been retained. Parquet floors, period fireplaces, and stained-glass windows evoke the past. The hotel is only a 2-minute walk from the royal château and is close to the former home of Leonardo da Vinci.

1 mail Saint Thomas, Amboise 37400. www.manoir-saint-thomas.com. ✆ **02-47-23-21-82.** Fax 02-47-23-24-96. 10 units. 90€–190€ double; 250€–340€ suite. AE, MC, V. **Amenities:** Outdoor pool; room service. *In room:* A/C, TV, hair dryer, minibar, free Wi-Fi. Closed Jan.

Where to Eat

For gourmet dinning, the restaurants at **Le Choiseul** and **Le Fleuray** are both excellent (for reviews of both hotels, see "Where to Stay," above).

Brasserie de l'Hôtel de Ville ☺ FRENCH In the town's historic core, a short walk from the château, this bustling Paris-style brasserie has enjoyed a solid reputation since the early 1990s. Expect a noisy environment focused on rows of banquettes, hassled waiters, and steaming platters that emerge relatively quickly from the overworked kitchen. Menu items include a full range of old-fashioned cuisine that locals may remember from their childhoods, like sole meunière, grilled beefsteak with french fries, *pot-au-feu,* and calves' liver.

1 and 3 rue François, 1er. ✆ **02-47-57-26-30.** Reservations recommended. Main courses 7€–18€; fixed-price menu 15€–26 €; children's menu 6.90€. AE, MC, V. Daily noon–2pm and 7–9:30pm.

CHENONCEAUX

224km (139 miles) SW of Paris; 26km (16 miles) E of Tours

A Renaissance masterpiece, the **Château de Chenonceau ★★★** (✆ **02-47-23-90-07;** www.chenonceau.com) is best known for the dames de Chenonceau, who once occupied it. (The village, whose year-round population is less than 300, is spelled with a final *x,* but the château isn't.)

In 1547, Henri II gave Chenonceau to his mistress, Diane de Poitiers. For a time, this remarkable woman was virtually queen of France, infuriating Henri's dour wife, Catherine de Médicis. Diane's critics accused her of using magic to preserve her celebrated beauty and to keep Henri's attentions from waning. Apparently, Henri's love for Diane continued unabated, and she was in her 60s when he died in a jousting tournament in 1559.

When Henri died, Catherine became regent (her eldest son was still a child) and forced Diane to return the jewelry Henri had given her and to abandon her beloved home. Catherine added her own touches, building a two-story gallery across the bridge—obviously inspired by her native Florence.

Chenonceau is one of the most remarkable castles in France because it spans an entire river. The way the waters of the Cher surge and foam beneath its vaulted medieval foundations has been described as mystical. Many visitors consider this their favorite château in all of France.

Gobelin tapestries, including one depicting a woman pouring water over the back of an angry dragon, cover many of the château's walls. The chapel contains a marble *Virgin and Child* by Murillo, as well as portraits of Catherine de Médicis in black and white. There's even a portrait of the stern Catherine in the former bedroom of her rival, Diane de Poitiers. In François I's Renaissance bedchamber, the most interesting portrait is that of Diane as the huntress Diana.

The women of Chenonceau is the subject of the **Musée de Cire (Wax Museum),** located in a Renaissance-era annex a few steps from the château. Open the same hours as the château, you can purchase a combination ticket including entrance to the château and the museum for 13€ for adults, 10€ ages 7 to 17, free for 6 and under. The highlight of the "Galerie des Dames" is the collection of period costumes worn by the wax effigies.

Garden at the Château de Chenonceau.

The château is open daily 9am to 8pm July and August; 9am to 7pm for the last two weeks of March; 9am to 6:30pm in June, September, and October; 9am to 5pm the rest of the year. Admission is 11€ for adults and 8€ for students and children 7 to 17. Allow 2 hours to see this château.

Essentials

GETTING THERE About a dozen daily **trains** run from Tours to Chenonceaux (trip time: 30 min.), costing 6.10€ one-way. The train deposits you at the base of the château; from there, it's an easy walk. For information, call ✆ **36-35** or visit www.voyages-sncf.com. If you're **driving,** from the center of Tours, follow the signs to the D40 east, which will take you to the signposted turnoff for Chenonceaux.

VISITOR INFORMATION The **Syndicat d'Initiative** (tourist office), 1 rue du Dr-Bretonneau (✆ **02-47-23-94-45**), is open year-round.

Where to Stay

Auberge du Bon-Laboureur ★★ This inn, within walking distance of the château, is your best bet for a comfortable night's sleep and exceptional Loire Valley cuisine. Founded in 1786, the hotel maintains the flavor of that era, thanks to thick walls, solid masonry, and a scattering of antiques. Most guest rooms open out onto the garden, which features formally planted roses. Menu choices in the restaurant include crayfish with chopped tomatoes and basil, and confit of lamb; the kitchen uses fresh produce direct from the hotel's garden. The prix-fixe menu at lunch is 30€; dinner menus run from 48€ to 85€.

6 rue du Dr-Bretonneau, Chenonceaux 37150. www.amboise.com/laboureur. ✆ **02-47-23-90-02.** Fax 02-47-23-82-01. 25 units. 120€–160€ double; 210€–280€ suite. AE, MC, V. Closed mid-Nov to mid-Dec and Jan 7–Feb 14. **Amenities:** Restaurant; bar; outdoor pool; room service. *In room:* A/C, TV, hair dryer, free Wi-Fi.

La Roseraie ★ If charm is what you are after, you will be very happy at this friendly inn, where cheerful rooms are individually decorated with lots of period prints and old-fashioned furniture. History has left its mark: Just after World War II, Churchill, Truman, and Eleanor Roosevelt all came through; a framed letter from Mrs. Roosevelt hangs in the cozy salon. The exceptionally helpful and enthusiastic owners also welcome guests at the restaurant, which features homemade foie gras, filet of sander in butter sauce, and a delicious invention—sliced rump steak with wine-marinated pears.

7 rue du Dr-Bretonneau, Chenonceaux 37150. www.hotel-chenonceau.com. ✆ **02-47-23-90-09.** Fax 02-47-23-91-59. 18 units. 65€–129€ double. AE, DC, MC, V. Closed mid-Nov to mid-Mar. Free parking. **Amenities:** Restaurant; bar; outdoor pool; Wi-Fi in lobby and bar. *In room:* A/C, TV.

Le Relais Chenonceaux Like the two other hotels listed above, this one is the center of the village and just a short walk to the château. The building has a dormer roof and an inviting courtyard filled with flowers in summer. Inside, exposed beams and an old fireplace decorate the restaurant, which serves traditional Loire Valley cuisine. There is also an on-site crêperie for light meals. The rustic bedrooms are personalized and comfortable, and also tidily maintained.

10 rue du Docteur Brettoneau, Chenonceaux 37150. www.chenonceaux.com. ✆ **02-47-23-98-11.** Fax 02-47-23-84-07. 24 units. 50€–68€ double. MC, V. Closed mid-Nov to Jan. **Amenities:** Restaurant; bar. *In room:* TV, free Wi-Fi.

Where to Eat

La Roseraie (see above) has a very good restaurant.

Au Gâteau Breton TRADITIONAL FRENCH This pretty 18th-century inn was once a grocery store run by an "immigrant" from the distant land of Brittany. Just a short walk from the château, today this restaurant makes a refreshing stop for dinner or tea. Gravel paths run among beds of pink geraniums and lilacs, and bright umbrellas adorn the red tables. In cool months, meals are served in the rustic dining rooms. Worthwhile dishes include homey favorites like *boudin* (blood sausage) with apples, *poulet Tourangelle* (sautéed chicken with mushroom and cream sauce), and steak with *beurre maitre d'hôtel* (butter mixed with parsley, garlic, and lemon).

16 rue du Dr-Bretonneau. ✆ **02-47-23-90-14.** www.restaurant-gateau-breton.com. Reservations required July–Aug. Main courses 14€–18€; fixed-price menus 15€–27€. MC, V. Apr–Sept daily noon–2:30pm, and 7–10pm; Nov–Mar daily noon–2:30pm.

TOURS ★

232km (144 miles) SW of Paris; 113km (70 miles) SW of Orléans

Though it doesn't have a major château, Tours (pop. 137,000), at the junction of the Loire and Cher rivers, is known for its food and wine. Many of its buildings were bombed in World War II, and 20th-century apartment towers have taken the place of châteaux. However, because Tours is at the doorstep of some of the most magnificent châteaux in France, it makes a good base from which to explore. Pilgrims en route to Santiago de Compostela in northwest Spain once stopped here to pay homage at the tomb of St-Martin, the "Apostle of Gaul," who was bishop of Tours in the 4th century. One of the most significant conflicts in European history, the 732 Battle of Tours, checked the Arab advance into Gaul. In the 15th century, French kings started setting up shop here, and Tours became the capital of France for over 100 years.

Most Loire Valley towns are rather sleepy, but Tours is where the action is, with busy streets and cafes. A quarter of the residents are students, who add a vibrant touch to a soulless commercial enclave. Allow a morning or an afternoon to see Tours.

Essentials

GETTING THERE There are as many as 14 high-speed TGV **trains** per day departing from Paris's Gare Montparnasse and arriving at St-Pierre des Corps station, 6km (3¾ miles) east of the center of Tours, in an hour. Free *navettes,* or shuttle buses, await on your arrival to take you to the center of town (the Tours Centre train station). There are also a limited number of conventional trains that depart from Gare d'Austerlitz and arrive in the center of Tours, but they take twice as long (about 2¼ hr.). One-way fares range from 32€ to 56€. For information, call ✆ **36-35** or visit www.voyages-sncf.com. If you're **driving,** take highway A10 to Tours.

GETTING AROUND It's easy to walk from one end of central Tours to the other, and many of the good hotels are near the train station. For taxi service, call **Taxi Radio** (✆ **02-47-20-30-40**). You can rent a car at **Avis** (✆ **02-47-20-53-27;** www.avis.fr), located in the Tours Centre train station, or **Europcar,** at the St-Pierre des Corps station (✆ **02-47-63-28-67;** www.europcar.fr). You can rent a bike at **Detours de Loire,** 35 rue Charles Gilles (✆ **02-47-61-22-23;** www.locationdevelos.com), at a cost of 14€ per day. A deposit is required.

Outdoor dining in Tours.

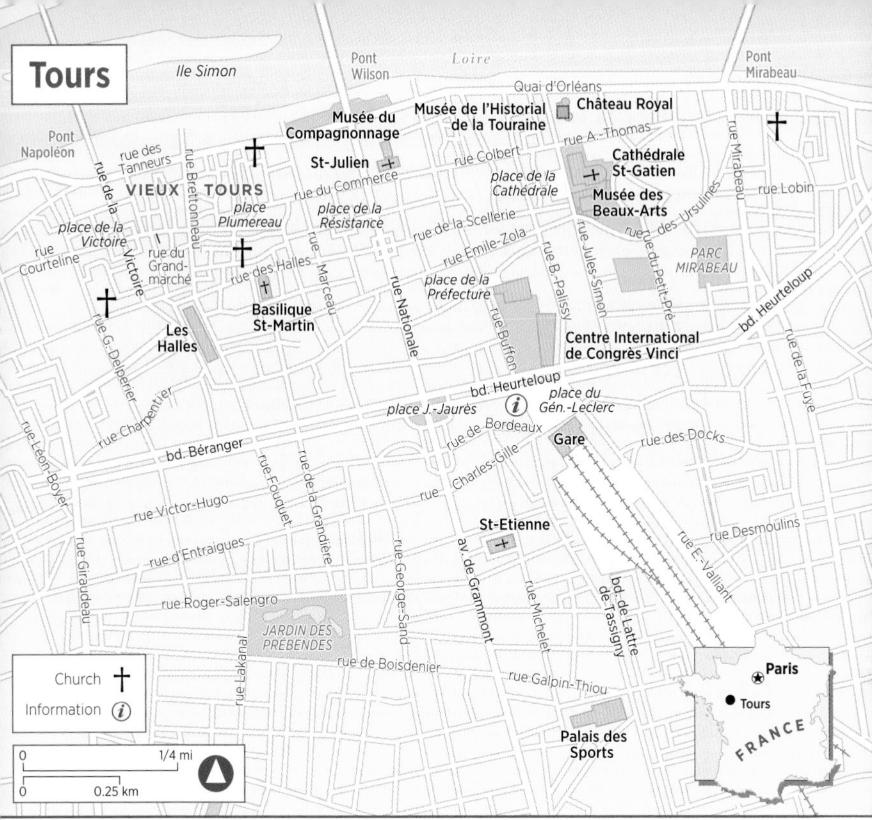

VISITOR INFORMATION The **Office de Tourisme** is at 78–82 rue Bernard-Palissy (✆ **02-47-70-37-37;** www.ligeris.com).

Exploring the City

The heart of town is **place Jean-Jaurès.** The principal street is **rue Nationale,** running north to the Loire River. Head west along rue du Commerce and rue du Grand-Marché to Vieux Tours/Vieille Ville (Old Town).

Cathédrale St-Gatien This cathedral honors a 3rd-century evangelist and has a Flamboyant Gothic facade flanked by towers with bases from the 12th century. The lanterns date from the Renaissance. The choir is from the 13th century, with new additions built in each century through the 16th. Sheltered inside is the handsome 16th-century tomb of Charles VIII and Anne de Bretagne's two children. Some of the glorious stained-glass windows are from the 13th century.

5 place de la Cathédrale. ✆ **02-47-70-21-00.** Free admission. Daily 9am–7pm.

Musée des Beaux-Arts This fine provincial museum in the Palais des Archevêques is worth a visit just to see its lovely rooms and gardens. There are old masters here as well, including works by Rubens, Delacroix, Rembrandt, and Boucher. The sculpture collection includes works by Houdon and Bourdelle.

18 place François Sicard. ✆ **02-47-05-68-73.** www.tours.fr/culture/musees/bxarts. Admission 4€ adults, 2€ seniors and students, free for children 12 and under. Wed–Mon 9am–6pm. Bus: 3.

FUN-FILLED WAYS TO GET around

For an overview of Tours, its monuments, and its layout (with commentary in French and a brochure in English), ride through the streets of the city aboard a simulated train with rubber wheels. It operates from Easter to mid-October daily at 10 and 11am, and on the hour from 2 to 6pm. Tickets, available at the tourist office or onboard, cost 6€ for adults and 3€ for children 11 and under. Rides (about 50 min.) begin and end in front of the tourist office, 78–82 rue Bernard-Palissy (✆ **02-47-70-37-37**).

An old-fashioned alternative is a ride on one of the horse-drawn carriages *(les calèches)* operated by **Fil Bleu** (✆ **02-47-66-70-70**). A pair of slow-moving workhorses pull the wagonlike conveyances, which hold up to 10 passengers, through the city's medieval neighborhoods. There's no commentary. Tickets cost 1.30€ per person. May through September and December, rides leave from Place François Sicard Tuesday to Saturday at 10 and 11am, and 3, 4, and 5pm; and on Sunday at 3, 4, and 5pm.

Shopping: To Market We Go

In the pedestrian area of rue de Bordeaux, from the train station to rue Nationale, you'll find dozens of mall-type shops and department stores selling clothes, shoes, jewelry, leather goods, and the like. Up rue Nationale toward the river are more shops and upscale boutiques, and a small mall with chain stores. If you turn left on rue du Commerce toward the old town center, you can explore the streets and courtyards for regional specialties, books, toys, and crafts. A hotbed for antiques is east of rue Nationale (toward the cathedral), along rue de la Scellerie.

Of the more than 30 markets here, the most animated are the **gourmet market (Marché Gourmand),** the first Friday of each month, 4 to 10pm, place de la Résistance; the **antiques market,** the first and third Friday of the month in the pedestrian zone on rue de Bordeaux, and on the fourth Sunday of the month, a larger version of the event with more *brocante* than genuine antiques; the **flower market,** Wednesday and Saturday 8am to 6pm, boulevard Béranger; and the **craft market (Marché Artisanal),** Saturday 9am to 1pm, place des Halles. The covered market, **Les Halles et Grand Marché,** with a huge selection of fresh local meat, cheese, and produce, is at place Gaston-Pailhou Tuesday through Saturday 6am to 1pm and 3 to 7pm, and Sunday 6am to 1pm.

Where to Stay

Best Western Le Central Off the main boulevard, this old-fashioned hotel is within walking distance of the train station, the river, and the cathedral. Despite its central location, there is plenty of greenery here: The back of the hotel looks out on a leafy garden, and the front is set off by a lawn. The decor is classic and conservative, and blends well with the 19th-century building. Half of the guest rooms have tub/showers, the others only showers.

21 rue Berthelot, Tours 37000. www.bestwesterncentralhoteltours.com. ✆ **800/528-1234** in the U.S. and Canada, or 02-47-05-46-44. Fax 02-47-66-10-26. 37 units. 93€–155€ double; 195€–250€ suite. AE, DC, MC, V. Parking 10€. **Amenities:** Bar; babysitting; room service. *In room:* A/C, TV, hair dryer, minibar, free Wi-Fi.

Hôtel de l'Univers ★ This grand old 19th-century hotel was recently upgraded to four-star status and is the best in the town center. Its midsize rooms, outfitted in a conservative contemporary style, have monochromatic and tasteful soft-color schemes. The bathrooms, with shower and tub, have also been renewed. On weekdays, the hotel fills with business travelers; on most weekends, it offers reduced rates.

5 bd. Heurteloup, Tours 37000. www.hotel-univers.fr. ✆ **02-47-05-37-12.** Fax 02-47-61-51-80. 85 units. 198€–270€ double; 364€–398€ suite. AE, DC, MC, V. Parking 15€. **Amenities:** Restaurant; bar; room service. *In room:* A/C, TV, hair dryer, minibar, free Wi-Fi.

Hôtel du Manoir On a quiet street near the train station, this 19th-century residence is a comfortable and affordable place to stay. The cheerful reception area reflects the quality of the rooms. Though small to average in size, all units have windows that let in lots of light and afford views of the neighborhood or the hotel courtyard. Most have simple furnishings.

2 rue Traversière, Tours 37000. http://hotel.manoir.tours.voila.net. ✆ **02-47-05-37-37.** Fax 02-47-05-16-00. 20 units. 65€–75€ double. AE, MC, V. Parking 7€. *In room:* TV, hair dryer, free Wi-Fi.

Where to Eat

Restaurants can be pricey, but you can keep costs low at **La Souris Gourmande,** 100 rue Colbert (✆ **02-47-47-04-80;** http://lasourisgourmande.com), where the chef is respected for the diversity of his cheese selection. Try it in half a dozen fondues. You may be asked to join a communal table. Main courses cost 13€ to 15€. At the raffish but cheerful bistro **Le Lapin qui Fume,** 90 rue Colbert (✆ **02-47-66-95-49**), a fixed-price menu costs 11€ to 14€ at lunch and 17€ to 24€ at dinner.

EXPENSIVE

La Roche le Roy ★★ MODERN FRENCH Alain Couturier, one of the hottest chefs in town, blends new and old techniques in a gabled 18th-century manor south of the town center. Couturier's repertoire includes brill baked in a spice bread crust, foie gras with caramelized apples, bass with champagne cream sauce, and *matelote* (stew) of eel with Vouvray wine. His masterpiece is suprême of pigeon with "roughly textured" sauce. For dessert, try a warm orange soufflé flavored with Grand Marnier.

55 rte. St-Avertin. ✆ **02-47-27-22-00.** www.rocheleroy.com. Reservations recommended. Main courses 25€–38€. AE, MC, V. Wed–Sat noon–1:30pm and 7:30–9:30pm. Closed 2 weeks in Feb and 3 weeks in Aug. From the center of town, take av. Grammont south (follow signs to St-Avertin–Vierzon).

MODERATE

Rive Gauche TRADITIONAL FRENCH Having recently changed chefs, this gourmet restaurant now touts "responsible gastronomy," which takes into consideration both taste and environmental impact. The talented young chef, Gaëtan Evrard, uses his lively imagination and high-quality local and/or artisinal products to create surprising dishes like steamed Loire mullet with crushed apples, herring caviar, and Zubrowka vodka, or Racan pigeon in Lapsang Souchong tea. Dessert includes an award-winning *nougat de Tours,* a light almond cake, served warm and topped with apricot sherbet. You can savor these delicacies in either of the two cozy dinning rooms or, in warm weather, outdoors on the terrace.

23 rue du Commerce. ✆ **02-47-05-71-21.** www.tours-rivegauche.com. Reservations required. Main courses 19€–26€; fixed-price menu 26€–69€. AE MC, V. Daily 12:30am–2pm and 7:30–10pm.

INEXPENSIVE

La Brasserie Buré TRADITIONAL FRENCH A 5-minute walk east of the center of Tours, this old-fashioned brasserie specializes in shellfish and regional recipes. It has a busy bar and a front terrace, with tables inside on the street level and mezzanine. The four-page menu offers a profusion of possibilities: a wide choice of grilled meats, including steak au poivre; foie gras and smoked salmon; and a tempting array of desserts.

1 place de la Résistance. ✆ **02-47-05-67-74.** Main courses 15€–23€; fixed-price menu 20€–30€. AE, DC, MC, V. Daily noon–3pm and 7pm–midnight. Bus: 1 or 5.

Le Petit Patrimoine TRADITIONAL FRENCH This pocket-size, long-established restaurant exudes a powerful, albeit quirky and idiosyncratic, appeal. Outfitted in a rustic and old-fashioned style that might have been inspired by someone's early-20th-century grandmother, it has exposed ceiling beams, old masonry walls, and a sense of respect for old-fashioned French aesthetics and values. Your hosts, each a distinct personality known by clients as either independent-minded or curmudgeonly, depending on their mood of the moment, will propose dishes that include a savory *matelote* of veal with baby vegetables, a salad of *rillons* (a meat byproduct made from bacon), and grilled beefsteaks with goat cheese.

58 rue Colbert. ✆ **02-47-66-05-81.** Reservations recommended. Main courses 14€; fixed-price menu 12€–14€ lunch, 18€–25€ dinner. MC, V. Tues–Sat noon–2pm and 7–10pm.

Where to Stay & Eat Nearby

Château d'Artigny ★★★ This is perhaps the grandest address in the Loire Valley. About 1.5km (1 mile) west of the hamlet of Montbazon and 15km (9¼ miles) south of Tours, the château was built between 1912 and 1920 for perfume and cosmetics king François Coty, who lived and entertained lavishly. Set in a forest, overlooking formal gardens, the château combines Jazz Age ostentation and 18th-century French aesthetics. The drawing room and corridors are furnished

Château-Hopping Made Easy

Several tour companies in Tours arrange full- and half-day visits to nearby castles, and three of them offer mini bus tours that leave daily from the tourist office. Acco-Dispo (✆ 06-82-00-64-51; www.accodispo-tours.com), Saint-Eloi Excursions (✆ 06-70-82-78-75; http://saint-eloiexcursions.com), and Quart de Tours (✆ 06-30-65-52-01; www.quartdetours.com) all offer mini bus tours that depart around 9am; you can reserve on the tourist office website (see above) or contact them directly. Costs range from 20€ to 50€ per person, depending on the company and how many castles you want to see. The price does not include meals or admission to the châteaux, but participation in the tour qualifies you for reduced group rates. Keep in mind that less is sometimes more when it comes to castle viewing; after two or three, you may not be able to remember which was which.

with fine antiques, Louis XV–style chairs, and bronze statuary. The grounds contain acres of parks and a large garden with a reflecting pool. Guest rooms are outfitted in period style, with many antiques, comfortable mattresses, and all the perks of upscale country living. Only 31 units are in the main building; the others are in four annexes—a former chapel, gatehouse, mill, and staff dormitory.

Rte. des Monts (D17), Montbazon 37250. www.artigny.com. ✆ **02-47-34-30-30.** Fax 02-47-34-30-39. 65 units. 170€–320€ double; 490€ junior suite. AE, DC, MC, V. From Tours, take N10 south for 11km (6¾ miles) to Montbazon, and then take D17 1.5km (1 mile) southeast. **Amenities:** Restaurant; bar; babysitting; exercise room; outdoor pool; room service; sauna; spa; 2 tennis courts. *In room:* TV, hair dryer, minibar, free Wi-Fi (in some).

Château de Beaulieu ★★ At this 18th-century estate, about 5km (3 miles) south of Tours, you can experience the lifestyle of another era. Beyond the entrance, a double-curving stairway leads to the reception hall. Guest rooms have mahogany and chestnut furniture, decorative fireplaces, and chic modern bathrooms. Nine are in the château (we recommend these); the others, a bit more sterile, are in a turn-of-the-20th-century pavilion a stone's throw away. All have elegant beds outfitted with comfortable mattresses.

67 rue de Beaulieu, Joué-les-Tours 37300. www.chateaudebeaulieu37.com. ✆ **02-47-53-20-26.** Fax 02-47-53-84-20. 19 units. 105€–170€ double. AE, MC, V. From Tours, take av. de Grammont south, and turn right on bd. Winston Churchill, and then left on av. de Pont Cher, and right on rue de Beaulieu. **Amenities:** Restaurant; bar; bike rental. *In room:* A/C, TV, hair dryer, minibar, free Wi-Fi.

Tours After Dark

Long a student town, Tours has a lively young population. Even during summer, when most students have left, a youthful crowd rules the hot spots. **Place Plumereau** (often shortened to "place Plume"), a square of medieval buildings, houses a concentration of restaurants and bars. In the warmer months, the square explodes with tables, which fill with people who like to people-watch (and be watched themselves). In addition to the bars and clubs around the place Plumereau, an even trendier street, **rue Colbert,** has emerged as a hip and fashionable strip. Rue Colbert lies in the heart of Tours, midway between the place Plumereau and the cathedral.

The hottest place in town is **L'Excalibur,** 35 rue Briçonnet (✆ **02-47-64-76-78**), with an electro beat and video system. A clientele of all ages, many from the surrounding countryside, heads to **Le Pyms,** 170 av. de Grammont (✆ **02-47-66-22-22;** www.lepyms.com), where there are two spaces, one playing '80s nostalgia and the other contemporary electro.

And if you're gay, relatively energetic, and like to dance, check out the town's most popular gay bar and disco, **Le G.I.,** 13 rue Lavoisier (✆ **02-47-66-29-96;** www.giclub.fr). Positioned on a dark street in a safe but somewhat rundown neighborhood, it attracts a local, mostly male crowd that packs the place on weekends.

LOCHES ★★

258km (160 miles) SW of Paris; 40km (25 miles) SE of Tours

Forever linked to legendary beauty Agnès Sorel, Loches is an exquisite village, situated on the banks of the Indre. Sitting high on a bluff overlooking the valley,

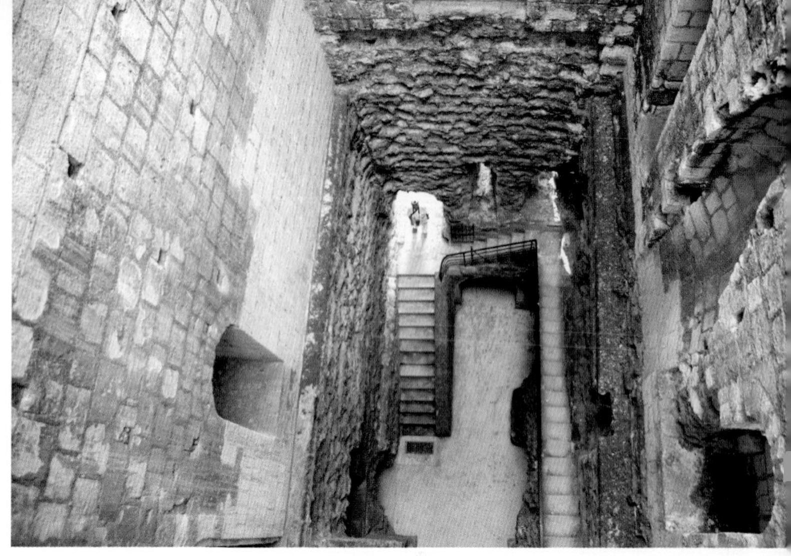

Dungeon at Loches.

the château and its satellite buildings form a complex called the **Cité Royale ★**. The House of Anjou, from which the Plantagenets descended, owned the castle from 886 to 1205. The kings of France occupied it from the mid–13th century until Charles IX became king in 1560.

Château de Loches ★★, 5 place Charles-VII (✆**02-47-59-01-32;** www.chateau-loches.fr), is remembered for the *belle des belles* (beauty of beauties) Agnès Sorel, who lived there in the 15th century. Maid of honor to Isabelle de Lorraine, she was singled out by Charles VII, who was so enamored of his mistress that he gave her the chateau to live in. She bore the king three daughters and had great influence on him until her mysterious death. Afterward, Fouquet painted her as a practically topless Virgin Mary, with a disgruntled Charles VII looking on. (The original is in Antwerp; the château has a copy.) The château also contains the oratory of Anne de Bretagne, decorated with ermine tails. One of its outstanding treasures is a triptych of *The Passion* (1485) from the Fouquet school.

The huge and ancient keep, or *donjon,* of the comtes d'Anjou was built in the 11th century and turned into a prison by Louis XI. The Round Tower contains rooms used for torture; a favorite method involved suspending the victim in an iron cage. In the 15th century, the duke of Milan, Ludovico Sforza, was imprisoned in the Martelet and painted frescoes on the walls to pass the time; he died here in 1508.

You can visit the château and the keep without a guide daily. It's open April to September from 9am to 7pm, and October to March 9:30am to 5pm.

Tickets to the château and the dungeon cost 7€ for adults, 4.50€ for students and children 12 to 18. Children 11 and under enter free.

The tomb of Agnès Sorel rests nearby at the Romanesque **Collégiale St-Ours (Collegiate Church of St-Ours),** 1 rue Thomas-Pactius (✆**02-47-59-02-36**), which was erected in the 11th and 12th centuries. Sculpted figures of saints and animals decorate the portal. Stone pyramids *(dubes)* surmount the nave; the carving on the west door is exceptional. The church is open daily from 9am to 7pm, except during mass; admission is free.

Finally, you may want to walk the ramparts and enjoy the view of the town, including a 15th-century gate and Renaissance inns.

Allow 3 hours to see Loches.

Essentials

GETTING THERE Six to 10 **buses** run daily from Tours, run by the SNCF railway; the 50-minute trip costs 8.40€ one-way. For schedules, call ✆ **02-47-05-30-49** or visit www.voyages-sncf.com. If you're **driving** from Tours, take N143 southeast to Loches.

VISITOR INFORMATION The **Office de Tourisme** is near the bus station on place de la Marne (✆ **02-47-91-82-82;** www.loches-tourainecotesud.com).

Where to Stay & Eat

Loches is short on inns and good restaurants. If you're here for lunch, we recommend the 19th-century **Hôtel George-Sand,** 39 rue Quintefol (✆ **02-47-59-39-74;** www.hotelrestaurant-georgesand.com), for its Touraine cuisine, including filet of pikeperch from the Loire. It also rents 19 rooms; doubles go for 65€ to 130€.

Hotel de France ★ This charming hotel was a postal relay station until the mid–19th century. In 1932, it gained three floors and became an inn. Before the turn of the 21st century, management upgraded and redecorated the guest rooms, added new beds, and restored the small bathrooms. The most tranquil rooms overlook the courtyard. You can dine in the wood-paneled dining room or under the parasols in the courtyard.

6 rue Picois, Loches 37600. http://h.france.loches.free.fr. ✆ **02-47-59-00-32.** Fax 02-47-59-28-66. 17 units. 62€–90€ double. AE, DC, MC, V. Parking 5€. Closed Jan 5 to early Feb and mid-Nov to mid-Dec. **Amenities:** Restaurant; bar; free Internet; room service. *In room:* TV.

Le Château de Reignac ★★ 🎁 The former château of the Marquis de la Fayette has been entirely renovated and is today one of the most luxurious châteaux in the Loire. You can explore the landscaped grounds with their ancient trees, have a drink in a plush 18th-century living room, or relax in the book-lined library as you listen to your favorite opera. The antiques-filled bedrooms, each sumptuously furnished, were named for famous people in French history, each a guest who had stayed here with the marquis. Gourmet-level food is served in the evening along with wine from the Touraine. A stay here is like wandering back to a more elegant age.

19 rue Louis de Barberin, Reignac-sur-Indre 37310. www.lechateaudereignac.com. ✆ **02-47-94-14-10.** Fax 02-47-94-12-67. 13 units. 172€–202€ double; 252€ junior suite; 354€ family suite for 4. AE, MC, V. 15km (9¼ miles) north of Loches. **Amenities:** Restaurant for guests; room service; Wi-Fi in common areas. *In room:* Hair dryer.

VILLANDRY

253km (157 miles) SW of Paris; 32km (20 miles) NE of Chinon; 18km (11 miles) W of Tours; 8km (5 miles) E of Azay-le-Rideau

The 16th-century-style gardens of the Renaissance **Château de Villandry** ★★★ (✆ **02-47-50-02-09;** www.chateauvillandry.com) are celebrated throughout

Touraine. A trio of superimposed cloisters with a water garden on the highest level, they were restored by the Spanish doctor and scientist Joachim Carvallo, great-grandfather of the present owner.

The grounds contain 17km (11 miles) of boxwood sculpture, which the gardeners cut to style in only 2 weeks each September. Every square of the gardens is like a geometric mosaic. The borders symbolize the faces of love: tender, tragic (represented by daggers), and crazy (with a labyrinth that doesn't get you anywhere). Pink tulips and dahlias suggest sweet love; red, tragic; and yellow, unfaithful. All colors signify crazy love. The vine arbors, citrus hedges, and walks keep six men busy full-time. One garden contains all the French vegetables except the potato, which wasn't known in France in the 16th century.

A feudal castle once stood at Villandry. In 1536, Jean Lebreton, François I's chancellor, built the present château, whose buildings form a U and are surrounded by a moat. Near the gardens is a terrace from which you can see the small village and its 12th-century church. A tearoom on-site, **La Doulce Terrasse** (✆ **02-47-50-02-10;** www.chateauvillandry.com; closed mid-Nov to mid-Feb), serves regional cuisine, including hot dishes, freshly baked bread, homemade ice cream, and cocktails made from fresh fruit.

Admission to the gardens, including a guided tour of the château, costs 9.50€ for adults, 5.50€ for children 8 to 18, and is free for children 7 and under. Visiting the gardens separately, without a guide, costs 6.50€ for adults and 4€ for children 8 to 18. The gardens are open daily 9am to between 5 and 7:30pm, depending on the hour of sunset; the château is open daily from 9am to between 4:30 and 6:30pm, depending on a complicated seasonal schedule. Tours are conducted in French; leaflets are available in English. Allow 1½ hours to see Villandry.

Essentials

GETTING THERE There are three daily **buses** from Tours that operate from July to October only; the trip takes about 30 minutes and costs 1.70€. For bus

Château de Villandry.

information, call ✆ **02-47-05-30-49** or visit www.touraine-filvert.com. Villandry has no train service. The nearest connection from Tours is at the town of Savonnières; the trip takes around 15 minutes and costs 3.10€ one-way. For information, call ✆ **36-35** or visit www.voyages-sncf.com. From Savonnières, you can walk along the Loire for 4km (2½ miles) to reach Villandry, rent a **bike** at the station, or take a **taxi.** You can also **drive,** following D7 from Tours.

VISITOR INFORMATION The **Office de Tourisme** is located in a kiosk in front of the hotel Le Cheval Rouge (see below), in the center of town (✆ **02-47-50-12-66;** www.villandry-tourisme.com).

Where to Stay & Eat

Le Cheval Rouge MODERN FRENCH The well-known dining stopover near the château extends a congenial welcome. The conservatively decorated dining room lies about 91m (298 ft.) from the banks of the Cher. Specialties include bream flavored with vanilla, scallops flambéed with whiskey, roast lamb with thyme, and veal with *pleurotes,* a type of wild mushroom. The inn also rents 41 rooms, all with free in-room Wi-Fi. A double is 47€ to 62€.

9 rue Principale, Villandry 37510. www.lecheval-rouge.com. ✆ **02-47-50-02-07.** Fax 02-47-50-08-77. Reservations recommended. Main courses 15€–18€; fixed-price menu 20€–40€. AE, DC, MC, V. Daily noon–2:30pm and 7–9pm.

LANGEAIS

259km (161 miles) SW of Paris; 26km (16 miles) W of Tours

On December 6, 1491, 15-year-old Anne de Bretagne was wed to Charles VIII at Langeais, permanently attaching Brittany to France. It was the castle's golden hour.

Château de Langeais ★★ This is a medieval fortress, a formidable gray pile that dominates the town. It's one of the few châteaux actually on the Loire. The facade is forbidding, but once you cross the drawbridge, you'll find the apartments so richly decorated that they soften the effect. The original castle was built in the 10th century. Fulk III (972–1040), count of Anjou, sometimes called The Black Falcon, erected the first keep, the ruins of which can still be seen. The present structure was built in 1465. The interior is well preserved and furnished, thanks to Jacques Siegfried, who not only restored it over 20 years, but also bequeathed it to the Institut de France in 1904.

The rooms re-create the ambience of a regal residence of the late Middle Ages, rich with ornamental fireplaces and tapestries. A remarkable 15th-century "millefleurs" tapestry decorates the Chambre de la Dame, and seven superb tapestries known as the *Valiant Knights* cover the walls of the Salle des Preux.

The Banquet Hall features a mantelpiece carved to resemble a fortress, complete with crenellated towers. The Wedding Hall includes a re-creation of the marriage of Anne de Bretagne and Charles VIII with lavishly costumed wax figures. In the Luini Room is a large 1522 fresco by that artist, removed from a chapel on Lake Maggiore, Italy. It depicts Saint Francis of Assisi and Saint Elizabeth of Hungary with Mary and Joseph. The Byzantine Virgin in the drawing room is thought to be an early work of Cimabue, the Florentine artist. Allow 1½ hours to go through the château.

Langeais 37130. ✆ **02-47-96-72-60.** www.chateau-de-langeais.com. Admission 8.50€ adults, 7.20€ students and ages 18–25, 5€ for children 10–17, free for 9 and under. Daily Apr–June and Sept to mid-Nov 9:30am–6:30pm; mid-Nov to Jan 10am–5pm; Feb–Mar 9:30am–5:30pm; July–Aug 9am–7pm.

View from the Château de Langeais.

Essentials

GETTING THERE Several **trains** per day stop here en route from Tours or Saumur. The one-way fare from Saumur is 7.30€, the one-way fare from Tours 5€. Transit time from both cities is around 20 minutes. For schedules and information, call ✆ **36-35** or visit www.voyages-sncf.com. If you're **driving** from Tours, take D952 southwest to Langeais.

VISITOR INFORMATION The **Office de Tourisme** is at place du 14-Juillet (✆ **02-47-96-58-22;** www.tourisme-langeais.com).

Where to Stay & Eat

Hotel Errard Hosten ★ This ivy-draped country inn in the center of town was built in 1853. In 2002, it added a neighboring house, creating a hotel–restaurant complex. The restaurant, which has received many honors, is elegant and formal, while the hotel that houses it is a bit more relaxed. Guest rooms are rustic and comfortable, and some (particularly the suites in the annex) are surprisingly large. Most of the well-maintained tiled bathrooms have tub/showers. Guests dine indoors or at tables in the open courtyard under umbrellas and flowering trees. The *menu de prestige* includes *matelote* of eel with Bourgueil red wine, and Touraine pigeon with honeyed ginger. For a standout dessert, try pear mousse with Jamaican pepper ice cream.

2 rue Gambetta, Langeais 37130. www.errard.com. ✆ **02-47-96-82-12.** Fax 02-47-96-56-72. 10 units. 69€–79€ double; 95€–112€ apt. AE, MC, V. Parking 5€. Closed Dec–Jan. **Amenities:** Restaurant; bar. *In room:* TV, free Internet.

AZAY-LE-RIDEAU

261km (162 miles) SW of Paris; 21km (13 miles) SW of Tours

Its machicolated towers and blue-slate roof pierced with dormers shimmer in the moat, creating a reflection like a Monet painting. The defensive medieval look is all for show: The Renaissance **Château d'Azay-le-Rideau ★★**, rue Pineau, Azay-le-Rideau 37190 (✆ **02-47-45-42-04;** www.monuments-nationaux.fr), was created as a residence at an idyllic spot on the Indre River. Gilles Berthelot, François I's finance minister, commissioned the castle, and his wife, Philippa, supervised its construction. They didn't have long to enjoy their elegant creation: In 1527,

Berthelot was accused of misappropriation of funds and forced to flee, and the château reverted to the king. He didn't live here, but granted it to Antoine Raffin, one of his high-ranking soldiers. It became the property of the state in 1905.

Before you enter, circle the château and note the perfect proportions of the crowning achievement of the Renaissance in the Touraine. Check out its most fancifully ornate feature, the bay enclosing a grand stairway with a straight flight of steps.

From the second-floor Royal Chamber, look out at the gardens. This lavish bedroom housed Louis XIII when he came through in 1619. The private apartments are lined with rich tapestries dating from the 16th and 17th centuries and feature examples of rare period furniture, like the Spanish *bargueno,* a carved wooden chest that held writing materials.

The château is open daily in July and August 9:30am to 7pm, April to June and September 9:30am to 6pm, and October to March 10am to 12:30pm and 2 to 5:30pm. Admission is 8€ for adults, 5€ for ages 18 to 25, and free for children 17 and under. Allow 2 hours for a visit.

In July and August, there is a guided outdoor tour/performance that features actors in period dress, animals, recorded music, and lights beaming on the exterior of the château. The tour, which lasts about 1½ hours, begins at 9:15 and 10:20pm. Tickets are 10€ for adults, 6€ for ages 12 to 25, and free for children 11 and under.

Essentials

GETTING THERE To reach Azay-le-Rideau, take the **train** from Tours or Chinon. From either starting point, the trip time is about 30 minutes; the one-way fare is 4.60€ from Chinon, 5.20€ from Tours. For the same fare, the SNCF railway also operates a bus between Tours and Azay; the trip takes 50 minutes. For schedules and information, call ✆ **36-35** or visit www.voyages-sncf.com. If you're **driving** from Tours, take D751 southwest to Azay-le-Rideau.

VISITOR INFORMATION The **Office de Tourisme** is on place de L'Europe (✆ **02-47-45-44-40;** www.ot-paysazaylerideau.com).

Château d'Azay-le-Rideau.

Where to Stay & Eat

L'Aigle d'Or ★ TRADITIONAL FRENCH This excellent restaurant is set in a century-old house. Located in the village center, the service is professional, the welcome charming, and the food the best in Azay. In a dining room accented with ceiling beams, a fireplace, and pastel colors, you can savor dishes including foie gras with pears

For Literary Fans: An Ode to Balzac

Seven kilometers (4¼ miles) east of Azay-le-Rideau (take D17), you can visit **Saché,** the hometown of Honoré de Balzac. Here he wrote several of his novels, including *The Lily of the Valley* and *Père Goriot.* He declared that his affection for the Touraine was like "the love of the artist for his art." Of interest to fans is the **Musée Balzac,** in the 19th-century Château de Saché, Saché 37190 (✆ **02-47-26-86-50;** www.musee-balzac.fr). The small château contains the writer's bedrooms, preserved as they were when he lived here. A collection of Balzac's notes, first editions, etchings, letters, and cartoons are on display, as is a copy of Rodin's sculpture of the writer. The castle and museum are open daily April to June (and Sept) 10am to 6pm, July and August 10am to 7pm; closed Tuesdays October to March, when its opening hours are 10am to 12:30pm and 2 to 5pm. Admission is 4.50€ for adults, 3€ for seniors and students, and free for children 6 and under.

and *blanquette* (stew) of Loire Valley whitefish prepared with local white wine. Desserts include baked apple with rice pudding mousse, and chocolate cake with sour cherry coulis. In summer, the party expands onto an outdoor terrace.

10 av. Adélaïde-Riché. ✆ **02-47-45-24-58.** Reservations recommended. Main courses 12€–24€; fixed-price menus 27€–52€. V. Mon–Tues and Thurs–Sat noon–1:30pm and 7:30–9pm.

Le Grand Monarque The ivy that covers the exterior of this hotel—less than 150m (492 ft.) from the château—seems to protect it from the modern world. The large guest rooms are outfitted with antiques; ancient exposed beams adorn the lobby ceiling. Units in the annex aren't as well decorated but are more tranquil; those looking out on the wide courtyard are particularly quiet.

The restaurant features dishes like a brochette of crayfish with sesame sauce, suprême of *sandre* in shallot-flavored broth, and galette of pigs' feet *en confit.* Fixed-price menus range from 26€ to 33€. During warmer months, you can dine out on the courtyard terrace.

3 place de la République, Azay-le-Rideau 37190. www.legrandmonarque.com. ✆ **02-47-45-40-08.** Fax 02-47-45-46-25. 24 units. 70€–140€ double. AE, MC, V. Parking 10€. Closed Dec to mid-Jan. **Amenities:** Restaurant; bar; babysitting; room service. *In room:* TV, hair dryer, free Wi-Fi.

CHINON ★★

283km (175 miles) SW of Paris; 48km (30 miles) SW of Tours; 31km (19 miles) SW of Langeais

In the film *Joan of Arc,* Ingrid Bergman identified the dauphin as he tried to conceal himself among his courtiers. This took place in real life at the Château de Chinon, one of the oldest fortress-châteaux in France. Charles VII centered his government at Chinon from 1429 to 1450. In 1429, with the English besieging Orléans, the Maid of Orléans prevailed upon the dauphin to give her an army. The rest is history. The seat of French power stayed at Chinon until the end of the Hundred Years' War.

Today Chinon remains a tranquil village known mainly for its delightful red wines. After you visit the attractions, we recommend taking a walk along the Vienne River; definitely stop to taste the wine at one of Chinon's terraced cafes. Allow 3 hours to see Chinon.

Essentials

GETTING THERE The SNCF runs about seven **trains** and four **buses** every day to Chinon from Tours (trip time: 45 min. by train; 1 hr., 15 min. by bus). For schedules and information, call ✆ **36-35** or visit www.voyages-sncf.com. Both buses and trains arrive at the train station, which lies at the edge of the very small town. If you're **driving** from Tours, take D751 southwest through Azay-le-Rideau to Chinon.

VISITOR INFORMATION The **Office de Tourisme** is at place Hofheim (✆ **02-47-93-17-85;** www.chinon-valdeloire.com).

Exploring the Town & the Château

On the banks of the Vienne, the town of Chinon consists of winding streets and turreted houses, many built in the 15th and 16th centuries in the heyday of the court. For the best view, drive across the river and turn right onto quai Danton. From this vantage point, you'll be able to see the castle in relation to the village and the river. The most typical street is rue Voltaire, lined with 15th- and 16th-century town houses. At no. 44, Richard the Lion-Hearted died on April 6, 1199, from a wound suffered during the siege of Chalus in Limousin. The Grand Carroi, in the heart of Chinon, served as the crossroads of the Middle Ages.

Château de Chinon ★★ The château, which was more or less in ruins, has undergone a massive excavation and restoration effort that started in 2003 and so far has resulted in beautifully restored ramparts, castle keep, and royal apartments, which now look more or less as they did in the good old days. After being roofless for 200 years, the apartments now sport pitched and gabled slate roofs and wood floors, and the keep is once again fortified. The restoration, while not exact (due to the state of the original building), gives the overall impression of

IN PURSUIT OF THE grape

Chinon is famous for its wines, which crop up on prestigious lists around the world. Supermarkets and wine shops throughout the region sell them; families that have been in the business longer than anyone can remember maintain the two most interesting stores. At **Caves Plouzeau,** 94 rue Haute-St-Maurice (✆ **02-47-93-32-11;** www.plouzeau.com), the 12th-century cellars were dug to provide building blocks for the foundations of the château. The present management dates from 1929; bottles of red or white wine cost from 6€ to 12€. You're welcome to climb down to the cellars. They are open for wine sales and visits April to September Tuesday to Saturday 11am to 1pm and 3 to 7pm.

The cellars at **Couly-Dutheil,** 12 rue Diderot (✆ **02-47-97-20-20;** www.coulydutheil-chinon.com), are suitably medieval; many were carved from rock. This company produces largely Chinon wines (mostly reds), and it's proud of the Bourgueil and St-Nicolas de Bourgueil, whose popularity in North America has grown in recent years. Tours of the caves and a *dégustation des vins* (wine tasting) require an advance call and cost 4€ to 6€ per person. Visits are conducted April to September Monday to Friday 9am to noon and 1:45 to 5:45pm.

what the castle looked like around the time of Joan of Arc's visit. The buildings are separated by a series of moats, adding to its medieval look. A new building has been construction on the foundations of the Fort of St-George, which serves as an entrance hall and museum, displaying new archeological finds discovered during the restoration, as well as objects and documentation that recount the story of Joan of Arc, Charles VII, and the history of the castle.

Btw. rue St-Maurice and av. Francois Mitterrand. ✆ **02-47-93-13-45.** Admission 7€ adults, 4.50€ students, free for children 12 and under. Apr–Sept daily 9am–7pm; Oct–Mar daily 9:30am–5pm.

Musée Rabelais–La Devinière The most famous son of Chinon, François Rabelais, the earthy and often bawdy Renaissance writer, lived in town on rue de la Lamproie. (A plaque marks the spot where his father practiced law and maintained a home and office.) This site, just outside the hamlet of Seuilly, 5.5km (3½ miles) west of Chinon, was an isolated cottage at the time of his birth. It was maintained, because of local superstition and custom, for the sole purpose of delivering the children of the Rabelais clan into the world.

The museum has three floors of exhibition space, each focusing on an aspect of Rabelais, his times, and his role in Chinon. In two neighboring buildings, you'll find exhibits on aspects of life during the Middle Ages, including an unusual display on medicinal plants.

La Devinière, just outside of Seuilly off the N751. ✆ **02-47-95-91-18.** www.monuments-touraine.fr. Admission 4.50€ adults, 3€ students, free for children 11 and under. Apr–June Wed–Mon 10am–12:30pm and 2–6pm; July–Aug daily 10am–7pm; Sept Wed–Mon 10am–12:30pm and 2–6pm; Oct–Mar Wed–Mon 10am–12:30pm and 2–5pm. From Chinon, follow the road signs pointing to Saumur and the D117.

Where to Stay

Hostellerie Gargantua ★ This 15th-century building was once a courthouse where the father of François Rabelais worked as a lawyer in the 15th century. Art historians admire the building's early Renaissance staircase and its chiseled-stone details. The comfortably furnished guest rooms feature high ceilings and canopy beds, and a few have stone fireplaces and/or views of the castle. Try to stop here for a meal, served in a medieval hall. You can sample Loire *sandre* prepared with Chinon wine or duckling with dried pears and smoked lard, followed by a medley of seasonal red fruits in puff pastry.

73 rue Haute St-Maurice, Chinon 37500. www.hotel-gargantua.com. ✆ **02-47-93-04-71.** Fax 02-47-93-08-02. 7 units. 55€–81€ double. AE, MC, V. **Amenities:** Restaurant; bar. *In room:* TV, free Wi-Fi.

Hôtel Diderot ★ 🎁 Within a 5-minute walk of the town's historic core, this is a comfortable hotel with strands of ivy climbing romantically up its stone front. Although the foundations date from the 14th century, the building was radically altered in the 1700s; today you'll see remnants of thick wall and ceiling beams throughout the public rooms and in some of the guest rooms. Rooms are midsize to spacious, outfitted in Henry II or Napoleon III style, usually with big windows letting in maximum sunlight. One of the architectural highlights is a magnificent 15th-century fireplace in the breakfast room, where you'll enjoy as many as 52 kinds of jams and jellies as part of your morning ritual. The congenial hosts' enthusiasm for the charms of their home town is contagious.

4 rue du Buffon, Chinon 37500. www.hoteldiderot.com. ✆ **02-47-93-18-87.** Fax 02-47-93-37-10.

27 units. 55€–82€ double. AE, DC, MC, V. Parking 7€. Closed 1st 2 weeks of Dec and last week of Jan through first week of Feb. **Amenities:** Bar. *In room:* TV, hair dryer, free Wi-Fi.

Hôtel Le Plantagenet This hotel, an erstwhile 19th-century mansion in the center of town, opens onto views of the river Vienne and lies close to the medieval heart of Chinon. A recent change of ownership has brought renovations and a general freshening up; rooms are midsize and filled with character, each tastefully and comfortably furnished. The grace note of the hotel is its private garden and terrace, where you can enjoy a drink. Some rooms, just as good as those in the main building, are in an annex manor house, the Maison Bourgeoise.

12 place Jeanne d'Arc, Chinon 37500. www.hotel-plantagenet.com. ✆ **02-47-93-36-92.** Fax 02-47-98-48-92. 32 units. 66€–81€ double. AE, DC, MC, V. Parking 7€. **Amenities:** Bar; tearoom. *In room:* A/C (in 6 units), TV, hair dryer, free Wi-Fi.

Where to Eat

L'Oceanic SEAFOOD/FRENCH As its name implies, this restaurant specializes in fresh seafood, even though Chinon is inland. The specialties are changed daily, based on what's fresh and good at the marketplace. A particularly delicious meal may include cassoulet of lobster and scallops with vanilla-flavored butter, carpaccio of sea scallops with fried leeks and herb-flavored vinaigrette, ray with Camembert sauce, and roasted filets of codfish with Münster cheese cream sauce. If you don't like fish, the owners prepare delicious steak.

13 rue Rabelais. ✆ **02-47-93-44-55.** Reservations required. Main courses 18€–32€; fixed-price menu 24€–35€. MC, V. Tues–Sun noon–1:30pm; Tues–Sat 7:30–9:30pm.

Where to Stay & Eat Nearby

Château de Marçay ★★★ This property began in the 1100s as a fortress and took its present form during the Renaissance. The centerpiece of the wine-producing hamlet of Marçay, it's sumptuously decorated. The main building houses the more opulent lodgings; a handful of less expensive, less dramatic rooms are in an annex a short walk away. Menu specialties change with the season at the restaurant, and the chef works hard to maintain high standards. The garden terrace and elegantly rustic dining room afford a panoramic view.

Marçay, Chinon 37500. www.chateaudemarcay.com. ✆ **02-47-93-03-47.** Fax 02-47-93-45-33. 33 units. 100€–215€ double; 230€–290€ suite. AE, DC, MC, V. Closed Jan 15–Mar 15. Take D116 for 7km (4¼ miles) southwest of Chinon. **Amenities:** Restaurant; bar; outdoor pool; room service; tennis court. *In room:* TV, hair dryer, minibar, Wi-Fi.

Manoir de la Giraudière Built during the mid-1600s, this elegant manor house resembles a small château because of its use of *tuffeau* (the beige stone used in residences of many of the French monarchs). In a 2.4-hectare (6-acre) park surrounded by hundreds of acres of fields and forests, this midrange establishment offers classic decor and modern comforts. Each good-size room comes with a fine bed and quality linen. Air-conditioning isn't necessary because the thick walls act as natural insulation against heat and cold. A small on-site restaurant serves light meals.

15 rue de la Giraudiere, Beaumont-en-Veron 37420. www.giraudiere.com. ✆ **02-47-58-40-36.** Fax 02-47-58-46-06. 24 units. 50€–135€ double; 100€–130€ apt. AE, DC, MC, V. Head 5km (3 miles) west of Chinon along D749 toward Bourgueil. **Amenities:** Restaurant; bar. *In room:* TV, hair dryer, free Wi-Fi.

Chinon After Dark

A charming bar and nighttime hangout is **Le Café Français,** 37 place du Général-de-Gaulle (✆ **02-47-93-32-78;** www.cafefrancais.fr). Behind the Hotel de Ville (town hall), it attracts many good-looking singles. There's a modest admission charge for occasional concerts.

USSÉ

295km (183 miles) SW of Paris; 14km (8¾ miles) NE of Chinon

At the edge of the dark forest of Chinon in Rigny-Ussé, **Château d'Ussé** ★ (✆ **02-47-95-54-05;** www.chateaudusse.fr) was the inspiration for Perrault's legend of *The Sleeping Beauty (La Belle au bois dormant).* Conceived as a fortress, the complex of steeples, turrets, towers, and dormers was erected at the dawn of the Renaissance on a hill overlooking the Indre River. The terraces, laden with orange trees, were laid out in the 18th century. When the need for a fortified château passed, the north wing was demolished to open up a greater view.

The château was later owned by the duc de Duras and then by Mme. de la Rochejacquelin; its present owner, the marquis de Blacas, has opened many rooms to the public. The visit begins in the Renaissance chapel, with its sculptured portal and handsome stalls. You then proceed to the royal apartments, furnished with tapestries and antiques. One gallery displays an extensive collection of swords and rifles. A spiral stairway leads to a tower with a panoramic view of the river and a waxwork Sleeping Beauty waiting for her prince to come.

The château is open daily from mid-February to March 10am to 6pm, April to August 10am to 7pm, and September to November 10am to 6pm; closed the rest of the year. Entrance costs 13€ for adults, 4€ for students and children 8 to 16, and is free for children 7 and under. Allow 1½ hours to visit the castle and its grounds. The château is best visited by car or on an organized bus tour from Tours. If you're driving from Tours or Villandry, follow D7 to Ussé.

Where to Stay

Le Clos d'Ussé ★ 🎁 Although most visitors make Ussé a day trip, this little hotel across the street from the castle makes a good overnight stop. The Duchemin family offers well-maintained rooms that are midsize and comfortably furnished. The least expensive rooms are small and without in-suite bathrooms; the others have full facilities with either shower or bathtub. The friendly owners are experts on the lore of the castle.

7 rue Principale, on D7, Rigny-Ussé 37130. ✆ **02-47-95-55-47.** Fax 02-47-95-55-47. 7 units. 35€–65€ double. DC, MC, V. Closed Nov–Feb. **Amenities:** Restaurant; free Wi-Fi. *In room:* TV, hair dryer, no phone.

FONTEVRAUD-L'ABBAYE ★★

304km (188 miles) SW of Paris; 16km (10 miles) SE of Saumur

You'll find the Plantagenet dynasty buried in the **Abbaye Royale de Fontevraud** (✆ **02-41-51-73-52;** www.abbaye-fontevraud.com). The kings, whose male line ended in 1485, were also the comtes d'Anjou, and they wanted to be buried in their native soil.

In the 12th-century Romanesque church—with four Byzantine domes—are the remains of two English kings or princes, including Henry II of England, the first Plantagenet king, and his wife, Eleanor of Aquitaine, the most famous woman of the Middle Ages. Her crusading son, Richard the Lion-Hearted, was also entombed here. The Plantagenet line ended with the death of Richard III at the 1485 Battle of Bosworth. The tombs fared badly during the Revolution, when mobs desecrated the sarcophagi and scattered their contents on the floor.

Château d'Ussé.

More intriguing than the tombs is the octagonal **Tour d'Evraud,** the last remaining Romanesque kitchen in France. Dating from the 12th century, it contains five of its original eight *apsides* (half-rounded indentations originally conceived as chapels), each crowned with a conically roofed turret. A pyramid tops the conglomeration, capped by an open-air lantern tower pierced with lancets.

Robert d'Arbrissel, who spent much of his life as a recluse, founded the abbey in 1099. Aristocratic ladies occupied one part; many, including discarded mistresses of kings, had been banished from court. The four youngest daughters of Louis XV were educated here. Since 1975, the abbey has also functioned as a cultural center, offering expositions, concerts, and seminars.

Admission is 8.40€ in summer for adults or 7€ in winter. Free for ages 25 and under. Hours are April to June and September to October daily 9:30am to 6pm, July and August daily 9:30am to 7pm, November to December daily 10am to 5:30pm, and February to March Tuesday through Sunday 10am to 5:30pm. The abbey is closed in January. Allow ½ hour for the abbey.

Essentials

GETTING THERE If you're **driving,** take D147 about 4km (2½ miles) from the village of Montsoreau. In season, you can take a **bus** (Line 1) from Saumur; schedules vary according to school holidays—call (✆ **02-41-51-11-87**) or visit the bus company's website, www.agglobus.fr, to download the schedule. The one-way fare for the 30-minute trip is 1.35€.

VISITOR INFORMATION The **Office de Tourisme,** allée Ste-Catherine (✆ **02-41-51-79-45**), within the compound of the medieval abbey, is open only from Easter to September 30.

Where to Stay

Hôtel Abbaye Royale de Fontevraud ★ 🎁 This unusual hotel is set on 11th-century foundations within the perimeter of the Abbaye Royale in one-time monks' cells. It became a hotel in 1990. The guest rooms are well maintained and monastically simple, with white walls, modern furniture, and exposed sections of cream-colored *tuffeau,* the easy-to-carve rock used to build the abbey during the early Middle Ages.

Le Prieuré St-Lazare, rue St-Jean de l'Habit, Fontevraud-l'Abbaye 49590. www.hotelfp-fontevraud.com. ✆ **02-41-51-73-16.** Fax 02-41-51-75-50. 52 units. 65€–145€ double; 190€ suite. AE, MC, V. Closed Nov 16–Mar 15. **Amenities:** Restaurant; bar; babysitting; free Wi-Fi. *In room:* TV, hair dryer.

Abbaye Royale de Fontevraud.

Where to Eat

The **Hôtel Abbaye Royale de Fontevraud** (see above) has a good restaurant.

La Licorne ★ MODERN FRENCH For the perfect combination of medieval history and culinary sensuality, visit the abbey and then dine at this 35-seat restaurant on a linden-lined walkway between the abbey and a nearby parish church. Its symmetrical proportions and neoclassical pilasters, built in the 1700s just before the French Revolution, evoke the *ancien régime* at its most graceful and opulent. In summer, guests sit in the garden or the elegantly rustic dining room. The menu almost always includes filet of beef flavored with smoked pork and shallots, crayfish-stuffed ravioli with basil-flavored morel sauce, and luscious desserts such as a warm chocolate tart with pears and lemon-butter sauce.

Allée Ste-Catherine. ✆ **02-41-51-72-49.** www.la-licorne-restaurant.com. Reservations required. Main courses 18€–36€; fixed-price menu 27€–55€. AE, MC, V. Nov–Apr Tues–Sun noon–2pm; Tues and Thurs–Sat 7–9pm; May–Oct daily noon–2pm and 7–9pm. Closed 1 week in Dec.

SAUMUR

299km (185 miles) SW of Paris; 53km (33 miles) SE of Angers

Saumur is in a region of vineyards, where the Loire separates to encircle an island; it makes one of the best bases for exploring the western Loire Valley. A small but thriving town, it doesn't entirely live off its past: Saumur produces some 100,000 tons per year of the mushrooms the French adore. Balzac left us this advice: "Taste a mushroom and delight in the essential strangeness of the place." The cool tunnels for the *champignons* also provide the ideal resting place for the celebrated sparkling wines of the region. Enjoy both of these local favorites at a neighborhood cafe.

Essentials

GETTING THERE **Trains** run frequently between Tours Centre and Saumur. Some 20 trains per day arrive from Tours (trip time: 30–40 min.); the one-way fare is about 11€. Over a dozen trains per day pull in from Angers (trip time: 20–30 min.), costing 8€ one-way. From the station, take bus A into town. For schedules and information, call ✆ **36-35** or visit www.voyages-sncf.com. If you're **driving** from Tours, follow D952 or the A85 autoroute southwest to Saumur.

VISITOR INFORMATION The **Office de Tourisme** is on place de la Bilange (✆ **02-41-40-20-60;** www.ot-saumur.fr).

Exploring the Area

Of all the Loire cities, Saumur remains the most bourgeois; perhaps that's why Balzac used it for his classic characterization of a smug little town in *Eugénie Grandet*. Saumur is also famous as the birthplace of the *couturière* Coco Chanel.

The men of Saumur are among the best equestrians in the world. Founded in 1768, the city's riding school, **Cadre Noir de Saumur ★**, avenue de l'Ecole Nationale d'Equitation (✆ **02-41-53-50-50;** www.cadrenoir.fr), is one of the grandest in Europe, rivaling Vienna's. The stables house some 350 horses. Mid-February to October, tours (7€ adults, 5€ children) begin at 9:30 to 11am and 2 to 4pm from Monday afternoon to Saturday afternoon. Tours depart about every 20 minutes. Tours last about 1 hour. Some 48km (30 miles) of specialty tracks wind around the town—to see a rider carry out a curvet is a thrill. The performances peak during the **Carrousel de Saumur ★★** on the last 2 Saturdays and Sundays in July.

The area surrounding the town has become famous for its delicate sparkling wines. In the center of Saumur, you can wander the many aisles of **La Maison du Vin,** quai Lucien Gauthier (✆ **02-41-38-45-83;** www.vinsvaldeloire.fr), and choose from a large stock direct from the many surrounding vineyards.

An alternative is to travel east of Saumur to the village of St-Hilaire, where you'll find a host of vineyards. One of the better ones is **Veuve Amiot,** 21 rue Jean-Ackerman (✆ **02-41-83-14-14;** www.veuveamiot.fr), where you can tour

Riding at Cadre Noir de Saumur.

the wine cellars, taste different vintages, and buy bottles and gift boxes right in the showroom.

Regrettably, **Château de Saumur,** the main reason for visiting the town, is closed for extensive renovations, with no announced opening date. For the moment, for a small fee (3€ adult, 2.50€ children 7–16, free under 7), you can visit the exterior and enjoy the panorama from the terrace. A selection of equestrian statues is on display, as well as panels recounting the history of the château. Entry Tuesday to Sunday April to June and September to October 10am to 5:30pm, July and August 10am to 6pm.

Where to Stay

Hôtel Anne d'Anjou ★ This 18th-century building was constructed as a family mansion; its magnificent stairwell below a *trompe l'oeil* ceiling has been designated an historic monument. The rooms in the back overlook the château, and the front faces the Loire. Five units still have their original decor, ranging from Louis XVI to Empire. The hotel operates Les Menestrels, one of the most prestigious restaurants in Saumur. It offers creative fixed-price menus for 35€ to 65€. The restaurant is in a 16th-century structure with a vaulted cellar, opening onto landscaped gardens.

32–33 quai Mayaud, Saumur 49400. www.hotel-anneanjou.com. ✆ **02-41-67-30-30.** Fax 02-41-67-51-00. 42 units. 105€–170€ double; AE, DC, MC, V. Parking 10€. **Amenities:** Restaurant; bar; babysitting; room service. *In room:* TV, hair dryer, minibar, free Wi-Fi.

Hôtel St-Pierre ★ Nestled among tiny winding streets and built against the Eglise St-Pierre, this hotel overflows with character. Appointments include finely upholstered antiques, half-timbered walls, beamed ceilings, stone fireplaces, and spiral staircases. Guest rooms are individually decorated in the same rich style; even the bathroom walls showcase custom tile designs. Overall, the hotel is an appealing middle-bracket choice in a historic location. The intimate breakfast room opens onto a small garden terrace.

Rue Haute-Saint-Pierre, Saumur 49400. www.saintpierresaumur.com. ✆ **02-41-50-33-00.** Fax 02-41-50-38-68. 14 units. 100€–160€ double. AE, DC, MC, V. **Amenities:** Babysitting; room service. *In room:* A/C, TV, hair dryer, minibar, free Wi-Fi.

Le Prieuré ★★★ This one of the grandest addresses in the region, a bastion of comfort, charm, and grace. The 12th-century priory is in a 24-hectare (59-acre) park 8km (5 miles) from town. The hotel has a steep roof, dormer windows, and a large peaked tower. It provides gracious, comfortable rooms; two of the most beautiful are in a 10th-century chapel. The least expensive (and less desirable) rooms are in an outlying pavilion. The Grand Salon features an ornately carved stone fireplace, crystal chandeliers, oak furniture, and a bar with a fleur-de-lis motif.

From the dining room, you'll enjoy a magnificent view of the Loire—it's truly beautiful at sunset. The chef's oeuvre includes filet of beef with heritage vegetables, brill with ginger, and filet of rabbit with pumpkin gnocchi. Even if you're not a guest, consider dining here. Fixed-price menus cost 33€ to 70€ at dinner, and 24€ to 31€ at lunch.

Chênehutte-les-Tuffeaux, Saumur 49350. www.grandesetapes.fr. ✆ **02-41-67-90-14.** Fax 02-41-67-92-24. 36 units. 130€–275€ double; 345€ suite. AE, DC, MC, V. **Amenities:** Restaurant; bar; babysitting; outdoor pool; room service; tennis court. *In room:* TV, hair dryer, minibar, free Wi-Fi.

Les Terrasses de Saumur Although it was built relatively recently, this hotel has many of the architectural details (a steep slate roof, a U-shaped design ringing a formal courtyard) of a much older building. A recent renovation has resulted in sleek, modern rooms in warm colors; the best have private balconies overlooking the Loire Valley. There's also a large heated outdoor swimming pool, a new spa with sauna and steam room, rambling green lawns, and plenty of parkland dotted with benches, tables, and chairs. The restaurant features a stylish menu with seasonal dishes and ingredients; fixed-price menus range from 28€ to 38€.

2 rue des Lilas, St-Hilaire-St-Florent, Saumur 49400. www.lesterrassesdesaumur.fr. ✆ **02-41-67-28-48.** Fax 02-41-67-13-71. 20 units. 70€–120€ double; 120€–160€ suite. AE, MC, V. **Amenities:** Restaurant; bar; outdoor pool; room service; sauna; spa. *In room:* A/C (in some), TV, hair dryer, minibar, free Wi-Fi.

Where to Eat

Le Prieuré and Hôtel Anne d'Anjou's **Les Menestrels** (see above) serve excellent cuisine.

Le Gambetta ★★ MODERN FRENCH This is not the least expensive restaurant in Saumur, but if you want to savor cutting-edge cuisine made with top-quality ingredients, it's the place to go. Since Mickaël Pihours took over the kitchen in 2006, the restaurant has received a coveted Michelin star. The cuisine is creative and absolutely delicious—the menu includes dishes like bass with almond and ginger sauce, served with cannelloni stuffed with Bigorre pork and free-range lamb Gremolata served with bulgur pilaf and olive caponata. Try the duck foie gras served with orange and ground, roasted cacao beans. Evidence of the chef's roots can be found on the dessert menu—his scrumptious Far Breton (a classic cake from Brittany) is filled with apples, caramel, and salted butter.

12 rue Gambetta. ✆ **02-41-67-66-66.** www.legambetta.com Reservations recommended. Main courses 19€–30€; fixed-price menus 29€–69€. Tues and Thurs–Sun noon–2pm; Tues and Thurs–Sat 7–9pm. Closed 2 weeks in Jan, 3 weeks in Aug.

ANGERS ★★★

288km (179 miles) SW of Paris; 89km (55 miles) E of Nantes

Once the capital of Anjou, Angers straddles the Maine River at the western end of the Loire Valley. Though it suffered extensive damage in World War II, it has been restored, blending provincial charm with a suggestion of sophistication. The bustling regional center is often used as a base for exploring the château district to the west. Young people, including some 30,000 college students, keep this vital city of 155,700 jumping until late at night. Allow 3 hours to see the attractions at Angers.

Essentials

GETTING THERE High-speed **trains** make the 1½ hour trip every hour from Paris's Gare Montparnasse; the cost is 28€ to 61€ one-way. From Tours, about 10 trains per day make the 1-hour trip; a one-way ticket is 17€. The Angers train station is a convenient walk from the château. For schedules and information, call ✆ **36-35** or visit www.voyages-sncf.com. From Saumur, there are direct **bus** connections (1½ hr.); call ✆ **08-20-16-00-49** (.12€ per min.) or visit www.angoubus.fr for schedules. If you're **driving** from Tours, take the A85 autoroute west and exit at Angers Centre.

VISITOR INFORMATION The **Office de Tourisme,** 7 place Kennedy (✆ **02-41-23-50-00;** www.angers-tourisme.com), is opposite the entrance to the château.

Château d'Angers.

Exploring the Town

If you have time for shopping, wander to the pedestrian zone in the center of town. Its boutiques and small shops sell everything from clothes and shoes to jewelry and books. For regional specialties, head to **Maison du Vin de l'Anjou,** 5 bis place Kennedy (✆ **02-41-88-81-13;** www.vinsdeloire.fr), where you can learn about the area's vineyards and buy a bottle or two for gifts or a picnic.

Cathédrale St-Maurice ★★ The cathedral dates mostly from the 12th and 13th centuries; the main tower is from the 16th century. The statues on the portal represent everybody from the Queen of Sheba to David at the harp. The tympanum depicts Christ Enthroned. The stained-glass windows from the 12th through the 16th centuries have made the cathedral famous. The oldest one illustrates the martyrdom of St. Vincent; the most unusual is of St. Christopher with the head of a dog. The 12th-century nave, a landmark in cathedral architecture, is a work of harmonious beauty. If you're interested in a guided tour, call the church's presbytery at the number below. Tours are conducted erratically, often by an associate of the church, and usually with much charm and humor. The tours are available in French, English (offered July–Aug), and Italian.

Place Freppel. ✆ **02-41-87-58-45.** Free admission; donations appreciated. Daily 9am–7pm.

Château d'Angers ★★★ The château, dating from the 9th century, was the home of the comtes d'Anjou. The notorious Black Falcon lived here, and in time, the Plantagenets took up residence. From 1230 to 1238, the outer walls and 17 enormous towers were built, creating a fortress. King René favored the château, and during his reign, a brilliant court life flourished until he was forced to surrender to Louis XI. Louis XIV turned the château into a prison. In World War II, the Nazis used it as a munitions depot, and the Allies bombed it in 1944.

Visit the castle to see the **Apocalypse Tapestries ★★★**. They weren't always so highly regarded—they once served as a canopy to protect orange trees and were also used to cover the damaged walls of a church. Woven in Paris by Nicolas Bataille from cartoons by Jean de Bruges around 1375 for Louis I of Anjou, they were purchased for a nominal sum in the 19th century. The series of 77 sections, illustrating the Book of St. John, stretches 100m (328 ft.).

In 2009, the roof of the Logis Royal burned in an electrical fire and the château suffered damage (fortunately, the tapestries are housed in a separate building and were untouched). The Logis, which includes the royal apartments, is currently closed for repairs, but you can still tour the fortress, including the courtyard, ramparts, windmill tower, and 15th-century chapel, and see the tapestries. Once you've paid the entrance fee, you can take an hour-long guided tour focusing on the architecture and history of the château, or a tour devoted to the Apocolypse Tapestries. Both are available only in French; a self-guided tour with audioguides is available in English.

2 promenade du Bout-du-Monde. ✆ **02-41-86-48-77.** www.monuments-nationaux.fr. Admission 6€ adults, 5€ seniors and students 18–25, free for children 16 and under. Sept–Apr daily 10am–5:30pm; May–Aug daily 9:30am–6:30pm.

Musée Jean Lurçat ★★ The town's most intriguing museum is in the Ancien Hôpital St-Jean, founded in 1174 to care for the sick. The museum is known for its famous tapestry, *Le Chant du Monde (The Song of the World),* designed by Jean Lurçat and executed in 10 panels between 1957 and 1966. It depicts an abstract conglomeration of beneficent suns, popping champagne bottles, and life cycles of birth and death. You can visit a 17th-century dispensary, with earthenware jars and trivets still on its wooden shelves, and see everything from a Romanesque cloister with a secret garden to a pewter vessel from 1720 that once contained an antidote for snakebites.

4 bd. Arago. ✆ **02-41-24-18-45.** www.musees.angers.fr. Admission 4€ adults, free for 25 and under. June–Sept daily 10am–6:30pm; Oct–May Tues–Sun 10am–noon and 2–6pm.

Where to Stay

Hôtel d'Anjou Beside a park, this hotel built in 1846 is the best choice for overnighting in the area. Although comparable in price to the quality Hôtel de France, it has more upscale appointments and amenities, along with a better restaurant, La Salamandre (see "Where to Eat," below). The guest rooms closer to the ground have higher ceilings and are more spacious.

1 bd. de Maréchal Foch, Angers 49100. www.hoteldanjou.fr. ✆ **800/528-1234** in the U.S. and Canada, or 02-41-21-12-11. Fax 02-41-87-22-21. 53 units. 85€–193€ double. AE, DC, MC, V. Parking 8.50€. **Amenities:** Restaurant; bar. *In room:* TV, minibar, free Wi-Fi.

L'Hôtel de France For a good night's sleep near the railway station, this comfortable 19th-century hotel is your best bet. Run by the Bouyer family since 1893, the rooms are decorated in light shades of cream and beige, nicely furnished and well maintained. Room rates go up 15€ to 25€ per night when trade shows are in town.

8 place de la Gare, Angers 49100. www.hoteldefrance-angers.com. ✆ **02-41-88-49-42.** Fax 02-41-87-19-50. 55 units. 80€–140€ double. AE, DC, MC, V. Parking 7€. **Amenities:** Restaurant; bar; room service. *In room:* A/C, TV, hair dryer, minibar, free Wi-Fi.

Where to Eat

La Salamandre ★ CLASSIC FRENCH The salamander was the symbol of Renaissance king François I. In this formal, elegant restaurant, you'll see portraits of and references to that cunning strategist everywhere. Beneath massive sculpted ceiling beams, beside a large wooden fireplace, you'll enjoy the most impeccable service and best food in town. Shining examples include grilled bass in basil sauce, lobster stew, sautéed filet of beef and fresh foie gras with a reduction of red Anjou wine, and roasted and flambéed partridge. The restaurant is in a hotel but not owned by the hostelry.

A Toast with the Home-Brew—Cointreau

Another libation unique to Angers is Cointreau. **La Carée Cointreau,** 2 bd. des Bretonnières (© **02-41-31-50-50;** www.cointreau.fr), is in the suburb of St-Barthèlemy, a 10-minute drive east of the town center. If you call ahead to reserve, you can take a 1½-hour guided tour of the distillery and then visit the showroom, where you can sample and stock up on the fruity liqueur. Hours are variable; tours run on Saturdays only from October to April, and Tuesday through Saturday the rest of the year (9.80€ adult, 3.60€ children 12–17, free 11 and under).

Two brothers in Angers were confectioners who set out to create a drink of "crystal-clear purity." Today some 13 million bottles of Cointreau are consumed annually. Packaged in a square bottle with rounded corners, Cointreau is made from twice-distilled alcohol from the peels of two types of oranges, bitter and sweet. The factory has turned out the drink since 1849. Cointreau flavors such drinks as the Cosmopolitan and the Sidecar.

In the Hotel d'Anjou, 1 bd. du Maréchal Foch. © **02-41-88-99-55.** www.restaurant-lasalamandre.fr. Reservations recommended. Main courses 21€–38€; fixed-price menu 28€–48€. AE, DC, MC, V. Daily noon–2pm and Mon–Sat 7:30–9:30pm.

Provence Caffè PROVENÇAL This restaurant celebrates the herbs, spices, and especially the seafood of Provence. The chic decor includes bundles of herbs and souvenirs of the Mediterranean. The chef delights diners with such dishes as risotto served with rabbit and basil, and grilled salmon with Provençal herbs.

9 place du Ralliement. © **02-41-87-44-15.** www.provence-caffe.com. Reservations recommended. Main courses 15€; fixed-price menu 16€–32€. MC, V. Tues–Sat noon–2pm and 7–10pm.

Angers After Dark

If you head to **place du Ralliement** or **rue St-Laud,** with its many bars and cafes, you'll find yourself in the center of Angers's nightlife. For a great night of beer drinking with friends, go to **Le Kent,** 7 place Ste-Croix (© **02-41-87-88-55**). The Irish pub serves some 50 beers and 70 brands of whiskey. If a night of dancing seems the perfect antidote to a day of château gazing, consider **Le Boléro,** 38 rue St-Laud, adjacent to the place de Ralliement (© **02-41-88-61-19**). At the disco **Studio 49,** 8 place Vigan (© **02-41-48-15-28;** www.lestudio49.com), the bar specializes in rum drinks, and the entrance fee is 10€, including a beverage.

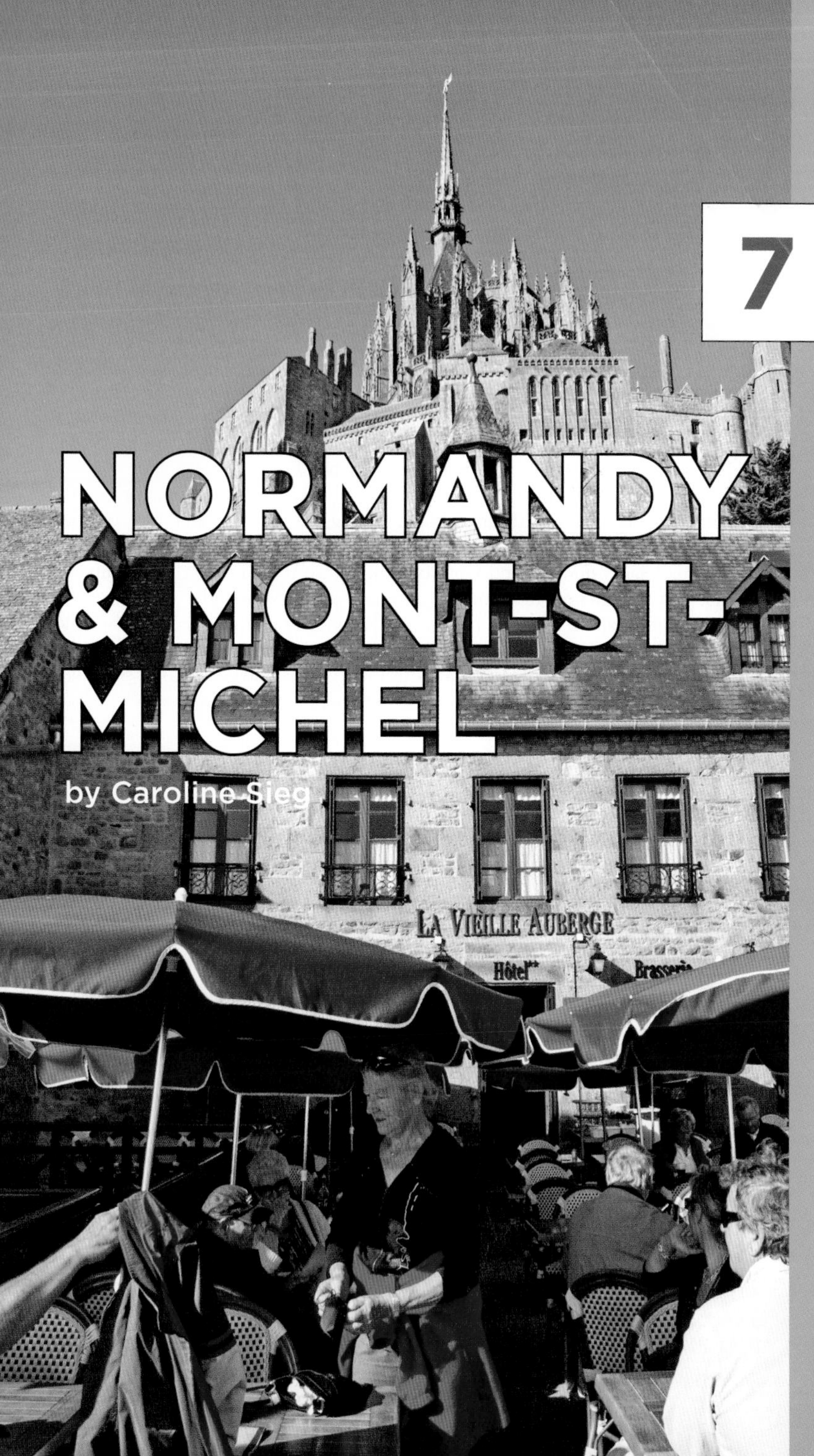

7

NORMANDY & MONT-ST-MICHEL

by Caroline Sieg

Ten centuries have passed since the Vikings invaded Normandy. The early Scandinavians came to seize the land, but they stayed to cultivate it. The Normans produced great soldiers, none more famous than William the Conqueror, who defeated King Harold at the Battle of Hastings in 1066. The English and the French continued to battle for centuries.

The invasion of June 6, 1944, ravaged much of Normandy. The largest armada ever assembled was responsible for regaining control of Europe from the Nazis. Today many visitors come to Normandy to see the D-day beachheads.

Some of this province may remind you of a Millet landscape, with cattle grazing in fields and wood-framed houses alongside modern buildings. Not far from the Seine is the hamlet where Monet painted his waterlilies. Here and there are stained-glass windows and Gothic architecture that survived the bombardments; however, many great buildings were leveled. Normandy's wide beaches attract families, and in August, the Deauville sands draw the chicest of the chic from Europe and North America. The resort towns of Deauville and Trouville are part of the region known as La Côte Fleurie (the Flower Coast), so called because of the profusion of flowers that grow there in the summer.

ROUEN ★★★

135km (84 miles) NW of Paris; 89km (55 miles) E of Le Havre

The capital of Normandy and the fifth-largest port in France, Rouen is a hub of commerce. It's a bustling, vibrant place, bursting with activity generated by

Rouen. PREVIOUS PAGE: **Mont-St-Michel.**

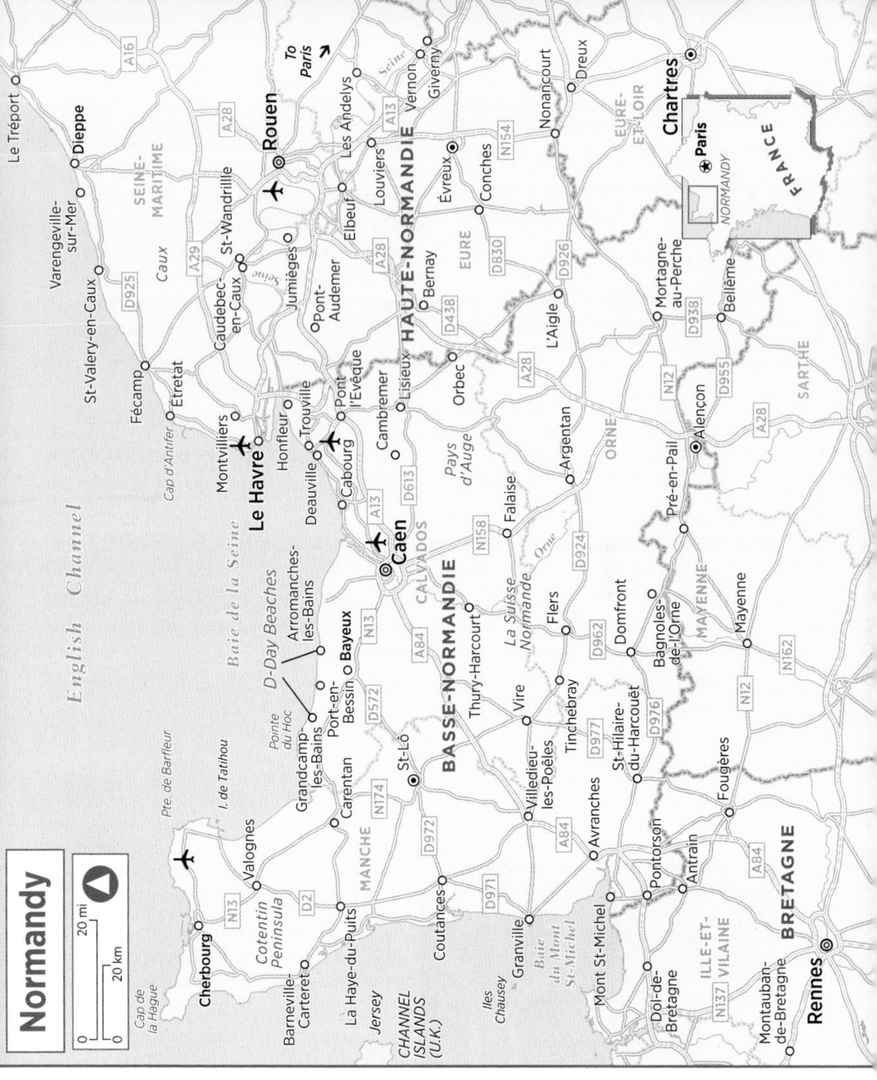

the industries connected to the port and the students at nearby universities and art schools. Former occupants include the writers Pierre Corneille and Gustave Flaubert, Claude Monet (who endlessly painted Rouen's Cathédrale de Notre-Dame), and Joan of Arc ("Oh, Rouen, art thou then my final resting place?"). Today it's a city of half a million people.

Victor Hugo called Rouen "the city of a hundred spires." Half of it was destroyed during World War II, mostly by Allied bombers, and many Rouennais were killed. During the reconstruction of the old quarters, some of the almost-forgotten crafts of the Middle Ages were revived. The city on the Seine is rich in historical associations: William the Conqueror died here in 1087, and Joan of Arc was burned at the stake on place du Vieux-Marché in 1431.

As in Paris, the Seine splits Rouen into a **Rive Gauche (Left Bank)** and **Rive Droite (Right Bank).** The old city is on the right bank.

> **A 4-Day Normandy Itinerary**
>
> **On your first day, head for Rouen and explore its old town and cathedral. On your second day, go to Caen, William the Conqueror's seat of government. Stay in Caen or in Bayeux, where you can see the local cathedral and the Bayeux tapestry. On your third day (from Caen or Bayeux), explore the D-day beaches. On your fourth day, continue west toward the ancient island-abbey of Mont-St-Michel.**

Essentials

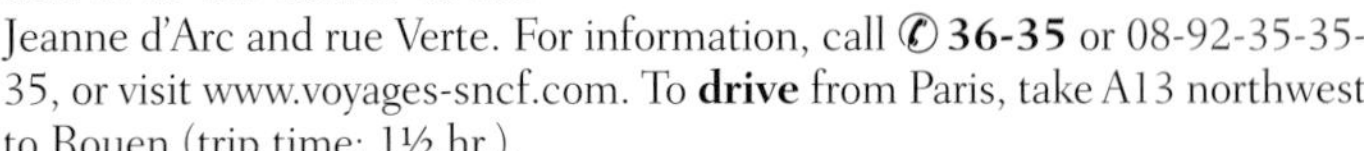

GETTING THERE From Paris's Gare St-Lazare, **trains** leave for Rouen about once an hour (trip time: 1½ hr.). The one-way fare is 20€. The station is at the corner of rue Jeanne d'Arc and rue Verte. For information, call ✆ **36-35** or 08-92-35-35-35, or visit www.voyages-sncf.com. To **drive** from Paris, take A13 northwest to Rouen (trip time: 1½ hr.).

GETTING AROUND The **Métro** is part of the city's MétroBus system (✆ **02-35-52-52-52**). It has one north–south line. The most central stations in Old Rouen are Palais de Justice and Gare (Rue Verte). Tickets cost 1.40€ per ride and are good for bus transfers within 1 hour of entering the Métro. Buy tickets from kiosks or automated machines.

VISITOR INFORMATION The **Office de Tourisme** is at 25 place de la Cathédrale (✆ **02-32-08-32-40;** www.rouentourisme.com).

Seeing the Sights

Cathédrale Notre-Dame de Rouen ★★★ Monet immortalized Rouen's cathedral (particularly the facade, with its galaxy of statues) in his paintings. The main door, **Porte Central,** is embellished with sculptures (some decapitated) depicting the Tree of Jesus. The 12th-century Porte St-Jean and Porte St-Etienne flank it. Consecrated in 1063, the cathedral, a symphony of lacy stonework, was reconstructed after suffering damage in World War II. Two towers distinguish it: **Tour de Beurre** was financed by the faithful who were willing to pay for the privilege of eating butter during Lent. Containing a carillon of 56 bells, the **Tour Lanterne (Lantern Tower)**—built in 1877 and using 740 tons of iron and bronze—rises to almost 150m (492 ft.).

Cathédrale Notre-Dame de Rouen.

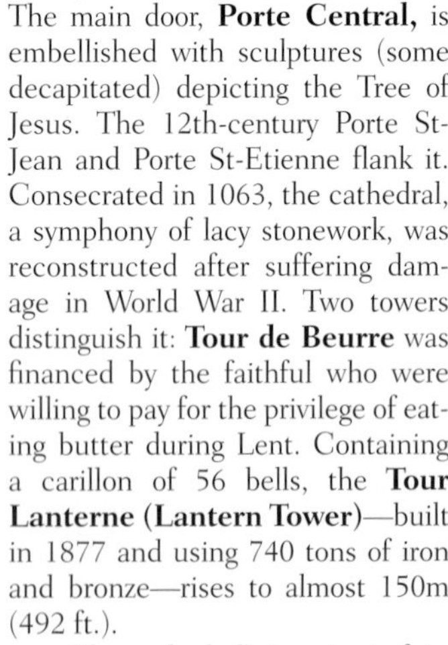

The cathedral's interior is fairly uniform. The choir is a masterpiece, with 14 soaring pillars. The Booksellers' Stairway, in the north

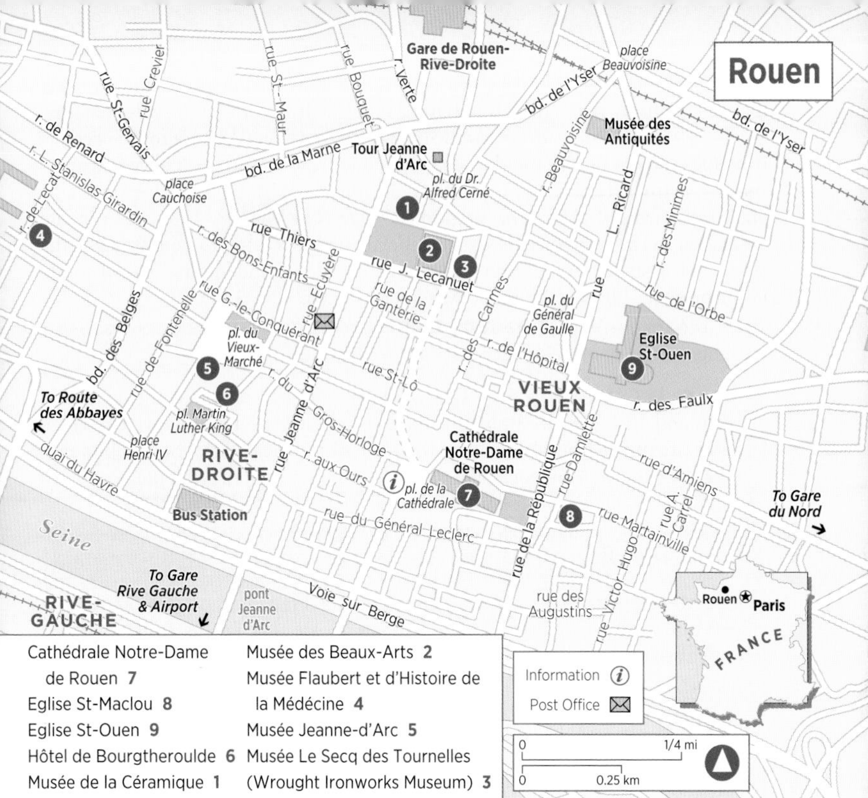

wing of the transept, is adorned with a stained-glass rose window that dates, in part, from the 1500s. The 13th-century chancel is beautiful, with simple lines. Especially interesting is the **Chapelle de la Vierge,** adorned with Renaissance tombs of the cardinals d'Amboise. Also entombed is the heart of Richard the Lion-Hearted, a token of his affection for the people of Rouen.

Behind the cathedral is the **Palais de l'Archevêché (Archbishop's Palace),** which was bombed in the war. Now it stands naked against the sky. The broken arches and rosette windows witnessed the trial of Joan of Arc in 1431, and her rehabilitation was proclaimed here in 1456.

Place de la Cathédrale. ✆ **02-35-71-71-60.** www.cathedrale-rouen.net. Free admission. Mon 2–6pm; Tues–Sat 7:30am–noon and 2–6pm; Sun 8am–6pm. Closed during Mass and on bank holidays.

Eglise St-Maclou ★★ St-Maclou was built in the Flamboyant Gothic style, with a step-gabled porch and cloisters, and is known for the 16th-century panels on its doors. Our favorite (to the left) is the Portail des Fontaines (Portal of the Fonts). The church was built in 1200, rebuilt in 1432, and consecrated in 1521; its lantern tower is from the 19th century. It sits on a square full of old Norman crooked-timbered buildings. Inside, pictures dating from June 4, 1944, document St-Maclou's destruction and its subsequent restoration.

3 place Barthélémy, behind the cathedral. ✆ **02-35-71-28-09.** Free admission. Apr–Oct daily 10am–noon and 2–6pm; Nov–Mar daily 10am–noon and 2–5:30pm.

Eglise St-Ouen ★★ This church is the outgrowth of a 7th-century Benedictine abbey. Flanked by four turrets, its 115m (377-ft.) octagonal lantern tower is called "the ducal crown of Normandy." The church represents the work of 5 centuries. Its nave is from the 15th century, its choir from the 14th (with 18th-c. railings), and its stained glass from the 14th to the 16th. On May 23, 1431, Joan of Arc was taken to the cemetery here, and officials sentenced her to be burned at the stake unless she recanted. She signed an abjuration, condemning herself to life imprisonment, but that sentence was later revoked.

Place du Général-de-Gaulle. ✆ **02-32-08-31-01.** Free admission. Mar–Oct Tues–Sun 10am–noon and 2–6pm; Nov–Feb Tues–Sun 10am–noon and 2–5:30pm.

Musée de la Céramique ★★ One of the great treasures here is the collection of 17th- and 18th-century Rouen faïence (opaquely glazed earthenware), which has a distinctive red hue because of the color of the local clay. The exhibits provide a showcase for Masseot Abaquesne, the premier French artist in faïence. An exceptional display is devoted to chinoiserie from 1699 to 1745.

94 rue Jeanne d'Arc. ✆ **02-35-07-31-74.** Admission 2.30€ adults, 1.55€ students, free for children 17 and under. Wed–Mon 10am–1pm and 2–6pm.

Musée des Beaux-Arts ★★★ This is one of France's most important provincial museums, with more than 65 rooms of art that ranges from medieval primitives to contemporary paintings. You'll find portraits by David and works by Delacroix and Ingres (seek out his *La Belle Zélie*). A Gérard David retable (altarpiece), *La Vierge et les saints (The Virgin and the Saints)*, is a masterpiece. One salon is devoted to Géricault, including his portrait of Delacroix. Other works here are by Veronese, Velázquez, Caravaggio, Rubens, Poussin, Fragonard, and Corot, and by Impressionists such as Monet, including several paintings of the Rouen cathedral.

Esplanade de Marcel Duchamp. ✆ **02-35-71-28-40.** Admission 4€ adults, 2.50€ students, free for children 17 and under. Mon and Wed–Sun 10am–6pm.

Musée Flaubert et d'Histoire de la Médécine Gustave Flaubert, author of *Madame Bovary,* was born in the director's quarters of Rouen's public hospital (his father was the director) in 1821. The room in which he was born is intact. You'll see the glass door that separated the Flauberts from the ward and its patients. Family furniture and medical paraphernalia are also displayed.

51 rue de Lecat. ✆ **02-35-15-59-95.** Admission 3€ adults, 1.50€ for students and ages 18–25, free for children 17 and under. Tues 10am–6pm; Wed–Sat 10am–noon and 2–6pm.

Musée Jeanne-d'Arc The life and the martyrdom of Joan of Arc, France's national heroine, are the focus here. In a vaulted cellar, dioramas, waxworks, and commentary in four languages tell the story of her life—from Domrémy, where she was born, to Rouen, where she was burned at the stake. The museum also contains a research library that concentrates on her life and the politics of her era. Visitors can hear, without charge, recorded narration on hand-held devices.

33 place du Vieux-Marché. ✆ **02-35-88-02-70.** www.jeanne-darc.com. Admission 4€ adults, 2.50€ students and children 17 and under. Apr–Sept daily 9:30am–7pm; Oct–Mar daily 10am–noon and 2–6:30pm.

Musée Le Secq des Tournelles (Wrought Ironworks Museum) ★ Housed in the 15th-century Eglise St-Laurent, this museum showcases ironwork, a Norman art form. Its collection ranges from what a critic once called "forthright masculine forging to lacy feminine filigree, from Roman keys to the needlepoint balustrade that graced Mme. de Pompadour's country mansion." The collection displays some 14,000 pieces.

2 rue Jacques-Villon. ✆ **02-35-88-42-92.** Admission 2.30€ adults, 1.55€ students, free for children 17 and under. Wed–Mon 10am–1pm and 2–6pm.

A Ride on "the Little Train"

The rubber-wheeled Petit Train (✆ 02-32-18-40-23) is the most fun way to see this ancient city. The 40-minute tours leave from the front of the tourist office, 25 place de la Cathédrale (✆ 02-32-08-32-40). Departures are daily at 10 and 11am and 2, 4, and 5pm. Tickets cost 6.50€ for adults and 4.50€ for children 12 and under. The train operates from April 1 to mid-October, with limited service over the Christmas holidays.

Place du Vieux-Marché ★ Joan of Arc was executed for heresy at the Old Marketplace. Tied to a stake, she was burned on May 30, 1431. Her ashes were gathered and tossed into the Seine. A modern church with stained-glass windows from St-Vincent sits in the center of a monumental complex in the square; beside it, a bronze cross marks the position of St. Joan's stake.

Rue du Gros-Horloge ★★ The "Street of the Great Clock" runs between the cathedral and place du Vieux-Marché. Now a pedestrian mall, it's named for an ornate gilt Renaissance clock mounted on an arch, Rouen's most popular monument. The arch bridges the street and connects to a Louis XV fountain with a bevy of cherubs and a bell tower. At night the bells still toll a curfew.

Shopping

Rouen was once one of France's major producers of the fine decorative ceramic ware known as ***faïence de Rouen.*** Examples of both antique and contemporary faïence abound, and it's worth picking up one or two pieces. For contemporary faïence, your best bet is **Faïencerie Carpentier Augy,** 26 rue St-Romain (✆ **02-35-88-77-47**). The well-known studio sells reproductions of historical styles in an array of colors.

Another Rouen specialty is ***les coffret de Rouen.*** The little hand-painted wooden boxes were all the rage during the 18th and 19th centuries. The original versions continue to be popular, but watch out for modern forgeries.

Rouen is also an antiques capital, with more than 80 vendors in the Old Town. The best hunting ground is in Vieux Rouen (the Old Town), along **rue Eau-de-Robec, place Barthélémy, rue Damiette,** and **rue St-Romain.** The city has two **flea markets,** on Saturday and Sunday at place St-Mare, and on Thursday at place des Emmurés. Medium- and large-scale auctions take place year-round at **Les Salles des Ventes** and 20 rue de la Croix-de-Fer (✆ **02-35-71-54-48**).

Other antiques shops worth visiting are **Michel Bertran,** 108 rue Molière (✆ **02-35-98-24-06**), with a good selection of 18th- and 19th-century paintings, especially by School of Rouen Impressionists; **Etienne Bertran,** 110 rue Molière (✆ **02-35-70-79-96**), with its collection of antique books dating to the 16th century; and **Patrick Chasset,** 12 rue de la Croix-de-Fer (✆ **02-35-70-59-97**), for toys and cards from the 1700s and 1800s, as well as bottles and glassware. You'll find watercolors by local artists, as well as antique Norman and English engravings.

Lovers of chocolate will discover a veritable paradise at **La Chocolatière,** 18 rue Guillaume-le-Conquérant (✆ **02-35-71-00-79**). The specialty that has attracted local gourmets for as long as anyone can remember is a praline-layered *paillardises,* rich in velvety chocolate that many readers describe as sinful.

Where to Stay

MODERATE

Hôtel de Dieppe The Gueret family has run this Best Western property, across from the train station, since 1880. Although it has been modernized, it's still a traditional French inn. The only problem might be noise, but double-glazed windows help, and the area quiets down after the last train from Paris arrives around 10:30pm. Rooms are compact, with comfortable beds. Half the guest rooms have a full bathroom, the rest just a shower. In **Le Quatre Saisons,** the adjoining rotisserie, you can enjoy dishes such as duckling *à la presse* (pressed duck) and sole poached in red wine.

Place Bernard-Tissot, Rouen 76000. www.hotel-dieppe.fr. ✆ **800/528-1234** in the U.S. and Canada, or 02-35-71-96-00. Fax 02-35-89-65-21. 41 units. 99€–120€ double. AE, DC, MC, V. Parking 5€. **Amenities:** Restaurant; bar; room service. *In room:* TV, hair dryer, free Wi-Fi.

INEXPENSIVE

Alive Hôtel De Québec In the historic core, this budget hotel stands close to the cathedral and its surrounding antiques shops. It is a very typical Norman city hotel, without any grand design, but offering affordable, comfortable rooms. Bedrooms are generally small, but each is well kept and many open onto a view of a garden. Suitable for families, some units have both a double bed and a single bed.

18–24 rue Québec, Rouen 76000. www.hotel-rouen.com. ✆ **02-35-70-09-38.** Fax 02-35-15-80-15. 38 units. 55€–60€ double; 68€–74€ triple. AE, MC, V. **Amenities:** Breakfast room. *In room:* TV, hair dryer, free Wi-Fi.

Hôtel Cardinal Not only is this hotel ideally located, it's also affordable. It's across from the cathedral (imagine waking up to a view of the majestic structure and the surrounding half-timbered buildings), in the middle of a neighborhood known for antiques, art galleries, and fine dining. With so much to do in the area, you won't mind the hotel's simplicity. Rooms are business-class plain with built-in furnishings and a small bathroom with tub or shower.

1 place de la Cathédrale, Rouen 76000. www.cardinal-hotel.fr. ✆ **02-35-70-24-42.** Fax 02-35-89-75-14. 18 units. 66€–86€ double; 86€–116€ triple or family room. MC, V. Parking 6€ nearby. Closed mid-Dec to mid-Jan. **Amenities:** Room service. *In room:* TV, hair dryer, free Wi-Fi.

Hôtel de la Cathédrale Built around a timbered and cobble-covered courtyard, this hotel is on a pedestrian street midway between the cathedral and the Eglise St-Maclou, opposite the Archbishop's Palace where Joan of Arc was tried. The remodeled rooms are well maintained and tastefully furnished, accessible by both stairs and an elevator. Breakfast is the only meal served.

12 rue St-Romain, Rouen 76000. www.hotel-de-la-cathedrale.fr. ✆ **02-35-71-57-95.** Fax 02-35-70-15-54. 26 units. 70€–98€ double. AE, MC, V. Parking 10€ nearby. **Amenities:** Tea lounge; babysitting; room service. *In room:* TV, hair dryer, free Wi-Fi.

Hôtel du Vieux Carré ★ In a restored half-timbered 18th-century house, this is one of the most charming and tranquil lodgings in Rouen. After inspecting too many impersonally furnished hotels, we found this one a surprise and a delight. Patrick Beaumont, the enthusiastic and much-traveled owner, has tastefully decorated the midsize guest rooms in comfortable rustic fashion. Unusual for central Rouen, its restaurant opens onto a flower-filled courtyard.

34 rue Ganterie, Rouen 76000. www.vieux-carre.fr. ✆ **02-35-71-67-70.** Fax 02-35-71-19-17. 13 units. 58€–65€ double. AE, MC, V. **Amenities:** Restaurant (lunch only); tearoom/cafe. *In room:* TV, free Wi-Fi.

Where to Eat

Gill ★★★ MODERN FRENCH The best restaurant in town sits beside the traffic of the Seine's quays. The minimalist decor, with high-tech lighting and accessories, is an appropriate backdrop for the sophisticated cuisine of Gilles Tournadre. Who can resist ravioli stuffed with foie gras and served in a bouillon sprinkled with fresh truffles? How about terrine of artichoke with fresh truffles or roasted white turbot with fresh asparagus flavored with Parmesan? The best items on the menu are pan-fried foie gras of duckling served with caramelized turnips and a turnip-green salad; a salad of crayfish tails with tomato-and-black-pepper chutney; and the most famous and popular specialty, Rouen-style pigeon with vegetables floating in densely concentrated consommé.

9 quai de la Bourse. ✆ **02-35-71-16-14.** www.gill.fr. Reservations required far in advance. Main courses 30€–57€; business lunch 38€; fixed-price dinner 95€. AE, DC, MC, V. Tues–Sat noon–1:45pm and 7:30–9:30pm. Closed Aug and 2 weeks in Apr.

Les Nymphéas ★★★ MODERN FRENCH One of the most appealing restaurants in Rouen bears the name of a painting by Monet (*Water Lilies*). The setting is a 16th-century half-timbered house that fits gracefully into the centrally located neighborhood (place du Vieux-Marché). The restaurant features sophisticated, savory cuisine. It's celebrated for its warm foie gras with cider sauce; wild duckling Rouennais style, served with wild mushrooms and caramelized onions; and *civet* (stew) of lobster with Sauternes. An award-winning dessert that evokes the Norman countryside is a warm soufflé flavored with apples and Calvados.

7 rue de la Pie. ✆ **02-35-89-26-69.** www.lesnympheas-rouen.com. Reservations required. Main courses 24€–55€; fixed-price menu 40€–70€. AE, MC, V. Tues–Sat 12:15–2pm and 7:30–9:45pm. Closed late Aug to mid-Sept.

Pascaline TRADITIONAL FRENCH This informal bistro is often filled with regulars and has been a favorite since its opening in 1880. The decor hasn't changed much since. The cheapest fixed-price menus are among the best bargains in town. Menu items include seafood dishes such as pavé of monkfish with roughly textured mustard sauce, breast of duck cooked in beer, and savory *pot-au-feu maison* (house stew). Don't come for refined cuisine—you should expect hearty, time-tested favorites.

5 rue de la Poterne. ✆ **02-35-89-67-44.** www.pascaline.fr. Reservations recommended. Main courses 10€–20€; fixed-price menu 13€–29€. AE, MC, V. Daily noon–2:30pm and 7–11pm.

Rouen After Dark

For highbrow entertainment, **Théâtre des Arts,** 7 rue du Dr.-Rambert (✆ **02-35-71-41-36**), presents ballet, opera, and classical music. **Théâtre des Deux Rives,** 48 rue Louis-Ricard (✆ **02-35-89-63-41**), presents plays in French. **Théâtre des Arts/Opéra Léonard de Vinci,** 7 rue du Dr-Rambert (✆ **02-35-**

Finding Old Normandy in Calvados Country

For a taste of old Normandy, motorists heading from Rouen to Deauville should stop in Pont-Audemer, 50km (31 miles) west of Rouen. On the banks of the River Risle, Pont-Audemer is in the heart of Calvados country. In spite of war damage, Pont-Audemer retains much of its old look, especially if you wander its historic streets, rue de la Licorne (unicorn) and rue de la République. Along rue de la République, look for Eglise St-Ouen, dating from the 11th century.

71-41-36), has a busy schedule of classical and contemporary opera. A variety of concerts takes place at **Eglise St-Ouen,** place du Général-de-Gaulle. For information about who's playing, contact the tourist office.

Much of the nightlife, especially pubs, centers on place du Vieux-Marché. **La Bohème,** 18 rue St-Amand (✆ **02-35-71-53-99;** www.laboheme-discotheque.com), is a small discothèque with a cozy, publike ambience. Many students meet at the **Underground Pub,** 26 rue des Champs-Maillets (✆ **02-35-98-44-84**), which has a street-level bar and an underground bar fitted with wood and British bric-a-brac.

WINE BAR **Le P'tit Zinc,** 20 place du Vieux-Marché (✆ **02-35-89-39-69**), is a bistro-style wine bar with early-1900s decor and one of the best wine selections in town. Of course, you can order Norman cider as well.

HONFLEUR ★★

201km (125 miles) NW of Paris; 63km (39 miles) NE of Caen

At the mouth of the Seine opposite Le Havre, Honfleur is one of Normandy's most charming fishing ports. Having escaped major damage in World War II, the working port looks like an antique. Thanks to the pont de Normande, the bridge that links Honfleur to Le Havre, visitors flock here. Honfleur is 500 years older than Le Havre, dating from the 11th century. Artists, including Daubigny, Corot, and Monet, have long favored this township.

Essentials

GETTING THERE If you're **driving** from Pont l'Evêque or other points south (including Paris), D579 leads to the major boulevard, rue de la République. Follow it to the town center. Driving time from Paris is 2 to 2½ hours.

There's no direct **train** service into Honfleur. From Paris, take one of the dozen or so daily trains from Gare St-Lazare to Deauville for 30€ one-way. From there, bus no. 20 makes the 25-minute ride to Honfleur; the one-way fare is about 2.15€. From Rouen, take the train to Le Havre and transfer to bus no. 50, which costs 4.10€ each way, for the 30-minute ride to Honfleur. Several **buses** run daily between Caen and Honfleur (trip time: 2 hr.); the one-way fare is 7.20€. For information, call **Bus Verts du Calvados** (✆ **08-10-21-42-14**).

VISITOR INFORMATION The **Office de Tourisme** is on quai Lepaulmier (✆ **02-31-89-23-30;** www.ot-honfleur.fr).

Seeing the Town

Begin your tour, which should take about an hour, at place de la Porte-de-Rouen. Stroll along the **Vieux Bassin,** the old harbor, taking in the fishing boats and narrow, slate-roofed houses. On the north side of the basin, the former governor's house, **Lieutenance,** dates from the 16th century. Nearby is the **Eglise Ste-Catherine,** place Ste-Catherine (✆ **02-31-89-11-83**), constructed of timber by 15th-century shipbuilders. The church's wooden belfry is on the other side of the street. The church is open July and August daily from 8am to 8pm, September through June daily 8:30am to noon and 2 to 6pm.

Maisons Satie Opened in 1998, this high-tech museum honors Honfleur's native son Erik Satie in the house where he was born in 1866. Satie was a "complete artist": He became most famous for his music, but he was also a painter and acted as a muse and inspiration to Picasso, Braque, Cocteau, Debussy, Ravel, and Stravinsky. This is not a traditional museum. The walk-through exhibitions incorporate sound, light, and recordings of Satie's compositions. Visitors wear high-tech helmets that transmit sound, which allows for a degree of play and experimentation in some of the exhibits.

67 bd. Charles V. ✆ **02-31-89-11-11.** Admission 5.10€ adults, 3.60€ ages 10–17, free for children 9 and under. May–Sept Wed–Mon 10am–7pm; Oct–Apr Wed–Mon 11am–6pm. Closed Jan–Feb 15.

Musée d'Ethnographie et d'art populaire This place celebrates the unique cultural and aesthetic contributions of Normandy to the rest of Europe. You'll find old furniture, lace headdresses, embroidery, candle-making equipment, and farm implements, as well as several rooms outfitted with period art and antiques.

Quai St-Etienne. ✆ **02-31-89-14-12.** Admission 3.50€ adults, 2.10€ students and children 10–18, free for children 9 and under. July–Aug daily 10am–noon and 2–6:30pm; Apr–June and Sept Tues–Fri 10am–noon and 2–6pm; Oct to mid-Nov and mid-Feb to Mar Tues–Fri 2–5:30pm, Sat–Sun 10am–noon and 2:30–5:30pm.

Honfleur.

Musée Eugène-Boudin This museum showcases a good collection of works by the painters who flocked to this port when Impressionism was new. The largest assortment is of the pastels and paintings of Boudin.

Place Erik-Satie. ✆ **02-31-89-54-00.** Admission 5.30€ adults, 3.80€ students and children 10 and over. Mar 15–Sept Wed–Mon 10am–noon and 2–6pm; Oct–Mar 14 Wed–Mon 2:30–5:30pm, Sat–Sun 10am–noon and 2:30–5:30pm. Closed Jan to mid-Feb, July 14, and Christmas.

NaturoSpace Inaugurated in 1999 on the western outskirts of town, adjacent to the seacoast, Honfleur's modern attraction displays the flora and butterfly life of some of the most exotic climates on Earth. Designed like an enormous greenhouse bursting with tropical plants and butterflies, it contains a labyrinth of walkways that cut through Normandy's approximation of a tropical rainforest. Most visitors spend about an hour in this environment, which is in distinct contrast to the old Norman ethnicity that's otherwise associated with Honfleur.

Bd. Charles V. ✆ **02-31-81-77-00.** www.naturospace.com. Admission 7.80€ adults, 6€ students and children 13 and under, family package 30€. Apr–June and Sept daily 10am–1pm and 2–7pm; Feb–Nov 10am–1pm and 2–5:30pm; July–Aug daily 10am–7pm.

Where to Stay

Restaurant/Hôtel L'Absinthe (see "Where to Eat," on p. 315) also rents rooms.

Castel Albertine ★ 🎁 Management takes great care to maintain the character of this home of Albert Sorel, a 19th-century historian and scholar. The impressive house, of red brick and rose-hued stone, is a 3-minute walk from the port. It is a handsome, welcoming hotel. All of the individually decorated rooms have floor-to-ceiling windows that open onto views of gardens and trees. Bathrooms are small but tidily kept, with either a tub or a shower.

19 cours Albert-Manuel, Honfleur 14600. www.honfleurhotels.com. ✆ **02-31-98-85-56.** Fax 02-31-98-83-18. 27 units. 80€–150€ double. MC, V. Parking 10€. Closed Jan. **Amenities:** Bar; babysitting; room service; sauna. *In room:* TV, hair dryer, free Wi-Fi.

La Ferme St-Siméon ★★★ An old farmhouse is the focal point of this 17th-century half-timbered slate hotel, one of Normandy's most elegant and prestigious inns. It's in the hills above Honfleur, about 1.5km (1 mile) from the old port. The shimmering water of the English Channel draws artists to the hilltop inn, said to be where Impressionism was born in the 19th century. Much of the hotel has terra-cotta floors, carved wood, and copper and faïence touches. Guest rooms, which are formal and comfortable, have fabric-covered walls. Some rooms contain exposed half-timbering or ceiling beams; others hold canopy-covered beds. Most have antique or heirloom furnishings. Bathrooms are beautifully maintained; about half have tub/showers.

20 rue Adolphe-Marais, Honfleur 14600. www.fermesaintsimeon.fr. ✆ **02-31-81-78-00.** Fax 02-31-89-48-48. 34 units. 220€–450€ double; 550€–850€ suite. AE, MC, V. **Amenities:** Restaurant; bar; babysitting; indoor pool; room service; sauna; spa. *In room:* TV, hair dryer, minibar, free Wi-Fi.

Le Manoir de Butin ★ Surrounded by well-landscaped grounds, this villa château evokes a more gracious era at the turn of the 20th century. The villa's half-timbered and dormers–styled structure suggest the frivolity of late-19th-century seaside architecture in Normandy. The bedrooms are some of the most intimate and cozy in the area, each with beautiful furnishings, often with a poster bed along with marble-clad bathrooms. *Fin de siècle* architectural details include a grand staircase, bay or bow windows, and wooden balconies.

Phare du Butin, Honfleur 14600. www.hotel-lemanoir.fr. ✆ **02-31-81-63-00.** Fax 02-31-89-59-23. 10 units. 120€–360€ double. AE, MC, V. Closed Nov and mid-Dec to Jan. **Amenities:** Restaurant; room service. *In room:* TV, minibar, free Wi-Fi.

Les Maisons de Léa ★★ A sense of old-fashioned coziness abounds here. In 1900, the hotel owners converted a 16th-century fish market and added plumbing and partitions between what are now comfortable, warmly decorated guest rooms. Rooms have individual color schemes and canopy-covered beds. The accommodations, though modest, are perfect for an overnight stop. All bathrooms contain showers, but only about a third have tubs.

Place Ste-Catherine, Honfleur 14600. www.lesmaisonsdelea.com. ✆ **02-31-14-49-49.** Fax 02-31-89-28-61. 30 units. 145€–205€ double; 205€–295€ suite. AE, MC, V. Bus: 20 or 50. **Amenities:** Snack bar; babysitting; room service (breakfast only). *In room:* TV, hair dryer, free Wi-Fi.

Where to Eat

La Terrasse et l'Assiette ★★ TRADITIONAL FRENCH Outfitted "in the Norman style" with heavy beams and lots of exposed brick, the gourmet citadel of Honfleur attracts an upscale international clientele. Dishes include crayfish with sautéed vermicelli and truffles, an omelet studded with chunks of lobster, unctuous fried foie gras served with lentils, and braised scallops with a purée of Brussels sprouts and smoked-ham sauce. Leave room for *petit gateau moelleux au chocolat* (very moist chocolate-fudge cake). In summer, if the weather is agreeable, ask for a table on the terrace, overlooking the historic Eglise Ste-Catherine.

8 place Ste-Catherine. ✆ **02-31-89-31-33.** www.laterrasseetlassiette.com. Reservations recommended. Main courses 26€–40€; fixed-price menu 32€–54€. AE, MC, V. Wed–Sun noon–2pm and 7:30–9pm. Closed Jan.

Restaurant/Hôtel L'Absinthe ★★ TRADITIONAL FRENCH This tavern, named for the drink preferred by many 19th-century writers, is known for its beautiful decor, extravagant portions, and well-prepared cuisine. Rooms in the 16th-century building have beamed ceilings, parquet floors, and furniture that matches the architectural grandeur. The restaurant consists of two dining rooms (one from the 15th c. with exposed beams and exposed stone, and one from the 17th c. with a stately fireplace). The menu changes frequently. The best menu items include foie gras with caramelized ginger and apples, and sea bass roasted with laurel leaves and red wine.

If you're taken with the place, you can rent a room or the suite. A double runs 115€ to 185€, and the suite goes for 250€. Parking costs 12€.

10 quai de la Quarantaine, Honfleur 14600. ✆ **02-31-89-39-00.** Fax 02-31-89-53-60. www.absinthe.fr. Reservations required. Main courses 26€–48€; fixed-price menu 34€–65€. AE, DC, MC, V. Daily 12:15–3pm and 7:15–10pm. Closed Nov 15–Dec 17.

DEAUVILLE ★★★

206km (128 miles) NW of Paris; 47km (29 miles) NE of Caen

Deauville has been associated with the rich and famous since the duc de Morny, Napoleon III's half-brother, founded it as an upscale resort in 1859. In 1913, it entered sartorial history when Coco Chanel launched her career here, opening a boutique selling tiny hats that challenged the fashion of huge-brimmed hats loaded with flowers and fruit. (Coco's point of view: "How can the mind breathe under those things?")

Essentials

GETTING THERE There are 6 to 10 daily **rail** connections from Paris's Gare St-Lazare (trip time: 2 hr., 15 min.); prices start at 30€ one-way. The rail depot lies between Trouville and Deauville, south of town. Take a taxi from the station. **Bus Verts du Calvados** (✆ **08-10-21-42-14;** www.busverts.fr) serves the Normandy coast from Caen to Le Havre. To **drive** from Paris (trip time: 2½ hr.), take A13 west to Pont L'Evêque, and then follow N177 east to Deauville.

VISITOR INFORMATION The **Office de Tourisme** is on place de la Mairie (✆ **02-31-14-40-00;** www.deauville.org).

SPECIAL EVENTS For a week in September, the **Deauville Festival of American Film** (✆ **02-31-14-40-00;** www.festival-deauville.com) honors movies made in the United States. Actors, producers, directors, and writers flock here and briefly eclipse the high rollers at the casinos and the horse-racing and polo crowd.

Exploring the Resort

Coco Chanel cultivated a tradition of elegance that survives in Deauville and in its smaller and less prestigious neighbor Trouville, on the opposite bank of the Toques (see the next section). Don't expect flash; in its way, restrained and ever-so-polite Deauville is the most British seaside resort in France.

However, in its heart, Deauville is less English than French. It has even been dubbed "Paris's 21st arrondissement." The crowds here tend to be urban and hip. Deauville is stylish and not (by anyone's definition) inexpensive.

With its golf courses, casinos, deluxe hotels, La Touques and Clairefontaine racetracks, regattas, a yachting harbor, polo grounds, and tennis courts, Deauville is a formidable contender for the business of the upper class. Looking for a charming place to stroll? Head for boutique-lined **rue Eugène-Colas, place Morny** (named for the resort's founder), and **place du Casino.**

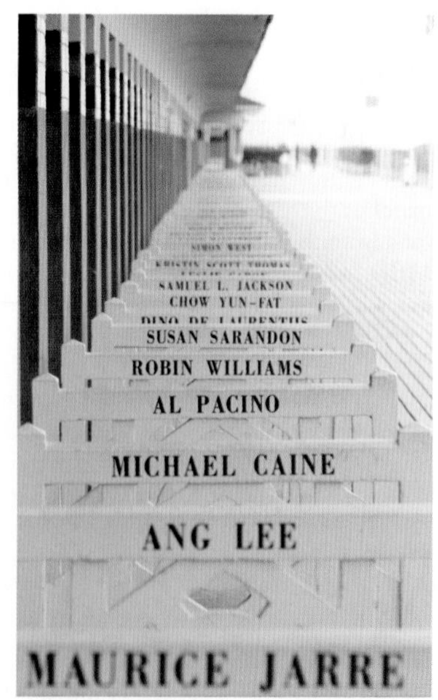

Les Planches, Deauville.

BEACHES Expect to spend time on Deauville's boardwalk, **Les Planches,** a promenade running parallel to the beach. Beaux Arts and half-timbered Norman-inspired buildings line its edges. In summer, especially August, parasols dot the beach and oiled bodies cover seemingly every inch of sand. The resort's only beach is **Plage de Deauville,** a strip that's part of La Côte Fleurie.

If you're looking for a gay and nude beach, you can go to **Merville-France-Ville,** 39km (24 miles) from Deauville toward Caen. But considering how permissive most Deauville fans are, many gay travelers feel perfectly comfortable here.

Access to every beach in Normandy is free; in Deauville, you'll pay from 2€ per hour for parking in any of the many public lots beside the sea.

The **Piscine Municipale,** boulevard de la Mer (✆ **02-31-14-02-17**), is a large indoor seawater pool. Depending on the season, bathers pay 4€ to 5€ per person. Hours are July and August daily 9:30am to 7:30pm, June and September daily 10am to 7pm, and October to December and February to May daily 10:30am to 7pm.

HORSE RACES/POLO You can watch horses every day from late June to early October. There's either a race at 2pm or a polo match at 3pm. The venues are the **Hippodrome de Deauville La Touques,** boulevard Mauger (✆ **02-31-14-20-00**), in the heart of town near the Mairie de Deauville (town hall); and the **Hippodrome de Deauville Clairefontaine,** route de Clairefontaine (✆ **02-31-14-69-00**), within the city limits, 2km (1¼ miles) west of the center.

Shopping

This seaside town has a pedestrian shopping area between the polo field and the port; the main drags are **rue Mirabeau, rue Albert-Fracasse,** and the west end of **avenue de la République.** The leading shops, selling some of the world's most elegant merchandise (with prices to match), cluster on **rue Eugène-Colas, place Morny,** and **place du Casino.** At **La Cave de Deauville,** 48 rue Mirabeau (✆ **02-31-87-35-36;** www.cave-de-deauville.com), you'll find a wide selection of apple ciders, Calvados, and the apple aperitif known as *pommeau.*

For an overview of the bounty of the fertile Norman soil, head for the **Marché Publique** (open-air market) in the place du Marché, adjacent to place Morny. From July to mid-September, it's open daily 8am to 1pm. The rest of the year, market days are Tuesday, Friday, Saturday, and occasionally Sunday. In addition to fruits, vegetables, poultry, cider, wine, and cheese, you'll find cookware, porcelain tableware, and cutlery.

Where to Stay

EXPENSIVE

Hôtel du Golf Barrière ★★★ ☺ Golfers gravitate to this half-timbered hotel created by the Lucien Barrière chain in the late 1980s. The location, in the hills above Deauville, about 3km (1¾ miles) from the center of town, creates an aura of country-club tranquillity. Outfitted in English country house style, it's one of the few hotels in Normandy with its own golf course. If the links aren't your thing, you might consider the Normandy or Royal hotels (reviewed below, and all three Lucien Barrière properties). The children's center and activities program are the best in Deauville. Rooms come in a wide range of sizes; those in back open onto the links, those in front have better views of the Channel. The best rooms, called "prestige luxe," feature antique-style furnishings, French windows, and spacious bathrooms and balconies.

At New-Golf Club, Mont Canisy, St-Arnoult Deauville 14800. www.lucienbarriere.com. ✆ **02-31-14-24-00.** Fax 02-31-14-24-01. 178 units. 245€–620€ double; 495€–655€ junior suite. AE, DC, MC, V. Closed mid-Nov to mid-Mar. From Deauville, take D278 south for 2.5km (1½ miles). **Amenities:** 2 restaurants; bar; babysitting; children's center; exercise room; 27-hole golf course; massage; heated outdoor pool; room service; rooms for those w/limited mobility; sauna; smoke-free rooms; 3 tennis courts. *In room:* TV, hair dryer, minibar, Wi-Fi.

Normandy Barrière ★★★ ☺ This is the most famous hotel in Deauville, a legendary place that dates back to the Edwardian age. The Anglo-Norman design includes half-timbering, dovecotes, turrets, and gables; the 1912 building resembles a cozy but stately English country house. A renovation updated all the rooms, public areas, and security systems. Because of its extensive facilities for children, including a nursery and babysitting, it attracts upscale families with children—although that doesn't interfere with the hotel's image as a chic nest for French celebrities. During the Deauville Festival of American Film, it attracts French stars, the press, and jury members. Originally built to house well-heeled gamblers from the nearby casino, it continues to draw the gambling crowd today.

38 rue Jean-Mermoz, Deauville 14800. www.lucienbarriere.com. ✆ **02-31-98-66-22.** Fax 02-31-98-66-23. 298 units. 319€–719€ double; 700€–1,020€ suite. AE, DC, MC, V. Parking 30€ in garage. **Amenities:** Restaurant; children's dining room; bar; babysitting; exercise room; heated outdoor pool; room service; steam room; 2 tennis courts. *In room:* TV, hair dryer, minibar, Wi-Fi (8€ per hr.).

Royal-Barrière ★★★ The Royal adjoins the casino and fronts a park near the Channel. It rises like a palace, with columns and exposed timbers. Although it doesn't have the insider cachet of the Normandy Barrière (see above), it is a grander and more opulent hotel. It's a member of Leading Hotels of the World, and its architecture evokes an Edwardian-era grand palace hotel. The hotel was built in 1913 on architectural principles conceived by Gustav Eiffel (an iron skeleton supports walls and ceilings). Post-millennium, the hotel concluded a 5-year renovation program that included virtually every aspect of the establishment, including elegant bathrooms with tubs and showers. The decor of the guest rooms, conceived by megadesigner Jacques Garcia, is a reinterpretation of Directoire and Napoleon III styles. During the Deauville Festival of American Film, the U.S. stars stay here.

Bd. Eugène-Cornuché, Deauville 14800. www.lucienbarriere.com. ✆ **02-31-98-66-33.** Fax 02-31-98-66-34. 290 units. 330€–750€ double; 685€–1,065€ suite. AE, DC, MC, V. Closed Nov to early Mar. **Amenities:** 2 restaurants; bar; health club; heated outdoor pool; room service; sauna. *In room:* TV, hair dryer, minibar, Wi-Fi (8€ per hr.).

INEXPENSIVE

Hôtel Ibis Built in the 1980s as part of the nationwide chain, the Ibis is on the periphery of Deauville about 1km (½ mile) from the casino. The modern building, overlooking the harbor, is one of the best bargains in town. Rooms are comfortable and tidy, but decorated in dull chain style. The small tiled bathrooms contain showers and the restaurant offers a traditional French menu.

9–10 quai de la Marine, Deauville 14800. www.hotelibis.com. ✆ **02-31-14-50-00.** Fax 02-31-14-50-05. 95 units. 76€–175€ double; 120€–185€ duplex suite for 2–6 people. AE, DC, MC, V. Parking 10€. **Amenities:** Restaurant; bar; babysitting. *In room:* A/C, TV, free Wi-Fi.

Hôtel Le Trophée This modern replica of a half-timbered medieval building is in the middle of Deauville, 150m (492 ft.) from the beach. The small rooms have contemporary furniture and private balconies overlooking the shopping streets.

Bathrooms are also small. A sun terrace on the roof provides a bird's-eye view of the town and a more private tanning area than the beach. If you plan to eat here, enjoy at least one meal under the stars in the patio courtyard garden. The hotel has also transformed what was a private house, immediately across the street, into an annex, creating an additional 15 suites.

81 rue du Général-Leclerc, Deauville 14800. www.letrophee.com. ✆ **02-31-88-45-86.** Fax 02-31-88-07-94. 35 units. 59€–159€ double; 145€–238€ suite. AE, DC, MC, V. Parking 10€. **Amenities:** Restaurant; babysitting; exercise room; heated outdoor pool; sauna; steam bath. *In room:* TV, hair dryer, minibar, Wi-Fi (20€ per day).

L'Augeval ★ Across from the racetrack and just blocks from the beach and casino, this hotel mixes city flair and country charm. The former private villa was built in the early 1900s and sits amid well-kept lawns and gardens. The cozy rooms range from medium to spacious, and each has at least one high-quality antique. Some units have Jacuzzis.

15 av. Hocquart-de-Turtot, Deauville 14800. www.augeval.com. ✆ **02-31-81-13-18.** Fax 02-31-81-00-40. 52 units. 95€–110€ double; 222€–333€ suite. AE, DC, MC, V. Parking 8€. **Amenities:** Bar; babysitting; exercise room; small heated outdoor pool; room service. *In room:* TV, hair dryer, minibar, free Wi-Fi.

Where to Eat

Chez Miocque TRADITIONAL FRENCH This hip cafe near the casino and the boutiques does a bustling business at its sidewalk tables. The place serves hearty brasserie-style food, including succulent lamb stew with spring vegetables, filet of skate with cream-based caper sauce, and steaks. Portions are filling, and the atmosphere can be lively. The dish of the day is always from the sea.

81 rue Eugène-Colas. ✆ **02-31-88-09-52.** Reservations recommended. Main courses 19€–43€. AE, MC, V. July–Sept daily 9am–midnight; mid-Feb to June and Oct–Dec Fri–Mon noon–4pm and 7–11:30pm.

Le Ciro's Barrière ★★★ FRENCH/SEAFOOD Hot on the resort's social scene, Le Ciro's serves Deauville's best seafood. It's expensive but worth it. If you want a bit of everything, ask for the *plateau de fruits de mer,* brimming with lobster and shellfish. For an elaborate appetizer, we recommend lobster salad with truffles. Marmite of scallops with sweet sauterne wine and saffron makes a superb main course. The collection of Bordeaux wine is exceptional. The ambience is airy, stylish, and evocative of the Belle Epoque heyday of Deauville.

Promenade des Planches. ✆ **02-31-14-31-31.** Fax 02-31-88-32-02. Reservations required. Main courses 23€–54€; fixed-price menu 29€. AE, DC, MC, V. Thurs–Mon 12:30–2:45pm and 7:30–9:30pm. Closed 2 weeks in Jan.

Le Spinnaker ★ NORMAN Owner-chef Pascal Angenard's charming yellow-and-blue restaurant features regional cuisine. The satisfying specialties include terrine of foie gras with four spices, roast lobster with cider vinegar and cream-enriched potatoes, slow-cooked veal flank, and hot apple tart. Pascal recommends roast turbot flavored with shallots *en confit.* A fine array of wines can accompany your meal. On some nights, a dish here or there might not be sublime, but most are excellent.

52 rue Mirabeau. ✆ **02-31-88-24-40.** www.spinnakerdeauville.com. Reservations required. Main courses 20€–50€; fixed-price menu 38€–52€. AE, DC, MC, V. Wed–Sun noon–1:30pm and 7:30–10pm. Closed June 21–28, Nov 15–30, and Jan 2–31.

Deauville After Dark

Opened in 1912, the **Casino de Deauville,** rue Edmond-Blanc (✆ **02-31-14-31-14;** www.lucienbarriere.com), is one of France's premier casinos. Its original Belle Epoque core has been expanded with a theater, a nightclub, three restaurants, and an extensive collection of slot machines (*machines à sous*). The casino distinguishes areas for slot machines from more formal locales containing such games as roulette, baccarat, blackjack, and poker. The slots are open daily from 11am to 2am (to 3am Fri and 4am Sat) and have no dress code; access to this area is free. The areas containing *les jeux traditionnels* (traditional games) are open daily at 4pm and close between 3 and 4am, depending on business and the day of the week. Entrance is free, and you must present a passport or identity card to gain admission. The most interesting nights are Friday and Saturday, when the cabaret theater and all the restaurants are open. The theater presents glittering, moderately titillating shows at 10:30pm on Friday and Saturday. Admission is 25€ Friday, rising to 29€ on Saturday. Dinner and the show costs 55€ to 59€.

If it's a dance club you're looking for, head to the high-energy **Y Club,** 14 bis rue Désiré-le-Hoc (✆ **02-31-88-30-91**), which charges a cover of 15€. For salsa, merengue, and reggae, visit **Brok Café,** 14 av. du Général-de-Gaulle (✆ **02-31-81-30-81**). If you want to re-create the restrained but decadent ambience of the 1970s, consider **Le Régine's,** inside Deauville's casino, rue Edmond-Blanc (✆ **02-31-14-31-96**).

Dancing Les Planches, Le Bois Lauret, Blonville (✆ **02-31-87-58-09**), 4km (2½ miles) from Deauville, is a club where you'll find up-to-date music, a dance floor, and even an indoor swimming pool near an indoor/outdoor bar. It's open from 11pm until dawn every Friday and Saturday night.

TROUVILLE ★★

206km (128 miles) NW of Paris; 43km (27 miles) NE of Caen

Across the Touques River from the fashionable (and expensive) Deauville, Trouville feels more like a fishing port. The town is similar to Honfleur, but with fewer boutiques and art galleries. Don't expect the grand atmosphere of Deauville; Trouville is more low-key. It's also less dependent on resort euros; when the bathers leave its splendid sands, Trouville continues to thrive—its resident population of fishermen sees to that.

Essentials

GETTING THERE There are **rail** connections from Gare St-Lazare in Paris to Trouville (see the "Deauville" section, earlier in this chapter). **Bus Verts du Calvados** (www.busverts.fr) links Trouville, Deauville, and the surrounding region with the rest of Normandy. For bus information, call the **Gare Routière** (✆ **08-10-21-42-14**). If you're traveling by **car** from Deauville, drive west along D180.

VISITOR INFORMATION The **Office de Tourisme** is at 32 quai Fernand-Moureaux (✆ **02-31-14-60-70;** www.trouvillesurmer.org).

Exploring the Town

In the heyday of Napoleon III, during the 1860s, *boulevardiers* (men about town) used to bring their wives and families to Trouville and stash their mistresses

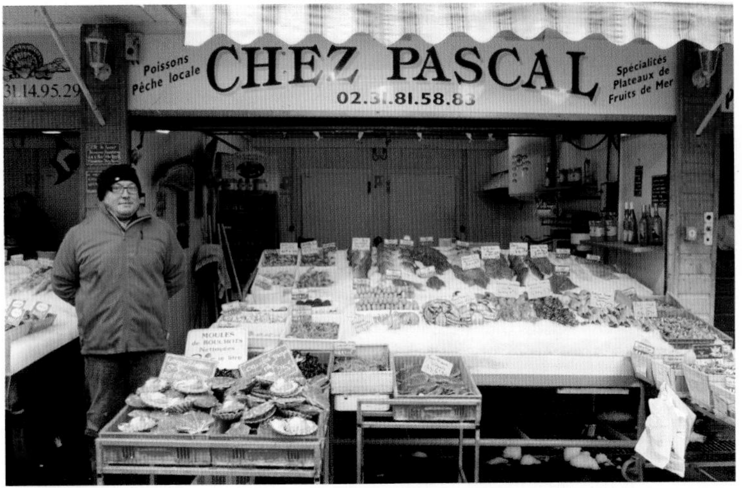

Seafood on offer in Trouville.

in Deauville. Deauville was just coming into existence; it's a planned city, with straight avenues and a sense of industrial-age orderliness. By contrast, the narrow, labyrinthine alleyways of Trouville hint at its origins as a medieval fishing port.

Our recommendation? Explore Trouville, enjoying its low-key charm, and when you tire of it, join the caravan of traffic that heads across the river to the bright lights and glamour of Deauville.

Les Planches is a stretch of seafront boardwalk dotted with concessions on one side and overlooking the sea on the other. In midsummer, expect lots of flesh sprawled on the sands in various states of undress. There's only one beach, **Plage de Trouville** (though when you've tired of it, you only have to cross the river to reach the Plage de Deauville). On Trouville's seafront is the **Piscine de Trouville,** promenade des Planches (✆ **02-31-14-48-10**), an indoor freshwater pool that gets very crowded in summer. Depending on the season, bathers pay 6€ to 7€ per person. Hours are July and August daily 9:30am to 7:30pm, June and September daily 10am to 7pm, and October to May daily 10:30am to 7pm.

Where to Stay

Best Western Hostellerie du Vallon ★ The best place to stay in town is this modern hotel constructed in a traditional Norman style. Lying a short walk from the beach, the hotel is far more affordable than so many of the properties at neighboring Deauville. Well run and spacious, it boasts a modern interior with such facilities as an indoor swimming pool, which makes it a good year-round choice. Many of the attractively and comfortably furnished bedrooms open onto private balconies with a view.

12 rue Sylvestre Lassere, Trouville 14360. www.hostellerie-du-vallon.com. ✆ **02-31-98-35-00.** 62 units. 120€–180€ double; 200€–260€ junior suite. AE, DC, MC, V. **Amenities:** Bar; exercise room; Jacuzzi; indoor pool; sauna; steam room. *In room:* TV, hair dryer, minibar.

Le Beach Hotel Although a poor relation to the palaces of Deauville, Le Beach Hotel provides comfort at more affordable prices. The seven-story hotel emerges from a lackluster lot only 45m (148 ft.) from the beach. Its average-size rooms have modern furniture and comfortable beds, plus views of Trouville harbor; most bathrooms have showers only.

1 quai Albert-1er, Trouville 14360. ✆ **02-31-98-12-00.** Fax 02-31-87-30-29. 110 units. 105€–220€ double. AE, DC, MC, V. Parking 9€. **Amenities:** Restaurant; bar; babysitting; indoor pool; room service. *In room:* TV, minibar, free Wi-Fi.

Where to Eat

La Petite Auberge NORMAN For a quality meal, head to this Norman bistro a block from the casino. Try cream of cauliflower soup with scallops or a *pot-au-feu Dieppoise* featuring filet of sole, scallops, monkfish, and salmon beautifully simmered together. You can also order grilled beef and chicken thighs braised in cider. Because the bistro seats only 30, reservations are vital in summer.

7 rue Carnot. ✆ **02-31-88-11-07.** Reservations required. Main courses 22€–33€; fixed-price menu 33€–55€. MC, V. Thurs–Mon noon–2:30pm and 7:15–9:30pm.

Les Vapeurs ★★ FRENCH/SEAFOOD This Art Deco brasserie, one of the most popular on the Norman coast, is frequented by stylish Parisians on *le week-end*. Established in 1926, it has been called the Brasserie Lipp of Normandy. The windows face the port, and in warm weather you can dine at sidewalk tables. Seafood—a wide range of shrimp, mussels laced with cream, crinkle-shelled oysters, and fish—is the specialty. Sauerkraut is also popular.

162 bd. Fernand-Moureaux. ✆ **02-31-88-15-24.** www.lesvapeurs.fr. Reservations recommended. Main courses 14€–33€. AE, MC, V. Mon–Fri noon–10:30pm; Sat–Sun noon–12:30am.

Trouville After Dark

If the casino in Deauville is too stuffy for you, you'll feel more comfortable in its smaller, less architecturally distinctive sibling in Trouville, **Casino Barrière de Trouville,** place du Maréchal-Foch (✆ **02-31-87-75-00;** www.lucienbarriere.com). It has more of a New Orleans–style environment, with a blues and jazz bar that schedules live music Friday and Saturday night, and a small-scale replica of Bourbon Street. Entrance to the slot machines is free. Entrance to the more formal area—with roulette, blackjack, and craps—costs 14€ per person. You must present a passport or identity card to gain admission. The formal area is open Sunday through Thursday 8pm to 2am, Friday 8pm to 3am, and Saturday 8pm to 4am. The rest of the casino is open daily from 10am. Men aren't required to wear jackets and ties, but tennis shoes are not allowed.

CAEN ★

238km (148 miles) NW of Paris; 119km (74 miles) SE of Cherbourg

Situated on the banks of the Orne, the port of Caen suffered great damage in the 1944 invasion of Normandy. Nearly three-quarters of its buildings, 10,000 in all, were destroyed, though the twin abbeys founded by William the Conqueror and his wife, Mathilda, were spared. The city today is essentially modern and has many broad avenues and new apartment buildings. Completely different from Deauville and Trouville, the capital of Lower Normandy is bustling, congested, and commercial; it's a major rail and ferry junction. The student population of 30,000 and the hordes of travelers have made Caen more cosmopolitan than ever.

Essentials

GETTING THERE From Paris's Gare St-Lazare, 12 **trains** per day arrive in Caen (trip time: 1 hr., 50 min.–2½ hr.). One-way fares start at 32€ to 47€. One-way fares from Rouen (trip time: 1 hr., 45 min.) start at 23€. To **drive** from Paris, travel west along A13 to Caen (driving time: 2½–3 hr.).

VISITOR INFORMATION The **Office de Tourisme** is on place St-Pierre in the 16th-century Hôtel d'Escoville (✆ **02-31-27-14-14;** www.tourisme.caen.fr).

Exploring the City

Abbaye aux Dames Founded by Mathilda, wife of William the Conqueror, this abbey embraces Eglise de la Trinité, which is flanked by Romanesque towers. Its spires were destroyed in the Hundred Years' War. The 12th-century choir houses the tomb of Queen Mathilda; note the ribbed vaulting.

Place de la Reine-Mathilde. ✆ **02-31-06-98-98.** Free admission. Daily 2–5:30pm. Free guided 1-hr. tour of choir, transept, and crypt (in French) daily 2:30 and 4pm.

Abbaye aux Hommes ★★ Founded by William and Mathilda, this abbey is adjacent to the Eglise St-Etienne, which you enter on place Monseigneur-des-Hameaux. During the height of the Allied invasion, residents of Caen flocked to St-Etienne for protection. Twin Romanesque towers 84m (276 ft.) tall dominate the church; they helped earn Caen the appellation "city of spires." A marble slab inside the high altar marks the site of William's tomb. The Huguenots destroyed the tomb in 1562—only a hipbone was recovered. During the French Revolution, the last of William's dust was scattered to the wind. The hand-carved wooden doors and elaborate wrought-iron staircase are exceptional. From the cloisters, you get a good view of the two towers of St-Etienne.

Esplanade Jean-Marie-Louvel. ✆ **02-31-30-42-81.** Obligatory tours (in French, accompanied by broken-English translation) 2.40€ adults, 1.20€ students, free for children 17 and under. Daily 8:30am–12:30pm and 1:30–7:30pm (2:30–7:30pm Sun). Tours daily 9:30 and 11am, and 2:30 and 4pm. Ticket office for tours daily 8am–4pm.

Abbaye aux Hommes.

Le Château de Caen This complex was built on the ruins of a fortress erected by William the Conqueror in 1060. Enter the grounds at esplanade de la Paix. The gardens are ideal for strolling and, from the ramparts, a panoramic view of Caen unfolds. Within the compound are two museums. The **Musée de Normandie** (✆ **02-31-30-47-60;** www.musee-

AN excursion TO THE FORBES CHÂTEAU

Built by François Mansart between 1626 and 1636, the **Château de Balleroy ★**, between Bayeux and Caen, has been owned by the Forbes family for more than 3 decades. The late Malcolm Forbes was an internationally known balloonist, and his dream of opening the world's first balloon museum has been fulfilled at the château. Today it is the venue for the biannual international ballooning festival.

The museum, in a converted stable, is filled with artifacts related to the history of ballooning. The château also contains many period rooms that abound with elegant art and antiques. Admission to the museum and castle is 8€ for adults or 6€ for students and children 7 to 18, and free for those 6 and under; entrance to just the grounds costs 3€ for everyone. Visiting times are from mid-March to mid-October Wednesday to Monday 10am to noon and 2 to 6pm (July–Aug hours are 10am–6pm).

The museum (✆ **02-31-21-60-61;** www.chateau-balleroy.com) lies at F-14490 Balleroy outside the village of Balleroy. To reach it from Caen (40km/25 miles), head west along N13, cutting south at the junction with D572, and follow the road to Balleroy, where the château is signposted.

de-normandie.caen.fr) displays artifacts from Normandy, including archaeological finds, along with a collection of regional sculpture, paintings, and ceramics. Admission is free, and it's open Wednesday to Monday 9:30am to 6pm. Also within the walls is the **Musée des Beaux-Arts** (✆ **02-31-30-47-70;** www.ville-caen.fr/mba), with a collection of works—though not their finest—by old masters including Veronese and Rubens. Admission is free except for temporary exhibits costing 3€ to 5€. It's open Wednesday through Monday from 9:30am to 6pm.

Le Mémorial de Caen (Caen Memorial) The memorial is a 15-minute drive away from the Pegasus Bridge and 15 minutes from the landing beaches. The museum presents a journey through history from 1918 to the present. It's an ideal place to relax. You can walk through International Park, have a meal or drink at the restaurant, or browse through the boutique. Expect to spend at least 2½ hours at this site—anyone intrigued by 20th-century European history will be fascinated. One wing is dedicated to a depiction of the American and global role after World War II. Its photo documentaries and exhibits illustrate the Cold War, the construction and collapse of the Berlin Wall, and the assault of military weapons (especially nuclear testing) on the environment.

Esplanade Général Dwight-Eisenhower. ✆ **02-31-06-06-45.** www.memorial-caen.fr. Admission Apr–Sept 18€ adults, 15€ students and children 10–18; Oct–Mar 17€ adults, 14€ students and children 10–18; free to World War II veterans, those with war disabilities, war widows, and children 9 and under. Daily 9am–7pm (until 8pm mid-July to mid-Aug). Closed Jan 4–26.

Shopping

Caen has some good boutique-lined shopping streets, including **boulevard du Maréchal-Leclerc, rue St-Pierre,** and **rue de Strasbourg. Antiques** hunters should check out the shops along rue Ecuyère and rue Commerçantes, and the antiques show at the **Parc des Expositions,** rue Joseph-Philippon (✆ **02-31-29-99-99**), in early May. The **markets** at place St-Sauveur on Friday morning and place Courtonne on Sunday morning also sell secondhand articles.

For custom-built reproduction antique furniture, visit **La Reine Matilde,** 47 rue St-Jean (✆ **02-31-85-45-52**); it also sells decorative items, including a selection of bed linens and curtains. **Le Chocolaterie Hotot,** 13 rue St-Pierre (✆ **02-31-86-31-90**), has a cornucopia of chocolate products, as well as local jams and jellies. At **Le Comptoir Normand,** 7 rue de Geôle (✆ **02-31-86-34-13**), you'll find many regional items, including Calvados and various charcuterie products, such as tripe in the style of Caen.

For objets d'art and paintings, check out **L'Atelier,** 33 rue Montoir-Poissonnerie (✆ **02-31-44-49-38**), which showcases the work of local painters. To browse through inventories of wine and *eaux-de-vie* from throughout France, head for **Nicolas,** 10 rue Bellivet (✆ **02-31-85-24-19**).

Where to Stay

Holiday Inn Caen City Centre ★ This is the best hotel in town, with a flavor that's both French and international. Across from the racecourse, the hotel predates World War II. Rooms are predictable, comfortable, and well maintained. Americans visiting the D-day beaches favor the cozy bar.

Place du Maréchal-Foch, Caen 14000. www.holiday-inn.com. ✆ **800/465-4329** in the U.S., or 02-31-27-57-57. Fax 02-31-27-57-58. 88 units. 115€–165€ double. AE, DC, MC, V. **Amenities:** Restaurant; bar; babysitting; room service. *In room:* A/C (in some), TV, hair dryer, minibar, free Wi-Fi.

Hôtel des Quatrans This agreeable, unpretentious hotel was rebuilt after World War II, and thanks to continual renovations, it's one of Caen's best bargains. Don't expect luxury: The hotel has four floors of old-fashioned rooms that offer basic amenities, including small, shower-only bathrooms. A buffet breakfast, available in the breakfast room or delivered to your room, is the only meal served.

17 rue Gémare, Caen 14300. www.hotel-des-quatrans.com. ✆ **02-31-86-25-57.** Fax 02-31-85-27-80. 47 units. 65€ double; 75€ triple. MC, V. Parking free. **Amenities:** Restaurant; bar. *In room:* TV, hair dryer, free Wi-Fi.

Hôtel Kyriad This hotel is a reliable bargain. The original was destroyed during a World War II bombing raid. Rebuilt several years later, it's surrounded by a commercial area of shops and restaurants, as well as more tranquil pedestrian streets. The hotel provides bedrooms in attractive color schemes such as soft yellows and reds. There's no restaurant, but an independent grill-style restaurant across the street offers inexpensive breakfast plans for hotel guests.

1 place de la République, Caen 14000. ✆ **02-31-86-55-33.** Fax 02-31-79-89-44. 47 units. 57€–90€ double. AE, MC, V. Parking 7€. **Amenities:** Bar. *In room:* A/C, TV, hair dryer, free Wi-Fi.

Where to Eat

Le Carlotta FRENCH/SEAFOOD This is a well-established brasserie, one of the best known in town, with a high-volume turnover and a penchant for seafood. With an Art Deco decor, it's a bustling venue. Tried-and-true menu items include platters of shellfish, especially oysters; strips of duck breast with parsley sauce; braised oxtail with truffles and mashed potatoes; and roasted shoulder of lamb *en*

A Proustian Remembrance of "Balbec"

Torn from the pages of Marcel Proust's *Remembrance of Things Past,* the resort of "Balbec" was really Cabourg, 24km (15 miles) northeast of Caen. Fans still come to this Second Empire resort, much of which looks as it did in the Belle Epoque. Guests can check into the 1907 Grand Hotel, promenade Marcel Proust, 14390 Cabourg (✆ 02-31-91-01-79; fax 02-31-24-03-20; www.mercure.com), a holdover from the opulent days of the 19th century and now part of the Mercure chain. One room, La Chambre Marcel Proust, has been restored from a description in *Remembrance.* A double costs from 158€ to 360€, with a suite going for 425€ to 625€.

confit, served with Middle Eastern spices and mashed potatoes. Desserts usually include a homemade version of tiramisu and a gratin of seasonal berries.

16 quai Vendeuvre. ✆ **02-31-86-68-99.** www.lecarlotta.fr. Reservations recommended. Main courses 18€–28€; set menus 23€–36€. AE, MC, V. Mon–Sat noon–2pm and 6–10:30pm.

Le p'tit B FRENCH/NORMAN A growing number of local diners are enthusiastic about this place, which is set in a 17th-century house in the center of town. Its fixed-price menu, with loads of good choices, is a great deal. You might begin with *terrine maison* or a slice of Norman-style Camembert tart, followed by a seafood brochette.

15 rue de Vaugueux. ✆ **02-31-93-50-76.** Reservations recommended. Main courses 14€–18€; fixed-price lunch 16€; fixed-price dinner 29€. AE, DC, MC, V. Daily noon–2:30pm and 7pm–midnight.

Caen After Dark

Take a walk down rue de Bras, rue St-Pierre, and the north end of rue Vaugueux to size up the action. If you want to connect with the hip 18-to-35 crowd, go to **Le Chic,** rue des Prairies St-Gilles (✆ **02-31-94-48-72**), where disco music begins at 10:30pm. **Le Carré,** 32 quai Vendeuvre (✆ **02-31-38-90-90**), is a disco that caters to patrons over 27 with rock 'n' roll, cutting-edge techno, and a goodly assortment of music from the '70s and '80s. Upstairs, there's the hip and often charming Bar de Nuit.

Intensely connected to the hip and trendy night-soul of Caen is an Irish-style pub, **O'Donnell's,** 20 quai Vendeuvre (✆ **02-31-85-51-50**). It's the site of televised European soccer matches and live Irish rock 'n' roll shows. The live music is every Friday night; otherwise, a DJ rules the night. It's open Monday through Wednesday 4:30pm to 2:30am, Thursday through Saturday 4:30pm to 4am, and Sunday 4:30pm to midnight.

BAYEUX ★★

267km (166 miles) NW of Paris; 25km (16 miles) NW of Caen

The *ducs de Normandie* sent their sons to this Viking settlement to learn the Norse language in the 9th century. Bayeux has changed a lot since then but was spared from bombardment in 1944. This was the first French town liberated, and the citizens gave de Gaulle an enthusiastic welcome when he arrived on June 14. The town is filled with timbered houses, stone mansions, and cobblestone streets.

Visitors wanting to explore sites associated with "the Longest Day" flood the town, because many memorials (not to mention the beaches) are only 9.5 to 19km (6–12 miles) away. Shops line the cozy little streets. Many sell World War II memorabilia, and more postcards and T-shirts than you'll ever need.

Essentials

GETTING THERE Twelve **trains** depart daily from Paris's Gare St-Lazare. The 2½-hour trip to Bayeux costs 35€. Most trains stop in Caen. Travel time between Caen and Bayeux is about 20 minutes and costs 5.80€. To **drive** to Bayeux from Paris (trip time: 3 hr.), take A13 to Caen and E46 west to Bayeux.

VISITOR INFORMATION The **Office de Tourisme** is at pont St-Jean (✆ **02-31-51-28-28;** www.bayeux-bessin-tourism.com).

SPECIAL EVENTS The town goes wild on the first weekend in July during **Fêtes Médiévales;** the streets fill with wine and song during 2 days of medieval revelry. For information, call ✆ **02-31-92-03-30.**

Seeing the Sights

Musée de la Tapisserie de Bayeux ★★★ The most famous tapestry in the world is actually an embroidery on linen, 69m (226 ft.) long and .5m (20 in.) wide, depicting 58 scenes in eight colors. Contrary to legend, it wasn't made by Queen Mathilda, the wife of William the Conqueror, but was probably commissioned in Kent and created by unknown embroiderers between 1066 and 1077. The first mention of the embroidery was in 1476, when it decorated the nave of the Cathédrale Notre-Dame de Bayeux.

Housed in a Plexiglas case, the embroidery tells the story of the conquest of England by William the Conqueror, including such scenes as the coronation of Harold as the Saxon king of England, Harold returning from his journey to Normandy, the surrender of Dinan, Harold being told of the apparition of a comet (a portent of misfortune), William dressed for war, and the death of Harold. The decorative borders include scenes from *Aesop's Fables*.

Admission to the museum includes access to an annex whose collections are not as spectacular. The **Collections Baron Gérard** is housed in **Le Musée de l'Hôtel du Doyen,** 6 rue Lambert le Forestier (✆ **02-31-92-14-21**). Exhibitions feature examples of regional lacework, porcelain, and religious and secular paintings, many of them created within this region.

Centre Guillaume-le-Conquérant, 13 rue de Nesmond. ✆ **02-31-51-25-50.** www.tapisserie-bayeux.fr. Admission 7.80€ adults, 3.80€ students, free for children 9 and under. Mar 15–Nov 15 daily 9am–6:30pm; off season daily 9:30am–12:30pm and 2–6pm.

A section of the Bayeux Tapestry.

Musée Memorial de la Bataille de Normandie This museum deals with the military and human history of the Battle of Normandy (June 6–Aug 22, 1944). In a low-slung building designed like a bunker are 132m (433 ft.) of window and film displays, plus a diorama. Wax soldiers in uniform, along with the tanks and guns used to win the battle, are on exhibit. Across from the museum, the **Commonwealth Cemetery** (✆ **03-21-21-77-00**) lies on the northwestern perimeter of Bayeux, containing 4,144 graves of soldiers from throughout the British Commonwealth, all of them killed during the Battle of Normandy.

Bd. Fabian Ware. ✆ **02-31-51-46-90.** Admission 6.50€ adults, 3.80€ students and children, free for children 9 and under. May–Sept 15 daily 9:30am–6:30pm; Sept 16–Apr daily 10am–12:30pm and 2–6pm.

Notre-Dame de Bayeux ★★ This cathedral was consecrated in 1077 and partially destroyed in 1105. Romanesque towers from the original church rise on the western side. The central tower is from the 15th century. The nave is a fine example of Norman Romanesque style. The 13th-century choir, a perfect example of Norman Gothic style, is rich in sculpture and has Renaissance stalls. The crypt was built in the 11th century and then sealed, its existence unknown until 1412.

Rue du Bienvenu. ✆ **02-31-92-14-21.** Admission 4€, free ages 14 and under. Daily 8:30am–6pm (to 7pm July–Aug).

Where to Stay

Best Western Grand Hôtel de Luxembourg ★ After Le Lion d'Or (see below), this Best Western is the area's finest hotel. The restored interior has terrazzo floors; the decor combines neoclassical and Art Deco design. Rooms range in size from small to medium and have been overhauled with an eye to modern comfort, including fine bed linens. All units come with small bathrooms with showers, and more than half also have tubs.

25 rue des Bouchers, Bayeux 14400. www.hotel-luxembourg-bayeux.com. ✆ **800/528-1234** in the U.S. and Canada, or 02-31-92-00-04. Fax 02-31-92-54-26. 27 units. 80€–125€ double; 115€–180€ suite. AE, MC, V. Parking 9€. **Amenities:** Restaurant; bar; room service. *In room:* TV, free Wi-Fi.

Churchill ★ Open from March to November, this hotel lies in the heart of the medieval town, close to the famous tapestry and the cathedral. Excursions for the D-day beaches leave from the square behind the hotel, and a shuttle to Mont-St-Michel can also be arranged. The staff is among the most accommodating in town. Their midsize bedrooms are personalized, each comfortably furnished on an individual basis. Of course, their deluxe rooms are the way to go, unless you're economizing, in which case you'll find their standard units most adequate.

14 rue St-Jean, Bayeux 14400. www.hotel-churchill.fr. ✆ **02-31-21-31-80.** 32 units. 100€–110€ standard double; 150€–168€ deluxe double. MC, V. **Amenities:** Free Internet. *In room:* TV, hair dryer.

Hôtel d'Argouges This government-rated three-star hotel consists of a pair of 18th-century town houses, set across a garden from one another, with exposed beams, thick walls, and sloping ceilings. Rooms are comfortable, intimate, and cozy, with old-fashioned furniture and modern conveniences. Breakfast is the only meal served, but at least three restaurants are within a 2-minute walk. In good weather, you can wander in the garden.

21 rue St-Patrice, Bayeux 14402. ✆ **02-31-92-88-86.** Fax 02-31-92-69-16. www.hotel-dargouges.com. 28 units. 70€–130€ double; 150€–295€ suite. MC, V. Parking 5€. **Amenities:** Bar; babysitting; room service. *In room:* TV, hair dryer, free Internet.

Le Lion d'Or ★★★ This old-world hotel is the oldest and most nostalgic in town, dating from 1928. The property, built in 1734, has an open courtyard with lush flower boxes decorating the facade. As befits an old inn, rooms come in various shapes and sizes. The midsize bathrooms are well equipped; each has a shower, and more than half have tubs. Guests are required to take at least one meal here, but that shouldn't be a problem—the traditional cuisine is delicious. The restaurant serves lots of reasonably priced wines.

71 rue St-Jean, Bayeux 14400. www.liondor-bayeux.fr. ✆ **02-31-92-06-90.** Fax 02-31-22-15-64. 28 units. 115€–195€ double. AE, DC, MC, V. Parking 8€. **Amenities:** Restaurant; bar; babysitting; exercise room. *In room:* TV, minibar, free Wi-Fi.

Where to Eat

Le Pommier ★ NORMAN One of the most appealing restaurants in Bayeux's historic zone occupies an 18th-century building. Ceiling beams and exposed masonry enhance the trio of dining rooms. The establishment is devotedly Norman, with cuisine that reflects the region's long tradition of baking with apples (the name translates as "The Apple Tree") and cream (though its use is limited, to make the food a bit healthier). The health-conscious staff is proud that the dishes "aren't drowned in gravies and sauces." Menu items evolve with the seasons. You can usually expect dishes such as rabbit stew braised in cider and a platter that contains two kinds of fish, served with chitterling sausage and a sauce of cream and chitterling drippings.

38 rue des Cuisiniers. ✆ **02-31-21-52-10.** Fax 02-31-21-06-01. www.restaurantlepommier.com. Reservations recommended. Main courses 16€–25€; fixed-price menus 23€–39€. AE, MC, V. Apr–Sept daily noon–2:30pm and 7–9:30pm; Oct–Mar Mon–Sat noon–2pm and 7–9:30pm. Closed mid-Dec to mid-Jan.

THE D-DAY BEACHES ★★

Arromanches-les-Bains: 272km (169 miles) NW of Paris, 11km (6¾ miles) NW of Bayeux; Grandcamp-Maisy (near Omaha Beach): 299km (185 miles) NW of Paris, 56km (35 miles) NW of Caen

During a rainy week in June 1944, the greatest armada ever—soldiers and sailors, warships, landing craft, tugboats, jeeps—assembled along the southern coast of England. At 9:15pm on June 5, the BBC announced to the French Resistance that the invasion was imminent, signaling the underground to start dynamiting the railways. Before midnight, Allied planes began bombing the Norman coast. By 1:30am on June 6 ("the Longest Day"), members of the 101st Airborne were parachuting to the ground on German-occupied French soil. At 6:30am, the Americans began landing on the beaches, code-named Utah and Omaha. An hour later, British and Canadian forces made beachheads at Juno, Gold, and Sword.

The Nazis had mocked Churchill's promise in 1943 to liberate France "before the fall of the autumn leaves." When the invasion did come, it was swift, sudden, and a surprise to the formidable "Atlantic wall." Today veterans walk with their children and grandchildren across the beaches where "Czech hedgehogs," "Belgian grills," pillboxes, and "Rommel asparagus" (all military barriers or structures) once stood.

Essentials

GETTING THERE The best way to get to the D-day beaches is to **drive.** Public transportation is unreliable. The trip takes about 3 hours from Paris. Take A13 west to Caen, and continue west along A13 to Bayeux. From Bayeux, travel north along D6 until you reach the coast at Port-en-Bessin. From here, D514 runs along the coastline; most D-day sites are west of Port-en-Bessin. Parking is not a problem, and most of the designated areas along the roadway are free. It's best to visit on a weekday, because weekends (especially in summer) can be crowded with tourists and sunbathers.

Bus service from Bayeux is uneven and usually involves long delays. **Bus Verts** (✆**08-10-21-42-14;** www.busverts.fr) runs to Port-en-Bessin and points west, and bus no. 75 offers service year-round to Arromanches and other points in the east. Bus no. 70 travels west (June–Sept only) from Bayeux toward Omaha Beach and the American cemetery.

If you don't have a car, the best way to see the D-day beaches is on a **tour. Normandy Tours,** Hotel de la Gare, Bayeux (✆**02-31-92-10-70;** www.normandy-landing-tours.com), runs a 4- to 5-hour tour (in English) to Arromanches, Omaha Beach, the American Military Cemetery, and Pointe du Hoc for 48€ adults and 40€ students and seniors. **D-Day Tours,** 52 rte. de Porte en Bessin, Bayeux (✆**02-31-51-70-52;** www.normandy webguide.com), conducts tours with a bit more pizazz and guides who speak better English. A half-day trip costs 45€ for adults and 40€ for students; a full-day trip is 75€ for adults and 65€ for students. The company picks you up at your hotel in Bayeux. A final option, **Battlebus** (✆**02-31-22-28-82;** www.battlebus.fr), leads a full-day tour encompassing all sites and beaches that were pivotal during the D-day landing and Battle of Normandy; cost is 85€ per person. Most participants have found this latter option the best tour of all—simultaneously riveting, exhausting, and stimulating.

VISITOR INFORMATION The **Office de Tourisme,** 4 rue du Maréchal-Joffre, Arromanches-les-Bains (✆**02-31-21-47-56**), is open year-round.

Reliving the Longest Day

Start your exploration at the seaside resort of **Arromanches-les-Bains.** In June 1944, this was a fishing port until the 50th British Division took it. A mammoth prefabricated port known as Winston was towed across the Channel and installed to supply the Allied forces. "Victory could not have been achieved without it," Eisenhower said. The wreckage of that artificial harbor is just off the beach,

Americans Return to Normandy

The **Normandy American Visitor Center,** opened at 14710 Colleville-sur-Mer (✆ **02-31-51-62-00;** www.abmc.gov), dedicated to those heroes of World War II who liberated mainland France from the Nazis, tells the story of the 9,387 Americans buried on French soil. The center relates that dramatic story through narrative text, photos, films, interactive displays, and artifacts. Admission is free. The center is open April 15 through September 15 daily 9am to 6pm, and off season daily 9am to 5pm.

Sand yachts at Omaha Beach.

Plage du Débarquement. Musée du Débarquement, place du 6-Juin (✆ **02-31-22-34-31;** www.normandy1944.com), in Arromanches, features maps, models, a cinema, photographs, and a diorama of the landing, all with English commentary. Admission is 6.50€ for adults and 4.50€ for students and children. From June to August, hours are daily 9am to 7pm; September Monday to Saturday 9am to 6pm, Sunday 10am to 6pm; October and March daily 9:30am to 12:30pm and 1:30 to 5:30pm; November to December and February daily 10am to 12:30pm and 1:30 to 5pm; April Monday to Saturday 9am to 12:30pm and 1:30 to 6pm, Sunday 10am to 12:30pm and 1:30 to 6pm; and May Monday

reliving THE ALLIED INVASION OF NORMANDY

One of the most evocative ways to re-create the sensations that the combat troops felt just prior to their invasion of Normandy involves signing up for a waterborne tour. Maintained by **Les Vedettes de Normandie,** and entitled "Balades sur les plages du Débarquement," the tour offers prerecorded English-language commentary on a cassette player, live commentary from a French-language guide, and boats with a capacity of 200 sightseers at a time. Commentary focuses on the physicality of the Norman coastline; the region's construction, shipping, and fishing industries; and the historic events associated with the invasion of Normandy by Allied troops in 1944.

Between mid-April and mid-October, boats depart between one and three times a day, with a schedule that varies with the tides, the season, the day of the week, and French national holidays. All tours depart from the harborfront quays of the hamlet of Port-en-Bessin. Tours lasting 90 minutes each, and which cost 15€ per participant, focus on either Arromanches or Omaha beaches. Lasting 3 hours, tours (at 23€) focus on Omaha Beach and the Pointe du Hoc. There's no discount for children. For information about departure times and reservations, contact *Les Vedettes de Normandie,* Ste. H.C., bd. De Général de Gaulle Point de Cabourg, 14160 Dives-sur-Mer (✆ **02-31-43-86-12**).

Normandy American Cemetery.

to Saturday 9am to 7pm, Sunday 10am to 7pm. It's closed December 24 to 26, December 31, and the month of January.

Moving along the coast, you'll arrive at **Omaha Beach,** where you can still see the war wreckage. "Hanging on by their toenails," the men of the 1st and 29th American Divisions occupied the beach that June day. The code name Omaha became famous; until then, the beaches had been called St-Laurent, Vierville-sur-Mer, and Colleville. A monument commemorates the heroism of the invaders. Covering some 70 hectares (173 acres) at Omaha Beach, the **Normandy American Cemetery** (**✆02-31-51-62-00;** www.abmc.gov) is filled with crosses and Stars of David in Lasa marble. The remains of 9,387 American military were buried here on territory now owned by the United States, a gift from the French nation. Admission is free. The cemetery is open daily 9am to 5pm, the visitor center until 6pm (both are closed Christmas and New Year's Day).

Farther along the coast, you'll see the jagged lime cliffs of the **Pointe du Hoc.** A cross honors a group of American Rangers, led by Lt. Col. James Rudder, who scaled the cliffs using hooks to get at the pillboxes (gun emplacements). The scars of war are more visible here than at any other point along the beach. Farther along the Cotentin Peninsula is **Utah Beach,** where the 4th U.S. Infantry Division landed at 6:30am. The landing force was nearly 3km (1¾ miles) south of its intended destination, but Nazi defenses were weak. By midday the infantry had completely cleared the beach. A U.S. monument commemorates their heroism.

Nearby, you can visit the hamlet of **Ste-Mère-Eglise,** which was virtually unknown outside of France before paratroopers dropped from the sky. In Ste-Mère-Eglise is Kilometer 0 on the Liberty Highway, marking the first of the milestones the American armies reached on their way to Metz and Bastogne.

Where to Stay & Eat at Grandcamp-Maisy

Hôtel Duguesclin TRADITIONAL FRENCH We recommend this Norman inn for lunch or even an overnight stay. The fish soup, grilled scallops, Norman sole (when it's available), and grilled turbot with white butter are excellent.

Everything tastes better with the dining room's country bread and Norman butter.

The hotel rents 23 simple, comfortable rooms, all with bathroom, phone, and TV. Accommodations have a shower or tub (sometimes both). A double costs 45€ to 66€.

4 quai Crampon, Grandcamp-Maisy 14450. ✆ **02-31-22-64-22.** Fax 02-31-22-34-79. Reservations recommended. Main courses 12€–33€; fixed-price menu 15€–35€. AE, MC, V. Daily noon–2pm and 7–9pm.

La Marée NORMAN Set beside the port, this small, nautically decorated restaurant serves mostly fish and only fish caught in the English Channel or within a reasonable distance out in the Atlantic, guaranteeing a local culinary experience. During nice weather, the dining room expands onto a terrace.

5 quai Henri Chéron. ✆ **02-31-21-41-00.** Reservations required. Main courses 18€–22€; fixed-price menus 14€–25€. AE, MC, V. Daily 12:30–2:30pm and 7–9:30pm. Closed Jan 1–Feb 7.

Where to Stay at Arromanches

Hôtel de la Marine A hotel has stood on this spot since 1837, although the one you see today wins over any of its earlier incarnations when it comes to comfort and style. The hotel directly faces the beach that played a keynote role during the U.S. invasion of Normandy and offers many of the charming details of a Norman private country estate. Bedrooms are rustically outfitted with colorful fabrics and solid, traditional furnishings. The restaurant appeals even to nonguests. It's open daily noon to 2pm and 7 to 9:30pm, and serves set-price, thoroughly French meals priced at 22€ to 35€ each.

1 quai du Canada, Arromanches les Bains 14117. www.hotel-de-la-marine.fr. ✆ **02-31-22-34-19.** Fax 02-31-22-98-80. 33 units. 72€–178€ double. Rates include breakfast and dinner. AE, MC, V. Free parking. **Amenities:** Restaurant; bar. *In room:* A/C, TV, hair dryer, free Wi-Fi.

MONT-ST-MICHEL ★★★

324km (201 miles) W of Paris; 129km (80 miles) SW of Caen; 76km (47 miles) E of Dinan; 48km (30 miles) E of St-Malo

Massive walls measuring more than half a mile in circumference surround one of Europe's great attractions, the island of Mont-St-Michel. Connected to the shore by a causeway, it crowns a rocky islet at the border between Normandy and Brittany. The rock is 78m (256 ft.) high.

Grand Rue.

Essentials

GETTING THERE The most efficient way to reach Mont-St-Michel is to **drive.** From Caen, follow A84 southwest to Pontorson,

Mont-St-Michel.

continuing a few more kilometers to Avranches; from there, merge onto D43, following signs to its end at Mont-St-Michel. Total driving time from Paris is about 4½ hours.

There are no direct trains between Paris and Mont-St-Michel. We suggest taking the high-speed **TGV train** from Paris's Gare Montparnasse to Rennes, where you can transfer to the **bus** run by the **SNCF** (**© 36-35** or 08-92-35-35-35; www.voyages-sncf.com) for the 75-minute trip to Mont-St-Michel. Depending on the season, two to five buses a day run to Rennes for 12€ per person. Another company, **Les Courriers Bretons** (**© 02-99-19-70-70;** www.lescourriersbretons.fr), also operates buses that make the 75-minute ride to Mont-St-Michel from St-Malo two to five times a day for 13€ per person.

VISITOR INFORMATION The **Office de Tourisme** is in the Corps de Garde des Bourgeois (the Old Guard Room of the Bourgeois), at the left of the town gates (**© 02-33-60-14-30;** www.ot-montsaintmichel.com). The tourist office is open daily year-round except Christmas and New Year's Day.

Exploring Mont-St-Michel

You'll have a steep climb up Grande Rue, lined with 15th- and 16th-century houses, to reach the **abbey** (**© 02-33-89-80-00;** www.monuments-nationaux.fr). Those who make it to the top can begin their exploration of the Marvel of the West. In the 8th century, St. Aubert, the bishop of Avranches, founded an oratory on this spot. A Benedictine monastery, founded in 966 by Richard I, replaced it. That burned in 1203. Philip Augustus financed the building of an abbey in the 13th century.

Ramparts encircle the church and a three-tiered ensemble of 13th-century buildings called **La Merveille** that rise to the pointed spire of the abbey church. This terraced complex is one of Europe's most important Gothic monuments, a citadel in which the concept of an independent France was nurtured during the darkest years of the English occupation of Aquitaine.

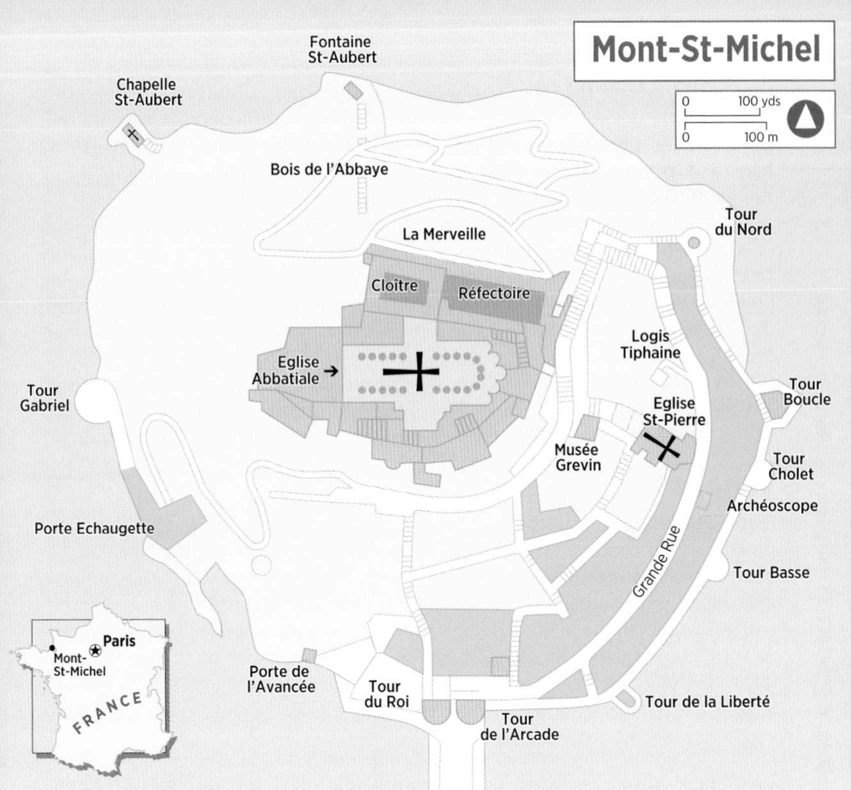

On the second terrace of La Merveille is one of Mont-St-Michel's largest and most beautiful rooms, a 13th-century hall known as the **Salle des Chevaliers.**

Crowning the mountain's summit is the **Eglise Abbatiale** (not to be confused with the parish church, Eglise St-Pierre, lower on the mountain). Begun in the 11th century, the abbey church consists of a Romanesque nave and transept, plus a choir in Flamboyant Gothic style. The rectangular refectory dates from 1212, and the cloisters with their columns of pink granite are from 1225.

The abbey is open daily May through September 9am to 7pm, and October to April 9:30am to 5:30pm. From June to September, it's also open Monday to Saturday 9pm to 1am (last entrance at midnight). Mass begins at 12:15pm Tuesday to Sunday. Entrance during daytime or nighttime tours includes a group tour, but you can also wander on your own. Year-round, day or night visits, with or without the tour, cost 8.50€ for adults, 5€ for students and ages 18 to 25, and free for children 17 and under.

Guided tours in French depart at intervals of 30 to 45 minutes, depending on the season. There are usually two to four English-language tours per day. Everything is closed New Year's Day, May 1, and Christmas.

Archeoscope, chemin de la Ronde (✆ **02-33-89-01-85**), is a small theater that presents *L'Eau et La Lumière (Water and Light),* celebrating the legend and lore of Mont-St-Michel and its role as a preserver of French medieval nationalism. The 30-minute shows begin every 30 to 60 minutes between 9:30am and 5:30pm. An unusual diversion is the adjacent **Musée de la Mer,** Grande

Rue (✆ **02-33-89-02-02**). It showcases marine crafts throughout history; the ecology of the local tidal flats; and illustrations of the French government's ongoing project intended to reactivate the tidal cleansing of the nearby marshes. **Musée Grevin (Musée Historique de Mont-St-Michel),** chemin de la Ronde (✆ **02-33-89-02-02**), traces the history of the abbey.

A museum that's worth a visit is the **Logis Tiphaine,** Grande Rue (✆ **02-33-89-02-02**), a 15th-century home originally under the control of the Duguesclin family, noted defenders of the fortress from English intrigue. In the building, next to the Eglise St-Pierre, you'll find furniture and accessories from that era, and a sense of pride at the fortress's durability as a bastion of all things French.

A combined ticket for all four of these attractions costs 16€ for adults and 13€ for students, 9€ ages 10 to 18. Free 9 and under. Other than the Archeoscope, whose hours are noted above, the museums are open daily from 9am to 5pm.

Where to Stay & Eat

Hôtel du Mouton-Blanc Occupying a pair of buildings, parts of which date from the 14th century, this inn stands between the sea and the basilica and has hosted guests since the 1700s. Rooms are small but cozy. Eight are in a comfortable annex, where all units have small bathrooms with showers. The seven better-equipped units in the main building have bathrooms with both tubs and showers. A rustic Norman-style dining room sits on a terrace overlooking the sea. Popular dishes include omelets with seafood, and two marvelous versions of lamb.

Grande Rue, Mont-St-Michel 50116. ✆ **02-33-60-14-08.** Fax 02-33-60-05-62. 15 units. 90€ double; 118€ suite. AE, MC, V. **Amenities:** Restaurant; bar. *In room:* TV.

La Mère Poulard NORMAN This country inn is a shrine to those who revere the omelet that Annette Poulard created in 1888, when the hotel was founded. It's under the same ownership as the more rustic Les Terrasses Poulard (see below). Annette Poulard's secret has been passed on to the inn's operators: The beaten eggs are cooked over an oak fire in a long-handled copper skillet. The frothy mixture creates more of an open-fire soufflé than an omelet. Other specialties are *agneau du pré salé* (lamb raised on the saltwater marshes near the foundations of the abbey) and an array of fish, including lobster.

Grande Rue, Mont-St-Michel 50116. www.mere-poulard.fr. ✆ **02-33-89-68-68.** Fax 02-33-89-68-69. Reservations recommended. Main courses 34€–45€; fixed-price lunch 55€–79€; fixed-price dinner 39€–85€. AE, DC, MC, V. Daily noon–10pm.

Les Terrasses Poulard This inn consists of two village houses, one medieval, the other built in the 1800s. It's one of the best in town, with an English-speaking staff, cozy rooms, comfortable beds, and neatly maintained shower-only bathrooms. The rates depend on the view: the main street, the village, or the medieval ramparts. The largest and most expensive rooms have fireplaces. The restaurant offers a sweeping view over the bay to accompany its seafood and regional Norman specialties.

Grande Rue, Mont-St-Michel 50116. www.terrasses-poulard.com. ✆ **02-33-89-02-02.** Fax 02-33-60-37-31. 29 units. 125€–200€ double. AE, DC, MC, V. **Amenities:** Restaurant. *In room:* TV, minibar, free Wi-Fi.

8

BRITTANY

by Joe Ray

Brittany is the great arm of France, reaching into the sea. In this ancient northwestern province, Bretons cling to their traditions and have a deep connection with the sea surrounding the peninsula that has forged their identity. Deep in l'Argoat (the lush, green interior), many older Bretons live in stone farmhouses as their grandparents did, and on special occasions the women wear starched-lace headdresses. The Breton language is spoken, but the Welsh and Cornish understand it better than the French.

Nearly every village and hamlet has its own pardon, a religious festival that can attract thousands of pilgrims in traditional dress. The best known are on May 19, at Treguier (honoring St-Yves); on the second Sunday in July, at Locronan (honoring St-Ronan); on July 26, at St-Anne-d'Auray (honoring the "mothers of Bretons"); and on September 8, at Le Folgoet (honoring *ar foll coat*—"idiot of the forest").

Traditionally, the province is divided into Haute-Bretagne and Basse-Bretagne. Promontories, coves, and beaches stud the rocky coastline, some 1,207km (748 miles) long. The interior is a land of hamlets, farmhouses, and moors covered with yellow broom and purple heather.

Brittany is a resort region. Many families visit for the beaches. British tourists frequent Dinard, although the water can be choppy and cold, with high waves. La Baule in the south is warmer, with a great beach, restaurants, and the best hotels in the region.

We suggest first-time visitors stick to the coast, where you can see salt-meadow sheep grazing. If you're coming from Mont-St-Michel, you can use St-Malo, Dinan, or Dinard as a base. Visitors from the château country of the Loire can explore the coastline of southern Brittany.

ST-MALO ★★★

414km (257 miles) W of Paris; 69km (43 miles) N of Rennes; 13km (8 miles) E of Dinard

Built on a granite rock in the Channel, St-Malo is joined to the mainland by a causeway. It's popular with the English, especially Channel Islanders, and its warm brown sands give it a modest claim to being a beach resort. The peninsula curves around a natural harbor that comprises several smaller basins. The walled city radiates outward from the town's château and its spiritual centerpiece, the Cathédrale St-Vincent, both of which lie near the peninsula's tip. The curse of St-Malo is the swarm of tour buses and their passengers engulfing the narrow streets. But there's plenty of charm here, having been virtually rebuilt after damage during World War II. The challenge is to appreciate that charm while contending with so many other travelers on the same pursuit.

PREVIOUS PAGE: **Scallops from the region.**

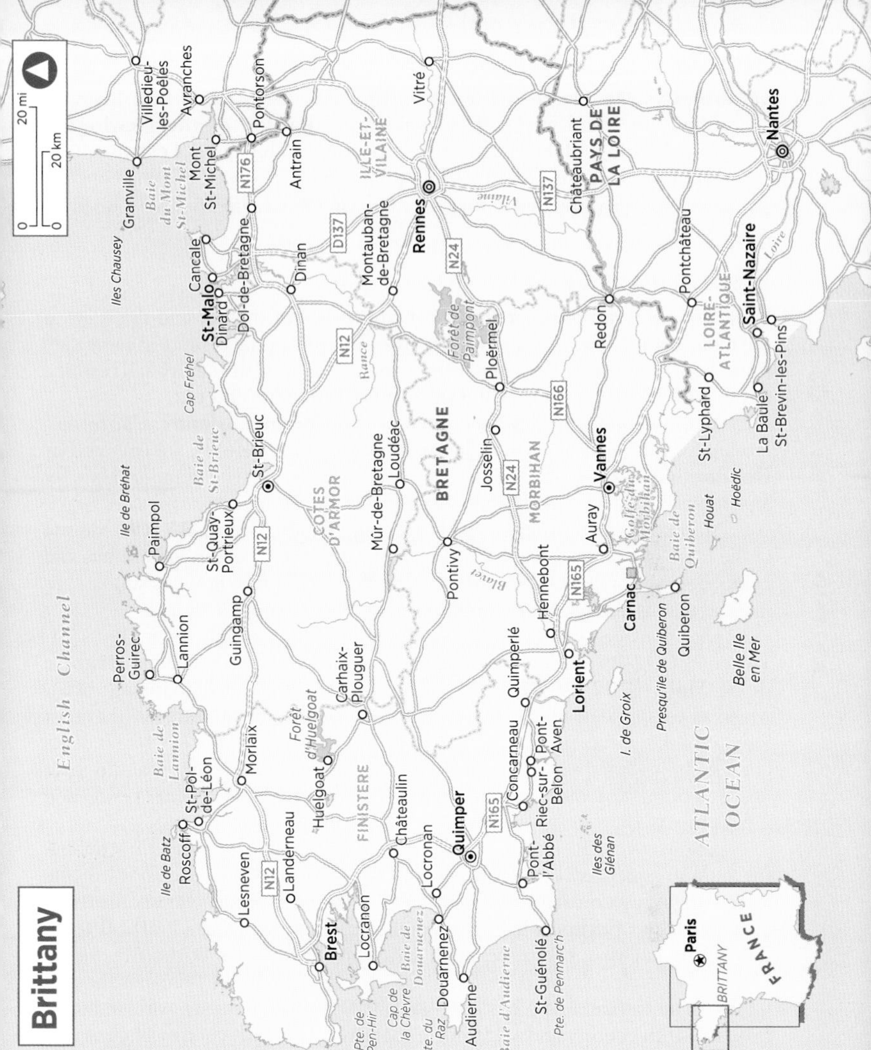

Essentials

GETTING THERE From Paris's Gare Montparnasse, about 14 TGV **trains** per day make the journey; a one-way ticket costs around 61€ to 77€. Two of these trains are nonstop, making the journey in 2¾ hours; other, less direct trains take 4 hours. For information, call ✆ **36-35** or 08-92-35-35-35. If you're **driving** from Paris, take A13 west to Caen and continue southwest along N175 to the town of Miniac Morvan. From there, travel north on N137 directly to St-Malo. Driving time is 4 hours from Paris.

VISITOR INFORMATION The **Office de Tourisme** is on esplanade St-Vincent (✆ **08-25-13-52-00;** www.saint-malo-tourisme.com). You must show a passport to take the car-ferry trips and tours to the Channel Islands or Les Iles Anglo-Normandes.

SPECIAL EVENTS One of the most important Breton *pardons* is at St-Malo, usually the third weekend in January: the **Pardon of the Newfoundland Fishing Fleet (Pardon de St-Ouen).** The town's **Festival de la Musique Sacrée,** from mid-July to mid-August, stages evening concerts twice a week presented in the cathedral. Call ✆ **02-99-56-05-38** for more information.

Exploring the City

Walk along the **ramparts ★★★** for the best view of the bay and the islets at the mouth of the Rance. These walls were built over several centuries; some date from the 14th century. They were reconstructed in the 17th century and restored in the 19th. You can begin at the 15th-century **Porte St-Vincent.**

At the harbor, you can book tours of the **Channel Islands.** Car ferries, leaving for the English island of Jersey from March to October, are operated by **Condor** (✆ **08-25-13-51-35;** www.condorferries.com). The round-trip fare for a pedestrian without a car from St-Malo is 55€.

At low tide, a 15-minute stroll leads to the **Ile du Grand-Bé ★★**, the site of the tomb of Chateaubriand, who was born in St-Malo, "deserted by others and completely surrounded by storms." The tomb, marked by a cross, is simple, unlike the man it honors, with a stunning view of the Emerald Coast.

The "Bastille of the West," the **Château de St-Malo ★★**, Porte St-Vincent (✆ **02-99-40-71-57**), and its towers shelter the **Musée d'Histoire de St-Malo** (✆ **02-99-40-71-57**). It abounds with insights into the role of St-Malo, as well as souvenirs of the pirates Duguay-Trouin and Surcouf, the most famous of the privateers. Admission costs 5.20€ for adults and 2.60€ for students and children 17 and under. It's open April through October daily 10am to noon and 2 to 6pm, November through March Tuesday to Sunday 10am to noon and 2 to 6pm.

After you visit the château, try to carve out some time for wandering through the narrow streets and alleyways of St-Malo's historic core. Memories of the town's origins as a medieval fishing village confront you at nearly every turn.

St-Malo's **Cathédrale St-Vincent,** 12 rue St-Benoît (✆ **02-99-40-82-31**), is known for its nave vault dating from 1160. It's of the Angevin or Plantagenet style, elegantly marking the transition between Romanesque and Gothic. The cathedral also has a Renaissance facade (the west), with additions from the 18th century and a 15th-century tower. The 14th-century choir is surmounted by a triforium with trefoiled arches and flanked by chapels. Admission is free, and it's open June through August Monday to Saturday 9:45am to 7pm, Sunday 9:30am to 6pm (Sept–May closed noon–2pm).

BEACHES Along the coast, long stretches of sand intersperse with rocky outcroppings that suggest fortresses protecting Brittany from Atlantic storms. You can swim wherever you like, but beware of the very strong undertow. If you're staying in St-Malo, the two best beaches are **Plage de Bon Secours,** near the northern tip of the Vieille Ville (Old Town), and **La Grande Plage du Sillon,** a longer stretch of sand at the eastern perimeter of the Vieille Ville.

SHOPPING If you're in St-Malo on Tuesday or Friday between 8am and 1pm and want to experience a great Breton **market,** head for the Halle au Blé, in the heart of the old city. You can't miss the activity, the bustle, and the hawking

St-Malo's ramparts.

of country-fresh produce, cheese, fish, and dozens of household items, including dishware, cooking utensils, and handicrafts.

For **boutique shopping,** head to rue St-Vincent, rue Porcon, rue Broussais, rue Georges Clemenceau, rue des Merciers, rue Ste-Barbe, rue Ville Pépin, and rue de Dinan. You'll find everything from the trendy to the trashy. Check out **Marin-Marine,** 5 Grand Rue (✆ **02-99-40-90-32**), for quality men's and women's fashions that include great Breton wool sweaters, one of the town's best buys. Rue Clemenceau and rue Ville Pépin lie within the 19th-century neighborhood known as **St-Servan,** less than 1km (½ mile) southwest from the medieval core of St-Malo. To reach that district, take bus no. 2 from the center of St-Malo.

For last-minute souvenirs, stop by **Aux Délices Malouins,** 12 rue St-Vincent (✆ **02-99-40-55-22**). This shop also specializes in regional pastries, cookies, and chocolates.

For Breton handicrafts, try **Le Comptoir de Bretagne,** 6 rue Broussais (✆ **02-99-40-57-01**). In addition to hand-painted stoneware, books, and Gaelic CDs, you'll find Breton lace, Celtic souvenirs, and food items such as almond-flavored pastries and sugarcoated *galettes.* Other shops offering crafts such as Breton pottery include **La Manne Bretonne,** 2 place Guy la Chambre (✆ **02-23-18-28-20**), and **La Trinitaine,** 2 rue Broussais (✆ **02-23-18-32-37**).

Where to Stay

While some hotels inside the city walls are up to snuff, many are a bit run down. It may be a better, more pleasant bet to stay along the Plage du Sillon and walk the 10 minutes along the beach into town.

Hotel Alba ★ ☺ For those who want to stay outside the walls near the beach, this boutique hotel is a winning choice, with rooms opening onto panoramic views of the English Channel. Guest rooms are small but attractively decorated in earthy tones, with contemporary furnishings; some are large enough for families. In fair weather, guests gather on the sunny terrace or else enjoy a drink at night from the scenic bar. The best rooms have an ocean view and a private balcony.

17 rue des Dunes, St-Malo 35400. www.hotelalba.com. ✆ **02-99-40-37-18.** Fax 02-99-40-96-40. 22 units. 125€–171€ double; 200€ family room. DC, MC, V. Free parking. **Amenities:** Bar; room service. *In room:* TV, hair dryer, free Wi-Fi.

Hôtel Beaufort A neighbor to the Hotel Alba (see above), recent renovations and new ownership have given this hotel modern amenities while retaining a seaside home feel. Rooms have spectacular beach and sunset views, and some rooms have a bed for a third person. The entire hotel is smoke-free.

25 chausée du Sillon, St-Malo 35400. www.hotel-beaufort.com. ✆ **02-99-40-99-99.** Fax 02-99-40-99-62. 22 units. 141€–211€ double. AE, DC, MC, V. Parking 15€. **Amenities:** Bar; babysitting. *In room:* TV, hair dryer, free Wi-Fi.

Hôtel Elizabeth ★ Adjacent to the medieval ramparts of the old town, this stone-sided hotel was built in the 17th century as a baronial private home. Traditional artifacts and antiques evoke old-time Brittany at its most authentic. The cozy, renovated guest rooms have mellow-grained paneling and comfortable but unpretentious period-reproduction furniture. There is a new annex that has less expensive (and less interesting) rooms. Breakfast, the only meal available, is served in a cellar under stout antique ceiling beams.

2 rue des Cordiers, St-Malo 35400. www.hotel-elizabeth.fr. ✆ **02-99-56-24-98.** Fax 02-99-56-39-24. 17 units. 75€–145€ double. DC, MC, V. Limited parking: 15€. **Amenities:** Bikes available. *In room:* TV, hair dryer, minibar, free Wi-Fi (only in main bldg. rooms).

Hôtel France et Chateaubriand The birthplace of Chateaubriand, inside the walls of old St-Malo, is a good example of Napoleon III architecture. Recent renovations to half the rooms creates an odd Jekyll-and-Hyde feeling between modern and dated—you'll pay more to be up-to-date. Twenty rooms have panoramic ocean views. In the chic bar with gold-trimmed Corinthian columns, you can chat over drinks and occasionally listen to the pianist play the baby grand.

Place Chateaubriand, St-Malo 35412. www.hotel-fr-chateaubriand.com. ✆ **02-99-56-66-52.** Fax 02-99-40-10-04. 83 units. 98€–171€ double. AE, DC, MC, V. Parking 15€. **Amenities:** Restaurant; cafe; bar; babysitting; room service. *In room:* TV, hair dryer, free Wi-Fi.

Where to Eat

Hôtel France et Chateaubriand (see above) has one of the finest dining rooms in town.

La Brasserie du Sillon ★ SEAFOOD/FRENCH Choosing a restaurant inside the old city can feel like a crapshoot. Walk in front of this beachside brasserie, and you'll know you're in for something good. Several prix-fixe menus offer excellent values. Along with beautiful shellfish platters, try the skate with brown butter served with capers and walnuts, or go all out for sole meunière. Meat dishes are on level with the seafood. Try the profiteroles.

3 chaussée du Sillon. ✆ **02-99-56-10-74.** Reservations recommended. Main courses 13€–25€; fixed-price menus 25€–40€. AE, MC, V. Daily 12–2pm; Sun–Thurs 7–10pm; Fri–Sat 7–10:30pm.

Le Chalut ★★ SEAFOOD/FRENCH The interior might be a bit kitschy, but this restaurant is the place to go for fresh fish. The flavorful cuisine, based on fresh ingredients, includes a tart with layers of salmon and scallops, sprinkled with lime juice; John Dory with wild mushrooms, essence of lobster, and fresh coriander; and succulent line-caught sea bass with sherry sauce and braised endive. For dessert, try gateau of bitter chocolate with almond paste, or homemade ice cream flavored with malt whiskey.

8 rue de la Corne-de-Cerf. ✆ **02-99-56-71-58.** Reservations required. Main courses 23€–29€; fixed-price lunch and dinner menus 25€–70€. AE, MC, V. Wed–Sun noon–1:30pm and 7–9:30pm.

CANCALE'S FAMOUS oysters

Welcome to oyster heaven. Cancale—which looks across the bay to Mont-St-Michel—is the oyster capital of France. It is a quintessential French pleasure to toss back a dozen while sitting on a sea wall, flipping the shells back into the sea. Oysters are ordered by size—No. 5s are tiny, 30-45 grams are medium, and 0s are whoppers that clock in at more than 150 grams. In Brittany, look for *plates,* "flat" oysters considered the finest in France. Though there are dozens of restaurants along the waterfront, the vendors on the water down below the Rue des Parcs will sell you a shucked dozen on a plate that you return when you're done. To make a meal out of it, head to the nearby Breizh Café (at 7 quai Thomas; ✆ **02-99-89-61-76**) for spot-on and often inventive sweet and savory crèpes.

St-Malo After Dark

For an evening of gambling, head to **Le Casino Barrière,** 2 chaussée du Sillon (✆ **02-99-40-64-00**). You can also order dinner, sometimes accompanied by live music. A passport must be presented.

For dancing, consider **L'Escalier,** La Buzardière (✆ **02-99-81-65-56**), open Thursday to Saturday midnight to 5am. The cover doesn't exceed 13€. You'll need a car or taxi, since the club is in the countryside 5km (3 miles) east of town. A disco, **Le 109,** 3 rue des Cordiers (✆ **02-99-56-81-09**), is in a vaulted cellar that's at least 300 years old. It isn't as fashionable as L'Escalier, but it's accessible without a car. It's open Tuesday to Sunday 8pm to 3am, charging a cover of 10€ after midnight, including a first drink.

On weekends, in search of nightlife, many young Bretons head for Rennes, but if you're interested in seeing the town's biggest disco, check out **Le Klub,** at L'Etanchet, just outside the hamlet of Pleurtuit (✆ **02-99-88-81-17**). Housed in an isolated farmhouse on the outskirts of St-Malo, it contains a bar, a dance floor, and a revolving series of lights that evoke a 1980s disco. It's open Thursday, Friday, and Saturday nights, and on the evening before national holidays. Cover is 11€ and includes the first drink.

Popular bars include **L'Aviso,** 12 rue du Point du Jour (✆ **02-99-40-99-08**), which specializes in beers from everywhere. **Pub Saint Patrick,** 24 rue Sainte-Barbe (✆ **02-99-56-66-90**), serves 50 different Irish whiskeys, along with Breton beers and regularly scheduled concerts. Also appealing is **La Caravelle,** 95 bd. de Rochebonne (✆ **02-99-56-39-83**), a piano bar 2km (1¼ miles) east of St-Malo, with a fine view of the sea.

DINARD ★★

417km (259 miles) W of Paris; 23km (14 miles) N of Dinan

Dinard (not to be confused with its inland neighbor, Dinan) sits on a rocky promontory at the top of the Rance River, opposite St-Malo. Ferries ply the waters between the two resorts. Victorian Gothic villas, many now hotels, overlook the sea, and gardens and parks abound. Though a few eyesore buildings seem to have gotten in under a snoozing architectural board, there's historic architecture, too; for a look at what the Edwardians admired, go down the pointe de la Vicomte at the resort's southern tip or stroll along the promenade and watch the emerald-blue waters bash into the shore.

One of France's best-known resorts, Dinard offers well-sheltered bathing and healthful sea air in La Manche ("The Sleeve," as the French call the English Channel).

Essentials

GETTING THERE If you're **driving,** take D186 west from St-Malo to Dinard. SNCF **trains** go only as far as St-Malo; from there, take bus no. 16, which departs from the St-Malo rail station daily for the 30-minute ride to Dinard. The one-way fare is 1.80€. **Buses** arrive from many large cities in Brittany, including Rennes. For information, call **illenoo** (✆ **08-25-13-81-30**). Between April and October, **Compagnie Corsaire,** Gare Maritime de la Bourse, St-Malo (✆ **02-23-18-15-15**), operates ferryboats from St-Malo to Dinard. The trip takes 10 minutes and costs 4.30€ one-way. A **taxi** to Dinard from St-Malo is another option; it costs 22€ during the day and 30€ after 7pm and on holidays. For information, call ✆ **06-84-92-55-73.**

VISITOR INFORMATION The **Office de Tourisme** is at 2 bd. Féart (✆ **02-99-46-94-12;** fax 02-99-88-21-07; www.ot-dinard.com).

SPECIAL EVENTS From early June to mid-September, *musique-et-lumière* adds the drama of floodlights and recorded jazz, pop, or classical music to walks along the city's flowered seafront promenade du Clair de Lune.

Enjoying the Resort

A 10-minute walk from the town's historic core to the Pointe du Moulinet encircles most of the old town and encompasses views as far away as St-Malo.

BEACHES & SWIMMING Dinard's main beach is **Plage de l'Ecluse** or **La Grande Plage,** the strip of sand between the peninsulas that defines the edges of the old town. Favored by families and vacationers, it's crowded on hot days. Smaller and more isolated is **Plage de St-Enogat** (you pass through the village of St-Enogat on the 20-min. hike east from Dinard). **Plage du Prieuré,** a 10-minute walk from the center, has a few trees that shade the sand. Because there's such a difference between high and low tides, the municipality has built swimming pool–style basins along the Plage de L'Ecluse and the Plage du Prieuré beaches to catch seawater during high tide. Most people walk along the salt flats at low tide to bathe in the sea.

Looking for a pool that's covered, heated, filled with seawater, and open year-round? Head for the **Piscine Olympique,** boulevard du Président-Wilson (✆ **02-99-46-22-77**), next to the casino. Entrance is 4.50€ for adults, 3.50€ for children 5 to 16, and free for children 4 and under. From July to mid-September, it's open Monday to Saturday 10am to 12:30pm and 3 to 7:30pm, Sunday 10am to 12:30pm and 3 to 6:30pm. The rest of the year, it runs on a varying schedule according to the needs of school groups and swim teams.

SHOPPING For shops and boutiques, concentrate on rue du Maréchal-Leclerc, rue Levavasseur, and boulevard Féart. In the 15th-century house containing **Atelier du Prince Noir,** 70 av. George-V (✆ **02-99-46-29-99**), you'll find paintings and sculptures by some of the most talented artists in France.

The gallery is closed from October to April. Another worthwhile destination is **L'Ancien Temple,** 29 rue Jacques-Cartier (✆ **09-50-63-04-52**), in a former Protestant church. The high-ceilinged showrooms feature upscale porcelain, stoneware, kitchen utensils, gift items, and fresh flowers.

Where to Stay

Didier Méril (see "Where to Eat," below) also rents rooms.

Grand Hôtel Barrière de Dinard ★ A member of the Lucien Barrière chain, Dinard's largest hotel dates from 1858. Its location, a 2-minute walk from the town center, commands an excellent view of the harbor. It rises in two wings, separated by a heated indoor pool. Most rooms have balconies and are equipped with traditional furnishings and cloth-covered walls. The inviting bar is a popular spot before and after dinner.

46 av. George-V, Dinard 35801. www.lucienbarriere.com. ✆ **02-99-88-26-26.** Fax 02-99-88-26-27. 90 units. 290€–480€ double. AE, DC, MC, V. Closed late Nov to early Mar. **Amenities:** Restaurant; bar; babysitting; fitness center; hammam; indoor pool; room service; rooms for those w/limited mobility; sauna; smoke-free rooms; spa. *In room:* TV, hair dryer, minibar, Wi-Fi (10€ per day).

Hôtel Printania ★ Originally built in 1920, and a longtime favorite of nostalgia buffs, writers, and artists, the family-owned Printania lies a 5-minute walk from the beaches. On August 15, 1944, a bombing raid damaged the hotel. Terraces and a glassed-in veranda with potted palms highlight the main villa. The guest rooms contain antiques and Breton decorations. Some have Breton *lits clos*—Brittany-style beds which surround the occupant with either curtains or paneled wood doors. Every room is different, so tour around to find one you enjoy.

5 av. George-V, Dinard 35800. www.printaniahotel.com. ✆ **02-99-46-13-07.** Fax 02-99-46-26-32. 56 units. 80€–149€ double; 180€–220€ suite. DC, MC, V. Closed mid-Nov to mid-Mar. **Amenities:** 3 restaurants; bar. *In room:* TV, hair dryer, free Wi-Fi.

Villa Reine-Hortense ★★ This beachside hotel was built in 1860 as a retreat for one of the Russian-born courtiers of Queen Hortense de Beauharnais, daughter of Josephine de Beauharnais (who married Napoleon) and mother of Napoleon III. It offers glamorously outfitted public salons and guest rooms decorated in either Louis XV or Napoleon III style. Most units have private balconies. One high-ceilinged room (no. 4) has Hortense's silver-plated bathtub, dating from the early 1800s. Breakfast (16€) is the only meal served.

19 rue de la Malouine, Dinard 35800. www.villa-reine-hortense.com. ✆ **02-99-46-54-31.** Fax 02-99-88-15-88. 8 units. 150€–245€ double; 320€–395€ suite. AE, DC, MC, V. Closed Oct to mid-Apr. **Amenities:** Bar. *In room:* TV, hair dryer, free Wi-Fi.

Where to Eat

Another choice is the restaurant at the **Grand Hôtel Barrière de Dinard** (see above).

Didier Méril ★ FRENCH/BRETON The finest dining room in town offers tables opening onto the panoramic view of the Bay of Prieuré. Filled with designer furniture, it offers traditional fare in spite of its contemporary look. Located in the historic center of Dinard, the restaurant edges close to the beach. Chef Didier Méril takes full advantage of the local seafood and vegetables from neighboring farmland. He also offers the finest and most varied wine list in the area. In good

AN idyll ON AN ILE

Ile de Bréhat is home to some 350 hearty folk who live most of the year in isolation—until the summer crowds arrive. The tiny island (actually two islands, Ile Nord and Ile Sud, linked by a bridge, Le Pont Vauban) is in the Golfe de St-Malo, north of Paimpol. A visit to Bréhat is an adventure, even to the French. The only settlement on the islands is Le Bourg, in the south. The only bona fide beach is a strip of sand at Guerzido.

Walking is the primary activity, and it's possible to stroll the footpaths around the island in a day. Cars other than police and fire vehicles aren't allowed. Tractor-driven carts carry visitors on an 8km (5-mile) circuit of Bréhat's two islands, charging 13€ for the 45-minute jaunt. A number of places rent bikes, but they aren't necessary.

The rich flora here astonishes many visitors, who get off the ferry expecting a wind-swept island, only to discover a more Mediterranean clime. Flower gardens are in full summer bloom, though both the gardens and houses appear tiny because of the scarcity of land. At the highest point, Chapelle St-Michel, you'll be rewarded with a panoramic view.

The tourist office, place du Bourg, Le Bourg (✆ **02-96-20-83-16**), is open Monday to Saturday mid-June to mid-September.

To reach Paimpol, **drive** west on D768 from Dinard to Lamballe, then take E50 west to Plérin and D786 north to Paimpol. To reach the island, take D789 4km (2½ miles) north of Paimpol, where the peninsula ends at the Pointe de l'Arcouest. From Paimpol, 6 to 10 **ti'bus** buses make the 10-minute run to the point for a one-way fare of 2€. Then catch one of the **ferries** operated by **Les Vedettes de Bréhat** (✆ **02-96-55-79-50;** www.vedettesdebrehat.com). Ferries depart about every 30 minutes in summer, around seven times per day in the off season; the round-trip costs 9€. Visitors in April, May, June, and September will find the island much less crowded than in July and August. Cars are not allowed on the ferry.

weather, tables are placed on a sea-bordering terrace. Try such tasty specialties as sweetbread with lemon, foie gras with caramelized apples, roast pigeon with cabbage, and lobster flavored with cognac. John Dory, sea bass, and turbot are regularly featured, depending on the catch of the day.

The restaurant also rents six stylish bedrooms, some with bay views; the simplest rents for 85€, the best for 160€.

1 place du Gen. de Gaulle. ✆ **02-99-46-95-74.** www.restaurant-didier-meril.com. Reservations required. Main courses 20€–45€; fixed-price menu 29€–65€. AE, DC, MC, V. Daily noon–2:30pm and 7–9:30pm.

Dinard After Dark

Like many of Brittany's seaside towns, Dinard has a casino, **Le Casino Barrière,** 4 bd. du Président-Wilson (✆ **02-99-16-30-30**). It's liveliest from Easter to late October for games including roulette, blackjack, and slot machines. Hours are Sunday through Thursday from 11am to 3am, Friday and Saturday from 11am to 4am. Admission is free. There are several restaurants within walking distance. An alternative outside of the casino is **La Suite,** Zone Artisanale La Mare (✆ **02-**

99-46-46-46), a nightclub and disco that has earned the loyalty of many residents, thanks to a good selection of wine and an amiable ambience. It lies on the outskirts of town on the road to St-Malo.

In the evenings from June to September, the **promenade du Clair-de-Lune** attracts a huge crowd of strollers for the *musique-et-lumière,* when the buildings, flowers, and Alfred Hitchcock statue along the promenade are illuminated and musical groups of just about every ilk—from rock to blues to jazz—perform.

DINAN ★★★

396km (246 miles) W of Paris; 52km (32 miles) NW of Rennes

Once a stronghold of the ducs de Bretagne, Dinan is one of the best-preserved towns in Brittany. It's noted for its *maisons à piliers,* houses built on stilts over the sidewalks. The 18th-century granite dwellings provide a sharp contrast to the medieval timbered houses that droop and sway romantically in this walled town with a once-fortified château. Dinan (pop. 12,000) is one of Brittany's prettiest towns. There's tourist bustle on a busy day, but it's hard not to be moved by a walk atop the ramparts or a visit to the basilica.

Essentials

GETTING THERE Dinan has a railway station, but few SNCF **trains** stop here. Railway passengers usually travel to Rennes or St-Malo and then transfer to one of the **buses** (about five a day from each) that line up in front of the railway stations. The one-way train fare from Rennes is 4.10€, from St-Malo 2.60€. For information about bus service to Dinan, call the town's Gare Routière, adjacent to the railway station, about 1km (½ mile) west of the center (✆ **08-10-22-22-22**). If you're **driving** from Dinard, take highway D166 south to Dinan.

VISITOR INFORMATION The **Office de Tourisme** is at 9 rue du Château (✆ **02-96-87-69-76;** fax 02-96-87-69-77; www.dinan-tourisme.com).

SPECIAL EVENTS The most activity occurs on the third weekend of July, during the **Fêtes des Remparts,** held in even-numbered years (2012 is the next one). Duels from the age of chivalry are staged, and locals don medieval apparel for carousing in the streets of the city's historic core.

Exploring the Town

For a panoramic view of the valley, head for the **Jardin Anglais (English Garden),** a terraced garden that huddles up to the ramparts. A Gothic-style bridge spans the Rance River; damaged in World War II, it has since been restored. Dinan's most typical and one of its most appealing streets is the sloping **rue du Jerzual,** flanked with some buildings dating from the 15th century. The street ends at the **Porte du Jerzual,** a 13th- and 14th-century gate. **Rue du Petit-Fort** and place des Merciers contain a number of 15th-century *maisons.*

Dominating the city's ramparts, **Château Musée de Dinan,** rue du Château (✆ **02-96-39-45-20**), contains a 14th-century keep and a 15th-century tower, built to withstand sieges. In the stones, you'll see the space for the portcullis and the drawbridge. Inside you can view an exhibition on the architecture and art of the city, including sculpture from the 12th to the 15th centuries. Admission is 4.40€ for adults, 1.75€ for children 12 to 18, and free for children 11 and under. It's open June to September daily 10am to 6:30pm, October to May daily 1:30 to 5:30pm (closed Jan).

Tour de l'Horloge (Clock Tower), on rue de l'Horloge (✆ **02-96-87-58-72**), boasts a clock made in 1498 and a bell donated by Anne de Bretagne in 1507. You'll have a view of Dinan from the 23m (75-ft.) belfry. Admission is 2.95€ for adults, 1.90€ for children 12 to 18, and free for children 11 and under. The tower is open daily July to September 10am to 6:30pm, and Easter to June and October daily 2 to 6:30pm. Closed October to Easter.

The heart of Bertrand du Guesclin, who defended the town when the duke of Lancaster threatened it in 1359, is entombed in a place of honor in the **Basilique St-Sauveur,** place St-Sauveur (✆ **02-96-39-06-67**). Note the basilica's Romanesque portals and ornamented chapels. It's open daily from 9am to 6pm, but call ahead.

Dinan.

REGIONAL CRAFTS Dinan has attracted craftspeople and artists for at least 20 years. The densest concentration of studios is along the **rue du Jerzual, rue de la Chaux,** and **rue l'Apport,** where art objects are crafted from glass, wood, silk, leather, and clay. Our favorite shopping street is Jerzual. Other good streets include **place des Merciers** and **place des Cordeliers.** You may be able to buy an item directly from the artisan, but it's more efficient to visit galleries that sell objects by an assortment of the artisans. One of the best is **Galerie St-Sauveur,** 12 rue de l'Apport (✆ **02-96-85-26-62**), where wide cross-sections of paintings and crafts help provide perspective on the arts in Dinan. St-Sauveur specializes in avant-garde paintings and sculptures by living artists.

Where to Stay

Hôtel Arvor 🏷 ☺ This is a comfortable, relatively inexpensive hotel in a 14th-century Jacobin convent under new ownership. Despite dormlike hallways, rooms are inviting and continually redone, including a suite that sleeps six. The result is comfortable guest rooms with small bathrooms. They retain none of their original medieval characteristics, but provide a cozy haven in one of Dinan's oldest neighborhoods. Breakfast (7€) is the only meal served, but many inviting restaurants lie within a short walk.

5 rue Pavie, Dinan 22100. www.hotelarvordinan.com. ✆ **02-96-39-21-22.** Fax 02-96-39-83-09. 23 units. 72€–85€ double. MC, V. Closed Jan. *In room:* TV, hair dryer, free Wi-Fi.

Hôtel d'Avaugour ★★ ☺ Set on the town ramparts, this is one of the town's best hotels. It's hard to believe that a pair of gutted stone-fronted buildings has been transformed into an up-to-date hotel. Guest rooms are decorated in a style that reflects the historical charm of the area. Midsize bathrooms all have tubs. Half the units overlook the square; the others face the large and wonderful garden. A vast breakfast, for 14€, is the only meal served.

1 place du Champs-Clos, Dinan 22100. www.avaugourhotel.com. ✆ **02-96-39-07-49.** Fax 02-96-85-43-04. 24 units. 160€–198€ double; 220€–280€ suite. MC, V. Closed Nov–Mar 1. *In room:* TV, hair dryer, free Wi-Fi.

Where to Eat

L'Auberge du Pélican ★ FRENCH/BRETON This traditional restaurant's decor is contemporary but the food is often based on time-honored recipes, all of which are homemade, even the bread. Our favorite dish is the casserole of fresh fish served daily with *beurre blanc,* a sauce made with vinegar, white wine, shallots, and butter. Succulent scallops from the bay are also a worthy choice for seafood lovers. The chef prepares meat and poultry dishes equally well, particularly the *magret de canard* (duck breast) with figs and a tender, well-flavored filet of beef with mushrooms. For a lighter meal, the busy, solid Creperie Ahna is just around the corner on rue de la Poissonniere.

3 rue Haute Voie. ✆ **02-96-39-47-05.** Reservations recommended. Main courses 14€–28€; fixed-price menus 19€–60€. AE, MC, V. July–Aug daily noon–2pm and 7–10pm; Sept–June Tues–Sun noon–2pm, Tues–Wed and Fri–Sun 7–9:30pm. Closed Jan.

ON THE OUTSKIRTS

Jean-Pierre Crouzil ★★ 🎁 BRETON/NORMAN Those who think there's nothing left to discover on the Breton coast can drive to this restaurant tucked away in the hamlet of Plancoët, 28km (17 miles) from St-Malo and 17km (11 miles) from Dinan. A smooth beginning is *foie gras en terrine* in sauterne wine jelly. The most lavish dish is lobster roasted in Calvados, which imparts a rich, aromatic flavor. We are fond of the duck served in thick, rosy slices; farmhouse quail; and *pigonneaux de nid au porto* (squab in potato baskets with port-wine sauce). The chef also prepares turbot with beurre blanc and scallops in dishes that change depending on his inspiration for the evening.

20 Les Quais, Plancoët. ✆ **02-96-84-10-24.** www.crouzil.com. Reservations required. Fixed-price menus 35€–130€. AE, MC, V. Wed–Sun noon–1:30pm; Wed–Sat 7:30–9:15pm. Closed 3 weeks in Jan. From Dinan, take rue des Rouairies west and follow signs to Plancoët.

Dinan After Dark

The densest concentration of cafes and bars in Dinan lines the **rue de la Cordonnerie,** nicknamed *la rue de la soif* ("the street where you go when you're thirsty") by long-ago sailors.

QUIMPER ★★

570km (353 miles) W of Paris; 205km (127 miles) NW of Rennes

The town that pottery built, Quimper, at the meeting of the Odet and Steir rivers, is the historic capital of Brittany's most traditional region, La Cornouaille. Today its faïence decorates tables from Europe to the United States. Skilled artisans have been turning out Quimperware since the 17th century, using bold provincial designs. Inquire at the tourist office (see below) to tour one of the ateliers. Today Quimper is rather smug and bourgeois, home to some 67,000 *Quimperois,* who walk narrow streets spared from World War II damage.

Essentials

GETTING THERE Speedy TGV trains take only 4½ hours from the Montparnasse station in Paris. The one-way fare is 75€. For information, call ✆ **36-35** or 08-92-35-35-35. If you're **driving,** the best route is from Rennes: Take E50/N12 west to just outside the town of Montauban, continue west along N164 to Châteaulin, and head south along N165 to Quimper.

VISITOR INFORMATION The **Office de Tourisme** is on place de la Résistance (✆ **02-98-53-04-05;** www.quimper-tourisme.com).

SPECIAL EVENTS For 6 days in mid- to late July, the **Festival de Cornouaille** adds a traditional flavor to the nightlife scene with Celtic and Breton concerts throughout the city. For information, contact the Office de Tourisme.

Exploring the Town

In the summer, the tourist office organizes a 90-minute walking tour of the city *(des circuits de ville).* It costs 5.20€. Tours in French depart daily except Sunday at 4:30pm from in front of the tourist office.

In some quarters, Quimper maintains its old-world atmosphere, with footbridges spanning the rivers. At place St-Corentin is the **Cathédrale St-Corentin ★★** (✆ **02-98-95-06-19**), characterized by two towers that climb 75m (246 ft.). The cathedral was built between the 13th and15th centuries; the spires were added in the 19th. Inside, note the 15th-century stained glass. It's open September to June daily 9:45am to noon and 1:30 to 6:30pm, daily in July and August 9:45am to 6:30pm, except during Sunday morning services.

Also on the square is the **Musée des Beaux-Arts ★★**, 40 place St-Corentin (✆ **02-98-95-45-20**). The collection includes work by Rubens, Boucher, Fragonard, and Corot, plus an exceptional exhibit from the Pont-Aven school (Bernard, Gaugin, Sérusier, Lacombe, Maufra, Denis). Admission is 4.50€ for adults, 2.50€ for ages 12 to 26, and free for children 11 and under. The museum is open July and August daily from 10am to 7pm; April to June and September and October Monday and Wednesday to Sunday 10am to noon and 2 to 6pm; and November to March Monday and Wednesday to Saturday 10am to noon and 2 to 6pm, Sunday 2 to 6pm.

Musée Departemental Breton, 1–3 rue Roi Gradlon (✆ **02-98-95-21-60**), is in the medieval Palais des Eveques de Cornouaille (Palace of the Bishops of Cornwall), adjacent to the cathedral. The museum showcases the evolution of Breton costumes, with examples of local handicrafts, archaeology, and furniture. It is open June through September daily 9am to 6pm, October through May Tuesday to Saturday 9am to noon and daily 2 to 5pm. Admission is 4€ for adults, 2.50€ for ages 18 to 25, and free for children 17 and under.

Shopping

When artisans from Rouen settled in Quimper, the city became forever associated with ceramics. It produces the most recognized and most popular French porcelain. Typical are chunky white pieces painted with blue-and-yellow Breton figures, fruits, and flowers. The most popular feature a male *Breton* or a female

Quimper.

Bretonne, both in profile and in traditional Breton costume. Today that 19th-century design is copyrighted and fiercely protected.

The best shopping streets are **rue Kéréon** and **rue du Parc,** where you'll find Breton products including pottery, dolls and puppets, clothing made from regional cloth and wool, jewelry, lace, and beautiful Breton costumes.

One of three sites that produce stoneware is open for tours. Monday to Friday 9am to 4:30pm, five to seven tours a day depart from the visitor information center of **HB-Henriot Faïenceries de Quimper,** rue Haute, Quartier Locmaria (✆ **02-98-90-09-36;** www.hb-henriot.com). Tours in English, French, or both last 40 to 45 minutes and cost 5€ for adults, 2.50€ for children 8 to 14, and are free for children 7 and under. On-site, a store sells the most complete inventory of Quimper porcelain in the world. You can invest in first-run (nearly perfect) pieces or slightly discounted "seconds," with almost imperceptible flaws. Everything can be shipped.

For other Breton pottery and pieces of the faïence once heavily produced in this area, visit **François le Villec,** 4 rue Roi-Gradlon (✆ **02-98-95-31-54**). Here you'll find quality tablecloths, linens, and other household linens.

Another good choice for Breton items is **La Galerie le Cornet à Dés,** 1 rue Ste-Thérêse (✆ **02-98-53-37-51**). It stocks hand-painted porcelain and antique and contemporary paintings, mostly of Quimper landscapes.

Where to Stay

Hôtel Gradlon The town's most consistently reliable hotel is this 19th-century landmark. The frequently renovated hotel has a modern annex a few steps away. The decor is simple, angular, and solid, with framed posters of Breton landscapes and monuments, a nice courtyard, lots of varnished-wood trim, and a fireplace near the bar. Guest rooms are simple and comfortable. Breakfast, for 9€, is the only meal served.

30 rue de Brest, Quimper 29000. www.hotel-gradlon.com. ✆ **02-98-95-04-39.** Fax 02-98-95-61-25. 20 units. 101€–135€ double; 135€–175€ suite. AE, DC, MC, V. Parking 10€. Closed mid-Dec to mid-Jan. Pets 9€. **Amenities:** Bar. *In room:* TV, hair dryer, free Wi-Fi.

Hôtel Kregenn The best hotel in town boasts spacious, stylish rooms that are a real value. This family-run establishment under the Best Western umbrella might not be terribly Breton, but it's not so modern that it lacks a soul. Breakfast, for 13€, is the only meal served, though light items can be requested at any time. The hotel is smoke-free.

11–15 rue des Réguaires, Quimper 29000. www.hotel-kregenn.fr. ✆ **02-98-95-08-70.** Fax 02-98-53-85-12. 32 units. 105€–180€ double. AE, DC, MC, V. Parking 7€. Pets 15€. **Amenities:** Bar; limited room service. *In room:* TV, hair dryer, Internet.

Where to Eat

Ambroisie ★ ☺ BRETON/FRENCH Although it's surpassed by Les Acacias (see below), this restaurant remains one of the most respected and sought-after in Quimper. A 5-minute walk north of the cathedral, the airy ocher-and-gold dining room has contemporary furniture and large paintings in a style inspired by the English neosurrealist Francis Bacon. Menu items incorporate Breton traditions, with an occasional contemporary twist. The finest examples include a crusty buckwheat galette stuffed with spiced crabmeat, braised scallops with asparagus and citrus sauce, and filet of John Dory on an artfully contrived bed of vegetable ragout.

49 rue Elie Fréron. ✆ **02-98-95-00-02.** www.ambroisie-quimper.com. Reservations recommended. Fixed-price menu 36€–58€; children's menu 15€. MC, V. Tues–Sun noon–1:30pm; Tues–Sat 7:30–9:15pm.

Les Acacias ★ ☺ BRETON/SEAFOOD This is Quimper's leading restaurant, focusing on seafood and very fresh fish, with a few meat dishes, including game. Your meal may include roasted crayfish with sweet spices, delectable smoked John Dory perfumed with algae, fondant of pigs' feet with exotic mushrooms, or roast pigeon with baby vegetables. Customers rave about the dessert specialty of local strawberries marinated in spiced wine. The wine list features 150 to 200 mostly French vintages.

88 bd. Creac'h Gwen. ✆ **02-98-52-15-20.** Reservations recommended. Main courses 27€–60€; fixed-price menu 28€–45€; children's menu 12€. MC, V. Sun–Fri 12:30–2:30pm; Mon-Fri 8pm–9:30 pm. Closed May 1–7. From Quimper, drive 2km (1¼ miles), following signs to Benodet.

Where to Stay & Eat Nearby

In an orchard district 13km (8 miles) from Quimper, the sleepy village of **La Forêt-Fouesnant** produces the best cider in the province and is home to one of Brittany's finest manors.

Manoir du Stang ★★★ To get to this 16th-century ivy-covered manor, you travel down a tree-lined avenue, through a stone gate, and into a courtyard. On your right is a formal garden; stone terraces lead to 10 hectares (25 acres) of woodland. M. and Mme. Hubert provide gracious lodging in period rooms. Guests stay in the main building or in the even older but less desirable annex, which has a circular stone staircase. Your room is likely to be furnished with silk and fine antiques; each midsize bathroom comes with a combination tub/shower. One luxury perk is that a maid brings you breakfast on a tray each morning.

La Forêt-Fouesnant 29940. www.manoirdustang.com. ✆ **02-98-56-96-38.** Fax 02-98-56-97-37. 22 units. 65€–142€ double. AE, MC, V. Free parking. Closed mid-Sept to mid-May. Drive 1.5km (1 mile) north of the village center and follow signs from N783; access is by private road. **Amenities:** Bar. *In room:* Hair dryer, free Wi-Fi.

Quimper After Dark

You will likely hear singing at the steadfastly Celtic bar **Céili Pub** before you find it at 4 rue Aristide-Briand (✆ **02-98-95-17-61**). It has lots of polished wood, regional music, and happy people—join in a game of darts with one of the regulars. Two animated pubs with modern recorded music and a lot of innate Breton/Celtic pride are **O Patchwork,** place Pierre de Ronsard (✆ **02-98-95-05-72**), and **An Poitin Still,** 2 av. Libération (✆ **02-98-90-02-77**), the latter featuring Irish music Fridays at 10pm. Both are favorites of the young, the restless, and the *Vive La Bretagne* fervor, especially during soccer matches.

The young and stylish flock to **Les Naïades Discothèque,** boulevard Creac'h Gwen (✆ **02-98-53-32-30**), where you can dance to the latest tunes. It sometimes charges a cover.

CONCARNEAU ★★

539km (334 miles) W of Paris; 93km (58 miles) SE of Brest

This port is a favorite of painters, who never tire of capturing the subtleties of the fishing fleet. It's also our favorite of the coast communities—primarily because it doesn't depend on tourists. Its canneries produce most of the tuna in France. Walk along the quays, especially in the evening, and watch the Breton fishers unload their catch; later, join them for a pint of cider in the taverns.

Essentials

GETTING THERE There's no **rail** service to Concarneau. If you're **driving,** the town is 21km (13 miles) southeast of Quimper along D783. A **bus** (✆ **08-10-81-00-29**) runs from Quimper to Concarneau (trip time: 30 min.); the one-way fare is 2€. The bus from Resporden, site of another SNCF railway station, runs about eight times per day (trip time: 20 min.) for a fare of 2€.

VISITOR INFORMATION The **Office de Tourisme** is on quai d'Aiguillon (✆ **02-98-97-01-44;** www.tourismeconcarneau.fr).

Exploring the Area

The town is built on three sides of a natural harbor whose innermost sheltered section is the **Nouveau Port.** In the center of the harbor is the heavily fortified **Ville Close,** an ancient hamlet surrounded by ramparts, some from the 14th century. From the quay, cross the bridge and descend into the town. Souvenir shops have taken over, but don't let that spoil it. You can spend an hour wandering the alleys, gazing up at the towers, peering at the stone houses, and stopping in secluded squares.

For a splendid view of the port, walk the **ramparts.** They're open to pedestrians daily 10am to 7:30pm, with seasonal variations.

Also in the old town is a fishing museum, **Musée de la Pêche,** 3 rue Vauban (✆ **02-98-97-10-20**). The 17th-century building has ship models and exhibits tracing the development of the fishing industry; you can also view the ship *Hemerica*. Admission is 6€ for adults and 4€ for students and children 14 and under. It's open April through October daily 10am to 6pm (July–Aug until 7:30pm).

BEACHES Concarneau's largest, most beautiful beach, popular with families, is **Plage des Sables Blancs,** near the historic core. Within a 10-minute walk are **Plage de Cornouaille** and two small beaches, **Plage des Dames** and **Plage de Rodel,** where you'll find fewer families with children. The wide-open **Plage du Cabellou,** 5km (3 miles) west of town, is less crowded than the others.

SEA EXCURSIONS Boat rides are usually fine between June and September but can be treacherous the rest of the year. During midsummer, you can arrange deep-sea fishing with the captain of the ***Santa Maria*** (✆ **06-62-88-00-87**). For excursions along the coastline of southern Brittany, contact **Vedettes Glenn** (✆ **02-98-97-10-31**) or **Vedettes de l'Odet** (✆ **02-98-57-00-58**).

Where to Stay

Hôtel des Halles The tourist board gives only two stars to this cement-sided 1960s-era hotel, which is short on historical charm. Yet it's affordable, warm, and ecofriendly, with guest rooms that are cozier than you may expect. The frequently upgraded rooms have wood paneling and shower-only bathrooms. The location, a short distance from the fortifications encircling the town's historic core, is convenient. The city's covered food market, Les Halles (daily 8am–1pm), is a short walk away. Breakfast is the only meal served. The entire hotel is smoke-free.

Rue Charles Linement, Concarneau 29900. www.hoteldeshalles.com. ✆ **02-98-97-11-41.** Fax 02-98-50-58-54. 25 units. 64€–84€ double. AE, MC, V. Parking 6€. Small pets accepted free. Closed weekends in Jan and weekends late Nov to early Dec. *In room:* TV, hair dryer, free Internet.

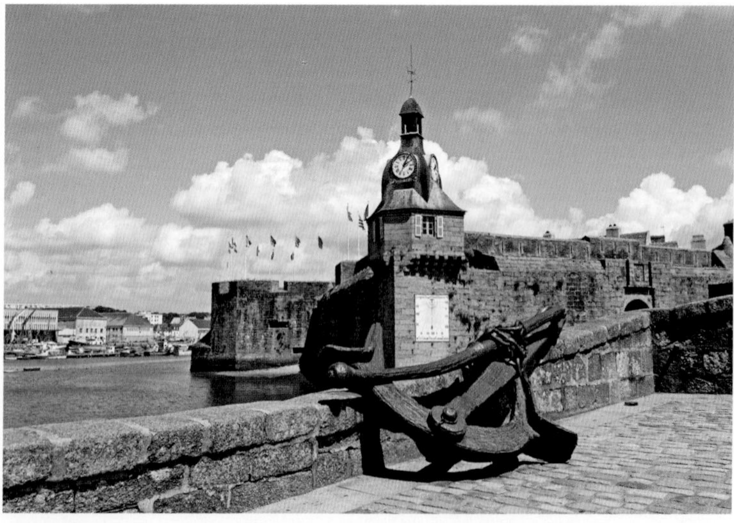

Concarneau.

Where to Eat

La Coquille ★ SEAFOOD/TRADITIONAL FRENCH This 4-decade-old restaurant occupies one end of a stone-sided harbor-side building; guests dine in a trio of rooms with stone walls, ceiling beams, and century-old oil paintings from the School of Pont-Aven. Seafood is the focus at La Coquille, and much of what is on the menu is offered simply because the fish is so fresh and succulent. Try the abalone salad or sautéed scallops with caramelized endives. The service is bistro style, with a cheerful, old-fashioned panache enhanced by the harbor view.

1 rue du Moros, at Nouveau Port. ✆ **02-98-97-08-52.** www.lacoquille-concarneau.com. Reservations required Sat–Sun and in summer. Main courses 21€–39€; fixed-price menu 29€–45€. AE, DC, MC, V. Tues–Sun noon–1:30pm; Tues–Sat 7:30–9:30pm.

Le Vauban FRENCH/SEAFOOD It's always best not to mess with a good thing, especially fish. The owner is a former fisherman, which gives him a bead on where to get the good stuff, and his wife, the chef, makes the best of what they get. Tasty oysters are served with a tangy sourdough bread (instead of a traditional brown bread) and churned butter. Try ground cuttlefish rolled around algae and salmon, sprinkled with paprika—a mouthful of smoky sea. There's a pleasant bar and gentle, more sophisticated dining room hidden in the back.

10 rue Vauban. ✆ **02-98-97-34-93.** Reservations recommended. Main courses 9.90€–24€; set-price menus 16€–19€. MC, V. Wed–Sun noon–2pm and 7–9:30pm. Closed mid-Jan to mid-Feb.

PONT-AVEN ★★

522km (324 miles) W of Paris; 32km (20 miles) SE of Quimper; 16km (10 miles) S of Concarneau

Paul Gauguin loved this village, with its white houses along the gently flowing Aven River. In the late 19th century, many painters followed him here, including Maurice Denis, Paul Sérusier, and Emile Bernard. The theories and techniques developed at the time have been known ever since as the School of Pont-Aven. It has the potential to be a large tourist draw yet remains modest and pleasant.

Essentials

GETTING THERE If you're **driving** from Quimper, go southeast on N165 and follow signs into Pont-Aven. From Quimperlé, head west along D783. SNCF **trains** stop at Quimperlé, where you can transfer to between four and six daily **buses** for the 30-minute ride to Pont-Aven. The one-way fare is 2€. For train information, call the Pont-Aven tourist office (see below) or ✆ **08-92-35-35-35,** or visit www.voyages-sncf.com.

VISITOR INFORMATION The **Office de Tourisme** is at 5 place de l'Hôtel-de-Ville (✆ **02-98-06-04-70;** www.pontaven.com).

Exploring the Area

The 16th-century **Chapelle de Trémalo,** lieu-dit Trémalo (✆ **02-98-06-01-68**), lies 1.2km (¾ mile) north of the town center. Severely dignified and set on private lands, which still belong to descendants of the Plessis-Nizon family that originally built and consecrated the chapel in 1532, it contains a wooden crucifix that inspired two of Gauguin's best-known paintings, *The Yellow Christ* (displayed today in a museum in Buffalo, New York) and his *Self-Portrait with* *the Yellow Christ* (displayed today in the Musée d'Orsay in Paris). The elderly caretakers of this place unlock it every morning at 10am and close it at 5pm (6pm July–Aug). The location is signposted, and entrance is free. The chapel, incidentally, still defines itself as a place of worship, and masses are conducted from time to time. Plunk a coin or two into a machine to briefly illuminate the interior—otherwise, midday sunlight from the windows is sufficient.

Where to Stay & Eat

Le Moulin de Rosmadec ★★★ TRADITIONAL FRENCH For a charming setting, nothing in Brittany compares to this 15th-century stone mill. Meals are served in a bi-level dining room with antique furnishings or, in good weather, on a flower-filled "island" terrace. The owners serve carefully prepared specialties such as ragout of freshwater crayfish. Among the proficiently prepared dishes are *croustillant de pigeon* (crisply baked pigeon in puff pastry) and grilled lobster with two butters. Well worth ordering is stir-fried crayfish in its natural juices. M. Sébillau's brother Franck recently opened **Sur Le Pont** (✆ **02-98-60-16-16**), which is open on Thursday, when the Moulin is closed. Franck learned his trade at some of the best restaurants in Paris, giving the cuisine a modern touch that goes with the decor. Try the angler fish with leeks and ginger butter, or the pigeon *à la plancha*.

The Moulin rents four comfortable double rooms for 90€ to 120€. Each has a TV and a tidy bathroom with tub and shower. Because of the location at the end of a cul-de-sac, the accommodations are quiet and calm. Closed Thursday.

Pont-Aven 29123. ✆ **02-98-06-00-22.** www.moulinderosmadec.com. Reservations recommended. Main courses 30€–50€; fixed-price menu 38€–76€; *menu tradition* (with oysters and lobster) 76€. MC, V. Fri–Wed 12:30–2pm and 7:30–9pm. Closed Nov 11–Dec 18 and Feb.

In the Footsteps of Gauguin

In 1886, Paul Gauguin blazed the trail to the Breton village of Pont-Aven, and in time, lesser artists followed. One of Gauguin's most memorable works, *The Yellow Christ,* exemplified the credo of the School of Pont-Aven. Breaking from mainstream Impressionism, Pont-Aven artists emphasized purer colors ("as true as nature itself"). They shunned perspective and simplified human figures.

The tourist office offers a walking-tour guide that directs you on a trail once trod by the artists who drew inspiration from the sea and landscapes of this region.

Musée Municipal de Pont-Aven, place de l'Hôtel de Ville (✆ 02-98-06-14-43), provides one of the best overviews of the 19th-century painters. Expect muted greens and blues and lots of Breton patriotism as interpreted through the most famous artistic movement to emerge from Brittany. Admission is 4.50€ for adults, 2.50€ for people under 26, and free for children 17 and under. Prices go up 1.50€ when larger exhibits are on display from June to October. The museum is open in July and August daily 10am to 7pm, September to March daily 10am to noon and 2 to 6pm, and April to June daily 10am to 12:30pm and 2 to 6:30pm. *Note:* The museum will be completely or partially closed for renovations in 2012–13, so call ahead.

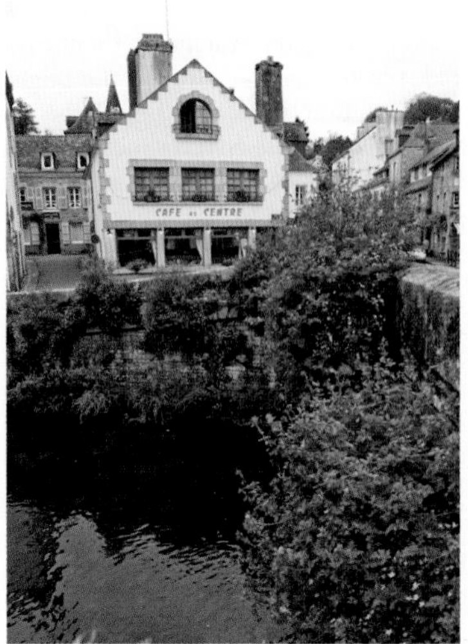
Pont-Aven.

Where to Stay & Eat Nearby

On the outskirts of the once-fortified town of **Hennebont,** 56km (35 miles) southeast of Concarneau, is the most delightful hotel in all of southern Brittany.

Château de Locguénolé ★★★ This country estate is owned by the same family that ran it some 5 centuries ago. Following a devastating fire, the 15th-century château was rebuilt in its present form in 1805. A Relais & Châteaux member since 1970, with views over coastline and an inlet, it's filled with antiques, tapestries, and paintings. Guest rooms vary in size and style, but each has a harmonious color scheme and, season permitting, sprays of flowers. The converted maids' rooms are smaller yet still charming; some units are in a converted 1720 Breton cottage.

Rte. de Port-Louis en Kervignac, Hennebont 56700. www.chateau-de-locguenole.com. ✆ **02-97-76-76-76.** Fax 02-97-76-82-35. 22 units. 129€–185€ double; 250€–500€ suite. AE, DC, MC, V. Closed Jan 2 to mid-Feb. From Hennebont, follow signs to château, 4km (2½ miles) south. **Amenities:** Restaurant; babysitting; outdoor pool; room service; 2 saunas. *In room:* TV, hair dryer, minibar, free Wi-Fi.

CARNAC ★★

486km (301 miles) W of Paris; 37km (23 miles) SE of Lorient; 100km (62 miles) SE of Quimper

Aside from being a seaside resort, Carnac is home to the hundreds of huge stones in the **Field of Megaliths ("Les Alignements")** that date from Neolithic times. Scholars have debated their purpose for centuries, although most suggest they had astronomical or religious significance to the people of the area. One theory is that some of the stones marked burial sites. In all, the town contains 2,732 menhirs (monumental stones), some of them rising to heights of 20m (66 ft.). They stand in 11 more or less straight lines in at least three separate fields.

Even if Carnac didn't possess these monuments, its pine-studded sand dunes would be worth the trip. Protected by the Quiberon Peninsula, **Carnac-Plage** is a family resort and camping hotspot beside the ocean and along the waterfront boulevard de la Plage. And in May and June, the fields—especially around the megaliths—are resplendent with heather and golden broom.

Essentials

GETTING THERE **Driving** is the most convenient way to get to Carnac. From Pont-Aven, travel east along N165, passing through Hennebont. At the intersection with D768, continue south along the signposted road to Carnac. From Lorient, take N165 east to Auray and turn south on D768 to Carnac.

Links to Carnac by public transport are inconvenient, as there's no SNCF railway station in town. Instead, travelers, depending on the origin of their train and the season, get off the SNCF network at either Quiberon or Auray, two nearby towns, both of which lie on the SNCF lines. An additional option, available only between June and August, involves getting off in the hamlet of Plouharnel-Carnac, 3km (1¾ miles) from Carnac.

From any of the above-mentioned towns, **buses** make between two and seven departures per day for the center of Carnac. One-way transit into Carnac by bus from any of the above-mentioned hamlets is 2€ per person. Know in advance that the SNCF itself will usually advise you, when you buy your ticket to Carnac from other points throughout France, which of the above-mentioned hamlets is the most convenient for your descent.

For information about rail transits throughout the region, call ✆ **08-92-35-35-35.** For more information about bus transit from any of the above-mentioned hamlets into Carnac, call ✆ **02-97-47-29-64.**

VISITOR INFORMATION The **Office de Tourisme,** 74 av. des Druides in Carnac-Plage (✆ **02-97-52-13-52;** www.carnac.fr), is open year-round, closed Sunday.

Exploring the Area

Out of fear of vandalism, the local tourist authorities have fenced in the **megaliths** and now allow visitors to wander freely among the menhirs *only* between October and March, when the park is open daily from 10am to 5pm, and when entrance is free. From April to September, the park can be visited only as part of a rigidly controlled 1-hour guided tour, priced at 4.50€ per person (4€ for students or anyone 18–24; under 18 are free). Tours are usually in French but, depending on the perceived need, may include some additional commentary in English; during high season, there may even be an all-English-language tour offered, but nothing is guaranteed. The only way to be sure involves calling the Parc's Visitor Center *(Maison des Mégalithes)* for a rundown on the tours that will be arranged on the day of your intended visit.

Field of Megaliths.

At Carnac Ville, **Musée de Préhistoire,** 10 place de la Chapelle (✆ **02-97-52-22-04**), displays collections from 450,000 B.C. to the 8th century. Admission is 5€ for adults, 2.50€ for children 6 to 18, and free for children 5 and under. Hours are as follows: July and August daily 10am to 6pm; October to March Wednesday to Monday 10am to 12:30pm and 2 to 5pm; April, May, June, and September Wednesday to Monday 10am to 12:30pm and 2 to 6pm.

The center of Carnac is about .8km (½ mile) from the sea. From the main square, rue du Tumulus leads north from the center of town to the **Tumulus St-Michel,** a Celtic burial chamber 1.2km (¾ mile) from the center (it is closed to the public).

NANTES ★★★

385km (239 miles) W of Paris; 325km (202 miles) N of Bordeaux

Nantes is Brittany's largest town and one of the most vibrant cities in France. The mouth of the Loire is 48km (30 miles) away, and here it divides into several branches. Nantes is a busy port that suffered great damage in World War II. It's best known for the Edict of Nantes, issued by Henri IV in 1598, which guaranteed religious freedom to Protestants (it was later revoked). Many famous people, from Molière to Stendhal, have lived here. But Nantes hardly rests on its illustrious past. Now home to high-tech industries, it has some 30,000 college students and a population of half a million.

Built on the largest of three islands in the Loire, the city expanded in the Middle Ages to the northern edge of the river, where its center lies today. The most prominent building, the **Château des Ducs de Bretagne,** rises high above the wide boulevard quai de la Fosse.

Despite a lackluster reputation, Nantes has taken on a kind of Atlantic Coast chic. Impressive revitalization is changing the city, as once-dreary industrial suburbs are being transformed into places you'd actually like to visit.

The most outstanding example of that is the compound **Le Lieu Unique,** 2 rue de la Biscuiterie, a former biscuit factory converted into a venue for art exhibitions, a restaurant, a bar/cafe, and fashionable shops. For the restaurant, see **Le Lieu Unique,** below. At one end of this boulevard is the train station; at the other are the promenades beside the Loire.

Essentials

GETTING THERE The **TGV** (fast train) from Paris's Gare Montparnasse takes about 2 to 2½ hours to get to Nantes and costs about 70€. For information, call ✆ **36-35** or 08-92-35-35-35. Nantes's **Gare SNCF,** 27 bd. de Stalingrad, is a 5-minute walk from the town center. If you're **driving,** take A11 for 385km (239 miles) west of Paris. The trip takes about 4 hours. **Aéroport Nantes-Atlantique** (✆ **02-40-84-80-00**) is 12km (7½ miles) southeast of town. **Air France** (✆ **36-54**) offers daily flights from Paris. A shuttle bus between the airport and the Nantes train station takes 25 minutes and costs 7€. A taxi from the airport costs 30€ and takes about 20 minutes.

VISITOR INFORMATION The **Office de Tourisme** is at 3 cours Olivier de Clisson, with another at 2 Place Saint-Pierre (✆ **08-92-46-40-44;** fax 02-40-89-11-99; www.nantes-tourisme.com). Both offices plan to move in 2012; consult their website for the new address.

Exploring the City

At the tourist office, you can buy a **Pass Nantes,** which allows you to enter museums and ride any of the city's public conveyances, including buses, trams, and some of the boats (summer only) that cruise along the river Erdre through the town. The pass costs 18€ for 1 day, 28€ for 2 days, and 36€ for 3 days, and comes with an audio guide and walking tour possibilities.

Cathédrale St-Pierre ★★ Begun in 1434, this cathedral wasn't finished until the end of the 19th century, but it remained architecturally harmonious—a rare feat. Two square towers dominate the facade; more impressive is the 100m-long (328-ft.) interior. Its *pièce de résistance* is Michel Colomb's Renaissance tomb of François II, duc de Bretagne and his second wife, Marguerite de Foix. Also noteworthy is the tomb of Gen. Juchault de Lamoricière, a Nantes native and a great African campaigner; sculptor Paul Dubois completed the tomb in 1879. After a 1972 fire destroyed the roof, the interior was restored. The white walls and pillars contrast with the rich colors of the stained-glass windows; helpful signs explain the significance of most objects. The 11th century crypt is open only Saturday and Sunday 3 to 6pm.

Place St-Pierre. ✆ **02-40-47-84-64.** Free admission. Daily 8:30am–6:15pm.

Château des Ducs de Bretagne ★★ Between the cathedral and the Loire is Nantes's second major sight, where the Edict of Nantes was signed. The castle was constructed in the 9th or 10th century, enlarged in the 13th century, destroyed, and rebuilt into its present shape by François II in 1466. His daughter, Anne de Bretagne, continued the work. Large towers and a bastion flank the castle, which contains a symmetrical section (the Grand Gouvernement) built during the 17th and 18th centuries. The duchesse du Berry, royal courtesan, was imprisoned here, as was Gilles de Retz (aka "Bluebeard"), one of France's most notorious mass murderers. The castle's rich collections were shaped into a museum of the history of Nantes from the 17th century to the present. About 30 rooms are devoted to a depiction of the history of one of France's most important ports. Included are many evocative objects, including scaled-down models of the city during different eras. The museum charges admission, but you can visit the courtyard of the château and parade along the ramparts for free.

4 place Marc-Elder. ✆ **08-11-46-46-44.** www.chateau-nantes.fr. Ramparts free daily 10am–7pm (until 9pm July–Aug). Museum 5€ adults, 3€ students 25 and under, free for children 17 and under. Sept–June Tues–Sun 10am–6pm; July–Aug daily 10am–7pm.

Musée des Beaux-Arts de Nantes ★ In one of western France's most interesting provincial galleries, you'll find an unusually fine collection of sculptures

The Secret Garden of Nantes

Two blocks east of the cathedral, you can visit one of France's most beautiful gardens, the Jardin des Plantes, boulevard Stalingrad, adjacent to Gare SNCF (✆ 02-40-41-90-09). The northern entrance is close to the Musée des Beaux-Arts; the southern border is across from the train station. Admission is free. It is open daily at 8:30am, closing at 5:30pm in the winter, 6:30pm in the spring and fall, and at 8pm from late March to late October.

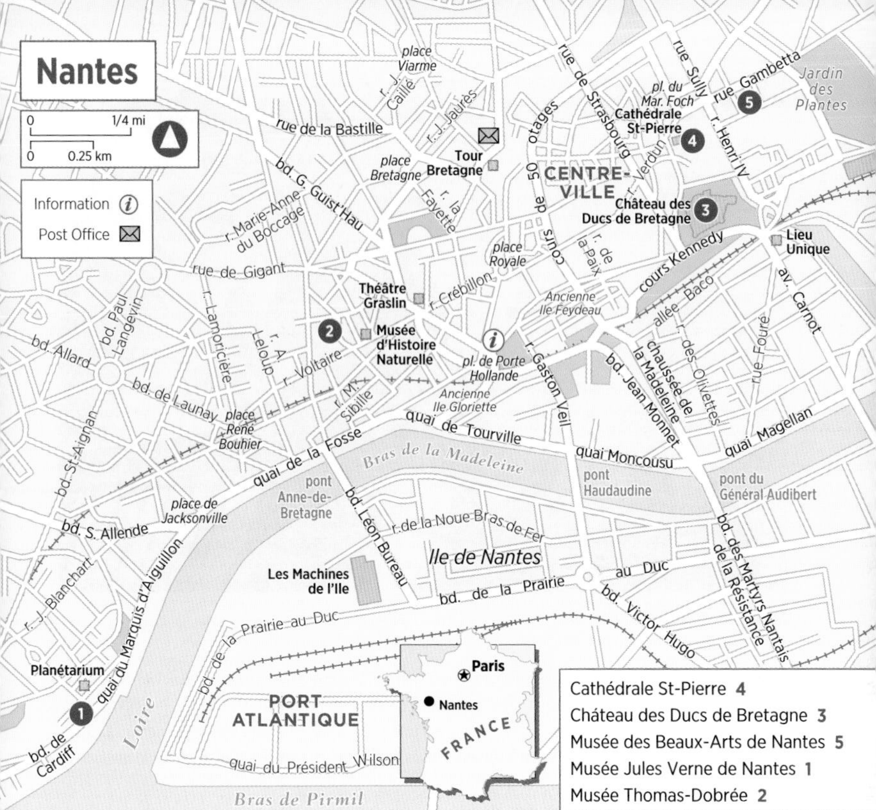

and paintings from the 12th to the late 19th centuries. The street level is devoted to mostly French modern or contemporary art created since 1900, with special emphasis on painters from the 1950s and 1960s.

10 rue Georges Clemenceau. ✆ **02-51-17-45-00.** Admission 3.50€ adults, 2€ students 19–26, free for children 18 and under. Wed–Mon 10am–6pm.

Musée Jules Verne de Nantes The novelist Jules Verne (*Journey to the Center of the Earth, Around the World in Eighty Days*) was born in Nantes in 1828. This museum is filled with memorabilia and objects inspired by his writings, from ink spots to a "magic" lantern with glass slides. Fans also seek out Verne's house at 4 rue de Clisson in the Ile-Feydeau, which is privately owned and not open to the public. In a historic, mostly 18th-century neighborhood in the heart of the town, the house was named after an island (l'Ile Feydeau) that became part of "mainland" Nantes after the river was diverted into a series of canals during the 18th century.

3 rue de l'Hermitage. ✆ **02-40-69-72-52.** Admission 3€ adults, 1.50€ for students, 18 and under are free. Wed–Sat and Mon 10am–noon and 2–6pm; Sun 2–6pm.

Musée Thomas-Dobrée This 19th-century neo-Romanesque mansion was built by Thomas Dobrée, an important collector and traveler. It stands in the town center, adjacent to the 15th-century manor of Jean V, where the bishops of Nantes occasionally lived. You'll see Dobrée's eclectic collection, gathered during

Shopping at passage Pommeraye.

the height of France's Gilded Age, including prehistoric and medieval antiquities, Flemish paintings from the 15th century, ecclesiastical relics, paintings by masters such as Dürer, art objects from India, and the Dobrée family jewels. The collection and building were deeded to the Département de Loire-Atlantique after the death of M. Dobrée in 1894.

18 rue Voltaire. ✆ **02-40-71-03-50.** Admission 3€ adults and 1.50€ seniors, students, and children. Tues–Fri 1:30–5:30pm; Sat–Sun 2:30–5:30pm.

Shopping

Nantes overflows with shops and boutiques. The principal shopping streets are rue du Calvaire, rue Crébillon, rue Boileau, rue d'Orléans, rue de la Marne, rue de Verdun, and passage Pommeraye. Most of these encompass the shopping districts around place Graslin, place Royale, the château, and the cathedral. One of the prime areas for antiques is around place Aristide-Briand and rue Mercoeur.

Interesting antiques dealers include **Ecritoire Antiquités Poidras,** 12 rue Jean-Jaurès (✆ **02-40-47-78-18**), offering 18th- and 19th-century furniture and decorative pieces such as historic mantels.

For unusual gifts, check out the stores of two master artisans: **Maison Devineau,** 4 rue de la Belle Image (✆ **02-40-47-19-59**), which brings the art of waxworking to a new level, "growing" bushels of fruits, flowers, and vegetables from liquid wax; and **Gautier Debotte,** 9 rue de la Fosse (✆ **02-40-48-23-19**), a historic boutique established in 1823 with the town's best chocolates.

Where to Stay

Hôtel de France ★ Classified by the government as a historic monument, this well-run, beautifully maintained hotel dates from the 1700s and has the feeling of a '70s spy flick set. Many of the accommodations are decorated with reproductions of Louis XV– or Louis XVI–style furnishings. The comfortable midsize guest rooms have small bathrooms with a tub and a shower. A few of the guest rooms are quite spacious, with high ceilings. The hotel is a 3-minute walk from the pedestrian zone.

24 rue Crébillon, Nantes 44000. www.oceaniahotels.com. ✆ **02-40-73-57-91.** Fax 02-40-69-75-75. 74 units. 124€–154€ double; 194€ suite. AE, DC, MC, V. Free parking. Pets 15€. **Amenities:** Restaurant; bar; room service. *In room:* TV, free Wi-Fi.

Hôtel Graslin In 1944, the pilot of an American bomber misjudged the wind factor while trying to bomb a German ship in the port of Nantes, and to everyone's horror, a then-antique hotel was blasted and virtually incinerated. In its place, built shortly after the war, came this five-story, beige-fronted structure. Its interior was completely renovated, based on the conservative modern taste of its owner, M. LeMoine. The comfortable, midsize rooms are well furnished and

THE WILD, WILD coast

Follow the D768 south from Carnac onto the peninsula (formerly an island) connected to the mainland by a narrow strip of alluvial deposits, and you'll come to the port of **Quiberon,** with its white-sand beach. You'll probably see the rugged Breton fishers hauling in their sardine catch.

This entire coast—the **Côte Sauvage,** or Wild Coast—is dramatic and rugged; the ocean breaks with fury against the reefs. Winds, especially in winter, lash the dunes, shaving the short pines that grow here. On the landward side, the beach is calm and relatively protected.

Sixteen kilometers (10 miles) west of Brittany's shoreline is **Belle-Ile-en-Mer,** an outpost of sand, rock, and vegetation. For information, contact the **Office de Tourisme,** Quai Bonnelle Le Palais (✆ **02-97-31-81-93**). Depending on the season, 5 to 15 ferries depart daily from Port Maria in Quiberon (✆ **08-20-05-61-56**). The trip takes 45 minutes; a round-trip ticket costs 30€ for adults, 19€ for those 24 and under, and free for children 4 and under. In summer, you must reserve space for your car, as well as for passengers. The ferry docks at **Le Palais,** a fortified 16th-century port that is the island's window to mainland France. Despite a scattering of hotels and seasonal restaurants, the island feels blissfully isolated. A drive around the periphery is about 56km (35 miles).

You'll find excellent accommodations in **Port de Goulphar,** on the southern shore on an inlet framed by cliffs. The standout is the 39-unit Relais & Châteaux property **Castel Clara,** Port de Goulphar, 56360 Bangor (www.castel-clara.com; ✆ **02-97-31-84-21;** fax 02-97-31-51-69). Ideal service and first-class cuisine add to the sense of peace. The rooms are comfortable, with TVs and balconies facing the sea. The hotel also has a terrace with a solarium around a heated seawater pool.

Depending on the season, rates range from 155€ to 380€ in a double, 290€ to 590€ in a suite. The hotel is closed from mid-December to mid-February. For meals, try **La Table de La Desirade,** Petit Cosquet, Bangor (✆ **02-97-31-70-70**), which uses fresh, locally sourced ingredients. Try the cockles and zucchini between layers of potato rosettes and drizzled with foie gras–enriched meat *jus.* Mains range from 24€ to 28€, with prix-fixe menus from 30€ to 82€.

tidily maintained, with funky shag rugs. Breakfast is served downstairs, and there are "at least 50" restaurants within a relatively short walking distance.

1 rue Piron, Nantes 44000. www.hotel-graslin.com. ✆ **02-40-69-72-91.** Fax 02-40-69-04-44. 47 units. 79€–109€ double. AE, MC, V. Parking 3€. Pets 6€. *In room:* TV, hair dryer, free Wi-Fi.

L'Hôtel Within sight of the château and the cathedral, this hotel is, for the price, a perfect base in Nantes. Built in the 1980s, the place is neat and modern but maintains an inviting atmosphere. Firm beds, rich colors, and contemporary furnishings fill the hotel, and renovations are frequent. Some units have private patios overlooking the château, while others open onto a garden and terrace. Each neatly tiled bathroom has a tub or shower. The softly lit breakfast room has terrace views.

6 rue Henri IV, Nantes 44000. www.nanteshotel.com. ✆ **02-40-29-30-31.** Fax 02-40-29-00-95. 31 units. 110€–160€ double. AE, MC, V. Parking 9€. **Amenities:** Room service. *In room:* A/C, TV, hair dryer, free Wi-Fi.

Where to Eat

L'Atlantide ★★★ MODERN FRENCH On the fourth floor of the complex that houses the city's chamber of commerce, this panoramic restaurant, with views over the semi-industrial landscape, serves the finest cuisine in the area. World-renowned designer Jean-Pierre Wilmotte created the nautical-looking enclave with lots of mirrors, but Jean-Yves Guého's innovative cooking is what draws patrons. Menu items are steeped in the traditions of both the Loire Valley and the Breton coast. An excellent dessert is bananas braised in local beer. The cellar is known for some of the finest vintages of Loire Valley wine anywhere, with an emphasis on Anjous and Muscadets.

Centre des Salorges, 16 quai Ernest Renaud. ✆ **02-40-73-23-23.** www.restaurant-atlantide.net. Reservations required. Main courses 23€–58€; fixed-price lunch 30€, dinner 60€–95€. AE, MC, V. Mon–Fri noon–2pm; Mon–Sat 8–9:45pm. Closed Aug and Dec 23–Jan 3.

La Cigale FRENCH/SEAFOOD This is Nantes's most historic and charming brasserie, decorated in a jaw-dropping Belle Epoque style that has changed little since the place opened in 1895 across from the landmark Théâtre Graslin. Menu items may include platters of fresh shellfish, *confit des cuisses de canard* (duck confit), and fresh scallops with green peppers and emulsified butter. The sprawling restaurant is usually quite loud, and the staff members tend to be overworked.

4 place Graslin. ✆ **02-51-84-94-94.** www.lacigale.com. Reservations recommended. Main courses 16€–23€; fixed-price menu 14€–28€. MC, V. Daily 7:30am–12:30am. Bus: 11 or 34.

Le Lieu Unique FRENCH/BRETON The chief attraction of this restored biscuit factory is this restaurant and bar, which has become a major nighttime rendezvous spot for the young people of Nantes. In an atmospheric setting, diners can order from a market-fresh menu. At least three fish dishes are featured nightly, including, perhaps, pickerel in a white butter sauce or grilled sea bream with lentils. Sea bass also appears regularly on the menu with wild rice. Other dishes are likely to include a honey-flavored *magret* of duckling or roast lamb flavored with thyme juice. For dessert, you might order roast pineapple with vanilla ice cream or a crème brûlée.

Le Lieu Unique, 2 rue de la Biscuterie. ✆ **02-51-72-05-55.** www.lelieuunique.com. Reservations recommended. Main courses 10€–17€; fixed-price lunch 12€, dinner 15€–27€. MC, V. Mon–Sat noon–2pm; Tues–Thurs 7–11pm; Fri–Sat 7pm–midnight.

Les Oubliettes FRENCH As part of the restoration of the château at Nantes, a luncheon restaurant was installed with an ancient atmosphere with a large fireplace and an outdoor terrace. The walls are made from *tuffaud,* the local stone. Affordable fixed-price menus are offered, with good-tasting, classic French dishes served, including such appetizers as a terrine of duckling foie gras or a salad of tomatoes, mozzarella, and anchovies with fresh basil. A fish of the day is usually served with *beurre Nantais* (a sauce with butter, vinegar, white wine, shallots, and herbs). Also, veal piccata appears regularly on the menu, as does beef pâté. For dessert, you might opt for strawberries with sabayon, chocolate mousse, or a Grand Marnier soufflé.

Château des Ducs de Bretagne, 4 place Marc-Elder. ✆ **02-51-82-67-04.** www.lesoubliettes.fr. Reservations recommended. Fixed-price menus 14€–19€. MC, V. Thurs–Sun 10am–4pm.

Nantes After Dark

When the sun goes down, the town turns into one big party. On **place du Bouffay, place du Pilori,** and **rue Kervégan,** you'll find lots of cafes and pubs, many with live music and fun people. A younger crowd rules **rue Scribe.**

The hippest location in Nantes, and the town's leading cultural center, is **Le Lieu Unique,** 2 rue de la Biscuiterie (✆ **02-51-82-15-00**). Converted from a 19th-century biscuit factory, the venue offers presentations ranging from plays (in French) to art exhibitions. Admission is free to the dimly lit, concrete-floored bar at ground level, which is frequented by students and artists who pack the dance floor. Beer is cheap, only 2.50€ a mug. The bar is open Monday 11am to 8pm, Tuesday and Wednesday 11am to 1am, Thursday 11am to 2am, Friday and Saturday 11am to 3am, and Sunday 3 to 8pm.

Catch some live blues, jazz, or rock at **L'Univers Café,** 16 rue Jean-Jacques-Rousseau (✆ **02-40-73-49-55**), or techno and disco at **L.C. Club,** 21 quai des Antilles (✆ **02-40-47-68-45**), open all night. A great piano bar with a dance floor and occasional jazz concerts is **Le Tie Break,** 1 rue des Petites-Ecuries (✆ **06-82-16-89-60**).

The pump-it-up dance scene has a huge following of everyone from students to seniors. The over-30 crowd heads to the vintage 1970s gay-friendly disco **L'Evasion,** 3 rue de l'Emery (✆ **02-40-47-99-84**). Other discos include **Le Royal Club Privé,** 7 rue des Salorges (✆ **02-40-69-11-10**). Don't wear jeans to any of these places, and be prepared to pay 15€ to 20€ to get in.

The favorite with gays and lesbians is **Le Petit Marais,** 15 rue Kervégan (✆ **02-40-20-15-25**), where people meet and talk in a friendly atmosphere that welcomes everything from leather to lace. **Le Temps d'Aimer,** 14 rue Alexandre-Fourny (✆ **02-40-89-48-60**), is mixed and gay-friendly. This disco with its small dance floor attracts a sophisticated crowd. Cover is around 15€.

9

THE CHAMPAGNE COUNTRY

by Caroline Sieg

In about 3 days, you can take the Autoroute de l'Est (N3) from Paris and explore a region of cathedrals, historic battlefields, great food, and vineyards, topping your tour with a glass or two of bubbly. On the Routes du Champagne, you can drive to the wine-producing center of Epernay and on to Reims, 145km (90 miles) northeast of Paris. After visiting Reims and its cathedral, you can head toward Verdun, of World War I fame.

LA FERTÉ-SOUS-JOUARRE

66km (41 miles) E of Paris; 82km (51 miles) SW of Reims

The little town of La Ferté-sous-Jouarre and the village of Jouarre are twin communities—you can't tell where one ends and the other begins. Although La Ferté-sous-Jouarre, which took its name from a now-gone 10th-century fortress, played a role in French history, it is of little interest today and is worth a visit chiefly for the lodging at Château des Bondons (see below).

In the village of Jouarre, 3km (1¾ miles) south of La Ferté-sous-Jouarre, you can visit a 12th-century Benedictine abbey and explore one of the oldest crypts in France. At the **Tour et Crypt de l'Abbaye de Jouarre,** 6 rue Montmorin (✆**01-60-22-64-54**), those interested in medieval history will appreciate the documents referring to the Royal Abbey of Jouarre, as well as the stones in the Merovingian crypt, which evoke the 7th century. There's also a collection of prehistoric artifacts, remnants of the Roman occupation, and sculptural fragments. Each of these monuments is a medieval treasure. Entrance to the crypt costs 4.50€ for adults and 4€ for students and children 17 and under. Entrance to the tower is included. One floor above the crypt, a small-scale museum, **Musée Briard,** showcases the medieval history of the region of Brie. Entrance to the museum costs 2.50€ for adults and 2€ for children.

The crypt is the star of the three attractions, the tower somewhat less famous and evocative. All three sites are open Wednesday to Monday but can be visited only on guided tours, lasting 30 to 45 minutes. From April to October, tours leave every hour on the hour from 10:15am to 5:15pm.

Essentials

GETTING THERE If you're **driving,** take N3 along the Marne. About 10 **trains** per day make the 55-minute run from Paris's Gare de l'Est, stopping at La Ferté-sous-Jouarre. From there, take a taxi 3km (1¾ miles) south to Jouarre and its abbey. For train reservations and schedules, call ✆**36-35** or 08-92-35-35-35, or visit www.voyages-sncf.com.

VISITOR INFORMATION The **Office de Tourisme** in Jouarre is on rue de la Tour, adjacent to the tower and the abbey (✆**01-60-22-64-54;** fax 01-60-22-65-15; www.tourisme-jouarre.com).

FACING PAGE: **Champagne's rolling hills.**

Tour et Crypt de l'Abbaye de Jouarre.

Where to Stay

Château des Bondons ★★ Surrounded by a 7-hectare (17-acre) park and forest, this château dates from the French Revolution. The doomed Louis XVI and Marie Antoinette were brought here following their arrest at Varennes in June 1791 (they were then taken to Paris and executed). Not much of the furniture is original to the building; a country aesthetic, complete with chintz upholstery and antiques, characterizes the public areas. As befits a château, guest rooms come in a variety of shapes, but they are all comfortable, filled with old and new furnishings.

47–49 rue des Bondons, La Ferté-sous-Jouarre 77260. www.chateaudesbondons.com. ✆ **01-60-22-00-98.** Fax 01-60-22-97-01. 14 units. 120€–160€ double; 160€–240€ suite. AE, DC, MC, V. Follow signs to Montménard; take D70 for 2.5km (1½ miles) east of the town center. **Amenities:** Restaurant; bar; room service. *In room:* TV, hair dryer, Jacuzzi (in some suites), minibar, free Wi-Fi.

Where to Eat

Château des Bondons (see above) has a restaurant.

Le Plat d'Etain TRADITIONAL FRENCH This homelike, conservative restaurant caters to the gastronomic needs of art history lovers who make the pilgrimage to see the famous Merovingian crypt, which is nearby. It has exposed ceiling beams, lacy curtains, and tokens of old-fashioned France. The food might remind locals of the style of cuisine once prepared by their grandmothers. The best examples include *blanquette de veau* (veal stew), boeuf bourguignon, and whatever is seasonal and appeals to the whims of the chef. The restaurant also rents 18 simply furnished bedrooms, costing 62€ to 68€ for a double.

6 place Auguste-Tinchant, Jouarre. ✆ **01-60-22-06-07.** Reservations recommended. Main courses 18€–27€; fixed-price menus 19€–49€. MC, V. Daily noon–2pm; Mon–Thurs and Sat 7:30–9pm.

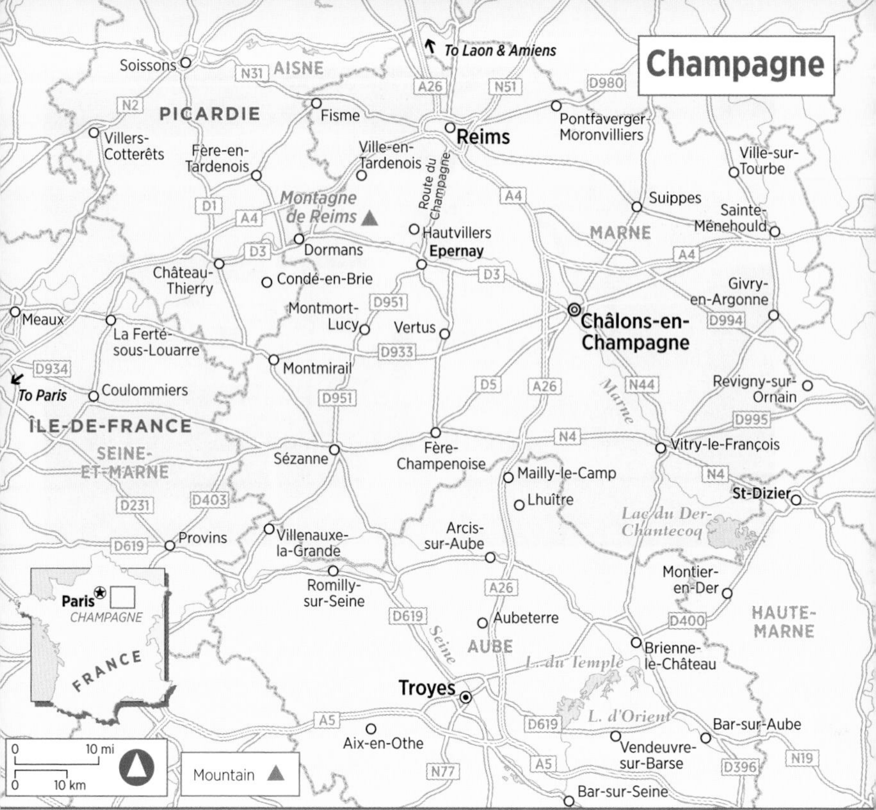

CHÂTEAU-THIERRY

90km (56 miles) E of Paris; 9.5km (6 miles) SW of Reims

An industrial town on the Marne's right bank, Château-Thierry contains the ruins of a castle believed to have been constructed for the Frankish king Thierry IV. Château-Thierry gained fame for being the farthest point the German offensive reached in 1918. Under heavy bombardment, the Second and Third Divisions of the U.S. Expeditionary Force aided French troops. The battlefields of the Marne are just west of town; thousands of Allied soldiers who died in World War I are buried here. Atop Hill 204 is a monument honoring American troops.

The poet and fable writer Jean de la Fontaine (1621–95) was born here, in a stone-sided house built in 1452. Today it contains one of France's most-visited literary shrines, the **Musée Jean-de-la-Fontaine,** 12 rue Jean de la Fontaine (**✆ 03-23-69-05-60;** www.musee-jean-de-la-fontaine.fr). Located a few steps from place de l'Hôtel-de-Ville, it contains a collection of his mementos, editions of his works published over many centuries, and a trio of rooms outfitted with furniture from the 17th through 19th centuries. Each room centers on some aspect of the effect of de la Fontaine on those centuries. Copies of his fables (allegorical barnyard stories depicting the foibles of humans) and *contes* (short stories a lot racier than the fables) are for sale in the bookshop. The museum is open Tuesday to Sunday 9:30am to noon and 2 to 5:30pm. Admission is 3.60€

Musée Jean-de-la-Fontaine.

for adults, 2.20€ for students, and 1.80€ for children 17 and under; it's free to everyone on Wednesday.

If you're interested in World War I, head 8km (5 miles) northwest of Château-Thierry to the **Bois de Belleau (Belleau Wood).** The Battle of Belleau Wood marked the second clash between American and German troops in World War I and demonstrated the bravery of the U.S. soldiers. After a 2-week struggle, the Second Division of the U.S. Expeditionary Force under Maj. Gen. Omar Bundy took the woods. Though the Germans suffered many losses and some 1,650 prisoners were taken, U.S. casualties were appalling—more than 8,000 American troops were wounded, killed, or missing. In 1923, the battleground was dedicated as a memorial to the men who gave their lives here. The **American cemetery,** also known as Le Cimetière de Belleau (✆ **03-23-70-70-90**), contains 2,288 graves. You'll also see a chapel that was damaged in World War II. Entrance is free; it's open daily 9am to 5pm.

Essentials

GETTING THERE If you're **driving,** take A4 southwest from Reims or northeast from La Ferté-sous-Jouarre. There are **trains** from Paris's Gare de l'Est (16€ one-way) and Reims (12€ one-way); each trip takes 1 hour. For information, call ✆ **36-35** or 08-92-35-35-35.

VISITOR INFORMATION The **Office de Tourisme** is at 11 rue Vallée (✆ **03-23-83-10-14;** fax 03-23-83-14-74; www.otsichateau-thierry.com).

Where to Stay

Ile-de-France This modern hotel is the leading choice in an area of not-so-hot options. In a park overlooking the Marne Valley, near the ruins of the town's château, the four-story structure boasts balconies and dormers, a view of the town, and well-maintained guest rooms.

Rte. de Soissons, Château-Thierry 02400. www.hotel-iledefrance.fr. ✆ **03-23-69-10-12.** Fax 03-23-83-49-70. 32 units. 90€ double; 140€–190€ suite. AE, DC, MC, V. **Amenities:** Restaurant;

bar; babysitting; fitness center; indoor pool; room service; rooms for those w/limited mobility; smoke-free rooms; spa. *In room:* TV, hair dryer, free Wi-Fi.

Where to Eat

Les Fabliaux TRADITIONAL FRENCH Outfitted in a conservatively modern and cozy style, and accented with framed illustrations based on the short fables of La Fontaine, this restaurant is widely respected in the district for its well-prepared, traditional French food. Outfitted in pastel colors, it offers a menu that includes snails poached in garlic butter, curried rack of lamb with almond butter, and sea bass with asparagus-studded risotto. The restaurant also rents simply furnished bedrooms that nonetheless are equipped with TVs, minibars, and Wi-Fi, costing 58€ to 64€ for a double. Technically, it lies in the suburb of Brasles, about 45m (148 ft.) northwest of the boundary of Chateau-Thierry, very close to that city's historic core.

3 av. de Château-Thierry, Brasles. ✆ **03-23-83-23-14.** www.les-fabliaux.com. Main courses 15€–17€; set-price menus 20€–47€. AE, MC, V. Sun–Fri noon–2pm; Mon–Sat 7:30–9pm.

CONDÉ-EN-BRIE ★

89km (55 miles) E of Paris; 24km (15 miles) W of Epernay

West of Epernay, **Château de Condé ★**, rue du Château, Condé-en-Brie 02330 (✆ **03-23-82-42-25;** www.chateaudeconde.com), was bequeathed to the comte de Sade in 1814 and remained in his family until 1983. The name gained notoriety from the works of the marquis, an innovative writer (*Justine, Juliette, The 120 Days of Sodom*) whose sexual practices as described in his works gave us the word "sadism."

Enguerrand of Coucy built the castle in the late 12th century. A part of the old keep—two big rooms with great chimneys and thick walls—survives. Cardinal de Bourbon, a member of the royal family, reconstructed the castle in the Renaissance style early in the 16th century. His nephew, Louis de Bourbon, called himself the prince de Condé, most likely because he had many fond childhood memories of the place. After sustaining damage in the 18th century, the château was rebuilt for the marquis de La Faye. The Italian architect Servandoni invited artists Boucher and Watteau to do frescoes and paintings, which you can see today. Servandoni decorated the largest room, making it a theater for music and entertainment. The present castle is exceptional, with its paintings, woodwork, chimneys, and so-called Versailles floor.

In 1994, the new owners, the de Rocheforts, discovered several Watteau frescoes behind mirrors installed during the 18th century. Now, at the push of a button, the mirrors open to reveal the previously hidden treasures.

Admission is 9.50€ for adults, 4.50€ for children 6 to 12, and free for children 5 and under. The castle is open only during the afternoon, and only between mid-April and mid-October, Tuesday to Sunday from 2:30 to 5:30pm. Visits are self-guided, conducted with the help of a free leaflet outlining the history of the building and some of its most important features. Families with children sometimes opt to collectively follow a self-guided treasure hunt, whereby the gift at the end of the hunt is a key that opens a treasure chest loaded with candy and simple toys.

If you're **driving** between Château-Thierry and Epernay on N3, head south at Dormans and follow the signs to Condé-en-Brie.

REIMS ★★★

143km (89 miles) E of Paris; 45km (28 miles) NW of Châlons-en-Champagne

Reims (pronounced "rahns"), an ancient Roman city, was important when Caesar conquered Gaul. French kings came here to be crowned, and it's said that the French nation was born here in A.D. 498. Joan of Arc escorted Charles VII here in 1429, kissing the silly man's feet. But don't let its ancient background mislead you: As you approach Reims, you'll pass through prefabricated suburbs that look like eastern European apartment-house blocks. There are gems in Reims, including the cathedral, but you must seek them out.

Most visitors come to Reims because it's the center of a winegrowing district; its bubbly is present at celebrations all over the world. The city (pop. 200,000) is filled with swank restaurants, ritzy champagne houses, large squares, and long, tree-lined avenues. The champagne bottled here has the lightest and most subtle flavor in the world. Make an effort to linger, and explore the vineyards and wine cellars, the Gothic monuments, and the battlefields.

Essentials

GETTING THERE If you're **driving** from Paris, take A4 east. **Trains** depart from Paris's Gare de l'Est every 1½ hours (trip time: 45 min.); the one-way fare is 30€ to 38€. Five trains per day arrive from Strasbourg (trip time: 2 hr.; 48€ one-way). For information, call ✆ **08-36-35-35-35** or visit www.voyages-sncf.com.

VISITOR INFORMATION The **Office de Tourisme** is at 2 rue Guillaume-de-Machault (✆ **03-26-77-45-00;** fax 03-26-77-45-19; www.reims-tourisme.com).

Exploring the City

Basilique St-Rémi ★★ This church dates from 1007, making it the oldest in Reims. Though an example of classic medieval French masonry, it's often unfavorably compared to the more spectacular cathedral. Within the complex is the former royal abbey of St-Rémi, who, as the guardian of the holy ampula, used to anoint the kings of France. The abbey now functions as a museum, with an extensive collection covering the history of Reims, regional archaeology, and military history. Architect Louis Duroché designed the majestic ornamental front of the main quadrangle and the Grand Staircase (1778), where you can admire a portrait of the young Louis XV in his coronation robes. The church also contains a Romanesque nave leading to a magnificent choir crowned with pointed arches. The nave, the transepts, one of the towers, and the aisles date from the 11th century; the portal of the south transept is in early-16th-century Flamboyant Gothic style. Some of the stained glass in the apse is from the 13th century. The tomb of St. Rémi is elaborately carved with Renaissance figures and columns.

Place Chanoine Ladame, Basilique. ✆ **03-26-85-31-20.** Free admission. Daily 8am–7pm. Musée: ✆ **03-26-85-23-36.** Admission 3€ adults, free for children 16 and under. Mon–Fri 2–6:30pm; Sat–Sun 2–7pm.

Cathédrale Notre-Dame de Reims ★★★ One of the world's most famous cathedrals was restored after World War I, funded largely by contributions from John D. Rockefeller; it escaped World War II relatively unharmed. Built on the

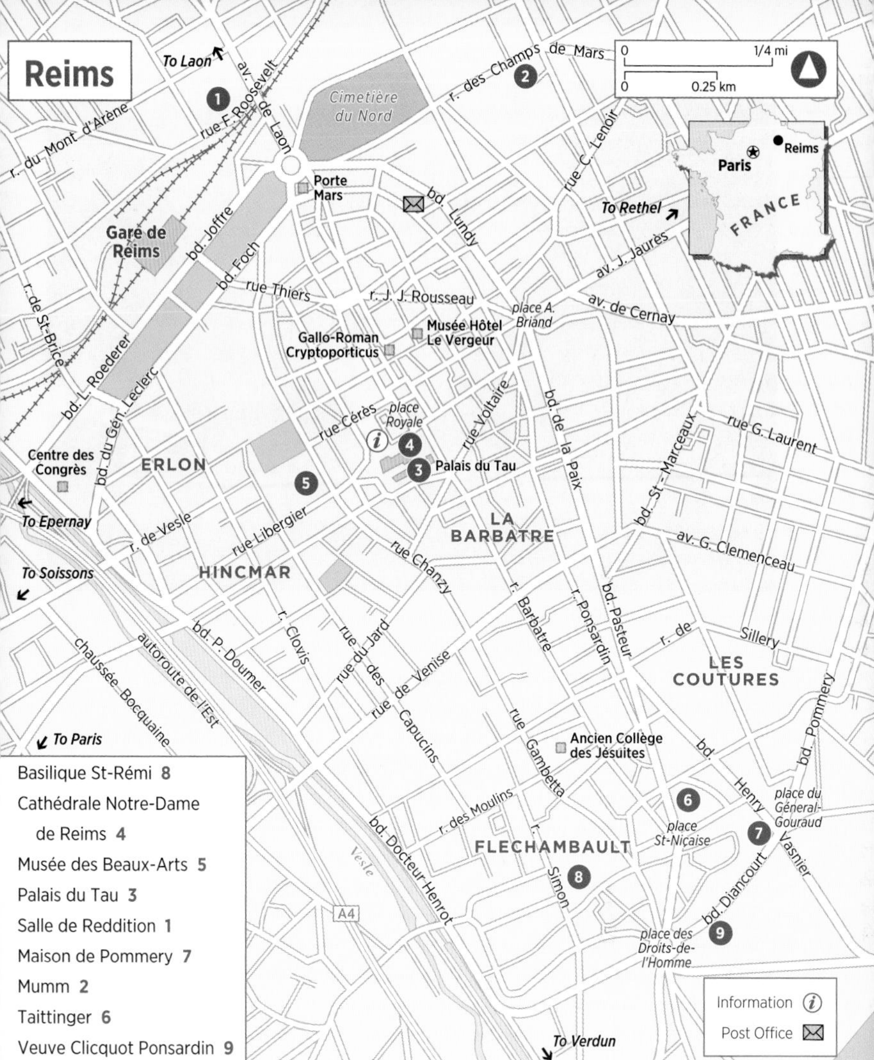

site of a church that burned in 1211, it was intended as a sanctuary where French kings would be anointed. St-Rémi, the bishop of Reims, baptized Clovis, the king of the Franks, here in A.D. 496. All the kings of France from Louis the Pious in 815 to Charles X in 1825 were crowned here.

Laden with statuettes, the cathedral has three spectacular western facade portals. A rose window above the central portal is dedicated to the Virgin. The right portal portrays the Apocalypse and the Last Judgment; the left, martyrs and saints. At the western facade's northern door is a smiling angel. Lit by lancet windows, the immense nave has many bays.

Place du Cardinal-Luçon. ✆ **03-26-35-36-00.** Free admission. Daily 7:30am–7:30pm.

Cathédrale Notre-Dame de Reims.

Musée des Beaux-Arts Housed in the 18th-century buildings belonging to the old Abbaye St-Denis, this fine provincial gallery contains more than a dozen portraits of German princes by both "the Elder" and "the Younger" Cranach; the museum has owned this collection since it opened in 1795. You can see the *toiles peintes* (light painting on rough linen) that date from the 15th and 16th centuries and depict the *Passion du Christ* and *Vengeance du Christ*. Paintings and furniture from the 17th and 18th centuries are in the salles Diancourt and Jamot-Neveux. There's an excellent series of 27 of Corot's tree-shaded walks.

8 rue Chanzy. ✆ **03-26-47-28-44.** Admission 3€ adults, free for students and children 17 and under; free to all 1st Sun of every month. Wed–Mon 10am–noon and 2–6pm. Closed Jan 1, May 1, July 14, Nov 1 and 11, and Dec 25.

Salle de Reddition On May 7, 1945, the Germans surrendered to General Eisenhower in this structure, which was once a schoolhouse near the railroad tracks. Maps of the rail routes line the walls of the rooms, exactly as they did on the day of surrender.

12 rue Franklin-D-Roosevelt. ✆ **03-26-47-84-19.** Admission 3€ adults, free for children 17 and under. Wed–Mon 10am–noon and 2–6pm. Closed May 1 and July 14.

Exploring the Champagne Cellars ★★

Many of the champagne cellars of Reims extend for miles through chalky deposits. During the German siege of 1914 and throughout the war, people lived and even published a daily paper in them. The cellars are open year-round but are most interesting during the fall grape harvest. After that, the wine is fermented in vats in the caves and then bottled with a small amount of sugar and natural yeast. The yeast feeds on the sugar and causes a second fermentation that produces those fabulous bubbles. The winegrowers wait until the sparkle has "taken" before they move the bottles to racks or pulpits. For about 3 months, *remueurs* (migrant workers) turn them every day, which brings the impurities (dead yeast cells and other matter) toward the cork. Eventually, the sediments are removed and the wine is given its proper dosage (sugar dissolved in wine), depending on the desired sweetness. The process takes 4 or 5 years and takes place in caves that are 30m (98 ft.) deep, where the temperature is a constant 50°F (10°C).

Mumm Founded in 1827, Mumm welcomes visitors with a video that explains how champagne is made. An in-house museum exhibits casks and illustrates the ancient role of the vintner. On a 1-hour tour, a guide will lead visitors into a labyrinth of tunnels and storage cellars in the chalky bedrock; they contain a vast inventory—almost 25 million bottles—of slowly fermenting champagne. The more expensive tours contain oeneological insights and tastings.

34 rue du Champ-de-Mars. ✆ **03-26-49-59-70.** www.mumm.com. Reservations required. Tours (in English) 8€–20€ adults, free for children 15 and under. Mar–Oct daily 9–11am and 2–5pm; out of season, phone ahead for tours.

Pommery Among the most-visited cellars are those under the Gothic-style buildings and gardens of the Pommery, all set atop a dazzling hilltop. But the fun's not up there: A magnificent 116-step stairway leads to a maze of galleries dug into the chalk. The complex is more than 18km (11 miles) long and about 30m (98 ft.) below ground, set within Gallo-Roman quarries. Various stages of champagne making are shown, and the end product is for sale in the gift shop; also check the website for occasional art exhibits on the premises.

Place du Général-Gouraud. ✆ **03-26-61-62-55.** www.pommery.com. Reservations required. Admission 10€, free for children 11 and under. Daily 9:30am–7pm Apr to mid-Nov, Sat–Sun 10am–6pm mid-Nov to Mar.

Taittinger Taittinger is a grand *marque* of French champagne, one of the few still controlled by members of the family that founded it (in 1930). It's one of the most visitor-friendly champagne houses. The Romanesque cellars were dug from the site of Gallo-Roman chalk mines in use from the 4th to the 13th centuries. Tours—including a film, a guided cellar visit, anecdotes about Reims and the champagne-making process, and Taittinger family lore—last about an hour and include everything from how a corking machine works to the science behind sediment removal. By the end, you'll know how champagne is made, from A to Z.

9 place St-Nicaise. ✆ **03-26-85-84-35.** www.taittinger.com. Admission 10€ adults, free for children 11 and under. Mid-Mar to mid-Nov daily 9:30am–noon and 2–5pm; mid-Nov to mid-Mar Mon–Fri 9:30am–1pm and 2–4:30pm.

Mumm champagne cellar.

Veuve Clicquot–Ponsardin One of the most memorable and successful logos in France shows a 19th-century matriarch, Nicole Ponsardin, outfitted in dowdy but expensive finery. She remained firmly in control of the *maison de champagne* that bears her name from 1866 (when her husband died) to 1895. You can visit some of the 26km (16 miles) of underground galleries as part of guided tours that last 75 to 90 minutes.

1 place des Droits-de-l'Homme. ✆ **03-26-89-53-90.** www.veuve-clicquot.com. Reservations required. Admission 13€, free for 15 and under. Apr–Oct Mon–Sat 10am–6pm; Nov 2–Dec 22 and Jan 12–Mar Mon–Fri 10am–6pm.

Shopping

The city's main shopping district is around the cathedral. Nearby streets to browse are the long **rue de Vesle,** the **cours Langlet,** and **place Drouet d'Erlon.**

You'll want to include champagne on your shopping list. Many people opt to visit one of the major houses in town; others drive along the **Routes du Champagne.** This is where you'll find the smaller champagne makers. When you're making the rounds, know that most houses prefer that you take the tour and not just stop in the shop. If you do take the tour, you'll at least get a glass of bubbly at the end. Bottles are priced individually, but you can get discounts if you buy three or six bottles. If you're looking for a good deal, you may want to buy at a store in town, such as **a Grande Boutique du Vin,** 3 place Léon-Bourgeois (✆ **03-26-40-12-12**). It stocks one of the most comprehensive inventories of champagne in Reims, with 150 types of bubbly from more than 100 companies. They include many superb brands for 15€ to 38€ per bottle, which are virtually never advertised in North America. Excellent lesser-known brands include Deutz, Billecart Salmon, Henriot, Guy Charlemagne, and Erick de Sousa. Staff members speak English.

Another specialty is the light, delicious little pink cookie known as *biscuit de Reims.* The best place to find this treat is **La Maison Fossier/Biscuits Fossier,** 25 cours Langlet (✆ **03-26-47-59-84**). For chocolate and candied specialties, try **La Petite Friande,** 15 cours Langlet (✆ **03-26-47-50-44**), where you can purchase liqueur-filled chocolate champagne bubbles and corks.

Parc des Expositions (✆ **03-26-84-69-69**), route de Châlons-en-Champagne (4km/2½ miles east of Reims), plays host to a flea market the first Sunday of every month except July and August. On the first weekend of April, there's a huge "Euro" flea market, with more than 500 vendors, in the same location. The organization responsible for these events is **Artcom/Puces de Reims,** 82 rue Jacquart (✆ **03-26-02-04-06**).

Where to Stay

EXPENSIVE

Grand Hôtel des Templiers ★★ This chic hotel a short walk from the cathedral is small, but it's your best inner-city bet. In a restored 1800s mock-Gothic house, antiques, ornate ceilings, and hand-carved woodwork create an inviting ambience. The guest rooms maintain the 19th-century atmosphere, with color-coordinated fabrics and bold-print wall coverings. Each comes with a quality bed and well-maintained bathroom, most often with both tub and shower.

22 rue des Templiers, Reims 51100. ✆ **03-26-88-55-08.** Fax 03-26-47-80-60. 17 units. 190€–280€ double; 350€ suite. AE, DC, MC, V. Bus: H. **Amenities:** Bar; indoor heated pool; sauna. *In room:* A/C, TV, hair dryer, minibar, free Wi-Fi.

Les Crayères ★★★ In Reims, there's no better place to stay or dine than here, one of the finest châteaux in eastern France. Located in a 7-hectare (17-

acre) park, it has 5.5m (18-ft.) ceilings, paneling, and luxurious furnishings. The guest rooms, with terraces and all the amenities, are individually decorated in a country manor style and usually available when a champagne mogul isn't in residence. The bathrooms hold deluxe toiletries and tub/showers. The restaurant is the greatest in the region (p. 378).

64 bd. Henri-Vasnier, Reims 51685. www.lescrayeres.com. ✆ **03-26-82-80-80.** Fax 03-26-82-65-52. 20 units. 345€–620€ double. AE, DC, MC, V. Closed Jan. **Amenities:** Restaurant; bar; babysitting; room service; tennis court. *In room:* A/C, hair dryer, minibar, free Wi-Fi.

MODERATE

L'Assiette Champenoise ★★ About 3km (1¾ miles) southwest from Reims in the suburb of Tinqueux, this is the second-best hotel and restaurant in the area. Built in the 1970s among century-old trees, it occupies part of a former Norman estate, standing in a 1.6-hectare (4-acre) park. The well-maintained rooms are attractively furnished in a mix of French traditional and modern style. Many visitors come here just for the rustic dining room. Chef Arnaud Lallement's cuisine covers a medley of classics, some with an innovative twist. Try John Dory with ragout of vegetables, suckling veal with seven vegetables, or grilled duck liver with fondue of tomatoes. Homemade foie gras is always a reliable starter.

40 av. Paul-Vaillant-Couturier, Tinqueux 51430. www.assiettechampenoise.com. ✆ **03-26-84-64-64.** Fax 03-26-04-15-69. 55 units. 160€–240€ double; 310€ suite. AE, DC, MC, V. Free parking. From Reims, take A4 west toward Paris and exit at SORTIE 22–TINQUEUX; av. Paul-Vaillant-Couturier will lead you directly to Tinqueux. **Amenities:** Restaurant; bar; indoor pool; sauna. *In room:* TV (in some), hair dryer, minibar, free Wi-Fi.

INEXPENSIVE

Best Western Hôtel de la Paix Located between the train station and the cathedral, this is the only modern hotel in France with a medieval chapel (built for Benedictine nuns in the 1200s) overlooking its garden and pool. Constructed in 1946, it has been enlarged since then. The rooms in this pleasant chain hotel are contemporary and well maintained, and many are air-conditioned. Furnishings are a bit sterile, but the beds are comfortable and most bathrooms have tub/showers. The hotel's restaurant (✆ **03-26-47-00-45**) serves excellent meals daily at lunch and dinner. The cuisine may include sauerkrauts, fish, grills, oysters, and casseroles.

9 rue Buirette, Reims 51100. www.hotel-lapaix.fr. ✆ **800/528-1234** in the U.S. and Canada, or 03-26-40-04-08. Fax 03-26-47-75-04. 169 units. 155€–210€ double; 350€ suite. AE, DC, MC, V. Parking 10€. Bus: G or H. **Amenities:** Restaurant; bar; exercise room; indoor pool; room service; sauna. *In room:* A/C, TV, hair dryer, minibar, free Wi-Fi.

Grand Hôtel du Nord This 1920s hotel is a former relay station for the postal service. The high-ceilinged guest rooms are decorated in comfortable contemporary style. The hotel lies in a pedestrian-only zone in Reims's historic core, a 10-minute walk from the cathedral and just steps from the rail station. Two steps from the entrance, lively place Drouet-d'Erlon has many boutiques, cafes, and cinemas. The hotel is also near the cathedral, the basilica, and various museums.

75 place Drouet-d'Erlon, Reims 51100. www.hotel-nord-reims.com. ✆ **03-26-47-39-03.** Fax 03-26-40-92-26. 50 units. 65€–80€ double. AE, DC, MC, V. Take A4 (A26) to Reims-Centre. Bus: G or H. **Amenities:** Smoke-free rooms. *In room:* TV, hair dryer.

Mercure Reims Cathédrale ★ This chain hotel from the 1970s sits on the banks of the Marne Canal, a 5-minute walk from the town center and the cathedral. It's near the entrance to the highway A4, so it's easy to find. The good-size rooms have all the modern conveniences, including bathrooms with tubs and showers; some have views of a waterway. Furnishings are standard motel style.

31 bd. Paul-Doumer, Reims 51100. www.mercure.com. ✆ **03-26-04-78-23.** Fax 03-26-84-49-84. 126 units. 124€–179€ double; 165€–209€ suite. AE, DC, MC, V. Parking 11€. **Amenities:** Restaurant; bar; babysitting; room service. *In room:* A/C, TV, hair dryer, minibar, free Wi-Fi.

Where to Eat

L'Assiette Champenoise (see p. 377) has an excellent restaurant.

Le Jamin FRENCH Airy; clean; well respected; outfitted in a pleasantly contemporary, noncontroversial style; and a fixture in Reims for more than a decade, this restaurant describes itself as "semi-gastronomique" and, as such, offers reasonable prices for some remarkably stylish food. The best examples include a salad composed of scallops, crayfish, and sweetbreads; St-Marcellin cheese, fried and served with pine nuts as a salad; and a "*declinaison* of duckling," whereby at least four different preparations (*rilletes, magret* both smoked and unsmoked, and terrine of duck liver) are assembled onto a single flavorful platter. Delectable main courses include roasted turbot in champagne sauce, stingray with garlic butter, and English-style calves' liver.

18 bd. Jamin. ✆ **03-26-07-37-30.** www.lejamin.com. Reservations recommended. Main courses 12€–19€; set menus 20€–35€. AE, MC, V. Tues–Sun noon–2:30pm; Tues–Sat 7:30–9:30pm. Closed last 2 weeks in Aug and last 2 weeks in Jan.

Le Millénaire ★★★ FRENCH Competing for supremacy in a town where the culinary competition is severe, Le Millénaire emerges near the very top. Set near the place Royale, it offers a contemporary setting with frequently changing art exhibitions. Its market-fresh cuisine is sublime, with the finest ingredients deftly handled by a skilled staff. A risotto is made with black truffles and shavings of parmesan, or else you can opt for the turbot in a champagne sauce with leeks. Sweetbreads are served with a foie gras ravioli, and yet another specialty is the roast lamb in a rosemary sauce.

4 rue Bertin. ✆ **02-26-08-26-62.** Reservations required. Main courses 32€–42€; fixed-price menus 30€–47€. AE, DC, MC, V. Mon–Fri noon–2pm and Mon–Sat 7–10pm.

Les Crayères ★★★ MODERN FRENCH There is no restaurant to equal this one in the entire champagne country—and the setting is elegant, too (p. 376). The restaurant installed in the château originated as a hyperupscale *maison bourgeoise* (actually a mini château) back in 1903. The cuisine here has always been a magnet for the champagne barons of the area, and the restaurant is the number-one choice for wine buyers from around the world. Launch your meal with ravioli stuffed with escargots, or sample another appetizer that is celestial in its taste—three different preparations of foie gras, including one presented au naturel. The wild turbot and the grilled lobster are ineffably delicate, and the roast duck with honey-vinegar sauce is earthy, regional, and a delight.

64 bd. Henri-Vasnier. ✆ **03-26-82-80-80.** Fax 03-26-82-65-52. Reservations required a few days in advance for weekday dinners, at least a month in advance for weekend dinners. Main

courses 50€–140€; fixed-price menus (including red bordeaux and champagne) 185€–305€; fixed-price lunch 70€. AE, DC, MC, V. Wed–Sun noon–1:30pm and 7–9:30pm.

Where to Stay & Eat Nearby

Château de Fère ★★ MODERN FRENCH This fabulous restaurant occupies a turreted 16th-century château in a park. The only restaurant in Champagne with superior cuisine is Les Crayères (see above). Begin in the garden, sipping an aperitif or a glass of champagne with juice from freshly crushed raspberries. Your meal may consist of specialties such as foie gras of duckling with confit of ginger and a sauce made from the dessert wine Muscats de Venise, nuggets of suckling lamb cooked in a truffle-and-parsley-flavored crust, and deliberately undercooked Scottish salmon in lemon-flavored sweet-and-sour sauce.

Also available are 26 guest rooms with minibars and TVs. Doubles are 150€ to 360€, suites 310€ to 420€.

Rte. de Fismes (D967), Fère-en-Tardenois 02130. www.chateaudefere.com. ✆ **03-23-82-21-13.** Fax 03-23-82-37-81. Reservations required. Main courses 34€–68€; fixed-price menu 36€–99€. AE, DC, MC, V. Wed–Sun 12:30–2pm; Tues–Sun 7:30–9:30pm. Closed Jan–Feb 15. From Reims (35 min.), take E46 northwest toward Soissons. At Fismes, take D367 toward Fère-en-Tardenois and follow signs to Château de Fère. About 2.5km (1½ miles) north of the restaurant, you'll see the ruins of a 12th-century castle, also called the Château de Fère.

Reims After Dark

Reims has the most vibrant nightlife in the region. The best place to start is **place Drouet-d'Erlon,** home to the city's premier clubs. This is a university town—for the most part, students rule the night. Just follow them to the best venues.

For a beer and a heavy dose of noise and rowdy students, head to the **Glue Pot,** 49 place Drouet-d'Erlon (✆ **03-26-47-36-46**). At **James Joyce Pub,** 80 place Drouet-d'Erlon (✆ **03-26-40-33-06**), a mixed-age crowd congregates in an Irish-style pub that has more than 120 types of beer. For a more sedate experience, try **L'Escale,** 132 rue Vesle (✆ **03-26-88-17-85**), where the atmosphere is more conducive to conversation with locals and other tourists.

The Route de Champagne

Whether for hiking or for biking, the Montagne de Reims or Route de Champagne is the best place to experience the beauty of this vineyard-studded region. Montagne de Reims is a forested plateau south of Reims, where the slopes produce the grapes used to make bubbly.

Armed with a map from the tourist office in Reims or Epernay, you can explore this area along trails called *sentiers de Grandes Randonnées,* along the top of the northern plateau of Montagne de Reims.

These trails are called GRs. Because you're not likely to have time to visit all of them, we recommend routes GR14 and GR141. They form a loop of some 50km (31 miles) around the plateau's eastern section, taking in such towns as Verzy. Several train stations along the way, including a convenient one at Verzy, offer opportunities to take you back to Reims or Epernay, should you tire before finishing the full loop.

The best dance floors in town are at **Le Vogue,** 93 bd. Général-Leclerc (✆ **03-26-47-34-29**), which attracts a mixed-age crowd (25–40); and **Le Soft,** 2 bis av. Georges-Clemenceau (✆ **03-26-35-78-19**), with its decor of old French cars placed like artwork against the brick walls and mirrors. Young gays and lesbians go to **Bar Lilas,** 75 rue des Courcelles (✆ **03-26-47-02-81**). Everybody wears jeans; the cover at any of these clubs ranges from free to 11€.

Comédie de Reims, chaussée Bocquaine (✆ **03-26-48-49-10**), has a varied schedule; tickets cost 12€ to 19€ for adults and 6€ to 8€ for children.

EPERNAY

140km (87 miles) E of Paris; 26km (16 miles) S of Reims

On the left bank of the Marne, Epernay rivals Reims as a center for champagne. Although it has only one-sixth Reims's population, Epernay produces nearly as much champagne, with an estimated 322km (200 miles) or more of cellars and tunnels. These caves are vast vaults cut into the chalk rock on which the town is built. Represented in Epernay are such champagne companies as Moët et Chandon (the largest), Pol Roger, Mercier, and de Castellane.

Epernay's main boulevards are the elegant residential avenue de Champagne, rue Mercier, and rue de Reims, all radiating from place de la République. Two important squares in the narrow streets of the commercial district are place Hughes-Plomb and place des Arcades.

Invading armies have destroyed or burned Epernay nearly two dozen times. Few of its buildings have survived. However, check out the neoclassical villas and Victorian town houses on avenue de Champagne.

Essentials

GETTING THERE If you're **driving** to Epernay from Reims, head south on E51. Eighteen **trains** per day arrive from Paris's Gare de l'Est (trip time: 1 hr., 15 min.); the one-way fare is 20€. From Reims, there are 16 trains per day (trip time: 25 min.; 5.60€ one-way). For information, call ✆ **08-92-35-35-35** or visit www.voyages-sncf.com. The major **bus** link is SDM Trans-Champagne (✆ **03-26-65-17-07** in Epernay), operating four buses per day Monday to Saturday between Châlons-en-Champagne and Epernay (trip time: 45 min.).

VISITOR INFORMATION The **Office de Tourisme** is at 7 av. de Champagne (✆ **03-26-53-33-00;** fax 03-26-51-95-22; www.ot-epernay.fr).

Exploring the Town

Boutiques and shops abound in the pedestrian district of **place des Arcades, rue du Général-Leclerc, rue St-Thibault, rue St-Martin,** and **rue Porte Lucas.** You'll find stores selling gifts, clothes, antiques, books, and regional food items.

For champagne, you can go to the individual houses along avenue de Champagne (see below) or try one of the stores that represent a variety of houses. Two of the best are **La Cave Salvatori,** 11 rue Flodoard (✆ **03-26-55-32-32**), and **Le Domaine des Crus,** 2 rue Henri Dunant (✆ **03-26-54-18-60**), known for a staggering array of champagnes.

For champagne gift items such as flutes and corks, as well as table decorations and linens, visit **De-ci-de-ca,** 34 rue du Général-Leclerc (✆ **03-26-**

55-67-68). **Fromm Jacques,** 33 rue St-Thibault (✆**03-26-55-25-64**), and **Camaieu,** 12 rue de Professeur Langevin (✆**03-26-51-83-83**), sell garden ornaments, souvenirs, and art objects commemorating the historic medievalism of Amiens.

Champagne de Castellane Across from Mercier (see below), this champagne house, unlike the two recommended below, gives you a closer view of how champagne is actually produced. You see workers doing it all—corking, labeling, even removing sediment. The museum on-site may be a bit dull, but the climb to the tower (237 steps) for a panoramic view of the area is not. The tower is from 1904 and has become the symbol of Epernay.

63 av. de Champagne. ✆ **03-26-51-19-19.** www.castellane.com. Tours 8€–18€, free for ages 16 and under. Apr–Dec daily 10am–noon and 2–6pm. Closed Sat–Sun Jan–Mar.

Mercier Mercier is near Moët et Chandon, and you can visit them both on the same day. Mercier conducts tours in English of its 18km (11 miles) of tunnels from laser-guided trains. The caves contain one of the world's largest wooden barrels, with a capacity of more than 200,000 bottles. No reservation is necessary if there are fewer than 10 in your group.

70 av. de Champagne. ✆ **03-26-51-22-22.** www.champagnemercier.fr. Admission 8€. Mid-Feb to mid-Nov Thurs–Mon 9:30–11:30am and 2–4:30pm.

Moët et Chandon Champagne Cellars One of the most prestigious champagne houses runs an informative tour, describing the champagne-making process and filling you in on champagne lore: Napoleon, a friend of Jean-Rémy Moët, used to stop by for thousands of bottles on his way to battle. The only time he didn't take a supply was at Waterloo—and look what happened there. At the end of the tour, you're rewarded with a glass of bubbly.

20 av. de Champagne. ✆ **03-26-51-20-20.** www.moet.com. Admission 14€–28€. Early May to early Nov daily 9:30–11:30am and 2–4:30pm; early Nov to Apr Mon–Fri 9:30–11:30am and 2–4:30pm. Closed Jan.

Moët et Chandon Champagne Cellars.

Where to Stay

Les Berceaux (see "Where to Eat," below) also rents rooms.

Le Clos Raymi Set inside a charming 19th-century structure once occupied by Monsieur Chandon (as in the champagne maker), guests are treated to sumptuous beds and antique furnishings, and made to feel at home. It's a short (10-min.) but pleasant walk from the center of town.

30 rue Joseph de Venoge, Epernay 51200. www.closraymi-hotel.com. ✆ **03-26-51-00-58.** 16 units. 110€–170€ double. AE, MC, V. Free parking. *In room:* TV, free Wi-Fi.

Royal Champagne ★★★ This hotel is constructed around an 18th-century relay station for the postal system. The establishment's historic core contains the reception area, bar, and dining facilities; guest rooms are in town house–style accommodations overlooking the nearby vineyards. The units are rustic and very comfortable, exemplifying the coziness of wine-country living. Each comes with a sumptuous bed with fine linen, plus a combination tub/shower.

The chef is known for classic dishes with an innovative twist. The food is exceptional, with specialties such as lobster ragout, John Dory with a purée of celery and truffle-flavored cream sauce, and roast lamb with garlic.

Champillon Bellevue 51160. www.royalchampagne.com. ✆ **03-26-52-87-11.** Fax 03-26-52-89-69. 25 units. 240€–375€ double; 355€–400€ suite. AE, DC, MC, V. Closed Dec 2–Feb 15. Drive 8km (5 miles) north from Epernay toward Reims on the rte. du Vignoble (N2051) to Champillon. **Amenities:** Restaurant; bar; babysitting; room service. *In room:* A/C, TV, hair dryer, minibar, free Wi-Fi.

Where to Eat

The food at **Royal Champagne** (see above) is excellent.

Les Berceaux ★★★ CHAMPENOISE Chef-owner Patrick Michelon serves generous portions of flavorful, conservative regional cuisine. The menu changes seasonally and always features fresh produce and superior cuts of fish, meat, and game. Particularly scrumptious are such dishes as Pyrénéan suckling lamb roasted on a spit; snails in champagne sauce; roast filet of John Dory; and galette of roasted and minced pigs' feet in puff pastry, served with potatoes. At an on-site wine bar, Bistrot le 7, you can sample an assortment of vintages by the glass. It showcases local wines, especially champagne. If Les Berceaux errs at all, it's that it tends to be a bit pretentious.

Available upstairs are 28 comfortable guest rooms, each with TV. A double with a tub/shower rents for 95€, or else 140€ in a junior suite.

13 rue des Berceaux, Epernay 51200. ✆ **03-26-55-28-84.** Fax 03-26-55-10-36. www.lesberceaux.com. Reservations recommended. Main courses 34€–72€; fixed-price menu 59€–69€. AE, DC, MC, V. Wed–Sun noon–2pm and 7–9pm. Closed early Feb to early Mar.

Epernay After Dark

Start out at the chic cafe and bar **Le Progrès,** 5 place de la République (✆ **03-26-55-22-72**). For a glass of wine or even Scotch (something you don't see enough of in this wine-crazed region), consider a visit to **Le Chriss Bar,** a nightclub at 40 rue de Sézanne (✆ **03-26-57-87-18**).

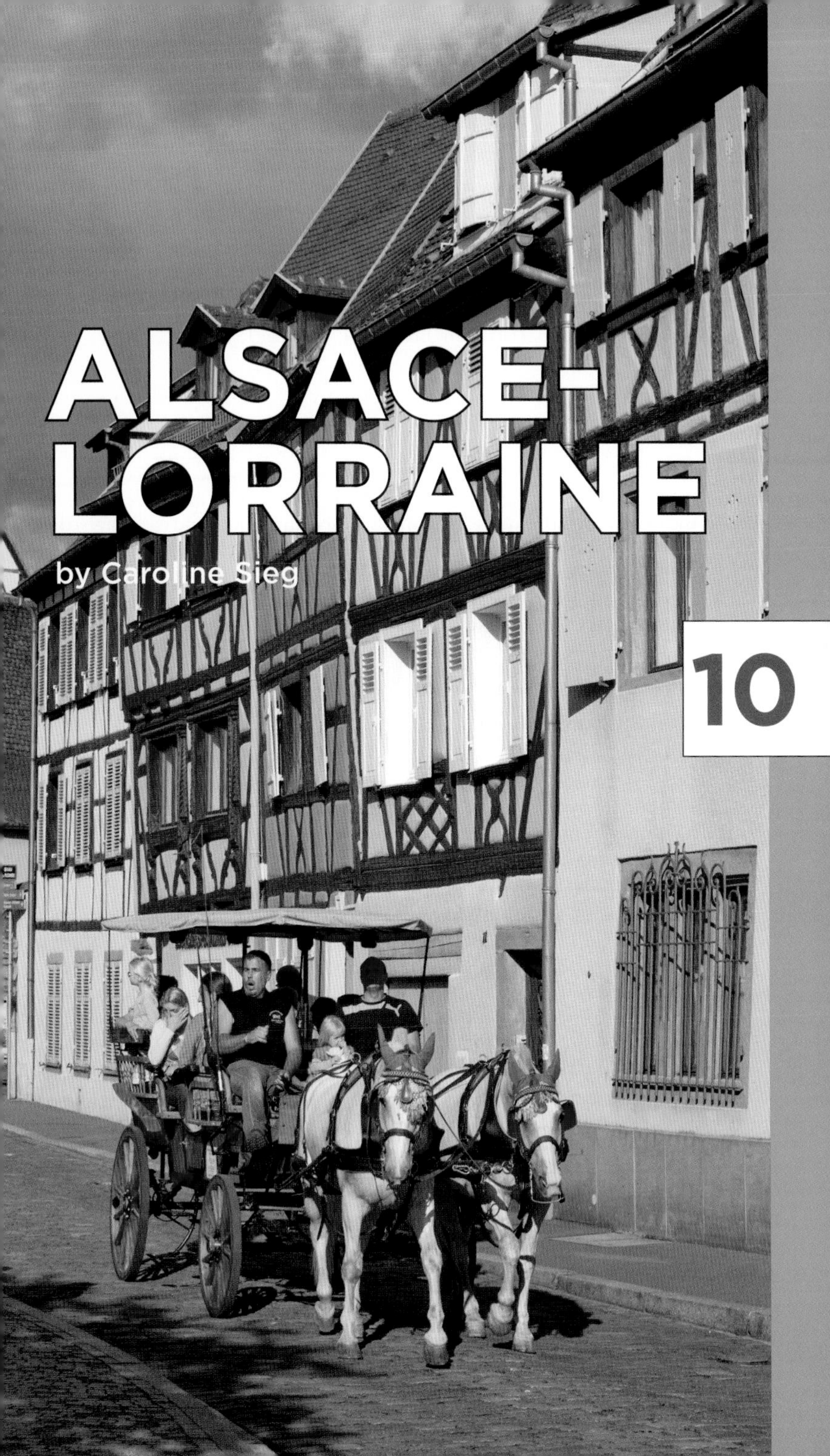

ALSACE-LORRAINE

by Caroline Sieg

10

The provinces of Alsace and Lorraine, with ancient capitals at Strasbourg and Nancy, have been the object of many disputes between Germany and France. Alsace has been called "the least French of French provinces," more reminiscent of the Black Forest across the Rhine. In fact, it became German from 1870 until after World War I and was ruled by Hitler from 1940 to 1944. These days, both provinces are back under French control, though they remain somewhat independent.

In the Vosges Mountains, you can follow La Route des Crêtes (Crest Road) or skirt the foothills, visiting the wine towns of Alsace. In its cities and cathedrals, the castle-dotted landscape evokes a past filled with military glory or defeat. Lorraine is Joan of Arc country, and many of its towns still suggest their medieval heritage.

No clear-cut line delineates Alsace from Lorraine. Alsace is more German. Lorraine, with its rolling landscape, appears more French in character.

STRASBOURG ★★★

488km (303 miles) SE of Paris; 217km (135 miles) SW of Frankfurt

Situated about 483km (300 miles) southeast of Paris and tucked in the elbow of northwest France, Strasbourg ping-ponged between Germany and France for centuries. Today this capital of wine-growing Alsace blends Teutonic might with a cosmopolitan flair. All canals and cobblestones, half-timbered houses and Gothic spires, this UNESCO World Heritage Site on the River Ill weaves fairy-tale charm with the European Parliament's political clout.

Things to Do The **Gothic Cathédrale Notre-Dame de Strasbourg** has beautiful 12th- to 14th-century stained-glass windows, but drop by at 12:30pm, when carved wooden figures whirl and change in its astronomical clock. **La Petite France** is an enchanting scene of half-timbered houses, canals, and medieval bridges. The sumptuous, rococo **Palais de Rohan** shelters the Musée des Beaux-Arts, with work by Rubens and Rembrandt. It's all contained on Grand Île, a designated UNESCO Heritage Site and an island ensconced within the city.

Shopping Delicate **ceramics and pottery** and high-quality **textiles** abound throughout Strasbourg's historic center; your best bets are around the Cathédrale and place des Halles; head to **Nappes d'Alsace** for Alsacian napkins, tea towels, and the like, or **Bastian** for 18th- and 19th-century ceramic tureens. In late November and December, the place de Cathédrale erupts with the magical **Marché de Noël** (Christmas Market), where you can purchase handmade ornaments and gifts and warm up with hot vin chaud (mulled wine).

Nightlife & Entertainment Each summer, the illuminated **place de la Cathédrale** and other outdoor venues in town come alive after dark with world-

PREVIOUS PAGE: **Alsatian buildings in Strasbourg.**

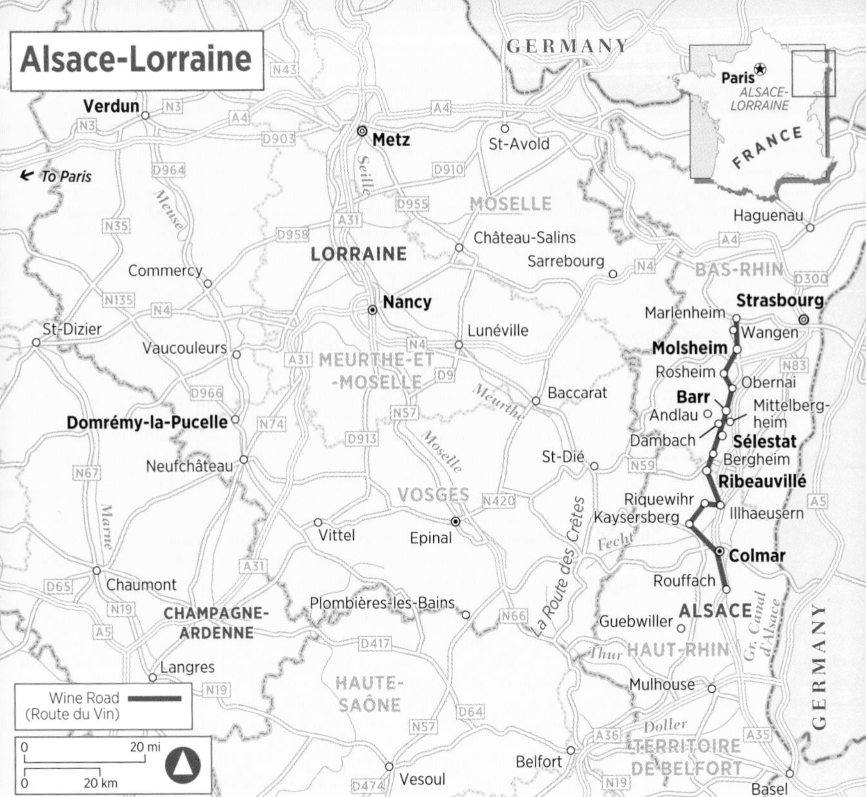

class drama, dance, and classical concerts. For innovative ballet and opera, make your way to **Opéra du Rhin,** while the **Orchestre Philharmonique de Strasbourg** performs at the Palais de la Musique et des Congrès, north of the center. Dance the night away at one of the biggest discos in the region, **Le Chalet,** a few miles north of the city.

Restaurants & Dining Strasbourg serves up a mix of hearty local staples with French finesse. Feast on **Flammekueche,** a thin, crispy tart often topped with cheese, ham, and/or mushrooms, and best sampled at one of the traditional restaurants lining place de la Cathédrale. Sip **Alsatian wine** such as Pinot Blanc on a riverside terrace in **La Petite France.** Experience the cozy, convivial Alsatian atmosphere at **Winstub Le Clu,** north of **place de la Cathédrale.**

Essentials

GETTING THERE The **Strasbourg-Entzheim Airport** (Aéroport International Strasbourg; ✆ **03-88-64-67-67;** www.strasbourg.aeroport.fr), 15km (9¼ miles) southwest of the city center, receives daily flights from many European cities, including Paris, London, Rome, Vienna, and Moscow. You can get from the airport to the town center by using **shuttle buses** and **city trams.** They run at 40-minute intervals all day long. The one-way cost is 3.60€. Take a shuttle bus to the south side of Strasbourg, to a junction point known as Baggersee. From there, you'll continue to the town center on tram line A. Combined travel time is between 35 and 40 minutes each way. For information, call ✆ **03-88-77-70-70.**

The superfast TGV train makes round-trips from Paris to Strasbourg, cutting travel time nearly in half to 2 hours, 20 minutes. At least 20 **trains** a day arrive from Paris's Gare de l'Est (trip time: 4 hr.); the one-way fare is 70€ to 90€. For information and schedules, call ✆ **36-35** or 08-92-35-35-35.

By **car,** the giant A35 crosses the plain of Alsace, with occasional references to its original name, the N83. It links Strasbourg with Colmar and Mulhouse.

VISITOR INFORMATION The **Office de Tourisme** is on 17 place de la Cathédrale (✆ **03-88-52-28-28;** fax 03-88-52-28-29; www.otstrasbourg.fr).

SPECIAL EVENTS **Wolf Music,** 24 rue de la Mésange (✆ **03-88-32-43-10;** http://wolf-musique.musicunivers.com), arranges ticket sales for two festivals: the **Festival of Classical Music** (✆ **03-88-15-29-29**), for 2 weeks in June, and the **Festival de Jazz** (✆ **03-88-15-29-29**), in early July. Both feature international artists and draw large crowds. Ticket prices range from 19€ to 70€ and go on sale in mid-April. The Association Musica (✆ **03-88-23-46-46;** www.festival-musica.org) organizes the **Festival International des Musiques d'Aujourd'hui.** It takes place from the end of September to the first week of October and combines contemporary music concerts with movies and modern opera performances. Tickets are 6€ to 19€ and go on sale at the end of June.

Exploring Strasbourg

Despite war damage, much remains of Old Strasbourg, including covered bridges and towers from its former fortifications, plus many 15th- and 17th-century dwellings with painted wooden fronts and carved beams.

The city's traffic hub is **place Kléber ★**, dating from the 15th century. Sit here with a tankard of Alsatian beer and get to know Strasbourg. The bronze statue in the center is of J. B. Kléber, born in Strasbourg in 1753; he became one of Napoleon's most noted generals and was buried under the monument.

La Petite France.

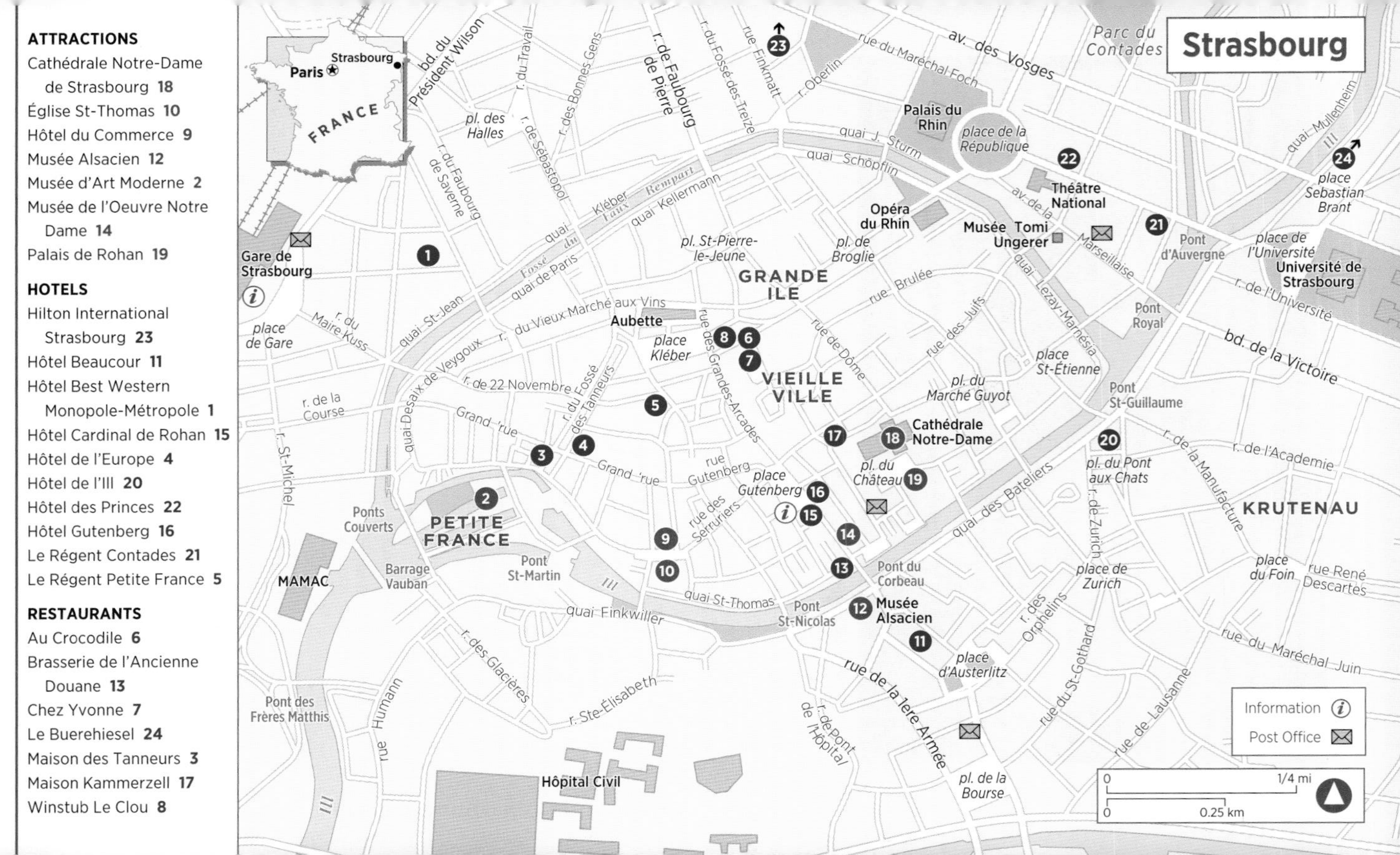

ATTRACTIONS
Cathédrale Notre-Dame de Strasbourg **18**
Église St-Thomas **10**
Hôtel du Commerce **9**
Musée Alsacien **12**
Musée d'Art Moderne **2**
Musée de l'Oeuvre Notre Dame **14**
Palais de Rohan **19**

HOTELS
Hilton International Strasbourg **23**
Hôtel Beaucour **11**
Hôtel Best Western Monopole-Métropole **1**
Hôtel Cardinal de Rohan **15**
Hôtel de l'Europe **4**
Hôtel de l'Ill **20**
Hôtel des Princes **22**
Hôtel Gutenberg **16**
Le Régent Contades **21**
Le Régent Petite France **5**

RESTAURANTS
Au Crocodile **6**
Brasserie de l'Ancienne Douane **13**
Chez Yvonne **7**
Le Buerehiesel **24**
Maison des Tanneurs **3**
Maison Kammerzell **17**
Winstub Le Clou **8**

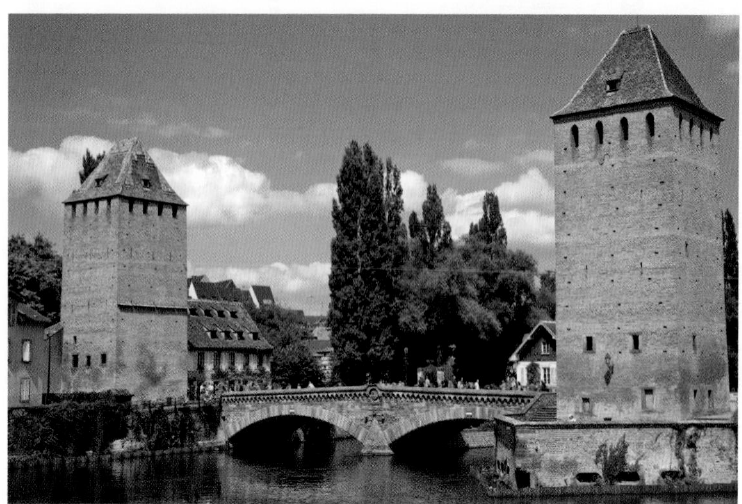

Ponts Couverts, one of Strasbourg's medieval bridges.

Apparently, his presence offended the Nazis, who removed the statue in 1940. This Alsatian bronze was restored to its proper place in 1945.

From here, take rue des Grandes-Arcades southeast to **place Gutenberg,** one of the city's oldest squares. The central statue (1840), by David d'Angers, is of Gutenberg, who perfected his printing press in Strasbourg in the winter of 1436 and 1437. The former town hall, now the **Hôtel du Commerce,** was built in 1582 and is one of the most significant Renaissance buildings in Alsace. The neighborhoods within a few blocks of the city's **cathedral** are loaded with medieval references and historical charm.

La Petite France ★★ is the most interesting quarter of Strasbourg. A virtual island, it's surrounded by scenic canals on four sides, and its 16th-century houses reflect in the waters of the Ill River. In "Little France," old roofs with gray tiles have sheltered families for ages, and the cross-beamed facades with roughly carved rafters are in typical Alsatian style. For a good view, walk along rue des Moulins, branching off from rue du Bain-aux-Plantes.

Cathédrale Notre-Dame de Strasbourg ★★★ The city's crowning glory is an outstanding example of Gothic architecture, representing a transition from

Exploring Strasbourg by Boat

One of the most romantic ways to spend time in Strasbourg is to take an excursion on the Ill River from the Palais de Rohan. The 75-minute cruises cost 8€ for adults and 4€ for children. They include recorded commentary in six languages. From mid-March to early November, rides depart at 30-minute intervals daily between 9:30am and 9pm, with hours extended to 10pm May to September. In November, departures are at 10:30am, 1, 2:30, and 4pm; in December, rides depart every half-hour from 9:30am to 5pm. For information, call Batorama, 9 rue de Nantes (✆ **03-88-84-13-13;** www.batorama.fr).

the Romanesque. Construction began in 1176. The pyramidal tower in rose-colored stone was completed in 1439; at 141m (462 ft.), it's the tallest one from medieval times. This cathedral is still in use. Religious ceremonies, particularly on feast days, meld perfectly with the architectural majesty. Individual tourists can visit the tower only in the summer (you may have to wait to climb it). The Office de Tourisme (see above) organizes tours for groups; call for the schedule.

Four large counterforts divide the **main facade ★★★** into three vertical parts and two horizontal galleries. Note the **rose window,** which looks like stone lace. The facade is rich in decoration: On the portal of the south transept, the *Coronation and Death of the Virgin* in one of the two tympanums is the finest such medieval work. In the north transept, see also the facade of the **Chapelle St-Laurence,** a stunning achievement of the late Gothic German style.

A Romanesque **crypt** lies under the chancel, which is covered with square stonework. The stained-glass window is the work of Max Ingrand. The **nave** is majestic, with windows depicting emperors and kings on the north Strasbourg aisle. Five chapels cluster around the transept, including one built in 1500 in the Flamboyant Gothic style. In the south transept stands the **Angel Pillar ★★**, illustrating the Last Judgment, with angels lowering their trumpets.

The **astronomical clock ★** was built between 1547 and 1574. It stopped during the Revolution, and from 1838 to 1842, the mechanism was replaced. Each day at 12:30pm, crowds gather to see its show of allegorical figures. On Sunday, Apollo drives his sun horses; on Thursday, you see Jupiter and his eagle. The body of the clock has a planetarium based on the theories of Copernicus. Close-up views of the clock are available Monday to Saturday noon to 12:30pm; tickets (2€ adults, 1.50€ ages 5–18 and students) go on sale in the south portal at 11:45am.

Place de la Cathédrale. ✆ **03-88-32-75-78** for times of services. Cathedral: Daily 7–11:20am and 12:35–7pm. Tower: ✆ **03-88-43-60-40.** Apr–Sept daily 9am–7:15pm; Oct–Mar daily 10am–5:15pm. Tower admission 4.60€ adults, 2.30€ children 17 and under and students.

Cathédrale Notre-Dame de Strasbourg.

Eglise St-Thomas Built between 1230 and 1330, this Protestant church houses five naves. It contains the **mausoleum ★★** of Maréchal de Saxe, a masterpiece of French art by Pigalle (1777).

Rue Martin-Luther (along rue St-Thomas, near pont St-Thomas). ✆ **03-88-32-14-46.** Free admission. Apr–Oct daily 10am–6pm; Nov–Dec & Mar daily 10am–5pm; Feb daily 2–5pm. Closed Jan.

Musée Alsacien ★ This museum occupies three mansions from the 16th and 17th centuries. It's like a living textbook of the folklore and customs of Alsace, containing arts, crafts, and tools of the old province.

23 quai St-Nicolas. ✆ **03-88-52-50-01.** Admission 5€ adults, 2.50€ students, free for children 17 and under. Wed–Fri and Mon noon–6pm; Sat–Sun 10am–6pm.

Musée d'Art Moderne In the heart of La Petite France, this is Strasbourg's showcase of modern European art. Don't take the word *modern* too literally—the collection dates from 1870 to the present. The layout of the museum starts with a historical section tracing the emergence of modern art and going forward to the 21st century. Other facilities include a graphic art and photography room, an art library, a museum shop, and a cafe-restaurant on the terrace.

1 place Jean-Hans Arp. ✆ **03-88-23-31-31.** Admission 6€ adults, 3€ students 24 and under and seniors, free for children 17 and under. Tues–Wed and Fri noon–7pm; Thurs noon–9pm; Sat–Sun 10am–6pm.

Musée de l'Oeuvre Notre-Dame ★★★ This museum illustrates the art of the Middle Ages and Renaissance in Strasbourg and Alsace. Some pieces were displayed in the cathedral, where copies have been substituted. The most celebrated is a stained-glass head of Christ from about the 11th century. There's also a window depicting an emperor from around 1200. The sculpture is of great interest, as are the works of Strasbourg goldsmiths from the 16th and 17th centuries. The winding staircase and interior are in the Renaissance style. The 13th-century hall contains sculptures from the cathedral, including the wise and foolish virgins from 1280.

3 place du Château. ✆ **03-88-52-50-00.** Admission 5€ adults, 2.50€ students, free for children 17 and under. Tues–Fri noon–6pm; Sat–Sun 10am–6pm.

Palais de Rohan ★★ This palace south of the cathedral was built from 1732 to 1742. It's an example of supreme elegance and proportion. Noted for its facades and rococo interior, it's one of the crowning design achievements in eastern France. On the first floor is a fine-arts museum (Musée des Beaux-Arts) with works by Rubens, Rembrandt, Van Dyck, El Greco, Goya, Watteau, Renoir, and Monet. On the street level is a decorative-arts museum that exhibits ceramics and the original machinery of the cathedral's first astronomical clock. Also on the premises are collections of artifacts excavated from nearby digs, focusing especially on art and utilitarian objects from the Roman and early medieval (Merovingian) eras.

2 place du Château. ✆ **03-88-52-50-00.** Admission for 1 museum 5€ adults, 2.50€ students, free for children 17 and under; combo ticket 6€ adults, 3€ students, free for children 17 and under. Wed–Mon noon–6pm.

Shopping

Strasbourg overflows with antiques shops, artisans, craftspeople, and beer makers. Every well-accessorized home in Alsace owns some of the napkins, aprons, tablecloths, and tea and bath towels of the Beauvillé textile mills. **Nappes d'Alsace,** 6 rue Mercière, near the cathedral (✆ **03-88-22-69-29**), has one of the widest selections of textiles in town.

Bastian, 22–24 place de la Cathédrale (✆ **03-88-32-45-93**), specializes in 18th- and 19th-century ceramic tureens that Alsace produced in abundance. Look for ragout pots in the forms of a cabbage, a trout, a boar's head, or a turkey, painted in bright colors. There's also a selection of Louis XV and Louis XVI furniture, crafted in the region during the 18th and 19th centuries following Parisian models from the same era.

Bastian's main competitor is **Ville et Campagne,** 23 quai des Bateliers (✆ **03-88-36-96-84**), housed in a Renaissance-style 17th-century building across from the Palais de Rohan. Standout items are polychromed Alsatian antiques (especially 18th- and 19th-c. armoires and chests), Louis- and Directoire-style furnishings, statues, and antique paintings.

One of the most appealing shops in Strasbourg is **Arts et Collections d'Alsace,** 4 place du Marché aux Poissons (✆ **03-88-14-03-77**), which sells copies of art objects and utilitarian ware from museums and private collections through Alsace. You'll see upscale gift items for the home and kitchen, made from pottery, stone, wrought iron, glass, copper, and carved wood. The shop also sells fabric by the yard.

A name in pottery that you're likely to encounter is **Soufflenheim,** a provincial rococo pattern—usually in blues and reds—named after the Alsatian village north of Strasbourg where the style originated. To get there, take N63 north of the center of Strasbourg for 24km (15 miles). In the village, ceramics and pottery have been made since the Bronze Age. Soufflenheim is home to at least a dozen outlets selling cake molds, tureens, saucers and cups, dinnerware, and more, usually in rustic patterns. One of the most prominent retailers is **Gérard Wehrling,** 64 rue de Haguenau (✆ **03-88-86-65-25**), known for pottery that can withstand the rigors of modern ovens, microwaves, and refrigerators.

If you're driving, you may want to check out the villages of Obernai, Illhaeusern, Ribeauvillé, and Schiltigheim. The last is beer-drinking territory; the others offer country wares and antiques.

Where to Stay

EXPENSIVE

Hilton International Strasbourg ★★★ The luxurious, seven-story steel-and-glass Hilton—the best hotel in the city—stands over a university complex opposite the Palais de la Musique et des Congrès. The decor incorporates five kinds of Iberian marble, much of it chosen to resemble the ruddy sandstone of the famous cathedral, which is visible from the hotel. The midsize guest rooms are decorated in standard international chain style—comfortable but not outstanding. They contain tasteful artwork and have spacious marble-trimmed bathrooms.

Av. Herrenschmidt, Strasbourg 67000. www.hilton-strasbourg.com. ✆ **800/445-8667** in the U.S. and Canada, or 03-88-37-10-10. Fax 03-88-25-55-03. 243 units. 175€–380€ double; from 465€ suite. AE, DC, MC, V. Parking 19€. Take the Strasbourg-Centre exit from the autoroute and follow signs to the Wacken, Palais des Congrès, and Palais de l'Europe. **Amenities:** 2 restaurants; 2 bars; babysitting; exercise room; room service. *In room:* A/C, TV, hair dryer, minibar, free Wi-Fi.

Le Régent Petite France ★★ This well-run hotel gives serious competition to the Hilton. Many guests choose it for its more comfortable rooms and atmosphere. This site was once an ice factory, and many of the old steam machines remain. The marble lobby sets the tone, with ice-cream colors and potted palms. Guest rooms come in various sizes, the best of which are quite spacious and open onto river views. The luxurious beds are among the city's finest, and the bathrooms are state of the art. The staff is one of the most professional in Strasbourg.

5 rue des Moulins, Strasbourg 67000. www.regent-petite-france.com. ✆ **800/223-5652** in the U.S. and Canada, or 03-88-76-43-43. Fax 03-88-76-43-76. 72 units. 178€–390€ double; 260€–786€ suite. AE, DC, MC, V. Parking 22€. **Amenities:** Restaurant; bar; babysitting; exercise room; room service; sauna. *In room:* A/C, TV, hair dryer, Jacuzzi (in suites), minibar, free Wi-Fi.

MODERATE

Hôtel Beaucour ★★ This hotel is geared toward business travelers, but anyone will find it ideal—it's the city's most tranquil lodging. At the end of a private street a few blocks east of the cathedral, within what used to be an umbrella factory, it occupies a 17th-century building with timbered ceilings. Every guest room contains a whirlpool tub. Furnishings are of standard international style, but comfortable. The hotel maintains an affiliation with at least two restaurants a short walk away. The concierge, who seems to know all the city's secrets, will make reservations for you.

5 rue des Bouchers, Strasbourg 67000. www.hotel-beaucour.com. ✆ **03-88-76-72-00.** Fax 03-88-76-72-60. 49 units. 116€–165€ double; 113€–220€ suite. AE, DC, MC, V. Parking 9€. **Amenities:** Babysitting. *In room:* TV, hair dryer, minibar, free Wi-Fi.

Hôtel Best Western Monopole–Métropole This hotel is on a quiet street near the train station. Its lobby features a scattering of antiques, among them a 17th-century armoire and a statue of a night watchman. An extension of the salon displays oil portraits of 18th-century Alsatian personalities and glass cases with pewter tankards and candlesticks. Breakfast (the only meal available) is served in the high-ceilinged Alsatian-style dining room. The guest rooms are comfortable, with crisp white linens and (in most) air-conditioning. Each unit is unique; some have Alsatian-style antiques.

16 rue Kuhn, Strasbourg 67000. www.bw-monopole.com. ✆ **800/528-1234** in the U.S. and Canada, or 03-88-14-39-14. Fax 03-88-32-82-55. 86 units. 100€–200€ double; 200€ suite. Rates include breakfast. AE, DC, MC, V. Parking 12€. **Amenities:** Bar; babysitting. *In room:* A/C (in most), TV, hair dryer, minibar, free Wi-Fi.

Hôtel Cardinal de Rohan ★ In the pedestrian zone steps from the cathedral, this five-story hotel is one of the city's best values and within walking distance of the Palais de Rohan. The 17th-century building was rebuilt shortly after World War II. It offers a choice of elegantly furnished rooms, the cheapest of which are small and have a French bed called a *matrimonial* (a standard double bed). Guest-room decor ranges from Louis XV to a regional Alsatian look with lots of wood paneling.

17–19 rue du Maroquin, Strasbourg 67060. www.hotel-rohan.com. ✆ **03-88-32-85-11.** Fax 03-88-75-65-37. 36 units. 75€–159€ double. AE, DC, MC, V. Parking 17€. **Amenities:** Babysitting. *In room:* A/C, TV, hair dryer, minibar, free Wi-Fi.

Hôtel de l'Europe Behind a half-timbered facade a 3-minute walk west of the cathedral, this is one of the best-located government-rated three-star hotels in town. Its roots go back to the 15th century, when it functioned as a coaching inn; it was enlarged with the annexation of an 18th-century house next door. Units run the gamut from modern to a half-timbered fantasy directly under the roof (room no. 404), where angled beams evoke the original construction.

38–40 rue du Fossé-des-Tanneurs, Strasbourg 67000. www.hotel-europe.com. ✆ **03-88-32-17-88.** Fax 03-88-75-65-45. 60 units. 75€–205€ double. AE, DC, MC, V. Parking 14€. **Amenities:** Babysitting; room service. *In room:* A/C, TV, hair dryer, minibar (in some), free Wi-Fi.

Hôtel des Princes A 15-minute walk from the center of town, the Hôtel des Princes enjoys a three-star government rating and is one of the best bargains in the city. Rooms are furnished comfortably but simply. Continental breakfast is the only meal served.

33 rue Geiler, Quartier du Conseil de l'Europe, Strasbourg 67000. www.hotel-princes.com. ✆ **03-88-61-55-19.** Fax 03-88-41-10-92. 43 units. 110€–140€ double. AE, MC, V. Closed Aug. **Amenities:** Babysitting; free Wi-Fi. *In room:* TV, minibar.

Le Régent Contades ★★ Our favorite moderately priced choice is this glorified B&B, in a five-story structure with dormers, close to the cathedral. Diplomats may consider it a secret, but word is out. The stylish hostelry has an intelligent, helpful staff. The guest rooms are furnished in a romantic style with a variety of monochromatic colors that include pink, blue, or soft browns or reds. Breakfast is the only meal served.

8 av. de la Liberté, Strasbourg 67000. www.regent-contades.com. ✆ **03-88-15-05-05.** Fax 03-88-15-05-15. 47 units. 105€–325€ double; 170€–560€ suite. AE, DC, MC, V. Parking 20€. **Amenities:** Bar; room service. *In room:* A/C, TV, hair dryer, minibar, free Wi-Fi.

INEXPENSIVE

Hôtel de l'Ill A 5-minute walk from the cathedral, this government-rated two-star hotel is a good deal. It was originally a restaurant which added rooms in the 1920s. In the 1990s, the property became a hotel only and gained a modern wing. An inviting, unpretentious place, it houses quiet, comfortably furnished rooms decorated in either modern or Alsatian traditional style. Two rooms at the rear have a private terrace or balcony opening onto a view of neighboring gardens. Each room comes with a tidily kept shower-only bathroom, but no amenities other than a phone (some have a TV). The breakfast room is decorated in Laura Ashley style—well, except for the cuckoo clock.

8 quai des Bateliers, Strasbourg 67000. www.hotel-ill.com. 27 units. ✆ **03-88-36-20-01.** Fax 03-88-35-30-03. 60€–80€ double. AE, MC, V. Parking 9€. **Amenities:** Free Wi-Fi. *In room:* A/C (in some), TV.

Hôtel Gutenberg ★ Just off place Gutenberg, this many-windowed hotel is both a bargain and a discovery. The mansion exudes old-fashioned charm—the sculptured walls date to 1745—yet is completely modern (with soundproofing). Many of the guest rooms, with flowery draperies and upholstered furniture, have wooden beams. The most romantic accommodations, evoking old France, are on the fifth floor under timbers.

31 rue des Serruriers, Strasbourg 67000. www.hotel-gutenberg.com. ✆ **03-88-32-17-15.** Fax 03-88-75-76-67. 42 units. 75€–135€ double. AE, MC, V. **Amenities:** Free Internet. *In room:* A/C (in some), TV.

Where to Eat

VERY EXPENSIVE

Au Crocodile ★★★ ALSATIAN A beautiful sky-lit restaurant, Au Crocodile serves the most inventive food in Strasbourg. An especially appealing feature is the fixed-price menus that revolve around creative themes, which have included Egypt and Victor Hugo. Some of the best dishes include sautéed scallops with purée of celery and Indian-style (Marsala-style) spiced butter sauce; delicate local freshwater whitefish *(sandre)* served in sauerkraut; and duck liver cooked in a salt crust. Our major problem comes only when the bill (*la note,* as the French say) arrives—especially when we indulge in the high-priced wines.

10 rue de l'Outre. ✆ **03-88-32-13-02.** www.au-crocodile.com. Reservations required. Main courses 39€–78€; fixed-price menu 35€–75€. AE, DC, MC, V. Tues–Sat noon–1:30pm and 7:30–9:30pm. Closed last 3 weeks of July and Dec 24–28.

Le Buerehiesel ★★★ MODERN FRENCH Also known as Le Restaurant Westermann, Buerehiesel is famous for its *cuisine moderne* and for its prime location in l'Orangerie, a park at the end of the allée de la Robertsau planned by the landscape artist Le Nôtre, who gave the park to Josephine during her marriage to Napoleon. The decor includes richly grained wooden ceilings and a conservatively modern design. The kitchen recycles heirloom recipes in innovative and exciting ways. Of special merit are foie gras of goose with truffles; frogs' legs fried with local herbs; ravioli stuffed with confit of onions; and steamed sea bass with a marinade of crisp, al dente vegetables and aromatic herbs. Appealingly old-fashioned, and prepared for only two diners at a time, is one of the Alsace's most classic recipes, *poularde baeckoffe:* Consisting of a top-quality Bresse hen that's slow-cooked in a covered ceramic dish, it comes in versions appropriate to both summer (with potatoes, artichoke hearts, and a confit of lemons) and winter (with leeks, potatoes, and truffles).

4 parc de l'Orangerie. ✆ **03-88-45-56-65.** www.buerehiesel.fr. Reservations required. Main courses 21€–39€; fixed-price menu 45€–90€. AE, DC, MC, V. Tues–Sat noon–2pm and 7–9:45pm. Closed 1st 3 weeks of Jan and 1st 3 weeks of Aug.

MODERATE

Chez Yvonne ★ FRENCH/ALSATIAN Journalists and other political dignitaries frequent this traditional Alsatian *winstub,* which has operated here since 1873. It's located near the cathedral in the middle of the historic core. The backdrop is in the traditional bistro style, with lots of wood and red-checked curtains. Steaming platters of well-prepared food emerge from the kitchen, including such appetizers as snails Alsatian or foie gras of the house. For a main course, opt for such temptations as hen cooked in Riesling and served with spaëtzle, or choucroute (sauerkraut) with pork products. Suckling pig is another one of the specialties.

10 rue du Sanglier. ✆ **03-88-32-84-15.** www.chez-yvonne.net. Reservations required. Main courses 14€–29€. AE, DC, MC, V. Daily noon–2:15pm and 6pm–midnight.

Maison des Tanneurs ★ ALSATIAN This longtime favorite, housed in a building from 1572, opened in 1949. The restaurant abounds with flowers and antiques that create a warm atmosphere, and has a terrace that opens onto the canal. The restaurant has been called "La Maison de la Choucroute" because its sauerkraut-and-pork platter is the finest in the area. But the chef prepares many other tasty dishes, including snails cooked Alsatian style with local white wine, a traditional version of Strasbourg foie gras, and guinea fowl stuffed with green peppers. We recommend crayfish tails in court bouillon and *coq au Riesling* (chicken cooked in white wine, with noodles).

42 rue du Bain-aux-Plantes. ✆ **03-88-32-79-70.** www.maison-des-tanneurs.com. Reservations required. Main courses 21€–24€; fixed-price lunch 20€–26€. AE, DC, MC, V. Tues–Sat noon–1:45pm and 7–10pm (also Sun noon–2pm in Dec). Closed 3 weeks in Jan.

Maison Kammerzell ★ ☺ ALSATIAN The gingerbread Maison Kammerzell is an attraction as well as a fantastic restaurant. The carved-wood framework was constructed during the Renaissance, the overhanging stories in 1589. We suggest *la choucroute formidable*, the Alsatian specialty prepared with goose fat, Riesling wine, and Strasbourg sausages. The owner, Guy-Pierre Baumann, also prepares homemade foie gras, guinea hen with mushrooms, medallion of young wild boar, and other regional dishes. A concession to modern cuisine is the chef's version of sauerkraut with fish. Families will want to take advantage of the free meals for children 9 and under at lunch, which makes the place popular with big broods. If you'd rather eat your sauerkraut in relative peace, come for dinner.

16 place de la Cathédrale. ✆ **03-88-32-42-14.** www.maison-kammerzell.com. Reservations required. Main courses 17€–26€; fixed-price menu 32€–48€. AE, DC, MC, V. Daily noon–2:30pm and 7–11pm.

INEXPENSIVE

Brasserie de l'Ancienne Douane ★ ALSATIAN This is the largest and most colorful dining spot in Strasbourg. The high-ceilinged rooms are somewhat formal, with Teutonic chairs and heavily timbered ceilings. Among the Alsatian specialties are the well-known "sauerkraut of the Customs officers" and the foie gras of Strasbourg. Onion pie and ham knuckle with potato salad and horseradish are also popular.

6 rue de la Douane. ✆ **03-88-15-78-78.** www.anciennedouane.fr. Reservations recommended. Main courses 16€–24€; fixed-price menu 25€–32€. AE, DC, MC, V. Daily 11:30am–2:30pm and 6:30–11pm.

Winstub Le Clou ★★ ALSATIAN With its long communal tables, this restaurant has a typical *Winstub* vibe (a *Winstub*—which literally means "wine room"—is a traditional Alsation restaurant oozing coziness and warmth). They specialize in typical Alsation fare, like Baeckoffe (a hearty meat stew) or *jambon en cruote* (ham wrapped with a crispy crust). One of their specialties is *choucroute en wädele*—Alsation sauerkraut with think hunks of ham. It's gut-filling comfort food in a convivial atmosphere.

3 rue de Chaudron. ✆ **03-88-32-11-67.** www.le-clou.com. Main courses 16€–24€; fixed-price menu 13€–18€. AE, MC, V. Mon–Tues and Thurs–Sat 11:30am–2:15pm; Mon–Sat 5:30–midnight.

Where to Stay & Eat Nearby

Many visitors head north 12km (7½ miles) to La Wantzenau, which has very good restaurants. From Strasbourg, take D468 along the west bank of the Rhine.

Relais de la Poste ★★★ FRENCH/ALSATIAN The leading restaurant in this citadel of fine dining is a cozy half-timbered 18th-century house in the heart of the little Alsatian village. The chefs depend on the changing seasons for their inspiration. They prepare traditional dishes with a modern twist, lighter versions of old favorites. Their succulent concoctions include boned and stuffed quail with a sauce of morels, and fried turbot *osso buco* with Szechuan peppercorn sauce. Two superb appetizers are fresh goose liver and game terrine.

The inn also rents 18 comfortably furnished guest rooms, each in a rustic style, for a double rate of 80€ to 150€.

21 rue du Général-de-Gaulle, La Wantzenau 67610. www.relais-poste.com. ✆ **03-88-59-24-80.** Fax 03-88-59-24-89. Main courses 26€–89€; fixed-price menu 50€–90€. AE, DC, MC, V. Tues–Fri and Sun noon–2pm; Tues–Sat 7–10pm. Closed 1st 2 weeks of Jan.

Strasbourg After Dark

A bastion of outdoor entertainment is **place de la Cathédrale,** where you can find an assortment of performers and artists. Dancers perform spontaneously against the illumination of the cathedral. From mid-July to early August, additional folk dances take place in La Petite France on Monday night in place des Tripiers, Tuesday in place Benjamin Zix, and Wednesday in place du Marché aux Cochons de Lait. Performance dates vary; check with the Office de Tourisme (✆ **03-88-52-28-29;** www.otstrasbourg.fr) for a schedule.

THE PERFORMING ARTS For opera and ballet, seek out the **Opéra du Rhin,** 19 place Broglie (✆ **03-88-75-48-23;** www.operanationaldurhin.fr); tickets cost 12€ to 78€. The **Orchestre Philharmonique de Strasbourg** performs at the Palais de la Musique et des Congrès, place de Bordeaux (✆ **03-69-06-37-00;** www.philharmonique-strasbourg.com). Tickets cost 20€ to 55€. The **Théâtre National de Strasbourg** plays a busy schedule at 1 av. de la Marseillaise (✆ **03-88-24-88-00;** www.tns.fr). Tickets cost 5.50€ to 25€.

CLUBS Head to the streets surrounding place de la Cathédrale: rue des Frères, rue des Soeurs, and rue de la Croix. **Jeannette et les Cycleux,** 3 rue des Tonneliers (✆ **03-88-23-02-71;** www.lenetdejeannette.com), is a wine bar with a jukebox playing rock 'n' roll and other hits from America in the 1950s. Entrance is free.

Le Seven, 25 rue des Tonneliers (✆ **03-88-32-77-77**), has a below-street-level dance floor that features all types of music except disco. The place packs in a stylish crowd ages 20 to 35.

One of the biggest and most visible discos in the region, **Le Chalet,** 376 rte. de Wantzenau (✆ **03-88-31-18-31**), lies 8km (5 miles) north of Strasbourg. The 8€ cover on Friday and 10€ cover on Saturday buys the first drink and access to two huge and distinctly different sections. One is designed for techno fans, another for less harsh dance music, with a good mix of disco classics. It's open 10pm to 4am Friday and Saturday. To get here, follow signs to Wantzenau.

LA ROUTE DU VIN (WINE ROAD) ★★★

The fastest route between Strasbourg and Colmar, 68km (42 miles) south, is N83. But if you have time, the famous Route du Vin makes a rewarding experience.

It rolls through 60 charming villages—don't miss one of the jewels of the route, Wangen (30km/19 miles from Strasbourg) which features a city gate crowned by a tower and twisting, narrow streets—one of the most typical of the wine towns. Along the way are inns where you can sample wine, take a leisurely meal, or spend the night.

The Wine Road runs along the Vosges foothills, with medieval towers and feudal ruins evoking faded pageantry. The vine-covered slopes sometimes reach a height of 435m (1,427 ft.), and an estimated 20,000 hectares (49,400 acres) of vineyards line the road. Some 30,000 families earn their living tending the grapes. The best time to go is for the harvest in September and October. The well-marked route starts at Marlenheim.

Marlenheim

This agreeable town, noted for its Vorlauf red wine, is 21km (13 miles) west of Strasbourg on N4. Even if you can't drive the full length of the Wine Road, you may want to visit for the excellent inn.

WHERE TO STAY & EAT

Le Cerf ★★★ In the heart of this medieval village, occupying a half-timbered building at least 300 years old, this hotel offers pleasantly furnished rooms adjoining an excellent restaurant. The elegant, esoteric, and upscale menu items include, depending on the mood of the chef, such dishes as a fricassee of crayfish and wild mushrooms, a gratin of mushrooms with Riesling, an exotic version of sauerkraut that supplements the normal roster of pork and sausage with smoked foie gras, and a roulade of lobster with spinach and a broth that's brewed from the lobster shells. Fixed-price menus range from 39€ to 125€. The restaurant (but not the hotel) is closed on Tuesday and Wednesday year-round.

30 rue du Général-de-Gaulle, Marlenheim 67520. www.lecerf.com. ✆ **03-88-87-73-73.** Fax 03-88-87-68-08. 14 units. 187€–240€ double; 297€–347€ suite. AE, DC, MC, V. Parking 14€. **Amenities:** Restaurant; free Wi-Fi. *In room:* A/C, TV, hair dryer.

BIKING THE wine road

To rent bikes, visit **Association Velo Emploi (Velocation),** 10 rue des Bouchers (✆ **03-88-24-05-61;** www.velocation.net). Subsidized by the city of Strasbourg, this place offers among the cheapest rentals anywhere. Half-day rentals cost 5€, full-day rentals 8€. It's open April to September daily 9:30am to 12:30pm and 1:30 to 7pm, and October through March Monday to Friday 10am to 12:30pm and 1 to 5pm. A security deposit of 200€ is required.

The Strasbourg tourist office provides maps showing bike routes that fan out from the city into the countryside, with emphasis on cycle lanes (*les pistes cyclables* in French) that prohibit cars. One of these is a 27km (17-mile) stretch that runs southwest from Strasbourg to the wine hamlet of Molsheim. It has a forest on one side, the banks of the Brûche River (a tributary of the Rhine) on the other, and little car traffic.

Mittelbergheim

Mittelbergheim, 43km (27 miles) from Strasbourg, is a special village. Houses in the Renaissance style border its **place de l'Hôtel-de-Ville.**

WHERE TO STAY & EAT

Winstub Gilg ★ This is an excellent inn. Though parts of the building date from 1614, its showpiece is a two-story stone staircase, classified as a historic monument. Medieval stonemasons who worked on the cathedral at Strasbourg carved it. Each attractively furnished guest room has a tub/shower. Chef Vincent Reuschlé attracts a loyal following with regional specialties such as onion tart, sauerkraut, and foie gras in brioche. Main courses include stewed kidneys and sweetbreads, duck with oranges, and, in season, roast pheasant with grapes. The hotel and restaurant close in January and from late June to early July. The rest of the year, the restaurant closes on Tuesday and Wednesday.

1 rte. du Vin, Mittelbergheim, Barr 67140. www.hotel-gilg.com. ✆ **03-88-08-91-37.** Fax 03-88-08-45-17. 15 units. 57€–87€ double. AE, DC, MC, V. **Amenities:** Restaurant; Wi-Fi in lobby. *In room:* TV.

Andlau

This gardenlike resort, 42km (26 miles) from Strasbourg, was the site of an abbey founded in 887 by the disgraced wife of Emperor Charles the Fat. It has now faded into history, but a church remains that dates from the 12th century. In the tympanum are noteworthy Romanesque carvings. The **Office de Tourisme,** 5 rue du Général-de-Gaulle (✆ **03-88-08-22-57;** www.pays-de-barr.com), is open Monday through Friday 9am to noon.

WHERE TO EAT

Au Boeuf Rouge TRADITIONAL FRENCH This bustling, unpretentious bistro has a busy bar and a comfortably battered dining room. Its menu of time-tested specialties includes homemade terrines, gamecock, fresh fish, and a tempting dessert cart. Noted chef Pierre Kieffer prepares a fabulous quenelle of brochet, a local whitefish, according to his grandmother's recipe. Although the fare is reliable and consistent, it isn't the most innovative cookery on the wine trail, excepting his seasonal version of wild boar with cassis sauce and spaëtzle. For dessert, try a slice of Baettelman, an Alsatian cake baked with apples and cherries. There's also a wine *stube* (tavern) on-site to the right as you enter. From March to October, you can sit on the terrace in front.

6 rue du Dr-Stoltz. ✆ **03-88-08-96-26.** Reservations recommended. Main courses 17€–37€; fixed-price menu 15€–25€. AE, DC, MC, V. Oct–July 12 Fri–Wed 11:30am–2:30pm, Fri–Tues 6–9:30pm; July 15–Sept daily 11:30am–2:30pm and 6–9:30pm. Closed 10 days in Feb and 3 weeks June–July.

Dambach

In the midst of its vineyards, Dambach (48km/30 miles from Strasbourg) is one of the delights of the Wine Road. The town, formally Dambach-la-Ville, has ramparts and three fortified gates. Its timbered houses are gabled with galleries, and many contain oriels. Wrought-iron signs still tell you if a place is a bakery or a butcher shop. A short drive from the town is the **Chapelle St-Sebastian,** with a 15th-century ossuary. The **Office de Tourisme** (✆ **03-88-92-61-00;** fax 03-88-92-47-11; www.dambach-la-ville.fr) is in La Mairie (town hall), place du Marché.

Ribeauvillé ★

At the foot of vine-clad hills, Ribeauvillé (87km/54 miles from Strasbourg) is picturesque, with old shop signs, pierced balconies, turrets, and flower-decorated houses. The town is noted for its Riesling and Gewürztraminer wines. See its Renaissance fountain and **Hôtel de Ville,** place de la Mairie, which has a collection of silver-gilt medieval and Renaissance tankards known as *hanaps.* For information, go to the tourist office at 1 Grand'rue (✆ **03-89-73-23-23;** www.ribeauville-riquewihr.com).

Guided tours showcase the *hanaps,* the building's architecture, and the history of the town. The free 90-minute tours run from May to September, on Sunday and Tuesday through Friday at 10 and 11am, and 2pm. On tour days at 3pm, the same guide leads a 90-minute walking tour of the town. Tours are in French, German, or halting English.

Also of interest in Ribeauvillé is the **Tour des Bouchers** (Butcher's Tower), built in stages from the 13th to the 16th century.

Every year on the first Sunday in September, visitors fill the town for its **Jour des Menetriers (Day of the Minstrels).** Beginning at 3pm and lasting almost 2½ hours, it features a parade of flute players from Alsace, the rest of France, Switzerland, and Germany, and as many as 600 parade participants. You can stand anywhere to watch the spectacle, but seats on the medieval stone benches line either side of the parade route.

WHERE TO STAY & EAT

Clos St-Vincent ★★★ This is one of the most elegant choices along Route du Vin. Most of the individually decorated guest rooms have a balcony or terrace, but you get much more than a view of the Haut-Rhin vineyards and summer roses. The rooms, ranging from medium to large, are furnished with grand comfort; each has a bed covered in fine linen and a bathroom with state-of-the-art plumbing and tub/shower. Some have air-conditioning. The Chapotin family's cuisine is exceptional: hot duck liver with nuts, turbot with sorrel, roebuck (in season) in hot sauce, and veal kidneys in pinot noir. The wines are smooth, especially the popular Riesling and Gewürztraminer.

Rte. de Bergheim, Ribeauvillé 68150. www.leclossaintvincent.com. ✆ **03-89-73-67-65.** Fax 03-89-73-32-20. 24 units. 135€–223€ double; 200€–255€ suite. AE, MC, V. Closed mid-Dec to mid-Mar. **Amenities:** Restaurant (dinner only Wed–Mon); bar; babysitting; Jacuzzi; indoor pool; room service; sauna. *In room:* TV, hair dryer, minibar, free Wi-Fi.

Kaysersberg ★★

Once a free city of the empire, Kaysersberg (93km/58 miles from Strasbourg) lies at the mouth of the Weiss Valley, between two vine-covered slopes; it's crowned by a castle ruined in the Thirty Years' War. From one of the many ornately carved bridges, you can see the city's medieval fortifications along the top of one of the nearby hills. Many of the houses are Gothic and Renaissance, and most have half-timbering, wrought-iron accents, leaded windows, and multiple designs carved into reddish sandstone.

In the cafes, you'll hear a combination of French and Alsatian. The age of the speaker usually determines the language—the older ones remain faithful to the dialect of their grandparents.

Dr. Albert Schweitzer was born here in 1875; his house is near the bridge over the Weiss. You can visit the **Musée du Docteur Schweitzer,** 126 rue du

Général-de-Gaulle (✆ **03-89-47-36-55**), from April to November daily from 9am to noon and 2 to 6pm. Admission is 2€ adults and 1€ for students and children 11 and under.

The **Office de Tourisme** is at 39 rue du Général-de-Gaulle (✆ **03-89-78-22-78;** fax 03-89-71-34-11; www.kaysersberg.com).

WHERE TO STAY & EAT

Le Chambard ★★★ FRENCH/ALSATIAN The regional cuisine here is so good, it's worth planning a stop. You'll recognize the restaurant by the gilded wrought-iron sign above the cobblestones. Exposed stone and polished wood accent the rustic interior. Regional specialties with Mediterranean influences attest to the mastery of the kitchen. The imaginative chef, Olivier Nasti, presents impeccably flavored and sophisticated cuisine. The restaurant is known for sauerkraut served with a host of (mostly smoked) pork specialties, as well as foie gras and pungent Münster cheese. Other choices include a "cake" of eggplant with goose foie gras, an upscale version of traditional Alsatian stew made with foie gras, and traditional Alsatian cake *(kugelhof)* with cinnamon-flavored ice cream. The cellar stocks the best local vintages.

A 20-room hotel annex (with an elegant spa) was built to match the other structures on the street. A double goes for 145€ to 200€, a suite from 240€.

9-13 rue du Général-de-Gaulle, Kaysersberg 68240. www.lechambard.com. ✆ **03-89-47-10-17.** Fax 03-89-47-35-03. Reservations required. Main courses 28€–42€; fixed-price menu 34€–100€. AE, MC, V. Thurs–Sun noon–2pm; Tues–Sun 7–9pm.

WHERE TO EAT

Au Lion d'Or FRENCH/ALSATIAN This 1521 building boasts an exceptionally beautiful decor. A carved lion's head adorns the oak door leading into the restaurant, which has a beamed ceiling, stone detailing, brass chandeliers, and a massive fireplace. If you eat at an outdoor table, you'll have a view of one of Alsace's prettiest streets. The classic Alsatian dishes include wild game, foie gras (which Alsatians claim to have invented), and yummy pork dishes, often with hams and sausage. Sauerkraut, served in its traditional meat-and-potato form or with fish, is an enduring specialty and a favorite with the loyal clientele.

66 rue du Général-de-Gaulle. www.auliondor.fr. ✆ **03-89-47-11-16.** Reservations required. Main courses 15€–24€; fixed-price menu 22€–36€. AE, MC, V. Thurs–Mon noon–2:30pm and 6:30–9:30pm.

Ammerschwihr

Ammerschwihr, 9km (5½ miles) north of Colmar (79km/49 miles from Strasbourg), is a good stop to cap off your Wine Road tour. Once a free city of the empire, the town was almost destroyed in 1944 and has been reconstructed in the traditional style. More and more travelers visit to sample the wine, especially Käferkopf. Check out the town's gate towers, 16th-century parish church, and remains of early fortifications.

WHERE TO STAY & EAT

A l'Arbre Vert ★ At least part of this hotel's charm derives from the close supervision of Joël and Evelyne Tournier, chef and *maître d'hôtel,* respectively, who represent at least three generations of attentive, family-managed service.

Clos St-Landelin.

Public rooms are delightful, loaded with regional artifacts and coziness. Guest rooms are well maintained with a shower-only bathroom. The restaurant, which is closed every Tuesday, is open to nonresidents and serves very good Alsatian specialties, including savory scallop of goose liver with pinot noir, cassoulet of snails with mushrooms, and crisp-baked salmon with leeks. Some of the best warm dessert soufflés in the region emerge steaming from the kitchens, many laden with whatever fresh fruit happens to be in season at the time. (In midwinter, look for a superb version with oranges, clementines, or lemons.)

7 rue des Cigognes, Ammerschwihr 68770. www.arbre-vert.net. ✆ **03-89-47-12-23.** Fax 03-89-78-27-21. 19 units. 55€–75€ double. Half-board 59€–69€ per person double. AE, DC, MC, V. Closed mid-Feb to mid-Mar and 2 weeks in Nov. **Amenities:** Restaurant; bar. *In room:* TV.

Aux Armes de France ★★★ FRENCH/ALSATIAN This is the best restaurant along the Wine Road. Although you can rent one of 10 rooms here (doubles go for 69€–84€), the real reason to come is the cuisine. In a flower-filled setting, Philippe Gaertner and his staff attract many French and German gourmets. A specialty is fresh foie gras served in its own golden aspic. Main courses include classics with imaginative variations, such as roebuck (in season) in hot sauce, and lobster fricassee with cream and truffles. Spicy duckling is savory, as is filet of sole with fresh noodles. Terrine of lobster and calf's head in aspic *(presskopf)*, which we've never seen in any other restaurant in France, is a particular enticement for adventurous gastronomes.

1 Grand'rue, Ammerschwihr 68770. www.aux-armes-de-france.com. ✆ **03-89-47-10-12.** Fax 03-89-47-38-12. Reservations required. Main courses 16€–66€; fixed-price menu 28€–50€. AE, DC, MC, V. Fri–Tues noon–2pm and 7:30–9pm.

Rouffach

Rouffach is south of Colmar. One of the highest of the Vosges Mountains, Grand-Ballon shelters the town from the winds that bring rain, which makes for a dry climate and a special grape. Make a beeline for the excellent vineyard **Clos St-Landelin** (✆ **03-89-78-58-00;** www.mure.com), on the Route du Vin, at the intersection of RN83 and route de Soultzmatt. A clerical estate from the 6th century until the Revolution, it has been celebrated over the centuries for the quality of its wine. Clos St-Landelin covers 21 hectares (52 acres) at the southern end of the Vorbourg Grand Cru area. Its steep slopes call for terrace cultivation.

The soil that produces these wines is anything but fertile. Loaded with pebbles, sand, and limestone, the high-alkaline earth produces low-yield, scraggly vines whose fruit goes into superb Rieslings, Gewürztraminers, and pinot noirs. Members of the Muré family have owned these vineyards since 1648. In their cellar is a 13th-century wine press, the oldest in Alsace, and one of only three like it in France. (The other two are in Burgundy.) The family welcomes visitors who want to tour the cellars and ask about the wine, which is for sale. It's open Monday to Friday 8am to 6:30pm, and Saturday 10am to 1pm and 2 to 6pm.

COLMAR ★★★

440km (273 miles) SE of Paris; 140km (87 miles) SE of Nancy; 71km (44 miles) SW of Strasbourg

One of the most attractive towns in Alsace, Colmar abounds with medieval and early Renaissance buildings, half-timbered structures, gables, and gracious loggias. Tiny gardens and wash houses surround many of the homes. Its old quarter looks more German than French, filled with streets of unexpected twists and turns. As a gateway to the Rhine country, Colmar is a major destination for travelers heading south from Strasbourg. Near the vine-covered slopes of the southern Vosges, it's the third-largest town in Alsace.

Colmar has been so well restored that it's Alsace's most beautiful city—you'd never guess Colmar was hard hit in two world wars.

Essentials

GETTING THERE If you're **driving,** take N83 from Strasbourg; trip time is 1 hour. Because of the narrow streets, we suggest that you park and walk. Leave the car in the Champ-de-Mars, or in the underground Place Rapp for a fee of around 1.20€ per hour, northeast of the railway station, and then walk a few blocks east to the old city; or park in the lot designated PARKING VIEILLE VILLE, accessible from rue de l'Est at the edge of the Petite Venise neighborhood, and walk a few blocks southeast to reach the old city. **Trains** link Colmar to Nancy, Strasbourg, and Mulhouse, as well as to Germany via Strasbourg, across the Rhine. Twenty-one trains per day arrive from Paris's Gare de l'Est (trip time: 4–6 hr.); the one-way fare is 68€. For information, call ✆ **36-35,** or 08-92-35-35-35 from outside France.

VISITOR INFORMATION The **Office de Tourisme** is at 4 rue Unterlinden (✆ **03-89-20-68-92;** fax 03-89-41-34-13; www.ot-colmar.fr).

For information on wines, vintages, and winery visits, contact the **CIVA** (Alsace Wine Committee), Maison du Vin d'Alsace, 12 av. de la Foire-aux-Vins (✆ **03-89-20-16-20**). It's usually open Monday to Friday 8am to noon and 2 to 5pm. Make arrangements far in advance.

SPECIAL EVENTS Alsatian **folk dances** on place de l'Ancienne-Douane begin at 8:30pm on Tuesday from mid-May to mid-September. If you want to listen to classical music, visit during the first 2 weeks in July for the **Festival International de Musique de Colmar** (✆ **03-89-20-68-97;** www.festival-colmar.com), which schedules 24 concerts in venues around the city, such as churches and public monuments. **Les Mardis de la Collégiale,**

at place de la Cathédrale (✆**06-71-06-50-18**), stages concerts every Tuesday at 8:45pm from the end of July to mid-September. Tickets for these events cost 10€ to 15€. You can get complete information on any of the events in town at the Office de Tourisme.

Exploring Colmar

Colmar is rich with historic houses, many half-timbered and, in summer, accented with geranium-draped window boxes. One of the most beautiful is **Maison Pfister,** 11 rue des Marchands, at the corner of rue Mercière, a 1537 building with wooden balconies. On the ground floor is a wine boutique owned by a major Alsace winegrower, **Muré,** proprietor of the vineyard Clos St-Landelin (✆**03-89-41-33-61**).

If you take pont St-Pierre over the Lauch River, you'll have an excellent view of Old Colmar and can explore **Petite Venise,** which is filled with canals.

SHOPPING Head for the old town of Colmar, particularly rue de Clefs, Grand'rue, rue des Têtes, and rue des Marchands.

Antiques abound, and you'll find a large grouping of stores in the old town, especially along rue des Marchands. Shops that deserve particular attention include **Geismar Dany,** 32 rue des Marchands (✆/fax **03-89-23-30-41**), specializing in antique painted furniture, and **Antiquités Guy Caffard,** 56 rue des Marchands (✆**03-89-41-31-78;** www.caffard-antiquites.com), with its mishmash of furniture, postcards, books, toys, bibelots, and the like. Also worth noting are **Lire & Chiner,** 36 rue des Marchands (✆**03-89-24-16-78;** www.lire-et-chiner.fr), and **Antiquité Arcana,** 13 place l'Ancienne Douane (✆**03-89-41-59-81**).

One of the most appealing stores is **Arts et Collections d'Alsace,** 1 rue des Tanneurs (✆**03-89-24-09-78**), which stocks copies of art objects and utilitarian wares of yesteryear. There are items for the home and kitchen, made from wrought iron, pottery, glass, copper, carved wood, and fabric.

WINERIES Because Colmar is one of the gateways to the wine-producing Rhine country, local wine is one of the best purchases you can make. If you don't have time to visit the vineyards along the Wine Road, stop in at **Cave du Musée,** 11 rue Kléber (✆**03-89-23-85-29**), for one of the largest selections of wines and liqueurs from the region and the rest of France.

You can drive to one of the most historic vineyards in Alsace-Lorraine. **Domaines Schlumberger** (✆**03-89-74-27-00;** www.domaines-schlumberger.com) lies 26km (16

Pretty home in Colmar.

miles) southwest of Colmar in Guebwiller. The cellars, established by the Schlumberger family in 1810, are an unusual combination of early-19th-century brickwork and modern stainless steel. These grapes become such famous wines as Rieslings, Gewürztraminers, muscats, sylvaners, and pinots (blanc, gris, and noir). Views of the vineyards and tasting rooms are available without an appointment, but group tours of the cellars are conducted only when a staff member is available. Call before you go to find out when that might be. The vineyard is closed 2 weeks in August and December 21 or 22 to January 2 (varies each year—call for details).

Eglise des Dominicains This church contains one of Colmar's most famous treasures: Martin Schongauer's painting *Virgin of the Rosebush,* or *Vierge au buisson de rose* (1473), all gold, red, and white, with fluttering birds. Look for it in the choir.

Place des Dominicains. ✆ **03-89-24-46-57.** Admission 1.50€ adults, 1€ students, .50€ ages 12–16, free for children 11 and under. Apr–Dec daily 10am–1pm and 3–6pm.

Eglise St-Martin ★ In the heart of Old Colmar is a collegiate church begun in 1230 on the site of a Romanesque church. It has a choir erected by William of Marburg in 1350 and a steeple that rises to 70m (230 ft.).

Place de la Cathédrale. ✆ **03-89-41-27-20.** Free admission. Daily 8am–7pm. Closed to casual visitors during Mass.

Musée Bartholdi Statue of Liberty sculptor Frédéric-Auguste Bartholdi was born in Colmar in 1834. This small memento-filled museum is in the house where he was born. It has Statue of Liberty rooms containing plans and scale models, and documents related to its construction and other works regarding U.S. history. Bartholdi's Paris apartment, with furniture and memorabilia, has been reconstructed here. The museum supplements its exhibits with paintings of Egyptian scenes that Bartholdi collected during his travels in 1856.

30 rue des Marchands. ✆ **03-89-41-90-60.** www.musee-bartholdi.com. Admission 5€ adults, 2.50€ students and children 12–18, free for children 11 and under. Wed–Mon 10am–noon and 2–6pm. Closed Jan–Feb, May 1, Nov 1, and Christmas.

Musée d'Unterlinden (Under the Linden Trees) ★★ This former Dominican convent (1232), the chief seat of Rhenish mysticism in the 14th and 15th centuries, became a museum around 1850, and it's been a treasure house of the art and history of Alsace ever since.

The jewel of its collection is the **Issenheim Altarpiece (Le Retable d'Issenheim)** ★★★, created by Würzburg-born Matthias Grünewald, "the most furious of realists," around 1515. His colors glow, and his fantasy will overwhelm you. One of the most exciting works in German art, it's an immense altar screen with two-sided folding wing pieces—designed to show the Crucifixion, then the Incarnation, framed by the Annunciation and the Resurrection. The carved altar screen depicts St. Anthony visiting the hermit St. Paul; it also shows the Temptation of St. Anthony, the most beguiling part of a work that contains some ghastly birds, weird monsters, and loathsome animals. The demon of the plague is depicted with a swollen belly and purple skin, his body blotched with boils; a diabolical grin appears on his horrible face.

Other attractions include the magnificent altarpiece (dating from 1470) of Jean d'Orlier by Martin Schongauer, a large collection of religious woodcarvings and stained glass from the 14th to the 18th centuries, and Gallo-Roman lapidary collections, including funeral slabs. The armory collection contains ancient arms from the Romanesque to the Renaissance, featuring halberds and crossbows.

1 rue d'Unterlinden. ✆ **03-89-20-15-58.** www.musee-unterlinden.com. Admission 7€ adults, 5€ students and children 12–17, free for children 11 and under. May–Oct daily 9am–6pm; Nov–Apr Wed–Mon 9am–noon and 2–5pm. Closed national holidays.

Where to Stay

Rooms are also available in **La Maison des Têtes** (see p. 406).

Grand Hôtel Bristol This 1926 red sandstone "grand hotel" right at the train station provides well-maintained rooms with both modern and provincial decor. Accommodations are rather standardized and not quite as grand as the name of the hotel suggests. Most of the tidy, midsize bathrooms have tub/showers.

7 place de la Gare, Colmar 68000. www.grand-hotel-bristol.com. ✆ **03-89-23-59-59.** Fax 03-89-23-92-26. 91 units. 96€–170€ double. AE, DC, MC, V. **Amenities:** 2 restaurants; bar; babysitting; room service; rooms for those w/limited mobility; smoke-free rooms. *In room:* A/C (in some), TV, hair dryer, minibar, free Wi-Fi.

Hostellerie Le Maréchal ★★ Three 16th-century houses make up this hotel, the most tranquil in town. You climb a wide staircase to reach the guest rooms, most of which are air-conditioned. In the east wing is a small, partially timbered room with a sloping ceiling. Accommodations are small but neatly organized, each with a tiled bathroom, most with tub/showers. The restaurant has a fireplace in winter; in summer, seating moves to the terrace, where you can enjoy a water view. Feast on stuffed quail, good beef and veal dishes, and lamb Provençal, all accompanied by Tokay and Alsatian wines.

4–6 place des Six-Montagnes-Noires, Colmar 68000. www.hotel-le-marechal.com. ✆ **03-89-41-60-32.** Fax 03-89-24-59-40. 30 units. 105€–225€ double; 255€ suite. AE, DC, MC, V. Parking 15€. **Amenities:** Restaurant; room service; smoke-free rooms. *In room:* TV, hair dryer, minibar, free Wi-Fi.

Le Colombier ★ Originally built as a half-timbered house in the 14th century, this building is among the town's finest hotels. Very old beams and masonry contrast pleasantly with contemporary lighting and furniture. The staff is engaging and helpful. If the government-rated three-star hotel had a restaurant (breakfast is the only meal served), it would surely earn four-star status. With the exception of the cozy unit beneath the steeply pitched pinnacle of the roof, all of the guest rooms have high ceilings; they vary in size and shape. Each contains comfortable appointments and fine linen, plus a small but tidy shower-only bathroom. Some rooms overlook the canals of Petite Venise; others open onto a half-timbered courtyard.

7 rue Turenne, Colmar 68000. www.hotel-le-colombier.fr. ✆ **03-89-23-96-00.** Fax 03-89-23-97-27. 28 units. 95€–190€ double; 205€–255€ suite. AE, DC, MC, V. Parking 10€. **Amenities:** Bar; room service. *In room:* A/C, TV, hair dryer, minibar, Wi-Fi (3.50€ per day).

Where to Eat

Chez Hansi ALSATIAN Set within two rooms of a half-timbered house dating from 1532, this is the most historic and most folklorically charming restaurant in a town that's loaded with worthy competitors. Even its name is a reference to the pen name (Hansi) of Jean-Jacques Waltz, a 19th-century illustrator who, in his artwork, elevated Alsatian kitsch to an art form rivaled in America by Norman

Rockwell. You'll find this hypertraditional place in the Vieille Ville, beneath massively beamed ceilings and a staff whose women are clad in dirndls. Come here for steaming and heaping platters of choucroute (sauerkraut garnished with pork products), foie gras, onion tarte, *pot-au-feu* that's redolent with gravy and chunks of beef, and, for the ultra-adventurous, calf's head (*tete de veau*) garnished with an apple in its mouth.

23 rue des Marchands. ✆ **03-89-41-37-84.** Reservations recommended. Main courses 17€–28€; prix-fixe menus 18€–50€. MC, V. Fri–Tues 11:45am–1:45pm and 6:45–9:30pm. Closed Jan.

La Maison des Têtes TRADITIONAL FRENCH This Colmar monument is the town's leading hotel and one of its top restaurants. It opens off a covered cobblestone drive and courtyard. The 17th-century house lies in the center of town, near the Unterlinden Museum. The dining rooms are decorated with aged-wood beams and paneling, Art Nouveau lighting fixtures, and stained-glass and leaded windows. Dishes include foie gras with truffles, choucroute, seasonal roebuck with morels and dried fruits, and fresh trout or Rhine salmon braised in Riesling. The Alsatian wines are sublime. There are also 21 nicely furnished rooms with minibars, safes, air-conditioning, and TVs; some have Jacuzzis. Rates are 91€ to 235€ for a double, 205€ to 270€ for a suite.

In the Hôtel des Têtes, 19 rue des Têtes, Colmar 68000. ✆ **03-89-24-43-43.** Fax 03-89-24-58-34. www.la-maison-des-tetes.com. Reservations required. Main courses 10€–29€; fixed-price menu 29€–75€; menu dégustation 65€. AE, DC, MC, V. Wed–Sun noon–2pm; Tues–Sat 7–9:30pm. Closed Feb.

Winstub Le Cygne ★★★ ALSATIAN Wander down this unassuming side street for simple but flavorful Alsatian fare in a wood-paneled room. Its quietly buzzing with locals most nights, who come for fare that tends to be a bit lighter than the average Winstub grub. They serve flammekueche in both savory and sweet variations (we love the simple ham and cheese version, and sweet tooths can't go wrong with the sugar and lemon version).

17 rue Edouard Richard, Colmar 68000. ✆ **03-89-23-76-26.** Main courses 10€–24€. AE, MC, V. Wed–Fri noon–2pm; Tues–Sat 7–midnight.

Where to Stay & Eat Nearby

Gourmets flock to **Illhaeusern,** 18km (11 miles) from Colmar, east of the N83 highway, to dine at the Auberge de l'Ill, one of France's great restaurants. The signs for the restaurant, beside the main highway, are difficult to miss.

Auberge de l'Ill ★★★ MODERN FRENCH This is the greatest restaurant in eastern France. Run by the Haeberlin family in their 19th-century farmhouse, Auberge de l'Ill combines the finest Alsatian specialties with *cuisine moderne* and classic offerings. You can enjoy your aperitif or coffee under the weeping willows in a beautiful garden with a river view. Chef Marc Haeberlin takes dishes of Alsatian origin and makes them into *grande cuisine*—freshwater eel stewed in Riesling, *matelotes* (small glazed onions) in Riesling, and an inventive foie gras. Two unsurpassed choices are braised slices of pheasant and partridge served with winey game sauce, chestnuts, wild mushrooms, and Breton cornmeal; and salmon soufflé. A divine starter is mousseline of frogs' legs with white-wine and chive sauce; you may follow that with mallard duckling lacquered with spices and served with a confit of red cabbage and figs. Some dishes require 24 hours' notice, so inquire when you make reservations.

You can spend the night in one of 13 rooms at the **Hôtel des Berges,** in a delightfully furnished, air-conditioned room overlooking the Ill River. The rates are 265€ to 300€ for a double, 350€ to 520€ for a suite, and 465€ for a decade-old cottage on the grounds.

Rue de Collonges, Illhaeusern 68970. www.auberge-de-l-ill.com. ✆ **03-89-71-89-00.** Fax 03-89-71-82-83. Reservations required (1 week in advance for summer weekends). Main courses 46€–140€; fixed-price menu 122€–158€. AE, DC, MC, V. Wed–Sun noon–2pm and 7–9pm. Closed 1st week of Jan and early Feb to mid-Mar.

Colmar After Dark

Head for the seductive **La Fiesta/Le Cotton Club,** place de la Gare (✆**03-89-23-43-04**). Popular and busy, this nightclub consists of two strikingly different venues: On street level, La Fiesta is a bar with lots of suds, margaritas, and a busy after-work scene. Upstairs there's a cocktail lounge with a dance floor and a calmer, more urban (think Paris or Berlin) ambience. For a mellow atmosphere, try the piano bar **Louisiana Club,** 3A rue Berthe-Molly (✆**03-89-24-94-18**), where you can groove to authentic blues and jazz.

LA ROUTE DES CRETES ★★★

From Basel, Switzerland, to Mainz, Germany, a distance of some 242km (150 miles), the Vosges Mountains stretch along the west side of the Rhine Valley, bearing a similarity to the Black Forest of Germany. Many German and French families spend their summer vacation exploring the Vosges. Travelers with less time may want to settle for a quick look at the ancient mountains that once formed the boundary between France and Germany. They are filled with tall hardwood and fir trees, and a network of twisting roads with hairpin curves traverses them. The depths of the mountain forests are the closest France comes to wilderness.

Exploring the Area

You can explore the mountains by heading west from Strasbourg, but there's a more interesting route from Colmar. La Route des Crêtes (Crest Road) begins at **Col du Bonhomme,** west of Colmar. The French High Command created it during World War I to carry supplies over the mountains. From Col du Bonhomme, you can strike out on this magnificent road, once the object of bitter fighting but today a series of panoramic vistas, including one of the Black Forest.

By **Col de la Schlucht,** 62km (38 miles) west of Colmar, you'll have climbed 1,472m (4,828 ft.). Schlucht is a summer and winter resort, one of the most beautiful spots in the Vosges, with a panoramic view of the Valley of Münster and the slopes of Hohneck. As you skirt the edge of this glacier-carved valley, you'll be in the midst of a land of pine groves with a necklace of lakes. You may want to turn off the main road and go exploring in several directions; the scenery is that tempting. But if you're still on the Crest Road, you can circle **Hohneck,** one of the highest peaks, at 1,590m (5,215 ft.), dominating the Wildenstein Dam of the Bresse winter-sports station.

At **Markstein,** you'll come to another resort. From here, take N430 and then D10 to **Münster,** where the savory cheese is made. You'll go via the Petit-Ballon, a landscape of forest and mountain meadows with grazing cows. Finally,

Grand-Ballon, at 1,400m (4,592 ft.), is the highest point you can reach by car in the Vosges. Get out of your car and go for a walk; if it's a clear day, you'll be able to see the Jura, with the French Alps beyond.

Along La Route des Cretes.

Where to Stay & Eat in Munster

Au Chêne Voltaire This chalet-style inn, built in 1939, lies in an isolated section of the forest. Most of the modern, no-frills rooms are in a building separate from the rustic core that contains the popular restaurant, which is open to the public (closed Wed–Thurs). The hotel isn't a destination; it's just good to keep in mind if you need to rest for the night before pressing on in the morning. Each unit comes with a small shower-only bathroom, a balcony, and clean, comfortable, no-nonsense furniture. Set-price menus in the dining room go for 12€ to 25€.

Rte. du Chêne-Voltaire, Luttenbach, Münster 68140. http://au-chene-voltaire.fr. ✆ **03-89-77-31-74.** Fax 03-89-77-45-71. 20 units. 38€–65€ double. AE, MC, V. Take D10 less than 2.5km (1½ miles) southwest from the center of Münster. **Amenities:** Free Internet; outdoor pool; sauna. *In room:* TV.

NANCY ★★★

370km (229 miles) E of Paris; 148km (92 miles) W of Strasbourg

Nancy, in France's northeast corner, was the capital of old Lorraine. The city was built around a fortified castle on a rock in the swampland near the Meurthe River. A canal a few blocks east of the historic center connects the Marne to the Rhine.

The city is serenely beautiful, with a history, cuisine, and architecture all its own. It once rivaled Paris as the center for the design and production of Art Nouveau. Nancy has three faces: the medieval alleys and towers around the old Palais Ducal where Charles II received Joan of Arc, the rococo golden gates and fountains, and the dull modern sections.

With a population of more than 100,000, Nancy remains the hub of commerce and politics in Lorraine. Home to a large university, it's a center of mining, engineering, metallurgy, and finance. Its 30,000 students, who have a passion for *le cool jazz,* keep Nancy jumping at night.

Essentials

GETTING THERE The fast **TGV train** from Paris's Gare de l'Est arrives in Nancy after just 90 minutes, making the city a virtual commute from Paris. Many Parisians now visit for *le weekend.* The one-way fare ranges between 50€

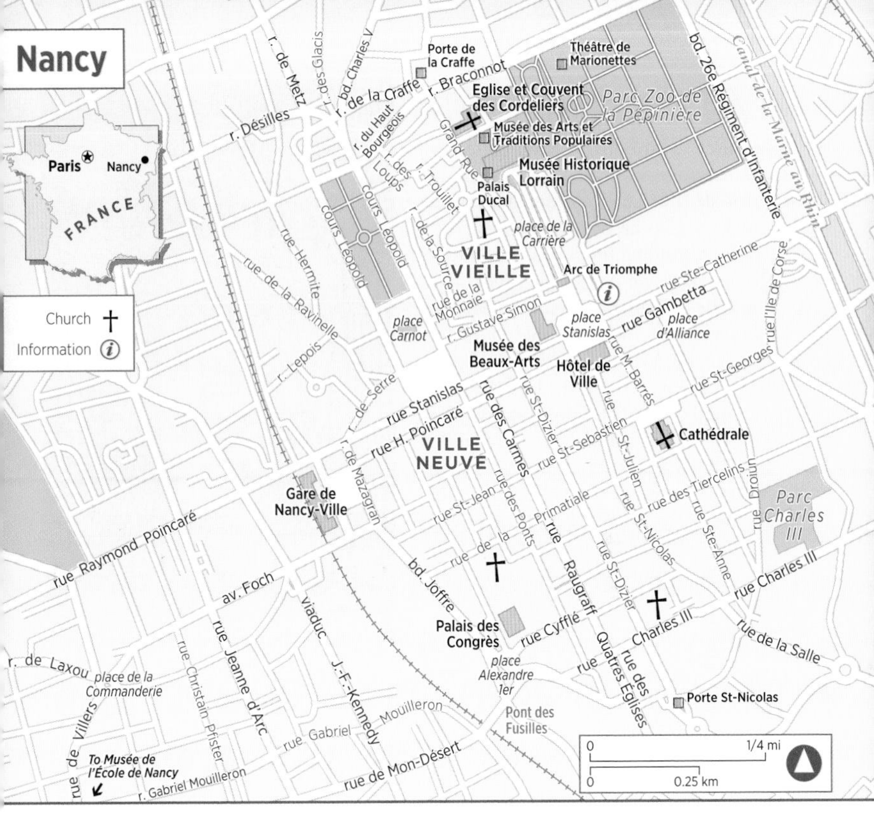

and 57€. Trains from Strasbourg arrive in Nancy every hour, a one-way fare costing 20€ to 28€. For information and schedules, call ✆ **36-35,** or 08-92-35-35-35 from outside France. If you're **driving** to Nancy from Paris, follow N4 east (trip time: 4 hr.).

VISITOR INFORMATION The **Office de Tourisme** is at place Stanislas (✆ **03-83-35-22-41;** fax 03-83-35-90-10; www.ot-nancy.fr).

SPECIAL EVENTS Serious jazz lovers come to town for 2 weeks in October to attend **Jazz Pulsations** (✆ **03-83-35-40-86;** www.nancyjazzpulsations.com). Some kind of performance takes place every night around sundown in a tent in the Parc de la Pépinière, a very short walk from the place Stanislas. Tickets cost 10€ to 35€.

Exploring Nancy

A **Passe-Musée** is a combination ticket that allows entrance to three of the town's most visited attractions, all for a net price of 10€ per person (another 14€ pass gives access to six museums in town), with no discounts for students or children. Included in the pass is access to the Musée de l'Ecole de Nancy, the Musée des Beaux-Arts, and the Musée Historique Lorraine (which is also known as the Musée des Arts et Traditions Populaires). Ask about the ticket at the tourist office.

Place Stanislas.

The most monumental square in eastern France, and the heart of Nancy, is **place Stanislas ★★★**, named for Stanislas Leszczynski, the last of the ducs de Lorraine, ex-king of Poland, and father-in-law of Louis XV. His 18th-century building programs transformed Nancy into one of Europe's most palatial cities. The square stands between Nancy's two most notable neighborhoods: the **Ville Vieille** (Old Town), in the medieval core in the northwest, centered on the cathedral, Grande-Rue, and the labyrinth of narrow, meandering streets that funnel into it; and the **Ville Neuve,** in the southwest. Built in the 16th and 17th centuries, when streets were laid out in straight lines, Ville Neuve centers on rue St-Jean.

Place Stanislas was laid out from 1752 to 1760 according to the designs of Emmanuel Héré. Its ironwork gates are magnificent. The square is fabled for the brilliant and fanciful railings, the work of Jean Lamour. His gilded railings with flowery decorations and crests evoke Versailles. The entire plaza is an all-pedestrian zone.

The **Arc de Triomphe,** constructed by Stanislas from 1754 to 1756 to honor Louis XV, adjoins the place de la Carrière, a tree-lined promenade leading to the 1760 **Palais du Gouvernement.** This governmental palace adjoins the **Palais Ducal,** built in 1502 in the Gothic style with Flamboyant Gothic balconies.

Musée de l'Ecole de Nancy ★ In a turn-of-the-20th-century building is a museum displaying the works of Emile Gallé, the greatest artist of the Nancy style. See Gallé's celebrated "Dawn and Dusk" bed and, our favorite, the "Mushroom Lamp." Works by Eugène Vallin, another outstanding artist, are also on display.

36–38 rue Sergent-Blandan. ✆ **03-83-40-14-86.** www.ecole-de-nancy.com. Admission 4€ adults, 2.50€ students, free for children 17 and under. Free for students on Wed. Wed–Sun 10am–6pm.

Musée des Beaux-Arts ★★ Built in the 1700s, this is an outstanding regional museum, encompassing the Collection Galilée, works displayed in Paris between 1919 and 1930. It houses a rare Manet portrait of the wife of Napoleon III's dentist—remarkable because of its brilliance and intensity. There are also works by Delacroix, Utrillo, Modigliani, Boucher, and Rubens. Italians such as Perugino, Caravaggio, Ribera, and Tintoretto are represented as well.

3 place Stanislas. ✆ **03-83-85-30-72.** www.iac-nancy.com. Admission 6€ adults, 4€ students and children. Free for students on Wed. Wed–Mon 10am–6pm.

Musée Historique Lorraine ★★★ This is one of France's great museums, covering the art and history of the Lorraine region from ancient times. The first floor devotes an entire room to Jacques Callot, an engraver born in Nancy in 1592. Galerie des Cerfs displays tapestries. You'll see a collection of 17th-century masterpieces by Jacques Bellange, Jacques Callot, Georges de la Tour, and Claude Deruet, dating from when the duchy was known as a cultural center.

Until the Revolution, this was a Franciscan convent. Franciscans were known as Cordeliers—hence the name of the church that adjoins the museum. The Flamboyant Gothic **Eglise des Cordeliers ★** is the burial site of the dukes of Lorraine. The most notable of the burial monuments are those of René II (1509; attributed to the sculptor Mansuy Gauvain) and a reclining statue of his second wife, Philippa of Gueldres, by Ligier Richier. The limestone rendering of Philippa is one of Nancy's most stunning examples of Renaissance portraiture. The octagonal Chapel of the Dukes (1607) holds the baroque sarcophagi.

In the Palais Ducal, 64 Grande-Rue. ✆ **03-83-32-18-74.** Admission 6€ adults, 4€ students and children 12–18, free for children 11 and under (combo ticket for Palais Ducal and Eglise des Cordeliers). Free for students 1st Sun of each month. Tues–Sun 10am–12:30pm and 2–6pm.

Shopping

Many of Nancy's antiques shops specialize in Art Nouveau. Visit **Denis Rugat,** 13 rue Stanislas (✆ **03-83-35-20-79**), for the best pieces. Another good outlet is **Galerie d'Art International,** 17 rue Amerval (✆ **03-83-35-06-83;** www.galerie-art-international.com). Both stock inventories of Lalique crystal, brightly colored vases, and enameled boxes made with a technique known locally as *les émaux de Longwy,* plus an assortment of glass-shaded lamps. You'll find more glass and crystal by Daum, at more reasonable prices, than virtually anywhere else in France. The company's premier outlet is **Boutique Daum,** 14 place Stanislas (✆ **03-83-32-21-65;** www.daum.fr), where the most perfect specimens from the Daum factory are sold at prices that are usually about 30% less than what you'd pay in other glass galleries in France. Each piece, a work of art in its own right, is signed "Daum." In contrast, and for prices that are about 30% to 40% less than what's sold in the above-mentioned boutique, you can head to Daum's factory outlet, **Magasin d'Usine Daum,** 17 rue Cristallerie (✆ **03-83-30-80-24**), a 5-minute walk from the place Stanislas. Their "slightly flawed" factory seconds are gift-wrapped and sold, each signed with the more enigmatic (and less prestigious) "Nancy."

Where to Stay

All Seasons Nancy Centre Gare Near the back of the railway station, this hotel was built after World War II and has an annex just around the corner. Guests select this efficiently operated, government-rated two-star hotel for its reasonable prices and central location. It provides comfortable but not particularly plush guest rooms, outfitted in contemporary style with a monochromatic color scheme. The hotel has a pleasant garden. Breakfast is the only meal served.

3 rue de l'Armée-Patton, Nancy 54000. www.all-seasons-hotels.com. ✆ **03-83-40-31-24.** Fax 03-83-28-47-78. 85 units. 74€–100€ double. AE, MC, V. Parking 6.50€. **Amenities:** Bar. *In room:* A/C, TV, hair dryer, free Wi-Fi.

Grand Hôtel de la Reine ★★★ This is the grandest hotel in Nancy. The 18th-century mansion was built simultaneously with the monumental square that contains it. The hotel is one of the showplaces of the Concorde chain, which operates such bastions of luxury as Paris's Hôtel de Crillon. The Louis XV–style guest rooms are appointed with draped testers over comfortable beds, Venetian-style chandeliers, and gilt-framed mirrors. All accommodations contain roomy bathrooms with tub/showers. Units overlooking place Stanislas are expensive. If you can live without a view, some suites (those overlooking the hotel's back and sides) are cheaper than the most expensive double. The elegant and very grand Stanislas restaurant serves classic and modern dishes.

2 place Stanislas, Nancy 54000. www.hoteldelareine.com. ✆ **800/777-4182** in the U.S. and Canada, or 03-83-35-03-01. Fax 03-83-32-86-04. 42 units. 125€–260€ double; 300€ suite. AE, DC, MC, V. Parking 16€. **Amenities:** Restaurant; bar; babysitting; room service. *In room:* A/C, TV, hair dryer, minibar, free Wi-Fi.

Hotel D'Haussonville ★★ This grand town house originally dating from the 1500s has been magnificently restored and is today the finest B&B in Nancy. Standing in the town's medieval heart, the hotel is an elegant, tranquil choice. Of course, it's a bit old-fashioned, but its antique charm is appreciated by many discerning guests seeking an old Lorraine ambience. The midsize-to-spacious bedrooms are a bit plush, with parquet flooring, antiques, and fireplaces. Bathrooms are thoroughly modernized and clad in marble. Each room has a special name, ranging from "Ming" to "Nairobi."

9 rue Mgr. Trouillet, Nancy 54000. www.hotel-haussonville.fr. ✆ **03-83-35-85-84.** Fax 03-83-32-78-96. 7 units. 140€–230€ double. AE, DC, MC, V. Closed most of Aug and 1st 2 weeks of Jan. **Amenities:** Breakfast room. *In room:* TV.

Where to Eat

While exploring the city, you can stop for food and wine at the minuscule **Le V'Four,** 10 rue St-Michel (✆ **03-83-32-49-48**), where set menus are priced from 26€ to 40€. A special fixed-price lunch is 18€. The best version of the celebrated quiche Lorraine (the egg, ham, and cheese tart) is sold at **Nathalie Lalonde,** 3 rue Stanislas (✆ **03-83-51-67-08**), a tradition since 1901.

The macaroon, that almond cookie so beloved by foodies, was said to have been invented in Nancy by Benedictine nuns. Their original recipe is followed at **Soeurs Macarons,** 21 rue Gambetta (✆ **03-83-32-24-25**). You might end your sightseeing day by calling at the century-old brasserie, **L'Excelsior,** 50 rue Henri Poincare (✆ **03-83-35-24-57**), a period piece from 1911 with stained-glass windows and polished brass chandeliers. Just a block from the rail station, it serves Lorraine specialties with fresh oysters, a delight in season.

The Other Centre Pompidou

In spring 2010, amidst much fanfare, Paris's Centre Pompidou unveiled a futuristic, brand-spanking new outpost in Metz, the capital city of Alsace's neighboring region, Lorraine. In addition to a theater and performance auditorium, the prime draw is its contemporary museum, where you'll encounter modern art from the 20th and 21st centuries. This newbie, a satellite of the Centre Pompidou in Paris (see p. 103), features rotating exhibits from the National Modern Art Museum (housed inside the Paris original). The easiest way to get to Metz is by taking a train from Nancy. Trains fun every 20 minutes and take 35-55 minutes (9.80€ one-way). The museum is located at 1 parvis des Droits de l'Homme (✆ 03-87-15-39-39; www.centrepompidou-metz.fr; admission 7€ adults, free for seniors and those 26 and under).

Pompidou Metz.

Le Capucin Gourmand ★★ TRADITIONAL FRENCH This is the leading grand restaurant of Nancy, within a 5-minute walk of place Stanislaus, and has a warm, cozy decor with tones of gray and wood paneling. On our last visit, we savored such creations as minced scallops and truffles pressed into patties and served with a walnut-oil vinaigrette; a "marble" of foie gras with exotic mushrooms; and a turbot steak that was "clothed" in baby vegetables. A signature dish is a civet of rabbit *à la royale*—in a sauce of its own blood mixed with red wine and just a hint of bitter chocolate. For dessert, a "passion of chocolate" came with baked fresh figs marinated in honey and served with a yogurt-flavored ice cream.

31 rue Gambetta. ✆ **03-83-35-26-98.** www.lecapu.com. Reservations required. Main courses 28€–38€; fixed-price menu 30€–78€. AE, MC, V. Tues–Fri and Sun noon–2pm; Tues–Sat 7:30–10pm.

Les Pissenlits (The Dandelions) TRADITIONAL FRENCH At this cost-conscious brasserie, the food is simple but flavorful and artfully prepared. Chef Jean-Luc Mengin's specialties are likely to include *matelote* of freshwater zander with shallots, dandelion salad with bacon and creamy vinaigrette, and aiguillettes of duckling with spice-flavored honey sauce. The chef's wife, Danièle, is one of the few accredited female wine stewards in France. Art Nouveau antiques, many of them crafted in Nancy, fill the dining room.

27 bis rue des Ponts. ✆ **03-83-37-43-97.** www.les-pissenlits.com. Reservations recommended. Main courses 14€–17€; fixed-price menu 18€–40€. MC, V. Tues–Sat 11:45am–2:30pm and 7:15–10:30pm.

Nancy After Dark

As night approaches, most of the student population heads to the Old Town. **Blue Note Why Not,** 3 rue des Michottes (✆ **03-83-30-31-18**), has a room for rock performances, a piano bar, a lounge with a fireplace and comfy armchairs, and a rowdy beer hall. It's open Wednesday through Sunday. Entrance is free except on Friday and Saturday night, when there's a 12€ cover. Women enter free on those nights before 12:30am.

Nancy's most popular dance club is **Les Caves du Roy,** 9 place Stanislas (✆ **03-83-35-24-14**), where a techno crowd flails around in a chrome-and-metallic space. It's open Tuesday to Thursday 11pm to 4am, Friday 11pm to 5am, Saturday midnight to 6:15am.

The hottest nightclub in the region is a converted warehouse in the suburb of Vandoeuvre, 4km (2½ miles) south of the center of town. **Le Circus,** 42 rue Jean-Mermoz (✆ **03-83-57-53-85;** www.circusmedia.fr; for many events, you can print out a "pass" from their website that gives free or discounted access), sits near the town's wholesale food market (le Marché en Gros). It features fire-eaters, jugglers, and techno music. Expect up to 2,000 revelers on a Friday or Saturday night, when the cover is 11€ and includes the first drink; it's open from 11pm to 5am.

DOMRÉMY-LA-PUCELLE

443km (275 miles) SE of Paris; 10km (6¼ miles) NW of Neufchâteau

Most often visited on a day trip, Domrémy is a plain village that would have slumbered in obscurity, but for the fact that Joan of Arc was born here in 1412. Today it's a pilgrimage center attracting tourists from all over the world.

A residence traditionally considered her family's house is known as **Maison Natale de Jeanne d'Arc,** 2 rue de la Basilique (✆ **03-29-06-95-86**). Here you can see the chamber where she was born. A museum beside the house shows a film depicting St. Joan's life. The house is open April to September Wednesday to Monday 10am to 6pm, and October to March Wednesday to Monday 10am to noon and 2 to 5pm. Admission is 3€ for adults, free for children 9 and under. The house is closed in January.

Adjacent to the museum, on rue Principale, is **Eglise St-Rémi;** repairs and partial reconstructions have masked its 12th-century origins. All that remain from the age of Joan of Arc are a baptismal font and some stonework. On a slope of the Bois-Chenu 1.5km (1 mile) uphill from the village is a monument steeped

Maison Natale de Jeanne d'Arc.

in French nationalism, the **Basilique du Bois-Chenu.** It was begun in 1881 and consecrated in 1926. To reach it, follow signs from the center and along rue de la Basilique.

Essentials

GETTING THERE If you're **driving,** take N4 southeast of Paris to Toul, and then A31 south toward Neufchâteau/Charmes. Then take N74 southwest (signposted in the direction of Neufchâteau). At Neufchâteau, follow D164 northwest to Coussey. From there, take D53 into Domrémy.

There is no railway station in Domrémy—you must take one of four **trains** daily going to either Nancy or Toul, where you can make bus and rail connections to Neufchâteau, 9.5km (6 miles) away. You can also take a **taxi,** MBM Assistance 88 (✆ **03-29-06-12-13**), for about 100€ each way.

VERDUN ★★

261km (162 miles) E of Paris; 66km (41 miles) W of Metz

Built on both banks of the Meuse and intersected by a series of canals, Verdun has an old section, the Ville Haute, on the east bank, which includes the cathedral and Episcopal palace. Today stone houses on narrow cobblestone streets give Verdun a medieval appearance. However, most visitors come to see the famous World War I battlefields, 3km (1¾ miles) east of the town, off N3 toward Metz.

Essentials

GETTING THERE Two **trains** arrive daily from Paris's Gare de l'Est; you'll have to change at Châlons-en-Champagne. Several daily trains also arrive from Metz, after a change at Conflans. The one-way fare from Paris is 33€ to 40€; from Metz, it's 13€. For train information and schedules, call ✆ **36-35** or 08-92-35-35-35. Driving is easy; Verdun is several miles north of the Paris-Strasbourg autoroute (A4).

VISITOR INFORMATION The **Office de Tourisme** is on place de la Nation (✆ **03-29-84-18-85;** fax 03-29-83-99-93; www.verdun-tourisme.com). It's closed on bank holidays.

Touring the Battlefields

At this garrison town in eastern France, Maréchal Pétain said, "They shall not pass!" And they didn't. Verdun is where the Allies held out against a massive assault by the German army in World War I. Near the end of the war, 600,000 to 800,000 French and German soldiers died battling over a few miles along the muddy Meuse between Paris and the Rhine. Two monuments commemorate these tragic events: Rodin's *Defense* and Boucher's *To Victory and the Dead.*

The local tourist office provides maps and advice on two carefully delineated, and separate, tours of the brutal and bloody battlefields that helped define World War I. They include the "Circuit Champs de Bataille Rive Droite," which encompasses the better-known battlegrounds on the River Meuse's right bank. They also have maps for two self-guided tours. The first, whose estimated length is about 4 hours, includes, on the Meuse's right bank, a 32km (20-mile) run, taking in **Fort Vaux,** where Raynal staged a heroic defense after sending his last

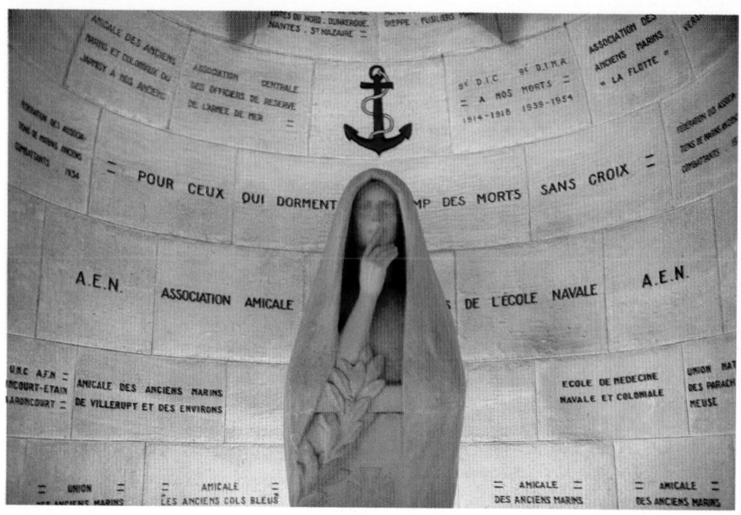

Ossuaire de Douaumont.

message by carrier pigeon. After passing a **French cemetery** of 16,000 graves—an endless field of crosses—you arrive at the **Ossuaire de Douaumont,** where the bones of those blown to bits were embedded. Nearby, at the **Fort de Douaumont,** the "hell of Verdun" was unleashed. From the roof, you can look out at a vast field of corroded tops of "pillboxes." Then you proceed to the **Tranchée des Baïonettes (Trench of Bayonets).** Bayonets of French soldiers entombed by a shell burst form this unique memorial.

Within a few paces of the Tranchée des Baïonettes, you'll see the premises of the **Mémorial de Verdun** (built around 1967), Fleury Devant Douaumont (✆ **03-29-84-35-34;** www.memorial-de-verdun.fr), a museum that commemorates the weapons, uniforms, photographs, and geography of one of the bloodiest battles of World War I. From February to mid-December, it's open daily 9am to noon and 2 to 6pm. Entrance is 7€ for adults and students, 3.50€ for children 8 to 16, free for children 7 and under.

The second self-guided tour, known as **"Circuit Champs de Bataille Rive Gauche"** (or "Circuit de l'Argonne"), also requires about 4 hours, and during its 97km (60 miles), it focuses on mostly outdoor sites, as opposed to the monuments and museums that are included in the tour's first 2 hours. It takes in the **Butte de Montfaucon,** a hill on which Americans erected a memorial tower, and the **Cimetière Américain at Romagne,** with some 15,000 graves.

Because public transportation is inadequate, only visitors with cars should attempt to make these circuits.

11

BURGUNDY

by Joe Ray

Castles rising from vineyards and medieval churches mark the landscape of Burgundy, the land of the good life for those who savor fine cuisine and wine in historic settings. Burgundy was once an independent province; its Valois dukes spread their might across Europe from 1363 to 1477. In preserving its independence, Burgundy weathered many struggles, notably under Charles the Bold, always in conflict with Louis XI. When Charles died in 1477, Louis annexed the duchy. Burgundy later suffered more upheaval, including damage to its cities during the Franco-Spanish wars that began in 1636. Peace finally held in 1678.

The ducs de Bourgogne are but a memory, but they left a legacy of vintage red and white wines to please and excite the palate. The major winegrowing regions of Burgundy are Chablis, Côte de Nuits, Côte de Beaune, Côte de Chalon, Mâconnais, and Nivernais.

AUXERRE ★★

154km (95 miles) SE of Paris; 148km (92 miles) NW of Dijon

Auxerre was founded by the Gauls and enlarged by the Romans. On a hill overlooking the Yonne River, it's the capital of Lower Burgundy and home to many vineyards, some of which produce Chablis. Joan of Arc spent several days here in 1429. Napoleon met Maréchal Ney here in 1815, on the former emperor's return from Elba. Louis XVIII had sent Ney to stop Napoleon, but Ney embraced him and turned his army against the king. For that, Ney was later shot.

This city is a sleepy, pleasant place with beautifully preserved *colombage* buildings. Its 40,000 residents will admit that not a lot happens here—and that's how they like it.

Essentials

GETTING THERE Visitors often **drive** here because Auxerre is near A6/E1 (the Autoroute du Soleil). There are nine trains per day from Paris (Gare de Bercy; trip time: 1½ hr.), and the fare is 25€ one-way. For train information, call ✆ **08-92-35-35-35.**

VISITOR INFORMATION The **Office de Tourisme** is at 1–2 quai de la République (✆ **03-86-52-06-09;** www.ot-auxerre.fr).

Exploring Auxerre

The railway station is at the eastern edge of town, about 1.5km (1 mile) from the historic center. Most of Auxerre is on the western bank of the Yonne. Its heart is

PREVIOUS PAGE: **Harvesting wine in Burgundy.**

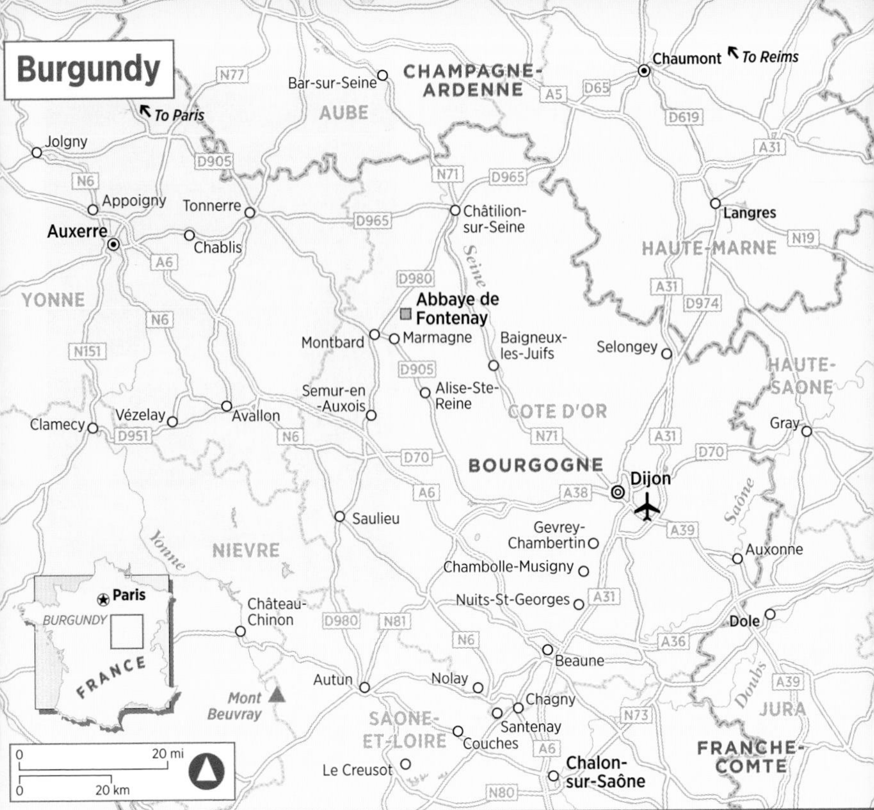

between place du Maréchal-Leclerc (near the Hôtel de Ville [city hall]) and the Cathédrale St-Etienne.

Cathédrale St-Etienne ★★ Pay a visit to the Flamboyant Gothic Cathédrale St-Etienne, begun in the 13th century but not completed until the 16th. The front facade is remarkable, with sculptured portals. The stained glass, some of it original, is famous. In the crypt, which is all that remains of the Romanesque church that stood on this site, you can see 11th-century frescoes.

Daily from June to August at 10pm (9:30pm in Sept) a 70-minute sound-and-light show relates the history of the church. It's presented in English, French, and German, and costs 5€ for adults and is free for children 12 and under.

Place St-Etienne. ✆ **03-86-52-23-29.** Free admission to church. Admission 1.90€ to treasury, 3€ to crypt. Cathedral daily 7:30am–6pm (till 5pm All Saints Day–Palm Sunday), and Sun openings at 8:30. Crypt and treasury Palm Sunday–All Saints Day Mon–Sat 9am–6pm, Sun 2–6pm; All Saints Day–Palm Sunday Mon–Sat 10am–5pm, Sun 2–6pm.

Where to Stay

Hôtel Le Maxime Attractive, high-ceilinged rooms, many with views of the river or the old city, highlight this family-run hotel. Most units retain their original wall and ceiling beams. Built as a private villa in 1855, the gracious, old-fashioned inn has been a hotel since 1900. A thorough renovation has upgraded the accommodations. You can take breakfast in your room or in the quiet salon, amid

Oriental rugs, polished paneling, and a sense of the gentility of an earlier era.

2 quai de la Marine, Auxerre 89000. www.lemaxime.com. ✆ **03-86-52-14-19.** Fax 03-86-52-21-70. 27 units. 92€–106€ double; 140€–212€ suite. AE, DC, MC, V. Parking 8€. **Amenities:** Bar. *In room:* A/C, TV, hair dryer, minibar, free Wi-Fi.

Auxerre.

Hôtel Normandie Inside this three-story hotel and former tea salon, antique furnishings complement modern amenities. The tranquil, comfortably furnished rooms open onto garden views; each unit is different. Most bathrooms come with showers only, many multijet, but some have tubs. Breakfast (9€) is the only meal served.

41 bd. Vauban, Auxerre 89000. www.hotelnormandie.fr. ✆ **03-86-52-57-80.** Fax 03-86-51-54-33. 47 units. 69€ double; 79€–125€ family room. AE, DC, MC, V. Parking 7€. **Amenities:** Bar; exercise room; room service; sauna. *In room:* A/C, TV, hair dryer, minibar, free Wi-Fi.

Le Parc des Maréchaux ★★ FRENCH A gem that outshines the competition, this was a Napoleon III–style private residence in the 19th century, set in its own .4-hectare (1-acre) park. The most secluded choice in the area, it's on the western outskirts of town, surrounded by century-old trees. The decor in the public areas and the lounge is French Empire; the style of the guest rooms is less consistent—a mixture of contemporary and Empire. The only available meal is breakfast, but the staff will serve hot food, on special request, in your room or in one of the salons.

6 av. Foch, Auxerre 89000. www.hotel-parcmarechaux.com. ✆ **03-86-51-43-77.** Fax 03-86-51-31-72. 25 units. 97€–113€ double; 134€–168€ triple or quad. AE, DC, MC, V. **Amenities:** Heated outdoor pool; room service. *In room:* A/C, TV, minibar, free Wi-Fi.

Where to Eat

Le Jardin Gourmand ★★ FRENCH The most sophisticated restaurant in town specializes in *cuisine moderne du marché* (modern market cuisine), employing the freshest ingredients to create artfully presented menus that change, often radically, eight times a year. The setting is an 1870 house a 10-minute walk from the cathedral with seating for just 17. In summer, an awning shades a pleasant terrace. Pierre Boussereau and Olivier Laplaine are devoted to cultivating fresh salad greens and herbs in their garden, and use them to garnish such platters as carpaccio of duck liver. Other tasty dishes include veal loin with white truffle sauce, and duckling confit with a fresh carrot salad. Roast young boar is served with pears and pumpkin in a red wine sauce, or you can order John Dory in an oyster sauce.

56 bd. Vauban. ✆ **03-86-51-53-52.** www.lejardingourmand.com. Reservations required. Main courses 25€–66€; fixed-price menu 49€ lunch, 70€–100€ dinner. MC, V. Thurs–Mon noon–1:45pm and 7:30–9:15pm. Closed 4 weeks throughout the year (consult the website for dates).

Where to Stay & Eat Nearby

La Côte Saint Jacques ★★★ FRENCH/BURGUNDIAN This is one of the top Relais & Châteaux members in France, with a 300-year-old foundation, a clientele that has included Catherine Deneuve and several French presidents, and a well-ingrained sense of comfort and culinary style. Chef Jean Michel Lorain's specialties include sea scallops roasted with caramelized spices, braised endive, and zabaglione; exotic mushrooms, foie gras, terrine of Brittany oysters; and smoked sea bass served with Sevruga caviar.

La Côte Saint Jacques also offers 32 opulent rooms that are air-conditioned, contemporary, very comfortable, and decorated with individual color schemes and parquet floors. Ten less expensive, non-air-conditioned rooms lie on an older site. An underground tunnel, fashioned from rocks salvaged from old buildings, connects the two sections. Doubles start at 190€, and suites run from 510€ to 640€.

14 Faubourg de Paris (N6), Joigny 89300. www.cotesaintjacques.com. ✆ **03-86-62-09-70.** Fax 03-86-91-49-70. Reservations required. Main courses 30€–100€; fixed-price lunch about 170€, dinner 145€–215€. AE, DC, MC, V. Daily 12:15–2pm and 7:30–9:45pm. Hotel and restaurant closed Jan 5–29. From Auxerre, head north on N6 (toward Sens) for 27km (17 miles). **Amenities:** Restaurant; fitness room; indoor pool; sauna. *In room:* TV, minibar, free Wi-Fi.

La Lucarne aux Chouettes ★★ 🎁 FRENCH You may remember Leslie Caron—she was that French gamin who won our hearts by sexily pirouetting with Gene Kelly in *An American in Paris* in 1951 and, later, in 1958, portraying a Parisian courtesan-in-training in *Gigi*. She was more recently seen playing a widow who found passion in *Chocolat* (2000). In this village 46km (29 miles) north of Auxerre, she took some 17th-century buildings and turned them into a small inn. The whole is now under new ownership that has brought La Lucarne up-to-date.

Quai Bretoche, Villenueve-sur-Yonne 89500. www.lalucarneauxchouettes.fr. ✆ **03-86-87-18-26.** Fax 03-86-87-22-63. 4 units. 55€ double; 99€ triple or duplex. AE, MC, V. **Amenities:** Restaurant. *In room:* TV, hair dryer, Wi-Fi.

VÉZELAY ★★

217km (135 miles) SE of Paris; 52km (32 miles) S of Auxerre

Vézelay, a living museum of French antiquity, stands frozen in time. For many, the town is the high point of a trip through Burgundy. Because it contained what was believed to be the tomb of St. Mary Magdalene, that "beloved and pardoned sinner," it was one of the great pilgrimage sites of the Christian world.

Today the medieval charm of Vézelay is widely known throughout France, and visitors virtually overrun the town in summer. The hordes are especially thick on July 22, the official day of homage to La Madeleine.

Essentials

GETTING THERE If you're **driving** from Paris, take A6 south to Auxerre, then continue south along N151 to Clamecy and turn east on D951 to Vézelay. Eight **trains** a day travel from Paris Gare de Bercy via Auxerre to Sermizelles, taking 2½ hours and costing about 28€ one-way. You'll need to take a short taxi ride from there into town.

VISITOR INFORMATION The **Office de Tourisme** is at 12 rue St-Etienne (✆ **03-86-33-23-69;** fax 09-70-62-05-62; www.vezelaytourisme.com).

Exploring the Town

On a hill 108m (354 ft.) above the countryside, Vézelay is known for its ramparts and houses with sculptured doorways, corbeled staircases, and mullioned windows. The town began as an abbey founded by Girart de Roussillon, comte de Bourgogne. Pope John VIII consecrated the abbey in 878.

On March 31, 1146, St. Bernard preached the Second Crusade here; in 1190, the town was the rendezvous point for the Third Crusade, drawing such personages as Richard the Lion-hearted and King Philippe-Auguste of France. Later, St. Louis of France came here several times on pilgrimages.

Park outside the town hall and walk through the medieval streets lined with 15th-, 16th-, and 18th-century houses and flower-filled gardens. If you're in the mood to shop, head for rue St-Etienne and rue St-Pierre. You'll find an assortment of stores selling religious books and statuary, including **La Pierre d'angle,** place de la Basilique (✆ **03-86-33-29-14**). **Galerie Lieber,** 14 rue St-Etienne (✆ **03-86-33-33-90**), specializes in handmade jewelry, using semiprecious and precious stones in both heavy and delicate settings of silver and gold, including some African and Asian items. You may also want to pick up a bottle or two of Vézelay wine at **La Cave Henry de Vézelay,** route de Nanchèvres, St-Père-sous-Vézelay (✆ **03-86-33-29-62**).

Basilique Ste-Madeleine ★★ Built in the 12th century, France's largest and most famous Romanesque church is only 9m (30 ft.) shorter than Notre-Dame de Paris. When you enter the narthex, a vestibule of about 370 sq. m (3,983 sq. ft.), raise your eyes to the doorway depicting Christ giving the apostles the Holy Spirit. From the Romanesque nave, with its traverse arches in white-and-gray stone, you'll see the light Gothic chancel. You can visit the Carolingian crypt, where the tomb of Mary Magdalene formerly rested and which now contains some of her relics. There's a panoramic view from the back terrace.

Place de la Basilique, Vézelay 89450. ✆ **03-86-33-39-50.** Free admission. Daily 8am–7pm.

Where to Stay

L'Espérance (see "Where to Eat," below) also rents luxurious rooms.

Le Compostelle This pleasant hotel is the best of Vézelay's more affordable inns. It's in the center of town, up the hill leading to the basilica, in a late-19th-century building that was transformed into a hotel in 1991. It's reminiscent of an English country house. Guest rooms are midsize and comfortably furnished, with small, shower-only bathrooms. Breakfast is the only meal served.

Place du Champ de Foire, Vézelay 89450. www.lecompostellevezelay.com. ✆ **03-86-33-28-63.** Fax 03-86-33-34-34. 18 units. 64€ double. AE, MC, V. Closed Nov 29 to mid-Feb. **Amenities:** Bar. *In room:* TV, free Wi-Fi.

Basilique Ste-Madeleine.

Poste et Lion d'Or ★ This local favorite is filled with character and tradition. On the main square, at the bottom of the hill that rises to the basilica, this hotel was built in the 17th century as a postal station. With a terrace, garden, and small restaurant, the Poste et Lion d'Or is first-class lodging with surprisingly reasonable rates. The functional guest rooms are conservatively outfitted—in some cases, in a vaguely Louis XVI style. Other than L'Espérance (see below), it's the finest address in town.

Place du Champ-de-Foire, Vézelay 89450. www.laposte-liondor.com. ✆ **03-86-33-21-23.** Fax 03-86-32-30-92. 38 units. 82€–96€ double; 149€–164€ suite. AE, DC, MC, V. Parking 6€. Closed Jan–Feb. **Amenities:** Restaurant; bar. *In room:* A/C, TV, free Wi-Fi.

Where to Eat

La Bougainville ★ BURGUNDIAN Not all of us can afford to dine at L'Espérance (see below), so La Bougainville is a more affordable alternative. This elegantly decorated antique house, complete with fireplace, serves as a backdrop for such regional specialties as *oeufs en meurette* (eggs poached in red wine and served with red-wine sauce) or a platter of oysters. After that, you can plunge into *filet de boeuf bourguignon* (beef cooked in burgundy, here with crème fraîche and escargots). The restaurant is also adept at concocting game dishes, such as venison with chestnuts or a delightful hare stew. For dessert, the specialty is *success aux noisettes avec nectarines rôti pralinée* (hazelnut cakes with roasted nectarines and praline ice cream).

28 rue St-Etienne. ✆ **03-86-33-27-57.** Reservations required. Main courses 10€–30€; fixed-price menus 22€–29€. MC, V. Thurs–Mon noon–2pm and 7–9pm. Closed mid-Nov to mid-Feb.

L'Espérance ★★★ MODERN FRENCH No other restaurant in Burgundy is as frequently assessed and gossiped about as this one. The restaurant has the feel of an old-fashioned farm and bakery, with Napoleon III decor. Located in a fertile valley, it emanates both Burgundian wholesomeness and Parisian chic. Flagstone floors and big windows overlooking a garden complement the superb cuisine. Menu items change frequently but are likely to include *cromesquis de foie gras* (in the form of a cube that melts in your mouth), potato galette with caviar, turbot en croûte, and roasted and caramelized filet of veal. The overworked staff struggles valiantly with the traffic generated by the place's fame.

On the premises are 28 well-maintained and comfortable guest rooms in three historic buildings. The accommodations epitomize French country living at its best. Doubles cost 150€ to 300€, apartments 300€ to 450€.

St-Père-sous-Vézelay, Vézelay 89450. ✆ **03-86-33-39-10.** Fax 03-86-33-26-15. www.marc-meneau-esperance.com. Reservations recommended. Main courses 80€–120€; fixed-price lunch 95€ with wine, dinner 150€–210€ without. AE, DC, MC, V. Thurs–Sun noon–2pm; Wed–Mon 7:30–9:30pm. Closed mid-Jan to early Mar.

AVALLON ★

214km (133 miles) SE of Paris; 52km (32 miles) SE of Auxerre; 96km (60 miles) NW of Dijon

This fortified town sits behind ancient ramparts, upon which you can stroll. A medieval atmosphere permeates Avallon, where you'll find many 15th- and 16th-century houses. At the town gate on Grande Rue Aristide-Briand is a 1460 clock tower. The Romanesque **Eglise St-Lazare** dates from the 12th century and has fantastic doorways, an artfully lit interior, and impressive woodwork. The church, open daily from 8am to 7pm, is said to have received the head of St. Lazarus in 1000, thus turning it into a pilgrimage site. Today Avallon is a destination mainly for its fabulous food.

Essentials

GETTING THERE If you're **driving,** travel south from Paris along A6 to Auxerre; from Auxerre, take N6 south to Avallon. Four **trains** arrive daily from Paris Gare de Bercy (trip time: 1½ hr.; 31€ one-way). Bus service from Dijon takes 2 hours and costs 1.50€ one-way; purchase tickets on the bus. For bus and train information, call ✆ **08-00-10-20-04.**

VISITOR INFORMATION The **Office de Tourisme** is at 6 rue Bocquillot (✆ **03-86-34-14-19;** www.avallonnais-tourisme.com).

Eglise St-Lazare.

Where to Stay

Château de Vault-de-Lugny ★★★ Between Avallon and Vézelay is this 16th-century moat-encircled château, with a fortress tower and peacocks on the grounds. It emphasizes service, with two staff members to every guest. The accommodations are sumptuous, with canopy beds, antique furnishings, and fireplaces. Luxurious bathrooms hold tub/showers. You can order cocktails in the salon and then eat dinner by candlelight. Fresh ingredients are the hallmark of the cuisine here. A special bourguignon meal of typical regional dishes is offered nightly.

11 rue du Chateau, Vault-de-Lugny 89200. www.lugny.fr. ✆ **03-86-34-07-86.** Fax 03-86-34-16-36. 16 units. 210€–650€ (king's bedroom); 470€–550€ suite. AE, DC, MC, V. Closed mid-Nov to mid-Apr. Take D957 from Avallon, turn right in Pontaubert (after the church) and follow signs; Vault-de-Lugny is about 3km (1¾ miles) away. **Amenities:** Restaurant; bar; babysitting; indoor pool; room service, free Wi-Fi. *In room:* TV, hair dryer, minibar.

Moulin des Ruats ★ 🎁 This enchanting country inn sits on the banks of the Cousin. Constructed as a flour mill in the 17th century, it has been a family hotel since 1924. Some guest rooms have exposed beams and intimate alcoves. Each contains a small bathroom with a shower, and some have tubs as well. Try for a room with a balcony overlooking the river. The elegant dining room serves prix-fixe menus ranging from healthy to traditional fare, complemented by a fine wine list and a terrace. The restaurant and accommodations are equally atmospheric and impressive.

9, rue des Isles Labaumes, Avallon 89200. www.moulindesruats.com. ✆ **03-86-34-97-00.** Fax 03-86-31-65-47. 25 units. 82€ double. AE, DC, MC, V. Closed mid-Nov to mid-Feb. Take D427 3km (1¾ miles) outside town. **Amenities:** Restaurant; bar; free Wi-Fi. *In room:* TV.

Where to Eat

Les Capucins BURGUNDIAN Warm colors and fresh flowers brighten this restaurant, which is just a 12-minute stroll from the heart of town. It's on the ground floor of a little hotel that rents 19 air-conditioned guest rooms for 55€ to 60€ for doubles. Free Wi-Fi is offered in every room. New chef Eric Moiteaux has big shoes to fill and fashions dishes such as sautéed veal kidney with Dijon mustard.

6 av. du President Paul Doumer, Avallon 89200. ✆ **03-86-34-06-52.** Fax 03-86-34-58-47. www.avallonlescapucins.com. Main courses 12€–24€; fixed-price menu 14€–36€. AE, MC, V. Daily noon–2pm and 7–9:30pm.

AUTUN ★★

293km (182 miles) SE of Paris; 85km (53 miles) SW of Dijon; 48km (30 miles) W of Beaune; 60km (37 miles) SE of Auxerre

Deep in Burgundy, Autun is one of the oldest towns in France. In the days of the Roman Empire, it was called "the other Rome." Some relics still stand, including the remains of the largest theater in Gaul, the Théâtre Romain. It was nearly 150m (492 ft.) in diameter and could hold some 15,000 people. Outside the town, you can see the tower of the 24m-high (79-ft.) Temple de Janus.

Autun is a thriving provincial town of 18,000, but because it's off the beaten track, the hordes go elsewhere. Still, it has its historical associations—Napoleon studied here in 1779 at the military academy (today the Lycée Bonaparte).

Essentials

GETTING THERE If you're **driving,** take D944 south from Avallon to Château-Chinon. Follow D978 east into Autun. Rail links to Autun are awkward. Four trains a day from Paris's Gare de Lyon run to Montchanin–Le Creusot, 40km (25 miles) south of Autun (37€–58€ one-way). From there, take a 45-minute bus connection to Autun. In Autun, **buses** arrive at a parking lot by the railway station on avenue de la République (1.50€ one-way). For bus information, call ✆ **08-00-07-17-70.** For railway information, call the station in Autun (✆ **03-85-52-78-97**) or SNCF (✆ **03-80-42-11-00**).

VISITOR INFORMATION The **Office de Tourisme** is at 13 rue du Genéral Demetz (✆ **03-85-86-80-38;** fax 03-85-86-80-49; www.autun-tourisme.com).

Seeing the Sights

Autun was once an important link on the road from Lyon to Boulogne. A legacy of that period is the 17m-high (56-ft.) **Porte d'Arroux,** once the city gate, which has two archways now used for cars and smaller ones used for pedestrians. Also exceptional is the **Porte St-André (St. Andrew's Gate),** northwest of the Roman theater. Rising 20m (66 ft.), it has four doorways and is surmounted by a gallery of 10 arcades.

Cathédrale St-Lazare ★★ On the highest point in Autun, the cathedral was built in 1120 to house the relics of St. Lazarus. On the facade, the tympanum in the central portal depicts the Last Judgment—a triumph of Romanesque sculpture. Inside, a painting by Ingres depicts the martyrdom of St. Symphorien, who was killed in Autun. In the 1860s, Viollet-le-Duc, who restored many monuments in France, had to double the size of some of the columns supporting the roof to avoid a collapse. New capitals matching the Romanesque style of the originals were crafted to top the new columns. The original capitals are on display, more or less at eye level, in the Salle Capitulaire, a flight above street level; especially noteworthy are *La Reveil des Mages (The Awakening of the Magi)* and *La Fuite en Egypte (The Flight into Egypt)*.

Place St-Louis. ✆ **03-85-52-12-37.** Daily 9am–7pm.

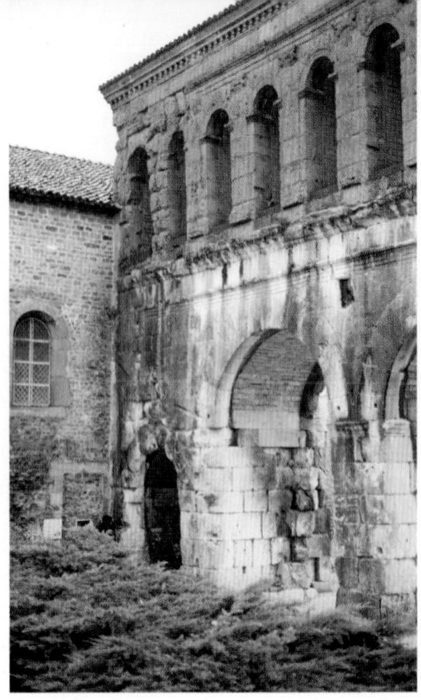

Porte St-André.

Musée Rolin ★ This 15th-century mansion was built for a famous lawyer, Nicolas Rolin (b. 1380). An easy walk from the cathedral, the museum displays a collection of Burgundian Romanesque sculpture, as well as paintings and archaeological mementos. From the original Rolin collection are *Nativity,* by the Maître de Moulins, and a statue that's a 15th-century masterpiece, *Our Lady of Autun La Vierge d'Autun,* also known as *La Vierge Bulliot,* after the benefactor who returned the original statue to the cathedral in 1948).

3 rue des Bancs. ✆ **03-85-52-09-76.** Admission 4€ adults, 2€ students and children. Apr–Sept Mon and Wed–Sun 9:30am–noon and 1:30–6pm; Oct–Mar Wed–Mon 10am–noon and 2–5pm (2:30pm reopening on Sun).

Nearby Attractions

After visiting Autun (if you have a car), you can tour one of Burgundy's finest wineries: **Domaine Maurice Protheau,** Château d'Etroyes, in Mercurey, 40km (25 miles) southeast along D978 (✆ **03-85-45-10-84**). Among the selections are at least two *appellations contrôlées* (a regulation system that ensures a wine has been produced where the bottles says under a varying set of rules), so you'll have a chance to immerse yourself in the subtle differences among reds (both pinot noirs and burgundies), whites, and rosés produced under the auspices of Rully and Mercurey. The headquarters of the winery, founded in the 1740s, is a château built in the 1700s and early 1800s. Free tours of the cellars are offered, in French and halting English, daily from 10am to noon and 2 to 7pm (call ahead to confirm). A *dégustation des vins* (wine tasting) and the opportunity to haul a bottle or two away costs 4€.

Three kilometers (1¾ miles) away, you can visit the **Château de Rully,** site of the **Domaine de la Bressande** (✆ **03-85-87-20-89**), a well-respected producer of white and some red burgundies. Originally built in the 12th century as a stronghold for the comte de Ternay, it offers tours, but the owner prefers that you visit as part of a group. Individuals can visit in July and August Wednesday through Sunday at 2, 4, and 5pm, but this offering is more limited than the group tour. The cost ranges from 4€ to 8€.

Where to Stay & Eat

Hôtel les Ursulines ★ The best hotel in Autun, the Ursulines offers comfortable rooms with views of the countryside and the Morvan mountains. Built in the 1600s as a convent, it gained a comfortable annex in 2000 that holds about half the rooms. Accommodations vary in shape and size—ask to see rooms in the 300 section whose recent remodel best reflects the historic design. The hotel is known for its cuisine, and despite recent chef changes and a dated dining room, it remains a solid value with fixed-price menus costing from 39€ to 79€.

14 rue Rivault, Autun 71400. www.hotelursulines.fr. ✆ **03-85-86-58-58.** Fax 03-85-86-23-07. 43 units. 71€–81€ double; 145€–171€ suite. AE, DC, MC, V. Parking 7€. **Amenities:** Restaurant; bar; babysitting. *In room:* A/C (in some), TV, hair dryer, minibar, free Wi-Fi.

BEAUNE ★★

316km (196 miles) SE of Paris; 39km (24 miles) SW of Dijon

This is the capital of the Burgundy wine country and one of the best-preserved medieval cities in the district, with a girdle of ramparts. Its history spans 2,000 years. Beaune was a Gallic sanctuary, then a Roman town. Until the 14th century, it was the residence of the ducs de Bourgogne. When the last duke, Charles the Bold, died in 1477, Louis XI annexed Beaune.

Essentials

GETTING THERE If you're **driving,** note that Beaune is a few miles from the junction of four highways—A6, A31, A36, and N6. Beaune has good railway connections with Dijon, Lyon, and Paris. From Paris's Gare de Lyon, there are 2 TGV **trains** per day (trip time: 2 hr.; 35€–60€ one-way), with many more possibilities via a transfer in Dijon; from Lyon, 10 trains per day (trip time: 1½ hr.; 18€–35€ one-way); and from Dijon, 26 trains per day (trip time: 35 min.; 7€ one-way). For train information and schedules, call ✆ **08-10-20-04.**

VISITOR INFORMATION The **Office de Tourisme** is at 6 bd. Perpreuil (✆ **03-80-26-21-30;** fax 03-80-26-21-39; www.beaune-tourism.com).

SPECIAL EVENTS Beaune comes to life during the weekend preceding the third Sunday in November, when wine buyers and oenophiles from the world over descend on the old town for a 3-day festival and wine auction called **Les Trois Glorieuses.** The town is packed with wineries offering dégustations priced from 20€ to 35€ for "several" glasses each of a different vintage—and with tourists visiting the labyrinth of caves and wine cellars. With all the free spirits (both kinds), visitors crowding the streets can be more than a bit tipsy.

Burgundy by Bike

The best way to see this golden land is by bike. Near the Beaune Rail Station, Bourgogne Randonnées, 7 av. du 8 Septembre (✆ 03-80-22-06-03; www.bourgogne-randonnees.com), rents bikes for 18€ per day.

Exploring the Town

North of the Hôtel-Dieu, the **Collégiale Notre-Dame,** place du Général Leclerc (✆ **03-80-24-77-95**), is an 1120 Burgundian Romanesque church. Some remarkable tapestries illustrating scenes from the life of the Virgin Mary are on display in the sanctuary. You can view them from Easter to mid-November.

The best **shopping** streets are rue de Lorraine, rue d'Alsace, rue Maufoux, and place de la Madeleine. For smaller boutiques, stroll down the pedestrian rue Carnot and rue Monge. For flea market antiques, concentrate your efforts around **Quartier du Camp Americain,** 3km (1¾ miles) northeast of the center of Beaune.

Beaune is one of the best towns in the region for sampling and buying Burgundy wines. You can tour, taste, and buy at **Marché aux Vins,** rue Nicolas-Rolin (✆ **03-80-25-08-85**), housed in a 14th-century church. Entrance is 10€. Its cellars are in and among the ancient tombs, under the floor of the church. A well-stocked competitor, stocking most of the vintages of Burgundy, is **Cordelier,** 6 rue de l'Hôtel-Dieu (✆ **03-80-25-08-20**). Another cellar, **Caves Patriarche Père et Fils,** 7 rue du Collège (✆ **03-80-24-53-78**), is under the former Convent of the Visitandines, with cellars from the 13th, 16th, and 17th centuries.

Musée de l'Hôtel-Dieu ★★ One of the town's most visible antique buildings is the Hôtel-Dieu. It thrived during the Middle Ages under an order of nuns associated with the famous vineyards of Aloxe-Corton and Meursault. It functioned as a hospital until 1970, and some sections still hold a retirement home. The Musée de l'Hôtel-Dieu displays Flemish-Burgundian art such as Rogier van der Weyden's 1443 polyptych ***The Last Judgment*** **★★★**. In the Salle des Pauvres (Room of the Poor), you'll find painted, broken-barrel, timbered vaulting and mostly authentic furnishings.

Rue de l'Hôtel-Dieu. ✆ **03-80-24-47-00.** Admission 6.70€ adults, 2.80€ ages 10–18, free for children 9 and under. Apr–Nov 19 daily 9am–6:30pm; Nov 20–Mar daily 9–11:30am and 2–5:30pm.

Musée des Beaux-Arts Along with a rich Gallo-Roman archaeological section, this museum has paintings from the 16th to the 19th centuries, including Flemish primitives, and pieces by Felix Ziem, a precursor of the Impressionists. Sculptures from the Middle Ages and the Renaissance are also on display.

6 bd. Perpreuil (Porte Marie de Bourgogne). ✆ **03-80-24-98-70.** Admission (includes Musée du Vin de Bourgogne) 5.50€ adults, 3.50€ students and children, free for children 15 and under. Apr–Oct daily 11am–1pm and 2–6pm; Nov–Mar Wed–Mon 11am–1pm and 2–6pm.

Musée du Vin de Bourgogne ★ Housed in the former mansion of the ducs de Bourgogne, this museum traces the evolution of the region's winemaking. The collection of tools, objets d'art, and documents is housed in 15th- and 16th-century rooms. On display in the 14th-century press house is a collection of wine presses.

Rue d'Enfer. ✆ **03-80-22-08-19.** Admission 5.50€ adults, 3.50€ students and children, free for children 15 and under. Apr–Nov daily 9:30am–6pm; Dec–Mar Wed–Mon 9:30am–5pm.

Musée de l'Hôtel-Dieu.

Where to Stay

Hôtel de la Poste ★ Outside the town fortifications, La Poste's origins as an inn go back to 1660; it was radically restored in the 1990s and has been upgraded every year since. The rooms overlook the ramparts or the vineyards, and some have brass beds. Specialties at the restaurant range from chicken fricassee with tarragon to sole in court bouillon with *beurre blanc*.

1-5 bd. Georges-Clemenceau, Beaune 21200. www.hoteldelapostebeaune.com. ✆ **03-80-22-08-11.** Fax 03-80-24-19-71. 36 units. 165€ double; 290€–550€ suite. AE, DC, MC, V. Parking 10€. **Amenities:** 2 restaurants (closed Tues); bar; room service. *In room:* A/C, TV, hair dryer, free Wi-Fi.

Hôtel Le Cep ★★★ This former residential mansion in the town center is a great spot for oenophiles, fit for the ducs de Bourgogne. Each antiques-filled guest room is individually decorated and named after a Grand Cru wine of the Côte-d'Or vineyards. On the grounds are two of the loveliest arcaded courtyards in Beaune, one from the 16th century, another from the 14th century. A tower housing one of the city's most beautiful stone staircases rises from here. A former wine cellar is the breakfast room. One of Beaune's finest restaurants, Loiseau des Vignes, run by the Bernard Loiseau group, is part of the hotel, featuring a stunning 70 wines by the glass.

27 rue Jean-Francois Maufoux, Beaune 21200. www.hotel-cep-beaune.com. ✆ **03-80-22-35-48.** Fax 03-80-22-76-80. 64 units. 134€ double; 294€–500€ suite. AE, DC, MC, V. Parking 15€. **Amenities:** Exercise room, restaurant; room service. *In room:* A/C, TV, hair dryer, minibar, free Wi-Fi.

L'Hostellerie de Bretonnière This is the best bargain in town. It's well run, has quiet rooms, and is a 5-minute walk from the center of town. The inn was built as a postal relay station around 1900 and became a hotel in 1950. In 2004, management enlarged the hotel with a seven-unit garden annex containing only duplex suites, each rustically outfitted in a style that evokes the traditions of rural Burgundy. The accommodations in the rear are the most tranquil, though most visitors prefer those overlooking the garden. Rooms are small but adequate for an overnight, and some have bathtubs. Continental breakfast is available for 9.50€.

43 rue de Faubourg Bretonnière, Beaune 21200. www.hotelbretonniere.com. ✆ **03-80-22-15-77.** Fax 03-80-22-72-54. 32 units. 56€–59€ double; 100€–110€ duplex suite. AE, DC, MC, V. Free parking. **Amenities:** Bar. *In room:* A/C (in some), TV, hair dryer, Wi-Fi (3€ per day).

L'Hôtel de Beaune ★★ Marble, mahogany, teak, and Italian stucco abound in this luxurious hotel, which opened in 2002. Behind the 19th-century exterior, its guest rooms are tastefully furnished and comfortable. Each of the rooms is individually decorated, with lustrous yellow-and-orange quilts on beds of royal size. The hotel maintains an extraordinarily comprehensive wine cellar that, on advance notice, visitors can examine. Wines inside are for sale, either for consumption within the hotel's bar or for takeaway.

3–5 rue Samuel Legay, Beaune 21200. www.lhoteldebeaune.com. ✆ **03-80-25-94-14.** Fax 03-80-25-94-13. 7 units. 170€–370€ double. AE, DC, MC, V. Closed Dec 8–Jan 5. **Amenities:** Restaurant; bar; babysitting; room service. *In room:* A/C, TV, hair dryer, Internet (10€ per day).

Where to Eat

Hôtel de la Poste (see "Where to Stay," above) has a good restaurant.

Bistro de L'Hotel ★ FRENCH/BURGUNDIAN A lot of the movers and shakers of the wine industry patronize this elegant bistro, where summer diners can enjoy the terrace. The chef and owner, Johan Björklund, is from Sweden, but he invites favorable comparison to some of the finest chefs of Burgundy. He is known for taking advantage of the best of regional produce, including a divine Bresse chicken carved tableside. His fixed-price menu is always a good recommendation, or else you can order a la carte. This restaurant has the town's finest sole meunière, served for two.

In L'Hotel de Beaune, 3–5 rue Samuel Legay. ✆ **03-80-25-94-10.** Reservations recommended. Main courses 35€–65€; fixed-price menu 40€. AE, DC, MC, V. Daily 12:30–2pm and 7–10pm, closed Sun lunch. Closed Dec 20–Jan 4.

Jardin des Remparts ★★★ MODERN FRENCH Just outside the city's medieval wall, this 1930s-era Art Deco *maison bourgeoise* is the finest restaurant in Beaune. Two pale-yellow-and-green dining rooms open onto a terrace overlooking the garden. Happily, prices for the well-regarded cuisine are a bit lower than you may expect. Menu items are adventurous and creative, and include whitefish baked in a mushroom crust, and pigeon roasted with licorice and softened caramel.

10 rue de l'Hôtel-Dieu. ✆ **03-80-24-79-41.** Reservations recommended. Main courses 30€–42€; fixed-price menu 28€–90€. MC, V. Tues–Sat noon–1:30pm and 7–9pm. Closed Dec 1–Jan 15.

Ma Cuisine ★ 🎁 BURGUNDIAN Open only 4 days a week, Ma Cuisine enjoys a reputation for well-prepared regional food and an impressively varied wine cellar. The restaurant attracts local residents, many of them wine producers. Your old-fashioned meal may begin with a platter of thin-sliced cured ham with parsley, or compote of rabbit with fresh tarragon. Main courses include spit-roasted and deboned pigeon or garlicky beef bourguignon. Desserts are 19th-century French brasserie favorites: thin-sliced apple or pear tart, crème brûlée, almond cake. The setting, a much-renovated 15th-century stable, is appropriately historic.

Passage Ste-Hélène. ✆ **03-80-22-30-22.** Reservations recommended. Main courses 15€–35€; fixed-price menu 24€. MC, V. Mon–Tues and Thurs–Fri noon–1:30pm and 7–9:30pm.

Relais de Saulx ★ FRENCH In a 200-year-old stone-trimmed building named after one of the region's ancient and noble families, Relais de Saulx is decorated with heavy timbers and all the accouterments you'd expect from one of the region's most respected restaurants. The kitchen prepares traditional Bourguignon cuisine and up-to-date adaptations. Staples are Bresse chicken with morel sauce, scallops with truffle sauce, and roast duck with sauces and garnishes that vary according to the season.

6 rue Louis Very. ✆ **03-80-22-01-35.** Reservations recommended. Main courses 15€–20€; fixed-price menu 18€–33€. MC, V. Tues and Fri–Sat noon–2pm; Mon–Sat 7–9:30pm. Closed 1 week in Feb, 2 weeks in Aug, and 1 week in early Dec.

Where to Stay & Eat Nearby

Hostellerie de Levernois ★ FRENCH Under Jean Croet and his sons, this became one of the most celebrated restaurants of regional France. Now chef Philippe Auge is in charge, and the restaurant is charting a new path. Auge creates grand cuisine in a stone-sided 17th-century *maison bourgeoise* in a 3.2-hectare (8-acre) park. The snails in risotto are a pure delight, and the menu changes with the seasons. Chickens for roasting come from Bresse and are acclaimed as the best in France.

The inn rents 26 carefully decorated rooms in a well-designed modern annex. They have TV, air-conditioning, and (in most) tub/showers. Doubles cost 135€ to 185€; the suites go for 280€ to 400€, with free Wi-Fi offered in the rooms.

Rue du Golf, Levernois 21200. www.levernois.com. ✆ **03-80-24-73-58.** Fax 03-80-22-78-00. Reservations required. Main courses 35€–48€; fixed-price dinner 68€–103€. AE, DC, MC, V. Mon–Sat 7–9:30pm; Sun noon–2pm and 7–9:30pm. Nov–Apr closed Wed. Closed late Jan to mid-Mar. Take D970 south of Beaune for 3km (1¾ miles), following signs for LONS LE SAUNIER.

Beaune After Dark

If you're in the mood for an ale or two, try the English-style **Pickwick's Pub,** 2 rue Notre-Dame (✆ **03-80-22-55-92**). **Le Bout du Monde,** 7 rue du Faubourg Madeline (✆ **03-80-23-04-52**), has a beautiful courtyard and offers occasional concerts, theme nights, a wine bar, and tapas.

DIJON ★★★

312km (193 miles) SE of Paris; 320km (198 miles) NE of Lyon

Dijon is known overseas mainly for its mustard. Located in the center of the Côte d'Or, it's the ancient capital of Burgundy. Here great wine accompanies good food. Between meals, you can enjoy the art and architecture.

Your first impression, especially if you arrive at the rail station, can be misleading. You may think Dijon is a dreary modern city, but press on to its medieval core, and you'll discover old streets and buildings that have been restored. Mayor François Rebsamen was elected on a platform that mixed aspects of socialist, communist, and Greenpeace rhetoric. He is committed to the verdancy of Dijon.

Essentials

GETTING THERE The best way to reach Dijon is by **driving.** From Paris, follow A6 southeast to Pouilly-en-Auxois, and then go east along A38 into Dijon. Dijon also has excellent rail and bus connections to the rest of Europe. At least 10 TGV **trains** arrive from Paris's Gare de Lyon each day (trip time: 1 hr., 45 min.); the one-way fare is 42€ to 56€. Trains arrive from Lyon every hour (trip time: 2 hr.; 26€–30€ one-way). For information, call ✆ **08-92-35-35-35.**

VISITOR INFORMATION The **Office de Tourisme** is at Cour de la Gare (✆ **08-92-70-05-58;** www.dijon-tourism.com).

SPECIAL EVENTS From mid-June to the end of July, the streets of Dijon experience a lively renaissance when **Estivade** (✆ **03-80-74-51-51**) comes to town. The festival uses the city's streets as a stage for folk dances, music, and theater. It's always a big hit. You can get a schedule of events from the city tourist office (see above) or La Mairie (the town hall; ✆ **03-80-74-53-74**).

Seeing the Sights

One of the most historic buildings in this ancient province is the **Palais des Ducs et des Etats de Bourgogne,** which symbolizes the independent (or semi-independent, depending on the era) status of this fertile region. Capped with an elaborate tile roof, the complex is arranged around a trio of courtyards. The oldest section, only part of which you can visit, is the **Ancien Palais des Ducs de Bourgogne,** erected in the 12th century and rebuilt in the 14th. The newer section is the **Palais des Etats de Bourgogne,** constructed in the 17th and 18th centuries for the Burgundian parliament. Today the palace is *la mairie* (the town hall); all of its newer section and much of its older section are reserved for the municipal government and not open to the public. However, there's a fine museum, the **Musée des Beaux-Arts** (see below).

On N5, 1.5km (1 mile) west from the center of town, stands the **Chartreuse de Champmol,** the Carthusian monastery built by Philip the Bold as a burial place; it's now a psychiatric hospital. Much of it was destroyed during the Revolution. The Well of Moses in the gardens was designed by Sluter at the end of the 14th century, and the Gothic entrance is superb. Admission 3.50€ adults and 2.50€ students (Nov–Mar 9:30am–12:30pm and 2–5pm; Apr–Oct 9:30am–12:30pm and 2–5:30pm).

The **Musée Archéologique,** 5 rue du Dr-Maret (✆ **03-80-48-83-70;** www.musees-bourgogne.org), contains findings unearthed from Dijon's archaeological digs. A medieval nunnery, **L'Ancien Couvent des Bernardines,** 17 rue Ste-Anne (✆ **03-80-44-12-69**), is home to two museums. The chapel holds the Musée d'Arts Sacrés, devoted to art from regional churches, and the cloister contains the **Musée de la Vie Bourguignonne** (also known as the Musée Perrin de Puycousin), which exhibits folkloric costumes, farm implements, and some 19th- and early-20th-century storefronts from Dijon's center. Admission is free to all three of these museums. (Hours are Oct–Apr Wed–Mon 9am–noon and 2–6pm, and May–Sept 9am–12:30pm and 1:30 to 6pm.)

Musée des Beaux-Arts ★★ The part of the old palace that you can visit contains one of France's oldest and richest museums. It showcases exceptional sculpture, ducal kitchens from the mid-1400s (with great chimney pieces), a collection of European paintings from the 14th to the 19th centuries, and modern French paintings and sculptures. Take special note of the Salle des Gardes, the banquet hall of the old palace built by Philip the Good (Philippe le Hardi). The tomb of Philip the Bold was created between 1385 and 1411 and is one of the best in France: A reclining figure rests on a slab of black marble, surrounded by 41 mourners.

In the Palais des Ducs et des Etats de Bourgogne, cour de Bar. ✆ **03-80-74-52-09.** Free admission. Temporary expositions cost around 2€ each (free Sun). May–Oct Wed–Mon 10am–6pm; Nov–Apr Wed–Mon 10am–5pm.

Musèe des Beaux-Arts.

Musée Magnin This museum was built in the 19th century as the home of an arts-conscious member of the *grande bourgeoisie.* The city of Dijon inherited the building and its contents following the death of the family's last descendant. It contains an eclectic display of 19th-century antiques and art objects, as well as a collection of paintings accumulated or painted by the former owners.

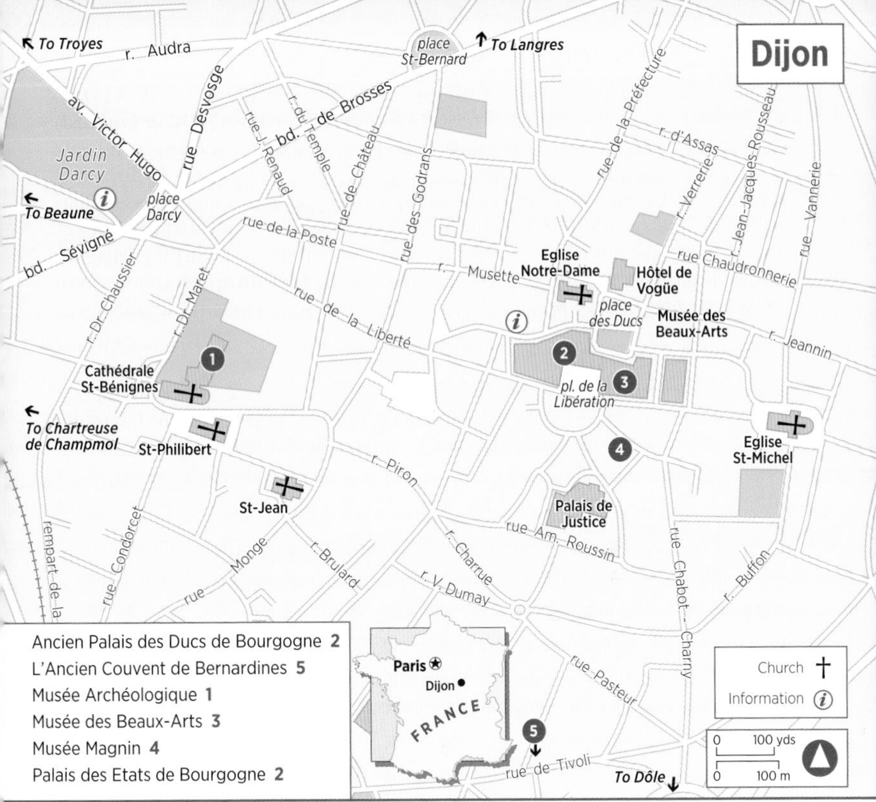

4 rue des Bons-Enfants. ✆ **03-80-67-11-10.** www.musee-magnin.fr. Admission 3.50€ adults, 2.50€, free for ages 26 and under. Tues–Sun 10am–noon and 2–6pm.

Shopping

Your shopping list may include robust regional wines, Dijon mustard, antiques, and the blackcurrant liqueur, cassis (try a splash with white wine for a kir, or use champagne for a kir royale). The best shopping streets are rue de la Liberté, rue du Bourg, rue Bossuet, and (for antiques) rue Verrerie. The market at **Les Halles Centrales,** rue Odebert, sells fruits, vegetables, and foodstuffs on Tuesday, Thursday, and Friday from 8am to noon, and Saturday from 8am to around 5pm. A separate endeavor that specializes in used clothing, kitchen utensils, housewares, and flea-market castoffs operates along the market's periphery Tuesday, Thursday, and Friday 8am to noon, and Saturday 8am to around 5pm.

For the ideal picnic lunch, begin at **La Boutique Maille,** 32 rue de la Liberté (✆**03-80-30-41-02**), where you can purchase many varieties of the world-famous mustard. Follow with a visit to the **Crémerie Porcheret,** 18 rue Bannelier (✆**03-80-30-21-05**), to pick up several regional cheeses, including *citeaux,* made by the brothers at a nearby monastery. Finish your journey at one of the three locations of **Mulot et Petitjean,** 1 place Notre-Dame, 16 rue de la Liberté, or 13 place Bossuet (✆**03-80-30-07-10**), where you can pick up a pastry (especially gingerbread) for dessert.

For antiques, try **Monique Buisson,** 21 rue Verrerie (✆ **03-80-30-31-19**), which offers a good collection of regional furniture from the 1700s, or **Dubard,** 25 bis rue Verrerie (✆ **03-80-30-50-81**), for 19th-century garden ornaments and contemporary upholstery fabric. Also appealing is **Antiquaires Golmard,** 3 rue Auguste-Comte (✆ **03-80-67-14-15**), which specializes in objects originating on private estates in the region. This store is flexible about trading antiques with individuals and other dealers, making it something of a clearinghouse for unusual antiques from throughout Europe. **Le Consortium,** 16 rue Quentin (✆ **03-80-68-45-55**), is one of Dijon's most interesting modern-art galleries.

Where to Stay

Hostellerie du Chapeau-Rouge ★ This Dijon landmark, which has an acclaimed restaurant, combines modern conveniences and stylish furnishings and is a good value. Most of the bathrooms have Jacuzzis, others have large showers. Because no other hotel restaurant in town serves comparable food, you may want to visit here even if you're not a guest. The restaurant features innovative fare with French and Asian influences.

5 rue Michelet, Dijon 21000. www.chapeau-rouge.fr. ✆ **03-80-50-88-88.** Fax 03-80-50-88-89. 29 units. 115€–150€ double; 239€ suite. AE, DC, MC, V. Parking 13€. **Amenities:** Restaurant; bar; room service. *In room:* A/C, TV, hair dryer, minibar, free Wi-Fi.

Hôtel de La Cloche ★ Legends associated with this site date from the 15th century, but the building evokes a late-19th-century grand hotel, complete with high ceilings and the modernized decor favored by Napoleon III. Located between the train station and the town center, it features pink-and-gray marble floors, modern guest rooms with tub/showers, and an elegant lobby bar.

14 place Darcy, Dijon 21000. www.hotel-lacloche.com. ✆ **03-80-30-12-32.** Fax 03-80-30-04-15. 68 units. 240€–260€ double; 320€–800€ suite. AE, DC, MC, V. **Amenities:** Restaurant; bar; babysitting; exercise room; room service; sauna. *In room:* A/C, TV, hair dryer, minibar, free Wi-Fi.

Hôtel Wilson ★ 🎁 Our favorite nest in Dijon, opening onto a pleasant square, this *ancien relais de poste* (coaching inn) dates from the 17th century and has been tastefully restored. Although it has been modernized and decorated with Burgundian wood furniture, many of the old wood ceiling beams have been exposed, adding authentic charm. Units have small bathrooms, some with tubs.

1 rue de Longvic, Dijon 21000. www.wilson-hotel.com. ✆ **03-80-66-82-50.** Fax 03-80-36-41-54. 27 units. 82€–91€ double. AE, MC, V. Parking 9€. **Amenities:** Bar. *In room:* A/C (in some), TV, hair dryer, free Wi-Fi.

Dijon's namesake mustard.

SIDE trips FROM DIJON

Head northwest from Dijon on A38 into the Vallée de l'Ouche, alongside the Burgundy Canal. At pont de Pany, on the outskirts of Sombernon, exit onto a local highway (D905) and continue northwest. On your left lies the lake of Grosbois. The scenery is typical of agricultural France, with isolated farms, woods, and pastures.

Pass through Vitteaux; just before the next village, Posanges, stands a feudal château. You can't visit it, but it's worth a picture. Continue on D905 until you come to a railroad crossing. On your left is another old castle, now part of a private farm. The next village you reach along D905 is Pouillenay. Follow the signs for a short detour to the hamlet of **Flavigny-sur-Ozerain.** Park your car outside the walls and walk through the old streets.

Leave Flavigny and follow signs for a few miles on country roads to **Alise-Ste-Reine,** the site of what was once Alésia, the camp of the Gallic chieftain Vercingetorix. Alise-Ste-Reine was named after a local Christian who was decapitated for refusing to marry a Roman governor. In the town center stands a statue of Vercingetorix crafted by Millet. You can explore the ruins of a Roman-Gallic town, **Les Fouilles d'Alésia,** and **Le Musée d'Alésia.**

After Alise-Ste-Reine, you can head back to the village of Les Laumes, a railroad center. Before entering the village, make a U-turn to the right and take N454 to Baigneux-les-Juifs. After the village of Grésigny, you'll see a farm-fortress surrounded by water on your left.

Go 1.5km (1 mile) farther and turn right toward the **Château de Bussy-Rabutin** (✆ **03-80-96-00-03**). Roger de Rabutin ridiculed Louis XIV's court, for which he spent 6 years in the Bastille prison. The château, with two towers, has survived mostly intact. The gardens and park are attributed to Le Nôtre. It's open Tuesday to Sunday from 9:15am to noon and 2 to 5pm (6pm from mid-May to mid-Sept). Admission is 7€ for adults, 4.50€ for students 18 to 25, and free for those 17 and under.

Return to Grésigny, turn right before the farm-fortress, and then go left. Outside the village, turn right toward Menetreux Le Pitois. Here you're off the main road and into the real countryside. Back on D905, head to **Montbard,** hometown of George-Louis Leclerc, comte de Buffon, one of the 18th century's great naturalists and author of *L'Histoire Naturelle,* a 44-volume encyclopedia. The scientist's home is open to visitors, and a mini museum, **Musée Buffon** (✆ **03-80-92-50-42**), is dedicated to his life and work. It's open only from March to October Wednesday through Sunday from 10am to noon and 2 to 5pm. The **Hôtel de l'Ecu,** 7 rue Auguste Carré (✆ **03-80-92-11-66**), serves moderately priced meals in an 18th-century postal relay station; prix-fixe menus cost 21€ to 52€. The inn also rents 23 simply furnished yet comfortable bedrooms, costing 78€ to 90€ a night in a double. Closed February 20 to March 9.

Continue east 9.5km (6 miles) to Marmagne, then turn left on D32, and head toward the **Abbaye de Fontenay** (✆ **03-80-92-15-00;** www.abbayedefontenay.com). Isolated in a valley, Fontenay is one of Europe's most unspoiled 12th-century Cistercian abbeys. It is open mid-November to mid-April daily 10am to noon and 2 to 5pm; mid-April to mid-November daily 10am to 6pm. Admission is 9€ for adults, 4.20€ for children and students, and free for children 6 and under.

Le Jacquemart In the center of Old Dijon is one of the town's most affordable hotels. A building from the 1900s was completely restored, yet retains its steep stairwell and high ceilings. It's furnished in a comfortable, provincial style, with immaculate bathrooms and crisp bed linens. There is no elevator or air-conditioning, but the welcome is genuine. Some of the accommodations are large enough to house three or four guests. Breakfast is available for 6€.

32 rue Verrerie, Dijon 21000. www.hotel-lejacquemart.fr. ✆ **03-80-60-09-60.** 3 units. 66€–68€ double; 74€ triple; 81€ quad. AE, MC, V. Parking 5€. **Amenities:** Breakfast room. *In room:* TV, hair dryer, free Wi-Fi.

Where to Eat

Hostellerie du Chapeau-Rouge (see "Where to Stay," above) has a marvelous restaurant.

Le Pré aux Clercs ★★★ BURGUNDIAN/FRENCH In an 18th-century house across from the Palais des Ducs, this is one of Burgundy's finest restaurants, with a reputation that dates to 1833. Chef-owner Jean-Pierre Billoux, assisted by his wife, Marie-Françoise, and their son, Alexis, prepare meals that consistently win acclaim. Menu items, served beneath an intricately beamed ceiling, may include langoustines prepared with aged sherry vinegar, or roasted duckling with gingerbread stuffing. The array of wines will delight any connoisseur.

13 place de la Libération. ✆ **03-80-38-05-05.** www.jeanpierrebilloux.com. Reservations required. Main courses 25€–45€; fixed-price lunch 35€, dinner 50€ and 95€. AE, MC, V. Tues–Sun noon–1:45pm; Tues–Sat 7:30–9:30pm. Closed 10 days in Aug.

Les Oenophiles ★ FRENCH You enter this elegant, grand restaurant through an antique courtyard. Stone walls surround a dining room decorated with Oriental carpets and Louis XII chairs. New chef Vincent Bourdon serves traditional food that's hearty and satisfying, in a style somewhere between old-fashioned and conservatively modern. Specialties include foie gras in puff pastry, served with fruited wine; and marinated scallops and shrimp prepared tempura style. For more casual fare, the **Autre Entrée** bistro is run out of the same kitchen. On the premises is the modern 32-room Hotel Philippe-le-Bon. Rooms have minibars, air-conditioning, and TVs. Rates for a double are 80€ to 88€, or 130€ to 159€ for a suite.

18 rue Ste-Anne, Dijon 21000. ✆ **03-80-30-73-52.** Fax 03-80-30-95-51. Reservations required. Main courses 18€–30€; fixed-price dinner 39€–59€. AE, MC, V. Mon–Sat noon–1:30pm and 7–9:30pm.

Stéphane Derbord ★★★ FRENCH Given the prices and acclaim of this restaurant, customers have a right to expect perfection—and they get it. Stéphane Derbord is the most sought-after restaurant in Dijon. Stéphane's charming wife presides over the cozy dining room. Saône River *sandre* (a local whitefish) is steamed and served with crayfish and pike dumplings, and chicken is roasted to perfection and served with spicy gravy. Chef Derbord recommends the *filet de boeuf,* "the emblem of our region," with a pinot noir reduction and organic potatoes.

10 place Wilson. ✆ **03-80-67-74-64.** www.restaurantstephanederbord.fr. Reservations required. Main courses 35€–44€; fixed-price menu 43€–88€. AE, DC, MC, V. Wed–Sat noon–1:45pm; Mon–Sat 7:30–9:45pm. Closed 1 week in Jan and 2 weeks in Aug.

Where to Eat Nearby

Restaurant des Gourmets ★★ FRENCH This restaurant is reason enough to journey to a charming medieval village 6km (3¾ miles) south of Dijon. In a modern room overlooking a garden, you can enjoy a seasonal menu that may include main-course delights such as John Dory with paprika. The cellar contains more than 600 wines; many are burgundies from lesser-known, small-scale wineries.

8 rue Puits-de-Têt, Marsannay-la-Côte 21160. ✆ **03-80-52-16-32.** www.les-gourmets.com. Reservations recommended. Main courses 22€–34€; fixed-price menus 25€–95€. AE, DC, MC, V. Wed–Sun noon–1:30pm and 7–9:30pm. Closed 2 weeks in Aug. Drive 9.5km (6 miles) south of Dijon on N74, following the signs for Beaune and then Marsannay-la-Côte.

Dijon After Dark

Begin your evening at one of the cafes or brasseries lining place Zola, rue des Godrans, place du Théâtre, or place Darcy, such as the **Concorde,** 2 place Darcy (✆ **03-80-30-69-43**); **Brasserie du Théâtre,** 1 bis place du Théâtre (✆ **03-80-31-91-49**); or **La Comédie,** 3 place du Théâtre (✆ **03-80-67-11-62**). These spots fill up with young people who start the night with a drink and a look around.

If you prefer a 30s-to-40s crowd that likes to mingle in the low-key atmosphere of a piano bar, try **Hunky Dory,** 5 av. Foch (✆ **03-80-53-17-24**); **Le Messire,** 3 rue Jules-Mercier (✆ **03-80-30-16-40**); or **Le Cintra,** 13 av. Foch (✆ **03-80-53-19-53**), which also has a little disco. For the boisterous (and often sloshed) atmosphere of an Irish pub, head over to **Le Kilkenny,** 1 rue Auguste-Perdrix (✆ **03-80-30-02-48**). Appealing to a more sedate crowd is **Le Chat Noir,** 20 av. Garibaldi (✆ **03-80-73-39-57**), which emphasizes slower, more romantic music.

The opera season in Dijon stretches from the middle of October to May. The city's premier venue is the **Grand Théâtre de Dijon,** 2 rue Longepierre (✆ **03-80-60-44-00**); call ahead for information on operas, operettas, dance recitals, and concerts. The city's second-most visible cultural venue is the **Théâtre National Dijon-Bourgogne,** rue Danton (✆ **03-80-68-47-47**). Tickets for performances at either theater range from 15€ to 40€.

SAULIEU ★

250km (155 miles) SE of Paris; 76km (47 miles) NW of Beaune

Saulieu is interesting, but its food put it on the international map. The town (pop. 3,000) has enjoyed a reputation for cooking since the 17th century. Even Mme. de Sévigné praised it in her letters. So did Rabelais.

The main sight is the **Basilique St-Andoche,** place de la Fontaine (✆ **03-80-64-07-03**), which has some interesting decorated capitals. Next door, in the **Musée François-Pompon,** place du Docteur, at rue Sallier (✆ **03-80-64-19-51**), you can see works by François Pompon (d. 1930), the sculptor of animals whose works are featured in Paris's Musée d'Orsay. Pompon's large statue of a bull stands on a plaza off N6 at the entrance to Saulieu. Also in the museum are archaeological remnants from the Gallo-Roman era, sacred medieval art, and old tools illustrating aspects of life in Burgundy several centuries ago. Admission is 4€ for adults and 2.50€ for children 12 to 16. It's closed in January and February.

Essentials

GETTING THERE If you're **driving,** head along N80 from Montbard or N6 from Paris or Lyon. The **train** station is northeast of the town center. Passengers coming from Paris sometimes opt to take the TGV from the Gare de Lyon, getting off in Montbard, 48km (30 miles) to the north. From Montbard, a series of **buses** timed to the arrival of the TGV carry passengers on to Saulieu about three times a day for a one-way fare of 1.50€. For bus information, call Transco (✆ **03-80-97-42-00**); for rail information, call ✆ **36-35.**

VISITOR INFORMATION The **Office de Tourisme** is at 24 rue d'Argentine (✆ **03-80-64-00-21;** www.saulieu.fr).

Where to Stay & Eat

Château Les Roches ★★ Twelve kilometers (7 ½ miles) east of Saulieu, reached along the A38, stands this imposing country residence in a medieval hilltop village, with panoramic views of the countryside. This magnificent house, decorated in exquisite taste, was built by a judge at the turn of the 20th century as an abode for his mistress. The face of that long-ago mistress can be found on the hand-painted ceiling panels in the dining room. The architect borrowed freely from styles in Austria, Switzerland, and Germany. Public rooms are adorned with original wood paneling, high ceilings, and intricate plasterwork. Bedrooms are spacious and furnished with a sumptuous mix of antique and contemporary furnishings, half with showers, half with bathtubs. A Burgundy wine-tasting course is offered daily for 35€.

Rue de Glanot, Mont Saint-Jean 21320. www.lesroches-burgundy.com. ✆ **03-80-84-32-71.** 6 units. 129€–169€ double. Rates include breakfast. MC, V. **Amenities:** Restaurant (Mon and Fri); set-menu dinner Thurs and Sat; exercise room; room service (breakfast only). *In room:* Free Wi-Fi.

Le Relais Bernard Loiseau ★★ This former stagecoach stop with one of the best-known restaurants in France is an excellent choice. If you want to stay overnight, you'll find guest rooms with everything from Empire to Louis XV decor. You'll sleep on a comfortable mattress, on a bed that's likely to be 200 years old.

The 2003 suicide of its famous chef, Bernard Loiseau (rumored to be despondent at the thought of losing a Michelin star), shocked the culinary world. Loiseau's wife, Dominique, and staff are carrying on admirably under Chef Patrick Bertron, who was culinary disciple of Loiseau for 20 years. The cooking remains in his style: less traditional, emphasizing maximum taste with no excess fat or sugar. All the great Burgundies are on the wine list. A fixed-price lunch costs 66€ to 185€, with a fixed-price dinner going for 120€ to 185€.

2 rue Argentine, Saulieu 21210. www.bernard-loiseau.com. 32 units. ✆ **03-80-90-53-53.** Fax 03-80-64-08-92. 175€–255€ double; 375€–450€ suite. AE, MC, V. Closed Jan 4–Feb 15. **Amenities:** Restaurant; bar; exercise room; indoor and outdoor pools; room service; sauna; spa. *In room:* A/C (in some), TV, hair dryer, minibar, free Wi-Fi.

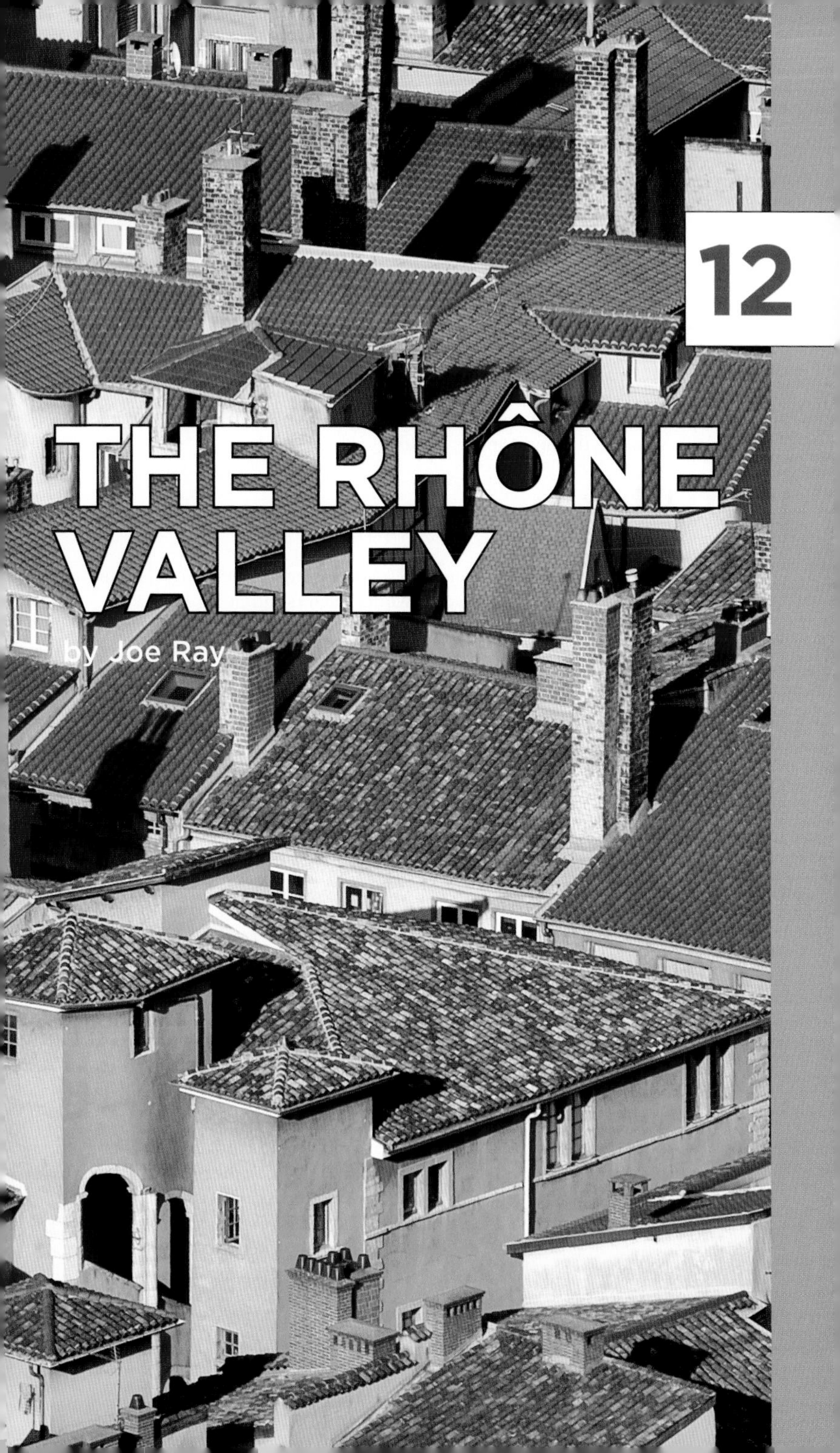

12

THE RHÔNE VALLEY

by Joe Ray

The Rhône is as mighty as the Saône is peaceful, and these rivers form a part of the countryside that most travelers experience only briefly as they rush to the Riviera on the Mediterranean Express. This land of mountains and rivers is Beaujolais country, filled with Roman ruins, castles, and the Grand Canyon of France. It's also home to Lyon, a fabulous stop for gourmets.

The district brims with time-mellowed inns and stylish restaurants serving cuisine that's among the finest in the world.

LYON ★★★

431km (267 miles) SE of Paris; 311km (193 miles) N of Marseille

Whether you're high atop Fourvière Hill, meandering in Vieux Lyon, or climbing the slopes of the Croix-Rousse, you'll witness Lyon's intriguing history over the last 2,000 years. At the confluence of the Rhône and Saône rivers, the city is well deserving of its UNESCO status. In Lyon, long known for its silk industry, old weavers' workshops lie next to boutiques that sell modern-day silk creations. This is also the city that consistently knocks Paris off its culinary block, and there's an enthusiasm among chefs and foodies here unseen anywhere else in France.

Things to Do Wander the narrow cobblestone lanes of Vieux Lyon that date from the Middle Ages, and search for traboules—corridors that connect two streets through a building or courtyard. Learn about the history of Lyon, and that of its beloved Guignol puppet, at the Musée Gadagne. In the Fourvière neighborhood, visit the two Roman theaters, remnants of the ancient Roman city of Lugdunum. The spectacular Festival of Lights in December showcases light shows by professional artists from around the world.

Shopping For boutiques and art galleries, shop in **Vieux Lyon** and the area around rue de la République. In the 18th century, Lyon was renowned throughout Europe for its **silk** industry, and today you can get your own silk scarves at the **Hermès** boutique or choose from a treasure of touchable textiles at **Le Comptoir des Couleurs.** To bring home something with history, head for **antiques** shops concentrated around rue Auguste-Comte near place Bellecour. Get some of the best **wines** in France at **Antic Wine** on the Rue du Boeuf.

Restaurants & Dining Lyon is France's gastronomic capital, and chef Paul Bocuse its longtime star. Just outside of town, his **L'Auberge du Pont de Collonges** is the focus of many a foodie's pilgrimage. Local specialties are plentiful and vary from the creamy *cervelle de canut* (fromage blanc with herbs) to Bresse chicken and sturdy, sublime offal dishes. Whether you dine with famous chefs or in modest *bouchons* such as **Les Adrets,** you'll have a meal to remember.

PREVIOUS PAGE: **Lyon rooftops.**

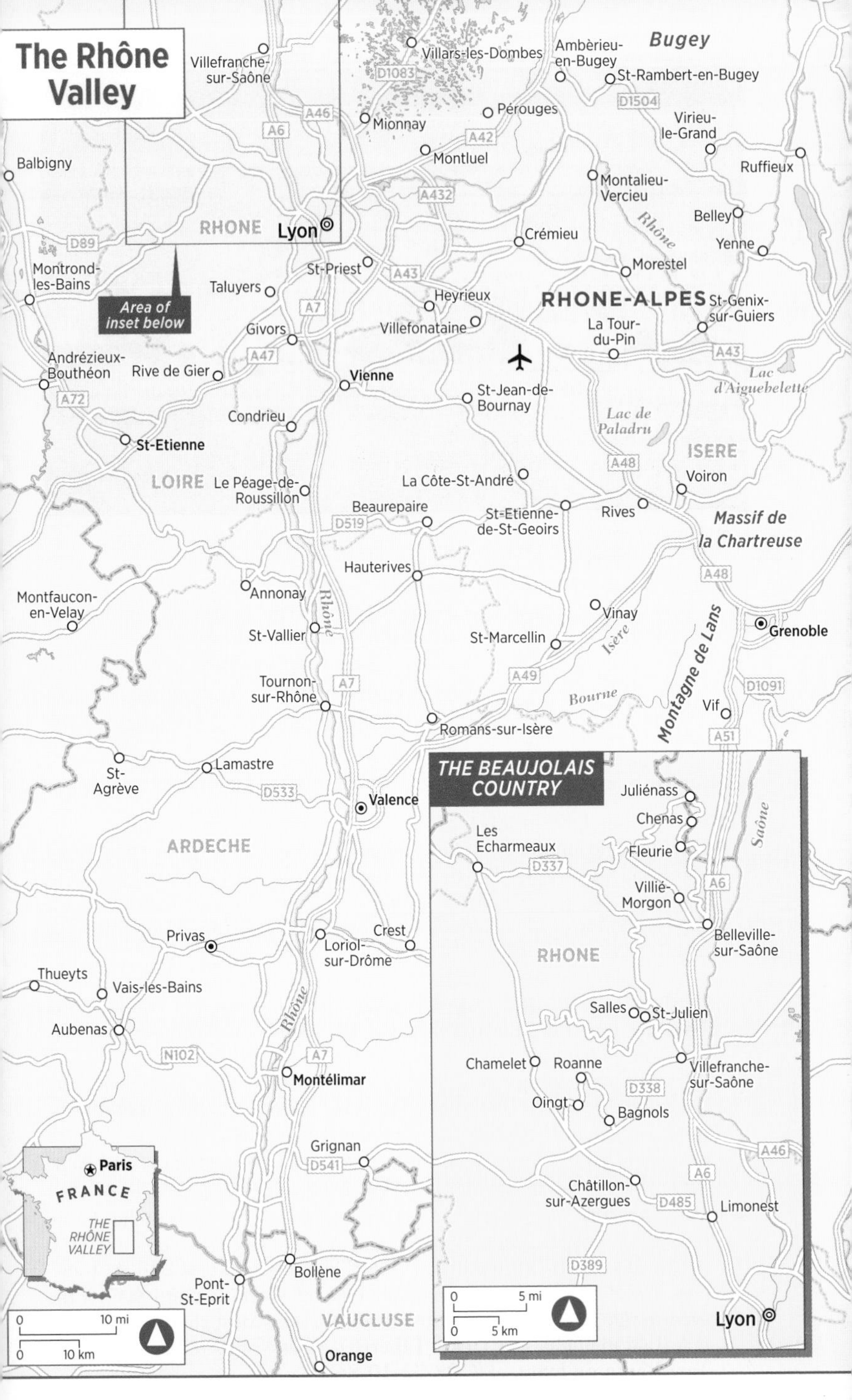

The Rhône Valley
Villefranche-sur-Saône
Villars-les-Dombes
Ambèrieu-en-Bugey
Bugey
St-Rambert-en-Bugey
D1083
D1504
A46
A6
Mionnay
Pérouges
A42
Virieu-le-Grand
Montluel
Ruffieux
Balbigny
Montalieu-Vercieu
A432
Rhône
Belley
RHONE
Lyon
D89
Crémieu
Yenne
Montrond-les-Bains
St-Priest
A43
Morestel
Taluyers
Heyrieux
RHONE-ALPES
St-Genix-sur-Guiers
Area of inset below
A7
Givors
Villefonataine
La Tour-du-Pin
A47
A43
Andrézieux-Bouthéon
Rive de Gier
Vienne
Lac d'Aiguebelette
St-Jean-de-Bournay
A72
Condrieu
Lac de Paladru
St-Etienne
ISERE
A48
LOIRE
Le Péage-de-Roussillon
La Côte-St-André
Voiron
Beaurepaire
St-Etienne-de-St-Geoirs
Rives
Massif de la Chartreuse
D519
Hauterives
A48
Annonay
Montfaucon-en-Velay
Vinay
Grenoble
St-Vallier
St-Marcellin
Isère
Montagne de Lans
A49
Tournon-sur-Rhône
A7
D1091
Bourne
Vif
Romans-sur-Isère
A51
St-Agrève
Lamastre
D533
Valence
ARDECHE
Privas
Crest
Loriol-sur-Drôme
Thueyts
Vais-les-Bains
Aubenas
N102
A7
Montélimar
Grignan
D541
Paris
FRANCE
THE RHÔNE VALLEY
Bollène
Pont-St-Esprit
VAUCLUSE
Orange
0 10 mi
0 10 km
THE BEAUJOLAIS COUNTRY
Juliénass
Chenas
Les Echarmeaux
Fleurie
Saône
D337
A6
Villié-Morgon
Belleville-sur-Saône
RHONE
Salles
St-Julien
Chamelet
Roanne
Villefranche-sur-Saône
D338
Oingt
Bagnols
A46
A6
Châtillon-sur-Azergues
D485
Limonest
D389
0 5 mi
0 5 km
Lyon

Lyon along the Rhône.

Nightlife & Entertainment Grab the weekly guide *Lyon-Poche* at a newsstand for a list of events and venues around town. The Opéra de Lyon presents opera, concerts, and ballets in a modernized version of the 19th-century opera house. Dance the night away at popular **Le First Tendency**, a disco housed in the old Les Brotteaux train station. Wind down your evening in a cozy wine bar, such as **La Cave des Voyageurs**, and sample the best from Burgundy, Beaujolais, and the Rhône Valley.

Essentials

GETTING THERE If you're arriving from the north by **train,** don't get off at Lyon's first station, Gare La Part-Dieu; continue to Gare de Perrache, where you can begin sightseeing. The high-speed TGV takes only 2 hours from Paris; the one-way fare is 60€ to 80€. Lyon makes a good stopover en route to the Alps or the Riviera. For information, call ✆ **08-92-35-35-35** or visit www.voyages-sncf.com.

By **plane,** it's a 45-minute flight from Paris to Aéroport Saint-Exupéry (✆ **08-26-80-08-26**), 25km (16 miles) east of the city. A 30-minute **tram** links the airport to the city center for 13€. **Taxis** cost about 40€ and take the same amount of time.

If you're **driving** from Paris, head southeast on A8/E1 into Lyon. From Nice, head west on E1/A7 toward Aix-en-Provence, continuing northwest toward Avignon. Bypass the city and continue north along the same route into Lyon. From Grenoble or the French Alps, head northwest on A48 to A43, which will take you northwest into Lyon.

GETTING AROUND A network of Métro lines, trams, and buses branches out to serve the city. A *plan de poche* (pocket map) is available at any office of **TCL** (✆ **08-20-42-70-00;** www.tcl.fr), which handles all forms of mass transport. Tickets are valid on all forms of public transport, costing 1.60€ for the average ride or else 14€ for a *carnet* of 10 tickets. Most short-time visitors may want to purchase a **Ticket Liberté** day pass for 4.80€. For a cab, call **Taxi Radio de Lyon,** at ✆ **08-72-10-86-86.**

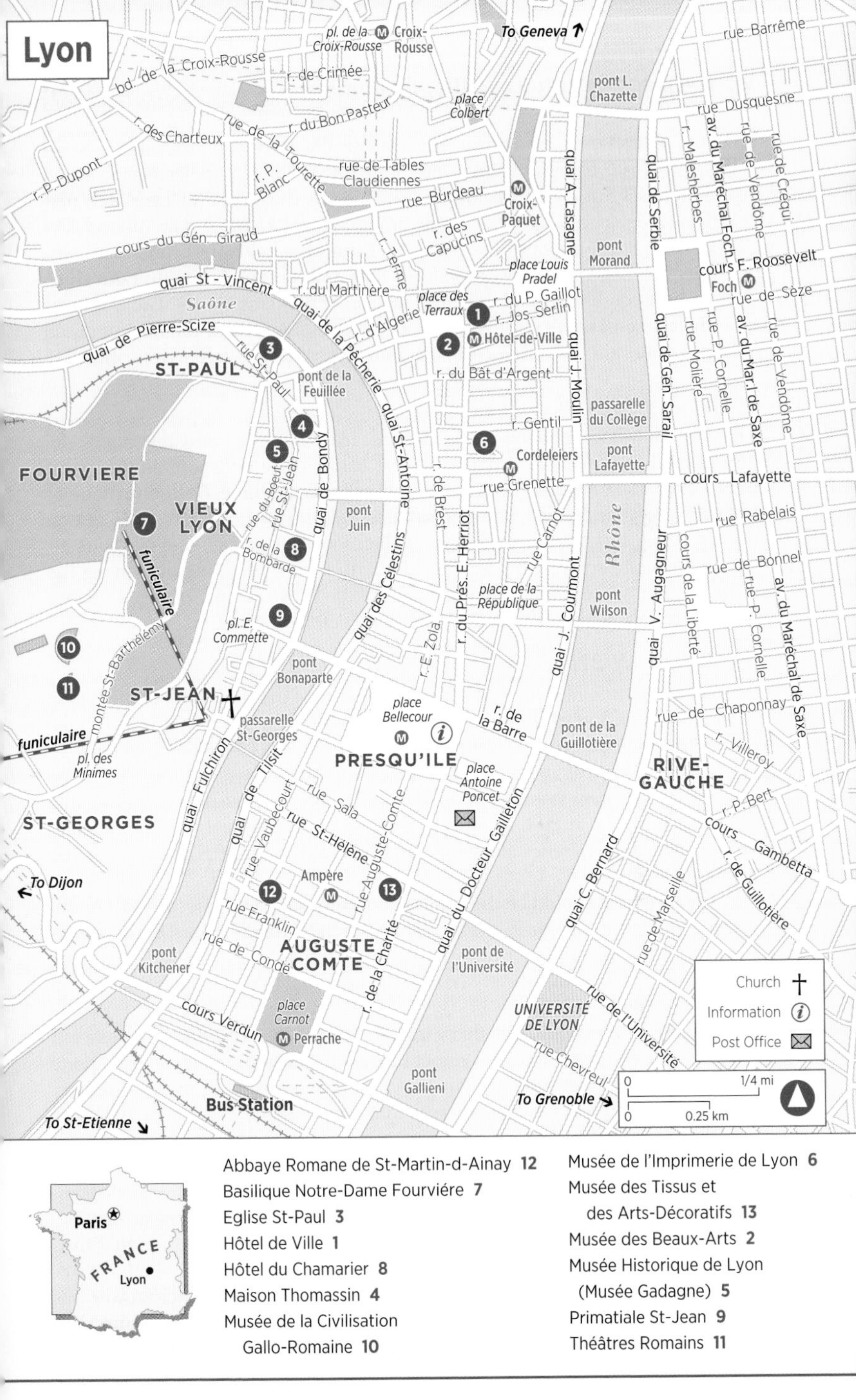
Lyon
To Geneva
pl. de la Croix-Rousse
Croix-Rousse
bd. de la Croix-Rousse
r. de Crimée
rue Barrême
pont L. Chazette
place Colbert
r. du Bon Pasteur
r. des Charteux
rue de la Tourette
rue Dusquesne
r. P. Dupont
r. P. Blanc
rue de Tables Claudiennes
rue Burdeau
Croix-Paquet
quai A. Lasagne
quai de Serbie
r. Malesherbes
av. du Maréchal Foch
rue de Vendôme
rue de Créqui
cours du Gén. Giraud
r. des Capucins
r. Terme
pont Morand
place Louis Pradel
cours F. Roosevelt
Foch
rue de Sèze
quai St-Vincent
r. du Martinère
place des Terraux
r. du P. Gaillot
r. Jos. Serlin
Saône
quai de la Pêcherie
r. d'Algerie
quai de Pierre-Scize
Hôtel-de-Ville
quai J. Moulin
quai de Gén. Sarail
rue Molière
rue P. Corneille
av. du Mar.l de Saxe
rue de Vendôme
ST-PAUL
rue St-Paul
pont de la Feuillée
r. du Bât d'Argent
passarelle du Collège
r. Gentil
quai St-Antoine
FOURVIERE
rue du Boeuf
rue St-Jean
quai de Bondy
Cordeleiers
pont Lafayette
cours Lafayette
rue Grenette
r. de Brest
VIEUX LYON
pont Juin
rue Carnot
Rhône
rue Rabelais
r. de la Bombarde
funiculaire
quai des Célestins
r. du Prés. E. Herriot
place de la République
quai J. Courmont
pont Wilson
quai V. Augagneur
cours de la Liberté
rue de Bonnel
rue P. Corneille
av. du Maréchal de Saxe
pl. E. Commette
montée St-Barthélémy
r. E. Zola
pont Bonaparte
ST-JEAN
passarelle St-Georges
place Bellecour
r. de la Barre
pont de la Guillotière
rue de Chaponnay
r. Villeroy
pl. des Minimes
PRESQU'ILE
place Antoine Poncet
RIVE-GAUCHE
quai Fulchiron
quai de Tilsit
rue Sala
rue Vaubecourt
rue St-Hélène
rue Auguste-Comte
quai du Docteur Gailleton
quai C. Bernard
r. P. Bert
cours Gambetta
r. de Guillotière
ST-GEORGES
To Dijon
Ampère
rue Franklin
rue de Marseille
pont Kitchener
rue de Condé
AUGUSTE COMTE
r. de la Charité
pont de l'Université
cours Verdun
place Carnot
Perrache
UNIVERSITÉ DE LYON
rue de l'Université
rue Chevreul
pont Gallieni
Church
Information
Post Office
To Grenoble
0
1/4 mi
0
0.25 km
Bus Station
To St-Etienne
Paris
FRANCE
Lyon
Abbaye Romane de St-Martin-d-Ainay 12
Basilique Notre-Dame Fourviére 7
Eglise St-Paul 3
Hôtel de Ville 1
Hôtel du Chamarier 8
Maison Thomassin 4
Musée de la Civilisation Gallo-Romaine 10
Musée de l'Imprimerie de Lyon 6
Musée des Tissus et des Arts-Décoratifs 13
Musée des Beaux-Arts 2
Musée Historique de Lyon (Musée Gadagne) 5
Primatiale St-Jean 9
Théâtres Romains 11

VISITOR INFORMATION The **Office de Tourisme** is on place Bellecour (✆ **04-72-77-69-69;** fax 04-78-42-04-32; www.lyon-france.com).

SPECIAL EVENTS Festivals take place practically every day, especially in summer. Music festivals reign supreme, with the most popular occurring on France's **Fête de la Musique,** which turns the streets of Lyon into performance spaces for local bands around June 21. For 4 days around December 8, the spectacular **Fête des Lumières** lights up Lyon's churches, monuments, and neighborhoods. In June and July, the **Nuits de Fourvière** festival combines music, theater, dance, and cinema in the Gallo-Roman theaters on Fourvière hill—prices depend on the act and can be purchased by phone at ✆ **04-72-32-00-00** (info at www.nuits-de-fourviere.org).

Exploring the City

The city sprawls over many miles, divided, like Paris, into *arrondissements.* Its heart straddles the Saône, around the east bank's place Bellecour and the west bank's Primatiale St-Jean. Begin your tour of Lyon at **Place Bellecour,** one of France's largest and most charming squares. A statue of Louis XIV looks out on the encircling 18th-century buildings. Urban sociologists are proud of Lyon's efforts to decorate some of its drab facades with *trompe l'oeil* murals. Among the most frequently cited works are the facade of the Musée Tony Garnier, 4 rue des Serpollières, 8e, and the fresco "des Lyonnais célèbres" in the 2e.

IN VIEUX LYON ★★★

From place Bellecour, walk across pont Bonaparte to the right bank of the Saône River and **Vieux Lyon.** (From elsewhere in the city, you can take bus 28 or take the Métro to Vieux Lyon.) Covering about a square mile, Old Lyon contains an amazing collection of medieval and Renaissance buildings, which helped the city attain UNESCO status in 1998. After years of existence as a slum, the area is now fashionable, attracting antiques dealers, artisans, weavers, sculptors, and painters who depict scenes along the **rue du Boeuf,** one of the most interesting streets for exploring.

Your first stop should be the cathedral, **Primatiale St-Jean** (p. 445). North of the cathedral is the most historically and architecturally evocative neighborhood of Old Lyon, with narrow streets, spiral stairs, hanging gardens, soaring towers, and unusual courtyards whose balconies seem to perch precariously atop medieval pilings or columns.

One architectural aspect that's unique to Lyon is its *traboules,* a series of short covered passageways that connect longer avenues running parallel to one another. Scattered throughout Vieux Lyon, they're capped with vaulted masonry ceilings. They often open unexpectedly into flower-ringed courtyards. Ask for a map at the tourist office.

Try to see the Gothic arcades of the 16th-century **Maison Thomassin,** place du Change, and the 16th-century **Hôtel du Chamarier,** 37 rue St-Jean, where Mme. de Sévigné lived. You can admire these buildings from the outside, but you are not allowed to enter. The neighborhood also contains **Eglise St-Paul,** 3 place Gerson (✆ **04-78-28-34-45**), consecrated in A.D. 549. Rebuilding began in 1084 after its destruction by the Saracens. Its octagonal lantern tower was completed in the 1100s, and the rest of the premises in the 13th century. You can visit Monday to Saturday noon to 6pm, Sunday 2 to 6pm, and admission is free. The tourism office offers guided *traboule* tours for 10€—call ahead for times.

Musée Historique de Lyon (Musée Gadagne) ★ This museum is in the Hôtel de Gadagne, an early-16th-century residence that has just completed a mammoth 10-year restoration. You'll find interesting Romanesque sculptures on the ground floor. Other exhibits include 18th-century Lyonnais furniture and pottery, antique ceramics from the town of Nevers, a pewter collection, and numerous paintings and engravings of Lyon.

In the same building is the **Musée de la Marionette** (same phone and hours), which has three puppets by Laurent Mourguet, creator of Guignol, the best-known French marionette character. The museum also displays marionettes from other parts of France (Amiens, Lille, and Aix-en-Provence) and from around the world.

Musée de la Marionette.

1 place du Petit-Collège. ✆ **04-78-42-03-61.** Admission (including Musée de la Marionette) 8€ adults, free students and children 17 and under. Wed–Sun 11am–6:30pm.

Primatiale St-Jean ★ This cathedral was built between the 12th and the 15th centuries, and its exceptional stained-glass windows date from the same era. Its apse is a masterpiece of Lyonnais Romanesque architecture. A highlight is the Flamboyant Gothic chapel of the Bourbons. On the front portals are medallions depicting the signs of the zodiac, the Creation, and the life of St. John. The cathedral's 16th-century clock is intricate and beautiful. It announces the hour daily at noon, 2, 3, and 4pm in grand style: A rooster crows, and angels herald the event. The treasury is in a wing called **La Manécanterie.** Entrance is free, and hours are Tuesday to Saturday 10am to noon and 2 to 6pm. The wing of the cathedral that houses the treasury is noted for the beauty and severe dignity of its 12th-century Romanesque facade. Its origins date to the 11th century, when it was established as a music school.

Place St-Jean. ✆ **04-78-92-82-29.** Free admission. Tues–Sun 9:30am–noon and 2–6pm.

IN FOURVIERE HILL ★

Rising to the west of Vieux Lyon is **Colline de Fourvière** (**Fourvière Hill;** www.fourviere.org). The wooded hill—home to numerous convents, colleges, and hospitals; two Roman theaters; and a superb Gallo-Roman museum—affords a panoramic vista of Lyon. You can see the city's many bridges across the two rivers, and the rooftops of the medieval town. In clear weather, you can even view the countryside extending to the snowcapped Alps.

Enthroned on the hill's summit is the 19th-century **Basilique Notre-Dame de Fourvière,** 8 place de Fourvière (✆ **04-78-25-13-01**), rising fortresslike with four octagonal towers and crenelated walls. Colored mosaics cover its interior, and an ancient chapel adjoins the church. A gilded statue of the Virgin surmounts the belfry. Admission is free; it's open daily 8am to 7pm.

Jardin du Rosaire extends along the hillside between the basilica and the 13th-century Primatiale St-Jean. It's open daily 6:30am to 9:30pm and promises a scenic walk. You'll see a vast shelter for up to 200 pilgrims. The area can also be reached via a pair of cable-driven **funiculars** that run every 10 minutes from a point immediately adjacent to the Métro station in Vieux Lyon to the top of Fourvière Hill. Priced at 2.40€ each way, they run daily between 5am and midnight.

Théâtres Romains, 7 rue du Cirque and 1 Montée de Fourvière (✆ **04-74-85-39-23**), a Roman theater-odeum complex, is in a park south of the basilica. The theater is the most ancient in France, built by order of Augustus from 17 to 15 B.C. and expanded during the reign of Hadrian. The odeum, reserved for musical performances, was once sumptuously decorated; its orchestra floor still contains mosaics of marble and porphyry. The third building was dedicated in A.D. 160 to the goddess Cybele, or Sibella. Only the building's foundations remain. The site is open from 7am until sunset, and entrance is free. Performances are given at both theaters in June and July during Les Nuits de Fourvière, when dance recitals, concerts, and plays are staged atop Fourvière Hill; prices depend on the performance—make reservations at ✆ **04-72-32-00-00.**

An altar dedicated to a bull cult and a marble statue of a goddess are on display in the **Musée de la Civilisation Gallo-Romaine,** 17 rue Cléberg (✆ **04-72-38-49-30**), near the archaeological site. The museum's collection of Gallo-Roman artifacts is the finest in France outside Paris. The site is open Tuesday through Sunday 10am to 6pm. Admission is 7€ adults, 4.50€ students, free for ages 17 and under. Entrance is free on Thursday. Guides are available on Sundays and holidays at 3pm.

Théâtres Romains.

ELSEWHERE AROUND THE CITY

In addition to the sites below, you can visit Lyon's oldest church, the 1107 **Abbaye Romaine de St-Martin-d'Ainay,** 11 rue Bourgelat (✆ **04-72-40-02-50**), south of place Bellecour, near place Ampère. Admission is free; hours are daily 8:30am to noon and 2:30 to 6pm. The rue de l'Hôtel-de-Ville extends north from place Bellecour to **place des Terreaux,** dominated by one of the most beautiful of Europe's city halls, the 1746 **Hôtel de Ville.** Its outside is dark and severe; the brilliant interior is closed to the public.

L'Institut & Musée Lumière Film buffs from all over the world come here. The famous Lumière family, including Antoine (1840–1911), Auguste (1862–1954), and Louis (1864–1948), once lived in Lyon. The brothers were chemists, industrialists, and motion-picture pioneers. In Lyon, they founded a factory for producing photographic plates, paper, and chemicals. They invented the Lumière process of color photography and the Cinématographe, an early motion picture camera, in 1895. They produced films, including *La Sortie des Usines Lumière,* released in 1895 and considered the first movie. The complex is dedicated to the memory of the innovators and is a living museum of cinema. Early films are shown, and books, photos, posters, and pre-cinematographic and cinematographic equipment are on display.

25 rue du Premier Film. ✆ **04-78-78-18-95.** www.institut-lumiere.org. Admission 6€ adults, 5€ students and children 7–18, free for children 6 and under. Tues–Sun 11am–6:30pm. Métro: Montplaisir-Lumière.

Musée de l'Imprimerie de Lyon Occupying a 15th-century mansion, this museum is devoted to Lyon's role in the world of printing. Exhibits include a page from a Gutenberg Bible, 17th- to 20th-century presses, 16th- to 19th-century woodcuts, and engravings. This is one of the most important printing museums in Europe, along with those at Mainz and Antwerp. It has a collection of books from "all epochs," including *incunabula,* books printed before Easter 1500.

13 rue de la Poulaillerie. ✆ **04-78-37-65-98.** Admission 5€ adults, free for 26 and under. Wed–Sun 9:30am–noon and 2–6pm.

Musée des Beaux-Arts ★★ On the south side of place des Terreaux stands the Palais des Arts (also called the Musée de St-Pierre). The former Benedictine abbey was built between 1659 and 1685 in the Italian baroque style. Today it is home to the Musée des Beaux-Arts, which has an outstanding collection of paintings and sculpture. You enter through a courtyard graced with statuary and shade trees, and the ground floor showcases an array of 14th-century paintings. The collection also includes Etruscan, Egyptian, Phoenician, Sumerian, and Persian art. Of special note is Perugino's altarpiece. The top floor holds one of France's richest 19th-century collections, with works by artists from Veronese, Tintoretto, and Rubens to Braque, Bonnard, and Picasso. Be sure to see Joseph Chinard's bust of Mme. Récamier, the Lyon beauty who charmed Napoleonic Paris by merely reclining, and the Fantin-Latour masterpiece *Reading.*

20 place des Terreaux. ✆ **04-72-10-17-40.** Admission 6€ adults, 4€ for students and children. Wed–Thurs and Sat–Mon 10am–6pm; Fri 10:30am–6pm.

Musée des Tissus et des Arts-Décoratifs ★★★ In the 1739 Lacroix-Laval mansion by Soufflot (architect of the Panthéon in Paris), the Musée des Arts-Décoratifs contains furniture and objets d'art from the 17th and 18th centuries.

The medieval and Renaissance periods are also represented. Look for a five-octave clavecin by Donzelague, the 18th-century creator of musical instruments.

Next door, in the 1730 Palais de Villeroy, is an even more interesting collection. On view are 2,000 years of priceless fabrics from around the world. Some of the finest fabrics made in Lyon from the 18th century to the present are displayed. The 15th- and 16th-century textiles embroidered with religious motifs are noteworthy, as are the 17th-century Persian carpets. Look for the partridge-motif brocade from Marie Antoinette's bedchamber at Versailles, as well as a 150-color brocaded satin woven for Queen Victoria, which is decorated with birds of paradise and orchids.

34 rue de la Charité. ✆ **04-78-38-42-00.** Admission 7€ adults, 4.50€ students, free for children 11 and under. Tues–Sun 10am–noon and 2–5:30pm. Métro: Ampère.

OUTSIDE THE HEART OF THE CITY

One of Lyon's grandest archaeological sites is **Amphithéâtre des Trois-Gauls,** rue du Jardin-des-Plantes, Croix-Rousse (no phone), near the city's northern perimeter. You can view the site only from the outside. At the time of its construction, it was the centerpiece of Condate, a Gallic village that predated the arrival of the Romans by centuries. Various accounts have members of Gallic tribes meeting here in the earliest example of a parliamentary system. Based on that information, France's 2,000th anniversary was celebrated in Lyon in 1989.

On the opposite side of the Rhône, you can explore Lyon's largest public park and garden, the 105-hectare (259-acre) **Parc de la Tête d'Or** (✆**04-78-89-02-03**). Its largest entrance is on boulevard des Belges. It opened in 1857 and has all the fountains, pedestrian walkways, and statues you'd expect. Surrounded by wealthy neighborhoods, the park has a lake, a zoo, a botanic garden with greenhouses, and a rose garden with some 100,000 plants. It's open daily 6:30am to 10pm (until 8:30pm Oct–Apr). Entrance is free.

At Rochetaillée-sur-Saône, 11km (6¾ miles) north of Lyon on D433, the **Musée Français de l'Automobile "Henri Malartre"** is in the Château de Rochetaillée, 645 rue du Musée (✆**04-78-22-18-80**). The château was built in 1131 on even older foundations and rebuilt in the 1400s. The curators are proud of the majestic 15th-century staircase, the Romanesque gateway that's part of the original 12th-century design, and a policy that permits photography, smoking, and any motorcycle-fetish garb you care to wear while admiring the collection of vehicles. The collection includes 100 cars dating to 1890, 65 motorcycles from 1903 and after, and 40 bicycles from 1818 and later. Admission to the museum and château is 6€ adults, and free for ages 25 and under. It is open Tuesday through Sunday 9am to 5pm (until 7pm July–Aug). From Lyon, take bus no. 40 or 70.

Shopping

The third-largest city in France offers an array of retail outlets. For boutiques, art galleries, and artists' studios, head to Vieux Lyon and the area around rue de la République, rue Victor Hugo, rue Mercière, and quai St-Antoine. Antiques dealers concentrate around rue Auguste-Comte as it approaches place Bellecour. Also consider venturing to the **Cité des Antiquaires,** 117 bd. Stalingrad (✆**04-72-69-00-00**), with more than 100 dealers spread over two floors, and merchandise from the 18th century to the 1950s. It's open Thursday through Sunday from 10am to 7pm.

Lyon is a bastion of fashion. The densest concentrations of retail shops are along rue Emile Zola, rue de Président-Herriot, and place Kléber. For chic women's couture that rivals anything you'll find in Paris, try **George Rech,** 59 rue du Président-Herriot (✆ **04-78-37-82-90**). More than 235 shops and boutiques fill the largest shopping center in Lyon, the **Centre Commercial de la Part-Dieu,** 17 rue du Dr-Bouchut (✆ **04-72-60-60-62**). Although Lyon is not the major silk center that it used to be, it is home to several silk manufacturers. You'll see a good selection of silk scarves, ties, sashes, and squares at **Hermès,** 96 rue du Président-Herriot (✆ **04-78-42-25-14**). For exquisite jewelry, visit **Joïa** at 4 rue Childebert (✆ **04-72-77-56-66**).

Bernachon, 42 cours Franklin-Roosevelt (✆ **04-78-24-37-98**), is home to Lyon's best chocolates and pastries. Here you'll find 30 varieties of bite-size pastries known as mini-gâteaux, 30 varieties of petits fours, and even dark, rich chocolates lightly dusted with 24-karat gold. The Bernachon store houses a small restaurant and tearoom, **Bernachon Passion** (✆ **04-78-52-23-65**). For wine, visit **Antic Wine,** one of the best and most amusing wine shops in France, at 18 Rue du Boeuf (✆ **04-78-37-08-96**).

Where to Stay

Alain Chapel (p. 451) also rents rooms.

EXPENSIVE

Hôtel la Cour des Loges ★★★ This luxury hotel in Old Lyon occupies four connected houses dating from the 15th and 16th centuries. Among its allures are a rooftop bar and garden, an indoor pool, and a magnificent loggia-ringed courtyard. Most of its beautifully furnished rooms and suites face gardens, the square, or a large, sunny lobby. The size and configuration of the rooms vary, but all are lavishly decorated. Most of the immaculate tiled bathrooms have both tub and shower. The staff, Lyon's savviest, is courteous and efficient.

2–8 rue du Boeuf, Vieux Lyon 69005. www.courdesloges.com. ✆ **04-72-77-44-44.** Fax 04-72-40-93-61. 61 units. 204€–240€ double; 505€–618€ suite. AE, DC, MC, V. Parking 35€. Métro: St-Jean. **Amenities:** 2 restaurants; bar; indoor pool; room service; sauna. *In room:* A/C, TV, hair dryer, minibar, free Wi-Fi.

Villa Florentine ★★★ Conveniently located in Vieux Lyon, this Relais & Châteaux hotel is as stunning as the Cour des Loges (see above). One of the great city hotels along the Rhône, it is a bastion of taste and luxury. The views from the lounges, terraces, and guest rooms are the most panoramic in town. Converted from a 17th-century convent, the building retains many of its original Italianate architectural details. The accommodations are spacious and comfortable, decorated in a style that blends modern Italian design with Renaissance reproductions. A nine-unit annex, just across the street, features rooms and suites that are a bit larger and more modern than those within the hotel's original core.

25 montée Saint Barthélemy, Lyon 69005. www.villaflorentine.com. ✆ **04-72-56-56-56.** Fax 04-72-40-90-56. 28 units. 250€ double; 415€–465€ junior suite; 515€–565€ suite. AE, DC, MC, V. Parking 18€. **Amenities:** Restaurant; bar; babysitting; exercise room; heated outdoor pool; room service; sauna; mini spa. *In room:* A/C, TV, hair dryer, minibar, free Wi-Fi.

MODERATE

Hôtel Globe et Cécil Near place Bellecour, this hotel is a good value, thanks to its location and attentive, friendly staff. Built as a private mansion during

France's 19th-century Gilded Age, it became a hotel in 1875. Today the calm, family-run, six-story property (with elevator) is a government-rated three-star staple. Some of the individually decorated rooms are old-fashioned and charmingly dowdy; others are more modern and efficient. Many restaurants are nearby.

21 rue Gasparin, Lyon 69002. www.globeetcecilhotel.com. 60 units. ✆ **04-78-42-58-95.** Fax 04-72-41-99-06. 140€–170€ double. Rates include breakfast. AE, DC, MC, V. Métro: Bellecour. **Amenities:** Room service. *In room:* A/C, TV, hair dryer, free Wi-Fi.

Le Phénix Hotel ★★ Overlooking the Saône in Vieux Lyon, this hotel dates in part from the 16th century, when it was a meeting place for theatrical troupes. Today the old structure has been joined with other buildings to create this atmospheric choice with its original Florentine architectural design. Tradition has been respected, but modern touches have been added in all the bedrooms. Rooms are intimate and decorated in warm colors with stylish furnishings; bathrooms have tub/showers.

7 quai de Bondy, Lyon 69005. ✆ **04-78-28-24-24.** Fax 04-78-28-62-86. 36 units. 85€–150€ double. AE, DC, MC, V. Parking 15€. **Amenities:** Bar; room service. *In room:* TV, hair dryer, minibar, free Wi-Fi.

INEXPENSIVE

Collège Hôtel The accommodations here, which adopt a tongue-in-cheek theme of a university dorm, are not the spartan affair you might expect; in fact, they are comfortable and include a number of attractive features. Located on the right bank of the Saône within the heart of Vieux Lyon, Collège Hôtel offers 39 small but well-furnished bedrooms with immaculate linens and a choice of modern bathrooms (the best ones are the corner units with hand-held showers, and the top two floors have stunning city views). Many of the trendy, all-white bedrooms open onto private terraces or balconies. Each floor has a 1960s vintage refrigerator from which "boarders" can help themselves to free nonalcoholic drinks. Best of all is the rooftop garden terrace with a "gym" that humorously reflects the French distaste for exercise. As soon as night falls, the hotel's 130 windows light up as part of a unique light show, enhancing the magnificent 1930s facade.

5 place Saint Paul, Lyon 69005. www.college-hotel.com. ✆ **04-72-10-05-05.** Fax 04-78-27-98-84. 39 units. 125€ double. AE, MC, V. Parking 15€. **Amenities:** Bar (w/an impressive selection of wines by the glass); library. *In room:* A/C, TV, free Wi-Fi.

Hôtel Bayard The foundations of this dignified townhouse date from the 16th century. Guest rooms are decorated in romantic French style with creative modern touches. Each room is outfitted in a style inspired by a period of French history. Most of the compact bathrooms have showers and tubs. You enter the hotel through a narrow hallway and climb one flight of stairs to the reception area. Don't be put off by the staff members, who may appear detached.

23 place Bellecour, Lyon 69002. www.hotelbayard.fr. ✆ **04-78-37-39-64.** Fax 04-72-40-95-51. 22 units. 79€–159€ double. AE, MC, V. Parking 20€ (call ahead). Métro: Bellecour. *In room:* TV, hair dryer, free Wi-Fi.

Hôtel Saint Paul "Two-star rating, four-star service" says the Saint Paul's owner, referring the French hotel rating system. He's not kidding; along with city knowledge to rival the concierges a few doors down at the Cour des Loges, the people who work here clearly love Lyon and are happy to give you a full, friendly rundown on where to go and what to do, particularly when it comes to food. Rooms, some with exposed ceiling beams or vaulted ceilings, are simply furnished while still allowing a sense of place.

6 rue Lainière, Lyon 69005. www.hotelsaint-paul.com. ✆ **04-78-28-13-29.** Fax 04-72-00-97-27. 20 units. 75€ double. AE, DC, MC, V. Métro: Hôtel de Ville. *In room:* TV, hair dryer, free Wi-Fi.

Where to Eat

The food in Lyon is among the finest in the world—with prices to match. However, we've found that a person of moderate means can often afford the most reasonable fixed-price menu even in the priciest establishments, and many smaller establishments are racing to fill the quality/price gap. *Bouchons,* Lyon's version of the bistro, featuring hearty fare like pike quenelles, tripe, and other offal, are a city hallmark, and though the quality of the genre may be in decline, there are still many outlets to find the food they've made famous.

VERY EXPENSIVE

Alain Chapel ★★ MODERN FRENCH This Relais Gourmand property occupies a 19th-century postal station that has evolved into a comfortable, stylish restaurant and lodging. Alain Chapel was one of the world's premier chefs, and after his death, many claimed that the reputation of his restaurant would falter. That hasn't been the case. Chef Philippe Jousse, who trained under Chapel, helps maintain Lyon's status as a gastronomic capital. Menu items served within a rustically antique-looking setting change with the seasons but are likely to include lobster salad with pigeon necks and black truffles; Bresse chicken cooked in a pig's bladder, stuffed with foie gras, and drizzled with foie gras sauce; puff pastry with apples and vanilla-flavored bourbon sauce and champagne-flavored sorbet; and a particularly appealing assortment of unusual local cheeses, charmingly presented.

Alain Chapel also has 12 beautiful guest rooms; a double runs 130€ to 150€.

60 rte. de Bourg, Mionnay 01390. ✆ **04-78-91-82-02.** Fax 04-78-91-82-37. www.alainchapel.fr. Reservations required. Main courses 42€–60€; fixed-price lunch Wed–Thurs 58€; fixed-price dinners start at 130€ and depend on the market. AE, DC, MC, V. Wed–Thurs and Sat–Sun noon–1pm; Wed–Sun 7:30–10pm. Closed Jan and 1 week in Aug. Take N83 20km (12 miles) north of Lyon.

Les Loges ★ FRENCH This hotel restaurant originated with lofty ambitions, a celebrity chef, and a flurry of promotion. In 2003, it dropped the pretense and gradually evolved into a desirable—albeit not particularly cutting-edge—dining room. Chef Anthony Bonnet's flavorful food is beautifully prepared and served in generous portions—well-executed fare that you'd expect from a top-notch steakhouse or hotel dining room. It's a stunning candlelit setting with Renaissance-era stone walls, wrought iron, and ornate crystal chandeliers. You may begin with seared foie gras or marinated scallops and continue with lamb with shallots *confit,* or roasted quail in a succulent mixture of herbs and its own juices. Finish with cheese from master cheesemonger Hervé Mons.

In the Hôtel la Cour des Loges, 6 rue du Boeuf. ✆ **04-72-77-44-44.** Reservations recommended. Main courses 35€–39€; fixed-price menu 68€–85€. AE, DC, MC, V. Tues–Sat 7:30–9:30pm; Sun 12:30–2:30pm.

Paul Bocuse ★★★ LYONNAIS Whether the namesake chef is on-site or not, the standards of this restaurant continue to reach for the skies. Paul Bocuse is one of the world's most famous chefs, and serious Parisian foodies take the TGV from Paris just to dine at this citadel of haute cuisine. He specializes in regional cuisine, though long ago he was the leading exponent of nouvelle cuisine (which he later called "a joke"). Because Bocuse, who is now in his 80s, is gone at least part of the time, other chefs carry on with the mass production (for up to 180 diners) of the signature dishes that the master created. There isn't a lot of room for variation. Tired of the conventional facades of most French restaurants, Bocuse commissioned a local artist to paint the history of French cuisine. The tale begins in the 1700s and proceeds through the years to its "defining moment"—a depiction of Bocuse himself.

You can begin your meal with the famous black-truffle soup and then try one of the most enduring dishes in the Bocuse repertoire: Bresse chicken cooked in a pig's bladder. Other options include roast pigeon in puff pastry with baby cabbage leaves, and red snapper served in a potato casing.

40 quai de la Plage, Pont de Collonges, Collonges-au-Mont-d'Or. ✆ **04-72-42-90-90.** www.bocuse.fr. Reservations required as far in advance as possible. Main courses 48€–84€; fixed-price menu 130€–220€. AE, DC, MC, V. Daily noon–1:30pm and 8–9:30pm. Closed Christmas and New Year's Day. Take N433 9km (5½ miles) north of Lyon.

MODERATE

Les Adrets LYONNAIS How this place stays under the radar is a mystery. Chef Jean-Luc Wesolowski has created a hidden institution in the heart of Lyon, adeptly blending the best of *bouchon* and high-end bistro fare that is an impressive value. Try poached eggs with cèpes in cream or creamy pumpkin soup with tiny scallops. Follow them with grilled turbot with a veal *jus,* or duck breast with roasted peaches. At 16€ including wine, the lunch prix fixe is one of Lyon's best deals.

30 rue du Boeuf. ✆ **04-78-38-24-30.** Reservations recommended. Main courses 13€–20€; fixed-price lunch with wine 16€, dinner 23€-45€. MC, V. Daily noon–2:30pm and 7pm–midnight. Mon–Fri noon–1:30pm and 7–9:30pm. Closed Aug. Métro: Cordelier.

M Restaurant ★★ FRENCH Chef/owner Julien Gautier is the darling of Lyon food critics, the most hard-to-please in France, teasing new tastes and flavors from the Rhône region's pungent foodstuffs. He continues to extend his repertoire and tantalize palates in his ultramodern dining room with colorful chairs and parquet flooring set off by a candelabrum created by famed Lyon designer Alain Vavry. Each plate that emerges from the kitchen seems to burst with flavor. Try the boneless chicken with foie gras, sweetbreads, and pickled vegetables appetizer. "It's all subject to change," says a smiling Gautier. "When I do one dish too long, I go crazy."

47 av. Foch. ✆ **04-78-89-55-19.** Reservations required. Main courses 18€–25€; fixed-price menu 24€–34€. AE, DC, MC, V. Mon–Fri noon–2pm and 7:30–10pm. Closed Aug 1–25 and 1 week in Feb.

INEXPENSIVE

Brasserie Georges ★ FRENCH With reasonable prices, an almost unbeatable dining room, and a list of brasserie classics that residents travel in from the suburbs for, visiting Georges is a must. It's the oldest brasserie in Lyon (founded in 1836) and probably the largest in Europe (with 450 seats). Turn-of-the-20th-

beaucoup DE BOCUSE

A resurgence of interest in chef Paul Bocuse swept across Lyon when Bocuse bought **Brasserie le Nord ★**, 18 rue Neuve, de Mon Plaisir (✆ **04-78-27-29-34**), where he had worked as a teenager. Its prices (20€–30€ for a main course) signaled that the last of the great chefs had finally decided to go for the mass market.

It's one of the most popular places in Lyon for traditional Lyonnais cuisine. A short while later, Bocuse opened a clone of Le Nord, **Brasserie le Sud,** 11 place Antonin Poncet (✆ **04-78-42-82-41**), where the culinary venue celebrates all points south (including Provence and, to a lesser degree, French-speaking North Africa) with a Mediterranean-inspired diet that includes tagines and couscous, and a color scheme of vivid blues and yellows. In 1998, he endorsed the opening of **Brasserie de l'Est,** 14 place Jules-Ferry (✆ **04-37-24-25-26**), a large, bustling place offering Pan-French cuisine and a noisy and animated ambience that evokes the *brasseries de gare* of faraway Paris. And finally, the Bocuse empire rounded out the four directions of the compass with the establishment of its final bistro, **La Brasserie de l'Ouest,** 1 Quai du Commerce (✆ **04-72-29-12-82**). Actually, its venue is more like the wild, wild American West (that is, California) than you may have expected. There's a hint of Pacific Rim cuisine here, and its layout is described as "American style," with an open kitchen, wide-open vistas, and a bustling theatricality. Each of the five is open for lunch and dinner daily. The latest to open is **La Brasserie d'Argençon,** 40 allée Pierre de Coubertin (✆ **04-72-73-72-73**), adjacent to the town's biggest soccer stadium, La Stade Gerland.

century French poet Lamartine still owes the restaurant 40 francs for a meal he consumed 100 years ago. If you thrill to nest where the proud and mighty have already nested, you can ask specifically for a table that is identified with a plaque as having hosted Ernest Hemingway, the Lumière brothers, Edith Piaf, Rodin, Jean-Paul Sartre, or Jules Verne. Other, more recent guests have included the Dalai Lama and former president Jacques Chirac. Specialties include roast beef, snails in garlic butter, heaping platters of choucroute, and grilled meats.

30 cours Verdun. ✆ **04-72-56-54-54.** www.brasseriegeorges.com. Main courses 15€–25€; fixed-price menus 20€–22€. AE, DC, MC, V. Daily 11:30am–11:15pm (until 12:15am Fri–Sat). Closed May 1. Métro: Perrache.

Café des Fédérations 🎁 FRENCH/LYONNAIS This is one of the busiest bistros in Lyon and sometimes the most amusingly raucous. Catering to the office-worker crowd, it's operated with panache by a team of hardworking employees who would probably perform beautifully in the trenches of a war zone. The fixed-price menus offer a selection of appetizers, main courses, and desserts. Each evokes old-time Lyonnais cuisine at its least pretentious, with such options as a green salad with bacon and croutons; eggs *en meurette* (poached in red wine); pork chops; and *andouillette* (tripe sausage) or other kinds of sausages, often served with a creamy potato gratin.

8 rue Major-Martin. ✆ **04-78-28-26-00.** Reservations recommended. Fixed-price lunch 19€, dinner 24€. V. Mon–Sat noon–2pm and 8–9:30pm. Closed 1 week in Jan. Métro: Hôtel-de-Ville.

Lyon After Dark

This cosmopolitan hub offers many entertainment and culture options. At any newsstand, pick up a copy of the weekly guide *Lyon-Poche,* which lists happenings and venues around town, from bars to classical concerts.

For the theater or opera buff, Lyon's **Théâtre des Célestins,** place des Célestins (✆ **04-72-77-40-00**), is the premier venue for comedy and drama, and the **Opéra,** place de la Comédie (✆ **08-26-30-53-25**), always has lively and diverse offerings. **Halle Tony Garnier,** 20 place Antonin Perrin (✆ **04-72-76-85-85**), originated as a 19th-century food market. The immense space with excellent acoustics is known for concerts, trade fairs, and art exhibitions.

The best pub in town is the **Smoking Dog,** 16 rue Lainerie (✆ **04-78-28-38-27**), a happy neighborhood bar with a mixed-age crowd.

The best of the former cargo boats parked on the Rhône is **Le Sirius,** Berges du Rhône, 4 quai Augagneur (✆ **04-78-71-78-71;** www.lesirius.com; Métro: Buillotière). An under-35 crowd packs the ship for dancing to the sounds of Lyon's best DJs on the lower-level floor. There's also an outdoor deck for fair weather. Sometimes big musical acts are booked here, at which time various cover charges are imposed. It's open Tuesday through Saturday from 6pm to 3am. **Le First Tendency,** 13 place Jules Ferry (✆ **04-78-52-90-72;** Métro: Brotteaux), is one of Lyon's most famous dance clubs, housed in the old Les Brotteaux train station.

As you may have expected in a city the size of Lyon, there are a scattering of busy and popular gay bars. Popular spots for men include **La Ruche,** 22 rue Gentil, 2e (✆ **04-78-37-42-26;** Métro: Cordelier); and **Le Forum,** 15 rue des Quatres Chapeaux, 2e (✆ **04-78-37-19-74;** Métro: Cordelier), in the city's historic core. One lesbian bar enjoying a certain vogue is **Le Domaine,** 9 rue du Jardin des Plantes (✆ **04-72-98-85-33;** www.ledomainebar.fr). Attracting a young, vibrant crowd, it's open daily 6pm to 3am.

THE BEAUJOLAIS COUNTRY ★★

The vineyards of Beaujolais start about 40km (25 miles) north of Lyon. This wine-producing region is small—64km (40 miles) long and less than 16km (10 miles) wide—yet it's one of the most famous in France. It's known throughout the world because of the Beaujolais wine craze that began in Paris some 30 years ago. In an average year, this region produces more than 190 million bottles of wine. Some 180 châteaux are scattered throughout this part of France. At many of them, you can sample and buy bottles of Beaujolais.

This region is a colorful and prosperous rural area, with vineyards on hillsides, winegrower's cottages, and historic houses and castles. It has been called the "Land of the Golden Stones," but don't expect architectural monuments.

Unlike Alsace, with its Route du Vin, the Beaujolais country doesn't have a defined route. You can branch off in any direction, stopping at whatever point or wine cellar intrigues you. Don't be worried about losing your way after meandering off the A6 superhighway. This is one of the easiest parts of eastern France to negotiate, with clear road signs. If you're in doubt, simply follow the signs to the region's capital and commercial center, Villefranche-sur-Saône.

If you're pressed for time, you can tie the highlights together in a one-way drive, beginning at Villefranche-sur-Saône, known as **Villefranche,** which you can reach from A6 between Mâcon and Lyon. (If you're heading north to south, follow the drive in reverse order, beginning in Juliénas, also off A6.)

Start in Villefranche. After an excursion west on D38 to **Bagnols-en-Beaujolais,** return to Villefranche. From here, take the meandering D504 and D20, which make sharp bends toward the east en route to **St-Julien-sous-Montmelas.** From St-Julien, take D19 to **Salles-en-Beaujolais.** From Salles, take D62 and D19 to **Belleville-sur-Saône.** Then follow D37 and D68 to **Villié-Morgon.** From Villié-Morgon, take D68 and D266 to **Juliénas.**

Villefranche-sur-Saône: Capital of Beaujolais

Go to the **Office du Tourisme,** 96 rue de la Sous-Prefecture, not far from the marketplace (✆ **04-74-07-27-50;** www.villefranche-beaujolais.fr), for a booklet on the Beaujolais country. It includes a map and itineraries, and lists the wine-tasting cellars open to the public. It also lists and details some 30 villages.

Bagnols-en-Beaujolais

To reach Bagnols from Villefranche, head west on D38.

WHERE TO STAY & EAT

Château de Bagnols-en-Beaujolais ★★★ This is lordly living on a grand scale. France's premier château hotel, this one-time Renaissance ruin has been restored by 400 artisans. It has been taken over by a British chain that owns such hotels as Lady Astor's former home, Cliveden, in England. As such, it attracts large numbers of British oenophiles. Antiques, paintings, and art, much from the 17th and 18th centuries, fill the mansion. The individually decorated guest rooms are sumptuous, with antique beds, period velvets, embroidered linen sheets, and down pillows; one unit is named for Mme. de Sévigné, who spent a restless night here in 1673. The bathrooms have tiled floors, brass fittings, and luxurious tubs. La Salle des Gardes, the dining area with cathedral-worthy stonework, serves elegant Beaujolais fare.

Place du Chateau, Bagnols 69620. www.chateaudebagnols.fr. ✆ **04-74-71-40-00.** Fax 04-74-71-40-49. 21 units. 235€–535€ double; from 350€–760€ suite. AE, DC, MC, V. **Amenities:** Restaurant; lounge; outdoor pool; room service. *In room:* TV, hair dryer, Wi-Fi (15€ per day).

St-Julien-sous-Montmelas

This charming village is 11km (6¾ miles) northwest of Villefranche (take D504, then D20). Claude Bernard, the father of physiology, was born here in 1813. His small stone house—now the **Musée Claude-Bernard** (✆ **04-74-67-51-44**)—exhibits the scholar's mementos, instruments, and books. Except for March, the museum is open year-round Wednesday to Saturday 2 to 6pm, Sunday 10am to noon and 2 to 6pm. Admission is 5€ for adults, 4€ for students, and 3€ for ages 16 and under.

Beaujolais Country landscape.

Salles-en-Beaujolais

Eglise de Salles Arbuissonnas ★ (✆ **04-74-03-40-88**) was begun in A.D. 1090 and completed in the 1700s. The religious hideaway is mostly Romanesque, with an occasional Gothic overlay, especially in its doorways. Connoisseurs of Romanesque architecture will love the golden ocher color of the limestone. Notice the Salle Capitulaire and its garden (reached by a side entrance), where the capitals of columns from throughout the building's history are on display; also note the one-armed clock above the altar. The church is open May to September daily 9am to 6pm, and October to April daily 9am to 5pm. Admission is free. From St-Julien, take D19 a short distance to Salles.

Belleville-sur-Saône

For an excellent dining experience, drive north from Salles on D19 and D62 to Belleville-sur-Saône.

WHERE TO EAT

Le Rhône au Rhin ★ MODERN FRENCH This out-of-the-way restaurant lies (1km/½ mile north of the village of Belleville-sur-Saône) in a converted antique house, as a refuge from the more congested regions. As you try the flavorful cuisine, you may surrender to the chef's escapist dream. The decor is contemporary and comfortable, outfitted in warm tones of brown and soft orange. Menu items change with the seasons but may include terrine of foie gras, scallops, or farm-raised chicken with morel mushrooms.

10 av. du Port. ✆ **04-74-66-16-23.** Reservations recommended. Main courses 18€–27€; fixed-price lunch 17€, dinner 18€–42€. MC, V. Tues–Sun noon–2pm; Tues and Thurs–Sat 7–9pm.

Villié-Morgon

For another wine tour in the Beaujolais country, we suggest driving west from Belleville-sur-Saône on D37, and then north on D18 to Villié-Morgon. The village and the surrounding region contain around 250 wine producers. Their product, at its best, is usually judged among the best Beaujolais wines in France.

In the basement of the **Château de Fontcrenne,** immediately adjacent to the Hôtel de Ville, is the **Caveau de Morgon** (✆ **04-74-04-20-99;** www.morgon.fr). It assembles and "marries" a selection of the Villié-Morgon region's best wines into a well-respected brand name (Caveau de Morgon) whose savvy marketing benefits winegrowers and consumers alike. Whatever you do, don't use the word *blend* to describe this company's product; the word is usually received with something akin to horror. The cellar is open for tours and sales daily 10am to noon and 2 to 6:15pm in winter, 10am to 12:15pm and 2 to 7:15pm in summer. You'll pay a nominal charge—1€ per glass, 7€ per bottle—for wine you consume. Admission is free. Closed first 3 weeks of January.

ROANNE

390km (242 miles) SE of Paris; 87km (54 miles) NW of Lyon

This industrial town on the left bank of the Loire is a popular excursion from Lyon and Vichy because it's home to one of France's greatest three-star restaurants, La Maison Troisgros (see "Where to Stay & Eat," below).

In a neoclassical mansion built at the end of the 18th century, **Musée Joseph Déchelette,** 22 rue Anatole-France (✆ **04-77-23-68-77**), showcases an exceptional collection of Italian and French earthenware from the 16th through 20th centuries, as well as Roanne earthenware. Hours are Wednesday to Monday 10am to noon and 2 to 6pm. On Sunday, the museum is open only in the afternoon, and on Saturday there is no noontime break. Admission is 4.50€ for adults, 2.50€ for students, free for ages 25 and under, and free for everyone on Wednesday afternoon.

Essentials

GETTING THERE **Trains** and some **buses** serve Roanne from nearby cities, notably Lyon, but the train is much more convenient. By train, Roanne lies 3 hours from Paris and 1 hour and 10 minutes from Lyon; for information, call ✆ **08-92-35-35-35** or visit www.voyages-sncf.com. If you're **driving,** follow N7 northwest from Lyon to Roanne. From Paris, follow A6 south to Nemours and continue southwest on N7.

VISITOR INFORMATION The **Office de Tourisme** is at place Maréchal de Lattre-de-Tassigny (✆ **04-77-71-51-77;** www.leroannais.com).

Where to Stay & Eat

La Maison Troisgros ★★★ FRENCH/LYONNAIS This Relais & Châteaux property is one of the top 10 restaurants in France. It attained that reputation in the 1950s and has since factored into the itineraries of globe-trotting foodies, visiting heads of state, and wealthy people touring the region. Come here with respect for the French *grande bourgeoisie* and the appeal of French culinary finesse. The place is too conservative and devoted to impeccably tailored service for anything radical or provocative.

Decorated in neutral colors and lined with contemporary artwork, the restaurant features superb cuisine at astronomical prices. The current keepers of the flame celebrate the bounty of the Lyonnais countryside. Some of the best dishes are sautéed foie gras served with marinated eggplant; oysters in turnips; king prawns with truffles; and boned monkfish with herbs and butter. To finish the meal, ask for one of the region's best assortments of cheese or perhaps a praline soufflé.

The hotel also rents 16 traditionally furnished rooms; a double costs 195€ to 570€, each with free Wi-Fi.

Place Jean Troisgros, Roanne 42300. www.troisgros.com. ✆ **04-77-71-66-97.** Fax 04-77-70-39-77. Reservations required. Main courses 60€–150€; fixed-price menu 90€ lunch, 160€–195€ dinner. AE, DC, MC, V. Thurs–Mon noon–1:30pm and 7:30–9pm. Closed Mon afternoons btw. Oct and Mar, 2 weeks in Feb, and 2 weeks in Aug.

Where to Stay & Eat Nearby

In the nearby village of **Le Coteau,** you'll find several worthy restaurants. These two are our favorites. To get there, take N7 3km (1¾ miles) south from the center of Roanne.

Auberge Costelloise ★★ FRENCH This is the place to head when you can't afford the dazzling but expensive food at Troisgros. Chef Christophe Suchon provides what this region needs: an attractive restaurant with fine cuisine and reasonable prices. The restaurant is adjacent to the banks of the headwaters of the Loire, in a dining room ringed with paintings and wood paneling. Choose one of the fixed-price menus, which change weekly. The well-planned menu focuses on fish. *Daurade* (bream) comes in garlic-flavored cream sauce, and red snapper is enhanced by Provençal pistou. You can order fine vintages of Burgundian wines by the pitcher.

2 av. de la Libération, Le Coteau 42120. ✆ **04-77-68-12-71.** www.auberge-costelloise.fr. Reservations required. Main courses 11€–32€; fixed-price lunch 19€–26€, dinner 26€–59€. AE, MC, V. Wed–Sun noon–1:30pm and 7:45–9:30pm. Closed mid-July to mid-Aug.

Hôtel-Restaurant des Lys TRADITIONAL FRENCH This *restaurant avec chambres* dates from around 1900, with many renovations and reconstructions since the turn of the millennium. Bedrooms are uncomplicated, contemporary, and well maintained, each with private bathroom, TV, and phone—a kind of afterthought for the well-prepared but reasonably priced cuisine that emerges from the kitchens. Doubles, with breakfast included, cost from 78€ to 98€, including free Wi-Fi. Menu items focus on the tried-and-true repertoire of French classics, including baked goat's cheese on a base of braised leeks, smoked salmon, sea bass filet, and a duckling confit with red berries.

133 av. de la Libération, Le Coteau 42120. www.hotel-des-lys.com. ✆ **04-77-68-46-44.** Fax 04-77-72-23-50. Reservations recommended. Main courses 10€–15€; set-price menus 17€–25€. AE, DC, MC, V. Mon–Thurs 7–9:30pm. Closed 3 weeks in Aug.

PÉROUGES ★★

464km (288 miles) SE of Paris; 35km (22 miles) NE of Lyon

Saved from demolition by a courageous mayor in 1909 and preserved by the government, this thousand-person village of craftspeople often attracted movie crews: *The Three Musketeers* (1973) and *Monsieur Vincent* (1948) were filmed here. Films had not been made here since the 1970s, since French film production moved primarily to Eastern Europe, but that has changed recently. The town sits on what has been called an "isolated throne," atop a hill northeast of Lyon.

Follow rue du Prince, once the main business street, to place des Tilleuls, at the center of which is the **Arbre de la Liberté (Tree of Liberty),** planted in 1792 to commemorate the Revolution. Nearby, in a 14th-century building, is the **Musée du Vieux-Pérouges,** place de la Halle (✆ **04-74-61-00-88**), displaying such artifacts as hand looms. It's open Easter to October daily 10am to noon and 2 to 6pm; off season, Saturday and Sunday 10am to noon and 2 to 6pm. Admission is 4€, free ages 11 and under. The price includes access to the museum and, through adjoining doors, to one of the finest houses in the village, the **Maison des Princes de Savoie,** with a watchtower **(La Tour de Guet)** and a replica of a 13th-century garden, the **Jardin de Hortulus.** The **Saint Marie Madeleine** church is supremely peaceful.

Wander through town, soaking in the atmosphere of a stone village that's remained virtually unchanged.

Essentials

GETTING THERE It's easiest to **drive** to Pérouges, though the signs for the town, especially at night, are confusing. From Lyon, take route 84 northeast and exit near Meximieux.

VISITOR INFORMATION The **Tourist Office** (**Syndicat d'Initiative,** Cité de Pérouges; ✆ **04-74-46-70-84;** www.perouges.org) lies adjacent to the entrance of this very small village. It's closed in winter.

Where to Stay & Eat

Ostellerie du Vieux-Pérouges ★★ This is a treasure in a restored group of 13th-century timbered buildings. Town mayor Thibaut and his family run a museum-caliber inn furnished with cupboards housing pewter plates, iron lanterns hanging from medieval beams, refectory dining tables, and stone fireplaces. The midsize to spacious guest rooms are completely up-to-date, with modern amenities, yet they have an old-fashioned atmosphere and style that recall medieval France.

The restaurant's food is exceptional, especially when accompanied by the local sparkling wine, Montagnieu, which has been compared to Asti Spumante. Specialties include Bresse chicken in morel-studded cream sauce, filet of carp stuffed *à l'ancienne* with pike, and *panache Pérougien* (an omelet stuffed with creamed morels and served with shrimp and crayfish cream sauce). By far the best-selling dessert is a crepe known as a *galette pérougienne à la crème,* made from a century-old recipe. After dinner, ask for a glass of Ypocras, a unique liqueur made from a recipe dating from the Middle Ages. Fixed-price menus range from 35€ to 62€.

Place des Tilleuls, Pérouges 01800. www.hostelleriedeperouges.com. ✆ **04-74-61-00-88.** Fax 04-74-34-77-90. 28 units. 124€ double; 190€–210€ triple or quad. AE, MC, V. **Amenities:** Restaurant; bar; room service. *In room:* TV, hair dryer, free Wi-Fi.

BOURG-EN-BRESSE

425km (264 miles) SE of Paris; 61km (38 miles) NE of Lyon

The ancient capital of Bresse, this farming and business center on the border between Burgundy and the Jura offers fabulous food.

Essentials

GETTING THERE Bourg-en-Bresse is accessible by **train** from Paris, Lyon, and Dijon. Seven TGV (fast) trains arrive from Paris's Gare de Lyon daily (trip time: 2 hr.). From Lyon (45–60 min.), more than 10 trains arrive per day. From Dijon (2 hr.), eight trains arrive daily. For information, call ✆ **08-92-35-35-35** or visit www.voyages-sncf.com. If **driving** from Lyon, take A42 or N83 for the 40-minute trip; from Dijon (2 hr.), follow A31 to Mâcon and take A40 to Bourg-en-Bresse.

VISITOR INFORMATION The **Office de Tourisme** is at 6 av. Alsace-Lorraine (✆ **04-74-22-49-40;** www.bourgenbressetourisme.fr).

Seeing the Sights

If you have time, visit the **Eglise Notre-Dame,** rue Notre-Dame, off place Carriat. Begun in 1505, it contains some finely carved 16th-century stalls. If you'd like to wander around town, check out the 15th-century houses on rue du Palais and rue Gambetta.

Monastère Royal de Brou ★★ Art lovers will want to stop at the Eglise de Brou to see its magnificent royal tombs. One of the great artistic treasures of France, this Flamboyant Gothic monastery was built between 1506 and 1532 (the three cloisters between 1506 and 1512, the church between 1513 and 1532) for Margaret of Austria, the ill-fated daughter of Emperor Maximilian. Over the ornate Renaissance doorway, the tympanum depicts Margaret and her "handsome duke," Philibert, who died after he caught a cold on a hunting expedition. The nave and its double aisles are admirable. Look for the ornate rood screen, decorated with basket-handle arching. Ask a guide for a tour of the choir, which is rich in decorative detail; Flemish sculptors and local craftsmen made the 74 choir stalls of oak in just 2 years.

The tombs are the church's treasure. The Carrara marble statues are of Philibert and Margaret. Another tomb is that of Marguerite de Bourbon, mother of Philibert and grandmother of François I, who died in 1483. See also the stained-glass windows inspired by a Dürer engraving and an alabaster retable (altarpiece) depicting *The Seven Joys of the Madonna*. The monastery occasionally hosts modern art expositions.

63 bd. de Brou. ✆ **04-74-22-83-83.** Admission to church, cloisters, and museum 7€ adults, 4.50€ students, free for children 5 and under. June–Sept daily 9am–6pm; Apr–June daily 9am–12:30pm and 2–6pm; Oct–Mar daily 9am–noon and 2–5pm. Closed Jan 1, May 1, Nov 1 and 11, and Christmas.

Where to Stay

Hôtel de France Most of the town's hotels are now run by chains, and this is the best of the bunch. It's also the nicest hotel in town, hosting everything from tourists to film crews (Charlotte Gainsbourg is reported to have been seen here recently). The hotel blends modern and regional styles, and many rooms have baths.

19 place Bernard, Bourg-en-Bresse 01000. www.bestwestern-hoteldefrance.com. ✆ **04-74-23-30-24.** Fax 04-74-23-69-90. 45 units. 85€–120€ double. AE, MC, V. Parking 8€. **Amenities:** Bar; restaurant. *In room:* TV, hair dryer, minibar, free Wi-Fi.

Le Logis de Brou This four-story property has landscaped grounds and is near the road fronting the monastery. Each guest room is basic but comfortable; some have bathtubs. Jacqueline and Gérard Roger run a fine inn and employ an especially helpful staff.

132 bd. de Brou, Bourg-en-Bresse 01000. www.logisdebrou.net. ✆ **04-74-22-11-55.** Fax 04-74-22-37-30. 30 units. 71€ double. AE, MC, V. Free parking. **Amenities:** Bar. *In room:* TV, hair dryer (in some), free Wi-Fi.

Where to Eat

Auberge Bressane ★★ TRADITIONAL FRENCH Bresse poultry is the best in France, and chef Jean-Pierre Vullin specializes in succulent *volaille de Bresse,* served five ways, including a delectable version in cream sauce with morels. You also may enjoy gâteau of chicken liver, frogs' legs with garlic and chervil, pike quenelles with crayfish, or grilled sea bass with fennel, accompanied by regional wines such as Seyssel and Montagnieu.

166 bd. de Brou. ✆ **04-74-22-22-68.** Reservations recommended. Main courses 15€–42€; fixed-price menus 29€–71€. AE, DC, MC, V. Wed–Mon noon–2pm and 7:15–9:30pm.

Au Chalet de Brou ★★ TRADITIONAL FRENCH You'll find flavorful and relatively inexpensive food at this unpretentious restaurant across from the village's famous monastery. Specialties include a "cake" of chicken livers served

Monastère Royal de Brou.

with essence of tomato; frogs' legs in parsley sauce; and at least a half-dozen kinds of Bresse chicken, served with your choice of morel-flavored cream sauce, raspberry vinegar, or chardonnay sauce. Purists may opt for it simply grilled, in order to appreciate the unadorned flavor of the bird in its own drippings. Dessert may be an apple tart presented, according to your choice, hot or cool.

168 bd. de Brou. ✆ **04-74-22-26-28.** Reservations recommended. Main courses 11€–28€; fixed-price menu 16€–45€. AE, MC, V. Tues–Wed and Fri–Sun 7–9:30pm. Closed Mon, Thurs, Nov 15–Dec 15, 1 week in Feb, and July 2–10.

VIENNE ★★

489km (303 miles) SE of Paris; 31km (19 miles) S of Lyon

Gastronomes know Vienne because it's the home of one of France's leading restaurants, La Pyramide. Even if you can't afford the haute cuisine, you may want to visit. It's a wine center and Burgundy's southernmost town.

Essentials

GETTING THERE **Trains** connect Vienne with the rest of France. Trips require a transfer in Lyon, 20 minutes away. For information, call ✆ **08-92-35-35-35** or visit www.voyages-sncf.com. **Buses** from Lyon arrive about eight times a day, making many stops and taking about an hour; for information, contact Vienne's Gare Routière (✆ **08-00-86-98-69**), adjacent to the railway station. The one-way bus or train fare from Lyon is about 6€. If you're **driving** from Lyon, take the N7.

VISITOR INFORMATION The **Office de Tourisme** is at cours Brillier (✆ **04-74-53-80-30;** fax 04-74-53-80-31; www.vienne-tourisme.com).

SPECIAL EVENTS In the first 2 weeks of July, Vienne attracts some of the biggest names in jazz for the annual **Festival du Jazz à Vienne.** Tickets range from 30€ to 40€. You can get tickets and information from the **Théâtre Antique de Vienne,** 4 rue du Cirque (✆ **04-74-78-87-87;** www.jazzavienne.com).

Seeing the Sights

Vienne contains many antique buildings, making it a *ville romaine et médiévale.* Near the center of town on place du Palais is the **Temple d'Auguste et de Livie,** built on the orders of the Roman emperor Claudius and turned into a "temple of reason" during the French Revolution. Another outstanding monument is the **Pyramide du Cirque Romain,** part of the Roman circus. Rising 16m (52 ft.), it rests on a portico with four arches and is sometimes called the tomb of Pilate.

Take rue Clémentine to the **Cathédrale St-Maurice ★★**, place St-Maurice (✆ **04-74-85-60-28**), which dates from the 12th century and wasn't completed until the 15th. It has three aisles but no transepts. Its west front is built in the Flamboyant Gothic style, and inside are many fine Romanesque sculptures. The cathedral is open daily 8am to 5pm (until 6pm Apr–Aug); admission is free.

In the south part of town is the **Eglise St-Pierre ★**, place St-Pierre (✆ **04-74-85-20-35**). A landmark with origins in the 5th century, it's one of the oldest medieval churches in France. Inside, the **Musée Lapidaire** (✆ **04-74-85-20-35**) displays architectural fragments and sculptures from excavations. The museum is open April to October Tuesday to Sunday 9:30am to 1pm and 2 to 6pm; November to March Tuesday to Friday 9:30am to 12:30pm and 2 to 5pm, Saturday and Sunday 1:30 to 5:30pm. Admission is 2.60€ for adults, 1.90€ for students, and free for children 17 and under. The museum is closed New Year's Day, May 1, November 1, November 11, and Christmas.

A **Roman Theater (Théâtre Romain) ★**, 7 rue du Cirque (✆ **04-74-85-39-23**), has been excavated east of town at the foot of Mont Pipet. Theatrical spectacles were once staged here for an audience of thousands. You can visit September and October Tuesday to Sunday 9:30am to 1pm and 2 to 6pm; January to March and November and December Tuesday to Friday 9:30am to 12:30pm and 1:30 to 5:30pm, Saturday and Sunday 1:30 to 5:30pm; and April to August daily 9:30am to 1pm and 2 to 6pm. Admission is 6€ for a day pass.

Detail at the Cathédrale St-Maurice.

If you have about an hour for a side trip, in Hauterives, south of Vienne, you'll find one of the world's strangest pieces of architecture. The **Palais du Facteur Cheval,** or **Palace of the Mailman Cheval** (✆ **04-75-68-81-19;** www.facteurcheval.com), the lifelong work of French postman Ferdinand Cheval, is built of stone and concrete and elaborately decorated, often with clamshells. It's an eccentric palace of fantasy and a tribute to the aesthetic value, or mania, of the individual. The work was finished in 1912, when Cheval was 76. Admission is 5.60€ for adults, 4.60€ students, and 4€ for children 6 to 16. The palace is open in July and August daily 9:30am to 12:30pm and 1:30 to 7pm; April, May, June, and September daily 9:30am to 12:30pm and 1:30 to 6:30pm; February, March, October, and November daily 9:30am to 12:30pm and 1:30 to 5:30pm; and December and January daily 9:30am to 12:30pm and 1:30 to 4:30pm.

Where to Stay

La Pyramide (see below) also offers rooms.

Hostellerie Beau-Rivage This place originated around 1900 as a simple inn that served food and wine to fishermen who traveled from Lyon to the well-stocked waters of this section of the Rhône. It has evolved into a stylish, nostalgic enclave. The rooms are well furnished; some are larger than you may expect. Most come with a tub/shower.

The Rhône passes by the dining terrace. The traditional cuisine is exceptional. Try downy-textured pike quenelles, and delicious suprême of pigeon on a platter with onion confit, roasted foie gras, and turnips. The Côtes du Rhône wines complement the food well. Fixed-price menus range from 38€ to 82€.

2 rue du Beau Rivage, Condrieu 69420. www.hotel-beaurivage.com. ✆ **04-74-56-82-82.** Fax 04-74-59-59-36. 30 units. 145€ double; 270€ suite. DC, MC, V. From Vienne, cross the Rhône on N86 and head south 12km (7½ miles); pass through Condrieu and, on the southern outskirts, look for signs on the left. **Amenities:** Restaurant; bar. *In room:* A/C, TV, hair dryer, minibar, free Wi-Fi.

Where to Eat

La Pyramide ★★★ MODERN FRENCH This is the area's premier place to stay or dine, and for many, it's the preferred stopover between Paris and the Riviera. The restaurant perpetuates the memory of a superb chef, Fernand Point, who died in 1955. Through the continuing efforts of Patrick Henriroux, many of Point's secrets, especially his sauces, have been preserved. Menus change seasonally, but the cuisine is always imaginative. The cheese platter is wonderful, and desserts are as artfully caloric, and as stylish, as anything else in the Rhône Valley.

The hotel offers 25 charming, air-conditioned guest rooms, each with minibar, TV, and free Wi-Fi. Doubles go for 200€, suites for 390€ to 420€, and there's also new, more affordable bistro, **L'Espace PH3,** on-site.

14 bd. Fernand Point, Vienne 38200. ✆ **04-74-53-01-96.** Fax 04-74-85-69-73. www.lapyramide.com. Reservations required. Main courses 41€–92€; fixed-price weekday lunch with wine 61€; fixed-price lunch and dinner menu 115€–172€. AE, DC, MC, V. Thurs–Mon 12–1:30pm and 7:30–9:30pm. Closed mid-Feb to mid-Mar and 1 week in mid-Aug.

Les Saveurs du Marché FRENCH This bustling, high-turnover, and slightly rowdy restaurant is known to many of the hardworking laborers of Vienne, who come here for inexpensive lunchtime meals and for slightly more leisurely and intricate food at night. It's within a 10-minute walk south of the town center. Along one wall is a massively paneled bar. Menu items change with the seasons and the availability of raw ingredients. Expect good value and a sense of cheerful informality.

34 cours de Verdun. ✆ **04-74-31-65-65.** www.lessaveursdumarche.fr. Reservations recommended. Main courses 16€–20€. Fixed-price lunch 14€, dinner 19€–38€. DC, MC, V. Mon–Fri noon–1:45pm and 7:30–9:30pm. Closed mid-July to mid-Aug.

VALENCE ★

671km (416 miles) SE of Paris; 100km (62 miles) S of Lyon

Valence stands on the left bank of the Rhône between Lyon and Avignon. A former Roman colony, it later became the capital of the Duchy of Valentinois, set up by Louis XII in 1493 for Cesare Borgia. Today Valence is a market town and distribution point for Rhône Valley fruit and vegetable producers. It's fitting that François Rabelais, who wrote of gargantuan appetites, spent time here as a student.

Visitors can climb the ruined château atop the white stone **Mont Crussol.** The ruins date from the 12th century. Valence is still the home of the Arsenal, one of France's oldest gunpowder factories.

The major sight is the **Cathédrale St-Apollinaire,** place de Ormeaux (✆ **04-75-44-90-45**), consecrated by Urban II in 1095 and much restored since. Built in the Auvergnat-Romanesque style, the cathedral is on place des Clercs in the center of town. The choir contains the tomb of Pope Pius VI, who died a prisoner here in the 18th century. It's open daily from 8am to 7pm.

Adjoining the cathedral is the **Musée Municipal,** 4 place des Ormeaux (✆ **04-75-79-20-80;** www.musee-valence.org), noted for its nearly 100 red-chalk drawings by Hubert Robert done in the 18th century. The museum is currently closed but slated to reopen in early 2013. Call ahead for hours.

Essentials

GETTING THERE **Trains** run from Lyon, Grenoble, and Marseille. For information, call ✆ **08-92-35-35-35.** If you're **driving** from Lyon, take A7 south. From Grenoble, follow E711 to outside the town of Voreppe, go southwest along E713, and follow W532 into Valence. From Marseille, follow A7 north.

VISITOR INFORMATION The **Office de Tourisme** is at 11 bd. Bancel (✆ **08-92-70-70-99;** fax 04-75-44-90-41; www.valencetourisme.com).

Where to Stay & Eat

Hôtel-Restaurant Pic ★★★ FRENCH This is the least-known of France's great restaurants, even though it ranks among the top 10. The cooking and the wine list (featuring regional selections such as Hermitage, St-Péray, and Côtes du Rhône) are exceptional. The villa has a courtyard and a dining room with big tables and ample chairs. Chef Anne-Sophie Pic has been called a fireball in the kitchen, bringing modern (often Asian) touches to classical dishes. Her appetizers, such as chicken skewered on twigs of aromatic rosemary, are a delight. For a main dish, you may select such dishes as sea bass with caviar, duck liver from Landes with black truffles, or a classic tournedos of beef Charolais. Pic pays

Mont Crussol.

special attention to fresh vegetables, including fava beans and baby spinach. The desserts are rapturous, from grapefruit sorbet to cold orange soufflé. Menu items change with the seasons.

The on-site brasserie, **Le 7** (© **04-75-44-53-86**), serves more affordable regional food without a lot of culinary fuss. Pic also rents 15 individually decorated guest rooms. They cost 330€ for a double, 440€ to 890€ for a suite.

285 av. Victor-Hugo. © **04-75-44-15-32.** Fax 04-75-40-96-03. www.pic-valence.com. Reservations required in restaurant. Restaurant: Set lunch 90€–330€, dinner 210€–330€. MC, V. Tues–Sat noon–1:30pm and 7:30–9:30pm. Brasserie: Main courses 19€–29€; prix-fixe lunch and dinner 30€. Daily 12:30–2:30pm and 8–10pm. Closed Jan.

THE ARDÈCHE ★★★

The Ardèche occupies the eastern flank of the Massif Central region, a landscape of jagged, much-eroded granite-and-limestone highlands. Although it defines itself as Le Midi—its southern border lies less than 40km (25 miles) from Avignon and 48km (30 miles) from Nîmes—its culture and landscape are more rooted in the rugged uplands of France's central highlands.

Through its territory flow the streams and rivers that drain the snow and rain of the Massif Central. They include rivers such as the Ligne, Fontolière, Lignon, Tanargue, and, most important, Ardèche. They flow beside, around, and through rocky ravines, feudal ruins, and stone-sided villages perched in high-altitude sites originally chosen for ease of defense in medieval times.

The most famous and visited section of the Ardèche is its southern extremity, with granite-sided ravines 300m (984 ft.) deep, gouged by millions of springtime floodings of the Ardèche River—no wonder it's called the Grand Canyon of France. This area draws thousands of tourists, often with their children, who take driving tours along the highways flanking the ravines.

THE grand canyon OF FRANCE

The ebbs and flows of the Ardèche, France's fastest-flowing river, have created the Grand Canyon of France. Littered with alluvial deposits, strewn in ravines whose depth can exceed 285m (935 ft.), the river's final 58km (36 miles), before the waters dump into the Rhône, are one of the country's most unusual geological areas. A **panoramic road (D290)** runs along a rim of these canyons, providing views over an arid landscape of grasses, trees, hardy shrubs, and some of the most distinctive deposits of granite, limestone, and basalt in Europe.

The beautiful driving route, which you can traverse in a few hours even if you stop for sightseeing (follow signs directing you along well-marked footpaths), stretches north to south between the towns of Vallon-Pont-d'Arc and Pont St-Esprit. The meandering corniche roads are a challenge. Beware of other vehicles weaving frighteningly as drivers and passengers admire the scenery and snap photos.

We recommend that you stop in the southern Ardèche to admire the gorges only briefly. It's better to spend the night in the less touristy northern reaches. The northern Ardèche, in the 45km (28 miles) of hills and valleys separating the hamlets of Vals-les-Bains and Lamastre, is a soft and civilized wilderness, with landscapes devoted to grape growing, shepherding, and hill trekking. For your overnight stop, we suggest you continue north to the more picturesque towns of Vals-les-Bains or Lamastre.

If you want to kayak in the gorges, go between early April and late November, when the waters are green and sluggish and safer than they are during the winter and spring floods. In Vallon-Pont-d'Arc, you'll find at least three dozen rental agencies for everything from plastic kayaks to horses. One of the best, **Aventure Canoës,** place du Marché (B.P. 27), Vallon-Pont-d'Arc 07150 (✆ **04-75-37-18-14;** www.aventure-canoes.fr), rents canoes and kayaks. A 3-hour *mini-descente* costs around 16€ per person for use of a canoe or kayak. The ride will take you along a 6.5km (4-mile) route from Vallon-Pont-d'Arc to the downstream hamlet of Chames. A full-day *grande descente* along the 31km (19-mile) downstream route from Vallon-Pont-d'Arc to St-Martin d'Ardèche costs around 26€ per person. A 2-day trip by canoe or kayak costs 48€ per person. Prices include transport by minivan back to Vallon-Pont-d'Arc at the end of the ride. Lunch is not included, so bring your own. Picnic fixings are available at dozens of bakeries and delicatessens near each point of origin.

Vals-les-Bains

43km (27 miles) W of Montélimar; 138km (86 miles) SW of Lyon

In a depression of the valley of the Volane River, Vals-les-Bains (pop. 3,500) is surrounded by about 150 springs whose existence was discovered around 1600. Scientists have never understood why each spring contains a different percentage of minerals: Most contain bicarbonate of soda, some are almost tasteless, and one—La Source Dominique—has such a high percentage of iron and arsenic that it's poisonous. Waters from Dominique are piped away from the town; others are funneled into a Station Thérmale adjacent to the town's casino.

In the park outside the Station Thérmale, a *source intermittante* erupts, Old Faithful style, to a height of around 7.5m (25 ft.) every 6 hours or so. Small crowds gather for eruptions usually at 5:30 and 11:30am, and 5:30 and 11:30pm (1 hr. earlier for all when clocks are changed in the winter).

Other than the scenery, this summertime town's most unusual site is about 23km (14 miles) south, beside the highway to Privas. The 16th-century entrance gate of a ruined feudal château stands here. The views over the confluence of two ravines and the valley are worth the detour.

WHERE TO STAY

Grand Hôtel des Bains This family-run enterprise is the largest and most authentic hotel in town, with slate floors in the lobby and long, tall hallways. The central wing was built in 1870 in anticipation of a visit from Empress Eugénie. Alas, Eugénie, finding she was comfortable in the nearby resort of Vichy, canceled her visit and died shortly thereafter. Though catering slightly to tour groups, the eco-friendly hotel has a cordial staff and well-maintained, conservatively furnished rooms, most with both tub and shower.

3 montée de l'Hôtel-des-Bains, Vals-les-Bains 07600. www.hotel-des-bains.com. ✆ **04-75-37-42-13.** Fax 04-75-37-67-02. 65 units. 70€–90€ double; 140€–157€ suite. AE, DC, MC, V. Closed Nov–Mar. **Amenities:** Restaurant; bar; 2 outdoor pools; room service. *In room:* TV, hair dryer, free Wi-Fi (in some).

Hôtel Helvie Though the casino that owns and runs this pleasant hotel has ruined a beautiful Belle-Epoque building housing it, they've done an admirable restoration of the nearby Helvie. Rooms, many of which look up the valley and onto the beautiful municipal pool, are calm, with pleasant period furnishings. Bathrooms are modern, and most have tub/showers.

Vallon-Pont-d'Arc.

5 rue Claude Expilly, Vals-les-Bains 07600. www.hotel-helvie.com. ✆ **04-75-94-65-85.** Fax 04-75-37-47-63. 45 units. 70€–90€ double; 120€–150€ suite. AE, MC, V. **Amenities:** Restaurant; bar; pool. *In room:* TV, hair dryer, free Wi-Fi. Closed 2 weeks in Mar.

WHERE TO EAT

Restaurant Mireille TRADITIONAL FRENCH This tiny (26-seat) restaurant occupies a space below vaulted stone ceilings that for centuries sheltered a herd of goats. Known for its earthy warmth, the restaurant serves an ambitious menu of carefully crafted cuisine. Choices range from homemade foie gras and house-smoked salmon to a duck confit in mille-feuille. There's a refreshingly strong emphasis on seasonal vegetables.

3 rue Jean-Jaurès. ✆ **04-75-37-49-06.** Reservations recommended in summer. Main courses 12€–18€; fixed-price menus 17€–27€. AE, MC, V. Sept–June Thurs–Tues noon–2pm, Thurs–Sat and Mon 7–9pm; July–Aug daily noon–2pm and 7–9:30pm. Closed 1 week in both Feb and Nov.

Lamastre

42km (26 miles) N of Vals-les-Bains; 30km (19 miles) W of Valence

Many connoisseurs of Ardèche architecture view Lamastre as the most unaltered and evocative village in the district. Its most important site is its church, in Macheville, the upper part of the village. Built of pink Romanesque stone, it encompasses portions that date from the 12th century, and it's a frequent site of weddings. Most visitors use the town as a base for hikes through the surrounding hills and valleys. Brown-and-white signs marks each trail.

WHERE TO STAY & EAT

Château d'Urbilhac ★ Its history is rich and illustrious, and if you ask them, the congenial owners of this massive stone palace will recite dates, names, and conflicts that date from France's wars of religion during the 16th century. For nearly 30 years, this high-altitude château and its 30 hectares (74 acres) of forest functioned as an upscale hotel with an equally upscale restaurant. Today Mme. Aillaud creates a Provençal-influenced cuisine with many vegetables from their garden; meals are available only to residents and their invited guests, who should make a point to sample at least one meal here. One of the high points is the pool, a 24m-long (79-ft.) watery rectangle that overlooks the valley of the River Doux. Bedrooms are high ceilinged and lavish, furnished with 19th- and early-20th-century antiques. An adjacent house is available for longer-term rental.

Rue de Vernoux, Lamastre 07210. www.chateaudurbilhac.fr. ✆ **04-75-06-42-11.** Fax 04-75-06-52-75. 6 units. 160€ double. Rates include breakfast. Dinner 38€ extra per person. MC, V. From the center of Lamastre, drive 2km (1¼ miles) southeast along Rte. de Vernoux-en-Vivarois. **Amenities:** Restaurant; bar; outdoor pool; sauna; tennis court. *In room:* Free Wi-Fi. Closed last 2 weeks of both Dec and Mar.

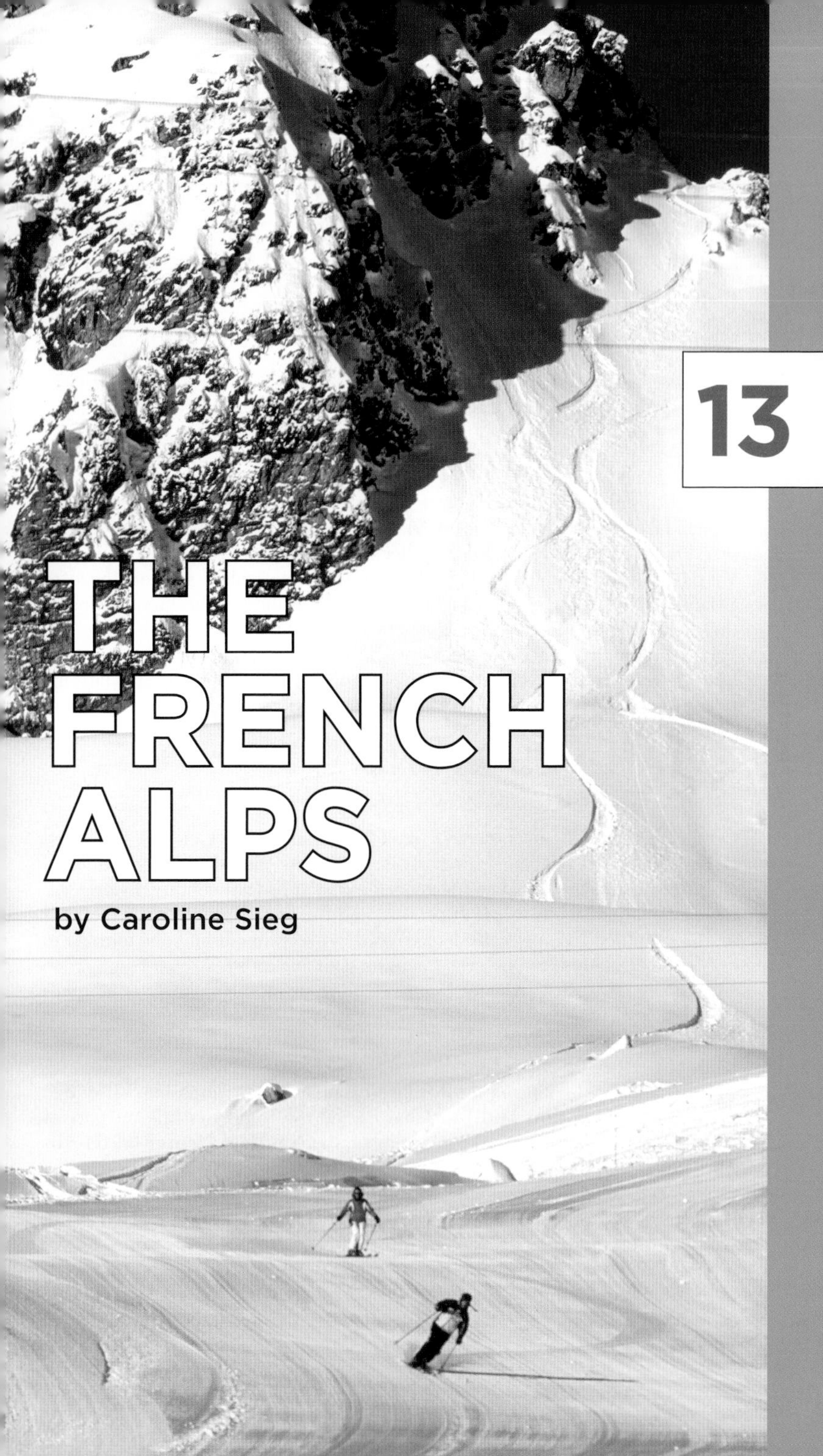

13

THE FRENCH ALPS

by Caroline Sieg

No part of France has more dramatic scenery than the Alps; the western ramparts of the mountains and their foothills are truly majestic. From the Mediterranean to the Rhine, they stretch along the southeastern flank of France. The skiing here is the best in Europe. Some resorts are legendary, such as Chamonix–Mont Blanc, the capital of Alpine skiing, with its 19km (12-mile) Vallée Blanche run. Mont Blanc, at 4,810m (15,777 ft.), is the highest mountain in Western Europe.

Most of this chapter covers the area known as the Savoy (Savoie), taking in the French lake district and the largest Alpine lake, Lac Léman (Lake Geneva).

From January to March, skiers flock to Chamonix–Mont Blanc, Megève, Val d'Isère, and Courchevel 1850; from July to September, spa fans head to Evian-les-Bains and Aix-les-Bains. Grenoble, the capital of the French Alps, is the gateway. Grenoble lies 30 minutes by car from the Grenoble–St-Geoirs airport, 40 minutes from the Lyon-Satolas international airport, and 90 minutes from Geneva's Cointrin airport. The city is connected to the Paris-Lyon-Marseille motorway on the west and to the Chambéry-Geneva motorway on the east.

EVIAN-LES-BAINS ★★★

576km (357 miles) SW of Paris; 42km (26 miles) NE of Geneva

On the château-dotted southern shore of Lac Léman (Lake Geneva), Evian-les-Bains is one of the leading spa resorts in France. Its lakeside promenade, lined with trees and lawns, has been fashionable since the 19th century. Evian's waters became famous in the 18th century, and the first spa buildings were built in 1839. Bottled Evian is considered useful in everything from baby formula to salt-free diets and is seen as a treatment for gout and arthritis.

In the days when Marcel Proust came to enjoy the Belle Epoque grandeur, Evian was the haunt of the very rich. Proust modeled his "Balbec baths" on Evian's. Today the spa, with its promenade and elegant casino, attracts a broader range of guests—it's not just for the rich anymore.

In addition to its **spa buildings,** Evian holds an imposing **Ville des Congrès (Convention Hall)** that has earned the resort the title of "City of Conventions." From late April to September, the **Nautical Center** (✆ **04-50-75-02-69**) on the lake is a popular attraction; it has a 115m (377-ft.) pool with a diving stage, solarium, restaurant, bar, and children's paddling pool.

The major excursion from Evian is a boat trip on Lake Geneva offered by the **Compagnie Générale de Navigation (CGN),** a Swiss outfit whose agent is in Evian. Call the port office directly at ✆ **04-50-70-73-20.** A round-trip ticket from Evian to Lausanne in Switzerland costs 23€, 12€ for children. Contact the company or head for the Office de Tourisme (see "Visitor Information," below)

PREVIOUS PAGE: **Skiers in the French Alps.**

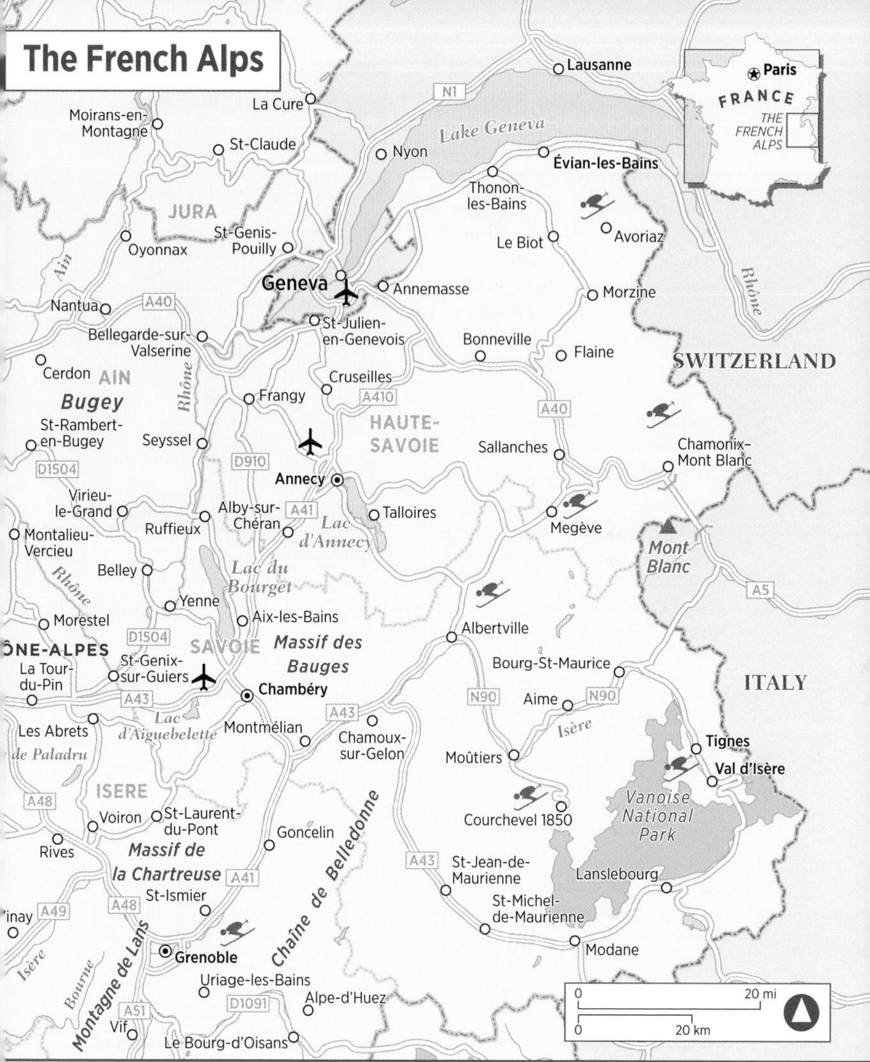

for other prices and hours. If you want to see it all, you can tour both Haut-Lac and Grand-Lac. The most popular trip is the crossing from Evian to Ouchy-Lausanne, Switzerland (the port for Lausanne), on the north side.

Crescent-shaped **Lake Geneva (Lac Léman)** is the largest lake in central Europe. Covering about 362 sq. km (141 sq. miles), the lake is formed by the Rhône River and is noted for its exceptional blue color.

Essentials

GETTING THERE The best way to approach Evian-les-Bains by **train** from the French Alps is to the gateway city of Annecy. (Many trains from other parts of France and Switzerland require transfers to the railway junction of Belle garde.) The one-way fare from Annecy is 15€. For train information and schedules, call ✆ **36-35** or 08-92-35-35-35.

Popular **ferries (CGN)** leave Geneva from quai du Mont-Blanc, at the foot of the rue des Alpes, or from Le Jardin Anglais. From May 28 to September 21, one ferry a day departs Geneva at 9am, arriving in Evian at 11:45am. The return trip leaves Evian at 5:50pm daily and reaches Geneva at 8:45pm. A first-class, one-way ticket costs 49€, a second-class ticket 36€. For ferry information and schedules, call ✆ **0848/811-848** or 04-50-70-73-20, or visit www.cgn.ch.

Evian-les-Bains.

If you're **driving** from Geneva (trip time: 50 min.), take N5 east along the southern rim of the lake. From Paris, take A6 south. Before Mâcon, you'll see signs pointing to the turnoff for Thonon-Evian. From Thonon, N5 leads to Evian. Trip time is about 5½ hours, which can vary depending on traffic.

VISITOR INFORMATION The **Office de Tourisme** is on place d'Allinges (✆ **04-50-75-04-26;** fax 04-50-75-61-08; www.eviantourism.com).

Taking the Waters at Evian

The clear, cold waters at Evian, legendary for their health and beauty benefits, attract a clientele that possesses both the time and the money to appreciate them.

The most luxurious way to immerse yourself in the resort's hydro-rituals is to check into either of these hotels, both of which maintain private spa facilities open only to well-heeled guests: **Hôtel Royal,** boulevard de Royal, or **Hôtel**

Driving the Route des Grandes Alpes

Evian can be a starting point for the 741km (459-mile) drive to Nice along the **Route des Grandes Alpes** ★★★. One of Europe's great drives, it links Lake Geneva with the Riviera, crossing 35 passes along the way. Leaping from valley to valley, it's open from end to end only in summer (many passes are closed in winter).

You can make the drive in 2 days, but why hurry? The charm of this journey involves stopping at scenic highlights along the way, including Chamonix, Megève, and Val d'Isère. The most dramatic pass is the **Galibier Pass (Col du Galibier),** at 2,645m (8,676 ft.), which marks the dividing line between the northern and southern parts of the French Alps.

En route to Nice, you'll pass to such towns as St-Veran (1,959m/6,426 ft.), the highest community in Europe; Entrevaux, once a fortress town marking the border between Upper Provence and the Alps; and Touet-sur-Var, a village filled with tall, narrow houses constructed directly against the towering rocky slope.

Hôtel Ermitage.

Ermitage, avenue du Léman (contact for both ✆ **04-50-26-85-00;** www.royalparcevian.com). They offer the most expensive packages and are adept at pampering patrons' bodies, souls, and egos.

More reasonably priced are the spa facilities at **Les Thermes Evian,** place de la Libération (✆ **04-50-75-02-30;** www.lesthermesevian.com). This public spa is adjacent to Débarcadère (the dock), just uphill from the edge of the lake. The hotel spas are more likely to emphasize beauty regimes and stress therapies; the public facility offers a broader range of services, including tanning, massage, and skin and beauty care (but no facilities for overnight guests).

You can indulge yourself with a daylong *thermale,* which provides access to exercise rooms and classes, saunas, steam baths, water from the Evian springs, and two massage sessions. Depending on the program you select, you will spend 60€ to 175€. You can also spend up to 130€ extra per day on additional massage, health, and beauty regimes. The spa is open Monday to Saturday, usually from 9am to 7pm.

Where to Stay

The **Hôtel-Restaurant Le Bourgogne** (see below) also rents rooms.

Hôtel de la Verniaz et ses Chalets ★★★ This glamorous country house stands on a hillside with a view of woods, water (Lac Léman), and the Alps. The antique-filled rooms are in either the main house or one of the separate chalets; the chalets have their own gardens and more privacy but cost a small fortune. Throughout the hotel, you'll find comfortable, even plush accommodations. Main courses in the hotel restaurant run from 25€ to 30€; fixed-price menus, 25€ to 75€.

Av. D'Abondance, à Neuvecelle Eglise, Evian-les-Bains 74500. www.verniaz.com. ✆ **800/735-2478** in the U.S. and Canada, or 04-50-75-04-90. Fax 04-50-70-78-92. 36 units. 110€–295€ double; 269€–370€ suite; 285€–610€ chalet. AE, DC, MC, V. Closed mid-Nov to mid-Feb. **Amenities:** Restaurant; bar; babysitting; outdoor pool; room service; 2 tennis courts. *In room:* TV, hair dryer, minibar, free Wi-Fi.

Where to Eat

Hôtel-Restaurant Le Bourgogne ★ TRADITIONAL FRENCH Come here for a delectable meal, impeccable service, an attractive setting, and excellent wine. Featured regional wines are Crépy and Rousette. Menu choices in the restaurant are likely to include the house version of foie gras, beef served with morels or a peppercorn sauce, and a poached version of *omble chevalier* (tiny local whitefish) with whiskey sauce.

The inn also offers 30 comfortable rooms with TVs for 75€ to 110€ double.

73 rue Nationale, Evian-les-Bains 74500. www.hotel-evian-bourgogne.com. ✆ **04-50-75-01-05.** Reservations required. Main courses 20€–28€; fixed-price menu 12€–46€. AE, DC, MC, V. Tues–Sun noon–2pm; Tues–Sat 7–10pm. Closed Jan.

ANNECY ★★★

538km (334 miles) SE of Paris; 56km (35 miles) SE of Geneva; 140km (87 miles) E of Lyon

Lac d'Annecy is the jewel of the Savoy Alps. The resort of Annecy, which is the region's capital, makes the best base for touring the Haute-Savoie. Once a Gallo-Roman town, the seat of the *comtes* de Genève, Annecy opens onto one of the best views of lakes and mountains in the French Alps. Since the 1980s, Annecy has become a booming urban center that has managed to preserve its natural setting. In summer, its lakefront promenade is crowded and active.

Essentials

GETTING THERE If you're **driving,** Annecy is near several highways: From Paris, take A6 southeast to Beaune and connect with A6/N6 south to Mâcon-Nord. Then follow A40 southeast to Seyssel, connecting with N508 going southeast to Annecy. Allow at least 5 hours. From Geneva, follow A40W to St-Julien and take RN201 south toward Annecy. Trip time is 30 minutes.

A car is useful but not essential in the Alps. Annecy has rail links with Paris and Lyon. Nine **trains** arrive daily from Lyon (trip time: 5 hr.), with a one-way fare costing 22€ to 40€. About six trains daily arrive from Paris's Gare de Lyon (trip time: around 5 hr., transfer at Lyon or Bellegarde); the fare is 77€ to 96€ one-way. For information, call ✆ **36-35** or 08-92-35-35-35.

There's also a nearby **airport** (✆ **04-50-27-30-06**) in the hamlet of Meythet (Aéroport Annecy-Haute-Savoie-Mont-Blanc), with service on Air France from Paris's Orly airport.

VISITOR INFORMATION The **Office de Tourisme** is at 1 rue Jean-Jaurès (✆ **04-50-45-00-33;** fax 04-50-51-87-20; www.lac-annecy.com).

Seeing the Sights

Built around the river Thiou, Annecy has been called the Venice of the Alps because of the canals that cut to the old part of town, **Vieil Annecy.** You can explore the arcaded streets where Jean-Jacques Rousseau arrived in 1728.

After seeing Annecy, consider a trek to the **Gorges du Fier ★★** (✆ **04-50-46-23-07;** www.gorgesdufier.com), a dramatic river gorge 9.5km (6 miles) to the west. To reach it, take a train or bus from Annecy's rail station to Poisy. From the station, go about 1.5km (1 mile), following the clearly marked signs. This striking gorge is one of the most interesting sights in the French Alps. A gangway takes you to a gully 3 to 10m (9¾–33 ft.) wide, cut through the rock by torrents of water; you'll hear the roar of the river at the bottom. Emerging from this labyrinth, you'll be greeted by a huge expanse of boulders. You can visit the gorge from June 15 to September 10 daily 9:30am to 7:15pm (last trip at 6:25pm), and from March 15 to June 14 and September 11 to October 15 daily 9:30am to 6:15pm (last trip at 5:25pm). The site is closed to the public October 16 to March 14. A hike to its well-signposted depths takes less than an hour and costs 4.90€ for adults, 2.70€ for children 7 to 15; it's free for kids 6 and under.

You can also take a cruise on the ice-blue lake for which the town is famous. Tours of **Lac d'Annecy,** conducted from February to December, last an hour and cost 12€. An English-speaking guide points out the sights. Tours depart between one and six times a day, depending on the season. Inquire at the Office de Tourisme (see above), or call the **Compagnie des Bateaux du Lac d'Annecy** (✆ **04-50-51-08-40;** www.annecy-croisieres.com).

Gorges du Fier.

Lac d'Annecy.

Château de Montrottier Within walking distance of the gorges, in the hamlet of Montrottier, is the 13th- and 14th-century Château de Montrottier. A one-time feudal citadel partially protected by the rugged geology around it, the château's tower offers a panoramic view of Mont Blanc. A small museum features items collected by a local dilettante, showcasing pottery, Asian and African costumes, armor, tapestries, and lace antiques, as well as some bronze bas-reliefs from the 16th century.

Lovagny 74330. ✆ **04-50-46-23-02.** www.chateaudemontrottier.com. Admission 7€ adults, 6.20€ students, 4.50€ children 7–15, free for children 6 and under. Mar 15–May 31 Wed–Mon 2–6pm; June–Aug daily 2–7pm; Sept Wed–Mon 2–6pm; Oct daily 2–6pm.

Le Palais de l'Ile This is the town's most potent and most frequently photographed visual symbol. Built before the 18th century and connected to the "mainland" of Annecy via a bridge, it resembles a miniature château, surrounded by water, despite its long-term use as a prison (and certainly a very cold one) for local malefactors.

3 passage de l'Ile. ✆ **04-50-33-87-30.** Admission 3.50€ adults, 1.20€ students and persons 12–25, free for children 11 and under. June–Sept daily 10:30am–6pm; Oct–May Wed–Mon 10am–noon and 2–5pm.

Musée Château d'Annecy This forbidding gray-stone monument, whose 12th-century pinnacle is known as the Queen's Tower, dominates the resort. The château contains a museum of regional artifacts that include Alpine furniture, religious art, oil paintings, and modern works. One section is devoted to the geology and marine life of the region's deep, cold lakes.

Place du Château. ✆ **04-50-33-87-30.** Admission 4.80€ adults, 2.50€ ages 12–25, free for children 11 and under. June–Sept daily 10:30am–6pm; Oct–May Wed–Mon 10am–noon and 2–5pm.

Where to Stay

La Maison de Marc Veyrat (see "Where to Eat," p. 476) also rents rooms.

The Lure of the Hills

The Office de Tourisme (see p. 474) distributes free pamphlets that describe about a dozen easy, family-oriented hiking and biking excursions in the forests around Annecy. More experienced hikers may wish to pick up a free map with a detailed set of challenging walks.

Walks in both categories last 2 to 6 hours. Some begin in the center of Annecy; others require a trip by car or bus from one of several towns in the area—such as Saint-Jorioz or Sevrier, to the west, or Talloires, to the east—to the excursion's origination point. A travel agency in Annecy, **Agence Crolard,** place de la Gare (✆ **04-50-51-74-62**), sells bus tickets to the destinations around Annecy and Lac d'Annecy and Lac Léman. It also arranges excursions by minibus to sites of panoramic interest in July and August (✆ **04-50-45-00-56** for information about these excursions).

Hôtel du Nord A government-rated two-star hotel in the center of Annecy, minutes from the train station and Lac d'Annecy, the du Nord is one of the town's better bargains. Guests appreciate the modernity of the soundproof rooms; 20 come with showers only, others with tub and shower. The helpful staff speaks English and can direct you to reasonably priced restaurants nearby. Breakfast is the only meal served.

24 rue Sommeiller, Annecy 74000. www.annecy-hotel-du-nord.com. ✆ **04-50-45-08-78.** Fax 04-50-51-22-04. 30 units. 69€–90€ double. MC, V. *In room:* A/C (in some), TV, dataport.

Hôtel La Demeure de Chavoire ★★ One of the most charming accommodations in the area is at Chavoires, about 3km (1¾ miles) east of Annecy. It's intimate and cozy, decorated with well-chosen Savoy antiques. Large doors lead to the gardens overlooking the lake. The guest rooms have names rather than numbers, and each is uniquely decorated with wood beams. Thoughtful service makes this a deserving selection, and it's more tranquil than the hotels in the center of Annecy. The staff will direct you to nearby restaurants.

71 rte. d'Annecy, Veyrier-du-Lac 74290. www.demeuredechavoire.com. ✆ **04-50-60-04-38.** Fax 04-50-60-05-36. 13 units. 126€–195€ double; 225€–275€ suite. AE, DC, MC, V. Parking 10€. From Annecy, follow signs to Chavoires and Talloires. **Amenities:** Bar; tearoom; babysitting; room service; spa. *In room:* TV, hair dryer, minibar, free Wi-Fi.

Where to Eat

La Maison de Marc Veyrat ★★★ MODERN FRENCH Famous throughout France for owner Marc Veyrat-Durebex's excellent and unusual cuisine, this world-class and horrendously priced restaurant occupies a romanticized version of a Savoyard château at the edge of a lake in the village of Veyrier-du-Lac, 1.5km (1 mile) south of Annecy. Guests dine in a posh room with ceiling frescoes.

The chef has been dubbed *l'enfant terrible* of upscale Alpine cuisine. He offers a unique dining experience, marked by an almost ritualistic etiquette, but the waitstaff advises you on the order in which the meal should be eaten. For example, a "declination of local cheeses," consisting of three large ravioli, each stuffed with a different cheese—a mild cow cheese, a pungent goat cheese, and a very strong blue—is eaten in ascending order of strength. Desserts include a miniature chestnut cake served with essence of truffles.

The *auberge* rents 11 expensive and beautifully furnished rooms. Rates are 260€ to 670€ for a double; a suite costs from 700€ to 880€.

13 vieille rte. des Pensières, Veyrier-du-Lac 74290. © **04-50-60-24-00.** Fax 04-50-60-23-63. www.marcveyrat.fr. Reservations required. Main courses 75€–138€; fixed-price dinner 485€. AE, DC, MC, V. Sat–Sun noon–1:30pm; Wed–Sun 7:30–9pm. Closed Nov to mid-June. From Annecy's lakefront bd., follow signs to Veyrier-du-Lac, Chavoires, and Talloires.

Le Belvédère FRENCH/SEAFOOD This is one of the most appealing reasonably priced restaurants in town. On a belvedere above Annecy, about 1.5km (1 mile) west of the town center, it provides views that extend up to 8km (5 miles) over mountains and lakes. Menu items include a salad of Breton lobster with freshwater crayfish and strips of foie gras, a platter containing scallops and red mullet with shellfish-flavored butter sauce, and an unusual pairing of foie gras with a purée of figs and vanilla-flavored bourbon sauce. Dessert may be a selection of tropical-flavored sorbets.

The 10 simple guest rooms are much less opulent than the restaurant. Rooms go for 110€ to 145€ double.

7 chemin du Belvédère, Annecy 7400. © **04-50-45-04-90.** www.belvedere-annecy.com. Reservations recommended. Main courses 16€–40€; fixed-price menus 28€ lunch and 42€–85€ dinner. AE, MC, V. Thurs–Tues 12:15–1:30pm; Mon and Thurs–Sat 7:30–9:30pm. Closed Jan. From downtown Annecy, follow signs leading uphill to Le Semnoz.

Where to Eat Nearby

Auberge du Père-Bise ★★★ FRENCH Since the 1950s, when it attracted starlets and millionaires, Auberge du Père-Bise has radiated style and charm. A chalet built in 1901, it's one of France's most acclaimed—and expensive—restaurants. It is located in Talloires, about 13 km (8 miles) from Annecy. In fair weather, you can dine under a vine-covered pergola and enjoy the view of mountains and the lake. The kitchen excels at dishes such as delicate young lamb, and gratin of crayfish tails.

The inn also offers 34 air-conditioned guest rooms with minibars, TV, and free Wi-Fi. Rates are 240€ to 400€ for a double and 580€ to 680€ for a suite. Reserve at least 2 months in advance, especially in summer.

Rte. du Port, bord du Lac, Talloires 74290. © **04-50-60-72-01.** Fax 04-50-60-73-05. www.pere-bise.com. Reservations required. Main courses 38€–104€; fixed-price menu 78€–178€. AE, DC, MC, V. Daily noon–2pm and 7–9pm. Closed mid-Nov to mid-Feb.

Annecy After Dark

In the old town, you'll find bars, cafes, pubs, and (in warmer months) street dances, fairs, and even carnivals. A calmer alternative is an evening of theater or dance at the **Théâtre d'Annecy,** 1 rue Jean-Jaurès (© **04-50-33-44-00;** www.bonlieu-annecy.com); tickets cost 15€ to 50€.

If a long day has left you thirsty, try the traditional Irish pub **Le Captain Pub,** 11 rue Pont-Morens (© **04-50-45-79-80**), with hearty ales on tap. **Le Vieux Necy,** 3 rue Filaterie (© **04-50-45-01-57**), attracts a younger, more boisterous crowd.

The best piano bar in town is **Le Duo,** 104 av. de Genève (© **04-50-57-01-46**). It's ideal for quiet conversation. For the most elegant evening on the town, head to the **Casino de l'Impérial,** 33 av. d'Albigny (© **04-50-09-30-**

00), part of the Belle Epoque–style Impérial Palace hotel on a peninsula jutting into Lac d'Annecy. Entrance to the gaming rooms is free; you must present a passport. The casino is open Sunday to Thursday noon to 2am, and Friday and Saturday noon to 4am.

AIX-LES-BAINS ★★★

535km (332 miles) SE of Paris; 34km (21 miles) SW of Annecy; 16km (10 miles) N of Chambéry

On the eastern edge of Lac du Bourget, modern Aix-les-Bains is the most fashionable (and largest) spa in eastern France. The hot springs, which provided comfort to the Romans, are said to be useful for treating rheumatism.

Essentials

GETTING THERE Some 20 **trains** per day arrive from Paris (trip time: 4 or 5 hr.); the one-way fare is 74€ to 90€. Ten daily trains pull in from Annecy (trip time: 30 min.; 7.10€–10€ one-way). For information and schedules, call ✆ **36-35** or 08-92-35-35-35. For information on **bus** routes in and around the French Alps, including the status of service from Nice to Aix, call the Gare Routière in Chambéry (✆ **04-79-69-11-88**). If you're **driving** to Aix-les-Bains from Annecy, follow RN 201 south.

VISITOR INFORMATION The **Office de Tourisme** is on place Maurice-Mollard (✆ **04-79-88-68-00;** fax 04-79-88-68-01; www.aixlesbains.com).

Seeing the Sights

Aix is well equipped for visitors, with flower gardens, a casino (the Palais de Savoie), a racecourse, a golf course, and Lac du Bourget, which has a beach. **Thermes d'Aix-les-Bains** (✆ **04-79-35-38-50;** www.thermaix.com) lies in the center of town, near the casino, the Temple of Diana, and the Hôtel de Ville (town hall). Closer to the lake, a string of flower beds and ornamental shrubs border the town's waterside promenades, where you can take a lovely stroll.

Steamboats take visitors on a beautiful 4-hour **boat ride** on Lac du Bourget. The trip travels most of the length of the Canal de Savière (which links the lake with the Rhône) between early February and mid-December daily or four times a week, depending on the season. Prices for boat rides range from 14€ to 15€. For departure times, which change almost weekly throughout the season, contact the ferry operator, **Les Bateaux d'Aix** (✆ **04-79-63-45-00**). Boats depart from the piers of Grand Port, 3km (1¾ miles) northwest of the center. You can also take a bus ride from Aix to the town of **Revard,** at 1,524m (4,999 ft.), which affords a panoramic view of Mont Blanc. For information, contact **Trans Savoie** (✆ **04-79-68-32-90**).

Abbaye d'Hautecombe ★★ This is the spiritual centerpiece of the French Alps and the mausoleum of many princes of the House of Savoy. It was built by a succession of monks, beginning in the 1100s, from the Cîteaux, Cistercian, and Benedictine orders. The abbey stands on a promontory over the western edge of Lac du Bourget, almost directly across the water from Aix-les-Bains. Before the 1500s, at least 40 members of the royal family of the Savoy were buried here.

After years of neglect, the church was reconstructed and embellished during the 19th century by Charles-Felix, king of Sardinia, in the Troubadour Gothic style. The fervently religious ecumenical community (Communaute du Chemin

Neuf) occupying the abbey organizes seminars, welcomes short- and medium-term devotees, and perpetuates the site's tradition of worship. Pilgrims are welcome to attend daily Mass at noon.

Self-guided half-hour tours with recorded narration, in English and French, depart at 6-minute intervals during open hours. You can drive to the abbey or take a 30-minute boat ride. Four steamers per day leave the landing stage at Aix-les-Bains; the round-trip fare is 13€ for adults and 8€ for children 11 and under.

St-Pierre de Curtille 73310. ✆ **04-79-54-58-80.** Tours 3€, free for ages 17 and under. Wed–Mon 10am–noon and 2–5pm.

Musée Faure This is the town's most interesting museum, with a modern-art collection that includes sculptures by Rodin and works by Degas, Corot, and Cézanne. It's on a hill overlooking the lake and the town.

10 bd. des Côtes 73310. ✆ **04-79-61-06-57.** Admission 4.60€ adults, 2.30€ students, free for children 15 and under. Wed–Mon 10am–noon and 1:30–6pm (Nov–Feb Wed–Sun).

Where to Stay

Hostellerie Le Manoir ★ This architecturally interesting site—a 19th-century stable until the present owners transformed it into a hotel—includes paths weaving to turn-of-the-20th-century gardens with outdoor furniture under shade trees. The decor in the midsize-to-spacious guest rooms is old fashioned—with antique and provincial furniture—yet up-to-date, each different from its neighbors. The government rates the Ariana (see below) higher because of its superior facilities, but the Manoir has more French charm and personality. You can order breakfast or dinner on a terrace bordering the garden. Most of the public and guest rooms open onto terraces.

37 rue Georges-1er, Aix-les-Bains 73105. www.hotel-lemanoir.com. ✆ **04-79-61-44-00.** Fax 04-79-35-67-67. 73 units. 99€–169€ double; 179€ suite. AE, DC, MC, V. Parking 8.50€. **Amenities:** Restaurant; bar; exercise room; Jacuzzi; indoor pool; room service; sauna. *In room:* TV, hair dryer, free Wi-Fi.

Where to Eat

Brasserie de la Poste FRENCH Since the mid-1960s, from a position in the heart of town, immediately across from the railway station and the post office, this cozy brasserie serves bountiful, cost-conscious meals to locals and savvy visitors. The interior is outfitted in tones of dark bordeaux and hardwood paneling, waiters are attentive and hardworking, and food is doled out in generous portions. Long-standing specialties include slabs of buttery foie gras, cheese-laden *fondues Savoyardes,* frogs' legs in garlic butter, pepper steaks with french fries, and sautéed crayfish.

32 av. Victoria. ✆ **04-79-35-00-65.** Main courses 9€–21€; fixed-price menus 12€–31€. AE, DC, MC, V. Tues–Sun noon–2:30pm; Tues–Sat 7–10pm.

Restaurant du Casino Grand Cercle (Koupol') FRENCH No other setting in Aix-les-Bains provides a taste of glamour and glitter like this Beaux Arts restaurant in the town casino. The restaurant occupies a corner of the area reserved for blackjack and roulette, giving diners a close-up view of the gamblers testing their luck. The food is not elaborate; the menu offers conservative but flavorful dishes of veal, beef, and chicken, with a scattering of terrines, soups, and salads. A passport is required for visitors to enter the casino. The slots are open Sunday

Grand Casino.

to Thursday 11am to 3am, and Friday and Saturday 11am to 4am; the gaming rooms are open Tuesday to Thursday 8pm to 3am, and Friday and Saturday 8pm to 4am. This site can also be your after-dark choice, as the compound includes a nightclub, Club Casino; a pub, Murphy's; and a piano bar, Le Colisée.

Rue du Casino. ✆ **04-79-35-16-16.** Reservations recommended. Fixed-price menu 12€–21€. AE, DC, MC, V. Daily noon–2pm and 7–11pm.

GRENOBLE

567km (352 miles) SE of Paris; 55km (34 miles) S of Chambéry; 103km (64 miles) SE of Lyon

The ancient capital of the Dauphine, Grenoble is the commercial, intellectual, and tourist center of the Alps. It's a major stop for travelers, including those driving between the Riviera and Geneva.

A sports capital in winter (it hosted the 1968 Winter Olympic Games) and summer, it attracts many foreign students; its university has the largest summer-session program in Europe. Founded in 1339, the University of Grenoble has a student body of some 50,000. The city (pop. 405,000) is also home to four other universities with a large contingent of English and American students, giving the city a cosmopolitan air.

Essentials

GETTING THERE An important rail and bus junction, Grenoble is easily accessible from Paris and all the cities in this chapter. About 11 **trains** per day arrive from Paris Gare de Lyon (trip time: 3½ hr.); the one-way fare is 74€ to 97€. Trains arrive almost every hour from Chambéry (trip time: 30 min.; 10€ one-way). For information, call ✆ **36-35** or 08-92-35-35-35.

Until 2004, Grenoble's airport accepted Air France flights from Paris and the rest of Europe. But when Air France transferred all of its inbound flights to nearby Lyon, air traffic to the airport in Grenoble virtually dried up. Flights arrive to Grenoble from London and Bristol (England). **EasyJet** and **British Airways** fly in only September to April, but **Ryanair** also flies in summer. For more information, contact Grenoble's **Aéroport Grenoble-Isère** (✆ **04-76-65-48-48**), 41km (25 miles) northwest of the city center. A shuttle bus meets every flight and takes passengers to and from Grenoble's center; the cost is 4.10€ each way. A taxi (✆ **04-76-65-46-18**) to the town center costs 70€ to 100€.

For information on flying into Lyon, see chapter 12. **Satobus** (✆ **04-72-68-72-17** or 04-76-27-89-29) meets most flights at the Lyon airport and takes passengers to Grenoble. Travel time is an hour; the fare is 20€ each way, 15€ students, and 10€ ages 4 to 12.

If you're **driving,** take A6 from Paris to Lyon and then continue on A48 into Grenoble. Depending on conditions, the drive should take 6 to 7 hours.

VISITOR INFORMATION The **Office de Tourisme** is at 14 rue de la République (✆ **04-76-42-41-41;** fax 04-76-00-18-98; www.grenoble-isere-tourisme.com). For information about public transportation in Grenoble, call ✆ **04-76-20-66-66.**

Seeing the Sights

Grenoble lies near the junction of the Isère and Drac rivers. Most of the city is on the south bank of the Isère, though its most impressive monument, the **Fort de la Bastille,** stands on a rocky hilltop on the north bank. A cable car will carry you from the south bank across the river to the top of the fort. The center of Grenoble's historic section is the **Palais de Justice** and **place St-André.** The more modern part of town is southeast, centered on the contemporary **Hôtel de Ville** (town hall) and the nearby **Tour Perret.**

Begin at **place Grenette,** where you can enjoy a drink or an espresso at a cafe. Don't miss the **place aux Herbes** and the **place St-André,** in the very heart of the *centre ville.* Place St-André, dating from the Middle Ages, is the most evocative square in old Grenoble, with the Palais de Justice on one side and the Eglise St-André on the other. The Palace of Justice was built in many stages. The brick church went up in the 13th century. Two great streets for strolling and browsing are rue de la Poste, in the medieval core, and rue J-J-Rousseau, a 5-minute walk southwest of the city.

Enjoy a ride on the **Téléphérique-Grenoble-Bastille** (✆ **04-76-44-33-65;** www.bastille-grenoble.fr), cable cars that take you over the banks of the

Grenoble's cable cars.

Isère River and its valley. Check the website for the cable car's operating hours, which vary by day and month. A round-trip ticket costs 6.50€ for adults, 5€ for students, and 4€ for ages 5 to 18. It's closed for a period during the month of January (btw. 4 days and 2 weeks). At the belvedere where you land, you'll have a view of the city, the mountains, and the remains of the Fort de la Bastille. Come for the view, not the fort. You can walk up in an hour or so if you're an Olympic athlete; the beginning of the route is signposted to the west of place St-André. We suggest you take the *téléphérique* to the top and then stroll down along the footpath, Montée de Chalmont, that winds to Alpine gardens and past old ruins before reaching a cobblestone walk that leads to the old town.

Musée Dauphinois ★ Housed in the 17th-century convent Ste-Marie-d'en-Haut and enhanced by the convent's cloister, gardens, and baroque chapel, this museum lies across the Isère in the Ste-Marie-d'en-Haut section of town. A collection of ethnographic and historical mementos of the Dauphine region is on exhibit, along with folk arts and crafts. This place is a quick course on life in the Alps: No other museum gives such a detailed view of the people. Furnishings, tools, artifacts, and replicas of Alpine settings are on display. Check out the special exhibition on skiing, tracing the development of the sport from its origins to the 21st century's high-tech innovations.

30 rue Maurice-Gignoux. ✆ **04-57-58-89-01.** www.musee-dauphinois.fr. Free admission. June–Sept Wed–Mon 10am–7pm; Oct–May Wed–Mon 10am–6pm. Closed New Year's Day, May 1, and Christmas.

Musée de Grenoble ★★★ Founded in 1796, this is one of the country's oldest art museums. It was the first French museum outside of Paris to focus on modern art, a fact appreciated by Picasso, who donated his *Femme Lisant* in 1921. The collection includes Flemish and Italian Renaissance works, but the Impressionist paintings generate the most interest. Note Matisse's *Intérieur aux aubergines* and Léger's *Le Remorqueur.* Ernst, Corot, Klee, Bonnard, Gauguin, Monet—they're all here. On display are a number of older paintings and sculptures, along with artifacts and relics from Greek, Egyptian, and Roman times, including a well-preserved mosaic. The artistic highlight is a sculpted door panel from the 1400s, depicting Jacob and his sons. A collection of 20th-century sculptures occupies the François Mitterrand Esplanade and the Albert Michallon Park surrounding the museum.

5 place de Lavalete. ✆ **04-76-63-44-44.** www.museedegrenoble.fr. Admission 5€ adults, 3€ seniors and students, free for children 17 and under. Free for everyone on 1st Sun of each month. Wed–Mon 10am–6:30pm.

Where to Stay

Hôtel d'Angleterre Tulip Inn Grenoble In the center of town, this hotel features tall windows and wrought-iron balconies, and opens onto a pleasant square with huge chestnut trees. The stylish salons boast wood-grained walls and ceilings and tropical plants. Some guest rooms look out on the Vercors Massif. Most of the small to midsize units are comfortably furnished and come with shower-only bathrooms; some have Jacuzzi tubs. Breakfast is the only meal served.

5 place Victor-Hugo, Grenoble 38000. www.hotel-angleterre-grenoble.com. ✆ **04-76-87-37-21.** Fax 04-76-50-94-10. 62 units. 110€–185€ double. AE, DC, MC, V. Free parking. **Amenities:** Room service. *In room:* A/C, TV, hair dryer, minibar, free Wi-Fi.

Park Hôtel Concorde ★★ This is the most opulent and prestigious hotel in Grenoble, a government-rated four-star legend that welcomes most of the important politicians and entertainment-industry moguls who visit the region. On the lower four floors of a mid-1960s tower mostly devoted to private condominiums, it's a short drive south of Grenoble's commercial center and close to City Hall. Each guest room is decorated differently, with a blend of dignified (sometimes antique) furniture, state-of-the-art lighting, and modern upholstery.

10 place Paul-Mistral, Grenoble 38027. www.park-hotel-grenoble.fr. ✆ **04-76-85-81-23.** Fax 04-76-46-49-88. 50 units. 240€–360€ double; from 450€ suite. AE, DC, MC, V. Parking 16€. Tram: A to Chavant. **Amenities:** Restaurant; bar; babysitting; room service. *In room:* A/C, TV, hair dryer, minibar, free Wi-Fi.

Where to Eat

Auberge Napoleon ★★★ FRENCH No other restaurant in France boasts as intense an association with Napoleon Bonaparte, but that's less important to diners than the fact that the restaurant is the finest in the Grenoble area. In 1815, Napoleon spent the night here at the beginning of a 100-day reign that ended with his defeat by Wellington at the Battle of Waterloo. You'll find enough subtle references to the history of France, from the Revolution to around 1820, to keep a student of French history busy throughout the superb meal. The restaurant seats only 23, in a plush, manicured dining room with upholstered walls and about 20 contemporary floral still lifes by renowned Grenoblois artist Martine Poller. We'd vote the bouillabaisse here as the best in the Alps. Try velvety-smooth crayfish-and-shrimp cream soup or duck foie gras terrine. The chef makes a superb filet of beef in game sauce.

7 rue de Montorge. ✆ **04-76-87-53-64.** www.auberge-napoleon.fr. Reservations recommended. Main courses 22€–36€; fixed-price menu 35€–72€. AE, DC, MC, V. Mon–Sat 7:30–10pm. Closed May 1–15, July 13–14, and Aug 10–25.

Café de la Table Ronde FRENCH This is the second-oldest cafe in France, after the more famous Procope in Paris. Founded in 1739, the cafe has attracted such luminaries as Stendhal and Sarah Bernhardt. It is said to be the spot where Pierre Choderlos de Laclos conceived the plot for his 1784 novel *Les Liaisons Dangereuses.* The menu offers both regional and national cuisine—the ingredients always fresh. We gravitate to *le poisson du jour* (fresh fish of the day), although the *fondue Savoyarde* with charcuterie is a winter delight, as is the Alpine ham. The cafe conducts concerts and poetry readings.

7 place St-André. ✆ **04-76-44-51-41.** www.restaurant-tableronde-grenoble.com. Main courses 10€–23€; fixed-price menus 25€–30€. AE, DC, MC, V. Apr–Oct daily 8am–11pm; off season Mon–Sat 8am–11pm, Sun 1–3pm.

Grenoble After Dark

To get things started, walk to **place St-André, place aux Herbes,** or **place de Gordes.** On a good night, these squares overflow with young people, and the energy level builds in anticipation of an explosion of dancing and partying.

Join fun-loving crowds of students at **Le Couche Tard,** 1 rue Palais (✆ **04-76-44-18-79**), and the **London Pub,** 11 rue Brochene (✆ **04-76-44-41-90**).

Le Styx, 6 place Claveyson (✆ **04-76-44-09-99**), is attuned to cutting-edge music from such centers as London and Los Angeles. Expect a mix of hip-hop, R&B, soul, and techno, but be prepared for anything. The dance floor is too small, but it's popular anyway. Young office workers head here after 5pm to sample some of the 70 different cocktails, but beer and pastis are the drinks of choice.

The town's most animated gay disco is **Le Georges V,** 124 cour Berriat (✆ **04-76-84-16-20**), which is open Wednesday from 9pm, Thursday to Sunday from 11:30pm (closing times vary).

COURCHEVEL 1850 ★★

633km (392 miles) SE of Paris; 52km (32 miles) SE of Albertville; 97km (60 miles) SE of Chambéry

Courchevel has been called a resort of "high taste, high fashion, and high profile," a chic spot where multimillion-dollar chalets sit on pristine pine-covered slopes. Skiers and geographers know it as part of Les Trois Vallées, sometimes called "the skiing supermarket of France." The resort, with 150km (93 miles) of ski runs in Courchevel and 604km (374 miles) of ski runs in the Trois Vallées around it, employs as many workers in winter as in summer, many of whom do nothing more than manicure and maintain the slopes. Courchevel 1850 has excellent resorts and hotels—with price tags to match—so it draws the super-rich. Travelers on average budgets should avoid it and head for more reasonably priced resorts, especially Chamonix (see "Chamonix–Mont Blanc," later in this chapter).

Courchevel consists of four planned ski towns, each designated by its elevation in meters. They are the less fashionable Courchevel 1300 (Le Prez), Courchevel 1550, Courchevel 1650, and, crowning them all, Courchevel 1850. Courchevel maintains three ski schools with a staff of 700 instructors, a labyrinth of chairlifts, and more than 200 ski runs, which are excellent in the intermediate and advanced categories.

Courchevel 1850 is the most attractive ski mecca in the French Alps. It's also the focal point of a chair-hoist network crisscrossing Les Trois Vallées region. At the center of one of the largest ski areas in the world, Courchevel sits at the base of a soaring amphitheater whose deep snowfalls last longer than those at most other resorts because it faces north. Expect reliable snow conditions, perfectly groomed runs, vertical cliffs, and enough wide runs to appease the intermediate skier. The glacier skiing draws experts from around the world.

SKI PASSES A 1-day pass (lift ticket) for Courchevel costs 39€, and a 1-day pass to Les Trois Vallées goes for 47€. A 3-day pass costs 118€ for Courchevel, 165€ for Les Trois Vallées.

Essentials

GETTING THERE If you're **driving** from Paris, take A6 to Lyon, then A42 to Chambéry, and then A430 to Albertville. At Albertville, take N90 to Moutiers and then follow the narrow roads 915 and 75 into Courchevel. Courchevel 1850 is the last stop on a steep Alpine road that dead-ends at the village center. Roads are open year-round, but driving can be treacherous during snowstorms. To go any higher, you'll have to take a cable car from the center of town. Most visitors drive here (you'll need snow tires and chains), but some buses link the city to railway junctions farther down the mountain.

The nearest **train** station is in Moutiers Salins. From Paris's Gare de Lyon, five trains per day leave for Moutiers. The high-speed TGV covers the distance from Paris to Chambéry in about 3 hours. In Chambéry, transfer for Moutiers. From the station in Moutiers, a 1-hour **bus** trip completes the journey to Courchevel. There are five buses per day Monday to Friday and 15 per day on Saturday and Sunday, costing from 10€ to 14€.

The nearest international **airport** is at Geneva. From there, you can catch a bus to Courchevel. There are three buses per day Monday to Friday and eight on Saturday and Sunday. The 4-hour ride costs 70€ one-way. From the airport at Lyon, there are three to five buses a day to Courchevel; the 4-hour trip costs 65€ one-way.

VISITOR INFORMATION The **Office de Tourisme,** at La Croisette in the heart of town (✆ **04-79-08-00-29;** fax 04-79-08-15-63; www.courchevel.com), provides information on skiing and each of the four Courchevel ski towns.

Where to Stay

Courcheneige ☺ This hotel is at the heart of the slopes—you can practically ski from your doorstep. Built like a chalet, with balconies, the hotel has its own ski shop. Guest rooms mostly open onto views of the mountain ranges, including l'Aiguille du Fruit. Most of the midsize bathrooms have tub/showers. Some rooms are large enough for a family of five. Courcheneige is always warm and cozy, especially in the art-filled, elegantly decorated public rooms. The Alpine and international cooking is excellent; meals are sometimes served on the terrace.

Rue Nogentil, Courchevel 1850 73120. www.courcheneige.com. ✆ **04-79-08-02-59.** Fax 04-79-08-11-79. 85 units. 175€–315€ double; 210€–570€ suite for 2. Rates include half-board. AE, MC, V. Parking 11€. **Amenities:** Restaurant; 2 bars; babysitting; exercise room; Jacuzzi; sauna; free shuttle bus to ski lifts. *In room:* TV, hair dryer, free Wi-Fi (in some).

Skiing at Courchevel 1850.

Hôtel Bellecôte ★★ This seven-story chalet, with direct access to the slopes, is known for its collection of unusual antiques. Bored with traditional Alpine motifs, the founder scoured the bazaars of Aghanistan and the Himalayas for objects that lend exotic warmth to the wood-sheathed walls and ceilings. Guest rooms are outfitted with lots of varnished paneling, plush accessories, and carved wooden objects from the Far or Middle East. The hotel has its own ski-rental shop.

Full meals in the elegant dining room include cassoulet of sweetbreads with flap mushrooms, frogs' legs Provençal, and chicken with morels.

Rue de Bellecôte, Courchevel 1850 73120. www.hotels-restaurants-courchevel.com. ✆ **04-79-08-10-19.** Fax 04-79-08-17-16. 54 units. 275€–380€ double; 490€–565€ suite for 2. Rates include half-board. AE, DC, MC, V. Closed mid-Apr to Dec 20. **Amenities:** Restaurant; bar; babysitting; exercise room; Jacuzzi; indoor pool; room service; sauna; free Wi-Fi in lobby. *In room:* TV, hair dryer, minibar.

Le Chabichou ★★ This is one of the town's finest hotels, within easy walking distance of many bars and clubs, and boasting a superb restaurant of the same name (see below). Most of the guest rooms in the gingerbread-trimmed chalet are large and well furnished; their daring modern design may not appeal to everyone, however. Beds offer grand Alpine comfort, with quality mattresses and fine linens.

Rue des Chenus, Courchevel 1850 73120. www.chabichou-courchevel.com. ✆ **04-79-08-00-55.** Fax 04-79-08-33-58. 42 units. 470€–830€ double; from 600€ suite for 2. Rates include half-board. AE, DC, MC, V. Parking 30€. Closed May–June and Sept to mid-Dec. **Amenities:** Restaurant; bar; babysitting; exercise room; room service; sauna; spa. *In room:* TV, hair dryer, minibar, free Wi-Fi.

Where to Eat

Chalet des Pierres FRENCH/SAVOYARD This is the best of the lunch restaurants scattered across the slopes. Accented with weathered planking and warmed by open hearths, it sits in the middle of the Des Verdons ski slope, a few paces from the path of whizzing skiers. Lunch can be served on a terrace, but most visitors gravitate to the two-story interior, where blazing fireplaces, hunting trophies, and a hip international crowd contribute to the place's charm. Items include air-dried Alpine meat and sausages, the best french fries in Courchevel, pepper steak, and *fondue Savoyarde.* Two appealing dishes are the Beaufort cheese tart and a leg of lamb that's suspended, the traditional way, from a string in the chimney and left to slowly cook in the smoke from the smoldering fire.

Au Jardin Alpin. ✆ **04-79-08-18-61.** www.chaletdepierres.com. Reservations required. Main courses 35€–52€. AE, MC, V. Daily noon–4:30pm. Closed late Apr to mid-July and mid-Aug to early Dec.

La Bergerie TRADITIONAL FRENCH Its uneven flagstone steps, stacks of firewood, and weathered pine logs and planks testify to La Bergerie's origins as an 1830s shepherd's hut. The ambience is sports oriented and outdoorsy. Well-prepared menu items include scallops in shallot butter, fondue bourguignon, raclette made with cheese from small-scale producers in Switzerland, and cheesy Savoyard pasta with ham. An especially refined platter that usually meets with success is pâté of salmon smoked, poached, grilled, and served with lemon-and-caviar crème fraîche.

Rte. de Nogentile. ✆ **04-79-08-24-70.** Reservations required. Main courses 17€–31€ lunch; fixed-price menu 35€–45€ dinner. AE, MC, V. Restaurant daily noon–3pm; Tues–Sat 8–10pm. Bar and cafe daily 10am–midnight. Closed late Apr to mid-Dec.

Le Bateau Ivre ★★★ MODERN FRENCH This restaurant, one of the greatest in the French Alps, occupies two floors of a hotel in the upper reaches of the resort. The paneled room has parquet floors and big windows that afford a view over the town and its slopes. Enjoyable dishes include *les oeufs cassées* (literally, "broken eggs"), an elegant house specialty accented with roasted crayfish tails and truffles. Also look for frogs' legs in garlic-flavored cream sauce, grilled red snapper with balsamic vinegar and fresh vegetables, polenta with escalopes of foie gras in vinaigrette, and succulent rack of lamb with olives and artichoke hearts.

In the Hôtel Pomme-de-Pin, quartier Les Chenus. ✆ **04-79-00-11-71.** Reservations required. Main courses 35€–110€; fixed-price menu 90€–190€. AE, DC, MC, V. Sat–Sun 12:30–2:15pm; daily 7:30–10pm. Closed Easter to mid-Dec.

Le Chabichou ★★★ MODERN FRENCH This is the second-best restaurant in town (only Le Bateau Ivre, above, is better). Le Chabichou is on the second floor of the hotel of the same name; big windows showcase a view of the slopes. The cuisine includes a number of superlative dishes, such as soup made from "fish from the lake," *magret* of duckling with honey sauce, divine lobster salad, red mullet with vinaigrette sauce, and velvety risotto with giant prawns.

In Le Chabichou hotel, quartier Les Chenus. ✆ **04-79-08-00-55.** Reservations required. Main courses 42€–60€; fixed-price lunch 35€, dinner 70€–160€. AE, DC, MC, V. Daily 12:30–2pm and 7:15–9:30pm. Closed May–June and Sept–Nov.

Courchevel After Dark

A chic but seasonal resort, Courchevel offers nightlife that roars into the wee hours in midwinter but melts away with the snow. The area around **La Croisette** (the departure point for most of the lifts) contains lots of restaurants, bars, and clubs that come and go.

Les Caves de Courchevel, Porte de Courchevel (✆ **04-79-08-12-74**), attracts an upscale crowd. A mock Tyrolean facade of weathered wood hides a club evoking a medieval cloister, with stone arches and columns. From December to April, Les Caves is open nightly for drinks from 11pm to 5am. Also appealing is **Piggy's Pub,** rue de la Croisette (✆ **04-79-08-00-71**), where stiff drinks and recorded music contribute to the sensation that you're far, far away from the French Alps. **Rhumerie Le Kalico,** Au Forum (✆ **04-79-08-20-28;** www.lekalico.com), is the closest thing in town to a British pub; it's open from December to April only.

CHAMONIX–MONT BLANC ★★★

613km (380 miles) SE of Paris; 82km (51 miles) E of Annecy

At an altitude of 1,027m (3,369 ft.), Chamonix is the historic capital of Alpine skiing. This is the resort to choose if you're not a millionaire. Site of the first Winter Olympic Games, in 1924, Chamonix is in a valley almost at the junction of France, Italy, and Switzerland. Skiers the world over know its 20km (12-mile) **Vallée Blanche run,** one of the most rugged, and the longest, in Europe.

With exceptional equipment—gondolas, cable cars, and chairlifts—Chamonix is among Europe's major sports resorts, attracting an international crowd with lots of English and Swedish skiers. Thrill seekers also flock here for mountain climbing and hang gliding. An old-fashioned mountain town, Chamonix has a breathtaking backdrop, **Mont Blanc ★★★**, Western Europe's highest mountain, at 4,734m (15,528 ft.).

The 11km (6¾-mile) **Mont Blanc Tunnel** (✆**04-50-55-39-36**) has made Chamonix a major stop along one of Europe's busiest highways. The tunnel is the easiest way to the mountains to Italy; motorists stop here even if they aren't interested in skiing or mountain climbing. For vehicles originating in France, the round-trip toll for a car and its passengers is 33€ one-way, 41€ round-trip. The return half of the round-trip ticket must be used within 7 days of issue. For information, call ✆**04-50-55-55-00.**

Chamonix sprawls in a narrow strip along both banks of the Arve River. Its casino, rail, and bus stations, and most restaurants and nightlife are in the town center. Cable cars reach into the mountains from the town's edge. Locals refer to Les Praz, Les Bossons, Les Moussoux, Argentière, and Les Pélérins as satellite villages within greater Chamonix, although, technically, Chamonix refers to only a section around place de l'Eglise.

Essentials

GETTING THERE Most (but not all) **trains** coming from other parts of France or Switzerland require a transfer in such nearby villages as St-Gervais (in France) or Martigny (in Switzerland). Passengers change trains in either of these villages before continuing on by train to Chamonix. Passengers from Aix-les-Bains, Annecy, Lyon, Chambéry, Paris, and Geneva pass to those villages. There are six daily connections from Paris (trip time: 7 hr.); the one-way fare is 84€ to 102€. From Lyon, there are six relatively complicated rail links per day (trip time: 4 hr.). A one-way fare costs 36€, with transfers at Bellegarde and St-Gervais. For more information and schedules for trains throughout France, call ✆**36-35** or 08-92-35-35-35.

Year-round, two to six buses a day run from the Geneva airport; the one-way fare is 37€. Buses arrive and depart from a spot adjacent to the railway station. For information, call **Cie S.A.T.** (✆**04-50-53-01-15;** www.sat-montblanc.com).

If you're **driving,** you probably won't have to worry about road conditions: Because Chamonix lies on a main road between Italy and the Mont Blanc Tunnel, conditions are excellent year-round. Even after a storm, roads are quickly cleared. From Paris, follow A6 toward Lyon, and then take A40 toward Geneva. Before Geneva, turn south along A40, which runs to Chamonix.

GETTING AROUND Within Chamonix, a local network of small buses (*navettes,* usually painted yellow and blue) make frequent runs from points in town to many of the *téléphériques* (cable cars) and villages up and down the valley. The price of a lift ticket usually includes the fare. Daily ski passes cost 37€ to 47€, depending on the areas you specify. For information, contact **Chambus** (✆**04-50-53-05-55;** www.chamonix-bus.com).

VISITOR INFORMATION Chamonix's **Office de Tourisme** is on place du Triangle-de-l'Amitié (✆**04-50-53-00-24;** fax 04-50-53-58-90; www.chamonix.com).

Skiing

With the highest mountain in Western Europe, this is an area for the skilled skier. Regrettably, the five main ski areas are not connected by lifts (you must return to the resort and take a different lift to ski a different area), and lines at the most popular areas are the longest in the Alpine world. Weather and snow conditions create crevasses and avalanches that may close sections for days and even threaten parts of the resort.

Skiing is not actually on Mont Blanc, but on the shoulders and slopes across the valley facing the giant. Vertical drops can be spectacular, with lift-serviced hills rising to as high as 3,150m (10,332 ft.). Glacier skiing begins at 3,740m (12,267 ft.). This is not for beginners or timid intermediate skiers, who should head for Les Houches or Le Tour. World-class skiers come here to face the challenges of the high snows of Brévent, La Flégère, and especially Les Grands Montets, a fierce north-facing wall of snow about 3 city blocks wide.

Seeing the Area by Cable Car

The belvederes accessible from Chamonix by cable car or mountain railway are famous. For information, contact **Compagnie du Mont-Blanc,** 35 place de la Mer de Glace (✆ **04-50-53-22-75**).

In town, you can board a cable car for the **Aiguille du Midi ★★★** and on to Italy—a harrowing full-day journey. The first stage, a 9-minute run to Plan des Aiguilles at an altitude of 2,263m (7,423 ft.), isn't so alarming. But the second stage, to the Aiguille du Midi station at 3,781m (12,402 ft.), may make your heart leap, especially when the car rises 600m (1,968 ft.) between towers. At the summit, you'll be about 100m (328 ft.) from Mont Blanc's peak. You'll have a commanding view of the aiguilles of Chamonix and Vallée Blanche, the largest glacier in Europe (15km/9¼ miles long and 6km/3¾ miles wide), and of the Jura and the French, Swiss, and Italian Alps.

You leave the tram station along a chasm-spanning narrow bridge leading to the third cable car and the glacial fields beyond. Or you can end your journey at Aiguille du Midi and return to Chamonix; this excursion takes half a day. Generally, the cable cars operate year-round: in summer daily 7am to 5pm, leaving at least every 10 minutes, and in winter daily 8:30am to 3:30pm, leaving every 10 minutes. The first stage, to Plan de L'Aiguille, costs 13€ round-trip. The complete round-trip from Chamonix to Aiguille du Midi goes for 40€.

You can also cross over high mountains and pass jagged needles of rock and ice bathed in dazzling light. The final trip to **Pointe Helbronner,** Italy—at 3,407m (11,175 ft.)—does not require a passport if you want to leave the station and descend on two more cable cars to the village of Courmayeur. From there, you can go to nearby Entrèves to dine at **La Maison de Filippo** (✆ **01-65-86-97-97;** www.lamaison.com), a "chalet of gluttony." The round-trip from Chamonix to Pointe Helbronner is 60€; the cable car operates from mid-May to mid-October only.

Another cableway takes you up to **Le Brévent ★★★**, at 2,485m (8,151 ft.). From here, you'll have a first-rate view of Mont Blanc and the Aiguilles de Chamonix. The round-trip excursion takes about 1½ hours. Cable cars operate year-round from 8am to 5pm. Summer departures are at least every 15 minutes. A round-trip costs 23€.

Another journey takes you to **Le Montenvers ★★★** (✆ **04-50-53-12-54**), at 1,883m (6,176 ft.). Access is not by cable car, but on a **cog railway**

Mont Blanc.

known as the **Train Montenvers–Mer de Glace.** It departs from the Gare Montenvers–Mer de Glace, behind Chamonix's Gare SNCF, near the center of town. At the end of the run, you'll have a view of the 6.5km-long (4-mile) *mer de glace* ("sea of ice," or glacier). Immediately east of the glacier, Aiguille du Dru is a rock climb notorious for its difficulty. The trip takes 1½ hours, including a return by rail. Departures are 8am to 6pm in summer, until 4:30pm in the off season; service usually operates year-round. The round-trip fare is 24€.

You can also visit a cave, **La Grotte de Glace,** hollowed out of the *mer de glace;* a cable car connects it with the resort of Montenvers, and the trip takes 3 minutes. The train, cable car, and visit to the cave cost 24€.

Where to Stay

Chalet Hôtel Le Chantel A 30-minute walk west of the city hall, this white-stucco B&B evokes a Swiss chalet, with dark-stained wood, balconies, and mountain panoramas. It benefits from the care and attention of its owners, who have added touches you'd expect in a private home. The cozy, knotty-pine-paneled rooms are small but homey, without many amenities; each has a comfortable bed and a compact shower-only bathroom.

391 rte. des Pecles, Chamonix 74400. www.skiambiance.co.uk. ✆ **04-50-53-06-69.** Fax 04-50-55-52-42. 8 units. 96€–124€ double. Rates include breakfast. MC, V. Free parking. **Amenities:** Breakfast lounge. *In room:* No phone, free Wi-Fi.

Hôtel de l'Arve Originally a cafe around the turn of the 20th century, this place is now a comfortable hotel. Most of its stucco facade dates from the 1960s. The interior is simple, with childproof, much-used furniture and accessories. Furnishings in the small to medium guest rooms are functional, and the compact bathrooms contain shower stalls. This is a simple place that offers a friendly welcome, an appreciation for the outdoors, and views of the Arve River from many rooms. The setting is convenient, a 5-minute walk from the town hall.

60 impasse des Anémones, Chamonix 74400. www.hotelarve-chamonix.com. ✆ **04-50-53-02-31.** Fax 04-50-53-56-92. 37 units. 63€–120€ double. AE, DC, MC, V. Closed mid-Oct to Dec 17. **Amenities:** Restaurant; exercise room; sauna. *In room:* TV, free Wi-Fi (in some).

Where to Eat

Bartavel ITALIAN The place is a sporty, informal pizzeria and brasserie. Service is a bit rough, but that's part of its style. Decorated much like a tavern in Italy, this restaurant serves a range of pastas, salads, soups, and rib-sticking platters designed to go well with cold air and high altitudes. Beer and wine flow liberally. Bartavel attracts many outdoor enthusiasts who appreciate its copious portions and reasonable prices.

26 cours du Bartavel. ✆ **04-50-53-97-19.** Main courses 14€–30€; pasta and pizzas 8.50€–12€. MC, V. Daily 11:30am–11:30pm.

Le Chaudron ★ TRADITIONAL FRENCH You'll find fancier places in town, but for good value, honest cooking, and fine mountain ingredients, Le Chaudron is near the top of our list. Chef Stephan Osterberger cooks in front of you, and you're sure to appreciate his specialties, which include house-style sweetbreads, rabbit stew with juniper berries, and fondues. The cellar is filled with well-chosen wines, including Château Mouton-Rothschild and Château Latour.

79 rue des Moulins. ✆ **04-50-53-40-34.** Reservations recommended. Main courses 15€–35€; fixed-price menu 20€–35€. MC, V. Daily 7–10:30pm. Closed May–June and Oct–Nov.

Restaurant Albert 1er ★★★ MODERN FRENCH This stalwart features a trio of cozily decorated dining rooms, with bay windows opening onto views of Mont Blanc and walls accented by rustic artifacts and antique farm implements. Begin with a broth *(fumet)* of wild mushrooms garnished with ravioli stuffed with foie gras. Main courses include bison steak with green-peppercorn sauce, superb pan-fried scallops with risotto and lobster sauce, and foie gras with truffled chicken rillettes. In summer, dine alfresco in the garden.

In the Hameau Albert 1er hotel, 38 rte. du Bouchet. ✆ **04-50-53-05-09.** Reservations recommended. Main courses 43€–160€; fixed-price dinner 76€–160€; fixed-price lunch 56€. AE, DC, MC, V. Fri–Mon 12:30–2pm; Thurs–Tues 7:30–9:30pm. Closed mid-May to June 5 and early Nov to early Dec.

Restaurant Les Jardins du Mont-Blanc ★ FRENCH This stellar restaurant centers on a pentagonal fireplace. Specialties change seasonally but may include *omble chevalier* (lake fish) meunière, rack of lamb roasted with herbs (for two), and sinful desserts such as a mousse of apples and white chocolate. The excellent cellar contains more than 500 wines, many reasonably priced. In summer, you can lunch next to the pool in the garden. There's music in the adjacent piano bar every night.

In the Hôtel Mont-Blanc, 62 allée du Majéstic. ✆ **04-50-53-05-64.** Reservations required. Main courses 25€–30€; fixed-price menu 36€–79€. AE, MC, V. Summer daily noon–2:30pm and 7–10pm. Closed for lunch in winter. Closed Oct–Nov.

Chamonix After Dark

Nightlife in Chamonix runs the gamut from classical to riotous. You'll find the most bars and pubs along rue des Moulins and rue Paccard. Chamonix's most popular disco is **Le Garage,** avenue de l'Aiguille du Midi (✆ **06-33-76-86-00;** www.nightclubgarage.com). Open nightly during the height of winter and summer high seasons, but only Thursday to Sunday during rainy months, it's outfitted with a modern format, very artfully "designed" with lots of chrome, steel, and glass. Clientele here could include just about anyone, reflecting the changing hordes of skiers and mountaineers who swarm to Chamonix at regular intervals. Entrance ranges from 5€ to 15€. The **casino,** 12 place H-B-de-Saussure (✆ **04-50-53-07-65**), has slot machines and roulette and blackjack tables.

VAL D'ISÈRE ★★

665km (412 miles) SE of Paris; 118km (73 miles) E of Albertville; 130km (81 miles) E of Chambéry

In an open valley, Val d'Isère (1,820m/5,970 ft. above sea level) was originally a hunting station for the ducs de Savoie. It's now a center of some of Europe's most spectacular skiing. Less snobbish than Courchevel and less old fashioned than Megève, it's a youthful, rather brash resort where virtually everyone comes to enjoy outdoor pursuits. Its fans compare it favorably to Chamonix, which—despite the allure of nearby Mont Blanc and superb skiing—seems to be burdened with longer lift lines and a less accessible layout of ski lifts and slopes.

Essentials

GETTING THERE & GETTING AROUND **Driving** is the preferred way to get to Val d'Isère. Most motorists come from Albertville, accessible by superhighway from Paris. From Albertville, follow signs to Moutiers, then take RN202 to Bourg-St-Maurice (58km/36 miles) and continue another 31km (19 miles) to Val d'Isère. The meandering RN202 is panoramic and breathtaking—for its views and its lack of guardrails along some sections. During snowfalls, chains on tires are required. When you get to the resort, we strongly advise you to park your car and not use it again until you leave. Parking problems are legendary, and without chains, you'll risk getting stuck during snowfalls. You can walk virtually anywhere in town faster than you can drive.

Two dozen red-and-white Train Rouge free **shuttle buses,** each with a capacity of 100 people and their equipment, connect the hamlets at either end of the valley (La Daille and Le Fornet) to the center. The central terminus is the Rond-Point des Pistes. In summer, service is available only in July and August.

Parking lots and garages scattered around the valley are clearly marked. Each charges 14€ per day, 81€ per week, depending on the season and the size of your car.

Nearby **airports** include Cointrin, outside Geneva (✆ **04122/717-7111** or 04122/717-7105); Lyon-St-Exupéry (✆ **08-26-80-08-26**); Grenoble (✆ **04-76-65-48-48**); and Chambéry (✆ **04-79-54-49-54**). Bus and limo service is available from these airports; contact Cars Martin (✆ **04-79-06-00-42**).

The nearest **train** station is at Bourg-St-Maurice (✆ **3635**), an Alpine village 31km (19 miles) west of Val d'Isère. For train information, also call ✆ **36-35.** From there, Cars Martin (✆ **04-79-68-32-96;** www.altibus.com) **buses** depart 4 to 10 times a day, depending on the season. The one-way fare is 13€. Or you can take a **taxi** from Bourg-St-Maurice that costs about 80€ for up to four passengers. Call **Altitude Taxis** (✆ **06-07-41-11-53;** www.altitude-espace-taxi.com) or arrange pickup in advance with your hotel.

VISITOR INFORMATION The resort's **Office de Tourisme,** rue Principale, Val Village (✆ **04-79-06-06-60;** fax 04-79-06-04-56; www.valdisere.com), is a font of information on outdoor activities. The widest spectrum of information on sports is available from the **Club des Sports (Sports Department),** route de la Balme, Quartier Balme B.P. 61, 73152 Val d'Isère (✆ **04-79-06-03-49;** www.valsport.org).

Outdoor Pursuits on & off the Slopes

Don't expect a pristine Alpine village. In Val d'Isère, traffic roars to the town center. Clusters of cheap restaurants, crêperies, and more than 125 stores and outlets line the road. Since 1983, some of the worst of the town's architectural sins have been corrected, thanks to tighter building codes and greater emphasis on traditional chalet-style architecture.

Access to Val d'Isère, less than 9.5km (6 miles) from the Italian border, is inconvenient and time consuming, and parking is a nightmare during busy seasons. But despite the commercialism, the town hums with the sense that its visitors are here to enjoy skiing. And few other European resorts can boast as logical a layout for a far-flung collection of ski slopes.

Val d'Isère is the focal point for a network of satellite resorts scattered around the nearby valleys, including the architecturally uninspired **Tignes** (2,066m/6,776 ft. above sea level), whose layout is divided into four resort-style villages. The most stylish and prosperous of the villages is **Val Claret;** less fortunate and successful are **Tignes le Lac, Tignes les Boisses,** and **Tignes les Brévières.**

Guarding one entrance to Val d'Isère is **La Daille,** a resort of mostly high-rise condominiums and timeshares. At the other end of town is the medieval hamlet of **Le Fornet,** the departure point for gondolas crossing a mountain ridge to the Pissaillas Glacier and another network of ski trails, the Système de Solaise.

All of these satellites lack the cachet and diversity of Val d'Isère's nightlife and dining. Public transport (the Train Rouge; see "Getting There & Getting Around," above) can pick you up and deposit you at the departure point to the terminus of virtually any ski lift or trail in the region.

Val d'Isère is legendary for its "death-defying" chutes and its off-piste walls. These slopes are for experts, but the intermediate skier will also find open snowfields. The best place for intermediates is Tignes, with its wide variety of runs, including the Grande Motte (3,345m/10,972 ft.). Skiers find enough variety here to stay 2 weeks and never revisit the slopes that stretch

Le Fornet.

from the Pissaillas Glacier far above Val d'Isère to Tignes Les Brévières, four valleys away.

There are only a few marked expert runs; the more accessible off-piste areas lure experts from all over Europe and the United States. Most of these runs can be reached after short traverses from the Bellevarde, Solaise, and Fornet cable cars in Val d'Isère and the Grande Motte cable car in Val Claret.

In winter, half-day, full-day, and 2-day **ski passes** (lift tickets) sell for 32€, 44€, and 76€, respectively.

At least a dozen **ski schools** flourish in winter. One of the largest and busiest is the **Ecole de Ski Français,** or French National Ski School (✆ **04-79-06-35-76;** www.esf.net), with 250 guides and teachers. Somewhat more personal is **Snow Fun** (✆ **04-79-06-16-79;** www.snowfun.com), with 60 guides. Purists usually gravitate to **Top Ski,** galerie des Cimes (✆ **04-79-06-14-80;** www.topskival.com), a small but choice outfit with 24 extremely well-trained guides catering exclusively to Alpine connoisseurs who want to ski off-piste (away from the officially recognized and maintained trails).

Officially, the resort's sports activities slow down or stop altogether between early May and late June, and from early September to mid-November.

Where to Stay

The staff at **Val Hôtel** (✆ **04-79-06-18-90;** fax 04-79-06-11-88), the resort's central reservations network, can book accommodations for you.

Hôtel Altitude This oft-modernized chalet dates from the 1970s, when it was built in Savoyard style. The Altitude is comfortable and cozy, a short walk south of the town center, so you'll be able to escape the crowds. Many guests return each year, occupying elegantly appointed guest rooms with quality beds and fine linens.

Rte. de la Balme, Val d'Isère 73150. www.hotelaltitude.com. ✆ **04-79-06-12-55.** Fax 04-79-41-11-09. 40 units. Winter 145€–170€ double; off season 103€–108€ double. Rates include half-board. AE, DC, MC, V. Closed May 5–June 30 and late Aug to Dec 1. **Amenities:** Restaurant; bar; babysitting; health club; outdoor pool; room service; sauna. *In room:* TV, hair dryer, free Wi-Fi.

Hôtel Christiania ★ This 1949 lodging (rebuilt in 1991) features *Sputnik*-style furniture in a sunken lobby ringed with exposed stone, varnished pine, and blazing fireplaces; guest rooms are outfitted with pine trim and Alpine touches. Some accommodations contain sleeping lofts or bunk beds.

B.P. 48, Val d'Isère 73152. www.hotel-christiania.com. ✆ **04-79-06-08-25.** Fax 04-79-41-11-10. 69 units. 319€–358€ double; from 478€ suite. Rates include half-board. AE, DC, MC, V. Closed late Apr to Dec 5. **Amenities:** Restaurant; bar; babysitting; exercise room; massage; indoor pool; room service; sauna; spa. *In room:* TV, hair dryer, free Wi-Fi.

Where to Eat

La Grande Ourse FRENCH This Savoyard charm-filled wooden house, built in 1937, oozes coziness, with flickering candles and a blazing fireplace, and has the resort's most intriguing mural, a depiction of the zodiac on the ceiling of its richly paneled main dining room. Menu items at lunch include grilled meats, pastas, and salads; evening menus offer more sophisticated fare, such as fricassee of guinea fowl with fondant of foie gras, roast rack of lamb with herbs, large pockets of lobster-stuffed ravioli with lobster sauce, and Savoyard fondue with three cheeses.

B.P. 57, Val d'Isère 73150, Sur le Front de Neige, adjacent to the church. ✆ **04-79-06-00-19.** www.grande-ourse.com. Reservations recommended at dinner. Main courses 13€–26€ lunch, 22€–32€ dinner; fixed-price menu 25€ lunch, 49€ dinner. AE, DC, MC, V. Daily noon–3pm; Wed–Mon 7:30–9:30pm. Closed mid-May to Nov.

La Vieille Maison ★ 🎁 SAVOYARD This former farmhouse is one of the valley's oldest chalets. Constructed in 1780, it has lots of exposed stone and old-fashioned style. Menu items are based on Savoyard themes, with hearty cold-weather dishes such as fondues and raclettes, many of which are prepared only for two to four diners. Menu items include *tartiflette,* a succulent dish made from Reblochon cheese, potatoes, onions, butter, and lardons; game dishes, including wild boar steak; and such local freshwater fish as *omble chevalier* in white-wine sauce. Hands-on diners sometimes opt for "La Viande à l'Auze"—a superhot slab of rock is placed on your table so you can sizzle your beef strips yourself.

Vieux Village de la Daille. ✆ **04-79-06-11-76.** www.resto-lavieillemaison.fr. Reservations recommended. Main courses 20€–24€; fixed-price menu 33€. MC, V. Mon–Sat 7–9:30pm. Closed May–June and Oct–Nov.

Val d'Isère After Dark

Most bars are in the town's pedestrian zone or adjacent to rue Principale. **Café Face,** rue Principale (✆ **04-79-06-29-80**), draws an attractive crowd and plays the best music. Its most fun alternative, **Dick's Tea Bar** (✆ **04-79-06-14-87;** www.dicksteabar.com), just off rue Principale and opposite the Hôtel Christiania, is the wildest après-ski joint in Val d'Isère. Inside you'll find a rustic and cozily appointed timber-and-stone interior (including an Internet cafe) where you can drink as merrily and as uninhibitedly as you want and—after around 9pm—dance, dance, dance. Although a cover charge of 10€ is imposed after midnight, the bar is open every day during winter from 9am (for breakfast) to 4am. Hours vary during off season, but even during the slowest period, the place is usually open on Friday and Saturday nights. Smaller and more intimate, without dancing, is a bar that has a neighborhood feel, two pool tables, and lots of English-speaking patrons: **Le Petit Danois,** behind the bus station, off rue Principale (✆ **04-79-06-27-97;** www.lepetitdanois.com).

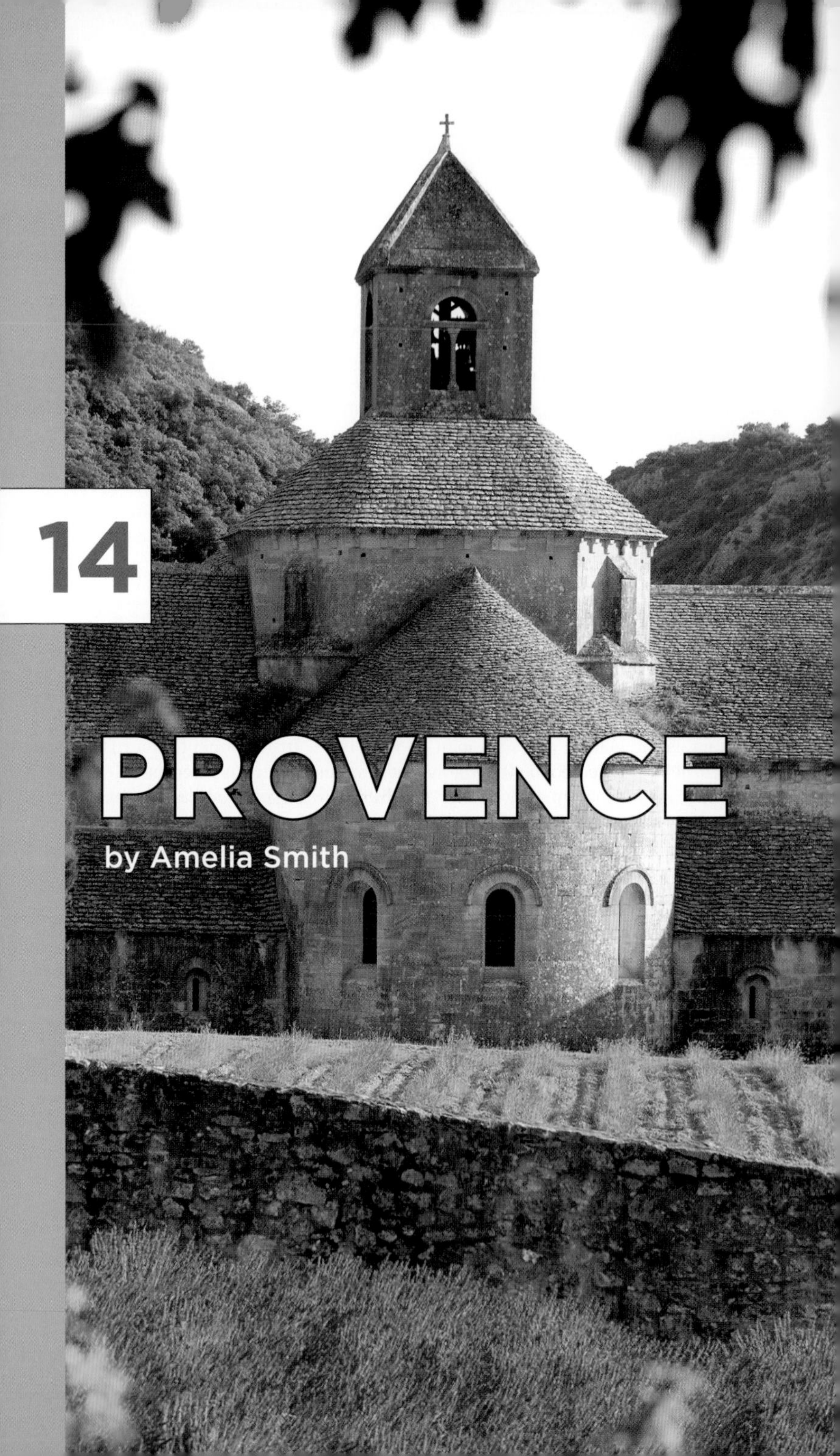

14

PROVENCE

by Amelia Smith

The ancient Greeks left their vines, the Romans their monuments and fortresses, but it was the 19th-century Impressionists who most shaped the romance of Provence today. Cezanne, Chagall, van Gogh, and countless others were drawn to the unique light and vibrant colors brought forth by what van Gogh called "the transparency of the air"—a phenomenon some say is due to the mighty Mistral wind that sweeps through the region.

Provence, perhaps more than any other part of France, blends past and present in a quiet, almost melancholy way. It has its own language and customs, and some of its festivals go back to medieval times. The region is bounded on the north by the Dauphine River, on the west by the Rhône, on the east by the Alps, and on the south by the Mediterranean. In chapter 15, we focus on the part of Provence known as the Côte d'Azur, or the French Riviera.

For more detailed coverage, see *Frommer's Provence & the Riviera.*

ORANGE ★★

659km (409 miles) S of Paris; 54km (33 miles) NE of Nîmes; 117km (73 miles) NW of Marseille; 31km (19 miles) N of Avignon

Antiquity-rich Orange (pop. 30,600) was not named for citrus fruit, but as a dependency of the Dutch House of Orange-Nassau during the Middle Ages. It is home to two UNESCO world heritage sites: Europe's third-largest triumphal arch and best-preserved Roman theater. Louis XIV, who once considered moving the theater to Versailles, said, "It is the finest wall in my kingdom."

The juice that flows from around Orange today goes into wine. The town is at the heart of the Côtes-du-Rhône appellation, making it an excellent base for tasting (ask the tourist office for a list of wineries).

Essentials

GETTING THERE Orange sits on major rail and highway arteries. Trains arrive daily from Avignon (trip time: 20 min.; 5.50€ one-way) and Marseille (trip time: 1 hr., 30 min.; 22€ one-way). From Paris, Orange can be reached in 3¼ hours via the TGV; the fare is 90€. For rail information, call ✆ **36-35;** www.voyages-sncf.com. For bus routes, contact the **Gare Routière,** place Pourtoules, behind the Théâtre Antique (✆ **04-90-34-15-59**). If you're **driving** from Paris, take A6 south to Lyon, then A7 to Orange. The 684km (424-mile) drive takes 5½ to 6½ hours.

VISITOR INFORMATION The **Office de Tourisme** is at 5 cours Aristide-Briand (✆ **04-90-34-70-88;** fax 04-90-34-99-62; www.otorange.fr).

SPECIAL EVENTS Taking advantage of the dramatic setting and acoustics of the Théâtre Antique, **Les Chorégies d'Orange** features opera and classical

FACING PAGE: **Abbaye Nôtre-Dame de Sénanque, Gordes.**

music performances for 2 to 3 weeks starting in mid-July. For information or tickets, contact the office at 18 place Sylvain, adjacent to the theater (© **04-90-34-24-24;** fax 04-90-11-04-04; www.choregies.asso.fr).

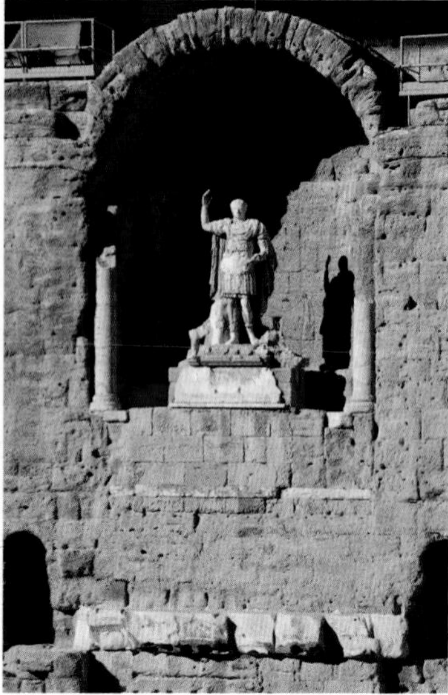
Théâtre Antique.

Exploring the Town

The carefully restored **Théâtre Antique ★★★**, rue Madeleine Roch (© **04-90-51-17-60;** www.theatre-antique.com), dates from the days of Augustus. Built into the side of a hill, it once held 9,000 spectators in tiered seats. Nearly 105m (344 ft.) long and 38m (125 ft.) high, it's open daily February 9:30am to 4:30pm; March and October 9:30am to 5:30pm; April, May, and September 9am to 6pm; and June to August 9am to 7pm. Admission is 8€ for adults and 6€ for students and children 17 and under. Audioguides are available.

Across the street, at the site of a ruined temple, the **Musée Municipal d'Orange,** place du Théâtre-Antique (© **04-90-51-17-60**), displays paintings, friezes, and artifacts from local archaeological digs. A ticket to the theater also admits you to the museum. Hours are November to February 9:30am to 4:30pm; March and October 9:30am to 5:30pm; April, May, and September 9am to 6pm; and June to August 9am to 7pm.

The imposing **Arc de Triomphe ★**, avenue de l'Arc-de-Triomphe, comprises a trio of arches held up by Corinthian columns embellished with military and maritime emblems. Also built during the reign of Augustus, it was once part of the original town's fortified walls.

The hilltop park on the **Colline St-Eutrope,** accessible by stairs behind the theater, offers a panoramic view of Orange and the surrounding landscape.

Where to Stay

Hôtel Arène ★ 🎁 On a leafy pedestrian street in the center of the historic district, this Best Western's bull's-eye location is a big draw. The complex consists of four antique town houses joined together to offer 35 rooms. "Provençal" rooms are modestly furnished with French-style decor, while those on the Executive Floor are larger, with newer bathrooms. Try to get a room with a balcony opening onto the old square in front; they have more personality. The staff is among the more courteous and helpful in town.

Place de Langes, Orange 84100. www.hotel-arene.fr. © **04-90-11-40-40.** Fax 04-90-11-40-45. 35 units. 70€–145€ double; 190€ junior suite. AE, DC, MC, V. Parking 9€. **Amenities:** 2 restaurants; in-room breakfast. *In room:* A/C, TV, hair dryer, minibar, free Wi-Fi.

Hotel Ibis Orange Centre If you're visiting Orange for a day on your way to somewhere else and have a car, this is a good alternative for comfort away from

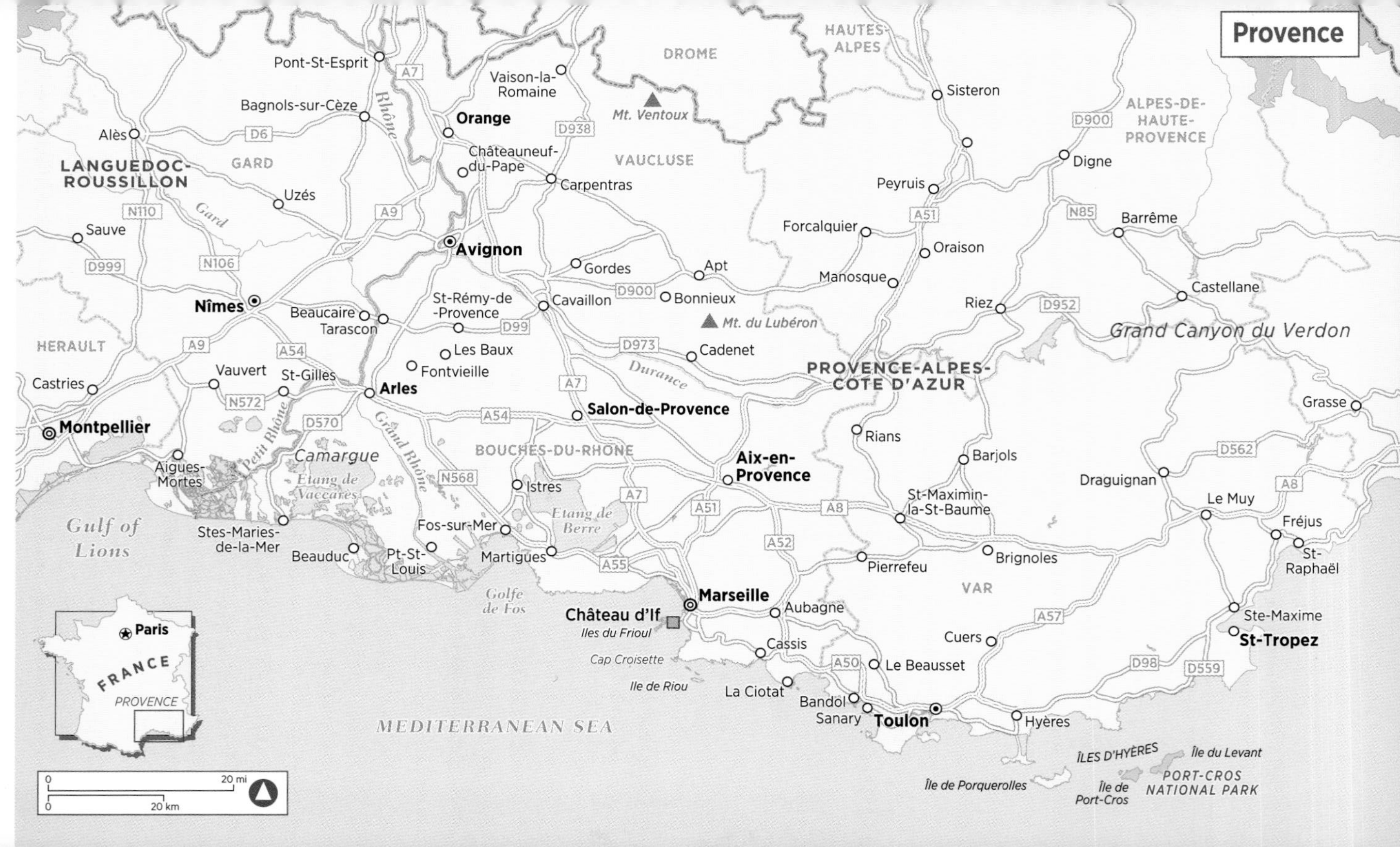
Provence
HAUTES-ALPES
DROME
ALPES-DE-HAUTE-PROVENCE
VAUCLUSE
LANGUEDOC-ROUSSILLON
GARD
HERAULT
PROVENCE-ALPES-COTE D'AZUR
BOUCHES-DU-RHONE
VAR
Pont-St-Esprit
Vaison-la-Romaine
Mt. Ventoux
Sisteron
Bagnols-sur-Cèze
Orange
Alès
Châteauneuf-du-Pape
Digne
Carpentras
Peyruis
Uzés
Gard
Rhône
Sauve
Avignon
Forcalquier
Barrême
Oraison
Gordes
Apt
Manosque
Bonnieux
Castellane
Nîmes
Beaucaire
Tarascon
St-Rémy-de-Provence
Cavaillon
Riez
Mt. du Lubéron
Grand Canyon du Verdon
Les Baux
Cadenet
Fontvieille
Durance
Castries
Vauvert
St-Gilles
Arles
Grasse
Salon-de-Provence
Montpellier
Petit Rhône
Rians
Camargue
Grand Rhône
Aigues-Mortes
Barjols
Aix-en-Provence
Etang de Vaccarès
Draguignan
Istres
St-Maximin-la-St-Baume
Le Muy
Gulf of Lions
Etang de Berre
Fréjus
Stes-Maries-de-la-Mer
Fos-sur-Mer
Beauduc
Pt-St-Louis
Martigues
Pierrefeu
Brignoles
St-Raphaël
Golfe de Fos
Marseille
Château d'If
Iles du Frioul
Aubagne
Ste-Maxime
Cuers
St-Tropez
Cassis
Cap Croisette
Le Beausset
Ile de Riou
La Ciotat
Bandol
Sanary
Toulon
Hyères
MEDITERRANEAN SEA
ÎLES D'HYÈRES
Île du Levant
Île de Porquerolles
Île de Port-Cros
PORT-CROS NATIONAL PARK
A7
A9
A51
A54
A8
A52
A55
A57
A50
D6
D938
D900
D999
D99
D973
D570
D952
D562
D98
D559
N110
N106
N572
N568
N85
Paris
FRANCE
PROVENCE
0
20 mi
0
20 km

the crowds. In a handful of chain hotels just off the A7/A9 interchange, it's about a 20-minute walk from the center of town (but definitely a taxi ride from the train station). What the hotel lacks in old-world charm, it makes up for in convenience: parking, a swimming pool, and a simple restaurant.

Rte. de Caderousse, Orange 84100. www.accorhotels.com. ✆ **04-90-34-35-35.** Fax 04-90-34-96-47. 72 units. 55€–85€ double. AE, DC, MC, V. Free parking. **Amenities:** Restaurant; bar; outdoor pool. *In room:* A/C, TV, free Wi-Fi.

Where to Eat

Au Petit Patio PROVENÇAL This agreeable little restaurant has gained a steady stream of fans since it opened its doors in 2009. The "patio" refers to the small outdoor dining area, which is tucked away rather than on the street like at most other restaurants in town. At the height of summer, you may prefer the colorful, air-conditioned dining room, however. Artfully presented Provençal specialties include eggplant terrine with tomato-basil coulis and veal filet with morels. The service is laid-back and efficient. An excellent value.

58 cours Aristide Briand. ✆ **04-90-29-69-27.** Reservations recommended. Main courses 15€–18€; fixed-price menu 24€–35€. MC, V. Mon–Sat noon–1:30pm and 7pm–9:30pm (closed Wed evening).

Le Parvis PROVENÇAL In a rather austere dining room, classic Provençal cuisine is served based on the freshest ingredients available from land or sea. Try braised sea bass with fennel and asparagus, lamb chops with goat cheese, or, for dessert, olive oil ice cream with wine-marinated figs. The staff is efficient and polite. There is a children's menu, but the hushed atmosphere could be a challenge for families.

55 cours Pourtoules. ✆ **04-90-34-82-00.** Reservations required. Main courses 17€–26€; fixed-price menu 26€–42€; children's menu 10€. AE, MC, V. Tues–Sun noon–2:30pm; Tues–Sat 7pm–11pm. Closed last 3 weeks in Nov.

Exploring the Area

Just 13km (8 miles) south along the A9 is **Châteauneuf-du-Pape,** a prestigious appellation known for its bold and spicy red wines. Spend a day visiting the village's numerous tasting rooms, winding your way up to the ruins of a castle that served as a summer residence for Pope John XXII. A pleasant option for lunch is Le Verger des Papes, 4 rue du Château (✆ **04-90-83-50-40;** www.vergerdespapes.com). Steps away from the castle, it serves grilled specialties or pasta on an outdoor terrace with stunning views of the Rhône Valley. The set-price lunch menu is 29€.

Where to Stay & Eat Nearby

Château de Rochegude ★★ A true 12th-century castle—whose former residents include a pope and a dauphin—this Relais & Châteaux member sits at the edge of a hill surrounded by 10 hectares (25 acres) of parkland. Fabrics and furniture influenced by 18th- and 19th-century local traditions create an atmosphere of authentic elegance in the rooms, which range from cozy to spacious. All the bathrooms have tub/showers. The gastronomic restaurant offers an ample selection of regional wines. You can also enjoy meals by the pool or on one of many tucked-away terraces. Fixed-price lunches cost 26€ to 35€, fixed-price dinners 39€ to 89€.

SHOPPING FOR *brocante* IN PROVENCE

In France, there's a wide gap between true antiques and old knickknacks, and it's wise to know the difference. For serious purchases, stick to well-established *antiquaires,* found in almost every town and city. If you're looking for more affordable treasures and enjoy flea markets, what you really want is a *brocante.* These are usually held outside on specific days (the markets in Cannes are a good example; see chapter 15). Furniture and objects can also be found in warehouses known as *depot-ventes.*

A village that specializes in *brocante* is **Isle-sur-la-Sorgue,** situated 23km (14 miles) east of Avignon, 11km (6¾ miles) north of Cavaillon, and 42km (26 miles) south of Orange. The **Foire à la Brocante** is held on Saturdays, Sundays, and Mondays; on Sundays there's also a food market. The activity starts at 9am and finishes around 6pm. If you're driving, try for a parking space in the free Parking Portalet adjacent to the fairgrounds. The *brocante* is on the near side of the river, a little farther downstream, where you'll find warehouses filled with dealers and loot.

Isle-sur-la-Sorgue's Office de Tourisme is at place de la Liberté (✆ **04-90-38-04-78;** www.oti-delasorgue.fr).

Place du Château, Rochegude 26790. www.chateauderochegude.com. ✆ **04-75-97-21-10.** Fax 04-75-04-89-87. 25 units. 170€–430€ double; 350€–540€ suite. AE, DC, MC, V. Parking 7€. Closed Sun and Mon Nov 1–Mar 31. Take D976 13km (8 miles) north of Orange, following signs toward Gap and Rochegude. **Amenities:** Restaurant; bar; outdoor pool; room service; tennis court. *In room:* A/C, TV, minibar, free Wi-Fi.

AVIGNON ★★★

691km (428 miles) S of Paris; 83km (51 miles) NW of Aix-en-Provence; 98km (61 miles) NW of Marseille

In the 14th century, Avignon was the capital of Christendom. What started as a temporary stay by Pope Clement V in 1309, when Rome was deemed too dangerous, became a 67-year golden age. The cultural and architectural legacy left by the six popes who served during this period makes Avignon one of Europe's most beautiful medieval destinations.

Today this walled city of some 89,000 residents is a major stop on the route from Paris to the Mediterranean. In recent years, it has become known as a cultural center, thanks to its annual international performing arts festivals and wealth of experimental theaters and art galleries. To make the most of the many galleries, museums, and the papal complex, plan to spend at least 2 days here.

Essentials

GETTING THERE The fastest and easiest way to get here is to **fly** from Paris's Orly Airport to **Aéroport Avignon-Caumont** (✆ **04-90-81-51-15;** www.avignon.aeroport.fr), 8km (5 miles) southeast of Avignon (trip time: 1 hr.). Taxis from the airport to the center cost approximately 25€. Call ✆ **04-90-82-20-20.** From Paris, TGV **trains** from Gare de Lyon take 2 hours and 40 minutes and arrive at a modern station 10 minutes from town by shuttle bus. The one-way fare is between 65€ and 90€, depending on the date and time. Trains arrive frequently from Marseille (trip time: 80 min.; 19€ one-way) and Arles (trip time: 20 min.; 8€ one-way), arriving at either the TGV or Avignon's central station. For rail information, call ✆ **36-35** (www.voyages-sncf.com). The regional **bus** routes go from Avignon to Arles (trip time: 1 hr., 20 min.; 6.80€ one-way) and Aix-en Provence (trip time: 1 hr., 15 min.; 15 € one-way). The bus station at Avignon is the **Gare Routière,** 5 av. Monclar (✆ **04-90-82-07-35**). If you're **driving** from Paris, take A6 south to Lyon, and then A7 south to Avignon.

To explore the area by bicycle, **Provence Bike,** 52 bd. St-Roch (✆ **04-90-27-92-61;** www.provence-bike.com), rents different models for around 10€ to 25€ per day. A deposit of 150€ to 450€, in cash or a credit card imprint, is required. It is possible to reserve a bike online.

VISITOR INFORMATION The **Office de Tourisme** is at 41 cours Jean-Jaurès (✆ **04-32-74-32-74;** fax 04-90-82-95-03; www.ot-avignon.fr).

SPECIAL EVENTS The international **Festival d'Avignon,** held for 3 weeks in July, focuses on avant-garde theater, dance, and music. Tickets cost 13€ to 38€. Prices for rooms and meals skyrocket during this period, so make reservations well in advance. Contact the **Bureaux du Festival,** Espace Saint-Louis, 20 rue du Portail Boquier, Avignon 84000 (✆ **04-90-27-66-50;** www.festival-avignon.com). An alternative and edgier festival, the **Avignon Off,** takes place in July, with theater performances in various improbable venues. For information, contact the **Bureaux du Off,** 5 rue Ninon Vallin, Avignon 84000 (✆ **04-90-85-13-08;** www.avignonleoff.com).

Exploring the Town

Every French child knows the ditty *"Sur le pont d'Avignon, l'on y danse, l'on y danse"* ("On the bridge of Avignon, we dance, we dance"). The bridge in question, **Pont St-Bénézet ★★** (✆ **04-90-27-51-16**), was constructed between 1177 and 1185. Once spanning the Rhône and connecting Avignon with Villeneuve-lèz-Avignon, it is now a ruin, with only 4 of its original 22 arches remaining (half of it fell into the river in 1669). On the third pillar is the **Chapelle St-Nicolas,** its first story in Romanesque style, the second in Gothic. The remains of the bridge are open November through March daily 9:30am to 5:45pm, mid-March through June and mid-September through October daily 9am to 7pm, July to mid-September daily 9am to 8pm, and August daily 9am to 9pm. Admission is 4.50€ for adults, 3.50€ for seniors and students, and free for children 7 and under. Entrance to the chapel is included.

Pont St-Bénézet.

Cathédrale Notre-Dame des Doms Near the Palais des Papes, this majestic 12th-century cathedral contains the elaborate tombs of popes Jean XXII and Benoît XII. Crowning the top is a 19th-century gilded statue of the

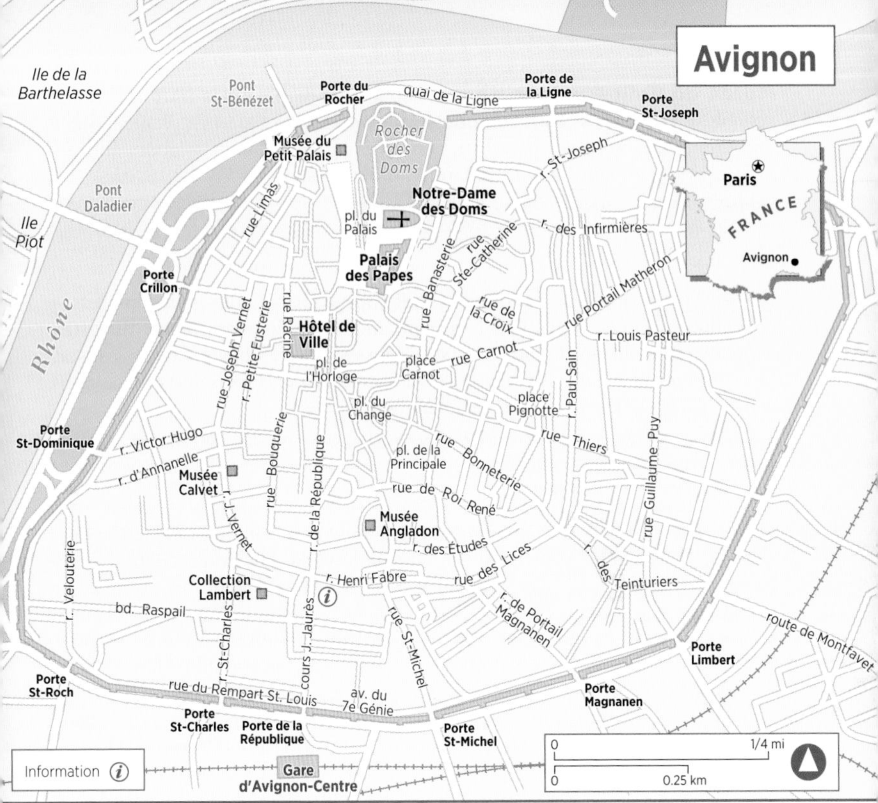

Virgin. From the cathedral, enter the **Promenade du Rocher-des-Doms** to stroll its garden and enjoy the view across the Rhône to Villeneuve-lez-Avignon.

Place du Palais. ✆ **04-90-82-12-21.** Free admission. Mon–Sat 8:30am–6pm; Sun 10am–6pm. Hours may vary according to religious ceremonies.

La Fondation Angladon-Dubrujeaud ★★ The magnificent art collection of Jacques Doucet (1853–1929), the Belle Epoque dandy and designer of Parisian haute couture, is on view here. Doucet and his wife collected the early works of artists including Picasso, Max Jacob, and van Gogh. Wandering through their former home, you'll see rare antiques; 16th-century Buddhas; Louis XVI chairs designed by Jacob; and canvases by Cézanne, Sisley, Degas, and Modigliani.

5 rue Laboureur. ✆ **04-90-82-29-03.** www.angladon.com. Admission 6€ adults, 3€ students and children 15–18, 1.50€ children 7–12. Tues–Sun 1–6pm. Closed Tues in winter.

Musée Calvet ★ Based on the collection of native son Esprit Calvet, who bequeathed a lifetime's worth of acquired art and artifacts to the city upon his death, this is Avignon's premier fine art museum. The 18th-century mansion displays dozens of sculptures and paintings, including works by Vernet, David, Corot, Manet, and Soutine, plus a collection of ancient silverware. Look for a copy of Bosch's *Adoration of the Magi,* plus sculptures by Camille Claudel.

65 rue Joseph-Vernet. ✆ **04-90-86-33-84.** www.musee-calvet.org. Admission 6€ adults, 3€ students, free for children 12 and under. Wed–Mon 10am–1pm and 2–6pm. Closed New Year's Day, May 1, and Christmas.

Musée du Petit-Palais ★ This museum exhibits paintings from the Italian schools of the 13th to 16th centuries, with works from Florence, Venice, Siena, and Lombardy. Salons display 15th-century paintings done in Avignon, and several galleries contain Roman and Gothic sculptures.

Place du Palais des Papes. ✆ **04-90-86-44-58.** www.petit-palais.org. Admission 6€ adults, 3€ students, free for children 12 and under. Wed–Mon 10am–1pm and 2–6pm. Closed New Year's Day, May 1, and Christmas.

Musée Lapidaire A 17th-century Jesuit college chapel houses this impressive collection of Greek, Egyptian, Etruscan, and Gallo-Roman artifacts that grew from the original Calvet collection (see "Musée Calvet," above). Gargoyles, statues, and broken pillars, as well as everyday items such as tools and ornate vases, are on display in the nave and side chambers.

27 rue de la République. ✆ **04-90-85-75-38.** www.musee-calvet.org. Admission 2€ adults, 1€ students 13–18, free for children 12 and under. Wed–Mon 10am–noon and 2–6pm. Closed New Year's Day, May 1, and Christmas.

Palais des Papes ★★★ Dominating Avignon from a hilltop is one of the most famous, or notorious, palaces in the Christian world. Headquarters of a schismatic group of cardinals who came close to destroying the authority of the popes in Rome, this fortress is the city's most popular monument. Because of its massive size, you may be tempted to opt for a guided tour—but these can be monotonous. The audioguide included in the price of admission should suffice.

A highlight is the Chapelle St-Jean, known for its frescoes of John the Baptist and John the Evangelist, attributed to the school of Matteo Giovanetti and painted between 1345 and 1348. The **Grand Tinel (Banquet Hall)** is about 41m (134 ft.) long and 9m (30 ft.) wide; the pope's table stood on the south side. The walls of the **Pope's Bedroom,** on the first floor of the Tour des Anges, are painted with foliage, birds, and squirrels. The **Studium (Stag Room)**—the

Palais des Papes.

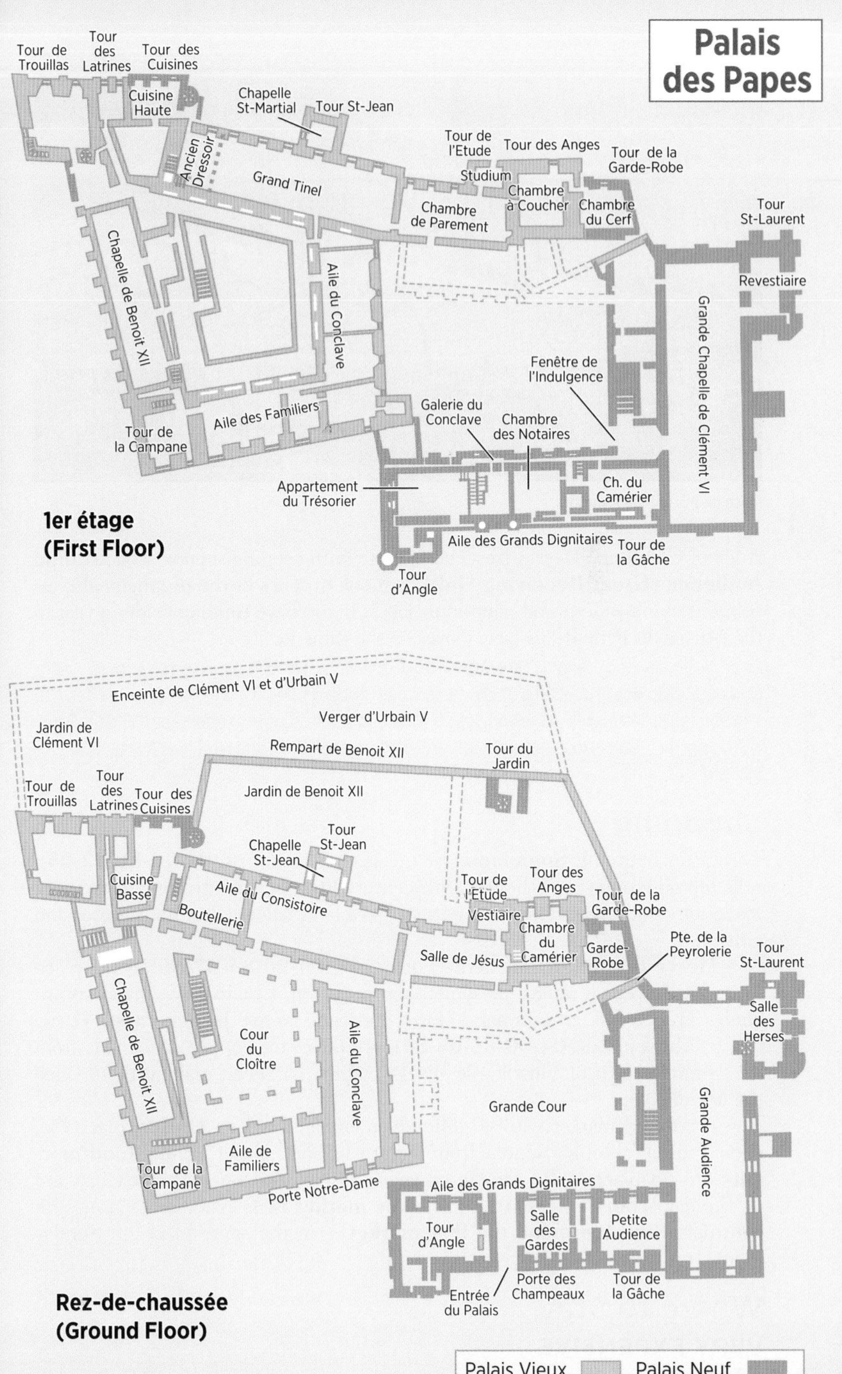
Palais des Papes
Tour de Trouillas
Tour des Latrines
Tour des Cuisines
Cuisine Haute
Chapelle St-Martial
Tour St-Jean
Ancien Dressoir
Grand Tinel
Tour de l'Etude
Tour des Anges
Tour de la Garde-Robe
Studium
Chambre à Coucher
Chambre de Parement
Chambre du Cerf
Tour St-Laurent
Revestiaire
Chapelle de Benoit XII
Aile du Conclave
Grande Chapelle de Clément VI
Fenêtre de l'Indulgence
Galerie du Conclave
Chambre des Notaires
Aile des Familiers
Tour de la Campane
Appartement du Trésorier
Ch. du Camérier
Aile des Grands Dignitaires
Tour de la Gâche
Tour d'Angle
1er étage (First Floor)
Enceinte de Clément VI et d'Urbain V
Verger d'Urbain V
Jardin de Clément VI
Rempart de Benoit XII
Tour du Jardin
Tour de Trouillas
Tour des Latrines
Tour des Cuisines
Jardin de Benoit XII
Tour St-Jean
Chapelle St-Jean
Cuisine Basse
Aile du Consistoire
Boutellerie
Tour de l'Etude
Tour des Anges
Tour de la Garde-Robe
Vestiaire
Chambre du Camérier
Garde-Robe
Pte. de la Peyrolerie
Tour St-Laurent
Salle de Jésus
Salle des Herses
Chapelle de Benoit XII
Cour du Cloître
Aile du Conclave
Grande Cour
Grande Audience
Aile de Familiers
Tour de la Campane
Porte Notre-Dame
Aile des Grands Dignitaires
Tour d'Angle
Salle des Gardes
Petite Audience
Porte des Champeaux
Tour de la Gâche
Entrée du Palais
Rez-de-chaussée (Ground Floor)
Palais Vieux
Palais Neuf

Place de l'Orloge in Avignon.

study of Clement VI—was frescoed in 1343 with hunting scenes. The **Grande Audience (Great Receiving Hall)** contains frescoes of the prophets, also attributed to Giovanetti and painted in 1352. If you have time, consider a visit to the Musée du Petit-Palais (see above), in the same location.

Place du Palais des Papes. ✆ **04-90-27-50-00.** www.palais-des-papes.com. Admission (including audioguide) 11€ adults, 8.50€ seniors and students, free for children 8 and under. Mar 1–14 9am–6:30pm; Mar 15–June and Sept 16–Oct daily 9am–7pm; July and Sept 1–15 daily 9am–8pm; Aug 9am–9pm; Nov–Feb daily 9:30am–5:45pm; Christmas and New Year's Day 10:30am–5:45pm.

Shopping

The chain boutique **Souleiado,** 19 rue Joseph-Vernet (✆ **04-90-86-32-05**), sells reproductions of 18th- and 19th-century Provençal fabrics by the meter or made into clothing and linens. There is also a large selection of housewares and gifts.

Hervé Baume, 19 rue Petite Fusterie (✆ **04-90-86-37-66**), is the place to buy a Provençal table—or something to put on it. A massive inventory includes French folk art and hand-blown hurricane lamps. **Jaffier-Parsi,** 42 rue des Fourbisseurs (✆ **04-90-86-08-85**), is known for copper saucepans from the Norman town of Villedieu-les-Poêles, which has been making them since the Middle Ages.

A covered market with 40 different merchants is **Les Halles,** place Pie, open Tuesday through Sunday from 6am to 1:30pm. Other smaller **food markets** are on place de la Méditerranée on Friday, and on place St-Chamand on Sunday (both 8am–1pm). The **flower market** is on place des Carmes on Saturday (8am–1pm), and the **flea market** is in the same place on Sunday (6am–1pm).

Where to Stay

VERY EXPENSIVE

Hôtel d'Europe ★★★ This deluxe property, in operation since 1799, has welcomed luminaries from Charles Dickens to Jacqueline Kennedy. The entrance is through a shady courtyard dominated by a gurgling fountain, where dining is possible in warmer months. Antiques fill the grand hall and salons, and the good-size guest rooms are handsomely decorated with period furnishings. Two top-floor suites offer private terraces with views of the Palais des Papes. Overall, accommodations are comfortable, with spacious, well-equipped bathrooms. The restaurant, specializing in traditional French and Provençal cuisine, is one of the best in Avignon.

14 place Crillon, Avignon 84000. www.heurope.com. ✆ **04-90-14-76-76.** Fax 04-90-14-76-71. 44 units. 210€–540€ double; 720€–920€ suite. AE, DC, MC, V. Parking 16€. **Amenities:** Restaurant; bar; babysitting; room service. *In room:* A/C, TV, hair dryer, minibar, free Wi-Fi.

La Mirande ★★★ In the heart of Avignon behind the Palais des Papes, this 700-year-old townhouse is one of France's greatest small hotels. In 1987, Achim and Hannelore Stein transformed it into a haven of opulence. On display are 2 centuries of decorative art, ranging from the 1700s *Salon Chinois* to the *Salon Rouge,* with striped red walls. The rooms are breathtaking, with hand-printed wall fabrics, antiques, and huge bathtubs. Number 20 is the most sought after—its lavish premises open onto the garden. The restaurant deserves its Michelin star.

4 place de la Mirande, Avignon 84000. www.lamirande-avignon.com. ✆ **04-90-14-20-20.** Fax 04-90-86-26-85. 21 units. 310€–540€ double; 660€–970€ suite. AE, DC, MC, V. Parking 25€. **Amenities:** Restaurant; bar; babysitting; room service. *In room:* A/C, TV, hair dryer, minibar, free Wi-Fi.

EXPENSIVE

Hôtel Clarion Cloître St-Louis ★ Steps from the main train station, this hotel is in a former Jesuit school built in the 1580s. Many of the original features remain, including the baroque facade, wraparound arcades, and soaring ceiling vaults. Though the guest rooms are modern and functional—in line with what you would expect from a chain hotel—the dining area made from a glassed-in section of the cloisters makes an impression.

20 rue du Portail Boquier, Avignon 84000. www.cloitre-saint-louis.com. ✆ **800/CLARION** [252-7466] in the U.S., or 04-90-27-55-55. Fax 04-90-82-24-01. 80 units. 210€–280€ double; 250€–320€ suite. AE, DC, MC, V. Parking 12€–15€. **Amenities:** Restaurant; bar; outdoor pool; room service. *In room:* A/C, TV, hair dryer, minibar, free Wi-Fi.

MODERATE

La Banasterie ★ 🎁 Just a short walk from the papal palace, this charismatic B&Bs is run by Françoise and Jean-Michel, who left Paris to open it and share their passion for all things chocolate. The cozy and elegant bedrooms are beautifully furnished, and some have balconies or terraces. All are named for varieties of chocolate or the Aztec god credited with bringing chocolate to humans as a divine gift. You're offered a decadently rich cup of cocoa before retiring. In the morning, a copious continental breakfast (included in the rate) is left in a basket on your door.

11 rue de la Banasterie, 84000 Avignon. www.labanasterie.com. ✆ **06-87-72-96-36.** 5 units. 100€ double; 170€ suite. MC, V. **Amenities:** Breakfast room. *In room:* AC, TV, hair dryer, free Wi-Fi.

Mercure Pont d'Avignon 🏷 This modern chain hotel is one of the best in Avignon, and good value for money. Its strong point is the location, just 3 minutes from the Palais des Papes. Rooms are well equipped and functional; what they lack in style, they make up for in comfort. Bathrooms are small, but most contain tub/showers. A breakfast buffet is the only meal served.

Quartier de la Balance, rue Ferruce, Avignon 84000. www.accorhotels.com. ✆ **04-90-80-93-93.** Fax 04-90-80-93-94. 87 units. 125€–170€ double; 250€ suite. Children 15 and under stay free in parent's room. AE, DC, MC, V. Parking in nearby garage 8.20€. **Amenities:** Bar. *In room:* A/C, TV, hair dryer, minibar, free Wi-Fi.

INEXPENSIVE

Hôtel d'Angleterre This three-story Art Deco structure in the heart of Avignon is the city's best budget hotel, with the advantage of being located inside the city walls and close to the train station. It was built in 1929 in gray stone, emulating the style that local builders imagined was characteristic of English houses. The rooms are on the small side but comfortably furnished; most have compact shower-only bathrooms. Breakfast is the only meal served.

29 bd. Raspail, Avignon 84000. www.hoteldangleterre.fr. ✆ **04-90-86-34-31.** Fax 04-90-86-86-74. 39 units. 60€–85€ double. AE, MC, V. Free parking. Closed mid–Dec to mid–Jan. *In room:* A/C, TV, free Wi-Fi.

Hôtel de l'Atelier This 16th-century property across the river in Villeneuve-lez-Avignon derives its name from the weaving machines that produced fabrics here during the 1950s (*atelier* means "workshop"). Since 2003, it has been the domain of Gérard and Annick Burret, who outfit their rooms in a refined and nostalgic style. Each of the accommodations, some with high beamed ceilings, comes with a neatly tiled bathroom with shower or bathtub. A rear garden with potted fruit trees and the lounge's stone fireplace complete the romantic atmosphere. Continental breakfast is the only meal served.

5 rue de la Foire, Villeneuve-lez-Avignon 30400. www.hoteldelatelier.com. ✆ **04-90-25-01-84.** Fax 04-13-33-71-41. 23 units. 59€–140€ double; 97€–170€ triple. AE, MC, V. Parking 9€ in nearby garage. *In room:* TV, hair dryer, free Wi-Fi.

Hôtel le Colbert On a tiny residential street close to the tourist office, this small hotel is known for its eclectic ambience, great breakfasts, and especially helpful owners. Rooms have modern conveniences and are decorated in vibrant colors with an assortment of avant-garde posters; they have showers only. There is no elevator, but a coin laundry just a few steps away. The postage stamp–sized back garden is the perfect place to sit with a coffee and street map and plan your day.

7 rue Agricol Perdiguier, Avignon 84000. ✆ **04-90-86-20-20.** Fax 04-90-85-97-00. www.avignon-hotel-colbert.com. 14 units. 70€–126€ double. AE, MC, V. Closed Nov–Feb. *In room:* A/C, TV, hair dryer, free Wi-Fi.

Where to Eat

Hôtel d'Europe and **La Mirande** (see above) offer excellent dining.

Christian Etienne ★★★ PROVENÇAL The stone house containing this restaurant was built in 1180, around the same time as the Palais des Papes next door. Etienne's fixed-price menus center on featured ingredients such as duck or lobster; the pricier tasting menu relies on his imagination for unique combinations. In summer, look for the vegetable (not vegetarian) menu entirely based on ripe tomatoes, the main course a mousse of lamb, eggplant, tomatoes, and herbs. The a la carte menu includes innovative desserts such as jellied beets with green pepper coulis and lemongrass sorbet. The dining room contains early-

16th-century frescoes honoring the marriage of Anne de Bretagne to the French king in 1491.

10 rue Mons. ✆ **04-90-86-16-50.** www.christian-etienne.fr. Reservations required. Main courses 30€–50€; fixed-price lunch 31€–125€, dinner 65€–125€. AE, DC, MC, V. Tues–Sat noon–1:15pm and 7:30–9:15pm.

Hiély-Lucullus ★★ FRENCH Before Christian Etienne (see above), this Relais Gourmand property reigned supreme in Avignon. It's still a worthy competitor, with young brothers Laurent and Gérald Azoulay having taken over to update the restaurant's slightly stuffy reputation. Fresh ingredients are imported daily and cooked to perfection, resulting in dishes such as grilled scallops with black truffles and celery purée, and roast hare. The recipe for *marmite de pecheur au saffron* (fish stew) dates back to the restaurant's original 1938 menu. An impressive wine list includes a good selection of Côtes du Rhônes.

5 rue de la République. ✆ **04-90-86-17-07.** Reservations required. Main courses 28€–35€; fixed-price menu 40€–90€. AE, MC, V. Thurs–Tues noon–1:30pm and 7:30–9:30pm. Closed Thurs and Sat lunch.

La Fourchette PROVENÇAL An upscale bistro serving innovative cuisine at a moderate price, La Fourchette is open only on weekdays. Its homey decoration (with collected items arranged on the walls) and large bay windows create a pleasant atmosphere. Among the dishes created by the sixth-generation chef: fresh sardines flavored with citrus, haddock-filled ravioli, and beef stew à l'Avignonnaise. It's popular with locals, so reservations are a must.

17 rue Racine. ✆ **04-90-85-20-93.** Fixed-price lunch 25€–31€, dinner 31€. MC, V. Mon–Fri 12:15–1:45pm and 7:15–9:45pm. Closed 3 weeks in Aug.

L'Isle Sonnante ★ PROVENÇAL There are only 20 seats in this little gem steps away from the Palais des Papes, though a few tables are added for terrace dining in summer. Chef Boris Chevtchenko transforms market-fresh produce into dishes such as ravioli with foie gras, rabbit with olives, and calamari risotto with saffron. The cuisine is in tune with the cozy, elegant dining area, where Anne Chevtchenko serves as *maîtresse d'hôtel.* Save room for the dessert cart, which offers up to 10 delicacies prepared daily. The wine list is dedicated exclusively to Côtes du Rhone.

7 rue Racine. ✆ **04-90-82-56-01.** Reservations essential. Main courses 22€–30€; fixed-price menu 25€–45€. AE, DC, MC, V. Tues–Sat noon–2pm and 7–9:30pm.

Avignon After Dark

Le Grand Café, 4 rue des Escaliers-Sainte-Anne (✆ **04-90-86-86-77**), is a restaurant-bar-cafe and one of the town's most popular watering holes. Behind the Palais des Papes, it's in an entertainment complex in a former military supply warehouse. The beautiful people frequent **Les Ambassadeurs,** 27 rue Bancasse (✆ **04-90-86-31-55;** www.lesambassadeurs.fr), an upscale dance club. The **Red Zone DJ bar,** 27 rue Carnot (✆ **04-90-27-02-44;** www.redzonedjbar.com), offers a different musical theme every night (salsa, electronic, and more). **83 Vernet,** 83 rue Joseph Vernet (✆ **04-90-85-99-04;** www.83vernet.fr), switches from restaurant into dance club mode around 10pm, under the high-ceilinged hallways and stone courtyards of a former 1363 Benedictine convent.

Behind the Hôtel d'Europe, the bar and disco **L'Esclave,** 12 rue de Limas (✆ **04-90-85-14-91**), is a focal point of the city's gay community.

GORDES ★★★

720km (446 miles) S of Paris; 38km (24 miles) E of Avignon; 77km (48 miles) N of Aix-en-Provence; 92km (57 miles) N of Marseille

Everything about Gordes is rocky—from the low walls flanking the hilltop access road, to the tiered houses clinging to the cliffside, to its *rues caladés* (streets paved with local river stones). From afar, it is a pastiche of beiges, grays, and terra cotta that blushes golden at sunrise and sunset.

The village unwinds downhill from the Château de Gordes, the Renaissance rehabilitation of a 12th-century fortress. The windows in its four machicolated towers still bear grooves from the bows and arrows used to protect Gordes during Gallo-Roman times, when it was a border town.

Gordes.

Today Gordes is more likely to be invaded by easels. Its austere beauty has drawn many artists, including Marc Chagall and Hungarian Victor Vasarely, who spent summers here gathering inspiration for his geometric abstract art.

Essentials

GETTING THERE Gordes is not easily reached via public transportation. The closest train station is Cavaillon, where trains arrive from the Avignon central station (trip time: 35 min.; 6.30€ one-way). Buses leave from the Cavaillon SNCF station and arrive at place du Château in Gordes (trip time: 35 min.; 1.50€ one-way). For rail information, call ✆ **36-35;** www.voyages-sncf.com. For information on bus routes, contact the Gordes tourist office (✆ **04-90-72-02-75**). Another option is to take a 1-day coach tour from either Avignon or Aix-en-Provence. **Autocars Lieutaud** (✆ **04-90-86-36-75;** www.cars-lieutaud.fr) offers this service in Avignon, as does the tourist office in Aix-en-Provence (✆ **04-42-16-11-61;** www.aixenprovence tourism.com).

By car, Gordes is a 38km (24-mile) drive from Avignon via A7. Take exit 25 for Cavaillon; at the village of Coustellet, follow the signs to Gordes.

VISITOR INFORMATION The **Office de Tourisme** is at the Place du Château (✆ **04-90-72-02-75;** fax 04-90-72-04-39; www.gordes-village.com).

Exploring the Town

Caves du Palais St. Firmin ★ Steep Gordes lacks an abundance of surface area, so early settlers burrowed into the rock itself. Below the Palace of St. Firmin is an underground network of crude rooms and stairways, on seven levels, that over the centuries housed the village's production of olive oil and grain, among other industries. Though the tunnels are adequately lit, children are provided with a small headlamp to give them the feeling of being true explorers.

2 rue de la République. ✆ **04-90-27-49-66.** Admission 4€ adults, 12€ families. Jan Tues–Sun 10am–noon and 2–5pm; Mar–Apr and Oct–Dec 2–5pm; May–Sept 2:30–6:30pm. Closed Feb, New Year's Day, May 1, Nov 1, and Christmas.

Château de Gordes Housed inside the Château (and the only way to see its interior) is a museum dedicated to the work of contemporary Flemish painter Pol Mara (1920–98), a former resident of Gordes. The visit begins with a Renaissance-era spiral staircase to the third floor. Over 200 of the artist's works are displayed chronologically as you make your way back downstairs to the *Salle d'Honneur,* dominated by a monumental 16th-century chimney—the largest of its kind in Europe.

Place du Château. ✆ **04-90-72-02-75.** Admission 4€ adults, 3€ children 10–17. Daily 10am–noon and 2–6pm. Closed New Year's Day and Christmas.

Village des Bories ★ Bories are beehive-shaped dwellings made of intricately stacked stone—and not one ounce of mortar. They date back as far as the Bronze Age and as recently as the 18th century in Provence. An architectural curiosity, their thick walls and cantilevered roofs beg the question: How did they do that? The Village des Bories is the largest extant group of these structures in the region, comprising 30 huts grouped according to function (houses, stables, bakeries, tanneries, and more). Traditional objects and tools are on display, along with an exhibit on the history of dry stone architecture in France and around the world.

1.5km (1 mile) west of Gordes on the D2. ✆ **04-90-72-03-48.** Admission 6€ adults, 4€ children. Daily 9am to sundown.

Where to Stay

VERY EXPENSIVE

Hôtel Les Bories & Spa ★ During a stay here, you're sure to rub elbows with the pampered and privileged. The hotel is known for its extensive spa; it's not

Village des Bories.

unusual to see blissed-out, bathrobed guests padding back to their rooms after a treatment. There is a large heated indoor whirlpool, as well as an outdoor pool overlooking the Cavaillon plain. The best way to describe the guest rooms is very white—but this is set off nicely by the lavender, orange flowers, and silvery plants of the aromatic garden seen from the windows and private terraces. Enjoy Michelin-starred cuisine in the restaurant or on the terrace at twilight in summer.

Rte. de l'Abbaye de Senanque, Gordes 84220. www.hotellesbories.com. ✆ **04-90-72-00-51.** Fax 04-90-72-01-22. 29 units. 200€–434€ double; 503€ or 820€ suite. AE, MC, V. Free parking. **Amenities:** Restaurant; bar; room service; indoor/outdoor swimming pools; rooms for those w/limited mobility; sauna; spa services; steam room. *In room:* A/C, TV, hair dryer, minibar, free Wi-Fi.

EXPENSIVE

Le Mas des Romarins The main terrace of this small hotel affords a postcard-perfect view of the village, 10 minutes away on foot. This means an opportunity to catch the natural light playing across the stone facades at dawn and dusk. The unpretentious guest rooms, a bit small, are in either the original *mas* or a 19th-century stone workshop. Upper rooms have a view; those on the ground floor have a private terrace or garden. A small lap pool, surrounded by low stone walls and fragrant brush, offers respite from the summer heat. The guests-only restaurant serves Provençal cuisine outside or next to the fireplace, depending on the season. Buffet breakfast for two is included in the rate.

Rte. de l'Abbaye de Senanque, Gordes 84220. www.masromarins.com/francais. ✆ **04-90-72-12-13.** Fax 04-90-72-13-13. 13 units. 99€–170€ double ; 174€–208€ suite. MC, V. Free parking. Closed mid-Nov to mid-Dec, Jan–Feb. **Amenities:** Restaurant; outdoor pool. *In room:* A/C, TV, hair dryer, minibar.

MODERATE

La Ferme de la Huppe ★ 🎁 Ten minutes down the road from Gordes, within 30 minutes of other famous Luberon villages such as Bonnieux and Roussillon, this former silk worm farm was remodeled into a casually elegant hotel. Its authenticity has been preserved thanks to the use of materials salvaged from old properties in the area. Arranged on different levels, the guest rooms are named after different functions—The Stable, Hay Loft, Wine Cellar, and so on. Though slightly dark, they are very tastefully decorated, with wooden furniture, real quilts, and modern bathrooms. The carefully tended garden and pool are romantically lit at night. Make sure to reserve the restaurant, which is open to the public. Expertly prepared dishes such as partridge with chestnut cream, and lamb with thyme and artichoke ravioli mean it's almost always full.

R.D. 156, Les Pourquiers, Gordes 84220. www.lafermedelahuppe.com. ✆ **04-90-72-12-25.** Fax 04-90-72-25-39. 10 units. 105€–138€ double; 175€–185€ suite. Breakfast (mandatory) 15€ per person. Free parking. DC, MC, V. **Amenities:** Restaurant; outdoor pool. *In room*: A/C, TV, hair dryer, minibar, free Wi-Fi.

INEXPENSIVE

L'Auberge de Carcarille Three kilometers (1¾ miles) from the center of Gordes, the heart of this modest hotel is its well-respected restaurant, which draws locals as well as guests. The dry stone main building is hidden at the end of long driveway with manicured trees, housing spacious, attractively decorated

THE LAST HOME OF Albert Camus

Author of *The Stranger,* among many other works, Algerian-born Albert Camus (1913-60) moved to France at the age of 25. A member of the French Resistance, he was first known as a political journalist before being recognized as a philosopher. He was awarded the Nobel Prize for Literature in 1958 "for his important literary production, which with clear-sighted earnestness illuminates the problems of the human conscience in our times."

That same year, drawn by its "solemn and austere landscape despite its bewildering beauty," Camus and his wife moved to Lourmarin. Just 2 years later, Camus was killed in a car accident south of Paris. According to his wishes, he was buried in the village cemetery.

In 1999, French president Nicolas Sarkozy—with whom Camus would have had little in common philosophically or politically—proposed moving the writer's ashes to the Pantheon in Paris, to rest aside literary giants such as Alexander Dumas, Victor Hugo, and Emile Zola. His descendants politely declined.

rooms that all have private terraces or balconies and access to a large swimming pool. The rates for this type of property are extremely reasonable, though the management is hoping you'll choose the more expensive half-board option (two meals per day for two people). If you're staying a few days, consider paying full price in the restaurant, to have the flexibility of sampling others in the region. As with La Ferme de La Huppe (see above), the hotel's position is a great base for exploring the Luberon (picnic baskets can be provided on request).

Rte. d'Apt (D2), Gordes 84220. www.auberge-carcarille.com. ✆ **04-90-72-02-63.** Fax 04-90-72-05-74. 20 units. 72€–112€ double. Half-board 116€–206€ double. AE, MC, V. Free parking. **Amenities:** Restaurant; outdoor pool; Wi-Fi in public areas. *In room:* A/C, TV, hair dryer.

Where to Eat

L'Artegal PROVENÇAL Due to its location on the place du Château, one might mistake this restaurant for a tourist trap. Not so. It serves well-conceived dishes such as sea bass with fresh herbs, duck with honey, and spinach-stuffed lamb, as well as lunchtime salads that are copious and meal-worthy. Dining is inside or outside with a view of the castle (busier during the day but tranquil at night). Prices may be higher than what one is used to for this type of restaurant—perhaps understandable when you consider the difficulty of delivering fresh and varied ingredients to such a hard-to-reach location. In season, try the strawberry gazpacho for dessert.

Place du Château, 84220 Gordes. ✆ **04-90-72-02-54.** Main courses 16€–22€; fixed-price menu 24€–35€. MC, V. Noon–1:45pm and 7:15–8:45pm. Closed mid-Jan to mid-Mar.

Un Jour, Charlotte ★ MEDITERRANEAN Serge and Muriel Alvarez run this eclectic restaurant and photo space. Uncomplicated but refined Mediterranean cuisine here highlights organic ingredients and herbs from their garden. Plates include white truffle ravioli with Parmesan shavings, tapenade-marinated rabbit, and supreme of guinea hen with morel mushrooms and local potatoes. Serge is the photographer—his work decorates the walls, as well as a nearby studio.

Because of its laid-back, artsy atmosphere (there is also a side wedding flower business, so beautiful buds are everywhere), the restaurant is popular with in-the-know locals. In good weather, there is outdoor dining under a 100-year-old plane tree. Reservations are advised.

Hameau Les Imberts, 84220 Gordes. ✆ **04-90-72-61-98.** www.unjourcharlotte.fr. Reservations recommended. Main courses 15€–22€; fixed-price menu 29€. MC, V. Daily (dinner only) 7:30–10pm. Closed Jan–Mar.

Exploring the Area

Gordes is part of the Parc Naturel Régional du Luberon, made up of three mountain ranges and their common valley. Author Peter Mayle brought attention to the area with his "A Year in Provence" series extolling the virtues of picturesque villages such as Bonnieux, Lourmarin, and Menerbes, where Mayle restored his first French home. Most of these are within 12km (7½ miles) of each other, making the Luberon well worth an afternoon's drive.

Abbaye Nôtre-Dame de Sénanque One of the prettiest sights in the Luberon—indeed, in all of Provence—is the Abbaye Nôtre-Dame de Sénanque when the lavender is in bloom. Five kilometers (3 miles) down the road from Gordes, it was built by Cistercian monks in 1148. Eight monks live on the premises today. The structure is noted for its simple architecture and unadorned stone—though standing in a sea of purple, from June to late July, it's dramatic indeed.The abbey is open daily to visitors. A gift shop sells books and items made by the resident monks, as well as lavender honey.

Abbaye Notre-Dame de Sénanque, 84220 Gordes. ✆ **04-90-72-17-92.** www.senanque.fr. Admission 7€ adults, 5€ students, 3€ children 6–18, 20€ families. Days and hours vary; call or see website.

ST-RÉMY-DE-PROVENCE ★

710km (440 miles) S of Paris; 24km (15 miles) NE of Arles; 19km (12 miles) S of Avignon; 10km (6¼ miles) N of Les Baux

Though Nostradamus, the physician and astrologer, was born here in 1503, most associate St-Rémy with Vincent van Gogh, who committed himself to a local asylum in 1889 after cutting off his left ear. *Starry Night* was painted during this period, as were many versions of *Olive Trees* and *Cypresses.*

Come to sleepy St-Rémy not only for its history and sights, but also for an authentic experience of daily Provençal life. The town springs into action on Wednesday mornings, when stalls bursting with the region's bounty, from wild-boar sausages to olives, elegant antiques to local crafts and bolts of French country fabric, huddle between the sidewalk cafes beneath the plane trees.

Essentials

GETTING THERE A regional bus, the Cartreize, runs four to nine times daily between Avignon's Gare Routière and St-Rémy's place de la République (trip time: 50 min.; 3.10€ one-way). For bus information, call ✆ **08-11-88-01-13** or see www.lepilote.com. If you're driving, head south from Avignon along D571.

VISITOR INFORMATION The **Office de Tourisme** is on place Jean-Jaurès (✆ **04-90-92-05-22;** fax 04-90-92-38-52; www.saintremy-de-provence.com).

Ruines de Glanum.

Seeing the Sights

Ruines de Glanum ★★ A Gallo-Roman settlement thrived here during the final days of the Roman Empire. Its monuments include a triumphal arch from the time of Julius Caesar; garlanded with sculptured fruits and flowers, it dates from 20 B.C. and is the oldest in Provence. Another interesting feature is the baths, which, back in the day, had separate chambers for hot, warm, and cold. You can see entire streets and foundations of private residences from the 1st-century town, plus some remains from a Gallo-Greek town of the 2nd century B.C.

Rte. des Baux-de-Provence. ✆ **04-90-92-23-79.** http://glanum.monuments-nationaux.fr. Admission 7€ adults, 4.50€ students, free for 18 and under. Apr–Aug daily 9:30am–6:30pm; Sept Tues–Sun 9:30am–6:30pm; Oct–Mar Tues–Sun 10am–5pm. From St-Rémy, take D5 1.5km (1 mile) south, following signs to Les Antiques.

St-Paul de Mausole ★ This former monastery and clinic is where Vincent van Gogh was confined from 1889 to 1890. It's now a psychiatric hospital for women; you can't see the artist's actual cell, but the Romanesque chapel and cloisters are worth a visit in their own right. Van Gogh depicted their circular arches and beautifully carved capitals in some of his paintings. The site is east of D5, a short drive north of Glanum (see below). A bust of van Gogh is outside the church.

Rte. des Baux-de-Provence. ✆ **04-90-92-77-00.** Admission 4€ adults, 3€ students, free for children 12 and under. Apr–Oct daily 9:30am–7pm; Oct–Dec and Feb–Mar daily 10:15am–4:45pm.

Shopping

St-Rémy is a decorator's paradise, with many antiques shops and fabric stores on the narrow streets of the old town and surrounding boulevards. **Broc de Saint Ouen,** route d'Avignon (✆ **04-90-92-28-90**), is a 6,000-sq.-m (64,583-sq.-ft.) space, open every day from 9am to 8pm, selling everything from architectural salvage to furniture, to *tchotchkes*. The town's famous market is held Wednesday mornings; on Saturday mornings, a small vegetable market is held near the Eglise St-Martin.

Where to Stay

EXPENSIVE

Château des Alpilles ★★★ For luxury and refinement, this is the only hotel in the area that can equal the Vallon de Valrugues (see below). It sits in the center of a magnolia-studded park 2km (1¼ miles) from the center of St-Rémy. Built by the Pichot family in 1827, it counted Chateaubriand among its guests. Françoise Bon converted the mansion in 1980, with the aim of creating a "house for paying friends." The rooms combine antiques, plush upholstery, whimsical accessories such as porcelain panthers flanking one of the mantels, and travertine-trimmed bathtubs. Units in the 19th-century annex are equally comfortable.

RD 31, St-Rémy-de-Provence 13210. www.chateaudesalpilles.com. ✆ **04-90-92-03-33.** Fax 04-90-92-45-17. 21 units. 185€–325€ double; 260€–355€ suite. AE, DC, MC, V. Closed early Jan to mid-Mar. **Amenities:** Restaurant; bar; outdoor pool; room service; sauna; 2 tennis courts. *In room:* A/C, TV, hair dryer, minibar, free Wi-Fi.

Hostellerie du Vallon de Valrugues ★★★ Surrounded by a park, this hotel has the best accommodations and restaurant in town. Constructed in the 1970s, it resembles an ancient Roman villa. Rooms are tastefully decorated in neoclassical style; many were renovated in 2010. All have huge, comfortable beds and marble bathrooms. Activities include a putting green, horseback riding, and bicycles. The restaurant's terrace is as appealing as its cuisine; its Italian-influenced dishes have earned Chef Marc de Passorio a Michelin star. Fixed-price menus are 58€ to 98€. A less formal bistro is open in the afternoons.

9 Chemin Canto-Cigalo, St-Rémy-de-Provence 13210. www.vallondevalrugues.com. ✆ **04-90-92-04-40.** Fax 04-90-92-44-01. 52 units. 190€–310€ double; 250€–1,200€ suite. AE, MC, V. Closed 3 weeks in Jan. **Amenities:** 2 restaurants; bar; babysitting; bikes; exercise room; golf putting green; horseback riding; outdoor pool; room service; sauna; tennis court. *In room:* A/C, TV, hair dryer, minibar, free Wi-Fi.

Hôtel les Ateliers de l'Image This is one of the most unusual hotels in the region. Dedicated to the art of photography, it manages to successfully combine an authentic Provençal setting with low-key, high-tech chic. The bar and less expensive guest rooms are in a building that was originally a movie theater. The more luxurious rooms and restaurant fill the radically restored premises of a 19th-century building that was the town's first hotel. In both buildings, accommodations are stylish and airy, outfitted with minimalist wood and metal furniture and, of course, photographs. Many rooms look out on the surrounding 1-hectare (2½-acre) park and faraway foothills. Four units are duplex suites, each with a private steam bath, and one is a "tree house" supported by the branches of a century-old plane tree. The restaurant, **Le Provence,** fuses French and Asian flavors. The unique bar (see "St-Rémy After Dark," below) is a nighttime draw.

36 bd. Victor Hugo, St-Rémy-de-Provence 13210. www.hotelphoto.com. ✆ **04-90-92-51-50.** Fax 04-90-92-43-52. 32 units. 165€–400€ double; 400€–600€ duplex suite. AE, DC, MC, V. Closed end of Oct to early Mar. **Amenities:** Restaurant; bar; babysitting; 2 outdoor pools; room service. *In room:* A/C, TV, hair dryer, free Wi-Fi.

MODERATE

La Maison du Village ★★ 🎁 This meticulously restored 18th-century town house in the center of St-Rémy appears regularly in French decorating magazines. Welcoming and quietly chic, it comprises five suites with wrought-iron beds and tasteful fabrics, each named after its dominating color: beige, raspberry, violet, and so on. The luxurious bathrooms feature old-fashioned, free-standing bathtubs large enough for a romantic duo. On request, the innkeepers serve organic meals in the family-style dining room or the "secret garden" out back. You can even do your gift shopping on the premises—a corner of the lobby sells France's famous Diptyque brand of perfumes and scented candles (try fig or anise).

10 rue du 8 Mai 1945, St-Rémy-de-Provence 13210. www.lamaisonduvillage.com. ✆ **04-32-60-68-20.** Fax 04-32-60-68-21. 5 units. 170€–210€ double. MC, V. **Amenities:** Lounge. *In room:* A/C, TV, free Wi-Fi.

INEXPENSIVE

L'Amandière This simple hotel is one of the best deals in the region. It's probably best suited to drivers, though the center of St-Rémy is only 10 minutes away on foot. Basic but pleasant rooms come with a bath or shower, balcony or terrace, depending on which you choose. Guests have access to a swimming pool, and there is an exercise trail nearby. There is no restaurant, but breakfast is served in various indoor and outdoor seating areas. A good option if you're just passing through or prefer to spend your travel budget on gourmet restaurants (rates are at least a third of what you'd pay at some of the local favorites).

Av. Théodore Aubanel, Plaisance du Touch, St-Rémy-de-Provence 13210. www.hotel-amandiere.com. ✆ **04-90-92-41-00.** Fax 04-90-92-48-38. 25 units. 62€–75€ double. AE, MC, V. Free parking. **Amenities:** Outdoor pool; Wi-Fi in public area. *In room:* TV, hair dryer.

Where to Eat

The **Hostellerie du Vallon de Valrugues** (see above) offers excellent dining.

Grain de Sel PROVENÇAL Don't let this restaurant's location on the town's main street deter you. It is a haven of good taste, in both decoration and cuisine. The chic dining area is a mix of Baroque and modern, with cushy sofas and ambient lighting. A sashimi-like plate is among the starters; main dishes include sea bass with fennel, duck comfit, and beef filet with foie gras and morel mushrooms. *Grandes assiettes* allow you to sample small portions of some of the best the kitchen has to offer. Despite its decidedly non-Provençal feel, some say it's the best restaurant in town.

25 bd. Mirabeau. ✆ **04-90-92-00-89.** www.graindesel-resto.com. Reservations recommended. Main courses 24€–38€; grand plates 27€ and 29€. AE, MC, V. Thurs–Mon (closed Thurs lunch). Closed 3 weeks in Nov and 1 week in June.

La Maison Jaune ★★ FRENCH/PROVENÇAL One of the most enduringly popular restaurants in St-Rémy is in the former residence of an 18th-century merchant. Today, in a pair of dining rooms occupying two floors, you'll appreciate cuisine prepared and served with flair by François and Catherine Perraud. In nice weather, additional seats are on a terrace overlooking the Hôtel de Sade. Menu items include pigeon roasted in wine and honey; braised artichoke hearts with white wine and tomatoes; mussel soup with fennel; and roast rack of lamb served with tapenade of black olives and anchovies.

15 rue Carnot. ✆ **04-90-92-56-14.** www.lamaisonjaune.info. Reservations required. Fixed-price menu 38€–68€. MC, V. Tues–Sun noon–1:30pm; Tues–Sat 7:30–9pm. Closed Nov–Jan.

St-Remy After Dark

Le Cocktail Bar, in the Hôtel les Ateliers de l'Image, 36 bd. Victor Hugo (✆ **04-90-92-51-50**), is an unusual destination in this laid-back town. In a former Art Deco movie theater, it is open June to September daily 5pm to 2am.

ARLES ★★

744km (461 miles) S of Paris; 36km (22 miles) SW of Avignon; 92km (57 miles) NW of Marseille

On the banks of the Rhône River, Arles (pop. 52,000) attracts art lovers, archaeologists, and historians. To the delight of visitors, many of the vistas van Gogh painted so luminously remain. Here the artist was inspired to paint even his own bedroom (*Bedroom in Arles,* 1888).

The Greeks are said to have founded Arles in the 6th century B.C. In the 1st century, Julius Caesar established a Roman colony (controversy continues over whether a bust bearing his likeness recovered from the Rhône as recently as 2008 is authentic). Constantine the Great named Arles the second capital of his empire in 306 A.D., when it was known as "the little Rome of the Gauls." The city was incorporated into France in 1481.

Arles is not as charming as, say, Aix-en-Provence, but it's still well worth a visit, with first-rate museums, excellent restaurants, and summer festivals. Its position on the river means it is a gateway to the Camargue (see chapter 16), giving the town a healthy dose of Spanish influence.

Essentials

GETTING THERE Trains run almost every hour between Arles and Avignon (trip time: 20 min.; 6.70€ one-way), Marseille (trip time: 45 min.; 14€), and Nîmes (trip time: 25 min.; 7.70€ one-way). Be sure to take local trains from city center to city center, not the TGV, which, in this case, takes more time. For rail information, call ✆ **36-35** or go to www.voyages-sncf.com. There are **buses** from Aix-en-Provence (trip time: 1 hr., 30 min.; 9.20€ one-way) and other major towns; for information, call ✆ **08-11-88-01-13** or see www.lepilote.com. If **driving,** head south along D570 from Avignon.

For bicycles, head to **Europebike Provence** (✆ **06-38-14-49-50;** www.europbike-provence.fr), which rents bikes from 14€ per day. Pickup is from several locations around Arles, and they deliver to certain hotels. It is possible to reserve online.

VISITOR INFORMATION The **Office de Tourisme** is on esplanade Charles-de-Gaulle (✆ **04-90-18-41-20;** fax 04-90-18-41-29; www.arlestourisme.com).

Exploring the Town

The **Place du Forum,** shaded by plane trees, stands around the old Roman forum. The Café de Nuit, immortalized by van Gogh, once stood on this square. You can see two Corinthian columns and fragments from a temple at the corner of the Hôtel Nord-Pinus. Three blocks south is **Place de la République,** dominated by a 15m-tall (49-ft.) blue porphyry obelisk.

Place du Forum.

One of the city's great classical monuments is the Roman **Théâtre Antique ★★**, rue du Cloître (✆ **04-90-49-59-05**). Augustus began the theater in the 1st century; only two Corinthian columns remain. The *Venus of Arles* was discovered here in 1651. The theater is open May through

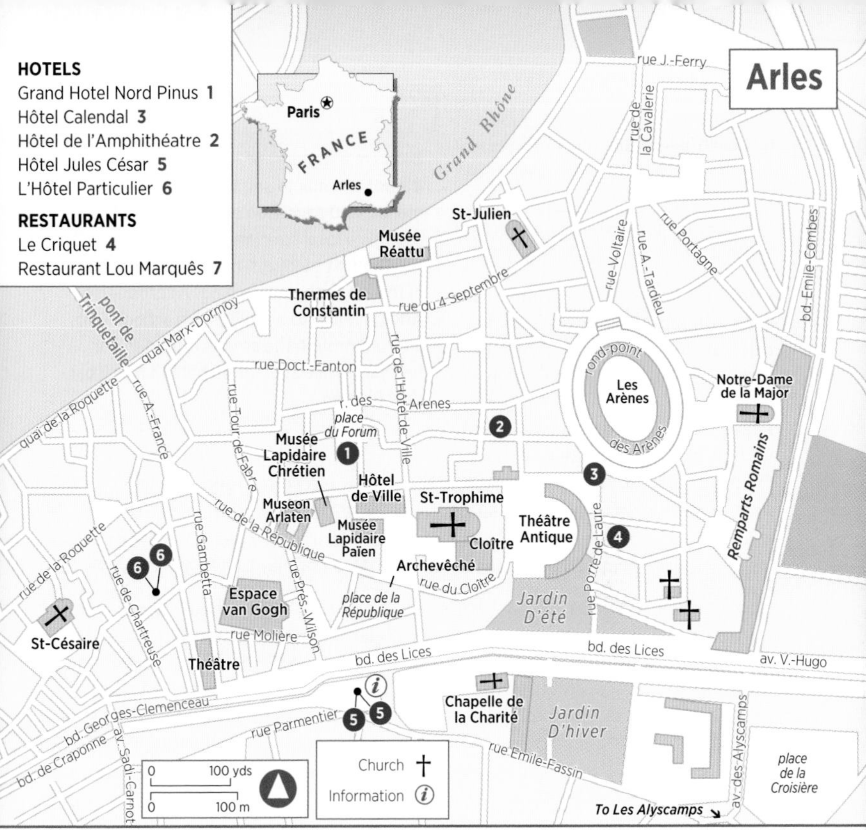

September daily 9am to 7pm; March, April, and October daily 9am to 6pm; and November through February daily 10am to 5pm. Closed public holidays. Admission is 6€ for adults, 4.50€ for students and children 12 to 18, and free for children 11 and under. The same ticket admits you to the nearby **Amphitheater (Les Arènes) ★★**, rond-pont des Arènes (✆ **04-90-49-59-05**), also built in the 1st century. Sometimes called Le Cirque Romain, it seats almost 25,000. For a good view, climb the three towers that remain from medieval times, when the amphitheater was turned into a fortress. Hours are the same as those for the Théâtre Antique.

Today *corridas* are held on Easter weekend, during the Festival of Arles in July and on 1 weekend in September. The bull is killed only during the Easter *corrida;* expect a few protestors. During the others, the bull is spared. The Easter event begins at 11am, others around 5pm. A seat on the stone benches of the amphitheater costs 17€ to 96€. Tickets are usually available a few hours beforehand at the ticket office on Les Arenes d'Arles (1 Rond Point Arenes). For information or advance tickets, contact ✆ **08-91-70-03-70** or www.arenes-arles.com.

Eglise St-Trophime ★ This church is noted for its 12th-century portal, one of the finest achievements of the southern Romanesque style. Frederick Barbarossa was crowned king of Arles here in 1178. In the pediment, Christ is surrounded by the symbols of the Evangelists. The cloister, in Gothic and Romanesque styles, is noted for its medieval carvings.

East side of place de la République. ✆ **04-90-96-07-38.** Free admission to church; cloister 3.50€ adults, 2.60€ students and children 12–18, free for children 11 and under. Daily 10am–noon and 2–5pm.

Les Taureaux

Bulls are a big part of Arlesien culture. It's not unusual to see bull steak on local menus, and *saucisson de taureau* (bull sausage) is a local specialty.

The first bullfight, or *corrida,* took place in the amphitheater in 1853. Appropriately, Arles is home to a bullfighting school. Bulls are run through the streets during major festivals, while spectators behind metal barriers look on.

Les Alyscamps ★ Perhaps the most memorable sight in Arles, this once–Roman necropolis became a Christian burial ground in the 4th century. Mentioned in Dante's *Inferno,* it is today lined with poplars and studded with ancient sarcophagi. Arlesiens escape here to enjoy a respite from the heat.

Rue Pierre-Renaudel. ✆ **04-90-49-59-05.** Admission 3.50€ adults, 2.60€ children 12–18, free for children 11 and under. Nov–Feb daily 10am–noon and 2–5pm; Mar–Apr and Oct daily 9am–noon and 2–6pm; May–Sept daily 9am–7pm. Closed New Year's Day, May 1, Nov 1, and Christmas.

Musée de l'Arles et de la Provence Antiques ★★ About 1km (½ mile) south of the town center within a hypermodern setting built in 1995, you'll find one of the world's most famous collections of Roman Christian sarcophagi, plus sculptures, mosaics, and inscriptions from the Augustinian period to the 6th century A.D. Eleven detailed models show ancient monuments of the region as they existed in the past.

Presqu'île du Cirque Romain. ✆ **04-90-18-88-88.** Admission 6€ adults, 4.50€ students and children 17 and under. Wed–Mon 10am–6pm. Closed New Year's Day, May 1, Nov 1, and Christmas.

Musée Réattu ★ This collection, which belonged to the local painter Jacques Réattu, includes etchings and drawings by Picasso. Other pieces are by Alechinsky, Dufy, and Zadkine.

10 rue du Grand-Prieuré. ✆ **04-90-49-37-58.** Admission 4€ adults, 3€ students and children 12–18, free for children 11 and under. July–Sept Tues–Sun 10am–7pm; Oct–July Tues–Sun 10am–12:30pm and 2–6:30pm. Closed 3 weeks in Jan, New Year's Day, May 1, Nov 1, and Christmas.

Where to Stay

VERY EXPENSIVE

L'Hôtel Particulier ★★★ Occupying an 18th-century pavilion, this was the last of the private town houses built in the center of Arles. It may not be as grand as the Jules César (see below), but its distinctive elegance has made it a formidable challenger, even though Le Particulier is a fraction of the size. Behind a monumental gate, you'll encounter ancient yew trees and a courtyard with teak lounges and a limestone-built *bassin* containing a lap pool. Each bedroom is decorated individually in cool, neutral tones with Provençal antiques, elegantly draped fabrics, and designer knickknacks. Gourmet dining is available in the crisp white dining room or outside.

4 rue de la Monnaie, 13200 Arles. www.hotel-particulier.com. ✆ **04-90-52-51-40.** Fax 04-90-96-16-70. 15 units. 239€–319€ double; 289€–429€ suite. AE, DC, MC, V. Parking 19€. **Amenities:** Restaurant; outdoor pool; room service; small spa. *In room:* A/C, TV, minibar, free Wi-Fi.

EXPENSIVE

Grand Hôtel Nord-Pinus ★ Depending on your taste, you'll find this legendary hotel either steeped in history and nostalgia—or just plain quirky. On the site of a bakery at the turn of the 20th century, it sits on a tree-lined square in the heart of Arles. The public spaces are crammed with antiques and memorabilia. The guest rooms, up an ornate staircase with wrought-iron balustrades, are glamorous, even theatrical, graced with rich upholsteries and linens. The designer Christian Lecroix recently redecorated the third floor. Many bullfighters, artists, and actors have stayed here; their photographs, as well as a collection of safari photos by Peter Beard, are hung throughout.

14 place du Forum, Arles 13200. www.nord-pinus.com. ✆ **04-90-93-44-44.** Fax 04-90-93-34-00. 26 units. 170€–310€ double; 570€ suite. AE, DC, MC, V. Parking 17€. **Amenities:** Restaurant; bar; room service. *In room:* A/C, TV, hair dryer, free Wi-Fi.

Hôtel Jules César ★★★ This 17th-century Carmelite convent is now a stately hotel with one of the best restaurants in town (see "Where to Eat," below). Although it's in a noisy neighborhood, most rooms face the unspoiled cloister. Throughout, you'll find a blend of neoclassical architecture and modern amenities. The decor is luxurious, with antique Provençal furnishings. The interior rooms are the most tranquil and the darkest, though enlivened by bright fabrics. Most of the downstairs units are spacious; those upstairs are small but have a certain old-world charm. Rooms in the modern extensions are comfortable but lack character.

9 bd. des Lices, Arles Cedex 13631. www.hotel-julescesar.fr. ✆ **04-90-52-52-52.** Fax 04-90-52-52-53. 58 units. 160€–250€ double; 300€–385€ suite. AE, DC, MC, V. Parking 13€. **Amenities:** Restaurant; outdoor pool; bar; babysitting; room service. *In room:* TV, hair dryer, minibar, Wi-Fi (10€ per hr.).

MODERATE

Hôtel Calendal ★ Because of everything it offers, the Calendal is a favorite in its price category. On a quiet square near the arena, it provides high-ceilinged accommodations decorated in bright colors. Most rooms have views of the hotel's garden, filled with palms and palmettos. Each unit comes with a compact shower-only bathroom. There is a spa on-site, as well as a boutique selling regional products.

5 rue Porte de Laure, Arles 13200. www.lecalendal.com. ✆ **04-90-96-11-89.** Fax 04-90-96-05-84. 38 units. 119€–169€ double; 159€–169€ triple; 139€–169€ quad. AE, DC, MC, V. Parking 8€. **Amenities:** Cafe; bar; spa. *In room:* A/C, TV, hair dryer, free Wi-Fi.

Hôtel de l'Amphitheatre Originally built in the 1600s, this hotel is ideally situated between the Roman amphitheater and the Théâtre Antique (though the entrance is on a tiny side street that can be a little tough to find). Its Old World atmosphere is enhanced by hand-hewn wood ceiling beams, bright fabrics, soft lighting, reproductions of Provençal furniture, and bedrooms that, in some cases, have views over the terra-cotta roofs of historic Arles. A favorite is the Belvedere Suite, whose windows offer 360-degree views over the town. Only breakfast is served, but many dining options lie within a short walk.

5–7 rue Diderot, Arles 13200. www.hotelamphitheatre.fr. ✆ **04-90-96-10-30.** Fax 04-90-93-98-69. 28 units. 55€–95€ double; 125€–155€ suite. AE, MC, V. Parking 5.50€. **Amenities:** Breakfast room. *In room:* A/C, TV, fridge, hair dryer, free Wi-Fi.

Mistral, Two Ways

Born north of Arles, Frédéric Mistral (1830-1914) dedicated his life to defending and preserving the original Provençal language known as Occitan. A poet who won the Nobel Prize for his epic work *Mirèio* and overall contributions to French literature, Mistral joined with six other Provençal writers in 1854 to found Félibrige, an association for the promotion of Occitan language and literature. He is the author of *Lo Tresor dóu Félibrige,* the most comprehensive dictionary of the Occitan language to this day.

Many think Mistral lent his name to the notorious glacial wind that roars through Provence every year. However, in this case, *mistral* is the Occitan word for "master"—and those who experience the phenomenon regularly say it's a cruel one. Tearing through the Rhône River Valley toward the Mediterranean, the Mistral reaches speeds of 100km (62 miles) per hour and can blow up to 100 days per year. Most of these occur in winter, but it is also common in the spring and, in unlucky years, can persist until early summer.

Where to Eat

L'Hôtel Particulier (see above) offers excellent dining.

Le Criquet ★ PROVENÇAL/SEAFOOD This tiny restaurant, on two floors, is two streets south of the amphitheater and, therefore, removed from the crowds. The atmosphere is dyed-in-the-wool Provençal. Though it excels in seafood specialties such as fish soup or shellfish with garlic aioli, there are meat-based options such as *civet de taureau* (bull stew). A showstopper is the *Bourride de Calanques,* a variation on *bouillabaisse* prepared with all white fish, including monkfish. The service is quick, efficient, and polite; some English is spoken.

21 rue Porte de Laure. ✆ **04-90-96-80-51.** Reservations recommended. Main courses 15€–22€; fixed-price menu 16€–22€. MC, V. Tues–Sat noon–2:30pm and 7–11pm. Closed Oct 1–Mar 31.

Restaurant Lou Marquès ★★ PROVENÇAL Lou Marquès, at the Hôtel Jules-César, has the best reputation in town. Seating is in the formal wood-paneled dining room or on the terrace. The cuisine features creative twists on Provençal specialties. A first course could be crème brulée of foie gras and celeriac, or chilled Provençal melon soup. As a main course, try Camargue risotto with roasted langoustines and black truffles. Desserts include unique combinations such as pineapple prepared with balsamic vinegar and black olives.

At the Hôtel Jules César, 9 bd. des Lices. ✆ **04-90-52-52-52.** Reservations recommended. Main courses 26€–34€; fixed-price lunch 21€–28€, dinner 28€–60€. AE, DC, MC, V. Mon–Fri and Sun noon–1:30pm; Mon–Sat 7–9:30pm.

Arles After Dark

Because of its relatively small population (around 52,000), Arles doesn't offer as many nightlife options as Aix-en-Provence, Avignon, Nice, or Marseille. The town's most appealing choice is the bar–cafe–music hall **Le Cargo de Nuit,** 7 av. Sadi Carnot (✆ **04-90-49-55-99;** www.cargodenuit.com). Open Wednesday to Saturday, it has live music—salsa, jazz, rock—and then club dancing until 3am. Cover ranges from 8€ to 25€.

LES BAUX ★★★

720km (446 miles) S of Paris; 18km (11 miles) NE of Arles; 85km (53 miles) N of Marseille

Les Baux de Provence is the kind of natural/manmade monument often featured in aerial films. Its situation and geology are extraordinary. Cardinal Richelieu called the massive, 245m-high (804-ft.) rock rising from a desolate plain "a nesting place for eagles." A eagle's-eye view of the outcropping would be part moonscape, dotted with archaeological ruins and a vast plateau, and part civilization, with boxy stone houses stacked like cards on the rock's east side. The combination is so cinematic that it seems like a living movie set.

Baux, or *baou* in Provençal, means "rocky spur." The power-thirsty lords who ruled the settlement took this as their surname in the 11th century, and by the Middle Ages had control of 79 other regional fiefdoms. After they were overthrown, Les Baux was annexed to France with the rest of Provence, but Louis XI ordered the fortress demolished. The settlement experienced a rebirth during the Renaissance, when structures where restored and lavish residences built, only to fall again in 1642 when, wary of rebellion, Louis XIII ordered his armies to destroy it once and for all.

Today the fortress compound is nothing but ruins, but fascinating ones. The surrounding countryside, including Le Val d'Enfer (the Valley of Hell), has its own mysterious allure. The area gives its name to Bauxite, discovered here in 1821 by French geologist Pierre Berthier.

Now the bad news: Because of its dramatic beauty, plus a number of quaint shops and restaurants in the village, Les Baux is virtually overrun with visitors. It's not unlike Mont-St-Michel in this respect.

Essentials

GETTING THERE Les Baux is best reached by car; there is no rail service. From Arles, take the express highway N570 northeast until you reach the turnoff for a secondary road (D17), which will lead you northeast to Fontvieille. From there, follow the signs east into Les Baux. By **train,** most passengers get off at Arles, then take a 35-minute local bus (2€ one-way). For bus information, call ✆ **08-11-88-01-13** or see www.lepilote.com. You can also book 1-day coach tours through **Autocars Lieutaud** (✆ **04-90-86-36-75;** www.cars-lieutaud.fr) in Avignon or the tourist office in Aix-en-Provence (✆ **04-42-16-11-61;** www.aixenprovencetourism.com).

VISITOR INFORMATION The **Office de Tourisme** (✆ **04-90-54-34-39;** fax 04-90-54-51-15; www.lesbauxdeprovence.com) is on Maison du Roy, near the northern entrance to the old city.

Exploring the Town

The ghostly ruins cover an area of 7 hectares (17 acres), much larger than the village itself. Consider visiting them early in the morning before the sun gets too strong, then repair to one of the village restaurants during the hottest part of the day. By afternoon, everything may be so overrun with tourists that you'll choose to escape.

The **Château des Baux** and medieval compound are accessed via the 15th-century **Hôtel de la Tour du Brau,** which also houses the **Musée du Château des Baux.** Beneath the high vaulted ceilings of this former bourgeois residence are historical exhibits that will help you understand the ruins. Models of the fortress explain how the site has evolved architecturally.

Beyond this building are replicas of wooden military equipment that would have been used in the 13th century. Built to scale—that is to say, enormous— are a battering ram, *trebuchet* (the largest in France), and other catapults capable of firing huge boulders every few minutes. From April to September, these are fired every day at 11am and 1, 3, and 5pm.

Other stopping points include the **Chapel of St-Blaise** (inside which a film of aerial views of Provence is shown), a windmill, the skeleton of a hospital built in the 16th century, and a cemetery. The **Tour Sarrazin,** named because it was used to spot Saracen invaders coming from the south, yields a sweeping view.

Les Baux ruins.

Admission to the Château, including the museum and access to the ruins, is 7.50€ for adults, 5.50€ children 7 to 17 from October to March. The rest of the year, it is 8.50€ for adults, 6.50€ children 7 to 17, and on weekends during this period 9€ for adults, 7.50€ children 7 to 17. Open daily in spring from 9am to 6:30pm, summer from 9am to 8:30pm, autumn from 9:30am to 6pm, and winter from 9:30am to 5pm. For information, contact ✆ **04-90-54-55-56** or www.chateau-baux-provence.com.

Eglise St-Vincent This church was constructed in stages between the 12th and 16th centuries. Its oldest nave comprises three troglodyte chapels. To the left of the building is a circular tower known as the *Lanterne des Morts* (Lantern of the Dead), after the old custom of lighting a flame inside whenever a resident of Les Baux died. The modern stained-glass windows were a gift from Prince Rainier III of Monaco when he was the marquis des Baux during the 1980s. Today Prince Albert fills the honorary/ceremonial duties associated with that role. If anything, you're more likely to see Princess Caroline, who has a private home in nearby St-Rémy-de-Provence.

Place St-Vincent. No phone. Free admission. Daily 9am–5pm (until 7pm June–Aug).

Musée des Santons Housed in the **Ancien Hôtel de Ville,** this museum is dedicated to the traditional wooden crèche figurines of Provence. It exhibits Neapolitan pieces from the 17th and 18th centuries, 19th-century *santons* with papier-mâché faces and glass sulfur eyes made by Carmelite nuns, and scenes illustrating the traditions of Provence and Les Baux. A documentary film on the making of the figurines is shown.

Place Louis Jou. ✆ **04-90-54-34-39.** Daily 10am–5pm.

The Yves Brayer Museum Inside the 16th-century Hôtel de Porcelet, this museum is devoted to the works of figurative painter Yves Brayer (1907–90). A native son, he became famous for his paintings of everyday life between World War I and World War II—landscapes of Italy, Morocco, and Spain, and bullfighting scenes. He also created the frescoes inside the **Chapelle des Pénitents Blancs,** on place St-Vincent just down the street. Brayer is buried in the village cemetery.

Intersection of rue de la Calade and rue de l'Eglise. ✆ **04-90-54-36-99.** www.yvesbrayer.com. Admission 5€ adults, free 18 and under. Daily Apr–Sept 10am–12:30pm and 2–6:30pm; Oct–Mar Wed–Mon 10am–12:30pm and 2–5pm. Closed Jan and Feb.

Where to Stay

La Riboto de Taven (p. 526) rents rooms.

VERY EXPENSIVE

La Cabro d'Or ★★★ This is the lesser-known sibling of the nearby Oustau de Baumanière (see below). You'll find some of the most comfortable accommodations in the region here, with a Michelin-starred restaurant. Set in a vast, well-manicured garden, the original building is an 18th-century farmhouse, while the dining room is situated in another building from the same period (meals are also served on the terrace). The massive ceiling beams are works of art in their own right. Guest rooms evoke authentic Provence with art and antiques; some have views over the tranquil countryside. Unlike the Oustau de Baumanière, the annexes in this hotel are not nearly as impressive as the original buildings.

Les Baux de Provence 13520. www.lacabrodor.com. ✆ **04-90-54-33-21.** Fax 04-90-54-45-98. 31 units. 170€–370€ double; 340€–530€ suite. AE, DC, MC, V. Closed mid-Nov to mid-Dec. **Amenities:** Restaurant; babysitting; outdoor pool; 2 tennis courts. *In room:* A/C, TV, hair dryer, minibar, free Wi-Fi.

Oustau de Baumanière ★★★ Ask a French person to name the top three must-stays in France, and this one is likely to make the list. Raymond Thuilier bought the main building, a remote 14th-century farmhouse, in 1945 and transformed it into a hotel that became a hotspot for the glitterati during the 1950s. Today the Relais & Châteaux member is managed by his grandson, who was born the year the hotel opened. Though not as exclusive now, l'Oustau's dramatic location at the base of the Val d'Enfer—under 10 minutes from the village of Les Baux on foot—contributes to its lasting magic. Guest rooms are elegantly furnished in 16th and 17th century style and include large sitting areas. If there's no vacancy in the main building, the hotel will assign you to one of the annexes. Request Le Manoir, the most appealing, next to the less-frequented of the hotel's two swimming pools. The faithful return not least for the two-star Michelin restaurant.

Les Baux, Maussane-les-Alpilles 13520. www.oustaudebaumaniere.com. ✆ **04-90-54-33-07.** Fax 04-90-54-40-46. 30 units. 205€–440€ double; 325€–625€ suite. AE, DC, MC, V. Closed 1st week of Jan to 1st week of Feb. Restaurant closed Jan–Mar Wed and Thurs lunch. **Amenities:** Restaurant; babysitting; 2 outdoor pools; room service; spa. *In room:* A/C, TV, hair dryer, minibar, free Wi-Fi.

EXPENSIVE

Auberge de la Benvengudo ★ In a quiet location about 1.5km (1 mile) south of town, this elegant *auberge* is a 19th-century farmhouse surrounded by sculptured shrubbery and parasol pines. The property has an outdoor pool, tennis court, and terrace filled with the scent of lavender and thyme. About half the rooms are in the original building, above the gourmet restaurant, and the rest in an attractive stone-sided annex. All are sunny and well maintained. Each has a private terrace or balcony, and some have antique four-poster beds. The hotel can prepare picnic baskets to take along on your sightseeing trips.

Vallon de l'Arcoule, rte. d'Arles, Les Baux 13520. www.benvengudo.com. ✆ **04-90-54-32-54.** Fax 04-90-54-42-58. 26 units. 105€–200€ double; 155€–370€ suite. AE, MC, V. Free parking. Closed Nov 1–Mar 15. Take RD78 for 1.5km (1 mile) southwest of Les Baux, following signs to Arles. **Amenities:** Restaurant; babysitting; outdoor pool; room service; tennis court. *In room:* A/C, TV, hair dryer, Wi-Fi (4€ per day).

Where to Eat

La Cabro d'Or and **Oustau de Baumanière** (see above) offer excellent dining.

La Riboto de Taven ★★★ PROVENÇAL Known for its flawless cuisine and market-fresh ingredients, this is one of the great restaurants of the area. When the Novi family opened guest rooms, they decided to stop chasing the favor of picky reviewers and focus completely on pleasing their clientele. It was a good decision, for today you can enjoy award-winning cuisine in an intimate family atmosphere free of food snobs. The heady perfumes of Provence characterize the cuisine, which can include sea bass in olive oil, lamb en croûte with olives, or, in late autumn and winter, medallions of venison served with caramelized root vegetables. The menu changes every day and always features an intelligent and tasteful use of local ingredients and produce.

The hotel is located in and around the 1835 *mas* the family has owned for nearly 2 decades. Accommodations include four rooms within the thick walls of the main farmhouse and two troglodyte suites carved into the grottoes at the far end of the fragrant garden. There is also a swimming pool.

Vallon de la Fontaine, Les Baux 13520. ✆ **04-90-54-34-23.** Fax 04-90-54-38-88. www.riboto-de-taven.fr. Reservations required. Fixed-price menu 56€. AE, MC, V. Thurs–Tues 7:30–9:30pm. Hotel: 6 units. 180€–230€ double; 255€–300€ suite. **Amenities:** Outdoor pool. *In room:* A/C, TV, hair dryer, minibar, free Wi-Fi. Closed Jan–Mar.

AIX-EN-PROVENCE ★★

760km (471 miles) S of Paris; 84km (52 miles) SE of Avignon; 34km (21 miles) N of Marseille; 185km (115 miles) W of Nice

One of the most surprising things about Aix is its size. Guidebooks and travel programs proclaim it the very heart of Provence, evoking a sleepy town filled with flowers and fountains. Which it is—in certain quarters. But Aix is also a bustling judicial center and university town of nearly 143,000 inhabitants (the Université d'Aix dates from 1413).

Founded in 122 B.C. by Roman general Caius Sextius Calvinus, who named the town Aquae Sextiae, after himself, Aix originated as a military outpost. Its former incarnations include a civilian colony, the seat of an archbishop, and official residence of the medieval counts of Provence.

Paul Cézanne, Aix's most celebrated son, immortalized the countryside in his paintings. Just as he saw it, the Montagne Ste-Victoire looms over the town today, though a string of high-rises now interrupts the landscape.

Time marches on, but there are still plenty of decades-old, family-run shops on the narrow streets of the old town. A lazy summer lunch at one of the flashy cafes on the cours Mirabeau is an experience not to be missed.

Dining alfresco in Aix-en-Provence.

Essentials

GETTING THERE **Trains** arrive daily from Marseille (trip time: 40 min.; 7€ one-way), Nice (trip time: 3–4 hr.; 34€ one-way), and Cannes (trip time: 3 hr., 30 min.; 31€ one-way). High-speed TGV trains from Paris and Marseilles arrive at the modern station at Vitrolles, 5.5km (3½ miles) west of Aix. For rail information, call ✆ **36-35** or see www.voyages-sncf.com. Bus transfers to the center of Aix cost 3.60€ one-way. There are **buses** from Marseille, Avignon, and Nice; for information, call ✆ **08-11-88-01-13** or see www.lepilote.com. If you're **driving** to Aix from Avignon or other points north, take A7 south to RN7 and follow it into town. From Marseille or other points south, take A51 north.

To explore the region by bicycle, head for **Aixprit Vélo,** 20 rue Fernand Dol (✆ **04-42-21-24-05;** www.aixpritvelo.com). Here you can rent 10-speed racing bikes or more durable mountain bikes from 10€ per half-day to 80€ per week. You must leave a credit card deposit of 200€ to 300€, depending on the bike. It is possible to reserve online.

VISITOR INFORMATION The **Office de Tourisme** is at 2 place du Général-de-Gaulle (✆ **04-42-16-11-61;** fax 04-42-16-11-62; www.aixenprovence tourism.com).

SPECIAL EVENTS The **Festival International d'Art Lyrique & de Musique,** created in 1948 (✆ **08-20-92-29-23;** www.festival-aix.com), in late July, features music and opera from all over the world.

Exploring the Town

Aix's main street, **Cours Mirabeau ★**, is one of Europe's most beautiful. A double row of plane trees shades it from the Provençal sun and throws dappled sunlight onto its rococo fountains. Shops and sidewalk cafes line one side; 17th- and 18th- century sandstone *hôtels particuliers* (mansions) take up the other. The street begins at the 1860 fountain **La Rotonde,** on place de la Libération, which honors Mirabeau, the revolutionary and statesman. Boulevard Carnot and Cours Sextius circle the heart of the old quarter (Vieille Ville) containing the pedestrian zone.

Atelier de Cézanne Cézanne was the major forerunner of cubism. This house, surrounded by a wall and restored by American admirers, is where he worked. It remains much as Cézanne left it in 1906, "his coat hanging on the wall, his

Aix Through the Eyes of Cézanne

One of the best experiences in Aix is a walk along the well-marked *route de Cézanne* (D17). From the east end of cours Mirabeau, take rue du Maréchal-Joffre across boulevard Carnot to boulevard des Poilus, which becomes avenue des Ecoles-Militaires and finally D17. The stretch between Aix and the hamlet of Le Tholonet is full of twists and turns where Cézanne often set up his easel. The route makes a lovely 5.5km (3½-mile) stroll. Le Tholonet has a cafe or two where you can refresh yourself while waiting for one of the frequent buses back to Aix.

easel with an unfinished picture waiting for a touch of the master's brush," as Thomas R. Parker wrote.

9 av. Paul-Cézanne (outside town). ✆ **04-42-21-06-53.** Admission 5.50€ adults, 2€ students and children 12 and under. Apr–June and Sept daily 10am–noon and 2–6pm; July–Aug daily 10am–6pm; Oct–Mar daily 10am–noon and 2–5pm. Closed New Year's Day, May 1, and Christmas, and Sun Dec–Feb.

Cathédrale St-Sauveur ★ The cathedral of Aix is dedicated to Christ under the title St-Sauveur (Holy Savior or Redeemer) and dates from the 4th and 5th centuries. Its pièce de résistance is a 15th-century Nicolas Froment triptych, *The Burning Bush*. One side depicts the Virgin and Child; the other, Good King René and his second wife, Jeanne de Laval.

Place des Martyrs de la Résistance. ✆ **04-42-23-45-65.** Free admission. Daily 8am–noon and 2–6pm. Mass Sun 10:30am and 7pm.

Cathédrale St-Sauveur.

Musée des Tapisseries ★ Three series of tapestries from the 17th and 18th centuries line the gilded walls of this former archbishop's palace. The prelates decorated the palace with *The History of Don Quixote*, by Natoire; *The Russian Games*, by Leprince; and *The Grotesques*, by Monnoyer. The museum also exhibits rare furnishings from the 17th and 18th centuries.

28 place des Martyrs de la Résistance. ✆ **04-42-23-09-91.** Admission 3.20€ adults, free for ages 25 and under. Apr 15–Oct 15 Wed–Mon 10am–6pm; Oct 16–Apr 14 Wed–Mon 1:30–5pm. Closed Jan, May 1, and Dec 25–26.

Shopping

Opened more than a century ago, **Bechard,** 12 cours Mirabeau (✆**04-42-26-06-78**), is the most famous bakery in town. They specialize in the famous *Calissons d'Aix,* a candy made from ground almonds, preserved melon, and fruit syrup.

Founded in 1934 on a busy boulevard just east of the center of town, **Santons Fouque,** 65 cours Gambetta, route de Nice (✆ **04-42-26-33-38**), stocks more than 1,900 traditional *santons* (crèche figurines).

For a range of truly useful souvenirs, including copper pots and pocket knives by famous French forgers such as Laguiole, try **Quincaillerie Centrale,** 21 rue de Monclar (✆ **04-42-23-33-18**), a hardware/housewares store that's been offering a little bit of everything since 1959.

Where to Stay

VERY EXPENSIVE

La Villa Gallici ★★★ This elegant inn, which originated in the 18th century as a private home, is the most stylish hotel in town. The rooms are chic but homey, thanks to soft furnishings in dozens of different Provençal fabrics. Some have a private terrace or garden, and each comes with a tub/shower. The villa sits in a large, enclosed garden with a swimming pool. It's a 5-minute walk to the town center.

Av. de la Violette, Aix-en-Provence 13100. www.villagallici.com. ✆ **04-42-23-29-23.** Fax 04-42-96-30-45. 19 units. 230€–680€ double; 420€–945€ suite. AE, DC, MC, V. Free parking. Closed Jan. **Amenities:** Restaurant; bar; babysitting; outdoor pool; room service. *In room:* A/C, TV, hair dryer, minibar, free Wi-Fi.

28 à Aix ★★★ The owners of this sophisticated *hotel particulier* have created an oasis of charm, tranquillity, style, and comfort, just steps away from the cours Mirabeau. A cozy town house created from a restored 17th-century mansion, it houses only four rooms, each decorated in a well-executed mix of sumptuous and modern. Enjoy light lunches and pastries near the fireplace or outside in the intimate garden.

28 rue du 4 Septembre, Aix-en-Provence 13100. www.28-a-aix.com. ✆ **04-42-54-82-01.** Fax 04-42-53-10-13. 4 units. 250€–500€ double. Rates include breakfast. MC, V. Parking 20€. **Amenities:** Breakfast lounge; in-room breakfast. *In room:* A/C, TV, hair dryer, minibar, free Wi-Fi.

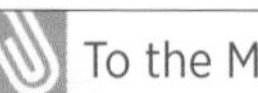

To the Markets We Will Go

Aix offers the best markets in the region. Place Richelme holds a fruit-and-vegetable market every morning from 8:30am to 12:30pm. Come here to buy exquisite products such as olives, lavender, local cheeses, and fresh produce. There's a flower market every day, with the same hours, at either place Richelme or place des Prêcheurs (the former on Tues, Thurs, and Sat; the latter on Mon, Wed, Fri, and Sun). The fish market is daily in the morning on place Richelme.

EXPENSIVE

Hôtel Cézanne ★★ Colorful and chic, Aix's finest boutique hotel pays homage to Provence and the paintings of Cézanne. Conceived by one of the designers of both Villa Gallici and 28 à Aix (see above), the Cézanne could be considered a younger, hipper cousin, with details such as mother-of-pearl-inlaid walls and elaborate tile in some of the bathrooms. Bedrooms are spacious and filled with light; amenities include rain showers and free cold drinks in the minibar. Breakfast, served until noon, might include smoked salmon and champagne. Modern art is on display in the public spaces, which include a bar.

40 av. Victor Hugo, Aix-en-Provence 13100. www.hotelaix.com/cezanne. ✆ **04-42-91-11-11.** Fax 04-42-91-11-10. 55 units. 185€ double; 250€ junior suite; 320€ suite. AE, MC, V. Free parking, by reservation. **Amenities:** Bar. *In room:* A/C, TV, hair dryer, minibar, free Wi-Fi.

MODERATE

Grand Hôtel Nègre Coste This hotel, an 18th-century former town house, is so popular with the musicians who flock to Aix for the summer festivals that it's difficult to get a room. Such popularity is understandable. Flowers cascade from jardinières, and 18th-century carvings surround the windows. Inside there's a wide staircase, marble portrait busts, and a Provençal armoire. The medium-size soundproof rooms contain interesting antiques. The higher floors overlook cours Mirabeau or the old city. Each unit comes with a compact bathroom with shower; some have tubs as well.

33 cours Mirabeau, Aix-en-Provence 13100. www.hotelnegrecoste.com. ✆ **04-42-27-74-22.** Fax 04-42-26-80-93. 37 units. 90€–180€ double. AE, DC, MC, V. Parking 10€. *In room:* A/C, TV, hair dryer, minibar, free Wi-Fi.

Hôtel des Augustins ★ Converted from the 12th-century Grands Augustins Convent, this hotel has retained its ribbed-vault ceilings, stained glass, stone walls, and terra-cotta floors. The reception desk is in a chapel, and paintings and watercolors decorate the public rooms. The convent won a spot in history by sheltering an excommunicated Martin Luther on his return from Rome. Rooms are outfitted in a restrained contemporary style, with dark-wood furniture and high ceilings. Breakfast is the only meal served.

3 rue de la Masse, Aix-en-Provence 13100. www.hotel-augustins.com. ✆ **04-42-27-28-59.** Fax 04-42-26-74-87. 29 units. 99€–250€ double. AE, MC, V. *In room:* A/C, TV, hair dryer, minibar, free Wi-Fi.

INEXPENSIVE

Hôtel du Globe A good budget option for a city where expensive is the norm. A short walk from the Cathédrale St-Sauveur and the old town, this hotel is about 20 minutes from the city center. Rooms are basic but clean; at the press of a button, an automatic shade descends to shield them from sun or unwanted noise. Bathrooms are on the small side. Some rooms have balconies, and a rooftop terrace is open to all. The staff is especially helpful and will do everything to ensure a pleasant stay.

74 cours Sextius, Aix-en-Provence 13100. ✆ **04-42-26-03-58.** Fax 04-42-26-13-68. 13 units. 74€–85€ double. AE, DC, MC, V. Parking 9.80€. **Amenities:** Breakfast in room. *In room:* A/C, TV, free Wi-Fi.

Hôtel St. Christophe The brasserie attached to this hotel was purchased in 1936 as a garage. It was made into a restaurant and art gallery that featured local artists such as Marcel Arnaud. Arnaud's family now runs the hotel and brasserie; his paintings decorate the premises. Regular rooms are unassuming, with time-worn Art Deco decor, and have tubs rather than showers. Superior rooms, recently renovated, have more contemporary furnishings with fully modern bathrooms. The hotel's location near the Rotonde fountain and the cours Mirabeau is a plus.

2 av. Victor Hugo, Aix-en-Provence 13100. ✆ **04-42-26-01-24.** Fax 04-42-38-53-17. 67 units. 89€–117€ double; 169€ suite. AE, DC, MC, V**. Amenities:** Restaurant. *In room:* A/C, TV, free Wi-Fi.

Where to Eat

EXPENSIVE

Le Clos de la Violette ★★★ MODERN FRENCH This innovative restaurant is a few steps from La Villa Gallici (see "Where to Stay," above) in an elegant neighborhood that most visitors reach by taxi. The Provençal villa has an octagonal reception area, several serenely decorated dining rooms, and tables outside. The seasonal, creative cuisine highlights the flavors of Provence. A tempting example is an appetizer of grilled eggplant with foie gras and Serrano ham. Roasted filet of lamb is served with goat cheese gnocchi and spinach shoots. For dessert, try tiramisu with lemon, olive oil, and thyme sorbet.

10 av. de la Violette. ✆ **04-42-23-30-71.** www.closdelaviolette.fr. Reservations required. Main courses 44€–48€; fixed-price lunch 50€; tasting menu 130€. AE, MC, V. Tues–Sat noon–1:30pm and 7:30–9:30pm.

MODERATE

Brasserie Les Deux Garçons PROVENÇAL Few come here for the food alone—though it's not bad, just standard. The draw is the nostalgia and atmosphere of a brasserie founded in 1792 and frequented by the likes of Emile Zola, Cézanne, Picasso, and Winston Churchill. In winter, the upstairs piano bar is one of the coziest spots in Aix, attracting jazz lovers. In summer, linen-draped tables spill onto the cours Mirabeau. Provençal fare includes *daube de boeuf* (stewed beef marinated in a garlic purée), wild rabbit, soupe de poisson, and fresh fruits and vegetables of the season.

53 cours Mirabeau. ✆ **04-42-26-00-51.** www.les2garcons.fr. Reservations recommended. Main courses 18€–36€; fixed-price menu 25€. AE, MC, V. Daily 11am–3pm and 7pm–2am.

Chez Maxime GRILLS/PROVENÇAL In the heart of Aix's pedestrian zone, this likeable restaurant offers an informal ambience of bordeaux-colored banquettes, salmon-colored walls, and tables that spill out onto the pavement when the weather is warm. There's a succulent array of grilled meat and fish, as well as a *marmite de la mer* (seafood stew) laced with saffron. Also appealing is house-made foie gras with figs or, for dessert, orange-blossom-flavored crème brulée. The wine list features dozens of vintages, many of them esoteric bottles from the region. The knowledgeable sommelier is helpful.

12 place Ramus. ✆ **04-42-26-28-51.** www.restaurant-chezmaxime.com. Reservations recommended. Main courses 12€–15€; fixed-price lunch 14€, dinner 19€–24€. MC, V. Tues–Sat noon–2pm and 7–10pm.

Le Mille Feuille ★ PROVENÇAL This small restaurant and tea shop is one of Aix's best-kept secrets. It was opened by two former staff of the l'Oustau de Baumanière in les Baux. The talented Nicolas Monribot is a pastry chef by training and also a musician, which shows through in his melodious savory dishes such as cream of Jerusalem artichoke soup, roasted lamb with soft polenta, and monkfish with orange-flavored curry. The tea shop is open every day and serves lunch, but dinner is offered only Thursday through Saturday nights. You'll be competing with some serious local fans, so be sure to reserve in advance. If you don't manage to get in, be sure to stop by during the day and treat yourself to a consolation pastry.

8 rue Rifle-Rafle. ✆ **04-42-96-55-17.** Dinner reservations essential. Main courses 15€; fixed-price dinner menu 23€. MC, V. Daily noon–2pm and Thurs–Sat 7–10:30pm. Tea shop daily 9am–7pm.

Aix After Dark

An establishment that manages to be convenient and hip at the same time lies almost directly across from the city's tourist office. Open daily 8am until at least 2am, **La Rotonde,** place Jeanne d'Arc (✆ **04-42-91-61-70**), is a bar, cafe, and rendezvous point for friends and business associates throughout the day and evening. Students meet up at **Le Sextius Bar,** 13 cours Sextius (✆ **04-42-26-07-21**), to kick off their evenings.

Under-30s who like thumping electronic beats head for **Le Mistral,** 3 rue Frédéric-Mistral (✆ **04-42-38-16-49;** www.mistralclub.fr), where techno and house music blares long and loud for a cover charge of around 16€ to 20€ (females enter free on Tues). **Le Divino,** 4039 Rte. de Sisteron (✆ **04-42-21-28-28;** www.divino.fr), draws a lively gay/straight crowd for dancing until 6am (cover charge 8€–16€).

For jazz produced by a changing roster of visiting musicians, head for the **Scat Club,** 11 rue de la Verrerie (✆ **04-42-23-00-23**), the preferred venue for patrons in their late 30s and 40s.

Last but certainly not least is the **Joïa Glam Club** (✆ **06-80-35-92-94;** www.discotheque-aixenprovence.com), route de l'Enfant, in the hamlet of Les

Milles, 8km (5 miles) south of Aix (follow the signs to Marseille). There is also a shuttle bus from La Rotonde in Aix proper—probably a safer bet anyway. Onsite is a restaurant, several bars, an outdoor swimming pool, and indoor/outdoor dance floor. Be forewarned that there are long lines on Fridays (when females get in free) and Saturdays. Entrance usually costs 12€ to 18€, unless you're a star or self-confident enough to schmooze the doorman.

MARSEILLE ★★

776km (481 miles) S of Paris; 203km (126 miles) SW of Nice; 32km (20 miles) S of Aix-en-Provence

Marseille, with nearly 1.5 million inhabitants, competes with Lyon for the title of second-largest city in France. It is, in fact, the oldest, founded as a port by the Greeks in the 6th century B.C.

Alexandre Dumas called teeming Marseilles "the meeting place of the entire world." It's an industrial city with many faces, both figuratively and literally. A view from high up reveals the colorful Vieux Port, with its elegant old buildings, boat-filled harbor, and the Mediterranean beyond, or just as likely an ocean of concrete comprising business districts and tenement suburbs. The city is sprawling and slumlike in many respects, but also a place of unique sounds, smells, and sights unlike any other in France.

Marseille is twice the size of Paris, and its age-old problems include a drug industry, smuggling, unemployment, the Mafia, and racial tension (a quarter of the population is of North African descent). Nevertheless, there is strong city pride and an eye toward the future, as evidenced by the recently completed multimillion-euro tramway installation and ongoing extension of the Métro system.

Essentials

GETTING THERE **Marseille-Provence Airport** (✆ **04-42-14-14-14**), 27km (17 miles) northwest of the city center, receives international flights from all over Europe. From the airport, blue-and-white shuttle buses *(navettes)* make the trip to Marseille's St-Charles rail station, near the Vieux-Port, for 8.50€. The shuttle buses run daily every 20 minutes from 5am until midnight; the trip takes 25 minutes. For information, call **08-92-70-08-40** or see www.marseille.aeroport.fr.

Marseille has **train** connections from all over Europe, with especially good connections to and from Italy. The city is the terminus for the TGV bullet train, which departs almost every hour from Paris's Gare de Lyon (trip time: 3 hr., 30 min.; 60€–100€ one-way). For rail information, call ✆ **36-35** or see www.voyages-sncf.com. **Buses** serve the **Gare Routière,** rue Honnorat (✆ **08-91-02-40-25**), adjacent to the St-Charles railway station. Several buses run daily between Aix-en-Provence and Marseille (trip time: 30 min.; 5€ one-way). If you're **driving** from Paris, follow A6 south to Lyon, and then continue south along A7 to Marseille. The drive takes about 8 hours. From Provence, take A7 south to Marseille.

GETTING AROUND Parking and car safety can be problematic enough that your best bet is to park in a garage and rely on public transportation.

Métro lines 1 and 2 both stop at the main train station, Gare St-Charles, place Victor Hugo. Line 1 runs north and south in the downtown area; Line 2 makes a U-shaped circuit from the suburbs into the city and back again. Also with two lines, the new tramway services the Canabière and continues out to the suburbs. Individual tickets are 1.50€; they're valid on Métro, tram, and bus lines for up to 60 minutes after purchase. If you plan to take public transport several times during your stay, buy a **Carte Liberté,** valid for either 5 rides for 6.30€ or 10 rides for 13€. Maps and transit information are also available at **Espace Info** kiosks, located at strategic points throughout the city, usually in or near Métro stations. Public transit maps are downloadable from the Régie des Transport de Marseilles (**© 04-91-91-92-10;** www.rtm.fr).

The major arteries divide Marseille into 16 *arrondissements.* As in Paris, the last two digits of a postal code tell you in which one an address is located.

Call **© 04-91-02-20-20** for a taxi.

VISITOR INFORMATION The **Office de Tourisme** is at 4 la Canebière (**© 08-26-50-05-00;** fax 04-91-13-89-20; www.marseille-tourisme.com; Métro: Vieux-Port).

Seeing the Sights

Many travelers never visit the museums, preferring to absorb the life of the city on its busy streets and at its cafes, particularly those along the main street, **La Canebière.** Known as the "Can of Beer" to World War II GIs, it is the heart and soul of Marseille—and the seediest main street in France. Lined with hotels, shops, and restaurants, it is saturated with sailors from every nation and people of every nationality.

La Canebière joins the **Vieux-Port ★★**, dominated by the massive neoclassical forts of St-Jean and St-Nicolas. The harbor is filled with fishing craft and yachts, and ringed by seafood restaurants. For a panoramic view, head to the **Parc du Pharo,** a promontory facing the entrance to the Vieux-Port. From the terrace of the Château du Pharo, built by Napoleon III, you can clearly see Fort St-Jean and the old and new cathedrals.

One of the most efficient, and easiest, ways to see Marseille's centrally located monuments is aboard the fleet of **Le Grand Tour Buses** (**© 04-91-91-05-82;** www.marseillelegrand tour.com). Each bus is painted white, blue, and yellow, and sports an open-air deck that you'll either appreciate for its unobstructed view or avoid because of its exposure to the blasting heat of the midsummer sun. The buses run every month but January; more run between March and mid-November (about eight per day, usually 10am to 6 or 7pm) than the rest of the year (four per day, usually every other hour

Daily catch at Vieux-Port.

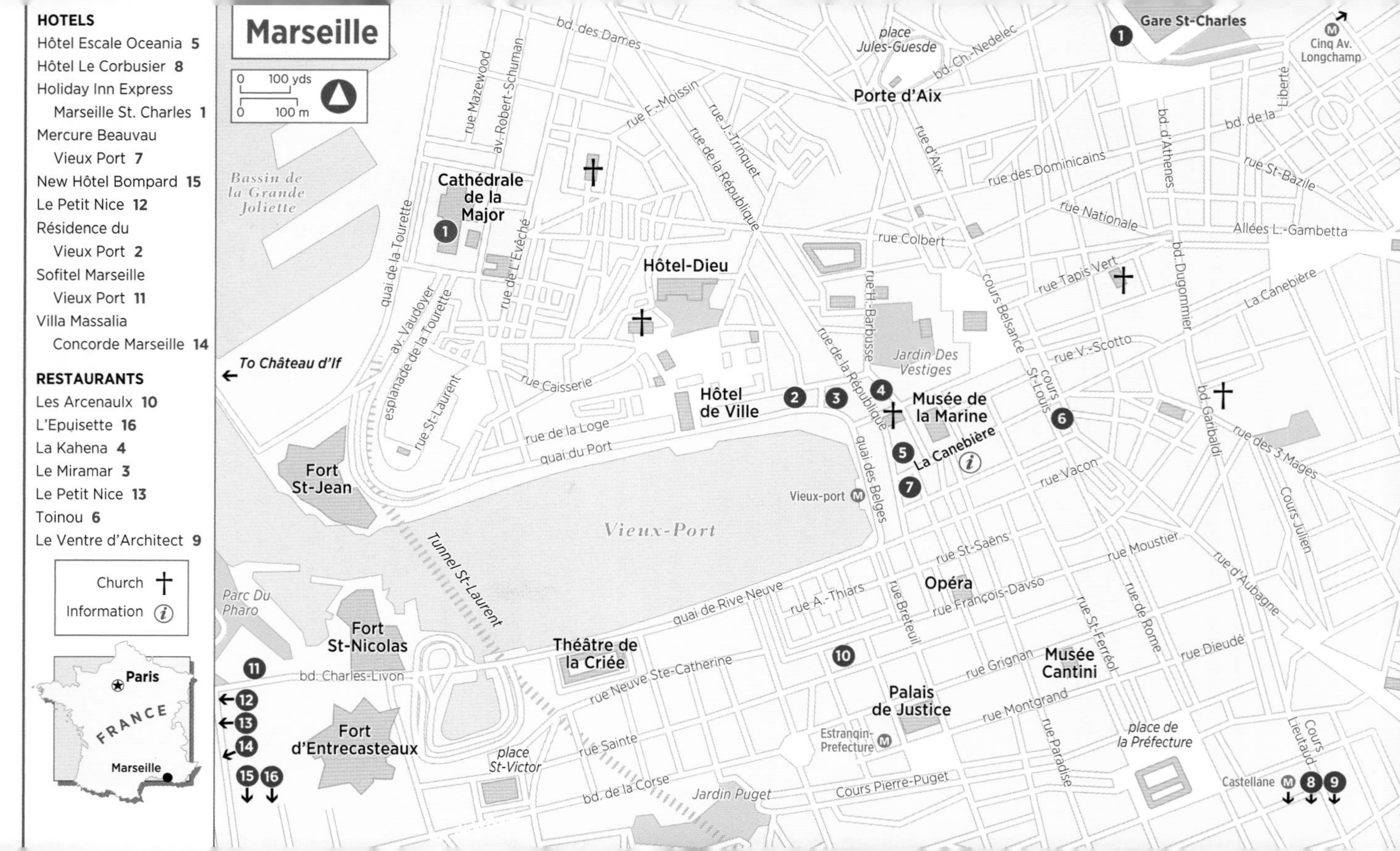
Marseille
HOTELS
Hôtel Escale Oceania 5
Hôtel Le Corbusier 8
Holiday Inn Express Marseille St. Charles 1
Mercure Beauvau Vieux Port 7
New Hôtel Bompard 15
Le Petit Nice 12
Résidence du Vieux Port 2
Sofitel Marseille Vieux Port 11
Villa Massalia Concorde Marseille 14
RESTAURANTS
Les Arcenaulx 10
L'Epuisette 16
La Kahena 4
Le Miramar 3
Le Petit Nice 13
Toinou 6
Le Ventre d'Architect 9
Church
Information
Paris
FRANCE
Marseille
0 100 yds
0 100 m
Bassin de la Grande Joliette
To Château d'If
Cathédrale de la Major
Hôtel-Dieu
Hôtel de Ville
Porte d'Aix
place Jules-Guesde
Gare St-Charles
Cinq Av. Longchamp
Musée de la Marine
La Canebière
Jardin Des Vestiges
Vieux-Port
Vieux-port
Fort St-Jean
Fort St-Nicolas
Fort d'Entrecasteaux
Parc Du Pharo
Tunnel St-Laurent
Théâtre de la Criée
Opéra
Musée Cantini
Palais de Justice
Estrangin-Prefecture
place de la Préfecture
place St-Victor
Jardin Puget
Castellane
bd. des Dames
rue Mazewood
av. Robert-Schuman
rue F.-Moissin
rue J.-Trinquet
rue de la République
rue d'Aix
bd. Ch.-Nedelec
rue des Dominicains
rue Nationale
rue Colbert
bd. d'Athenes
bd. de la Liberté
rue St-Bazile
Allées L.-Gambetta
rue Tapis Vert
bd. Dugommier
La Canebière
rue V.-Scotto
cours Belsance
cours St-Louis
rue H.-Barbusse
bd. Garibaldi
rue des 3 Mages
Cours Julien
rue Vacon
quai de la Tourette
rue de L'Evêché
av. Vaudoyer
esplanade de la Tourette
rue St-Laurent
rue Caisserie
rue de la Loge
quai du Port
quai des Belges
rue St-Saëns
rue Moustier
rue d'Aubagne
rue A.-Thiars
rue Breteuil
rue François-Davso
rue St-Ferréol
rue de Rome
rue Dieudé
quai de Rive Neuve
rue Grignan
rue Montgrand
rue Paradise
rue Neuve Ste-Catherine
bd. Charles-Livon
rue Sainte
bd. de la Corse
Cours Pierre-Puget
Cours Lieutaud

La Marseillaise

Few know that France's national anthem was actually composed in Strasbourg. Originally titled "War Song of the Army of the Rhine," it was written in 1 night by army captain Claude-Joseph Rouget de Lisle in 1792. That same year, revolutionaries from Marseille (who had been given printed copies) marched into Paris singing it. In their honor, the song became known as "La Marseillaise" and was quickly adopted as the rallying cry of the French Revolution. It was officially declared the national anthem of France in 1795, only to be banned by Napoleon during the Empire, Louis XVIII in 1815, and Napoleon III in 1830. The anthem was reinstated for good in 1879.

10am–6pm). A 1-day pass costs 18€ for adults and 15€ for seniors and students with proper ID; the fare for children ages 4 to 11 is 8€. Two-day passes are available. You can hop off at any of 16 different stops en route and back on to the next bus in the day's sequence, usually arriving between 1 and 2 hours later, depending on the season.

The motorized **Trains Touristiques de Marseille** (✆ **04-91-25-24-69;** www.petit-train-marseille.com; Métro: Vieux-Port) make circuits around town. Year-round, train no. 1 makes a 70-minute round-trip to Basilique Notre-Dame-de-la-Garde and Basilique St-Victor. From Easter to October, train no. 2 makes a 60-minute round-trip of old Marseille by way of the cathedral, Vieille Charité, and the Quartier du Panier. Both trains make a 30-minute stop for sightseeing. The trains depart from quai des Belges at the Vieux-Port. The fare for train no. 1 is 7€ for adults and 4€ for children; train no. 2 is 1€ less for both.

Boat tours to the Calanques, a series of limestone cliffs, fjords, and rocky promontories taking up the coast for 20 km (12 miles) southeast of Marseille, are popular. Many tour operators with different prices and formulas (for example, 3 calanques in 45 min., or 8 in 2 hr.) can be found on the quai des Belges at the Vieux-Port.

You can also take a 25-minute motorboat ride to the **Château d'If,** a national monument built by François I as a fortress to defend Marseille. Alexandre Dumas used it as a setting for the fictional adventures of *The Count of Monte Cristo.* Its most famous association—with the legendary Man in the Iron Mask—is also apocryphal. The château is open Tuesday to Sunday from mid-September through March, daily from April to mid-September 9:30am to 5:30 pm. Entrance to the island is 5€ adults, free for those 25 and under (✆ **04-91-59-02-30** for information). Boats leave approximately

Basilique Notre-Dame-de-la-Garde.

every 45 to 60 minutes, depending on the season; the round-trip transfer is 10€. For information, contact the **Frioul If Express** (✆**04-91-46-54-65;** www.frioul-if-express.com; Métro: Vieux-Port), daily 8:30am to 5:30pm.

If you're driving, continue from the old port to the **corniche Président-J.-F.-Kennedy,** a 4km (2½-mile) promenade. You'll pass villas and gardens and have a good view of the Mediterranean. To the north is the **Port Moderne,** the "Gateway to the East." Its construction began in 1844, and a century later the Germans destroyed it.

Abbaye St-Victor ★ This semifortified abbey was built above a crypt from the 5th century, when St. Cassianus founded the church and abbey. You can visit the crypt, which also reflects work done in the 10th and 11th centuries.

Place St-Victor. ✆ **04-96-11-22-60.** Admission to crypt adults 2€, children 1. Church and crypt daily 9am–7pm. Head west along quai de Rive-Neuve (near the Gare du Vieux-Port). Métro: Vieux-Port.

Basilique Notre-Dame-de-la-Garde This landmark church crowns a limestone rock overlooking the southern side of the Vieux-Port. It was built in the Romanesque-Byzantine style popular in the 19th century and topped by a 9m (30-ft.) gilded statue of the Virgin. Visitors come for the view—best at sunset—from its terrace. Spread out before you are the city, the islands, and the sea.

Rue Fort-du-Sanctuaire. ✆ **04-91-13-40-80.** www.notredamedelagarde.com. Free admission. Daily 7am–7pm. Métro: Vieux-Port. Bus: 60.

Cathédrale de la Major One of the largest cathedrals (some 135m/443 ft. long) built in Europe in the 19th century, this massive structure has almost swallowed its 12th-century predecessor, built on the ruins of a temple of Diana. Its striped exterior is in a bastardized Romanesque-Byzantine style with domes and cupolas; the intricate interiors include mosaic floors and red-and-white marble banners.

Place de la Major. ✆ **04-91-90-53-57.** Free admission. Hours vary. Métro: Vieux-Port.

Musée Cantini The temporary exhibitions in this *hôtel particulier* (private mansion) are often as good as the permanent collection. The museum is dedicated to modern art, specifically fauvism, cubism, surrealism, and abstraction, with masterpieces by Picasso, de Stael, Ernst, and others. It also owns a selection of works by important young international artists.

19 rue Grignan. ✆ **04-91-54-77-75.** Admission 3€ adults, 2€ seniors, free for children 18 and under. Oct–May Tues–Sun 10am–5pm; June–Sept Tues–Sun 11am–6pm. Métro: Estrangin/Préfecture.

Musée d'Archéologie Méditerranéenne Antiquities from all periods and civilizations of the Mediterranean basin are represented here, going all the way back to the Iron Age. Rooms are dedicated to the Near East, Cyprus, Greece, Etruria, and Rome. The Egyptian collection is the most extensive outside of Paris.

2 rue de la Charité. ✆ **04-91-14-58-59.** Admission 3€ adults, 2€ seniors, free for children 18 and under. Oct–May Tues–Sun 10am–5pm; June–Sept Tues–Sun 11am–6pm. Métro: Joliette. Bus: 35, 49, 55, or 83. Tram: République-Dames.

Musée Grobet-Labadié ★ After the death of music professor Louis Grobet from the Spanish flu, his wealthy wife, Marie Labadié, bequeathed their house and its rare contents to the city in 1919. Here you'll see Louis XV and Louis XVI furniture, as well as an outstanding collection of medieval Burgundian and Provençal sculpture. Other exhibits showcase 17th-century Gobelin tapestries; 15th- to 19th-century German, Italian, French, and Flemish paintings; and 16th- and 17th-century Italian and French faïence.

140 bd. Longchamp. ✆ **04-91-62-21-82.** Admission 3€ adults, 2€ seniors, free for children 18 and under. June–Sept Tues–Sun 11am–6pm; Oct–May Tues–Sun 10am–5pm. Closed public holidays. Métro: Cinq Avenues. Bus: 81. Tram: Longchamp.

Shopping

Only Paris and Lyon can compete with Marseille for its breadth and diversity of merchandise. Your best bet is a trip to the **Vieux-Port** and its surrounding streets, crowded with stores of all kinds.

On the rue Paradis, rue Saint Ferréol, and rue de Rome, you'll find many of the same upscale fashion boutiques found in Paris. There is also a Galeries Lafayette, France's largest chain department store. For more bohemian wear, try **cours Julien** and **rue de la Tour** for richly brocaded and beaded items on offer in North African boutiques.

For unique souvenirs, head to **Ateliers Marcel Carbonel,** 47 rue Neuve-Ste-Catherine (✆ **04-91-13-61-36;** www.santonsmarcelcarbonel.com). This 70-year-old business specializes in *santons,* clay figurines meant for Christmas nativities. In addition to personalities you may already know, the carefully crafted pieces depict Provençal common folk such as bakers, blacksmiths, and milkmaids. More than 600 figurines sell for 10€ and up.

Navettes, small cookies that resemble boats, are a Marseillaise specialty. Flavored with secret ingredients that include orange zest and orange flower water, their origin is subject to debate. Some associate them with the legend of *Les Trois Maries*—Mary Magdalene, Mary Salome and Mary Jacobe—who reportedly came ashore with St. Lazarus near Marseille to Christianize ancient Provence. Others say they commemorate the 13th-century tradition of parading a statue of the Virgin from the Abbaye St-Victor through the streets of Marseille. In any case, the cookies were invented in 1791 and are still sold at **Le Four des Navettes,** 136 rue Sainte (✆ **04-91-33-32-12;** www.fourdesnavettes.com), for around 15€ per dozen.

A sampling of the best markets in Marseille: The **Capucins Market** (Mon–Sat 8am–7pm), place des Capucins, has fruit, herbs, fish, and food products; there is a fish market at **Quai des Belges** (daily 8am–1pm) on the old port; **Allées de Meilhan,** on La Canebière (Tues and Sat 8am–1pm), sells flowers year-round (from the last Sun in Nov to Dec, vendors sell *santons* in the same location daily 8am–7pm). On **cours Julien** near Notre-Dame du Mont, you'll find a market with fruits, vegetables, and other foods (Tues, Thurs, and Sat 8am–1pm); stamps (Sun 8am–1pm); and secondhand goods (3rd Sun of the month 8am–1pm). Also on cours Julien, there are old-book vendors every other Saturday (8am–1pm), organic products (Wed 8am–1pm), and a flower market (Sat and Wed 8am–1pm).

Where to Stay

VERY EXPENSIVE

Le Petit Nice ★★★ This is the most prestigious address in Marseille. It opened in 1917, when the Passédat family joined two villas in a secluded area below a main street paralleling the beach. The spacious Marina Wing across from the main building offers rooms individually decorated in an antique style, opening onto sea views. The rooms in the main house are more modern and avant garde. Four units are inspired by the cubist movement, with posh geometric appointments and bright colors. The triple Michelin-starred restaurant is beautiful, if pricey, with a view of the Mediterranean and the Calanques. In summer, dinner is served in the garden facing the sea.

Corniche Président-J.-F.-Kennedy/Anse-de-Maldormé, Marseille 13007. www.petitnice-passedat.com. ✆ **04-91-59-25-92.** Fax 04-91-59-28-08. 16 units. 195€–640€ double; 610€–1,090€ suite. AE, DC, MC, V. Free parking. Métro: Vieux-Port. **Amenities:** Restaurant; bar; babysitting; free bikes; outdoor pool; room service. *In room:* A/C, TV, hair dryer, minibar, free Wi-Fi.

Sofitel Marseille Vieux Port ★★★ Though this five-star hotel lacks the cachet of Le Petit Nice, it is the highest-rated lodging in the city. A glistening modern palace, it stands above the embankments of the old port. Some guest rooms have panoramic views of the Vieux-Port; others look out on the boulevard. Rooms are chic, elegant, and well appointed; all are fairly generous in size. This hotel and its less expensive sibling, the Novotel Vieux Port, are in the same building—the Sofitel is on the upper floors—and share a staff and dining facilities. It's about a 15-minute walk to the city center.

36 bd. Charles-Livon, Marseille 13007. www.accorhotels.com. ✆ **04-91-15-59-00.** Fax 04-91-15-59-50. 134 units. 180€–550€ double; 800€–1,500€ suite. AE, DC, MC, V. Parking 18€. Métro: Vieux-Port. **Amenities:** Restaurant; bar; babysitting; outdoor pool, room service; spa. *In room:* A/C, TV, hair dryer, minibar, free Wi-Fi.

EXPENSIVE

Mercure Beauvau Vieux Port ★★ Although completely restored and up-to-date, this is the oldest hotel in Marseille, having hosted Frédéric Chopin and George Sand in the 19th century. It is decorated in the various epoch styles of France, including Louis XIII, Napoleon III, and Empire—above par for what one would expect from a hotel in the Mercure chain. The bedrooms are well furnished and comfortable; suites come with terraces. The two-story duplex suite is a good choice for families. There is no restaurant on-site, but many are available nearby. The hotel bar overlooks the port.

4 rue Beauvau, Marseille 13001. www.accorhotels.com. ✆ **04-91-54-91-00.** Fax 04-91-54-15-76. 73 units. 178€–300€ double; 430€–650€ suite. AE, DC, MC, V. Parking 20€. **Amenities:** Bar; breakfast room. *In room:* A/C, TV, hair dryer, minibar, free Wi-Fi.

Villa Massalia Concorde Marseille ★ Near the Borély racetrack and Parc Chanot, this hotel lies in an upmarket residential district of the city. It's close to several sandy beaches and is targeted at business travelers. Vacationers will find its location, 30 minutes from downtown Marseille by vehicle or Métro, either frustrating or a plus. Contemporary and elegant, the hotel is decorated with fine natural details, including real oak, leather, and feather bedding. Bedrooms are sleek and modern, with the latest gadgets and luxury toiletries. The concierge can arrange for day trips, including to the Calanques.

17 place Louis Bonnefon, Marseille 13008. www.concorde-hotels.com. ✆ **04-91-72-90-00.** Fax 04-91-72-90-01. 140 units. 164€–325€ double; 305€–690€ suite. AE, DC, MC, V. **Amenities:** Restaurant; bar; exercise room; outdoor pool; room service; spa. *In room:* A/C, TV, hair dryer, minibar, free Wi-Fi.

MODERATE

Hôtel Escale Oceania The exterior of this hotel evokes the grandeur of 19th-century life in Marseille. It's on the Canabière, less than 2 blocks from the Vieux-Port. The sun and mistrals of many seasons have battered its Beaux Arts facade, still impressive thanks to ornate corbels and cornices. By contrast, the guest rooms are modern, with up-to-date amenities. Consider taking an inside room rather than an outside one; the location can be noisy, and you may appreciate quiet more than a view. Breakfast is the only meal served, but the neighborhood offers many dining options.

5 la Canebière, Marseille 13001. ✆ **04-91-90-61-61.** Fax 04-91-90-95-61. 45 units. 140€–160€ double; 200€ suite. AE, DC, MC, V. Parking in nearby public lot 16€. **Amenities:** Business facilities. *In room:* A/C, TV, hair dryer, free Wi-Fi.

Hôtel le Corbusier ★ The radical designs of Swiss-born architect Le Corbusier (aka Charles-Edouard Jeanneret, 1887–1965) have long been associated with Marseille. Between 1952 and 1954, he designed La Cité Radieuse, a nine-story building that combines shops and apartments for 1,500 residents. The plans included a hotel, which, beginning in 1959, opened its doors on the building's third and fourth floors.

The current owners, Alban and Dominique Gérardin, are dedicated to the combination of expressionism and functionalism for which Le Corbusier was known. They've retained a handful of the studios' original kitchens for their design value alone (they're not functional) and outfitted the rooms with the kind of spartan and functional furniture, lighting fixtures, and accessories of which the architect would have approved. The hotel's location 2km (1¼ miles) south of Vieux-Port means you'll have to access most of the city's attraction by Métro or vehicle.

On the 3rd and 4th floors of La Cité Radieuse, 280 bd. Michelet, Marseille 13008. www.hotellecorbusier.com. ✆ **04-91-16-78-00.** Fax 04-91-16-78-28. 21 units. 98€–124€ double; 135€ suite. MC, V. Bus: 21. **Amenities:** Restaurant; bar; exercise room; jogging track; wading pool for children. *In room:* A/C, TV, fridge, Wi-Fi (4€ per hr.).

New Hôtel Bompard This tranquil retreat, built after World War II, lies atop a cliff along the corniche, about 3km (1¾ miles) east of the Vieux-Port. Partly because of its garden, it may remind you of a well-appointed apartment complex. A separate Provençal *mas* houses four large rooms that are more luxurious and atmospheric than those in the main building. Some have canopy beds, and all come with large bathrooms featuring tub/showers. Rooms in the main building are less expensive, more modern, and streamlined, but not terribly romantic.

2 rue des Flots Bleus, Marseille 13007. www.new-hotel.com. ✆ **04-91-99-22-22.** Fax 04-91-31-02-14. 49 units. 120€–149€ standard double; 145€–215€ Provençal *mas* double. AE, DC, MC, V. Free parking. **Amenities:** Restaurant; bar; outdoor pool. *In room:* A/C, TV, hair dryer, minibar, free Wi-Fi.

Résidence du Vieux Port Recently renovated, this hotel opens onto a panoramic view of the old port and Notre-Dame de la Garde. It also lies within walking distance of many of the major attractions of the city, and there is a tour bus stop just outside. Its selling point is the loggia-style terraces that come with many of the midsize rooms and suites; rooms in the annex are considerably less expensive but do not have a view. Some may find the primary color scheme off-putting, especially in the modern brasserie attached to the hotel.

18 quai du Port, Marseille 13002. www.hotelmarseille.com. ✆ **04-91-91-91-22.** Fax 04-91-56-60-88. 50 units. 180€–200€ double; 260€–290€ suite. AE, DC, MC, V. Métro: Vieux-Port. **Amenities:** Cafe; bar; room service. *In room:* A/C, TV, hair dryer, minibar, free Wi-Fi.

Where to Eat

Le Petit Nice (see above) offers exceptional dining.

Le Miramar ★★★ SEAFOOD After Le Petit Nice (see above), Le Miramar offers the grandest dining in Marseille. Bouillabaisse aficionados flock here to savor a version that will surely be a culinary highlight of your trip. The Miramar's presentation bears no resemblance to the original rough-and-tumble recipe favored by local fishermen, a way of using the least desirable portion of their catch—Le Miramar's involves lots of labor and just as much costly seafood. Saffron-infused soup is accompanied by fresh fish waiting to be poached in it; the final product is eaten with *rouille,* a sauce made with garlic, olive oil, and egg yolks, flavored with cayenne and saffron. The setting is a room with frescoes of underwater life and big windows that open onto the Vieux-Port, linked to a terrace that overlooks Notre-Dame-de-la-Garde.

12 quai du Port. ✆ **04-91-91-10-40.** Reservations recommended. Main courses 31€–45€; bouillabaisse from 58€ per person (minimum 2). AE, DC, MC, V. Tues–Sat noon–2pm and 7–10pm. Métro: Vieux-Port.

L'Espuisette ★★ SEAFOOD/MEDITERRANEAN This Michelin-starred restaurant is perched on a rocky outcropping in the tiny fishing port of Vallon des Auffes, 2.5km (1½ miles) south of the Vieux Port along the corniche. Serenely decorated in blue and white, the dining room is separated into intimate spaces by long drapes. A large mirror reflects an unobstructed view of the sea and the Château d'If. The menu is changed three times a year, though classics such as *bouillabaisse* and *bourride* are always available. Examples of other dishes: red mullet with sea urchin risotto, lamb shoulder with spices and bacon, and monkfish *osso bucco* with young violet artichokes. If you're willing to go a little out of your way, you'll be rewarded with a memorable meal in what could just be the most romantic restaurant in Marseille.

Vallon des Aufes, Marseille 13007. ✆ **04-91-52-17-82.** Reservations required. Main courses 42€–48€; fixed-price dinner 60€–145€. AE, MC, V. Tues–Sat 12:15–2:30pm and 7:30–9:30pm). Closed Aug.

Le Ventre de l'Architect FRENCH With a westward-facing view of the sea and the sunset, this is the restaurant associated with the Hôtel Le Corbusier (see "Where to Stay," above). "The Architect's Belly" offers both an architecturally historic setting and visually bold menu items that are imaginative, colorful, and—if you understand a bit of French—described in ways that would have pleased a 19th-century Impressionistic poet. A "pillow" of foie gras is "draped" with slices of Serrano ham; a "waltz" of jumbo shrimp with scallops is served with pink risotto, and so on. Other dishes include beef medallions with cured ham and veal chops with braised endives and purple potato purée.

In the Hotel le Corbusier, on the 3rd floor of La Cité Radieuse, 280 bd. Michelet. ✆ **04-91-16-78-23.** www.leventredelarchitecte.com. Main courses 24€–60€; fixed-price lunch 28€, dinner 60€. DC, MC, V. Tues–Sat noon–2pm and 8–10pm.

La Kahena TUNISIAN This is one of the busiest and most respected Tunisian restaurants in a city that's loaded with worthy competitors. Established in 1976 and set close to the Vieux-Port, it takes its name from a 6th-century-B.C. Tunisian princess who was legendary for uniting all the Berber tribes of North Africa. Served in two rooms, the menu includes *méchouia,* a succulent version of roasted lamb; and 10 varieties of couscous, including versions with lamb, chicken, fish, spicy sausages known as *merguez,* and a "complete" version with a little bit of everything.

2 rue de la République. ✆ **04-91-90-61-93.** Reservations recommended. Main courses 12€–15€. MC, V. Daily noon–2:30pm and 7:30–10:30pm. Métro: Vieux-Port.

Les Arcenaulx ★ PROVENÇAL At the Vieux Port, this restaurant is interesting for three reasons. One, it's housed in a former weapons arsenal built by the navy of Louis XIV. Two, its tables share space with hundreds of books (it's inside what is now a bookstore and publishing house owned by Jeanne Laffitte, who was instrumental in conserving the building itself). Three, run by Laffitte and her sister, Sabine, the restaurant offers excellent cuisine with a Marseillais accent, such as roasted pigeon or duckling with caramelized quince; roasted scallops with hearts of violet artichokes; and assorted *petites légumes farcies* (Provençal vegetables stuffed with chopped meat and herbs).

25 cours d'Estienne d'Orves. ✆ **04-91-59-80-30.** www.les-arcenaulx.com. Reservations recommended. Main courses 18€–34€; fixed-price menu 27€–57€ ; children's menu 10€. AE, DC, MC, V. Mon–Sat noon–2pm and 8–11pm. Métro: Vieux-Port.

Toinou SEAFOOD In a massive building that overshadows every other structure nearby, this landmark restaurant serves more shellfish than any other restaurant in Marseille. They even deliver. There's no question where your meal comes from—the fish market is just outside the door. Dining rooms are on three floors, served by a waitstaff who are true *Marseillais,* from their accents right down to their attitudes. Don't come here unless you're really fond of shellfish, over 40 species of which can be served raw or cooked. The wine list is extensive, with attractively priced whites from such regions as the Loire Valley.

3 cours St-Louis. ✆ **08-11-45-45-45.** www.toinou.com. Reservations recommended. Shellfish by 6 or the dozen 2€–22€; fixed-price platter for 2 people 30€, or 76€ with lobster. DC, MC, V. Daily 11:30am–11:30pm. Métro: Vieux-Port.

Marseille After Dark

For an amusing and relatively harmless exposure to the town's saltiness, walk around the **Vieux-Port,** where cafes and restaurants angle their sightlines for the best view of the harbor.

L'Escale Borély, avenue Mendès-France, is 20 minutes south of the town center (take bus 83 or 19). With a dozen bars and cafes, plus restaurants of every possible ethnicity, you'll be spoiled for choice. The animated promenade buzzes at night, and there is a Ferris wheel. There is the potential for conversation with friendly strangers. It's a hint of Santa Monica in Marseille.

Unless the air-conditioning is powerful, Marseille's dance clubs produce a lot of sweat, especially **Le Passe Temps,** 6 rue Fortia (✆ **06-77-02-22-46**), a small club that accommodates only 80 people. Music aficionados praise the playlist here, and it's open from midnight till dawn. You can also try the nearby **Trolley Bus,** 24 quai de Rive-Neuve (✆ **04-91-54-30-45;** www.letrolley.com), known for techno, house, hip-hop, jazz, and salsa.

For jazz right on the port, head to **La Caravelle,** 34 quai du Port (✆ **04-91-90-36-64;** www.lacaravelle-marseille.fr; Métro: Vieux-Port), a dinner club that serves a different flavor almost every night, including *manouche,* the French gypsy style most associated with Django Reinhardt. **Le Paradox,** 127 rue d'Aubagne (✆ **04-91-63-14-65;** www.leparadox.fr; Métro: Notre-Dame du Mont/cours Julien 127), is a restaurant and concert venue featuring a wide variety of indie musicians playing everything from folk to rock, to world music, starting at around 10pm. At least once a month, there is a DJ night, focusing mainly on funk.

More animated is **l'Exit,** 12 quai de Rive-Neuve (✆ **04-91-54-29-43;** Métro: Vieux-Port), a bar/disco with a terrace that profits from Marseille's sultry nights, and two floors of seething nocturnal energy (happy hour starts at 7pm). A flashy and fantastical club that's appealing for both its dance floor and its cabaret acts is **Le Circus,** 5 rue du Chantier (✆ **04-91-33-77-22;** www.lecircus.net; Métro: Vieux-Port). A fee of 10€ to 15€ gets you into the action; don't be surprised to see jugglers and trapeze artists. Dinner cabaret nights start at 39€ per person. For the retro set, the club dedicates Sunday afternoons to old-fashioned *thés-dansants* (tea dances) to mostly accordion music. A cover of 12€ includes beverages.

The **New Can Can,** 3–5 rue Sénac (✆ **04-91-48-59-76;** www.newcancan.com), is a lively, sprawling bar-and-disco that identifies itself as a gay venue but draws many straight folks too. On Thursday and Sunday nights, there are cabaret performances at 2am. Fridays and Saturdays are themed nights with names like "French Kiss" and "Special Blondes" (Madonna, Britney, and Gaga, whether you worship them or just want to dress like them). Open Thursday through Sunday from midnight until dawn, there is no cover charge except on Friday and Saturday (15€).

TOULON

839km (520 miles) S of Paris; 120km (74 miles) SW of Cannes; 65km (40 miles) E of Marseille

This fortress and town is France's principal naval base, headquarters of the Mediterranean fleet. It tends to get lumped in with Marseille as a port town on the seedier side, but recent efforts and renewal have greatly improved its reputation (one should still take care in certain neighborhoods at night). Its beautiful harbor is surrounded by hills and crowned by forts, protected on the east by a breakwater and on the west by the great peninsula of Cap-Sicié. Its prettiest beach, the **Plage du Mourillon,** is 2km (1¼ miles) east of town. Toulon's outer roads are known as the Grande Rade, its inner streets as the Petite Rade.

A bit of trivia: During the Roman Empire, Toulon (then called Telo) was known for providing the purple used to dye the imperial finery of its leaders. The color was extracted from shells along the coast.

Essentials

GETTING THERE & GETTING AROUND **Trains** arrive from Marseille about every 20 to 30 minutes (trip time: 1 hr.; 11€ one way). If you're on the Riviera, trains arrive frequently from Nice (trip time: 1 hr., 45 min.; 24€ one-way) and Cannes (trip time: 1 hr., 15 min.; 19€ one-way). For rail information, call ✆ **36-35** or see www.voyages-sncf.com.

Three **buses** per day arrive from Aix-en-Provence (trip time: 1 hr., 15 min.; 11€ one-way). For information, contact **Lignes Express Régionales Provence-Alpes-Côte d'Azur** (✆ **08-21-20-22-03;** www.info-ler.fr). If you're **driving** from Marseille, take A50 east to Toulon. When you arrive, park your car and get around on foot; the Vieille Ville (old town) and most attractions are easy to reach. A municipal **bus** system serves the town (see www.reseaumistral.com); the tourist office can give you a bus map.

VISITOR INFORMATION The **Office de Tourisme** is at 12 place Louis Blanc (✆ **04-94-18-53-00;** fax 04-94-18-53-09; www.toulontourisme.com).

Exploring the Town

Toulon has its fair share of monuments and museums, but you may find yourself content to just wander around, especially in fine weather. There are lovely tucked-away squares and beautifully restored fountains (notably in the old quarter), and a surprising number of large *trompe l'oeil* murals.

Vieux Toulon, between the harbor and boulevard de Strasbourg, gives an idea of the port's glory days. The **Cathédrale Ste-Marie-Majeure** (✆ **04-94-92-28-91**) is located here. Built in the Romanesque style in the 11th and 12th centuries, and expanded in the 17th, its nave is Gothic, while the belfry and facade are from the 18th century. It's open daily from 7:30am to noon and 2:30 to 7pm. A lively food market, **Le Marché du cours Lafayette,** also takes place in Vieux Toulon Tuesday through Sunday from 8am to 1pm on the streets around cours Lafayette.

The **Opera du Toulon,** place Victor Hugo, is considered one of the most beautiful opera houses in France. Built between 1860 and 1862, it seats 1,800 and is noted for its excellent acoustics. Some 50,000 spectators per year attend its operas and other performances. For information or tickets, call ✆ **04-94-92-70-78** or see www.operadetoulon.fr.

Musée de la Marine, Quai de Norfolk (✆ **04-94-02-02-01;** www.musee-marine.fr), contains figureheads and ship models, including two large 18th-century vessels, and the control panel of the Clemenceau aircraft carrier. Its collection retraces the history of the port, conditions onboard convict ships, the daily life of sailors, and maritime expeditions to the Far East. The museum is open daily July and August 10am to 6pm, September to June Wednesday to Monday 10am to 6pm. Admission is 5.50€ for adults, 4€ for students, free for ages 17 and under.

Musée d'Art de Toulon, 113 bd. du Maréchal-Leclerc (✆ **04-94-36-81-00**), displays works from the 16th century to the present. There's a good collection of Provençal and Italian paintings and religious works. The latest acquisitions include New Realism pieces and minimalist art. It's open Tuesday to Sunday from noon to 6pm; admission is free.

If you're driving, consider a sunset drive along the **corniche du Mont-Faron.** This scenic boulevard along the lower slopes of Mont Faron affords beautiful views of the port, the town, the cliffs, and the distant Mediterranean.

The **Memorial du Débarquement en Provence,** Mont Faron (✆ **04-94-88-08-09**), documents the Allied landings in Provence in 1944. It's open October to April Tuesday to Sunday 10am to 1pm and 2 to 5:30pm, May and

Musée de la Marine.

June Tuesday to Sunday 10am to 1pm and 2 to 6:30pm, and July to September daily 10am to 1pm and 2 to 6:30pm. Admission is 3.80€ for adults and 1.55€ for children 8 to 18.

Where to Stay

Best Western La Corniche Just a few minutes' walk from the Plage du Mourillon and across the boulevard from the small fishing port of Saint-Louis, this chain hotel overlooks the bay and the Iles d'Hyeres. The public areas are decorated in the colors of Provence, but the guest rooms are in tones of beige, making the most of the endless blue seen from the windows. All are well equipped with modern amenities and bathrooms. The buffet breakfast room has a panoramic view, but breakfast can also be delivered to your room on request.

17 Littoral Frédéric Mistral, Corniche du Mourillon, Toulon 83000. www.cornichehotel.com. ✆ **04-94-41-35-12.** Fax 04-94-41-24-58. 28 units. 120€–180€ double. AE, DC, MC, V. **Amenities:** Bar; room service. *In room*: A/C, TV, hair dryer, minibar, free Wi-Fi.

Grand Hotel de La Gare Opposite the railway and bus stations in the town center, this hotel is a 20-minute walk to the ferry terminal. It's especially convenient for anyone arriving late on the TGV from Paris or needing to catch one early the next morning. Guest rooms are clean and functional, with quite a bit of laminated wood. The bathrooms are up-to-date and windows are soundproofed.

14 bd. Tesse, Toulon 83000. www.grandhotelgare.com. ✆ **04-94-24-10-00.** Fax 04-94-22-34-82. 38 units. 77€–83€ double; 96€–120€ triple or quad. AE, DC, MC, V. **Amenities:** Breakfast room. *In room:* A/C, TV, hair dryer, minibar (in some), free Wi-Fi.

Where to Eat

Au Sourd ★ SEAFOOD This restaurant takes its name, "The deaf one," from its original owner, a former soldier who lost his hearing after an injury in the Crimean War. That's right, the Crimean War—the restaurant opened its doors in 1862. An institution in Toulon, it's housed in an old building on a pedestrian street near the Opera. The cuisine is thoroughly modern, however. Dishes such as John Dory with vermouth and lavender honey feature on the menu alongside grilled fresh-caught fish and classics such as *friture royale* (France's answer to fish and chips, with many different options, including calamari, smelt, and sardines). The present chefs make the finest *bouillabaisse* and *bourride* in the area.

10 rue Molière. ✆ **04-94-92-28-52.** www.ausourd.com. Reservations recommended. Main courses 12€–55€; fixed-price lunch 27€, dinner 27€. AE, MC, V. Tues–Sat noon–2pm and 7:15–10pm.

Le Pointiliste ★★ FRENCH/PROVENÇAL Chef Christophe Janvier, formerly of Michelin-starred classics such as the Moulin de Mougins and La Bastide St-Antoine in Grasse, decided to open his own little restaurant in Toulon, and by all accounts, it is a hit. Tucked away on a side street away from the more expensive (and usually less reliable) marina restaurants, the dining room is coolly modern and the welcome warm. Foie gras ravioli with mousse of Jerusalem artichokes and truffle shavings, roasted monkfish with white bean purée and pistou, and lamb shoulder with lemon/thyme potatoes are just three imaginative dishes that make this spot well worth your time. Selections on the ample wine list are not overly priced.

43 rue Picot. ✆ **04-94-71-06-01.** www.lepointilliste.com. Reservations required. Main courses 18€–38€; fixed-price menus 35€–55€. AE, MC, V. Mon–Sat (closed Sat and Mon for lunch).

Toulon After Dark

The temporary home of thousands of sailors is bound to have a nightlife scene that's earthier, and a bit raunchier, than those of equivalent-size towns elsewhere. A rough-and-ready bar that offers stiff drinks, live music, and billiards is **Le Bar 113,** 113 av. de Infanterie de la Marine (**© 04-94-03-42-41**). For more of a pub atmosphere, head to the **Bar à Thym,** 32 bd. Cuneo (**© 04-94-41-90-10**), for live music and dozens of varieties of whiskey and beer. Another popular pub is **Molly Bloom,** 18 rue Anatole France (**© 04-94-46-40-24**). Toulon is also home to one of the region's best-known gay discos, **Boy's Paradise,** 1 bd. Pierre-Toesca (**© 04-94-09-35-90**), near the train station.

ILES D'HYÈRES ★

39km (24 miles) SE of Toulon; 119km (74 miles) SW of Cannes

Off the Riviera in the Mediterranean, a small group of islands encloses the southern boundary of the Hyères anchorage. During the Renaissance, they were called the Iles d'Or (Golden Islands), named for the glow the rocks give off in sunlight. Nothing today hints at their turbulent past, when they were attacked by pirates and Turkish galleys, or saw Allied landings during World War II.

As you might expect, their location only half an hour from the French coast means the islands are packed with tourists in summer. Thousands of day-trippers arrive, often with children, for a day of sun, sand, and people-watching.

If you have time for only one island, choose the beautiful, more lively Ile des Porquerolles. The Ile de Port-Cros is quieter—and perhaps better for an overnight stay in order to take advantage of the great hiking, biking, and snorkeling that would be too rushed for a 6-hour day trip. As for the Ile du Levant, 80% belongs to the French army and is used for missile testing; the majority of the remainder is a nudist colony.

Essentials

GETTING TO ILE DE PORQUEROLLES Ferries leave from several points along the Côte d'Azur. The most frequent, most convenient, and shortest trip is from the harbor of La Tour Fondue on the peninsula of Giens, a 32km (20-mile) drive east of Toulon. Depending on the season, there are 5 to 19 departures per day. The round-trip fare for the 15-minute crossing is 17€ for adults, 15€ for children 4 to 10. For information, call the **Transports Maritimes et Terrestres du Littoral Varois,** La Tour Fondue, Giens 83400 (**© 04-94-58-21-81;** www.tlv-tvm.com). The next-best option is the ferry from Toulon operated by the **Bateliers de la Côte d'Azur** (**© 04-94-05-21-14;** www.bateliersdelacotedazur.com), but only between April and October (trip time: 30 min.; 23€ adults, 16€ children 4–11 round-trip). Another option is **Les Vedettes Ile d'Or & Le Corsaire** (**© 04-94-71-01-02;** www.vedettesilesdor.fr). They depart from the *Gare Maritime* in either Le Lavandou (trip time: 40 min.; 33€ adults, 25€ children 4–11 round-trip) or Cavalaire (trip time: 25 min.; 37€ adults, 30€ children 4–11 round-trip).

GETTING TO ILE DE PORT-CROS The most popular ferry route to the island is the 35-minute crossing that departs from Le Lavadou 3 to 7 times daily, depending on the season (25€ adults, 21€ children 4–11 round-trip). For information, contact **Les Vedettes Ile d'Or & Le Corsaire** (**© 04-94-**

71-01-02; www.vedettesilesdor.fr). The company also runs a ferry once daily from Cavalaire during July and August (trip time: 1 hr.; 29€ adults, 24€ children 4–11 round-trip). The **Transports Maritimes et Terrestres du Littoral Varois** and **Bateliers de la Côte d'Azur** (see above) also service the Ile de Port-Cros. The former also stops at the Ile de Levant.

VISITOR INFORMATION Other than temporary, summer-only kiosks without phones that distribute brochures and advice near the ferry docks in Porquerolles and Port-Cros, there are no tourist bureaus on the islands. The offices in Hyères and Toulon try to fill in the gaps. Contact the **Office de Tourisme,** 3 av. Ambroise Thomas, Hyères (© **04-94-01-84-50**), or the **Office de Tourisme,** 12 place Louis Blanc, Toulon (© **04-94-18-53-00**). Information can also be found at www.porquerolles.com.

Ile de Porquerolles ★

This is the largest and westernmost of the Iles d'Hyères. It has a rugged south coast, but the northern strand, facing the mainland, has some sandy beaches. The island is about 8km (5 miles) long and 2km (1¼ miles) wide, and is 4.8km (3 miles) from the mainland. The permanent population is only 400.

The island is said to receive 275 days of sunshine annually. The landscape is one of rocky capes, pine forests twisted by the mistral, sun-drenched vineyards, and pale ocher houses. The **place d'Armes,** former site of the garrison, is home to several quaint cafes—your best bet for lunch if you're just here for a day trip.

The Ile de Porquerolles has a violent history of raids, attacks, and occupation by everyone from the Dutch and the English to the Turks and the Spaniards. Ten forts, some in ruins, testify to its fierce past. The most ancient is **Fort Ste-Agathe,** built in 1531 by François I. In time, it was a penal colony and a retirement center for soldiers of the colonial wars.

In 1971, the French government purchased a large part of the island and turned it into a national park and botanical garden, where you can see indigenous trees such as fig, mulberry, and olive, as well as plants that attract butterflies.

WHERE TO STAY & EAT

Hotel et Residence Les Medes ★ This hotel is 400m (1,312 ft.) from Courtade Beach and only a short walk from the wharf. Simple guest rooms and apartments are available; all come with a kitchenette, and some have bunk beds for children. The more desirable units open onto private terraces with a view. Guests gather in the lounge, with its bar, fireplace, and public Internet. Main courses in the simple restaurant range from 16€ to 23€ and include local seafood with Asian accents (fish and scallop ceviche with mango, sesame-peanut crusted prawns) and Moroccan-style tagine. There is a coin laundry nearby, making this hotel a good choice for families.

2 rue de la Douane, Porquerolles 83400. www.hotel-les-medes.fr. © **04-94-12-41-24.** Fax 04-94-58-32-49. 95€–223€ double ; 172€–468€. MC, V. Closed Nov 8–Dec 26. **Amenities:** Restaurant; bar. *In room:* A/C, TV, free Wi-Fi.

Mas du Langoustier ★★ In a large park on the island's western tip—secluded from most of the tourists—this tranquil resort hotel is an old *mas* with a view of a lovely pine-ringed bay. Employees greet guests in minivan by the jetty. The rooms, in antique Provençal style, are the most elegantly decorated on the island. Bathrooms are roomy, and most have tub/showers. Should you visit for a

Beach at Ile de Porquerolles.

meal, the gourmet restaurant is the finest on the Hyères, featuring dishes such as steamed *loup de mer* (sea bass) with artichoke hearts, or olive-crusted lamb filet. The hotel's second restaurant is for guests only (half-board is mandatory). The Langoustier is only luxury hotel on the islands—a fact reflected by its rates.

Porquerolles 83400. www.langoustier.com. ✆ **04-94-58-30-09.** Fax 04-94-58-36-02. 50 units. 180€–290€ double; from 269€ suite. Rates include half-board. DC, MC, V. Closed Oct to late Apr. **Amenities:** 2 restaurants; bar; babysitting; outdoor pool; tennis court. *In room:* A/C, TV, minibar.

Ile de Port-Cros ★

The most mountainous island of the archipelago, Port-Cros has been a French national park since 1963. It's just 5km (3 miles) long and 2km (1¼ miles) wide. Though the island was devastated by a fire in 1892, today it's blanketed with pine forests and subtropical vegetation (birders flock here to observe nearly 100 different species). A hiker's paradise, it also has a number of well-marked trails. The most popular and scenic is the ***sentier botanique.*** The more adventurous and athletic take the 10km (6.25-mile) ***circuit historique*** (and pack their lunch). There is even a 274m (899-ft.) "underwater trail" along the coast where you can snorkel past laminated signs identifying the plants and fish you'll see along the way.

WHERE TO STAY & EAT

Le Manoir de Hélène ★ This is the only bona fide hotel on the Ile de Port-Cros. Originally, it was the grandiose home of the family that owned the island (the hotel is run by their descendants). Today it consists of an 18th-century whitewashed and turreted main building, plus an annex containing most of the guest rooms. Accommodations are basic, but the point is to take advantage of your surroundings—by hiking around the island or lounging by the pool, surrounded by eucalyptus trees. Half-board is mandatory; the dinner menu includes fresh local fish, regional cheeses, and homemade desserts.

Ile de Port-Cros 83400. lemanoir.portcros@wanadoo.fr. ✆ **04-94-05-90-52.** Fax 04-94-05-90-89. 22 units. 170€–210€ double; 200€–235€ suite. MC, V. Closed Oct–Apr. **Amenities:** Restaurant; bar; outdoor pool; room service. *In room:* A/C, hair dryer.

THE FRENCH RIVIERA

by Tristan Rutherford

15

Each resort on the Riviera, also known as the Côte d'Azur (Azure Coast), offers its own unique flavor and charms. This fabled real estate, less than 201km (125 miles) long and located between the Mediterranean and a trio of mountain ranges, has long attracted the jet set with its clear skies, blue waters, and a carefree cafe culture.

A trail of modern artists captivated by the light and setting has left a rich heritage: Matisse at Vence, Cocteau at Menton and Villefranche, Picasso at Antibes and seemingly everywhere else, Léger at Biot, Renoir at Cagnes, and Bonnard at Le Cannet. The finest collection of artworks is at the Foundation Maeght in St-Paul-de-Vence.

A century ago, winter and spring were considered high season on the Riviera. In recent decades, July and August have become the most crowded months, and reservations are imperative. The region basks in over 300 days of sun per year, and even December and January are often clement and bright.

The ribbonlike corniche roads stretch across the western Riviera from Nice to Menton. They have been depicted in scores of films, including Cary Grant's *To Catch a Thief* and Robert de Niro's *Ronin*. The Alps literally drop into the Mediterranean here, and roads were carved along the way. The lower road, the 32km (20 miles) long Corniche Inférieure, takes in the resorts of Villefranche, Cap-Ferrat, Beaulieu, Monaco, and Cap-Martin. The 31km (19-mile) Moyenne Corniche (Middle Rd.) winds in and out of mountain tunnels and takes in the picture-perfect village of Eze. Napoleon built the Grande Corniche—the most panoramic—in 1806. La Turbie is the principal town along the 32km (20-mile) stretch, which reaches more than 480m (1,574 ft.) high at Col d'Eze.

Note: For more extensive coverage of this region, check out *Frommer's Provence & the Riviera.*

ST-TROPEZ ★★

874km (542 miles) S of Paris; 76km (47 miles) SW of Cannes

An air of hedonism runs rampant in this sun-kissed town, but Tropezian style is blissfully understated—not in-your-face. St-Tropez attracts artists, novelists, and the film colony each summer, with a flamboyant parade of humanity trailing behind. In winter it morphs back into a boho fishing village, albeit one studded with modern art galleries and some of the best restaurants along the coast.

The Brigitte Bardot movie *And God Created Woman* put St-Tropez on the tourist map. Yet more decadent tourists, baring almost all on the peninsula's white-sand beaches, followed in her wake. In 1995, Bardot pronounced St-Tropez dead, "squatted by a lot of no-goods, drugheads, and villains." But 1997 saw her return, followed in recent years by celebrity A-listers including Oprah, Keith Richards, Jack Nicholson, Paris Hilton, Jay-Z, and Beyoncé.

PREVIOUS PAGE: **The beach and Promenade des Anglais, Nice.**

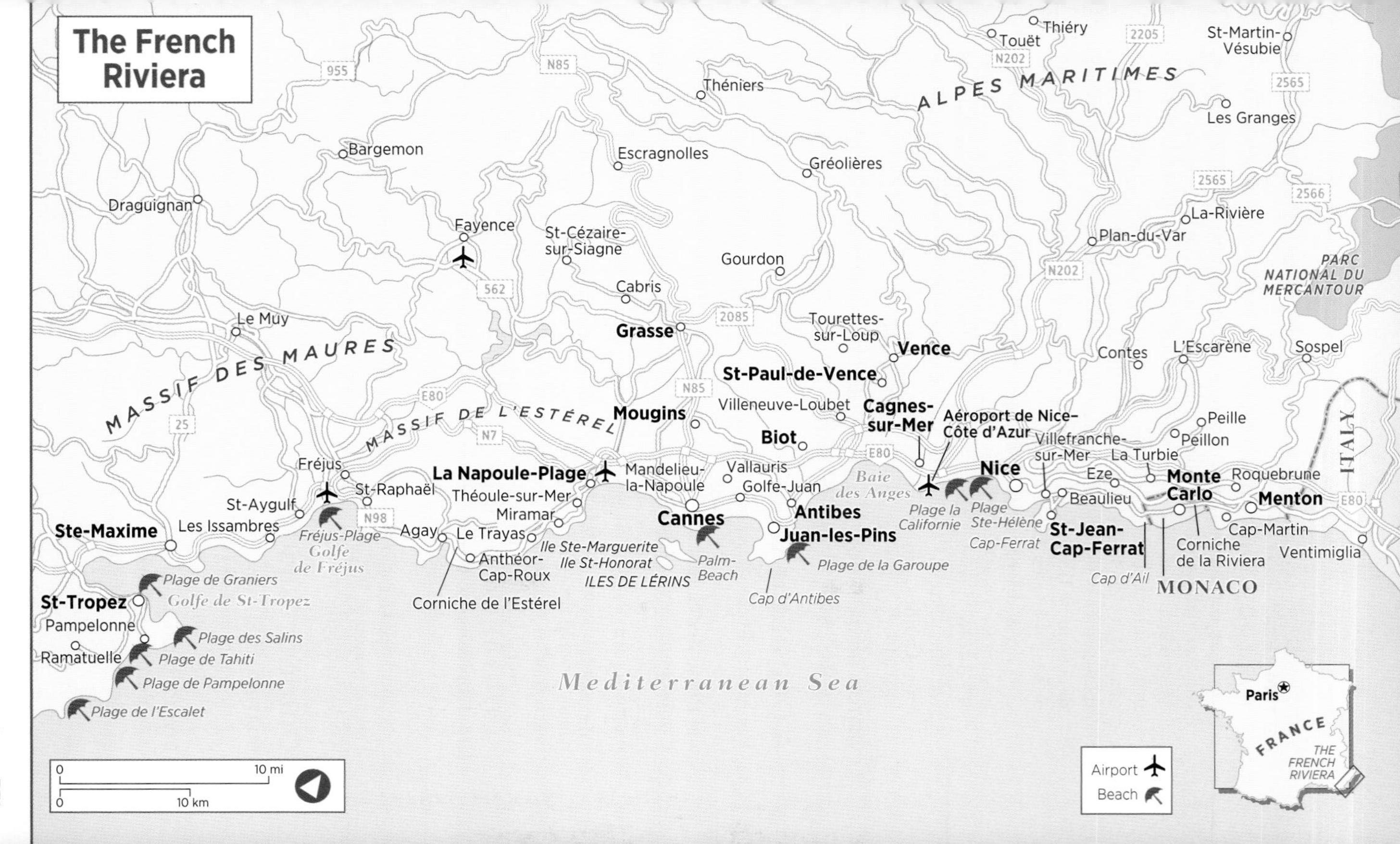
The French Riviera
ALPES MARITIMES
MASSIF DES MAURES
MASSIF DE L'ESTÉREL
PARC NATIONAL DU MERCANTOUR
ITALY
MONACO
FRANCE
Paris
THE FRENCH RIVIERA
Mediterranean Sea
Airport
Beach
0
10 mi
0
10 km
Thiéry
Touët
St-Martin-Vésubie
Théniers
Les Granges
Bargemon
Escragnolles
Gréolières
Draguignan
La-Rivière
Plan-du-Var
Fayence
St-Cézaire-sur-Siagne
Gourdon
Cabris
Le Muy
Grasse
Tourettes-sur-Loup
Vence
Contes
L'Escarène
Sospel
St-Paul-de-Vence
Mougins
Villeneuve-Loubet
Cagnes-sur-Mer
Aéroport de Nice-Côte d'Azur
Peille
Peillon
Biot
Villefranche-sur-Mer
La Turbie
Fréjus
La Napoule-Plage
Mandelieu-la-Napoule
Vallauris
Baie des Anges
Nice
Eze
Monte Carlo
Roquebrune
St-Raphaël
Théoule-sur-Mer
Golfe-Juan
Beaulieu
Menton
St-Aygulf
Miramar
Cannes
Antibes
Plage la Californie
Plage Ste-Hélène
Ste-Maxime
Les Issambres
Fréjus-Plage
Agay
Le Trayas
Juan-les-Pins
St-Jean-Cap-Ferrat
Cap-Martin
Golfe de Fréjus
Anthéor-Cap-Roux
Ile Ste-Marguerite
Ile St-Honorat
ILES DE LÉRINS
Palm-Beach
Plage de la Garoupe
Cap-Ferrat
Corniche de la Riviera
Ventimiglia
Cap d'Ail
Plage de Graniers
St-Tropez
Golfe de St-Tropez
Corniche de l'Estérel
Cap d'Antibes
Pampelonne
Plage des Salins
Ramatuelle
Plage de Tahiti
Plage de Pampelonne
Plage de l'Escalet
955
N85
N202
2205
2565
2566
562
2085
E80
25
N7
N98

Essentials

GETTING THERE The nearest rail station is in St-Raphaël, a neighboring resort. **Boats** depart (✆ **04-94-95-17-46;** www.bateauxsaintraphael.com) from its Vieux Port for St-Tropez (trip time: 50 min.) every 15 minutes in high summer, reducing to twice-daily sailings in winter. The one-way fare is 14€. Year-round, 10 to 15 Varlib **buses** per day leave from the Gare Routière in St-Raphaël (✆ **04-94-44-52-70;** www.varlib.fr) for St-Tropez. The trip takes 1½ to 2½ hours, depending on the bus and the traffic, which during midsummer is usually horrendous. A one-way ticket costs 2€. Buses run directly to St-Tropez from Toulon and Hyères, and from the nearest airport, at Toulon-Hyères, 56km (35 miles) away.

If you **drive,** note that parking in St-Tropez is very difficult, especially in summer. For parking, follow the signs for **Parking des Lices** (✆ **04-94-97-34-46**), beneath place des Lices, or **Parking du Nouveau Port,** on waterfront avenue Charles de Gaulle (✆ **04-94-97-74-99**). To get here from **Cannes,** drive southwest along the coastal highway (RD98), turning east when you see signs pointing to St-Tropez.

VISITOR INFORMATION The **Office de Tourisme** is on quai Jean-Jaurès (✆ **04-94-97-45-21;** fax 04-94-97-82-66; www.ot-saint-tropez.com).

A Day at the Beach

The hottest Riviera beaches are at St-Tropez. The best for families are closest to the center, including **Plage de la Bouillabaisse, Plage des Graniers,** and **Plage des Salins.** More daring is the 5km (3-mile) crescent of **Plage de Pampelonne,** about 10km (6¼ miles) from St-Tropez. Here around 35 hedonisitic beach clubs dot the sand, including cash-only **La Voile Rouge** (✆ **04-94-79-84-34**), where champagne is regularly sprayed over diners. Equally decadent **Club 55** (✆ **04-94-55-55-55;** www.club55.fr) is a former Bardot hangout, while American-run **Nikki Beach** (✆ **04-94-79-82-04;** www.nikki-beach.com) is younger and more understated, but nevertheless painfully chic. All-gay **Aqua Club** (✆ **04-94-79-84-35**) and bare-all **Plage de Tahiti** (✆ **04-94-97-18-02;** www.tahiti-beach.com) are extremely friendly. Way more relaxed are **Tropicana** (✆ **04-94-79-83-96**) and **Plage des Jumeaux** (✆ **04-94-55-21-80;** www.plagedesjumeaux.com), the latter drawing many families with young kids.

You'll need a car, bike, or scooter to get from town to Plage de Pampelonne. Parking is around 10€ for the day. More than anywhere else on the Riviera, topless bathing is the norm.

Outdoor Pursuits

BOATING In St-Tropez port, **Octopussy** (✆ **04-94-56-53-10;** www.octopussy.fr) rents boats 5 to 16m (16–52 ft.) long. Larger ones come with a captain at the helm. Prices begin at 320€ per day.

DIVING Multilingual scuba tuition and equipment hire is available from the **European Diving School** (✆ **04-94-79-90-37;** www.europeandivingschool.com), on Plage de Pampelonne. Regular dives, including all equipment, cost 37€.

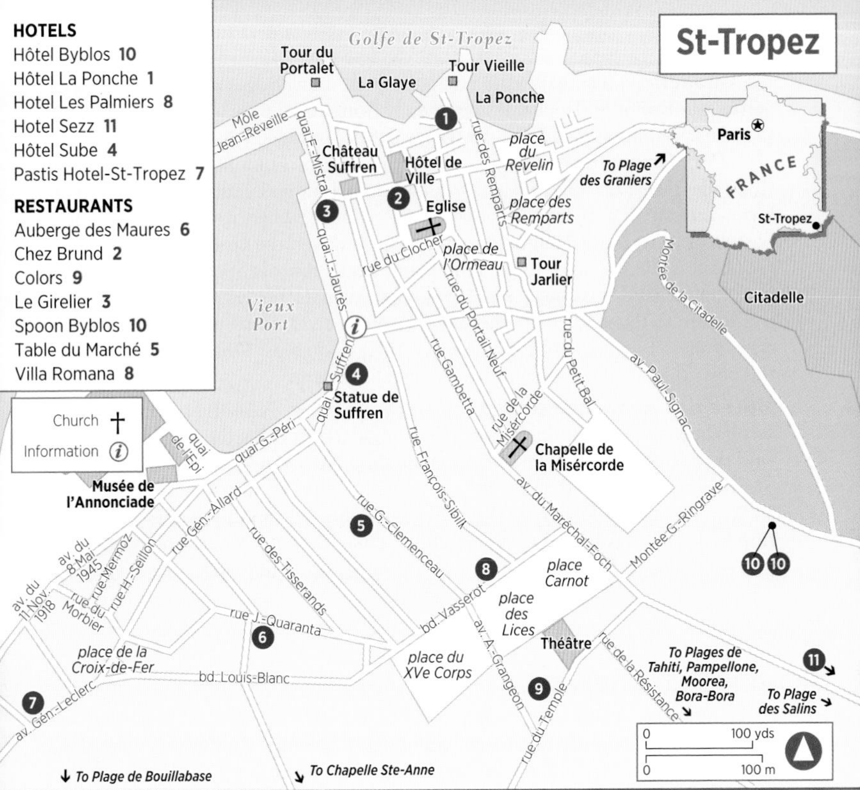

Shopping

St-Tropez is awash with stylish shops. The merchandise is mostly Mediterranean, breezy, and sophisticated. Chic labels include Hermès, Sonia Rykiel, and Dior. There are also scores of one-off designers around the Vieille Ville (old town), on rue Gambetta, and near place des Lices, which also hosts an excellent **outdoor market,** Marché Provençal, with food, clothes, and *brocante* on Tuesday and Saturday mornings. **Galeries Tropéziennes,** 56 rue Gambetta (✆**04-94-97-02-21**), packs loads of leather, designer clothes, and shoe stores into its showrooms near place des Lices.

Exploring the City

At the foot of St-Tropez's yacht-filled port lies the bronze **Statue de Suffren,** paying tribute to Vice Admiral Pierre André de Suffren. This St-Tropez native was one of greatest sailors of 18th-century France and fought in the Franco-American wars against the British in the 1780s.

In the old town, one of the most interesting streets is **rue de la Miséricorde.** It's lined with stone houses that hold boutiques and evokes medieval St-Tropez better than any other in town. At the corner of rue Gambetta is **Chapelle de la Miséricorde,** with a blue, green, and gold tile roof. Towering above town is the **Citadelle,** a fortified castle complete with drawbridges and stunning views across the Bay of St-Tropez. It's open daily from 10am to 6:30pm (until 5:30pm Oct–Mar). Admission is 2.50€; entrance is free for those 8 and under.

Port Grimaud ★ makes an interesting outing. From St-Tropez, drive 4km (2¾ miles) west on A98 to Route 98, and then 1.5km (1 mile) north to the Port Grimaud exit. If you approach the village at dusk, when it's bathed in Riviera pastels, it looks like a 16th-century hamlet. However, the vision is a mirage: Port Grimaud is the dream of its promoter, architect François Spoerry, who carved it out of marshland and dug canals. Flanking the canals, fingers of land extend from the square to the sea. The homes are Provençal style, many with Italianate window arches. Boat owners can anchor at their doorsteps. One newspaper called the port "the most magnificent fake since Disneyland."

Musée de l'Annonciade (Musée St-Tropez) ★★ Near the harbor, this museum showcases one of the Riviera's finest modern art collections of post-Impressionist masters. Many of the artists, including Paul Signac, painted the port of St-Tropez, a backdrop that lies right outside the building. The collection includes such works as Van Dongen's *Women of the Balustrade* and paintings and sculpture by Bonnard, Matisse, Braque, Dufy, Utrillo, Seurat, Derain, and Maillol.

Quai de l'Epi le Port. ✆ **04-94-17-84-10.** Admission 6€ adults, 4€ children 11 and under. June–Sept daily 10am–noon and 2–6pm; Oct and Dec–May Wed–Mon 10am–noon and 2–7pm. Closed Nov.

Where to Stay

VERY EXPENSIVE

Hôtel Byblos ★★★ The builder said he created "an anti-hotel, a place like home." That's true—if your home resembles a palace in Beirut and has salons decorated with Phoenician gold statues from 3000 B.C. On a hill above the harbor, this complex has intimate patios and courtyards. It's filled with antiques and rare objects such as polychrome carved woodwork and marquetry floors. Every room is unique, and all have elegant beds. Unusual features might include a fireplace on a raised hearth or a bed recessed on a dais. The rooms range in size from medium to spacious, often with high ceilings and antiques or reproductions. Some units have such special features as four-posters with furry spreads or sunken whirlpool tubs. Le Hameau, a stylish annex, contains 10 duplex suites built around a small courtyard with an outdoor spa. Some rooms have balconies overlooking an inner courtyard; others open onto a flowery terrace.

Av. Paul Signac, St-Tropez 83990. www.byblos.com. ✆ **04-94-56-68-00.** Fax 04-94-56-68-01. 91 units. 400€–950€ double; from 750€ suite. AE, DC, MC, V. Parking 30€. Closed Nov–Mar. **Amenities:** 2 restaurants; 2 bars; nightclub; babysitting; concierge; exercise room; massage; outdoor pool; room service; sauna; spa. *In room:* A/C, TV, hair dryer, minibar, free Wi-Fi.

Hôtel Sezz ★★ ☺ This designer dream took on the mantle of St-Tropez's newest and hippest hotel with the opening of 35 wow-factor suites in 2010. Accomplished French hotelier Shahé Kalaidjian has combined practical architecture (curved bedroom ceilings that draw eyes skyward) with smile-inducing additions (secluded outdoor showers with rainforest heads). The resulting atmosphere, no doubt aided by the vast palm-lined pool with huge concrete stepping stones, is laid-back, beachy, and communal, although those craving luxurious privacy can doze in their own secret grassy garden that lies to the rear of each unit. Sunrise yoga and open-air massage are the order of the day at the Payot Spa. The restaurant Colette sprouts from inside the glass cube dining room and creeps right around the pool. Dining under the innovative eye of rising star Jerome Roy is a delight. Light, summery dishes (think tomato salad with Campari ice cubes) were created in tandem with Parisian restaurant ace Pierre Gagnaire.

Rte Des Salins, Saint Tropez 83990. www.hotelsezz-sainttropez.com. ✆ **04-94-55-31-55.** Fax 04-94-55-31-51. 37 units. 330€–850€ double; from 1,400€ suite. AE, DC, MC, V. Free parking. Closed mid-Oct to Mar. **Amenities:** 1 restaurant; 1 bar; babysitting; bikes; concierge; exercise room; massage; outdoor pool; room service; sauna; free shuttle to beach; spa. *In room:* A/C, TV, hair dryer, minibar, free Wi-Fi.

Pastis Hôtel-St-Tropez ★★ Bestselling author Peter Mayle, whose writings have drawn thousands to visit Provence, occasionally drops by this boutique hotel. Here he is welcomed by two expat Brits, John and Pauline Larkin, who took a portside Provençal house and transformed it into a chic little inn. They have decorated it in a sophisticated eclectic style, even featuring their collection of framed album artwork that includes the Sex Pistols and the Rolling Stones. Guests can mingle as they sip an aperitif by the pool in the courtyard. You get the feeling that you're staying in a private home when you lodge here, one discreetly decorated with a fantastic eye for design. Like the guest-only lounge, the rooms are furnished in an inspired mix, and each unit comes with a spacious bathroom as well as (in most of the rooms) a balcony or breakfast terrace. Some accommodations are large enough for extra beds or cots. Indian rugs, Chinese armoires, and beds adorned with Provençal *boutis* spreads enhance the warm, intimate ambience.

61 av. du Général Leclerc, St-Tropez 83990. www.pastis-st-tropez.com. ✆ **04-98-12-56-50.** Fax 04-94-96-99-82. 10 units. 175€–650€ double. AE, MC, V. Free parking. Closed Dec. **Amenities:** Outdoor pool. *In room:* A/C, TV, minibar, free Wi-Fi.

EXPENSIVE

Hôtel La Ponche ★ The same family has run this hotel overlooking the port for more than half a century. The cozy nest has long been a favorite of ours, as it's the most discreet, most charming, and least celebrity-flashy establishment downtown, making Byblos (see above) look nouveau riche and a bit strident in comparison. It's filled with the original airy paintings of Jacques Cordier, who died in 1978. Each floor holds two or three rooms, all of which are well equipped and open onto sea views. Sun-colored walls with subtle lighting lend a homey feeling. The beds are elegantly appointed with linen and quality mattresses, and the midsize to large bathrooms have tub/showers or a shower only. There's also a convivial attached restaurant with outdoor terrace, specializing in *fruits des mer.*

Port des Pécheurs, St-Tropez 83990. www.laponche.com. ✆ **04-94-97-02-53.** Fax 04-94-97-78-61. 18 units. 225€–510€ double; 360€–655€ suite. AE, MC, V. Parking 25€. Closed Nov to mid-Feb. **Amenities:** Restaurant; bar; babysitting; room service. *In room:* A/C, TV, hair dryer, minibar, free Wi-Fi.

MODERATE

Hôtel Les Palmiers Accompanied by a verdant garden, this pleasant and practical three-star hotel was created in 1955 with the union of two once-separate houses, the older of which dates from the late 18th century. One of the best things about it is its location directly astride place des Lices in the center of St-Tropez. Bedrooms are simple and compact, and outfitted in a modernized

Provençal theme highlighted with blue, soft orange, and ocher. Christian Guerin is the extroverted owner. There's a bar on the premises, but no restaurant.

24–26 bd. Vasserot (place des Lices), St-Tropez 83991. www.hotel-les-palmiers.com. ✆ **04-94-97-01-61.** Fax 04-94-97-10-02. 25 units. 72€–230€ double. AE, MC, V. **Amenities:** Room service. *In room:* A/C, TV, hair dryer, minibar, free Wi-Fi.

Where to Eat

Auberge des Maures ★ PROVENÇAL One of our favorite restaurants lies close to one end of the all-pedestrian rue Allard. The stone-sided building, highlighted with Provençal murals, has a rollaway roof and garden seating (both experienced during nice weather). The open kitchen affords views of the staff preparing Provençal specialties, including stuffed zucchini blossoms and *gigot d'agneau* lamb with rosemary confit, and *petits farcis* (stuffed vegetables). The Salinesi family takes pride in using seasonal, all-fresh ingredients.

4 rue du Docteur Boutin. ✆ **04-94-97-01-50** www.aubergedesmaures.fr. Reservations recommended. Main courses 40€–60€; fixed-price menu 49€. AE, DC, MC, V. Daily 7:30pm–1am. Closed mid-Nov to Mar.

Le Girelier PROVENÇAL At this portside restaurant, the blue-and-white color scheme has become a trademark. They serve grilled fish in many versions, as well as bouillabaisse (only for two). Also on the menu are brochette of monkfish, a kettle of spicy mussels, and *pipérade* (a Basque omelet with pimientos, garlic, and tomatoes).

Quai Jean-Jaurès. ✆ **04-94-97-03-87.** www.legirelier.fr. Main courses 21€–50€; fixed-price menu 39€. AE, DC, MC, V. Daily noon–6pm and 7–11pm. Closed Nov–Mar.

Le Table du Marché ★ MODERN FRENCH This is French superchef Christophe Leroy's patisserie-brasserie concept, and, boy, does it work well. Shoppers from the local boutiques stop for coffee and point out their cake of choice in the tearoom-style front dining room. It's more formal at the rear, where diners may sit in front of a glass window and watch the team engineer unshowy yet sophisticated starters like Vietnamese chicken rolls or a modern take on Caesar salad. The petite menu of mains is heartier yet similarly unfussy. Try flash-fried fillet of beef, or lamb with preserved lemon. Foodies can join the chefs in

FRENCH boules

Second only to charging around St-Tropez's medieval Citadelle, a game of *pétanque*, or French boules, is seriously cool for kids. Hop to Le Café (✆ **04-94-97-44-69**), one of many alfresco bars in place des Lices, and request a handful of *pétanque* boules to toss around the tree-dappled square. The game was created down the coast and is about as Provençal as it gets. Pick up some tips by watching the locals first. Games begin with a toss of the jack, or *bouchon.* Teams then take turns to throw. Whoever is farthest away keeps trying to get closest to the ball, with any remaining balls tossed in at the end. A point is awarded for each steel ball that's closer to the jack than any balls from the opposing team.

making a four-course lunch (book 2 days in advance, minimum five persons) for 100€ per person. The truly lazy can have platters of foie gras canapés, quiches, terrines, and salads couriered out to their yacht.

38 rue Georges Clemenceau. ✆ **04-94-97-85-20.** www.christophe-leroy.com. Reservations recommended. Main courses 18€–32€; fixed-price menu 29€. AE, MC, V. Daily 12:30–3pm and 7–11pm; 7:30am–11pm for drinks or patisserie.

Pizzeria Bruno ITALIAN This cozy hole-in-the wall diner has been whipping out peerless pizzas from its wood-fired oven since 1959. Even Bardot was once a regular. A limited menu of grilled meats and steaks also features, as do five top-notch salads including Niçoise and *aux coquilles Saint-Jacques,* the latter brimming with warm scallops, green beans, potato, and onion. While the flavors and prices rank among St-Tropez's best, the stool and banquette seating is far from the most comfortable in town.

2 rue de l'Eglise. ✆ **04-94-97-05-18.** Main courses 10€–18€. AE, MC, V. Daily noon–2pm and 7:30pm–midnight. Closed Oct–Apr.

Spoon Byblos ★★ FRENCH/INTERNATIONAL Originally launched in Paris, Spoon's Riviera incarnation draws special inspiration from Catalonian, Andalusian, and Moroccan cuisine. It also offers more than 300 wines from around the world. It's terribly fashionable, as you might expect, given its location in one of the world's hippest hotels. Diners are advised to concentrate on the imaginative cuisine (split into signature Spoon Origin dishes and even more inventive Spoon Now dishes) rather than the self-conscious sense of chic. The restaurant opens onto a circular bar made of blue-tinted glass and polished stainless steel. Dig into shrimp and squid consommé with a hint of jasmine and orange, spicy king prawns on a skewer, or spit-roasted John Dory.

In the Hôtel Byblos, av. Paul-Signac. ✆ **04-94-56-68-20.** Reservations required. Main courses 34€–49€; fixed-price menu 89€. AE, DC, MC, V. Daily 8–11pm. Closed Nov to mid-Apr.

St-Tropez After Dark

On the lobby level of the Hôtel Byblos, **Les Caves du Roy,** avenue Paul-Signac (✆ **04-94-97-16-02**), is the most self-consciously chic nightclub in St-Tropez. Entrance is free, but drink prices are eye-wateringly high. Any riff-raff (or paparazzi, for that matter) are kept away from the beautiful people by owner Jean de Colmont. It's open nightly from Easter to late September from 11:30pm until dawn. **Le Papagayo,** in the Résidence du Nouveau-Port, rue Gambetta (✆ **04-94-97-95-95**), is one of the largest nightclubs in town. The decor was inspired by the psychedelic 1960s. Entrance is around 20€ and includes one drink, although those dining at the attached restaurant can routinely sneak in free. Adjacent to Le Papagayo is **Le VIP Room,** in the Résidence du Nouveau-Port (✆ **04-94-97-14-70**), a younger yet similarly chic version of Les Caves du Roy. Cocktails hover between 15€ and 20€.

Le Pigeonnier, 13 rue de la Ponche (✆ **04-94-97-84-26**), rocks, rolls, and welcomes a mostly gay or lesbian crowd between 20 and 50. Most of the socializing revolves around the long, narrow bar, where patrons from all over Europe chatter. There's also a dance floor. **L'Esquinade,** 2 rue de Four (✆ **04-94-56-26-21**), is the habitual sweaty follow-on club.

Below the Hôtel Sube, **Café de Paris,** sur le Port (✆ **04-94-97-00-56**), is one of the most popular—and most friendly—hangouts in town. It has 1900s-style globe lights, an occasional 19th-century bronze artifact, masses of artificial flowers, and a long zinc bar. **Café Sénéquier,** sur le Port (✆**04-94-97-00-90**), is historic, venerable, snobbish by day, and off-puttingly stylish by night.

CANNES ★★★

905km (561 miles) S of Paris; 163km (101 miles) E of Marseille; 26km (16 miles) SW of Nice

When Coco Chanel came here and got a suntan, returning to Paris bronzed, she shocked the milk-white society ladies—who quickly began to copy her. Today the bronzed bodies, clad in nearly nonexistent swimsuits, line the beaches of this chic resort and continue the late fashion designer's example. A block back from the famed promenade de la Croisette are the boutiques, bars, and bistros that make Cannes the Riviera's capital of cool.

Essentials

GETTING THERE By **train,** Cannes is 15 minutes from Antibes, 35 minutes from Nice, and 50 minutes from Monaco. The TGV from Paris reaches Cannes in an incredibly scenic 5 hours. The one-way fare from Paris is 50€ to 100€. For rail information and schedules, call ✆**36-35** or visit www.voyages-sncf.com. **Rapide Côte d'Azur,** place de l'Hôtel de Ville, Cannes (✆**04-93-85-64-44;** www.rca.tm.fr), provides bus service to Nice via Antibes and Cagnes-sur-Mer every 20 minutes during the day (trip time: 1½ hr.). The one-way fare is 1€.

Nice **international airport** (✆**08-20-42-33-33;** www.nice.aeroport.fr) is a 30-minute drive east. **Buses** pick up passengers at the airport every 30 minutes during the day (hourly at other times) and drop them at the Gare Routière, place de l'Hôtel de Ville (✆**04-93-45-20-08**). The one-way fare is 16€.

By **car** from Marseille, take A51 north to Aix-en-Provence, continuing along A8 east to Cannes. From Nice, follow A8 southwest to Cannes.

VISITOR INFORMATION The **Office de Tourisme** is at 1 bd. de la Croisette (✆**04-92-99-84-22;** fax 04-92-99-84-23; www.cannes.travel). There is an additional office by the train station.

SPECIAL EVENTS Cannes is at its most frenzied in mid-May during the **International Film Festival** at the Palais des Festivals, on promenade de la Croisette. It attracts not only film stars (you can touch the cement molds of their handprints), but also seemingly every photographer in the world. You have a better chance of being named prime minister of France than you do of attending one of the major screenings. (Hotel rooms and tables at restaurants are equally scarce during the festival.) But the people-watching is fabulous. If you find yourself here at the right time, you can join the thousands who line up in front of the Palais des Festivals, where the premieres are held. With paparazzi shouting and gendarmes holding back fans, the guests parade along the red carpet, stopping for a moment to strike a pose. *C'est Cannes!*

You may be able to get tickets for some of the lesser films. For information, see "France Calendar of Events" in chapter 2, or visit **www.festival-cannes.com**.

From international regattas and galas to *concours d'élégance* (an extravagant car show), summertime fireworks, winter ballet, and even a Mimosa

Festival (focusing on flowers and local handicrafts) in February, something's always happening at Cannes.

A Day at the Beach

Beachgoing in Cannes has more to do with exhibitionism than actual swimming. Plage de la Croisette extends between the Vieux Port and the Port Canto. The beaches along this billion-dollar stretch of sand are *payante,* meaning entrance costs 15€ to 30€. You don't need to be a guest of the Noga Hilton, Martinez, or Carlton to use the beaches associated with these high-end hotels (see "Where to Stay"), and there are heaps more buzzing beach clubs dotted around, including sassy 3.14 Beach (✆ **04-93-94-25-43**).

Why should you pay a fee at all? Well, it includes a full day's use of a mattress, a chaise longue (the seafront is more pebbly than sandy), and a parasol, as well as easy access to freshwater showers. There are also outdoor restaurants and bars (some with organic menus, others with burgers and sushi) where no one minds if you appear in your swimsuit. Every beach allows topless bathing, and you're likely to find the same forms of décolletage along the entire strip.

Looking for a free public beach without renting chaises or parasols? Head for **Plage du Midi,** sometimes called Midi Plage, just west of the Vieux Port, or **Plage Gazagnaire,** just east of the Port Canto. Here you'll find families with children and lots of caravan-type vehicles parked nearby.

Outdoor Pursuits

BICYCLING & MOTOR SCOOTERING Despite the summertime traffic, the flat landscapes between Cannes and satellite resorts such as La Napoule are well suited for riding a bike or motor scooter. At **Daniel Location,** 7 rue Suffern (✆ **04-93-99-90-30;** www.daniel-location-2roues.com), *vélos tout terrain* (mountain bikes) cost 12€ a day. Motorized bikes and scooters cost 35€ per day; renters must be at least 16 years old. For larger scooters, you must present a valid driver's license. Another purveyor of bikes is **Mistral Location,** 4 rue Georges Clemenceau (✆ **04-93-39-33-60;** www.mistral-location.com), which charges 16€ per day.

BOATING Several companies around Cannes's vieux port rent boats of any size, with or without a crew, for a day, a week, or even longer. An outfit known for short-term rentals of small craft, including motorboats, sailboats, and canoes, is **Elco Marine,** 110 bd. du Midi (✆ **04-93-47-12-62;** www.elcomarine.fr).

GOLF Cannes is ringed by 10 golf courses, almost all within a 20-minute drive. The Old Course, route de Golf, Mandelieu (✆ **04-92-97-32-00;** www.golfoldcourse.com), is a leafy gem dating from 1891. Greens fees start at 100€, with big reductions for lunch deals and afternoon tee-offs. The prestigious Royal Mougins Golf Club, 424 av. du Roi, Mougins (✆ **04-92-92-49-69;** www.royalmougins.fr), also boasts a gourmet restaurant and spa. Greens fees start at 175€, half-price for nine holes.

TENNIS Some resorts have their own courts. The city of Cannes also maintains 16 synthetic courts and 6 clay-topped ones at the **Garden Tennis Club,** 99 av. Maurice Chevalier (✆ **04-93-47-29-33**). You'll pay 12€ to 15€ per hour, depending on the court and the time you want to play, plus 3.50€ per hour for floodlights.

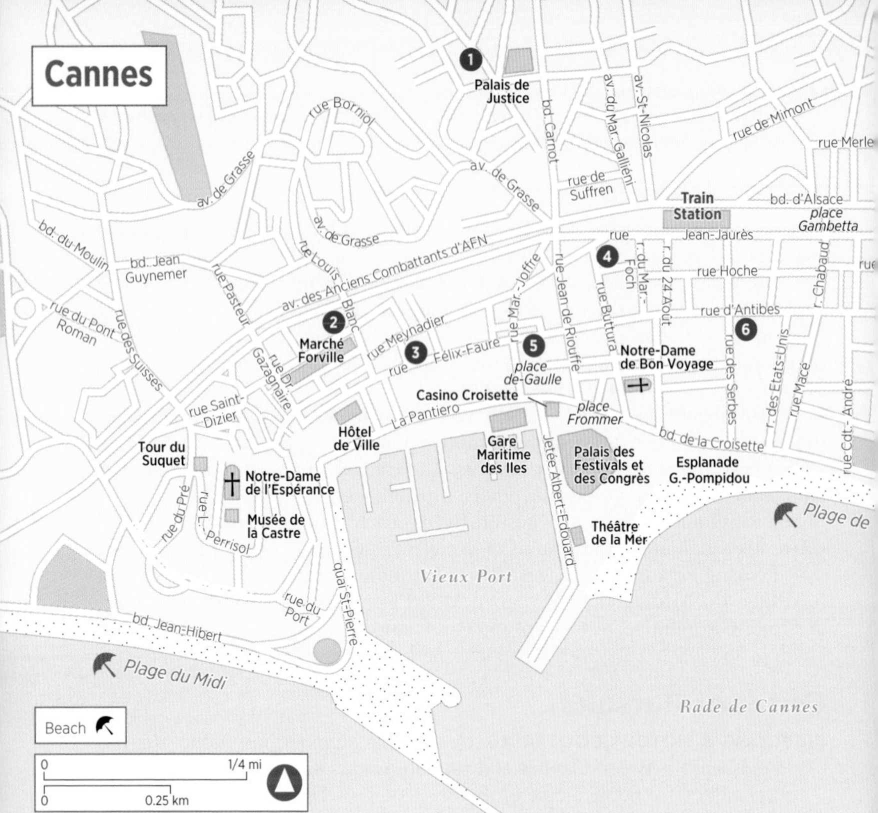

Shopping

Cannes achieves a blend of resort-style leisure, glamour, and media glitz more successfully than many of its neighbors. You'll see every big-name designer you can think of (Saint-Laurent, Rykiel, and Hermès), plus a legion of one-off designer boutiques and shoe stores. There are also real-people shops; resale shops for star-studded castoffs; flea markets for fun junk; and a fruit, flower, and vegetable market.

BOOKS **Ciné-Folie,** 14 rue des Frères-Pradignac (**✆04-93-39-22-99**), is devoted entirely to film. Called *La Boutique du Cinema,* it is the finest film bookstore in the south of France; vintage film stills and movie posters are also for sale. **Wally's English Bookshop,** 11 rue Bivouac Napoleon (**✆04-93-99-40-08;** www.cannesenglishbookshop.com), stocks locally based classics from Peter Mayle and Carol Drinkwater, plus bestselling novels, travel guides, and maps.

DESIGNER SHOPS Most of the big names in fashion, for both men and women, line **promenade de la Croisette,** also known as **La Croisette,** the main drag running along the sea. Among the most prestigious are **Dior,** 38 La Croisette (**✆04-92-98-98-00**), and **Hermès,** 17 La Croisette (**✆04-93-39-08-90**). The stores are in a row, stretching from the Hôtel Carlton almost to the Palais des Festivals, with the best names closest to the **Gray-d'Albion,** 38 rue des Ferbes (**✆04-92-99-79-79**), which is both a mall

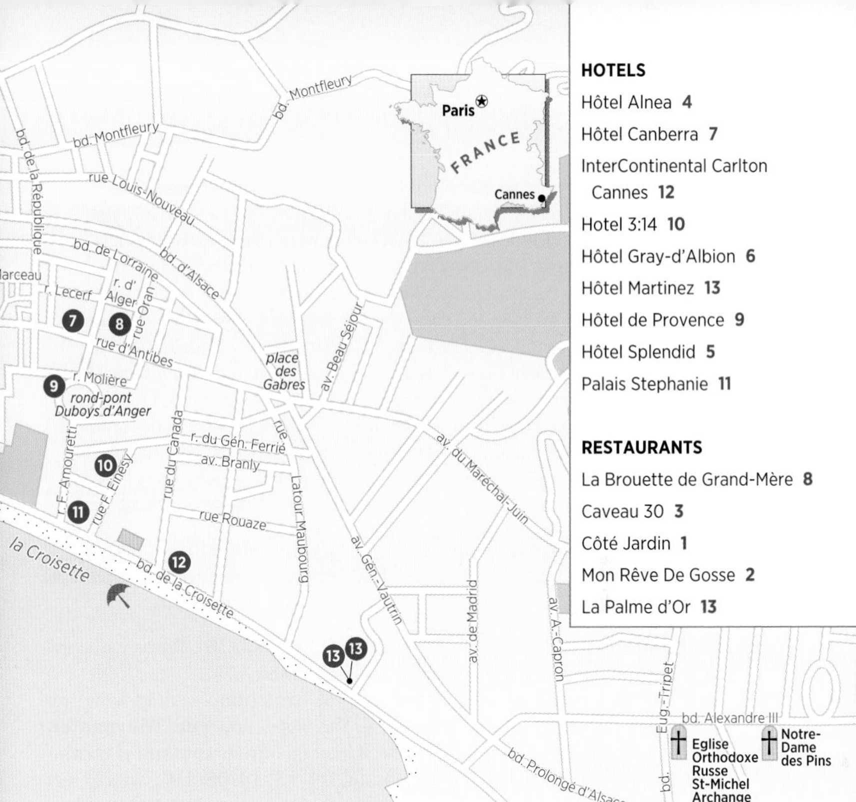

and a hotel (how convenient). Near the train station, department store **Galeries Lafayette** has all the labels crammed into one smallish space at 6 rue du Maréchal-Foch (✆ **04-97-06-25-00**).

Young hipsters should try **Bathroom Graffiti,** 52 rue d'Antibes (✆ **04-93-39-02-32**), for sexy luggage, bikinis, and designer homeware. The rue d'Antibes is also brilliant for big brand bargains including Zara and MaxMara, as well as one-off boutiques.

FLEA MARKETS Cannes has two regular flea markets. Casual, dusty, and increasingly filled with castaways from estate sales, **Marché Forville,** just north of the vieux port, is a stucco structure with a roof and a few arches but no walls. From Tuesday to Sunday, it's the fruit, vegetable, and flower market that supplies the dozens of grand restaurants in the area. Monday is *brocante* day, when the market fills with dealers selling everything from Grandmère's dishes to bone-handled carving knives.

On Saturdays, from 8am to 12:30pm, a somewhat disorganized and busy **Marché aux Fleurs** takes place outdoors along the edges of the allée de la Liberté, across from the Palais des Festivals.

FOOD The **Marché Forville** and the surrounding streets are unsurprisingly the best places to search for picnic supplies. For bottles of Côtes de Provence, try **Cave du Marché,** 5 rue Forville (✆ **04-93-99-60-98**). It also serves up glasses of local rosé and olive crostini on tables outside. **La Compagnie**

SEEING CANNES FROM A petit train

One of the best ways to get your bearings in Cannes (and to get an idea of the difference btw. the city's new and old neighborhoods) is to climb aboard a white-sided Petit Train touristique de Cannes. The diesel-powered vehicles roll through the streets on rubber tires. They operate every day from 10am to between 7 and 11:30pm, depending on the season. Two itineraries are offered: For views of glittery modern Cannes, board the train at a designated spot in front of either of the town's two casinos for a ride along La Croisette and its side streets. For a ride through the narrow streets of Vieux Cannes (Le Suquet), board the train at a clearly designated site on the seaward side of La Croisette, opposite the Hôtel Majestic. Both tours depart every 30 to 60 minutes. They last around 45 minutes, depending on traffic, and cost 7€ for adults and 3€ for children 9 and younger, depending on the tour. A combination ticket to both tours (good on separate days, if you prefer) costs 10€ for adults and 5€ for children 9 and under. For details, call ✆ **06-22-61-25-75** or check out www.cannes-petit-train.com.

des Saumons, 12 Marché Forville (✆ **04-93-68-33-20**), brims with caviar, bottles of fish soup, and slabs of smoked salmon.

The street with the greatest density of emporiums selling wine, olives, herbs, cheese, bread, and oils is the appealing **rue Meynadier,** which leads east from Marché Forville. Heading farther east still is charming **Cannolive,** 16–20 rue Vénizelos (✆ **04-93-39-08-19**), which was founded in 1880 by ancestors of the current owners, the Raynaud family. It sells Provençal olives and their byproducts—tapenades that connoisseurs refer to as "Provençal caviar," black "olives de Nice," and green "olives de Provence," as well as three grades of olive oil from regional producers.

Seeing the Sights

For many visitors, Cannes might as well consist of only one street, the **promenade de la Croisette**—or just La Croisette—curving along the coast and split by islands of palms and flowers.

A port of call for cruise liners, the grand hotels, apartments, and boutiques that line the seafront are the first things that visitors arriving by ship will see. Many of the bigger hotels, some dating from the 19th century, indulge their guests with exclusive beach clubs on the sand. Above the harbor, the old town of Cannes sits on Suquet Hill, where you'll see the 14th-century **Tour de Suquet,** which the English dubbed the Lord's Tower.

Nearby is the **Musée de la Castre ★**, in the Château de la Castre, Le Suquet (✆ **04-93-38-55-26**). It displays paintings, sculpture, and works of decorative art. The ethnography section includes objects from all over the world, including spears from the South Seas and Mayan pottery. There's also a gallery devoted to relics of Mediterranean civilizations, from the Greeks to the Romans, from the Cypriots to the Egyptians. The best part, however, is climbing the 101 steps of the museum's viewing tower: The views across the Riviera are astounding. The museum is open daily in July and August 10am to 7pm, September to March Tuesday to Sunday 10am to 1pm and 2 to 5pm, April to June Tuesday to

Sunday 10am to 1pm and 2 to 6pm. Admission is 3.40€ adults, 2.20€ ages 18 to 25, free 17 and under.

Ferrying to the Iles de Lerins ★★

Bobbing in the shimmering Mediterranean across the bay from Cannes, the Lérins Islands are the major excursion from the port. For access to Ile Ste-Marguerite, head for the quai Laubeuf on the western side of the port, where ferryboats operated by **Trans-Côte d'Azur** (✆ **04-92-98-71-30;** www.trans-cote-azur.com) whiz passengers back and forth year-round at intervals of between every 15 and 75 minutes, depending on the season. For access to Ile St-Honorat, head for the same quay, to the ferryboats operated by **Transports Planaria** (✆ **04-92-98-71-38;** www.cannes-ilesdelerins.com). Boats depart daily year-round at intervals of between 30 and 90 minutes, depending on the season. Round-trip transport to both islands costs 12€ per adult, 6€ for children 5 to 10, and free for children 4 and under.

ILE STE-MARGUERITE

This island was named after St-Honorat's sister, Ste-Marguerite, who lived here with a group of nuns in the 5th century. Today it's one big botanical garden ringed by crystal clear sea. Cars, cigarettes, and all other pollutants are banned, making it the ultimate escape from the Riviera commotion. From the dock, you can stroll along the island (signs point the way) to Fort Royal, built by Spanish troops from 1635 to 1637 and used as a military barracks and parade ground until World War II. The infamous "Man in the Iron Mask" was allegedly imprisoned here, and you can follow the legend back to his horribly spooky cell.

Musée de la Mer, Fort Royal (✆ **04-93-38-55-26**), traces the history of the island, displaying artifacts of Ligurian, Roman, and Arab civilizations, plus the remains discovered by excavations, including paintings, mosaics, and ceramics. The museum is open June to September daily 10am to 5:45pm, and October to May Tuesday to Sunday 10:30am to 1:15pm and 2:15 to 4:45pm (closing at 5:45pm Apr–May). Admission is 3.20€ for adults, free for students and children 17 and under.

Boat en route to the Iles de Lerins.

ILE ST-HONORAT ★★

Only 1.6km (1 mile) long, the Ile St-Honorat is much quieter than neighboring Ste-Marguerite. But in historical terms, it's much richer than its island sibling and is the site of a monastery whose origins date from the 5th century. The **Abbaye de St-Honorat ★**, Les Iles de Lérins, Cannes 06400 (✆ **04-92-99-54-00;** www.abbayedelerins.com), is a combination of medieval ruins and early-20th-century ecclesiastical buildings, and is home to a community of about 25 Cistercian monks. The monks transform the island's herbs, vines, and honey into a wealth of organic products, including lavender oil and wine. All can be purchased in the monastery shop. There is also an excellent lunch-only seafood restaurant, **La Tonnelle** (✆ **04-92-99-54-00**). It's closed from mid-November to mid-December. And no, it's not the monks who cook.

Most visitors content themselves with a wander through the pine forests on the island's western side, a clamber around the ruined monastery on the island's southern edge, and a sunbath on its seaweed-strewn beaches.

Where to Stay

VERY EXPENSIVE

Hôtel Martinez ★★★ When this Art Deco masterpiece was built in the 1930s, it rivaled any other lodging along the coast in sheer size. Over the years, however, it fell into disrepair. But in the '80s, the hotel and its restaurants were given a Belle Epoque makeover and returned to their former luster. The suite-laden penthouse floor has become most sought-after in town following a recent restyling. Several more suites look out over the sea from the first floor, including the Suite des Oliviers, a pleasure palace of upholstered silk bedsteads, a sauna, crystal chandeliers, and a 250-sq.-m (2,691-sq.-ft.) terrace with its own Jacuzzi. All units have full marble bathrooms, wood furnishings, and writing desks. The Martinez also possesses ZPlage (a beach club for the glitterati), plus a seventh-floor spa with products by Lancaster and Sothy, a water-skiing school, a kids'

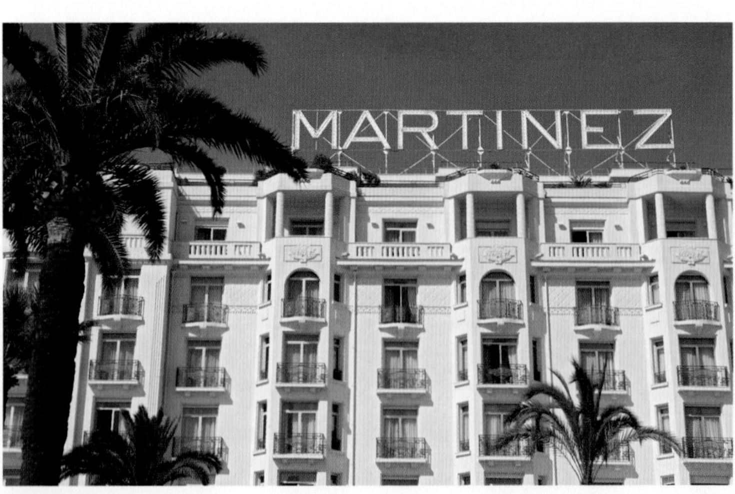

Hôtel Martinez.

club, a very cool bar for grown-ups, and one of the finest restaurants in the South of France (La Palme d'Or, p. 567).

73 bd. de la Croisette, Cannes 06406. www.hotel-martinez.com. ✆ **04-92-98-73-00.** Fax 04-93-39-67-82. 412 units. 610€–890€ double; from 2,900€ suite. AE, DC, MC, V. Parking 39€. **Amenities:** 3 summer restaurants, 2 winter restaurants; bar; babysitting; private beach; children's center; concierge; exercise room; outdoor pool; room service; sauna; spa. *In room:* A/C, TV, hair dryer, minibar, free Wi-Fi.

InterContinental Carlton Cannes ★★★ Here you'll see vehicles of every description dropping off huge amounts of baggage and fashionable guests. The twin gray domes at either end of the facade are often the first things recognized by starlets planning their grand entrances, grand exits, and grand scenes in the hotel's public and private rooms. Built in 1912, the Carlton once attracted the most prominent members of Europe's *haut monde.* Today the hotel is more democratic; however, in summer (especially during the film festival), the vast public rooms still fill with all the voyeuristic and exhibitionistic fervor that seems so much a part of the Riviera. Guest rooms are obscenely plush. The entire seventh floor is dedicated to luxurious suites, including the Grace Kelly suite, with multiple bedrooms and a set of personal photos donated by Prince Albert of Monaco in 2010; and the Sir Sean Connery suite, which has a spa room inside one of the Carlton's cupolas and, in a James Bond–esque touch, a private lift.

58 bd. de la Croisette, Cannes 06400. www.intercontinental.com. ✆ **04-93-06-40-06.** Fax 04-93-06-40-25. 343 units. 190€–1,050€ double; from 625€ suite. AE, DC, MC, V. Parking 38€. **Amenities:** 3 summer restaurants; 1 winter restaurant; 2 bars; health club; room service. *In room:* A/C, TV, hair dryer, minibar, free Wi-Fi.

EXPENSIVE

Hôtel Gray-d'Albion ★★ The smallest of the major hotels epitomizes contemporary luxury and friendly intimacy. Its location a block from the beach straddling the rue d'Antibes makes it a justifiably popular bet for shoppers and families. The happening beach club, with its waterskiing school, jet ski hire, and speedboat rides, makes it a hit with kids, too. The medium-size rooms have benefited from a recent renovation. They blend contemporary and traditional furnishings in a pleasing medley of brown and cream shades. Each unit has a balcony, but the views aren't notable, except from the eighth and ninth floors, where most of the executive rooms and suites look out to sea.

38 rue des Serbes, Cannes 06400. www.lucienbarriere.com. ✆ **04-92-99-79-79.** Fax 04-93-99-26-10. 208 units. 168€–448€ double; from 228€ suite. AE, DC, MC, V. Closed Dec. **Amenities:** Restaurant; bar; babysitting; room service. *In room:* A/C, TV, hair dryer, minibar, free Wi-Fi.

Hotel 3:14 ★ This is the only hotel in Cannes that was designed following feng shui principles and that serves all-organic cuisine. This incredibly playful establishment also has a Disney-esque design ethic: Each floor is themed around a different continent, which will appeal to romantic couples and holidaying families alike. "Africa" rooms are Lion King meets Arabian nights: red, purple, and gold drapes and cushions with art from the Serengeti. "Asia" occupies the fifth floor, where a zenlike geometry coupled with patchouli and jasmine scents lends a calming edge to each room. The top-floor terrace and spa area hosts yoga, massage, an outdoor pool, and hammam quarters. More painfully hip is the Cink bar and Mediterranean restaurant. Just 50m (164 ft.) away, on La Croisette, is 3:14's supercool beach club (Paris Hilton was a recent visitor).

5 rue François Einesy, Cannes 06400. www.3-14hotel.com. ✆ **04-92-99-70-00.** Fax 04-92-99-72-12. 96 units. 155€–355€ double; from 560€ suite. AE, DC, MC, V. **Amenities:** Restaurant; bar; babysitting; concierge; outdoor pool; room service; spa. *In room:* A/C, TV, hair dryer, minibar, free Wi-Fi.

MODERATE

Hôtel Canberra ★★ An oasis of calm midway between La Croisette and the rue d'Antibes, its unique location allows guests to lounge and sunbathe around a small swimming pool in calm and privacy. Both public areas and rooms are the epitome of design-led sophistication. Tradition and Privilege rooms (the latter are poolside) have soft, marbled carpets and funky, retro chairs. Terrace Privilege rooms have deck chairs in the sun. Suites boast sofas and period prints from Cannes's elegant past.

20 rue d'Antibes, Cannes 06400. www.hotel-cannes-canberra.com. ✆ **04-97-06-95-00.** Fax 04-92-98-03-47. 35 units. 150€–310€ double; 220€–500€ suite. AE, DC, MC, V. Parking 25€. **Amenities:** 2 summer restaurants; 1 winter restaurant; bar; babysitting; health club; outdoor pool. *In room:* A/C, TV, hair dryer, minibar, free Wi-Fi.

Hôtel Splendid ★ Opened in 1871 and sympathetically renovated over the following decades, this hotel is a favorite of scholars, politicians, actors, and musicians. But don't expect boutique: The Splendid is fabulously retro and *très* French. The ornate white building with wrought-iron accents looks out onto the sea, the old port, and a park. La Croisette is just a minute's walk south. Rooms are appointed with antique furniture and paintings; about 15 have kitchenettes. Each comes with a good bed and a small but tidy bathroom. The more expensive rooms have sea views.

4-6 rue Félix-Faure, Cannes 06400. www.splendid-hotel-cannes.fr. ✆ **04-97-06-22-22.** Fax 04-93-99-55-02. 62 units. 128€–264€ double. Rates include breakfast. AE, MC, V. **Amenities:** Babysitting; room service. *In room:* A/C, TV, hair dryer, free Wi-Fi.

INEXPENSIVE

Hôtel Alnea A class act packed with fun and flavor, but books up weeks in advance. The small but perfectly formed Alnea correctly advertises itself as being 1 minute from the Palais des Festivals, 2 minutes from La Croisette, and 5 minutes from Le Suquet. Stylish rooms are divided into two sizes. Pichtoune rooms are petite, to say the least, but Confort class rooms have enough space to swing a few shopping bags around. Both overflow with art and color.

20, rue Jean de Riouffe, Cannes 06400. www.hotel-alnea.com. ✆ **04-93-68-77-77.** Fax 09-63-49-97-89. 14 units. 60€–98€ double. AE, MC, V. *In room:* A/C, TV, free Wi-Fi.

Hôtel de Provence Built in the 1930s, this hotel is small and unpretentious—a contrast to the intensely stylish, larger hotels in the immediate area. Most of the rooms have private balconies, and many overlook the shrubs and palms of the hotel's walled garden. Guest rooms are modern and simple, with wooden parquet floors and simply tiled bathrooms. For Cannes, they represent a real bargain. In warm weather, breakfast is served under the flowers of an arbor.

9 rue Molière, Cannes 06400. www.hotel-de-provence.com. ✆ **04-93-38-44-35.** Fax 04-93-39-63-14. 30 units. 87€–127€ double; 107€–177€ suite. AE, MC, V. Parking: 16€. **Amenities:** Bar; room service. *In room:* A/C, TV, hair dryer, minibar, Wi-Fi (10€ for 3 hr.).

Where to Eat

VERY EXPENSIVE

La Palme d'Or ★★★ MODERN FRENCH The ultimate dining experience in Cannes is this double-Michelin-starred restaurant, commanding panoramic sea views from the second floor of the Hotel Martinez. Top chef Christian Sinicropi has presided over the inventive cuisine for more than a decade. He routinely greets diners at their table to best assess their culinary desires before wowing them over six, seven, or eight courses. Although the food is the true star, a celebrity fan base has put this on the see-and-be-seen circuit. Menu items change with the seasons but are likely to include warm foie gras with fondue of rhubarb; or crayfish, clams, and squid marinated in peppered citrus sauce. Intriguing bites on the tasting menus may include olive-flavored marshmallows, beetroot sorbet, and bread made with squid ink. The service is worldly without being stiff.

In the Hôtel Martinez, 73 bd. de la Croisette. ✆ **04-92-98-74-14.** www.hotel-martinez.com. Reservations required. Main courses 51€–120€; fixed-price menu 90€–180€. AE, DC, MC, V. Tues–Sat 12:30–2pm and 8–10pm. Closed Jan–Feb.

MODERATE

Le Caveau 30 ★ SEAFOOD Bow-tied staff balancing huge trays of *fruits de mer* on beds of ice sum up this age-old establishment. Le Caveau 30 is a timeless brasserie devoted to excellent service and top-notch but well-priced seafood and harbor-fresh fish. The Belle Epoque is evoked by the decor: hexagonal crystal chandeliers, red banquettes, and heavy white crockery. Dining spreads onto a smart outdoor terrace from Easter to October. Best value is the two prix-fixe menus. The cheaper option includes red mullet terrine and oysters for starters, grilled sea bass and seafood spaghetti for mains. The more expensive opens with stuffed mussels and crab tartare; mains include monkfish kabobs and heavenly roast cod.

45 av Félix Faure. ✆ **04-93-39-06-33.** www.lecaveau30.com. Main courses 16€–38€; fixed-price menu 24€–36€. AE, MC, V. Tues–Sun 7–11:30pm.

Mon Rêve De Gosse ★★ MODERN FRENCH Since his move from the Michelin-starred La Palme d'Or restaurant in 2010, food critics have been watching the rise of 30-year-old chef Ludovic Ordas with piqued interest. In his tiny new restaurant by the Marché Forville, Ordas dishes up cutting-edge French cuisine with an emphasis on fine local ingredients, all lovingly prepared in a small, open kitchen. Lip-smackingly good meals are a fraction of the cost of those in more famed restaurants, in part as Ordas eschews pricey meats in favor of pigeon, oxtail, and the like. Dishes can include slow-roasted suckling pig on a ricotta-and-leek mash, and flash-fried marinated scallops with aioli and Jerusalem artichokes. A hearty recommendation for a convivial culinary voyage.

11 rue Louis Blanc. ✆ **04-93-39-68-08.** www.monrevedegosse.com. Reservations recommended. Main courses 15€–25€. AE, DC, MC, V. Wed–Mon noon–2pm and 7–10:30pm.

INEXPENSIVE

Côté Jardin ★ PROVENÇAL Set near the courthouse (Palais de Justice) in the heart of commercial Cannes, this restaurant attracts loyal locals because of its unpretentious ambience and its reasonably priced and generous portions. You're offered three different choices as seating options: on the street-level glassed-in veranda, at a table amid the flowering shrubs of the garden terrace, or upstairs within the cozy Provençal dining room. Classic French menu items include scallops in a basil cream, bavette of beef with shallots, roast cod, and saffron mussels.

12 av. St-Louis. ✆ **04-93-38-60-28.** Reservations required, especially in summer. Fixed-price menus 22€–38€. AE, DC, MC, V. Tues–Sat noon–2pm and 7:30–10pm. Closed last week in Oct, 1st week in Nov.

La Brouette de Grand-Mère 🎁 TRADITIONAL FRENCH Few other restaurants in Cannes work so successfully at establishing a cozy testimonial to old-fashioned French cooking. Memories are evoked through dishes that include a savory meat-and-potato stew known as *pot-au-feu,* roasted rabbit in a mushroom sauce, and chicken casserole cooked with beer. Traditional starters may include sausage links, terrines, and baked potatoes stuffed with smoked fish roe and served with a small glass of vodka. Set in the heart of town just behind the Carlton, the place offers two dining rooms, each outfitted in Art Deco style in tones of deep red and soft violet, plus an outdoor terrace.

9 bis rue d'Oran. ✆ **04-93-39-12-10.** Reservations recommended. Fixed-price menu, including aperitif with half-bottle of wine, 35€. AE, MC, V. Daily 7–10pm; Sun noon–2pm. Closed 1 week in June.

Cannes After Dark

Cannes is invariably associated with easygoing permissiveness, filmmaking glitterati, and gambling. If the latter is your thing, Cannes has some world-class casinos loaded with high rollers, voyeurs, and everyone in between. The better established is the **Casino Croisette,** in the Palais des Festivals, Esplanade Lucien Barrière (✆ **04-92-98-78-50;** www.lucienbarriere.com). A well-respected fixture in town since the 1950s, a collection of noisy slot machines it is most certainly not.

Its main competitor is the newer **Palm Beach Casino,** place F-D-Roosevelt, Pointe de la Croisette (✆ **04-97-06-36-90**), on the southeast edge of La Croisette. Inaugurated in 1933 and rebuilt in 2002, it attracts a younger crowd with a summer-only beachside poker room, a beach club with pool, a restaurant, and a disco that runs until dawn. Both casinos maintain slots that operate daily 11am to 5am. Smarter dress is expected for the *les grands jeux* salons (for (blackjack, roulette, craps, poker, and chemin de fer), which open nightly 8pm to 4am.

After-dark diversions continue to grow, with a strip of sundowner bars stretching along rue Félix Faure. Most are chic, some have happy hour cocktails, and several have DJs after dinner. It's best to walk by and take your pick. Nearby is **Chokko,** 15 rue Frères Pradignac (✆ **04-93-39-62-70**), where killer cocktails are served by haughty waiting staff. Dance floor–filling tunes get everyone on their feet after 10pm. Less showy is **Morrison's Irish Pub,** 10 rue Teisseire (✆ **04-92-98-16-17**), which has become the meeting place for visiting yachties and the expat community. There's a DJ on Thursday, Friday, and Saturday in the attached **Morrison's Lounge** club.

The **Bar l'Amiral,** in the Hôtel Martinez, 73 La Croisette (✆ **04-92-98-73-00**), is where deals go down during the film festival. Directors, producers, stars, press agents, screenwriters, and wannabes crowd in here at festival time. The bow-tied barmen have won several world championship cocktail mixing trophies. Places around the bar come complete with a nametag of the star that once propped it up, Humphrey Bogart among them.

Gay and lesbian bar **Le Vogue,** 20 rue du Suquet (✆**04-93-39-99-18**), is a welcoming first stop on Cannes's scene. It's open daily from 7pm until 2:30am. A similar ambience prevails at **Zanzibar,** 85 rue Félix-Faure (✆**04-93-39-30-75**), every evening, although the pace picks up a beat at midnight and throbs until 4am. Another gay option is **Disco Le Sept,** 7 rue Rouguière (✆**04-93-39-10-36**), where drag shows appear nightly at 1:30am. Entrance is free, except on weekends, when it's 16€ (includes a drink). A lot of straights go here, too.

Cannes's most uplifting option is gay-friendly club **Le Nightlife,** 52 rue Jean-Jaurès (✆**04-93-39-20-50**). It was reoutfitted late in 2008 with white walls, a busy bar, occasional fashion shows, and lots of randomly scheduled parties that last until dawn.

MOUGINS

903km (560 miles) S of Paris; 11km (6¾ miles) S of Grasse; 8km (5 miles) N of Cannes

This former fortified town on the crest of a hill provides an alternative for those who want to be near the excitement of Cannes but not in the midst of it. Picasso discovered the tranquil maze of flower-filled streets in the company of his muse, Dora Marr, and photographer, Man Ray, in 1935. In time, Jean Cocteau, Paul Eluard, Fernand Léger, Isadora Duncan, and even Christian Dior called Mougins home.

Mougins now preserves the quiet life in a postcard-perfect manner. Real estate prices are among the highest on the Riviera, and the wealthy residents support a dining scene that punches well above its weight. The Etoile des Mougins food festival held each September is a highbrow gastronomic love-in featuring Michelin-starred chefs from across Provence. The town's artsy legacy has blessed the town with several must-see galleries plus the new Museum of Classical Art, which opened in spring 2011.

Essentials

GETTING THERE The best way to get to Mougins is to **drive.** From Nice, follow E80/A8 west and then cut north on Route 85 into Mougins. From Cannes, head north of the city along N85.

In 2005, the French railway, **SNCF,** reactivated an antique rail line stretching between Grasse (the perfume capital) and Cannes, linking the hamlet of Mouans-Sartoux en route. Mouans-Sartoux lies only 457m (1,499 ft.) from the center of Mougins. Rail service costs 2.80€ one-way from either Cannes or Grasse to Mouans-Sartoux. There are **trains** every hour. By bus, **Société Tam** (✆**08-00-06-01-06;** www.cg06.fr) runs

One of the beautiful fountains in Mougins.

buses between Cannes and Grasse. Bus no. 600 stops in Val-de-Mougins, a 10-minute walk from the center of Mougins. One-way fares from either Cannes or Grasse cost 1€. Given the complexities of a bus transfer from Cannes, it's a lot easier just to pay 30€ to 40€ for a **taxi** to haul you and your possessions northward from Cannes.

VISITOR INFORMATION The **Office de Tourisme** is at 15 av. Jean-Charles-Mallet (✆ **04-93-75-87-67;** fax 04-92-92-04-03; www.mougins.fr).

Seeing the Sights

Chapelle Notre-Dame de Vie The chapel, once painted by Churchill, lies 1.5km (1 mile) southeast of Mougins. It was built in the 12th century and reconstructed in 1646. The priory next door is even more famous. It was Picasso's studio and private residence for the last 12 years of his life. It's still a private home occupied intermittently by the Picasso heirs.

Chemin de la Chapelle. Admission free.

Musée d'Art Classique de Mougins ★ In a typically Mougins twist, the town's fascinating new museum shows Egyptian, Greek, and Roman artifacts from across Provence and the Mediterranean, alongside works from the Renaissance and modern day. Classically inspired sculptures, drawings, and canvases from Matisse, Dufy, Cézanne, Henry Moore, and Antony Gormley are thus transposed against pieces from a bygone age. The juxtaposition of an ancient statue of Venus right next to a Venus sculpture by Yves Klein and a *Birth of Venus* print by Andy Warhol gets our vote.

5 rue des Mûriers. ✆ **04-92-28-01-56.** www.mouginsmusee.com. Admission 17€ adults, 12€ children 17 and under. Apr–Oct daily 9:30am–8:30pm; Nov–Mar daily 9:30am–7pm.

Musée de la Photographie André Villers ★ Mougins is awash with art. A great place to start is this permanent collection of photography by Picasso's friend André Villers. Villers chronicled his friend's Mougins years in black-and-white photos, some scarily prescient, others hilarious (the photo showing Picasso sitting down for breakfast in his trademark Breton shirt pretending he has croissants for fingers will surely raise a smile). Temporary photography exhibitions fill the remaining floors of this traditional village house.

Porte Sarrazine. ✆ **04-93-75-85-67.** Free admission. Tues–Fri 10am–12:30pm and 2–7pm; Oct Sat–Sun 11am–7pm.

Where to Stay

Le Moulin de Mougins (see "Where to Eat," on p. 571) offers rooms and suites.

Le Mas Candille ★★ This 200-year-old Provençal *mas* (farmhouse) is bathed in five-star luxury. Thoroughly renovated in 2005, it gained six high-end villa suites in 2009. The public rooms contain many 19th-century furnishings, and some open onto the vast gardens that are awash with lavender and olives, and dotted with sculptures. Rooms are individually decorated in different styles, including Japanese, medieval, French colonial, and Provençal. Its restaurant offers prix-fixe lunch and evening menus (each fairly priced, considering the quality on offer), which include dishes such as red mullet and mussels with quince jelly; and scallop tart with ceps, Jerusalem artichokes, and Tio Pépé cappuccino. The inventive spa uses Shiseido products and offers cocooning weekends for two.

Bd. Clément Rebuffel, Mougins 06250. www.lemascandille.com. ✆ **04-92-28-43-43.** Fax 04-92-28-43-40. 51 units. 245€–445€ double; from 650€ suite. AE, DC, MC, V. **Amenities:** 2 restaurants; bar; exercise room; 2 outdoor pools; room service; spa. *In room:* A/C, TV, hair dryer, minibar, free Wi-Fi.

Royal Mougins ★ Guests rave about this luxurious country resort 1.5km (1 mile) west of outside Mougins for the golf, spa, and food, in that order. The 18-hole course, created in 1993, is broken by streams and waterfalls, and offers preferential rates for guests. The rest of the grounds are an organized chaos of olives, succulents, yuccas, and pine, all interspersed with giant sun-loungers covered in cushions. It's frequented by a wealthy local and European clientele. The indoor/outdoor spa performs microdermabrasion for men and "royal facials" for women. A smart restaurant overlooks the 18th green. It uses fabulously lavish, not to mention expensive, ingredients. Sumptuous suite-only rooms come with a private outdoor sun terrace in Deluxe and Premium categories.

Bd. Clément Rebuffel, Mougins 06250. www.royalmougins.fr. ✆ **04-92-92-49-69.** Fax 04-92-92-49-72. 46 units. 210€–550€ suite. AE, DC, MC, V. **Amenities:** Restaurant; bar; exercise room; room service; spa. *In room:* A/C, TV, hair dryer, minibar, free Wi-Fi.

Where to Eat

Le Mas Candille is noted for its sublime cuisine; you may want to call to reserve a table.

Le Moulin de Mougins ★★ FRENCH Once this address was arguably the most celebrated dining spot on the Riviera when it was the domain of Roger Vergé, now long retired but formerly one of France's top chefs. The current chef does an admirable job filling Vergé's very large shoes, without all the hype. Like Vergé, he employs market-fresh ingredients in his "cuisine of the sun," a reference to Provence's sun-drenched countryside. Dishes are earthy yet incredibly upscale, often with modern twists on culinary traditions from both Provence and other regions of the country. Some of the chef's best-known creations include pan-fried foie gras, carpaccio of scallops, and a truly delectable filet of sole stuffed with prawns.

The inn has six rooms and five suites. Each is individually designed, modern, and extremely luxurious. Double rooms cost 150€ to 200€, suites 200€ to 350€.

Notre-Dame de Vie, Mougins 06250. ✆ **04-93-75-78-24.** Fax 04-93-90-18-55. www.moulindemougins.com. Reservations required. Main courses 44€–58€; fixed-price menu 49€–160€ lunch, 90€–180€ dinner. AE, DC, MC, V. Wed–Sun noon–2pm and 7:30–10pm.

GRASSE ★

906km (562 miles) S of Paris; 18km (11 miles) N of Cannes; 9.5km (6 miles) N of Mougins; 23km (14 miles) NW of Antibes

Grasse, a 20-minute drive from Cannes, is the most fragrant town on the Riviera. Surrounded by jasmine and roses, it has been the capital of the perfume industry since the Renaissance. It was once a famous resort, attracting such royals as Queen Victoria and Princess Pauline Borghese, Napoleon's lascivious sister.

Today some three-quarters of the world's essences are produced here from foliage that includes violets, daffodils, wild lavender, and jasmine. It takes 10,000 flowers to produce just over 1 kilogram of jasmine petals. Almost a ton of petals is needed to distill 1 liter of essence. The quaint town, which formed the backdrop for the 2006 movie *Perfume,* has several free perfume museums where visitors can enroll in workshops to create their own scent.

Essentials

GETTING THERE **Trains** run to Grasse from Nice, Cannes, and all stations in between. It deposits passengers a 10-minute walk south of town. From here, a walking trail or shuttle bus leads visitors into the center. One-way train tickets cost 3.80€ from Cannes and 8.80€ from Nice. For train schedules and more information, call ✆ **36-35** or visit www.voyages-sncf.com. **Buses** pull into town every 30 to 60 minutes daily from Cannes (trip time: 50 min.). The one-way fare is 1€. There are also about 14 buses every day from Nice (trip time: 1 hr.). The one-way fare is around 1€. They arrive at the Gare Routière, place Notre Dame des Fleurs (✆ **04-93-36-37-37**), a 5-minute walk north of the town center. Visitors arriving by **car** take A8, which funnels in traffic from Monaco, Aix-en-Provence, and Marseille.

VISITOR INFORMATION The **Office de Tourisme** is at place du cours Honoré Cresp (✆ **04-93-36-66-66;** fax 04-93-36-86-36; www.grasse.fr).

Seeing the Sights

Musée International de la Parfumerie ★ This architectural wonder opened in 2008 and serves as a neat lesson on Grasse's scented history. It runs through the raw materials, trade routes, innovation, and marketing of both perfume's beginnings and its modern-day megabrands.

2 bd. du Jeu de Ballon. ✆ **04-93-36-80-20.** www.museesdegrasse.com. Admission 4€ adults, 2€ ages 11–18. June–Sept daily 10am–7pm (until 9pm Sat); Oct–May Wed–Mon 11am–6pm. Closed Nov.

Parfumerie Fragonard ★ One of the best-known perfume developers is named after an 18th-century French painter. This factory has the best villa, the best museum, and the best tour. An English-speaking guide will show you how "the soul of the flower" is extracted. After the tour, you can explore the museum, which displays bottles and vases that trace the industry back to ancient times. If you're shopping for perfume and want to skip the tour, that's entirely acceptable, too.

20 bd. Fragonard. ✆ **04-93-36-44-65.** www.fragonard.com. Free admission. Mar–Oct daily 9am–6pm; Nov–Feb daily 9am–12:30pm and 2–6pm.

Parfumerie Fragonard.

Parfumerie Molinard This firm is well known in the United States, where its products are sold at Saks, Neiman Marcus, and

Bloomingdale's. In the factory, you can witness the extraction of the essence from the flowers. You'll also learn all the details of the process of converting flowers into essential oils. You can admire a collection of antique perfume bottle labels and see a rare collection of perfume *flacons* by Baccarat and Lalique.

60 bd. Victor Hugo. ✆ **04-93-36-01-62.** www.molinard.com. Free admission. Apr–Sept daily 9am–6:30pm; Oct–Mar Mon–Sat 9am–noon and 2–6:30pm.

Villa Musée Fragonard ★ The setting is an 18th-century aristocrat's town house with a magnificent garden in back. The collection displayed here includes the paintings of Jean-Honoré Fragonard, who was born in Grasse in 1732; his sister-in-law, Marguerite Gérard; his son, Alexandre; and his grandson, Théophile. Alexandre decorated the grand staircase. Curiously, this is the least-visited museum in town but is surely one of the loveliest.

23 bd. Fragonard. ✆ **04-97-05-58-00.** Free admission. June–Sept daily 10am–7pm; Oct and Dec–May Wed–Mon 11am–6pm. Closed Nov.

Where to Stay

Hôtel La Bellaudière Part of the respected Logis de France chain, this unpretentious family-run hotel is 3km (1¾ miles) east of the town center in the hills above Grasse. The stone-sided farmhouse was constructed in stages beginning 400 years ago, with most of what you see today built in the 1700s. Guest rooms are simple but dignified and outfitted with Provençal motifs. Many boast views of the sea. A garden terrace is lined with flowering shrubs, and guests are genuinely welcomed by the hosts. Fixed-price meals in the dining room cost 25€ each. Triples and quad rooms also available.

78 av. Pierre Ziller. www.labellaudiere.com. ✆ **04-93-36-02-57.** Fax 04-93-36-40-03. 17 units. 60€–145€ double. AE, DC, MC, V. Free parking. **Amenities:** Restaurant; Internet; room service. *In room:* TV, free Wi-Fi.

Where to Eat

For inexpensive dining, you can head for **Hôtel La Bellaudière** (see above).

La Bastide St-Antoine (Restaurant Chibois) ★★★ FRENCH/PROVENÇAL La Bastide St-Antoine offers one of the grandest culinary experiences along the Riviera. Jacques Chibois and his restaurant have attracted national attention since 1996. In a 200-year-old Provençal farmhouse surrounded by 2.8 hectares (7 acres) of trees and shrubbery, the restaurant serves a sophisticated array of dishes. Exquisite examples are oysters flavored with yucca leaves, a terrine of foie gras with celery, roasted suckling lamb with a fricassee of fresh vegetables and basil, and roast pigeon risotto with artichokes and truffles. Desserts may include strawberry soup with spice wine or ice cream made with olives and a hint of olive oil. The chef also does wonders with wild duck.

You can stay in the attached five-star accommodations of nine rooms and seven suites, decorated in upscale Provençal style. They have air-conditioning, free Wi-Fi, hair dryers, minibars, and TVs. Outside there's a pool, jogging track, and boules court. Doubles cost 240€ to 415€, suites from 460€.

48 av. Henri-Dunant. ✆ **04-93-70-94-94.** Fax 04-93-70-94-95. www.jacques-chibois.com. Reservations required. Main courses 40€–75€; fixed-price lunch Mon–Sat 59€–190€, dinner 145€–190€. AE, DC, MC, V. Daily noon–2pm and 8–9:30pm.

BIOT ★

918km (569 miles) S of Paris; 9.5km (6 miles) E of Cagnes-sur-Mer; 6.5km (4 miles) NW of Antibes

Biot has been famous for its pottery since merchants began to ship earthenware jars to Phoenicia and throughout the Mediterranean. Settled by Gallo-Romans, Biot has a long, war-torn history, but somehow the potters persevered at their ancient craft. Biot is also where Fernand Léger painted until the day he died. A magnificent collection of his work is on display at a museum just outside town.

Essentials

GETTING THERE The **bus** lines no. 7 and no. 10 from Antibes's Gare Routière, place Guynemer (✆ **04-93-34-37-60**), direct to Biot are way more convenient than the train. Tickets cost 1€. To **drive** to Biot from Nice, take N7 west. From Antibes, follow N7 east.

VISITOR INFORMATION The **Office de Tourisme** is at 46 rue St-Sébastien (✆ **04-93-65-78-00;** fax 04-93-65-78-04; www.biot.fr).

Exploring the Town

If you have time, explore the village. Begin at **place des Arcades,** where you can see the 16th-century gates and the remains of the town's ramparts. **Eglise de Biot,** place des Arcades (✆ **04-93-65-00-85**), dates from the 15th century. It's the work of Italian immigrants who resettled the town after the Black Death. The church is known for two stunning 15th-century retables (altarpieces): the red-and-gold *Retable du Rosaire,* by Ludovico Bréa, and *Christ aux Plaies,* by Canavesio.

Musée d'Histoire Locale et de Céramique Biotoise, 9 rue St-Sebastien (✆ **04-93-65-54-54**), has assembled the best works from local artists, potters, ceramists, painters, and silver- and goldsmiths. Hours are May to September Wednesday to Sunday 10am to 6pm, October to April Wednesday to Sunday 2 to 6pm. Admission is 2€, free ages 16 and under.

In the late 1940s, glassmakers created a bubble-flecked glass known as *verre rustique.* It comes in brilliant colors such as cobalt and emerald, and is displayed in many store windows on the main shopping street, **rue St-Sebastien.** Nearby is **Galerie Jean-Claude Novaro,** place des Arcades (✆ **04-93-65-60-23**), run by a master glass blower whose colorful creations beguile and tempt.

Bonzaï Arboretum de la Côte d'Azur Privately owned and maintained by members of the Okonek family, this arboretum and showroom contains the largest collection of bonsai in France. Most of the potted trees were crafted from local fig, almond, oak, and even apple trees. Especially noteworthy are bonsai versions of rare tropical cypresses and tropical figs, some as tall as 2m (6½ ft.), loaded with aerial root systems and miniaturized trunks and branches. A 5-minute walk from the Musée National Fernand-Léger.

299 Chemin de Val de Pôme, Biot 06410. 3km (1¾ miles) south of Biot. ✆ **04-93-65-63-99.** http://museedubonsai.free.fr. Admission 4€ adults, 2€ students. Wed–Mon 10am–noon and 2–6pm.

Musée National Fernand Léger ★★ Léger's widow assembled this collection and donated it to the French government after the artist's death in 1955. This museum is a light-filled rich celebration of paintings, ceramics, tapestries, and sculptures. It opened in 1960, an event that was attended by long-term friends

Picasso and Chagall. The collection shows the artist's bright, jazzy pieces, which abound with cranes, acrobats, scaffolding, railroad signals, and buxom nudes. Temporary exhibitions are held on the ground floor and are habitually excellent. The shabby-chic alfresco cafe in the grounds serves cheap *pichets* of wine on mismatched tables, no doubt as the artist would have wanted.

Chemin du Val-de-Pôme (on the eastern edge of town, beside the road to the rail station). ✆ **04-92-91-50-20.** www.musee-fernandleger.fr. Admission 5.50€ adults, 4€ ages 12–18, free 17 and under. Wed–Mon 10am–6pm.

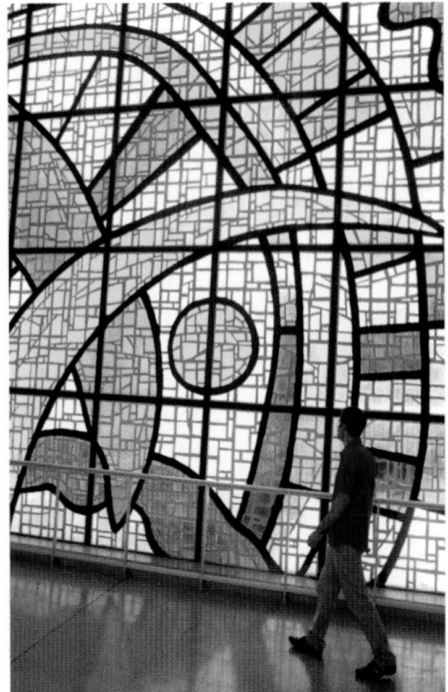

Musée National Fernand Léger.

Where to Eat

Le Jarrier ★ PROVENÇAL This enduringly excellent restaurant in Biot was built 300 years ago as a pottery for the *jarres* used to transport and store olive oil and wine. One of its two dining rooms has its walls removed every summer and becomes an open-air terrace with views over the valley. The cuisine is an idiosyncratic and modernized interpretation of Provençal staples. Examples include rabbit bouillabaisse with garlic *confit;* several versions of risotto, many of them vegetarian; *daurade* (sea bream) served with herb-laden vinaigrette; and Challons duckling with lavender-honey sauce.

30 passage de la Bourgade. ✆ **04-93-65-11-68.** www.lejarrier-restaurant.com. Reservations recommended. Main courses 22€–40€; fixed-price lunch 19€–29€, dinner 40€–84€. AE, MC, V. Daily 12:30–2:30pm and 7:30–10pm.

Les Terraillers ★★★ MODERN MEDITERRANEAN This stone-walled restaurant is .8km (about ½ mile) south of Biot, in a 16th-century studio for the production of clay pots and ceramics. Over the years, it has become a reliable favorite of many a restaurant critic, with its elegant display of modern Provençal cooking. Stunningly presented dishes include swordfish fillet seared with ginger and coriander, local lamb served with "virtual vegetables" constructed from semolina, and roast scallops atop celery branches and preserved lemon. Justifiably popular.

11 rte. du Chemin-Neuf. ✆ **04-93-65-01-59.** www.lesterraillers.com. Reservations required. Main courses 38€–43€; fixed-price lunch 39€–55€, dinner 65€–110€. AE, MC, V. Dec–Oct Fri–Tues noon–2pm and 7–10pm. Take rte. du Chemin-Neuf, following signs to Antibes.

JUAN-LES-PINS ★★

913km (566 miles) S of Paris; 9.5km (6 miles) S of Cannes

This suburb of Antibes is a resort which flourished during the 1920s under American property developer Frank Jay Gould. In the 1930s, Juan-les-Pins drew a chic summer crowd as the Riviera "season" flipped from winter respites to the hedonistic pursuit of summer sun, sea, and sensuality. It has been attracting the young and the young-at-heart from across Europe and the U.S. ever since. F. Scott Fitzgerald decried Juan-les-Pins as a "constant carnival." If only he could see it now . . . .

Essentials

GETTING THERE Juan-les-Pins is connected by **rail** and bus to most other Mediterranean coastal resorts, including Nice (trip time: 30 min.; 4.40€ one-way). For rail information and schedules, call ✆ **36-35** or visit www.voyages-sncf.com. **Buses** arrive from Nice and its airport at 40-minute intervals throughout the day. A bus leaves for Juan-les-Pins from Antibes at place Guynemer (✆ **04-93-34-37-60**) daily every 20 minutes and costs 1€ one-way (trip time: 10 min.). To **drive** to Juan-les-Pins from Nice, travel along N7 south; from Cannes, follow the signposted roads.

VISITOR INFORMATION The **Office de Tourisme** is at 51 bd. Charles-Guillaumont (✆ **04-97-23-11-10;** fax 04-97-23-11-09; www.antibesjuanlespins.com).

SPECIAL EVENTS The town offers some of the best nightlife on the Riviera, and the action reaches its height during the annual 10-day **Festival International de Jazz** (www.jazzajuan.fr) in mid-July. It attracts jazz, blues, reggae, and world music artists who play nightly on the beachfront Parc de la Pinède. Recent performers have included George Benson, Maceo Parker, and B. B. King. Tickets cost 25€ to 65€ and can be purchased at the Office de Tourisme in both Antibes and Juan-les-Pins.

A Day at the Beach

Part of the reason people flock here is for the town's wealth of sandy beaches, all lapped by a calm bay. Juan-les-Pins also basks in a unique microclimate, making it one of the warmest places on the Riviera to soak up the sun, even in winter. **Plage de Juan-les-Pins** is the most central beach, although quieter stretches of sand wrap around the Cap d'Antibes and include family-friendly **Plage de la Salis** and chic **Plage de la Garoupe.** If you want to stretch out on a sun lounger, go to any of the beach bar concessions that line the bay, where you can rent a mattress for around 12€ to 20€. Topless sunbathing and overt shows of cosmetic surgery are the norm.

Watersports

If you're interested in scuba diving, try **Easy Dive,** Port Gallice (✆ **04-93-61-41-49;** www.easydrive.fr). A one-tank dive costs 30€ to 55€, including all equipment. **Sea kayaking, pedalos, parascending,** and **donuts** are available at virtually every beach in Juan-les-Pins. **Water-skiing** was invented at the Hôtel des Belles-Rives in the 1920s, and this is still a great place to try out the sport. A 10-minute session costs around 30€, 1 hour goes for 110€.

Where to Stay

VERY EXPENSIVE

Hôtel Belles-Rives ★★★ Once a holiday villa occupied by Zelda and F. Scott Fitzgerald, this luxurious hotel is one of the Riviera's most fabled addresses. It was the scene of many a drunken brawl in the 1920s, a history illustrated in Fitzgerald's semi-autobiographical novel *Tender Is the Night.* It later played host to the illustrious, such as the duke and duchess of Windsor, Josephine Baker, and Edith Piaf. As befits a hotel of this age, rooms come in a variety of shapes and sizes, from small to spacious; each has a luxurious bathroom filled with Occitane beauty products. The lower terraces hold garden dining rooms, a waterside aquatic club with a snack bar and lounge, as well as a jetty. There is also a private beach and a dock.

33 bd. Edouard Baudoin, Juan-les-Pins 06160. www.bellesrives.com. ✆ **04-93-61-08-70.** Fax 04-93-61-76-60. 43 units. 148€–673€ double. AE, DC, MC, V. Free parking. Closed Jan–Feb. **Amenities:** 2 summer restaurants; 1 winter restaurant; 2 bars; room service. *In room:* A/C, TV, hair dryer, minibar, free Wi-Fi.

MODERATE

Hôtel des Mimosas This elegant 1870s-style villa sprawls in a subtropical garden on a hilltop, a 10-minute walk to Juan-les-Pins sandy public beach. The decor is a mix of high-tech and Italian-style comfort, with antique and modern furniture. Guest rooms come in a variety of shapes and sizes—some are tiny. Try for one of the four rooms with a balcony or one of the nine rooms with a terrace. A pool sits amid huge palm trees. The hotel gets fully booked in summer, so reserve as far in advance as possible.

Rue Pauline, Juan-les-Pins 06160. www.hotelmimosas.com. ✆ **04-93-61-04-16.** Fax 04-92-93-06-46. 34 units. 95€–150€ double. AE, MC, V. Free parking. Closed Oct–Apr. From the town center, drive .4km (¼ mile) west, following N7 toward Cannes. **Amenities:** Bar; outdoor pool; room service; free Wi-Fi. *In room:* A/C, TV, hair dryer, minibar.

INEXPENSIVE

Hôtel La Marjolaine A stone's throw from Juan-les-Pins train station and a 3-minute stroll to the beach. Granted, the decor of this century-old villa hasn't changed much since the 1980s, but rooms are clean, homey, and easily the best value in town. Most have exposed ceiling beams, hefty Provençal furniture, and solid wooden beds. The south-facing terrace ideal for taking breakfast outdoors in sunny days. A friendly welcome is assured.

15 rue du Dr Fabre, Juan-les-Pins 06160. ✆ **04-93-61-06-60.** Fax 04-93-61-02-75. 12 units. 65€–95€ double. AE, MC, V. Free parking. Closed Jan–Feb. **Amenities:** Bar. *In room:* A/C, TV, hair dryer, free Wi-Fi.

Where to Eat

Le Bijou Plage FRENCH/PROVENÇAL This upscale brasserie has flourished beside the seafront promenade since 1923. The marine-style decor includes lots of varnished wood and bouquets of flowers. Menu items include excellent bouillabaisse, grilled sardines, risotto with John Dory and truffled butter, steamed mussels with *sauce poulette* (frothy cream sauce with herbs and butter), and a supersize *plateau des coquillages et fruits de mer* (shellfish and seafood). This informally elegant establishment spills out onto a private beach with cocktail bar. Sand-in-toes outdoor tables are also available.

Bd. du Littoral. ✆ **04-93-61-39-07.** Reservations recommended. Main courses 20€–40€; fixed-price menu 22€–46€. AE, DC, MC, V. Daily noon–2:30pm and 7–10:30pm.

Le Perroquet ★ PROVENÇAL Known as the best restaurant in town for the last decade or so, this restaurant's ambience is carefully synchronized to the resort's casual and carnival-like summer aura. It's across from the Parc de la Pinède and is decorated with depictions of every imaginable form of parakeet, the restaurant's namesake. Look for savory fish dishes, at their best when grilled simply with olive oil and basil, and served with lemons. A worthwhile appetizer is the *assortiment Provençale,* which includes tapenade of olives, marinated peppers, grilled sardines, and stuffed vegetables. The set lunch menu changes daily and is especially good value.

Av. Georges-Gallice. ✆ **04-93-61-02-20.** Reservations recommended. Main courses 16€–31€; fixed-price lunch 18€; fixed-price dinner 26€–36€. AE, MC, V. Daily noon–2pm and 7–10:30pm. Closed early Nov to Dec 26.

Juan-les-Pins After Dark

Try your luck at the roulette wheel or poker tables at **Eden Casino,** boulevard Baudoin, in the heart of Juan-les-Pins (✆ **04-92-93-71-71**). Slot machines are open every day 10am to 5am; gaming tables from 9pm. A photo ID is required, preferably in the form of a passport.

For a faux-tropical-island experience, head to **Le Pam Pam,** route Wilson (✆ **04-93-61-11-05**), a time-honored establishment where guests sip rum and people-watch while reggae beats float around the bar. More modern is **La Reserve,** av. Georges Gallice (✆ **04-93-61-20-06**), where a younger crowd sips pastis and rosé on leopard-print seats under a large plane tree.

If you prefer high-energy partying, you're in the right place. The entire Riviera descends upon Juan-les-Pins's many discos every night in summer, and it's best to follow the crowds to the latest hotspot. **Le Village,** 1 bd. de la Pinède (✆ **04-92-93-90-00**), is one of the more established clubs and boasts an action-packed dance floor with DJs spinning the latest dance sounds. The cover charge is 10€, more for themed evenings.

ANTIBES & CAP D'ANTIBES ★★

913km (566 miles) S of Paris; 21km (13 miles) SW of Nice; 11km (6¾ miles) NE of Cannes

On the other side of the Baie des Anges (Bay of Angels) from Nice is the pretty port of Antibes. The town has a quiet charm unique on the Côte d'Azur. Its harbor is filled with fishing boats and pleasure yachts, and its winding streets are packed with promenading locals and well-dressed visitors. A pedestrianized port and several car-free squares make it a family-friendly destination, too. There's also an excellent covered market located near the harbor, open every morning except Mondays.

Spiritually, Antibes is totally divorced from Cap d'Antibes, a peninsula studded with the villas of the super-rich. But the less affluent are welcome to peek at paradise, and a lovely 6km (3¾ miles) coastal path rings the headland, passing picnic and diving spots en route.

Essentials

GETTING THERE **Trains** from Cannes arrive at the rail station, place Pierre-Semard, every 20 minutes (trip time: 15 min.); the one-way fare is 2.60€. Trains from Nice arrive at the rate of 25 per day (trip time: 20 min.); the one-way fare is 4€. For rail information, call ✆ **36-35** or visit www.voyages-sncf.com. The **bus** station, La Gare Routière, place Guynemer (✆ **04-93-34-37-60**), receives buses from throughout Provence. Bus fares to Nice, Cannes, Grasse, and Cagnes-sur-Mer cost 1€ one-way.

If you're **driving,** follow E1 east from Cannes and take the turnoff to the south for Antibes, which will lead to the historic core of the old city.

Harbor at Antibes.

Antibes's bustling market.

From Nice, take E1 west until you come to the turnoff for Antibes. The Cap d'Antibes is clearly visible from most parts of the Riviera. To drive here from Antibes, follow the coastal road, boulevard Leclerc, south—you can't miss it.

VISITOR INFORMATION The **Office de Tourisme** is at 11 place du Général-de-Gaulle (✆ **04-97-23-11-11;** fax 04-97-23-11-12; www.antibesjuanlespins.com).

Seeing the Sights

Musée Napoleonien ☺ In this stone-sided fort and tower on the Cap d'Antibes, built in stages in the 17th and 18th centuries, you'll find an interesting collection of Napoleonic memorabilia, naval models, and paintings. A toy-soldier collection depicts various uniforms, including one used by Napoleon in the Marengo campaign. A wall painting on wood shows Napoleon disembarking at Golfe-Juan on March 1, 1815, to start his 100 days' march to Paris. In contrast to Canova's Greek-god image of Napoleon, a miniature pendant by Barrault reveals the general as he really looked, with pudgy cheeks and a receding hairline. In the rear rotunda is one of the many hats worn by the emperor. You can climb to the top of the tower for a view of the coast that's worth the admission price alone.

Batterie du Graillon, bd. J.-F.-Kennedy. ✆ **04-93-61-45-32.** Admission 3€ adults; 1.50€ seniors, students, and ages 19–25; free for children 18 and under. Mid-June to mid-Sept Tues–Sat 10am–6pm; mid-Oct to mid-May Tues–Sat 10am–4:30pm.

Musée Picasso ★★ On the ramparts above the port is the Château Grimaldi, once the home of some princes of the Grimaldi family, who ruled the city from 1385 to 1608. Today it houses one of the world's greatest Picasso collections. The

Musée Picasso.

Spanish artist came to town after the war in 1946 and lived and worked in the château at the invitation of the municipality. When he departed, he gifted all the work he'd completed to the château museum: 23 paintings, 80 pieces of ceramics, 44 drawings, 32 lithographs, 11 oils on paper, 2 sculptures, and 5 tapestries. In addition, a gallery of contemporary art exhibits Léger, Miró, Ernst, and Calder, among others. An expansive outdoor terrace offers views over the Cap d'Antibes, which Picasso aficionados may recognize from his paintings.

Place du Mariejol. ✆ **04-92-90-54-20.** Admission 6€ adults, 3€ students and seniors, free for ages 18 and under. Mid-June to mid-Sept Tues–Sun 10am–6pm; mid-Oct to mid-May Tues–Sun 10am–noon and 2–6pm.

Where to Stay

VERY EXPENSIVE

Hôtel du Cap-Eden Roc ★★★ Legendary for the glamour of both its setting and its clientele, this Second Empire hotel, opened in 1870, is surrounded by a maze of manicured gardens. It's like a country estate, with spacious public rooms, marble fireplaces, paneling, chandeliers, and upholstered armchairs. Accommodation is among the most sumptuous on the Riviera. Guest rooms benefited from a thorough renovation in 2011, with sleek modern fittings, MP3 docking stations, and LED screens in every room. Even though the guests snoozing by the pool—blasted out of the cliff at enormous expense—appear artfully undraped during the day, evenings are upscale, with lots of emphasis on clothing and style. The stunning Restaurant Eden Roc spills out onto a panoramic sea view terrace. The Bellini Bar is the summertime meeting place of the stars. Casual visitors normally won't even get a look in, especially during the Cannes Film Festival and Monaco Grand Prix. However, the hotel is less elitist than it once was, and even bowed to the masses by accepting credit cards a few years ago (before that it was cash only).

Bd. J-F-Kennedy, Cap d'Antibes 06600. www.edenroc-hotel.fr. ✆ **04-93-61-39-01.** Fax 04-93-67-13-83. 67 units. 490€–990€ double; 1,100€–1,820€ suite. AE, DC, MC, V. Closed mid-Oct to mid-Apr. Bus: A2. **Amenities:** 2 restaurants; 2 bars; babysitting; exercise room; massage; outdoor pool; room service; sauna. *In room:* A/C, TV, hair dryer, free Wi-Fi.

EXPENSIVE

Cap d'Antibes Beach Hotel Since 2009, this chic Miami-style hotel has been drawing in the discerningly wealthy. Ultramodern and oh-so-stylish rooms are soaked in sunshine and draped in luxurious fabrics. Most have private terraces or, at the very least, extensive balconies. An indoor/outdoor spa and massage center leads onto a raised infinity pool. The entire package nuzzles up against a chichi beach club, which the hoi polloi may also access. The open-air Le Cap restaurant is based here. Serious diners may also try the award-winning cooking at Le Pêcheurs, a more formal, more inventive restaurant on-site.

Cap d'Antibes Beach Hotel, Cap d'Antibes 06160. www.ca-beachhotel.com. ✆ **04-92-93-13-30.** 27 units. 390€–500€ double; 1,300€–2,100€ suite. AE, DC, MC, V. Parking 25€. Closed Nov–Mar. **Amenities:** 2 restaurants; bar; babysitting; exercise room; outdoor pool; room service; spa. *In room:* A/C, TV, hair dryer, minibar, free Wi-Fi.

MODERATE

Le Bosquet ★ This fabulous villa midway along the Cap d'Antibes is as far removed from the Riviera bustle as you can get. A leafy, unkempt garden laps up against the pink-hued main building, which is 2½ centuries old. This houses the four boutique guest rooms. All are utterly charming: The Chambre Sable has traditional *tomette* floors and antique fittings; the Chambre Galet has a large bathroom and sitting area, and is large enough for a family.

14 chemin des Sables, Cap d'Antibes 06160. www.lebosquet06.com. ✆ **04-93-67-32-29.** 4 units. 90€–200€ double. MC, V. Free parking. Closed Nov–Jan. **Amenities:** Bar. *In room:* A/C, TV, hair dryer, fridge, free Wi-Fi.

INEXPENSIVE

Hôtel Beau Site This white stucco villa with a tile roof and heavy shutters is surrounded by eucalyptus trees, pines, and palms. Located off the main road a 7-minute walk from the beach, it has a low wall of flower turns and wrought-iron gates. The interior is like a country inn, with oak beams and antiques. Guest rooms are comfortable and well maintained, and bathrooms are small. Some even have a sea view.

141 bd. J-F-Kennedy, Cap d'Antibes 06150. www.hotelbeausite.net. ✆ **04-93-61-53-43.** Fax 04-93-67-78-16. 27 units. 80€–155€ double; 160€–225€ suite. AE, DC, MC, V. Bus: A2. Closed Nov–Feb. **Amenities:** Bar; babysitting; bikes; pool; room service. *In room:* A/C, TV, hair dryer, free Wi-Fi.

La Jabotte ★ Only 54m (177 ft.) from the beach, this one-story villa with a trio of bungalows is built around a citrus garden. Yves, Claude, and Tommy are gracious hosts, welcoming you into their cozy environment, where they serve breakfast on the terrace with homemade jams, freshly squeezed orange juice, and "the surprise of the morning." Each day the bar proposes a different aperitif. Bedrooms are small but elegantly decorated, with rich colors, original paintings, and an intriguing hodgepodge of furnishings. Accommodation is frequently themed, ranging from birds to angels. Many of the paintings and ceramics on display are also for sale.

13 av. Max Maurey, Cap d'Antibes 06160. www.jabotte.com. ✆ **04-93-61-45-89.** 18 units. 82€–135€ double. MC, V. Limited free parking. Closed Nov to mid-Feb. **Amenities:** Garden; room service (breakfast only). *In room:* A/C, TV (in some), free Wi-Fi.

Where to Eat

The Zelda and Scott Fitzgerald of today head for the **Eden Roc Restaurant** at the Hôtel du Cap–Eden Roc for grand service and grand cuisine. The excellent restaurants at the **Cap d'Antibes Beach Club** (see "Where to Stay," on p. 581) are also open to the public.

Bistro La Rustic FRENCH/PIZZA A family-run restaurant where grandmother mans the kitchen while grandson fields the outdoor tables on buzzing place Nationale. Cuisine, simple as it is, is based around a wood-fired oven. Delicious chargrilled steaks, half-chickens, and breasts of duck are cooked to perfection, the latter on a shovel (which makes it easier to whip it out of the stove at the last minute). Platters of prawns, salads filled with lardons, and melon with ham make up the appetizer menu. One of the author's picks for a great value traditional feast.

33 place Nationale. ✆ **04-93-34-10-81.** Main courses 9€–17€; fixed-price menu 13€–18€. MC, V. Daily noon–3pm and 7–11pm.

La Taverne du Saffranier PROVENÇAL Earthy and irreverent, this brasserie in a century-old building serves a changing roster of Provençal specialties. Zany art is hung up the walls of the car-free square that the restaurant occupies, making this spot a favorite of bohemian locals (who are all actually wealthy in this part of the world). It's also great for kids, as they may run around at leisure. Menu examples include a platter of *petits farcis* (stuffed vegetables), a mini bouillabaisse for single diners, savory fish soup, and an assortment of grilled fish (including sardines) that's served only with a dash of fresh lemon.

Place du Saffranier. ✆ **04-93-34-80-50.** Reservations recommended. Main courses 18€–28€; fixed-price menu 25€. MC, V. Tues–Sun noon–2pm; Tues–Sat 7–10:30pm. Closed mid-Nov to mid-Feb.

Restaurant de Bacon ★★★ SEAFOOD The Eden Roc restaurant at the Hôtel du Cap is more elegant, but Bacon serves the best seafood around and has done so for over 6 decades. Surrounded by ultraexpensive residences, this restaurant on a rocky peninsula offers a panoramic coast view. Bouillabaisse aficionados claim that Bacon offers the best in France. In its deluxe version, saltwater crayfish float atop the savory brew; we prefer the simple version, where a waiter adds the finishing touches at your table. If bouillabaisse isn't to your liking, try fish soup with garlic-laden rouille sauce, fish terrine, sea bass, or John Dory, or see what's on offer on the two fixed-price menus.

Bd. de Bacon. ✆ **04-93-61-50-02.** www.restaurantdebacon.com. Reservations required. Main courses 45€–145€; fixed-price lunch 49€–79€, dinner 79€. AE, DC, MC, V. Wed–Sun noon–2pm; Tues–Sun 8–10pm. Closed Nov–Feb.

CAGNES-SUR-MER ★

918km (569 miles) S of Paris; 21km (13 miles) NE of Cannes

Cagnes-sur-Mer has two visitor-friendly centers. Perched on a hill overlooking the Riviera, **Haut-de-Cagnes** is one of the most stunning hill villages on the Riviera. At the foot of the hill is an old fishing port and beach resort, **Cros-de-Cagnes,** which lies midway between Nice and Antibes.

For years Haut-de-Cagnes attracted the French literati, including Simone de Beauvoir. A colony of painters also settled here; Renoir said the village was "the place where I want to paint until the last day of my life." His museum is the highlight of any visit to the area. The coastal racecourse is one of the most fun-packed in France, with evening races all summer.

Essentials

GETTING THERE The **train** station, Gare SNCF, lies in Cagnes-Ville (the nondescript commercial part of town) at avenue de la Gare. It serves trains that run along the Mediterranean coast, with arrivals every 30 minutes from both Nice (trip time: 10 min.; 2.60€ one-way) and Cannes (trip time: 25 min.; 4€ one-way). For rail information, call ✆ **36-35** or visit www.voyages-sncf.com. **Buses,** costing 1€ from Nice and Cannes, stop at Cagnes-Ville and at Les Collettes, within walking distance of both Cros-de-Cagnes and the Renoir Museum. For information, contact **Ligne d'Azur** (✆ **08-10-06-10-06;** www.lignedazur.com). The climb from Cagnes-Ville to Haut-de-Cagnes is strenuous; a free minibus runs daily about every 15 minutes year-round from place du Général-de-Gaulle in the center of Cagnes-Ville to Haut-de-Cagnes. By **car** from any of the coastal towns, follow the A8 coastal highway, exiting at Cagnes/Sur-Mer/Cros-de-Cagnes.

VISITOR INFORMATION The **Office de Tourisme** is at 6 bd. Maréchal-Juin, Cagnes-Ville (✆ **04-93-20-61-64;** fax 04-93-20-52-63; www.cagnes-tourisme.com).

SPECIAL EVENTS The verdant gardens of the Renoir Museum are the site, for 2 days in mid-March, of an **Olive Festival (La Fête de l'Olivier).** Highlights include olive oil tasting and gourmet food samples from local restaurants. Entrance is free.

Exploring the Towns

Cros-de-Cagnes, a part of Cagnes-Sur-Mer, is known for its 4km (2½ miles) of beach, the **Plages de Cros-de-Cagnes.** It's covered with light-gray pebbles smoothed by centuries of wave action.

The orange groves and fields of carnations of the upper village of Haut-de-Cagnes provide a beautiful setting for the narrow flower-filled streets and 17th- and 18th-century homes. Head to the top, where you can enjoy the view from **place du Château** and have lunch or a drink at a pavement cafe.

Château-Musée Grimaldi (Musée de l'Olivier & Musée d'Art Moderne Méditerranéen) ★ Château-Musée was a fortress built in 1301 by Rainier Grimaldi I, a lord of Monaco and a French admiral (his portrait is in the museum). In the early 17th century, the castle was converted into a gracious Louis XIII château, which now contains two museums. The Museum of the Olive Tree shows the steps involved in cultivating and processing the olive. The Museum of Mediterranean Modern Art displays works by Kisling, Carzou, Dufy, Cocteau, and Seyssaud, plus temporary exhibits. In one salon is an interesting *trompe l'oeil* fresco, *La Chute de Phaeton*. The tower affords a view of the Côte d'Azur.

7 place Grimaldi. ✆ **04-92-02-47-30.** Admission to both museums 4€ adults, 2€ students, free for children 17 and under. May–Sept Wed–Mon 10am–noon and 2–6pm; Oct–Apr Wed–Mon 10am–noon and 2–5pm.

Musée Renoir & Les Collettes ★★ Les Collettes has been restored to its appearance when the great Impressionist painter Renoir lived here, from 1908 until his death in 1919.

The house was built in 1907 in an orange grove. You can explore the drawing room and dining room on your own before going up to the artist's bedroom. In his atelier are his wheelchair, easel, and brushes. The terrace of Mme. Renoir's bedroom faces stunning views over Cap d'Antibes and Haut-de-Cagnes. On a wall hangs a photograph of one of Renoir's sons, Pierre, as he appeared in the 1932 film *Madame Bovary.* Although Renoir is best remembered for his paintings, in Cagnes he began experimenting with sculpture, a form he found easy to manage, given his growing arthritis. The museum has 20 portrait busts and portrait medallions, most of which depict his wife and children. For many, the orange groves, olive plantation, and unkempt gardens that so inspired the artist are a definite highlight.

19 chemin des Collettes. ✆ **04-93-20-61-07.** Admission 4€ adults, 2€ students, free for ages 18 and under. May–Oct Wed–Mon 10am–noon and 2–6pm; Nov–Apr Wed–Mon 10am–noon and 2–5pm.

Where to Stay

IN CAGNES-SUR-MER

Appart'e A friendly, well-run option that won't break the bank. This fine little hotel is set back from the beach at Cros-de-Cagnes. Rooms have benefited from a recent overhaul and have modern fittings, from comfy beds to high-powered showers. They range from tiny singles to suites capable of fitting a family of five, the latter with a kitchenette thrown in. All are simply furnished, all have a balcony or terrace, and some have sea views.

3 av. de la Serre, Cagnes-sur-Mer 06800. www.hotel-aeva.fr. ✆ **04-93-73-39-52.** Fax 04-93-08-07-26. 23 units. 80€–120€ double; 120€–190€ suite. AE, DC, MC, V. Free parking. **Amenities:** Bar. *In room:* TV, minibar, free Wi-Fi.

IN HAUT-DE-CAGNES

Le Cagnard ★★ Several 13th-century houses were joined in the 1960s to form this understated, glamorous property. The dining room is covered with frescoes, and there's a vine-draped terrace. The rooms and salons are furnished with antiques such as provincial chests, armoires, and Louis XV chairs. Each room has its own style: Some are duplexes, others have terraces and views of the countryside. The luxurious bathrooms are spacious, with tub/showers. The award-winning cuisine in the attached restaurant is reason enough to make the trip.

Rue du Pontis-Long, Le Haut-de-Cagnes, Cagnes-sur-Mer 06800. www.le-cagnard.com. ✆ **04-93-20-73-21.** Fax 04-93-22-06-39. 23 units. 100€–145€ double; 150€–220€ suite. AE, DC, MC, V. Free parking. **Amenities:** Restaurant; bar; babysitting; room service. *In room:* A/C, TV, hair dryer, minibar, free Wi-Fi.

Where to Eat

In Haut-de-Cagnes, the hotel **Le Cagnard** (see above) has a remarkable restaurant.

IN HAUT-DE-CAGNES

Fleur de Sel FRENCH/PROVENÇAL Energetic owners Philippe and Pascale Loose run this charming restaurant in a 200-year-old stone-sided house in the center of the village. In two ocher-toned dining rooms outfitted with Provençal furniture and oil paintings, you'll enjoy the kind of cuisine that Philippe learned during stints at some of the grandest restaurants of France. Dining is best sampled over the three fixed-price menus, which take 2 hours or more to munch through. Dishes include baby lobster with black truffle oil and filet of beef braised in a soft local red wine, Bellet.

85 Montée de la Bourgade. ✆ **04-93-20-33-33.** www.restaurant-fleur-desel.com. Reservations recommended. Main courses 20€–36€; fixed-price menus 32€–66€. MC, V. Thurs–Tues noon–2pm and 7:30–10pm.

Josy-Jo ★★ TRADITIONAL FRENCH Le Cagnard (see p. 584) has a more elegant setting, but the food here is comparable. Behind a 200-year-old facade covered with vines and flowers, this ever-popular restaurant was the home and studio of Modigliani and Soutine during their hungriest years. Paintings cover the walls, and the Bandecchi family runs everything smoothly. The menu features grilled meats and a variety of fish. You can enjoy brochette of *gigot* of lamb with kidneys, calves' liver, homemade terrine of foie gras of duckling, stuffed Provençal vegetables, and an array of salads.

2 rue Planastel. ✆ **04-93-20-68-76.** www.restaurant-josyjo.com. Reservations required. Main courses 15€–25€; fixed-price lunch 25€–35€. AE, MC, V. Tues–Sat 12:30–2:30pm and 7:30–10:30pm. Closed mid-Nov to Dec.

ST-PAUL-DE-VENCE ★★

926km (574 miles) S of Paris; 23km (14 miles) E of Grasse; 28km (17 miles) E of Cannes; 31km (19 miles) N of Nice

Of all the hilltop villages of the Riviera, St-Paul-de-Vence is by far the most famous and the most chic. It gained popularity in the 1920s, when artists including Picasso, Chagall, and Matisse frequented the town, trading their paintings for hospitality at the Colombe d'Or hotel. Contemporary art is now the town's principal attraction, and the winding streets are studded with galleries and museums. Circling the town are magnificent old ramparts (allow about 30 min. to circle them) that overlook flowers and olive and orange trees. From the north ramparts, you can look out on Baou de St-Jeannet, a sphinx-shaped rock that was painted into the landscape of Poussin's *Polyphème*.

Essentials

GETTING THERE The nearest **rail** station is in Cagnes-sur-Mer. Some 20 **buses** per day leave from Nice's Gare Routière, dropping passengers off in St-Paul-de-Vence (1€ one-way), then in Vence. For information, contact Ligne d'Azur (✆ **08-10-06-10-06;** www.lignedazur.com). If you're **driving** from Nice, take the coastal A8 highway east, turn inland at Cagnes-sur-Mer, and follow signs north to St-Paul-de-Vence.

VISITOR INFORMATION The **Office de Tourisme** is at 2 rue Grande (✆ **04-93-32-86-95;** fax 04-93-32-60-27; www.saint-pauldevence.com).

Exploring the Town

Note: Driving a car in St-Paul's old town is prohibited, except to drop off luggage at your hotel.

If you phone at least a day (and sometimes a few hours) in advance, the local tourist office can arrange any of several distinctly themed walking tours of the town's historic core, as well as to some of the town's outskirts. Most tours last for about an hour and are priced at 5€ each; all of them depart from the tourist office. Depending on your interests, tours may highlight the city's history and architecture, the artists who lived here and the works they created, and even the lessons and lore of the French pastime of *pétanque* (also known as *boules*), wherein a practice session with seasoned locals is included as part of the experience.

St-Paul-de-Vence.

The pedestrian-only **rue Grande** is the most evocative street, running the length of St-Paul. Most of the stone houses along it are from the 16th and 17th centuries, and many still bear the coats of arms placed there by the original builders. Today most of the houses are antiques shops, arts-and-crafts galleries, and souvenir and gift shops; some are still artists' studios.

The village's chief sight is the **Collégiale de la Conversion de St-Paul ★**, constructed in the 12th and 13th centuries and much altered over the years. The Romanesque choir is the oldest part, containing some remarkable stalls carved in walnut in the 17th century. Look to the left as you enter: You'll see the painting *Ste-Cathérine d'Alexandrie,* which has been attributed to Tintoretto. The **Trésor de l'Eglise** is one of the most beautiful in the Alpes-Maritimes, with a spectacular ciborium. Look also for a low relief of the *Martyrdom of St-Clément* on the last altar on the right. It's open daily 9am to 6pm (to 7pm July–Aug). Admission is free.

Near the church is the **Musée d'Histoire de St-Paul,** place de l'Eglise (✆ **04-93-32-41-13**), a museum in a village house that dates to the 1500s. A collection of rather silly dioramas illustrates the history of the village. It's open from April to September daily 11am to 1pm and 3 to 6pm, and October to March daily from 2pm to 5pm. Admission is 3€ adults, 2€ students and children 5 to 18, and free for children 4 and under. The same ticket grants entrance to the awe-inspiring **Chapelle des Pénitents Blanc** (same hours), just across the street. The artist Folon, who worked on his masterpiece until his death in 2005, decorated the church using modern plaster effects and mosaics. The vast interior is alive with airy frescoes and sunny paintings. It opened to the public in 2008.

Foundation Maeght ★★★ This avant-garde building houses one of the most famed modern art museums in Europe. On a hill in pine-studded woods, the Foundation Maeght is like Shangri-La. Nature and the creations of men and women blend harmoniously in this unique achievement of the architect José Luis Sert. Its white concrete arcs give the impression of a giant pagoda.

A stark Calder sculpture rises like some futuristic monster on the lawn. In a courtyard and beyond, the bronze works of Giacometti, marble statues by Miró, and mosaics by Chagall form a surrealistic garden. Sculpture is displayed inside, but the museum is at its best in a natural setting of terraces and gardens. It's built on several levels, its many glass walls providing an indoor-outdoor vista. The foundation, a gift "to the people" from Aimé and Marguerite Maeght, also provides a showcase for new talent. On the property are a library, a cinema, a cafeteria, and a magnificent museum store.

Outside the town walls. ✆ **04-93-32-81-63.** www.fondation-maeght.com. Admission 14€ adults, 9€ students and ages 10–18, free for children 9 and under. July–Sept daily 10am–7pm; Oct–June daily 10am–6pm.

Where to Stay

La Colombe d'Or rents deluxe rooms (p. 588).

EXPENSIVE

Hôtel Le St-Paul ★★★ Converted from a 16th-century Renaissance residence and retaining many original features, this luxurious hideaway is in the heart of the village. The guest rooms, decorated in sophisticated Provençal style, have sumptuous beds and midsize bathrooms with tub/showers. Sitting on the balcony of room no. 30 will help you understand why Renoir, Léger, Matisse, and Picasso were inspired by Provence. Many rooms have a view of the valley with the Mediterranean in the distance. The Michelin-starred restaurant has a flower-bedecked terrace sheltered by 16th-century ramparts and a superb dining room with vaulted ceilings.

86 rue Grande, St-Paul-de-Vence 06570. www.lesaintpaul.com. ✆ **04-93-32-65-25.** Fax 04-93-32-52-94. 16 units. 300€–330€ double; 370€–620€ suite. AE, DC, MC, V. Closed mid-Dec to Jan 25. Free parking. **Amenities:** Restaurant; bar; babysitting; room service; 3 tennis courts; free Wi-Fi. *In room:* A/C, TV, hair dryer, minibar.

Le Mas de Pierre ★ The newest addition to St-Paul's accommodation scene is a vision of Provençal elegance with a dash of boutique charm thrown in. It's located about 2km (1¼ miles) from the village center. Of all the five-star hotels in the area, this spot is the most family friendly and the least stuffy. Eating in jeans and a jacket inside the superb Table de Pierre restaurant, or outside on its poolside terrace, is completely acceptable. The surrounding gardens loop around the pool and are dotted with wooden cabanas, each with a linen canopy roof that

Foundation Maeght.

can be pulled shut for a mischievous snooze. The "enchanted garden" contains a collection of orchids in an ancient glasshouse, hidden away next to the hotel's vegetable plot.

2320 route de Serres, St-Paul-de-Vence 06570. www.lemasdepierre.com. ✆ **04-93-59-00-10.** Fax 04-93-59-00-59. 48 units. 230€–570€ double; 345€–770€ suite. AE, DC, MC, V. Free parking. **Amenities:** Restaurant, bar; outdoor pool; spa. *In room:* A/C, TV, hair dryer, free Wi-Fi.

MODERATE

Hostellerie des Messugues ★ Visitors wishing to escape the hordes head to this idyllic retreat set in a flowery park with a sizeable swimming pool. Only a few steps from the Maeght Foundation, the hotel offers a countrylike environment, though close to the action, only 1km (½ mile) from the village center. Bedrooms are small to midsize but attractively furnished and most comfortable.

Domaine des Gardettes, St-Paul-de-Vence 06570. ✆ **04-93-32-53-32.** Fax 04-93-32-94-15. 15 units. 95€–170€ double. AE, DC, MC, V. Free parking. Closed Nov–Mar. **Amenities:** Breakfast room; outdoor pool; room service. *In room:* A/C, TV, hair dryer, free Wi-Fi.

Hotel Le Hameau ★ This romantic Mediterranean villa is on a hilltop on the outskirts of St-Paul-de-Vence, on the road to Colle-sur-Loup. Built as a farmhouse in the 1920s and enlarged and transformed into a hotel in 1967, it contains high-ceilinged rooms with every period detail. They range from the tiny Traveler's Rooms (perfect for a night's pit stop in the area), to Provençal suites with double sinks in the bathroom and ancient stone floors. View of the surrounding hills and valleys are remarkable. There is also a vineyard and a sunny terrace with fruit trees, flowers, and a pool.

528 rte. de la Colle (D107), St-Paul-de-Vence 06570. www.le-hameau.com. ✆ **04-93-32-80-24.** Fax 04-93-32-55-75. 17 units. 105€–170€ double; 230€–280€ suite. AE, DC, MC, V. Closed Nov 15–Feb 15. From the town, take D107 about 1km (½ mile), following the signs south of town toward Colle-sur-Loup. **Amenities:** Bar; outdoor pool; free Wi-Fi. *In room:* A/C, TV, hair dryer.

Where to Eat

The dining room at the **Hôtel Le St-Paul** (p. 587) features exceptional cuisine based on market-fresh ingredients.

La Colombe d'Or ★ PROVENÇAL For more than a decade, "The Golden Dove" has been St-Paul's most celebrated restaurant—not for cutting-edge cuisine or exotic experiments, but for its remarkable art collection. You can dine amid Mirós, Picassos, Klees, Dufys, Utrillos, and Calders. In fair weather, everyone vies for a seat on the terrace. Begin with smoked salmon or foie gras from Landes if you've recently won at the casino. If not, you can opt for a soup made with fresh seasonal vegetables. The house specials are Bellini Champagne cocktails and simple roast chicken, neither of which will break the bank.

The guest rooms (13 doubles, 12 suites) contain French antiques and Provençal accessories. They're in the original 16th-century stone house and in two wings added in the 1950s, one of which stretches into the garden next to the pool. Some units have exposed stone and ceiling beams; all are luxurious, with air-conditioning, minibars, and TVs. Prices are 250€ for a double, 430€ for a suite, including free Wi-Fi.

1 place du Général-de-Gaulle, St-Paul-de-Vence 06570. ✆ **04-93-32-80-02.** Fax 04-93-32-77-78. www.la-colombe-dor.com. Reservations required. Main courses 17€–35€. AE, DC, MC, V. Daily noon–2pm and 7:30–10pm. Closed Nov–Dec and Jan 10–20.

VENCE ★

926km (574 miles) S of Paris; 31km (19 miles) N of Cannes; 24km (15 miles) NW of Nice

Travel into the hills northwest of Nice—across country studded with cypresses, olive trees, and pines, where carnations, roses, oleanders, and other flowers grow in profusion—and Vence comes into view. Outside the town, along boulevard Paul-André, olive presses carry on their age-old duties. The main attraction here is the **Vieille Ville (Old Town),** a working town center with a blissful medieval backdrop. Visitors pose for photographs on place du Peyra in front of the **Vieille Fontaine (Old Fountain),** a feature in several films. If you're wearing sturdy shoes, the old town's narrow streets are worth poking around, particularly the cathedral on place Godeau.

Of great interest to art fans is the **Château de Villeneuve Fondation Émile Hugues,** 9 place du Frêne (✆**04-93-24-68-52;** www.museedevence.com), a temporary exhibition space dedicated to modern greats. Recent shows have included artists such as Matisse, Cézanne, Jean-Michel Basquiat, and Cy Twombly. Hours are Tuesday to Sunday 10am to 12:30pm and 2 to 6pm. Admission is 5€, 2.50€ for students and children 16 and under.

Vence's main draw, however, lies just outside the fortified main town. The Chapelle du Rosaire represents one of Matisse's most remarkable achievements.

Essentials

GETTING THERE Frequent **buses** (94 or 400) originating in Nice take 45 minutes to reach Vence; the one-way fare is 1€. For information, contact the **Compagnie SAP** (✆**04-93-58-37-60**). The nearest **rail** station is in Cagnes-sur-Mer, about 10km (6¼ miles) southwest from Vence. From there, about 20 buses per day priced at 1€ make the trip to Vence. For train information, call ✆**36-35** or visit www.voyages-sncf.com. To **drive** to Vence from Nice, take N7 west to Cagnes-sur-Mer, and then D236 north to Vence.

VISITOR INFORMATION The **Office de Tourisme** is on place Grand-Jardin (✆**0493-58-06-38;** www.ville-vence.fr).

Vieille Fontaine, Vence.

A Matisse Masterpiece

Chapelle du Rosaire ★★ It was a beautiful golden autumn along the Côte d'Azur. The great Henri Matisse was 77, and after the turbulence of World War II, he set out to design his masterpiece. Matisse created the Chapelle du Rosaire for the Dominican nuns of Monteils. (Sister Jacques-Marie, a member of the order, had nursed him back to health after a serious illness.) From the front, you might find the structure unremarkable and pass it by—until you spot a 12m (39-ft.) crescent-adorned cross rising from a blue-tile roof.

Matisse wrote: "What I have done in the chapel is to create a religious space . . . in an enclosed area of very reduced proportions and to give it, solely by the play of colors and lines, the dimensions of infinity." The light picks up the subtle coloring in the simply rendered leaf forms and abstract patterns: sapphire blue, aquamarine, and lemon yellow. In black-and-white ceramics, St. Dominic is depicted in only a few bold strokes. The most remarkable design is in the black-and-white-tile Stations of the Cross, with Matisse's self-styled "tormented and passionate" figures. The bishop of Nice came to bless the chapel in the late spring of 1951, when the artist's work was completed. Matisse died 3 years later.

Av. Henri-Matisse. ✆ **04-93-58-03-26.** Admission 3€ adults, 1.50€ children 16 and under; contributions to maintain the chapel are welcome. Mon, Wed, and Sat 2–5:30pm; Tues and Thurs 10–11:30am and 2–5:30pm. Closed mid-Nov to mid-Dec.

Where to Stay

VERY EXPENSIVE

Le Château du Domaine St-Martin ★★★ If you're heading into the hill towns above Nice and you seek luxury and refinement, this is the address for you. The château, in a 14-hectare (35-acre) park with terraced gardens, was built in 1936 and has been continuously upgraded ever since. The main building holds the standard units; suites are in the tile-roofed villas. You can walk through the gardens on winding paths lined with tall cypresses, past the chapel ruins and olive trees. The spacious rooms are distinctively decorated, and the large rose-colored bathrooms have tub/showers. The classic restaurant has a view of the coast and serves superb French cuisine under the command of Yannick Franques. A protégé of Alain Ducasse, Franques was awarded his second Michelin star in 2010.

Av. des Templiers B.P. 102, Vence 06140. www.chateau-st-martin.com. ✆ **04-93-58-02-02.** Fax 04-93-24-08-91. 39 units, 6 villas. 360€–570€ double; 450€–840€ suite. AE, DC, MC, V. Closed mid-Nov to mid-Feb. From the town center, follow signs toward Coursegoules and Col-de-Vence for 1.5km (1 mile) north. **Amenities:** Restaurant; bar; babysitting; outdoor pool; room service; spa; 2 tennis courts. *In room:* A/C, TV, hair dryer, free Wi-Fi.

MODERATE

La Maison du Frêne ★ 🎁 In the heart of Vence, this Provençal guesthouse, now an elegant retreat, was once a private home in the 18th century. Vence has far more lavish and luxurious retreats, but none with this snug, cozy comfort—all revolving around a modern art theme, with pop-art designs and playful touches everywhere. Guest rooms are midsize to spacious. An old ash tree planted in front of the house during the reign of François I and the manse itself have been the subject of countless paintings. The original architecture has been preserved, although all the modern comforts have been added. The reception area contains original sculptures and paintings, and it's linked to the country kitchen, where delicious homemade breakfasts are prepared.

1 place du Frêne, Vence 06140. www.lamaisondufrene.com. ✆ **04-93-24-37-80.** 4 units. 145€–185€. MC, V. Parking 13€. **Amenities:** Dinner upon request in winter. *In room:* A/C, TV (on request), free Wi-Fi.

INEXPENSIVE

Auberge des Seigneurs ★ This 400-year-old stone hotel gives you a taste of old Provence. Decorative objects and antiques are everywhere. The guest rooms are well maintained, but the management dedicates its energy to the restaurant. Nevertheless, the Provençal-style rooms are comfortable, with lots of exposed paneling and beams. Two have decorative fireplaces. The small, tiled bathrooms contain showers. The restaurant is in a stone building that used to be the kitchen of the Château de Villeneuve, where François I spent part of his youth. The specialty is grills prepared on an open spit in view of the dining room, which holds a long wooden table and an open fireplace with a row of hanging copper pots and pans.

1 rue de Docteur Biret, Vence 06140. www.auberge-seigneurs.com. ✆ **04-93-58-04-24.** 5 units. 85€–95€ double. DC, MC, V. Closed mid-Dec to mid-Jan. **Amenities:** Restaurant; bar; room service. *In room:* Hair dryer, free Wi-Fi.

Where to Eat

Auberge des Seigneurs and **Le Château du Domaine St-Martin** (see reviews for all in "Where to Stay," above) offer excellent dining.

La Farigoule PROVENÇAL In a century-old house that opens onto a rose garden, this restaurant specializes in Provençal cuisine and is generally regarded as one of the most genial establishments in town. Menu items are traditional but flavorful: They include roast pigeon in a truffle-laden cassoulet; scallop and foie gras risotto; and classic roast lamb with local herbs and potatoes. In the summer, you can dine in the rose garden.

15 av. Henri-Isnard. ✆ **04-93-58-01-27.** Reservations recommended. Main courses 25€–29€; fixed-price menus 30€–40€. MC, V. Wed–Mon noon–2pm and 7:30–10pm. Closed mid-Nov to mid-Dec.

NICE ★★★

929km (576 miles) S of Paris; 32km (20 miles) NE of Cannes

Nice is known as the "Queen of the Riviera" and is the largest city on this fabled stretch of coast. It's also one of the most ancient, founded by the Greeks, who called it Nike (Victory). By the 19th century, Russian aristocrats and the British upper class—led by Queen Victoria herself—were flocking here. But these days, it's not as chichi as Cannes or St-Tropez. In fact, of all the major French resorts, Nice is the most down-to-earth, with an emphasis on fine dining and high culture. Indeed, it hosts more museums than any other French city outside of Paris.

It's also the best place to base yourself on the Riviera, especially if you're dependent on public transportation. You can go to San Remo, a glamorous town over the Italian border, for lunch and return to Nice by nightfall. From Nice airport, the second largest in France, you can travel by train or bus along the entire coast to resorts such as Antibes, Juan-les-Pins, and Monaco.

Because of its brilliant sunshine and liberal attitude, Nice has long attracted artists and writers, among them Dumas, Nietzsche, Flaubert, Hugo, Sand, and Stendhal. Henri Matisse, who made his home in Nice, said, "Though the light is intense, it's also soft and tender." The city averages 300 sunny days a year.

Essentials

GETTING THERE **Trains** arrive at Gare Nice-Ville, avenue Thiers (✆ **36-35;** www.voyages-sncf.com). From there you can take trains to Cannes for 6.10€, Monaco for 3.40€, and Antibes for 4€, with easy connections to Paris, Milan, and anywhere else along the Mediterranean coast.

Buses to and from Monaco (100), Cannes (200), and all points in between serve the main bus station, or **Gare Routière,** 5 bd. Jean-Jaurès (✆ **08-92-70-12-06**).

Transatlantic and intercontinental flights land at **Aéroport Nice–Côte d'Azur** (✆ **08-20-42-33-33**). From there, municipal bus nos. 98 and 99 depart at 20-minute intervals for Gare Routière (see above) and Gare Nice-Ville, respectively; the one-way fare is 4€. A **taxi** from the airport into the city center will cost between 30€ and 40€ each way. Trip time is about 25 minutes.

Book market at Place du Palais-de-Justice.

Ferryboats operated by **Trans-Côte d'Azur** (✆ **04-92-98-71-30;** www.trans-cote-azur.com), on quai Lunel on Nice's port, link the city with Ile Ste-Marguerite (see "Ferrying to the Iles de Lerins," p. 563) in July and August, and St-Tropez from June to September.

VISITOR INFORMATION Nice maintains three **tourist offices.** The largest and most central is at 5 promenade des Anglais, near place Masséna (✆ **08-92-70-74-07;** www.nicetourisme.com). Additional offices are in the arrivals hall of the Aéroport Nice–Côte d'Azur and the railway station on avenue Thiers. Any office can make a hotel reservation (but only for the night of the day you show up), for a modest fee.

GETTING AROUND Most local buses serve the main bus station, or **Gare Routière,** 10 av. Félix-Faure (✆ **08-92-70-12-06**), a very short walk from place Masséna. Municipal buses charge 1€ for rides within greater Nice. The same ticket can be used on Nice's tramway, which connects the Gare Routière with Gare Nice-Ville and northern Nice. Tickets can be purchased at tobacco shops or at electronic kiosks around the city.

Nice is very walkable, and no point of interest downtown is more than a 10-minute walk from place Massena, including the seafront Promenade, Old Town, and harbor.

A recent addition to the transport scene is **Vélo Bleu** (www.velobleu.org), a bike-sharing scheme with over 90 stations throughout the city. However, registering for the scheme on the electronic stands takes a degree of patience. A more human place to rent both bikes and scooters is **Energy Scoot,** 2 rue St-Phillipe (✆ **04-97-07-12-64**), just behind the Negresco.

Open Monday to Saturday 9am to noon and 2 to 7pm, it charges from 10€ per day for a bike, or from 30€ per day for a 50cc scooter. A valid driver's license and deposit are required.

One of the most fun ways to quickly gain an overview of Nice involves boarding a **Nice–Le Grand Tour** (✆ **04-92-29-17-00;** www.nicelegrandtour.com) double-decker bus. Every day of the year, between 9:30am and 6:50pm, one of a flotilla of this company's buses departs from a position adjacent to the Jardins Albert I. The panoramic 90-minute tour takes in the harbor, the museums of Cimiez, the Russian church, and the promenade. Per-person rates for the experience are 20€ for adults, 18€ for students, and 5€ for children 4 to 11. Participants can get off at any of 14 stops en route and opt to reboard any other buses, which follow at 40-minute intervals, after they've explored the neighborhood. Advance reservations aren't necessary, and commentary is piped through to headsets in seven different languages.

Another easy way to see the city is by the small **Train Touristique de Nice** (✆ **06-08-55-08-30;** www.trainstouristiquesdenice.com), which also departs from the Jardins Albert I. The 40-minute ride passes many of Nice's most-heralded sites, including place Masséna, promenade des Anglais, and quai des Etats-Unis. Departing every 30 minutes, the train operates daily 10am to 5pm (until 6pm Apr–May and Sept, until 7pm June–Aug). The round-trip price is 7€ for adults and 4€ for children 9 and under.

Possibly the coolest way to get around Nice is by Segway, the two-wheeled electronic scooters. Bespoke tours are run by **Mobilboard, 2 rue Halévy** (✆ **04-93-80-21-27;** www.mobilboard.com). Children 18 and under must be accompanied by an adult.

SPECIAL EVENTS The **Nice Carnaval** (www.nicecarnaval.com) draws visitors from all over Europe. The "Mardi Gras of the Riviera" runs from mid-February to early March, celebrating the return of spring with 3 weeks of parades, *corsi* (floats), *veglioni* (masked balls), confetti, and battles in which young women toss flowers at the audience.

The **Nice Festival du Jazz** (www.nicejazzfest.fr) runs for a week in mid-July, when jazz, funk, and reggae artists perform amid the ancient ruins of Arène de Cimiez. Recent performers have included Herbie Hancock, Kris Kristofferson, and Toots and the Maytals.

A Note on Nice Buses

If you plan to use the city's buses, consider buying a 1- or 7-day pass, available from tobacco stands and newspaper kiosks throughout the city. The pass allows unlimited transit on any municipal buses that run along the coast, the airport bus, and Nice's tramway. The price is 4€ for a 1-day pass. For additional information, call Ligne d'Azur (✆ 08-10-06-10-06; www.lignedazur.com). The most useful lines are the no. 15 that runs up to the Matisse and Chagall museums in Cimiez, and lines no. 11 and 52 that run along the Promenade des Anglais.

Exploring the City

In 1822, Nice's orange crop had an awful year. The workers faced a lean time, so the English residents employed them to build the **promenade des Anglais ★★**, today a wide boulevard fronting the bay, split by "islands" of palms and flowers and stretching for about 7km (4¼ miles) all the way to the airport. Along the beach are rows of grand cafes, the Musée Masséna, villas, and the city's most glamorous hotels.

Crossing this boulevard in the tiniest bikinis are some of the world's most attractive bronzed bodies. They're heading for the **beach.** Tough on tender feet, *le plage* is made not of sand, but of pebbles (and not small ones, either).

Rising sharply on a rock at the eastern end of the promenade is **Le Château,** where the ducs de Savoie built their castle, which was torn down in 1706. The hill has since been turned into a wonderful public park complete with a waterfall, cafes, and a giant children's play area. To reach the site and take in the view, board an elevator from the quai des Etats-Unis; the fit can walk up one of five sets of steep steps. The park is open daily from 8am to dusk. At the north end of Le Château is the famous old **graveyard** of Nice, known primarily for lavish monuments that form their own enduring art statement. It's one of the largest in France.

Continuing east from "the Rock" (the site of Le Château), you reach the **Vieux Port,** or harbor, where the restaurants are even cheaper and are filled with locals. While lingering over a drink at a sidewalk cafe, you can watch the boats depart for Corsica. The harbor was excavated between 1750 and 1830. Since then, it has gained an outer harbor, protected by two jetties, and is great for a stroll around.

The "authentic" Niçoise live in **Vieille Ville ★**, the old town, beginning at the foot of the Rock and stretching to place Masséna. Sheltered by sienna-tiled roofs, many of the Italianate facades suggest 17th-century Genoese palaces. The old town is a maze of narrow streets, teeming with local life and studded with the least expensive restaurants in Nice. Buy an onion pizza (*pissaladière*) from a vendor. Many of the buildings are painted a faded Roman gold, and their banners are laundry flapping in the sea breezes.

While here, try to visit the **Marché aux Fleurs.** This flower market lies on the **cours Saleya,** the old town's principal walkway, which is filled with alfresco restaurants and cafes. A flamboyant array of carnations, violets, roses, and birds of paradise, the market operates Tuesday to Sunday 8am to 6pm in summer, and 8am until between 2 and 4pm in winter, depending on the vendors' remaining inventory and energy level. On Monday the same space is occupied by a superb antiques market, with vendors carting wares from across France and Italy.

Cathédrale Orthodoxe Russe St-Nicolas à Nice.

Nice's newly pedestrianized centerpiece is **place Masséna,** with pink buildings in the 17th-century Genoese style and fountains with water jets. Stretching from the main square to the promenade is the **Jardin Albert-1er,** with an open-air terrace and a Triton Fountain. With palms and exotic flowers, it's the most relaxing oasis in town.

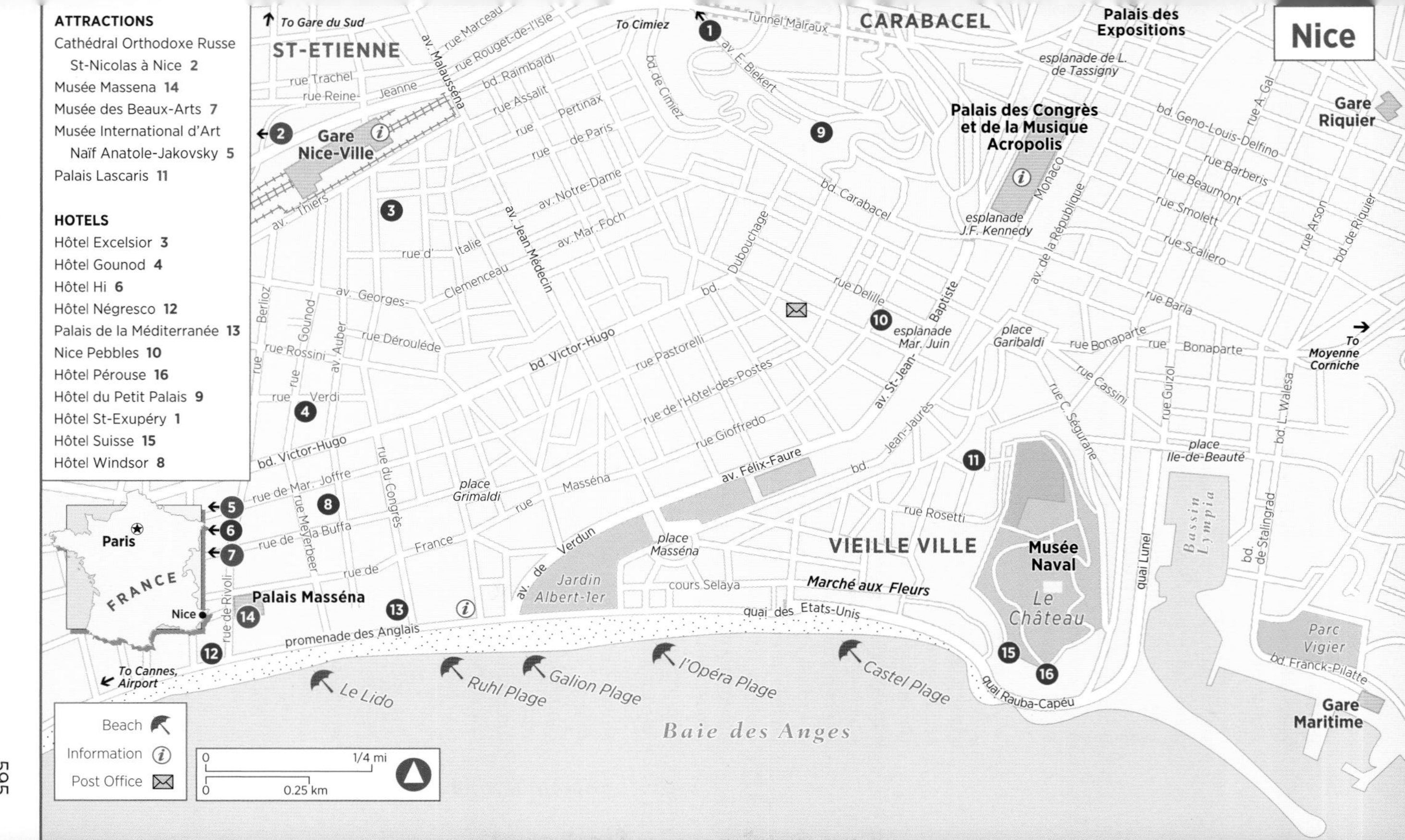

Nice
ATTRACTIONS
Cathédral Orthodoxe Russe St-Nicolas à Nice 2
Musée Massena 14
Musée des Beaux-Arts 7
Musée International d'Art Naïf Anatole-Jakovsky 5
Palais Lascaris 11
HOTELS
Hôtel Excelsior 3
Hôtel Gounod 4
Hôtel Hi 6
Hôtel Négresco 12
Palais de la Méditerranée 13
Nice Pebbles 10
Hôtel Pérouse 16
Hôtel du Petit Palais 9
Hôtel St-Exupéry 1
Hôtel Suisse 15
Hôtel Windsor 8
Beach
Information
Post Office
0 1/4 mi
0 0.25 km
To Gare du Sud
To Cimiez
To Moyenne Corniche
To Cannes, Airport
ST-ETIENNE
CARABACEL
VIEILLE VILLE
Gare Nice-Ville
Gare Riquier
Gare Maritime
Palais des Expositions
Palais des Congrès et de la Musique Acropolis
Palais Masséna
Musée Naval
Le Château
Marché aux Fleurs
Jardin Albert-1er
Parc Vigier
Bassin Lympia
Baie des Anges
Le Lido
Ruhl Plage
Galion Plage
l'Opéra Plage
Castel Plage
promenade des Anglais
quai des Etats-Unis
quai Rauba-Capéu
quai Lunel
place Masséna
place Grimaldi
place Garibaldi
place Ile-de-Beauté
esplanade J.F. Kennedy
esplanade Mar. Juin
esplanade de L. de Tassigny
Tunnel Malraux
av. E. Biekert
bd. de Cimiez
bd. Carabacel
av. Jean Médecin
bd. Victor-Hugo
av. Félix-Faure
av. St-Jean-Baptiste
bd. Jean-Jaurès
av. de la République
av. Malausséna
av. Thiers
av. de Verdun
rue de France
rue Masséna
rue de Rivoli
cours Selaya
rue Rosetti
rue C. Ségurane
rue Cassini
rue Bonaparte
rue Guizol
bd. L. Walesa
bd. de Stalingrad
bd. Franck-Pilatte
bd. Geno-Louis-Delfino
rue Barberis
rue Beaumont
rue Smolett
rue Scaliero
rue Barla
rue Arson
bd. de Riquier
rue A. Gal
FRANCE
Paris
Nice

Cathédrale Orthodoxe Russe St-Nicolas à Nice ★ Ordered and built by none other than Tsar Nicholas II, this cathedral is the most beautiful religious edifice of the Orthodoxy outside Russia and a perfect expression of Russian religious art abroad. It dates from the Belle Epoque, when some of the Romanovs and entourage turned the Riviera into their stomping ground (everyone from grand dukes to ballerinas walked the promenade). The cathedral is richly ornamented and decorated with icons. You'll spot the building from afar because of its collection of ornate onion-shaped domes. During church services on Sunday morning, the building closes to tourist visits.

Av. Nicolas-II (off bd. du Tzaréwitch). ✆ **04-93-83-94-08.** www.acor-nice.com. Admission 3€ adults, 2€ students, free for children 12 and under. May–Sept daily 9am–noon and 2:30–6pm; Oct–Apr daily 9:30am–noon and 2:30–5pm. From the central rail station, head west along av. Thiers to bd. Gambetta, and then go north to av. Nicolas-II.

Musée des Beaux-Arts ★★ This collection is housed in the fabulous former residence of the Ukrainian Princess Kotchubey. It is devoted to the masters of the Second Empire and the Belle Epoque, with an extensive collection of 19th-century French experts. Many of the canvases depict the South of France. The gallery of sculptures includes works by J. B. Carpeaux, Rude, and Rodin. Note the important collection by a dynasty of painters, the Dutch Vanloo family. One of its best-known members, Carle Vanloo, born in Nice in 1705, was Louis XV's premier *peintre*. A fine collection of 19th- and 20th-century art includes works by Ziem, Raffaelli, Boudin, Guillaumin, and Sisley. Armed robbers broke into the museum 5 minutes before closing on a quiet summer Sunday in 2007, stealing a Monet canvas in the process.

33 av. des Baumettes. ✆ **04-92-15-28-28.** www.musee-beaux-arts-nice.org. Free admission. Tues–Sun 10am–6pm. Bus: 3, 8, 9, 10, 12, 22, or 23.

Musée International d'Art Naïf Anatole-Jakovsky (Museum of Naive Art) ★ This museum is in the beautifully restored Château Ste-Hélène in the Fabron district. The museum's namesake, for years one of the world's leading art critics, once owned the 600-piece collection of colorful collages, far-out sculptures, and 3-D artworks. Its playful nature and surrounding gardens make it one of the few art galleries in Nice that will appeal to children. Artists from over 25 countries are represented by everything from primitive painting to 20th-century works.

Château St-Hélène, av. de Fabron. ✆ **04-93-71-78-33.** Free admission. Wed–Mon 10am–6pm. Bus: 9, 10, or 23; 10-min. walk.

Musée Masséna ★★★ Reopened to the public in 2008 after a seemingly endless renovation, this is Nice's key museum. It is surrounded by carefully planted gardens and housed in a Belle Epoque villa with traces of the White House about it. Housed inside is a potted history of the French Riviera. A timeline traces the first Victorian visitors to the roaring 1920s. Costumes from the age, train tickets from London to Nice, and portraits of the holidaying rich bring the past to life. Of additional note are the paintings and objets d'art dedicated from the Masséna family, a noble set of locals who constructed the villa and married themselves off to various European royals.

65 rue de France. ✆ **04-93-91-19-10.** Free admission. Wed–Mon 9am–6pm.

Palais Lascaris ☺ The baroque Palais Lascaris in the city's historic old town is associated with the Lascaris-Vintimille family, whose recorded history dates back over 7 centuries. Built in the 17th century, it contains elaborately detailed ornaments and suits of armor. An intensive restoration by the city of Nice in 1946 brought back its original beauty, and the palace is now classified as a historic monument. The most elaborate floor, the *étage noble,* retains many of its 18th-century panels and plaster embellishments. A pharmacy, built around 1738 and complete with many of the original accessories, is on the ground floor.

15 rue Droite. ✆ **04-93-62-72-40.** Free admission. Wed–Mon 10am–6pm.

Nearby Attractions in Cimiez ★★

In the once-aristocratic hilltop quarter of Cimiez, 5km (3 miles) north of Nice, Queen Victoria wintered at the Hôtel Excelsior and brought half the English court with her. Founded by the Romans, who called it Cemenelum, Cimiez was the capital of the Maritime Alps province. Excavations have uncovered the ruins of a Roman town, and you can wander the dig sites, which are shaded with olive trees. The arena was big enough to hold at least 5,000 spectators, who watched contests between gladiators and wild beasts. It now plays host to Nice's Jazz Festival each July. To reach this suburb and its attractions, take bus no. 15 from place Masséna.

Monastère de Cimiez (Cimiez Convent) ★ The convent embraces a church that owns three of the most important works by the locally prominent Bréa brothers, who painted in the late 15th century. In a restored part of the convent where some Franciscan friars still live, the Musée Franciscain is decorated with 17th-century frescoes. Some 350 documents and works of art from the 15th to the 18th centuries are on display. The magnificent gardens are a photographer's dream. You'll have a panoramic view of Nice and the Baie des Anges. Artists Matisse and Dufy are buried in the cemetery.

Place du Monastère. ✆ **04-93-81-00-04.** Free admission. Museum Mon–Fri 8:30am–12:30pm and 2:30–6:30pm. Church daily 9am–6pm.

Musée Matisse ★★ This museum in a beautiful old Italian villa honors Henri Matisse, one of the 20th century's greatest painters. He came to Nice for the light and made the city his home, living in the Hotel Beau Rivage and on the cours Saleya, and dying in Cimiez in 1954. Seeing his playful nude sketches today, you'll wonder how early critics could have denounced them as "the female animal in all her shame and horror." Most of the pieces in the museum's permanent collection were painted in Nice (you may recognize a few of the backdrops). These include *Nude in an Armchair with a Green Plant* (1937), *Nymph in the Forest* (1935–42), and a chronologically arranged series of paintings from 1890 to 1919. The most famous of these is *Portrait of Madame Matisse* (1905), usually displayed near a portrait of the artist's wife by Marquet, painted in 1900. There's also an assemblage of designs he prepared as practice sketches for Matisse's final masterpiece, his *Chapel at Vence.* Also here are *The Créole Dancer* (1951), *Blue Nude IV* (1952), and around 50 dance-related sketches he did between 1930 and 1931.

In the Villa des Arènes-de-Cimiez, 164 av. des Arènes-de-Cimiez. ✆ **04-93-81-08-08.** www.musee-matisse.nice.org. Free admission. Wed–Mon 10am–6pm.

Musée National Message Biblique Marc Chagall.

Musée National Message Biblique Marc Chagall ★★ In the hills of Cimiez, this handsome museum, surrounded by pools and a garden, is devoted to Marc Chagall's treatment of biblical themes. Born in Russia in 1887, Chagall became a French citizen in 1937 and painted with astonishing light and color until his death in St-Paul-de-Vence in 1985. The artist and his wife donated the works—the most important Chagall collection ever assembled—to France in 1966 and 1972. On display are 450 of his oils, drawings, pastels, lithographs, sculptures, and ceramics; a mosaic; three stained-glass windows; and a tapestry. Chagall decorated a concert room with brilliantly hued stained-glass windows.

Av. du Dr.-Ménard. ✆ **04-93-53-87-20.** www.musee-chagall.fr. Admission 8.50€ adults, 5.50€ students, free for children 17 and under. May–Oct Wed–Mon 10am–6pm; Nov–June Wed–Mon 10am–5pm.

Outdoor Pursuits

BEACHES Along Nice's seafront, beaches extend uninterrupted for more than 7km (4¼ miles), going from the edge of Vieux-Port (the old port, or harbor) to the international airport. Tucked between the public areas are several rather chic private beaches. Many of these beach bars provide mattresses and parasols for 12€ to 20€. The coolest clubs include Hi Beach (✆ **04-97-14-00-83;** www.hi-beach.net), which has a sushi bar, weights room, and swing chairs; and Castel Plage (✆ **04-93-85-22-66;** www.castelplage.com), which is a celebrity hangout in summer. The most family friendly, with its giant pile of outdoor toys, is Opera Plage (✆ **04-93-62-31-52**).

SCUBA DIVING The best outfit is the **Centre International de Plongée (CIP) de Nice,** 14 quai des Dock (✆ **04-93-89-42-44;** www.cip-nice.com). A *baptême* (dive for first-timers) costs 45€. A two-tank dive for experienced divers, equipment included, is 140€; appropriate diver's certification is required.

Shopping

Nice's densest concentrations of clothes, shoes, and electronic shops are around **rue Masséna** and **avenue Jean-Médecin.** Both are great for hip French brands. For more high-end couture, the streets around **place Magenta,** including **rue de Verdun, rue Paradis,** and **rue Alphonse Karr** are a credit card's worst nightmare. A shop of note is **Cotelac,** 12 rue Alphonse Karr (✆ **04-93-87-31-59**), which sells chic women's clothing.

Men should try **Façonnable,** 7–9 rue Paradis (✆ **04-93-87-88-80**). This is the original site of a chain with several hundred branches worldwide. The look is youthful and conservatively stylish. Find men's suits, overcoats, sportswear, and jeans in this branch, and an outlet for women's wear (Façonnable Femmes) immediately across the street at 10 rue Paradis (✆ **04-93-88-06-97**).

The winding streets of Nice's old town are the best place to find local crafts, ceramics, gifts, and foodie purchases. If you're thinking of indulging in a Provençale *pique-nique,* **Nicola Alziari,** 318 bd. Madeleine (✆ **04-93-44-45-12**), will provide everything from olives, anchovies, and pistous to aiolis and tapenades. It's one of Nice's oldest purveyors of olive oil, with a house brand that comes in several strengths and flavors. Also for sale are objects crafted from olive wood.

For arts and crafts, **Plat Jérôme,** 34 rue Centrale (✆ **04-93-62-17-09**), stocks varnished pottery. Many artists' studios and galleries line the surrounding side streets near old town's cathedral in the old town. The best selection of Provençal fabrics is at **Le Chandelier,** 7 rue de la Boucherie (✆ **04-93-85-85-19**), where you'll see designs by two of the region's best-known producers of cloth, Les Olivades and Valdrôme.

Nice is also known for its **street markets.** In addition to the flower market, **Marché aux Fleurs** (see "Exploring the City," above), the main flea market, **Marché à la Brocante,** also at cours Saleya, takes place Monday 8am to 5pm. Another flea market on the port, **Les Puces de Nice,** place Robilante, is open Tuesday to Saturday 9am to 6pm.

Also in the harbor is **Confiserie Florian du Vieux-Nice,** 14 quai Papacino (✆ **04-93-55-43-50**). Opened in 1949 by Joseph Fuchs, the grandfather of the present English-speaking owners, their specialty is glazed fruit crystallized in sugar or artfully arranged into chocolates. Look for exotic jams (rose-petal preserves, mandarin marmalade) and the free recipe leaflet, as well as candied violets, verbena leaves, and rosebuds. Back near the opera house, one of the oldest chocolatiers in Nice, **Confiserie Auer,** 7 rue St-François-de-Paule (✆ **04-93-85-77-98**), was established in 1820. Since then, few of the original decorative accessories have changed. The shop specializes in chocolates, candies, and fruits confits, the signature Provençal goodies.

Where to Stay

VERY EXPENSIVE

Hôtel Negresco ★★★ The Negresco, on the seafront in the heart of Nice, is one of the Riviera's superglamorous hotels. This Victorian wedding-cake hotel is named after its founder, Henry Negresco, and has hosted each era's superstars, from The Beatles to Michael Jackson. The hotel's decorators scoured Europe to gather antiques, tapestries, and art for the ritzy interior and domed central salon. Most of the rooms were given a thorough makeover in early 2011, mixing sea views with state-of-the-art wetrooms and contemporary furniture. The entire fifth floor is now dedicated to VVIPs (that's right, "very, very important persons") and has a private luncheon area and bar. Dining is among the best in town, with the Michelin-starred Chantecler and the funky brasserie-style Rotonde, which was also given a thorough makeover in 2011. Despite the changes, the staff still wear 18th-century costumes and are as fawningly polite as ever.

37 promenade des Anglais, Nice Cedex 06007. www.hotel-negresco-nice.com. ✆ **04-93-16-64-00.** Fax 04-93-88-35-68. 146 units. 245€–475€ double; from 690€ suite. AE, DC, MC, V. Free parking. **Amenities:** 2 restaurants; bar; babysitting; exercise room; massage; room service. *In room:* A/C, TV, hair dryer, minibar, free Wi-Fi.

Palais de la Méditerranée ★★★ This glittering seaside palace on the promenade des Anglais reigned from 1929 to the late 1970s as the chicest hotel in Nice. In its heyday, the hotel's theater stage hosted everyone from Maurice Chevalier to American chanteuse Josephine Baker. But in 1978, it was shuttered up, a sad tale involving the probable murder of heiress Agnès Le Roux, who was a major shareholder in the establishment. In 2004, it reopened with great fanfare. The complete restoration left its Art Deco facade intact, but the interior of this place was gutted. It was turned into a marble palace, with glamorous touches such as plush hallways and such modern amenities as a heated outdoor swimming pool. Also kept in the renovation were the hotel's monumental chandeliers and stained-glass windows. Bedrooms, midsize to grandly spacious, are outfitted in a tasteful modern decor. Ninety of the bedrooms also open onto sea views. The hotel's casino was also restored to its former glory.

13–15 promenade des Anglais, Nice 06011. www.lepalaisdelamediterranee.com. ✆ **04-92-14-77-00.** Fax 04-92-14-77-14. 188 units. 180€–610€ double; from 710€–2,100€ suite. AE, DC, MC, V. **Amenities:** 2 restaurants; bar; babysitting, casino; exercise room; 2 pools (indoor and outdoor); room service; solarium; Turkish bath; watersports equipment/rentals. *In room:* A/C, TV, hair dryer, minibar, free Wi-Fi.

EXPENSIVE

Hôtel Hi ★ 🎁 The Japanese word *hi* describes the black mottling on the back of an ornamental carp, which has traditionally been associated with good luck. An architectural and decorative statement, this hotel occupies a former boarding house that dates to the 1930s. Spearheaded by Matali Crasset, a one-time colleague of Philippe Starck, a team of architects and engineers created one of the most aggressively avant-garde hotels in the south of France. The angular seven-story hotel opened in 2003. Each of the nine high-tech room concepts is different. They range from white-on-white to birch-wood veneer and acid green, to cool violet and gray. The unconventional layouts may include a bathtub tucked behind a screen of potted plants or elevated to a position of theatrical prominence. Electronic gizmos include state-of-the-art MP3 docks and power showers. The Hi's highly regarded beach club and spa are hip hangouts in their own right.

3 av. des Fleurs, Nice 06000. www.hi-hotel.net. ✆ **04-97-07-26-26.** Fax 04-97-07-26-27. 38 units. 269€–489€ double; from 440€ suite. AE, DC, MC, V. Parking 24€. Bus: 23. **Amenities:** Organic restaurant; 24-hr. bar and snack bar; rooftop swimming pool; Turkish bath. *In room:* A/C, TV, free Wi-Fi.

La Pérouse ★★ 🎁 Once a prison, La Pérouse has been reconstructed and is now a spectacular and unique Riviera hotel. Set on a cliff, it's built right in the gardens of the ancient château hill, with a secluded swimming pool almost carved out of the rock. No hotel aside from the adjoining Hotel Suisse affords a better view over both the old city and the Baie des Anges. Inside it resembles an old Provençal home, with low ceilings, white walls, and antique furnishings. The lovely, spacious rooms are beautifully furnished, often with Provençal fabrics. Most have balconies overlooking the bay. The bathrooms are large, clad in Boticino marble, and hold tubs and showers.

11 quai Rauba-Capéu, Nice 06300. www.hotel-la-perouse.com. ✆ **04-93-62-34-63.** Fax 04-93-62-59-41. 65 units. 135€–495€ double; 490€–1,700€ suite. AE, DC, MC, V. Parking 25€. **Amenities:** Restaurant (mid-May to mid-Sept); bar; babysitting; exercise room; Jacuzzi; outdoor pool; room service; sauna. *In room:* A/C, TV, hair dryer, minibar, free Wi-Fi.

MODERATE

Hôtel du Petit Palais This whimsical hotel occupies a mansion built around 1890; in the 1970s, it was the home of the actor and writer Sacha Guitry (a name that's instantly recognized in millions of French households). It lies about a 10-minute drive from the city center in the Carabacel district near the Musée Chagall. Many of the Art Deco and Italianate furnishings and Florentine moldings and friezes remain intact. The preferred rooms, and the most expensive, have balconies that afford sea views during the day and sunset views at dusk. Bathrooms are small and tidy, and each has a shower and tub. Breakfast is served in a pretty salon or outdoors in the garden.

17 av. Emile-Bieckert, Nice 06000. www.petitpalaisnice.com. ✆ **04-93-62-19-11.** Fax 04-93-62-53-60. 25 units. 115€–230€ double. AE, DC, MC, V. Parking 10€. **Amenities:** Bar; babysitting; room service. *In room:* A/C, hair dryer, minibar, free Wi-Fi.

Hôtel Suisse ★ Along with the Hotel Pérouse, this offers the most splendid views in Nice, panning over the sea and promenade des Anglais to the Alpes-Maritimes mountains beyond. But unlike its adjoining rival hotel, it offers a less expensive, more low-key, but equally comfortable experience. It also has six inexpensive rooms facing the chateau hill to the rear. Standard rooms are very small but are contemporary, comfy, and extremely bright, with lush fabrics and floor-to-ceiling windows. Balcony rooms are a little larger and have a petite outdoor spot from which to sit and gaze out to sea.

15 Quai Raubà Capéù, Nice 06000. www.hotel-nice-suisse.com. ✆ **04-92-17-39-00.** Fax 04-93-85-30-70. 42 units. 115€–199€ double. AE, DC, MC, V. Nearby parking. Amenities: Babysitting; Jacuzzi; outdoor pool; room service; spa. In room: A/C, TV, hair dryer, minibar, free Wi-Fi.

Hôtel Windsor ★ One of the most arts-conscious hotels on the Riviera is in a *maison bourgeoise* built by disciples of Gustav Eiffel in 1895. It's near the Negresco and the promenade des Anglais. Each unit is a unique decorative statement by a different artist. The heir and scion of the longtime owners, the Redolfi family, commissioned manifestations of his mystical and mythical visions after years of traveling through Asia, Africa, and South America. In the "Ben" room, for example, the Provençal artist of the same name painted verses of his own poetry, in tones of blue, orange, yellow, and green, on a white background. You can take your chances or select a room based on the photos on the hotel website. Most units have a combination tub/shower. The fifth floor holds the health club, steam room, and sauna. The garden contains scores of tropical and exotic plants, a tiny pool, and, to top it off, a parrot who chirps away as happily as the guests.

11 rue Dalpozzo, Nice 06000. www.hotelwindsornice.com. ✆ **04-93-88-59-35.** Fax 04-93-88-94-57. 54 units. 90€–185€ double. AE, DC, MC, V. Parking 11€. **Amenities:** Restaurant; bar; babysitting; health club; outdoor pool; room service; sauna; smoke-free rooms. *In room:* A/C, TV, hair dryer, minibar.

Nice Pebbles ★ We cannot recommend this apartment rental company highly enough. Nice Pebbles manages around 50 high-class properties in the city's premier zones, including the old town and harbor, and along the promenade des Anglais. All of its properties are carefully selected, presumably to minimize any complaints or hassles. Its stock is thus in excellent condition and has first-class amenities (generally MP3 docks, high-definition TVs, and designer bathrooms). Sizes vary from one-bedroom properties with large terraces, to large seaview places sleeping 10 or more guests. When booked by the week, prices work out much more competitively than a hotel, especially when traveling with a family. Booking can be made online, although due to high demand, reservations are best made as far in advance as possible.

23 rue Gioffredo, Nice 06000. www.nicepebbles.com. ✆ **09-52-78-27-65.** 44 units. 90€–350€ per apt. MC, V. **Amenities:** Babysitting. *In apartments:* A/C (generally in all), TV, hair dryer, free Wi-Fi.

INEXPENSIVE

Hôtel Excelsior The Excelsior's ornate corbels and stone pediments rise grandly a few steps from the railway station. This much-renovated 19th-century hotel has modern decor and rooms outfitted in tones of Provençal ocher, blue, and brown that have seen a lot of wear but are still comfortable. They have small shower-only bathrooms. Furnishings, for the most part, are functional and conservative. Some rooms have balconies, and there are family rooms with kitchenettes available. There's also a garden. The beach is a 15-minute walk through the shopping streets of Nice.

19 av. Durante, Nice 06000. www.excelsiornice.com. ✆ **04-93-88-18-05.** Fax 04-93-88-38-69. 42 units. 57€–220€ double. AE, DC, MC, V. Bus: 99. *In room:* A/C, TV, hair dryer, free Wi-Fi.

Hôtel Gounod ★ A top choice in the city center, this hotel is a 5-minute walk from the sea. It was built around 1910 in a neighborhood where the street names honor composers. Ornate balconies, a domed roof, and an elaborate canopy of wrought iron and glass embellish the Gounod. The attractive lobby and adjoining lounge are festive and stylish, with old prints, copper flowerpots, and antiques. The high-ceilinged guest rooms won't win any luxury hotel awards, but are clean are quiet; most overlook the gardens of private homes. The tiled bathrooms are small but efficiently organized, mainly with shower units. Guests have free unlimited use of the pool and Jacuzzi at the Hôtel Splendid next door.

3 rue Gounod, Nice 06000. www.gounod-nice.com. ✆ **04-93-16-42-00.** Fax 04-93-88-23-84. 45 units. 90€–160€ double; 140€–260€ suite. AE, DC, MC, V. Parking 17€. Closed Nov 20–Dec 20. Bus: 98. **Amenities:** Babysitting; free Internet; Jacuzzi; outdoor pool; room service; spa. *In room:* A/C, TV, hair dryer, minibar.

Villa Saint-Exupéry This former Carmelite monastery has been completely renovated and turned into an award-winning hostel for young and old alike. It's busy year-round with seasoned travelers on a budget, artists, musicians, families, hikers, and, of course, students on summer break. The restored and comfort-filled villa offers standard hotel rooms (some with kitchenette), as well as some dormitory accommodations at youth hostel tariffs. Echoing its past life, the former chapel preserved its stained-glass windows. There is also a bar with all drinks at 1€, free Wi-Fi, free luggage storage, free breakfast, and a barbeque area. Guests are also welcome to use a fully equipped kitchen. A new sister hostel offering the same facilities, **Villa Saint Exupéry Beach,** 6 rue Sacha Guitry, opened downtown opposite Galleries Lafayette in late 2010.

22 av. Gravier, Nice 06100. www.villahostels.com. ✆ **04-93-84-42-83.** Fax 04-92-09-82-94. 60 units. 27€–40€ per person in a single or twin-bedded room; 16€–30€ per person for dormitory bed. Rates include continental breakfast. MC, V. Free parking. **Amenities:** Bar; cooking facilities; free Wi-Fi. *In room:* Kitchenettes (in some).

Where to Eat

VERY EXPENSIVE

Le Chantecler ★★★ TRADITIONAL/MODERN FRENCH This is Nice's most prestigious, most formal, and most commended restaurant. Its walls are decked with panels removed from a château in Pouilly-Fuissé, rich tapestries hang from the ceilings, and bow-tied multilingual waiters anticipate your every move. The menu is revised each week to include the most sophisticated and creative dishes in the city. Dishes may include turbot filet served with purée of broad beans, sun-dried tomatoes, and asparagus; flash-fried sea bass served with baked red onion confit; and a melt-in-your-mouth fantasy of marbled hot chocolate drenched in almond-flavored cream sauce.

In the Hôtel Negresco, 37 promenade des Anglais. ✆ **04-93-16-64-00.** Reservations required. Main courses 48€–80€; fixed-price lunch 50€–130€, dinner 90€–130€. AE, MC, V. Wed–Sun 12:30–1:45pm and 7:30–10pm. Closed Jan.

EXPENSIVE

Aphrodite ★★ MODERN FRENCH Chef David Faure became the first chef to supplant molecular cuisine on the traditional citizens of Nice—an act that garnered him his first Michelin star in 2010. But for Faure, this experimental branch of gastronomy is more flavorful than fancy, and his mantra that "good ingredients equals good food" has him calling at the city's markets most days. His least expensive set meal has a reinvention of the classic dish salade Niçoise, and foie gras turned into a maki roll dotted with salmon eggs. The priciest menu allows diners to soak their wild prawns in liquid nitrogen—at the table—before a dessert of strawberry samosas. A 25€ lunch menu encourages budget gastronomes too.

10 bd Dubouchage. ✆ **04-93-85-63-53.** www.restaurant-aprodite.com. Reservations recommended. Main courses 25€–40€; fixed-price dinner 39€–98€. AE, DC, MC, V. Mon–Sat noon–2pm and 7:30–11pm.

MODERATE

Brasserie Flo TRADITIONAL FRENCH This is Nice's most bustling brasserie, and one of the few places in town in which to try traditional bistro cooking from northern France. Smartly dressed waiters dish up simple but well-executed French classics in an early-1900s former theater (the chefs cook in the kitchen "on stage") near place Masséna. Frescoes from the original building were left in place during a renovation in 2011 and still cover the high ceiling. The place is brisk, stylish, reasonably priced, and fun. And as Flo is part of an upscale chain, waiters are mostly multilingual and are used to visitors. Menu items include an array of grilled fish, Alsatian-style choucroute, steak with pepper sauce, and platters of fresh oysters and shellfish.

2–4 rue Sacha-Guitry. ✆ **04-93-13-38-38.** Reservations recommended. Main courses 18€–40€; fixed-price menu 23€–38€. AE, DC, MC, V. Daily noon–2:30pm and 7–11pm. Bus: 1, 2, or 5.

L'Ane Rouge ★★ PROVENÇAL Facing the old port and occupying an antique building—the owners have carefully retained its ceiling beams and stone walls—this is one of the city's best-known seafood restaurants. In the two modern yet cozy dining rooms, you can enjoy traditional specialties such as bouillabaisse, *bourride* (stew), filet of John Dory with roulades of stuffed lettuce leaves, mussels stuffed with bread crumbs and herbs, and sea bream sautéed in local Bandol wine. Service is commendable.

7 quai des Deux-Emmanuels. ✆ **04-93-89-49-63.** www.anerougenice.com. Reservations recommended. Main courses 24€–48€; fixed-price dinner 35€–68€. AE, DC, MC, V. Fri–Tues noon–2pm and Thurs–Tues 7–10:30pm. Closed early Feb to late March. Bus: 30.

Le Safari ★ PROVENÇAL/NIÇOISE Highly recommended for its honest prices and solid cooking, this establishment has been in business for over 50 years. Diners can choose the alfresco terrace on the bustling cours Saleya in spring or summer, or they may cozy up inside around the wood-fired oven in winter. Menu items include a pungent *bagna cauda,* which calls for diners to immerse vegetables in a sizzling brew of hot oil and anchovy paste; grilled peppers bathed in olive oil; *daube* (stew) of beef; and an omelet with *blettes* (tough but flavorful greens). The unfortunately named *merda de can* (dog poop) is gnocchi stuffed with spinach, and a lot more appetizing than it sounds. Even the pizzas and bottles of inexpensive house wine are commendable.

1 cours Saleya. ✆ **04-93-80-18-44.** Reservations recommended. Main courses 12€–30€. AE, DC, MC, V. Daily noon–11pm.

La Zucca Magica ★ VEGETARIAN/ITALIAN The chef at this popular harborside restaurant has been named the best Italian chef in Nice. That this honor should go to a vegetarian restaurant was the most startling part of the news. Chef Marco, who opened his restaurant in 1997 after cooking for many years in Rome, certainly has a fine pedigree—he's a relative of the late Luciano Pavarotti. He serves refined cuisine using recipes from Italy's Piedmont region and updating them with no meat or fish. The red-and-green decor (the colors of Italy) will put you in the mood for the creative cuisine. You'll have to trust Marco, though, because everyone is served the same meal based around a set fixed-price menu, normally comprising five or six courses. You can count on savory cuisine using lots of herbs, Italian cheeses, beans, and pasta.

4 bis quai Papacino. ✆ **04-93-56-25-27.** www.lazuccamagica.com. Reservations recommended. Fixed-price lunch 20€, dinner 29€. No credit cards. Tues–Sat 12:30–2pm and 7–9:30pm.

INEXPENSIVE

Flaveur ★★ MODERN FRENCH This chic little diner was set up by three young men with a passion in 2009. Tired with the regular restaurant trade, they wanted to create something with novel tastes, far-out decor, and memorable service, all laced with a good splash of self-belief. As the restaurant's name suggests, the end flavors are sublime. Cuts of beef are paired with aubergine caviar, steak tartare is blended with panisse chips, and local seafood is placed on a bed of cauliflower and grilled taragon. Servings are as artistically displayed as they are generous. Excellent value lunchtime set menus allow for gourmet bites on a budget.

25 rue Gubernatis. ✆ **04-93-62-53-95.** www.flaveur.net. Reservations recommended. Main courses 12€–35€; fixed-price lunch 16€–24€, dinner 35€–60€. MC, V. Tues–Fri noon–2pm and 7:30–11pm; Sat 7:30–11pm.

Nice After Dark

Nice has some of the most active nightlife and cultural offerings along the Riviera. Big evenings out usually begin at a cafe or bar; take in a restaurant, opera, or film; and finish in a club. At kiosks around town, you can pick up a copy of *La Semaine des Spectacles,* which outlines the week's diversions.

The major cultural center on the Riviera is the **Opéra de Nice,** 4 rue St-François-de-Paule (✆ **04-92-17-40-00;** www.opera-nice.org), built in 1885 by Charles Garnier, fabled architect of the Paris Opéra. It presents a full repertoire, with emphasis on serious, often large-scale operas. In one season you might see *Tosca, Les Contes de Hoffmann,* Verdi's *Macbeth,* Beethoven's *Fidelio,* and *Carmen,* as well as a *saison symphonique,* dominated by the Orchestre Philharmonique de Nice. The opera hall is also the major venue for concerts and recitals. Tickets are available (to concerts, recitals, and full-blown operas) right up until the day of performance. You can show up at the box office (Mon–Sat 10am–5:30pm, Sun 10am–6pm) or buy tickets in advance online. Tickets run from 10€ for seats up in the gods, to 100€ for front-and-center seats on opening night.

Cabaret du Casino Ruhl, in Casino Ruhl, 1 promenade des Anglais (✆ **04-97-03-12-22**), is Nice's answer to the more ostentatious glitter of Monte Carlo and Las Vegas. It includes just enough flesh to titillate. The casino contains an area exclusively for slot machines, open daily from 10am to 4am; entrance is free. A more formal gaming room (jacket required, but not a tie) offering blackjack, baccarat, and chemin de fer opens from 3pm. A more chic alternative is the **Casino in the Palais de Mediterranée,** 15 promenade des Anglais (✆ **04-92-14-68-00;** www.casinomediterranee.com), which offers a similar experience daily from 10am.

At the hip end of the spectrum is **Smarties,** 10 rue Defly (✆ **04-93-62-30-75**), a cool cocktail lounge with great DJs. The old town's most happening spot is currently **Villa,** 7 rue Raoul Bosio (✆ **04-93-87-99-45**), whose house aperitif is the wickedly named Putain de le Palais: crushed strawberries topped with champagne. More laid-back for cocktails, conversation, and understated cool is **Bliss,** 12 rue de l'Abbaye (✆ **04-93-16-82-38**).

The party spirit is best lapped up at **Chez Wayne's,** 15 rue de la Préfecture (✆ **04-93-13-46-99**), where dancing on the tables to raucous cover bands is the norm. Another adjacent bar with roughly equivalent decor, clientele, and sports priorities is **Le Master Home Bar,** 11 rue de la Prefecture (✆ **04-95-85-51-64**). **La Bodeguita,** 14 rue Chavin (✆ **04-93-92-67-24**), serves tapas, wine by the glass, and lots of beer, and re-creates some of the sun-and-salsa motifs of nightlife at its best in the Caribbean and South America.

GAY NIGHTLIFE

A trend-conscious gay bar in Nice is **Le Klub,** 6 rue Halevy (✆ **04-93-16-87-26;** www.leklub.net), near the Casino Ruhl. Entrance costs between 10€ and

20€, and includes one drink. Expect a hard-dancing, high-energy crowd of mostly gay men, many of them under 35, as well as lots of straight people who come for the house tunes and nonstop dancing.

VILLEFRANCHE-SUR-MER ★

935km (580 miles) S of Paris; 6.5km (4 miles) E of Nice

Soaking up the sun in a big blue bay, Villefranche's beauty is legendary. Its medieval old town literally tumbles downhill into the shimmering sea. It's little wonder than countless artists made this beachy getaway their home, or that it's served as the backdrop for countless movies. About 6.5km (4 miles) east of Nice, it's the first town you reach along the Lower Corniche.

Essentials

GETTING THERE **Trains** arrive from all the Côte d'Azur's coastal resorts from Cannes to Monaco every 30 minutes or so. For rail information and schedules, call ✆ **36-35** or visit www.voyages-sncf.com. Ligne d'Azur (✆ **08-10-06-10-06;** www.lignedazur.com) maintains a **bus** service at 15-minute intervals aboard line no. 100 from Nice to Monte Carlo via Villefranche. One-way fares costs 1€. Buses deposit their passengers just above the old town, almost directly opposite the tourist information office. Many visitors **drive** via the Corniche Inférieure (Lower Corniche).

VISITOR INFORMATION The **Office de Tourisme** is on Jardin François-Binon (✆ **04-93-01-73-68;** fax 04-93-76-63-65; www.villefranche-sur-mer.com).

Exploring the Town

Villefranche's long curve of beach, **plage des Marinières,** is the principal attraction to most visitors. From here, **quai Courbet** runs along the sea to the colorful old town. This quay runs past scores of bobbing boats and is lined with waterside restaurants.

Old-town action revolves around **place Amélie Pollonnais.** This delightful square is shaded by palms and spread with the chairs and table of six easygoing restaurants. A Sunday antiques market also takes places here. People from across the Riviera come to root through vintage posters, silverware, 1930s jewelry, and ex-hotel linens.

The painter, writer, filmmaker, and well-respected dilettante Jean Cocteau left a fine memorial to the town's inhabitants. He spent a year (1956–57) painting frescoes on the 14th-century walls of the Romanesque **Chapelle St-Pierre,** quai Courbet (✆ **04-93-76-90-70**). He presented it to "the fishermen of Villefranche in homage to the Prince of Apostles, the patron of fishermen." In the apse is a depiction of the miracle of St. Peter walking on the water, not knowing that an angel supports him. Villefranche's busty local women, in their regional costumes, are honored on the left side of the narthex. Admission is 2.50€, free for ages 15 and under. In summer, it is open daily 10am to noon and 3 to 7pm; off-season hours are daily 10am to noon and 2 to 6pm.

A short coastal path leads from the car park below place Amélie Pollonnais to the **16th century citadelle.** This castle dominates the bay, and its ramparts can be wandered around at leisure.

Where to Stay

Hôtel Welcome ★ The Welcome was a favorite of author and filmmaker Jean Cocteau and is still the best hotel in town. Every room in this modernized six-story villa has shutters, a balcony, and a view over the bay. Rooms range from midsize to spacious and are comfortably furnished, each with a small bathroom and most with a combination tub/shower. The sidewalk cafe is the focal point of town life. The on-site wine bar has an open fireplace.

1 quai Amiral-Courbet, Villefranche-sur-Mer 06231. www.welcomehotel.com. ✆ **04-93-76-27-62.** Fax 04-93-76-27-66. 36 units. 105€–255€ double; 215€–425€ suite. AE, DC, MC, V. Parking 25€. **Amenities:** Bar; babysitting; room service. *In room:* A/C, TV, hair dryer, minibar, free Wi-Fi.

Where to Eat

La Mère Germaine FRENCH/SEAFOOD This is the best of the string of restaurants stretching along the quay from the tiny port. Plan to relax over lunch while watching fishermen repair their nets. Mère Germaine opened the place in the 1930s, and these days a descendant, Remy Blouin, handles the cuisine, producing bouillabaisse celebrated across the Riviera. We recommend grilled sea bass with fennel, sole Tante Marie (stuffed with mushroom purée), lobster ravioli with shellfish sauce, and roast cod with chorizo sausage. Perfectly roasted *carré d'agneau* (lamb) is prepared for two.

Quai Courbet. ✆ **04-93-01-71-39.** Reservations recommended. Main courses 35€–48€; fixed-price menu 41€. AE, DC, MC, V. Daily noon–2:30pm and 7–10:30pm. Closed mid-Nov to Christmas.

ST-JEAN-CAP-FERRAT ★★

939km (582 miles) S of Paris; 9.5km (6 miles) E of Nice

Of all the oases along the Côte d'Azur, no other place has the snob appeal of Cap-Ferrat. It's a 15km (9¼-mile) promontory sprinkled with luxurious villas and outlined by sheltered bays, beaches, and sun-kissed coves. In the charming port of St-Jean, the harbor accommodates yachts, fishing boats, and a dozen low-key restaurants.

Essentials

GETTING THERE Many visitors drive or take a **taxi** from the rail station at nearby Beaulieu. Buses from the station at Beaulieu depart hourly for Cap-Ferrat; the one-way fare is 1€. There's also an hourly bus, the no. 81, from Nice. For bus information and schedules, contact Ligne d'Azur (✆ **08-10-06-10-06;** www.lignedazur.com). By **car** from Nice, take N7 east.

VISITOR INFORMATION The **Office de Tourisme** is on 59 av. Denis-Séméria (✆ **04-93-76-08-90;** fax 04-93-76-16-67; www.saintjeancapferrat.fr).

Seeing the Sights

One way to enjoy the scenery here is to wander on the public pathway that circles the entire peninsula. It winds past deserted coves and alongside the gardens of countless millionaire dwellings. The most scenic section runs from **plage de Paloma** to **pointe St-Hospice,** where a panoramic view of the Riviera

Villa Ephrussi de Rothschild.

landscape unfolds. You can also wander around the hamlet of **St-Jean,** a colorful fishing village with bars, bistros, and inns.

Villa Ephrussi de Rothschild ★★ Built by Baronne Ephrussi de Rothschild, this is one of the Côte d'Azur's legendary villas. Born a Rothschild, the baronne married a Hungarian banker and friend of her father. She died in 1934, leaving the Italianate building and its gardens to the Institut de France on behalf of the Académie des Beaux-Arts. The museum preserves the wealth of her collection: 18th-century furniture; Tiepolo ceilings; Savonnerie carpets; screens and panels from the Far East; tapestries from Gobelin, Aubusson, and Beauvais; Fragonard drawings; canvases by Boucher; Sèvres porcelain; and more. It's also hilarious to witness the sheer spending power of a young madame whose hero was Marie Antoinette. The gardens, set in French, Japanese, Spanish, and Florentine styles, with additional rose and exotic gardens, are a particular delight. An attractive tea salon overlooks the Bay of Villefranche.

1 av. de Rothschild. ✆ **04-93-01-33-09.** www.villa-ephrussi.com. Admission 10€ adults, 7.50€ students and children 7–18. Feb–June and Sept–Oct daily 10am–6pm; July–Aug daily 10am–7pm; Nov–Jan Mon–Fri 2–6pm, Sat–Sun 10am–6pm.

Hitting the Beach

The town's most visible and popular beaches are **plage Passable,** on the northeastern "neck" of the Cap-Ferrat peninsula, close to where it connects to the French mainland; and **plage de Paloma,** near the peninsula's southernmost tip, overlooked by the Chapelle St-Hospice. Both are lined with soft pebbles, although these are easy on sensitive feet. Both have classy beach bars and a restaurant apiece.

Where to Stay

EXPENSIVE

Grand Hôtel du Cap-Ferrat ★★★ This grande dame hotel, set in vast gardens of semitropical trees and manicured lawns, reawakened in summer 2009 after an extravagant renovation. It has been the retreat of the international elite since 1908 and occupies the same celestial status as La Réserve de Beaulieu (p. 611). Parts of the exterior have open loggias and big arched windows; you can also enjoy the views from the elaborately flowering terrace over the sea. Accommodation is modern and unfussy. A handful of suites benefit from the recent addition of private plunge pools. Another new feature is the Cellu M6 spa, which spills outside into curtained cabanas, where massages and other treatments can take place. Le Cap, the hotel's acclaimed gourmet restaurant, is overseen by top chef Didier Anies. Admission to the pool (the first on the Riviera, and still apparently the largest) and the seaside Club Dauphin beach club incurs a hefty extra charge, even for guests.

71 bd. du Général-de-Gaulle, St-Jean-Cap-Ferrat 06230. www.grand-hotel-cap-ferrat.com. ✆ **04-93-76-50-50.** Fax 04-93-76-04-52. 73 units. 265€–980€ double; 580€–4,200€ suite. AE, DC, MC, V. Parking 35€. Closed Jan and Feb. **Amenities:** 3 restaurants; bar; babysitting; bikes; Olympic-size heated outdoor pool; room service; spa; 2 tennis courts. *In room:* A/C, TV, hair dryer, minibar, free Wi-Fi.

La Voile d'Or ★★ Established in 1966, the "Golden Sail" is a tour de force. It provides intimate luxury in a converted 19th-century villa at the edge of the little fishing port and yacht harbor, with a panoramic coast view. It's equal to the Grand Hôtel in every feature except cuisine, which is just a notch lower. The guest rooms, lounges, and restaurant open onto terraces. Accommodations are individually decorated, with hand-painted reproductions, carved gilt headboards, baroque paneled doors, parquet floors, antique clocks, and paintings. The luxurious bathrooms have tub/showers. Guests gather on the canopied terrace for lunch, and in a stately room with Spanish armchairs and white wrought-iron chandeliers for dinner.

31 av. Jean-Mermoz, St-Jean-Cap-Ferrat 06230. www.lavoiledor.fr. ✆ **04-93-01-13-13.** Fax 04-93-76-11-17. 45 units. 270€–480€ double; 610€–990€ suite. Rates include continental breakfast. AE, MC, V. Parking 25€. Closed Oct to mid-Apr. **Amenities:** 2 restaurants; bar; babysitting; exercise room; 2 saltwater outdoor pools; room service; sauna. *In room:* A/C, TV, hair dryer, free Internet, minibar.

MODERATE

Hôtel Brise Marine Built around 1878, this heavenly little villa with front and rear terraces sits on a hillside between St-Jean village and Paloma Plage. A long rose arbor, beds of subtropical flowers, palms, and pines provide an attractive setting. The atmosphere is casual and informal, and the rooms are comfortably but simply furnished. They have small, tiled bathrooms with shower and tub. You can have breakfast in the beamed lounge or under the rose trellis. The little corner bar serves afternoon drinks.

58 av. Jean-Mermoz, St-Jean-Cap-Ferrat 06230. www.hotel-brisemarine.com. ✆ **04-93-76-04-36.** Fax 04-93-76-11-49. 16 units. 140€–178€ double. AE, DC, MC, V. Parking 14€. Closed Nov–Jan. **Amenities:** Bar; room service. *In room:* A/C, TV, hair dryer, minibar, free Wi-Fi.

Where to Eat

Capitaine Cook ★ PROVENÇAL/SEAFOOD Next door to the fancy La Voile d'Or hotel (see "Where to Stay," above), a few blocks uphill from the center of the village, this restaurant specializes in seafood served in hearty portions. You'll have a panoramic view of the coast from the terrace; inside, the decor is maritime and rugged. Oysters, served simply on the half-shell or in several creative ways with sauces and herbs, are a specialty. Roasted catch of the day is the mainstay, but filet mignon is also popular.

11 av. Jean-Mermoz. ✆ **04-93-76-02-66.** Main courses 17€–30€; fixed-price menu 26€–31€. MC, V. Fri–Tues noon–2pm; Thurs–Tues 7:15–10pm. Closed mid-Nov to Dec.

Le Sloop FRENCH/PROVENÇAL A justifiably popular bistro specializing in harbor-fresh seafood. Outfitted in blue and white inside and out, it sits at the edge of the port, overlooking the yachts in the harbor. A meal may begin with a carpaccio of sea bass dotted with capers, or perhaps tartare of salmon with aioli and lemon crepes. You may follow with a filet of bream served with red-wine sauce, or a mixed fish fry of three kinds of Mediterranean fish, bound together with olive oil and truffles. Low-key celebrities who holiday nearby have been known to drop in for lunch on the outdoor terrace.

Au Nouveau Port. ✆ **04-93-01-48-63.** www.restaurantsloop.com. Reservations recommended. Main courses 22€–26€; fixed-price menu 30€. AE, MC, V. Thurs–Tues noon–2pm; Thurs–Mon 7–10pm. Closed mid-Nov to mid-Dec.

BEAULIEU-SUR-MER ★★

939km (582 miles) S of Paris; 9.5km (6 miles) E of Nice; 11km (6¾ miles) W of Monte Carlo

Beaulieu-sur-Mer is a Belle Epoque resort cradled between a bustling pleasure harbor and the beach-lined base of Cap-Ferrat. Its casino and fine restaurants have attracted *bonnes vivantes* since the days of Riviera tourism began. Like many of the more classic resorts along the Côte d'Azur, it is popular with old money holidaymakers and the wintering wealthy.

Essentials

GETTING THERE Most visitors **drive** from Nice on the coastal highway. **Trains** connect Beaulieu with Nice, Monaco, and the rest of the Côte d'Azur every 30 minutes. For **rail** information, call ✆ **36-35** or visit www.voyages-sncf.com. **Bus** line no. 100 from Nice to Monte Carlo also passes through Beaulieu. One-way fares costs 1€.

VISITOR INFORMATION The **Office de Tourisme** is on place Georges Clemenceau (✆ **04-93-01-02-21;** www.beaulieusurmer.fr).

Fun on & off the Beach

Beaulieu has popular public beaches at both ends of town. The beaches aren't as rocky as those in Nice or other nearby resorts, but they're still closer to gravel than to sand. The longer of the two is **Petite Afrique,** just past the yacht harbor. It has a submerged diving platform, a beach bar, and a family-friendly atmosphere. The shorter is **Baie des Fourmis,** which lies beneath the casino at the foot of Cap-Ferrat.

The town is home to an important church, the late-19th-century **Eglise de Sacré-Coeur,** a quasi-Byzantine, quasi-Gothic mishmash at 13 bd. du Maréchal-Leclerc (✆ **04-93-35-70-45**). It's open daily 8am to 7pm. At the same address (same phone) is the 12th-century Romanesque chapel of Santa Maria de Olivo, used mostly for temporary exhibits of painting, sculpture, and civic memorabilia. Unlike the Eglise de Sacré-Coeur, the chapel is not an active house of worship and is open only for special exhibitions.

As you walk along the seafront promenade, you can see many stately Belle Epoque villas that evoke the days when Beaulieu was the height of fashion. Although you can't go inside, you'll see signs for **Villa Namouna,** which once belonged to Gordon Bennett, the owner of the *New York Herald,* and **Villa Léonine,** former home of the marquess of Salisbury.

Villa Kérylos.

For a memorable 90-minute walk, start north of boulevard Edouard-VII, where a path leads up the Riviera escarpment to **Sentier du Plateau St-Michel.** A belvedere here offers panoramic views from Cap-d'Ail to the Estérel. An hour-long alternative is the stroll along **promenade Maurice-Rouvier.** The promenade runs parallel to the water, stretching from Beaulieu to St-Jean. On one side you'll see the most elegant mansions in well-landscaped gardens, including the pink palace of former resident David Niven on place Niven; on the other, views of the Riviera landscape and the peninsular point of St-Hospice.

Villa Kérylos ★★ Jutting out into the Mediterranean is this replica of an ancient Greek residence, painstakingly designed and built by the archaeologist Theodore Reinach. A collection of Greek figurines and ceramics fills the cabinets, while an imposing line of larger-than-life statues line several walls. Also interesting is the reconstructed Greek furniture, much of which would be fashionable today. One curious mosaic depicts the slaying of the Minotaur and provides its own labyrinth. Outside, a series of walkways loops around by the sea.

Rue Gustave-Eiffel. ✆ **04-93-01-01-44.** www.villa-kerylos.com. Admission 8.50€ adults, 6.30€ seniors and children 7–18, free for children 6 and under. Mid-Feb to Oct daily 10am–6pm (until 7pm July–Aug); Nov to mid-Feb Mon–Fri 2–6pm, Sat–Sun 10am–6pm.

Where to Stay

EXPENSIVE

La Réserve de Beaulieu ★★★ This pink-and-white *fin de siècle* palace is one of the Cote d'Azur's most famous hotels. Here you can sit, have an (expensive) aperitif, and watch the sunset while a pianist plays Mozart. A number of the lounges open onto a courtyard with bamboo chairs, grass borders, and urns of flowers. Social life revolves around the main drawing room. Like Beaulieu's classic heritage, the clientele is older and more moneyed than in the Riviera's other glamorous hotels. The individually decorated guest rooms range widely in size and design, but all are large; all feature the most subtle of mod cons, such as Bang & Olufsen televisions and stereos, and push-button room service. Most overlook the Mediterranean, and some have a view of the mountains. Some have private balconies. With a name like Restaurant des Rois (*Restaurant of Kings*), it's obvious that the hotel's double Michelin-starred restaurant is very special, too.

5 bd. du Maréchal-Leclerc, Beaulieu-sur-Mer 06310. www.reservebeaulieu.com. ✆ **04-93-01-00-01.** Fax 04-93-01-28-99. 39 units. 240€–865 € double; 860€–3,320€ suite. AE, DC, MC, V. Parking 36€. Closed mid-Oct to mid-Dec. **Amenities:** Restaurant; bar; babysitting; exercise room; massage; outdoor pool; room service. *In room:* A/C, TV, hair dryer, minibar, free Wi-Fi.

INEXPENSIVE

Hôtel Le Havre Bleu This is a great bargain if you don't require a lot of services and amenities. Le Havre Bleu has one of the prettiest facades of any inexpensive hotel in town. In a former Victorian villa, the hotel has arched ornate windows and a front garden dotted with flowering urns. The impeccable guest rooms are comfortable, functional, and tidy, and all feature satellite television. Many have small outdoor terraces. Breakfast can be served alfresco.

29 bd. du Maréchal-Joffre, Beaulieu-sur-Mer 06310. www.lehavrebleu.com. ✆ **04-93-01-01-40.** Fax 04-93-01-29-92. 20 units. 63€–78€ double. AE, MC, V. Free parking. **Amenities:** Babysitting; room service. *In room:* A/C, TV, free Wi-Fi.

Inter-Hôtel Frisia Most of the Frisia's rooms, decorated in a modern style, open onto views of the harbor. The water-view units are the most expensive. All rooms have small bathrooms, with a combination tub/shower. Two spacious suites with kitchenettes are in free-standing villas near the hotel's main building. Public areas include a sunny garden and inviting lounges. English is widely spoken here, and the management makes foreign guests feel especially welcome. Breakfast is the only meal served, but many reasonably priced restaurants are nearby.

2 bd. Eugène-Gauthier, Beaulieu-sur-Mer 06310. www.frisia-beaulieu.com. ✆ **04-93-01-01-04.** Fax 04-93-01-31-92. 32 units. 57€–135€ double; 110€–195€ suite. AE, MC, V. Parking 9€. Closed Nov 13–Dec 17. **Amenities:** Bar; babysitting; room service; free Wi-Fi. *In room:* A/C, TV, hair dryer, minibar.

Where to Eat

The African Queen ★ FRENCH/INTERNATIONAL Superb food meets a raucous holiday crowd on Beaulieu's bustling port. This ever-popular institution is the meeting point of celebrities, yachties, and the painfully newly rich. The awesome salads are the most popular starters, and it's hard to eat a better bowl of greens on the entire Riviera. The remaining cuisine comes direct from the wood-fired oven: pizzas, fillets of steak, and the African Queen's classy take on the traditional burger.

Port de Plaisance. ✆ **04-93-01-10-85.** www.africanqueen.fr. Reservations recommended. Pizzas 11€–16€; main courses 14€–32€. MC, V. Daily noon–midnight. Closed Oct–Mar.

La Pignatelle FRENCH/PROVENÇAL Even in this expensive town, you can find an excellent, affordable Provençal bistro. Despite its relatively low prices, La Pignatelle prides itself on the fresh ingredients in its robust cuisine. Specialties include mushroom-stuffed ravioli with truffled cream sauce, succulent *soupe de poissons* from which the kitchen has labored to remove the bones, cassoulet of mussels, fricassee of sea bass with shrimp, and *petite friture du pays*, which incorporates small fish using old Provençal traditions.

10 rue de Quincenet. ✆ **04-93-01-03-37.** Reservations recommended. Main courses 9€–27€; fixed-price lunch 22€–32€, dinner 32€. MC, V. Fri–Tues noon–2pm and 7–9:30pm. Closed mid-Nov to mid-Dec.

Les Agaves ★★ MODERN FRENCH One of the most stylish restaurants in Beaulieu is in an early-1900s villa across the street from the railway station. It's also one of the most reliable and highly rated, despite its relatively moderate prices. Of note are curry-enhanced scallops with garlic-flavored tomatoes and parsley, lobster salad with mango, ravioli with flap mushrooms, chopped shrimp with Provençal herbs, and several preparations of foie gras. Filet of sea bass with truffles and champagne sauce is delectable. Les Agaves is a hit with visiting restaurant critics, actors, and the Monaco royal family.

4 av. Maréchal Foch. ✆ **04-93-01-13-12.** Reservations required. Main courses 24€–40€; fixed-price menu 38€. AE, MC, V. Daily 7–10pm. Closed Nov 15–Dec 20.

Beaulieu After Dark

Sir Winston Churchill was once a regular at the Art Deco **Grand Casino de Beaulieu,** 4 av. Fernand-Dunan (✆ **04-93-76-48-00**). The house still encourages jackets for men in its fancier areas. It requires that patrons show a passport. The slot machine section, where dress is more casual, is free to enter and doesn't require identification. Of note is the casino's summertime gaming room, where poker and roulette are played under the stars, just across from the Baie des Fourmis beach.

EZE & LA TURBIE ★★

942km (584 miles) S of Paris; 11km (6¾ miles) NE of Nice

The hamlets of Eze and La Turbie, 6.5km (4 miles) apart, are picture-perfect hill villages that literally cling to the mountains. Both have fortified medieval cores overlooking the coast, and both were built during the early Middle Ages to stave off raids from Saracen pirates. In Eze's case, it's now tour buses, not coastal raiders, that make daily invasions into town. Its impossibly cute streets contain galleries, boutiques, and artisans' shops. La Turbie is much more authentic and offers a welcome respite from the coast's summertime heat.

Eze is accessible on the Moyenne (Middle) Corniche, La Turbie by way of the Grande (Upper) Corniche. Both are spellbindingly pretty routes. Signs along the coastal road indicate the direction motorists should take to reach either village.

Aside from its pretty lanes, the leading attraction in Eze is the **Jardin d'Eze ★**, boulevard du Jardin-Exotique (✆ **04-93-41-10-30**), a showcase of exotic plants in Eze-Village, at the pinnacle of the town's highest hill. Admission is 5€ for adults, 2.50€ for students and ages 12 to 25, and free for children 11 and under. In July and August, it's open daily 9am to 8pm; the rest of the year, it opens daily at 9am and closes between 5 and 7pm, depending on the time of sunset.

La Turbie boasts a ruined monument erected by Roman emperor Augustus in 6 B.C., the **Trophée des Alps (Trophy of the Alps)** ★. It's near a rock formation known as La Tête de Chien, at the highest point along the Grand Corniche, 450m (1,476 ft.) above sea level. The Roman Senate ordered the creation of the monument, which many locals call La Trophée d'Auguste, to celebrate the subjugation of the people of the French Alps by the Roman armies.

Trophée des Alps.

A short distance from the monument is the **Musée du Trophée d'Auguste,** rue Albert-1er, La Turbie (✆ **04-93-41-20-84**), a mini-museum containing finds from digs nearby and information about the monument's restoration. Both the trophy enclosure and the museum are open Tuesday to Sunday mid-May to mid-September 9:30am to 1pm and 2:30 to 6:30pm, and mid-September to mid-June 10am to 1:30pm and 2:30 to 5pm. Admission to both sites is 4.20€ for adults and free for children 17 and under.

The **Office de Tourisme** is on place du Général-de-Gaulle, Eze-Village (✆ **04-93-41-26-00;** fax 04-93-41-04-80; www.eze-riviera.com).

Where to Stay

Hostellerie du Château de la Chèvre d'Or ★★★ This is one of the grandest resort hotels along the eastern Riviera, and a favorite of royalty and A-list celebrities. The miniature-village retreat was built in the 1920s in neo-Gothic style. The decor of the "Golden Goat" maintains its character while adding modern comfort. Each sumptuously decorated suite is essentially a grand apartment with an expansive view of the coastline. La Chèvre d'Or boasts a variety of restaurants dotted across its outdoor terraces serving classic French and Asian cuisine. The best is its fabulous signature restaurant, which boasts two Michelin stars. Even if you don't eat or spend the night, try to visit for a drink in the lounge, which has a panoramic view.

Rue du Barri, Eze-Village 06360. www.chevredor.com. ✆ **04-92-10-66-66.** Fax 04-93-41-06-72. 36 units. 280€–760€ double; 660€–2,900€ suite. AE, DC, MC, V. Closed Dec–Feb. **Amenities:** 4 restaurants; bar; babysitting; exercise room; outdoor pool; room service; sauna. *In room:* A/C, TV, hair dryer, minibar, free Wi-Fi.

Where to Eat

Le Troubadour FRENCH/PROVENÇAL The stone-fronted medieval house that contains this well-known restaurant has, since World War I, housed businesses that have included a bar, a delicatessen, and the local post office. Today, within three dining rooms, each accented with thick ceiling beams, you can order succulent and flavorful dishes that include braised rabbit served with warm hearts of artichoke, foie gras, and carrots; a delightful filet of John Dory with stuffed and deep-fried zucchini blossoms; and other dishes that each manage to showcase some aspect of the Mediterranean diet. You'll find the place close to the village church, in the upper heights of Eze Village.

4 rue du Brec, Eze Village. ✆ **04-93-41-19-03.** Reservations recommended. Main courses 22€–38€; fixed-price menus 39€–52€. MC, V. Tues–Sat 12:30–2pm and 7:30–9:30pm. Closed mid-Nov to mid-Dec.

MONACO ★★

939km (582 miles) S of Paris; 18km (11 miles) E of Nice

As a tableau on the Rock of Monaco explains, this sunny stretch of coast became the property of the Grimaldi clan in 1297 when one Francesco Grimaldi tricked his way into the fortress protecting the harbor. The dynasty has maintained something resembling independence ever since. In a fit of impatience, the French annexed it in 1793, but the ruling family recovered it in 1814.

Hemmed in by France on three sides and the Mediterranean on the fourth, this feudal anomaly is arguably the world's richest country per capita. And as almost everybody knows, the Monégasques do not pay taxes. Nearly all their country's revenue comes from banking, tourism, and gambling. Better still, in an astute feat of cunning, local residents aren't allowed to gamble away their inheritance, so visitors must bring a passport to play on the Principality's famed poker, roulette, and blackjack tables.

Monaco, or, more precisely, its capital of Monte Carlo, has for a century been a symbol of glamour. The 1956 marriage of Prince Rainier III to American actress Grace Kelly enhanced its status. She met the prince when she was in Cannes to promote *To Catch a Thief*. Their daughter Caroline was born in 1957; a son, Albert, in 1958; and a second daughter, Stephanie, in 1965. The Monégasques welcomed the birth of Caroline but went wild for Albert, a male heir. According to a 1918 treaty, Monaco would become an autonomous state under French protection, should the ruling dynasty become extinct. Though not always happy in her role, Princess Grace won the respect and admiration of her people. The Monégasques still mourn her death in a 1982 car accident on the Moyenne Corniche, near La Turbie.

In April 2005, Prince Rainier died after suffering ailing health for many years. Upon his father's death, Prince Albert became the reigning prince. Unlike his father's storybook marriage to Grace Kelly, Albert remained unmarried and heirless, even though he's admitted to having a son out of wedlock. (His illegitimate son cannot ascend to the throne.) Fortunately for the Grimaldi line, Albert proposed to his girlfriend, South African swimmer Charlene Wittstock, in 2010. As part of the marriage preparation she learned the Monégasque dialect and converted to Albert's Catholic faith. She assumed the title of Her Serene Highness when the couple tied the knot in July 2011.

The second-smallest state in Europe (Vatican City is the tiniest), Monaco consists of four parts. The old town, **Monaco-Ville,** on a promontory, "the Rock," 60m (197 ft.) high, is the seat of the royal palace and the government building, as well as the Oceanographic Museum. To the west, **La Condamine** is at the foot of the old town, forming its ritzy harbor and port sector. Up from the port (Monaco is steep) is **Monte Carlo,** once the playground of royalty and still the center for the wintering wealthy, the setting for the casino, and the luxurious hotels. The fourth part, **Fontvieille,** is a neat industrial suburb.

Monaco used to be slow in summer, but now July and August tend to be so crowded that it's hard to get a room. Dine alfresco, and you'll be passed by a motorcade of Bugattis, Lamborghinis, and Rolls Royces (regular Porches and Mercedes are considered parvenu here). As always, you can lose your shirt at the gaming tables year-round. "Suicide Terrace" at the casino, though not used as frequently as in the old days, is still a real temptation to many.

Once defined by Somerset Maugham as "370 sunny acres peopled with shady characters," Monaco has complemented its private banking income with high-tech industries, leisure dollars, and cultural tourism in recent years. New museums like the Villa Paloma and Villa Sauber have sprung up, and the dining scene is now superb (if on the expensive side). A new wave of celebrities have taken up (tax-free) residency, including Claudia Schiffer, Boris Becker, and Michael Schumacher.

Essentials

GETTING THERE Monaco has rail, bus, and highway connections from other coastal cities, especially Nice. There are no border formalities when entering Monaco from mainland France. The 19km (12 miles) **drive** from Nice takes around 30 minutes and runs along the N7 Moyenne Corniche. The pretty D6098 coast road takes a little longer. Ligne d'Azur (✆ **08-10-06-10-06;** www.lignedazur.com) runs a **bus** service at 15-minute intervals aboard line no. 100 from Nice to Monte Carlo. One-way bus transit from Nice costs 1€. **Trains** arrive every 30 minutes from Cannes, Nice, Menton, and Antibes. For more rail information, call ✆ **36-35** or visit www.voyages-sncf.com. Monaco's underground railway station (Gare SNCF) is on place St-Devote. A system of pedestrian tunnels, escalators, and elevators riddle the Principality, and such an underground walkway links the train station to Monte Carlo. If you'd rather take a **taxi** but can't find one at the station, call ✆ **08-20-20-98-98.**

CAM (✆ **97-70-22-22;** www.cam.mc) runs buses inside the Principality. Lines nos. 1 and 2 link Monaco-Ville with the Casino area. CAM's **shuttle boat** hops between the banks of Monaco's port every 20 minutes. The ride is great for kids and connects the Casino area with foot of Monaco-Ville. All CAM tickets cost 1€.

Monaco Dialing Tips

To call Monaco from within France, dial 00 (the access code for all international long-distance calls from France), followed by the **country code, 377;** and then the eight-digit local phone number. (Don't dial the 33 code; that's the country code for France.)

To call Monaco from North America, dial the international access code, 011; the country code, 377; and then the eight-digit Monaco number.

To call any other country from within Monaco, dial 00 (the international access code), then the applicable country code, and the number. For example, to call Cannes, you would dial 00, 33 (France's country code), 4 (the city code, without the zero), and the eight-digit number.

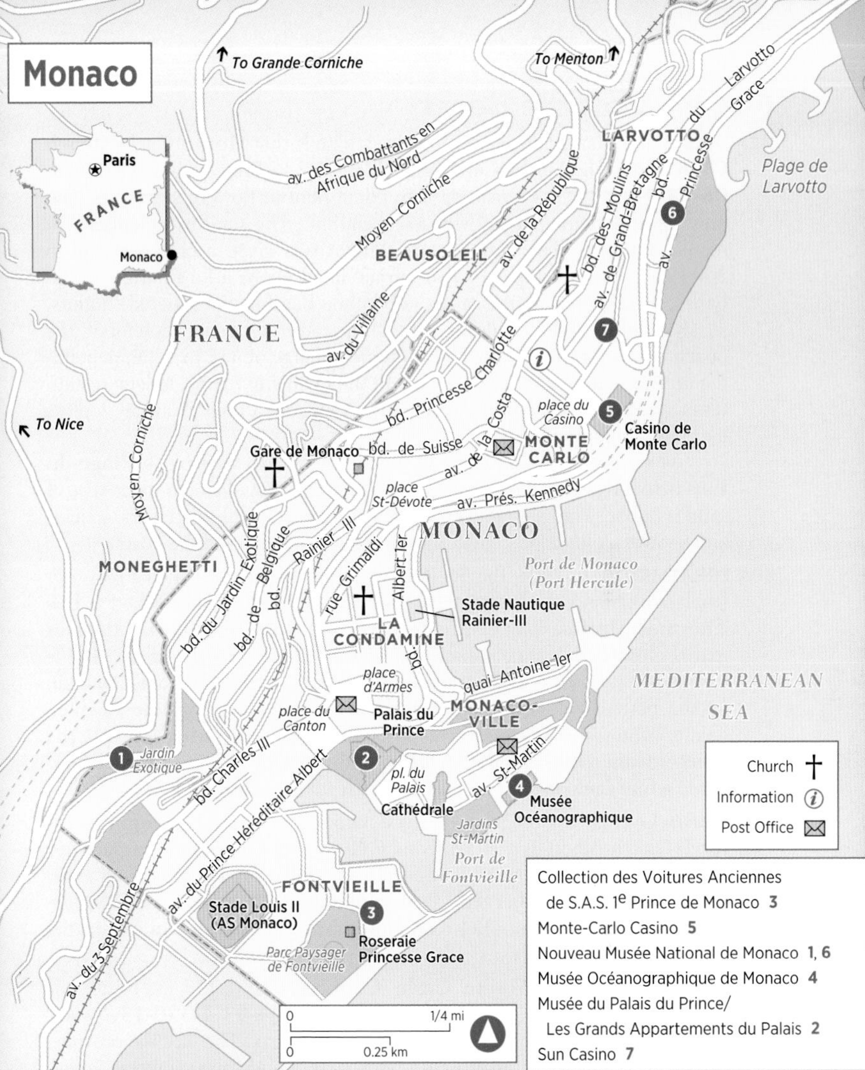

VISITOR INFORMATION The **Direction du Tourisme et des Congrés** office is at 2A bd. des Moulins (✆ **92-16-61-16;** fax 92-16-60-00; www.visitmonaco.com).

SPECIAL EVENTS Two of the most-watched **car-racing events** in Europe are in January (Le Rallye) and May (the Grand Prix). The **Monte-Carlo Masters** ATP tennis tournament (www.monte-carlorolexmasters.com) takes place in April. The **Monte-Carlo International Fireworks Festival** lasts all summer long. The skies above the harbor are lit up several times a week as millions of euros go up in smoke, courtesy of those who can assuredly afford it.

Fun on & off the Beach

BEACHES Just outside the border, on French soil, the **Monte-Carlo Beach Club** adjoins the Monte-Carlo Beach Hotel, 22 av. Princesse-Grace (© **98-06-54-54**). Princess Grace used to come here in flowery swimsuits, and now it's an integral part of Monaco social life. The sand is replenished at regular intervals. The entire establishment was given a chic overhaul in 2009 and now encompasses two mosaic-lined pools, a La Prairie spa, cabanas, two cool restaurants, and the Bambou Bar. Activities include donuts, jet skis, and parachute rides. As the temperature drops in September, the beach closes for the winter. The admission charge of 45€ to 120€, depending on the season, grants you access to the changing rooms, toilets, restaurants, and bar, along with use of a mattress for sunbathing. As usual, topless bathing is common.

More low-key swimming and sunbathing is also available at **Plage du Larvotto,** off avenue Princesse-Grace. Part of this popular man-made strip of sand is public. The other part contains private beach clubs with bars, snacks, and showers, plus a kids' club. A jogging track runs behind the beach.

SPA TREATMENTS In 1908, the Société des Bains de Mer launched a seawater (thalassotherapy) spa in Monte Carlo, inaugurated by Prince Albert I. **Les Thermes Marins,** 2 av. de Monte-Carlo (© **98-06-69-00;** www.thermesmarinsmontecarlo.com), is now one of the largest spas in Europe and is wellness at its most chic. Spread over four floors is a pool, Turkish hammam (steam bath), healthy restaurant, juice bar, tanning booths, fitness center, beauty center, and private treatment rooms. A day pass, giving access to the sauna, steam rooms, fitness facilities, and pools, costs 90€. Therapies include a four-handed *affusion* massage with warm seawater for 85€.

SWIMMING Overlooking the yacht-clogged harbor, the **Stade Nautique Rainier-III,** quai Albert-1er, at La Condamine (© **93-30-64-83**), a pool frequented by the Monégasques, was a gift from Prince Rainier to his subjects. It's open May to October daily 9am to 6pm (until 8pm July–Aug). Admission costs 5€ per person. Between November and April, it's an ice-skating rink.

TENNIS & SQUASH The **Monte Carlo Country Club,** 155 av. Princesse-Grace, Roquebrune–Cap Martin, France (© **04-93-41-30-15;** www.mccc.mc), has 21 clay and 2 concrete tennis courts. The 42€ fee provides access to a restaurant, health club with Jacuzzi and sauna, putting green, beach, squash courts, and well-maintained tennis courts. Guests of the hotels administered by the Société des Bains de Mer (Hôtel de Paris, Hermitage, Monte Carlo Bay, and Monte Carlo Beach Club) pay half-price. It's open daily 8am to 8 or 9pm, depending on the season.

Shopping

If you insist on the likes of Hermès, Gucci, and Lanvin, you'll find them cheek by jowl with the Hôtel de Paris and the casino, lining the streets leading to the Hôtel Hermitage. **Allée Serge-Diaghilev** is just that, an alley, but a very tiny one filled with designer shops.

Adonis, 35 av. Princess-Grace (© **93-50-57-04**), stocks this season's Jil Sander, Chloé, and Marni for this season's prices. For less expensive bags, head to designer outlet **Stock Griffe,** 5 bis av. St-Michel (© **93-50-86-06**). It slashes prices on Prada, Pucci, Escada, and the like. The place may be small, but not the discounts, some of which add up to an astonishing 90%. The prize for Monaco's hippest store goes to **Lull,** 29 rue de Millo (✆ **97-77-54-54**), which is awash with labels like Dries Van Noten and Raf Simmons. It has a clothes re-engineering workshop to the rear.

Boutique du Rocher, 1 av. de la Madone (✆ **93-30-91-17**), is the larger of two boutiques Princess Grace opened in 1966 as the official retail outlets of her charitable foundation. The organization merchandises Monégasque and Provençal handicrafts. A short walk from place du Casino, the shop sells carved frames for pictures or mirrors; housewares; gift items crafted from porcelain, textiles, and wood; toys; and dolls.

The Galeries du Métropole also has a few specialty shops worth visiting. Check out **Manufacture de Monaco** (✆ **93-50-64-63**) for glorious bone china and elegant tabletop items. Two doors away is a branch of the chic but often affordable French linen house **Yves Delorme** (✆ **93-50-08-70**). **Royal Food** (✆ **93-15-05-04**) is a gourmet grocery store, which you'll find down a set of curving stairs hidden in the side entrance of the mall; here you can buy food from France, Lebanon, and the United States, or stock up for *le pique-nique* or for day trips.

For real-people shopping, stroll **rue Grimaldi,** the principality's most commercial street, near the fruit, flower, and food market (see below); and **boulevard des Moulins,** closer to the casino, where you'll see glamorous boutiques. There's also a pedestrian thoroughfare with shops less forbiddingly chic than those along boulevard des Moulins: **Rue Princesse-Caroline** is loaded with bakeries, flower shops, and the closest thing you'll find to funkiness in Monaco. Also check out the **Formule 1** shop, 15 rue Grimaldi (✆ **93-15-92-44**), where everything from racing helmets to specialty key chains and T-shirts celebrates the roaring, high-octane racing machines.

MARKETS For a look at the heart and soul of the real Monaco, head to place des Armes for the **fruit, flower, and food market,** which starts daily at 7:30am. The indoor and outdoor market has a fountain, cafes, and hand-painted vegetable tiles beneath your feet. The outdoor market packs up at noon, and some dealers at the indoor market stay open until 2pm.

Seeing the Sights

Collection des Voitures Anciennes de S.A.S. le Prince de Monaco ☺ Prince Rainier III opened a showcase of his private collection of more than 100 vintage autos, including the 1956 Rolls-Royce Silver Cloud that carried the prince and princess on their wedding day. Monaco shopkeepers gave it to the royal couple as a wedding present. A 1952 Austin Taxi on display was once used as the royal "family car." Other exhibits are a "woodie" (a 1937 Ford station wagon Prince Louis II used on hunting trips); a 1925 Bugatti 35B, winner of the Monaco Grand Prix in 1929; a 1903 De Dion Bouton; and a 1986 Lamborghini Countach.

Les Terrasses de Fontvieille. ✆ **92-05-28-56.** www.palais.mc. Admission 6€ adults, 3€ students and children 8–14, free for children 7 and under. Daily 10am–6pm. Closed Christmas.

Les Grands Appartements du Palais ★ Most summer day-trippers want to see the home of Monaco's royal family, the Palais du Prince, which dominates the principality from the Rock. A tour of the Grands Appartements allows you a glimpse of the Throne Room and some of the art, including works by Bruegel and Holbein, as well as Princess Grace's state portrait. The palace was built in the 13th century, and part dates from the Renaissance. The ideal time to arrive is 11:55am, to watch the 10-minute **Relève de la Garde (Changing of the Guard).**

Place du Palais. ✆ **93-25-18-31.** www.palais.mc. Admission 7€ adults, 3.50€ children 8–14, free for children 7 and under. Daily Apr 10:30am–6pm; May–Sept 9:30am–6:30pm; Oct 10am–5:30pm. Closed Nov–Mar.

Musée Océanographique de Monaco ★★ ☺ Albert I, great-grandfather of the present prince, founded this museum in 1910. You'll see models of the ships aboard which he directed his scientific cruises from 1885 to 1914. Some of the exotic creatures he found on travels were unknown before he captured them. Skeletons of specimens, including a whale that drifted ashore in 1896, are on the main floor. An exhibition devoted to the discovery of the ocean is in the physical-oceanography room on the first floor. Underwater movies are shown in the lecture room. There is also a shark lagoon and over 90 aquariums re-creating tropical reefs, arctic zones, and jellyfish feeding grounds.

Av. St-Martin. ✆ **93-15-36-00.** www.oceano.mc. Admission 13€ adults, 6€ children 6–18, free for children 5 and under. Apr–June and Sept daily 9:30am–7pm; July–Aug daily 9:30am–7:30pm; Oct–Mar daily 10am–6pm.

Nouveau Musée National de Monaco ★★ The Villa Sauber and the Villa Paloma, two stunning new art spaces set in palatial former homes, opened in summer 2010. Both make up the Nouveau Musée National de Monaco although they are set on the other side of the city—well, country, actually—from each other. They explore contemporary art themes by way of paintings, sculpture, and installations. The exhibitions that have been carried in so far have been magnificent, and such is the pulling power of these state-backed galleries.

Villa Sauber, 17 av. Princess-Grace; Villa Paloma, 56 bd. du Jardin Exotique. ✆ **98-98-16-82.** www.nmnm.mc. Admission to both 6€ adults, 3€ children 6–18, free for children 5 and under. Daily 10am–6pm.

Where to Stay

VERY EXPENSIVE

Hôtel de Paris ★★★ On the resort's main plaza, opposite the casino, this is one of the world's most famous hotels. Elegant fabrics, classic accessories, and one of the finest restaurants in France (see Louis XV, p. 623) combine to make this a favorite of the world's most discerning travelers. The fabulous Art Nouveau lobby is fresh from a sympathetic renovation in 2011 and includes statues and crystal chandeliers. Leading off is Le Bar Americain, a classic wood-paneled watering hole lined with photos of Monaco's greatest patrons, among them Cary Grant and Grace Kelly. The guest rooms come in two principal styles: period and contemporary. Some units are enormous. Bathrooms are awash with marble and elegant brass fittings and are stocked with La Prairie products. Most fabulous of all are the Garnier Suite, which overlooks place du Casino and is the ultimate stage for watching the Formula One Grand Prix; and the Churchill Suite, overlooking the harbor, where the former British Prime Minister's furniture still resides. Additional restaurants include Michelin-starred Le Grill, which has an electronic roof that slides opens to the heavens, and the Côté Jardin, a Mediterranean restaurant spilling onto private gardens.

Musée Océanographique de Monaco.

Place du Casino, Monaco 98007. www.montecarloresort.com. ✆ **98-06-30-00.** Fax 98-06-59-56. 182 units. 425€–960€ double; from 775€ suite. AE, DC, MC, V. Valet parking 32€. **Amenities:** 3 restaurants (see "Where to Eat," below); bar; babysitting; concierge; exercise room; large indoor pool; room service; sauna; Thermes Marins spa offering thalassotherapy. *In room:* A/C, TV, hair dryer, minibar, Wi-Fi (20€ per day).

Hôtel Hermitage ★★ The Hermitage, with its wedding-cake facade, was the creation of Jean Marquet (who also created marquetry). This five-star cliff-top hotel has long been the most subtly elegant of all Monaco's most deluxe establishments. Since 2010, it has gone a stage further, thanks to the addition of a stylish new wine bar (Crystal) and modern gastronomic restaurant (Vistamar). A new courtyard garden was created in 2011. The main Beaumarchais lobby is a vision of timeless grace, with a lounge, tearoom, and boutiques. It's connected to the winter lobby—an additional public room under a glass cupola where breakfast is now served—by the mosaic-lined Prince's Corridor. Winding up several classic staircases are a series of decadent yet comfy guest rooms, plus private wings for those with a large entourage. Of the several jaw-dropping suites, our favorite is the one that boasts a glass staircase leading up to a private roof terrace overlooking the harbor (it has its own open-air Jacuzzi, too).

Square Beaumarchais, Monaco 98005. www.montecarloresort.com. ✆ **98-06-40-00.** Fax 98-06-59-70. 280 units. 385€–940€ double; from 640€ junior suite; from 1,600€ suite. AE, DC, MC, V. Parking 34€. **Amenities:** Restaurant; bar; babysitting; concierge; exercise room; large indoor pool; room service; sauna; Thermes Marins spa offering thalassotherapy. *In room:* A/C, TV, hair dryer, minibar, Wi-Fi (20€ per day).

EXPENSIVE

Fairmont Monte Carlo ★ A vision of modern opulence that hugs one of the most valuable pieces of real estate on the Côte d'Azur. The Fairmont is the pinnacle of comfortable luxury: Guests may wear casual dress at dinner yet still expect exemplary service from the multilingual team of staff. The hotel was architecturally daring when built in 1975: Some of its foundations were sunk into the seabed, and some of the Principality's busiest highways (including part of Monaco's F1 Grand Prix track) sweep beneath it. The resort is viewed as an integral part of Monégasque life, especially since its recent renovation, which was completed in 2010. It contains Monaco's highest concentration of restaurants, bars, and nightclubs including the Horizon Deck rooftop restaurant (open summer only) and the Saphir Bar (open 24 hr.); both have heart-stopping panoramic views that stretch all the way over the Italian border. The restaurant, L'Argentin, is a South American steakhouse, with a fabulous wine list and similar views. The guest rooms and suites are furnished in contemporary style with a maritime theme. Many benefit from sea views, terraces, and lashings of fine Italian marble.

12 av. des Spélugues, Monaco 98007. www.fairmont.com/montecarlo. ✆ **93-50-65-00.** Fax 93-30-01-57. 602 units. 249€–869€ double; from 1,500€ suite. AE, DC, MC, V. Parking 38€. **Amenities:** 3 restaurants; 2 bars; babysitting; concierge; health club; 2 outdoor pools; room service; spa. *In room:* A/C, TV, hair dryer, minibar, Wi-Fi (20€ per day or free if you enroll in the Fairfont President Club at no charge at check-in)..

Monte Carlo Bay Hotel & Resort ★★★ Occupying a 4-hectare (10-acre) Mediterranean garden, this is a plush garden of Eden in the principality. It's the most child-friendly and business-friendly of all the Monaco hotels. Vast lagoons, pools, exotic gardens, the Cinq Mondes spa, and an indoor pool covered with a monumental glass dome are linked by a network of teak footbridges. A network of five restaurants, bars, and a summer casino round out the complex. Of the beautifully furnished bedrooms, more than three-quarters of them open onto sea views. Rooms are decorated with white-oak furnishings, often sandstone floors, and soft Mediterranean pastels.

40 av. Princesse-Grace, Monaco 98000. www.montecarlobay.com. ✆ **98-06-02-00.** Fax 98-06-00-03. 334 units. 325€–800€ double; 830€–2,500€ suite. AE, DC, MC, V. Parking 30€. **Amenities:** 4 restaurants; 2 bars; nightclub; casino; disco; babysitting; concierge; exercise rooms; 3 pools (indoor, outdoor, and children's); spa. *In room:* A/C, TV, hair dryer, minibar, Wi-Fi (20€ per day).

MODERATE

Ni Hôtel ★ Monaco's newest, coolest offering occupies two grand apartments a few blocks back from the port. Guest rooms are minimalist creations with crisp white sheets, cubelike desks, and contemporary art on the walls. Duplex suites have kitchenettes, Nespresso machines, and an outdoor terrace. There are shades of overdesign in the hotel's starkness and layout, not least in the dark lobby, where staff have to continually warn guests about the changes in gradient. But overall, this is a fine, hip, well-priced addition to the local hotel scene.

1 bis rue Grimaldi, Monaco 98000. www.nihotel.com. ✆ **97-97-51-51.** Fax 97-97-51-52. 15 units. 150€–260€ double; from 350€ suite. AE, DC, MC, V. **Amenities:** Bar. *In room:* A/C, TV, hair dryer, minibar, free Wi-Fi.

INEXPENSIVE

Hôtel de France Not all Monégasques are rich, as a stroll along workaday rue de la Turbie will convince you. Here you'll find some of the cheapest accommodations and eateries in the high-priced Principality. This 19th-century hotel, 3 minutes from the rail station, has modest furnishings but is well kept and comfortable, and should benefit greatly from its thorough renovation in 2011, which was ongoing at the time of writing. The guest rooms and bathrooms are small, and each unit has a shower.

6 rue de la Turbie, Monaco 98000. www.monte-carlo.mc/france. ✆ **93-30-24-64.** Fax 92-16-13-34. 27 units. 110€–130€ double. Rates include breakfast. MC, V. **Amenities:** Bar; room service. *In room:* TV, hair dryer, free Wi-Fi.

Where to Eat

VERY EXPENSIVE

Le Louis XV ★★★ MEDITERRANEAN In the Hôtel de Paris, the Louis XV offers one of the finest dining experiences in southern France. Superstar chef Alain Ducasse oversees the refined but not overly adorned cuisine. The restaurant's head chef can be seen in Nice's market at dawn purchasing local cheeses, or wandering through the corridors of the Hôtel de Paris carrying white truffles purchased from over the Italian border. Everything is light and attuned to the seasons, with intelligent, modern interpretations of Provençal and northern Italian dishes. You'll find chargrilled breast of baby pigeon with sautéed duck liver, and an ongoing specialty known as Provençal vegetables with crushed truffles. All is served under a magnificent frescoed ceiling, which also includes the portraits of Louis XV's six mistresses. Service is easily best in the principality, and each diner routinely uses 50 individual pieces of cutlery.

In the Hôtel de Paris, place du Casino. ✆ **98-06-88-64.** Reservations recommended. Jacket and tie recommended for men. Main courses 80€–120€; fixed-price lunch 140€, dinner 210€–280€. AE, MC, V. Thurs–Mon 12:15–1:45pm and 8–9:45pm; also June–Sept Wed 12:15–1:45pm. Closed Feb 9–24.

EXPENSIVE

Beefbar ★ STEAK/FRENCH One patron said that this restaurant buzzes with a "polyglot crowd of dealmakers, socialites, and pre-club beauties," and so it does. A chic crowd comes to this elegant salon overlooking the Mediterranean to feast on everything from Argentine steaks to raw fish specials, the menu backed up by the best collection of Bordeaux in Monaco. The chef claims he selects only "the most noble pieces" from the slaughterhouses of the world, mostly from the United States, Argentina, and the Netherlands. The chef's Black Angus beef from Kansas is some of the best you are likely to find in the south of France. Noncarnivorous choices include shrimp tartare and asparagus gnocchi.

42 quai Jean-Charles Rey. ✆ **97-77-09-29.** www.beefbar.com. Reservations required. Main courses 21€–78€; fixed-price menu 39€–90€. AE, MC, V. Daily noon–2:30pm and 8–11pm.

Le Café de Paris ★ TRADITIONAL FRENCH Its *plats du jour* are well prepared, and its location, the plaza adjacent to the casino and the Hôtel de Paris, allows a front-row view of the comings and goings of the Principality's nerve center. Despite its very public location, this 1985 re-creation of old-time Monaco still attracts the stars and a sampling of Monte-Carlo old money. Hors d'oeuvre platters include steak tartare, carpaccio of beef, and gambas fricassée. Mains are mostly very classic: sautéed veal escalope, grilled sea bass and, as a very un-French addition, hamburger.

Place du Casino. ✆ **98-06-76-23.** Reservations recommended. Main courses 12€–40€; fixed-price menu 35€. AE, DC, MC, V. Daily 8am–2am.

INEXPENSIVE

Adagio ★ 🎁 MODERN ITALIAN This contemporary restaurant has been a hugely popular addition to Monaco's modern dining scene since autumn 2010. Smart wooden tables are set against lightly adorned white walls in a sunlight-filled dining room. Granted, it's a 10-minute hike north of the harbor, but Adagio's bargain set-lunch menu, complete with coffee and a generous slug of wine, has some locals calling it their second home. Simple starters include tuna and fresh fava bean salad, and *ravioli di verdure;* equally uncomplicated mains range from roast beef and green beans to *papillotes* of salmon.

1 rue Biovès. ✆ **97-98-15-56.** Main courses 12€–20€; fixed-price lunch 15€. AE, MC, V. Mon-Fri noon–2:30pm and 7:30–11pm; Sat 7:30-11pm.

Stella Polaris ITALIAN The Stella won't win any awards for haute cuisine, but for quality Italian cuisine at honest prices, it's hard to beat. And its open dining room, which spills out onto Monaco harbor and the Formula One Grand Prix racetrack, is surely prize-winning in itself. Freshly cooked pizzas, pastas, and grilled meats are served with inexpensive Italian red and white wines.

3 av. President Kennedy. ✆ **93-30-88-63.** Main courses 8€–17€; pizzas 9€–12€. MC, V. Daily noon–3pm and 7pm–midnight.

Monaco After Dark

CASINOS & CULTURE The **Monte-Carlo Casino,** place du Casino (✆ **98-06-20-00;** www.montecarlocasinos.com), is one the most famous in the world. Its creation by architect Charles Garnier (of Paris Opera house fame) in

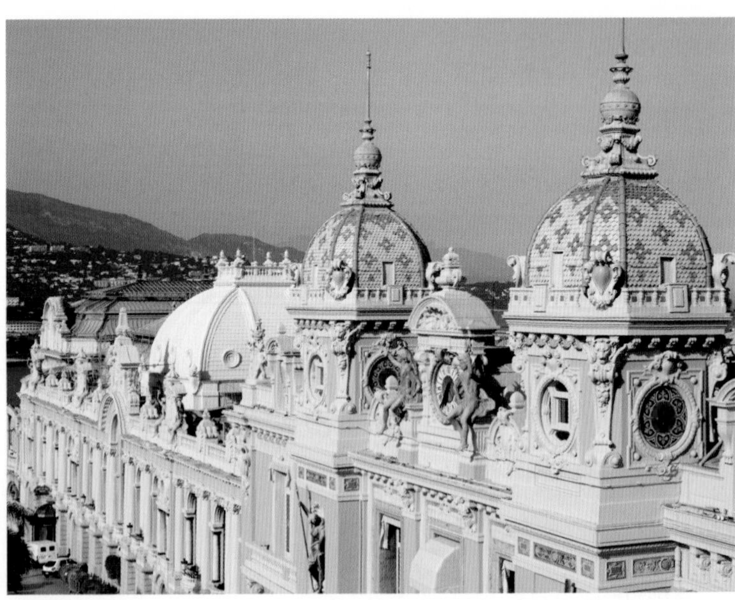

Monte-Carlo Casino.

1863 turned the tables for Monaco, turning a weary port into a world-class destination.

The building encompasses the casino and other areas for different kinds of entertainment, including a theater (Opéra de Monte-Carlo; see below) presenting opera, ballet, and jazz, plus the new Buddha Bar (see "Dancing & Drinking," below).

The casino's marble-floored **Atrium,** containing only slot machines, opens at 2pm Monday to Friday, noon on weekends. Doors for roulette and *trente et quarante* in the rococo **Salon Europe** open at the same time, or at 3pm for private players. Blackjack opens in the hallowed **Salle des Amériques** at 5pm (2pm weekends). The gambling continues until very late (or early), depending on the crowd. The casino classifies its "private rooms" as the more demure, nonelectronic areas without slots. To enter the casino, you must show a passport or other photo ID and be at least 18. After 8pm, the staff will insist that men wear jackets and neckties for entrance to the private rooms. Entrance costs 10€ to anywhere past the Atrium; 20€ to the Salons Privés. And entrance to the Les Salons Supers Privés? It's by invitation only (they've got our number).

No dress code or entry fee applies in the **Café de Paris Casino,** place du Casino (✆ **98-06-77-77**), across the square. Video gaming machines open at 10am, with roulette and blackjack tables in operation from 8pm.

The **Opéra de Monte-Carlo** (✆ **98-06-28-28;** www.opera.mc) is headquartered in the lavish, recently renovated Belle Epoque **Salle Garnier** of the casino. Tickets to the operas and other events scheduled inside range from 20€ to 120€. Tickets to events within the Salle Garnier are available from a kiosk outside the Café de Paris Casino; tickets can be purchased Tuesday to Saturday from 10am to 5:30pm.

The **Grimaldi Forum,** 10 av. Princesse-Grace (✆ **99-99-20-00;** www.grimaldiforum.com), is Monaco's live entertainment showpiece. It lines up big-name jazz acts, ballet, chamber music, rock, and even house music DJs. Regular exhibitions also take place here. Concert and performance tickets cost 20€ to 150€.

DANCING & DRINKING Monaco's three newest bars are currently its most hopping. **Buddha Bar** (✆ **98-06-19-19**), in the Monte-Carlo Casino complex, is bedecked with chinoiserie, Asian statues, and a raised DJ booth. It attracts a classy crowd from 7pm onward. Since 2009, **Ni Bar,** 1 bis rue Grimaldi (✆ **97-97-51-51**), has pulled in a trendy post-work crowd for two-for-one cocktails from 6 to 8pm, with DJs playing into the night. Head upstairs to the roof terrace in summer. **Café Llorca,** in the Grimaldi Forum, 10 av. Princesse-Grace (✆ **99-99-20-00**), opened in December 2010. It combines a smart bistro run by top Riviera chef Alain Llora, with an upscale bar overlooking the Mediterranean.

For sheer class, the new **Crystal Bar** (✆ **98-06-98-98**), inside the Hôtel Hermitage, pulls out all the stops. Elegant dress, vintage champagne, and the odd feather boa sets the scene. It opens from noon until 1am. Under the same management is timeless **Jimmy's,** in the Sporting d'Eté, avenue Princesse-Grace (✆ **92-16-22-77**), open nightly 11pm to 5am. It's a nightly blowout of champagne-laced celebrity culture and rocking music.

ROQUEBRUNE & CAP-MARTIN ★★

Roquebrune: 953km (591 miles) S of Paris, 7km (4½ miles) W of Menton, 58km (36 miles) NE of Cannes, 3km (1¾ miles) E of Monaco. Cap-Martin: 4km (2½ miles) W of Menton, 2.5km (1½ miles) W of Roquebrune.

Roquebrune, along the Grande Corniche, is a charming mountain village with vaulted streets. The views over the Mediterranean are immense. Artists' workshops and boutiques with their pricey merchandise line rue Moncollet.

Down the hill from Roquebrune, Cap-Martin is a pine-covered peninsula, long associated with the rich and famous since the empress Eugénie wintered here in the 19th century. In time, the resort was honored by the presence of Sir Winston Churchill, who came here often in his final years. The long, pebbly plage de la Buse lies underneath Roquebrune–Cap-Martin train station. Its tranquillity is disturbed only by the odd paraglider looping down to the beach from Roquebrune village.

Essentials

GETTING THERE To **drive** to Roquebrune and Cap-Martin from Nice, follow N7 east for 26km (16 miles). Cap-Martin has **train** and bus connections from the other cities on the coast, including Nice and Menton. For **railway** information and schedules, call ✆ **36-35** or visit www.voyages-sncf.com. To reach Roquebrune, you'll have to take a **taxi** or follow the hiking signs for 30 minutes uphill. For bus information, contact the Gare Routière in Menton (✆ **04-93-35-93-60**).

VISITOR INFORMATION The **Office de Tourisme** is at 218 av. Aristide-Briand, Roquebrune (✆ **04-93-35-62-87;** fax 04-93-28-57-00; www.roquebrune-cap-martin.com).

More than any other municipality in the region, Roquebrune and Cap-Martin have at least three guided walking tours of its attractions. The most popular of the three is a 90-minute guided tour of the old town, priced at 5€ for adults and 2€ for students. Tours depart whenever there are enough (at least five) participants to justify it. More esoteric tours, conducted for the most part exclusively in French, are tours of the municipality's wealth of public buildings, one of them a rather humble cabin, designed by world-famous architect Le Corbusier. It's conducted every Tuesday and Friday at 9:30am.

Seeing the Sights

IN ROQUEBRUNE

Exploring Roquebrune will take about an hour. You can stroll through its colorful streets, which retain their authentic feel. **Château de Roquebrune** (✆ **04-93-35-07-22**) was originally a 10th-century Carolingian castle; the present structure dates in part from the 13th century, although it was jazzed up by its wealthy British owner, Sir William Ingram, nearly a century ago. From the towers, there's a panoramic view along the coast. The interior is open in July and August daily 10am to 12:30pm and 3 to 7:30pm; April to June and September daily 10am to 12:30pm and 2 to 6:30pm; February, March, and October daily 10am to 12:30pm and 2 to 6pm; and November to January daily 10am to 12:30pm and 2 to 5pm. Admission is 3.70€ for adults, 2.70€ for seniors, 1.60€ students and children 7 to 11, and free for children 6 and under.

Sentier Le Corbusier.

Rue du Château leads to place William-Ingram. Cross this square to rue de la Fontaine and take a left. This leads you to the **Olivier millénaire** (millenary olive tree), one of the oldest in the world—it's at least 1,000 years old.

IN CAP-MARTIN

Once the exclusive domain of Belgian despot King Leopold II, Cap-Martin is still a fabulously rich spit of land. At its base, you can see the ruins of the **Basilique St-Martin,** a ruined priory constructed by the monks of the Lérins Islands in the 11th century. After pirate raids in later centuries, notably around the 15th century, it was destroyed and abandoned. Privately owned, it is not open to visitors.

You can also take one of the most scenic walks along the Riviera here, lasting about 2 hours. The coastal path, **Sentier Le Corbusier ★**, extends between Pointe du Cap-Martin to the eastern (meaning, the closest) frontier of Monaco. If you have a car, you can park it in the lot at avenue Winston-Churchill and begin your stroll. A sign labeled PROMENADE LE CORBUSIER marks the path. As you go along, you'll take in a view of Monaco set in a natural amphitheater. In the distance, you'll see Cap-Ferrat and, high above, Roquebrune. The scenic path ends at Monte-Carlo Beach and takes about 2 hours. Walkers can then take the line no. 100 bus back to their rough starting point. An alternative is to return on foot from either Monte-Carlo Beach or Roquebrune–Cap-Martin train station, following the walking signs back through the Parc des Oliviers, which occupies the central spine of Cap Martin.

16

LANGUEDOC-ROUSSILLON

by Alison Culliford

Languedoc is a loosely defined area encompassing the cities of Montpellier, Nîmes, Toulouse, and Carcassonne. It's one of the leading wine-producing areas of the world, and it's fabled for its art treasures.

Both Languedoc and Roussillon are old provinces of France, the first named for the language *(langue)* spoken by its occupants, called Occitan, and the second from the Roman name Ruscino. Languedoc covers the present-day *départements* (ministates) of Lozère, Gard, Hérault, and Aude, and Roussillon the Pyrénées Orientales, on the border with Spain. To the west, the city of Toulouse is in the Haute-Garonne *département* of the Midi-Pyrénées region.

The coast of Languedoc-Roussillon, from Montpellier to the Spanish frontier, might be called France's "second Riviera" (after the Côte d'Azur). This land of ancient cities has an almost continuous strip of sand stretching west from the Rhône toward the Pyrénées, covered by miles of sun-baking bodies in July and August.

The area around the regional capital of Perpignan is French Catalonia. Over its long history, it has known many rulers, passing back and forth between the kings of Aragón, Majorca, and France from the 13th to the 17th centuries. In 1659, it became part of Louis XIV's centralized kingdom. France firmly governs the land today, but cultural links with Spain are strong, and a high-speed rail link to Barcelona will bring the two Catalan cities even closer.

The Camargue is a marshy delta between two arms of the Rhône. South of Arles is cattle country. Black bulls are bred here for the bullfighting arenas of Arles and Nîmes. The cattle are herded by *gardians* (French cowboys), who ride white horses said to have been brought here by the Saracens. The whitewashed houses, plaited-straw roofs, plains, sandbars, and pink flamingos in the marshes make this area exotic.

As for wine, Hérault, Aude, and Garde are some of the largest wine producers in France. Most of this is ordinary table wine. A few, however, have been granted an Appellation d'Origine Contrôlée. Some of the best are Fitou, produced in the Hautes-Corbières district near Narbonne, and Minervois, from west and northwest of Narbonne.

NÎMES ★★★

721km (447 miles) S of Paris; 43km (27 miles) W of Avignon

Nîmes, the ancient Nemausus, is one of the finest places in the world for wandering among Roman relics. The city grew to prominence during the reign of Caesar Augustus (27 B.C.–A.D. 14). It possesses one of the best-preserved Roman amphitheaters in the world and a near-perfect Roman temple. The city is more like Provence than Languedoc, in which it lies. And there's a touch of Pamplona, Spain, in the festivals of the *corridas* (bullfights) at the arena. The Spanish influence is even more apparent at night, when its bodegas fill up, usually with students drinking sangria and listening to flamenco.

FACING PAGE: **Church of St-Sernin, in Toulouse's Old Town.**

By 1860, the togas of Nîmes's citizenry had long given way to denim, the cloth *de Nîmes.* An Austrian immigrant to Nîmes, Levi Strauss, exported the heavy fabric to California to make into work pants for gold-rush prospectors. The rest, as they say, is history.

Essentials

GETTING THERE The entire town center is now free of vehicular traffic. Nîmes has bus and train service from the rest of France and is near several autoroutes. It lies on the main **rail** line between Marseille and Bordeaux. Thirteen TGV trains arrive daily from Paris's Gare de Lyon; the one-way fare is 116€. For train information and schedules, call ✆ **36-35** or 08-92-35-35-35. If you're **driving,** take A7 south from Lyon to the town of Orange and connect to A9 into Nîmes.

VISITOR INFORMATION The **Office de Tourisme** is at 6 rue Auguste (✆ **04-66-58-38-00;** fax 04-66-58-38-01; www.ot-nimes.fr).

SPECIAL EVENTS The **Féria de Pentecôte,** a 5-day festival that revolves around the bull (and also includes plenty of drinking and merrymaking), is one of Europe's most popular festivals, attracting almost a million people each year. It takes place over Pentecost, which is 7 weeks after Easter, around the beginning of June. A second *féria,* **Féria des Vendanges,** celebrating the grape harvest, takes place the third weekend of September.

Every Thursday night during July and August, many of Nîmes's squares burst with music, crowds of pedestrians, and rich troves of paintings, crafts, used objects, and sculpture during **Les Jeudis de Nîmes** (Nîmes Thursdays).

Exploring the City

If you want to see all of the city's monuments and museums, consider buying the **Nîmes romaine** combined ticket, sold at the ticket counter of any of the local attractions. It provides access for a 3-day period to Maison Carrée, les Arènes de Nîmes, and Tour Magne. For more information, call **Culturespace** (✆ **04-66-21-82-56**). The fee is 9.90€ for adults, 7.70€ for children aged 7 to 17, and free for children 7 and under.

The pride of Nîmes is the **Maison Carrée ★★★**, place de la Maison Carrée (✆ **04-66-21-82-56**), built during the reign of Caesar Augustus. Consisting of a raised platform with tall Corinthian columns, it's one of Europe's most beautiful, best-preserved Roman temples. It inspired the builders of La Madeleine in Paris, as well as Thomas Jefferson. It schedules

Corinthian column at the Maison Carrée.

Languedoc-Roussillon
FRANCE
Paris
LANGUEDOC-ROUSSILLON
Gulf of Lions
Golfe d'Aigues-Mortes
Cap Leucate
SPAIN
ANDORRA
PYRENEES
PYRENEES ORIENTALES
LANGUEDOC-ROUSSILLON
MIDI-PYRENEES
MTS. DE LACAUNE
CÉVENNES NATIONAL PARK
VAUCLUSE
BOUCHES-DU-RHÔNE
GARD
HÉRAULT
AUDE
TARN
AVEYRON
ARIEGE
HAUTE-GARONNE
TARN-ET-GARONNE
The Camargue
Grand Rhône
Canal du Midi
Orange
Avignon
Cavaillon
Salon-de-Provence
Tarascon
Arles
Martigues
Fos-sur-Mer
Stes-Maries-de-la-Mer
Vauvert
Nîmes
Aigues-Mortes
Alès
La Grande Motte
La Baraque
Sauve
St-Martin-de-Londres
Castries
Montpellier
Le Vigan
Frontignan
Sète
Gignac
Mèze
Le Cap-d'Agde
Alzon
Le Caylar
Lodève
Clermont-l'Hérault
Pézenas
Agde
Valras-Plage
Nant
Millau
La Cavalerie
St-Affrique
Bédarieux
Béziers
Gruissan
Narbonne
Sigean
Port-Barcarès
Perpignan
Salses
Elne
Collioure
Port-Vendres
Banyuls-sur-Mer
Le Poujol-sur-Orb
Olargues
St-Pons-de-Thomières
St-Chinian
Lézignan-Corbières
Château de Peyrepertuse
Estagel
Millas
Le Boulou
Céret
St-Sernin-sur-Rance
Alban
Albi
Villefranche-d'Albigeois
Réalmont
Castres
Labruguière
Mazamet
Châteaux de Lastours
Capendu
Carcassonne
Rennes-le-Château
St-Paul-de-Fenouillet
Prades
Prats-de-Mollo-la-Preste
Cordes-sur-Ciel
Puylaurens
Castelnaudary
Limoux
Couiza
Quillan
Axat
Villefranche-de-Conflent
Olette
Font-Romeu
Llívia
Toulouse
Montauban
Autrieve
Pamiers
Foix
Tarascon
Ax-les-Thermes
A7
A9
A54
A750
A75
A61
A62
A64
A66
A68
N20
N112
N116
D999
0
20 km
20 mi

Amphithéâtre Romain de Nîmes.

cultural and art exhibits, presented beneath an authentically preserved roof. Admission is 4.50€ for adults or 3.70€ for students and children (free ages 9 and under). Open March daily 10am to 6pm; April, May, and September daily 10am to 6:30pm; June daily 10am to 7pm; July and August daily 10am to 8pm; October 10am to 1pm and 2 to 6pm; and November through February daily 10am to 1pm and 2 to 4:30pm.

Across the square stands its modern-day twin, the **Carré d'Art,** whose understated design by Norman Foster was inspired by (but doesn't overpower) the ancient monument. Inside is the **Musée d'Art Contemporain** (**© 04-66-76-35-70**), containing a permanent collection of art from 1960 to the present day and temporary exhibitions. It's open Tuesday through Sunday 10am to 6pm. The permanent collection is free; changing exhibitions cost 5€ for adults and are free for anyone aged 25 and under. Adults, too, gain free admission on the first Sunday of each month. Note that this building's terrace provides a panorama of most of the ancient monuments and medieval churches of Nîmes.

Scholars call it **Amphithéâtre Romain de Nîmes ★★★**, and locals refer to it as **Les Arènes de Nîmes.** The monument at place des Arènes (**© 04-66-76-72-77**) is a better-preserved twin of the one at Arles, and far more complete than Rome's Colosseum. It's two stories high—each floor has 60 arches—and was built of huge stones painstakingly fitted together without mortar. It once held more than 20,000 spectators who came to see gladiatorial combat and wolf or boar hunts. Today it's used for everything from ballet recitals to bullfights. Admission is 7.80€ for adults and 5.90€ for students and children 9 and under. Open March and October daily 9am to 6pm; April, May, and September daily 9am to 6:30pm; June 9am to 7pm; July to August daily 9am to 8pm; and November through February daily 9:30am to 5pm.

One of the most beautiful gardens in France, **Jardins de la Fontaine ★★**, at the end of quai de la Fontaine, was laid out in the 18th century using the ruins of a Roman shrine as a centerpiece. The garden is open from April to mid-September daily 7:30am to 10pm, and from mid-September to March daily 7:30am to 6:30pm. Within the garden are the ruined **Le Temple de Diane ★** and the

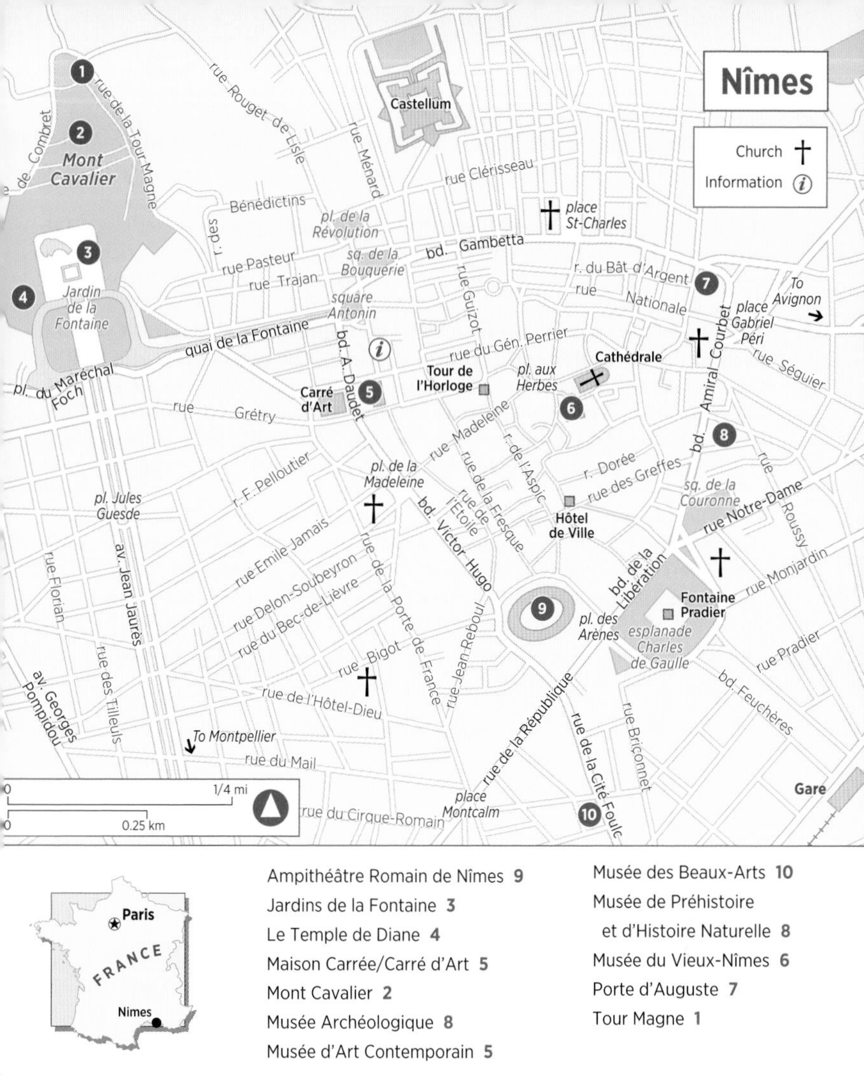

remains of some Roman baths. Over the park, within a 10-minute walk north of the town center, is **Mont Cavalier,** a low, rocky hill on top of which rises the sturdy bulk of the **Tour Magne** ★ (✆**04-66-67-65-56**), the city's oldest Roman monument. You can climb it for 2.70€ for adults and 2.30€ for students and children 9 and under. Its open March and October daily 9:30am to 1pm and 2 to 6pm; April and May daily 9:30am to 6pm; June daily 9am to 7pm; July and August 9am to 8pm; October 9:30am to 1pm and 2 to 6:30pm; and November through February 9:30am to 1pm and 2 to 4:30pm.

Nîmes is home to many museums. The largest and most respected, the **Musée des Beaux-Arts,** rue Cité-Foulc (✆**04-66-67-38-21**), contains French paintings and sculptures from the 17th to the 20th centuries, as well as Flemish, Dutch, and Italian works from the 15th to the 18th centuries. Seek out one of G. B. Moroni's masterpieces, *La Calomnie d'Apelle,* and a well-preserved Gallo-Roman mosaic. The museum is open Tuesday to Sunday 10am to 6pm. Admission is 5.20€ for adults and 3.80€ for students and children 10 to 16. Free for ages 9 and under.

If time allows, visit the **Musée du Vieux-Nîmes,** place aux Herbes (✆ **04-66-76-73-70**), housed in an Episcopal palace from the 1700s. It's rich in antiques, antique porcelain, and workday objects from the 18th and 19th centuries. Admission is free; hours are Tuesday to Sunday 10am to 6pm.

One of the city's busiest thoroughfares, **boulevard de l'Amiral-Courbet,** leads to the **Porte d'Auguste (Porte d'Arles)**—the remains of a gate built by the Romans during the reign of Augustus. About 45m (148 ft.) to the south are the **Musée de Préhistoire et d'Histoire Naturelle** (✆ **04-66-76-73-45**) and the **Musée Archéologique ★** (✆ **04-66-76-74-80**), in the same building, at 13 bis bd. l'Amiral-Courbet. Admission is free; hours are Tuesday to Sunday 10am to 6pm.

Outside the city, 23km (14 miles) northeast, the **pont du Gard ★** spans the Gard River; its huge stones, fitted together without mortar, stand as one of the region's most vivid reminders of the ancient glory. Consisting of three tiers of arches arranged into gracefully symmetrical patterns, it dates from about 19 B.C. Frédéric Mistral, national poet of Provence and Languedoc, recorded a legend alleging that the devil constructed the bridge with the promise that he could claim the soul of the first person to cross it. To visit it, take highway N86 from Nîmes to a point 3km (1¾ miles) from the village of Remoulins, where signs are posted.

The pont du Gard has a museum, **La Grande Expo du Pont du Gard** (✆ **04-66-37-50-99**). Four exhibits detail the bridge's construction, its function throughout the Middle Ages, and insights into its role as a symbol of the architectural savvy of ancient Rome. There's also a restaurant, cafe, and gift shop. It's open June to September daily 9:30am to 7pm, October daily 9:30am to 6pm, and November through February daily 9:30am to 5pm Admission is by way of a family ticket, which costs 15€ for up to five people.

During the month of August, artificial beaches are installed on the right bank of the Gardon near the bridge for **"Rendez-vous à la rivière,"** with lifeguards surveying river swimming, music, and food.

Shopping

Head to the center of town and **rue du Général-Perrier, rue des Marchands, rue du Chapître,** and the pedestrian **rue de l'Aspic** and **rue de la Madeleine.** A Sunday flea market runs from 8am to around 1pm in the parking lot of the **Stade des Costières,** site of most of the town's football (soccer) matches, adjacent to the southern edge of the Boulevard Périphérique that encircles Nîmes.

To appease your sweet tooth, go to just about any pastry shop in town and ask for the regional almond-based cookies called *croquants villaret* and *caladons.* They're great for a burst of energy or for souvenirs. *Santons,* wood or clay figurines sculpted into characters from Provençal country life, can be found at **Boutique Provençale,** 10 place de la Maison Carré (✆ **04-66-67-81-71**).

Where to Stay

Imperator Concorde ★★ This hotel, part of the Concorde chain, is the largest and finest in town, and is adjacent to Les Jardins de la Fontaine—it's the one with the pale-pink Italianate facade. In 2005, it underwent a major renovation that left it much improved. The artful and cozy good-size rooms have traditional or French furniture, with fluted or cabriole legs in one or another of the Louis styles. You can order a meal in the hotel's verdant rear gardens or in the high-ceilinged dining room, L'Enclos de la Fontaine.

15 rue Gaston Boissier, Nîmes 30900. www.hotel-imperator.com. ✆ **04-66-21-90-30.** Fax 04-66-67-70-25. 60 units. 140€–230€ double; 230€–290€ suite. AE, DC, MC, V. Parking 13€. **Amenities:** Restaurant; bar; babysitting; room service. *In room:* A/C, TV, hair dryer, minibar, free Wi-Fi.

New Hôtel La Baume ★ One of our favorite nests in Nîmes bears the name of the Marquis de la Baume, whose family built this 17th-century mansion. With an overall sense of grandeur, its best feature is the magnificent staircase that ornaments the interior courtyard. During the hotel conversion, the designers carefully preserved the original architecture, and the result is a winning combination of modern and traditional. In contrast to the stately exterior, the guest rooms are hypercontemporary, usually in tones of soft red, orange, and ocher, and the tiled bathrooms are in a postmodern style evocative of Philippe Starck's work.

21 rue Nationale, Nîmes 30000. www.new-hotel.com. ✆ **04-66-76-28-42.** Fax 04-66-76-28-45. 34 units. 140€ double; 170€ junior suite. AE, DC, MC, V. **Amenities:** Bar; room service. *In room:* A/C, TV, hair dryer, minibar, free Wi-Fi.

Where to Eat

The dining rooms at the **New Hôtel La Baume** and the **Imperator Concorde** (see above) are good choices.

Alexandre (Michel Kayser) ★★★ FRENCH/LANGUEDOCIENNE The most charming restaurant around is on the outskirts of Nîmes, 8km (5 miles) south of the center. It's the elegantly rustic domain of Michel Kayser, who adheres to classic tradition, with subtle improvements. His wife, Monique, assists him in the ultramodern dining room, which is outfitted in tones of soft red and ocher. Menu items are designed to amuse as well as delight the palate: *île flottante,* a playful update of old-fashioned floating island, with truffles and velouté of cèpe mushrooms; roasted pigeon stuffed with vegetable purée and foie gras; and filet of bull from the Camargue in red-wine sauce with Camarguais herbs.

Rte. de l'Aéroport de Garons. ✆ **04-66-70-08-99.** www.michelkayser.com. Reservations recommended. Main courses 44€–66€; fixed-price menus 64€–165€. AE, DC, MC, V. July–Aug Tues–Sat noon–1:30pm and 8–9:30pm; Sept–June Wed–Sun noon–1:30pm, Wed–Sat 8–9:30pm. Closed 2 weeks in Feb–Mar and 2 weeks end of Aug into Sept and 1st week of Jan. From town center, take rue de la République southwest to av. Jean-Jaurès; then head south and follow signs to the airport (toward Garons).

Wine Bar le Cheval Blanc TRADITIONAL FRENCH This mahogany-paneled place has leather banquettes evocative of an early-1900s California saloon. Choices include an array of salads and platters. At lunch you can order a quick menu, including an appetizer, a garnished main course, and two glasses of wine. Typical dishes are *magret* of duckling, top-notch beefsteaks, and fresh (usually grilled) fish. You can also enjoy lunch on the terrace in the courtyard. A restaurateur extraordinaire, Michel Hermet makes his own wine at vineyards that have been associated with his family for many generations. More than 300 other varieties of wine are in stock, 15 of which are available by the glass or by the pitcher.

1, place des Arènes. ✆ **04-66-76-19-59.** Main courses 8.50€–26€; fixed-price lunch 13€, dinner 16€–24€. AE, MC, V. Mon–Sat noon–2pm; Mon–Thurs 7–11pm; Fri–Sat 7pm–midnight.

Nîmes After Dark

Once warm weather hits, all sorts of activities take place at the arena, including open-air concerts and theater. The Office de Tourisme has a complete listing.

If you like hanging out with students and soldiers, head to **Café Le Napoleon,** 46 bd. Victor-Hugo (**✆04-66-67-20-23**). Popular with the intelligentsia is **Haddock Cafe,** 13 rue de l'Agau (**✆04-66-67-86-57**), which books occasional rock concerts.

Sexy, hip **La Comédie,** 28 rue Jean-Reboul (**✆04-66-76-13-66**), is hands-down the best for dancing and attracts a pretty crowd of youthful danceaholics. A little less flashy, but a lot more fun, **Lulu Club,** 10 impasse de la Curaterie (**✆04-66-36-28-20**), is the gay and lesbian stronghold in Nîmes. Open Thursday to Saturday, it's a magnet for hip and straight folk as well. A youth-oriented contender is **Le C-Cafe,** 20 rue de l'Etoile (**✆04-66-21-59-22**); open Thursday to Saturday at 11pm, it rocks 'n' rolls to music from L.A. to London.

Streets to explore on virtually any night of the week include **place de la Maison Carrée** and **boulevard Victor-Hugo.**

AIGUES-MORTES ★★

750km (465 miles) SW of Paris; 63km (39 miles) NE of Séte; 40km (25 miles) E of Nîmes; 48km (30 miles) SW of Arles

South of Nîmes, you can explore much of the Camargue by car. The most rewarding place to focus on is Aigues-Mortes, the city of the "dead waters." In the middle of swamps and lagoons, Aigues-Mortes is France's most perfectly preserved walled town. Louis IX and his crusaders once set forth from Aigues-Mortes, which was then a thriving port, the first in France on the Mediterranean. Now 6.5km (4 miles) inland from the sea, it stands on four canals. The **ramparts ★★**, which still enclose the town, were constructed between 1272 and 1300. The **Tour de Constance ★★** (**✆04-66-53-61-55**) is a model castle of the Middle Ages. At the top, which you can reach by elevator, a panoramic view of the marshes unfolds. Admission is 7€ for adults, 4.50€ for ages 18 to 25, and free for children 17 and under. The monument is open May to August daily 10am to 7pm, and September to April daily 10am to 5.30pm.

Aigues-Mortes's main appeal is the medieval feeling that permeates virtually every building, rampart, and cobble-covered street. The city's religious centerpiece is the **Eglise Notre-Dame des Sablons,** rue Jean-Jaurès (no phone). Constructed of wood in 1183, it was rebuilt in stone in 1246 in the ogival style. Its modern stained-glass windows were installed in 1980 as replacements for the badly damaged originals. The church is open May to September daily 8:30am to 6pm, and October to April daily 10am to 5pm.

Essentials

GETTING THERE Five **trains** and four **buses** per day connect Aigues-Mortes and Nîmes. Trip time is about an hour. For information and schedules, call **✆36-35,** or 08-92-35-35-35 from outside France. If you're **driving** to Aigues-Mortes, take D979 south from Gallargues, or A9 from Montpellier or Nîmes.

VISITOR INFORMATION The **Office de Tourisme** is at place St-Louis (**✆04-66-53-73-00;** fax 04-66-53-65-94; www.ot-aiguesmortes.fr).

Where to Stay

Restaurant Les Arcades (see "Where to Eat," on p. 638) also rents rooms.

Hostellerie des Remparts Opened about 300 years ago, this weather-worn inn lies at the foot of the Tour de Constance, adjacent to the medieval fortifications. Popular and often fully booked (especially in summer), it evokes the defensive atmosphere of the Middle Ages, albeit with charm and a sense of nostalgia. Narrow stone staircases lead to the small, simply furnished rooms. Breakfast is the only meal served.

FRANCE'S COWBOY COUNTRY: The Camargue

The Camargue, where the cowboys of France ride the range, is an alluvial plain inhabited by wild horses, fighting black bulls, roaming Gypsies, pink flamingos and gluttonous mosquitoes. You can explore the rugged terrain by boat, bike, horse, or jeep.

With the most fragile ecosystem in France, the Camargue has been a nature reserve since 1970. You cannot drive into the protected parts, and some are accessible only to the *Gardians,* the cowboys of the Camargue who guard the wild horses and small black bulls that are reared for the *course Camarguais,* a type of bull-fighting where men in white run through the area with nothing but a knuckle-duster to protect them. The *Gardians* wear large felt hats, and their ancestors may have been the first American cowboys, who sailed on French ships to the port of New Orleans, where they rode the bayous of Louisiana and east Texas, rounding up cattle—in French, no less.

There's no more evocative sight than the proud snow-white horses running at liberty through the marshlands, with hoofs so tough that they don't need shoes. The breed was brought here by the Arabs long ago, and it is said that their long manes and bushy tails evolved over the centuries to slap those pesky mosquitoes.

Exotic flora and fauna abound where the delta of the Rhône River empties into the Mediterranean. The bird life is the most luxuriant in Europe. The area, which resembles the Florida Everglades, is known for its colonies of pink flamingos *(Flamants roses).* They share living quarters with some 400 other bird species, including ibises, egrets, kingfishers, owls, wild ducks, swans, and ferocious birds of prey. The best place to see flamingo colonies is the area around Ginès, a hamlet on N570, 5km (3 miles) north of Camargue's capital, Stes-Maries-de-la-Mer.

Exploring the Camargue is best undertaken on the back of a Camarguais horse. The steeds can take you into the interior, which you couldn't see otherwise, fording waters to places where the black bulls graze and wild birds nest. You'll find two to three dozen stables (depending on the time of year) along the highway from Arles to Stes-Maries. Virtually all of them charge the same rate, 17€ per hour. The rides are aimed at the neophyte, not the champion equestrian. They're so easy that they're recommended even for those who have never been on a horse before.

6 place Anatole-France. www.hotel-camargue.fr ✆ **04-66-53-82-77.** Fax 04-66-53-73-77. 19 units. 60€–110€ double. AE, MC, V. **Amenities:** Restaurant; bar; room service. *In room:* A/C, TV.

Hôtel Les Templiers ★ The leading inn in town is a gem of peace and tranquillity. Protected by the ramparts built by St. Louis, king of France, this 17th-century residence has small to medium-size rooms decorated in Provençal style, with just enough decorative objects to lend a homelike aura. You can relax in the courtyard, where you can also enjoy breakfast. The establishment contains two restaurants, each featuring competent and traditional food. The less formal option is open for both lunch and dinner Wednesday through Monday; the more formal restaurant is open only for dinner Thursday through Sunday, or Tuesday through Sunday in July and August.

23 rue de la République. www.hotellestempliers.fr. ✆ **04-66-53-66-56.** Fax 04-66-53-69-61. 14 units. 125€–190€ double. MC, V. **Amenities:** 2 restaurants; bar; outdoor pool; room service. *In room:* A/C, TV, hair dryer, free Wi-Fi.

Where to Eat

Hôtel Les Templiers (see above) is also a good choice for dining.

Restaurant Les Arcades ★★ ☺ CAMARGUAISE There's no contest: This is the area's finest dining choice. Almost as old as the nearby fortifications, the place is especially charming on sultry days, when the thick masonry keeps the interior cool. The good, reasonably priced food is likely to include warm oysters, fish soup, fried stuffed zucchini flowers, grilled beefsteak from the Camargue, roasted monkfish in red-wine sauce, and grilled duckling. A Camargue gypsy guitarist plays flamenco on Fridays and Saturdays. The owner also rents nine large, comfortable rooms with air-conditioning and TVs. Doubles go for 96€ to 104€.

23 bd. Gambetta, Aigues-Mortes 30220. ✆ **04-66-53-81-13.** www.les-arcades.fr. Reservations recommended. Main courses 20€–30€; fixed-price lunch 20€, dinner 35€–45€; children's menu 14€. AE, DC, MC, V. Wed and Fri–Sun noon–2pm; Tues–Sun 7:30–10pm; daily July–Aug noon–2pm and 7:30–10pm. Closed 3 weeks in Mar and 2 weeks in Oct.

MONTPELLIER ★★

758km (470 miles) SW of Paris; 161km (100 miles) NW of Marseille; 50km (31 miles) SW of Nîmes

The capital of Languedoc-Roussillon, the ancient university city of Montpellier is renowned for its medical school, founded in the 13th century. Nostradamus qualified as a doctor here, and Rabelais studied at the school. Petrarch came to Montpellier in 1317 and stayed for 7 years.

Today Montpellier is a bustling metropolis with a population of 390,000, one of southern France's fastest-growing cities, thanks to an influx of new immigrants and the implantation of high-tech corporations. Although some suburbs are dreary, the city has a handsome core, with tree-flanked promenades, broad avenues, and historic monuments. Students make up a quarter of the population, giving the city a lively feel.

Essentials

GETTING THERE Some 12 **trains** per day arrive from Avignon (trip time: 1 hr.), 12 from Marseille (trip time: 1¾ hr.), one every 2 hours from Toulouse (trip time: 2 hr.), and 17 per day from Perpignan (trip time: 1½ hr.). Fourteen TGV trains arrive daily from Paris Gare de Lyon, taking less than 3½ hours. The one-way fare is 84€. For rail information, call ✆ **36-35** or 08-92-35-35-35.

If you're **driving,** Montpellier lies off A9.

VISITOR INFORMATION The **Office de Tourisme** is at 30 allée Jean de L. de Tassigny (✆ **04-67-60-60-60;** fax 04-67-60-60-61; www.ot-montpellier.fr).

SPECIAL EVENTS From June 24 to July 7 (approx.), classical and modern dancers leap into town for the **Festival International Montpellier Danse.** Tickets for performances cost 6€ to 30€ and can be purchased through the box office, 18 rue Ste-Ursule (✆ **08-00-60-07-40** or 04-67-60-83-60; www.montpellierdanse.com). During the last 3 weeks of July, the **Festival de Radio France et de Montpellier** presents orchestral music, jazz, and opera. Tickets run from free to 48€; call ✆ **04-67-61-66-81** for more information, or contact **Cité des Congrés Le Corum,** esplanade Charles de Gaulle (✆ **04-67-61-67-61;** www.festivalradiofrancemontpellier.com).

Exploring the Town

The expansive **place de la Comédie** is the living room of Montpellier, where you can admire the opera, the 18th-century "Fountain of the Three Graces," and watch students hurry to lectures from a cafe terrace. A former military parade ground spreads out from here, where you'll find the **Tourist Office**, **Musée Fabre,** and **Le Corum** convention and arts venue. Head up **rue de la Loge** to explore the Old Town.

At the top of the Old Town, you'll find the 17th-century **promenade du Peyrou ★★**, a terraced park with views of the Cévennes and the Mediterranean. The broad esplanade sits at the loftiest point in Montpellier. Opposite its entrance at the end of rue Foch is the **Arc de Triomphe,** erected in 1691 to celebrate the victories of Louis XIV. In the center of the promenade is an equestrian statue of the Sun King, and at the end is the **Château d'Eau,** a pavilion with Corinthian columns that is a monument to 18th-century classicism. Water travels here along a 15km-long (9¼-mile) conduit and an aqueduct. Just to the right of here is the cathedral and botanical gardens.

Cathédrale St-Pierre The town's spiritual centerpiece was founded in 1364. Once associated with a Benedictine monastery, the cathedral suffered badly during the religious wars of the 16th and 17th centuries. After 1795, the medical school occupied the monastery. Today it has a somewhat bleak western front with two towers and a canopied porch.

Place St-Pierre. ✆ **04-67-66-04-12.** Free admission. Mon–Sat 9am–noon and 2:30–7pm; Sun 9am–1pm.

Jardin des Plantes Paul Valéry met André Gide in the Jardin des Plantes, the oldest such garden in France. The botanical garden, filled with exotic plants and a handful of greenhouses, opened in 1593.

163 rue Auguste-Broussonnet (enter from bd. Henri-IV). ✆ **04-67-63-43-22.** Free admission. Apr–Sept Tues–Sun noon–8pm; Oct–Mar Tues–Sun noon–6pm.

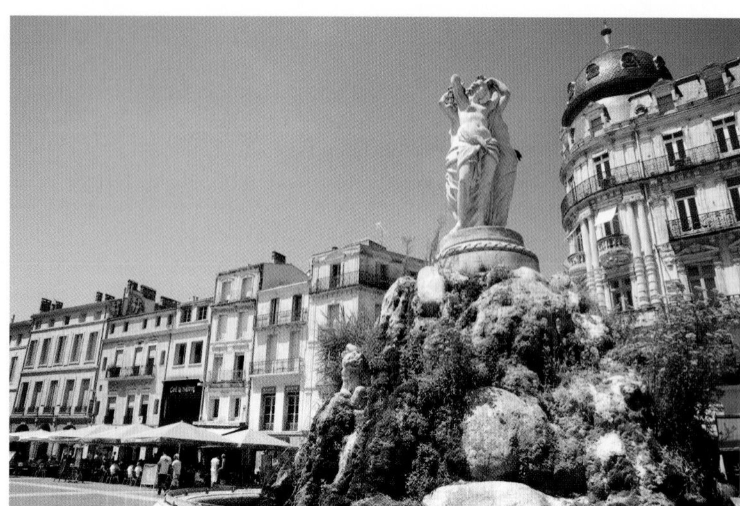

Place de la Comédie.

Musée Fabre ★★★ One of France's great provincial art galleries occupies the former Hôtel de Massilian, where Molière once played for a season. The collection originated when Napoleon sent Montpellier an exhibition of the Académie Royale in 1803. François Fabre, a Montpellier painter, contributed its most important works in 1825. After Fabre's death, other paintings from his collection were donated to the gallery, including Poussin's *Venus and Adonis* and Italian paintings such as *The Mystical Marriage of Saint Catherine*. After 2 years of renovations, the museum reopened in 2007 with expanded exhibition space, so more than 300 new works can now be displayed, including an entire wing devoted to abstract expressionist Pierre Soulages.

2 rue Montpellieret. ✆ **04-67-14-83-00.** Admission 6€ adults, 4€ ages 6–26, free for children 5 and under. Tues–Fri and Sun 10am–6pm; Wed 1–9pm; Sat 11am–6pm.

Where to Stay

Le Jardin des Sens (p. 642) also rents rooms.

Hôtel du Palais ★ This hotel in the heart of a neighborhood loaded with antiques dealers is one of the best bargains in town. Built in the late 18th century, Hôtel du Palais is at the top of the Old Town, amid a labyrinth of narrow streets and monumental plazas and parks. Much of the decor dates from around 1983, when the hotel was richly restored in a style that uses lots of fabrics, big curtains, and faux marble finishes on walls of public areas. Subsequent renovations have kept the property up-to-date. The guest rooms are relatively large and appealing, thanks to thoughtful placement of antique reproductions and good maintenance.

3 rue du Palais. www.hoteldupalais-montpellier.fr. ✆ **04-67-60-47-38.** Fax 04-67-60-40-23. 26 units. 68€–90€ double. MC, V. Parking 6.50€. **Amenities:** Room service. *In room:* A/C, TV, hair dryer, minibar, free Wi-Fi.

Hôtel Le Guilhem ★ Two 16th-century houses make up this oasis, located on a back street. In its transformation to a hotel, the connected buildings gained all the modern conveniences, including an elevator. Each room is furnished and decorated in individual style, with more than a hint of Laura Ashley design in the striped wallpaper and flowery spreads. Although the accommodations are small, they are tastefully furnished and comfortable. The day begins with a breakfast of freshly baked *pain au chocolat* and croissants served on a terrace overlooking the garden and the cathedral. The location is in the old town, an ideal base from which to explore the sights.

18 rue Jean-Jacques-Rousseau, Montpellier 34000. www.leguilhem.com. ✆ **800/528-1234** or 04-67-52-90-90. Fax 04-67-60-67-67. 35 units. 96€–192€ double. AE, DC, MC, V. Parking 6.50€ in nearby garage. **Amenities:** Room service. *In room:* A/C, TV, hair dryer, minibar, free Wi-Fi.

La Maison Blanche ★★ Few other hotels in the south of France so successfully emulate the gingerbread and French Creole ambience of old New Orleans. Suites are stylishly furnished in rattan and wicker with plenty of wood paneling, whereas standard guest rooms are outfitted with oak. Bathrooms are midsize to roomy. Parts of the interior, especially the dining room, may remind you of Louis XIII's France more than Louisiana, but overall, the setting in a verdant park (a 10-min. drive northeast of Montpellier's center) is as charming and unusual as anything else in town.

1796 av. de la Pompignane. www.hotel-maison-blanche.com. ✆ **04-99-58-20-70.** Fax 04-67-79-53-39. 35 units. 81€–132€ double; 165€–203€ suite. AE, DC, MC, V. Free parking. Take bd. d'Antigone east until you reach the intersection with av. de la Pompignane, and head north until you see the hotel on your right (trip time: 5 min.). **Amenities:** Restaurant; bar; outdoor pool; room service. *In room:* A/C, TV, hair dryer, minibar, free Wi-Fi.

Pullman Montpellier Antigone ★ In the heart of Montpellier, this angular, modern, glass-sheathed hotel is the city's top hotel for comfort and first-class amenities. In summer, it does quite a trade with visitors. A particularly appealing feature is the pool, which, along with a bar and breakfast room, occupies most of the top floor. The rooms are chain format but first class. The Antigone is a winning choice, with the most efficient staff in the city, and its bar is one of the coziest hideaways in town.

1 rue des Pertuisanes. www.pullmanhotels.com. ✆ **04-67-99-72-72.** Fax 04-67-65-17-50. 88 units. 153€ –193€ double. AE, DC, MC, V. Parking 3€–10€. **Amenities:** Restaurant; bar; exercise room; Jacuzzi; outdoor pool; room service. *In room:* A/C, TV, hair dryer, free Wi-Fi.

Where to Eat

La Compagnie des Comptoirs INTERNATIONAL Owned by the Poucel brothers (see below) and in a road adjacent to their Le Jardin des Sens, this restaurant manages to evoke the aesthetic and sense of internationalism of the late-19th-century French colonies in, say, India, North Africa, or Indochina. There's room inside for about 130 diners; a big terrace with flowering shrubs and a splashing fountain; and an ongoing emphasis on the kind of sunny, flavorful, and pungent cuisine you're likely to find around the edges of the Mediterranean. The best examples include a succulent version of tempura of crayfish; *accras* (beignets) of crab; grilled calamari with a confit of lemon; grilled steak from bulls from the Camargue, served with red wine sauce; and a winning collection of desserts. The lounge bar operates until around 1am.

51 av. de Nîmes. ✆ **04-99-58-39-29.** www.lacompagniedescomptoirs.com. Reservations recommended. Fixed-price menus 22€–28€. AE, DC, MC, V. Tues–Fri, Sun and Mon noon–2:30pm; Tues–Sun 8–11pm (1am for the lounge bar).

Le Grillardin FRENCH The best choice on this charming, tree-shaded square, Le Grillardin serves succulent grills such as the superb lamb shank, *filet de boeuf,* or veal steak, accompanied by wok-fried vegetables, green beans, or your own choice of vegetables (they are happy to accommodate menu changes). Fish choices such as scallops, monkfish, and sea bass are equally well prepared. Sit on the heated terrace and enjoy the chance to fraternize with Parisian émigrés who have discovered this idyllic spot.

2 pl. de la Chapelle Neuve. ✆ **04-67-66-24-33.** www.restaurantlegrillardin.com. Main courses 16€–22€; fixed-price lunch (weekdays) 23€, dinner 20€–28€. AE, MC, V. Mon, Thurs, Fri, Sun noon–2pm and 7–11pm; Sat 7–11pm.

Le Jardin des Sens ★★★ FRENCH This is one of the great restaurants of southern France. The chefs, twins Laurent and Jacques Pourcel, have taken Montpellier by storm, and their cuisine could involve almost anything, depending on where their imaginations roam. The rich bounty of Languedoc goes through a process designed to enhance its natural flavor. A starter may be ravioli stuffed with foie gras of duckling and flap mushrooms, floating in chicken bouillon fortified with truffles, broad beans, and crispy potatoes. Main courses of note are shelled lobster, pressed flat and served with duck meat and vanilla oil; and filet of pigeon stuffed with pistachios. A dessert specialty is gratin of limes with slices of preserved pineapple.

Le Jardin des Sens also rents 13 guest rooms, plus 2 suites, each designed in cutting-edge style by Bruno Borrione, a colleague of Philippe Starck. They cost 170€ to 280€ for a double and 310€ to 480€ for a suite.

11 av. St-Lazare. ✆ **04-99-58-38-38.** Fax 04-99-58-38-39. www.jardindessens.com. Reservations required. Main courses 45€–85€; fixed-price lunch Tues–Fri 45€; fixed-price dinner and Sat lunch 80€–170€. AE, MC, V. Mon–Sat noon–2pm and 8–10pm.

Les Vignes ★ PROVENÇAL/LANGUEDOCIENNE This small restaurant near the Préfecture building serves one of the finest regional cuisines in Montpellier. Walk down the stairs into a spectacular 13th-century arched dining room. Once here, you can enjoy the products of the land, including fresh thyme, olives, and other herbs. Bull from the Camargue is served, along with Provence lamb, as well as fish caught in the Mediterranean. Specialties include braised turbot with baby vegetables or wild shrimp cooked in pastis, and perhaps a mousselline of scallops with crayfish and red pepper. A selection from Languedoc vineyards accompanies most dishes.

2 rue Bonnier d'Alco. ✆ **04-67-60-48-42.** www.lesvignesrestaurant.com. Reservations recommended. Main courses 22€–16€; fixed-price lunch 14€–22€, dinner 28€–75€. AE, MC, V. Mon–Sat noon–1:30pm and 7:45–9:30pm.

Montpellier After Dark

After the sun sets, head for **place Jean-Jaurès, rue des Ecoles Laïques, place St Ravy,** or the more sophisticated area around **rue du Palais de Guilhems,** where you'll find the lounge bar **Les Pampilles** at no. 25 (✆ **06-88-23-59-63**).

Rockstore, 20 rue de Verdun (✆ **04-67-06-80-00;** www.rockstore.fr), draws lots of students with 1950s rock memorabilia and live concerts. Up a flight of stairs is its disco, which pounds out techno and rock. There is no cover, except on concert nights. For the best jazz and blues in town, check out **JAM,** 100 rue Ferdinand-de-Lesseps (✆ **04-67-58-30-30;** www.lejam.com). In a noisy, smoky, and even gritty space, its regular concerts attract jazz enthusiasts from miles around. Concert tickets average 10€ to 25€.

A modern, noisy, convivial disco, known throughout the region, is **Le Pacha,** 63 chemin du Mas de Gau, in the beachside suburb of Lattes (✆ **04-99-52-97-06**). It attracts drinkers and dancers ages 23 to 40. Le Pacha is open Thursday through Saturday beginning around 11pm; on Friday and Saturday, it charges a 10€ to 15€ cover, which includes one drink. Gays, lesbians and a club-loving crowd gather at the town's most animated bar and disco, **La Villa Rouge,** route de Palavas (✆ **04-67-06-50-54**), also in Lattes. Both clubs lie about 5km (3 miles) south of the town center.

NARBONNE ★

845km (524 miles) SW of Paris; 61km (38 miles) E of Carcassonne; 93km (58 miles) S of Montpellier

Narbonne was the first town outside Italy to be colonized by the Romans, which makes it an intriguing place. At that time, it was the largest town in Gaul after Lyon, and even today you can see evidence of the its former wealth. Some come for the beach, undoubtedly, but it also attracts history buffs and others drawn to memories of its glorious past.

Some 50,000 Narbonnais live in this sleepy backwater, and if many of the vineyards have been torn up for holiday homes around here, others are trying to raise the profile of their vineyards. You can visit vineyards in the surrounding area (the tourist office will advise you). If you want to go to the beach, head to the nearby village of **Gruisson** and its adjoining beach, Gruisson-Plage, or to the suburb of **St-Pierre la Mer** and its adjoining beach, Narbonne-Plage. Both are 15km (9¼ miles) south of Narbonne. Buses from the town are frequent, each marked with its destination.

Cathédrale St-Just.

Essentials

GETTING THERE Narbonne has rail, bus, and highway connections with other cities on the Mediterranean coast and with Toulouse. Rail travel is the most popular way to get here, with 23 **trains** per day arriving from Perpignan (trip time: 35 min.), 13 per day from Toulouse (trip time: 1¼ hr.), and 42 per day from Montpellier (trip time: 1 hr.). Most rail passengers arriving from Paris take the TGV directly to Narbonne (trip time: 4½ hr.). The one-way fare from Paris is 105€; from Montpellier, 15€. For rail information, call ✆ **36-35** or 08-92-35-35-35. If you're **driving,** Narbonne is at the junction of A61 and A9, easily accessible from either Toulouse or the Riviera.

VISITOR INFORMATION The **Office de Tourisme** is on 31 rue Jean Jaurès (✆ **04-68-65-15-60;** fax 04-68-65-59-12; www.mairie-narbonne.fr).

Exploring the Town

Starting with the oldest site, there's the **Horreum,** 7 rue Rouget de Lisle (✆ **04-68-32-45-30**), an underground warren of granaries and grain chutes built by the Romans in the 1st century B.C. Situated in the restored medieval quarter, it's now filled with attractive shops and restaurants. In the center of town, the huge palace and cathedral complex, built from the 12th to the 14th centuries, reveals vaunting ecclesiastical ambitions. The **Cathédrale St-Just et St-Pasteur,** rue Armand Gautier ★★ (✆ **04-68-32-09-52;** free admission; daily 9am–noon and 2–6pm), is just the chancel of the original cathedral plan, but it is still magnificent, decorated with 14th-century statues, stained glass, and Aubusson tapestries. Cloisters join it to the **Palais des Archevêques** (Archbishop's Palace), which contains several museums, including the **Archaeology Museum** and the **Museum of Art and History.** Additional sights include the **Donjon Gilles-Aycelin,** place de l'Hôtel-de-Ville (✆ **04-68-90-30-30**), a watchtower and prison from the late 13th century, with an observation platform offering a view of the cathedral, the plain, and the Pyrénées; and the **Maison Charles Trenet,** 13 av. Charles Trenet (✆ **04-68-90-30-65**), birthplace of the sentimental songwriter beloved of the French. There are pleasant walks by the canal, which is lined with 18th-century houses and *chais* (wine warehouses).

All Narbonne museums and the Horreum have the same opening hours and prices: Admission to one museum is 6€ (4€ students and children aged 10 to 17, children 9 and under free); a pass for all museums, the Donjon Gilles-Aycelin, the Cathedral treasure, and Charles Trenet's birthplace is 9€ (6€ students and children aged 10 to 17, children aged 9 and under free). They're open April to July 14 Wednesday to Monday from 10am to noon and from 2 to 5pm, July 15 to October 31 daily from 10am to 1pm and from 2:30 to 6pm, and November to March Wednesday to Monday from 2 to 5pm.

Where to Stay

Hôtel du Languedoc Despite frequent modernizations, the grand stone structure of this Belle Epoque hotel still stands out from the cityscape around it. Beside the canal du Rhône, it's the site of municipal meetings and social events, with high-ceilinged public rooms and a mishmash of decors. The rooms come in a variety of shapes and sizes, usually with some of the hotel's original wood furniture and pastel color schemes.

22 bd. Gambetta. www.hoteldulanguedoc.com. ✆ **04-68-65-14-74.** Fax 04-68-65-81-48. 40 units. 62€–77€ double; 95€ suite. AE, DC, MC, V. Parking 9€. **Amenities:** Bar/Breton-style crêperie; room service. *In room:* TV, hair dryer, free Wi-Fi.

La Résidence ★ Our favorite hotel in Narbonne is near the Cathédrale St-Just. The 19th-century La Résidence, converted from a stately villa, is comfortable and decorated with antiques. The rooms are midsize to spacious, tastefully furnished, and very well maintained. Most of the good-size bathrooms have tub/showers. The hotel doesn't have a restaurant but serves breakfast.

6 rue du 1er-Mai. www.hotelresidence.fr. ✆ **04-68-32-19-41.** Fax 04-68-65-51-82. 26 units. 76€–115€ double. AE, DC, MC, V. Parking 7.50€. Closed Jan 20–Feb 20. *In room:* A/C, TV, hair dryer, minibar, free Wi-Fi.

Where to Eat

La Table St-Crescent ★★★ FRENCH/LANGUEDOCIENNE This is one of the region's best-respected restaurants. It's just east of town, beside the road leading to Perpignan, in a complex of wine-tasting boutiques established by a local syndicate of growers. The chef delivers refined, brilliantly realized dishes, with sublime sauces and sophisticated herbs and seasonings. Menu items change four times a year based on the availability of seasonal ingredients and the inspiration of the owners. Some of the best main courses include sea bass marinated with olives, tuna tartare with roasted almonds, and chicken served with a truffle sauce.

In the Palais des Vins, 68 av. Général Leclerc, rte. de Perpignan. ✆ **04-68-41-37-37.** www.la-table-saint-crescent.com. Reservations recommended. Main courses 26€–41€; fixed-price lunch Tues–Fri 25€; fixed-price dinner and Sun lunch 48€–80€. AE, DC, MC, V. Tues–Fri and Sun noon–1:30pm; Tues–Sat 8–9:30pm.

COLLIOURE ★★

929km (576 miles) SW of Paris; 28km (17 miles) SE of Perpignan

A port established by the Greeks in 6000 B.C. and later owned by the kings of Majorca, Collioure is best known as the home of a colony of artists, including Derain, Dufy, Picasso, and Matisse. Attracting art lovers from all over the world, it still has some of the charm of a pre-Bardot St-Tropez.

Essentials

GETTING THERE Collioure has frequent **train** and bus service, especially from Perpignan (trip time: 20 min.). For train information and schedules, call ✆ **36-35** or 08-92-35-35-35. Many visitors **drive** along the coastal road (RN114) leading to the Spanish border.

VISITOR INFORMATION The **Office de Tourisme** is on place du 18-Juin (✆ **04-68-82-15-47;** fax 04-68-82-46-29; www.collioure.com).

Exploring the Town

The two curving ports sit on either side of the heavy masonry of the 13th-century **Château Royal,** place de 8-Mai-1945 (✆ **04-68-82-06-43**). It's of interest in its own right for its medieval fortifications, but between the months of May and September, it's also the home to a changing series of exhibitions by contemporary artists. Entrance costs the same regardless of whether there's an exhibition: 4€ for adults, 2€ students and children ages 12 to 18, and free for children 11 and under. In July and August, hours are daily 10am to 6:15pm; June and September, daily 10am to 5:15pm; October to May, daily 9am to 4:15pm.

The **Eglise de Notre-Dame-des-Anges,** rue de l'Eglise (✆ **04-68-82-06-43**), is the town's most famous monument; half lighthouse, half church, it

The beach at Collioure.

looks austere from the outside, but inside features a floor-to-ceiling altarpiece dripping with gold. The church is open daily from 9am to noon and 2 to 6pm. Also try to visit the **Musée Jean-Peské,** route de Port-Vendres (✆ **04-68-82-10-19**), home to a collection of works by artists who painted here. It's open in July and August daily 10am to noon and 2 to 6pm, and September to June Wednesday to Monday 10am to noon and 2 to 6pm. Admission is 2€ for adults, 1.50€ for children 12 to 16 and students, and free for children 11 and under. The **Chemin du Fauvisme** lists 20 stops where you can see reproductions of paintings by Matisse, Dérain, and other fauvists beside the actual scene they painted—and the colors that inspired this vibrant but short-lived movement are just as alive in the area today. Pick up a map at **Espace Fauve,** av. Camille Pelletan (✆ **04-68-98-07-16**).

Where to Stay

Casa Pairal ★ This pleasant family-operated hotel is in a 150-year-old house a very short walk from the port and beach. In the guest rooms, charming antiques blend with more modern pieces. The best doubles have *petit salons* plus small balconies. Breakfast is the only meal served, but there are many restaurants nearby. On sunny days, guests can take a dip in the pool, which sits in the shadow of century-old trees.

Impasse des Palmiers. www.hotel-casa-pairal.com. ✆ **04-68-82-05-81.** Fax 04-68-82-52-10. 27 units. 89€–187€ double; 184€–233€ suite. AE, DC, MC, V. Parking 14€. Closed Nov–Mar. **Amenities:** Outdoor pool; room service. *In room:* A/C, TV, hair dryer, minibar, free Wi-Fi.

Relais des 3 Mas et Restaurant La Balette ★★ This is the town's premier hotel and the restaurant of choice. In the decor of its beautiful rooms, the hotel honors the famous artists who lived at Collioure. The rooms, which have spacious bathrooms with Jacuzzis, open onto water views. Even if you aren't a guest, you may want to have a meal in the dining room and take in its vistas of the harbor. The cooking is inventive—often simple but always refined. Fixed-price menus cost 39€ to 90€ and are served Wednesday to Sunday at lunch and dinner.

Rte. de Port-Vendres, Collioure. www.relaisdes3mas.com. ✆ **04-68-82-05-07.** Fax 04-68-82-38-08. 23 units. 100€–460€ double; 190€–625€ suite. AE, MC, V. Free parking. Closed Dec–Feb. **Amenities:** Restaurant; babysitting; outdoor pool; room service; sauna; free Wi-Fi. *In room:* A/C, TV, hair dryer, minibar.

Where to Eat

Restaurant La Balette, at the Relais des 3 Mas (see p. 646), is the best hotel dining room in town.

Neptune ★★★ FRENCH/CATALAN This is the best restaurant in Collioure, but much to the credit of its owners and staff, it's easygoing and remarkably unpretentious. You'll find it on the southeastern edge of town in a salmon-toned Provençal *mas* (farmhouse). Main courses change with the seasons but may include grilled Mediterranean sea wolf; several versions of lobster; or rack of suckling lamb from the nearby salt marshes, served in orange sauce or an herb-flavored pastry crust.

9 rte. de Porte-Vendres. ✆ **04-68-82-02-27.** www.leneptune-collioure.com. Reservations recommended. Main courses 21€–54€; fixed-price menus 38€–79€. AE, MC, V. Wed–Mon noon–2pm and 7:30–9pm.

PERPIGNAN ★★

905km (561 miles) SW of Paris; 369km (229 miles) NW of Marseille; 64km (40 miles) S of Narbonne

Perpignan is a city on the verge of a new future. The former capital of the kingdom of Majorca and second city of Catalonia welcomes a new TGV (high-speed train) station in 2012, and by 2014 will be only 45 minutes from Barcelona, making it the center of a new Catalan cultural and business hub. Hopes for Perpignan's future are embodied in the Espace Méditerranée neighborhood that is being created around the Théâtre de l'Archipel arts complex designed by France's favorite architect, Jean Nouvel, with views of Mount Canigou from its golden tower.

Southern as it is, Perpignan will probably always retain the relaxed pace it is famous for. You'll have time to smell the flowers that grow here in great abundance. It also embodies the late-night culture and love of partying of its Spanish neighbors.

This is one of the sunniest places in France, but during summer afternoons in July and August, it's a cauldron. That's when many locals catch the 9.5km (6-mile) ride to the beach resort of Canet. Bus no. 1 runs from the center of Perpignan every 15 minutes in the summer and costs 4€. A young scene brings energy to Perpignan, especially along the quays of the Basse River, site of impromptu nighttime concerts, beer drinking, and the devouring of tapas, a tradition adopted from nearby Barcelona.

Essentials

GETTING THERE Five TGV **trains** per day arrive from Paris from both Austerlitz and Gare de Lyon (trip time: 5 hr.); others change at Montpellier; the one-way fare is 112€. There are also six trains from Marseille (trip time: 4 hr.; 42€ one-way). For rail information and schedules, call ✆ **36-35** or 08-92-35-35-35. If you're **driving** from the French Riviera, drive west along A9 to Perpignan.

VISITOR INFORMATION The **Office Municipal du Tourisme** is in the Palais des Congrès, place Armand-Lanoux (✆ **04-68-66-30-30;** fax 04-68-66-30-26; www.perpignantourisme.com).

SPECIAL EVENTS Perpignan is the only city in France to celebrate Holy Week in the same way as in Spain: with remarkable processions of penitents dressed in hooded gowns. The **Procession de la Sanch** leaves from Eglise St-Jacques on Good Friday morning and moves through the city center, accompanied by chants and the beating of drums. In the heat of July, **Les Estivales** (✆ **04-68-35-01-77;** www.estivales.com) causes the city to go on a 4-week cultural binge, with music, expositions, and theater.

The first 2 weeks of September, Perpignan is host to the most widely discussed celebrations of photojournalism in the industry, **Visa pour l'Image** (✆ **04-68-62-38-00;** www.visapourlimage.com). Photographs are exhibited in at least 10 sites of historical (usually medieval) interest. Entrance to the shows is free, and an international committee awards prizes.

Exploring the City

Place de la République is at the heart of the pedestrianized city center, whose inviting streets make it a good town for shopping. Catalan is the style indigenous to the area, and its influence is evident in the textiles, pottery, and furniture. A good selection of Catalan-inspired home-decorating items is found at **La Maison Quinta,** 3 rue des Grands-des-Fabriques (✆ **04-68-34-41-62;** www.maison-quinta.com). For one of the best selections of Catalan pieces, including pottery, furniture, carpets, and antiques, visit **Centre Sant-Vicens,** rue Sant-Vicens (✆ **04-68-50-02-18**), where about a dozen merchants sell ceramics, pottery, and art. You'll find it 4km (2½ miles) south of the town center; follow signs pointing to Enne and Collioure. All the flavor of Perpignan's colorful street life is found at the outdoor market **Marché Cassanyes,** place Cassanyes, selling fruit, vegetables, preserves, and cheap clothes. It happens daily from 7:30am to 1:30pm.

A 2-hour guided **walking tour** is a good way to see the attractions in the town's historic core. Tours begin at 5pm daily from mid-June to mid-September. The rest of the year, they start at 2:30pm on Wednesdays only. They depart from in front of the Palmarium tourist information point on Place Arago and cost 5€ per person. For more details, contact the tourist office (see above).

On the opposite bank of the Têt to the Le Castillet (see below), **Théâtre de l'Archipel** is scheduled to open in 2012 (www.theatredelarchipel.org). Landscaped, olive-filled gardens make this a perfect place for seeking shade on a summer afternoon.

Cathédrale St-Jean ★ The cathedral dates from the 14th and 15th centuries and has an admirable nave and interesting 17th-century retables (altarpieces). Leaving through the south door, you'll find on the left a chapel with the *Devost-Christ* (Devout Christ), a magnificent woodcarving depicting Jesus contorted with pain and suffering, with his head, crowned with thorns, drooping on his chest. Sightseeing visits are discouraged during Mass. On Good Friday, the statue is promenaded through the streets of the town center.

Place Gambetta/rue de l'Horloge. ✆ **04-68-51-33-72.** Free admission. Daily 7:30am–6:30pm. Closes at 5:30pm Dec–Feb.

Le Castillet ★ This crenelated red-brick building is a combination gateway and fortress from the 14th century. You can climb its bulky tower for a view of the town. Also here is the **Musée des Arts et Traditions Populaires Catalans** (also known as La Casa Païral), with exhibitions of Catalan regional artifacts and folkloric items, including typical dress. Check opening hours with the tourist office, as these may be subject to change.

Place de Verdun. ✆ **04-68-35-42-05.** Admission 4€ adults, 2€ students, free ages 18 and under. Tues–Sun 10am–6:30pm.

Musée des Beaux Arts Hyacinthe Rigaud Housed in an 18th-century *hôtel particulier,* the main collection of Perpignan's art museum is from native son Hyacinthe Rigaud, the official court painter of Versailles who painted four generations of Bourbons. Other artists who visited the area, including Picasso, Dufy, Maillol, and Miro, are represented, along with Catalan ceramics and 210 contemporary artists.

16 rue de l'Ange. ✆ **04-68-35-43-40.** Admission 4€ adults, free ages 18 and under. Tues–Sun 10:30am–6pm.

Palais des Rois de Majorque (Palace of the Kings of Majorca) ★ At the top of the town, the Spanish citadel encloses the Palace of the Kings of Majorca. The government has restored this structure, built in the 13th and 14th centuries, around a court encircled by arcades. You can see the old throne room, with its large fireplaces, and a square tower with a double gallery; from the tower, there's a fine view of the Pyrénées. A free guided tour, in French only, departs four times a day if demand warrants it.

Rue des Archers. ✆ **04-68-34-48-29.** Admission 4€ adults, 2€ students and children 12–18, free for children 11 and under. June–Sept daily 10am–6pm; Oct–May daily 9am–5pm.

Where to Stay

La Villa Duflot ★★★ This is the area's greatest hotel, yet its prices are reasonable for the luxury it offers. Located in a suburb 4km (2½ miles) from Perpignan, the Mediterranean-style dwelling is surrounded by a park of pine, palm, and eucalyptus. You can sunbathe in the gardens surrounding the pool and order drinks from the outside bar. The good-size guest rooms are spacious and soundproof, with Art Deco interiors. The restaurant is reason enough to stay. Try, for example, a salad of warm squid, a platter of fresh anchovies marinated in vinegar, or lasagna of foie gras with asparagus points. It's open daily noon to 2pm and 8 to 11pm, with main courses from 19€ to 25€, a weekday fixed-price lunch menu at 25€, and weekend menu at 27€.

Rond-Point Albert Donnezan, Perpignan 66000. www.villa-duflot.com. ✆ **04-68-56-67-67.** Fax 04-68-56-54-05. 24 units. 150€–190€ double; 210€–275€ suite. AE, DC, MC, V. From the center of Perpignan, follow signs to Perthus–Le Belou and A9, and travel 3km (1¾ miles) south. Just before you reach A9, you'll see the hotel. **Amenities:** Restaurant; 2 bars; babysitting; outdoor pool; room service. *In room:* A/C, TV, hair dryer, minibar, free Wi-Fi.

Park Hotel ★ This five-story, mid-'60s hotel facing the Jardins de la Ville provides well-furnished, soundproof rooms. Midsize to spacious, they are comfortably furnished with taste but not much flair; each comes with an average-size bathroom, and most have tub/showers. The restaurant, Le Chap', serves first-class Mediterranean cuisine. Post-nouvelle choices include roast sea scallops flavored with succulent sea urchin velouté, various lobster dishes, and penne with truffles. As an accompaniment, try one of the local wines—perhaps a Collioure or Côtes du Roussillon. Main courses cost between 19€ and 30€, and the restaurant is open for lunch Tuesday to Friday and dinner Tuesday to Saturday.

18 bd. Jean-Bourrat. www.parkhotel-fr.com. ✆ **04-68-35-14-14.** Fax 04-68-35-48-18. 69 units. 80€–140€ double; 180€–280€ suite. AE, DC, MC, V. Parking 10€. **Amenities:** Restaurant; bar; room service. *In room:* A/C, TV, hair dryer, minibar, free Wi-Fi.

Suitehotel Perpignan ★ Perpignan's newest hotel is right next to the Théâtre de l'Archipel and its exciting new district. Styled as a complex of 50 studio apartments, it offers everything an urban nomad could want: spacious (30-sq.-m./323-sq.-ft.) suites with both a bath and a shower; free Wi-Fi through the "Suitebox," which also offers free calls to French landlines, music, and video; a gym; an ironing room; and a bar and "boutique gourmande," where you can buy ready-meals to pop into your own microwave or luxurious snacks like mini boxes of foie gras. There are free massages from 7:30 to 9:30pm on Thursday nights. The contemporary decor, with rooms in soothing slate tones, strikes the right *Elle Decor* note and feels more like a hip bachelor pad than a business hotel.

23 Espace Mediterranée. www.suitehotel.com. ✆ **04-68-92-72-72.** Fax 04-68-64-11-54. 50 units. 110€–125€ suite. Free parking. AE, DC, MC, V. **Amenities:** Bar; gym; self-service meals. *In room:* A/C, TV, hair dryer, minibar, free Wi-Fi.

Where to Eat

The **Park Hotel** and **La Villa Duflot** (see p. 648) both have good restaurants.

L'Assiette Catalane CATALAN Known to virtually every resident of Perpignan for its well-prepared cuisine, this restaurant resembles something you'd expect across the Pyrénées in Spain. Hand-painted ceramic plates, rugby and flamenco posters, and antique farm implements cover the thick stone walls. Even the long, lively bar is inlaid with Iberian mosaics, and copies of works by Dalí and Picasso seem to stare back at you as you dine. Menu items include *parrillade de poissons*—a mixed fish grill cooked on a hot slab of iron that's brought directly to your table—and zarzuellas, paella, and tapas. Chicken with crayfish is another regional specialty. It seems appropriate to follow up with a portion of the flan *crème Catalane.*

9 rue de la République. ✆ **04-68-34-77-62.** www.assiettecatalane.com. Reservations recommended. Main courses 12€–18€; fixed-price lunch 8€–11€, dinner 16€–27€. MC, V. Mon–Sat noon–2pm; Tues–Sat 7:15–10:30pm.

Le Clos des Lys ★ FRENCH/CATALAN This well-recommended restaurant, in a stately building that sits apart from its neighbors, has an outdoor terrace overlooking a copse of cypresses and bubbling fountains. It's supervised by Jean-Claude Vila and Frank Seguret, respected chefs who have been finalists in several culinary competitions. The fixed-price menus vary widely in selection and cost. Dishes may include goat cheese in puff pastry, served with a reduction of banyuls dessert wine; filets of sea wolf fried with sesame seeds and served with eggplant mousse and tomato-flavored risotto; and tournedos of beef with a layer of foie gras, creamed morels, and soufflé potatoes.

660 chemin de la Fauceille. ✆ **04-68-56-79-00.** www.closdeslys.com. Reservations recommended. Main courses 28€–31€; fixed-price lunch 20€–79€, dinner 26€–79€. AE, DC, MC, V. Tues–Sun noon–2pm; Tues and Thurs–Sat 7pm–midnight. Closed 2 weeks in Feb. From the center of Perpignan, drive 2.5km (1½ miles) west, following rte. d'Espagne.

Perpignan After Dark

Perpignan shows its Spanish and Catalan side at night, getting lively only when other cities go to bed. The streets radiating from **place de la Loge** offer a higher concentration of bars and clubs than any other part of town.

You may begin at **Le Habana Bodegita-Club,** 5 rue Grande-des-Fabriques (✆ **04-68-34-11-00**), where salsa and merengue play and sunset-colored cocktails flow. Suds with an Irish accent are the attraction at **Le O'Shannon Bar,** 3 rue de l'Incendie (✆ **04-68-35-12-48**). **Le Cosy Club,** 4 rue du Théâtre (✆ **04-68-66-02-57**), is a piano bar where local jazzers play and a fun-loving crowd congregates over cocktails. It offers the elegance and warmth promised by its name, with a great bar and soothing lighting.

Nightclubs in Perpignan open around 11pm. **Le Napoli,** 3 rue place de Catalogne (✆ **04-68-51-25-02**), is a modern, mirror-sheathed space and may remind you of an airport waiting area without the chairs. (Yes, you'll have to stand up and mingle or dance, because there's almost nowhere to sit.) Another option for dancing is the **Uba-Club,** 5 bd. Mercader (✆ **04-68-34-06-70**), which has a smallish dance floor and, thankfully, some sofas and chairs.

During summer, the beachfront strip at the nearby resort of **Canet-Plage,** 12km (7½ miles) east of Perpignan's historic core, abounds with seasonal bars and dance clubs that come and go with the tourist tides.

CARCASSONNE ★★★

797km (494 miles) SW of Paris; 92km (57 miles) SE of Toulouse; 105km (65 miles) S of Albi

Evoking bold knights, fair damsels, and troubadours, the greatest fortress city of Europe rises against a background of the Pyrénées. Seen from afar, it suggests fairy-tale magic, but in its heyday in the Middle Ages, it wasn't so romantic. Shattering the peace and quiet were battering rams, grapnels, a mobile tower (inspired by the Trojan horse), catapults, flaming arrows, and the mangonel (a type of catapult).

Today the city that once served as a backdrop for the 1991 movie *Robin Hood, Prince of Thieves* is overrun with visitors and tacky gift shops. But the elusive charm of Carcassonne emerges in the evening, when thousands of day-trippers have departed and floodlights bathe the ancient monuments.

Essentials

GETTING THERE Carcassonne is a major stop for **trains** between Toulouse and destinations south and east. There are 17 trains per day from Toulouse (trip time: 1 hr.; 14€ one-way), 16 per day from Montpellier (trip time: 1½ hr.; 23€ one-way), and three per day from Marseille (trip time: 3 hr.; 45€ one-way). For rail information, call ✆ **36-35** or 08-92-35-35-35. If you're **driving,** Carcassonne is on A61 south of Toulouse.

VISITOR INFORMATION The **Office de Tourisme** has locations at 28 rue de Verdun (✆ **04-68-10-24-30;** fax 04-68-10-24-38; www.carcassonne-tourisme.com) and in the medieval town at Porte Narbonnaise (✆ **04-68-10-24-36**).

SPECIAL EVENTS The town's nightlife sparkles during its summer festivals. During the **Festival de Carcassonne** (www.festivaldecarcassonne.com), from mid-July to mid-August, concerts, modern and classical dance, operas, and theater fill the city, with big stars such as Bob Dylan appearing at the **Théâtre Jean Deschamps,** an amphitheatre seating 5,000 in La Cité. Tickets run 25€ to 65€ and can be purchased by calling ✆ **04-68-11-59-15** or 04-68-77-74-31. On July 14, **Bastille Day,** one of the best fireworks spectacles in France lights up the skies at 10:30pm. Over 6 weeks in July and August, the merriment and raucousness of the Middle Ages overtake the city during the **Spectacles Medievaux,** in the form of jousts, food fairs, and street festivals. For information, contact the **Office de Tourisme** (✆ **04-68-10-24-30;** www.carcassonne-tourisme.com).

Exploring the Town

Carcassonne consists of two towns: the **Bastide St-Louis** (also known as Ville Basse, or "Lower City") and the medieval **Cité.** The former has little of interest, but the latter is among the major attractions in France. The fortifications consist of the inner and outer walls, a double line of ramparts. The Visigoths built the inner rampart in the 5th century. Clovis, king of the Franks, attacked it in 506 but failed to breach the fortifications. The Saracens overcame the city in 728, but Pepin the Short (father of Charlemagne) drove them out in 752.

The epic medieval poems *Chansons de Geste* tell the tale of the origin of the town's name. During a siege by Charlemagne, the populace of the city was starving and near surrender until a local noblewoman, Dame Carcas, reputedly gathered up the last of their grain, fed it to a sow, and then tossed the pig over the ramparts. The pig burst, scattering the grain. Dame Carcas then ordered the trumpets sounded for a parley and cried, *"Carcas te sonne!"* (Carcas is calling you!) The Franks concluded that Carcassonne must have unlimited food supplies and ended their siege.

Carcassonne's walls were further fortified by the *vicomtes* de Trencavel in the 12th century and by Louis IX and Philip the Bold during the following century. By the mid–17th century, the city had lost its position as a strategic frontier, and the ramparts were left to decay. In the 19th century, the builders of the Lower Town began to remove the stone for use in new construction. But interest in the Middle Ages revived, and the government ordered Viollet-le-Duc (who restored Notre-Dame in Paris) to repair and, where necessary, rebuild the walls. Reconstruction continued until very recently. A small population lives inside the walls.

In the highest elevation of the Cité, at the uppermost terminus of rue Principale (rue Cros Mayrevielle), you'll find the **Château Comtal,** place du

Basilique St-Nazaire.

Château (✆ **04-68-11-70-70**), a restored 12th-century fortress that's open April through September daily 10am to 6:30pm, October through March daily 10am to 5pm. Entrance includes an obligatory 45-minute guided tour, in French and broken English. It's also the only way to climb onto the city's inner ramparts. The cost is 8.50€ for adults, 5€ ages 18 to 25, and free age 17 and under. The tour includes access to exhibitions that display the archaeological remnants discovered on-site, plus an explanation of the 19th-century restorations.

Another major monument in the fortifications is the **Basilique St-Nazaire★**, place de l'Eglise (✆ **04-68-25-27-65**), dating from the 11th to the 14th centuries and containing some beautiful stained-glass windows and a pair of rose medallions. The nave is in the Romanesque style, and the choir and transept are Gothic. The 16th-century organ is one of the oldest in southwestern France. The 1266 tomb of Bishop Radulphe is well preserved. The cathedral is open Monday through Saturday 9 to 11:45am and 1:45 to 6pm, Sunday 9 to 10:45am and 2 to 5pm. It closes slightly earlier in winter. Mass is celebrated on Sunday at 11am. Admission is free.

Shopping

Carcassonne has two distinct shopping areas. In the modern Lower City, the major streets for shopping, particularly if you're in the market for clothing, are **rue Clemenceau** and **rue de Verdun.** In the walled medieval city, the streets are chock-full of tiny stores and boutiques; most sell gift items such as antiques and local arts and crafts.

Stores worth visiting, all in the Cité, include **Comptoir des Vins,** 3 rue du Conte Roger (✆ **04-68-26-44-76**), where you'll find a wide selection of regional wines. Some antiques stores of merit are **Mme. Faye-Nunez,** 4 place du Château (✆ **04-68-47-09-45**), for antique furniture; **Antiquités Safi,** 26 rue Trivalle (✆ **04-68-25-60-51**), for paintings and art objects; and **Maison du Sud,** 13 porte d'Aude (✆ **04-68-47-10-06**), for home decoration.

Where to Stay

IN THE CITÉ

Hôtel de la Cité ★★★ Originally a palace for whatever bishop or prelate happened to be in power at the time, this has been the most desirable hotel in town since 1909. It's in the actual walls of the city, adjoining the cathedral. The Orient-Express Hotel group acquired the hotel in the '90s and fluffed it up to the tune of $3 million. You enter a long Gothic corridor-gallery leading to the lounge. Many rooms open onto the ramparts and a garden, and feature antiques or reproductions. A few accommodations contain wood headboards and four-poster beds. The ideal unit is no. 308, which opens onto the most panoramic view of the city. The hotel is renowned for its restaurant, **La Barbacane** (p. 654).

Place Auguste Pierre Pont. www.hoteldelacite.com. ✆ **04-68-71-98-71.** Fax 04-68-71-50-15. 61 units. 230€–395€ double; 445€–1,065€ suite. AE, DC, MC, V. Parking 21€. Closed Feb to mid-Mar. **Amenities:** 3 restaurants; bar; babysitting; outdoor pool; room service. *In room:* A/C, TV, hair dryer, minibar, free Wi-Fi.

AT THE ENTRANCE TO THE CITÉ

Best Western Le Donjon et Les Remparts ★★ This little hotel is big on charm and is the best value in the moderate price range. Built in the style of the old Cité, it has a honey-colored stone exterior with iron bars on the windows. The interior is a jewel, with elaborate Louis XIII–style furniture gracing the reception lounges. A newer wing contains additional rooms in medieval architectural style. Their furnishings are more severe, consistent with the medieval look of the nearby ramparts. The hotel also runs the nearby Brasserie Le Donjon. In summer, the garden is the perfect breakfast spot.

2 rue du Comte-Roger. www.hotel-donjon.fr. ✆ **04-68-11-23-00.** Fax 04-68-25-06-60. 62 units. 89€–159€ double; 150€–403€ suite. AE, DC, MC, V. Parking 10€. **Amenities:** Restaurant; bar; room service. *In room:* A/C, TV, hair dryer, minibar, free Wi-Fi.

IN VILLE-BASSE

Trois Couronnes ★★ This dependable modern hotel makes the most of its Lower City location by offering great views of the Cité and the Aude River from its 44 "panoramic" rooms and suite, and from the fourth-floor restaurant and bar. A government-rated three-star hotel, "Three Crowns" has some of the best facilities in town, including an indoor pool. The rooms are functionally comfortable, with tasteful furnishings. Service is top rate, and maintenance is good. Good regional cuisine is served in the on-site restaurant.

2 rue des Trois Couronnes. www.hotel-destroiscouronnes.com. ✆ **04-68-25-36-10.** Fax 04-68-25-92-92. 69 units. 95€–145€ double; 200€–240€ suite. AE, DC, MC, V. Parking 6€–9€. **Amenities:** Restaurant; bar; indoor pool; room service. *In room:* A/C, TV, hair dryer, minibar, free Wi-Fi.

Where to Eat

Brasserie Donjon, run by Le Donjon et Les Remparts hotel, is a good, affordable choice for meals, especially if you're visiting the Cité at lunchtime. In Ville-Basse, the moderately priced restaurant at **Trois Couronnes** (see above) serves well-prepared regional cuisine.

Au Jardin de la Tour INTERNATIONAL This restaurant and its verdant garden introduce greenery and charm into the city's medieval core. Rustic finds from local antiques fairs decorate the early-19th-century building. You can order from a large selection of salads, beef filet with morels, sushi, cassoulet, terrines of foie gras, and all kinds of grilled fish. The consistently good cooking relies on fresh ingredients deftly handled by a talented kitchen staff.

11 Porte-d'Aude. ✆ **04-68-25-71-24.** Reservations recommended in summer. Main courses 15€–25€; fixed-price menu 30€. MC, V. Tues–Sat noon–2pm and 7:30–10pm. Closed Nov 1–Dec 15.

La Barbacane ★ FRENCH Named after its medieval neighborhood, this restaurant enjoys equal billing with the celebrated hotel that contains it. Its soothing-looking dining room has green walls and lots of paneling. Menu items are based on seasonal ingredients, with just enough zest. Examples are green ravioli perfumed with squid and its own ink, crisp-fried cod with black olives, saltwater crayfish with strips of Bayonne ham, and organically fed free-range guinea fowl rubbed with vanilla and stuffed with truffles. A star dessert is the warm soufflé flavored with coffee from Ecuador and chocolate, served with peppermint sherbet.

In the Hôtel de la Cité, place de l'Eglise. ✆ **04-68-71-98-71.** www.hoteldelacite.com. Reservations recommended. Main courses 35€–65€; fixed-price menu 75€–160€. AE, DC, MC, V. Thurs–Mon 7:30–10pm. Closed Feb–Mar.

Carcassone After Dark

Carcassonne nightlife centers on **rue Omer-Sarraut** in La Bastide and **place Marcou** in La Cité. **La Bulle,** 115 rue Barbacane (✆ **04-68-72-47-70**), explodes with techno and rock dance tunes for an under-30 crowd that keeps the place hopping until 5am Wednesday to Sunday. The cover charge begins at 10€ per person. Another enduringly popular disco, 4km (2½ miles) southwest of town, is **Le Black Bottom,** route de Limoux (✆ **04-68-47-37-11**), which plays every conceivable kind of dance music Thursday through Sunday beginning at 11pm. Entrance costs 10€ on Saturday only.

CASTRES ★

728km (451 miles) SW of Paris; 42km (26 miles) S of Albi

On the bank of the Agout River, Castres is the gateway for trips to the Sidobre, the mountains of Lacaune, and the Black Mountains. Castres is one of France's most important wool-producing areas; the industry's origins in the region date to the 14th century. The town, with a current population of 50,000, was once a Roman military installation. A Benedictine monastery was founded here in the 9th century, and the town fell under the comtes d'Albi in the 10th century. During the wars of religion, it was Protestant.

Essentials

GETTING THERE From Toulouse, there are seven **trains** per day (trip time: 1¼ hr.); the one-way fare is 14€. For information, call ✆ **36-35** or 08-92-35-35-35. If you're **driving,** Castres is on N126 east of Toulouse and N112 south of Albi.

VISITOR INFORMATION The **Office de Tourisme** is at 2 place de la République (✆ **05-63-62-63-62;** fax 05-63-62-63-60; www.tourisme-castres.fr).

Exploring the Town

Eglise St-Benoît The town's most prominent church is an outstanding example of French baroque architecture. The architect Caillau began construction in 1677 on the site of a 9th-century Benedictine abbey, but the structure was never completed according to its original plans. Gabriel Briard executed the painting above the altar in the 18th century.

Place du 8-Mai-1945. ✆ **05-63-59-05-19.** Free admission. Mon–Sat 9am–noon and 2–6pm; Sun 8:30am–noon. Closed to casual visitors Sun Oct–May, except for religious services.

Musée Goya ★ The museum is in the town hall, an archbishop's palace designed by Mansart in 1669. Some of the spacious public rooms have ceilings supported by a frieze of the archbishop's coats of arms. The collection includes 16th-century tapestries and the works of Spanish painters from the 15th to the 20th centuries. Most notable are the paintings of Goya, all donated to the town in 1894 by Pierre Briguiboul, son of the Castres-born artist Marcel Briguiboul. *Les Caprices* is a study of figures created in 1799 after the illness that left Goya deaf. Filling much of an entire room, the work consists of symbolic images of demons and monsters, a satire of Spanish society.

In the Jardin de l'Evêché. ✆ **05-63-71-59-30.** Admission 3€ adults, free for children 18 and under. July–Aug daily 10am–6pm; Apr–June and Sept Tues–Sat 9am–noon and 2–6pm, Sun 10am–noon and 2–6pm; Oct–Mar Tues–Sat 9am–noon and 2–5pm, Sun 10am–noon and 2–5pm.

Painting by Francisco Pacheco at the Musée Goya.

Where to Stay

Hôtel Renaissance ★ Built in the 17th century as a courthouse, this had become a colorful but run-down hotel when it was restored in 1993. Today you'll see a dignified building with *colombages*-style half-timbering and a mixture of stone blocks and bricks. Some of the comfortable rooms have exposed timbers. Some rooms are in the style of Napoleon III, some are 18th-century Asiatic, and some are country-comfortable with safari-themed fabrics.

17 rue Victor-Hugo. www.hotel-renaissance.fr. ✆ **05-63-59-30-42.** Fax 05-63-59-21-38. 22 units. 65€–85€ double; 85€–120€ suite. AE, DC, MC, V. Parking 10€. **Amenities:** Restaurant; bar; room service. *In room:* A/C, TV, hair dryer, minibar, free Wi-Fi.

Where to Eat

Brasserie de l'Europe FRENCH/PROVENÇAL This modern brasserie is a good bet for solid cuisine. The rustic decor features English-inspired furnishings with lots of well-oiled wood paneling. The expansive menu includes a selection of regional platters as well as pizzas. There are also regional sausages served with purée of apples and cheese from the foothills of the Pyrénées. Other menu items include cassoulets and roasted Camembert cheese with Provençal herbs. The service is polite but pressed for time. Many visitors find it suitable for a simple noontime meal.

1 place Jean-Jaurès. ✆ **05-63-59-01-44.** Reservations recommended. Main courses 15€–19€; fixed-price lunch 14€–21€, dinner 22€. MC, V. Mon–Sat noon–2:30pm and 7–10:30pm.

La Mandragore ★ LANGUEDOCIENNE On an easily overlooked narrow street, this restaurant, named for a legendary plant with magic powers, occupies a small section of one of the many wings of the medieval château-fort of Castres. The decor is simple, with stone walls and tones of autumn colors. The regional cuisine is served with a smile. Among the best dishes are ravioli stuffed with truffles, snails, and pink garlic, flavored with basil; rack of suckling veal with exotic mushrooms; and *magret* of duckling with natural Canadian maple syrup. The owners are French citizens who lived in Montreal for 15 years and worked at a restaurant there.

1 rue Malpas. ✆ **05-63-59-51-27.** Reservations recommended. Main courses 12€–18€; fixed-price menu 13€ lunch, 18€–26€ dinner. DC, MC, V. Tues–Sat noon–2pm and 7–9pm. Closed 2 weeks in Sept and 2 weeks in Mar.

ALBI ★★★

697km (432 miles) SW of Paris; 76km (47 miles) NE of Toulouse

The "red city" (for the color of its bricks) of Albi straddles both banks of the Tarn River and is dominated by its 13th-century cathedral, which is at the center of a remarkable brick-built Episcopal city. The whole of this Medieval city center was added to UNESCO's World Heritage List in 2010. Toulouse-Lautrec was born in the Hôtel Bosc in Albi; it's still a private home and not open to visitors, but there's a plaque on the wall of the building, on rue Toulouse-Lautrec in the town center. The town's major attraction is a museum with a world-class collection of the artist's work.

Essentials

GETTING THERE Fifteen **trains** per day link Toulouse with Albi (trip time: 1 hr., 15 min.); the one-way fare is 12€. For rail information, call ✆ **36-35** or 08-92-35-35-35. If you're **driving** from Toulouse, take N88 northeast.

VISITOR INFORMATION The **Office de Tourisme** is in the Palais de la Berbie, place Ste-Cécile (✆ **05-63-49-48-80;** fax 05-63-49-48-98; www.albi-tourisme.fr).

Exploring the Town

Cathédrale Ste-Cécile ★★★ Fortified with ramparts and parapets, this 13th-century cathedral was built by a local lord-bishop after a religious struggle with the comte de Toulouse (the crusade against the Cathars). It holds three records: the largest brick-built cathedral in the world, the oldest Medieval depiction of the last judgment, and the largest surface area of Italian Renaissance frescos in France. Note the exceptional 16th-century rood screen with a unique suit of polychromatic statues from the Old and New Testaments. Free classical concerts take place in July and August on Wednesday at 5pm and Sunday at 4pm.

Near place du Vigan, in the medieval center of town. ✆ **05-63-43-23-43.** Cathédrale: Free admission. Choir and audioguide 3€ adults, free children 11 and under; Treasury 3€ adults, 2€ ages 12–25, free 11 and under. June–Sept daily 9am–6:30pm; Oct–May daily 9am–noon and 2–6:30pm.

Musée de Lapérouse Set on the opposite bank of the Tarn from the bulk of Albi's medieval core (take the Pont-Vieux to reach it), this museum honors the achievements of Albi's native son, Jean-François de Lapérouse, and tries to penetrate the mystery of his shipwreck off the Salomon Islands in 1788. Commissioned as an explorer by Louis XVI in the late 1600s, he mapped and charted the coastlines of Alaska, California, and China, bringing the French up to speed against England in its rush for colonies outside of Europe.

Square Botany Bay. ✆ **05-63-46-01-87.** www.laperouse-france.fr. Admission 3€ adults, 2€ students and ages 13–25, free for children 12 and under. Mar–June and Sept–Oct Tues–Sun

9am–noon and 2–6pm; July–Aug Mon–Fri 9am–noon and 2–6pm, Sat–Sun 10am–noon and 2–7pm; Nov–Feb Tues–Sun 10am–noon and 2–5pm.

Musée Toulouse-Lautrec ★★ The Palais de la Berbie (Archbishop's Palace) is a fortified structure dating from the 13th century. This museum contains the world's most important collection of the Toulouse Lautrec's paintings, more than 1,000 in all, with new extensions inaugurated in 2010 and a complete rehanging of the work. The collection began with the works left in his studio in Albi, which were bequeathed by his family in 1922, and the museum also owns paintings by Degas, Bonnard, Matisse, Utrillo, and Rouault.

Place Ste-Cécile. ✆ **05-63-49-48-78.** Admission 5.50€ adults, 2.50€ students, free for children 13 and under. July–Aug daily 9am–6pm; June and Sept daily 9am–noon and 2–6pm; Apr–May daily 10am–noon and 2–6pm; Mar and Oct Wed–Mon 10am–noon and 2–5:30pm; Nov–Feb Wed–Mon 10am–noon and 2–5pm. Closed New Year's Day, May 1, Nov 1, and Christmas.

Where to Stay

Hostellerie St-Antoine ★★ Some historians say this is one of the oldest continuously operated hotels in France. Originally a monastery and then a medieval hospital, the property became an inn in 1734 (when the present building was constructed). The same family has owned it for five generations; today the father-son team of Jacques and Jean-François Rieux manages it. Jacques's mother focused on Toulouse-Lautrec when designing the hotel, because her grandfather was a friend of the painter and was given a few of his paintings, sketches, and prints. Several are in the lounge, which opens onto a rear garden. The rooms have been delightfully decorated, with a sophisticated use of color, reproductions, and occasional antiques. They're generally spacious, furnished with French Provincial pieces. Even if you're not staying, visit the dining room. The Rieux culinary tradition is revealed in their traditional yet creative cuisine.

17 rue St-Antoine. www.saint-antoine-albi.com. ✆ **05-63-54-04-04.** Fax 05-63-47-10-47. 44 units. 125€–165€ double; 185€–225€ suite. AE, DC, MC, V. Parking 7€. **Amenities:** Restaurant (open only to groups); bar; babysitting; room service. *In room:* A/C, TV, hair dryer, minibar, free Wi-Fi.

Hôtel Chiffre This hotel in the city center was built as a lodging for passengers on the mail coaches that hauled letters and people across France. The renovated building retains the original porch that sheltered carriages from the rain and sun. The rooms are artfully cozy, with upholstered walls in floral patterns; some have views of the inner courtyard. The midsize bathrooms come with tub/showers or showers only. The hotel restaurant is popular among locals because of its good-value fixed-price menus. The menu, priced at 20€ to 27€ per person, consists of

Cathédrale-Ste-Cécile.

choices that were compiled after Toulouse-Lautrec's death by his friends. They remembered the way he'd often prepare the dishes himself during his dinner parties. Some of his favorite dishes included radishes stuffed with braised liver, suprême of *sandre* (fish), and duckling roasted with garlic.

50 rue Séré-de-Rivières. www.hotelchiffre.com. ✆ **05-63-48-58-48.** Fax 05-63-38-11-15. 39 units. 88€–112€ double; 200€ suite. AE, MC, V. Parking 9€. **Amenities:** Restaurant; bar; room service; free Wi-Fi. *In room:* A/C, TV, hair dryer.

Where to Eat

La Hostellerie St-Antoine has a wonderful restaurant, and Bateau Ivre at the **Hôtel Chiffre** is another worthy choice. See "Where to Stay," above.

Jardin des Quatre Saisons ★★ MODERN FRENCH The best food in Albi is served by Georges Bermond, who believes that menus, like life, should change with the seasons, which is how the restaurant got its name. In his two simple dining rooms, the service is always competent and polite. Fine-tuned menu items include delicious fricassee of snails garnished with strips of the famous hams produced in the nearby hamlet of Lacaune, and ravioli stuffed with pulverized shrimp and served with truffled cream sauce. Most delectable of all—an excuse for returning—is *pot-au-feu* of the sea, with three or four species of fish garnished with crayfish-cream sauce. The wine list is the finest in Albi.

19 bd. de Strasbourg. ✆ **05-63-60-77-76.** www.lejardindesquatresaisons.fr. Reservations recommended. Fixed-price menu 24€–35€. AE, DC, MC, V. Tues–Sun noon–2:30pm; Tues–Sat 7:30–10pm.

Le Lautrec TRADITIONAL FRENCH Part of this restaurant's charm derives from its associations with Toulouse-Lautrec—it lies across the street from his birthplace and is decorated with paintings by local artists. Also appealing is the rich patina of its interior brickwork. The skillfully prepared food items include scallops that come with rose oil and essence of shrimp, and roasted rack of lamb marinated in a brewed infusion of Provençal thyme. Hearty regional dishes—beloved by local diners—are a cassoulet of codfish, savory sweetbreads (an acquired taste for some), duckling *en confit,* and rabbit stew with vegetables.

13–15 rue Toulouse-Lautrec. ✆ **05-63-54-86-55.** www.restaurant-le-lautrec.com. Reservations recommended. Main courses 18€–38€; fixed-price lunch Tues–Fri 15€–17€; fixed-price lunch or dinner 18€–50€. AE, MC, V. Tues–Sun noon–2pm; Tues–Sat 7–9:30pm. Closed 1 week in Jan, 1 week in Aug, and 2 weeks in Nov.

CORDES-SUR-CIEL ★★

678km (420 miles) SW of Paris; 25km (16 miles) NW of Albi

This remarkable site is like an eagle's nest on a hilltop, opening onto the Cérou valley. In days gone by, celebrities such as Jean-Paul Sartre and Albert Camus considered this town a favorite hideaway. In low season, the population is only 1,050, but it swells to 10,000 in midsummer.

Through the centuries, Cordes has been known for its textile, leather, and silk industries. Even today, it's an arts-and-crafts city, and in many of the old houses on the narrow streets, artisans—blacksmiths, enamelers, graphic artists, weavers, engravers, sculptors, and painters—ply their trades. Park outside and then pass under an arch leading to the old town.

Essentials

GETTING THERE If you're **driving,** take N88 northwest from Toulouse to Gaillac, turning north on D922 into Cordes-sur-Ciel. If you're coming by **train,** get off in Cordes-Vindrac and walk, rent a bicycle, or take a taxi the remaining 3km (1¾ miles) west of Cordes. For train information, call ✆ **36-35** or 08-92-35-35-35. For a **minibus,** call Taxi Barrois (✆ **05-63-56-14-80**). The one-way fare is 4.15€ Monday through Saturday, rising to 6.65€ after 7pm and on Sunday. There's no regular bus service.

VISITOR INFORMATION The **Office de Tourisme** is at 8 place Jeanne Ramel-Cals (✆ **05-63-56-00-52;** fax 05-63-56-19-52; www.cordessurciel.eu).

Exploring the Town

Often called "the city of a hundred Gothic arches," Cordes contains numerous ***maisons gothiques*** ★★ of pink sandstone. Many of the doors and windows are fashioned of pointed (broken) arches that retain their 13th- and 14th-century grace. Some of the best-preserved ones line **Grande Rue Raymond VII,** also called **rue Droite.**

Eglise St-Michel The church, the most important historic building in town, dates from the late 13th century and has undergone many alterations. Most of the lateral design of the side chapels probably comes from the cathedral at Albi. Before being shipped here, the organ (dating from 1830) was in Notre-Dame in Paris.

Rue St-Michel. ✆ **05-63-56-00-25** (tourist office). Free admission. Summer tours daily 10:30am–12:30pm and 3–6:30pm.

Musée Charles-Portal Small, quirky, and relatively unvisited even by residents of Cordes, this somewhat sleepy museum is named after a nearby pass-through (the Painted Gate) that pierces the fortifications surrounding the city's medieval center. It's also named for Charles-Portal (d. 1936), a 1920s-era archivist of the Tarn region and a local historian. In a medieval house whose foundations date from the Gallo-Roman era, it contains artifacts of the textile industry, farming implements, samples of local embroidery, a reconstruction of an old peasant home, and a scattering of medieval pieces.

Porte des Ormeaux. ✆ **05-63-53-44-41.** Admission 2.50€ adults, 1.50€ students and ages 12–25, free for children 11 and under. July–Aug Wed–Mon 2–6pm; Apr–June and Sept–Oct only Sat–Sun 2–5pm.

Where to Stay & Eat

Hostellerie du Parc TRADITIONAL FRENCH This inn originated in the 18th century as a landowner's thick-walled home. Today, in a verdant park, the stone house holds this charming getaway *restaurant avec chambres*. It serves generous meals in a garden or paneled dining room. Specialties include homemade foie gras, duckling, *poularde* (chicken) *occitaine*, rabbit with cabbage leaves, and confit of roasted rabbit with pink garlic from the nearby town of Lautrec.

The hotel offers 13 comfortable and well-furnished rooms; a double costs 65€ to 75€. Each accommodation comes with free Wi-Fi.

Les Cabannes. www.hostellerie-du-parc.com. ✆ **05-63-56-02-59.** Fax 05-63-56-18-03. Reservations recommended. Main courses 14€–32€; fixed-price menu 28€–65€. AE, DC, MC, V. June–Oct daily noon–2pm and 7–9:30pm; off season Fri–Sun noon–2pm, Fri–Sat 7–10pm. Closed 3 weeks in Jan. From the town center, take rte. de St-Antonin (D600) for about 1km (½ mile) west.

Le Grand Ecuyer ★★★ MODERN FRENCH The medieval monument that contains this restaurant (the 15th-c. hunting lodge of Raymond VII, comte de Toulouse) is a national historic treasure. Chef Yves Thuriès's platters have made his dining room an almost mandatory stop for royalty visiting the area, but despite this, the restaurant remains intimate and unstuffy. Specialties include three confits of lobster, red mullet salad with fondue of vegetables, confit of pigeon with olive oil and rosemary, and noisette of lamb in chicory sauce. The dessert selection is nearly overwhelming. The hotel contains 12 rooms and 1 suite, all with antiques and modern comforts. Doubles cost 115€ to 165€; the suite is 265€. The same management owns two other, more affordable hotels in Cordes, and details of these are on their website.

Cordes-sur-Ciel.

Grand-Rue Raymond VIII, Haute de la Cité. www.thuries.fr. ✆ **05-63-53-79-50.** Fax 05-63-53-79-51. Reservations required. Main courses 28€–38€; fixed-price menu 43€–93€. AE, DC, MC, V. July–Aug Thurs–Sun noon–1:30pm, daily 7–9:30pm; Apr–June and Sept to mid-Oct Tues–Sun 7–9:30pm. Closed mid-Oct to Mar.

TOULOUSE ★★★

705km (437 miles) SW of Paris; 245km (152 miles) SE of Bordeaux; 97km (60 miles) W of Carcassonne

The old capital of Languedoc and France's fourth-largest city, Toulouse (known as La Ville Rose) has a cosmopolitan flavor. The major city of the southwest, filled with gardens and squares, it's the gateway to the Pyrénées. Most of Toulouse's fine old mansions date from the Renaissance, when this was one of the richest cities in Europe. Today Toulouse is an artistic and cultural hub and a high-tech center, home to two huge aircraft makers—Airbus and Aerospatiale. Also making the city tick is its great number of students: some 110,000 out of a total population of 800,000.

A city with a distinguished past, Toulouse is also a city of the future. The National Center for Space Research has been headquartered here for more than 3 decades. The first regularly scheduled airline flights from France took off from the local airport in the 1920s. Today Airbus planes are assembled in a gargantuan hangar in the suburb of Colombiers.

Essentials

GETTING THERE The Toulouse-Blagnac international **airport** lies in the city's northwestern suburbs, 11km (6¾ miles) from the center; for flight information, call ✆ **08-25-38-00-00. Air France** (✆ **08-20-80-28-02**) has about 25 flights a day from Paris and flies to Toulouse from London twice a day.

Some 5 TGV **trains** per day arrive from Paris Montparnasse (trip time: 5½ hr.; 86€ one-way), 14 trains from Bordeaux (trip time: 2 hr., 10 min.; 36€ one-way), and 8 from Marseille (trip time: 3½ hr.; 56€ one-way). For information, call ✆ **36-35** or 08-92-35-35-35. The **drive** from Paris takes 6 to 7 hours. Take A10 south to Bordeaux, connecting to A62 to Toulouse. The Canal du Midi links many of the region's cities with Toulouse by waterway.

VISITOR INFORMATION The **Office de Tourisme** is in the Donjon du Capitole in the Square de Gaulle (✆ **05-61-11-02-22;** fax 05-61-23-74-97; www.ot-toulouse.fr).

Exploring the City

In addition to the sights listed below, architectural highlights include the Gothic brick **Eglise des Jacobins ★★**, parvis des Jacobins (✆ **05-61-22-21-92**), in Old Toulouse, west of place du Capitole along rue Lakanal. The church and the restored convent, daring in its architecture and its use of palm tree–shaped vaults, form the largest extant monastery complex in France. It's open daily 9am to 7pm. Admission to most of the complex is free, but a visit to the cloisters costs 3€, free for 17 and under.

Small, charming, and dating mostly from the 18th century, **Notre-Dame la Daurade,** 1 place de la Daurade (✆ **05-61-21-38-32**), gets its name from the gilding that covers its partially baroque exterior. Its prized possession is a statue of the Black Virgin, about 1m (3¼ ft.) tall, to which some locals attribute quasi-mystical powers. The one you'll see today was crafted in 1807 as a replacement for a much older statue that was burned during the French Revolution. Admission is free, and Basilique Notre-Dame is open daily 8:30am to 6:30pm.

In civic architecture, **Le Capitole ★**, place du Capitole (✆ **05-61-22-34-12**), is an outstanding achievement and one of the most potent symbols of Toulouse. Built in a baroque style in 1753, it houses the **Hôtel de Ville** (City Hall), as well as the **Théâtre National du Capitole** (✆ **05-61-63-13-13**), which presents concerts, ballets, and operas. It's outfitted in an Italian-inspired 18th-century style with shades of scarlet and gold. Admission, which usually includes a view of the theater, is free. The Capitole complex is open Monday through Saturday 9am to 5pm, and until 7pm during holidays.

After all that sightseeing, head for **place Wilson,** a showcase 19th-century square (actually an oval) lined with fashionable cafes.

Basilique St-Sernin ★★★ Consecrated in 1096, this is the largest, finest, and most pure Romanesque church in Europe, containing the tombs of the Counts of Toulouse. Entering by the main west door, you can see the double side aisles that give the church five naves, an unusual feature in Romanesque architecture. An upper cloister forms a passageway around the interior. In the crypt (ask the custodian for permission to enter) are the relics of 128 saints, plus a thorn said to be from the Crown of Thorns. The old baroque retables (altarpieces) and shrine in the ambulatory have been reset; the relics here are those of the apostles and the first bishops of Toulouse.

Place St-Sernin. ✆ **05-61-21-80-45.** Free admission to church; combined admission to the crypt and ambulatory 2€. Church June–Sept Mon–Sat 8:30am–7pm, Sun 8:30am–7:30pm; Oct–May Mon–Sat 8:30am–6pm, Sun 8:30am–7:30pm. Crypt and ambulatory June–Sept Mon–Sat 10am–6pm, Sun 11:30am–6pm; Oct–May Mon–Sat 10am–noon and 2–5:30pm, Sun 2–5:30pm.

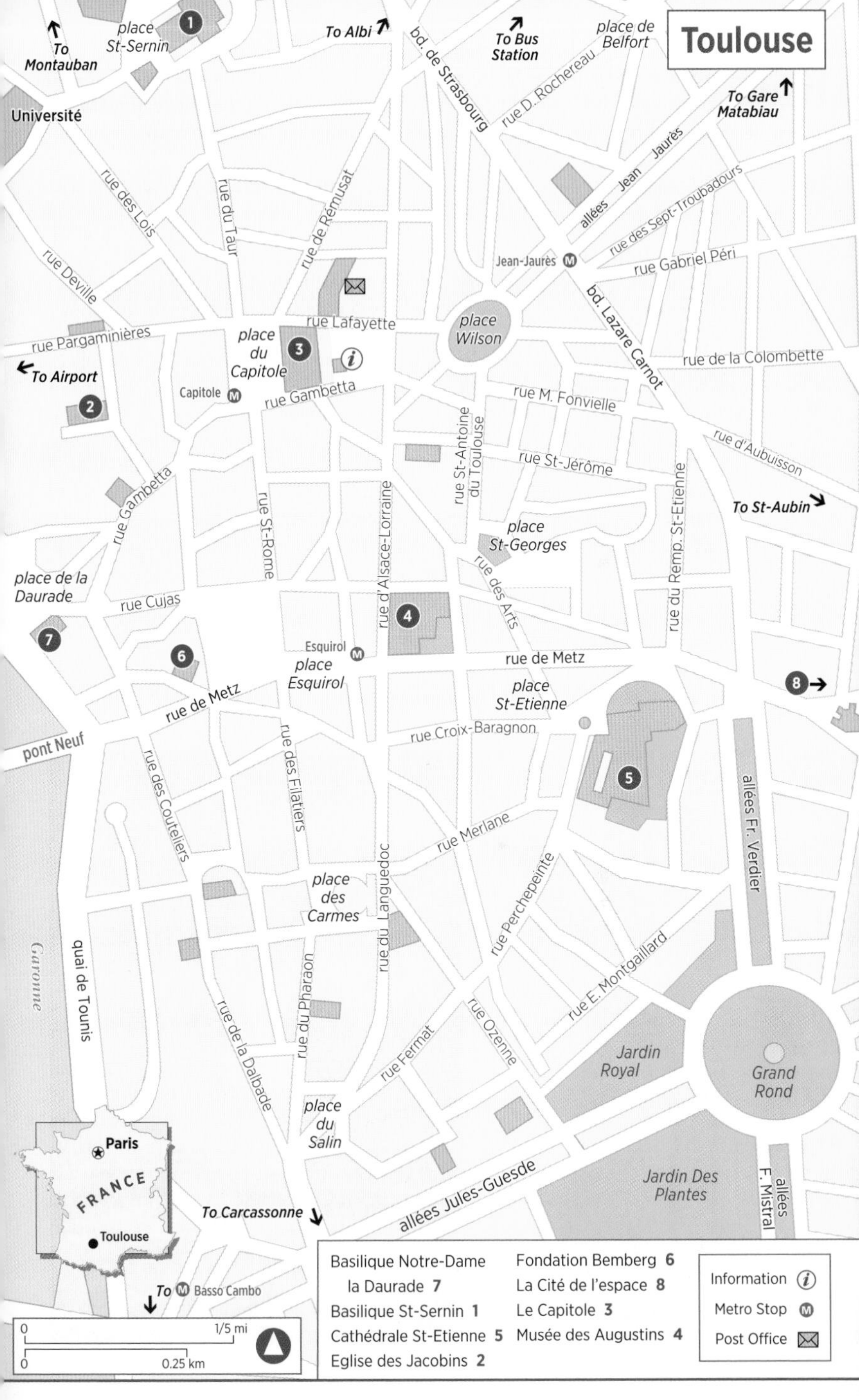
Toulouse
place St-Sernin
To Montauban
To Albi
bd. de Strasbourg
To Bus Station
place de Belfort
To Gare Matabiau
Université
rue D. Rochereau
allées Jean Jaurès
rue des Sept-Troubadours
rue des Lois
rue du Taur
rue de Rémusat
rue Deville
Jean-Jaurès
rue Gabriel Péri
bd. Lazare Carnot
rue Pargaminières
place du Capitole
rue Lafayette
place Wilson
To Airport
Capitole
rue Gambetta
rue de la Colombette
rue M. Fonvielle
rue St-Antoine du Toulouse
rue d'Aubuisson
rue St-Jérôme
rue Gambetta
rue St-Rome
rue d'Alsace-Lorraine
To St-Aubin
place St-Georges
rue du Remp. St-Etienne
place de la Daurade
rue Cujas
rue des Arts
Esquirol
place Esquirol
rue de Metz
place St-Etienne
rue de Metz
pont Neuf
rue Croix-Baragnon
rue des Couteliers
rue des Filatiers
allées Fr. Verdier
rue Merlane
place des Carmes
rue du Languedoc
rue Perchepeinte
Garonne
quai de Tounis
rue E. Montgaillard
rue de la Dalbade
rue du Pharaon
rue Ozenne
rue Fermat
Jardin Royal
Grand Rond
place du Salin
Paris
FRANCE
Toulouse
To Carcassonne
allées Jules-Guesde
Jardin Des Plantes
allées F. Mistral
To Basso Cambo
0
1/5 mi
0
0.25 km
Basilique Notre-Dame la Daurade 7
Basilique St-Sernin 1
Cathédrale St-Etienne 5
Eglise des Jacobins 2
Fondation Bemberg 6
La Cité de l'espace 8
Le Capitole 3
Musée des Augustins 4
Information
Metro Stop
Post Office

Cathédrale St-Etienne ★ Because it took so long to build (it was designed and constructed from the 11th–17th c.), some critics scorn this cathedral for its mishmash of styles. The rectangular bell tower is from the 16th century. A Gothic choir has been added to its unique ogival nave.

Place St-Etienne, at the eastern end of rue de Metz. ✆ **05-61-52-03-82.** Mon–Sat 8am–7pm; Sun 9am–7pm.

Fondation Bemberg Opened in 1995, this quickly became one of the city's most important museums. Housed in the magnificent Hôtel Assézat (built in 1555), the museum provides an overview of 5 centuries of European art, showcasing world-class paintings from the Renaissance to the late 19th century. The nucleus of the collection represents the lifelong work of German-French collector extraordinaire Georges Bemberg, who donated 331 works. The largest bequest was 28 paintings by Pierre Bonnard, including his *Moulin Rouge.* Bemberg also donated works by Pissarro, Matisse *(Vue d'Antibes),* and Monet, plus the fauves. The foundation also owns Canaletto's much-reproduced *Vue de Mestre.* The mansion houses the **Académie des Jeux-Floraux,** which, since 1323, has presented literary awards in the form of wrought-metal flowers to poets.

Place d'Assézat, rue de Metz. ✆ **05-61-12-06-89.** www.fondation-bemberg.fr. Admission 6€ adults, 3.50€ students and children 8–18, free for children 7 and under. Tues–Wed and Fri–Sun 10am–12:30pm and 1:30–6pm; Thurs 10am–12:30pm and 1:30–9pm.

La Cité de l'Espace ★ ☺ Some half a million visitors a year come here to learn what it's like to program the launch of a satellite or how to maneuver one in space. You learn, for example, how easy it is to lose a satellite by putting on

Le Capitole.

Basilique St-Sernin.

a burst of speed at the wrong point during a launch. Life-size structural models abound, including a model of an astronaut riding an exercise bike in zero gravity. On the grounds, you can walk through a replica of Russia's Mir space station. The place is both a teaching tool and a lot of fun to visit. The top floor focuses on exploration of the universe, with close-ups from flybys of the moons of Jupiter.

Av. Jean Gonord. ✆ **08-20-37-72-23.** www.cite-espace.com. Admission 20€–22€ adults, 15€ ages 5–15, free for children 4 and under. Feb, Mar, and Sept–Dec Tues–Fri 9:30am–5pm, Sat–Sun 9:30am–6pm; Apr–June Mon–Fri 9:30am–5pm, Sat–Sun 9:30am–6pm; July–Aug daily 9:30am–7pm. Closed Jan. Bus: 37 (Sat–Sun only). Follow N126 from the center of town to the E. Peripheral route and take exit 17.

Musée des Augustins ★★ The museum was established in this convent in 1793, shortly after the French Revolution, when revolutionary acts closed the institution—then one of the city's most important monasteries—and adapted it for public use. In addition to the fabulous paintings, a stroll through this place gives you the chance to view a 14th-century monastery in all its mystical splendor. This museum's 14th-century cloisters contain the world's largest and most valuable collection of Romanesque capitals. The sculptures and carvings are magnificent, and there are some fine examples of early Christian sarcophagi. On the upper floors is a large painting collection, with works by Toulouse-Lautrec, Gérard, Delacroix, and Ingres. The museum also contains several portraits by Antoine Rivalz, a local artist and major talent.

21 rue de Metz. ✆ **05-61-22-21-82.** www.augustins.org. Admission 3€, free for children 18 and under. Wed 10am–9pm; Thurs–Tues 10am–6pm. Closed New Year's Day, May 1, and Christmas.

Shopping

Head for **rue d'Alsace-Lorraine,** which is rich in clothing and housewares. At the well-stocked shopping mall, the **Centre Commercial St-Georges,** rue du Rempart St-Etienne, you can fill your suitcases with all kinds of glittery loot. For upscale boutiques, head to **rue Croix-Baragnon, rue des Arts,** and **rue St-Antoine du T.** The pearly gates of antiques heaven are on **rue Fermat.** More down-market antiques spread out each Saturday and Sunday 6am to 1pm during the weekly **flea market** adjacent to the Basilique St-Sernin. In addition to that, in the same spot, a *brocante* sale takes place on the first weekend (Fri–Sun) of each month from 8am to 1pm.

Violets grow in abundance in meadows on the outskirts of Toulouse. Two shops that sell everything related to violets include **Violettes & Pastels,** 10 rue St-Pantaléon (✆ **05-61-22-14-22**), and **Péniche Maison de la Violette,** 4 bd. Bonrepos (✆ **05-61-99-01-30**). Inventories include violet-scented perfume, and clothing—especially scarves—patterned with the dainty purple flower.

Péniche Maison de la Violette.

Where to Stay

EXPENSIVE

Grand Hôtel de l'Opéra ★★★ This is the most elegant oasis in Toulouse, and the owners have won several prestigious awards for transforming a 17th-century convent into a sophisticated hotel. The public rooms contain early-19th-century antiques and Napoleonic-inspired tenting over the bars. Some of the spacious and stylish guest rooms have urn-shaped balustrades overlooking formal squares, and all have high ceilings and modern amenities. The beds are elegantly attired in tasteful fabrics and soft pillows. The hotel restaurant, Les Jardins de l'Opéra (p. 667), is the town's most prestigious.

1 place du Capitole. www.grand-hotel-opera.com. ✆ **05-61-21-82-66.** Fax 05-61-23-41-04. 57 units. 190€–490€ double; 390€–490€ suite. AE, DC, MC, V. Parking 17€. Métro: Capitole. **Amenities:** Restaurant; brasserie; bar; room service; sauna. *In room:* A/C, TV, hair dryer, minibar, Wi-Fi (12€ per day).

MODERATE

Les Bains-Douches ★★ Small and intimate, Toulouse's best boutique hotel is the latest word in modernity. It is so sleek, it's almost self-consciously so, and its cocktail lounge has become a chic rendezvous spot. All the bedrooms are tasteful and stylish, the beds comfortable with fine linens, and the bathrooms reflect a designer's touch. A terrace opens up during the summer months.

4 and 4 bis rue du Point Guilheméry. www.hotel-bainsdouches.com. ✆ **05-62-72-52-52.** Fax 05-34-42-09-98. 22 units. 140€–330€ double; 160€–330€ suite. AE, MC, V. Parking 12€. **Amenities:** Breakfast room; room service. *In room:* A/C, TV, hair dryer, minibar, free Wi-Fi.

Mercure Wilson ★ Set behind a rather formal stone facade, this historic building operates a government-rated three-star hotel in the heart of Toulouse's historic core, a 5-minute walk southwest of the heartbeat place Wilson. Inside, some of the rooms radiate off a glassed-over interior courtyard that contains touches of wrought-iron filigree similar to what you'll find in Spain. Bedrooms are high-ceilinged and, despite the prevalence of angular, not particularly distinctive furniture, still evoke the building's origins as a well-heeled private home. Staff here isn't as helpful or well informed as that within this hotel's nearby competitor, the St-Claire Hôtel, but it's nonetheless a worthy and cost-effective choice.

6 rue Labéda. www.mercure.com. ✆ **05-34-45-40-60.** Fax 05-34-45-40-61. 95 units. 185€–195€ double; 215€–225€ family room for 2 adults and up to 2 children. AE, MC, V. Parking 11€. Métro: Place Jean-Jaurès or Capitole. **Amenities:** Restaurant; bar. *In room:* A/C, TV, hair dryer, free Wi-Fi.

INEXPENSIVE

Hotel de France ★ In the heart of Toulouse, this hotel in a restored historic monument from 1890 stands near the landmark squares Wilson and Capitole. Restaurants, cafes, cinemas, markets, and shops lie just a few feet from the hotel's doorstep. The midsize bedrooms combine charm, convenience, and comfort, and each is tastefully decorated, with a travertine-tiled bathroom. The facade may suggest the halcyon days of Belle Epoque, but the interior is sleekly modern, with splashes of sophistication in the decor.

5 rue Austerlitz. www.hotel-france-toulouse.com. ✆ **05-61-21-88-24.** Fax 05-61-21-99-77. 63 units. 69€ double; 86€ quad. AE, MC, V. **Amenities:** Breakfast room; room service. *In room:* A/C, TV, free Wi-Fi.

Where to Eat

EXPENSIVE

Chez Michel Sarran ★★★ MODERN FRENCH At the most stylish restaurant in Toulouse, you can enjoy the cuisine of master chef Michel Sarran. Sarran's wife, Françoise, oversees the three red, green, and violet dining rooms, in a building in the heart of town near the Novotel Centre. The food brings out the flavors of southern and southwestern France. Start with a warm soup of foie gras and oysters. Move on to a succulent version of poached sea bass served with a creamy polenta and lobster sauce; or perhaps a portion of roasted pigeon from the underpopulated Bigorre region of France, served in a stewpot with thyme and wine-roasted potatoes.

21 bd. Armand Duportal. ✆ **05-61-12-32-32.** www.michel-sarran.com. Reservations recommended. Main courses 36€–68€; fixed-price lunch 44€–165€, dinner 98€–165€. AE, DC, MC, V. Mon–Fri noon–1:45pm and 8–9:45pm (closed Wed for lunch). Closed Aug and 1 week around Christmas. Métro: Capitole.

Le 19 ★ MODERN FRENCH This high-profile cellar restaurant is one of the city's finest. It's 19 steps down from the street, in the high-ceilinged cellar of a medieval building once used for the storage of fish and the salts to preserve them. Inside, wood panels and carpeting contrast with its terra-cotta bricks. The delicate, creative menu items change with the seasons. Among delectable dishes are a terrine of deliberately undercooked foie gras, served with figs; cream of watercress soup with warm oysters; roasted shoulder of rabbit served in a stewpot with polenta and baby vegetables; and filet of curried duck breast with Asian-style vegetables. To end your meal, try a stir-fry of mandarin oranges flavored with balsamic vinegar, or saffron-flavored sabayon with ice cream made from unpasteurized milk.

19 descente de la Halle aux Poissons. ✆ **05-34-31-94-84.** www.restaurantle19.com. Reservations recommended. Main courses 20€–27€; fixed-price lunch 15€–19€, dinner 44€. AE, DC, MC, V. Wed–Sat noon–2pm; Mon–Sat 8–10:30pm. Métro: Esquirol.

Les Jardins de l'Opéra ★★★ FRENCH The entrance to the city's best restaurant is in the 18th-century Florentine courtyard of the Grand Hôtel de l'Opéra (p. 665). The dining area is a series of salons, several of which face a winter garden and a reflecting pool. A long-standing staple, praised by gastronomes, is ravioli stuffed with foie gras of duckling and served with essence of truffles. Equally appealing are carpaccio of lobster served with foie gras; tartare of sturgeon, mushrooms, and oysters; and spicy breast of pigeon with a "surprise" preparation of the bird's organs decorated with rosettes of zucchini. One of the most appealing desserts is figs poached in red banyuls wine, stuffed with homemade vanilla ice cream.

In the Grand Hôtel de l'Opéra, 1 place du Capitole. ✆ **05-61-23-07-76.** www.lesjardinsdelopera.com. Reservations required. All main courses 25€–42€; fixed-price lunch 29€–99€, dinner 29€–99€. AE, DC, MC, V. Tues–Sat noon–2pm and 8–10pm. Métro: Capitole.

Metropolitan ★★★ FRENCH This is a bright, modern restaurant, which is a showcase for one of Toulouse's most celebrated chefs, Jeremy Morin. Trained at the Hotel Meurice in Paris, Morin offers sublime dishes that are not only creative, but prepared with well-chosen ingredients. Try his scallops roasted with herb-studded ravioli and served with candied carrots, or else his lean roast filet of beef with pressed artichokes, foie gras, and a truffle vinaigrette. Another delight is saddle of rabbit flavored with grape juice. His roasted veal sweetbreads with truffles and Roman hazelnuts have won him deserved praise. The designer dining room contains a chic bar, and there's a small terrace draped with vines.

2 place Auguste Albert. ✆ **05-61-34-63-11.** www.metropolitan-restaurant.fr. Main courses 24€–50€; fixed-price lunch 25€–30€, dinner 39€–85€. AE, MC, V. Tues–Fri noon–2pm and Tues–Sat 8–10pm.

MODERATE

Emile ★ 🎁 TOULOUSIAN This special restaurant is in an old-fashioned house on one of Toulouse's most beautiful squares. In winter, meals are served upstairs overlooking the square; in summer, seating moves to the street-level dining room and flower-filled terrace. Menu choices include cassoulet Toulousian (cooked in goose fat), *magret* of duckling in traditional style, a medley of Catalonian fish, and a very fresh *parillade* (mixed grill) of fish with a pungently aromatic cold sauce of sweet peppers and olive oil. The wine list is filled with intriguing surprises.

13 place St-Georges. ✆ **05-61-21-05-56.** www.restaurant-emile.com. Reservations recommended. Main courses 20€–32€; fixed-price lunch 20€–30€, dinner 36€–55€. AE, DC, MC, V. Mid-May to Sept Tues–Sat noon–2pm, Mon–Sat 7–10:30pm; Oct to mid-May Tues–Sat noon–2pm and 7:30–10pm. Closed Dec 23–Jan 8. Métro: Capitole or Esquirol.

INEXPENSIVE

Le Bon Vivre ★ SOUTHWESERN FRENCH One of downtown Toulouse's most appealing bistros occupies the street level of a historic 18th-century mansion immediately adjacent to the Hôtel de Ville (Town Hall). Established in 2004, it provides cost-conscious dining within an environment surrounded by the pink-colored bricks of antique Toulouse. Menu items feature contemporary twists on time-tested French specialties, many of them heralded by workaday diners who appreciate the attractive ratios of value to quality. The best examples include an unusual version of macaroni studded with flap mushrooms, truffles, and foie gras; and a version of cassoulet (the specialty of France's southwest) that's made with both duck and pork.

15 bis place Wilson. ✆ **05-61-23-07-17.** www.lebonvivre.com. Reservations recommended. Main courses 17€–28€; fixed-price menus 29€–45€. AE, DC, MC, V. Mon–Fri 11:30am–2:30pm and Sat–Sun 11:30am–3pm; Sun–Tues 6:45–11:30pm; Wed–Sat 6:45pm–12:30am.

Le Colombier ★ TOULOUSIAN Don't tell your cardiologist—slip away to this bastion of regional cookery. Alain Lacoste arguably serves the best cassoulet in Toulouse and also lures with white beans in pork fat, red sausage, white sausage, and, of course, goose confit. His duck foie gras comes with figs and, of all things, gingerbread. Calves' sweetbreads are delectable with morels, and scallops are served in the Provençal style. Nearly all locals order the cassoulet; it's slow-cooked to perfection. The restaurant itself is a simple stone-and-brick dining room. With all this fat, you can cut it with the acidity of strawberry soup with lime sorbet. If not that, then opt for the apple "croustade."

14 rue Bayard. ✆ **05-61-62-40-05.** www.restaurant-lecolombier.com. Reservations recommended. Main courses 18€–30€; fixed-price menus 21€–49€. MC, V. Tues–Fri noon–2pm and Mon–Sat 7:15–10pm.

Toulouse After Dark

Toulouse's theater, dance, and opera are often on par with those found in Paris. To stay on top of the arts scene, pick up a copy of the free monthly magazine *Toulouse Culture* from the Office de Tourisme.

PERFORMING ARTS

The city's most notable theaters are **Théâtre du Capitole,** place du Capitole (✆**05-61-63-13-13**), which specializes in operas, operettas, and often works from the classical French repertoire; **Théâtre de la Digue,** 3 rue de la Digue (✆**05-61-42-97-79**), for ballets and works by local theater companies; and **Halle aux Grains,** place Dupuy (✆**05-61-63-13-13**). The home of the Orchestre du Capitole, Halle aux Grains is the venue for mostly classical concerts. **Théâtre Garonne,** 1 av. du Château d'Eau (✆**05-62-48-56-56**), stages everything from works by Molière to current dramas. Another important venue is **Théâtre Zenith,** 11 av. Raymond-Badiou (✆**05-62-74-49-49**), which has a large stage and seating capacity. It usually schedules rock concerts, variety acts, and musical comedies from other European cities. A smaller competitor, with a roughly equivalent mix of music, theater, and entertainment, is **Théâtre de la Cité,** 1 rue Pierre Baudis (✆**05-34-45-05-05**).

BARS & CLUBS

The liveliest squares to wander after dark are **place du Capitole, place St-Georges, place St-Pierre,** and **place Wilson.**

For bars and pubs, **La Tantina de Bourgos,** 27 rue de la Garonette (✆**05-61-55-59-29**), has a Latin flair that's popular with students; and the rowdier **Chez Tonton,** 16 place St-Pierre (✆**05-61-21-89-54**), has an *après-match* atmosphere, complete with the winning teams boozing it up. A popular bar that schedules both live and recorded music is **Monsieur Carnaval,** 34 rue Bayard (✆**05-61-99-14-56**), where there's lots of rocking and rolling *à la française* for the under-35 crowd. The busiest English-style pub in town, **Le Frog & Le Roast Beef,** 14 rue de l'Industrie (✆**05-61-99-28-57**), is often very crowded with the city's English-speaking community. **La Pelouse Interdite,** 72 av. des Etats-Unis (✆**05-61-47-30-40**), offers a charming restaurant and bar behind a simple, discreetly marked green door.

The town's trendiest nightclub is **Le Purple,** 2 rue Castellane (✆**05-62-73-04-67**). Set close to the Pullman, it has the longest lines, with the city's A-list wannabes.

Disco Le Maximo, 3 rue Gabrielle-Peri (✆**05-61-62-08-07**), starts hopping Tuesday to Saturday after 11pm and serves a distinctly French-inspired list of tapas. There's also a vaguely Iberian-looking establishment, **Bar La Bodega,** rue Gabriel-Peri (✆**05-61-63-03-63**), that's beer soaked and raucous. It's particularly interesting after one of the region's football (soccer) games.

The oldest and most deeply entrenched gay bar in Toulouse is **Shanghai Express,** 12 rue de la Pomme (✆**05-61-23-37-80**), a man's dance domain playing the latest in techno. Entrance is free, and it's open every night.

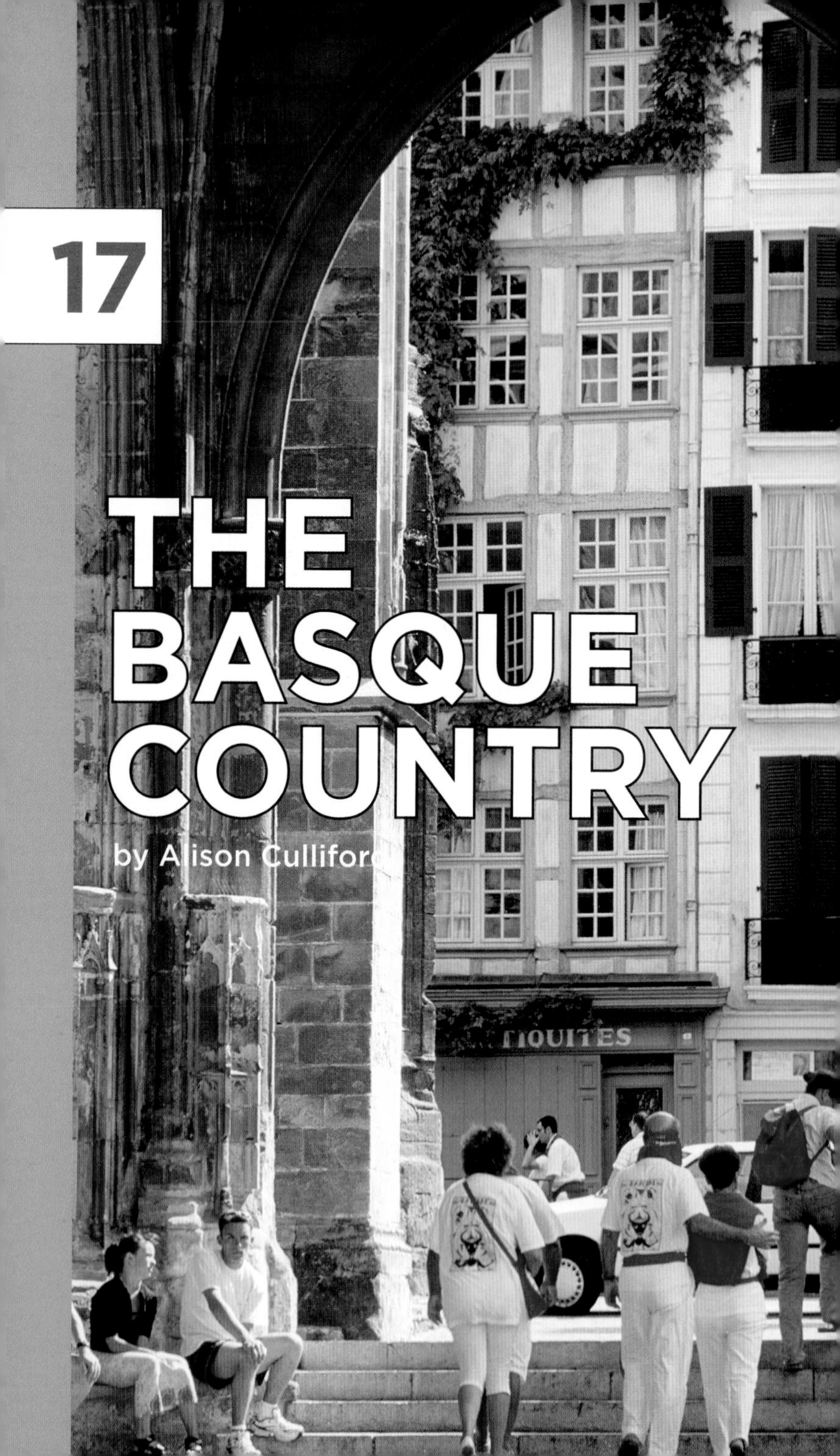

17

THE BASQUE COUNTRY

by Alison Culliford

A land rich in folklore, the Basque Country extends to the Spanish border in southwest France. The Basque capital, Bayonne, and the resorts, Biarritz and St-Jean-de-Luz, are on the coast, while Pau and Lourdes are the gateway to the Pyrénées.

The vast Pyrénéan region is a land of glaciers, summits, thermal baths, subterranean grottoes and caverns, winter-sports centers, and trout-filled mountain streams. **Pau** is a good base for excursions to the western Pyrénées.

PAU ★★★

768km (476 miles) SW of Paris; 196km (122 miles) SW of Toulouse

High above the banks of the Gave de Pau River, Pau is the most cosmopolitan city in the western Pyrénées and the capital of the Pyrénées-Atlantiques *département* (ministate). It was once the capital of the Béarn region, the land of the kings of Navarre, the most famous and beloved of whom was Henri IV, who was born in Pau. The British discovered Pau in the early 19th century, launching such practices as fox hunting, a custom that lingers. Even if you're just passing through, follow boulevard des Pyrénées, an esplanade erected on Napoleon's orders, for a famous panoramic view.

Essentials

GETTING THERE **Pau-Uzein airport** is 12km (7½ miles) north of town; call ✆**05-59-33-33-00** for flight information. There are good **train** connections from Biarritz (seven per day, taking 1 hr., 40 min.); the one-way fare is 18€. For train information, call ✆**36-35. Driving** to Pau is relatively easy because of its location along the N117 roadway, which is directly accessible from Toulouse. From Paris, take A10 south to Vierzon, changing to N20 south to Limoges, continuing on N21 south to Tarbes, and finally turning west along N117 to Pau.

VISITOR INFORMATION The **Office de Tourisme** is on place Royale (✆**05-59-27-27-08;** fax 05-59-27-03-21; www.tourismepau.com).

SPECIAL EVENTS In late May and early June, there's the **Grand Prix de Pau** (✆**05-59-27-31-89;** www.grandprixautomobilepau.com), when race cars compete for speed records in what may remind you of a small-scale replica of the Grand Prix in Monaco.

Exploring the City

The city center is 30m (98 ft.) up from the river and the railway station, and if you arrive by train, you'll have the pleasure of ascending in its historic **Funicular** from near the station to Place Royale. Restored in 2010 and more than a century old, it runs Monday to Saturday from 6:45am to 9:40pm and on Sundays from 1:30 to

FACING PAGE: **Cathedral and Basque houses in Bayonne, with people dressed for the July festival.**

8:50pm, and is free. Place Royale is in the center of the 2km-long (1¼-mile) **boulevard des Pyrénées,** a popular promenade since the 19th century for its views over palm-landscaped slopes to the distant mountains. At the eastern end is Parc Beaumont, where the **Palais Beaumont** (✆ **05-59-11-20-00;** www.pau-congres.com), built as a casino and winter garden, now hosts concerts, theater performances, and exhibitions; and at the western end is the **Château de Pau ★**, 2 rue du Château (✆ **05-59-82-38-00;** www.musee-chateau-pau.fr), dating from the 12th century and steeped in the Renaissance spirit of the bold Marguerite de Navarre, who wrote the bawdy *Heptaméron* at age 60. Inside are many souvenirs, including a crib made of a single tortoiseshell for Henri de Navarre, who was born here, and a splendid array of Flemish and Gobelin tapestries. The great rectangular tower, **Tour de Gaston Phoebus,** is from the 14th century. The château is open for visits mid-June to mid-September daily 9:30am to 12:30pm and 1:30 to 5:45pm, and mid-September to mid-June daily 9:30 to 11:45am and 2 to 5pm. Guided tours (conducted in French and English) depart at 15-minute intervals during open hours. Admission is 6€ for adults, 4.50€ for students 18 to 25, and free for ages 17 and under.

View in Pau.

The **Musée des Beaux-Arts ★**, 1 rue Mathieu-Lalanne (✆ **05-59-27-33-02**), displays a collection of European paintings, including Spanish, Flemish, Dutch, English, and French masters such as El Greco, Zurbarán, Degas, and Boudin. It's open Wednesday to Monday 10am to noon and 2 to 6pm. Admission is 4€ adults, 3.50€ students, and free for children 18 and under. Pau is also famous for its **Haras National** (National Stud), created by Napoleon, which is well worth a visit if you are equine minded. It's situated south of the Gave de Pau at 1 rue du Maréchal Leclerc (✆ **05-59-35-06-52;** www.haras-nationaux.fr). Guided visits Monday to Friday are at 10am, 2, and 4pm in July and August; 2 and 4pm in May, June, September, and October; and 2pm only November to April. Admission is 5€ for adults, 3€ for children 7 to 18, and free for ages 6 and under.

Shopping

Pau affords ample opportunities for you to buy authentic regional specialties, such as chocolates, sweet jams, and Basque antiques. The pedestrian **rue Serviez** and **rue des Cordeliers** harbor an array of boutiques and shops that carry these items, as do **rue Louis-Barthou** and **rue du Maréchal-Foch,** which are all around the central **place Georges Clemenceau.**

Pau is home to some of the best antiques shops in the region, such as **Antiquites Delan,** 4 rue Gassion (✆ **05-59-27-45-62** or 06-08-07-82-40). The area around the château is the antiques center.

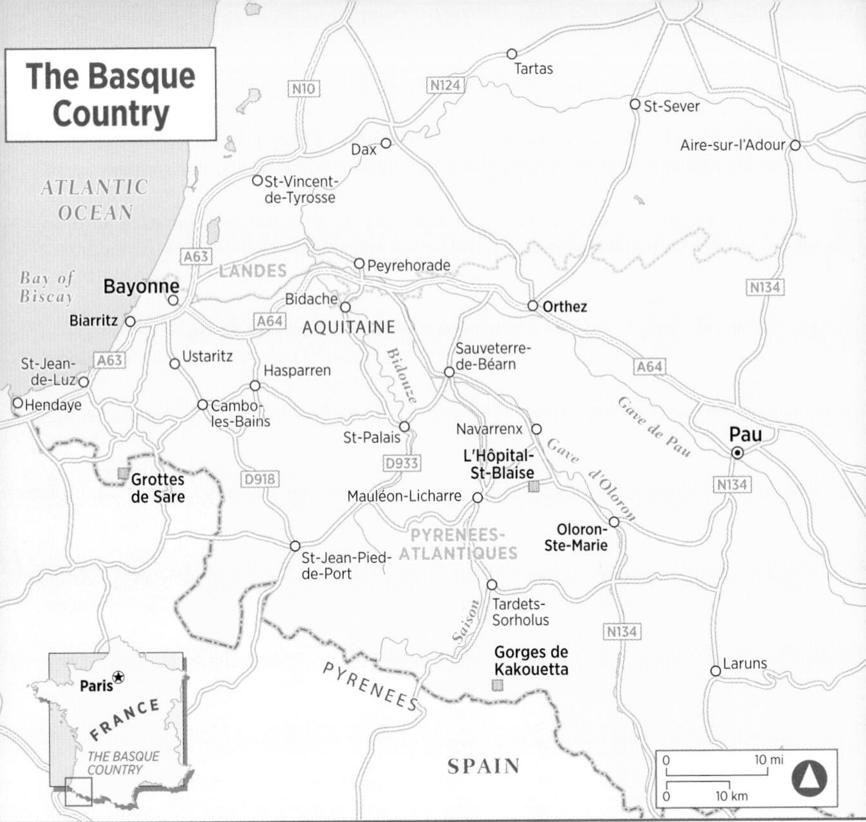

One of the best-known shops in Pau is **La Féerie Gourmande,** 48 rue du Maréchal Joffre (✆ **05-59-27-69-51**). The owner, M. Francis Miot, has been voted best jam and candy maker in France several times. If you're interested in seeing where his confections are made, head for the suburbs of Pau, about 1.5km (1 mile) southeast of the center, to the residential hamlet of Uzos. Here you'll find **Musée de la Confiture** (✆ **05-59-35-05-56**), where exhibits display the history of jams from medieval times to the present. It's open Monday to Saturday 10am to noon and 2 to 6pm; admission is 4.60€ adults and 3€ ages 3 to 12; closed in December.

Where to Stay

Best Western Hôtel Continental In a classic Haussmannian building with a rotunda (ask for a "rotunda" room to experience a room with no corners), the centrally located Continental is decorated with antiques and paintings. Many of the rooms are spacious. About 60 have midsize bathrooms with tub/showers; the rest have showers. Redecoration is being done room by room, and some look distinctly old-fashioned, so bear this in mind when booking.

2 rue du Maréchal-Foch, Pau 64000. www.hotel-continental-pau.com. ✆ **05-59-27-69-31.** Fax 05-59-27-99-84. 75 units. 72€–100€ double. AE, DC, MC, V. Free parking. **Amenities:** Restaurant; room service. *In room:* TV, hair dryer, minibar, free Wi-Fi.

Hôtel de Gramont In the heart of Pau, on a gracefully designed 18th-century plaza classified as a historic treasure, this hotel was built around 1880 in a style that complements the medievalism of the château nearby. Its management spent lots of money restoring the elegant woodwork in the street-level salons and decorated the guest rooms in a warm, contemporary style but incorporating antique (mostly English) furniture. Beds are very comfortable. About half of the medium-size bathrooms contain tub/showers; the others have showers. Many restaurants are a short walk away.

3 place Gramont, Pau 64000. www.hotelgramont.com. ✆ **05-59-27-84-04.** Fax 05-59-27-62-23. 34 units. 77€–126€ double; 140€–180€ suite. AE, DC, MC, V. Closed Dec 23–Jan 5. **Amenities:** Bar; billiards room. *In room:* A/C (some rooms), TV, minibar, free Wi-Fi.

Where to Eat

Au Fin Gourmet ★★ BASQUE This restaurant, in the Joantho gardens near the bottom of the funicular, is maintained by the sons of the retired founder, Clément Ithurriague. The postmodern, circular dining room opens onto a terrace for warm-weather dining. The cuisine is based on regional ingredients. Some of the best menu items include grilled scallops with fennel, preceded by an appetizer of foie gras with mushrooms. Rack of lamb with fresh herbs from the Pyrénées is an always-reliable choice.

24 av. Gaston-Lacoste. ✆ **05-59-27-47-71.** www.restaurant-aufingourmet.com. Reservations recommended. Main courses 22€–25€; fixed-price lunch 27€–76€, dinner 38€–76€. AE, DC, MC, V. Tues–Sun noon–2pm; Tues–Sat 7:30–9:30pm.

Chez Ruffet ★★ BEARNAISE The most famous restaurant in the region is on the southern outskirts of Pau, within an old-fashioned stone-built house with a slate roof and a bell tower. Many guests opt for the 80€ five-course menu, but guests in a group of four or more can opt for a 40€ menu where everyone eats the same thing. The choices change weekly, but examples of dishes served here include sea scallops that are first smoked, then grilled, and served with chicken-stuffed ravioli and a sweet pepper–and–mango sauce; braised sweetbreads with a butter-flavored cream sauce and vanilla-flavored brioches; and line-caught sea bass glazed with miso.

3 av. Charles Touzet, Jurançon. ✆ **05-59-06-25-13.** www.restaurant-chezruffet.com. Reservations required. Main courses 34€–42€; fixed-price lunch (Tues–Fri) 28€, dinner 40€ and 80€. AE, DC, MC, V. Tues–Sat noon–2pm and 7:30–10pm.

Restaurant Pierre ★★ BEARNAISE/MEDITERRANEAN There's a new look and new owners for this restaurant with a reputation as one of the best in Pau. Established in 1924, a 5-minute walk west of the château, the restaurant is divided into six salons seating between 5 and 40 people. The main dining room has green velvet *banquettes* arranged in a horseshoe. The new chef, Frédéric Narbout, has introduced a cuisine that goes by the trendy term "*bistronomique*" (a contraction of bistro and gastronomic). With the same attention to seasonal regional ingredients, it takes inspirations from around the Mediterranean, with, for instance, scallops *à la plancha* with sweet potatoes on the evening menu, and chicken tajine with dried fruits as the lunchtime dish of the day. The menus change every month. It also has an attractive adjacent bar, outfitted like the club room of a golf course.

16 rue Louis-Barthour. ✆ **05-59-27-76-86.** www.restaurant-chez-pierre.com. Reservations required. Main courses 11€ lunch, 19€ dinner; fixed-price lunch 14€–17€, dinner 24€–30€. AE, DC, MC, V. Mon–Sat noon–2pm; Tues–Sat 7:30–10pm. Closed 2 weeks in early Jan and 2 weeks in mid-Aug.

Pau After Dark

Whereas nightlife in Pau always centered on **Le Triangle,** an area in the town center that's flanked by the rue Emile Garet, rue Lespy, and rue Castetnau, in recent years, it's been augmented with a rash of openings along **boulevard des Pyrénées** near place Clemenceau. The best of the newcomers is **Le Winfield,** 20 bd. des Pyrénées (✆ **05-59-27-80-60**), a cafe-bar with contemporary design, a fun-loving clientele, and a fabulous terrace facing the Pyrénées. A beer costs around 3.50€.

Within the borders of Le Triangle, **Le Garage Bar,** at 47 rue Emile Garet (✆ **05-59-83-75-17;** www.legaragebar.com), has been going strong since 1993. Set within an old auto repair shop, it retains many of its original industrial-looking fixtures, plus a collection of antique traffic lights, road signs, and mopeds hanging from chains in the ceiling. Most people come here just for the bar, but if you want food, there's a selection of salads at 7€ and dishes including fish and chips, burgers, and steaks from 7.20€ to 11€. It's open Monday to Friday noon to 1:30am, Saturday and Sunday 3pm to 1:30am.

The new live music venue **Show Case Time,** 8–10 rue d'Arribes (✆ **05-59-06-94-62;** www.showcasetime.fr), has a full program of jams, slam, and concerts, ranging from rockabilly through salsa to jazz, blues, and indie. Entrance is usually free except on Fridays and Saturdays, when prices range from 5€ to 15€, depending on the band. Art is exposed on the walls of the lounge bar. It's open Tuesday to Saturday from 6pm to 2am.

The best of the town's nightclubs is **El Barrio Libre** (✆ **05-59-81-14-43;** www.elbarriolibre.com), located in a shopping center (Le Centre Commercial Quartier Libre) in the suburb of Lescar, about 8km (5 miles) south of Pau's historic core. Here a raucous, sports-oriented crowd of 20-somethings moves restlessly between the metallic, high-tech interior and a large terrace every Wednesday to Sunday from 10pm till at least 3am. There's a cover charge of 11€ per person. Its most viable competitor is within Pau's Le Triangle, **L'Esprit,** 11 place du Foirail (✆ **06-75-38-59-99**), patronized by usually attractive 20- to 30-somethings. Entrance, depending on the night of the week, ranges from free to 11€. It's open Wednesday to Saturday beginning around 10pm, getting busy at around 11pm and often going on until 5am.

BAYONNE ★★

770km (477 miles) SW of Paris; 184km (114 miles) SW of Bordeaux

Bayonne is the leading port and pleasure-yacht basin of the Côte Basque, divided by the Nive and Adour rivers. A cathedral city and the capital of the Pays Basque, it's characterized by narrow streets, quays, and ramparts. Enlivening the scene are bullfights, *pelote* (jai alai), and street dancing at annual fiestas. You may want to buy some of Bayonne's famous chocolate at one of the arcaded shops along rue du Port-Neuf, and then enjoy coffee at a cafe along place de la Liberté, the hub of town.

Essentials

Pont de Bayonne.

GETTING THERE Five TGV **trains** per day link Bayonne and Paris (trip time: 5 hr., 10 min.; 85€ one-way). Nine trains per day arrive from Bordeaux (trip time: 1 hr., 50 min.; 28€ one-way). For train information and schedules, call ✆ **36-35.**

There's a **bus** service from Biarritz, 15 minutes away. Bus no. 1 departs from Biarritz at 12-minute intervals throughout the daylight hours, depositing passengers on place de la Mairie in Bayonne; the one-way fare is 1€, and tickets can be bought on the bus. There's also bus service between Bayonne and outlying towns and villages not serviced by train. For bus information in Bayonne, call ✆ **05-59-59-04-61.**

Bayonne is near the end of the N117 roadway, easily accessible by **car** from Toulouse and other cities in the south of France. From Paris, take A10 south to Vierzon, and then N20 south to Limoges. Continue on N21 south to Tarbes, and turn west along N117 to Bayonne.

VISITOR INFORMATION The **Office de Tourisme** is on place des Basques (✆ **08-20-42-64-64;** fax 05-59-59-37-55; www.bayonne-tourisme.com).

SPECIAL EVENTS During the 4-day **Fête de Bayonne,** the last week in July, a frenzy of outdoor concerts and dancing fills the streets. The celebration is intense. For **free concerts** on fair-weather Thursday evenings in July and August, head to the gazebo on place de Gaulle, where styles range from jazz to traditional Basque. Contact the Office de Tourisme (see above) for more information.

Exploring the town

Vieux Bayonne, the old town, is inside the ramparts, on the left bank of the Nive. The early-13th-century **Cathédrale Ste-Marie** (✆ **05-59-59-17-82;** www.cathedrale-de-bayonne.fr.st) dominates this part of town on rue d'Espagne and rue des Gouverneurs. The spiny 19th-century steeples are the best-known landmarks in Bayonne. The cathedral is worth half an hour of your time and is a good retreat on a hot day. It was begun in 1258 when Bayonne was under English rule; it fell to the French in 1451. That explains the cathedral's ornamentation, mixing such elements as the English coat of arms (three lions) with the fleur-de-lis of France. Don't miss the gorgeous 14th-century cloisters. They're like a secret garden from the Middle Ages. The cathedral is open daily 7am to 12:30pm and 3 to 7pm.

Atelier de Chocolat de Bayonne Andrieu Bayonne's chocolate tradition began with the Jewish community that fled here from the Spanish Inquisition. Come to this industrial-looking neighborhood near the railway station for an insight into history and ingredients for one of the world's most sought-after confections, followed of course by a tasting.

7 allée de Gibéléou, Zone Artisanale Sainte-Croix. ✆ **05-59-55-70-23.** www.atelierduchocolat.fr. Entrance 5.60€ adults, 2.80€ children 4–12. July–Aug Mon–Sat 9:30am–6:30pm; Sept–June Mon–Sat 9:30am–12:30pm and 2–6pm.

Musée Basque ★★ Bayonne's major museum showcases the traditions, architecture, and decorative arts (including textiles and furniture) of the Basques in a state-of-the-art format that's more advanced and sophisticated than any equivalent museum in the Basque-speaking world.

37 quai des Corsaires. ✆ **05-59-59-08-98.** www.musee-basque.com. Admission 5.50€ adults, 3€ students and children 6–17, free for children 5 and under on Wed evenings July–Aug and the first Sun of every month; includes entrance to the Musée Bonnat (see below). July–Aug Wed 10am–9:30pm, Thurs–Tues 10am–6:30pm; Sept–June Tues–Sun 10am–6:30pm.

Musée Bonnat ★★ This museum owns one of the best collections of paintings in France. It's hardly the Louvre, but it encompasses hundreds of canvases (far too many to display in its limited space). A sampling of works from some of the greatest European masters is showcased. If anybody's the star, it's Peter Paul Rubens (1577–1640), who has an entire salon devoted to his paintings. The collection's strongest point is its 19th-century art. Otherwise, it's like Art History 101, with works by David, Degas, Goya, Ingres, Leonardo da Vinci, El Greco, Tiepolo, and Rembrandt—an overview of European art from the 13th to the 20th centuries. Check out the often-overlooked collection of antiquities in the basement, a museum within a museum with everything from Egyptian amulets to Greek vases.

5 rue Jacques-Lafitte. ✆ **05-59-59-08-52.** www.museebonnat.bayonne.fr. Admission 5.50€ adults, 3€ students and children 6–17, free for children 5 and under and the 1st Sun of every month. May–Oct Wed–Mon 10am–6:30pm; Nov–Apr Wed–Mon 10am–12:30pm and 2–6pm.

Shopping

Most of Bayonne's specialty shops and boutiques lie inside the ramparts of the old town, Grand Bayonne. The pedestrian streets of **rue Port Neuf** (aptly nicknamed the "street of chocolate shops"), **rue Victor-Hugo,** and **rue de la Salie** are major shopping destinations. For antiques, walk along the **rue des Faures** and the edges of **place Montaut,** behind the cathedral. Most of the modern shops and French chain stores are on **rue Thiers** and **quai de la Nive,** outside the old town. Visit **Maison Jean Vier** shop, carrefour Cinq Cantons (✆ **05-59-59-16-18**), to get your Basque bathroom, kitchen, and bed linens. **Cazenave,** 19 rue Port Neuf (✆ **05-59-59-03-16**), specializes in *chocolats de Bayonne,* which include rich, dark, strong chocolate nougats; stop in the tearoom here for warm chocolate mousse.

The accessories of one Basque tradition have become something of a fine art. In olden days, the *makhila* was used as a walking stick, a cudgel, or—when equipped with a hidden blade—a knife. Today carved *makhilas* are sold as collectors' items and souvenirs. For safety's sake, they almost never come with a blade. One of the best outlets in town is **Fabrication de Makhilas,** 37 rue Vieille Boucherie (✆ **05-59-59-18-20**). Another famous product of the Basque country is *jambon de Bayonne,* its cured hams, which taste best shaved into paper-thin slices and consumed with one of the region's heady red wines. An establishment that prepares and sells these hams is **Saloir et Séchoire à Jambon Pierre Ibaialde,** 41 rue des Cordeliers (© **05-59-25-65-30**), where the hams are sold either whole or in thin slices. Also available is an impressive roster of sausages, pâtés, and terrines.

Where to Stay

Best Western Grand Hôtel ★ The best chain hotel in town was originally built in 1835 on the ruins of a medieval Carmelite convent. Rooms were recently refurbished in a comfortable, contemporary style with quality beds. Each midsize bathroom has a tub and shower. There is an English club–style bar, and breakfast is served in a pleasant vaulted courtyard covered by a glass roof.

21 rue Thiers. www.bw-legrandhotel.com. © **800/528-1234** in the U.S. and Canada, or 05-59-59-62-00. Fax 05-59-59-62-01. 54 units. 140€–170€ double. AE, DC, MC, V. Parking 13€. **Amenities:** Restaurant (breakfast only); bar; room service. *In room:* A/C, TV, hair dryer, minibar, free Wi-Fi.

La Villa Bayonne ★★ If you can manage to get a room here, you'll enjoy a dreamy setting and the owners' personal touch. On a hill overlooking the River Nive, 900m (½ mile) from the town center, this lovely 1905 villa, surrounded by an Italianate garden, offers a peaceful stay. The rooms, either ground floor or in the eaves, are exquisitely decorated in mauve, gray, and gold, and the reception rooms make it feel like your own splendid home.

12 Chemin de Jacquette. www.bayonnne-hotel-lavilla.com. © **05-59-03-01-20.** 10 units. 90€–150€ double. AE, MC, V. Free parking. *In room:* A/C, TV, free Wi-Fi.

Where to Eat

Auberge du Cheval Blanc ★★ BASQUE The finest restaurant in Bayonne occupies a half-timbered Basque-style house built in 1715 in the heart of the historic center. Menu items vary with the season but may include slices of foie gras with caramelized endive and pine nuts, ravioli stuffed with wild boar and flavored with local red wine and confit of baby onions, and corn blinis with flap mushrooms. Dorado may be simmered in garlic and served with *crépinette de marmitako* (diced tuna with red and green peppers, bound in a pig's stomach). One of the best desserts is a Grand Marnier soufflé.

68 rue Bourgneuf. © **05-59-59-01-33.** Reservations recommended. Main courses 18€–35€; fixed-price menu 30€–80€. AE, MC, V. Tues–Fri and Sun noon–1:30pm; Tues–Sat 7:45–9:30pm. Closed Feb.

Brasserie de l'Aviron Bayonnais BASQUE Very few restaurants that we know of are as passionately associated with local sports teams as this one, housed in the headquarters of the rugby team Aviron Bayonnais. Near the river, a 10-minute walk from the cathedral, it occupies a second-story dining room that's modern, minimalist, and lined with photos of local athletes. Come here for two-fisted, no-nonsense platters of local charcuteries, among which, of course, will be paper-thin slices of *jambon de Bayonne;* garlicky tartines piled high with peppers, tomatoes, and onions; massive chunks of beefsteak prepared for two diners at a time; and oven-baked hake from nearby St-Jean-de-Luz prepared with olive oil and garlic "in the Spanish style."

In the Garage de la Nive, 1 rue Harry Owen Roe. © **05-59-58-27-27.** Reservations recommended. Main courses 15€–23€; set-price menu 30€. AE, DC, MC, V. Mon–Tues and Thurs–Sat 9am–2am; Wed 9am–3pm. Closed 2 weeks in Aug.

François Miura ★ FRENCH A few steps from the Eglise St-André, this restaurant occupies a late-19th-century cloister built for Visitandine nuns. The cuisine is the most eclectic and personalized in town. Menu items are sophisticated and composed with intelligence. They include flavorful, complicated dishes such as twice-cooked pigeon in regional wine stuffed with foie gras, and stuffed squid served with confit of pigs' feet flavored with squid ink and essence of crayfish. Less daring examples include warm calamari salad with two kinds of peppers, and braised rack of lamb with fresh vegetables and coriander sauce. Desserts may include a soufflé with pear liqueur.

24 rue Marengo. ✆ **05-59-59-49-89.** Reservations recommended. Main courses 19€–24€; fixed-price menus 21€–32€. AE, DC, MC, V. Thurs–Tues noon–2pm; Mon–Tues and Thurs–Sat 8–10pm.

La Cidrerie TTiPia ★ BASQUE This restaurant has become famous throughout Bayonne for its resuscitation of the cider-making traditions of the Basque country. Owned and managed by an amiable Basque nationalist known simply as Isabelle, it serves two brands of (mildly alcoholic) cider and a very limited array of old-fashioned Basque food. This is configured into a "one choice fits all" set-price menu whose four courses include omelets with morels, grilled steaks, and a slab of local goat's cheese with walnuts. This place gets boisterous and gregarious, with sports fans sometimes singing over their cups after important matches.

27 rue des Cordeliers. ✆ **05-59-46-13-31.** http://titipia.364.fr. Set-price menu 29€. MC, V. Tues–Sun noon–2pm; Mon–Sat 8–11pm (till midnight Fri–Sat).

Bayonne After Dark

Nightlife centers on the neighborhood known as Petit Bayonne, the town's historic core. **Rue des Tonneliers, rue Pannecau,** and **rue des Cordeliers** are the liveliest areas after dark. **Katie Daly's,** 3 place de la Liberté (✆ **05-59-59-09-14**), serves endless pints of Guinness; the drinkers really pile in on weekends. Expect a carefree group of rowdies and a lot of fun. For a taste of local color, try **Le Cabaret La Luna Negra,** rue des Augustins (✆ **05-59-25-78-05;** www.lunanegra.fr), where the 6€-to-10€ cover charge includes cabaret, jazz, or blues performances and popular French songs.

BIARRITZ ★★★

779km (483 miles) SW of Paris; 193km (120 miles) SW of Bordeaux

One of the most famous seaside resorts in the world, Biarritz was once a fishing village. Empress Eugénie and her husband, Napoleon III, put it on the map and started a constant stream of royal visitors. In the 1930s, the Prince of Wales (before and after his brief reign as Edward VIII) and Wallis Simpson did much to make Biarritz more fashionable as they headed south with these instructions: "Chill the champagne, pack the pearls, and tune up the Bugatti." Although those legendary days are long gone, the resort is still fashionable and has become the surfing capital of France, with plenty of surf shops, snack bars, and even some reasonably priced hotels.

Essentials

GETTING THERE Seventeen **trains** arrive daily from Bayonne (trip time: 10 min.), which has rail links with Paris and other cities in the south of France.

The one-way fare is 2.50€. The rail station is 3km (1¾ miles) south of the town center, in La Négresse. For information, call ✆ **36-35.** Bus no. 2 carries passengers from the station to the center of Biarritz; the one-way fare is 1€. You can also take a cab for around 15€ to 20€. If you're **driving,** Biarritz is at the end of the N117 roadway, the major thoroughfare for the Basque country. From Paris, take A10 south to Vierzon, and then N20 south to Limoges. Continue on N21 south to Tarbes, and then head west on N117.

VISITOR INFORMATION The **Office de Tourisme** is on square d'Ixelles (✆ **05-59-22-37-00;** fax 05-59-24-14-19; www.biarritz.fr).

SPECIAL EVENTS If you're in town in mid-September, check out the modern dance and ballet performances during the 9-day festival **Le Temps d'Aimer.** Tickets cost 40€ for adults or 15€ for ages 5 to 15 (free 4 and under). For reservations and ticket sales for the festival, contact the tourist office above. At the end of September, the **Festival Biarritz Amérique Latine** (www.festivaldebiarritz.com) is the most important Latin American film festival in the world. It's much more laid-back than Cannes—you'll find yourself rubbing shoulders or even salsaing with top Latin directors in the casino complex, where most events are held. Entry to the whole week's films is 55€, and single-film entry is 6€.

Biarritz is the surfing capital of France, and each year, in mid-July, cadres of enthusiasts descend on the town for the 5-day **Roxy Jam,** an event known as the **Women's International Festival of Long Board Surfing.** It's centered on the waves offshore from La Plage de la Côte Basque. For more information, contact the tourist office. Biarritz also has 10 golf courses within a short drive of the town. A good practice setting is the **Centre d'Entraînement d'Ilbarritz-Bidart,** avenue du Chateau, Bidart 64210 (✆ **05-59-43-81-30**); you can play 9 holes for 23€ to 36€. The **Biarritz Cup** is a nationwide competition attended by mostly French golfers in the third week in July at the Golf du Phare, avenue Edith-Cavell (✆ **05-59-03-71-80;** www.golfbiarritz.com). Information on both festivals is available from the tourist office.

A Day at the Beach

Along the seafront facing the Casino is the **Grande Plage.** During the Belle Epoque, this was where Victorian ladies promenaded under parasols and wide-brimmed veiled hats. Today's bathers are more likely to be in wetsuits or surfy combos.

Promenade du Bord de Mer, along the coast within the city limits, is still a major attraction. The paths are often carved into cliffs, and sections have been designed as rock gardens with flowers, turning the area into a public park. From here, you can head north to **Pointe St-Martin,** where you'll find more gardens and a staircase (look for the sign DESCENTE DE L'OCEAN) leading you to allée Winston-Churchill, a paved path going along **Plage Miramar.**

La Perspective de la Côte des Basques, a walk that goes up to another plateau, leads to one of the wildest beaches in France: **Plage de la Côte des Basques,** with breakers crashing at the base of the cliffs. This is where serious surfers head.

If you like your beaches calmer, the safest beach is the small, horseshoe-shaped **Plage du Port-Vieux,** along the path from plateau de l'Atalaye. Its tranquil waters, protected by rocks, make it a favorite with families.

Exploring the Town

Eglise St-Martin, rue St-Martin (✆**05-59-23-05-19**), is one of the few vestiges of the port's early boom days. In the 12th century, Biarritz grew prosperous as a whaling center. The mammals' departure from the Bay of Biscay marked a decline in the port's fortunes. The church dates from the 1100s and was restored in 1541 with a flamboyant Gothic chancel. It's in the town center between two of Biarritz's major arteries, rue d'Espagne and avenue de Gramont, and is open daily 8am to 7pm. Admission is free.

Biarritz's turning point came with the arrival of Queen Hortense, who spent lazy summers here with her two daughters. One of them, Eugénie, married Napoleon III in 1853 and prevailed on him to visit Biarritz the next year. The emperor fell under its spell and ordered the construction of the **Hôtel du Palais** (p. 682). The hotel remains the town's most enduring landmarks. When Biarritz's star started to wane in the 1950s, the municipality showed a great deal of foresight in buying the hotel and the equally monumental casino, the essence of Biarritz's fading glamour. In a commanding spot on Grande Plage, the hotel is worth a visit even if you're not a guest. You can view the palatial trappings of its public rooms.

Across from the Hôtel du Palais, the **Eglise Orthodoxe Russe,** 8 av. de l'Impératrice (✆**05-59-24-16-74**), was built in 1892 so that wintering Russian aristocrats could worship when they weren't enjoying champagne, caviar, and Basque prostitutes. It's noted for its gilded dome, the interior of which is the color of a blue sky on a sunny day. It can be visited only on weekends: Saturday 3 to 6pm and Sunday 4 to 7pm. After you pass the Hôtel du Palais, the walkway widens into **quai de la Grande Plage,** Biarritz's principal promenade. This walkway continues to the opposite end of the resort, where a final belvedere opens onto the southernmost stretch of beach. This whole walk takes about 3 hours. At the southern edge of Grande Plage, steps will take you to **place Ste-Eugénie,** Biarritz's most gracious old square. Right below place Ste-Eugénie is the colorful **Port des Pêcheurs** (fishers' port). Crowded with fishing boats, it has old wooden houses and shacks backed up against a cliff, along with small harborfront restaurants and cafes.

The rocky **plateau de l'Atalaye** forms one side of the Port des Pêcheurs. Carved on orders of Napoleon III, a tunnel leads from the plateau to an esplanade. Here a footbridge stretches over the sea to a rocky islet that takes its name, **Rocher de la Vierge (Rock of the Virgin),** from the statue crowning it. Alexandre-Gustave Eiffel (designer of the tower) directed construction of the footbridge. The walk out onto the edge of the rock, with crashing surf on both sides, is the most dramatic in Biarritz. You can see all the way to the mountains of the Spanish Basque country, far to the south.

Here you can visit the **Musée de la Mer,** 14 plateau de l'Atalaye (✆**05-59-22-33-34;** www.museedelamer.com), which houses 24 aquariums of fish native to the bay. The seals steal the show at their daily 10:30am and 5pm feedings. The museum also houses sharks that are fed on Tuesday and Friday at 11am and Wednesday and Sunday at 4:30pm. Admission is 8€ adults, 5.50€ students and children 4 to 16, and free for children 3 and under. It's open in July and August daily 9:30am to midnight, June and September daily 9:30am to 7pm, and October to May Tuesday to Sunday 9:30am to 12:30pm and 2 to 6pm.

Shopping

The major boutiques, with all the big designer names from Paris, are on **place Clemenceau** in the heart of Biarritz. From this square, fan out to **rue Gambetta, rue Mazagran, avenue Victor-Hugo, avenue Edouard-VII, avenue du Maréchal-Foch,** and **avenue de Verdun.** Look for the exceptional Biarritz chocolates and confections, and textiles from the Basque country.

The finest chocolatiers are **Pariès,** 1 place Bellevue (✆ **05-59-22-07-52**), where you can choose from seven kinds of *tourons* (nougats), ranging from raspberry to coffee; and **Henriet,** place Clemenceau (✆ **05-59-24-24-15**), where the house specialty is *rochers de Biarritz* (morsels of candied orange peel and roasted almonds covered in dark chocolate). At the other end of the gastronomic spectrum, try **Mille et Un Fromages,** 8 rue Victor Hugo (✆ **05-59-24-67-88**), specializing in, as the name suggests, French cheeses, as well as a host of hearty wines to accompany them.

Virtually every souvenir shop and department store in the region sells **espadrilles,** the canvas-topped, rope-bottomed slippers. A simple off-the-shelf model begins at around 15€, and made-to-order versions (special sizes and colors) rarely top 70€.

Where to Stay

Hôtel Atalaye For economy with a bit of style, head to this simple government-rated two-star lodging. In the heart of town on a tranquil spot overlooking the ocean, this early-20th-century hotel gets rather sleepy in winter. Rooms are well maintained and traditionally furnished; most of the small, tiled bathrooms have showers. Breakfast is provided anytime you request it. The location is right off place Ste-Eugénie near the beaches, lighthouse, and casino.

6 rue des Goelands, Plateau de L'Atalaye, Biarritz 64200. www.hotelatalaye.com. ✆ **05-59-24-06-76.** Fax 05-59-22-33-51. 25 units. 47€–92€ double; 67€–119€ triple. MC, V. Closed mid-Nov to mid-Dec and last week of Jan. *In room:* A/C, TV.

Hôtel du Palais ★★★ ☺ There is no finer hotel palace along the Basque coast. The Hôtel du Palais has been the grand playground for the international elite for over a century and has truly come into vogue again after opening its Spa Impérial in 2006. Of course, the hotel has elaborately furnished suites, but even the double rooms have period furniture and silk draperies, plus spacious private bathrooms. Try to get a room facing west, to enjoy the sunsets over the Basque coast.

1 av. de l'Impératrice, Biarritz 64200. www.hotel-du-palais.com. ✆ **800/223-6800** in the U.S. and Canada, or 05-59-41-64-00. Fax 05-59-41-67-99. 154 units. 375€–585€ double; 750€–1,800€ suite. AE, DC, MC, V. **Amenities:** 3 restaurants; bar; children's program and playground; exercise room; indoor pool and outdoor seawater pool; room service; sauna; spa. *In room:* A/C, TV, hair dryer, minibar, free Wi-Fi.

Mercure Plaza Hotel Near the casino and beach, this hotel is a gorgeous Art Deco monument. Built in 1928, it has remained virtually unchanged, except for discreet renovations, so it's classified as a historic monument and a civic treasure. Rooms retain their original Art Deco furnishings; they tend to be large and have high ceilings, and some open onto private terraces. Those overlooking the back and side cost less than those with seafront views. The hotel has direct access to the beach.

10 av. Edouard-VII, Biarritz 64200. www.groupe-segeric.com. ✆ **05-59-24-74-00.** Fax 05-59-22-22-01. 69 units. 127€–203€ double. AE, DC, MC, V. Parking 17€. **Amenities:** Bar; room service. *In room:* A/C, TV, hair dryer, minibar, Wi-Fi (15€ per day).

Sofitel Biarritz Le Miramar Thalassa ★★ Containing Biarritz's most prestigious thalassotherapy institute, this Sofitel has far-out '70s architecture based on the shape of a wave. Once inside, you can see the genius of it, as most rooms have balconies facing the setting sun on Miramar beach. You can leave the sliding doors open and be soothed to sleep by the sound of the waves. Many guests check in for a week of seawater treatments and don't balk at coming down to breakfast in their robes. Lunch and dinner, however, merit dressing as chef Robert Job produces very fine fare, in both a gastronomic and an équilibré menu. The quality of service is exemplary, particularly the old-school maître d' who's a veteran of the Hôtel du Palais.

13 rue Louison Bobet. www.sofitel.com. ✆ **800/SOFITEL** [763-4835] in the U.S. and Canada, or 05-59-41-30-00. Fax 05-59-24-77-20. 126 units. 275€–372€ double. AE, DC, MC, V. Parking 20€. **Amenities:** Restaurant; bar; outdoor pool; room service; spa. *In room:* A/C, TV, hair dryer, minibar, free Wi-Fi.

Where to Eat

The restaurant at **Château de Brindos** (see "Where to Stay & Eat Nearby," below) also serves excellent Franco-Basque cuisine.

Clos Basque ★★ BASQUE/FRENCH The best regional specialties are showcased here in this Basque kitchen known for its savory offerings from both the land and sea nearby. The creative cuisine varies with the season, the availability of ingredients, and the chef's inspiration on any given day. One of the best fish dishes is a local Atlantic whitefish known as maigre. Their codfish platter with chorizo and artichokes reflects inspiration from neighboring Spain.

12 rue Louis Barthou. ✆ **05-59-24-24-96.** Reservations recommended as far in advance in summer as possible. Main courses 13€ each; fixed-price menu 24€. MC, V. Tues–Sun noon–1:30pm and Tues–Sat 8–9:30pm. Closed June 25–July 6, Oct 22–Nov 9, and Feb 18–Mar 18.

Negresse & Co. ★ BASQUE/FRENCH This restaurant takes its name from a 19th-century slave who escaped from an American plantation by hiding in the bottom of a French ship returning home. She established an inn in Biarritz, which was used by Napoleon's army en route to Spain. Inside, the decor is somber and dignified, opening onto a summer terrace. At lunch, typical brasserie food is served. At dinner, the menu is more gastronomic. Menus change every month for the relatively young and fashionable crowd that flocks here.

44 rue Luis Mariano. ✆ **05-59-41-28-51.** www.negresseco.com. Reservations required. Lunch main courses 15€–18€; dinner main courses 20€; fixed-price lunch 13€, dinner 35€. AE, DC, MC, V. Mon–Fri noon–2:30pm and Tues–Sat 7–9:30pm.

Where to Stay & Eat Nearby

Château de Brindos ★★ This is one of the most architecturally and culturally unusual homes in the southwest of France, with a history entrenched in the Jazz Age. Built by an American heiress in 1920, it occupies 11 hectares (27 acres) of inland park and garden. With a facade inspired vaguely by the architecture of Spain, and an interior loaded with architectural remnants such as fireplaces and staircases from the Gothic age, this is the most romantic stopover on the Côte Basque.

1 allée du Château, Anglet 64600. www.chateaudebrindos.com. ✆ **05-59-23-89-80.** Fax 05-59-23-89-81. 29 units. 275€–600€ double; 250€–330€ suite. AE, DC, MC, V. From town center, follow AEROPORT signs; after the 2nd roundabout *(rond-point),* follow signs to château; it's about 2.5km (1½ miles) north of Biarritz. Closed last 2 weeks of Feb. **Amenities:** Restaurant; bar; exercise room; heated outdoor pool; room service; sauna. *In room:* A/C, TV, hair dryer, minibar, free Wi-Fi.

Biarritz After Dark

Start the night with a stroll around **Port des Pêcheurs,** an ideal spot for people-watching, with its sport fishermen, restaurants, and fascinating crowds.

Fortunes have been made and lost at **Le Casino Municipal,** 1 av. Edouard-VII (✆**05-59-22-77-77**), where you can easily catch gambling fever. The less formal section, containing only slot machines, is open daily 10am to 3am (until 4am Sat). Entrance is free, no ID is required, and there's no dress code. The more elegant section (for *les jeux de table,* or table games) is open Sunday to Thursday 8pm to 3am, Friday and Saturday 8pm to 4am. This section requires a passport or photo ID. "Correct" dress for this section means no shorts or sloppy attire—jackets for men aren't required.

The hippest nightclub in town is **Le Copa,** 24 av. Edouard-VII (✆**05-59-22-29-43;** www.lecopa.fr), which plays Latin (particularly Cuban) salsa, and virtually every other kind of dance music. **Le Play Boy,** 15 place Clemenceau (✆**05-59-24-38-46**), appeals to a diverse crowd ranging in age from 20 to 40. More appealing is **Disco Le Caveau,** 4 rue Gambetta (✆**05-59-24-16-17**), where a well-dressed and attractive crowd of gay and straight people mingle with ease. **Le Carré Coast,** 21 av. Edouard VII (✆**05-59-24-64-64**), is open nightly between 7:30pm and 4am June and September, but closed Sunday to Wednesday the rest of the year. It combines a view of the sea, an outdoor terrace, a minimalist decor with lots of burnished steel, and a dance floor. Entrance is free, but a whiskey with soda begins at around 10€.

ST-JEAN-DE-LUZ ★★

791km (490 miles) SW of Paris; 15km (9¼ miles) S of Biarritz

This Basque country tuna-fishing port and beach resort is ideal for a seaside vacation. St-Jean-de-Luz lies at the mouth of the Nivelle, opening onto the Bay of Biscay, with the Pyrénées in the background. Tourists have been flocking here since the 1920s, when H. G. Wells, Aldous Huxley, and friends "discovered" the town.

Essentials

GETTING THERE Eight to 10 **trains** per day arrive from Biarritz (trip time: 15 min.; 3€–5€ one-way), and 10 trains per day arrive from Paris (trip time: 5½ hr.; 88€ one-way). For train information and schedules, call ✆ **36-35. Buses** pulling into town from other parts of the Basque country arrive at the Gare Routière (✆**05-59-26-06-99**), in front of the railway station. St-Jean-de-Luz is a short **drive** from Biarritz along N10 south.

VISITOR INFORMATION The **Office de Tourisme** is on 20 bd. Victor Hugo (✆**05-59-26-03-16;** fax 05-59-26-21-47; www.saint-jean-de-luz.com).

SPECIAL EVENTS In July and August on Wednesday and Sunday after 10:30pm, people pile into place Louis-XIV to take part in **Toro de Fuego,** a celebration of the bull. Revelers take to the streets to dance and watch fireworks. The highlight of the festivities is a snorting papier-mâché bull carried around place Louis-XIV. Between June 22 and June 26, the city celebrates the **Festival of St-Jean *(Fêtes Patronales de la Saint Jean)*** with concerts and a series of food kiosks along the harborfront. For 4 days during the first half of October, a small film festival, **Festival International des Jeunes Réalisateurs** (✆**05-59-51-65-30**), showcases the work of filmmakers from southwestern France. For information about festivals, contact the Office de Tourisme (see above).

Grand Plage St-Jean-de-Luz.

Fun on & off the Beach

The major draw here is the gracefully curving stretch of the white-sand **La Grande Plage St-Jean-de-Luz;** it's one of the best beaches in France and, consequently, very crowded in July and August. The beach lies in a half-moon-shaped bay between the ocean and the source of the Nivelle River. St-Jean-de-Luz is also a **working port,** where garishly painted fishing boats jut right up to the shopping streets. Eating seafood recently plucked from the sea is one of the reasons to visit, especially when Basque chefs transform the big catch into intriguing platters. This port's many narrow streets flanked by old houses are great for strolling.

Exploring the Town

In the town's principal church, the 13th-century **Eglise St-Jean-Baptiste ★★**, at the corner of rue Gambetta and rue Garat (✆**05-59-26-08-81**), Louis XIV and the Spanish Infanta, Marie-Thérèse, were married in 1660. The interior is among the handsomest of all Basque churches. Surmounting the altar is a statue-studded gilded retable (altarpiece). The interior is open to visitors Monday to Saturday 9am to noon and 2 to 6pm, and Sunday 3 to 6:30pm.

Two houses are associated with the couple. **La Maison Louis XIV,** place Louis XIV (✆**05-59-26-01-56**), was the scene of royal wedding night. Built of chiseled gray stone between 1644 and 1648 beside the port, it is richly furnished with antiques and mementos. It's open daily for guided tours in July and August at 10:30am and 12:30, 2:30, and 6:30pm; and from April to June and September to October at 3, 4, and 5pm. Entrance is 5.30€. **La Maison de l'Infante,** 1 rue de l'Infante (✆ **05-59-26-36-82**), is where the Infanta lived at the time of her marriage. It was designed and built by wealthy weapons merchant Johannot de Haraneder. Its pink facade, made from bricks and local stones, evokes an Italian palazzo. Inside is a "grand" reception room with a 17th-century fireplace and ceiling beams richly adorned and painted. It is open only from June to October 15, Tuesday to Saturday from 11am to 12:30pm and 2:30 to 6:30pm, and Sunday and Monday from 2:30 to 6:30pm. Entrance is 2.50€.

Shopping

You'll find the best shopping along pedestrian **rue Gambetta** and around the Eglise St-Jean-de-Luz. There you can find anything from clothes and leather handbags to books and chocolates, to dishes and linens.

You can also ramble around the port, sip pastis in a harborfront cafe, and debate the virtues of the beret. Then scout out **Maison Adam,** 49 rue Gambetta (✆ **05-59-26-03-54**), which has sold almond-based confections from this boutique since 1660. Nearby **Confiserie Pariès,** 9 rue Gambetta (✆ **05-59-26-01-46**), is especially famous for its canougat, a soft and easily chewable caramel that literally melts, with explosions of flavor, in your mouth.

Where to Stay

Grand Hôtel Loreamar ★★★ This Belle Epoque beauty has been brought back to its original splendor. Spruce chintzes and impressionist paintings in the rooms and vintage trunks in the corridors evoke a more elegant age—one where you could nip down to the English-style bar and have a jazz-era cocktail perfectly mixed, just like today. The restaurant has a superb open kitchen where you can watch the chefs put finishing touches to the Basque-influenced cuisine. And then there's the spa, with direct access to the beach: an aesthetic delight with candlelight and watery ripples.

43 bd. Thiers. www.luzgrandhotel.fr. ✆ **05-59-26-35-36.** Fax 05-59-51-99-84. 55 units. 170€–320€ double; 590€–620€ suite. AE, DC, MC, V. Parking 20€. **Amenities:** Restaurant; bar; indoor pool; room service; spa. *In room:* A/C, TV, hair dryer, minibar, free Wi-Fi.

Hôtel Hélianthal ★ Efficient, well designed, and comfortable, this hotel dates from the early 1990s and offers a spa and healthy food. It sits atop a restaurant that has been a city monument since the 1920s. Unfortunately, none of the Art Deco–style rooms overlook the sea, but many have terraces, bay windows, or balconies. Each room has an immaculately kept bathroom with tub and shower. The big-windowed restaurant, L'Atlantique, offers a terrace overlooking the sea.

Place Maurice-Ravel. www.helianthal.fr. ✆ **05-59-51-51-00.** Fax 05-59-51-51-54. 100 units. 118€–248€ double. AE, DC, MC, V. Parking 6€–12€. **Amenities:** Restaurant; bar; babysitting; health club; pool; room service; sauna. *In room:* A/C, TV, hair dryer, minibar, free Wi-Fi.

Le Parc Victoria ★★ The most secluded and tranquil hotel at the resort is a white 19th-century villa, saved from destruction and lovingly restored. The chandelier-lit salon of the main building, decorated in Napoleon III fashion, sets the tone. Guest rooms hold antiques and comfortable, tasteful Art Deco furnishings, and marble-clad bathrooms. The restaurant's cuisine and wines are first class.

5 rue Cepé. www.parcvictoria.com. ✆ **05-59-26-78-78.** Fax 05-59-26-78-08. 20 units. 175€–340€ double; 290€–455€ suite. AE, DC, MC, V. Free parking. Closed mid-Nov to mid-Mar. **Amenities:** 2 restaurants; bar; babysitting; outdoor pool. *In room:* A/C, TV, hair dryer, minibar, free Wi-Fi.

Where to Eat

You may also like to check out L'Atlantique, the restaurant at the **Hôtel Hélianthal**, and Le Rosewood at the **Grand Hôtel Loreamar** (see p. 686).

Auberge Kaïku ★ BASQUE/FRENCH On a narrow street off place Louis-XIV, Auberge Kaïku is the best restaurant in town outside the hotels. The structure, with hand-hewn beams and chiseled masonry, dates from 1540 and is said to be the oldest in town. Examples of the cuisine are roast suckling Pyrénéan lamb, John Dory with fresh mint, filet of beef with essence of truffles, and duckling in honey.

17 rue de la République. ✆ **05-59-26-13-20.** Reservations recommended. Main courses 20€–25€; fixed-price lunch 25€, dinner 32€. MC, V. July–Aug daily 12:15–2pm and 7:30–10pm; Sept–June Thurs–Mon 12:15–2pm and 7–10pm.

Chez Kako BASQUE "Kako who?" you might ask. He's Jean-Claude Ascery (which translates from the Basque as "fox"), whose childhood nickname, Kako, is known to virtually every longtime resident of St-Jean-de-Luz. You'll find his rustic, artfully old-fashioned bodega within Les Halles, point of sale for the town's freshest meats and produce. Come here for beefsteaks prepared for two diners at a time, tapas, very fresh fish—especially hake—and slices of aromatic goat cheese from local farmsteads. There's a full list of French and Spanish wines, but many diners here prefer bottles of the moderately alcoholic local cider instead.

18 rue du Maréchal Harispe at the Place des Halles. ✆ **05-59-85-10-70.** Reservations recommended. Main courses 15€–20€; set-price menu 43€. AE, MC, V. Tues–Sat noon–2:30pm and 7:30–10pm (till 11pm Fri–Sat). Open Mon in summer.

Chez Maya BASQUE This small *auberge* is highly acclaimed for quality and value. The fixed-price menu is the best deal in town. The chefs cook as their grandparents did, preparing all the old favorites, such as squid cooked in its own ink and a local fish soup known as *morro.*

4 rue St-Jacques. ✆ **05-59-26-80-76.** Reservations recommended. Main courses 15€–22€; fixed-price menu 20€–29€. AE, DC, MC, V. Fri–Sun and Tues noon–2pm; Thurs–Tues 7–10pm. Closed Dec 19–Jan 25.

St-Jean-de-Luz After Dark

You can start by taking a walk along the promenade to watch the sunset. Around **place Louis-XIV,** you'll find a hotbed of activity at the cafes and bars. A fun spot in the center of town is **Pub du Corsaire,** 16 rue de la République (✆ **05-59-26-10-74**), for unpretentious merrymaking accompanied by copious amounts of alcohol and rock 'n' roll. The hot pickup joint that's crowded with scantily clad wannabe *vedettes, starlettes,* and *princesses* is **Le Brouillarta,** promenade de Jacques Thibaud (✆ **05-59-51-29-51**). There's a view of the sea, a crowd of tourists and locals whose age ranges from 18 to around 55, platters of Basque food priced at 8€ to 18€ per main course, and a separate bar area where, frankly, no one really cares if you ever migrate onward to dinner at all.

18

BORDEAUX & THE ATLANTIC COAST

by Margie Rynn

From La Rochelle to the Bordeaux wine district, the southwest of France is often just a quick stopover for visitors driving from Paris to Spain. However, this area is well worth a more in-depth visit for its Atlantic beaches, medieval and Renaissance ruins, Romanesque and Gothic churches, vineyards, and delightful inns serving splendid regional cuisine.

This intriguing region merits a detour inland to sample cognac in Cognac and to visit nearby art cities such as Poitiers and Angoulême. If you can manage it, allow a week here—enough time to sample the wine, savor the cuisine, and see some of the sights.

POITIERS ★★

333km (206 miles) SW of Paris; 177km (110 miles) SE of Nantes

Poitiers stands on a hill overlooking the Clain and Boivre rivers—a strategic location that tempted many conquerors. Everybody has passed through here—from Joan of Arc to Richard the Lion-Hearted. Charles Martel chased out the Muslims in A.D. 732 and altered the course of European civilization. Poitiers was the chief city of Eleanor of Aquitaine, who had her marriage to pious Louis VII annulled so she could wed England's Henry II.

For those interested in history, this is one of the most fascinating towns in France. The Battle of Poitiers was fought on September 19, 1356, between the armies of Edward the Black Prince and King John of France. It was one of the three great English victories in the Hundred Years' War, distinguished by the use of the longbow in the skilled hands of English archers.

After decades of slumber, the town came alive with the opening of **Futuroscope,** a cinema theme park in 1987, which now gets upward of 1.7 million visitors per year. The thriving student population (25,000 of Poitiers's 92,000 residents are students) adds vitality as well.

Essentials

GETTING THERE Frequent **rail** service is available from Paris, Bordeaux, and La Rochelle. Around 15 high-speed TGV trains arrive daily from Paris's Gare Montparnasse (trip time: 90 min.; 65€ one-way). Another 17 TGVs arrive daily from Bordeaux (trip time: 1¾ hr; 37€ one-way), and 12 regular trains arrive from La Rochelle (trip time: 1¾ hr.; 22€–23€one-way). For train information, call ✆ **36-35** or visit www.voyages-sncf.com. **Bus** service from Poitiers is so badly scheduled that it's virtually nonexistent. If you're **driving,** Poitiers is located on the A10 highway; from Paris, follow A10 south through the cities of Orléans and Tours, and on to Poitiers.

VISITOR INFORMATION The **Office de Tourisme** is at 45 place Charles de Gaulle (✆ **05-49-41-21-24;** www.ot-poitiers.fr).

FACING PAGE: **La Rochelle.**

SPECIAL EVENTS The liveliest time to visit is from mid-June to mid-September during **Poitiers l'Eté,** a festival of free live jazz, theater, opera, rock, and fireworks. Free concerts and theater pieces, both in and out of the streets, take place at various parks and churches around the city. Check with the tourist office for schedules.

Exploring the City

Baptistère St-Jean ★ From the cathedral, you can walk to the most ancient Christian monument in France. It was built as a baptistery in the early 4th century on Roman foundations and extended in the 7th century. It contains frescoes from the 11th to the 13th centuries and a collection of funerary sculpture.

Rue Jean-Jaurès. No phone. Admission 2€ adults, 1€ children 11 and under. July–Aug daily 10:30am–12:30pm and 3–6pm; Sept and Apr–May Wed–Mon 10:30am–12:30pm and 3–6pm; Oct–Mar Wed–Mon 2:30–4:30pm.

Cathédrale St-Pierre ★ In the eastern sector of Poitiers is the twin-towered Cathédrale St-Pierre, begun in 1162 by Henry II of England and Eleanor of Aquitaine on the ruins of a Roman basilica. The architecturally undistinguished cathedral was completed much later. The interior, 89m (292 ft.) long, contains some admirable 12th- and 13th-century stained glass.

Place de la Cathédrale. ✆ **05-49-41-23-76.** Free admission. Daily 8:30am–7:30pm (until 6pm in winter).

Eglise Notre-Dame-la-Grande ★★ This church, built in the Romanesque-Byzantine style and richly decorated, is from the late 11th century. See in particular its western front, dating from the mid–12th century. Surrounded by an open-air market, the facade, carved like an ivory casket, is characterized by pine cone–shaped towers. It was thoroughly cleaned and restored in 1996. Carvings on the doorway represent biblical scenes.

Place Charles de Gaulle. ✆ **05-49-41-22-56.** Free admission. Mon–Sat 9am–7pm; Sun noon–7pm.

Futuroscope ★★ ☺ This multimedia amusement park in a suburb of Poitiers is a wonderland of technology that lets you experience sounds, images, and sensations with the world's most advanced film-projection techniques and largest screens. The architecture is extraordinary—take a peek at the **Kinémax**, a 400-seat cinema shaped like a rock crystal covered with mirrors, or the **Cité du Numérique** (Digital City), a giant glass triangle with a huge white globe sitting in the middle. There are no less than six IMAX theatres here, projecting viewers into the heart of the action, as well as attractions that use "increased reality" 3-D technology, motion simulators, and sophisticated lighting effects.

Eglise Notre-Dame-la-Grande.

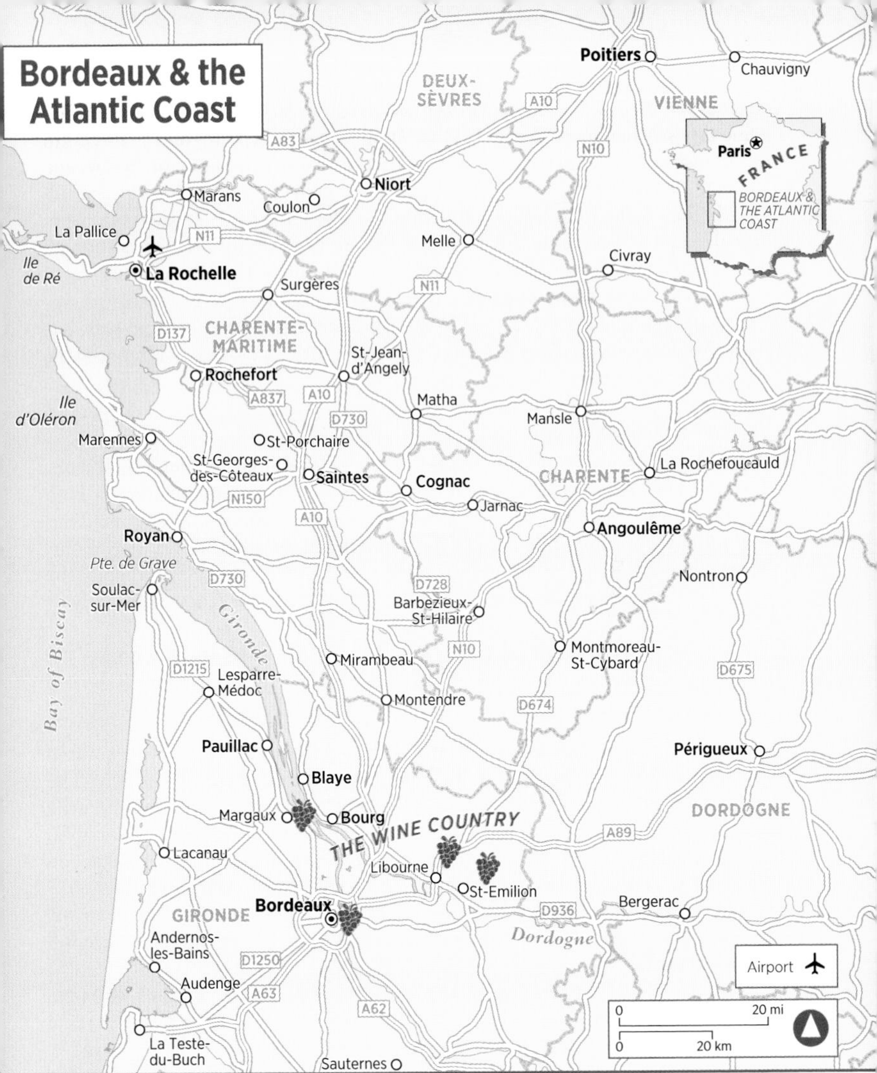

Attractions let you rocket deep into space, dive under the ocean, or fly up in the air for a virtual sky tour. New rides include a roller coaster following the wild adventures of a futuristic pizza delivery man, and an IMAX Arthur and the Minimoys escapade. In July and August every night until 10pm, *les nocturnes* are staged with illuminated fountains, lights, and recorded music.

The park's success is such that it has its own TGV train station with direct connections to Bordeaux, Paris, and other major cities, as well as a selection of hotels and restaurants (detailed on the website) so that you can stay overnight.

Jaunay-Clan. ✆ **05-49-49-30-80.** www.futuroscope.com. Admission 36€ adults, 33€ over 60, 27€ children 5–16, free for children 4 and under. Daily 10am–dusk. Bus: Vitalis line 1 and E direct from Poitiers Centre train station. Driving: From Poitiers, take D910 or A10 autoroute about 12km (7½ miles) north. Closed Jan to mid-Feb.

Musée Ste-Croix On the site of the old abbey of Ste-Croix, this museum has a fine arts section devoted mainly to painting—especially 16th- and 17th-century Flemish art and 19th-century salon painting. Works by Bonnard, Sisley, and Moreau are on display, as well as an impressive collection of sculptures, including Maillol, Rodin, and seven statues by Camille Claudel. A separate archaeological section documents the history of Poitou, from prehistoric times through the Gallo-Roman era and the Renaissance, to the end of the 19th century.

3 rue Jean-Jaurès. ✆ **05-49-41-07-53.** www.musees-poitiers.org. Admission 4€ adults, free for ages 17 and under. June–Sept Tues 10am–noon and 1:15–8pm, Wed–Fri 10am–noon and 1:15–6pm, Sat–Sun 10am–noon and 2–6pm; Oct–May Tues 10am–5pm, Wed–Fri 10am–noon and 1:15–5pm, Sat–Sun 2–6pm.

Where to Stay

Hôtel de l'Europe ★ Composed of several buildings, one of which dates from the 19th century, these comfortable lodgings offer a combination of both modern and fin-de-siècle style. The breakfast room features curlicue moldings and a grand fireplace, while most of the rooms are modern and sleek. Sixty rooms were fully renovated in 2009, some with a vaguely colonial or Asian theme; the older ones in the main building are smaller (and cheaper) and accessible only by staircase.

39 rue Carnot, Poitiers 86000. www.hotel-europe-poitiers.com. ✆ **05-49-88-12-00.** Fax 05-49-88-97-30. 88 units. 62€–98€ double. AE, MC, V. Parking 6€. Closed btw. Christmas and New Year's Day. **Amenities:** Room service. *In room:* TV, hair dryer, minibar (in some), free Wi-Fi.

Hôtel du Plat d'Etain One of the best bargains in Poitiers, this renovated hotel is on a narrow alley close to the landmark place du Maréchal-Leclerc. The much-renovated, much-simplified building dates from 1895. It's named after the medieval inn, the "Pewter Plate," that stood on the site. (That inn became infamous for unwittingly housing Ravaillac, the deranged zealot who fatally stabbed King Henri IV in 1610.) Rooms are compact and simply but comfortably furnished, in warm shades of gold, beige, and red. A few bargain-basement rooms have a sink in the room and shared toilet facilities in the hall, but most have full in-suite bathrooms.

7-9 rue du Plat-d'Etain, Poitiers 86000. www.poitiers-leplatdetain.com. ✆ **05-49-41-04-80.** Fax 05-49-52-25-84. 20 units. 31€–59€ double. AE, MC, V. Parking 5€. Closed last 2 weeks in Dec. *In room:* TV, minibar, free Wi-Fi.

Le Grand Hotel It's the most imposing Art Deco monument in town, with an exterior that is pure 1920s and bedrooms that have maintained the same style in spirit. With four stories and a location in the heart of the city's commercial core, it often hosts French actors and entertainers, thanks to a good reputation for solid quality and its proximity to the Théâtre National. There is an expansive terrace where breakfasts are served on clement summer mornings, overlooking a quiet inner courtyard. While there's no on-site restaurant, there are plenty nearby. Bedrooms, depending on what floor you're on, may have a modernized 1920s-inspired decor and monochromatic color schemes.

28 rue Carnot, Poitiers 86000. www.grandhotelpoitiers.fr. ✆ **05-49-60-90-60.** Fax 05-49-62-81-89. 47 units. 79€–89€ double; 116€ suite. AE, DC, MC, V. Parking 6€. **Amenities:** Bar; room service. *In room:* TV, hair dryer, minibar, free Wi-Fi.

Where to Eat

Alain Boutin ★ FRENCH/SEAFOOD Chef Boutin has awakened the sleepy taste buds of the town with his market-fresh cuisine combined with his culinary imagination. A regional influence enhances his clever dishes, especially when he uses produce of the area, as he does most effectively. You might begin with a shellfish soup flavored with saffron with a rouille sauce, followed by filet of zander or veal kidneys with a piquant sauce and zucchini flan. Located near the Jardins de Blossac, the restaurant has one large dining room, plus another smaller one seating only 15.

65 rue Carnot. ✆ **05-49-88-25-53.** www.alainboutin.com. Reservations required. Main courses 16€–30€; fixed-price menus 24€–35€. MC, V. Tues–Fri noon–1:30pm; Mon–Sat 7:30–9:30pm. Closed 1st week of Sept and 1st week of Jan.

Poitevin FRENCH Shoppers and office workers descend on this restaurant en masse at midday, but evening meals are less rushed. There are six cozy dining rooms: One contains an 18th-century fireplace transported here from a demolished building nearby; another abounds with butterflies (on the carpets, curtains, and napery, and mounted in frames). Menu items may include *mouclade Charentaise* (mussels in white wine–and-cream sauce); scallops with sauterne sabayon; and an unusual stewpot containing filets of eel and sole, served with lemon sauce. For dessert, try a semisoft slice of oozing chocolate cake.

76 rue Carnot. ✆ **05-49-88-35-04.** Reservations recommended. Main courses 16€–40€; fixed-price menu 24€–36€. AE, DC, MC, V. Daily noon–2pm; Mon–Sat 7–10pm. Closed 2 weeks at Easter, 3 weeks in late July and Aug, and 2 weeks at Christmas.

Vingélique ★ CLASSICAL FRENCH Established in the heart of historic Poitiers and contained within an ultramodern pair of fresco-ringed dining rooms, this highly recommended restaurant offers quality cuisine at very reasonable prices. The chef focuses on fresh produce from local sources to create dishes, which include lobster salad with avocados and lime; "barely cooked" scallops with a chantilly of herbs and a salad of wild greens; filet of sea bass with a sea urchin sauce; and sweetbreads with a foie gras sauce. The only dining choice here involves the set-price menus, but because of the wide choice of seasonally adapted dishes available, that is just fine.

37 rue Carnot. ✆ **05-49-55-07-03.** Reservations recommended. Lunch *plat du jour* with dessert 11€; set-price lunches and dinners 25€–37€. AE, MC, V. Mon–Sat noon–2pm and 7:30–10pm.

LA ROCHELLE ★★★

467km (290 miles) SW of Paris; 145km (90 miles) SE of Nantes; 183km (113 miles) N of Bordeaux; 142km (88 miles) NW of Angoulême

La Rochelle is a historic port and ancient sailors' city, formerly the stronghold of the Huguenots. It was founded as a fishing village in the 10th century on a rocky platform in the center of a marshland. Eleanor of Aquitaine gave La Rochelle a charter in 1199, freeing it from feudal dues. After becoming an independent city-state, the port capitalized on the wars between France and England. It was the departure point for the founders of Montreal. From the 14th to the 16th century, La Rochelle was one of France's great maritime cities. It became the principal port between France and the colony of Canada, but France's loss of Canada ruined its Atlantic trade.

La Rochelle.

As a hotbed of Protestant factions, it armed privateers to prey on Catholic vessels but was eventually besieged by Catholic troops, led by Cardinal Richelieu (with his Musketeers) and Jean Guiton. When Richelieu blockaded the port, La Rochelle bravely resisted. It took 15 months to starve the city into submission, during which time 25,000 citizens perished from hunger. On October 30, 1628, Richelieu entered the city and found only 5,000 survivors.

Today La Rochelle, a city of 147,000, is the cultural and administrative center of the Charente-Maritime *département* (administrative region). Its famous city lights have earned it the title "City of Light." While many of La Rochelle's sights are old, the city is riddled with high-rise condos and home to the largest pleasure-boat basin in Europe. In summer, the city is overrun with visitors.

Essentials

GETTING THERE The La Rochelle–Ile-de-Ré **airport** (✆ **05-46-42-86-70;** www.larochelle.aeroport.fr) is on the coast, 4km (2½ miles) north of the city. Take bus no. 7 or 47 to reach it; for information and schedules, call ✆ **05-46-34-84-58** or visit www.rtcr.fr. Six to eight **trains** from Bordeaux and Nantes arrive daily (trip time: 2 hr.; 26€–27€ one-way). There are direct TGVs from Paris's Gare Montparnasse (trip time: 3 hr.); the one-way fare is 56€ to 78€. For train information, call ✆ **36-35** or visit www.voyages-sncf.com. **Buses** leave from place de Verdun (✆ **05-46-00-95-15** for information). If you're **driving** to La Rochelle, follow A10 south from Poitiers to exit 33 toward La Rochelle/Niort/St-Maixent, and then take N11 west to the coast and La Rochelle.

VISITOR INFORMATION The **Office de Tourisme** is on Quai Georges Simenon, Le Gabut (✆ **05-46-41-14-68;** www.larochelle-tourisme.com).

SPECIAL EVENTS The busiest month is July; the **Festival International du Film de La Rochelle** rolls in at the beginning of the month. It attracts a huge following of fans, press, actors, directors, and, of course, paparazzi. Screenings are held around town; a pass for 10 screenings costs 45€. For information, contact the festival office, at 10 Quai Georges Simenon (✆ **05-46-52-28-96** or 01-48-06-16-66; www.festival-larochelle.org). For a week in mid-July, **Les Francofolies,** a festival of French-speaking music, features big names as well as not-so-famous groups, many of them international pop musicians. The town is overrun with groupies and fans, and a party atmosphere prevails. Tickets range from 20€ to 35€. Call ✆ **05-46-28-28-28** for details (www.francofolies.fr). The Office de Tourisme can also provide details on both festivals.

La Rochelle is also the site of the biggest showcase of boats and yachts in Europe, **Le Grand Pavois–Salon Nautique.** It's a 5-day extravaganza in mid-September. The action is based in and around La Rochelle's Port de Plaisance (better known as the Bassin des Yachts, or Yacht Basin). Sellers and buyers of boats and marine hardware, as well as weekend sailors from everywhere, usually attend. For information about dates and venues, call ✆ **05-46-44-46-39** or check www.grand-pavois.com.

Exploring the City

There are two sides to La Rochelle: the old and unspoiled town inside the Vauban defenses, and the tacky modern and industrial suburbs. Its **fortifications** have a circuit of 5.5km (3½ miles), with a total of seven gates.

The town, with its arch-covered streets, is great for strolling. The port is a fishing harbor and one of Europe's major sailing centers. Try to schedule a visit in time to attend a fish auction. The best streets for strolling, each with a 17th-century arcade, are **rue du Palais, la Rue du Temple, rue Chaudrier,** and **rue des Merciers,** with its ancient wooden houses (seek out the ones at nos. 3, 5, 8, and 17).

Aquarium de La Rochelle ★ La Rochelle's blockbuster crowd pleaser rises from a portside position near the Port des Minimes, north of the old city. Inside are guided walkways stretching over two floors of massive and bubbling seawater tanks loaded with approximately 10,000 species of flora and fauna from the oceans of the world, living in what look like natural habitats. It's hard to miss this place; there are signs for it all over town.

Bassin des Grands Yachts, Quai Louis Prunier, Le Vieux Port. ✆ **05-46-34-00-00.** www.aquarium-larochelle.com. 14€ adults, 11€ students and children 3–17, free for children 2 and under. English-language audio guide 3.50€. July–Aug daily 9am–11pm; Apr–June and Sept daily 9am–8pm; Oct–Mar daily 10am–8pm.

Hôtel de Ville (City Hall) ★ The town's 14th-century showcase is built in flamboyant Gothic style with battlements. Inside you can admire the Henry II staircase with canopies and the marble desk of the heroic Jean Guiton. You must visit as part of a guided tour (in French only); advance reservations are not necessary.

Place de la Mairie, in the city center. ✆ **05-46-51-51-51.** Admission 4€ adults, 1.50€ students and children 4–18, free for children 3 and under. Guided tours July–Aug daily 3 and 4pm; June and Sept daily 3pm; Oct–May Sat–Sun 3pm (and some holidays at 3 and 4pm).

Musée des Beaux-Arts ★ The museum is in an Episcopal palace built in the mid–18th century. The art spans the 15th to the

Money-Saving Museum Pass

You can buy a combination ticket good for entrance to the Musée des Beaux-Arts, Musée Orbigny-Bernon, Muséum d'Histoire Naturelle, and Musée du Nouveau-Monde. Available at any of the museums and the tourist office, it costs 12€, a big savings.

20th centuries, with works by Gustave Doré, Brossard de Beaulieu, Corot, and Fromentin. Twentieth-century pieces include works by Maillol and Léger.

28 rue Gargoulleau. ✆ **05-46-41-64-65.** www.ville-larochelle.fr. Admission 4€ adults, free for children 17 and under. Oct–Mar Mon and Wed–Fri 9:30am–12:30pm and 1:30–5:30pm, Sat–Sun 2:30–6pm; Apr–Sept Mon and Wed–Sat 10:30am–12:30pm and 2–6pm, Sun 2–6pm.

Muséum d'Histoire Naturelle Set within an enormous (2,500 sq. m/26,910 sq. ft.) once-private mansion in the heart of town, and reopened in 2007 after a 13-year closing, this museum stockpiles everything of interest, ethnographically and anthropologically speaking. Stuffed animals, African masks, maps of prehistoric migrational patterns, and everything brought back by La Rochelle's 17th-century traders from around the world are on display.

28 rue Albert 1er. ✆ **05-46-41-18-25.** www.museum-larochelle.fr. Admission 4€, free for 17 and under. Oct to mid-May Tues–Fri 9am–6pm, Sat–Sun 2pm–6pm; mid-May to Sept Tues–Fri 10am–7pm, Sat–Sun 2–7pm.

Musée du Nouveau-Monde ★ In an 18th-century town house rich with architectural details, this is one of the most intriguing museums in La Rochelle. It's rich with evidence of the city's prominent role in the colonization of Canada. The displays trace the port's 300-year history with the New World. Exhibits start with LaSalle's discovery of the Mississippi Delta in 1682 and end with the settling of the Louisiana territory. Other exhibits depict French settlements in the West Indies, including Guadeloupe and Martinique.

In the Hôtel Fleuriau, 10 rue Fleuriau. ✆ **05-46-41-46-50.** Admission 4€ adults, free for children 17 and under. Oct–Mar Mon and Wed–Fri 9:30am–12:30pm and 1:30–5:30pm, Sat–Sun 2:30–6pm; Apr–Sept Mon and Wed–Sat 10am–12:30pm and 2–6pm, Sun 2–6pm.

Musée Maritime This museum is comprised of eight permanently docked boats, two of which can be visited: a meteorological frigate and an antique *chalutier de peche* (fishing trawler). Exhibits evoke the grand days of La Rochelle as a maritime power and its commerce with the New World.

Quai Sénac de Meilhan. ✆ **05-46-28-03-00.** www.museemaritimelarochelle.fr. Admission 8€ adults, 5.50€ for students and children 4–16, free for children 3 and under. Apr–June and Sept daily 10am–6:30pm; July–Aug daily 10am–7pm.

Tour de la Chaîne During the 1300s, this tower was built as an anchor piece for the large forged-iron chain that stretched across the harbor, closing it against hostile warships. The exhibits focus on the history of the first migration to Canada.

Quai du Gabut. ✆ **05-46-34-11-81.** www.monuments-nationaux.fr. Admission, see box. Oct–Mar daily 10am–1pm and 2–5:30pm; Apr–Sept 10am–6:30pm.

Tour de la Lanterne ★ Built between 1445 and 1476, this was once a lighthouse but was used mainly as a jail as late as the 19th century. A low rampart connects the cylindrical tower to the Tour de

Saving Money Tower-Hopping

Instead of paying separate admissions to visit each historic tower of La Rochelle, you can purchase a three-tower global ticket for 8€ adults or 5€ ages 18 to 25; it's free for those 17 and under. It allows you to visit all three tours (though usually after two towers, only the most die-hard tower devotees press on). Should you wish to visit only one tower, you'll pay just 6€ for adults and 74€ for ages 18 to 25, free for 17 and under.

la Chaîne. During the Wars of Religion, 13 priests were tossed from its summit. You climb 162 steps to the top hold; in clear weather, the panoramic view extends all the way to Ile d'Oléron. On the way up, you can still see graffiti scrawled by former prisoners.

Opposite Tour St-Nicolas, quai du Gabut. ✆ **05-46-41-56-04.** Admission see above. Oct–Mar daily 10am–1pm and 2–5:30pm; Apr–Sept 10am–6:30pm.

Tour St-Nicolas.

Tour St-Nicolas ★ The oldest tower in La Rochelle, Tour St-Nicolas was built between 1371 and 1382. It originally guarded the town against surprise attacks. From its second floor, you can enjoy a view of the town and harbor; from the top, you can see only the old town and Ile d'Oléron.

Quai du Gabut. ✆ **05-46-41-74-13.** Admission see above. Oct–Mar daily 10am–1pm and 2–5:30pm; Apr–Sept 10am–6:30pm.

Where to Stay

Champlain–France-Angleterre ★★ Close to the major parks and the old port, this is the most gracious choice in La Rochelle. It's furnished with a winning combination of antiques and art objects, and has a genial staff. Rooms are tasteful and dignified; many have a nautical theme. One of the best aspects of the hotel is its romantic garden, brimming with flowers, shrubbery, and shade trees. Breakfast is the only meal served.

30 rue Rambaud, La Rochelle 17000. www.hotelchamplain.com. ✆ **800/528-1234** in the U.S. and Canada, or **05-46-41-23-99.** Fax 05-46-41-15-19. 40 units. 75€–140€ double; 140€–165€ suite. AE, DC, MC, V. Parking 7.50€. **Amenities:** Room service. *In room:* A/C, TV, hair dryer, minibar, free Wi-Fi.

Les Brises ★ This nautically decorated seaside hotel opposite the Port des Minimes, 1.5km (1 mile) north of the old city, offers a view of the sea and of a soaring 19th-century column dedicated to the Virgin. You can enjoy the view from the front balconies of the six-story building as well as the parasol-shaded patio. The immaculate rooms, which were completely renovated in 2008, have cherrywood furniture and comfortable beds.

1, Chemin de la Digue de Richelieu, La Rochelle 17000. www.hotellesbrises.cabanova.fr. ✆ **05-46-43-89-37.** Fax 05-46-43-27-97. 48 units. 80€–130€ double; 160€–210€ family room for 4. AE, DC, MC, V. Free parking. **Amenities:** Room service. *In room:* TV, hair dryer, free Wi-Fi.

Masqhotel ★ Near the train station and the old harborfront, this is the most sophisticated modern hotel in town, the creation of a local architect, Michel Dufour, who wanted to create an avant-garde building in his hometown. The design is cutting edge, and Dufour isn't afraid of orange or apple green. He wanted to decorate the hotel as if it were his own home—simple yet chic and subtle. In that, he succeeded admirably. From the lounge bar to the bedrooms, the hotel is high tech, with top-quality furnishings and bedding, plus a lounge bar.

17 rue de l'Ouvrage a Cornes, La Rochelle 17000. www.masqhotel.com. ✆ **05-46-41-83-83.** Fax 05-46-07-04-43. 76 units. 90€–170€ double; 149€–260€ suite. AE, DC, MC, V. **Amenities:** Bar; room service. *In room:* A/C, TV, hair dryer, free Wi-Fi.

Where to Eat

Bar/Bistro André SEAFOOD Seafood is an expensive item anywhere in France, but usually it's worth it. Here you can get a big meal even by choosing something from the lower end of the price scale. Traditional menu items include savory versions of fish soup; an unusual version of *cabillaud fumé* (home-smoked codfish) served with garlic-flavored cream sauce; curried mussels *(mouclade);* and a saltwater fish not very common in other parts of France, filet of *maîgre*, served with chive-flavored cream sauce.

5 rue St-Jean du Pérot/place de la Chaîne. ✆ **05-46-41-28-24.** www.barandre.com. Reservations recommended. Main courses 19€–32€. Fixed-price menus 18€–45€. AE, DC, MC, V. Daily noon–2:30pm and 7–10:30pm.

Chez Lulu FRENCH/INTERNATIONAL Located a 3-minute walk from La Rochelle's Old Port, this unpretentious and fun restaurant is owned by Betty Rechaux, who quit her job as a financial auditor in Paris to return to her hometown to open this place. She named it after her recently deceased grandmother, Lulu. Inside you'll sit on armchairs or sofas and may dine to the tune of a live pianist, who sometimes plays in the evenings. The best menu items include foie gras with figs and fig granita; medallions of lamb with pear, eggplant, and almond chutney; squid with a squid-ink risotto; and duck magret with black olive butter.

19 ter Place du Maréchal Foch. ✆ **05-46-50-69-03.** www.chezlulu.net. Main courses 17€; fixed-price menu 18€ lunch, 28€–38€ (dinner). MC, V. Mon–Sat noon–2pm and 7–10pm.

Comptoir des Voyages FRENCH/INTERNATIONAL This restaurant has a cost-conscious, lighthearted format that celebrates the cuisines of most of France's neighbors, its former colonies, and France itself. Surrounded by hardwood paneling and big windows, you'll have a choice of five starters, eight main courses, and six desserts. The frequently changing menu may include Martinique-style codfish fritters, lamb chops dredged in Indian spices, and buckwheat crepes stuffed with poached pears and Breton-style liqueur. Almost all the wines are from outside France.

22 rue St-Jean du Pérot. ✆ **05-46-50-62-60.** www.lecomptoirdesvoyages.com. Reservations recommended. Main courses 18€–25€; fixed-price menu 20€–28€. AE, DC, MC, V. Daily noon–2pm and 7:30–10pm.

Richard et Christopher Coutanceau ★★★ MODERN FRENCH This is not only the city's most glamorous and prestigious restaurant, but also one of the finest along the coast. Delectable cuisine is served in an airy dining room with big bay windows overlooking the adjacent beach and sea. Clearly an artist, Richard Coutanceau, the owner and genius chef, prepares "modernized" cuisine. For an appetizer, roasted frogs' legs come with crisp vegetables and bitter almond foam. The signature fish dish is line-caught sea bass cooked within its own crusty skin and served with chard and lardons. Among the meat dishes, you can sample boned pigeon bourguignon with vegetable minestrone, or medallions of venison with beets and stuffed dates in a cacao-flavored sauce.

Plage de la Concurrence. © **05-46-41-48-19.** www.coutanceaularochelle.com. Reservations required. Main courses 42€–62€; fixed-price menus 55€–95€. AE, DC, MC, V. Mon–Sat noon–1:30pm and 7:30–9:30pm.

La Rochelle After Dark

From July to September, head for **quai Duperré, cours des Dames,** and **cours des Templiers.** Once the sun starts to set, this becomes one big pedestrian zone peppered with street performers. It's a fun, almost magical area that sets the tone for the rest of the night.

sailing THE PORTS OF LA ROCHELLE

La Rochelle has always earned its living from the sea and from the ships that make its harbor their home. Four distinct harbors have grown up over the centuries, each a world unto itself, rich with local nuance and lore. They include the historic **Vieux-Port,** the **Port de Plaisance** (a modern yacht marina), the **Port de Pêche** (the fishing port), and the **Port de Commerce,** which is mostly used by large container ships.

The best way to appreciate them is to take a boat tour. Visit the tourist office (see "Essentials," earlier in this chapter), which acts as a clearinghouse for the outfitters (Croisières Inter-Iles, Navipromer, Ré Croisières). Tours combine a look at the modern facilities with a waterside view of the historic ramparts—which, despite their girth and height, did not protect the city's 17th-century Protestants from starvation and eventual annihilation.

The company with the most frequent departures is the **Croisières Inter-Iles** (© **08-25-13-55-00;** www.inter-iles.com). Every day from April to October, there are about a half-dozen cruises into each of the six ports. In winter, they're offered less frequently, usually only on school vacations. Tours last 70 to 180 minutes each, are conducted in French, and average 20€.

Another excellent waterborne outing—but only during the warmer months—involves taking a ferry from the Vieux-Port of La Rochelle to **Ile de Ré.** The island, 26km (16 miles) off the coast of La Rochelle and ringed with 69km (43 miles) of sandy beaches, holds nature preserves crisscrossed with biking and hiking paths. Croisières Inter-Iles (see above) serves the island. If you want to get here during July or August, and if you don't have a car, we recommend taking the ferry for a round-trip fare of 22€.

You can also drive your car across the bridge that connects the Ile de Ré to the French mainland. It's accessible from a point 3km (1¾ miles) south of La Rochelle. The toll is 17€ in summer, 9€ in winter. The local bus company, **Les Mouettes** (© **08-11-36-17-17;** www.lesmouettes-transports.com), offers 14 round-trips per day year-round (line 3), and charges 4.40€ one-way or 7.40€ round-trip from La Rochelle to several stops along the island.

COGNAC

478km (296 miles) SW of Paris; 37km (23 miles) NW of Angoulême; 113km (70 miles) SE of La Rochelle

The world enjoys 150 million bottles a year of the nectar known as cognac, which Victor Hugo called "the drink of the gods." It's worth a detour to visit one of the château warehouses of the bottlers. Martell, Hennessy, and Otard welcome visits from the public, as well as other worthy *maisons de négoce;* visits usually include free tastings.

Essentials

GETTING THERE Five **trains** per day arrive from Angoulême (trip time: 40 min.), and six trains pull in from Saintes (trip time: 20 min.). For train information and schedules, call ✆ **36-35** or visit www.voyages-sncf.com. There is limited **bus** service from Angoulême; the trip takes 50 minutes and costs 4.50€; call ✆ **05-45-95-95-99** or visit www.vtpc.fr for schedules. If you're **driving** to Cognac, the best route from Saintes (which lies along the major route A10) is N141 east.

VISITOR INFORMATION The **Office de Tourisme** is at 16 rue du 14-Juillet (✆ **05-45-82-10-71;** www.tourism-cognac.com).

SPECIAL EVENTS Cognac grapes are among the last picked in France. Harvest time usually begins in mid-October.

Cognac is home to several annual festivals, the best of which is **Cognac Blues Passions,** a jazz festival featuring performers from throughout France and the world, including stars like B. B. King, Liz McComb, and Taj Majal that takes place over 5 days in July. Most events cost between 30€ and 40€, although a *passeport* granting access to all the concerts in the venue sells for 130€. For information, call ✆ **05-45-36-11-81** or check www.bluespassions.com.

More closely tuned to French-speaking audiences is the annual **Coup de Chauffe/Festival du Théâtre de la Rue,** wherein for a 3-day period in September, street performers present social or political satires in the open air without any admission charges. Although a working knowledge of French is useful, many of the presentations are more "performance art" than traditional drama and can be appreciated for their visuals. For information, call ✆ **05-45-82-32-78** or visit www.avantscene.com.

Exploring the Town

Many visitors don't realize that this unassuming town of some 20,000 people is more than just a drink. Though the air is perfumed with the sweet scent from the distilleries, business goes on as usual in the cobbled streets, some of which still sport a few half-timbered houses from the Renaissance.

If you'd like to visit a distillery, go to its main office during regular business hours and request a tour, or visit the tourist office for assistance. On a tour, you'll see some brandies that have aged for as long as 50 or even 100 years. You can have a free taste and then purchase a bottle or two. As far as we're concerned, **Otard** offers the most informative and insightful tours, partly because of the sheer majesty of its headquarters, in the late-medieval **Château de Cognac,** 127 bd. Denfert-Rochereau (✆ **05-45-36-88-86;** www.otard.com). The tour is half historical overview of the castle, half a technical explanation of cognac production. Parts of the château are appropriately baronial (King François I was born here), and enormous other sections hold tens of thousands of bottles of cognac. Tours last about 1 hour and cost 8.50€ for adults, 4€ for students 12 to 18, and are free for children 11 and under. From April to October, tours depart at frequent intervals daily. During November to March, tours depart only Monday to Friday. Call the tourist office or the company several days in advance for exact schedules. The château lies within a 10-minute walk from the town center, near the Hôtel de Ville (city hall).

Cognac at Hennessy.

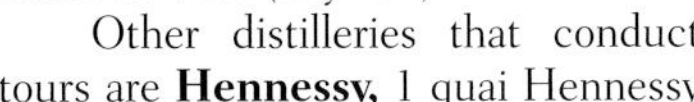

Other distilleries that conduct tours are **Hennessy,** 1 quai Hennessy (✆ **05-45-35-72-68;** www.hennessy.com; closed Jan–Feb); **Camus,** 21 rue de Cagouillet (✆ **05-45-32-70-14;** www.camus.fr; closed Oct–May); and **Martell,** place Edouard-Martell (✆ **05-45-36-33-33;** www.martell.com; closed Nov–Mar). **Rémy Martin** maintains a battered but authentic-looking wine storehouse in the countryside, at Domaine de Merpins, and a glossier, more media-hip information center and sales outlet in the heart of Cognac. Known as the **Maison Rémy Martin,** it's at 20 rue de la Société Vinicole (✆ **05-45-35-76-66;** www.visitesremymartin.com) and gives the most expensive tour of the lot. Priced at 25€, it punctuates its insights into the world of Rémy Martin with frequent dégustations of esoteric cognacs and lots of bite-sized canapés to accompany them. For connaisseurs, there are even more elaborate visits, at more elaborate prices. For all tours, call in advance for reservations.

If you're short on time, a good retail outlet is **La Cognathèque,** 8 place Jean-Monnet (✆ **05-45-82-43-31;** www.cognatheque.com), which prides itself on having the widest selection from all the region's distilleries, large and small (some 400 different cognacs), though you'll pay for the convenience of having everything under one roof.

No one ever accused the cognac industry of not knowing how to promote its products in its hometown. The **Musée des Arts de Cognac** lies in the town center, at place de la Salle Verte (✆ **05-45-36-21-10;** www.musees-cognac.fr). Within, you'll find exhibits showcasing everything associated with the cognac trade, from cultivation of grapes to bottle and barrel making, to insights into global marketing and sales. Entrance costs 4.80€ for adults, 3.50€ for students. Admission is free for anyone 17 and under. It's open as follows: July to August Tuesday to Sunday 10am to 6:30pm; May, June, and September Tuesday to Friday 11am to 6pm, and Saturday and Sunday 1 to 6pm; October to April Tuesday to Sunday 2 to 5:30pm.

Within a 15-minute walk lies the **Musée d'Art et l'Histoire de Cognac,** 48 bd. Denfert-Rochereau (✆ **05-45-32-07-25**), which has exhibits on popular arts and traditions, archaeological exhibits, and a fine art collection of paintings, sculpture, decorative arts, and furniture. Accessible with the same ticket that's valid for access to the above-noted Musée des Arts de Cognac (and vice versa), it's open as follows: July to August Wednesday to Monday 10am to 6:30pm; May, June, and September Monday, Wednesday, Thursday, and Friday 11am to 1pm and 2 to 6pm, and Saturday and Sunday from 1 to 6pm; October to April Wednesday to 2 to 5:30pm.

Cognac has two beautiful parks: the **Parc François-1er** and the **Jardin Public.** The Romanesque-Gothic **Eglise St-Léger,** rue de Monseigneur LaCroix (✆ **05-45-82-05-71**), is from the 12th century, and its bell tower is from the 15th. Admission is free; it's open daily 8am to 7pm.

Where to Stay

Domaine du Breuil ★★ This tranquil 19th-century manor house, studded with magnificent windows, is in a 7.2-hectare (18-acre) landscaped park 2 minutes from the center of Cognac. Rooms are simple but well furnished and well maintained. Cognac aficionados and those in town to do business with the factories head here for the hospitality, the well-appointed rooms, and the excellent cuisine from the southwest of France. The food is reason enough to visit, and, naturally, you'll finish your meal with a cognac in the bar to aid digestion.

104 rue Robert-Daugas, Cognac 16100. www.hotel-domaine-du-breuil.com. ✆ **05-45-35-32-06.** Fax 05-45-35-14-15. 24 units. 65€–120€ double. AE, MC, V. Free parking. Closed Dec 20–Jan 5. **Amenities:** Restaurant; bar; outdoor pool. *In room:* TV, hair dryer, minibar (in some), free Wi-Fi.

Hostellerie Les Pigeons Blancs ★ This stylish hotel is named after the white pigeons that nest in its moss-covered stone walls. The angular farmhouse with sloping tile roofs was built in the 17th century as a coaching inn. For many years, it was the home of the Tachet family, which transformed it into a hotel and restaurant in 1973. It's 1.5km (1 mile) northwest of the town center and offers elegant guest rooms outfitted in styles that range from Louis XV to Directoire. The restaurant serves modern French cuisine and is reviewed below.

110 rue Jules-Brisson, Cognac 16100. www.pigeons-blancs.com. ✆ **05-45-82-16-36.** Fax 05-45-82-29-29. 6 units. 85–105€ double. AE, MC, V. Free parking. **Amenities:** Restaurant; room service. *In room:* TV, hair dryer, free Wi-Fi.

Where to Eat

The restaurant at **Domaine du Breuil** (see "Where to Stay," above) serves worthwhile meals.

Hostellerie Les Pigeons Blancs ★★ MODERN FRENCH This restaurant, run by the Tachet family, has two elegant dining rooms with exposed ceiling beams and limestone fireplaces. Menu offerings depend on the availability of ingredients but may include warm oysters and shrimp in Chardonnay-flavored sauce, sautéed foie gras with cabbage and bacon, and filet of veal with morel sauce. The chef uses cognac vapors to steam many of his raw ingredients, including excellent line-caught sea bass with spices. Come with an appetite—there is no ordering a la carte here, though you are welcome to mix and match on the various two- and three-course fixed-price menus.

110 rue Jules-Brisson. ✆ **05-45-82-16-36.** Reservations recommended. Fixed-price menu 23€ lunch, 32€–58€ (dinner). AE, MC, V. Tues–Sun noon–2pm; Mon–Sat 7–9pm.

Where to Stay & Eat Nearby

Moulin de Cierzac ★ 🎁 This 19th-century former mill house sits beside a flowing stream at the southern periphery of a village (St-Fort-sur-le-Né) 13km (8 miles) south of Cognac. Loaded with character and charm, owner-chef Georges Renault's property is best known for its superb restaurant. Many diners do opt to spend the night, particularly after a wine-and-cognac-soaked dinner. The cuisine makes abundant use of local products, especially foie gras, vegetables, nuts, berries, lamb, and cognac. Come for dishes that include slow-cooked foie gras marinated in a mixture of cognac, sauterne, and white port. Also appealing are slow-cooked pork pâté flavored with cognac, pikeperch served with a compote of cabbage, and apple crumble.

The seven quaint, charmingly decorated guest rooms overlook a park that's traversed by a stream. They have big ceiling beams and TVs; the flowery decor evokes a British country house. The double rate is 53€ to 85€.

Rte. de Cognac, Cierzac 17520. www.moulindecierzac.com. ✆ **05-45-83-01-32.** Fax 05-45-83-03-59. Reservations recommended. Main courses 18€–35€; fixed-price menus 13€ (weekday lunch only) 30€–45€ (dinner). AE, MC, V. June–Sept Tues–Sun noon–2pm, daily 7–9pm; Oct–May Sun–Fri noon–2pm, Tues–Sat 7–9pm. Closed mid-Nov to Dec 3 and 2 weeks in Jan. From Cognac, drive 13km (8 miles) south of town, following the signs for Bordeaux and Barbezieux.

ANGOULÊME ★★

443km (275 miles) SW of Paris; 116km (72 miles) NE of Bordeaux

The old town of Angoulême hugs a hilltop between the Charente and Aguienne rivers. You can visit it on the same day you visit Cognac. The town has been a center for the French paper industry since the 17th century, a tradition that carries on today in the five remaining paper mills. These days, Angoulême (pop. 43,000) is probably best known for something that gets printed on that paper: comics. Authors, artists, and fans come from all over the world to attend the **Festival International de la Bande Dessinée,** one of the largest comic book/graphic novel gatherings on earth. Hard-bound comics, or *bandes dessinées,* not are only considered an art form in France (*"le 9eme art"*), but also are big business: They account for a big chunk of the French book market. These comics are not just for children—they cover everything from political humor to adventure stories, to personal memoirs and documentary reporting. The festival takes over the town for 3 days in January, when the latest books are presented, prizes are awarded, and contracts are signed. There are also lots of expositions and events for casual visitors. For more information, contact the festival (✆ **05-45-97-86-50;** www.bdangouleme.com) or the tourist office (see below). If you miss the festival, you can still explore this graphic world at the **Cité Internationale de la Bande Dessinée et de l'Image (CNBDI);** see "Exploring the Town," below.

Essentials

GETTING THERE There are about two TGV **trains** per hour (trip time: 55 min.) and a handful of regular trains (trip time: 1½ hr.) every day from Bordeaux; the one-way fare is 24€. There is also frequent train service from Saintes (trip time: 1 hr.) and Poitiers (trip time: 45 min.). From Paris's Montparnasse Station, some 15 TGV trains make the trip daily (trip time: 2 hr., 40 min.); the one-way fare is 65€. For train information and schedules, call ✆ **36-35**

or visit www.voyages-sncf.com. **Véolia** (✆ **05-45-95-95-99;** www.vtpc.fr) runs eight **buses** per day between Cognac and Angoulême. The trip takes 1 hour and costs 4.50€ each way. If you're **driving** from Bordeaux, take N10 northeast to Angoulême.

VISITOR INFORMATION The **Office de Tourisme** is at place des Halles (✆ **05-45-95-16-84;** www.angouleme-tourisme.com).

Exploring the Town

The hub of the town is **place de l'Hôtel-de-Ville.** The town hall was erected from 1858 to 1866 on the site of the palace of the ducs d'Angoulême, where Marguerite de Navarre, sister of François I, was born. All that remains of the palace are the 15th-century Tour de Valois and 13th-century Tour de Lusignan.

Cathédrale St-Pierre ★, 4 place St-Pierre, was built in the 11th and 12th centuries and restored in the 19th. Flanked by towers, its facade boasts 75 statues, each in a separate niche, representing the Last Judgment. This is one of France's most startling examples of Romanesque-Byzantine style. The 19th-century architect Abadie (designer of Sacré-Coeur in Paris) tore down the north tower and then rebuilt it with the original materials in the same style. In the interior, you can wander under a four-domed ceiling. It's open Monday to Saturday 9am to 7pm, Sunday 10am to 6:30pm.

As mentioned above, Angoulême is the European capital of comic book and graphic novel art. In addition to the festival, the city is now home of the **Cité Internationale de la Bande Dessinée et de l'Image,** 121 rue de Bordeaux (✆ **05-45-38-65-65;** www.cnbdi.fr), which has an exhibition space, a library and research center, and two screening rooms; it hosts seminars and lectures with famous authors, some of whom come to do residencies. It's open in July and August Tuesday to Friday 10am to 7pm, and Saturday and Sunday 2 to 7pm; and September to June Tuesday to Friday 10am to 6pm, and Saturday and Sunday 2 to 6pm. Entrance costs 6€ for adults, 4.50€ for students under 26, free for children 17 and under.

Comics on display at Cité Internationale de la Bande Dessinée et de l'Image

Finally, you can walk along the panoramic **promenade des Remparts ★**, a path that flanks the site of the long-gone fortifications that once surrounded the historic core of Angoulême. The most appealing section of the 3km (1¾-mile) walkway is the 1km (½-mile) section that connects the cathedral with Les Halles (the covered market). Views from here stretch over the hills that flank the River Charente almost 75m (246 ft.) below.

Where to Stay

Epi d'Or Hotel choices are limited in Angoulême, but these comfortable lodgings will do just fine for a short stay. Located in the center of town, this modern hotel offers clean, recently renovated rooms in cool shades of gray. Many rooms have balconies; all have new parquet floors. While those facing the busy street are soundproofed, serenity seekers should ask for a room facing the rear courtyard, which also have the advantage of being larger (if a little more expensive).

66 bd. René Chabasse, Angoulême 16000. www.hotel-epidor.fr. ✆ **05-45-95-67-64.** 33 units. 68€–73€ double. AE, MC, V. Free parking. **Amenities:** Bar. *In room:* TV, free Wi-Fi.

Where to Eat

La Cité FRENCH Set at the northern edge of Angoulême's medieval core, this small and intimate restaurant is pleasantly outfitted in tones of terra cotta and pale green. An enduring house specialty is seafood brochette, where crayfish, scallops, and mussels are spit-roasted and served with a creamy garlic sauce. Most of the menu is devoted to fish, but there are a handful of meat dishes on the menu.

28 rue St-Roch. ✆ **05-45-92-42-69.** Reservations recommended. Main courses 14€–16€; fixed-price menus 15€–29€. AE, MC, V. Tues–Sat noon–2pm and 7–10pm. Closed Aug.

La Ruelle ★★ FRENCH This first-class restaurant, in the oldest part of town, is Angoulême's best. Guillaume and Séverine Veyssière are the only shining lights in a dim culinary scene. Count on classic French recipes with a modern twist. The menu changes frequently, but some examples of its delights are filet of Limousin beef served with a pine needle bouillon and chocolate "surprise" served with orange and nougatine, and flambéed in Grand Marnier. The space was originally part of a pair of houses separated by a narrow alleyway *(une ruelle)*. Vestiges of the 17th-century structure are visible in the dining room's stonemasonry and painted ceiling beams.

6 rue Trois-Notre-Dame. ✆ **05-45-95-15-19.** www.restaurant-laruelle.com. Reservations recommended. Main courses 29€–38€; fixed-price menu 38€–60€. DC, MC, V. Tues–Sat noon–2pm and 7:30–10pm. Closed 1st week of Jan and 2 weeks at the end of July and beginning of Aug.

Where to Stay & Eat Nearby

Hostellerie du Maine Brun ★★ Originally a flour mill, this property is the premier place to stay and dine in this area. It's surrounded by 32 hectares (79 acres) of lowlands (including a garden, a creek, and open fields), about half of which are devoted to the production of cognac. These are the most luxurious accommodations around, larger than the lodgings at many competitors; each has a terrace. Rooms are individually decorated with 18th- and 19th-century French furniture. The restaurant serves splendid fare. Specialties include terrine of foie gras with cognac, and Porée charentaise, a combination of fish in a creamy Pineau wine sauce. Fixed-price menus range from 30€ to 40€.

RN 141, La Vigerie, Asnières-sur-Nouère 16290. www.hotel-maine-brun.com. ✆ **05-45-90-83-00.** Fax 05-45-96-91-14. 18 units. 120€–130€ double; 170€ suite. AE, DC, MC, V. Hotel and restaurant closed mid-Oct to mid-Apr. Take RN 141 7km (4¼ miles) west of Angoulême and turn right at Vigerie. **Amenities:** Restaurant; bar; outdoor pool; room service; free Wi-Fi. *In room:* TV, hair dryer, minibar.

BORDEAUX ★★★

578km (358 miles) SW of Paris; 549km (340 miles) W of Lyon

Elegant Bordeaux, capital of Aquitaine, is the hub for the legendary wine-growing region that includes *appelations* like St-Emilion and Médoc. You can visit many of the most famous vineyards and sample their wares. Wines aside, the city of Bordeaux is a treasure in itself. Its wide quays, which curve graciously around the Garonne River, have been given a new, car-free life and are now filled with public gardens, fountains, and playgrounds for both children and adults. Splendid plazas, like the Esplanade des Quinconces and Place de la Bourse, give way to narrow cobbled streets, 14th-century churches, and 18th- and 19th-century mansions, and an exquisite urban landscape that has been hailed as one of the aesthetic triumphs of western France.

Things to Do Let the neoclassical masks of Bacchus and Mercury on **place de la Bourse** lead you to **Quartier Saint Pierre**'s stately old merchants' houses. Or cross tree-lined **esplanade des Quinconces,** with its statues of Montaigne and Montesquieu, to antique shops and markets in the **Chartrons** district. Back in the historic center, the **Musée des Beaux Arts** displays the works of Titian, Delacroix, and Veronese. Standing 112m (374 ft.) tall, **Basilique St-Martin** provides sweeping panoramas over the city and the Garonne River, whose silvery waters link Bordeaux with the Atlantic.

Nightlife & Entertainment Sensible by day, Bordeaux rocks by night. Bars and bistros line the Garonne's **Quays,** leading well-dressed crews to the chic clubs on **Quai de Paludate,** while students guzzle cheap wine in grungy bars around **Place de la Victoire.** For something more sophisticated, the **Grand Théâtre** is a sumptuous neoclassical venue used for top-notch opera, dance, and theater. In the trendy **Bastide** district, just across the pont de Pierre (stone bridge), lights from Bordeaux's rows of mansions twinkle seductively.

Restaurants & Dining Sandwiched between the Atlantic Ocean and fertile land, Bordeaux gets the best of both worlds. Tantalize your taste buds with melt-in-your-mouth Arcachon oysters, tender Pauillac lamb, Aquitaine beef, Périgord truffles, prunes from Agen, and St-Emilion macaroons. The elegant **quays** are freckled with contemporary eateries, or take your pick along **rue St-Rémi** and **place du Parlement,** where French, Chinese, and Italian restaurants fight for space. For a Michelin-starred treat, **Le Chapon Fin** has been serving gourmet French cuisine since 1825.

Relaxation Nothing loosens muscles like Bacchus's old finest, and around Bordeaux, you're spoiled for choice. Escape the city to the verdant vineyards encircling **St-Emilion,** where gently trestled vines have grown since the 12th century and the village's postcard-perfect cobbles conceal an eerie troglodyte

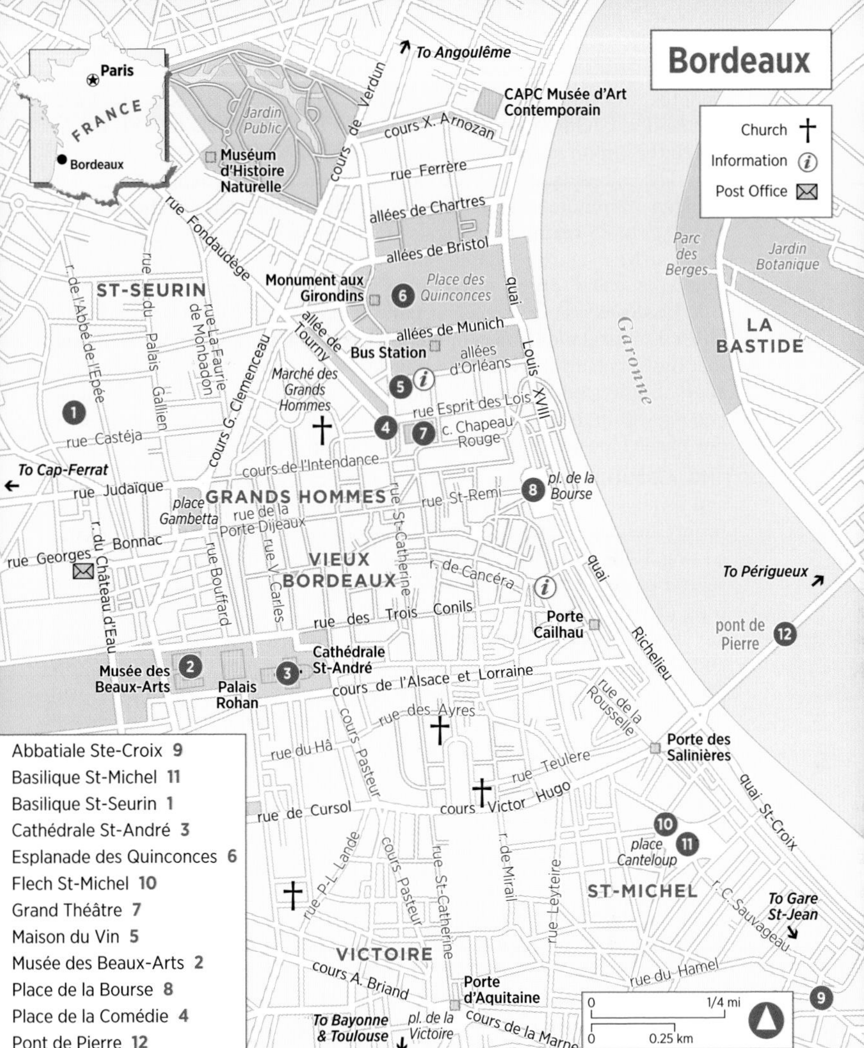

church. When the rolling hills beckon again, the great vineyards of **Médoc** (think châteaux Margaux, Lafite Rothschild, Latour, and Mouton Rothschild) produce some of the world's finest wines.

Essentials

GETTING THERE The local **airport,** Bordeaux–Mérignac (✆ **05-56-34-50-50** for flight information; www.bordeaux.aeroport.fr), is served by flights from European and North African cities like London, Madrid, Stockholm, and Casablanca, as well as many French destinations. It's 15km (9¼ miles) west of Bordeaux in Mérignac. Paris is an hour's flight away. A **shuttle bus** (Jet'Bus) connects the airport with the train station, departing every 45 minutes (trip time: 45 min.) and costing 7€ one-way for adults, 6€ for 25 and under. Children under 5 ride free. A taxi (✆**05-56-96-00-34**) between the airport and the train station costs about 45€.

The railway station, Gare St-Jean, is on the west bank of the river, within a 30-minute walk (or 5-min. taxi ride) of the center of the old town. Some 15 to 25 **trains** from Paris's Gare Montparnasse (trip time: 3 hr. by TGV) arrive each day. The one-way fare is 76€. For train information and schedules, call ✆**36-35** or visit www.voyages-sncf.com.

Bordeaux is easy to reach by **car.** From Paris, follow A10 south through Orléans, Tours, and Poitiers into Bordeaux (trip time: about 5 hr.). Be aware that the streets of Bordeaux are fraught with hazards: narrow 18th-century alleys, traffic jams, and simply too many cars and people. Easily available parking within the city's historic core is scarce. Whenever possible, head for one of the blue-and-white P signs that indicate public garages.

GETTING AROUND Three lines of a new modern tram system—labeled A, B, and C—have made traveling around Bordeaux easier than at any time in its history. Service is daily from 5am to 1am, with individual tickets (Tickarte) costing 1.40€, transfers included during a 1-hour period. There are also several passes: 1 day at Tickarte costs 4.10€, 5.20€ for 5 trips, 11€ for 10 trips, or 11€ for 1 week.

Once aboard, you must validate your Tickarte, which is sold in *tabacs* and other outlets. The combined bus-and-tram system (✆**05-56-57-88-88;** www.infotbc.com) serves both inner Bordeaux and its suburbs, with maps available at the train station. The most central information office is at 9 place Gambetta, open Monday to Friday 7am to 7pm and Saturday 9am to 6pm.

VISITOR INFORMATION The **Office de Tourisme** is at 12 cours du 30-Juillet (✆**05-56-00-66-00;** www.bordeaux-tourisme.com), with a branch office in the Gare St-Jean (✆**05-56-91-64-70**).

Exploring Bordeaux

Wine exporters welcome guests to sample wines and learn about the industry. In "The Wine Country," later in this chapter, we suggest a tour of the region. Plan your trip with maps, guides, and advice about local wines, available free from the **Maison du Vin (House of Wine),** 1 cours du 30-Juillet (✆**05-56-00-22-88;** www.vins-bordeaux.fr), opposite the tourist office (which also has a snazzy wine bar for some preliminary tasting). To make the rounds of the vineyards, consider alternative forms of transport: bus, bicycle, or even walking.

STROLLS THROUGH TOWN The prettiest and most historic neighborhood in Old Bordeaux is the "Golden Triangle," defined by cours Clemenceau, cours de l'Intendance, and les allées de Tourny. Since the new tram came to town, many of the streets are blissfully free of cars. You can traipse around the old town on your own, because it's fairly compact, or take advantage of the 2-hour **walking tour** the tourist office (see above) arranges daily at 10am Monday, Tuesday, Thursday, Friday, and Sunday. Conducted in both French and English, tours take in all the most important sites and begin at the tourist office. Cost is 8.50€ for adults, 7.50€ for students, 6€ for children 13 to 17, and free for children 12 and under. Reserve in advance and call to confirm. There are also a variety of other tours on offer through the tourist

Detail in Bordeaux's "Golden Triangle."

office—from a 2-hour bus tour (Sat and Wed at 10am) to an inline-skating excursion on car-free Sundays (the 1st Sun of each month at 2:30pm).

If you go it alone, your tour of Old Bordeaux can begin in the heart of this old city at **place de la Comédie,** which was once the site of a Roman temple. On this square, one of France's great theaters, **Grand Théâtre ★★**, place de la Comédie (✆ **05-56-00-85-95;** www.opera-bordeaux.com), the city's cultural symbol, was built between 1773 and 1780 as testimony to the burgeoning prosperity of Bordeaux's emerging bourgeoisie. This is one of the last remaining 18th-century theaters in the world, rivaling those of Naples, Stockholm, and Milan. A colonnade of 12 columns graces its facade. Surmounted on these are statues of goddesses and the Muses. If you'd like to visit the richly decorated interior, there are guided tours on Wednesdays and Saturdays at 2, 3:30, and 5pm. They cost 3€, and you can reserve ahead in person, by phone, or via Internet (see above).

From here, you can walk north to **esplanade des Quinconces.** It was laid out between 1818 and 1828, and covers nearly 12 hectares (30 acres). From here, you can stroll down the river and enjoy the gardens and fountains of the new promenade along the **quays** to the splendid **place de la Bourse ★**, which opens directly onto the Garonne. It was laid out between 1728 and 1755; the fountain of the Three Graces is at its center. Flanking the square are the Custom House and the Stock Exchange. On warm days, Bordelais (particularly the youngest ones) come here to splash through the huge 1-inch deep mirror of water that lies between the square and the river.

CHURCHES The largest and most ostentatious church in Bordeaux is the **Cathédrale St-André ★★**, place Pey-Berland (✆ **05-56-52-68-10**), near the southern perimeter of the old town. The sculptures on the 13th-century Porte Royale (Royal Door) are admirable; see also the 14th-century sculptures on the North Door. Separate from the rest of the church is the 47m (154-ft.) **Tour Pey-Berland** (✆ **05-56-81-26-25**), a belfry begun in the 15th century. Foundations date from 900 years ago. The church is open July to September daily 10 to 12:30am and 2:30 to 6pm. Off season, hours are Tuesday to Sunday 10am to noon and daily 2 to 6pm. The tower is open daily June to September 10am to 1:15pm and 2 to 6pm, October to May Tuesday to Sunday 10am to 12:30pm and 2 to 5:30pm. Tower admission is 5€ for adults and 3.50€ for those 25 and under. Free organ recitals are held in July and August on Tuesdays at 6:30pm.

Foremost among the "secondary" churches is the **Basilique St-Michel ★**, place St-Michel/Canteloup (✆ **05-56-94-30-50**). The church itself, constructed in stages from the 14th to the 16th centuries, is incredibly charming. More impressive is its bell tower, the **Fleche St-Michel ★**, across the street. This tower, erected in 1472, is the second-tallest stone tower in France (after the cathedral at Strasbourg), rising 112m (367 ft.). The basilica's hours vary, but it is usually open 10am to 6pm. The tower is open for visits June to September only, Tuesday to Friday 10am to 1pm and 2 to 7pm, and Saturday and Sunday 2 to 7pm, for 3.50€. You climb 228 steps to the top, where you have sweeping views over the port and the Garonne. During July and August, every Friday from 5 to 7pm, the bells in the tower are rung as part of a free carillon concert that can be heard throughout the neighborhood.

Another historic church is **Basilique St-Seurin,** place des Martyrs de la Résistance (✆**05-56-93-89-28**). Its most ancient sections, such as its crypt, date from the 5th century. See the porch left over from an earlier church; it has some capitals from the Romanesque era. In summer, hours are Tuesday to Sunday 8:30 to 6:30pm; off-season hours are Tuesday to Sunday 8:30am to 7:30pm. On Sunday, the basilica may shut down at 1pm.

Abbatiale Ste-Croix, place Pierre-Renaudel (✆**05-56-94-30-50**), gained attention in musical circles when its organ, a marvel built by a monk, Dom Bedos, was restored to its original working order in 1996. The church, a severe Romanesque structure from the 11th and 12th centuries, is revered for its stately dignity. In July and August, free organ concerts are presented Wednesday at 6:30pm; otherwise, the church is generally open daily 10am to 6pm.

MUSEUMS Admission to the permanent collections of all of Bordeaux's municipal museums (including the three below) is free. For an overview of the history and ethnography of the region, visit the **Musée d'Aquitaine ★**, 20 cours Pasteur (✆**05-56-01-51-00;** www.bordeaux.fr), which has a good collection of Gallo-Roman sculptures and artifacts, as well as displays and model ships detailing the maritime history of Bordeaux. The museum is open Tuesday to Sunday 11am to 6pm.

The **Musée des Beaux-Arts ★★**, 20 cours d'Albret, Jardin du Palais-Rohan (✆**05-56-10-20-56;** www.bordeaux.fr), has an outstanding collection from the 16th to the 20th centuries. Works by Perugina, Titian, Rubens, Veronese, Delacroix, and Marquet are on display. The museum is open Wednesday to Monday 11am to 6pm.

Housed in a stunning mansion built in 1779, the **Musée des Arts Décoratifs ★**, 39 rue Bouffard, (✆**05-56-10-14-00;** www.bordeaux.fr), has a significant collection of sculptures, paintings, furniture, ceramics, and other art objects dating primarily from the 18th and 19th centuries. Of particular interest are several "period rooms" set up to approximate the world of the rich aristocracy in the 18th century. This museum is open Wednesday to Monday 2 to 6pm.

BOAT RIDES The **pont de Pierre,** with 17 arches, stretches 478m (1,568 ft.) across the Garonne and is one of the most beautiful bridges in France. Built on orders of Napoleon I, the bridge proved so difficult to build that it wasn't finished until 1822, after he died. The bridge can be crossed on foot for a view of the quays and the port. For an even better view, we suggest a **tour of the port,** which lasts about 90 minutes and goes up the river and all around the harbor. The tours run from April to October and usually depart

Buying Wine in Bordeaux

If you've come to Bordeaux to buy wine, try to choose one that carries personal significance because you've visited the vineyard, or consult the experts at the wine shops. We recommend La Vinothèque, 8 cours du 30-Juillet (© 05-56-52-32-05; www.la-vinotheque.com), and Badie, 62 allées de Tourny (© 05-56-52-23-72). Some of the best red bordeaux wines come from small houses such as Château Lesparre, Beychac-et-Caillau, 39km (24 miles) north of Bordeaux (© 05-57-24-51-23); Château Bel Air, Naujan-et-Postiac, 40km (25 miles) east of Bordeaux (© 05-57-84-55-08); and Château les Bouzigues, Saintes Gemmes, 76km (47 miles) south of Bordeaux (© 05-56-61-80-77).

from the Quai des Chartrons, in the center of town. The cost is 15€ for adults and free for children 11 and under. For exact times and a description of other cruises, call the tourist office (see "Essentials," above) or **Bateaux "Ville de Bordeaux,"** Quai des Chartrons (**© 05-56-52-88-88;** www.bateaubordeaux.com). Ask about the occasional floating concerts at night.

Shopping

If you want antiques, head to **rue Bouffard, rue des Remparts,** and **rue Notre-Dame,** where you'll find an indoor market known as **Village Notre-Dame** (**© 05-56-52-66-13;** www.antiquitesbordeaux.com), housing about 30 antiques stands. Another destination is the neighborhood around **Eglise St-Michel,** particularly the passage St-Michel, a narrow alleyway a few steps from the church.

For fashion, go to the couture quarter around **place des Grands Hommes,** as well as **cours Georges-Clemenceau,** with its many trendy and classic emporiums. For the greatest concentration of shops, head to the **rue Ste-Catherine,** the longest pedestrian street in France. It has at least 100 boutiques, from the most luxurious to the cheapest. The **Allées de Tourny** are also rife with goodies, including **Cadiot-Badie,** 26 allées de Tourney (**© 05-56-44-24-22;** www.cadiot-badie.com), a must for serious chocoholics. Established in 1826, their chocolates are considered the best in Bordeaux.

Where to Stay

EXPENSIVE

The Regent Grand ★★★ Located opposite the Opéra National de Bordeaux, the Regent Grand has been restored to its former glory, bringing five-star luxury to the historic center. Rooms still evoke the 19th century, with their elegant damasks and reproduction period furniture. Black lacquer wrought-iron lamps and pleated silk shades add more elegance. Rooms have all the modern amenities, including flatscreen TVs and Bose radio systems. Enjoy market-fresh seafood in the supremely elegant dining room of Le Pressoir d'Argent, the hotel's acclaimed restaurant.

2–5 place de la Comédie, Bordeaux 33000. www.theregentbordeaux.com. **© 05-57-30-44-44.** 310€–450€ double; 485€–2,000 suite. AE, DC, MC, V. **Amenities:** Restaurant; bar; room service; spa. *In room:* A/C, TV, hair dryer, minibar, free Wi-Fi.

Seeko'O Hotel ★★ This daringly modern hotel makes a statement on the 18th-century quays of the Garonne. Its jagged glistening white exterior evokes a block of ice. It's got enough electronic gadgetry to launch itself into space—well, almost. The location of this surreal hotel is near the Quai des Chartrons, a once-seedy neighborhood that is now about as happening as it gets in Bordeaux. Bedrooms have been likened to a space-age bachelor pad, with some circular beds and color schemes of black and white with red splashes like a woman would "slash on" her lipstick. Most of the bedrooms are, in essence, junior suites, and bathtubs are designed for two.

54 quai de Bacalan, Bordeaux 33300. www.seekoo-hotel.com. ✆ **05-56-39-07-07.** 45 units. 199€–239€ junior suite; 390€ panoramic suite. AE, MC, V. Parking 10€. **Amenities:** Bar; room service; sauna, Turkish baths. *In room:* A/C, TV, hair dryer, minibar, free Wi-Fi.

MODERATE

Best Western Bordeaux Le Bayonne Etche-Ona ★ There's a touch of the Basque country at this hotel, where a 1930s aura has been retained and many features added, most notably soundproofing and comfortable furnishings, along with midsize bathrooms. Rooms are medium to generous in size. Many attractions, including restaurants, the cathedral, place de la Bourse, the quays, and the Grand Théâtre, are nearby. Breakfast is the only meal served.

15 cours de l'Intendance (entrances at 4 rue Martignac and 11 rue Mautrec), Bordeaux 33000. www.bordeaux-hotel.com. ✆ **05-56-48-00-88.** 61 units. 163€–215€ double; 275€–365€ suite. AE, DC, MC, V. **Amenities:** Bar; room service. *In room:* A/C, TV, hair dryer, minibar, free Wi-Fi.

Hôtel Tour Intendance ★★ This former mansion has been transformed into a cozy hotel that successfully blends modern comfort with the building's 18th-century charm. Rooms are light filled and airy, with lots of exposed stone walls and blonde wood. Antique wood beams support the ceiling in the breakfast room; terra-cotta tiles cover the floor. Located on a quiet side street off the Cours de l'Intendance, the hotel provides easy access to the historic center.

14–16 rue de la Vielle Tour, Bordeaux 33000. www.hotel-tour-indendance.com. ✆ **05-56-44-56-56.** Fax 05-56-44-54-54. 34 units. 108€–158€ double. AE, DC, MC, V. Parking 12€ overnight; during the day hourly rate 2.50€. *In room:* A/C, TV, hair dryer, free Wi-Fi.

Mercure Château Chartrons ★ Located in the up-and-coming Chartrons neighborhood about a 15-minute walk from place des Quinconces, this modern chain hotel has retained most of its Victorian facade. The medium-size rooms are decorated in warm, winey colors with contemporary furniture. The bar has an impressive array of local vintages available by the glass. The restaurant serves bistro-style fare.

81 cours St-Louis, Bordeaux 33300. www.mercure.com. ✆ **05-56-43-15-00.** Fax 05-56-69-15-21. 148 units. 90€–180€ double; 300€ suite. AE, DC, MC, V. Parking 10€. **Amenities:** Restaurant; bar; room service. *In room:* A/C, TV, hair dryer, minibar, free Wi-Fi.

INEXPENSIVE

Hôtel Continental ★ To get a certain class, charm, and elegance in Bordeaux at this price is a rarity. In the center of the "Golden Triangle," on a semipedestrian mall dotted with boutiques, this 18th-century town house wins new fans every year. You'll get a warm welcome and a fine dose of Bordelaise hospitality. Rooms, although a bit small (especially the singles), are warmly decorated and furnished, each with a compact bathroom; a few have tiny balconies. Breakfast is included in the price of the room.

10 rue Montesquieu, Bordeaux 33000. www.hotel-le-continental.com. ✆ **05-56-52-66-00.** Fax 05-56-52-77-97. 51 units. 96€–120€ double; 190€–209€ suite. AE, DC, MC, V. Parking 1.50€–2.50€. *In room:* A/C (in some), TV, hair dryer (in some), free Wi-Fi.

Hôtel de France ★ A mere 2-minute walk to the Grand Théâtre, this family-run hotel is about as central as it gets—and a whole lot cheaper than 90 percent of the lodging in the neighborhood. The friendly owners keep their rooms clean and simple, with white walls and modern bedsteads; the quiet side street ensures peace and tranquillity at night.

7 rue Franklin, Bordeaux 33000. www.hotel-france-bordeaux.fr. ✆ **05-56-48-24-11.** 20 units. 68€ double. AE, MC, V. *In room:* TV, free Wi-Fi.

Where to Eat

EXPENSIVE

La Tupina ★★ SOUTHWESTERN FRENCH One of Bordeaux's most talented chefs runs this cozy spot with a summer terrace near quai de la Monnaie. It's been called "a tribute to country kitchens and the grandmothers who cooked in them." Jean-Pierre Xiradakis's specialty is duck, so your meal may include *tournedos de canard,* and the kitchen often uses duck giblets, skin, and livers in salads. Other specialties are roasted shoulder of lamb *en confit* with garlic and white beans, and lamprey eel à la Bordelaise.

6 rue Porte de la Monnaie. ✆ **05-56-91-56-37.** www.latupina.com. Reservations recommended. Main courses 14€–55€; fixed-price lunch 18€–35€, dinner 60€. AE, DC, MC, V. Daily noon–2pm and 7–11pm.

Le Chapon-Fin ★★★ MODERN FRENCH Dating from 1825, this prestigious restaurant features an unusual decor that critics have referred to as "organic rococo." Crafted from distressed rocks into an Art Nouveau–style grotto, it soars almost 7.5m (25 ft.) to a skylight that floods the interior with light. Owner Nicolas Frion features artful renditions of classics like fresh duck foie gras with chutney and tamarind, Pauillac lamb grilled with peppers and mushrooms, and seared scallops served with cardamom-scented pineapple pulp. The restaurant is in one of the city's upscale neighborhoods, between place Gambetta and the Marché aux Grands Hommes.

5 rue Montesquieu. ✆ **05-56-79-10-10.** www.chapon-fin.com. Reservations required. Main courses 34€–44€; fixed-price menus 38€–90€. AE, DC, MC, V. Tues–Sat noon–1:30pm and 7:30–9:30pm.

Le Pavillon des Boulevards FRENCH Small, intimate, and charming, this award-winning restaurant provides sophisticated food for discerning customers. Menu items include Aquitaine caviar from local sturgeon, served with chestnut-flavored cream sauce and blue Breton lobster served with potato purée made with vanilla and sauternes wine. The cuisine is attuned to the changing seasons.

120 rue Croix-de-Seguey. ✆ **05-56-81-51-02.** www.lepavillondesboulevards.com. Reservations recommended. Main courses 38€–45€; fixed-price lunch 40€, dinner 80€. AE, MC, V. Tues–Fri noon–1:30pm; Mon–Sat 8–9:30pm. Closed 1st week in Jan and 3 weeks in Aug.

MODERATE

Fernand ★★ FRENCH You'll get a good dose of traditional bistro atmosphere at this seriously southwestern restaurant, located on the waterfront next to the place de la Bourse. Depending on the season, you'll find an excellent selection of the region's greatest hits: Pauillac lamb, lamprey, game, and a homemade foie gras. The chef specializes in fresh fish, oysters, and other shellfish straight from the day's market. Steaks come from the Blonde d'Aquitaine, a local race of prize-winning beef.

7 quai de la Douane. ✆ **05-56-81-23-40.** www.fernand-bordeaux.com. Reservations recommended. Main courses 20€–34€; fixed-price menus 16€–21€ lunch, 34€–48€ dinner. AE, MC, V. Mon–Sat noon–2:30pm and 7–11pm; Sun noon–3:30pm.

Le Mably ★ FRENCH In the heart of 18th-century Bordeaux, surrounded by art galleries and shops, this restaurant attracts gastronomes, hipsters, politicians, journalists, and locals who enjoy the elegant atmosphere of a 19th-century *brasserie de luxe*. The duck-intensive menu lists salad of duck necks stuffed with pistachios, confit of duckling, *magret* of duckling, and, of course, duck liver. Recommended nonduck items are veal kidneys with fresh coriander, blanquettes of veal, boeuf bourguignon, and several kinds of fresh fish. Pay special attention to the comprehensive wine list, rich in esoteric burgundies. There's additional seating on an outdoor terrace during warmer weather.

12 rue Mably. ✆ **05-56-44-30-10.** Reservations recommended. Main courses 15€–28€; fixed-price menu 23€–33€. AE, MC, V. Tues–Sat noon–2:30pm and 7:30–11pm. Closed 3 weeks in Aug.

Le Vieux Bordeaux ★ MODERN FRENCH Nearly a neighborhood institution, this restaurant ranks among the best in a highly competitive market. Specialties include soft-boiled eggs with Aquitaine caviar, grilled sea bass with sweet peppers and smoked ham, and pigeon with preserved lemons.

27 rue Buhan. ✆ **05-56-52-94-36.** www.le-vieux-bordeaux.com. Reservations recommended. Main courses 16€–40€; fixed-price lunch 20€, dinner 30€–52€. AE, DC, MC, V. Tues–Sat noon–2pm and 8–10pm. Closed last 2 weeks in Feb and 3 weeks in Aug.

INEXPENSIVE

Le Quai Zaco FRENCH/SPANISH Its solid stone walls were originally built 200 years ago as a warehouse, and just before it became a restaurant, it functioned as a sales outlet for sporting goods. Today it's a restaurant with a decor that accents the antique masonry with jazzy artwork, molded plastic chairs, and industrial-looking tables. The cuisine is derived from southwestern France and northern Spain, and it might include a platter of Pata Negra smoked ham, duck magret glazed with honey and orange caramel, or scallops in sea urchin sauce. Desserts are plentiful and imaginative.

80 quai des Chartrons. ✆ **05-57-87-67-72.** www.quaizaco.com. Reservations recommended. Main courses 16€–22€; fixed-price lunch 12€–15€, dinner 26€–36€. AE, MC, V. Mon–Fri noon–1:30pm; Mon–Sat 7:45–11pm.

L'O de l'Hâ ★ FRENCH/INTERNATIONAL This name is a play on both the French for "the great beyond" and the name of the cobbled street outside, which commemorates a long-gone medieval prison. Antique masonry, roughly textured plaster, and polished concrete decorate both fashionable dining rooms. Menu items are innovative and intriguing. Examples include butternut squash risotto with foie gras, and veal filet with parsnip purée and heritage vegetables. Friday and Saturday, a DJ spins disco from 8 until around 11pm.

5 rue du Hâ. ✆ **05-56-81-42-21.** www.odelha.fr. Main courses 18€–27€; fixed-price menus 22€–27€. MC, V. Tues–Fri noon–2pm; Tues–Thurs 8–10pm; Fri–Sat 8–11pm. Tram: A to Musée d'Aquitaine.

Bordeaux After Dark

Pick up a copy of *Clubs et Concerts* at the Office de Tourisme or *Bordeaux Plus* at a newsstand; both detail the goings-on in and around town.

Animated street life rules the inner core of Bordeaux by night. Head to **place de la Victoire, place St-Pierre, place du Parlement, place Camille Jullian,** and **place Gambetta;** the latter swarms with students. Night owls in Bordeaux gravitate toward quai du Paludate, where restaurants, bars, and discos remain open until the wee hours.

The hottest drinking spot in Bordeaux is **Le Calle Ocho,** rue des Piliers de Tutelle (✆ **05-56-48-08-68**), a red-and-black enclave of Cuban music, photographs, and posters, all of it richly lubricated with your choice of mojitos and some of the best-looking and most uninhibited people in town. It's open nightly from 6pm till dawn.

If you are feeling trendy and glamorous, try **La Casa Latina,** 59 quai Chartrons (✆ **05-57-87-15-80**), where merengue, salsa, and bachata might make you think that you've landed in the Dominican Republic or Brazil. For a more laid-back night on the town, **Café Populaire** (✆ **05-56-94-39-06**), or Café Pop, as it's known to locals, is a fun place to have a drink and mix with the natives. Filled with relics from the 1950s, it has music to keep you busy into the wee hours.

The leading gay bar, **BHV (Bar de l'Hôtel de Ville),** 4 rue de l'Hôtel de Ville (✆ **05-56-44-05-08**), is in the heart of town, across from the town hall, and is open Tuesday to Sunday 6pm to 2am. Drag shows take place from October to June on Sunday at 10:30pm.

A good choice for dancing is **La Plage,** 40 quai de Paludate (✆ **05-56-49-02-46**), with its 1970s decor and just as classic 25- to 45-year-old crowd.

THE WINE COUNTRY

The major Bordeaux wine districts are Graves, Médoc, Sauternes, Entre-deux-Mers, Libourne, Blaye, and Bourg. North of the city of Bordeaux, the Garonne River joins the Dordogne to form the Gironde, a broad estuary. Some 117,000 hectares (298,990 acres) of vines produce over 150 million gallons of wine a year, some of which are among the greatest reds in the world. (The white wines are less well known.)

Some of the famous vineyards welcome visitors, providing you don't arrive at the busy harvest time (Sept–Oct). However, most vineyards don't have a permanent staff to accommodate sightseers. Don't just show up—call first or check with local tourist offices about appropriate times to visit. A typical tour includes information about the winemaking process and a tour of the cellars. Most châteaux have historical artifacts on display. Tours end with a tasting, in which visitors 18 and older may participate.

Before heading out one of the many Wine Roads, or Routes des Vins, make sure you get a detailed map from the Bordeaux tourist office (see "Essentials" under the "Bordeaux" section, earlier in this chapter), because trails aren't always well marked.

Libourne

This is a sizable market town with a high-speed railway connection. At the junction of the Dordogne and Isle rivers, Libourne is roughly the center of the St-Emilion, Pomerol, and Fronsac wine districts. The center of town is in the form of a *bastide,* which was cutting-edge urban planning in the middle ages. This gridlike setup was perfect for both commerce and defense, and centered on a large town square lined with arcades. In Libourne, this square still contains some houses from the 16th century, including the lovely **Hôtel-de-Ville** (Town Hall). There is an open-air market on the square every Tuesday, Friday, and Saturday morning, one of the nicest in the region. You can also explore the remains of 13th-century ramparts. In the town center is the **Office de Tourisme,** 45 allée Robert Boulin (✆**05-57-51-15-04**), where you can get details on visiting the vineyards.

WHERE TO EAT

Chez Servais ★★ FRENCH The setting for our favorite restaurant in Libourne is an antique (probably 19th-c.) house whose sculpted facade occupies a prominent position in the town center. In the dining rooms—one small and intimate, the other more convivial—a hardworking, professional staff serves items from a menu that changes at least every 6 weeks. Our favorite dishes include sautéed foie gras with white grapes, scallops with salsify chips, and *magret* of duck with red seasonal berries.

14 place Decazes. ✆ **05-57-51-83-97.** Reservations recommended. Fixed-price menu 19€ lunch, 27€–49€ dinner. AE, MC, V. Tues–Sun 12:30–2pm; Tues–Sat 7:45–9:30pm. Closed 1 week in May and last 2 weeks in Aug.

Médoc ★

The Médoc, an undulating plain covered with vineyards, is one of the most-visited wine regions in southwestern France. Bordeaux and the Pointe de Grave mark its borders. Throughout the region are many châteaux producing grapes; only a handful of these, however, are of true star quality. The most-visited château is that of Mouton-Rothschild, said to be second only to Lourdes among attractions in southwestern France. Be advised that you cannot buy wine directly at most of the chateaux below.

EXPLORING THE AREA

Château Lafite-Rothschild This site is second in number of visitors only to the nearby Château Mouton-Rothschild. Count on spending at least an hour here. The *vinothèque* contains many vintage bottles, several dating from 1797. The Rothschilds purchased the château in 1868.

Rte. des Château, Pauillac. ✆ **05-56-59-26-83.** www.lafite.com. Tours by appointment only; minimum 2-week notice required. Free admission. Tours Mon–Fri 2 and 3:30pm. Closed Aug–Oct.

Château Margaux Known as the Versailles of the Médoc, this Empire-style château was built in the 19th century near the village of Margaux. The estate covers more than 263 hectares (650 acres), of which 80 hectares (198 acres) produce Château Margaux and Pavillon Rouge du Château Margaux; almost

12 hectares (30 acres) are devoted to producing Pavillon Blanc du Château Margaux. To see the vat rooms and wine cellars, make an appointment by e-mail, letter, or phone.

On D2, south of Pauillac, Margaux 33460. ✆ **05-57-88-83-83.** www.chateau-margaux.com. Vat rooms and wine cellars by appointment only, Mon–Fri. Closed Aug–Oct.

Château Mouton-Rothschild ★ Thousands of tourists usually visit this château, 1km (½ mile) north of Pauillac, one of many former homes of the baron Philippe de Rothschild and his American-born wife, Pauline. Today their daughter, Philippine de Rothschild, carries on their work. At press time, however, the château was undergoing extensive renovations, and all tours were suspended until at least 2012. Call or visit the website for more information regarding the reopening and future tour reservations.

Le Pouyalet, Pauillac 33250. ✆ **05-56-73-20-20.** www.bpdr.com. Tours by appointment only.

Société Duboscq Duboscq, a wine packager and wholesaler established in 1952, occupies the stately premises of the late-19th-century Château Haut-Marbuzet. Follow your visit to the cellars with a complimentary *dégustation des vins* (wine tasting). The château is 5 minutes north of Pauillac by car.

Château Haut-Marbuzet, St-Estephe 33180. ✆ **05-56-59-30-54.** Free admission. Mon–Sat 9am–noon and 2–5pm by appointment only. Tours in English on request.

WHERE TO STAY & EAT

Cordeillan-Bages ★★ In a region obsessed with fine wine and fine food, this emerges as the most consistently celebrated restaurant and hotel. The setting is a 18th-century mansion surrounded by vineyards. While most come for the restaurant, many also spend the night after indulging in wine with dinner. A la carte main courses go for 46€ to 70€; there's a 60€ fixed-price menu at lunch. Menu items may include a velouté of cockles and razor clams with seaweed and salmon roe, cod with French caviar and white beans, or rabbit with caramelized apples and wild mushrooms. For dessert, indulge in a cooked pear filed with liquid chocolate, or a sinful combination of caramel, peanuts, licorice, and yogurt sherbet. The spacious guest rooms are decorated with formal curtains, upholstered walls, a scattering of antiques, and an airy minimalism. About half are contemporary, with monochromatic color schemes; the rest are in traditional country house style.

Rte. D2, Pauillac 33250. www.cordeillanbages.com. ✆ **05-56-59-24-24.** Fax 05-56-59-01-89. 28 units. 199€–292€ double; 392€ junior suite; 517€ 2-bedroom apt for 4. AE, DC, MC, V. Closed Dec 15–Feb 14. **Amenities:** Restaurant; bar; exercise room; outdoor pool; room service; sauna. *In room:* TV, hair dryer, free Wi-Fi.

St-Emilion ★★

Surrounded by vineyards, St-Emilion is on a limestone plateau overlooking the valley of the Dordogne; a maze of wine cellars has been dug beneath the town. The wine made in this district has been called "Wine of Honor," and British sovereigns nicknamed it "King of Wines." The town, constructed mostly of golden stone and dating from the Middle Ages, is also known for its *macarons,* a light-as-air cookie made with almonds and egg whites.

St-Emilion maintains the ancient tradition of La Jurade, a society dedicated to maintaining the highest standard for the local wine and promoting and honoring it around the world. During the Jurade wine festival in September, members of this society wear silk hats and scarlet robes edged with ermine. ***Note:*** The town is jammed during the Jurade, and hotel prices tend to rise during the festival.

St-Emilion.

ESSENTIALS

GETTING THERE St-Emilion lies 35km (22 miles) northeast of Bordeaux, between Libourne, 8km (5 miles) away, and Castillon-la-Bataille, 11km (6¾ miles) away. **Trains** from Bordeaux make the 45-minute trip to St-Emilion 8 to 10 times per day; the one-way fare is 8.20€. Trains from other parts of France usually require transfers in either Bordeaux or Libourne, a 10-minute train ride from St-Emilion. For train information in St-Emilion, call ✆ **36-35** or visit www.voyages-sncf.com.

VISITOR INFORMATION The **Office de Tourisme** is on place des Créneaux (✆ **05-57-55-28-28;** www.saint-emilion-tourisme.com).

EXPLORING THE TOWN

At the heart of St-Emilion is the medieval **place du Marché,** also called **place de l'Eglise Monolithe,** between two hills. St-Emilion abounds with unusual monuments, some of them dug, for defensive reasons, into the limestone bedrock that adds such verve to the vineyards.

Foremost among the monuments is the **Eglise Monolithe ★**, place de l'Eglise Monolithe (✆ **05-57-55-28-28**), the largest underground church in Europe, carved by Benedictine monks during the 9th to 12th centuries. Three 14th-century bay windows mark its facade. A 14th-century sculpted portal depicts the Last Judgment and Resurrection of the Dead. The church is 11m (36 ft.) high, 20m (66 ft.) wide, and 38m (125 ft.) long. It can be visited only as part of an organized tour. The daily tours last 45 minutes, and English-language tours are regularly scheduled between April and October. Each tour includes a visit to the church, its **catacombs,** the 13th-century Chapelle de la Trinité, and its underground grotto—a site known as the Hermitage—where St-Emilion sequestered himself during the latter part of his life. The entire complex was kept alive during the heyday of its use by underground springs, which were surrounded in the 1500s by ornate balustrades (the monks charged admission). The tour, which lasts 45 minutes, costs 6.80€ for adults, 4.30€ for students, and is free for children 11 and under.

You can visit two additional monuments without an organized tour. The first is the **bell tower** *(clocher)* of the Eglise Monolithe (see above). It rises on place des Créneaux, near place de l'Eglise Monolithe. Built between the 1100s and the 1400s, it's the second-highest tower in the La Gironde region and, for years after its construction, was the only aboveground landmark that indicated the position of the underground church. You can climb the bell tower and take in the panoramic view daily between 9am and 6pm for a 1.25€ fee. To do this, go to the tourist office, where someone will give you a key to the tower door in exchange for an ID card. (When you return the key, you'll get your ID back.)

You may want to visit the **Château du Roi** (✆ **05-57-24-72-09**), founded by Henry III of the Plantagenet line during the 13th century. Don't expect a full-fledged castle. The tall *donjon,* or keep, was the first section built, and the construction that followed was either demolished or never completed. Until 1608, this building functioned as the town hall. From its summit, you can see as far away as the Dordogne. You can climb the tower (the procedure is the same as for visiting the bell tower) during daylight hours from April to October for 1.25€.

WHERE TO STAY & EAT

Hôtel Palais Cardinal ★ Though parts of the building date from the 13th century, when it was a cardinal's mansion, today this gracious inn is loaded with modern comforts. Carefully tended by the same family for five generations, rooms in these pleasant lodgings are swathed in warm colors and period prints, in keeping with the building's history. Comfort ranges from smaller rooms with views of the cobbled streets to larger, "luxury" rooms with views of the vineyards and marble bathrooms. All guests have equal access to the outdoor pool and the private garden, as well as to the dining room, which serves elegant regional classics (fixed-price menus are 28€–48€, with half-board rates available for hotel guests). The restaurant offers wine from the adjacent Clos de Sarpe, the hotel's very own vineyard.

Place du 11 Novembre 1918, St-Emilion 33330. www.palais-cardinal.com. ✆ **05-57-24-72-39.** Fax 05-57-74-47-54. 27 units. 88€–162€ double; 176€–216€ suite. AE, DC, MC, V. Free parking. Closed Dec–Mar. **Amenities:** Restaurant; outdoor pool. *In room:* TV, hair dryer, free Internet.

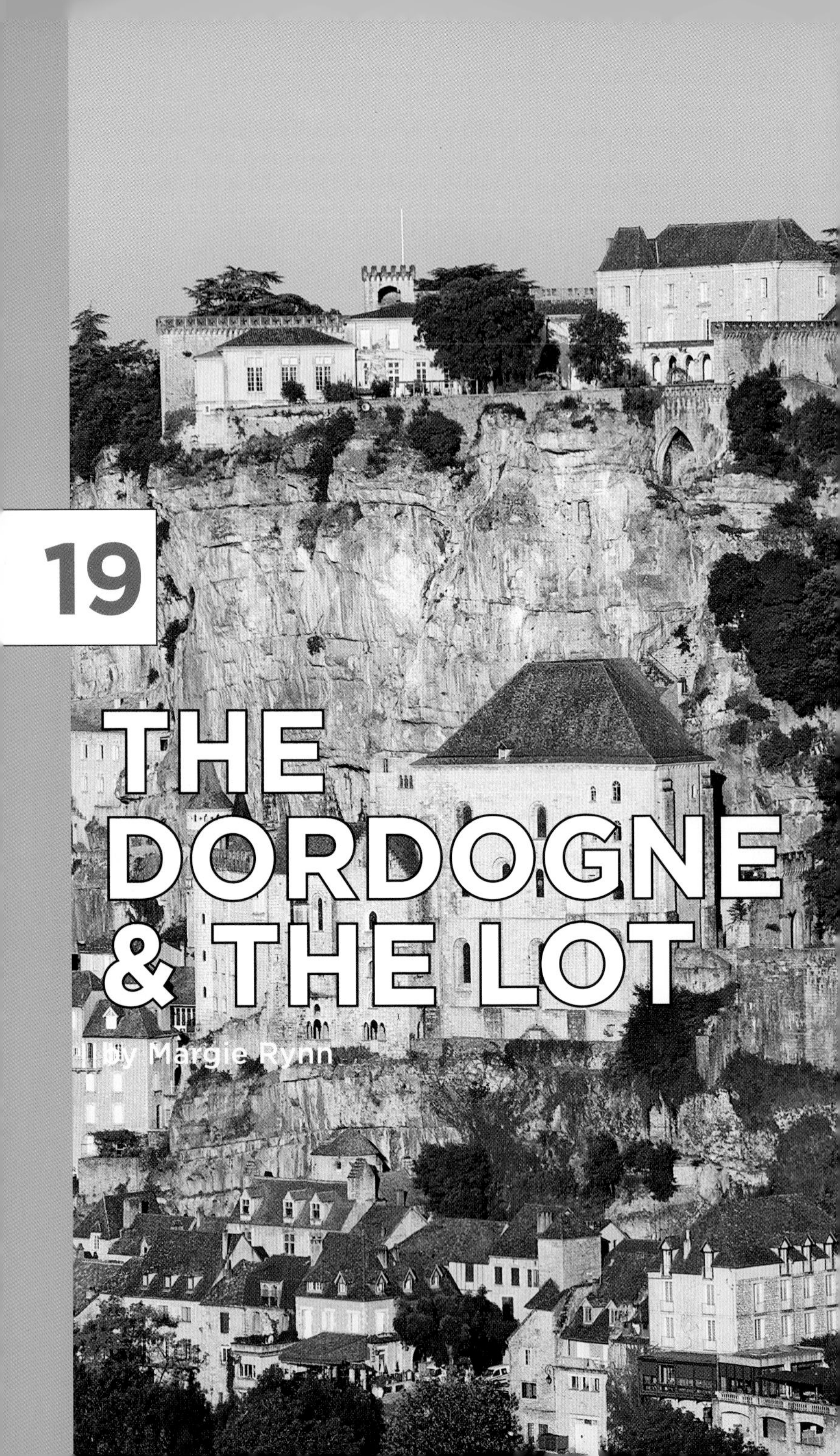

19

THE DORDOGNE & THE LOT

by Margie Rynn

Lovers of foie gras, truffles, and exceptional landscapes have always sought out the Dordogne and Périgord regions of France. Our first stop, Périgueux, was the capital of the old province of Périgord. After admiring Cro-Magnon artwork in prehistoric caves and taking in the beauty of the Dordogne Valley, we explore the lofty heights of Rocamadour and then visit Cahors, the ancient capital of Quercy.

Though the larger towns are inviting, the countryside is the main attraction here. Exquisite villages are, in some cases, literally carved into the limestone cliffs framing the Dordogne River. Medieval fortresses peer down from craggy bluffs. As evidenced by the stunning cave paintings they left behind, humans have been taken with this splendid natural setting since prehistoric times. Now it's your turn to take a few days to explore.

PÉRIGUEUX ★

485km (301 miles) SW of Paris; 85km (53 miles) SE of Angoulême; 113km (70 miles) NE of Bordeaux; 101km (63 miles) SW of Limoges

Capital of the old province of Périgord, Périgueux stands on the Isle River. In addition to its food products (foie gras and truffles reign supreme here), the town is known for its medieval and Renaissance architecture and its Gallo-Roman ruins. The city is divided into three sections: Le Puy St-Front (the medieval town), on the slope of the hill; the Cité (the old Roman town); and, to the west, the modern town.

Though Périgueux (pop. 29,600) is very pretty, it is basically a sleepy provincial town. Its attractions probably won't hold your interest for more than a day, but it's a gateway to the Dordogne Valley and the cave paintings at Les Eyzies.

Essentials

GETTING THERE At least a dozen **trains** per day arrive from Paris from either Montparnasse or Gare d'Austerlitz (trip time: 4–5 hr.; 85€ one-way), 12 direct trains from Bordeaux (trip time: 1½ hr.; 20€ one-way), 1 direct train from Lyon (trip time: 6 hr.; 57€ one-way), and 1 or 2 direct trains per hour from Limoges (trip time: 1 hr.; 15€ one-way). For train information, call ✆ **36-35** or visit www.voyages-sncf.com. If you're **driving** from Paris, take A10 south to Orléans and then A20 south to Vierzon, where you'll pick up the A89 to Périgueux.

VISITOR INFORMATION The **Office du Tourisme** is at 26 place Francheville (✆ **05-53-53-10-63;** www.tourisme-perigueux.fr).

You may want to rent a bike and explore the countryside; a map is available at the tourist office. Rent from **Cycles Cumenal,** 37 rte. de Bergerac (✆ **05-53-53-31-56;** http://cyclescums.ex-flash.com) for 12€ per day.

FACING PAGE: **Rocamadour.**

Exploring the Town & Environs

Périgueux.

Give yourself the time to amble through the **Puy St-Front,** Périgueux's well-preserved medieval quarter, rich with ancient houses, cobbled alleyways, and Renaissance facades. It's hard to miss the imposing **Tour Mataguerre,** a 15th-century tower that is all that's left of the city's fortifications. Follow the winding streets up to the **Cathedral St-Front** (see below) and the **Place de Coderc**, once a literal pigsty, and later the administrative center of the medieval town. Today there is an outdoor market here on Wednesdays and Saturdays from 8am to 1pm that snakes down to Place de la Cautre and the Hôtel de Ville.

Périgueux is a treasure-trove of Gallo-Roman antiquities. The most visible is the **Tour de Vésone,** a partially ruined site that stands 26m (85 ft.) tall, just southwest of town beyond the railway station. Here you'll see the remains of a Roman temple dedicated to the goddess Vesuna, but you can't enter the site. The remains of a large 1st-century Gallo-Roman villa were discovered next to the temple, and in 2003, a sleek new museum was opened, **Vesunna–Site-Musée Gallo Romain** (see below).

Nearby is the **Jardin des Arènes,** a public garden that holds a few remains of an amphitheater that held as many as 22,000 spectators back in the 2nd century. Near the arena are the ruins of the **Château Barrière,** rue Turenne, built in the 11th or 12th century on Roman foundations.

Gastronomy reigns supreme in Périgueux, especially when it comes to smooth, melt-in-your-mouth foie gras. Stores that sell this delicacy abound. One of the best is **La Maison Léon,** 9 place de la Clautre (**© 05-53-53-29-96;** www.maisonleon.fr). If you want an adventure, head for a goose farm that makes its own foie gras, such as **A la Ferme de Puy Gauthier,** about 15 minutes south of town in Marsaneix (**© 05-53-08-87-07;** http://puygauthier24.pages-perso-orange.fr) To get there, take the D2 and follow signs to Brive.

Truffles are another local specialty, and fans of this extremely expensive and delectable fungus come from far and wide, especially during the **Truffle Festival** (Fête de la Truffe), which takes place in mid-December. In July and August, there is a **truffle market** every Saturday from 10am to 1pm in place St-Silan.

Cathédrale St-Front ★ This 12th-century cathedral is one of the rare Byzantine-style churches to be found in France. Left in ruins after the Wars of Religion, it was restored with more than a few 19th-century flourishes by Paul Abadie, who, thus inspired, went on to design the Sacré-Coeur in Paris. With its five white domes and colonnaded turrets, St-Front evokes Constantinople. The cathedral's bell tower is one of the only authentic vestiges of the original church.

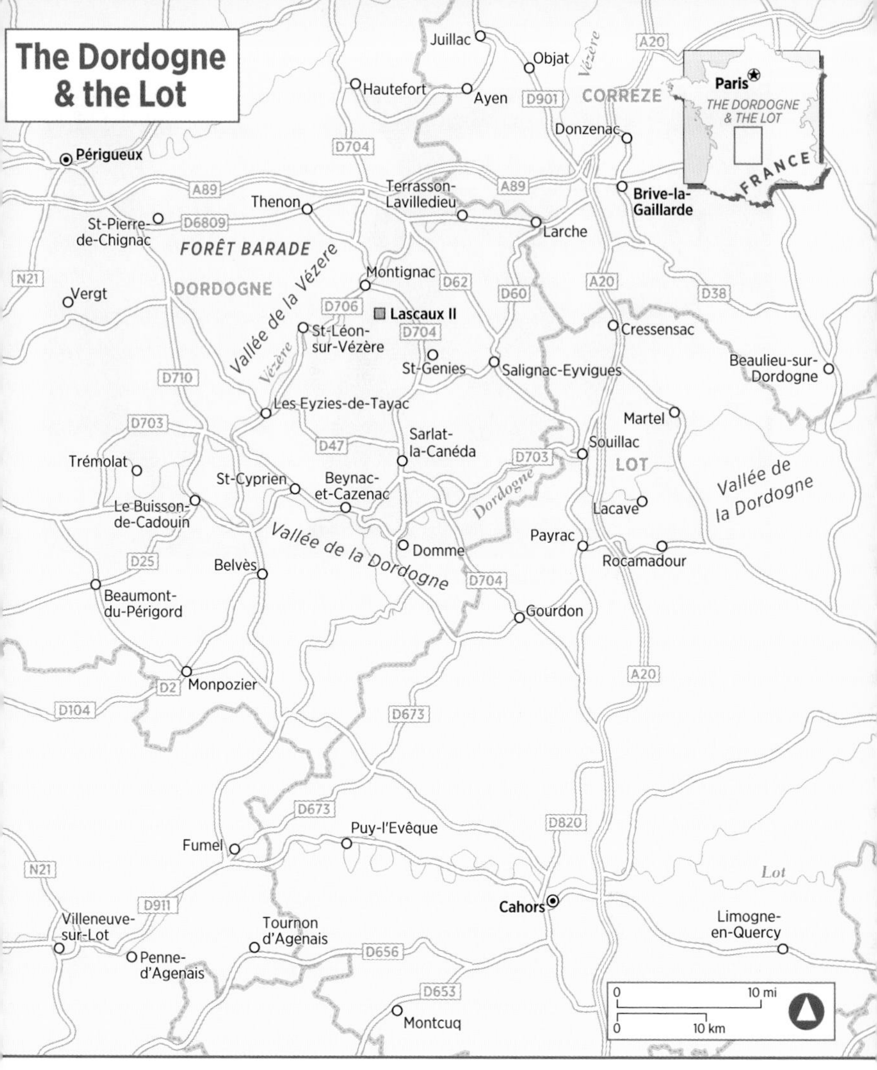

The interior is built on the plan of a Greek cross, unusual for a French cathedral. The recently restored cloisters, which date from the 9th century, can be visited for a fee of 1.50€.

Place de la Clautre. ✆ **05-53-53-23-62.** www.amiscathedralesaintfront.fr. Free admission. Daily 8am–7pm (closes at dusk in winter).

Eglise St-Etienne-de-la-Cité Périgueux's other remarkable church—this one in the Cité area—was a cathedral until 1669, when it lost its position to St-Front. The church was built in the 12th century but has been much damaged since. It contains a 12th-century bishop's tomb and a carved 17th-century wooden reredos depicting the Assumption of the Madonna.

10 av. Cavaignac. ✆ **05-53-06-48-10.** Free admission. Daily 8am–6pm.

Display at Musée d'Art et d'Archéologie du Périgord.

Musée d'Art et d'Archéologie du Périgord ★ Built on the site of an Augustinian monastery, this museum has an exceptional collection of prehistoric relics (one of the largest in France), as well as sculptures and medieval and Renaissance treasures. Many of the artifacts were recovered from digs in the Périgord region, which is rich in prehistoric remains.

22 cours Tourny. ✆ **05-53-06-40-70.** http://musee-perigord.museum.com. Admission 4€ adults, 2€ students, free for children 17 and under. Apr–Sept Mon and Wed–Fri 10am–5:30pm, Sat–Sun 1–6pm; Oct–Mar Mon and Wed–Fri 10am–5pm, Sat–Sun 1–6pm.

Musée Gallo-Romain Vesunna ★ One of the most talked-about museums in central France opened in July 2003 within a mostly glass shell that was designed by the renowned architect Jean Nouvel. A short walk from the center of Périgueux, it's positioned directly above excavations, which revealed an extensive, albeit ruined, ancient Roman villa, replete with mosaics and many of the workaday artifacts of everyday life in the ancient Roman provinces. Visitors will be intrigued by the juxtaposition of the hypermodern shell and the ancient artifacts within.

Rue du 26e Régiment d'Infanterie. ✆ **05-53-53-00-92.** www.perigueux.fr. Admission 6€ adults, 4€ students and children ages 6–25, free for children 5 and under. Oct–Mar Tues–Fri 9:30am–12:30pm and 1:30–5pm, Sat–Sun 10am–12:30pm and 2:30–6pm; Apr–June and Sept Tues–Fri 9:30am–5:30pm, Sat–Sun 10am–12:30pm and 2:30–6pm; July–Aug daily 10am–7pm. Closed 1st and 2nd week of Jan.

Where to Stay

The **Château des Reynats** (see "Where to Eat," p. 725) also has rooms.

Hôtel Bristol This modern hotel, the best in the town center, is centrally located and offers recently renovated comfortable rooms, often with sleek styling. It's your best bet in a town with a limited, lackluster selection. Bathrooms are a bit small but come with a combination tub/shower. Breakfast is the only meal served, but it's only a 5-minute walk to the town's best restaurants and major points of interest.

37–39 rue Antoine Gadaud, Périgueux 24000. www.bristolfrance.com. ✆ **05-53-08-75-90.** Fax 05-53-07-00-49. 29 units. 67€–79€ double. AE, MC, V. Free parking. Closed btw. Christmas and New Year's Day. **Amenities:** Room service. *In room:* A/C, TV, hair dryer, minibar, free Wi-Fi.

Where to Eat

Château des Reynats ★★ MODERN FRENCH This slate-roofed 19th-century manor has a yellow and soft-red Empire dining room in which you can enjoy the finest *cuisine du marché* in the entire region. Someone on the staff may relay stories of the role the château played during France's disastrous exit from its former department of Algeria, when it functioned as a kind of refugee center for French citizens booted off their estates. Menu items are likely to include salmon with caviar, foie gras with mango tartar, and a well-prepared version of scallops with velvety chestnuts.

BIKING & CANOEING DOWN THE Dordogne

The Dordogne's rivers meander through countryside that's among the most verdant and historic in France. This area is underpopulated but dotted with monuments, châteaux, 12th-century villages, and charming churches.

As you bike around, the rural character of the area unfolds before you. No château, hotel, or inn treats you disdainfully if you show up on two rather than four wheels. (*Au contraire,* the staff will probably offer advice on suitable bike routes.) If you're ever in doubt about where your handlebars should lead you, know that you'll rarely go wrong if your route parallels the riverbanks of the Lot, the Vézère, the Dordogne, or any of their tributaries. Architects and builders since the 11th century have added greatly to the visual allure of their watersides.

The SNCF makes it easy to transport a bike on the nation's railways. However, if you don't want to bring your own wheels on the train, there are plenty of rental shops throughout the region. (We recommend rentals in this chapter's sections on Périgueux and Les Eyzies-de-Tayac.)

Exploring the rivers by canoe is another option. Every summer, a flotilla of bathing-suited visitors can be seen paddling down the Dordogne; the Lot and the Vézère get less traffic and are also beautiful. The rivers tend to be shallow and lazy, perfect for a family outing.

Le Comité Départemental du Tourism, 25 rue du Président Wilson, Périgueux 24000 (✆ **05-53-35-50-24;** www.dordogne-perigord-tourisme.fr), provides information about all the towns in the *département* and will help you organize biking, hiking, kayaking, and canoeing trips. Two of the best outdoors outfitters are **Canoë Loisir,** Vitrac, 24200 (✆ **05-53-31-22-92;** www.canoes-loisirs.com), and **Adventure Plein Air,** St-Léon sur Vézère, 24290 (✆ **05-53-50-67-71;** www.canoevezere.com).

The château also rents 45 beautiful rooms. Thirteen of the rooms lie in the château, the other 37 in l'Orangerie, a guesthouse of comfort but less grand, of course, than the château. Rooms in the château range from 125€ to 200€ in a double, 230€ to 260€ in a suite, whereas doubles in the guesthouse go for 92€ to 104€.

Chancelade 24650. ✆ **05-53-03-53-59.** Fax 05-53-03-44-84. www.chateau-hotel-perigord.com. Reservations recommended. Main courses 33€–42€; fixed-price menu 28€ lunch, 42€–79€ dinner. MC, V. Tues–Fri 12:30–1:30pm; Mon–Sat 7:30–9pm. Closed (restaurant) first 3 weeks of Jan.

Perigueux After Dark

If the weather is clement, begin your evening with a stroll in the streets and alleyways surrounding **place St-Silain, place St-Louis,** and **place du Marché.** Each of those three areas boasts high concentrations of bars, restaurants, and nocturnal diversions. One of the town's best and most-frequented wine bars is **Le Cercle,** 18 cours Montaigne (✆**05-53-53-34-79;** www.hotelrestaurantlunivers.fr), whose cellar contains many excellent vintages.

For the high-energy crowd, the leading disco is **La Reg,** 16 rue Chancelier de l'Hôpital (✆**05-53-53-10-55**). It's open Wednesday to Saturday nights from midnight till dawn. An alternative is **l'Ubu,** 3 rue des Jacobins (✆**05-53-09-29-02**), where the DJ spins house, Latino, and Caribbean music Thursday to Saturday midnight till dawn. For drinks, dialogue, and endless cups of coffee, consider the **Café Le St-Louis,** place St-Louis (✆**05-53-53-53-90**).

LASCAUX (MONTIGNAC) ★★

496km (308 miles) SW of Paris; 47km (29 miles) SE of Périgueux

The **Caves at Lascaux,** 2km (1¼ miles) from the Vézère River town of Montignac in the Dordogne region, contain the most beautiful and most famous cave paintings in the world. Unfortunately, you can't view the actual paintings (the caves have been closed to the public to prevent deterioration), but a precise replica gives you a clear picture of the remarkable works.

Four boys looking for a dog discovered the caves in 1940. They opened to the public in 1948, quickly becoming one of France's major attractions and drawing 125,000 visitors annually. However, the hordes of tourists caused atmospheric changes in the caves, endangering the paintings. Scientists went to work to halt the destructive fungus plaguing the paintings, known as "the green sickness," and a detailed facsimile was constructed nearby for visitors.

Essentials

GETTING THERE By far, the easiest way to reach Montignac is to **drive** northeast from Les Eyzies on D65 for 19km (12 miles).

Rail service is to the neighboring hamlet of Condat-Le-Lardin, 9.5km (6 miles) northeast. From there, taxis (✆**05-53-51-80-46**) take visitors to Montignac for 20€. If no taxis are waiting, a railway station employee will call one for you. For train information, call ✆ **36-35** or visit www.voyages-sncf.com.

VISITOR INFORMATION The **Office de Tourisme** in Montignac is on place Bertrand-de-Born (✆**05-53-51-82-60;** www.tourisme-vezere.com).

Exploring the Caves & Other Attractions

Public visits to Lascaux I ceased in 1963. Permission to visit for research purposes is given only to qualified archaeologists, so unless you've got an advanced degree and good connections, you will have to make do with the facsimile. That said, Lascaux II is nothing to sniff at. Years of painstaking artistic and scientific labor went into re-creating the cave, including the use of prehistoric painting techniques and natural colorants. While some of the magic is lost, what you see is virtually identical to the real thing. For more virtual reality, you can visit the original cave online at an extensive site set up by the French government: www.lascaux.culture.fr.

Lascaux II ★★ A short walk downhill from the real cave is an impressive reproduction of the original, duplicated and molded in concrete above ground. The 39m-long (128-ft.) tunnel faithfully reproduces the section of the cave harboring 90 percent of the famous paintings, so you will get a good idea of what the "Sistine Chapel of Prehistory" looks like. You'll see majestic bulls, wild boars, stags, horses, and deer, the originals of which were painted by Cro Magnon peoples 15,000 to 20,000 years ago. No one has yet figured out exactly what purpose these paintings served, but the artistry of these prehistoric painters is startling. Try to show up as close to opening time as possible—the number of visitors per day is limited to 2,000, and tickets usually sell out by 2pm. During the winter, you can buy tickets directly at Lascaux II (remember, it's closed Mon in off season), but from April to October, you must purchase them from a kiosk adjacent to the Montignac tourist office, place Bertran-de-Born. You will be given a specific time for your guided visit; be sure to ask for a tour in English, if needed.

2km (1¼ miles) from Montignac, off D706. ✆ **05-53-51-95-03.** www.semitour.com. Admission 9€ adults, 6€ children 6–12, free for children 5 and under. July–Aug daily 9am–7pm; Oct to mid-Nov daily 10am–12:30pm and 2–6pm; mid-Feb to Mar Tues–Sun 10am–12:30pm and 2–5:30pm; Apr–June and Sept daily 9am–6pm. Closed mid-Nov to mid-Feb.

Lascaux cave paintings.

Le Thot ☺ This attraction includes a zoo with live animals that approximate those depicted on the walls of Lascaux, like Przewalski horses and European bison. Projection rooms show short films on the discovery of cave art at Lascaux, and exhibits explore prehistoric painting techniques and Cro Magnon life in the Dordogne. After your visit to Le Thot, walk out on the terrace for a view of the Vézère Valley and the Lascaux hills.

Thonac, 7km (4¼ miles) southwest of Montignac along D706 (follow the signs for Les Eyzies). ✆ **05-53-50-70-44.** www.semitour.com. Admission 7€ adults, 4.50€ children 6–12, free for children 5 and under. July–Aug daily 10am–7pm; Oct to mid-Nov daily 10am–12:30pm and 2–6pm; mid-Feb to Mar and mid-Nov to Dec Tues–Sun 10am–12:30pm and 2–5:30pm; Apr–June and Sept daily 10am–6pm. Closed Jan.

Site Préhistorique de Regourdou ☺ About 450m (1,476 ft.) uphill from Lascaux, a minor road branches off and runs through a forest until it reaches this site, discovered in 1954 by Roger Constant when he conducted an archaeological dig in front of his house. Found at the site was a sepulcher with a skeleton of a Neanderthal man and a bear and several other bear skeletons nearby, possibly evidence of a prehistoric bear cult. The house has been made into an archaeological museum; nearby, six semiwild bears roam around a naturalized habitat that's barricaded against humans. Depending on the time of year, you may be required to take a guided tour (available in English and French, at no extra cost).

✆ **05-53-51-81-23.** www.regourdou.fr. Admission 5€ adults, 3€ children 6–12, free for children 5 and under. July–Aug daily 10am–7pm; Sept–Nov and Feb–June daily 11am–6pm. Closed Dec to mid-Feb.

Where to Stay & Eat

Hostellerie la Roseraie ★ In the heart of the medieval village, this little charmer is both affordable and cozy. It was converted from a comfortable home built for one of the town merchants in the 19th century on the banks of the Vézère. The midsize bedrooms have individual character and well-kept bathrooms with either a tub or shower. Adding to the charm is a rose garden in back. There is a pleasant terrace to enjoy in the summer months, and the restaurant is one of the better choices in town, serving traditional French cuisine; fixed-price menus cost from 28€ to 49€.

11 place d'Armes, Montignac 24290. www.laroseraie-hotel.com. ✆ **05-53-50-53-92.** Fax 05-53-51-02-23. 14 units. 80€–180€ double; 200€–280€ family apt. AE, DC, MC, V. Parking 8€. Closed Nov–Easter. **Amenities:** Restaurant; bar; outdoor pool. *In room:* TV, hair dryer, Wi-Fi (in most; 3€ per 2 hr.).

Hôtel Le Relais du Soleil d'Or ★ In the heart of Montignac, this former postal relay station offers traditionally furnished rooms and a lush, landscaped garden. The larger, better-decorated accommodations with a more contemporary look lie in a modern annex built in the 1980s, a short walk from the original building. Units in the hotel's core are very comfortable, albeit a bit less stylish. The main restaurant serves traditional Dordogne fare such as foie gras with pears and spice bread, and duck *magret* prepared with three different gourmet mushrooms: cèpes, morels, and truffles. The less formal Le Bistrot offers salads, snacks, and simple platters. Set dinners in the main restaurant range from 27€ to 53€.

16 rue du 4-Septembre, Montignac 24290. www.le-soleil-dor.com. ✆ **05-53-51-80-22.** Fax 05-53-50-27-54. 32 units. 69€–179€ double. AE, DC, MC, V. Closed Feb. **Amenities:** 2 restaurants; bar; Internet; outdoor pool; room service; free Wi-Fi. *In room:* TV, hair dryer, minibar.

LES EYZIES-DE-TAYAC ★★★

533km (330 miles) SW of Paris; 45km (28 miles) SE of Périgueux

When prehistoric skeletons were unearthed here in 1868, the market town of Les Eyzies-de-Tayac (known as Les Eyzies) suddenly became an archaeologist's dream. This area in the Dordogne Valley was found to be one of the richest in the world in ancient sites and deposits. Some of the caves contain primitive drawings made 30,000 years ago. The most beautiful and most famous are at Lascaux (see above), but many caves around Les Eyzies are open to the public.

Essentials

GETTING THERE Local **trains** run from Le Buisson, 19km (12 miles) away. The several daily trains from Périgueux are more direct. For information, call ✆ **36-35** or visit www.voyages-sncf.com. To **drive** from Périgueux, start along D710 southeast to Le Bugue, and then follow the signs to Les Eyzies-de-Tayac.

VISITOR INFORMATION The **Office de Tourisme** (✆ **05-53-06-97-05;** www.tourisme-vezere.com) is open year-round at 19 rue de la Préhistoire (place de la Mairie).

Exploring the Area

Many of the caves in this area limit the number of daily visitors they admit; you can call ahead for reservations up to a year in advance. We recommend that you do so, especially if you plan to visit in the summer.

If you want to pedal around the countryside, you can rent bicycles at the tourist office. Prices begin at 10€ per half-day, 15€ per full day. A 20€ deposit is required; no credit cards are accepted.

Whether you're biking or driving, the loveliest villages in the **Dordogne Valley ★★★** include Sarlat-la-Canéda, 17km (11 miles) southeast of Les Eyzies, and La Roque-Gageac, 14 km (8¾ miles) south of Sarlat. Smaller villages, including Beynac-et-Cazenac, Castelnaud, Domme, and Montfort, lie beside the road that meanders through the Dordogne Valley. Throughout the region, routes are country roads marked only with signs leading to the above-mentioned destinations.

Make a special effort to stand in the shadow of the foreboding **Château de Beynac ★★**, Beynac-et-Cazenac (✆ **05-53-29-50-40**), a remarkably intact 12th-century fortress that peers out over the Dordogne Valley from a rocky crag. The fortress played an important role in the 100 Years War and at one point was seized by Richard the Lionhearted. The Grosso family, who live on-site, have been renovating the monument for almost 40 years, and they've done a amazing job; the castle has served as a backdrop in several movies, including Luc Besson's *Jean d'Arc*. The view alone is worth the hike up the hill; fans of knights in shining armor will surely appreciate the visit. It's open April through September daily 10am to 6:30pm, and October to March daily 11am to sundown. Free 1-hour guided tours (in French) begin once or twice an hour. Admission, with or without the tour, costs 7.50€, 4.30€ ages 12 to 16, and 3.20€ ages 5 to 11. There's a worthy restaurant in the nearby **Hôtel du Chateau** (✆ **05-53-29-19-20**), located on the river at the base of the chateau.

Grotte de Font-de-Gaume ★★ This is the last cave with multicolored prehistoric paintings that is still open to the public. Only 180 visitors are allowed per day, so be sure to reserve well in advance, particularly in the summer. You will be on a 45-minute guided tour (tours are limited to 12 persons, and make sure to request one in English when you reserve) through a rather narrow cave (claustrophobes beware). Discovered in 1901, the paintings and etchings in the cave date from the Magdalenian period (17,000–9,000 B.C.). While the paintings are not as spectacular as those at Lascaux, here you are seeing the real thing, including depictions of bison, mammoths, horses, and other animals. The knowledgeable guides will point out how prehistoric artists used the shape of the caves walls to make their paintings more lifelike. They may also show you some eerie prehistoric hand prints.

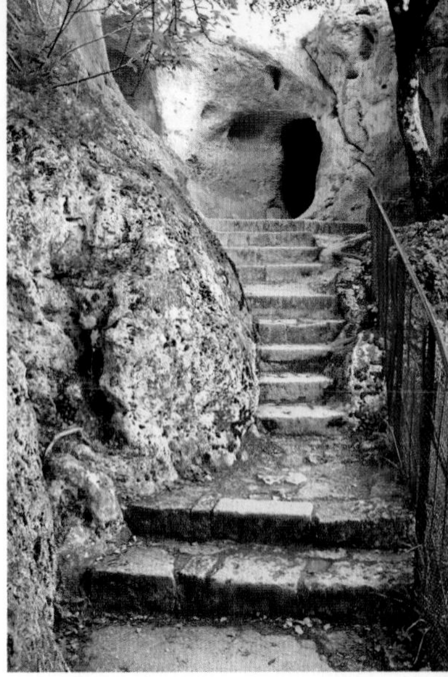

Grotte de Font-de-Gaume.

On D47, 1.5km (1 mile) outside Les Eyzies. ✆ **05-53-06-86-00.** http://eyzies.monuments-nationaux.fr/en. Admission 7€ adults, 4.50€ 18–25, free for ages 17 and under. May 15–Sept 15 Sun–Fri 9:30am–5:30pm; Sept 16–May 14 Sun–Fri 9:30am–12:30pm and 2–5:30pm.

Grotte des Combarelles ★ Discovered at the turn of the 20th century, this wide cave on the southeast edge of town has over 400 etchings of animals, including musk oxen, horses, bison, and aurochs (prehistoric oxen). Think of it as a gallery of Magdalenian art. Advance reservations are vital—only 60 visitors per day are admitted.

On D47, 17km (11 miles) north of Bergerac. ✆ **05-53-06-86-00.** http://eyzies.monuments-nationaux.fr/en. Admission 7€ adults, 4.50€ 18–25, free for ages 17 and under. May 15–Sept 15 Sun–Fri 9:30am–5:30pm; Sept 16–May 14 Sun–Fri 9:30am–12:30pm and 2–5:30pm.

Grotte du Grand-Roc ★ The artistic marvels here are all created by nature, not man; this cave is a geological wonder of crystals, stalagmites, and stalactites. The cave is about 1.5km (1 mile) northwest of Les Eyzies on the left bank of the Vézère (signs point the way on D47). There are no limits to visitors at this venue.

48 av. Préhistoirie, Les Eyzies 24620. ✆ **05-53-06-92-70.** www.semitour.com. Admission 7.50€ adults, 3.50€ children 6–12, free for children 5 and under. July–Aug daily 10am–7pm; Sept to mid-Nov and Easter–June Sun–Fri 10am–12:30pm and 2–6pm; mid-Nov to Dec and Feb–Mar Mon–Thurs 10am–12:30pm and 2–5:30pm. Closed Jan.

Musée National de la Préhistoire ★★ In the shadow of the limestone cliff that hovers above the village, this museum had a major overhaul in 2004 and is now set in a modern limestone building next to a fortress-castle from the 16th century. One of the largest collections of prehistoric artifacts in Europe ("only" 18,000 of its 5 million objects are on display), this museum traces 400,000 years of human history, from the origins to the end of the Ice Age (around 10,000

B.C.). Highlights include an exquisite **15,000-year-old etching of a bison** ★ carved on a bone, showing its head licking its flank; a **40,000-year-old skeleton** of a newborn; **Neanderthal jewelry;** and **stone tools** dating back 150,000 years. Also on display are the first replicas of the first-known human footprints, dating from around 3.6 million years ago.

The Scoop on Cave Tickets

To prevent deterioration of the art, a limited number of visitors are allowed into the caves of Les Eyzies-de-Tayac each day (specifically Font-de-Gaume and Combarelles). Tickets are available up to 3 months in advance, and we advise you to reserve that far ahead, if possible.

1 rue du Musée, Les Eyzies 24640. ✆ **05-53-06-45-45.** www.musee-prehistoire-eyzies.fr. Admission 5€ adults, 3.50€ 18–25, free for children 17 and under. July–Aug daily 9:30am–6:30pm; June and Sept Wed–Mon 9:30am–6pm; Oct–May Wed–Mon 9:30am–12:30pm and 2–5:30pm.

Where to Stay & Eat

Hôtel Le Moulin de la Beune ★ This is the best bet for the frugal traveler —a transformed 17th-century mill (complete with working waterwheel) just off the main street. The simple but cozy rooms are nicely decorated with homey touches; a small stream runs through the property, so if you open the window, you'll be lulled to sleep by the sound of splashing water. Ivy covers the outside of the hotel and the restaurant, Au Vieux Moulin, which serves elegant regional classics with set menus starting at 31€. In good weather, you can dine on a shaded terrace or just laze in a lounge chair next to the babbling brook.

2 rue du Moulin Bas, Les Eyzies-de-Tayac 24620. www.moulindelabeune.com. ✆ **05-53-06-94-33.** Fax 05-53-06-98-06. 20 units. 64€–79€ double. MC, V. Closed Nov–Apr. **Amenities:** Restaurant. *In room:* A/C, hair dryer.

Musée National de la Préhistoire.

Hôtel Le Centenaire ★★ This charm-filled oasis is even better known for its cuisine than for its accommodations. The good-size, comfortable rooms are conservatively modern, with period touches like reproduction antiques and small canopies over the beds. The verdant grounds include a shady terrace and an outdoor pool. Even if you're not a hotel guest, consider a visit to the restaurant, where fixed-price menus cost 35€ to 70€. Specialties include sautéed foie gras with homemade spice bread, sautéed scallops with truffle risotto, and veal fricassee with wild mushrooms.

Rocher de la Penne, Les Eyzies-Tayac-Sireuil 24620. www.hotelducentenaire.fr. ✆ **05-53-06-68-68.** Fax 05-53-06-92-41. 24 units. 120€–195€ double; 195€–215€ suite. AE, MC, V. Closed Jan to mid-Feb. **Amenities:** Restaurant; bar; exercise room; heated outdoor pool; room service; sauna. *In room:* TV, hair dryer, minibar, free Wi-Fi.

Hôtel Les Glycines ★ 🎁 We'd stay here just for the flower garden. Housed in a building that dates from 1862, this establishment offers regional cuisine, comfortable accommodations, and drinks on a veranda with a grape arbor. Rooms are done up in relaxing shades of beige, combining regional charm with designer style. Some rooms look out over the ample grounds, which include a pool and lots of the aforementioned flowers. Restaurant specialties include new twists on foie gras, cèpes, and truffles: braised *ris de veau* with black truffle juice; roast Quercy lamb with rosemary and artichokes; and grilled scallops with truffle polenta. Fixed-price menus range from 39€ to 95€. Many ingredients for the restaurant's dishes come from the hotel's impressive kitchen garden.

Rte. de Périgueux (D47), Les Eyzies-Tayac-Sireuil 24620. www.les-glycines-dordogne.com. ✆ **05-53-06-97-07.** Fax 05-53-06-92-19. 23 units. 95€–165€ double; 195€–235€ junior suite. AE, DC, MC, V. Closed Nov–Apr. **Amenities:** Restaurant; bar; babysitting; outdoor pool; room service. *In room:* A/C, TV, hair dryer, free Wi-Fi.

SARLAT-LA-CANÉDA ★★

9.5km (6 miles) E of Les Eyzies-de-Tayac; 530km (329 miles) SW of Paris; 60km (37 miles) NW of Cahors

The capital of Perigord Noir (Black Perigord), Sarlat is possibly the best-preserved medieval town in southwestern France, almost a living museum. Its inner core is filled with so many ancient buildings that it's like stepping back into another age as you wander past stone structures of ocher color along cobblestone streets.

Sarlat grew up around Benedictine abbey back in the 9th century and was awarded a city charter in 1299. The zenith of its fame came in the 14th century, when it was known as a bustling center of artisans, painters, and students. Old Sarlat, called **Vieille Ville** ★★★, the main reason to visit, is split by the 19th-century main street, **rue de la République,** which defines the commercial heart of town and is lined with shops and restaurants.

With more medieval buildings than in any town in France, Sarlat is often a movie backdrop. Robert Hossein's *Les Misérables* was shot here in 1982, as was Danny Huston's *Becoming Colette,* in 1991.

Essentials

GETTING THERE There are good direct train connections from Bordeaux (trip time: 2½ hr.), about four trains per day. Trains from Paris go to Souillac, about 30km (19 miles) by bus from Sarlat; buses run fairly frequently (trip time: 40 min.); visit www.ter-sncf.com/Regions/Aquitaine/fr for schedules. For train information and schedules, call ✆ **36-35** or visit www.voyages-sncf.com. The terminus in Sarlat lies 1km (½ mile) south of the old town. You can walk it in 15 minutes or else take a taxi.

Motorists **drive** the A10 autoroute from Paris, going by way of Poitiers, Angoulême, and Périgueux to reach Sarlat. Or you can take the A89 from Bordeaux. Sarlat lies 180km (112 miles) east of Bordeaux.

VISITOR INFORMATION The Office de Tourisme, 3 rue Tourny (✆ **05-53-31-45-45;** www.sarlat-tourisme.com), sells maps of the area and offers English-language tours from May to October.

SPECIAL EVENTS In the summer, the streets of Sarlat are bustling with people, many of whom come to attend the **Féstival des Jeux de Théâtre de Sarlat** (✆ **05-53-31-10-83;** www.festival-theatre-sarlat.com), a theater festival that runs from mid-July to the first week of August. During the month of August and into the first week of September, Sarlat also hosts the **Féstival de Musique du Périgord Noir** (✆ **05-53-51-61-61;** www.festivaldu perigordnoir.fr). The November film festival, **Le Féstival de Film de Sarlat** (✆ **05-53-29-18-13;** www.ville-sarlat.fr/festival), is the biggest such event in France after Cannes and Deauville.

Exploring the Town

Start your tour of Old Sarlat at **place du Peyrou** ★, and allow at least 2 hours to wander around. Opening onto place du Peyrou is the **Cathédral de Saint Sacerdos,** which enjoyed its greatest prestige when it was an Episcopal seat between 1317 and 1790. The cathedral has a Romanesque bell tower, but most of the structure dates from the 16th and 17th centuries. Much of the interior is in the late Gothic style. The structure stands to the right of the tourist office (see above). Leave by the south doorway.

Behind the cathedral is **Lanterne des Morts,** or "Lantern to the Dead" ★★, which was reputedly built in the 1100s to honor St. Bernard's pilgrimage to Sarlat. This is one of the finest examples of early medieval sepulchral architecture.

Also opening on place du Peyrou, **Maison de la Boétie** ★ stands opposite the cathedral. You can admire its facade, as it's the most charming Renaissance house in Sarlat. Dating from 1525, the house has mullioned windows and a painted gable. It was once inhabited by the town's most famous son, Etienne de la Boétie, who was born about the time the house was completed. A criminal magistrate, he had a lifelong friendship with Montaigne, who was at La Boétie's bedside when he died in 1563. That death inspired Montaigne's famous essay "Friendship."

The second square to visit is **Place du Marché aux Oies** ★, known for its bronze statue of three geese by Lalanne. For centuries, this market sold live fowl, and the statue commemorates that long-ago role. The most stunning Renaissance facade on this square belongs to the Hotel Chassaing.

One of Sarlat's most colorful medieval streets is **rue des Consuls** ★★, whose greatest buildings include **Hôtel Plamon,** its Gothic windows making it look like a church. Beyond the doorway of Plamon is a series of five arcades on the ground floor opening onto a covered market. A trio of Gothic bay windows on the second floor has been restored to its original appearance.

Rue Montaigne.

If you follow **Jardin des Enfeus** (behind the cathedral), you reach **rue Montaigne ★** where the great 16th-century philosopher was born and once lived. The buildings along this street are extremely photogenic.

Feel free to roam the back streets of Sarlat. You can allow yourself to get lost, as you'll invariably wind up back at **place de la Liberté,** in the center of town, and the 18th-century Hotel de Ville, or City Hall.

Sarlat is celebrated by French gastronomes for its foie gras and truffle market, **Le Marché aux Truffles et au Gras,** held at the bottom of rue Fénelon every Saturday from 9am to noon December to February. Sarlat is also known for its wines, and the best selection is found at **Julien de Savignac,** place Pasteur (✆ **05-53-31-29-20**).

Where to Stay

The most sumptuous way to live in and around Sarlat is at the **Château de Puymartin** (see above), which rents two of the most elegant guest rooms in the entire area. Surrounded by antiques, you get to live like a count (or countess) of medieval times, but with all the modern comforts. The cost of a double is 120€ to 150€ per night.

Hôtel des Récollets ★ West of rue de la République, you can enjoy some of Sarlat's medieval past by lodging in the old town at this time-honored hotel. It stands by Chapelle des Récollets, dating from the 16th century. Behind an ocher-colored stone facade, the hotel is centered on the early medieval cloister of the convent, an idyllic spot for breakfast. On a summer day, a generous breakfast is served here among the flowers. Rooms are simply but comfortably furnished.

4 rue Jean-Jacques Rousseau, Sarlat 24200. www.hotel-recollets-sarlat.com. ✆ **05-53-31-36-00.** Fax 05-53-30-32-62. 18 units. 49€–69€ double; 89€–99€ family rooms. MC, V. Parking 7€. *In room:* A/C, TV, free Wi-Fi.

Hôtel Restaurant La Couleuvrine Capped with crenellations and a formidable tower, this hotel occupies part of what was once Sarlat's barricades during the 12th and 13th centuries. Efforts have been made to preserve the medieval ambiance; exposed stone walls and beams abound. The cozy rooms are furnished with reproduction antiques; in some cases, they are rather small. Philippe and Isabelle Lebon-Henault, the cordial owners, maintain an on-site boutique loaded with samples of the region's gastronomic bounty, and both of the restaurants here are reviewed below. The hotel's name, incidentally, derives from the long cannon (*les couleuvrines*) that used to be fired at attackers from the hotel's crenellations. 1 place de La Bouquerie, Sarlat 24200. www.la-couleuvrine.com. ✆ **05-53-59-27-80.** Fax 05-53-31-26-83. 27 units. 58€–78€ double; 90€–114€ suite. AE, DC, MC, V. **Amenities:** 2 restaurants; bar, free Wi-Fi. *In room:* TV.

Plaza Madeleine ★ Having had a thorough makeover in 2009, this sleek hotel now offers contemporary design in a historic setting. Located at the northern entrance to medieval Sarlat, this grand 19th-century building harbors comfortable rooms furnished in neutral tones with splashes of color on the beds and period-style armchairs. Guests suffering from sightseeing fatigue can relax in the outdoor pool or make the most of the nifty spa, which features a sauna, Jacuzzi, and steam room. The hotel also caters to business travelers, as evidenced by the cozy restaurant's name: Au Bureau (At the Office), which is reviewed below. 1 place de la Petite-Rigaudie, Sarlat-la-Canéda 24200. www.hoteldelamadeleine-sarlat.com. ✆ **05-53-59-10-41.** Fax 05-53-31-03-62. 39 rooms. 98€–144€ double; 140€–163€ junior suite. AE, DC, MC, V. Parking 10€. **Amenities:** Restaurant; bar. *In room:* TV, hair dryer, minibar, free Wi-Fi.

La Maison des Peyrat ★ 🎁 Up a hill and away from the crowds that flock to Sarlat in summer, this is the most tranquil retreat in walking distance, lying only 1.6km (1 mile) from the center. The oldest section of this one-story stone structure dates from 1343, when it was a hospital for victims of the Black Death. Those unhappy memories are long gone now. In 1843, a local baron turned it into a hunting lodge. Today it's a small hotel and preserves much of its original character, with simply furnished bedrooms in pastel and rattan furnishings. Exposed beams and original artwork add to its character. On a terrace shaded by a massive chestnut tree, breakfast and dinner are served (for hotel guests only; dinner is 23€).

Abode of the Fabled Dame Blanche ("White Lady"), a Ghost

The Dordogne is riddled with châteaux and one of our favorites, Château de Puymartin ★★ (✆ 05-53-59-29-97; www.chateau-de-puymartin.com), lies 8km (5 miles) from Sarlat, found along the curvy road between Sarlat and Les Eyzies, the D47. Not only can you stay here (see below), but you can also visit it as a sight. The present owner, Countess de Montbron, shares her family home and will relate the story of the famous ghost, Dame Blanche, who, so it is said, has been seen wandering the castle at night. The château is furnished with family heirlooms and has been in the Montbron family since 1450. It can be visited daily April 8 to June and September 10am to noon and 2 to 6pm, July and August 10am to 6:30pm. In October, it is also open daily, but from 2:30 to 5pm. Admission is 7€ for adults, 5€ for students, and 3.50€ children 6 to 12.

Le Lac de la Plane, Sarlat 24200. http://maisondespeyrat.com. ✆ **05-53-59-00-32.** 10 units. 55€–100€ double. MC, V. Closed Nov 15–Apr 1. **Amenities:** Restaurant for hotel guests (dinner served Mon–Tues and Thurs–Sat); outdoor pool; free Wi-Fi. *In room:* TV, hair dryer.

Le Mas de Castel ★ Francine Charpenet Mottet has transformed the family farm into a tranquil retreat for guests who'd like to enjoy the countryside 3km (1¾ miles) south of the historic core of Sarlat. The hotel is surrounded by farms and rolling hills—noise is not a problem here. A Provençal theme runs throughout the decor; the larger "superior rooms" have a ground-floor terrace. All guests enjoy the garden and pool; next to the pool is a *borie,* a cone-roofed structure built without mortar. These dry stone huts, which have existed since ancient times, can be found throughout the south of France.

Route de Sudalissant, Sarlat 24200. http://hotel-lemasdecastel.com. ✆ **05-53-59-02-59.** Fax 05-53-28-25-62. 14 units. 50€–75€ double; 70€–100€ family room for 4. MC, V. Closed Nov–Mar. **Amenities:** Outdoor pool. *In room:* TV, hair dryer, free Wi-Fi.

Where to Eat

Au Bureau FRENCH BISTRO With a decor that resembles a cross between a pub and an old-fashioned gentlemen's club, this cozy restaurant, located in the Plaza Madeleine hotel (see above), offers well-executed bistro fare at very reasonable prices. Steak frites, grilled scallops, and fresh, meal-size salads head the menu, along with fun desserts like chocolate profiteroles and banana splits. There is a nice terrace for outdoor dining, as well as a full bar complete with colorful cocktails and Irish coffees.

1 place de la Petite-Rigaudie. ✆ **05-53-31-84-15.** www.aubureau-sarlat.fr. Reservations recommended on weekends. Main dishes 10€–15€; fixed-price menus 12€–14€ lunch, 21€ dinner. MC, V. Daily noon–2pm and 7–10pm.

Le Présidial DORDOGNE/FRENCH Its setting is a showstopper: a bulky Renaissance-era courthouse erected by King Henri II in 1558. Within an appropriately baronial dining room, or within a flowering garden, you'll select meals concocted from ingredients linked to the region, with ample use of foie gras, duckling, and truffles. Consider a pasta studded with sweetbreads and kidneys; roasted rack of spring lamb with mountain herbs; salmon in champagne sauce; medallions of veal in basil-flavored cream sauce; and some of the most succulent *mille-feuille* pastries in this part of France. Be warned that some diners have found the service lacking.

6 rue Landry. ✆ **05-53-28-92-47.** Reservations recommended. Set menus 35€–60€. AE, MC, V. Tues–Sat noon–1:30pm; Mon–Sat 7:30–10pm. Closed mid-Nov to Mar.

Le Quatre Saisons FRENCH Only in a town as rich in medieval monuments as Sarlat could a well-recommended restaurant be tucked into a 14th-century stone tower. You'll climb an exterior stairway to reach the dining room, which is outfitted in a minimalist contemporary style in tones of gray and soft orange. A separate corkscrew-style staircase leads upstairs to a terrace with additional tables and a view over town. Menu items might include foie gras with caramelized apples, lamb with an herb-cream sauce, and a moist chocolate cake served with licorice-flavored ice cream.

2 côte de Toulouse. ✆ **05-53-29-48-59.** www.4saisons-sarlat-perigord.com. Reservations recommended. Set-price menus 24€–48€. AE, DC, MC, V. Sept–June Thurs–Mon 12:15–1:30pm and 7:15–9:30pm; July–Aug daily 12:15–1:30pm and 7:15–9:30pm. Closed 1 week in Jan and 1 week in Mar.

Restaurant La Couleuvrine/Côté Bistrot La Couleuvrines ★ FRENCH The more formal dining room at this hotel (see review above) occupies a baronial hall with 13th-century stonework, massive ceiling beams, and a fireplace big enough to roast an ox. Menu items reflect local ingredients and might include a platter with both green and white asparagus and splashes of truffle-studded vinaigrette; foie gras of duckling with pear chutney; and a fricassee of scallops with prune liqueur and baby vegetables. Desserts usually include a brochette of fresh fruit with a creamy Sauterne-based sabayon.

If you happen to arrive at lunch, you'll be directed to "the Bistrot," where less complicated and less expensive platters of grilled fish and meat are featured, including meal-size salads and steaks with fried potatoes and creamy peppercorn sauce.

1 place de la Bouquerie, Sarlat 24200. ✆ **05-53-59-27-80.** Reservations recommended in the restaurant. Restaurant main courses 16€–29€; set menus 19€–32€; Bistrot main courses 10€–19€. AE, DC, MC, V. Restaurant daily 7:30–9pm; Sun noon–2pm. Bistro Mon–Sat noon–2pm.

ROCAMADOUR ★★★

541km (335 miles) SW of Paris; 66km (41 miles) SE of Sarlat-la-Canéda; 55km (34 miles) S of Brive; 63km (39 miles) NE of Cahors

Rocamadour reached the zenith of its fame and prosperity in the 13th century, when it was one of the most famous pilgrimage sites in Christendom. Countless miracles were said to have taken place there, thanks to the sacred aura of the Chapel of Notre-Dame and, specifically, the statue of the Black Madonna. Pilgrims still come here (in significantly smaller numbers), but most visitors are secular tourists who come to admire this spectacular village that seems to be carved into sheer rock. It's definitely worth a detour, even if it's out of your way. The setting is one of the most unusual in Europe: Towers, churches, and oratories rise in stages up the side of a cliff on the slope of the usually dry gorge of Alzou.

Rocamadour.

Only around 600 people live in the village year-round, but in the summer that numbers skyrockets during the day, when crowds of tourists arrive. For obvious logistical reasons, vehicles are prohibited in the town and there is a lot of stair climbing to do. The faint of heart or the mobility-impaired can take an elevator from the village at the base of the cliff up to the religious sanctuary, and from the religious sanctuary to the castle (see below). It's a short walk from the parking lot to the village.

Essentials

GETTING THERE The best way to reach Rocamadour is by **car.** From Bordeaux, travel east along A89 autoroute to Brive-la-Gaillarde, then take the A20 to exit 54 toward Gramat. Then continue on D840 and take the D673 south to Rocamadour.

Rocamadour and neighboring Padirac share a **train** station, **Gare de Rocamadour-Padirac,** that isn't really convenient to either—it's 4km (2½ miles) east of Rocamadour on N140. Trains arrive about five or six times a day from Brive in the north and Capdenac in the south; for transport from the station, your only option is to call a **taxi** (phone numbers posted at the station). For train information and schedules, call ✆ **36-35** or visit www.voyages-sncf.com. There is no **bus** service.

VISITOR INFORMATION The town maintains two separate **tourist offices,** one in the village Hôtel de Ville, rue Roland-le-Preux (✆ **05-65-33-62-59**), and another well-signposted branch office in l'Hospitalet, a small village in the heights that you will pass through on your way to Rocamadour (✆ **05-65-33-22-00;** www.rocamadour.com).

Exploring the Town

The **site** ★★★ of this gravity-defying village rises abruptly across the landscape. Its single street, lined with souvenir shops, runs along the side of a steep hill. It's best seen when approached from the road coming in from the tiny village of L'Hospitalet. Once in Rocamadour, you will want to get from the lower town (Basse Ville) to the town's **Cité Réligieuse,** a cluster of chapels and churches halfway up the cliff. The main way of getting from bottom to top is a narrow street/staircase that loops and twists its way upward. Called the "Chemin de la Croix," or the Stations of Christ, it was the route medieval penitents used to make their way to the sacred chapel—the most penitent did it on their knees.

For the unrepentant, and others who are loath to negotiate the town's steep inclines, the town maintains two elevators. One goes from Basse Ville to Cité Réligieuse, midway up the rocky heights of Rocamadour. The ride costs 2€ one-way, 3€ round-trip. The other goes from Cité Réligieuse to the panoramic medieval ramparts near the hill's summit; it costs 2.50€ one-way, 4€ round-trip.

For a superb **view**, head toward the **Château de Rocamadour,** which perches on a rock spur high above the town center. You can reach it by way of Chemin de la Croix or take the elevator. It was built in the 14th century and restored by the local bishops in the 19th century. Its interior is off-limits, except for guests of the church officials who live and work here. You can, however, walk along its panoramic **ramparts** ★★, which open at 8am daily year-round. Closing times vary, usually just before sunset and no later than 9pm in the summer. Admission to the ramparts costs 2€. ***Note:*** You must buy your entrance ticket at a machine; be sure to have exact change, or you will have made the trip up for nothing.

Cité Réligieuse ★★★ This cluster of chapels and churches is the town's religious centerpiece, visited by both casual tourists and devoted pilgrims. Site of many conversions, with mystical connotations that date to the Middle Ages, it's accessible from the town on the **Grand Escalier,** a stairway of 216 steps. Climbing the weathered steps will lead you to the **parvis des Eglises,** place St-Amadour, with seven chapels. Free tours are conducted by volunteers; schedules change frequently, according to holidays and church schedules. Two to five 1-hour tours take place each day (depending on the season); times are prominently posted at the entrance.

The three most important churches are detailed below.

Basilique St-Sauveur Set against the cliff, this small basilica was built in the Romanesque-Gothic style from the 11th to the 13th centuries. It's decorated with paintings and inscriptions recalling visits of celebrated persons, including Philippe the Handsome.

Chapelle Notre-Dame ★★ This is the "chapelle miraculeuse," the holy of holies, where St. Amadour is said to have carved out an oratory in the rock (who exactly St. Amadour was, however, is subject of debate). After caving in during the 15th century, it was rebuilt in flamboyant Gothic style, and it underwent various alterations in the 19th century, when it was restored. It shelters the venerated **Black Madonna** ★, a small sculpture carved out of wood that dates from the 12th century, depicting the Virgin seated with small but adult-looking Jesus on her knee. Hanging from the roof is a 9th-century **bell** that was rung when a miracle occurred. Outside, above the door leading to the chapel, is an iron sword stuck in the rock that is said to be **Durandal,** the sword of Roland, the legendary 8th-century knight.

Chapelle St-Michel ★ Sheltered by an overhanging rock on the outside of this Romanesque chapel are two impressive **12th-century frescoes** ★ representing the Annunciation and the Visitation. There are more frescoes inside, though many are damaged.

Free admission; donations appreciated. Suggested donation for tour 6€ adults, 3.50€ children 8–18. Daily 9am–11pm.

Where to Stay & Eat

Grand Hôtel Beau-Site ★ With its entrance evoking a medieval hall, this is one of the finest inns in the village. The stone walls were built in the 15th century by an Order of Malta commander, Jehan de Valon (1440–1516). Today the rear terrace provides a view of the Val d'Alzou. The reception area has heavy beams and a cavernous fireplace. Rooms (23 of which are in the air-conditioned main building, the rest in a less desirable annex) are comfortable and conservatively decorated; many have beautiful views, and some have spa bathtubs.

The restaurant serves regional cuisine prepared by the Menot family, which has owned the place for generations. Specialties include monkfish medallions with white beans and ginger, and duck magret with fig sauce. Dessert may be a slice of caramelized apple tart or Poire Belle Hélène (poached pears in chocolate sauce). Fixed-price menus cost 19€ at lunch and 26€ to 58€ at dinner.

Cité Médiévale, Rocamadour 46500. www.bw-beausite.com. ✆ **800/528-1234** in the U.S. and Canada, or 05-65-33-63-08. Fax 05-65-33-65-23. 38 units. 89€–145€ double. AE, DC, MC, V. Free parking. Closed mid-Nov to mid-Feb. **Amenities:** Restaurants; bar; free Internet; outdoor pool. *In room:* A/C, TV, hair dryer, free Wi-Fi.

Where to Stay & Eat Nearby

Château de La Treyne ★★ For a treat away from the tourist bustle, try this Relais & Châteaux property 20 minutes away, in Lacave. Built in the 14th and 17th centuries, this superb chateau sits on the edge of a particularly tranquil bend of the Dordogne River. Blessed with lush grounds and a classic French garden, the property is surrounded by 120 hectares (296 acres) of forest for hiking and truffle hunting. The spacious rooms feature Pierre Frey fabrics, antiques, and exposed beams; the more luxurious ones feel like private apartments from another era. The restaurant has been awarded a Michelin star for chef Andrieux's delectable creations, like langoustine risotto, foie gras in a spice crust, wild mushroom ravioli, and grilled Quercy lamb. If you've gone this far, you may as well indulge in an orange-rhubarb semolina roll with lemon-infused ice cream. Set menus are 48€ at lunch and 96€ to 138€ at dinner.

Lacave 46200. http://chateaudelatreyne.com. ✆ **05-65-27-60-60.** Fax 05-65-27-60-70. 16 units. 180€–420€ double; 480€–780€ suite. AE, DC, MC, V. Closed mid-Nov to Christmas and Jan to mid-Mar. Take the D32 and D247 from Rocamadour to Lacave. **Amenities:** Restaurant; bar, outdoor pool. *In room:* A/C, TV, hair dryer, minibar, free Wi-Fi.

Domaine de La Rhue ★ 🎁 This property's charming owners, Christine and Eric Jooris, gutted a 19th-century stable and turned it into a series of spacious and light-filled rooms, each simply but elegantly decorated in superb taste. Some have terraces, some have minibars, and all are equipped with compact bathrooms, mainly with shower units. On the lower level is an inviting reception and breakfast room with a welcoming fireplace. The Joorises, who speak English, are most helpful in directing you to the best places for dinner in the center of Rocamadour, a few minutes' drive away. Christine enjoys mapping out tours of nearby villages and plotting the best direction from which to approach each town or castle, to ensure a commanding view and to take advantage of afternoon sun for photographs. Eric is a pilot and can takes guests for a 45-minute hot-air balloon ride over the canyon of Rocamadour.

Rocamadour 46500. www.domainedelarhue.com. ✆ **05-65-33-71-50.** Fax 05-65-33-72-48. 14 units. 80€–160€ double. MC, V. Closed Nov–Easter. Follow D673, then N140 signposted RHUE for a total of 5km (3 miles) from town. **Amenities:** Outdoor pool; free Wi-Fi. *In room:* A/C (in some), hair dryer, minibar (in some), kitchenette (in some).

CAHORS ★

541km (335 miles) SW of Paris; 217km (135 miles) SE of Bordeaux; 89km (55 miles) N of Toulouse

The ancient capital of Quercy, Cahors was a thriving university city in the Middle Ages, and many antiquities from its illustrious past remain. Today Cahors is best known for the almost-legendary red wine that's made principally from the Malbec grapes grown in vineyards around this old city. Firm but not harsh, Cahors is one of the most deeply colored fine French wines.

Since the mid-1990s, the city of Cahors has funded the redesign and replanting of at least 21 municipal gardens, most of them laid out in medieval patterns, using historically appropriate plants. The most spectacular of these gardens lie immediately adjacent to Town Hall. Overall, they function as a magnet for horticultural societies throughout France.

Essentials

GETTING THERE To **drive** to Cahors from Toulouse, follow the A62 autoroute north to the junction with A20 and continue on A20 north into Cahors.

Trains serve Cahors from Toulouse, Brive, and Montauban. For train information and schedules, call ✆ **36-35** or visit www.voyages-sncf.com. There's infrequent **bus** service from some of the outlying villages, several of which are of historical interest, but it's vastly easier to drive.

VISITOR INFORMATION The **Office de Tourisme** is on place François-Mitterrand (✆ **05-65-53-20-65;** fax 05-65-53-20-74; www.tourisme-cahors.com).

SPECIAL EVENTS The **Festival du Blues** turns this town upside down for 3 days in mid-July, when blues groups, including some from the United States, descend. Most of the performances are free outdoor affairs along boulevard Gambetta. Main concerts are usually at the open-air **Théâtre des Verdures,** a courtyard in the heart of the medieval city. Tickets are 25€ to 39€. For exact dates and information, contact the Office de Tourisme (see above) or visit the site of **Cahors Blues Festival** (www.cahorsbluesfestival.com). You can buy tickets on the website or at any Fnac bookstore (www.fnac.fr)

Exploring the Area

The town is on a rocky peninsula almost entirely surrounded by a loop of the Lot River. It grew near a sacred spring that still supplies the city with water. At the source of the spring, the **Fontaine des Chartreux** stands by the side of **pont Valentré ★★** (also called pont du Diable), a bridge with a trio of towers. It's a magnificent example of medieval defensive design erected between 1308 and 1380 and restored in the 19th century. The pont, the first medieval fortified bridge in France, is the most eye-catching site in Cahors, with crenelated parapets, battlements, and pointed arches.

Pont Valentré.

Dominating the old town, the **Cathédrale St-Etienne ★**, 30 rue de la Chanterie (✆ **05-65-35-27-80**), was begun in 1119 and reconstructed between 1285 and 1500. It was the first cathedral in the country to have cupolas, giving it a Romanesque-Byzantine look. One remarkable feature is its sculptured Romanesque north portal, carved around 1135 in the Languedoc style. It's open daily from 9am to 7pm; in winter the cathedral is closed Sunday mornings. Adjoining the cathedral are the remains of a Gothic cloister from the late 15th century. The admission-free cloister is open during the same hours as the cathedral.

Where to Stay

Hôtel de France Hotel choices are limited in Cahors, but these 1970s-era lodgings, positioned midway between pont Valentré and the train station, provide some of the best rooms in the town center. They're well furnished and modern, if not particularly chic. Each unit comes with an average-size bathroom, most with a shower unit. Breakfast is the only meal served, but there are plenty of restaurants nearby.

252 av. Jean-Jaurès, Cahors 46000. www.hoteldefrance-cahors.fr. ✆ **05-65-35-16-76.** Fax 05-65-22-01-08. 39 units. 69€ double. AE, DC, MC, V. Parking 1.50€. *In room:* A/C, TV, hair dryer, minibar, free Wi-Fi.

Hôtel Terminus ★ On the avenue leading from the railway station into the heart of town, this hotel oozes turn-of-the-20th-century character with its original stone construction. Rooms are conservative yet tasteful, with floral prints, fresh flowers, and firm beds. On the premises is Le Balandre, the town's best restaurant, which specializes in regional dishes from the surrounding Périgord-Quercy district. Fixed-price menus are 18€ to 31€ at lunch and 36€ to 75€ at dinner. Even if you don't opt for a meal in its quaint dining room or on the outdoor terrace, you may want to stop into the 1920s-style bar for a drink.

5 av. Charles de Freycinet, Cahors 46000. www.balandre.com. ✆ **05-65-53-32-00.** Fax 05-65-53-32-26. 21 units. 70€–100€ double; 130€–160€ suite. AE, DC, MC, V. Parking free in courtyard, 7€ in garage. Closed last 2 weeks in Nov. **Amenities:** Restaurant; bar; room service; free Wi-Fi. *In room:* TV, hair dryer, minibar.

Where to Eat

Le Balandre, the restaurant at **Hôtel Terminus** (see above), serves well-recommended cuisine.

Le Rendez-Vous ★ FRENCH One of the most appealing restaurants in Cahors's historic core occupies the stone-walled, ocher-colored premises of a 13th-century private house. It turns out an array of well-prepared and reasonably priced dishes that guarantee an animated crowd. Menu items change with the season but may include fried foie gras with spice bread; a tart layered with anchovies and confit of onions; and superb farm-raised veal.

49 rue Clément Marot. ✆ **05-65-22-65-10.** Reservations recommended. Main courses 14€; fixed-price lunch 16€, dinner 22€. MC, V. Tues–Sat noon–2pm and 7:30–9:30pm.

L'O à la Bouche ★ MODERN FRENCH One of Cahors's best brasseries recently moved to a restored mansion from the turn of the 20th century in the center of town. Meals at this popular spot involve full fixed-price menus, each with a choice of at least four food items per category (that is, a minimum of four starters, four main courses, and four desserts). Menu items might include fresh trout from the Pyrenees served with leeks in vinaigrette, and medallions of chicken stuffed with cèpes. The wine list includes an excellent sampling of Cahors vintages.

56 allée Fénelon. ✆ **05-65-35-65-69.** Reservations recommended. Fixed-price menu 27€. MC, V. Tues–Sat noon–1:30pm and 7–9:30pm.

SIDE TRIP TO LIMOGES ★

396km (246 miles) S of Paris; 311km (193 miles) N of Toulouse; 93km (58 miles) NE of Périgueux

Limoges, the ancient capital of Limousin in west-central France, is world famous for its exquisite porcelain and enamel works. Enamel production is a medieval industry revived in the 19th century and still going strong. In fact, Limoges is the economic capital of western France. Occupying the Vienne's right bank, the town has historically consisted of two parts: La Cité (aka Vieux Limoges), with its narrow streets and old *maisons* on the lower slope, and La Ville Haute (aka "Le Château"), at the summit.

Essentials

GETTING THERE Limoges has good **train** service from most regional cities, with direct trains from Toulouse, Poitiers, and Paris. Ten trains depart daily from Paris's Gare d'Austerlitz for Limoges (trip time: 3 hr.; 52€ one-way). There are 12 trains a day from Périgueux (trip time: 1 hr.; 15€ one-way). For complete train information, call ✆ **36-35** or 08-92-35-35-35 (calls cost 0.34€ per min.) or visit www.voyages-sncf.fr. **Bus** transit in and out of the small towns and villages nearby can be arranged through the **Régie des Transports de la Haute-Vienne,** place des Charentes (✆ **05-55-10-31-10;** www.rdthv.com). If you're **driving** from Périgueux, take N21 north for the 1½-hour trip. If driving from Cahors, take A20 north for the 2-hour trip.

VISITOR INFORMATION The **Office de Tourisme** is at 12 bd. de Fleurus (✆ **05-55-34-46-87;** fax 05-55-34-19-12; www.tourismelimoges.com).

Exploring the Town

If you'd like to see an enameler at work or an operating porcelain factory, ask at the tourist office (see above) for a list of workshops, or go directly to the famous **Pavillon de la Porcelaine** (see below).

Thanks to the rich deposits of kaolin (known locally as "white gold") found near Limoges in the 18th century, more than 30 manufacturers of porcelain have set up operations through the years. Many maintain factory outlets, sometimes offering good-quality seconds at reduced prices. In the center of town, you'll find **Raynaud,** 14 ancienne rte. d'Aixe (✆ **05-55-01-77-65**), and **Porcelaines Philippe Deshoulières-Lafarge,** 77bis rue Armand Dutreix (✆ **05-55-50-33-43**). Largest of all, with the best publicity operation, is **Bernardaud,** 27 av. Albert-Thomas (✆ **05-55-10-55-91**), where a small-scale museum (focusing on past porcelain-related triumphs) and a tearoom adjoin the showroom.

Cathédrale St-Etienne The cathedral was begun in 1273 and took years to complete. The choir was finished in 1327, but work continued in the nave until almost 1890. The cathedral is the only one in the old province of Limousin built entirely in the Gothic style. The main entrance is through Porte St-Jean, which has carved wooden doors from the 16th century (constructed at the peak of the Flamboyant Gothic style). Inside, the nave appears so harmonious it's hard to imagine that its construction took 6 centuries. The rood screen is of particular interest, built in 1533 in the ornate style of the Italian Renaissance. The cathedral also contains some admirable bishops' tombs from the 14th to the 16th centuries.

Place de l'Evêché. ✆ **05-55-34-46-87.** Free admission. Mon–Sat 2:30–5pm, Sun 2:30–6pm.

Limoges.

Eglise St-Michel-des-Lions Two stone lions guard the entrance to this church. Constructed between the 14th and 16th centuries, it features a typically Limousin bell tower surmounted by a strange copper globe and splendid vaulting supported by slender pillars. Despite its name, the church is the center of the cult of St-Martial, a Limoges hometown bishop who died in the 3rd century. The church is the home of what's reputed to be his skull, stored in an elaborately enameled reliquary. Les Ostensions is a religious pilgrimage, established in 994, that occurs every 7 years from February to November. The skull, La Châsse de St-Martial—which some believers credit with healing powers—is removed from storage and exhibited as part of religious processions that attract as many as 100,000 devout adherents. The next such procession is scheduled for 2016.

Place St-Michel. ✆ **05-55-34-46-87.** Free admission. Mon–Sat 8am–6pm; Sun 8–11:45am and 4–6pm.

Musée des Beaux-Arts de Limoges Reopened at the end of 2010 with much fanfare, the former municipal museum has been renovated, with double its space and a new museography to live up to its new title as a museum of fine arts. The main part of the museum is housed in the 18th-century archbishops' palace, now joined by luminous modern galleries for temporary exhibitions. It is surrounded by the Jardins de l'Evêché, which offer a view of the Vienne and the 13th-century pont St-Etienne. The collections are divided into four parts: an outstanding collection of Limoges enamels from the 12th century to the present day; an Egyptian collection of 2,000 pieces; archaeology, sculptures, and stained glass from now-defunct abbeys; and fine art, including works by Auguste Renoir, who was born in Limoges.

1 place de l'Evêché. ✆ **05-55-45-98-10.** www.museebal.fr. Free admission to permanent collections; temporary exhibitions 5€ adults, 3€ age 18 and under. Apr–Sept Wed–Mon 10am–6pm; Oct–Mar Mon and Wed–Sat 10am–noon and 2–5pm, Sun 2–5pm.

Musée National de la Porcelaine Adrien-Dubouché ★★ This museum, in a 19th-century building, has the largest public collection of Limoges porcelain. Its 12,000 pieces illustrate the history of glassmaking and ceramics (porcelain, earthenware, stoneware, and terra cotta) throughout the ages. In France, its porcelain collection is second in quantity only to that of Sèvres. The main gallery contains whole dinner sets of noted figures and some contemporary Limoges ware.

Limoges porcelain.

8 bis place Winston-Churchill. ✆ **05-55-33-08-50.** www.musee-adriendubouche.fr. Admission 4.50€ adults, 3€ ages 6–18. Wed–Mon 10am–12:25pm and 2–5:40pm.

Pavillon de la Porcelaine–Musée Haviland Haviland has been exporting its porcelain to the United States and other countries since 1842, when a group of American entrepreneurs immigrated to France from Boston to found the first American-owned company ever established in Europe. Over the years, it has used the designs of artists such as Gauguin and Dalí. In the museum, you can see masterpieces as well as original pieces created for the U.S. White House. A video screening can tell you more about the manufacturing process, and a large shop also sells the porcelain.

40 av. John-Kennedy. ✆ **05-55-30-21-86.** www.haviland-limoges.com. Free admission. Mid-Mar to June daily 10am–1pm and 2–6:30pm; July–Aug daily 10am–6:30pm; Sept to mid-Mar Mon–Sat 10am–1pm and 2–6:30pm.

Where to Stay

Best Western Hotel Richelieu ★ Not far from the town center, this hotel in a 1930s building was recently renovated with an attractive contemporary decor using quality fabrics. Extras like free Wi-Fi, tea- and coffee-making in the room, slippers, and an exercise room make it a good value.

40 av. Baudin. www.hotel-richelieu.com. ✆ **05-55-34-22-82.** Fax 05-55-34-35-36. 43 units. 88€–118€ double. AE, DC, MC, V. **Amenities:** Bar; breakfast room; exercise room. *In room:* A/C, TV, hair dryer, minibar (in some), free Wi-Fi.

Mercure Limoges Royal Limousin What it lacks in individuality, this Mercure hotel makes up for in centrality. Rooms are generally quite spacious and comfortable. Accommodations on the noisier avenue Carnot side cost less than those on the quieter place de la République. There's no restaurant, but the staff can recommend several in the neighborhood.

Place de la République. www.mercure.com. ✆ **05-55-34-65-30.** Fax 05-55-34-55-21. 76 units. 90€–140€ double. AE, DC, MC, V. **Amenities:** Bar; breakfast room; room service. *In room:* A/C, TV, hair dryer, minibar, free Wi-Fi.

Where to Eat

Le Versailles FRENCH Set on a busy commercial boulevard near the center of town, this is a deeply entrenched staple of conservative French cuisine that's always mentioned as one of the town's most visible, most professional, and most consistent dining spots. The rooms that contain it haven't changed much (especially the wood paneling and mirrors) since it was built in 1928. Since the restaurant opened in 1932, it seems everybody in town has been here at least once.

Today the menu remains relatively conservative, but with long lists of flavorful and freshly made food.

20 place d'Aine. ✆ **05-55-34-13-39.** Reservations recommended. Main courses 15€–32€; set-price menus 17€ (weekday lunch), 24€ and 29€ (dinner). AE, MC, V. Daily noon–2:30pm and 7:30–11:30pm. Bus: 4 or 10.

Where to Stay & Eat Nearby

IN ST-MARTIN-DU-FAULT

La Chapelle St-Martin ★★★ This is the best place in the area if you enjoy early-1900s living and superb food in the tradition of the Relais & Châteaux group. The hotel is in a private park with two ponds. The tasteful rooms are individually decorated with a 19th-century theme, usually Directoire or Empire. The restaurant offers excellent French food, with fixed-price menus ranging from 45€ to 89€.

Nieul. 12km (7½ miles) northwest of Limoges taking D947 (rue de Bellac) for 1.5km (1 mile) then turning left onto D35 which will take you all the way there. www.chapellesaintmartin.com. ✆ **05-55-75-80-17.** Fax 05-55-75-89-50. 13 units. 125€–220€ double; 260€–390€ suite. AE, DC, MC, V. Free parking. Hotel closed Jan 1–Feb 5. Reserve well in advance. Restaurant Apr–June and Sept–Oct Tues–Sun 12–2pm and 7:30–10pm; July and Aug daily 12–2pm and 7:30–10pm; Nov–Mar Thurs–Sun 12–2pm, Tues–Sat 7:30–10pm **Amenities:** Restaurant; outdoor pool; room service; tennis court. *In room:* A/C (in some), TV, hair dryer, minibar, free Wi-Fi.

IN NIEUIL

Note: Don't confuse Nieuil with La Chapelle St-Martin (see above) at Nieul, with a slightly different spelling.

Château de Nieuil ★★ A perfect provincial château, this place comes with quite a pedigree. The château, built in the 16th century as a hunting lodge for François I, became the first château-hotel in France in 1937. Restored by the comte de Dampierre early in the 1800s after its destruction in the Revolution, it has remained in the antiques-collecting Bodinaud family since around 1900. Rooms are beautifully furnished and magnificently comfortable, with elegant bathrooms. Today 160 hectares (395 acres) of park and forest surround a series of beautifully maintained gardens.

The restaurant, La Grange aux Oies (the Goose Farm), is in a stone-walled annex constructed in the late 19th century as stables. The cuisine focuses on classic and regional recipes. Main courses cost 20€ to 28€, fixed-price menus are 46€ to 70€, and there is a kids' menu for 16€. Nonguests may dine here if they call ahead.

Nieuil. 64km (40 miles) west of Limoges, taking the N141 (signposted ANGOULEME) and turning right at the D739. www.chateaunieuilhotel.com. ✆ **05-45-71-36-38.** Fax 05-45-71-46-45. 14 units. 135€–280€ double; 265€–435€ suite. AE, DC, MC, V. Closed Nov–Apr. **Amenities:** Restaurant; bar; outdoor pool; room service; tennis court. *In room:* A/C, TV, hair dryer, minibar, free Wi-Fi.

20

PLANNING YOUR TRIP TO FRANCE

Of almost any destination in the world, flying into France is one of the most effortless undertakings in global travel. There are no shots to get, no particular safety precautions, no unusual aspects of planning a trip. With your passport, airline ticket, and enough money, you just go. Of course, before you lift off the ground in your native country, you can do some advance preparation. In the pages that follow, you'll find everything you need to know about the practicalities of planning your trip.

GETTING THERE

AIRPORTS

The two Paris airports—Orly (airport code: ORY) and Charles de Gaulle (airport code: CDG)—are about even in terms of convenience to the city's center, though taxi rides from Orly may take less time than those from de Gaulle. Orly, the older of the two, is 13km (8 miles) south of the center; Charles de Gaulle is 22km (14 miles) northeast. Air France serves Charles de Gaulle (Terminal 2C) from North America. U.S. carriers land at both airports.

Most airlines charge their lowest fares between November 1 and March 13. Shoulder season (Oct and mid-Mar to mid-June) is a bit more expensive, though we think it's the ideal time to visit France.

THE MAJOR AIRLINES

American Airlines (© **800/433-7300;** www.aa.com) has daily flights to Paris from Dallas–Fort Worth, Chicago, Miami, Boston, and New York.

British Airways (© **800/247-9297;** www.britishairways.com) offers flights from 18 U.S. cities to Heathrow and Gatwick airports in England. From there, you can connect to a British Airways flight to Paris.

Continental Airlines (© **800/231-0856;** www.continental.com) provides nonstop flights to Paris from Newark and Houston. Flights from Newark depart daily; flights from Houston depart four to seven times a week, depending on the season.

Delta Air Lines (© **800/221-1212;** www.delta.com) flies nonstop from Atlanta to Paris every evening and operates daily nonstop flights from Cincinnati and New York. Delta is the only airline offering nonstop service from New York to Nice.

US Airways (© **800/428-4322;** www.usairways.com) offers daily nonstop service from Philadelphia to Paris.

The French national carrier, **Air France** (© **800/237-2747;** www.airfrance.com), offers daily flights between Paris and such North American cities as Atlanta, Boston, Chicago, Cincinnati, Houston, Los Angeles, Mexico City, Miami, Montreal, New York, Newark, San Francisco, Toronto, and Washington, D.C.

PREVIOUS PAGE: **Musée d'Orsay in Paris.**

In 2004, Air France acquired control of KLM Royal Dutch Airlines, which led to the creation of **Air France–KLM,** the world's biggest airline in terms of revenue. KLM and Air France have coordinated their schedules and fares and are acting as a unit. The merger has led to better connections between flights.

FLIGHTS FROM AUSTRALIA & NEW ZEALAND

Getting to Paris from Australia is difficult because **Air France** (**© 02/92-44-21-00;** www.airfrance.fr) has discontinued direct flights. Qantas flies from Sydney to Singapore and other locations, with service to Paris. Consequently, on virtually any route, you have to change planes at least once and sometimes twice. **British Airways** (**© 1300/767-177;** www.britishairways.com) flies daily from Sydney and Melbourne to London, where you can catch one of several connecting flights to Paris. **Qantas** (**© 612/13-13-13;** www.qantas.com.au) can route passengers from Australia into London, where you make connections for the hop across the Channel. Qantas also flies from Auckland to Sydney and on to London.

GETTING THERE FROM THE U.K. & CONTINENTAL EUROPE

By Plane

From London, **Air France** (**© 0870/142-4343;** www.airfrance.com) and **British Airways** (**© 0844/493-0787** in the U.K.; www.britishairways.com) fly frequently to Paris; the trip takes 1 hour. These airlines operate up to 17 flights daily from Heathrow. Many travelers also fly out of the London City Airport in the Docklands.

Direct flights to Paris operate from other U.K. cities, such as Manchester and Edinburgh. Contact Air France, British Airways, or **British Midland** (**© 0870/607-0555;** www.flybmi.com). Daily papers often carry ads for cheap flights. Highly recommended **Trailfinders** (**© 0845/058-5858;** www.trailfinders.com) sells discount fares.

You can reach Paris from any major European capital. Your best bet is to fly on the national carrier, Air France, which has more connections into Paris from European capitals than any other airline. From Dublin, try **Aer Lingus** (**© 800/IRISH-AIR** [474-7424]; www.aerlingus.com), which schedules the most flights to Paris from Ireland. From Amsterdam, try **NWA/KLM** (**© 800/225-2525;** www.nwa.com).

By Train

Paris is one of Europe's busiest rail junctions, with trains arriving at and departing from its many stations every few minutes. If you're in Europe, you may want to go to Paris by train. The cost is relatively low—especially compared to renting a car.

Rail passes as well as individual rail tickets are available at most travel agencies or at any office of **Rail Europe** (**© 888/382-7245** in the U.S.; www.raileurope.com) or **Eurostar** (**© 800/EUROSTAR** [387-6782] in the U.S.; www.eurostar.com).

By Bus

Bus travel to Paris is available from London, as well as from many cities on the Continent. In the early 1990s, the French government established incentives for long-haul buses not to drive into the center of Paris. The arrival and departure point for Europe's largest operator, **Eurolines France,** 28 av. du Général-de-

Gaulle, 93541 Bagnolet (✆ **08-92-89-90-91;** www.eurolines.fr), is a 35-minute Métro ride from central Paris, at the terminus of line no. 3 (Métro: Gallieni), in the eastern suburb of Bagnolet. Despite this inconvenience, many people prefer bus travel.

Long-haul buses are equipped with toilets, and they stop at mealtimes for rest and refreshment.

Because Eurolines does not have a U.S. sales agent, most people buy their tickets in Europe. Any European travel agent can arrange the sale. If you're traveling to Paris from London, contact **Eurolines (U.K.) Ltd.,** 52 Grosvenor Gardens, Victoria, London SW1 0AU (✆ **0871/781-81-81;** www.national express.com for information or credit card sales).

By Car

The major highways into Paris are A1 from the north (Great Britain and Benelux); A13 from Rouen, Normandy, and northwest France; A10 from Bordeaux, the Pyrénées, the southwest, and Spain; A6 from Lyon, the French Alps, the Riviera, and Italy; and A4 from Metz, Nancy, and Strasbourg in the east.

By Ferry from England

Ferries and hydrofoils operate day and night, with the exception of last-minute cancellations during storms. Many crossings are timed to coincide with the arrival and departure of trains (especially those btw. London and Paris). Trains let you off a short walk from the piers. Most ferries carry cars, trucks, and freight, but some hydrofoils take passengers only. The major routes include at least 12 trips a day between Dover or Folkestone and Calais or Boulogne.

Hovercraft and hydrofoils make the trip from Dover to Calais, the shortest distance across the Channel, in just 40 minutes during good weather. The ferries may take several hours, depending on the weather and tides. If you're bringing a car, it's important to make reservations—space below decks is usually crowded. Timetables can vary depending on weather conditions and many other factors.

The leading operator of ferries across the channel is **P&O Ferries** (✆ **0871/664-5645** in the U.K.; www.poferries.com). It operates car and passenger ferries between Portsmouth, England, and Cherbourg, France (three departures a day; 4 hr., 15 min. each way during daylight hours; 7 hr. each way at night); and between Portsmouth and Le Havre, France (three a day; 5½ hr. each way). Most popular is the route between Dover, England, and Calais, France (25 sailings a day; 75 min. each way).

GETTING AROUND

BY PLANE

France has few domestic competitors. **Air France** (✆ **800/237-2747;** www.airfrance.com) is the primary carrier, serving about eight cities in France and eight others in Europe. Air travel time from Paris to almost anywhere in France is about an hour.

BY CAR

The most charming châteaux and country hotels always seem to lie away from the main cities and train stations. Renting a car is often the best way to travel around France, especially if you plan to explore it in depth.

But Europe's rail networks are so well developed and inexpensive that we recommend you rent a car only for exploring areas little serviced by rail, such as

Brittany, rural Burgundy, and the Dordogne. Or take trains between cities and rent a car on the days when you want to explore independently.

Driving time in Europe is largely a matter of conjecture, urgency, and how much sightseeing you do along the way. Driving time from Paris to Geneva is 5½ hours minimum. It's 2½ hours from Paris to Rouen, 3½ hours to Nantes, and 4 hours to Lyon. The driving time from Marseille to Paris (771km/478 miles) is a matter of national pride, and tall tales abound about how rapidly the French can do it. Flooring it, you may conceivably get there in 7 hours, but we always make a 2-day journey of it.

RENTALS To rent a car, you'll need to present a passport, a driver's license, and a credit card. You also have to meet the company's minimum-age requirement. (For the least expensive cars, this is 21 at Hertz, 23 at Avis, and 25 at Budget. More expensive cars may require that you be at least 25.) It usually isn't obligatory within France, but certain companies have asked for the presentation of an International Driver's License, even though this is becoming increasingly superfluous in Western Europe.

Note: The best deal is usually a weekly rental with unlimited mileage. All car-rental bills in France are subject to a 19.6% government tax. Though the rental company won't usually mind if you drive your car into, say, Germany, Switzerland, Italy, or Spain, it's often forbidden to transport your car by ferry, including across the Channel to England.

In France, **collision damage waiver (CDW)** is usually factored into the overall rate quoted, but you should always verify this, of course, before taking a car on the road. At most companies, the CDW provision won't protect you against theft, so if this is the case, ask about purchasing extra theft protection.

Automatic transmission is a luxury in Europe, so if you want it, you'll pay dearly.

Budget (✆ **800/472-3325;** www.budget.com) has about 30 locations in Paris and at Orly (✆ **01-49-75-56-05**) and Charles de Gaulle (✆ **01-48-62-70-22**). For rentals of more than 7 days, you can usually pick up a car in one French city and drop it off in another, but there are extra charges. Drop-offs in cities within an easy drive of the French border (including Geneva and Frankfurt) incur no extra charge; you can arrange drop-offs in other non-French cities for a reasonable surcharge.

Hertz (✆ **800/654-3001** in the U.S. and Canada; www.hertz.com) maintains about 15 locations in Paris, including offices at the city's airports. The main office is at 27 place St-Ferdinand, 17e (✆ **01-45-74-97-39;** Métro: Argentine). Be sure to ask about promotional discounts. **Avis** (✆ **800/331-1084** in the U.S. and Canada; www.avis.com) has offices at both Paris airports and an inner-city headquarters at 5 rue Bixio, 7e (✆ **01-44-18-10-50;** Métro: Ecole Militaire), near the Eiffel Tower.

National (✆ **800/CAR-RENT** [227-7368] in the U.S. and Canada; www.nationalcar.com) is represented in Paris by Europcar, one office is at 78 rue du Rocher, 8e (✆ **01-45-22-77-91;** Métro: St-Philippe du Roule). It has offices at both Paris airports and at about a dozen other locations. For the lowest rates, reserve in advance from North America.

Two U.S.-based agencies that don't have Paris offices but act as booking agents for Paris-based agencies are **Kemwel Drive Europe** (✆ **877/820-0668;** www.kemwel.com) and **Auto Europe** (✆ **888/223-5555;** www.

autoeurope.com). They can make bookings in the United States only, so call before your trip.

GASOLINE Known in France as *essence,* gas is expensive for those accustomed to North American prices. All but the least expensive cars usually require an octane rating that the French classify as *essence super,* the most expensive variety. Depending on your car, you'll need either leaded *(avec plomb)* or unleaded *(sans plomb)*.

Beware the mixture of gasoline and oil, called *mélange* or *gasoil,* sold in some rural communities; this mixture is for very old two-cycle engines.

Note: Sometimes you can drive for miles in rural France without encountering a gas station; don't let your tank get dangerously low.

DRIVING RULES Everyone in the car, in both the front and the back seats, must wear seat belts. Children 11 and under must ride in the back seat. Drivers are supposed to yield to the car on their right, except where signs indicate otherwise, as at traffic circles.

If you violate the speed limit, expect a big fine. Limits are about 130kmph (81 mph) on expressways, about 100kmph (62 mph) on major national highways, and 90kmph (56 mph) on country roads. In towns, don't exceed 60kmph (37 mph).

Note: It's illegal to use a cellphone while you're driving in France; you will be ticketed if you're stopped.

MAPS For France as a whole, most motorists opt for **Michelin map 989** (www.viamichelin.com). For regions, Michelin publishes a series of **yellow maps** that are quite good. Big travel-book stores in North America carry these maps, and they're commonly available in France (at lower prices). In this age of congested traffic, one useful feature of the Michelin map is its designations of alternative *routes de dégagement,* which let you skirt big cities and avoid traffic-clogged highways.

Another recommended option is *Frommer's Road Atlas Europe.*

BREAKDOWNS/ASSISTANCE A breakdown is called *une panne* in France. Call the police at © **17** anywhere in France to be put in touch with the nearest garage. Most local garages offer towing. If the breakdown occurs on an expressway, find the nearest roadside emergency phone box, pick up the phone, and put a call through. You'll be connected to the nearest breakdown service facility.

BY TRAIN

The world's fastest trains link some 50 French cities, allowing you to get from Paris to just about anywhere else in the country in hours. With 39,000km (24,180 miles) of track and about 3,000 stations, SNCF (French National Railroads) is fabled for its on-time performance. You can travel in first or second class by day and in couchette by night. Many trains have dining facilities.

INFORMATION If you plan to travel a lot on European railroads, get the latest copy of the *Thomas Cook Timetable of European Passenger Railroads.* This 500-plus-page book documents all of Europe's main passenger rail services with detail and accuracy. It's available online at www.thomascookpublishing.com.

In the United States: For more information and to purchase rail passes before you leave, contact **Rail Europe** (© **877/272-RAIL** [272-7245]; www.raileurope.com).

In Canada: Call Rail Europe at ✆ **800/361-RAIL** [361-7245].

In London: SNCF has offices at Rail Europe, 179 Piccadilly, London W1V 0BA (✆ **0870/584-8848**).

In Paris: For information or reservations, go online (www.sncf.fr). You can also go to any local travel agency. A simpler way to buy tickets is to use the *billetterie* (ticket machine) in every train station. If you know your PIN, you can use a credit card to buy your ticket.

FRANCE RAIL PASSES Working cooperatively with SNCF, Air Inter Europe, and Avis, Rail Europe (www.railfrance.com) offers three flexible rail passes to North Americans that can reduce travel costs considerably.

The **France Railpass** provides unlimited rail transport in France for any 3 days within 1 month, at $315 in first class and $269 in second. You can purchase up to 6 more days for an extra $48 per person per day. Children 4 to 11 travel for half-price.

The **France Rail 'n' Drive Pass,** available only in North America, combines good value on both rail travel and Avis car rentals. It is best used by arriving at a major rail depot and then striking out to explore the countryside by car. It includes the France Railpass (see above) and use of a rental car. A 2-day rail pass (first class) and 2 days' use of the cheapest rental car (with unlimited mileage) is $534 to $612 per person. The best deal if you're traveling in France with a friend—or even three or four friends—is the **France Saverpass,** granting 3 days of unlimited travel in a 1-month period. The cost is $268 per person first class or $231 second class. There's also a **France Youthpass** for travelers 25 or under, granting 3 days of unlimited train travel within a month. The cost is $233 in first class or $200 in second class. For those over 60, the **France Senior Pass** offers all the same features as the France Railpass, but with a savings. You get 3 days of unlimited train travel in 1 month for $288, with additional rail days costing $43 each. Travel days may be used consecutively or nonconsecutively.

A **France Rail Day Pass** allows you to take day trips from Paris to such cities as Lyon, Reims, Dijon, or Nantes. The cost is $162 in first class or $114 in second class. The pass grants you 1 day of unlimited travel in a 1-month period on the national rail network.

EURAILPASS The Eurailpass permits unlimited first-class rail travel in any country in western Europe except the British Isles (good in Ireland). Passes are available for purchase online (www.eurail.com) and at various offices/agents around the world. Travel agents and railway agents sell Eurailpasses. You can purchase them at the North American offices of CIT Travel Service, the French National Railroads, the German Federal Railroads, and the Swiss Federal Railways. It is strongly recommended that you purchase passes before you leave home, as not all passes are available in Europe; also, passes purchased in Europe will cost about 20% more. Numerous options are available for travel in France.

The **Eurail Global Pass** allows you unlimited travel in 20 Eurail-affiliated countries. You can travel on any of the days within the validity period, which is available for 15 days, 21 days, 1 month, 2 months, 3 months, and some other possibilities as well. Prices for first-class adult travel are $798 for 15 days, $1,034 for 21 days, $1,285 for 1 month, $1,813 for 2 months, and $2,236 for 3 months. Children 4 to 11 pay half fare; those 3 and under travel for free.

A **Eurail Global Pass Saver,** also valid for first-class travel in 20 countries, offers a special deal for two or more people traveling together. This pass costs $676 for 15 days, $878 for 21 days, $1,090 for 1 month, $1,541 for 2 months, and $1,908 for 3 months.

A **Eurail Global Youth Pass** for those 12 to 25 allows second-class travel in 18 countries. This pass costs $518 for 15 days, $671 for 21 days, $836 for 1 month, $1,179 for 2 months, and $1,457 for 3 months.

The **Eurail Select Pass** offers unlimited travel on the national rail networks of any three, four, or five bordering countries out of the 22 Eurail nations linked by train or ship. Two or more passengers can travel together for big discounts, getting 5, 6, 8, 10, or 15 days of rail travel within any 2-month period on the national rail networks of any three, four, or five adjoining Eurail countries linked by train or ship. A sample fare: For 5 days in 2 months, you pay $504 for three countries. **Eurail Select Pass Youth,** for travelers under 26, allows second-class travel within the same guidelines as Eurail Selectpass, with fees starting at $328. **Eurail Select Pass Saver** offers discounts for one or more people traveling together in first-class travel within the same guidelines as Eurail Select Pass, with fees starting at $428.

20 [FastFACTS] FRANCE

Area Codes All French telephone numbers consist of 10 digits, the first two of which are like an area code. If you're calling anywhere in France from within France, just dial all 10 digits. If you're calling from the United States, drop the initial 0 (zero). See "Telephones" later in this section for further information.

Business Hours Business hours in France are erratic. Most banks are open Monday through Friday from 9:30am to 4:30pm. Many, particularly in small towns, take a lunch break. Hours are usually posted on the door. Most museums close 1 day a week (often Tues), and they're generally closed on national holidays. Usual hours are from 9:30am to 5pm. Refer to the individual listings. Generally, offices are open Monday through Friday from 9am to 5pm, but always call first. In Paris or other big French cities, stores are open from 9, 9:30, or (often) 10am to 6 or 7pm, without a break for lunch. Some shops, delis, cafes, and newsstands open at 8am and close at 8 or 9pm. In some small stores, the lunch break can last 2 hours, beginning at 1pm. This is more common in the south than in the north.

Car Rental See "Getting There by Car," earlier in this chapter.

Cellphones See "Mobile Phones," later in this section.

Crime See "Safety," later in this section.

Customs **What you can bring into France:** Citizens of E.U. countries can bring in any amount of goods, as long as the goods are intended for their personal use and not for resale. Non-E.U. citizens are entitled to 200 cigarettes, 100 small cigars, 50 cigars, or 250g of tobacco duty-free. You can also bring in 2 liters of wine or beer and 1 liter of spirits (more than 22% alcohol). In addition, you can bring in 50g (1.76 oz.) of perfume.

What you can take out of France:

Australian Citizens A helpful brochure is available from the Australian Customs and Border Protection Service: *Know Before You Go,* online under "Information for Travelers." For more information, call the **Australian Customs Service** (✆ **1300/363-263,** or 612/6275-6666 if you're abroad; www.customs.gov.au). The duty-free allowance in Australia is A$900, or, for those 17 or younger, A$450. If you're returning with valuables you already own, you should file the "Goods Imported in Passenger Baggage" form.

Canadian Citizens For a clear summary of Canadian rules, ask for the booklet *I Declare,* issued by the **Canada Border Services Agency** (✆ **800/461-9999** in Canada, or 204/983-3500 from abroad; www.cbsa-asfc.gc.ca, under "Going on Vacation?"). Canada allows its citizens a C$750 exemption, and you're allowed to mail gifts to Canada from abroad valued at less than C$60 a day, provided they're unsolicited and don't contain alcohol or tobacco (write on the package "Unsolicited gift, under C$60 value"). All valuables, including serial numbers of valuables you already own, should be declared on the Y-38 form before departure from Canada.

New Zealand Citizens The answers to most questions regarding customs can be found on the website of the **New Zealand Customs Service** (✆ **0800/4-CUSTOMS** [0800/428-786], or 649/300-5399 from outside New Zealand; www.customs.govt.nz).The duty-free allowance for New Zealand is NZ$700. Fill out a certificate of export listing the valuables you are taking out of the country so that you can bring them back without paying duty.

U.K. Citizens When returning to the U.K. from an E.U. country such as France, you can bring in an unlimited amount of most goods. There is no limit on what you can bring back from an E.U. country, as long as the items are for personal use (this includes gifts) and you have already paid the duty and tax. However, if you bring in more than these levels, you may be asked to prove that the goods are for your own use. For information, contact **HM Revenue Customs** (✆ **0845/010-9000;** www.hmrc.gov.uk).

U.S. Citizens For specifics on what you can bring back and the corresponding fees, download the invaluable free pamphlet *Know Before You Go,* online at **www.cbp.gov**. Or contact the **U.S. Customs & Border Protection (CBP)** (✆ **877/CBP-5511** [227-5511], or 703/526-4200 for international calls). Returning U.S. citizens who have been away for 48 hours or more are allowed to bring back, once every 30 days, $800 worth of merchandise duty-free. You're charged a flat rate of duty on the next $1,000 worth of purchases, and any dollar amount beyond that is subject to duty at whatever rates apply. On mailed gifts, the duty-free limit is $200. To avoid having to pay duty on foreign-made personal items you owned before your trip, bring along a bill of sale, insurance policy, jeweler's appraisal, or receipt of purchase, or register items before you leave. You cannot bring fresh foodstuffs into the U.S.

Disabled Travelers Facilities for travelers in France, and nearly all modern hotels, provide accessible rooms. Older hotels (unless they've been renovated) may not provide elevators, special toilet facilities, or wheelchair ramps. The TGVs (high-speed trains) are wheelchair accessible; older trains have compartments for wheelchair boarding. If you visit the Paris tourist office's website (www.parisinfo.com) and click on "Paris Pratique," you'll find links to a number of guides and websites dedicated to travelers with disabilities. With the exception of Line 14 and several other stations, most Paris Métro lines do not have disabled access and are not always equipped with either escalators or elevators. Buses are a much better option for disabled visitors, as many lines are now equipped with lowering floors and space for wheelchairs. RER lines and some SNCF services are wheelchair accessible (call ✆ **08-10-64-64-64,** or look at www.infomobi.com for a useful disabled-access version of the Paris Métro map).

Doctors Doctors are listed in the Pages Jaunes (French equivalent of the Yellow Pages; www.pagesjaunes.fr) under "Médecins: Médecine générale." If you're using the website, you can search for a doctor by typing the town in the "Où" box. The minimum fee for a consultation is about 23€—for this rate, look for a doctor who is described as "conventionée secteur 1." The higher the "secteur," the higher the fee. **SOS Médecins** (✆ **36-24** or 01-47-07-77-77) makes house calls, which cost 70€ before 7pm and from 110€ after 7pm or on holidays (prices quoted are for people without French social security). See also "Emergencies" and "Health" later in this section.

Drinking Laws Supermarkets, grocery stores, and cafes sell alcoholic beverages. The legal drinking age is 18, but persons under that age can be served alcohol in a bar or restaurant if accompanied by a parent or legal guardian. The law regarding drunk driving is tough. Motorists are considered "legally intoxicated" if their blood-alcohol limit exceeds .05%. If it is under .08% (the limit in the U.K., Ireland, and some U.S. states) the driver faces a fine of 135€. Over .08%, and it could cost 4,500€ or up to two years in jail. If you cause an accident while driving drunk, the fine could be increased to 30,000€, and if you cause serious injury or death, you face 10 years in jail and a fine of up to 150,000€.

Driving Rules The French drive on the right. At junctions where there are no signposts indicating the right of way, cars coming from the right have priority. Many roundabouts now give priority to those on the roundabout. If this is not indicated, priority is for those coming from the right.

Drugstores You'll spot French *pharmacies* by looking for the green neon cross above the door. If your local pharmacy is closed, there should be a sign on the door indicating the nearest one open. You can also have the front-desk staff at your hotel contact the nearest Commissariat de Police; an agent there will have the address of a nearby pharmacy open 24 hours a day. *Parapharmacies* sell medical products and toiletries, but they don't dispense prescriptions. In Paris, one of the most central all-nighters is the **Pharmacie des Champs-Elysées** (84 av. des Champs-Elysées; Métro: George V; ✆ **01-45-62-02-41**). See also "Emergencies" and "Health" later in this section.

Electricity Electricity in France runs on 220 volts AC (60 cycles). Adapters or transformers are needed to fit sockets, which you can buy in branches of Darty, FNAC or BHV. Many hotels have two-pin (in some cases, three-pin) sockets for electric razors.

Embassies & Consulates If you have a passport, immigration, legal, or other problem, contact your consulate. Call before you go—they often keep odd hours and observe both French and home-country holidays.

The Embassy of **Australia** is at 4 rue Jean-Rey, 15e (✆ **01-40-59-33-00;** www.france.embassy.gov.au; Métro: Bir Hakeim), open Monday to Friday 9am to noon and 2 to 4pm.

The Embassy of **Canada** is at 35 av. Montaigne, 8e (✆ **01-44-43-29-00;** www.amb-canada.fr; Métro: Franklin-D-Roosevelt or Alma-Marceau), open Monday to Friday 9am to noon and 2 to 5pm.

The Embassy of **Ireland** is at 4 rue Rude, 16e (✆ **01-44-17-67-00;** www.embassyofireland.fr; Métro: Etoile), open Monday to Friday 9:30am to noon.

The embassy of **New Zealand** is at 7ter rue Léonard-de-Vinci, 16e (✆ **01-45-01-43-43;** www.nzembassy.com; Métro: Victor Hugo), open Monday to Thursday 9am to 1pm and 2 to 5:30pm, Friday 9am to 1pm and 2 to 4pm.

The Embassy of the **United Kingdom** is at 35 Rue du Faubourg St-Honoré, 8e (✆ **01-44-51-31-00;** http://ukinfrance.fco.gov.uk; Métro: Concorde or Madeleine), open Monday to Friday 9:30am to 1pm and 2:30 to 6pm.

The Embassy of the **United States,** 2 av. Gabriel, 8e (✆ **01-43-12-22-22;** http://france.usembassy.gov; Métro: Concorde), is open Monday to Friday 9am to 6pm.

Emergencies In an emergency while at a hotel, contact the front desk. Most staffs are trained in dealing with a crisis and will do whatever is necessary. If the emergency involves something like a stolen wallet, go to the police station in person. Otherwise, call ✆ **112** from a mobile phone, or call the fire brigade *(Sapeurs-Pompiers)* at ✆ **18;** they are trained to deal with all kinds of medical emergencies, not just fires. For an ambulance, call ✆ **15.** For the police, call ✆ **17.**

Etiquette & Customs Parisians like pleasantries and take manners seriously: Say "Bonjour, Madame/Monsieur" when entering an establishment and "Au revoir" when you depart. Always say "Pardon" when you accidentally bump into someone. With strangers, people who are older than you, and professional contacts, use *vous* rather than *tu* (*vous* is the polite form of the pronoun *you*).

Family Travel To locate accommodations, restaurants, and attractions that are particularly kid-friendly, look for the "Kids" icon throughout this guide.

Health For travel abroad, Non-E.U. nationals should consider buying medical travel insurance. For U.S. citizens, Medicare and Medicaid do not provide coverage for medical costs incurred abroad, so check what medical services your health insurance covers before leaving home. U.K. nationals will need a **European Health Insurance Card (EHIC)** to receive free or reduced-cost medical care during a visit to a European Economic Area (EEA) country or Switzerland (go to www.ehic.org.uk for further information).

Pack prescription medications in your carry-on luggage and carry them in their original containers, with pharmacy labels—otherwise, they won't make it through airport security. Carry the generic name, in case a local pharmacist is unfamiliar with the brand name.

For further tips on travel and health concerns, and a list of local English-speaking doctors, contact the **International Association for Medical Assistance to Travelers** (**IAMAT;** ✆ **716/754-4883** in the U.S., or **416/652-0137** in Canada; www.iamat.org). You can also find listings of reliable medical clinics overseas at the **International Society of Travel Medicine** (www.istm.org). See also "Doctors," "Drugstores," "Emergencies," and "Hospitals."

Holidays Major holidays are New Year's Day (Jan 1), Easter Sunday and Monday (late Mar/Apr), May Day (May 1), VE Day (May 8), Ascension Thursday (40 days after Easter), Pentecost/Whit Sunday and Whit Monday (seventh Sun and Mon after Easter), Bastille Day (July 14), Assumption Day (Aug 15), All Saints Day (Nov 1), Armistice Day (Nov 11), and Christmas Day (Dec 25). For more information on holidays, see "France Calendar of Events," p. 54.

Hospitals Dial ✆ **15** for medical emergencies. In Paris, the **American Hospital,** 63 bd. Victor-Hugo, in the suburb of Neuilly-sur-Seine (✆ **01-46-41-25-25**; www.american-hospital.org; Métro: Pont-de-Levallois or Pont-de-Neuilly; bus no. 82), operates a

24-hour emergency service. The bilingual staff accepts Blue Cross and other American insurance plans. Hospitals in other major cities include **Hôpital Rouen,** 1 rue de Germont (✆ **02-32-88-89-90;** www.chu-rouen.fr), in Rouen; **Hôpital Bretonneau,** 2 bd. Tonnellé (✆ **02-47-47-80-29;** www.chu-tours.fr), in Tours; **Hôpital Civil de Strasbourg,** 1 place de l'Hôpital (✆ **03-88-11-67-68;** www.chru-strasbourg.fr), in Strasbourg; **Hôpital Edouard Herriot,** 5 place Arsonval (✆ **08-20-08-20-69**), in Lyon; **Hôpital de Avignon,** 305 rue Raoul Follereau (✆ **04-32-75-33-33**), in Avignon; **Hôpital St-Roch,** 5 rue Pierre Dévoluy (✆ **04-92-03-33-33**), in Nice; and **CHU de Rangueil,** av. du Prof. Jean-Poulhes (✆ **05-61-32-25-33**), in Toulouse.

Hot Lines S.O.S. Help is a hotline for English-speaking callers in crisis at ✆ **01-46-21-46-46** (www.soshelpline.org). Open 3 to 11pm daily.

Internet & Wi-Fi In French cities, many hotels and cafes have Internet access, and Wi-Fi (pronounced *wee-fee*) is becoming increasingly common in cafes and public spaces. There are also hundreds of cybercafes all over France. To find cybercafes, check **www.cybercaptive.com** and **www.cybercafe.com**. A reasonably priced option in Paris is **Luxembourg Micro,** 81 bd. Saint-Michel, 5e (✆ **01-46-33-27-98;** Métro: Luxembourg; www.luxembourg-micro.com). It's open daily from 9am to 10pm.

Language English is increasingly understood in France, especially among younger people who have studied it in school. People are more likely to understand English in centers such as Paris and the Riviera than in the more remote provinces. Service personnel in hotels tend to speak English, at least at the front desk. For handy French words and phrases, as well as food and menu terms, refer to chapter 21, "Useful Terms & Phrases." A good phrasebook is *Frommer's French PhraseFinder & Dictionary.*

Legal Aid In an emergency, especially if you get into trouble with the law, your country's embassy or consulate will provide legal advice. See "Embassies & Consulates" on p. 756.

LGBT Travelers France is one of the world's most tolerant countries toward gays and lesbians. "Gay Paree" boasts a large gay population, with many clubs, restaurants, organizations, and services. Lesbian or bisexual women can pick up a copy of ***Lesbia.*** This publication and others are available at Paris's largest, best-stocked gay bookstore, **Les Mots à la Bouche,** 6 rue Ste-Croix-de-la-Bretonnerie, 4e (✆ **01-42-78-88-30;** www.motsbouche.com; Métro: Hôtel-de-Ville), which carries publications in both French and English. In addition, both www.paris-gay.com and www.gayvox.com have updated listings about the gay and lesbian scene and events.

Lost & Found To speed the process of replacing your personal documents if they're lost or stolen, make a photocopy of the first few pages of your passport and write down your credit card numbers. Leave this information with someone at home (to be called in an emergency) and your traveling companion. If your credit card is stolen, you can call **American Express** (call collect U.S. ✆ **336-393-1111**), **MasterCard** (✆ **08-00-90-13-87;** www.mastercard.com), or **Visa** (✆ **08-00-90-13-87;** www.visaeurope.com). In Paris, all lost objects—except those found in train stations or on trains—are taken to the **Bureau des Objets Trouvés** (36 rue des Morillons, 15e ✆ **08-21-00-25-25;** www.prefecture-police-paris.interieur.gouv.fr). It's better to visit in person than to call, but be warned that there are huge delays in processing claims. It's open from Monday to Thursday 8:30am to 5pm and Friday 8:30am to 4:30pm. Objects lost on the Métro are held by the station agents before being sent on to the Bureau des Objets Trouvés. If you lose something on a train or in a train station, go to the Lost Property office of the SNCF station in question.

Mail Most post offices in France are open Monday to Friday from 8am to 5pm and every Saturday from 8am to noon. Allow 5 to 8 days to send or receive mail from home. Stamps are also sold in *tabacs* (tobacconists). Tariffs depend on the weight and size of the letter or package, but more information can be found at www.laposte.fr.

Medical Requirements Unless you are arriving from an area of the world known to be suffering from an epidemic, especially cholera or yellow fever, inoculations or vaccinations are not required for entry in France.

Mobile Phones The three letters that define much of the world's wireless capabilities are **GSM** (Global System for Mobile Communications), a big, seamless network that makes for easy cross-border mobile phone use throughout Europe and dozens of other countries worldwide. You can use your mobile phone in France, provided it is GSM and triband or quad-band; just confirm this with your operator before you leave.

Using your phone abroad can be expensive, and you usually have to pay to receive calls, so it's a good idea to get it "unlocked" before you leave. This means you can buy a SIM card from one of the three French providers: **Bouygues Télécom** (www.bouygestelecom.fr), **Orange** (www.orange.fr), or **SFR** (www.sfr.fr). A SIM card with 5€ call credit costs about 10€. Alternatively, if your phone isn't unlocked, you can buy a cheap mobile phone. To top-up your phone credit, buy a Mobicarte from *tabacs,* supermarkets, and mobile phone outlets. Prices range from 5€ to 100€.

Money & Costs Frommer's lists exact prices in the local currency. The currency conversions quoted were correct at press time. However, rates fluctuate, so before departing, consult a currency exchange website such as www.oanda.com/convert/classic to check up-to-the-minute rates.

THE VALUE OF THE EURO VS. OTHER POPULAR CURRENCIES

EURO (€)	US$	C$	UK £	A$	NZ$
1	1.37	1.36	0.86	1.38	1.77

It's always advisable to bring money in a variety of forms on a vacation: a mix of cash, credit cards, and traveler's checks. You should also exchange enough petty cash to cover airport incidentals, tipping, and transportation to your hotel before you leave home, or withdraw money upon arrival at an airport ATM. In many international destinations, ATMs offer the best exchange rates. Avoid exchanging money at commercial exchange bureaus and hotels, which often have the highest transaction fees. ATMs are widely available in Paris, but if you're venturing into rural France, it's always good to have cash in your pocket.

Not just Paris, but all of France is a very expensive destination. To compensate, you can often find top-value food and lodging. Part of the cost is the value-added tax (VAT in English, TVA in French), which adds between 6% and 33% to everything. Rental cars (and fuel) are expensive, and flying within France costs more than within the U.S. Train travel is relatively inexpensive, especially with a rail pass. Prices in Paris and on the Riviera are higher than in the provinces. Three of the most visited areas—Brittany, Normandy, and the Loire Valley—have reasonably priced hotels and restaurants.

Visa (known as Carte Bleue in French) is the most common credit card in France, but most international credit cards are widely used. In an attempt to reduce credit card fraud, French credit cards are issued with an embedded chip and a PIN to authorize transactions. Non-French cards (which don't have a chip) do work, but they print a slip that requires a signature. This does mean, however, that they cannot be used in automated machines, such as those in Métro stations. There are still shops, restaurants, and bars, often family run, that don't accept credit or debit cards, so it's always good to both check in advance and have cash on you. The minimum amount you have to spend to use a credit or debit card is slowly decreasing, but in some shops and bars—again, often smaller businesses—it can be as high as 15€.

You can buy traveler's checks at most banks, and they are widely accepted in France, although, frankly, merchants prefer cash. They are offered in denominations of $20, $50, $100, $500, and sometimes $1,000. Generally, you'll pay a service charge ranging from 1% to 4%. The most popular traveler's checks are offered by **American Express, Visa,** and **MasterCard.** You can change traveler's checks at most post offices. If you carry traveler's checks, keep a record of their serial numbers separate from your checks, in the event that they are stolen or lost—you'll get your refund faster.

For help with currency conversions, tip calculations, and more, download Frommer's convenient Travel Tools app for your mobile device. Go to www.frommers.com/go/mobile/ and click on the Travel Tools icon.

Multicultural Travelers See "Safety," later in this section.

Newspapers & Magazines Only 20% of French people read a national paper. The most famous is the serious, center-left **Le Monde,** which is strong on both politics and economic issues. **Le Figaro** is more conservative and tends to favor lifestyle features over controversial issues. **Libération,** founded in the late 1960s by Jean-Paul Sartre and Simone de Beauvoir, has good news and arts coverage and is considered more left-wing.

English-language newspaper *International Herald-Tribune,* based in Paris and published Monday to Saturday, is distributed all over France and sold at newspaper kiosks and in the lobbies of first-class hotels. Copies of ***Time*** and ***Newsweek*** are also widely sold. A far larger selection of U.K. magazines and newspapers is available. London newspapers arrive in Paris an hour or so after publication.

Passports Citizens of the U.K., New Zealand, Australia, Canada, and the United States need a valid passport to enter France. The passport is valid for a stay of 90 days. To prevent international child abduction, E.U. governments have initiated procedures at entry and exit points. These often (but not always) include requiring documentary evidence of relationship and permission for the child's travel from the parent or legal guardian not present. Having such documentation on hand, even if not required, facilitates entries and exits. All children must have their own passports.

Allow plenty of time before your trip to apply for a passport; processing normally takes 3 weeks but can take longer during busy periods (especially spring). Keep in mind that if you need a passport in a hurry, you'll pay a higher processing fee.

For Residents of Australia: You can pick up an application from your local post office or any branch of Passports Australia. Visit the government website at www.passports.gov.au for more details.

For **Residents of Canada:** Passport applications are available at Passport Canada agencies throughout Canada. Forms and further information can be found at www.ppt.gc.ca).

For Residents of Ireland: You can apply for a passport using the Passport Express service at most post offices. Further information can be found at www.foreignaffairs.gov.ie.

For Residents of New Zealand: You can pick up a passport application at any New Zealand Passports Office or download it from their website, www.passports.govt.nz.

For Residents of the United Kingdom: To pick up an application for a passport, visit your nearest passport office or major post office, or download the forms from the website www.ips.gov.uk.

For **Residents of the United States:** Whether you're applying in person or by mail, you can download passport applications from the U.S. State Department website at http://travel.state.gov.

Police In an emergency, call ✆ **17** or **112** from a mobile anywhere in France.

Safety The most common menace, especially in large cities—particularly Paris—is the plague of pickpockets. Take precautions and be vigilant at all times: Don't take more money with you than necessary, keep your passport in a concealed pouch or leave it at your hotel, and ensure that your bag is firmly closed at all times. In cafes, bars, and restaurants, it's best not to leave your bag under the table or on the back of your chair. Keep it between your legs or on your lap, to avoid it being stolen. Never leave valuables in a car, and never travel with your car unlocked.

Much of the country, particularly central France, the northeast, Normandy, and Brittany, remains relatively safe, although no place in the world is crime-free. Those intending to visit the south of France, especially the Riviera, should exercise caution; robberies and muggings are more likely to occur here than in other parts of the country. It's best to check your baggage into a hotel and then go sightseeing instead of leaving it unguarded in the trunk of a car, which can easily be broken into. Marseille is among the most dangerous French cities.

In general, Paris is a safe city and it is safe to use the Métro late at night. However, certain Métro stations (and the areas around them) are best avoided at night: Châtelet-Les Halles, Gare du Nord, Barbès Rochechouart, and Strasbourg St-Denis. Violent incidents and robberies have been known on the RER, particularly RER B, so it is best to find alternative transport to and from the airport (such as buses or taxis) late at night or early in the morning. Also, around the major sites, it is quite common to be approached by a young Roma girl and asked if you speak English. It's best to avoid these situations, and any incident that might occur, by shaking your head and walking away.

Most nonwhite travelers won't experience any problems. Although there is a significant level of discrimination against West and North African immigrants, there has been almost no harassment of African-American tourists to Paris or France itself. **S.O.S. Racisme** (51 av. de Flandre, 19e (✆ **01-40-35-36-55;** www.sos-racisme.org) offers legal advice to victims of prejudice and will even intervene to help with the police.

Female travelers should not expect any more hassle than in other major cities, and the same precautions apply. Avoid walking alone at night and never get into an unmarked taxi. If you are approached in the street or on public transportation, it's best to avoid entering into conversation and walk away.

Senior Travel Many discounts are available to seniors—men and women over 60. Although they often seem to apply to residents of E.U. countries, it pays to announce at the ticket window of a museum or monument that you are 60 years old or more. You may not receive a discount, but it doesn't hurt to ask. "Senior," incidentally, is pronounced *seenyore* in France. Senior citizens do not get a discount for traveling on public transport in Paris, but there are senior discounts on national trains. Check out www.voyages-sncf.com for further information. Frommers.com offers more information and resources on travel for seniors.

Smoking Smoking is now banned in all public places in France, including cafes, restaurants, bars, and nightclubs.

Student Travel Student discounts are less common in France than other countries, but simply because young people under 26 are usually offered reduced rates. Some discounts apply only to residents of E.U. countries, but it's worth carrying ID to prove your age and announcing it when buying tickets. Look out for the **Ticket Jeune** when using the Métro in Paris. It can be used on a Saturday, Sunday, or bank holiday, and provides unlimited travel in zones 1 to 3 for 3.40€. SNCF also offer discounts for under-26-year-olds traveling on national trains (www.voyages-sncf.com).

Taxes As a member of the European Union, France routinely imposes a value-added tax (VAT in English; TVA in French) on most goods. The standard VAT is 19.6%, and prices that include it are often marked TTC (*toutes taxes comprises*, "all taxes included"). If you're not an E.U. resident, you can get a VAT refund if you're spending less than 6 months in France, you purchase goods worth at least 175€ at a single shop on the same day, the goods fit into your luggage, and the shop offers *vente en détaxe* (duty-free sales or tax-free shopping). Give them your passport and ask for a *bordereau de vente à l'exportation* (export sales invoice). This is then signed by the retailer and yourself. When you leave the country, you need to get all three pages of this invoice validated by France's customs officials. They'll keep one sheet, and you must post the pink one back to the shop. Once the shop receives its stamped copy, it will send you a *virement* (fund transfer) using the payment method you requested. It may take several months.

Telephones Public phones can still be found in France. They all require a phone card (known as a *télécarte*), which can be purchased at post offices, *tabacs,* supermarkets, SNCF ticket windows, Métro stations, and anywhere you see a blue sticker reading *"Télécarte en vente ici"* ("Phone card for sale here"). They cost 7.50€ for 50 calling units and 15€ for 120 units.

The country code for France is 33. To make a local or long-distance call within France, dial the 10-digit number of the person or place you're calling. Mobile numbers begin with 06. Numbers beginning with 0-800, 0-804, 0-805, and 0-809 are free in France; other numbers beginning with 8 are not. Most four-digit numbers starting with 10, 30, and 31 are free of charge.

For operator assistance and French directory inquiries, dial ✆ **12.**

Time France is on Central European Time, which is 1 hour ahead of Greenwich Mean Time. French daylight saving time lasts from the last Sunday in March to the last Sunday in October, when clocks are set 1 hour ahead of the standard time.

Tipping By law, all bills in **cafes, bars, and restaurants** say *service compris,* which means the service charge is included. However, it is customary to leave 1€ or 2€, depending on the quality of the service. **Taxi drivers** usually expect a 5% to 10% tip, or for the fare to be rounded up to the next euro. The French give their **hairdressers** a tip of about 15%, and if you go to the theater, you're expected to tip the **usher** about 2€.

Toilets If you're in dire need, duck into a cafe or brasserie to use the lavatory. It's customary to make a small purchase if you do so. Paris is full of gray-colored automatic street toilets, which are free to use and are washed and disinfected after each use. France still has some hole-in-the-ground squat toilets, so be warned.

VAT See "Taxes," earlier in this section.

Visas E.U. nationals don't need a visa to enter France. Nor do U.S., Canadian, Australian, New Zealand, or South African citizens for trips of up to 3 months. Nationals of other countries should make inquiries at the nearest French embassy or consulate before they travel to France. If Non-E.U. citizens wish to stay for longer than 3 months, they must apply to a French embassy or consulate for a long-term visa.

Visitor Information Before you go, your best source of information is the **French Government Tourist Office** (www.franceguide.com), which can be reached at the following addresses:

- **United States:** 825 Third Ave., 29th Floor, New York, NY 10022 (✆ **514/288-1904;** fax 212/838-7855); 205 N. Michigan Ave., Chicago, IL 60601 (✆ **514/288-1904**); or 9454 Wilshire Blvd., Ste. 715, Beverly Hills, CA 90212 (✆ **514/288-1904**)
- **Canada:** 1800 av. McGill College, Ste. 490, Montreal, QC H3A 2W9 (✆ **514/288-2026;** fax 514/845-4868)
- **United Kingdom:** 178 Piccadilly, London W1J 9AL (✆ **09068/244-123** [60p per min.]; fax 020/7493-6594)
- **Australia:** 25 Blight St., Sydney, NSW 2000 (✆ **02/9231-5244;** fax 02/9221-8682)

Water Drinking water is generally safe. If you ask for water in a restaurant, it'll be served bottled (for which you'll pay), unless you specifically request *l'eau de robinet* (tap water). Your waiter may ask if you'd like your water *avec gas* (carbonated) or *sans gas* (without bubbles).

Wi-Fi See "Internet & Wi-Fi," earlier in this section.

Women Travelers See "Safety," earlier in this section.

21

USEFUL TERMS & PHRASES

GLOSSARY OF FRENCH-LANGUAGE TERMS

It's often amazing how a word or two of halting French will change your hosts' dispositions in their home country. At the very least, try to learn a few numbers, basic greetings, and—above all—the life raft, *"Parlez-vous anglais?"* As it turns out, many French do speak passable English and will use it liberally if you demonstrate the basic courtesy of greeting them in their language. Go on, try our glossary out, and don't be bashful. *Bonne chance!*

BASICS

English	French	Pronunciation
Yes/No	Oui/Non	**wee/nohn**
Okay	D'accord	**dah-*core***
Please	S'il vous plaît	**seel voo *play***
Thank you	Merci	**mair-*see***
You're welcome	De rien	**duh ree-*ehn***
Hello (during daylight hours)	Bonjour	**bohn-*jhoor***
Good evening	Bonsoir	**bohn-*swahr***
Goodbye	Au revoir	**o ruh-*vwahr***
What's your name?	Comment vous appellez-vous?	**ko-mahn voo za-pell-ay-*voo*?**
My name is . . .	Je m'appelle . . .	**jhuh ma-*pell* . . .**
Happy to meet you	Enchanté(e)	**ohn-shahn-*tay***
Miss	Mademoiselle	**mad-mwa-*zel***
Mr.	Monsieur	**muh-*syuh***
Mrs.	Madame	**ma-*dam***
How are you?	Comment allez-vous?	**kuh-mahn tahl-ay-*voo*?**
Fine, thank you, and you?	Très bien, merci, et vous?	**tray bee-ehn, mare-ci, ay *voo*?**
Very well, thank you	Très bien, merci	**tray bee-ehn, mair-*see***
So-so	Comme ci, comme ça	**kum-*see*, kum-*sah***
I'm sorry/excuse me	Pardon	**pahr-*dohn***
I'm so very sorry	Désolé(e)	**day-zoh-*lay***
That's all right	Il n'y a pas de quoi	**eel nee ah pah duh kwah**

GETTING AROUND/STREET SMARTS

English	French	Pronunciation
Do you speak English?	Parlez-vous anglais?	**par-lay-voo ahn-*glay*?**
I don't speak French	Je ne parle pas français	**jhuh ne parl pah frahn-*say***
I don't understand	Je ne comprends pas	**jhuh ne kohm-*prahn* pas**
Could you speak more loudly/ more slowly?	Pouvez-vous parler un peu plus fort/plus lentement?	**poo-vay-voo par-lay un puh ploo for/ploo lan-te-*ment*?**

Could you repeat that?	Répetez, s'il vous plaît?	**ray-pay-*tay*, seel voo *play***
What is it?	Qu'est-ce que c'est?	**kess kuh *say*?**
What time is it?	Qu'elle heure est-il?	**kel uhr eh-*teel*?**
What?	Quoi?	**kwah?**
How? or What did you say?	Comment?	**ko-*mahn*?**
When?	Quand?	**kahn?**
Where is . . . ?	Où est . . . ?	**ooh eh . . . ?**
Who?	Qui?	**kee?**
Why?	Pourquoi?	**poor-*kwah*?**
Here/there	ici/là	**ee-*see*/lah**
Left/right	à gauche/à droite	**a goash/a drwaht**
Straight ahead	tout droit	**too drwah**
I'm American/Canadian/British	Je suis américain(e)/ canadien(e)/anglais(e)	**jhe sweez a-may-ree-*kehn*/can-ah-dee-*en*/ ahn-glay (*glaise*)**
Fill the tank (of a car), please	Le plein, s'il vous plaît	**luh plan, seel voo *play***
I'm going to . . .	Je vais à . . .	**jhe vay ah . . .**
I want to get off at . . .	Je voudrais descendre à . . .	**jhe voo-*dray* day-son-drah ah**
I'm sick	Je suis malade	**jhuh swee mal-*ahd***
airport	l'aéroport	**lair-o-*por***
bank	la banque	**lah bahnk**
bridge	pont	**pohn**
bus station	la gare routière	**lah gar roo-tee-*air***
bus stop	l'arrèt de bus	**lah-*ray* duh boohss**
by means of a bicycle	en vélo/par bicyclette	**ahn *vay*-low/par bee-see-*clet***
by means of a car	en voiture	**ahn vwa-*toor***
cashier	la caisse	**lah *kess***
cathedral	cathédral	**ka-tay-*dral***
church	église	**ay-*gleez***
dead end	une impasse	**ewn am-*pass***
driver's license	permis de conduire	**per-mee duh con-*dweer***
elevator	l'ascenseur	**lah-sahn-*seuhr***
stairs	l'escalier	**les-kal-*yay***
entrance (to a building or a city)	une porte	**ewn port**

English	French	Pronunciation
exit (from a building or a freeway)	une sortie	**ewn sor-*tee***
fortified castle or palace	château	**sha-*tow***
garden	jardin	**jhar-*dehn***
gasoline	du pétrol/de l'essence	**duh pay-*trol*/de lay-*sahns***
ground floor	rez-de-chausée	**ray-de-show-*say***
highway to . . .	la route pour	**la root por**
hospital	l'hôpital	**low-pee-*tahl***
luggage storage	consigne	**kohn-*seen*-yuh**
museum	le musée	**luh mew-*zay***
no entry	sens interdit	**sehns ahn-ter-*dee***
no smoking	défense de fumer	**day-*fahns* de fu-may**
on foot	à pied	**ah pee-*ay***
1-day pass	ticket journalier	**tee-kay jhoor-nall-ee-*ay***
one-way ticket	aller simple	**ah-*lay sam*-pluh**
police	la police	**lah po-*lees***
rented car	voiture de location	**vwa-*toor* de low-ka-see-on**
round-trip ticket	aller-retour	**ah-*lay*-re-*toor***
second floor	premier étage	**prem-ee-*ehr* ay-*taj***
slow down	ralentir	**rah-lahn-*teer***
store	le magasin	**luh ma-ga-*zehn***
street	rue	**roo**
subway	le Métro	**le *may*-tro**
telephone	le téléphone	**luh tay-lay-*phone***
ticket	un billet	**uh *bee*-yay**
ticket office	vente de billets	**vahnt duh bee-*yay***
toilets	les toilettes/les WC	**lay twa-*lets*/lay vay-*say***

NECESSITIES

English	French	Pronunciation
I'd like . . .	Je voudrais . . .	**jhe voo-*dray* . . .**
a room	une chambre	**ewn *shahm*-bruh**
the key	la clé (la clef)	**la *clay***

English	French	Pronunciation
I'd like to buy . . .	Je voudrais acheter . . .	**jhe voo-dray ahsh-*tay* . . .**
aspirin	des aspirines/des aspros	**deyz ahs-peer-*eens*/ deyz ahs-*prohs***
condoms	des préservatifs	**day pray-ser-va-*teefs***
dictionary	un dictionnaire	**uh deek-see-oh-*nare***
dress	une robe	**ewn robe**
envelopes	des envelopes	**days ahn-veh-*lope***
gift (for someone)	un cadeau	**uh kah-*doe***
handbag	un sac	**uh sahk**
hat	un chapeau	**uh shah-*poh***
magazine	une revue	**ewn reh-*vu***
map of the city	un plan de ville	**unh plahn de *veel***
matches	des allumettes	**dayz a-loo-*met***
necktie	une cravate	**eun cra-*vaht***
newspaper	un journal	**uh jhoor-*nahl***
phone card	une carte téléphonique	**Ewn cart tay-lay-fone-*eek***
postcard	une carte postale	**ewn carte pos-*tahl***
road map	une carte routière	**ewn cart roo-tee-*air***
shirt	une chemise	**ewn che-*meez***
shoes	des chaussures	**day show-*suhr***
skirt	une jupe	**ewn jhoop**
soap	du savon	**dew sah-*vohn***
socks	des chaussettes	**day show-*set***
stamp	un timbre	**uh *tam*-bruh**
trousers	un pantalon	**uh pan-tah-*lohn***
writing paper	du papier à lettres	**dew pap-pee-*ay a let*-ruh**
How much does it cost?	C'est combien? / Ça coûte combien?	**say comb-bee-*ehn*?/ sah coot comb-bee-*ehn*?**
That's expensive	C'est cher/chère	**say share**
That's inexpensive	C'est raisonnable/C'est bon marché	**say ray-son-*ahb*-bluh/ say bohn mar-*shay***
Do you take credit cards?	Est-ce que vous acceptez les cartes de credit?	**es-kuh voo zaksep-*tay* lay kart duh creh-*dee*?**

NUMBERS & ORDINALS

English	French	Pronunciation
zero	zéro	**zare-*oh***
one	un	**uh**
two	deux	**duh**
three	trois	**twah**
four	quatre	***kaht*-ruh**
five	cinq	**sank**
six	six	**seess**
seven	sept	**set**
eight	huit	**wheat**
nine	neuf	**nuf**
ten	dix	**deess**
eleven	onze	**ohnz**
twelve	douze	**dooz**
thirteen	treize	**trehz**
fourteen	quatorze	**kah-*torz***
fifteen	quinze	**kanz**
sixteen	seize	**sez**
seventeen	dix-sept	**deez-*set***
eighteen	dix-huit	**deez-*wheat***
nineteen	dix-neuf	**deez-*nuf***
twenty	vingt	**vehn**
twenty-one	vingt-et-un	**vehnt-ay-*uh***
twenty-two	vingt-deux	**vehnt-*duh***
thirty	trente	**trahnt**
forty	quarante	**ka-*rahnt***
fifty	cinquante	**sang-*kahnt***
sixty	soixante	**swa-*sahnt***
sixty-one	soixante-et-un	**swa-*sahnt*-et-*uh***
seventy	soixante-dix	**swa-sahnt-*deess***
seventy-one	soixante-et-onze	**swa-sahnt-et-*ohnze***
eighty	quatre-vingts	**kaht-ruh-*vehn***
eighty-one	quatre-vingt-un	**kaht-ruh-vehn-*uh***
ninety	quatre-vingt-dix	**kaht-ruh-venh-*deess***

English	French	Pronunciation
ninety-one	quatre-vingt-onze	**kaht-ruh-venh-*ohnze***
one hundred	cent	**sahn**
one thousand	mille	**meel**
one hundred thousand	cent mille	**sahn meel**
first	premier	***preh*-mee-ay**
second	deuxième	***duhz*-zee-em**
third	troisième	***twa*-zee-em**
tenth	dixième	***dees*-ee-em**
twentieth	vingtième	***vehnt*-ee-em**
thirtieth	trentième	***trahnt*-ee-em**
one-hundredth	centième	***sant*-ee-em**

THE CALENDAR

English	French	Pronunciation
Sunday	dimanche	**dee-*mahnsh***
Monday	lundi	***luhn*-dee**
Tuesday	mardi	***mahr*-dee**
Wednesday	mercredi	***mair*-kruh-dee**
Thursday	jeudi	***jheu*-dee**
Friday	vendredi	***vawn*-druh-dee**
Saturday	samedi	***sahm*-dee**
yesterday	hier	**ee-*air***
today	aujourd'hui	**o-jhord-*dwee***
this morning/this afternoon	ce matin/cet après-midi	**suh ma-*tan*/set ah-preh-mee-*dee***
tonight	ce soir	**suh *swahr***
tomorrow	demain	**de-*man***

INDEX

A

Abbatiale, Eglise (Mont-St-Michel), 335
Abbatiale Ste-Croix (Bordeaux), 710
Abbaye aux Dames (Caen), 323
Abbaye aux Hommes (Caen), 323
Abbaye de Fontenay (near Marmagne), 435
Abbaye de St-Honorat, 564
Abbaye d'Hautecombe, 478–479
Abbaye Nôtre Dame de Sénanque (Gordes), 514
Abbaye Romaine de St-Martin-d'Ainay (Lyon), 447
Abbaye St-Victor (Marseille), 537
Académie des Jeux-Floraux (Toulouse), 664
Acco-Dispo (Tours), 282
Accommodations, best, 12–16
Adonis (Monte-Carlo), 618
Adventure and wellness trips, 58–59
Adventureland (Disneyland Paris), 239
Aer Lingus, 749
Agence Crolard (Annecy), 476
Agnès b (Paris), 172
Aigues-Mortes, 636–638
Aiguille du Midi, 489
Air France, 748–750
Air travel, 748–750
Aix-en-Provence, 526–533
Aix-les-Bains, 478–480
A la Ferme de Puy Gauthier (Périgueux), 722
Albi, 657–659
Alise-Ste-Reine, 435
Allées de Meilhan (Marseille), 538
Allées de Tourny (Bordeaux), 711
Allée Serge-Diaghilev (Monte-Carlo), 618
Alliance Française, 60
Alsace-Lorraine, 64, 384–416
  cuisine, 50
Amboise, 271–275
American Airlines, 748
American cemetery (near Château-Thierry), 370
Ammerschwihr, 400–401
Amphitheater (Les Arènes; Arles), 519
Amphithéâtre des Trois-Gauls (Lyon), 448
Amphithéâtre Romain de Nîmes, 632
Ancien Hôtel de Ville (Les Baux), 524
Ancien Palais des Ducs de Bourgogne (Dijon), 432
Andlau, 398
Angel Pillar (Strasbourg), 389
Angers, 299–302
Angoulême, 703–706
Annecy, 474–478
An Poitin Still (Quimper), 353
Antebellum (Blois), 264
Antibes & Cap d'Antibes, 578–582
Antic Wine (Lyon), 449
Antiquaires Golmard (Dijon), 434
Antiques Show (Paris), 55
Antiquité Arcana (Colmar), 403
Antiquités Delan (Pau), 672
Antiquités Guy Caffard (Colmar), 403
Antiquités Safi (Carcassonne), 653
Antoine & Lili (Paris), 177
Apocalypse Tapestries (Angers), 300–301
Aqua Club (St-Tropez), 552
Aquarium de la Rochelle, 695
Aquarium du Val de Loire (near Amboise), 273
Arbre de la Liberté (Pérouges), 458
Arc de Triomphe
  Montpellier, 639
  Nancy, 410
  Orange, 498
  Paris, 107–108
Archbishop's Palace (Rouen), 307
Archeoscope (Mont-St-Michel), 335
Architecture, 37–41
The Ardèche, 465–466
The Ardennes, 64
Area codes, 754
Arles, 517–522
Armistice Day, 57
Arromanches-les-Bains, 330
Art, 35–37
Artcom/Puces de Reims, 376
Artcurial (Paris), 170
Arts et Collections d'Alsace
  Colmar, 403
  Strasbourg, 391
Astier de Villatte (Paris), 182
Astronomical clock (Strasbourg), 389
Atelier Brancusi (Paris), 104
Atelier de Cézanne (Aix-en-Provence), 527–528
Atelier de Chocolat de Bayonne Andrieu, 676–677
Atelier du Prince Noir (Dinard), 344
Ateliers Marcel Carbonel (Marseille), 538
The Atlantic Coast, 66–67
Au Lapin Agile (Paris), 190
Au Nain Bleu (Paris), 183
Auto Europe, 751–752
Autun, 425–427
Aux Délices Malouins (St-Malo), 341
Auxerre, 418–421
Avallon, 423–425
Aventure Canoës (Vals-les-Bains), 466
Avignon, 501–509
Avignon Off, 502
Avis, 751
Azay-le-Rideau, 288–290

B

Baccarat (Paris), 182
Bagnols-en-Beaujolais, 455
Baie des Fourmis (Beaulieu-sur-Mer), 610
Balenciaga (Paris), 172
Ballooning, 58
Ballroom (Fontainebleau), 233
Balzac, Honoré de, 296, 297
  Musée Balzac (Saché), 290
Baptistère St-Jean (Poitiers), 690
Bar à Thym (Toulon), 546
Bar à Vins-Restaurant Le Ducis (Versailles), 225
Barge cruises, 58–59
Bar Hemingway/Bar Vendôme (Paris), 187–188
Bar La Bodega (Toulouse), 669
Bar l'Amiral (Cannes), 568
Bar Lilas (Reims), 380
Barthélémy (Paris), 180
Basilique du Bois-Chenu (Domrémy-la-Pucelle), 415
Basilique du Sacré-Coeur (Paris), 116
Basilique Notre-Dame de Fourvière (Lyon), 445–446
Basilique Notre-Dame-de-la-Garde (Marseille), 536, 537
Basilique St-Andoche (Saulieu), 437
Basilique Ste-Madeleine (Vézelay), 422
Basilique St-Martin (Cap-Martin), 627
Basilique St-Michel (Bordeaux), 709

Basilique St-Nazaire (Carcassonne), 653
Basilique St-Rémi (Reims), 372
Basilique St-Sauveur
  Dinan, 348
  Rocamadour, 739
Basilique St-Sernin (Toulouse), 662
Basilique St-Seurin (Bordeaux), 710
Basque Country, 66, 671–687
Bastian (Strasbourg), 391
Bastide St-Louis (Carcassonne), 652
Bastille Day, 56
  Carcassonne, 651
Bastille neighborhood (Paris)
  accommodations, 205
  restaurants, 151–153
  shopping, 166
Bathroom Graffiti (Cannes), 561
Batofar (Paris), 191
Battle Gallery (Versailles), 222
Bayeux, 326–329
Bayonne, 675–679
Beaches. *See also specific beaches*
  Beaulieu-sur-Mer, 610
  Biarritz, 680
  Cagnes-sur-Mer, 583
  Cannes, 559
  Concarneau, 354
  Deauville, 316–317
  Dinard, 344
  Juan-les-Pins, 576
  Monaco, 618
  Nice, 594, 598
  St-Jean-Cap-Ferrat, 607–608
  St-Jean-de-Luz, 685
  St-Malo, 340
  St-Tropez, 552
  Toulon, 543
  Villefranche-sur-Mer, 606
Beaugency, 260–262
Beaujolais Country, 454–456
Beaulieu-sur-Mer, 610–613
Beaune, 427–431
Bechard (Aix-en-Provence), 528
Belleau Wood (near Château-Thierry), 370
Belle-Ile-en-Mer, 363
Belleville (Paris), 89
  accommodations, 205–206
  restaurants, 153–154
  shopping, 166
Belleville-sur-Saône, 455, 456
Bensimon (Paris), 173
Bernachon (Lyon), 449
Bernachon Passion (Lyon), 449
Bernardaud (Limoges), 743
BHV (Bar de l'Hôtel de Ville; Bordeaux), 715
Biarritz, 679–684
Biarritz Cup, 680
Bibliothéque Publique d'Information (Paris), 104
Bijoux Blues (Paris), 177
Bijoux Burma (Paris), 177
Biking
  Avignon, 502
  Burgundy, 427
  Cannes, 559
  The Dordogne, 725
  Forest of Fontainebleau, 234
  Loire Valley, 256
  tours, 59
  the Wine Road, 397
Biot, 574–575
Biot, Eglise de, 574
Black Madonna (Rocamadour), 739
Bliss (Nice), 605
Blois, 263–267
Blue Note Why Not (Nancy), 413
Boating (boat rentals)
  Cannes, 559
  Juan-les-Pins, 576
  St-Tropez, 552
Bocuse, Paul, 453
Bois-Chenu, Basilique du (Domrémy-la-Pucelle), 415
Bois de Belleau (near Château-Thierry), 370
Bois de Boulogne (Paris), 108–109
Bonpoint (Paris), 175
Bonton (Paris), 175
Bonzaï Arboretum de la Côte d'Azur (Biot), 574
Books, recommended, 41–44
Bordeaux, 66–67, 706–715
  exploring, 708–711
  getting there, 707–708
  visitor information, 708
Bordeaux and Atlantic Coast region, 689–719
Bordeaux wine country, 715–719
Boules, 556
Boulevard des Pyrénées (Pau), 672
The Bourbons, 29–30
Bourg-en-Bresse, 459–461
Bourgogne Randonnées (Beaune), 427
Boutique Daum (Nancy), 411
Boutique du Rocher (Monte-Carlo), 619
Boy's Paradise (Toulon), 546
Brasserie du Théâtre (Dijon), 437
British Airways, 748, 749
British Midland, 749
Brittany, 64, 338–365
  cuisine, 50
Brocante, 501
Broc de Saint Ouen (St-Rémy), 515
Brok Café (Deauville), 320
Buddha Bar (Monte-Carlo), 625
Budget, 751
Bullfights, Arles, 519, 520
Burgundy, 64, 418–438
  cuisine, 50–51
  suggested itinerary, 76–79
Business hours, 754
Bus travel, 749–750
Butte de Montfaucon (Verdun), 416

C

Cabaret du Casino Ruhl (Nice), 605
Cabourg, 326
Cadiot-Badie (Bordeaux), 711
Cadre Noir de Saumur, 297
Caen, 322–326
Caen Memorial, 324
Cafe Charbon (Paris), 188
Cafe de Flore (Paris), 163
Café de Paris Casino (Monte-Carlo), 625
Café de Paris (St-Tropez), 557–558
Cafe des Deux Moulins (Paris), 163
Café Face (Val d'Isère), 495
Café Le Napoleon (Nimes), 636
Café Le St-Louis (Périgueux), 726
Café Llorca (Monte-Carlo), 625
Café Populaire (Bordeaux), 715
Café Sénéquier (St-Tropez), 558
Cagnes-sur-Mer, 582–585
Cahors, 740–742
Calendar of events, 54–58
Calvados country, 312
The Camargue, 637
Camus, Albert, 513
Camus (Cognac), 701
Canal St-Martin (Paris), 88, 114
  accommodations, 201–203
  restaurants near, 147–150
  shopping, 166
Cancale, 343
Canet-Plage (near Perpignan), 651
Cannes, 558–569
  accommodations, 564–566
  beaches, 559
  getting there, 558
  nightlife, 568–569
  outdoor pursuits, 559
  restaurants, 567–568
  seeing the sights, 562–564
  shopping, 560–562
  visitor information, 558
Cannes Film Festival, 55
Cannolive (Cannes), 562
Canoeing, The Dordogne, 725
Cap d'Antibes, 578–582
Cap-Martin, 626, 627
Capucins Market (Marseille), 538
Carcassonne, 651–655
Carnac, 357–359

Carnac-Plage, 357
Carnaval, Nice, 54–55, 593
The Carolingians, 25
Carré d'Art (Nîmes), 632
Carrefour des Cascades (Paris), 109
Car rentals, 751
Carrousel de Saumur, 297
Carrousel du Louvre (Paris), 167
Car travel, 750–751
Casino Barrière
  Dinard, 346
  St-Malo, 343
Casino Barrière de Trouville, 322
Casino Croisette (Cannes), 568
Casino de Deauville, 320
Casino de l'Impérial (Annecy), 477–478
Casino in the Palais de Mediterranée (Nice), 605
Casino Municipal (Biarritz), 684
Casinos
  Beaulieu-sur-Mer, 613
  Biarritz, 684
  Cannes, 568
  Juan-les-Pins, 578
  Monaco, 624–625
  Nice, 605
Cassegrain (Paris), 183
Castres, 655–657
Cathédral de Saint Sacerdos (Sarlat-la-Canéda), 733
Cathédrale de la Major (Marseille), 537
Cathédrale de Notre-Dame (Paris), 100–102
Cathédrale Notre-Dame de Chartres, 228–230
Cathédrale Notre-Dame de Reims, 372–373
Cathédrale Notre-Dame de Rouen, 306–307
Cathédrale Notre-Dame des Doms (Avignon), 502–503
Cathédrale Notre-Dame de Senlis, 248
Cathédrale Notre-Dame de Strasbourg, 388–389
Cathédrale Orthodoxe Russe St-Nicolas à Nice, 596
Cathédrale St-André (Bordeaux), 709
Cathédrale St-Apollinaire (Valence), 464
Cathédrale St-Corentin (Quimper), 350
Cathédrale Ste-Cécile (Albi), 657
Cathédrale Ste-Croix (Orléans), 257–258
Cathédrale Ste-Marie (Bayonne), 676
Cathédrale Ste-Marie-Majeure (Toulon), 544
Cathédrale St-Etienne
  Auxerre, 419
  Cahors, 741
  Limoges, 743
  Toulouse, 664
Cathédrale St-Front (Périgueux), 722–723
Cathédrale St-Gatien (Tours), 279
Cathédrale St-Jean (Perpignan), 648
Cathédrale St-Just et St-Pasteur (Narbonne), 644
Cathédrale St-Lazare (Autun), 425–426
Cathédrale St-Maurice
  Angers, 300
  Vienne, 462
Cathédrale St-Pierre
  Angoulême, 704
  Montpellier, 639
  Nantes, 360
  Poitiers, 690
Cathédrale St-Sauveur (Aix-en-Provence), 528
Cathedrals, best, 10–11
Caveau de Morgon (Villie-Morgon), 456
Caveau des Oubliettes (Paris), 190
Cave de Marc & Sebastien (Orléans), 259
Cave du Marché (Cannes), 561
Cave du Musée (Colmar), 403
Caves at Lascaux, 726–728
Caves du Palais St. Firmin (Gordes), 510–511
Caves Patriarche Père et Fils (Beaune), 428
Caves Plouzeau (Chinon), 291
Cazenave (Bayonne), 677
Céili Pub (Quimper), 353
Cellphones, 759
Centre Commercial de la Part-Dieu (Lyon), 449
Centre Commercial (Paris), 177
Centre d'Entraînement d'Ilbarritz-Bidart (Biarritz), 680
Centre International de Plongée (CIP) de Nice, 598
Centre Pompidou
  Metz, 412
  Paris, 103–104
Centre Sant-Vicens (Perpignan), 648
107Rivoli (Paris), 170
Cézanne, Paul, 37
  Aix-en-Provence, 526
    Atelier de Cézanne, 527–528
Chambord, 262–263
Chamonix-Mont Blanc, 487–492
Champagne, Reims, 372, 374–376
Champagne country, 64, 367–382
Champagne de Castellane (Epernay), 381
Champs Elysées area (Paris), 85, 107–114
  accommodations, 197–201
  restaurants, 143–147
  shopping, 166
Chanel (Paris), 173
Changing of the Guard (Monaco), 620
Channel Islands, 340
Chantal Thomass (Paris), 176
Chantilly, 244–247
Chapelle de la Miséricorde (St-Tropez), 553
Chapelle de la Vierge (Rouen), 307
Chapelle de St-Hubert (Amboise), 272
Chapelle de St-Symphorien (Paris), 125–126
Chapelle des Anges (Paris), 126
Chapelle des Pénitents Blancs
  Les Baux, 525
  St-Paul-de-Vence, 586
Chapelle de Trémalo (Pont-Aven), 355–356
Chapelle du Rosaire (Vence), 589–590
Chapelle Notre-Dame de Vie (Mougins), 570
Chapelle Notre-Dame (Rocamadour), 739
Chapelle St-Laurence (Strasbourg), 389
Chapelle St-Michel (Rocamadour), 739
Chapelle St-Nicolas (Avignon), 502
Chapelle St-Pierre (Villefranche-sur-Mer), 606
Chapelle St-Sebastian (Dambach), 398
Charles de Gaulle Airport (Roissy; Paris), 81–82
  accommodations near, 214
Chartres, 227–232
Chartreuse de Champmol (Dijon), 432
Château Barrière (Périgueux), 722
Château Comtal (Carcassonne), 652–653
Château d'Amboise, 271–272
Château d'Angers, 300–301
Château d'Azay-le-Rideau, 288–289
Château d'Eau (Montpellier), 639
Château de Beynac (Beynac-et-Cazenac), 729
Château de Blois, 263–265
Château de Bussy-Rabutin, 435
Château de Caen, 323–324
Château de Chambord, 262
Château de Chantilly/Musée Condé, 245–246

Château de Chaumont, 269–270
Château de Chenonceau, 275–276
Château de Cheverny, 267
Château de Chinon, 291–292
Château de Cognac, 700–701
Château de Condé, 371
Château de Fontcrenne (Villie-Morgon), 456
Château de Gordes, 511
Château de Langeais, 287–288
Château de Loches, 284
Château de Montrottier, 475
Château de Pau, 672
Château de Pierrefonds (Compiègne), 250–251
Château de Puymartin (between Sarlat and Les Eyzies), 735
Château de Rambouillet, 226
Château de Rocamadour, 738
Château de Roquebrune, 626
Château de St-Malo, 340
Château de Saumur, 298
Château des Baux, 523–524
Château des Ducs de Bretagne (Nantes), 359, 360
Château de Valençay, 268–269
Château de Vaux-le-Vicomte, 235–236
Château de Versailles, 220–223
Château de Villandry, 285–286
Chateau de Villeneuve Fondation Émile Hugues (Vence), 589
Château d'If (Marseille), 536
Château du Clos-Lucé (Amboise), 272
Château Dunois (Beaugency), 260
Château du Roi (St-Emilion), 719
Château d'Ussé, 294
Château Lafite-Rothschild (Médoc), 716
Château Margaux (Médoc), 716–717
Château Mouton-Rothschild (Médoc), 717
Château Musée de Dinan, 347–348
Château-Musée Grimaldi (Musée de l'Olivier & Musée d'Art Moderne Méditerranéen; Cagnes-sur-Mer), 583
Châteauneuf-du-Pape, 500
Château Royal (Collioure), 645
Château-Thierry, 369–371
Châteaux and palaces, best, 7–8
Chaumont-sur-Loire, 269–271
Chemin du Fauvisme, 646
Chenonceaux, 275–277
Cheverny, 267–268
Chez Tonton (Toulouse), 669
Chez Wayne's (Nice), 605
Children, families with, 757
Chinese Museum (Fontainebleau), 233
Chinon, 290–294
Chokko (Cannes), 568
Christian Constant (Paris), 180
Christian Louboutin (Paris), 175
Christmas Fairs, 58
Cimetière Américain at Romagne (Verdun), 416
Cimetière de Montmartre (Paris), 117
Cimetière du Montparnasse (Paris), 135
Cimiez, 597
Cimiez Convent (Monastère de Cimiez), 597
Ciné-Folie (Cannes), 560
Cinéscénie de Puy du Fou, Son-et-Lumière, 55
5e Cru (Paris), 187
Citadelle, Villefranche-sur-Mer, 606
Citadelle (St-Tropez), 554
Citadium (Paris), 174–175
Cité de la Musique (Paris), 185
Cité des Antiquaires (Lyon), 448
Cité des Congrés Le Corum (Montpellier), 639
Cité des Sciences et de l'Industrie (Paris), 119–120
Cité du Numérique (Poitiers), 690
Cité Internationale de la Bande Dessinée et de l'Image (CNBDI; Angoulême), 703, 704
Cité Réligieuse (Rocamadour), 738, 739
Cité Royale (Loches), 284
Clarière de l'Armistice (Compiègne), 252
Claude Monet Foundation (Giverny), 243
Climate, 54
Clock Tower (Dinan), 348
Clos St-Landelin (Rouffach), 401–402
Club 55 (St-Tropez), 552
Cognac, 700–703
Cognac Blues Passions, 700
Cointreau, 302
Col de la Schlucht, 407
Col du Bonhomme, 407
Col du Galibier, 472
Colette (Paris), 177–178
Collection des Voitures Anciennes de S.A.S. Le Prince de Monaco, 619
Collections Baron Gérard (Bayeux), 327
Collégiale de la Conversion de St-Paul (St-Paul-de-Vence), 586
Collégiale Notre-Dame (Beaune), 427–428
Collégiale St-Ours (Loches), 284
Colline de Fourvière (Lyon), 445
Colline St-Eutrope (Orange), 498
Collioure, 645–647
Colmar, 402–407
Colmar International Festival, 56
Comédie de Reims, 380
Comédie-Française (Paris), 184–185
Comédie Française-Théâtre du Vieux-Colombier (Paris), 185
Commonwealth Cemetery (Bayeux), 328
Compagnie du Mont-Blanc, 489
Compiègne, 249–255
Comptoir des Vins (Carcassonne), 653
Concarneau, 353–355
Conciergerie (Paris), 104–105
Concorde (Dijon), 437
Condé-en-Brie, 371
Confiserie Auer (Nice), 599
Confiserie Florian du Vieux-Nice, 599
Confiserie Pariès (St-Jean-de-Luz), 686
Continental Airlines, 748
Cooking classes, 59
Cordelier (Beaune), 428
Cordeliers, Eglise des (Nancy), 411
Cordes-sur-Ciel, 659–661
Corniche du Mont-Faron (Toulon), 544
Corniche Président-J.-F.-Kennedy (Marseille), 537
Cotelac (Nice), 599
Côte Sauvage, 363
Couly-Dutheil (Chinon), 291
Coup de Chauffe/Festival du Théâtre de la Rue (Cognac), 700
Courchevel 1850, 484
Cours Julien (Marseille), 538
Cours Mirabeau (Aix-en-Provence), 527
Cours Saleya (Nice), 594
The Crazy Horse (Paris), 188
Credit cards, 760
Crémerie Porcheret (Dijon), 433
Crime and safety, 761
Croisières Inter-Iles (La Rochelle), 699
Cros-de-Cagnes, 582–585
Crussol, Mont, 464
Crystal Bar (Monte-Carlo), 625
Cuisine, 48–52
Culturespace (Nîmes), 630
Currency and currency exchange, 759–760
Customs regulations, 754–755

D

Dambach, 398
Daniel Location (Cannes), 559
D-day beaches, 330–332

Deauville, 315–320
Debit cards, 760
De-ci-de-ca (Epernay), 380–381
Degas, Edgar, 37
Dehillerin (Paris), 182
Delta Air Lines, 748
Denis Rugat (Nancy), 411
Deportation Memorial (Paris), 102–103
Dick's Tea Bar (Val d'Isère), 495
Didier Ludot (Paris), 176
Dijon, 431–437
Dinan, 347–349
Dinard, 343–347
Dior (Cannes), 560
Dior Joaillerie (Paris), 177
Diptyque (Paris), 183
Disabled travelers, 755–756
Disco Le Caveau (Biarritz), 684
Disco Le Maximo (Toulouse), 669
Disco Le Sept (Cannes), 569
Discoveryland (Disneyland Paris), 239
Discrimination, 761
Disneyland Paris, 237–242
Diving
  Nice, 598
  St-Tropez, 552
Doctors, 756
Domaine de Marie-Antoinette (Versailles), 222
Domaines Schlumberger (Colmar), 403–404
Dôme, Eglise du (Paris), 128
Dominicains, Eglise des (Colmar), 404
Domrémy-la-Pucelle, 414–415
Donjon Gilles-Aycelin (Narbonne), 644
The Dordogne, 67, 725
The Dordogne and Périgord regions, 721–746
Dordogne Valley, 729
Drinking laws, 756
Driving rules, 752, 756
Driving tours, best, 5–6
Drugstores, 756
Dubard (Dijon), 434

E

Easy Dive (Juan-les-Pins), 576
Eating and drinking, 48–52
Ecole de Ski Français (Val d'Isère), 494
Ecritoire Antiquités Poidras (Nantes), 362
Eden Casino (Juan-les-Pins), 578
Eglise. *See under First significant word (e.g. Jacobins, Eglise des . . .)*
Eiffel Tower neighborhood (Paris)
  accommodations, 211–212
  restaurants, 158–161
  shopping, 167
  sights and attractions, 126–134
Eiffel Tower (Paris), 90, 133–134
El Barrio Libre (Pau), 675
Elco Marine (Cannes), 559
Electricity, 756
Embassies and consulates, 756–757
Emergencies, 757
English Garden (Dinan), 347
Epernay, 380–382
Erès (Paris), 176
Esplanade des Quinconces (Bordeaux), 709
Estivade (Dijon), 431
Etienne Bertran (Rouen), 309
Etiquette & customs, 757
Eurailpass, 753–754
Eurolines France, 749–750
European Diving School (St-Tropez), 552
European Health Insurance Card (EHIC), 757
Eurostar, 749
Evian-les-Bains, 470–473
Experimental Cocktail Club (Paris), 188
Eze, 613–615

F

Fabrication de Makhilas (Bayonne), 677
Façonnable (Nice), 599
Faïencerie Carpentier Augy (Rouen), 309
Families with children, 757
Fauchon (Paris), 180–181
Female travelers, 761
Festival Biarritz Amérique Latine, 680
Festival d'Aix-en-Provence, 57
Festival d'Automne (Paris), 57
Festival d'Avignon, 56, 502
Festival de Carcassonne, 651
Festival de Jazz (Strasbourg), 386
Festival de la Musique Sacrée (St-Malo), 340
Féstival de Musique du Périgord Noir (Sarlat-la-Canéda), 733
Festival de Radio France et de Montpellier, 639
Festival de St-Denis (Paris), 55
Féstival des Jeux de Théâtre de Sarlat, 733
Festival du Jazz à Vienne, 461
Festival Interceltique de Lorient, 57
Festival International d'Art Lyrique & de Musique (Aix-en-Provence), 527
Festival International de la Bande Dessinée (Angoulême), 703
Festival International de Musique de Colmar, 402
Festival International des Jeunes Réalisateurs (St-Jean-de-Luz), 685
Festival International des Musiques d'Aujourd'hui (Strasbourg), 386
Festival International du Film de La Rochelle, 694
Festival International Montpellier Danse, 639
Festival of Classical Music (Strasbourg), 386
Festival of St-Jean (St-Jean-de-Luz), 685
Fête Chopin (Paris), 56
Fête de Bayonne, 676
Fête de la Truffe (Périgueux), 722
Fête de St-Sylvestre, 58
Fête des Lumières (Lyon), 58
Fêtes Médiévales (Bayeux), 327
Fêtes Patronales de la Saint Jean (St-Jean-de-Luz), 685
Field of Megaliths (Carnac), 357, 358
Fil Bleu (Tours), 280
Films, 44–46
Flaubert, Gustave, Musée Flaubert et d'Histoire de la Médécine (Rouen), 308
Flavigny-sur-Ozerain, 435
Flea market, Toulouse, 665
Flea markets
  Avignon, 506
  Cannes, 561
  Nice, 599
  Paris, 168–169
  Rouen, 309
Fleche St-Michel (Bordeaux), 709–710
FNAC (Paris), 182–184
Foire à la Brocante (Isle-sur-la-Sorgue), 501
Foire du Trône, (Paris), 55
Folies-Bergère (Paris), 189
Fondation Bemberg (Toulouse), 664
Fondation Cartier (Paris), 136
Fontainebleau, 232–235
Fontaine des Chartreux (Cahors), 741
Fontevraud-l'Abbaye, 294–296
Fontvieille (Monaco), 615
Food and cuisine, 48–52
Forest of Fontainebleau, 234
Forest of Rambouillet, 225–227
Formule 1 (Monte-Carlo), 619
Fort de Douaumont (Verdun), 416
Fort de la Bastille (Grenoble), 481
Fort Ste-Agathe (Ile de Porquerolles), 547
Fort Vaux, 415–416

Forum des Halles (Paris), 91
Foundation Maeght (St-Paul-de-Vence), 586–587
Fourviere Hill (Lyon), 445
Francis Kurkdjian (Paris), 183
François le Villec (Quimper), 351
The French Alps, 65, 470–495
French Open Tennis Championship (Paris), 55
The French Riviera (Côte d'Azur), 65–66, 550–627
French Trotters (Paris), 173
Frioul If Express (Marseille), 537
The Frog and the Princess (Paris), 188
Fromm Jacques (Epernay), 381
Funicular (Pau), 671–672
Futuroscope (Poitiers), 689, 690–691

G

Gaîté Lyrique (Paris), 105
Galerie d'Art International (Nancy), 411
Galerie du Vitrail (Chartres), 230
Galerie Jean-Claude Novaro (Biot), 574
Galerie Lieber (Vézelay), 422
Galerie St-Sauveur (Dinan), 348
Galeries Lafayette (Cannes), 561
Galeries Tropéziennes (St-Tropez), 553
Galibier Pass, 472
Galignani (Paris), 171
Gallery of François I (Fontainebleau), 232
Gardens of Versailles, 222
Garden Tennis Club (Cannes), 559
Gasoline, 752
Gauguin, Paul, 37
  Pont-Aven, 356
Gautier Debotte (Nantes), 362
Gay Pride Parade (Paris), 56
Gays and lesbians, 758
  Avignon, 509
  Cannes, 569
  Deauville, 317
  Nice, 605–606
  Paris, 193
  Toulon, 546
  Toulouse, 669
Geismar Dany (Colmar), 403
Geneva, Lake, 471–472
George Rech (Lyon), 449
Gérard Wehrling (Strasbourg), 391
Givenchy (Paris), 173
Giverny, 242–244
Glue Pot (Reims), 379
Golf, Cannes, 559
Gordes, 510–514
Gorges du Fier, 474
Grand-Ballon, 407–408
Grand Canyon of France, 466
Grand Casino de Beaulieu, 613
Grande Audience (Avignon), 506
Grande Boutique du Vin (Reims), 376
Grande Plage
  Biarritz, 680
  Dinard, 344
Grande Plage du Sillon (St-Malo), 340
Grande Plage St-Jean-de-Luz, 685
Grand Escalier (Rocamadour), 739
Grand Palais (Paris), 109, 112
Grands Appartements (Versailles), 220–221
Grand Théâtre (Bordeaux), 709
Grand Théâtre de Dijon, 437
Grand Tinel (Avignon), 504
Grand Trianon (Versailles), 222
Grasse, 571–573
Gray-d'Albion (Cannes), 560–561
Grenoble, 480–484
Grimaldi Forum (Monte-Carlo), 625
Grotte de Font-de-Gaume (Les Eyzies), 730
Grotte des Combarelles (near Bergerac), 730
Grotte du Grand-Roc (Les Eyzies), 730
Gruisson, 643

H

Haddock Cafe (Nimes), 636
Halle aux Grains (Toulouse), 669
Halle Tony Garnier (Lyon), 454
Hall of Mirrors (Versailles), 221
Haras National (Pau), 672
Haut-de-Cagnes, 582–585
HB-Henriot Faïenceries de Quimper, 351
Health concerns, 757
Hédiard (Paris), 181
Hennessy (Cognac), 701
Henriet (Biarritz), 682
Hermès
  Cannes, 560
  Lyon, 449
  Paris, 173
Hertz, 751
Hervé Baume (Avignon), 506
Hippodrome d'Auteuil (Paris), 109
Hippodrome de Deauville Clairefontaine, 317
Hippodrome de Deauville La Touques, 317
Hippodrome de Longchamp (Paris), 109
History of France, 20–35
Hohneck, 407
Holidays, 757
Holy Week, Perpignan, 647–648
Honfleur, 312–315
Horreum (Narbonne), 644
Horse-drawn carriages, Tours, 280
Horse racing, Deauville, 317
Hospitals, 757–758
Hôtel de la Tour du Brau (Les Baux), 523
Hôtel des Invalides/Napoleon's Tomb (Paris), 126, 128
Hôtel de Ville (City or Town Hall)
  La Rochelle, 695
  Libourne, 716
  Lyon, 447
  Ribeauvillé, 399
  Toulouse, 662
Hôtel du Chamarier (Lyon), 444
Hôtel du Commerce (Strasbourg), 388
Hôtel Groslot (Orléans), 258
Hôtel le Peletier de St-Fargeau (Paris), 106
Hôtel Plamon (Sarlat-la-Canéda), 733
Hot lines, 758
Hunky Dory (Dijon), 437
Hunting Museum (Senlis), 248

I

Ile de Bréhat, 346
Ile de France, 63
Ile de la Cité (Paris), 85
  accommodations, 195–197
  restaurants around, 141–143
  shopping, 166
  sights and attractions, 100–107
Ile de Porquerolles, 546–548
Ile de Port-Cros, 546, 548
Ile de Ré, 699
Ile du Grand-Bé, 340
Ile Ste-Marguerite, 563
Ile St-Honorat, 564
Ile St-Louis (Paris), 85
  accommodations, 195–197
  restaurants around, 141–143
  shopping, 166
  sights and attractions, 100–107
Iles de Lerins, 563
Iles d'Hyères, 546–547
Institut & Musée Lumière (Lyon), 447
Institut de Recherche et de Coordination Acoustique-Musique (Paris), 104
International Association for Medical Assistance to Travelers (IAMAT), 757
International Garden Festival (Château de Chaumont), 270
International Marathon of Paris, 55
International Ready-to-Wear Fashion Shows (Paris), 55
International Society of Travel Medicine, 757
Internet and Wi-Fi, 758
Isabel Marant (Paris), 174

Isle-sur-la-Sorgue, 501
Issenheim Altarpiece (Colmar), 404
Itineraries, suggested, 67–79
- for families, 73–76
- France in 1 week, 67–70
- France in 2 weeks, 70–73
- a wine lover's tour of Burgundy, 76–79

J

Jacobins, Eglise des (Toulouse), 662
Jaffier-Parsi (Avignon), 506
James Joyce Pub (Reims), 379
JAM (Montpellier), 642–643
Jardin Albert-1er (Nice), 594
Jardin Anglais (Dinan), 347
Jardin d'Acclimatation (Paris), 109, 112
Jardin de Hortulus (Pérouges), 458
Jardin des Arènes (Périgueux), 722
Jardin des Enfeus (Sarlat-la-Canéda), 734
Jardin des Plantes
- Montpellier, 639
- Nantes, 360
Jardin des Tuileries (Paris), 92, 94
Jardin d'Eze, 613
Jardin du Luxembourg (Paris), 124–125
Jardin du Palais Royal (Paris), 100
Jardin du Rosaire (Lyon), 446
Jardin Public (Cognac), 702
Jardins de la Fontaine (Nîmes), 632
Jazz Pulsations (Nancy), 409
JC de Castelbajac (Paris), 174
Jeannette et les Cycleux (Strasbourg), 396
Jean-Paul Hévin (Paris), 180
Jeff de Bruges (Blois), 264
Jeu de Paume (Paris), 94
Jimmy's (Monte-Carlo), 625
Joan of Arc
- Maison Natale de Jeanne d'Arc (Domrémy-la-Pucelle), 414
- Musée Jeanne-d'Arc (Rouen), 308
- Place du Vieux-Marché (Rouen), 309
- statue of
  - Compiègne, 250
  - Orléans, 257
Joïa Glam Club (Les Milles), 532–533
Joïa (Lyon), 449
Jouarre, 367
Jour des Menetriers (Strasbourg), 399
Juan-les-Pins, 575–578
Juliénas, 455
Julien de Savignac (Sarlat-la-Canéda), 734

K

Katie Daly's (Bayonne), 679
Kayaking, Juan-les-Pins, 576
Kaysersberg, 399–400
Kemwel Drive Europe, 751
Kiliwatch (Paris), 176
Kilomètre Zéro (Paris), 100
Kinémax (Poitiers), 690
Kiosque-Théâtre (Paris), 184

L

La Belle Hortense (Paris), 163–164
La Bodeguita (Nice), 605
La Bohème (Rouen), 312
La Boutique Maille (Dijon), 433
La Bulle (Carcassonne), 655
La Canebière (Marseille), 534
La Caravelle
- Marseille, 542–543
- St-Malo, 343
La Carée Cointreau (Angers), 302
La Casa Latina (Bordeaux), 715
La Cave Henry de Vézelay, 422
La Cave Salvatori (Epernay), 380
Lac d'Annecy, 474
Lac du Bourget, 478
La Chapelle des Lombards (Paris), 191
La Chocolatière (Rouen), 310
La Cité de l'Architecture et du Patrimoine (Paris), 112
La Cité de l'Espace (Toulouse), 664–665
La Cognathèque (Cognac), 701
La Comédie
- Dijon, 437
- Nimes, 636
La Compagnie des Saumons, 561–562
La Condamine (Monaco), 615
La Coupole (Paris), 164
La Croisette (Courchevel 1850), 487
La Daille, 493
Lafayette Maison (Paris), 179
La Féerie Gourmande (Pau), 673
La Ferté-sous-Jouarre, 367–368
La Fête de l'Olivier (Olive Festival; Cagnes-sur-Mer), 583
La Fiesta/Le Cotton Club (Colmar), 407
La Fondation Angladon-Dubrujeaud (Avignon), 503
La Galerie le Cornet à Dés (Quimper), 351
La Grande Expo du Pont du Gard (Nîmes), 634
La Grande Plage (Dinard), 344
La Grande Plage du Sillon (St-Malo), 340
La Grande Plage St-Jean-de-Luz, 685
La Grotte de Glace, 490
Lake Geneva, 471–472
Lalique (Paris), 182
La Maison de l'Infante (St-Jean-de-Luz), 686
La Maison du Vin (Saumur), 297
La Maison Fossier/Biscuits Fossier (Reims), 376
La Maison Léon (Périgueux), 722
La Maison Louis XIV (St-Jean-de-Luz), 685–686
La Maison Quinta (Perpignan), 648
La Manne Bretonne (St-Malo), 341
La Maroquinerie (Paris), 190
La Marseillaise, 536
Lamastre, 468
La Merveille (Mont-St-Michel), 334
L'Ancien Couvent des Bernardines (Dijon), 432
L'Ancien Temple (Dinard), 345
Langeais, 287–288
Language, 758
Language classes, 60
Languedoc-Roussillon, 66, 629–669
Lanterne des Morts (Sarlat-la-Canéda), 733
La Palette (Paris), 164
La Pelouse Interdite (Toulouse), 669
La Perspective de la Côte des Basques (Biarritz), 680
La Petite France (Strasbourg), 388
La Petite Friande (Reims), 376
La Pierre d'Angle (Vézelay), 422
La Plage (Bordeaux), 715
La Reg (Périgueux), 726
La Reine Matilde (Caen), 325
La Reserve (Juan-les-Pins), 578
La Rochelle, 693–699
La Rotonde (Aix-en-Provence), 527, 532
La Route des Crêtes, 407
La Route du Vin (between Strasbourg and Colmar), 396–406
La Ruche (Lyon), 454
La Salle de Bal (Fontainebleau), 233
Lascaux II, 727
Lascaux (Montignac), 726–728
Lassaussois Antiquités (Chartres), 230
La Suite (Dinard), 346–347
La Tantina de Bourgos (Toulouse), 669
L'Atelier (Caen), 325

Latin Quarter (Paris), 90
  accommodations, 206–213
  restaurants, 154–163
  shopping, 167
  sights and attractions, 120–136
La Tour César (Beaugency), 260
La Tour de Guet (Pérouges), 458
La Trinitaine (St-Malo), 341
La Turbie, 613–615
La Villa Rouge (Montpellier), 643
La Villette Jazz Festival (Paris), 57
La Villette (Paris), 117
Lavinia (Paris), 181
L'Aviso (St-Malo), 343
La Voile Rouge (St-Tropez), 552
L.C. Club (Nantes), 365
Le Baron (Paris), 191–192
Le Bar (Paris), 188
Le Bar 113 (Toulon), 546
Le Bataclan (Paris), 192
Le Black Bottom (Carcassonne), 655
Le Boléro (Angers), 302
Le Bon Marché (Paris), 178
Le Bout du Monde (Beaune), 431
Le Brévent, 489
Le Brouillarta (St-Jean-de-Luz), 687
Le Cabaret La Luna Negra (Bayonne), 679
Le Café Français (Chinon), 294
Le Calle Ocho (Bordeaux), 715
Le Capitole (Toulouse), 662
Le Captain Pub (Annecy), 477
Le Cargo de Nuit (Arles), 522
Le Carré (Caen), 326
Le Carré Coast (Biarritz), 684
Le Casino Municipal (Biarritz), 684
Le Castillet (Perpignan), 648–649
Le C-Cafe (Nimes), 636
Le Central (Paris), 193
Le 109 (St-Malo), 343
Le Cercle (Périgueux), 726
Le Chalet (Strasbourg), 396
Le Chandelier (Nice), 599
Le Château (Nice), 594
Le Chat Noir (Dijon), 437
Le Chic (Caen), 326
Le Chocolaterie Hotot (Caen), 325
Le Chriss Bar (Epernay), 382
Le Cintra (Dijon), 437
Le Circus
  Marseille, 543
  Nancy, 414
L'Eclaireur (Paris), 174
Le Cocktail Bar (St-Rémy), 517
Le Comptoir de Bretagne (St-Malo), 341
Le Comptoir Normand (Caen), 325
Le Consortium (Dijon), 434
Le Copa (Biarritz), 684
Le Cosy Club (Perpignan), 651
Le Couche Tard (Grenoble), 483
Le Cox (Paris), 193
Le Divino (Aix-en-Provence), 532
Le Domaine des Crus (Epernay), 380
Le Domaine (Lyon), 454
Le Duo (Annecy), 477
Le Duplex (Paris), 193
Le Féstival de Film de Sarlat, 733
Le Fornet, 493
Le Forum des Halles (Paris), 168
Le Forum (Lyon), 454
Le Four des Navettes (Marseille), 538
Le Frog & Le Roast Beef (Toulouse), 669
Legal aid, 758
Le Garage Bar (Pau), 675
Le Garage (Chamonix), 491–492
Le Georges V (Grenoble), 484
Léger, Fernand, Musée National (Biot), 574–575
Le Gibus (Paris), 190
Le G.I. (Tours), 283
Le Grand Café (Avignon), 509
Le Grand Pavois-Salon Nautique (La Rochelle), 695
Le Grand Tour Buses (Marseille), 534
Le Habana Bodegita-Club (Perpignan), 650–651
Le Kent (Angers), 302
Le Kilkenny (Dijon), 437
Le Klub (Nice), 605–606
Le Klub (St-Malo), 343
Le Legende de Buffalo Bill (Disneyland Paris), 242
Le Lieu Unique (Nantes), 359, 365
Le Marais (Paris), 85
  accommodations, 195–197
  restaurants, 141–143
  shopping, 166
  sights and attractions, 100–107
Le Marché aux Truffles et au Gras (Sarlat-la-Canéda), 734
Le Marché du Cours Lafayette (Toulon), 544
Le Master Home Bar (Nice), 605
Le Messire (Dijon), 437
Le Mistral (Aix-en-Provence), 532
Le Montenvers, 489–490
Le Musée d'Alésia, 435
Le Napoli (Perpignan), 651
Le Nightlife (Cannes), 569
Leonardo da Vinci
  Château du Clos-Lucé (Amboise), 272
  Mona Lisa (La Gioconda; Paris), 36, 98
  tomb of (Amboise), 272
Le O'Shannon Bar (Perpignan), 651
Le Pacha (Montpellier), 643
Le Palais (Belle-Ile-en-Mer), 363
Le Palais de l'Ile (Annecy), 475
Le Pam Pam (Juan-les-Pins), 578
Le Papagayo (St-Tropez), 557
Le Paradox (Marseille), 543
Le Passe Temps (Marseille), 542
Le Petit Danois (Val d'Isère), 495
Le Petit Journal Montparnasse (Paris), 191
Le Petit Marais (Nantes), 365
Le Pigeonnier (St-Tropez), 557
Le Play Boy (Biarritz), 684
Le Privilège (Chartres), 232
Le Prix du Jockey Club (Chantilly), 244
Le Procope (Paris), 164–165
Le Progrès (Epernay), 382
Le P'tit Zinc (Rouen), 312
Le Purple (Toulouse), 669
Le Pyms (Tours), 283
Le Raidd (Paris), 193
Le Régine's (Deauville), 320
Le Retable d'Issenheim (Colmar), 404
Le Royal Club Privé (Nantes), 365
Les Alignements (Carnac), 357, 358
Les Ambassadeurs (Avignon), 509
Les Arènes (Amphitheater; Arles), 519
Les Arènes de Nîmes, 632
Les Bacchantes (Paris), 187
Les Bateaux d'Aix, 478
Les Baux, 523–526
L'Escale Borély (Marseille), 542
L'Escale (Reims), 379
L'Escalier (St-Malo), 343
Les Catacombes (Paris), 135
Les Caves de Courchevel, 487
Les Caves du Roy
  Nancy, 414
  St-Tropez, 557
Les Chorégies d'Orange, 56, 497–498
L'Esclave (Avignon), 509
Les Egouts (Paris), 130–131
Les Estivales (Perpignan), 648
Le Seven (Strasbourg), 396
Le Sextius Bar (Aix-en-Provence), 532
Les Eyzies-de-Tayac, 729–732
Les Fouilles d'Alésia, 435
Les Francofolies (La Rochelle), 694–695
Les Galeries Lafayette (Paris), 178–179
Les Grandes Ecuries/Musée Vivant du Cheval (Chantilly), 246
Les Grandes Ecuries (Versailles), 222
Les Grands Appartements du Palais (Monaco), 619–620

Les Halles
Avignon, 506
Paris, 85, 91
accommodations, 194–195
restaurants, 137–141
shopping, 165–166
Les Halles Centrales (Dijon), 433
Les 24 Heures du Mans Moto, 55
Les 24 Heures du Mans Voitures, 56
Le Sirius (Lyon), 454
Les Mardis de la Collégiale (Colmar), 402–403
Les Mouettes (La Rochelle), 699
Les Naïades Discothèque (Quimper), 353
Les Nocturnes du Mont-St-Michel, 56
Le Soft (Reims), 380
Le 66 (Paris), 178
Les Pampilles (Montpellier), 642
Les Planches
Deauville, 316, 320
Trouville, 321
L'Esprit (Pau), 675
Les Puces de Nice (Nice), 599
L'Esquinade (St-Tropez), 557
Les Thermes Evian, 473
Les Thermes Marins (Monaco), 618
Les Trois Glorieuses, 57
Le Styx (Grenoble), 484
Le Sunset/Le Sunside (Paris), 191
Les Vedettes de Normandie (Port-en-Bessin), 331
Le Temple de Diane (Nîmes), 632–633
Le Temps d'Aimer (Biarritz), 680
Le Temps d'Aimer (Nantes), 365
Le Thot (Lascaux), 728
Le Tie Break (Nantes), 365
Le Triangle (Pau), 675
Le 3w Kafe, 193
L'Evasion (Nantes), 365
Le Velvet Jazz Lounge (Blois), 267
Le Vieux Necy (Annecy), 477
Le Village (Juan-les-Pins), 578
Le VIP Room (St-Tropez), 557
Le Vogue (Cannes), 569
Le Vogue (Reims), 380
Le Winfield (Pau), 675
L'Excalibur (Tours), 283
L'Exit (Marseille), 543
L'Habilleur (Paris), 176
L'Hendrix Café (Blois), 267
Libourne, 716
Librairie le Bail-Weissert (Paris), 171
Lido de Paris (Paris), 189
Lieutenance (Honfleur), 313
Limoges, 743–746
L'Institut & Musée Lumière (Lyon), 447
Lire & Chiner (Colmar), 403
Loches, 283–285
Logis du Roi (Amboise), 272
Logis Tiphaine (Mont-St-Michel), 336
Loire Valley, 63, 253–302
London Pub (Grenoble), 483
Lost and found, 758
Louisiana Club (Colmar), 407
Louis Vuitton (Paris), 175
Louis XV Staircase (Fontainebleau), 233
Lourmarin, 513
Louvre, accommodations, 194–195
Louvre area (Paris), shopping, 165–166
Louvre district (Paris), 36
restaurants, 137–141
Louvre Museum, 96
L'Ubu (Périgueux), 726
Lull (Monte-Carlo), 619
Lulu Club (Nimes), 636
L'Univers Café (Nantes), 365
Lyon, 440–454
accommodations, 449–451
exploring, 444–449
getting around, 442
getting there, 442
nightlife, 454
restaurants, 451–453
shopping, 448–449
visitor information, 444

M

Magasin d'Usine Daum (Nancy), 411
Mail, 759
Main Street, U.S.A. (Disneyland Paris), 239
Maison Adam (St-Jean-de-Luz), 686
Maison Baccarat (Paris), 182
Maison Carrée (Nîmes), 630
Maison Charles Trenet (Narbonne), 644
Maison de la Boétie (Sarlat-la-Canéda), 733
Maison de la Truffe (Paris), 181
Maison de l'Infante (St-Jean-de-Luz), 686
Maison des Princes de Savoie (Pérouges), 458
Maison Devineau (Nantes), 362
Maison du Sud (Carcassonne), 653
Maison du Vin
Bordeaux, 708
Saumur, 297
Maison du Vin de l'Anjou (Angers), 300
Maison Fabre (Paris), 175–176
Maison Fossier/Biscuits Fossier (Reims), 376
Maison Jean Vier (Bayonne), 677
Maison Léon (Périgueux), 722
Maison Louis XIV (St-Jean-de-Luz), 685
Maison Natale de Jeanne d'Arc (Domrémy-la-Pucelle), 414
Maison Pfister (Colmar), 403
Maison Quinta (Perpignan), 648
Maison Rémy Martin (Cognac), 701
Maisons Satie (Honfleur), 313
Maison Thomassin (Lyon), 444
Manet, Edouard, 37
Manufacture de Monaco (Monte-Carlo), 619
Manufacture Nationale de Sèvres (Paris), 182
Maps, 752
Marché à la Brocante (Nice), 599
Marché aux Fleurs
Nice, 594, 599
Paris, 168
Marché aux Puces de la Porte de Vanves (Paris), 168
Marché aux Puces St-Ouen de Clignancourt (Paris), 168–169
Marché aux Vins (Beaune), 428
Marché Ave du Président Wilson (Paris), 169
Marché Biologique (Paris), 169
Marché Cassanyes (Perpignan), 648
Marché des Enfants Rouges (Paris), 169
Marché Forville (Cannes), 561
Marché Notre-Dame (Versailles), 223
Marché Publique (Deauville), 317
Marin-Marine (St-Malo), 341
Markstein, 407
Marlenheim, 397
Marseille, 533–543
accommodations, 538–541
nightlife, 542–543
restaurants, 541
seeing the sights, 534–538
shopping, 538
traveling to, 533–534
visitor information, 534
Martell (Cognac), 701
Martin Pouret (Orléans), 258
The Massif Central, 67
Matisse, Henri, 37
Chapelle du Rosaire (Vence), 589–590
Musée Matisse (Cimiez), 597
Max Vauché (Blois), 264
Meals and dining customs, 51–52
Médoc, 716–717
Mémorial de Caen, 324
Mémorial des Martyrs Français de la Déportation de 1945 (Paris), 102–103

Mémorial de Verdun, 416
Memorial du Débarquement en Provence (Toulon), 544–545
Mercier (Epernay), 381
Merci (Paris), 178
Merville-France-Ville (Deauville), 317
Metz, 412
Michel Bertran (Rouen), 309
The Middle Ages, 25–27
Mille et Un Fromages (Biarritz), 682
Mistral, Frédéric, 522
Mistral Location (Cannes), 559
Mittelbergheim, 398
Mme. Faye-Nunez (Carcassonne), 653
Mobile phones, 759
Moët et Chandon Champagne Cellars (Epernay), 381
Molly Bloom (Toulon), 546
Monaco, 615–625
accommodations, 620–623
dialing tips, 616
getting there, 616
nightlife, 624–625
outdoor activities, 618
restaurants, 623–624
seeing the sights, 619–620
shopping, 618
special events, 617
visitor information, 617
Monaco Grand Prix de Formule, 55
Monaco-Ville, 615
Mona Lisa (Leonardo da Vinci; Paris), 98
Monastère de Cimiez (Cimiez Convent), 597
Monastère Royal de Brou (Bourg-en-Bresse), 459–460
Monet, Claude, 37
Foundation (Giverny), 243
Money and costs, 759–760
Monique Buisson (Dijon), 434
Monolithe, Eglise (St-Emilion), 718
Monsieur Carnaval (Toulouse), 669
Montbard, 435
Mont Blanc, 488
Mont Blanc Tunnel, 488
Mont Cavalier (Nîmes), 633
Mont Crussol, 464
Monte-Carlo Beach Club (Monaco), 618
Monte-Carlo Casino (Monaco), 624–625
Monte-Carlo Country Club (Monaco), 618
Monte-Carlo International Fireworks Festival (Monaco), 617
Monte-Carlo Masters (Monaco), 617
Monte-Carlo (Monaco), 615
Monte-Carlo Motor Rally, 54
Montmartre (Paris), 88, 114, 116
accommodations, 203–204
restaurants, 150–151
shopping, 166
Montparnasse (Paris), 91
accommodations, 212–213
restaurants, 161–163
shopping, 167
sights and attractions, 134–136
Montpellier, 638–643
Montrottier, 475
Mont-St-Michel, 333–338
Morabito (Paris), 176
Morrison's Irish Pub (Cannes), 568
Morrison's Lounge (Cannes), 568
Mougins, 569–571
Moulin, Jean, 227
Moulin Rouge (Paris), 189
Mulot et Petitjean (Dijon), 433
Münster, 407–408
Muré (Colmar), 403
Musée Alsacien (Strasbourg), 390
Musée Archéologique
Dijon, 432
Nîmes, 634
Musée Balzac (Saché), 290
Musée Bartholdi (Colmar), 404
Musée Basque (Bayonne), 677
Musée Bonnat (Bayonne), 677
Musée Briard (Jouarre), 367
Musée Buffon (Montbard), 435
Musée Calvet (Avignon), 503
Musée Cantini (Marseille), 537
Musée Carnavalet-Histoire de Paris, 103, 106
Musée Charles-Portal (Cordes-sur-Ciel), 660
Musée Château d'Annecy, 475
Musée Chinois (Fontainebleau), 233
Musée Claude-Bernard (St-Julien-sous-Montmelas), 455
Musée Condé, 245–246
Musée d'Aquitaine (Bordeaux), 710
Musée d'Archéologie Méditerranéenne (Marseille), 537
Musée d'Art Classique de Mougins (Mougins), 570
Musée d'Art Contemporain (Nîmes), 632
Musée d'Art de Toulon (Toulon), 544
Musée d'Art et d'Archéologie du Périgord (Périgueux), 724
Musée d'Art et d'Archéologie (Senlis), 249
Musée d'Art et l'Histoire de Cognac, 701–702
Musée d'Art Moderne de la Ville de Paris, 112–113
Musée d'Art Moderne (Strasbourg), 390
Musée Dauphinois (Grenoble), 482
Musée de Cire (Chenonceau), 276
Musée de Grenoble, 482
Musée de la Castre (Cannes), 562–563
Musée de la Céramique (Rouen), 308
Musée de la Civilisation Gallo-Romaine (Lyon), 446
Musée de la Confiture (Pau), 673
Musée de la Figurine Historique (Compiègne), 251
Musée de la Marine (Toulon), 544
Musée de la Marionette (Lyon), 445
Musée de la Mer
Biarritz, 681
Ile Ste-Marguerite, 563
Mont-St-Michel, 335–336
Musée de l'Annonciade (Musée St-Tropez), 554
Musée de la Pêche (Concarneau), 353–354
Musée de Lapérouse (Albi), 657–658
Musée de la Photographie André Villers (Mougins), 570
Musée de l'Arles et de la Provence Antiques, 520
Musée de l'Armée (Paris), 126, 128
Musée de la Tapisserie de Bayeux, 327
Musée de l'Automobile de Valençay, 269
Musée de la Vénerie (Senlis), 248
Musée de la Vie Bourguignonne (Dijon), 432
Musée de l'Ecole de Nancy, 410
Musée de l'Hôtel-Dieu (Beaune), 428
Musée de l'Hôtel du Doyen (Bayeux), 327
Musée de l'Imprimerie de Lyon, 447
Musée de l'Oeuvre Notre-Dame (Strasbourg), 390
Musée de l'Olivier & Musée d'Art Moderne Méditerranéen (Château-Musée Grimaldi; Cagnes-sur-Mer), 583
Musée de l'Orangerie (Paris), 94, 96
Musée de Normandie (Caen), 323–324
Musée Departemental Breton (Quimper), 350

Musée de Préhistoire (Carnac), 359
Musée de Préhistoire et d'Histoire Naturelle (Nîmes), 634
Musée des Arts de Cognac, 701
Musée des Arts Décoratifs
Bordeaux, 710
Paris, 96
Musée des Arts et Traditions Populaires Catalans (Perpignan), 648–649
Musée des Augustins (Toulouse), 665
Musée des Beaux-Arts
Beaune, 428
Bordeaux, 710
Caen, 324
Chartres, 230
Dijon, 432
La Rochelle, 695–696
Limoges, 744
Lyon, 447
Nancy, 410
Nantes, 360–361
Nice, 596
Nîmes, 633–634
Orléans, 258
Pau, 672
Quimper, 350
Reims, 374
Rouen, 308
Tours, 279
Musée des Beaux-Arts Hyacinthe Rigaud (Perpignan), 649
Musée des Equipages (Vaux-le-Vicomte), 236
Musée des Plans-Reliefs (Paris), 128
Musée des Santons (Les Baux), 524
Musée des Spahis (Senlis), 248–249
Musée des Tapisseries (Aix-en-Provence), 528
Musée des Tissus et des Arts-Décoratifs (Lyon), 447
Musée d'Ethnographie et d'Art Populaire (Honfleur), 313
Musée d'Histoire de St-Malo, 340
Musée d'Histoire de St-Paul (St-Paul-de-Vence), 586
Musée d'Histoire Locale et de Céramique Biotoise (Biot), 574
Musée d'Orsay (Paris), 131–132
Musée du Château des Baux, 523–524
Musée du Débarquement (Arromanches-les-Bains), 331–332
Musée du Docteur Schweitzer (Kaysersberg), 399–400
Musée du Louvre (Paris), 96–99
Musée du Nouveau-Monde (La Rochelle), 696
Musée d'Unterlinden (Colmar), 404
Musée du Petit-Palais (Avignon), 504
Musée du Quai Branly (Paris), 132
Musée du Second Empire (Compiègne), 251
Musée du Trophée d'Auguste (La Turbie), 614
Musée du Vieux-Nîmes, 634
Musée du Vieux-Pérouges, 458
Musée du Vin de Bourgogne (Beaune), 428
Musée Eugène-Boudin (Honfleur), 314
Musée Fabre (Montpellier), 640
Musée Faure (Aix-les-Bains), 479
Musée Flaubert et d'Histoire de la Médécine (Rouen), 308
Musée Français de l'Automobile "Henri Malartre" (Rochetaillée-sur-Saône), 448
Musée François-Pompon (Saulieu), 437
Musée Gadagne (Musée Historique de Lyon), 445
Musée Gallo-Romain Vesunna (Périgueux), 724
Musée Goya (Castres), 655
Musée Grevin (Mont-St-Michel), 336
Musée Grobet-Labadié (Marseille), 537–538
Musée Historique de Lyon (Musée Gadagne), 445
Musée Historique de Mont-St-Michel, 336
Musée Historique Lorrain (Nancy), 410–411
Musée International d'Art Naïf Anatole-Jakovsky (Museum of Naive Art; Nice), 596
Musée International de la Parfumerie (Grasse), 572
Musée Jean-de-la-Fontaine (Château-Thierry), 369
Musée Jean Lurçat (Angers), 301
Musée Jeanne-d'Arc (Rouen), 308
Musée Jean-Peské (Collioure), 646
Musée Joseph Déchelette (Roanne), 457
Musée Jules Verne de Nantes, 361
Musée Lambinet (Versailles), 223
Musée Lapidaire
Avignon, 504
Vienne, 462
Musée le Secq des Tournelles (Rouen), 308–309
Musée Magnin (Dijon), 432–433
Musée Maritime (La Rochelle), 696
Musée Masséna (Nice), 596
Musée Matisse (Cimiez), 597
Musée Memorial de La Bataille de Normandie (Bayeux), 328
Musée Municipal de Pont-Aven, 356
Musée Municipal d'Orange, 498
Musée Municipal (Valence), 464
Musée Napoleonien (Cap d'Antibes), 579
Musée National d'Art Moderne (Paris), 104
Musée National de la Porcelaine Adrien-Dubouché (Limoges), 744–745
Musée National de la Préhistoire (Les Eyzies), 730–731
Musée National de la Voiture (Compiègne), 251
Musée National des Arts Asiatiques-Guimet (Paris), 113
Musée National d'Histoire Naturelle (Paris), 121
Musée National du Château de Compiègne, 251
Musée National du Château de Fontainebleau, 232
Musée National du Moyen Age/ Thermes de Cluny (Paris), 121–122
Musée National Fernand Léger (Biot), 574–575
Musée National Message Biblique Marc Chagall (Nice), 598
Musée Océanographique De Monaco, 620
Musée Perrin de Puycousin (Dijon), 432
Musée Picasso (Cap d'Antibes), 579–580
Musée Rabelais-La Devinière (Chinon), 292
Musée Réattu (Arles), 520
Musée Renoir & Les Collettes (Cagnes-sur-Mer), 583–584
Musée Rodin (Paris), 132–133
Musée Rolin (Autun), 426
Musée Ste-Croix (Poitiers), 692
Musée St-Tropez (Musée de l'Annonciade), 554
Musée Thomas-Dobrée (Nantes), 361–362
Musée Toulouse-Lautrec (Albi), 658
Musée Vivant du Cheval (Chantilly), 246
Muséum d'Histoire Naturelle (La Rochelle), 696
Museum of Historical Figurines (Compiègne), 251

Museum of Naive Art (Musée International d'Art Naïf Anatole-Jakovsky; Nice), 596
Museums, best, 9–10
Music, 46–48
  tours, 60

N

Nancy, 408–414
Nantes, 359–365
Napoleon Bonaparte, 28–29, 97–98
Napoleon's Tomb (Paris), 128, 130
Nappes d'Alsace (Strasbourg), 391
Narbonne, 643–645
National, 751
National Automobile Museum (Compiègne), 251
NaturoSpace (Honfleur), 314
Nautical Center (Evian-les-Bains), 470
New Can Can (Marseille), 543
New Morning (Paris), 191
Newspapers and magazines, 760
New Year's Eve, 58
Ni Bar (Monte-Carlo), 625
Nice, 591–606
  accommodations, 599–603
  beaches, 598
  exploring, 593–598
  getting around, 592–593
  getting there, 592
  nightlife, 605–606
  restaurants, 603–605
  shopping, 599
  special events, 593
  visitor information, 592
Nice Carnaval, 593
Nice Festival du Jazz, 593
Nice Jazz Festival, 57
Nice-Le Grand Tour, 593
Nicola Alziari (Nice), 599
Nicolas (Caen), 325
Nicolas (Paris), 181
Nikki Beach (St-Tropez), 552
Nîmes, 629–635
Normandy, 63
  cuisine, 50
  suggested itinerary, 306
Normandy American Cemetery (Omaha Beach), 332
Normandy American Visitor Center (Colleville-sur-Mer), 330
Notre-Dame, Cathédrale (Paris), 100–102
Notre-Dame, Collégiale (Beaune), 427–428
Notre-Dame, Eglise
  Beaugency, 260–261
  Bourg-en-Bresse, 459
Notre-Dame de Bayeux, 328
Notre-Dame de Chartres, 228–230
Notre-Dame de Fourvière, Basilique (Lyon), 445–446
Notre-Dame-de-la-Garde, Basilique (Marseille), 536–537
Notre-Dame de Reims, Cathédrale, 372–373
Notre-Dame de Rouen, Cathédrale, 306
Notre-Dame-des-Anges, Eglise de (Collioure), 645–646
Notre-Dame des Doms, Cathédrale (Avignon), 502–503
Nôtre Dame de Sénanque, Abbaye (Gordes), 514
Notre-Dame de Senlis, 248
Notre-Dame des Sablons, Eglise (Aigues-Mortes), 636
Notre-Dame de Strasbourg, Cathédrale, 388–389
Notre-Dame de Vie, Chapelle (Mougins), 570
Notre-Dame La Daurade (Toulouse), 662
Notre-Dame-la-Grande, Eglise (Poitiers), 690
Nouveau Casino (Paris), 192
Nouveau Musée National De Monaco, 620
NWA/KLM, 749

O

Octopussy (St-Tropez), 552
O'Donnell's (Caen), 326
Olive Festival (La Fête de l'Olivier; Cagnes-sur-Mer), 583
Olivier millénaire (Roquebrune), 627
Omaha Beach, 332
O'Paris Pub (Versailles), 225
O Patchwork (Quimper), 353
Opéra Bastille (Paris), 185
Opéra de Monte-Carlo, 625
Opéra de Nice, 605
Opéra du Rhin (Strasbourg), 396
Opera du Toulon, 544
Opéra Garner (Paris), 114
Opéra Garnier (Paris), 88, 185–186
  accommodations, 201–203
Opéra (Lyon), 454
Opéra (Paris)
  restaurants, 147–150
  shopping, 166
Orange, 497–501
Orchestre Philharmonique de Strasbourg, 396
Orléans, 255–260
Orly airport, accommodations near, 213
Orly Airport (Paris), 81, 82
Orthodoxe Russe, Eglise (Biarritz), 681
Ossuaire de Douaumont (Verdun), 416
Otard (Cognac), 700

P

Paimpol, 346
Palace of the Kings of Majorca (Perpignan), 649
Palais Beaumont (Pau), 672
Palais de l'Archevêché (Rouen), 307
Palais de Rohan (Strasbourg), 390
Palais des Archevêques (Narbonne), 644
Palais des Ducs et des Etats de Bourgogne (Dijon), 431–432
Palais des Papes (Avignon), 504
Palais des Rois de Majorque (Perpignan), 649
Palais des Tuileries (Paris), 92, 94
Palais de Tokyo (Paris), 113
Palais Ducal (Nancy), 408, 410
Palais du Facteur Cheval (Hauterives), 463
Palais du Gouvernement, Nancy, 410
Palais du Luxembourg (Paris), 124–125
Palais Lascaris (Nice), 597
Palais Royal (Paris), 99–100
Palm Beach Casino (Cannes), 568
P&O Ferries, 750
Panthéon (Paris), 122, 124
Parc de Bagatelle (Paris), 109
Parc de la Tête d'Or (Lyon), 448
Parc de la Villette (Paris), 120
Parc des Expositions (Caen), 325
Parc des Expositions (Reims), 376
Parc des Mini-Châteaux (near Amboise), 273
Parc du Château Royal and Musées de La Vénerie et des Spahis (Senlis), 248
Parc du Pharo (Marseille), 534
Parc François-1er (Cognac), 702
Parc Monceau (Paris), 113–114
Pardon de St-Ouen (St-Malo), 340
Pardon of the Newfoundland Fishing Fleet (St-Malo), 340
Parfumerie Fragonard (Grasse), 572
Parfumerie Molinard (Grasse), 572–573
Pariès (Biarritz), 682
Paris, 80–214
  accommodations, 193–214
  arriving in, 81–83
  business hours, 165
  cafes, 163–165

entertainment and nightlife, 184–193
exploring, 91–136
layout, 83–84
neighborhoods in brief, 84–91
restaurants, 136–163
shopping, 165–183
visitor information, 83
Paris Auto Show, 57
Paris Convention and Visitors Bureau, 83
Paris Quartier d'Eté, 56–57
Parvis des Eglises (Rocamadour), 739
Passage de la Geôle (Versailles), 223
Passe-Musée (Nancy), 409
Pass Nantes, 360
Passports, 760–761
Patrick Chasset (Rouen), 309
Pau, 671–675
Pavillon de la Porcelaine-Musée Haviland (Limoges), 745
Péniche Maison de la Violette (Toulouse), 665
Père-Lachaise Cemetery (Paris), 117–119
Périgueux, 721–726
Pérouges, 458–459
Perpignan, 647–651
Perpignan Jazz Festival, 57
***Pétanque,* 556**
Petite Afrique (Beaulieu-sur-Mer), 610
Petite Venise (Colmar), 403
Petits Appartements (Versailles), 221
Petit Train (Rouen), 309
Petit Train touristique de Cannes, 562
Petit Trianon (Versailles), 222
Philippe Denies (Blois), 264
Picasso, Pablo, 37
Musée Picasso (Cap d'Antibes), 579–580
Pickwick's Pub (Beaune), 431
Pierre Hermé (Paris), 179
Piggy's Pub (Courchevel 1850), 487
Piscine de Trouville, 321
Piscine Municipale (Deauville), 317
Piscine Olympique (Dinard), 344
Place Amélie Pollonnais (Villefranche-sur-Mer), 606
Place Bellecour (Lyon), 444
Place d'Armes (Ile de Porquerolles), 547
Place de Coderc (Périgueux), 722
Place de la Bastille (Paris), 89
Place de la Bourse (Bordeaux), 709
Place de la Cathédrale (Strasbourg), 396
Place de la Comédie
Bordeaux, 709
Montpellier, 639
Place de la République
Arles, 518
Perpignan, 648
Place de l'Hôtel-de-Ville (Angoulême), 704
Place des Arcades (Biot), 574
Place des Vosges (Paris), 106
Place du Forum (Arles), 518
Place du Marché aux Oies (Sarlat-la-Canéda), 733
Place du Marché (place de l'Eglise Monolithe; St-Emilion), 718
Place du Vieux-Marché (Rouen), 309
Place Gutenberg (Strasbourg), 388
Place Kléber (Strasbourg), 386
Place Masséna (Nice), 594
Place Plumereau (Tours), 283
Place Stanislas (Nancy), 409–410
Plage de Bon Secours (St-Malo), 340
Plage de Cornouaille (Concarneau), 354
Plage de Deauville, 317
Plage de Juan-les-Pins, 576
Plage de la Bouillabaisse (St-Tropez), 552
Plage de la Côte des Basques (Biarritz), 680
Plage de la Garoupe (Juan-les-Pins), 576
Plage de la Salis (Juan-les-Pins), 576
Plage de l'Ecluse (Dinard), 344
Plage de Paloma (St-Jean-Cap-Ferrat), 608
Plage de Pampelonne (near St-Tropez), 552
Plage de Rodel (Concarneau), 354
Plage de St-Enogat (Dinard), 344
Plage des Dames (Concarneau), 354
Plage des Graniers (St-Tropez), 552
Plage des Jumeaux (St-Tropez), 552
Plage des Sables Blancs (Concarneau), 354
Plage des Salins (St-Tropez), 552
Plage de Tahiti (St-Tropez), 552
Plage de Trouville, 321
Plage du Cabellou (Concarneau), 354
Plage du Débarquement (Arromanches-les-Bains), 331–332
Plage du Larvotto (Monaco), 618
Plage du Midi (Cannes), 559
Plage du Mourillon (Toulon), 543
Plage du Port-Vieux (Biarritz), 680
Plage du Prieuré (Dinard), 344
Plage Gazagnaire (Cannes), 559
Plage Miramar (Biarritz), 680
Plage Passable (St-Jean-Cap-Ferrat), 608
Plages de Cros-de-Cagnes, 583
Planning your trip, 748–763
getting around, 750–754
getting there, 748–750
Plateau de l'Atalaye (Biarritz), 681
Plat Jérôme (Nice), 599
Poilâne (Paris), 179–180
Pointe du Hoc, 332
Pointe Helbronner (Italy), 489
Pointe St-Martin (Biarritz), 680
Poitiers, 689–693
Poitiers l'Eté, 690
Police, 761
Pommery (Reims), 375
Pont-Audemer, 312
Pont-Aven, 355–357
Pont de Pierre (Bordeaux), 710
Pont du Gard (Nîmes), 634
Pont Neuf (Paris), 103
Pont St-Bénézet (Avignon), 502
Pont Valentré (Cahors), 741
Pope's Bedroom (Avignon), 504
Porcelaines Philippe Deshoulières-Lafarge (Limoges), 743
Port de Commerce (La Rochelle), 699
Port de Goulphar, 363
Port de Pêche (La Rochelle), 699
Port de Plaisance (La Rochelle), 699
Port des Pêcheurs (Biarritz), 681, 684
Porte Central (Rouen), 306
Porte d'Arroux (Autun), 425
Porte d'Auguste (Porte d'Arles; Nîmes), 634
Porte St-André (Autun), 425
Porte St-Vincent (St-Malo), 340
Port Grimaud, 554
Port Moderne (Marseille), 537
Prieuré St-Mauritius (Senlis), 248
Primatiale St-Jean (Lyon), 444, 445
Princesse Tam-Tam (Paris), 177
Printemps (Paris), 179
Prix de l'Arc de Triomphe (Paris), 57
Prix Diane (Chantilly), 244
Prix Diane-Hermès, (Paris), 55
Prix du Jockey Club (Paris), 55
Procession de la Sanch (Perpignan), 648
Promenade des Anglais (Nice), 593–594

Promenade des Remparts (Angoulême), 705
Promenade du Bord de Mer (Biarritz), 680
Promenade du Clair-de-Lune (Dinard), 347
Promenade du Peyrou (Montpellier), 639
Promenade du Rocher-des-Doms (Avignon), 503
Promenade Maurice-Rouvier (Beaulieu-sur-Mer), 611
Proust, Marcel, 326
Provence, 65, 497–548
Pub du Corsaire (St-Jean-de-Luz), 687
Pub Saint Patrick (St-Malo), 343
Puy St-Front (Périgueux), 722
Pyramide du Cirque Romain (Vienne), 462

Q

Qantas, 749
Quai des Belges (Marseille), 538
Quart de Tours, 282
Quartier du Camp Americain (Beaune), 428
83 Vernet (Avignon), 509
Quiberon, 363
Quimper, 349–353
Quincaillerie Centrale (Aix-en-Provence), 529

R

Rabelais, François, Musée Rabelais-La Devinière (Chinon), 292
Rail Europe, 749, 752–753
Rambouillet, 225–227
Raynaud (Limoges), 743
Réciproque (Paris), 176
Red Zone DJ bar (Avignon), 509
Regions in brief, 62–67
Reims, 372–380
Relève de la Garde (Monaco), 620
Rémy Martin (Cognac), 701
Renoir, Pierre-Auguste, 37, 582–583
  Musée Renoir & Les Collettes (Cagnes-sur-Mer), 583–584
Restaurants, best, 16–18
Revard, 478
Revolution of 1789, 28–29
Rhône Valley, 64–65, 440–468
Rhumerie Le Kalico (Courchevel 1850), 487
Ribeauvillé, 399
Roanne, 456–458
Rocamadour, 737–740
Rocher de la Vierge (Biarritz), 681
Rochers d'Angennes, 227
Rock 'n' Roller Coaster (Disneyland Paris), 241
Rockstore (Montpellier), 642
Rodin, Auguste, 37
  Musée Rodin (Paris), 132–133
Roman Theater (Vienne), 462
Roquebrune, 626
Rouen, 304–312
Rouffach, 401–402
Route de Cézanne, 528
Route de Champagne, 376, 379
Route des Grandes Alpes, 472
Route du Vin (between Strasbourg and Colmar), 396–406
Roxy Jam (Biarritz), 680
Royal Chapel (Versailles), 221–222
Royal Food (Monte-Carlo), 619
Rue de la Miséricorde (St-Tropez), 553
Rue du Gros-Horloge (Rouen), 309
Rue Grande (St-Paul-de-Vence), 586
Rue Montaigne (Sarlat-la-Canéda), 734
Ruines de Glanum (St-Rémy), 515

S

Saché, 290
Sacré-Coeur, Eglise de (Beaulieu-sur-Mer), 611
Safety concerns, 761
St-Aignan (Orléans), 258
St-Andoche, Basilique (Saulieu), 437
St-André, Cathédrale (Bordeaux), 709
St. André (Chartres), 230
St. Andrew's Gate (Autun), 425
St-Apollinaire, Cathédrale (Valence), 464
St-Benoît, Eglise (Castres), 655
St-Blaise, Chapel of (Les Baux), 524
St-Corentin, Cathédrale (Quimper), 350
Ste-Catherine, Eglise (Honfleur), 313
Ste-Cécile, Cathédrale (Albi), 657
Sainte-Chapelle (Paris), 106–107
Ste-Croix, Cathédrale (Orléans), 257–258
Ste-Madeleine, Basilique (Vézelay), 422
Ste-Marie-Majeure, Cathédrale (Toulon), 544
Ste-Mère-Eglise (near Utah Beach), 332
St-Emilion, 717–719
St-Etienne, Cathédrale
  Auxerre, 419
  Cahors, 741
  Limoges, 743
  Toulouse, 664
St-Etienne, Eglise (Beaugency), 261
St-Etienne-de-la-Cité, Eglise (Périgueux), 723
St-Front, Cathédrale (Périgueux), 722–723
St-Gatien, Cathédrale (Tours), 279
St-Germain-des-Prés, accommodations, 208–211
St-Germain-des-Prés area (Paris), 90
  restaurants, 156–158
  shopping, 167
  sights and attractions, 124–134
St-Germain-des-Prés church (Paris), 125–126
St-Honorat, Abbaye de, 564
St-Jean, 608
St-Jean, Baptistère (Poitiers), 690
St-Jean, Cathédrale (Perpignan), 648
St-Jean-Baptiste, Eglise (St-Jean-de-Luz), 685
St-Jean-Cap-Ferrat, 607–610
St-Jean-de-Luz, 684–687
St-Julien-sous-Montmelas, 455
St-Just et St-Pasteur, Cathédrale (Narbonne), 644
St-Lazare, Cathédrale (Autun), 425–426
St-Lazare, Eglise (Avallon), 423–424
St-Léger, Eglise (Cognac), 702
St-Maclou, Eglise (Rouen), 307
St-Malo, 338–343
Saint Marie Madeleine (Pérouges), 458
St-Martin, Eglise
  Biarritz, 681
  Colmar, 404
St-Martin-d'Ainay, Abbaye Romaine de, 447
St-Maurice, Cathédrale
  Angers, 300
  Vienne, 462
St-Michel, Basilique (Bordeaux), 709–710
St-Michel, Eglise
  Bordeaux, 711
  Cordes-sur-Ciel, 660
St-Michel-des-Lions, Eglise (Limoges), 744
St-Nazaire, Basilique (Carcassonne), 653
St-Ouen, Eglise (Rouen), 308, 312
St-Ours, Collégiale (Loches), 284
St-Paul, Eglise (Lyon), 444–445
St-Paul de Mausole (St-Rémy), 515
St-Paul-de-Vence, 585–588

St-Pierre, Cathédrale
Angoulême, 704
Montpellier, 639
Nantes, 360
Poitiers, 690
St-Pierre, Chapelle (Villefranche-sur-Mer), 606
St-Pierre, Eglise
Chartres, 230
Vienne, 462
St-Pierre la Mer, 643
St-Rémi, Basilique (Reims), 372
St-Rémi, Eglise (Domrémy-la-Pucelle), 414
St-Rémy-de-Provence, 514–517
Saint Sacerdos, Cathédral de (Sarlat-la-Canéda), 733
St-Sauveur, Basilique
Dinan, 348
Rocamadour, 739
St-Sauveur, Cathédrale (Aix-en-Provence), 528
St-Sernin, Basilique (Toulouse), 662
St-Servan (St-Malo), 341
St-Seurin, Basilique (Bordeaux), 710
St-Sulpice (Paris), 126
St-Thomas, Eglise (Strasbourg), 390
St-Tropez, 550–558
St-Trophime, Eglise (Arles), 519–520
St-Vincent, Cathédrale (St-Malo), 340
St-Vincent, Eglise (Les Baux), 524
Salle de Reddition (Reims), 374
Salle des Chevaliers (Mont-St-Michel), 335
Salle Garnier (Monte-Carlo), 625
Salle Pleyel (Paris), 186
Salles Arbuissonnas, Eglise de (Salles-en-Beaujolais), 456
Salles-en-Beaujolais, 455, 456
Saloir et Séchoire à Jambon Pierre Ibaialde (Bayonne), 678
Salon Nautique de Paris, 58
Salons du Palais Royal, Shiseido (Paris), 183
Sandro Homme (Paris), 175
Santons Fouque (Aix-en-Provence), 529
Sarlat-la-Canéda, 732–737
Satie, Erik, Maisons Satie (Honfleur), 313
Saulieu, 437
Saumur, 296–299
Scat Club (Aix-en-Provence), 532
Scuba diving
Nice, 598
St-Tropez, 552
Seasons, 54
The Second Empire, 29–30
Senior travel, 761–762
Senlis, 247–249
Sennelier (Paris), 171
Sentier du Plateau St-Michel (Beaulieu-sur-Mer), 611
Sentier Le Corbusier (Cap-Martin), 627
7L (Paris), 171
Shakespeare and Company (Paris), 172
Shanghai Express (Toulouse), 669
Shiseido (Paris), 183
Showcase (Paris), 192
Show Case Time (Pau), 675
Site Préhistorique de Regourdou (Lascaux), 728
Skiing
Chamonix, 487–489
Courchevel 1850, 484
Val d'Isère, 494
Smarties (Nice), 605
Smoking, 762
Smoking Dog (Lyon), 454
Snow Fun (Val d'Isère), 494
Société Duboscq (Médoc), 717
Soirées aux Chandelles (Vaux-le-Vicomte), 236–237
Sonia Rykiel (Paris), 174
SOS Médecins, 756
S.O.S. Racisme, 761
Soufflenheim (Strasbourg), 391
Souleiado (Avignon), 506
Spectacles Medievaux (Carcassonne), 652
Spree (Paris), 178
Squash, Monaco, 618
Stade Nautique Rainier-III (Monaco), 618
Statue de Suffren (St-Tropez), 553
Stock Griffe (Monte-Carlo), 618–619
Strasbourg, 384–397
accommodations, 391–393
exploring, 386–390
getting there, 385
nightlife, 396
restaurants, 394–396
shopping, 390–391
special events, 386
visitor information, 386
Strasbourg-Entzheim Airport, 385–386
Stravinsky fountain (Paris), 104
Student travel, 762
Studio 49 (Angers), 302
Studium (Avignon), 504, 506

T

Taittinger (Reims), 375
Tapisserie Langlois (Blois), 264
Taxes, 762
Téléphérique-Grenoble-Bastille, 481–482
Telephones, 762
Temple d'Auguste et de Livie (Vienne), 462
Tennis
Cannes, 559
Monaco, 618
Théâtre Antique
Arles, 518–519
Orange, 498
Théâtre Antique de Vienne, 461
Théâtre d'Annecy, 477
Théâtre de Chartres, 232
Théâtre de la Cité (Toulouse), 669
Théâtre de la Digue (Toulouse), 669
Théâtre de l'Archipel (Perpignan), 648
Théâtre des Arts/Opéra Léonard de Vinci (Rouen), 311–312
Théâtre des Célestins (Lyon), 454
Théâtre des Deux Rives (Rouen), 311
Théâtre du Capitole (Toulouse), 669
Théâtre Garonne (Toulouse), 669
Théâtre Jean Deschamps (Carcassonne), 651
Théâtre National de Strasbourg, 396
Théâtre National Dijon-Bourgogne, 437
Théâtre National du Capitole (Toulouse), 662
Théâtre Romain (Vienne), 462
Théâtres Romains (Lyon), 446
Théâtre Zenith (Toulouse), 669
Thermes d'Aix-les-Bains, 478
Ticket Jeune, 762
Tignes, 493
Time zone, 762
Tipping, 762
Toilets, 763
Top Ski (Val d'Isère), 494
Toro de Fuego (St-Jean-de-Luz), 685
Toulon, 543–546
Toulouse, 661–669
Tour d'Argent (Paris), 104
Tour de Beurre (Rouen), 306
Tour de César (Paris), 104
Tour de Constance (Aigues-Mortes), 636
Tour de France, 56
Tour de Gaston Phoebus (Pau), 672
Tour de la Chaîne (La Rochelle), 696
Tour de la Lanterne (La Rochelle), 696–697

Tour de l'Horloge (Dinan), 348
Tour des Bouchers (Strasbourg), 399
Tour des Minimes (Amboise), 272
Tour de Suquet (Cannes), 562
Tour de Vésone (Périgueux), 722
Tour Eiffel (Paris), 90, 133–134
Tour et Crypt de l'Abbaye de Jouarre, 367
Tour Lanterne (Rouen), 306
Tour Magne (Nîmes), 633
Tour Mataguerre (Périgueux), 722
Tour Montparnasse (Paris), 136
Tour Pey-Berland (Bordeaux), 709
Tours, 277–283
Tour St-Fermin (Beaugency), 261
Tour St-Nicolas (La Rochelle), 697
Tour Sarrazin (Les Baux), 524
Trailfinders, 749
Train Montenvers-Mer de Glace, 490
Trains Touristiques de Marseille, 536
Train Touristique de Nice, 593
Train travel, 749, 752–754
Tranchée des Baïonettes (Verdun), 416
Trans-Côte d'Azur (Cannes), 563
Transports Planaria (Cannes), 563
Trench of Bayonets (Verdun), 416
Trésor de l'Eglise (St-Paul-de-Vence), 586
Trolley Bus (Marseille), 542
Trophée des Alps (La Turbie), 614
Tropicana (St-Tropez), 552
Trouville, 320–322
Truffle Festival (Périgueux), 722
Truffles, Périgueux, 722
Tumulus St-Michel (Carnac), 359

U

Uba-Club (Perpignan), 651
Underground Pub (Rouen), 312
Uniqlo (Paris), 174
US Airways, 748
Ussé, 294
Utah Beach, 332

V

Val Claret, 493
Val d'Isère, 492–495
Valençay, 268–269
Valence, 464–465
Vallée Blanche run (Chamonix), 487
Vals-les-Bains, 466–468
Van Cleef & Arpels (Paris), 177
Vaux-le-Vicomte, 235–237
Vence, 589–591
Verdun, 415–416
Verne, Jules, Musée Jules Verne de Nantes, 361
Versailles, 216–225
Veuve Amiot (Saumur), 297
Veuve Clicquot-Ponsardin (Reims), 375–376
Vézelay, 421–423
Vieil Annecy, 474
Vieille Fontaine (Vence), 589
Vieille Ville
  Nice, 594
  Sarlat-la-Canéda, 732
  Vence, 589
Vienne, 461–464
Vienne River, 290
Vieux Bassin (Honfleur), 313
Vieux Bayonne, 676
Vieux Lyon, 444–445
Vieux-Port
  La Rochelle, 699
  Marseille, 534, 542
  Nice, 594
Vieux Toulon, 544
Villa Ephrussi de Rothschild (St-Jean-Cap-Ferrat), 608
Village des Bories (near Gordes), 511
Village Notre-Dame (Bordeaux), 711
Village St-Paul (Paris), 171
Village Voice Bookshop (Paris), 172
Villa Kérylos (Beaulieu-sur-Mer), 611
Villa Léonine (Beaulieu-sur-Mer), 611
Villa Musée Fragonard (Grasse), 573
Villa Namouna (Beaulieu-sur-Mer), 611
Villandry, 285–287
Villa (Nice), 605
Ville Close (Concarneau), 353
Ville des Congrès (Evian-les-Bains), 470–471
Ville et Campagne (Strasbourg), 391
Villefranche-sur-Mer, 606–607
Villefranche-sur-Saône, 454, 455
Villié-Morgon, 455, 456
Vineyards and wineries. *See* Wineries and vineyards
Violettes & Pastels (Toulouse), 665
Visa pour l'Image (Perpignan), 648
Visas, 763
Visitor information, 763

W

Wagon de l'Armistice (Wagon du Maréchal-Foch; Compiègne), 251–252
Wally's English Bookshop (Cannes), 560
Walt Disney Studios (Disneyland Paris), 237, 241
Water, drinking, 763
Water-skiing, 576
Watersports, Juan-les-Pins, 576
Wax Museum (Chenonceaux), 276
Weather, 54
Willi's Wine Bar (Paris), 187
Wineries and vineyards
  Beaujolais, 454–456
  best, 11–12
  Bordeaux, 715–719
  Châteauneuf-du-Pape, 500
  Colmar, 403
  La Route du Vin (between Strasbourg and Colmar), 396–406
  Médoc, 716–717
  Saumur, 297–298
Wines and wine shops, 52–53
  Beaune, 428
  Bordeaux, 711
  Carcassonne, 653
  champagne, Reims, 372, 374–376
  Chinon, 290, 291
  Pont-Audemer, 312
  Sarlat-la-Canéda, 734
  Saumur, 297
Wolf Music (Strasbourg), 386
Women's International Festival of Long Board Surfing (Biarritz), 680
World War I, 30
  Verdun battlefields, 415–416
World War II, 30–31
  Bayeux, 326–327
    Musée Memorial de La Bataille de Normandie, 328
  D-day beaches, 330–332
  Mémorial des Martyrs Français de la Déportation de 1945 (Paris), 102–103
  Memorial du Débarquement en Provence (Toulon), 544–545
  Salle de Reddition (Reims), 374

Y

Y Club (Deauville), 320
Yves Brayer Museum (Les Baux), 524–525
Yves Delorme (Monte-Carlo), 619

Z

Zadig & Voltaire (Paris), 174
Zanzibar (Cannes), 569

PHOTO CREDITS

p. i © Kirsten Scully; p. iii, iv, v, vi, vii, viii © Kirsten Scully; p. 1 © Markel Redondo; p. 2 © Markel Redondo; p. 3 © Jessica Hauf; p. 4 © Oscar Pinal; p. 5 © Oscar Pinal; p. 6 © Matthieu Colin; p. 7 © Patrick Forget / SAGAPHOTO. COM / Alamy; p. 8, left © Markel Redondo; p. 8, right © Markel Redondo; p. 10 © Xaume Olleros; p. 11 © Anne Ackermann/Aurora; p. 12 © Markel Redondo; p. 13 © Courtesy Hotel Ritz, Photo by Fabrice Rambert; p. 14 © Courtesy Leading Hotels of the World, Hotel Negresco; p. 15, left © Courtesy Hotel Les Maisons de Lea; p. 15, right © Courtesy Hotel La Maison Blanche; p. 16, left © Courtesy Château de Locguénolé; p. 16, right © Courtesy Manoir Du Stang, Photo by A. Hubert; p. 17 © Xaume Olleros; p. 18 © Xaume Olleros; p. 19 © Alden Gewirtz; p. 25 © The British Library / Heritage / AGE Fotostock; p. 27 © SGM / AGE Fotostock; p. 28 © The Print Collector / Heritage / AGE Fotostock; p. 30 © RIA Novosti / Alamy; p. 31 © A H C / AGE Fotostock; p. 34 © Eric Feferberg / AFP / Getty Images; p. 38 © Kirsten Scully; p. 39, top © David R. Frazier Photolibrary, Inc. / Alamy; p. 39, bottom © Robert Harding Picture Library / SuperStock ; p. 41 © Markel Redondo; p. 43 © Bridgeman Art Library / SuperStock ; p. 45 © INTERFOTO / Alamy; p. 47 © The Art Archive / SuperStock ; p. 51 © Simon Reddy / Alamy; p. 52 © Markel Redondo; p. 61 © Kirsten Scully; p. 63 © Markel Redondo; p. 65 © Matthieu Colin; p. 66 © Art Kowalsky / Alamy; p. 68, left © Markel Redondo; p. 68, right © Oscar Pinal; p. 70 © J. D. Heaton / Picture Finders / AGE Fotostock; p. 72 © Kirsten Scully; p. 74, left © Alden Gewirtz; p. 74, right © Steve Vidler / SuperStock ; p. 79, right © Doug Pearson / Agency Jon Arnold Images / AGE Fotostock; p. 79, left © Matthieu Colin; p. 80 © Nicholas McInnes; p.92 © Nicholas McInnes; p.94 © Alden Gewirtz; p.98 © Markel Redondo; p. 102 © Nicholas McInnes; p. 105 © Markel Redondo; p. 107 © Markel Redondo; p. 108 © Markel Redondo; p. 112 © Alden Gewirtz; p. 113 © Markel Redondo; p. 116 © Markel Redondo; p. 118, left © Markel Redondo; p. 118, right © Markel Redondo; p. 120 © Elizabeth Blanchet; p. 121 © Markel Redondo; p. 124 © Markel Redondo; p. 125 © Markel Redondo; p. 130 © Arnaud Chicurel / Hemis / AGE Fotostock; p. 134 © Nicholas McInnes; p. 135 © Markel Redondo; p. 137 © Georgios Makkas; p. 164 © Markel Redondo; p. 167 © Jessica Hauf; p. 168 © Alden Gewirtz; p. 170 © Jessica Hauf; p. 172 © Markel Redondo; p. 179 © Markel Redondo; p. 180 © Alden Gewirtz; p. 185 © Courtesy Cité de la musique, Photo by P.-E. Rastoin; p. 186 © Markel Redondo; p. 189 © Markel Redondo; p. 192 © Oliver Knight / Alamy; p. 201 © Courtesy Hotel Banke; p. 203 © Courtesy Hotel Particulier; p. 206 © Markel Redondo; p. 215 © Markel Redondo; p. 220 © Markel Redondo; p. 221 © Markel Redondo; p. 225 © Markel Redondo; p. 228 © Markel Redondo; p. 233 © Markel Redondo; p. 236 © Photononstop / SuperStock ; p. 239 © David Jerome Ball / Impact / AGE Fotsotock; p. 243 © Markel Redondo; p. 245 © Charles Bowman / Robert Harding Picture Library Ltd / Alamy; p. 248 © Xaume Olleros; p. 250 © Xaume Olleros; p. 253 © Markel Redondo; p. 258 © Markel Redondo; p. 261 © Oscar Fdez. Santana / AGE Fotostock; p. 263 © Markel Redondo; p. 265 © Markel Redondo; p. 267 © Xaume Olleros; p. 271 © Xaume Olleros; p. 272 © Markel Redondo; p. 276 © Markel Redondo; p. 278 © Markel Redondo; p. 284 © Markel Redondo; p. 286 © Markel Redondo; p. 288 © Markel Redondo; p. 289 © CpC Photo / Alamy; p. 295 © Andre Lebrun / AGE Fotostock; p. 296 © Markel Redondo; p. 297 © ImagesEurope / Alamy; p. 300 © Markel Redondo; p. 303 © Oscar Pinal; p. 304 © Oscar Pinal; p. 306 © Oscar Pinal; p. 313 © Oscar Pinal; p. 316 © Andrew Wheeler; p. 321 © Andrew Wheeler; p. 323 © Andrew Wheeler; p. 327 © Oscar Pinal; p. 331 © Oscar Pinal; p .332 © Andrew Wheeler; p. 334 © blickwinkel / Alamy; p. 333 © Oscar Pinal; p. 337 © Andrew Wheeler; p. 341 © Oscar Pinal; p. 348 © Rene Mattes / Mauritius Images / AGE Fotostock; p. 351 © Oscar Pinal; p. 354 © Lothar Hinz / Zoonar GMBH / AGE Fotostock; p. 357 © Oscar Pinal; p. 358 © Oscar Pinal; p. 362 © Georgios Makkas; p. 366 © Markel Redondo; p. 368 © Xaume Olleros; p. 370 © Xaume Olleros; p. 274 © Markel Redondo; p. 375 © Markel Redondo; p. 381 © Markel Redondo; p. 383 © Matthieu Colin; p. 386 © Matthieu Colin; p. 388 © Matthieu Colin; p. 389 © Matthieu Colin; 401 © Courtesy René René; p. 403 © Matthieu Colin; p. 408 © Matthieu Colin; p. 410 © Matthieu Colin; p. 413 © Matthieu Colin; p. 414 © Xaume Olleros; p. 416 © Georgios Makkas; p. 417 © Kevin Galvin / AGE Fotostock; p. 420 © Bertrand Rieger / Hemis / AGE Fotsotock; p. 422 © Georgios Makkas; p.424 © Georgios Makkas; p. 426 © Georgios Makkas; p. 428 © Matthieu Colin; p .432 © Xaume Olleros; p. 434 © Matthieu Colin; p. 439 © Kirsten Scully; p. 442 © Kirsten Scully; p. 445 © Kirsten Scully; p. 446 © Kirsten Scully; p. 455 © Bernard Jaubert / AGE Fotostock; p. 461 © Kirsten Scully; p. 462 © Kirsten Scully; p.465 © Kirsten Scully; p. 467 © Kirsten Scully; p. 469 © Courchevel Tourisme/Jérome Kélagopian; p. 470 © Kirsten Scully; p.473 © Courtesy Evian Royal Resort, Photo by G. Trilard;

p. 475, right © Kirsten Scully; p. 475, left © Kirsten Scully; p. 480 © Kirsten Scully; p. 481 © Kirsten Scully; p.485 © Courchevel Tourisme / Patrick Pachod; p. 490 © Kirsten Scully; p. 493 © Kirsten Scully; p. 496 © Kirsten Scully; p. 498 © Kirsten Scully; p. 502 © Kirsten Scully; p. 504 © Kirsten Scully; p. 506 © Kirsten Scully; p. 510 © Kirsten Scully; p. 511 © Kirsten Scully; p. 515 © Kirsten Scully; p. 518 © Kirsten Scully; p. 524 © Kirsten Scully; p. 527 © Kirsten Scully; p. 528 © Kirsten Scully; p. 534 © Kirsten Scully; p. 536 © Kirsten Scully; p. 544 © Kirsten Scully; p. 548 © Matthieu Colin; p. 549 © Matthieu Colin; p. 563 © Matthieu Colin; p. 564 © Xaume Olleros; p. 569 © Valery Trillaud / AGE Fotsotock; p. 572 © Matthieu Colin; p. 575 © Matthieu Colin; p. 579, left © Robert Harding Picture Library / SuperStock ; p. 579, right © Matthieu Colin; p. 580 © Xaume Olleros; p. 586 © Kirsten Scully; p. 587 © Matthieu Colin; p. 589 © Kirsten Scully; p. 592 © Matthieu Colin; p. 594 © Kirsten Scully; p. 598 © Matthieu Colin; p. 608 © Matthieu Colin; p. 611 © Kirsten Scully; p. 614 © Kirsten Scully; p. 621 © Matthieu Colin; p. 624 © Matthieu Colin; p. 627 © Kirsten Scully; p. 628 © Georgios Makkas; p. 630 © Kirsten Scully; p. 632 © Kirsten Scully; p. 640 © Kirsten Scully; p. 643 © Kirsten Scully; p. 646 © Kirsten Scully; p. 652 © Kirsten Scully; p. 656 © Kirsten Scully; p. 658 © Kirsten Scully; p. 661 © Kirsten Scully; p. 664, left © Kirsten Scully; p. 664, right © Kirsten Scully; p. 666 © Kirsten Scully; p. 670 © Hemis / SuperStock; p. 672 © Kirsten Scully; p. 676 © Kirsten Scully; p. 685 © Kirsten Scully; p. 688 © Hemis / SupersStock; p. 690 © Markel Redondo; p. 694 © Markel Redondo; p. 697 © Markel Redondo; p. 701 © Markel Redondo; p. 704 © Courtesy CIBDI, Photo by Alberto Bocos Gil; p. 709 © Markel Redondo; p. 718 © Markel Redondo; p. 720 © Markel Redondo; p. 722 © Markel Redondo; p. 724 © Kirsten Scully; p. 727 © Kirsten Scully -- CHECK FILE for ACCURACY (might be French Gov't Organization); p. 730 © Kirsten Scully; p. 731 © directphoto.bz / Alamy; p. 734 © Kirsten Scully; p. 737 © Markel Redondo; p. 741 © Matthieu Colin; p. 744 © Brigitte Merz / Look / AGE Fotostock; p. 745 © Kirsten Scully; p. 747 © Markel Redondo; ;

> *I had crushes on friends of mine that were girls, but I didn't know that's what it was at the time. Looking back to my coming-out era in my early twenties, I realized, "Oh, that's what those feelings were back then." I didn't really understand them at the time, but it was clear to me once I kind of understood how to love someone else and experience what that felt like.*
>
> –Karla

For some, realizing and accepting their sexuality doesn't happen until they begin to see and meet other people who are not heterosexual.

> *I think it took me a long time because I just didn't see anyone who looked like myself. In middle school and high school, gay women were gym teachers. That wasn't me. I didn't relate to them. Whenever I dated a guy, something felt really uncomfortable about that. Then, when I saw someone who looked a lot like me, I felt like I could finally ask myself that question. I was in medical school, so I was twenty-five-ish. I worked under a physician who was a lesbian and a mom and very competent and successful. I realized I could be doing everything that I am doing now and that I could be gay. At that point, I said, "For two weeks, I will put on my gay glasses." For example, instead of thinking of what the guys are looking at, I will think about what the women are looking at and see if that felt more comfortable. Two weeks went by and another two weeks went by and I was like, "This feels right. This feels consistent and comfortable. This is me." After that month of letting myself see the world like that, I found it really surprising how comfortable it felt to be with a woman. I didn't date anyone for months and months after I sort of reached this new identity, but once I did, I was like, "This is totally right."*
>
> –Anne

Some gay and lesbian people date and marry someone of the opposite sex before realizing and accepting, at the age of twenty-five, that she was attracted to women.